With the purchase of a New Book*

You Can Practise What You Learned in Class Today.

*If you purchased a used book, see other side for access information.

Stock-Trak® Portfolio Simulation.

Learning to make good investment decisions comes from experience—experience making bad investment decisions. Get those bad decisions over with before managing real money by using the Stock-Trak® Portfolio Simulation included with this text. After all, learning to effectively manage real money and make investment decisions is what this text is all about.

Stock-Trak® gives students $500,000 in play money to trade stocks, options, futures, bonds, mutual funds, and international stocks (no other simulation offers so many!). Students can immediately apply investment material from the text or class by managing their Stock-Trak® portfolio, accessible online through the text's website at **www.mcgrawhill.ca/olc/jordan**.

If you bought a **new book**, you already have a subscription to Stock-Trak® (**it is included with this text**), so follow the directions on the other side of this card to set up your trading account today!

Professors: Use it as a Class.

Who picked the best stock? Who made the best trade? See the Online Stock-Trak® Instructor's Manual for information on Stock-Trak's® reporting system so you can see how your students and class do compared to others.

Students: Use it on your Own.

Your professor doesn't have to sign up in order for you to participate. See the reverse side of this card for information on how to activate your subscription. Stock-Trak® exercises at the end of the chapters briefly summarize key topics and trades and prompt you to try these out yourself!

Use it Right Away.

This text covers the basics early so you can start trading through Stock-Trak® within the first two weeks of class!

featuring stocks, options, futures, bonds, mutual funds & more

See other side for your unique Certificate Number.

With the purchase of a New Book*

You can access the

STOCK|TRAK

GLOBAL PORTFOLIO SIMULATIONS

featuring stocks, options, futures, bonds, mutual funds & more

www.stocktrak.com/cj

This card entitles the purchaser of a new textbook to one free STOCK-TRAK® account. To find out more about this offer, please visit the web page at www.stocktrak.com/cj. You will need the Certificate Number listed below to activate your account. **Please keep this card**.

- Manage an imaginary $500,000 portfolio.
- Test the investment techniques and strategies learned in class.
- Trade stocks, options, futures, mutual funds, bonds, and international stocks.
- Compete against your classmates or against individuals from around the world.

This is a limited time offer. This certificate is valid for one free STOCK-TRAK® account. See the web page for complete rules. This coupon may not be reproduced in any way. Void where prohibited.

Your Certificate Number is:

15052-68431

Second Edition

Fundamentals of
INVESTMENTS

Bradford D. Jordan
University of Kentucky

Thomas Miller
St. Louis University

Ayşe Yűce
Ryerson University

McGraw-Hill
Ryerson

Toronto Montréal Boston Burr Ridge, IL Dubuque, IA Madison, WI New York
San Francisco St. Louis Bangkok Bogotá Caracas Kuala Lumpur Lisbon London Madrid
Mexico City Milan New Delhi Santiago Seoul Singapore Sydney Taipei

To my parents, Şükrü and Ĵale Yüce.
AY

The McGraw·Hill Companies

Fundamentals of Investments
Second Canadian Edition

Copyright © 2009, 2006 by McGraw-Hill Ryerson Limited, a Subsidiary of The McGraw-Hill
Companies. Copyright © 2008, 2005, 2002, 2000 by McGraw-Hill Inc., a business unit of
The McGraw-Hill Companies All rights reserved. No part of this publication may be reproduced or
transmitted in any form or by any means, or stored in a data base or retrieval system, without the prior
written permission of McGraw-Hill Ryerson Limited, or in the case of photocopying or other
reprographic copying, a licence from The Canadian Copyright Licencing Agency (Access Copyright).
For an Access Copyright licence, visit www.accesscopyright.ca or call toll free to 1-800-893-5777.

ISBN-13: 978-0-07-097980-2
ISBN-10: 0-07-097980-4

1 2 3 4 5 6 7 8 9 10 TCP 0 9

Printed and bound in Canada

Care has been taken to trace ownership of copyright material contained in this text; however, the
publisher will welcome any information that enables them to rectify any reference or credit for
subsequent editions.

Vice President, Editor-in-Chief: Joanna Cotton
Sponsoring Editor: Kimberley Redhead
Senior Marketing Manager: Joy Armitage Taylor
Senior Developmental Editor: Maria Chu
Editorial Associate: Stephanie Hess
Supervising Editor: Graeme Powell
Copy Editor: Imogen Brian
Production Coordinator: Lena Mastromarco
Cover Design: Liz Harasymczuk
Cover Image: © See Tsay Yiap/Alamy
Interior Design: Liz Harasymczuk
Page Layout: SR Nova Pvt Ltd, Bangalore, India
Printer: Transcontinental Gagne

Jordan, Bradford D.
    Fundamentals of investments / Bradford D. Jordan, Thomas W.
Miller Jr., Ayse Yüce.—2nd Canadian ed.

First ed. by Charles J. Corrado, Bradford D. Jordan and Ayse Yüce.
Includes bibliographical references and indexes.
ISBN 978-0-07-097980-2

    1. Investments–Textbooks. I. Miller, Thomas W. II. Yüce, Ayse III. Title.

HG4521.J667 2008   332.6   C2008-902301-3

About the Authors

Bradford D. Jordan
Gatton College of Business and Economics, University of Kentucky

Bradford D. Jordan is Professor of Finance and holder of the Richard W. and Janis H. Furst Endowed Chair in Finance at the University of Kentucky. He has a long-standing interest in both applied and theoretical issues in investments, and he has extensive experience teaching all levels of investments. Professor Jordan has published numerous research articles on issues such as valuation of fixed-income securities, tax effects in investments analysis, the behaviour of security prices, IPO valuation, and pricing of exotic options. He is co-author of *Fundamentals of Corporate Finance, Sixth Edition,* and *Essentials of Corporate Finance, Fourth Edition,* two of the most widely used finance textbooks in the world.

Thomas W. Miller, Jr.,
John Cook School of Business, Saint Louis University

Tom Miller is the Associate Dean for Academic Programs and Professor of Finance at the John Cook School of Business at Saint Louis University. Professor Miller has a longstanding interest in derivative securities and investments and has published numerous articles on various topics in these areas. Professor Miller has been honored with many research and teaching awards. Professor Miller is a co-author (with David Dubofsky) of *Derivatives: Valuation and Risk Management* (Oxford University Press). Professor Miller's interests include golf, skiing, and American saddlebred horses.

Ayşe Yűce
Ryerson University

Ayşe Yűce is a Professor at Ryerson University. She received her B.Sc. from Bogaziçi University, her M.B.A. from the University of Southern Mississippi, and in 1994 her Ph.D. from Louisiana State University. She has taught various finance and accounting courses at Bilkent University, Wilfrid Laurier University, and the University of Northern British Columbia before joining Ryerson University. Her areas of expertise in teaching and in research are investments, international finance, and corporate finance. She has published articles in the Canadian Journal of Administrative Sciences, *European Journal of Finance, Applied Financial Economics, Emerging Markets and Finance,* and the *Russian and East European Finance and Trade*. She has a book on statistical properties and characteristics of Turkish stocks listed on the Istanbul Stock Exchange.

Table of Contents

PART 4   Portfolio Management 385

PART 5   Options and Futures 448

x Table of Contents

Preface

So why *did* we write this book?

As we toiled away, we asked ourselves this question many times, and the answer was always the same: *Our students made us.*

Traditionally, investments textbooks tend to fall into one of two camps. The first type has a greater focus on portfolio management and covers a significant amount of portfolio theory. The second type is more concerned with security analysis and generally contains fairly detailed coverage of fundamental analysis as a tool for equity valuation. Today, most texts try to cover all the bases by including some chapters drawn from one camp and some from another.

The result of trying to cover everything is either a very long book or one that forces the instructor to bounce back and forth between chapters. The result is frequently a noticeable lack of consistency in treatment. Different chapters have completely different approaches: some are computational, some are theoretical, and some are descriptive. Some do macroeconomic forecasting, some do mean-variance portfolio theory and beta estimation, and some do financial statements analysis. Options and futures are often essentially tacked on the back to round out this disconnected assortment.

The goal of these books is different from the goal of our students. Our students told us they come into an investments course wanting to learn how to make investment decisions. As time went by, we found ourselves supplying more and more supplemental materials to the texts we were using and constantly varying chapter sequences while chasing this elusive goal. We finally came to realize that the financial world had changed tremendously, and investments textbooks had fallen far behind in content and relevance.

What we really wanted, and what our students really needed, was a book that would do several key things:

- Focus on the students as investment managers by giving them information they can act on instead of concentrating on theories and research without the proper context.

- Offer strong, consistent pedagogy, including a balanced, unified treatment of the main types of financial investments as mirrored in the investment world.

- Organize topics in a way that would make them easy to apply—whether to a portfolio simulation or to real life—and support these topics with hands-on activities.

We made these three goals the guiding principles in writing this book. The next several sections explain our approach to each and why we think they are so important.

Who Is This Book For?

This book is aimed at introductory investments classes with students who have relatively little familiarity with investments. A typical student may have taken a principles of finance class and had some exposure to stocks and bonds, but not much beyond the basics. The introductory investments class is often a required course for finance majors, but students from other areas often take it as an elective. One fact of which we are acutely aware is that this may be the only investments class many students will ever take.

We intentionally wrote this book in a relaxed, informal style that engages the student and treats him or her as an active participant rather than a passive information absorber.

We think the world of investments is exciting and fascinating, and we hope to share our considerable enthusiasm for investing with the student. We appeal to intuition and basic principles whenever possible because we have found that this approach effectively promotes understanding. We also make extensive use of examples throughout, drawing on "real world" material and familiar companies wherever appropriate.

By design, the text is not encyclopedic. As the table of contents indicates, we have a total of 20 chapters. Chapter length is about 30–40 pages, so the text is aimed at a single-term course; most of the book can be covered in a typical quarter or semester.

Aiming the book at a one-semester course necessarily means some picking and choosing, both with regard to topics and depth of coverage. Throughout, we strike a balance by introducing and covering the essentials while leaving some of the detail to follow-up courses in security analysis, portfolio management, and options and futures.

How Does the Second Canadian Edition of This Book Expand upon the Goals Described Above?

Based on our students' feedback, we created a hands-on, easy-to-read investment book that teaches readers how to make investment decisions, how to form portfolios, and how to manage simulated portfolios of financial instruments.

To give some examples of new content:

- Chapter 1 contains the recent history of returns provided by Canadian financial instruments between 1983 and 2007. At the end of the chapter we discuss financial crashes.

- Chapter 2 introduces three-security portfolio return and variance formulas and examples. We discuss the importance of asset allocation in portfolio formation and management.

- Chapter 4 gives information on methods of obtaining futures contract and options contract price quotes using the Internet.

- Chapter 5 gives information on the recent changes regarding income trust fund proceeds and updates on Canadian mutual fund performance.

- Chapter 6 includes updated information about the major stock exchanges and extended coverage of the Toronto Venture Exchange.

- Chapter 7 contains a new section covering the residual income model and EVA.

- Chapter 8 has been expanded to include event studies, informed traders, insider trading, and illegal insider trading. New material includes the performance of professional money managers and stock market anomalies.

- Chapter 9 contains a substantial amount of new material on behavioural finance. In addition to a greatly expanded section on technical analysis, new material in this chapter includes prospect theory, overconfidence, misperceiving randomness, overreacting to chance events, sentiment-based risk, and limits to arbitrage.

- Chapter 11 continues to show methods of immunization by using the concepts of duration and convexity and uses more examples and problems.

- Chapter 12 extends the CAPM with a discussion of the Fama-French three-factor model.

- Chapter 14 now includes a discussion of option "moneyness."

- Chapter 15 covers using an online calculator to value stock options and it now has a section about hedging stock with stock options.

- Chapter 16 contains a new example of how to change the beta of a stock portfolio using stock index futures.
- Chapter 17 (which was Chapter 8) now includes a section about financial statement forecasting using the percentage of sales approach with a detailed case study that values Barrick Gold Corporation.
- Chapter 18 contains a new section on "make-whole" call provisions.
- Chapter 20 includes a new section on crosslisting by multinational companies.

For the Second Canadian edition, we aim to provide our students with information not only on Canadian securities and Canadian exchanges, but also on U.S. securities and U.S. exchanges. In the last chapter we provide information on the world exchanges and on the risk-return profile of international investment. The majority of our students indicated that they want to write CFA exams, so we added new problems and CFA questions. We created a series of questions that test understanding of concepts with no calculations involved. We have developed three different features which, we believe, enhance the student learning experience. First, we offer a block of questions called *What's on the Web?* These questions give students assignments to perform based on information they retrieve from various websites. Second, we added *Standard & Poor's* problems. These problems require the use of the educational version of Market Insight, which provides access to S&P's well-known Compustat database. They also provide instructors with an easy way to incorporate current, real-world data. Finally, in selected chapters, we have created spreadsheet assignments, which ask students to create certain types of spreadsheets to solve problems.

We emphasize the use of the Web in investments analysis, and we integrate Web-based content in several ways. First, wherever appropriate, we provide a commented link in the margin. These links send readers to selected, particularly relevant websites. Second, our *Work the Web* feature appears in most chapters. These boxed readings use screen shots to show students how to access, use, and interpret various types of key financial and market data. Finally, we have some end-of-chapter problems that rely on data retrieved from the Web.

We provide *Spreadsheet Analysis* exhibits. These exhibits illustrate directly how to use spreadsheets to do certain types of important problems, including such computationally intensive tasks as calculating Macauley duration, finding Black-Scholes-Merton option prices, and determining optimal portfolios based on Sharpe ratios. We provide readings from the *The Globe and Mail* and also from *The Wall Street Journal*.

How Is This Book Relevant to the Student?

Fundamental changes in the investments universe drive our attention to relevance. The first major change is that individuals are being asked to make investment decisions for their own portfolios more often than ever before. There is, thankfully, a growing recognition that traditional "savings account" approaches to investing are decidedly inferior. At the same time, the use of employer-sponsored "investment accounts" has expanded enormously. The second major change is that the investments universe has exploded with an ever-increasing number of investment vehicles available to individual investors. As a result, investors must choose from an array of products, many of which are very complex, and they must strive to choose wisely as well.

Beyond this, students are more interested in subjects that affect them directly (aren't we all). By taking the point of view of the student as an investor, we are better able to illustrate and emphasize the relevance and importance of the material.

Our approach is evident in the table of contents. Our first chapter is motivational; we have found that this material effectively "hooks" students and even motivates a semester-long discourse on risk and return. Our third chapter answers the student's next natural question: "How do I get started investing and how do I buy and sell securities?" The fourth chapter surveys the different types of investments available. After only four chapters, very early in the term, students have learned something about the risks and rewards of investing, how to get started investing, and what investment choices are available.

We close the first part of the text with a detailed examination of mutual funds. Without a doubt, mutual funds have become the most popular investment vehicles for individual investors. Given the size and enormous growth in the mutual fund industry, this material is important for investors. Even so, investments texts typically cover mutual funds in a cursory way, often banishing the material to a back chapter under the obscure (and obsolete) heading of "investment companies." Our early placement lets students explore right away a topic they have heard a lot about and are typically very interested in.

How Does This Book Allow Students to Apply the Investments Knowledge They Learn?

After studying this text, students will have the basic knowledge needed to move forward and actually act on what they have learned. We have developed two features to encourage making decisions as an investment manager. Learning to make good investment decisions comes with experience, while experience (regrettably) comes from making bad investment decisions. As much as possible, we press our students to get those bad decisions out of their systems before they start managing real money!

Not surprisingly, most students don't know how to get started buying and selling securities. We have learned that providing some structure, especially with a portfolio simulation, greatly enhances the experience. Therefore, we have a series of *Real World* boxes. These boxes (at the end of each chapter) usually describe actual trades for students to explore. The intention is to show students how to gain real experience with the principles and instruments covered in the chapter. The second feature is a series of *Stock-Trak* exercises that take students through specific trading situations using *Stock-Trak Portfolio Simulations.*

Because we feel that portfolio simulations are so valuable, we have taken steps to assist instructors who, like us, plan to integrate portfolio simulations into their courses. Beyond the features mentioned above, we have organized the text so that the essential material needed before participating in a simulation is covered at the front of the book. Most notably, with every new book, we have included a subscription to *Stock-Trak Portfolio Simulations. Stock-Trak* is the leading provider of investment simulation services to the academic community.

How Does This Book Maintain a Consistent, Unified Treatment?

In most investments texts, depth of treatment and presentation vary dramatically from instrument to instrument, stranding the student without an overall framework for understanding the many types of investments. We stress early on that there are essentially only four basic types of financial investments—stocks, bonds, options, and futures. In parts 2 through 6, our simple goal is to take a closer look at each of these instruments. We take a unified approach to each by answering these basic questions:

1. What are the essential features of the instrument?
2. What are the possible rewards?

3. What are the risks?

4. What are the basic determinants of investment value?

5. For whom is the investment appropriate and under what circumstances?

6. How is the instrument bought and sold, and how does the market for the instrument operate?

By covering investment instruments in this way, we teach the students which questions to ask when looking at any potential investment.

Unlike other introductory investments texts, we devote several chapters beyond the basics to the different types of fixed-income investments. Students are often surprised to learn that the fixed-income markets are so much bigger than the equity markets and that money management opportunities are much more common in the fixed-income arena. Possibly the best way to see this is to look at recent CFA exams and materials and note the extensive coverage of fixed-income topics. We have placed these chapters toward the back of the text because we recognize not everyone will want to cover all this material. We have also separated the subject into several shorter chapters to make it more digestible for students and to allow instructors more control over what is covered.

Acknowledgments

We have received extensive feedback from reviewers at each step along the way, and we are very grateful to the following dedicated scholars and teachers for their time and expertise:

Raymond Cox, University of Ontario Institute of Technology

Alex Faseruk, Memorial University of New Brunswick

Jim Fischer, Mount Royal College

Richard Hallison, University of Lethbridge

Shahriar Hasan, Thompson River University

Keith Jensen, Malaspina College

Pat Latham, Northern Alberta Institute of Technology

Eben Otuteye, University of New Brunswick

Charles Schell, University of Northern British Columbia

Kamal Smimou, University of Lethbridge

Larry Stubbs, British Columbia Institute of Technology

Zhao Sun, University of Saskatchewan

Francis Tapon, University of Guelph

We'd like to thank Helen Prankie, Humber Institute of Technology and Advanced Learning for the unenviable task of technical proofreading, and, in particular, careful checking of each calculation throughout the text.

We are deeply grateful to the select group of professionals who served as our development team on this edition: Kimberley Redhead, Sponsoring Editor; Maria Chu, Senior Developmental Editor; Joy Armitage Taylor, Senior Marketing Manager; Graeme Powell, Supervising Editor, and Imogen Brian, Copyeditor.

I want to especially thank to Vefa Goksel Buyukalpelli for his diligent and hard work as my research assistant and also for sharing the passion for the book.

Bradford D. Jordan

Thomas Miller

Ayşe Yüce

Pedagogical Features

We have included many pedagogical features in this text that will be valuable learning tools for your students. This walkthrough highlights some of the most important elements.

CHAPTER 3

Buying and Selling Securities

"Don't gamble! Take all your savings and buy some good stock and hold it till it goes up. If it don't go up, don't buy it."

—Will Rogers

You might wish to try Will Rogers's well-known stock market advice, but first you must know the basics of securities trading. Fortunately, trading is a relatively simple task, as attested to by the billions of shares of stocks that trade among investors on a typical day. Essentially, you begin the process by opening a trading account with a brokerage firm and then submitting trading orders. But you should know about some important details beforehand. ■

To help you get started, this chapter covers the basics of the investing process. We begin by describing how you go about buying and selling securities such as stocks and bonds. We then outline some of the most important considerations and constraints to keep in mind as you get more involved in the investing process.

Chapter Openers

These one-paragraph introductions for each chapter present facts and misconceptions that may surprise you. An explanation is more fully developed in the chapter.

Key Terms

Key terms are indicated in bold and defined in the margin. The running glossary in the margin helps students quickly review the basic terminology for the chapter.

Web Addresses

Websites are called out in the margins, along with a notation of how they relate to the chapter material.

Futures Contracts

futures contract
An agreement made today regarding the terms of a trade that will take place later.

In many ways, a futures contract is the simplest of all financial assets. A **futures contract** is just an agreement made today regarding the terms of a trade that will take place later. For example, suppose you know that you will want to buy 100 ounces of gold in six months. One thing you could do is to strike a deal today with a seller in which you promise to pay, say, $400 per ounce in six months for the 100 ounces of gold. In other words, you and the seller agree that six months from now, you will exchange $40,000 for 100 ounces of gold. The agreement that you have created is a futures contract.

With your futures contract, you have locked in the price of gold six months from now. Suppose that gold is actually selling for $450 per ounce in six months. If this occurs, then you benefit from having entered into the futures contract because you have to pay only $400 per ounce. However, if gold is selling for $350, you lose because you are forced to pay $400 per ounce. Thus, a futures contract is essentially a bet on the future price of whatever is being bought or sold. Notice that with your futures contract, no money changes hands today.

 You can download lots of basic futures info from the Education Centre at www.cbot.com

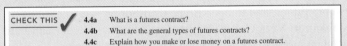

CHECK THIS ✓	4.4a	What is a futures contract?
	4.4b	What are the general types of futures contracts?
	4.4c	Explain how you make or lose money on a futures contract.

Check This!

Every major section in each chapter ends with questions for review. This feature helps students test their understanding of the material before moving on to the next section.

INVESTMENT UPDATES With Cash, Investors Must Find a Happy Medium

Cash doesn't pay much, but when stock markets around the world plunge, as they have recently, an investor begins to look longingly at assets that hold their value no matter what.

For the record, the past two weeks have taken S&P/TSX composite index down almost 7 percent. Around the world, almost every other market tumbled. There was nowhere to hide—except in cash.

The problem is, of course, that while cash holds its value in the short term, keeping it for the long run means giving up a great deal of potential gain in riskier but more profitable stocks and other assets.

Professional investors disdain cash as a long-term investment. "It is a performance drag," says Elizabeth Lunney, senior vice-president and portfolio manager for Fiduciary Trust Co. of Canada, a unit of Toronto-based Franklin Templeton Investments Corp.

Hanif Mamdani, chief investment officer at money manager Phillips Hager & North in Vancouver, points out that the long-term annual return on U.S. stocks is about 8 percent, bonds 4 to 5 percent and cash 3 percent.

to take advantage of buying opportunities in market downturns.

Investors differ in trading style, anticipated holding period and needs for cash in daily life. Moreover, there are times when stocks are expensive and a bigger weighting in cash is defensive. Probably the biggest factor though, is risk tolerance. As the accompanying pie chart shows, holding assets other than stocks reduces short-term risk. But the chart also shows that an increase in risk adds to potential gains.

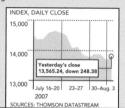

INDEX, DAILY CLOSE

Yesterday's close
13,565.24, down 248.38

July 16–20   23–27   30–Aug. 3
2007

SOURCES: THOMSON DATASTREAM

Investment Updates

These boxed readings, reprinted from various business press sources, provide additional real-world events and examples to illustrate the material in the chapter. Some articles highlight recent events, and others present events of more historical significance.

Work the Web

Various screenshots are showcased throughout the text to illustrate how to access specific features of selected websites.

WORK THE WEB

In order to participate in e-trading, investors should open an online account for electronic trading. After that they can go to the website of their broker and give buy or sell orders, track their accounts, and trade on margin. The following website shows an online trade for an investor at HSBC's InvestDirect site. The investor entered an order to buy 50 shares of Nortel Stock at market price. Once the investor hits Submit, the order will be entered and the broker will fulfill the order.

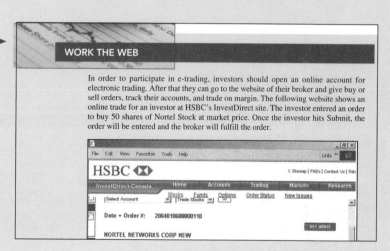

SPREADSHEET ANALYSIS

	A	B	C	D	E	F	G	H
1								
2		**Treasury Bill Price and Yield Calculations**						
3								
4	A Treasury bill traded on March 14, 2006, pays $100 on June 1, 2006. Assuming a							
5	discount rate of 6 percent, what are its price and bond equivalent yield?							
6	Hint: Use the Excel function TBILLPRICE and TBILLEQ.							
7								
8		$98.6833	= TBILLPRICE("3/14/2006","6/1/2006",0.06)					
9								
10		6.164%	= TBILLEQ("3/14/2006","6/1/2006",0.06)					
11								
12								
13	A credit card charges a nominal annual interest rate of 15 percent. With interest							
14	charged monthly, what is the effective annual rate (EAR) on this credit card?							
15	Hint: Use the Excel function EFFECT.							
16								
17		16.075%	= EFFECT(0.15,12)					
18								

Spreadsheet Analysis

Self-contained spreadsheet examples show students how to set up spreadsheets to solve problems—a vital part of every business student's education.

Numbered Examples

Separate numbered and titled examples are integrated throughout the chapters. Each example illustrates an intuitive or mathematical application in a step-by-step format.

CAUTION: INDEXES UNDER CONSTRUCTION

EXAMPLE 6.1

Suppose there are only two stocks in the market and the following information is given:

	Shares Outstanding	Price per Share Beginning of Year	Price per Share End of Year
Quark Co.	10 million	$10	$11
Bashir, Inc	20 million	$20	$25

Construct price- and value-weighted indexes and calculate the percentage changes in each.

The average share price rose from $15 to $18, or $3, so the price-weighted index would be up by 3 / 15 = 20 percent. Average total market value, in millions, rose from $250 to $305, so the value-weighted index rose by 55 / 250 = 22 percent.

$$\text{Percentage return} = \text{Dividend yield} + \text{Capital gains yield} \qquad (1.3)$$
$$= D_{t+1} / P_t + (P_{t+1} - P_t) / P_t$$
$$= (D_{t+1} + P_{t+1} - P_t) / P_t$$

Numbered Equations

Key equations are highlighted and numbered sequentially in each chapter for easy reference.

Figures and Tables

This text makes extensive use of real data and presents them in various figures and tables. Explanations in the narrative, examples, and end-of-chapter problems will refer to many of these exhibits.

TABLE 6.1 — **Stock Market Order Types**

Order Type	Buy	Sell
Market order	Buy at best price available for immediate execution.	Sell at best price available for immediate execution.
Limit order	Buy at best price available, but not more than the preset limit price. Forgo purchase if limit is not met.	Sell at best price available, but not less than the preset limit price. Forgo sale if limit is not met.
Stop order	Convert to a market order to buy when the stock price crosses the stop price from below.	Convert to a market order to sell when the stock price crosses the stop price from above. Also known as a "stop-loss."
Stop-limit order	Convert to a limit order to buy when the stock price crosses the stop price from below.	Convert to a limit order to sell when the stock price crosses the stop price from above.

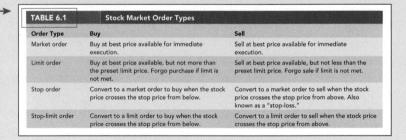

FIGURE 10.2 — **Money Market Interest Rates**

EXCHANGE RATES [+ MORE]	21/12/07	24/12/07	+/−	INFLATION [+ MORE]	10/07	11/07	+/−
$Can/US closing rate	0.9927	0.9850	−0.0077	Inflation-control target range	1–3	1–3	–
$Can/US noon rate	0.9944	0.9871	−0.0073	Total consumer price index**	2.4%	2.5%	+0.1
$US/Canada noon rate	1.0056	1.0131	+0.0075	Core consumer price index**	1.8%	1.6%	−0.2
CERI*	120.78	121.66	+0.88	INTEREST RATES [+ MORE]	12/12/07	19/12/07	+/−
MONEY MARKET [+ MORE]	20/12/07	21/12/07	+/−	Prime business rate	6.00%	6.00%	0.00
Overnight rate	4.2530%	4.2607%	+0.0077	Conventional mortgage, 5 year	7.39%	7.39%	0.00
Target for the overnight rate	4.25%	4.25%	0.00	BOND YIELDS [+ MORE]	20/12/07	21/12/07	+/−
Overnight repo rate (CORRA)	4.2446%	4.2670%	+0.0224	GoC marketable bonds, +10 yr	4.10%	4.17%	+0.07
Corporate paper, 1 month	4.61%	4.61%	0.00	GoC benchmark bonds, 3 yr	3.85%	3.92%	+0.07
Treasury bill, 1 month	3.70%	3.71%	+0.01				
Bankers' Acceptances, 1 month	4.58%	4.58%	0.00				

Source: Bank of Canada, http://www.bankofcanada.ca

Summary and Conclusions

Each chapter ends with a numbered summary that highlights the important points of the chapter. This provides a handy checklist for students when they review the chapter.

7.7 Summary and Conclusions

In this chapter, we examined several methods of fundamental analysis used by financial analysts to value common stocks. The methods examined were various dividend discount models, residual income models, and price ratio models. We saw that:

1. Dividend discount models value common stock as the sum of all expected future dividend payments, where the dividends are adjusted for risk and the time value of money.

2. The dividend discount model is often simplified by assuming that dividends will grow at a constant growth rate. A particularly simple form of the dividend discount model is the case in which dividends grow at a constant perpetual growth rate. The simplicity of the constant perpetual growth model makes it the most popular dividend discount model. However, it should be applied only to companies with stable earnings and dividend growth.

3. Dividend models require an estimate of future growth. We described the sustainable growth rate, which is measured as a firm's return on equity times its retention ratio, and illustrated its use.

4. Companies often experience temporary periods of unusually high or low growth, where growth eventually converges to an industry average. In such cases, analysts frequently use a two-stage dividend growth model.

Real World

This feature (at the end of each chapter) explains to students how they can apply the material they just learned. The *Real World* boxes encourage students—whether for practice, in a trading simulation, or with real money—to make investment decisions.

REAL WORLD

This chapter deals with various aspects of behavioural finance. How do you go about incorporating these concepts into the management of your portfolio? First, recall that one of the major lessons from this chapter is that, at times, you may be your own worst enemy when you are investing.

But suppose that you are able to harness your own psychological flaws that unduly influence your investment decisions. To profit from insights from behavioural finance, you might try to shift your portfolio to take advantage of situations where you perceive other market participants have incorrectly valued certain stocks, bonds, derivatives, market sectors, or even countries. Shifting portfolio weights to take advantage of these opportunities is called a "dynamic" trading strategy.

Here is one example of using a dynamic trading strategy. Consider a typical value/growth portfolio weight-shifting scheme. When there is a great deal of market overreaction, perhaps signalled by high market volatility, you would increase, or tilt, your relative portfolio weight toward value stocks. When there is a great deal of market underreaction, perhaps signalled by low market volatility, you would increase your relative weighting in

Chapter Review Problems and Self-Test

Students are provided with one to three practice problems per chapter with worked-out solutions to test their abilities in solving key problems related to the content of the chapter.

Chapter Review Problems and Self-Test

1. **The Perpetual Growth Model** Suppose dividends for Tony's Pizza company are projected to grow at 6 percent forever. If the discount rate is 16 percent and the current dividend is $2, what is the value of the stock?

2. **The Two-Stage Growth Model** Suppose the Titanic Ice Cube Co.'s dividend grows at a 20 percent rate for the next three years. Thereafter, it grows at a 12 percent rate. What value would we place on Titanic assuming a 15 percent discount rate? Titanic's most recent dividend was $3.

3. **Residual Income Model** Suppose Al's Infrared Sandwich Company has a current book value of $10.85 per share. The most recent earnings per share were $2.96 per share, and earnings are expected to grow at 6 percent forever. The appropriate discount rate is 8.2 percent. Assume the clean surplus relationship is true. Assuming the company maintains a constant retention ratio, what is the value of the company according to the residual income model if (a) there are no dividends, and (b) there are dividends of $1.00 per share?

4. **Price Ratio Analysis** The table below contains some information about the Jordan Air Co. Provide expected share prices using each of the three price ratio approaches we have discussed.

Test Your Investment Quotient

1. **Sustainable Growth** A company has a return on equity of ROE = 20 percent, and from earnings per share of EPS = $5, it pays a $2 dividend. What is the company's sustainable growth rate?
   a. 8 percent
   b. 10 percent
   c. 12 percent
   d. 20 percent

CFA® PROBLEMS

2. **Sustainable Growth** If the return on equity for a firm is 15 percent and the retention ratio is 40 percent, the sustainable growth rate of earnings and dividends is which of the following?
   a. 6 percent
   b. 9 percent
   c. 15 percent
   d. 40 percent

Test Your IQ

An average of 15 multiple-choice questions are included for each chapter, many of which are taken from past CFA exams. Answers to these questions appear in Appendix A.

Concept Questions

At the end of every chapter are 10–15 concept questions that further reinforce key concepts found throughout the chapter.

Concept Questions

1. **Dividend Discount Model** What is the basic principle behind dividend discount models?
2. **P/E Ratios** Why do growth stocks tend to have higher P/E ratios than value stocks?
3. **Earnings Yields** What is the earnings yield on a stock?
4. **Cash Flow** In computing the price-cash flow ratio, how is cash flow per share usually measured?
5. **Stock Valuation** Why does the value of a share of stock depend on dividends?
6. **Stock Valuation** A substantial percentage of the companies listed on the TSX don't pay dividends, but investors are nonetheless willing to buy shares in them. How is this possible given your answer to the previous question?
7. **Dividends** Referring to the previous two questions, under what circumstances might a company choose not to pay dividends?

Questions and Problems

1. **Dividend Valuation** CJ Industries will pay a regular dividend of $3.25 per share for each of the next four years. At the end of the four years, the company will also pay out a $50 per share liquidating dividend, and the company will cease operations. If the discount rate is 11 percent, what is the current value of the company's stock?
2. **Dividend Valuation** In the previous problem, suppose the current share price is $50. If all other information remains the same, what must the liquidating dividend be?
3. **Dividend Discount Model** Trust Bankers just paid an annual dividend of $2 per share. The expected dividend growth rate is 6 percent, the discount rate is 12 percent, and the dividends will last for 5 more years. What is the value of the stock? What if the dividends last for 10 more years? 30 years? 100 years?
4. **Dividend Discount Model** Apple Grove, Inc., will pay dividends for the next 10 years. The expected dividend growth rate for this firm is 7 percent, the discount rate is 14 percent, and the stock currently sells for $30 per share. How much must the most recent dividend payment have been?
5. **Dividend Growth Model** Suppose that McKenzie, Inc., just paid a dividend of $4.00 per share. The company will continue to pay dividends for the next 25 years, and then go out

Questions and Problems

A variety of problems (average of 20 per chapter) are included in each chapter to test students' understanding of the conceptual and mathematical elements. Each problem is labelled with the subject and the level—core or intermediate. Selected answers appear in Appendix B, and complete solutions are included in the Instructor's Manual.

S&P Problems

These optional end-of-chapter questions are problems directly incorporating the Educational Version of Market Insight, a service based on Standard & Poor's renowned Compustat® database. These problems provide you with an easy method of including current real-world data into your course. See page xxix for additional information.

STANDARD &POOR'S

S&P Problems
www.mcgrawhill.com/edumarketinsight

1. **Constant Perpetual Growth Model** Locate the information for Corel Corporation (CORL) If you follow the "Financial Hlts" link you will find the current stock price, most recent dividend, and the five-year growth rate for dividends. Assuming the five-year dividend growth rate is equal to the perpetual growth rate, what is the implied required return for Corel shareholders? Does this number make sense?
2. **Sustainable Growth** What is the sustainable growth rate for Inco Ltd (N)? Under "Excel Analytics" you will find a link for annual ratios. This report shows return on equity and the payout ratio. Calculate the sustainable growth rate for Inco each year for the past five years. Is the sustainable growth rate the same every year? Why or why not?

What's on the Web?

1. **Sustainable Growth Rate** You can find the home page for Magna International at www.magna.com. Go to this page and find the most recent annual report for Magna. Calculate the sustainable growth rate for each of the past two years. Are these values the same? Why or why not?

2. **Sustainable Growth Rate** Go to ca.finance.yahoo.com and get the information for Nova Chemical. Under the "Research" link you should find analysts' estimates for Nova's growth rate over the next five years. How does this compare to the industry, sector, and S&P 500 growth rates? Now find the EPS and dividends per share for Nova and calculate the sustainable growth rate. How does your number compare to analysts' estimates for the company? Why might these estimates differ?

3. **Perpetual Dividend Growth Model** Go to ca.finance.yahoo.com and find the following information for Noranda: the beta, the most recent annual dividend, and analysts' estimated growth rate. Next, find the three-month Treasury bill yield on ca.finance.yahoo.com. Assuming the market risk premium is 9 percent, what is the required return for Noranda? What is the value of Noranda stock using the perpetual dividend growth model? Does Noranda appear overpriced, underpriced, or correctly priced? Why might this analysis be inappropriate, or at least misleading?

What's on the Web

These end-of-chapter activities show students how to use and learn from the vast amount of financial resources available on the Internet.

Stock-Trak Exercises (Unique to this text)

This text is the only book that incorporates Stock-Trak Portfolio Simulations® exercises. Stock-Trak is one of the most successful trading simulations with over 30,000 post-secondary students having trading accounts each semester (see Supplements for more information). Go to the next level in teaching your students about investments management by encouraging your students to use this product. This section located at the text's Web site, www.mcgrawhill.ca/olc/jordan briefly summarizes topics from the chapter and asks students to perform certain trades as covered in the text.

Technology Solutions

Online Learning Centre

Increasingly students are studying online. That is why we offer an Online Learning Centre (OLC) that follows *Fundamentals of Investments* chapter by chapter. You don't have to build or maintain anything and it's ready to go the moment you and your students type in the URL:

www.mcgrawhill.ca/olc/jordan

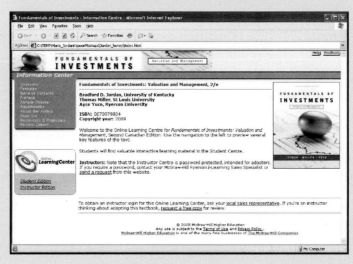

As your students study, they can refer to the OLC website for such benefits as:

- Online Quizzes
- Link to Stock-Trak®
- Stock-Trak Exercises
- Newsroom
- Finance Around the World
- Link to Standard & Poor's site

- Glossary and Key Terms
- Summary and Conclusions
- Real World
- Video Clips
- What's on the Web

Course Management

Content cartridges are available for course management systems such as **WebCT and Blackboard**. These platforms provide instructors with user-friendly, flexible teaching tools. Please contact your local McGraw-Hill Ryerson *i*Learning Sales Specialist for details.

We want to help bring your teaching to life using our products and services. We do this by integrating technology, events, conferences, training and more into services surrounding the textbook. We call it *i*Services. For more information, please contact your *i*Learning Sales Specialist.

Teaching, Learning and Technology Conferences Series

The educational environment has changed tremendously in recent years, and McGraw-Hill Ryerson continues to be committed to helping you acquire the skills you need to succeed in this new milieu. Our innovative Teaching, Technology and Learning Conference Series brings faculty together from across Canada with 3M Teaching Excellence award winners to share teaching and learning practices in a collaborative and stimulating environment. Pre-conference workshops on general topics, such as teaching large classes and technology integration, will also be offered. We will also work with you at your own institution to customize workshops that best suit the needs of your faculty.

Comprehensive Teaching and Learning Package

We have developed a number of supplements for both teaching and learning to accompany this text:

For Instructors

Instructor's Online Learning Centre (www.mcgrawhill.ca/olc/jordan)

The Online Learning Centre includes a password-protected website for instructors and downloadable supplements.

Instructor's Resource CD-ROM

The Instructor's Resource CD-ROM contains the following assets:

Instructor's Manual, *prepared by Ayşe Yüce,* Ryerson University. Developed to clearly outline the chapter material as well as provide extra teaching support, the first section of the Instructor's Manual includes an annotated outline of each chapter with suggested websites, references to PowerPoint slides, teaching tips, additional examples, and current events references. The second section contains complete worked-out solutions for the end-of-chapter questions and problems.

Test Bank, *prepared by Keith Cheung,* University of Windsor. With almost 1,500 questions, this Test Bank, in Rich Text Format, provides a variety of question formats (true-false, multiple-choice, fill-in-the blank, and problems) and levels of difficulty to meet any instructor's testing needs.

Microsoft® PowerPoint® Presentation

The PowerPoint package contains relevant figures and tables from the text, lecture outlines, and additional examples that you can customize for your lectures.

Standard & Poor's Educational Version of Market Insight

Mc Graw-Hill Ryerson and the Institutional Market Services division of Standard & Poor's are pleased to offer instructors and students optional access to the educational version of Standard & Poor's Market Insight. The Educational Version of Market Insight is a rich online resource that provides six years of fundamental financial data for over 1,000 companies in the database. S&P-specific problems can be found at the end of almost all chapters in this text. For more details on how to make this optional service available to your students please contact your local *i*learning sales specialist.

Stock-Trak® Portfolio Stimulation

Give your students investment management experience! McGraw-Hill Ryerson has partnered with *Stock-Trak* and is providing with each new text book, a one-semester subscription to the *Stock-Trak Portfolio Simulation. Stock-Trak* allows students to trade 500,000 dollars worth of stocks, options, futures, bonds, mutual funds, and international stocks—no other simulation offers all these types of securities! Instructors receive reports every week. All trades are done on the Web at *www.stocktrak.com/cj*. See this site for more information and refer to the card at the front of the text for your individual certificate number required to gain access to the site.

For Students

Student Online Learning Centre (www.mcgrawhill.ca/olc/jordan)

The Online Learning Centre prepared by Jim Fischer, Mount Royal College, includes online study material including Stock-Trak Exercises, self-grading quizzes, review material, video clips, and much more! There is also a link to *Finance Around the World,* a tremendous resource that takes students to important and popular finance websites throughout the world.

A Brief History of Risk and Return

"If you want to make money, go where the money is."

—Joseph Kennedy

Who wants to be a millionaire? Actually, anyone can retire as a millionaire. How? Consider this: Suppose you, at the age of 25, begin saving $3,000 per year. Forty years later, you retire at age 65. How much will you have? The answer might surprise you. If you earn 10 percent per year, you will have about $1.3 million. Are these numbers realistic? Based on the history of financial markets, the answer appears to be yes. For example, between 1983 and 2007, the Toronto Stock Index has yielded about 12.09 percent per year. ∎

The study of investments could begin in many places. After thinking it over, we decided that a brief history lesson is in order, so we start our discussion of risk and return by looking back at what has happened to investors in Canadian financial markets since 1983. In 1988, for example, the Canadian stock market lost 16.50 percent of its value. Then it reversed itself and gained 20 percent in 1989. More recently, in 2001, the market lost about 30 percent though it did rebound by almost 26 percent in 2005. For the period 2001 through 2002 the stock market lost value for two straight years. What lessons, if any, should investors learn from such shifts in the stock market? We explore the last two and a half decades of market history to find out.

Our primary goal in this chapter is to see what financial market history can tell us about risk and return. One of the most important things to get out of this discussion is a perspective on the numbers. What is a high return? What is a low return? More generally, what returns should we expect from financial assets such as stocks and bonds, and what are the risks from such investments? Beyond this, we hope that by studying what *did* happen in the past, we will at least gain some insight into what *can* happen in the future.

The history of risk and return is made day by day in global financial markets. The Internet is an excellent source of information on financial markets. Visit our website (at www.mcgrawhill.ca/college/jordan) for suggestions on where to find information on recent financial market events. We will suggest other sites later in the chapter.

Not everyone agrees on the value of studying history. On the one hand, there is philosopher George Santayana's famous comment, "Those who do not remember the past are condemned to repeat it." On the other hand, there is industrialist Henry Ford's equally famous comment, "History is more or less bunk." These extremes aside, perhaps everyone would agree with Mark Twain, who observed, with remarkable foresight, that "October. This is one of the peculiarly dangerous months to speculate in stocks in. The others are July, January, September, April, November, May, March, June, December, August, and February."

Two key observations emerge from a study of financial market history. First, there is a reward for bearing risk, and, at least on average, that reward has been substantial. That's the good news. The bad news is that greater rewards are accompanied by greater risks. The fact that risk and return go together is probably the single most important fact to understand about investments, and it is a point to which we will return many times.

1.1   Returns

We wish to discuss historical returns on different types of financial assets. First, we need to know how to compute the return from an investment. We will consider buying shares of stock in this section, but the basic calculations are the same for any investment.

Dollar Returns

If you buy an asset of any type, your gain (or loss) from that investment is called the *return* on your investment. This return will usually have two components. First, you may receive some cash directly while you own the investment. Second, the value of the asset you purchase may change. In this case, you have a capital gain or capital loss on your investment.[1]

To illustrate, suppose you purchased 100 shares of stock in Toronto Dominion Bank (TD) on January 1. At that time, TD was selling for $69 per share, so your 100 shares cost you $6,900. At the end of the year, you want to see how you did with your investment.

The first thing to consider is that over the year, a company may pay cash dividends to its shareholders. As a shareholder in TD, you are a part owner of the company, and you are entitled to a portion of any money distributed. So if TD chooses to pay a dividend, you will receive some cash for every share you own.

---

[1]As a practical matter, what is and what is not a capital gain (or loss) is determined by the Canada Revenue Agency. Even so, as is commonly done, we use these terms to refer to a change in value.

In addition to the dividend, the other part of your return is the capital gain or loss on the stock. This part arises from changes in the value of your investment. For example, consider these cash flows:

Our favourite investments website is Finance Yahoo! at ca.finance.yahoo. com
Visit this site and look around!

	Case 1	Case 2
Ending Stock Price	**$74.00**	**$65.00**
January 1 value	$6,900	$6,900
December 31 value	7,400	6,500
Dividend income	150	150
Capital gain or loss	500	−400

At the beginning of the year, on January 1, the stock is selling for $69 per share, and as we calculated above, your total outlay for 100 shares is $6,900. Over the year, Toronto-Dominion pays dividends of $1.50 per share. By the end of the year, then, you received dividend income of

$$\text{Dividend income} = \$1.50 \times 100 = \$150$$

As in Case 1, suppose that as of December 31, Toronto-Dominion was selling for $74, meaning that the value of your stock increased by $5 per share. Your 100 shares are now worth $7,400, so you have a capital gain of

$$\text{Capital gain} = (\$74.00 - \$69.00) \times 100 = \$500$$

On the other hand, if the price had dropped to, say, $65 (Case 2), you would have a capital loss of

$$\text{Capital loss} = (\$65.00 - \$69.00) \times 100 = -\$400$$

Notice that a capital loss is the same thing as a negative capital gain.

total dollar return
The return on an investment measured in dollars that accounts for all cash flows and capital gains or losses.

The **total dollar return** on your investment is the sum of the dividend and the capital gain (or loss):

$$\text{Total dollar return} = \text{Dividend income} + \text{Capital gain (or loss)}$$

In our first example here, the total dollar return is thus given by

$$\text{Total dollar return} = \$150 + \$500 = \$650$$

Overall, between the dividends you received and the increase in the price of the stock, the value of your investment increased from $6,900 to $6,900 + $650 = $7,550.

A common misconception often arises in this context. Suppose you hold on to your TD stock and don't sell it at the end of the year. Should you still consider the capital gain as part of your return? Isn't this only a "paper" gain and not really a cash gain if you don't sell it?

The answer to the first question is a strong yes, and the answer to the second is an equally strong no. The capital gain is every bit as much a part of your return as the dividend, and you should certainly count it as part of your return. The fact that you decide to keep the stock and don't sell (you don't "realize" the gain) is irrelevant because you could have converted it to cash if you had wanted to. Whether you choose to do so is up to you.

After all, if you insist on converting your gain to cash, you could always sell the stock and immediately reinvest by buying the stock back. There is no difference between doing this and just not selling (assuming, of course, that there are no transaction costs or tax consequences from selling the stock). Again, the point is that whether you actually cash out and buy pizzas (or whatever) or continue to hold the investment doesn't affect the return you actually earn.

Percentage Returns

It is usually more convenient to summarize information about returns in percentage terms than in dollar terms, because that way your return doesn't depend on how much you actually invested. With percentage returns the question we want to answer is: How much do we get *for each dollar* we invest?

To answer this question, let P_t be the price of the stock at the beginning of the year and let D_{t+1} be the dividend paid on the stock during the year. The following cash flows are the same as those shown earlier, except that we have now expressed everything on a per-share basis:

	Case 1	Case 2
Ending Stock Price	**$74.00**	**$65.00**
January 1 value	$69.00	$69.00
December 31 value	74.00	65.00
Dividend income	1.50	1.50
Capital gain or loss	5.00	−4.00

In our example, the price at the beginning of the year was $69 per share and the dividend paid during the year on each share was $1.50. If we express this dividend as a percentage of the beginning stock price, the result is the **dividend yield**:

$$\text{Dividend yield} = D_{t+1} / P_t \qquad (1.1)$$
$$= \$1.50 / \$69 = 0.02174 = 2.17\%$$

dividend yield The annual stock dividend as a percentage of the initial stock price.

This says that for each dollar we invested we received 2.17 cents in dividends.

The second component of our percentage return is the **capital gains yield**. This yield is calculated as the change in the price during the year (the capital gain) divided by the beginning price. With the $74 ending price, we get:

$$\text{Capital gains yield} = (P_{t+1} - P_t) / P_t \qquad (1.2)$$
$$= (\$74 - \$69) / \$69$$
$$= \$5 / \$69 = 0.0725 = 7.25\%$$

capital gains yield The change in stock price as a percentage of the initial stock price.

This 7.25 percent yield means that for each dollar invested we got 7.25 cents in capital gains.

Putting it all together, per dollar invested, we get 2.17 cents in dividends and 7.25 cents in capital gains for a total of 9.42 cents. Our **total percent return** is 9.42 cents on the dollar, or 9.42 percent. When a return is expressed on a percentage

total percent return The return on an investment measured as a percentage that accounts for all cash flows and capital gains or losses.

WORK THE WEB

To look up information on common stocks using the Web, you need to know the "ticker" symbol. You can look up ticker symbols in many places, including ca.finance.yahoo.com. Here we have looked up (using the "Symbol Lookup" link) and entered ticker symbols for some well-known "tech" stocks:

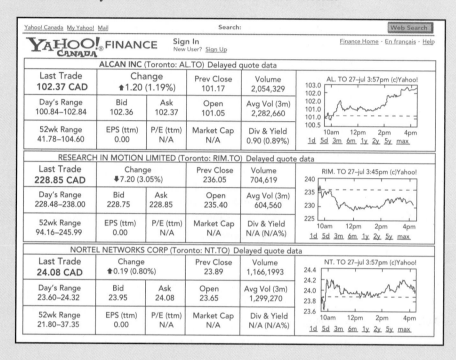

As you can see, we get the price for each stock, along with information about the change in price and volume (the number of shares traded).

basis, we often refer to it as the *rate of return*, or just "return," on the investment. Notice that if we combine the formulas for the dividend yield and capital gains yield, we get a single formula for the total percentage return:

$$\text{Percentage return} = \text{Dividend yield} + \text{Capital gains yield} \qquad (1.3)$$
$$= D_{t+1} / P_t + (P_{t+1} - P_t) / P_t$$
$$= (D_{t+1} + P_{t+1} - P_t) / P_t$$

To check our calculations, notice that we invested $6,900 and ended up with $7,550. By what percentage did our $6,900 increase? As we saw, we picked up $7,550 − $6,900 = $650. This is an increase of $650 / $6,900, or 9.42 percent.

CALCULATING PERCENTAGE RETURNS

EXAMPLE 1.1

Suppose you buy some stock for $25 per share. After one year, the price is $35 per share. During the year, you received a $2 dividend per share. What is the dividend yield? The capital gains yield? The percentage return? If your total investment was $1,000, how much do you have at the end of the year?

Your $2 dividend per share works out to a dividend yield of

$$\textbf{Dividend yield} = D_{t+1} / P_t$$
$$= \$2 / \$25$$
$$= 8\%$$

The per-share capital gain is $10, so the capital gains yield is

$$\textbf{Capital gains yield} = (P_{t+1} - P_t) / P_t$$
$$= (\$35 - \$25) / \$25$$
$$= \$10 / \$25$$
$$= 40\%$$

The total percentage return is thus 8% + 40% = 48%.

If you had invested $1,000, you would have $1,480 at the end of the year. To check this, note that your $1,000 would have bought you $1,000 / $25 = 40 shares. Your 40 shares would then have paid you a total of 40 × $2 = $80 in cash dividends. Your $10 per share gain would give you a total capital gain of $10 × 40 = $400. Add these together and you get $480, which is a 48 percent total return on your $1,000 investment.

Now that you know how to calculate returns on a hypothetical stock, you should begin looking at real stocks. The nearby *Work the Web* box describes how to get going. Meanwhile, in the next several sections, we will take a look at the returns that some common types of investments have earned over the last 25 years.

CHECK THIS

1.1a   What are the two parts of total return?

1.1b   Why are unrealized capital gains or losses included in the calculation of returns?

1.1c   What is the difference between a dollar return and a percentage return? Why are percentage returns usually more convenient?

1.2   The Historical Record

We now examine year-to-year historical rates of return on three important categories of financial investments. These returns can be interpreted as what you would have earned if you had invested in portfolios of the following asset categories:

1. Large-company stocks. The large-company stock portfolio is based on Toronto's S&P/TSX 60 Index, which contains 60 of the largest companies (in terms of total market value of outstanding stock) in Canada.

Annual historical financial market data can be downloaded at www.statcan.ca Another good site to examine financial performance of various investment instruments is the Globeinvestor site at www.globeinvestor.com

2. Canadian Treasury bills. This is a portfolio of Treasury bills (T-bills) with a three-month maturity.

3. Inflation data is obtained as changes in the consumer price indices from the Cansim database.

If you are not entirely certain what these investments are, don't be overly concerned. We will have much more to say about each in later chapters. For now, just take it as given that these are some of the things that you could have put your money into in years gone by. In addition to the year-to-year returns on these financial instruments, the year-to-year percentage changes in the Consumer Price Index (CPI) are also computed. The CPI is a standard measure of consumer goods price inflation.

Here is a bit of market jargon for you. A company's *total market capitalization* (or market "cap" for short) is equal to its stock price multiplied by the number of shares of stock. In other words, it's the total value of the company's stock. Large companies are often called "large-cap" stocks, and small companies are called "small-cap" stocks. We'll use these terms frequently.

A First Look

Figure 1.1 shows what happened to $1 invested in these different portfolios at the beginning of 1983 and held over the 25-year period ending in 2007.

Looking at Figure 1.1, we see that the S&P/TSX 60 index portfolio did the best overall. Every dollar invested grew to a remarkable $10.87 over the 25 years. At

FIGURE 1.1   **A $1 Investment in Different Types of Portfolios 1983–2007**

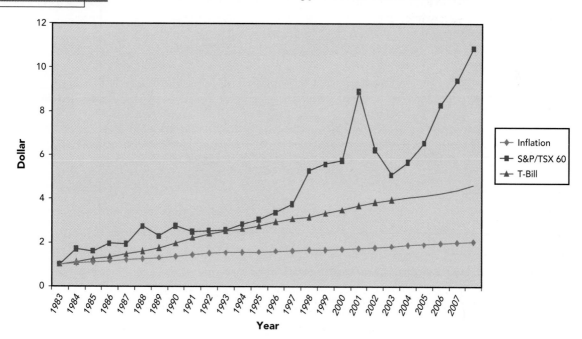

Source: Author calculations based on the data obtained from Datastream Database.

the other extreme, the T-bill portfolio grew to only $4.61. This is even less impressive when we consider the inflation over this period. As illustrated, the increase in the price level was such that $2.03 is needed just to replace the original $1.

Given the historical record, why would anybody buy anything other than stocks? If you look closely at Figure 1.1, you will probably see the answer—risk. The T-bill portfolio and long-term government bond portfolio grew more slowly than did the stock portfolio, but they grew more steadily.

What we see thus far is that there has been a powerful financial incentive for long-term investing. The real moral of the story is this: Get an early start!

A Closer Look

To illustrate the variability of different investments, Figures 1.2 through 1.4 plot the year-to-year percentage returns. You can see how predictably the Treasury bills (Figure 1.3) behaved compared to the stocks (Figure 1.2).

Looking at the graphs, we see, for example, that the largest single-year return for large stocks was 54.69 percent in 2000. In contrast, the largest Treasury bill return was 13.20 percent in 1990. For future reference, the actual year-to-year returns for the S&P/TSX 60, Treasury bills, and the CPI are shown in Table 1.1.

| FIGURE 1.2 | Year-to-Year Total Returns on Large-Company Stocks: 1983–2007 |

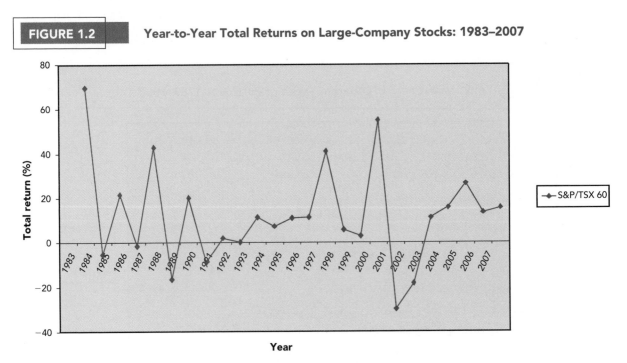

Source: Author calculations based on the data obtained from Datastream Database.

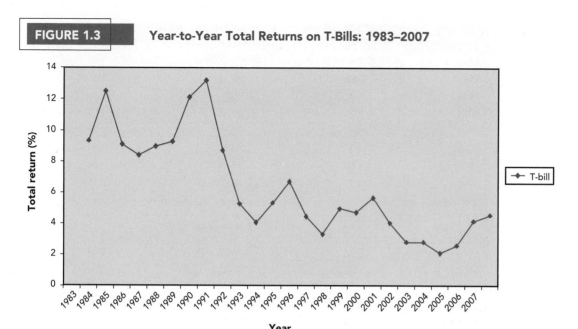

FIGURE 1.3   Year-to-Year Total Returns on T-Bills: 1983–2007

Source: Author calculations based on the data obtained from Datastream Database.

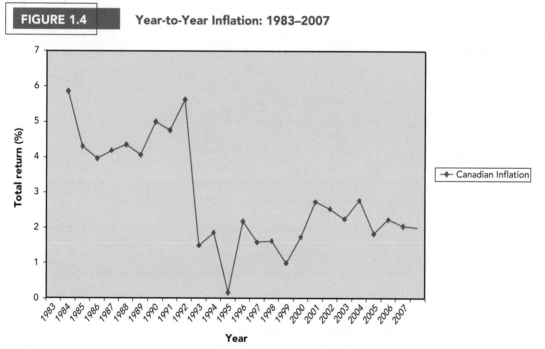

FIGURE 1.4   Year-to-Year Inflation: 1983–2007

Source: Author calculations based on the data obtained from Datastream Database.

TABLE 1.1	Year-to-Year Total Returns: 1983–2007		
Year	CPI/Inflation Rate	S&P/TSX 60	T-bill Annual Yield %
1983	5.86	69.33	9.31
1984	4.3	−5.51	12.5
1985	3.96	21.50	9.08
1986	4.18	−1.64	8.38
1987	4.34	42.66	8.94
1988	4.05	−16.50	9.26
1989	4.99	20.07	12.12
1990	4.76	−9.06	13.20
1991	5.62	2.06	8.68
1992	1.49	0.21	5.24
1993	1.86	11.23	4.06
1994	0.16	7.26	5.32
1995	2.17	11.05	6.68
1996	1.58	11.27	4.44
1997	1.62	40.81	3.29
1998	0.99	5.67	4.94
1999	1.73	2.98	4.71
2000	2.73	54.69	5.64
2001	2.53	−29.92	4.03
2002	2.25	−18.20	2.81
2003	2.77	11.14	2.81
2004	1.83	15.63	2.08
2005	2.23	26.44	2.59
2006	2.04	13.54	4.15
2007	2.01	15.60	4.54
Average	2.88	12.09	6.35
Std Dev.	1.52	22.43	3.26
Max.	5.86	69.33	13.20
Min.	0.16	−29.92	2.08

Source: Author calculations based on data obtained from Datastream Database.

CHECK THIS

1.2a With 20-20 hindsight, what was the best investment for the period 1983–2007?

1.2b Why doesn't everyone just buy stocks as investments?

1.2c What was the smallest return observed over the 25 years for each of these investments? Approximately when did it occur?

1.2d About how many times did large stocks (common stocks) return more than 30 percent? How many times did they return less than −20 percent?

1.2e What was the longest "winning streak" (years without a negative return) for large stocks?

1.2f How often did the T-bill portfolio have a negative return?

1.3 Average Returns: The First Lesson

As you've probably begun to notice, the history of financial market returns in an undigested form is complicated. What we need are simple measures to accurately summarize and describe all these numbers. Accordingly, we discuss how to go about condensing detailed numerical data. We start by calculating average returns.

Calculating Average Returns

The obvious way to calculate average returns on the different investments in Figures 1.2 to 1.4 is to simply add up the yearly returns and divide by 25. The result is the historical average of the individual values. For example, if you add the returns for large common stocks for the 25 years, you will get about 302.30 percent. The average annual return is thus 302.30 / 25 = 12.09 percent. You can interpret this 12.09 percent like any other average. If you picked a year at random from the 25-year history and you had to guess the return in that year, the best guess would be 12.09 percent.

Average Returns: The Historical Record and Comparison with U.S. Investment

Table 1.2 shows the average returns for the investments we have discussed. These averages don't reflect the impact of inflation. Notice that over the 25-year period the average inflation rate was 2.88 percent per year while the average return on Treasury bills exceeded the average rate of inflation by only 3.47 percent per year. At the other extreme, the return on large-cap common stocks exceeded the rate of inflation by a whopping 12.09% − 2.88% = 9.21%!

The nearby *Investment Updates* provides information on U.S. financial investment returns in bearish markets as well as 30-year annual long-term performance. U.S. large-company stocks provided 12.2 percent return which is approximately the same as Canadian large-company returns in the last 25 years.

Risk Premiums

Now that we have computed some average returns, it seems logical to see how they compare with each other. Based on our discussion above, one such comparison involves government-issued securities. These are free of much of the variability we see in, for example, the stock market.

The government borrows money by issuing debt securities, which come in different forms. The ones we focus on here are Treasury bills. Because these instruments have a very short investment life and because the government can always raise taxes or print money to pay its bills, at least in the short run, there is essentially no risk associated with buying them. Thus, we call the rate of return on such debt the **risk-free rate**, and we will use it as a kind of investing benchmark.

risk-free rate The rate of return on a riskless investment.

TABLE 1.2	Average Annual Returns: 1983–2007		
Investment	**Average**	**Maximum**	**Minimum**
Large Stocks	12.09	69.33	−29.92
Treasury Bills	6.35	13.20	2.08
Inflation	2.88	5.86	0.16

Source: Author calculations based on the data obtained from Datastream Database.

After 30 Years of Investing, Market Has No Sure Thing

The stock market exists to enrich investors, while utterly humiliating them. With great regularity, I receive e-mails from readers who are convinced that you should own only blue-chip companies, or only high-dividend stocks, or only technology companies. And all I can think about is the market's litany of once-sure things. It happens again and again. Hot stocks turn cold. Highflying stock funds crash and burn. Time-tested stock-picking strategies suddenly falter. To understand just how capricious the market can be, consider results from the past three decades.

As the Decades Turn

Take a look at the accompanying table (Swings and Roundabouts), which shows returns calculated by Baltimore's T. Rowe Price Associates using data from Chicago's Ibbotson Associates. In particular, focus on the performance of large, small and foreign stocks in each of the past three decades. I think of these as the three key stock-market sectors.

As you will see, large-company stocks—which are so beloved after their dazzling gains in the 1990s—didn't fare quite so well in the prior two decades. They ranked second behind foreign stocks in the 1980s and they lagged behind both small and foreign stocks in the 1970s. Similarly, small stocks ranked first in the 1970s, second in the 1990s and third in the 1980s. Meanwhile, foreign stocks were first in the 1980s, second in the 1970s and third in the 1990s.

In other words, none of the sectors consistently ranked as the top performer and all had periods of dreadful performance. Moreover, if you look at results for the 30 years through December 2001, there isn't a huge difference between the average annual returns for large, small and foreign stocks. Of course, if you were really clever, you would figure out which sector was going to be the decade's top performer, and then invest everything in

that sector. But I am not smart enough to make that sort of market call, and I don't think anybody else is, either.

Gerald Perritt, a money manager in Largo, Fla., and editor of the Mutual Fund Letter, a monthly newsletter, says he has lately met many investors who got themselves into financial trouble. All have one thing in common: They failed to diversify and instead made big investment bets that turned sour. "Diversification is good," Mr. Perritt says. "But if it's so good, why don't more people practice it? Return is the most visible element in the investing process. The least visible is risk. People see the return they miss by diversifying. We don't think about what will happen if a big bet goes in the wrong direction."

My hunch is that the current decade will be a lackluster one for blue-chip shares. Large-company stocks have been dazzling performers over the past two decades, and now they are burdened by lofty share price-to-earnings multiples and boast only skimpy dividend yields. Indeed, I suspect foreign and small stocks will prove to be the market's new darlings. But I am unwilling to invest based on such hunches. So what should an investor do? Owning a little bit of everything has worked well in the past, and it still seems like a mighty fine strategy to me.

Glancing at the performance of narrower market sectors strengthens the case for humility. In the past two years, three of the market's best-performing segments have been gold, bargain-priced "value" stocks and real-estate investment trusts, or REITs. Meanwhile, "growth" stocks, including once-sparkling technology shares, have been crushed. But look at the accompanying table to see results from earlier decades. Unfortunately, data aren't available for all time periods. Still, there are enough results to see how unpredictable market returns can be. Sure, value stocks were strong performers in 2000 and 2001. But they lagged behind growth stocks in the 1990s. True, REITs have generated great results recently. But they didn't do much better than intermediate-term

(continued)

risk premium The extra return on a risky asset over the risk-free rate; the reward for bearing risk.

A particularly interesting comparison involves the virtually risk-free return on T-bills and the risky return on common stocks. The difference between these two returns can be interpreted as a measure of the **risk premium** on the average risky asset. We call this the risk premium because it is the additional return we earn by moving from a risk-free investment to a typical risky one, and we interpret it as a reward for bearing risk.

The First Lesson

From the data in Table 1.2, we can calculate risk premiums for the three different categories of investments. The results are shown in Table 1.3. Notice that the risk

Swings and Roundabouts

All market sectors enjoy periods of dazzling gains. But none performs well all the time.

| | Bear Markets | | Long-Run Annual Performance | | | |
	1973–74	2000–01	1970s	1980s	1990s	30 Years*
Large-company stocks	−42.6%	−29.3%	5.9%	17.6%	18.2%	12.2%
Small-company stocks	−43.2	−19.4	11.5	15.8	15.1	14.9
Foreign markets	−35.2	−36.6	10.1	22.8	7.3	11.2
Growth stocks	NA	−42.2	NA	16.3	20.6	NA
Value stocks	NA	−13.4	NA	18.3	15.4	NA
Real-estate trusts	−52.6	35.2	NA	12.5	8.1	9.4
Intermediate bonds	4.9	19.4	7.0	11.9	7.2	8.5
Treasury bills	13.5	7.9	6.3	8.9	4.9	6.7
Gold	133.1	5.9	30.7	−2.5	−3.1	6.4

*Through December 31, 2001.

Note: All returns are annualized, except for the two bear markets, for which cumulative performance is shown.

NA: Not available.

government bonds in the 1990s. And gold? You have to go back to the 1970s to find a decent decade for the yellow metal.

When the Bear Growls

To get a handle on down-market performance, I had T. Rowe Price calculate returns for the two most-searing bear markets of recent decades, the 1973–74 debacle and the 2000–01 tech wreck. In both stock-market declines, gold, bonds and Treasury bills posted gains, even as other sectors were crushed. Clearly, if you want a little bear-market protection, these are good assets to own.

But how did different stock-market sectors fare? Consider the 1973–74 crash. The two hardest-hit sectors were REITs and small-company stocks. If you were worried about a bear market and you had taken your cues from the 1973–74 crash, you would have avoided

both sectors. Yet REITs, the hardest-hit sector in the 1973–74 crash, were the biggest winners in the recent bear market. Small-company stocks, meanwhile, didn't perform quite so impressively in the 2000–01 market decline. Nonetheless, they lost far less money than large-company stocks.

As the data make clear, there aren't many sure things in investing. But that doesn't mean you can't make good money over time. If you simply build a well-diversified portfolio and hang on for the long haul, history suggests you will be handsomely rewarded. "Here's a 30-year period that includes two grueling bear markets and one awful decade, the 1970s," notes Steven Norwitz, a T. Rowe Price vice president. "But if you invested through the whole period, you got pretty attractive returns."

Source: Jonathan Clements, The Wall Street Journal, April 28, 2002.

premium on T-bills is shown as zero in the table because they are our riskless benchmark. Looking at Table 1.3, we see that the average risk premium earned by the large-cap common stock portfolio is 12.09% − 6.35% = 5.74%. This is a significant reward. The fact that it exists historically is an important observation, and it is the basis for our first lesson: Risky assets, on average, earn a risk premium. Put another way, there is a reward, on average, for bearing risk.

Why is this so? Why, for example, is the risk premium for stocks so much larger than the risk premium for bonds? More generally, what determines the relative sizes of the risk premiums for the different assets? These questions speak to the heart of the

TABLE 1.3	Average Annual Returns and Risk Premiums: 1983–2007	
Investment	Average	Risk Premium
Large Stocks	12.09	5.74
Treasury Bills	6.35	0.00
Inflation	2.88	0.00

Source: Author calculations based on the data obtained from Datastream Database.

modern theory of investments, and we will discuss the issues involved many times in the chapters ahead. For now, part of the answer can be found by looking at the historical variability of returns of these different investments. So, to get started, we now turn our attention to measuring variability in returns.

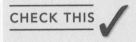

CHECK THIS

1.3a   What is a risk premium?

1.3b   What was the historical risk premium on common stocks?

1.3c   What is the first lesson from financial market history?

1.4   Return Variability: The Second Lesson

We have already seen that year-to-year returns on common stocks tend to be more volatile than returns on, say, T-bills. We now discuss how to measure this variability so we can begin examining the important subject of risk.

Frequency Distributions and Variability

To get started, we can draw a *frequency distribution* for large-company stock returns like the one in Figure 1.5. What we have done here is to count the number of times that an annual return on the large-company stock portfolio falls within each 10 percent range. For example, in Figure 1.5, the height of 5 for the bar within the interval of 0 percent to 10 percent means that 5 of the 25 annual returns are in that range. Notice also that most of the returns are in the −10 to 40 percent range.

FIGURE 1.5   **Frequency Distribution of Returns on Common Stocks: 1983–2007**

				2007					
				2006					
			1999	2004					
			1998	2003					
		1990	1994	1996	2005				
	2002	1986	1992	1995	1989		1997		
2001	1988	1984	1991	1993	1985		1987	2000	1983

−30   −20   −10   0   10   20   30   40   50   60

Source: Author calculations based on the data obtained from Datastream Database.

What we need to do now is to actually measure the spread in these returns. We know, for example, that the return on the S&P/TSX 60 index of common stocks in a typical year was 12.09 percent. We now want to know by how much the actual return differs from this average in a typical year. In other words, we need a measure of returns volatility. The **variance** and its square root, the **standard deviation**, are the most commonly used measures of volatility. We briefly review how to calculate these next. If you've already studied basic statistics, you should notice that we are simply calculating an ordinary sample variance and standard deviation, just as you may have done many times before.

variance A common measure of volatility.

standard deviation The square root of the variance.

The Historical Variance and Standard Deviation

Variance measures the average squared difference between the actual returns and the average return. The bigger this number is, the more the actual returns tend to differ from the average return. To illustrate how we calculate historical variance, suppose a particular investment had returns of 10 percent, 12 percent, 3 percent, and −9 percent over the last four years. The average return is $(10\% + 12\% + 3\% − 9\%) / 4 = 4\%$.

Notice that the return is never actually equal to 4 percent. Instead, the first return deviates from the average by $10\% − 4\% = 6\%$, the second return deviates from the average by $12\% − 4\% = 8\%$, and so on. To compute the variance, we square each of these deviations, add them up, and divide the result by the number of returns less one, or three in this case.[2] These calculations are summarized immediately below.

For an easy-to-read review of basic statistics, see www.robertniles. com/stats/

$$(10 − 4)^2 = 36$$
$$(12 − 4)^2 = 64$$
$$(3 − 4)^2 = 1$$
$$(−9 − 4)^2 = \underline{169}$$
$$270 \quad \rightarrow \quad \rightarrow \quad 270 / 3 = 90$$

To recap, we first calculate the differences between actual returns and their average by subtracting out 4 percent. Second, we square each difference. Third, we sum all squared deviations to get 270. Finally, we divide the sum of the squared deviations by $4 − 1 = 3$.

By these calculations we get $Var(R)$ or σ^2 (read this as "sigma squared"), which is the variance of the return:

$$Var(R) = \sigma^2 = 270 / (4 − 1) = 90$$

The standard deviation is the square root of the variance. So, if $SD(R)$ or σ stands for the standard deviation of return:

$$SD(R) = \sigma = \sqrt{90} = 9.487\%$$

The square root of the variance is used because the variance is measured in "squared" percentages and is hard to interpret. The standard deviation is an ordinary percentage, which here is 9.487 percent.

---

[2]The reason for dividing by $N − 1$ rather than simply N is based on statistical sampling theory, which is beyond the scope of this book. Just remember that to calculate a variance about a sample average divide the sum of squared deviations from the average by $N − 1$.

In general, if we have N historical returns, where N is some number, we can write the historical variance as:

$$Var(R) = [(R_1 - \overline{R})^2 + (R_2 - \overline{R})^2 + \ldots + (R_N - \overline{R})^2] / (N - 1) \qquad (1.4)$$

This formula tells us to do just what we did above: Take each of the N individual returns $(R_1, R_2, \ldots, R_N)$ and subtract the average return, $\overline{R}$; then square the results, and add them all up; finally, divide this total by the number of returns less one $(N - 1)$. The standard deviation is always the square root of $Var(R)$.

CALCULATING THE VARIANCE AND STANDARD DEVIATION

EXAMPLE 1.2

Calculate return averages, variances, and standard deviations for S&P/TSX 60 large-cap stocks and T-bills using data for the first five years in Table 1.1, 1983–1987.

First, calculate return averages as follows:

S&P/TSX Large Company Stocks	T-Bills
69.33	9.31
−5.51	12.50
21.50	9.08
−1.64	8.38
42.66	8.94
126.34	48.21
Average Return: 126.34 / 5 = 25.27	48.21 / 5 = 9.64

Using the averages above, calculate the squared deviations from the average returns and sum the squared deviations as follows:

S&P/TSX Large Company Stocks	T-Bills
$(69.33 - 25.27)^2 = 1941.46$	$(9.31 - 9.64)^2 = 0.11$
$(-5.51 - 25.27)^2 = 947.29$	$(12.50 - 9.64)^2 = 8.17$
$(21.50 - 25.27)^2 = 14.20$	$(9.08 - 9.64)^2 = 0.32$
$(-1.64 - 25.27)^2 = 724.04$	$(8.38 - 9.64)^2 = 1.59$
$(42.56 - 25.27)^2 = 302.48$	$(8.94 - 9.64)^2 = 0.49$
3929.47	10.68

Calculate return variances by dividing the sums of squared deviations by four, the number of returns less one.

S&P/TSX 60: 3929.4 / 4 = 982.37   **T-Bills: 10.68 / 4 = 2.67**

Standard deviations are then calculated as the square root of the variance:

S&P/TSX 60: $\sqrt{982.37} = 31.34$ **T-Bills: $\sqrt{2.67} = 1.63$**

Notice that the large-company stock portfolio had a volatility almost 15 times greater than the T-bills, which is not unusual during periods of market turbulence.

The Historical Record

Figure 1.6 summarizes much of our discussions of capital market history so far. It displays the average returns and standard deviations of annual returns. In Figure 1.6, notice, for example, that the standard deviation for the large stock portfolio (22.43 percent per year) is more than 6 times larger than the T-bill portfolio's standard deviation (3.26 percent per year).

Normal Distribution

normal distribution
A symmetric, bell-shaped frequency distribution that is completely defined by its average and standard deviation.

For many different random events in nature, a particular frequency distribution, the **normal distribution** (or *bell curve*), is useful for describing the probability of ending up in a given range. For example, the idea behind "grading on a curve" comes from the fact that exam scores often resemble a bell curve.

Figure 1.7 illustrates a normal distribution and its distinctive bell shape. As you can see, this distribution has a much cleaner appearance than the actual return distributions illustrated in Figure 1.5. Even so, like the normal distribution, the actual distributions do appear to be at least roughly mound shaped and symmetric. When this is true, the normal distribution is often a very good approximation.

Also, keep in mind that the distributions in Figure 1.6 are based on only 25 yearly observations, while Figure 1.7 is, in principle, based on an infinite number. So, if we had been able to observe returns for, say, 1,000 years, we might have filled in a lot of the irregularities and ended up with a much smoother picture. For our purposes, it is enough to observe that the returns are at least roughly normally distributed.

FIGURE 1.6

Historical Returns, Standard Deviations

Source: Author calculations based on the data obtained from Datastream Database.

	Average Return	Standard Deviation
Large-company stocks	12.09	22.43
Treasury bills	6.35	3.26
Inflation	2.88	1.52

FIGURE 1.7

The Normal Distribution Illustrated Returns Based on the Historical Return and Standard Deviation for a Portfolio of Large Common Stocks

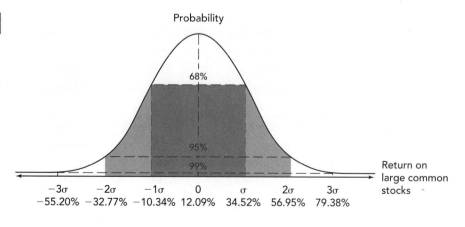

The usefulness of the normal distribution stems from the fact that it is completely described by the average and the standard deviation. If you have these two numbers, then there is nothing else to know. For example, with a normal distribution, the probability that we end up within one standard deviation of the average is about $^2/_3$. The probability that we end up within two standard deviations is about 95 percent. Finally, the probability of being more than three standard deviations away from the average is less than 1 percent. These ranges and the probabilities are illustrated in Figure 1.7.

To see why this is useful, recall from Figure 1.6 that the standard deviation of returns on the large common stocks is 22.43 percent. The average return is 12.09 percent. So assuming that the frequency distribution is at least approximately normal, the probability that the return in a given year is in the range of −10.34 percent to 34.52 percent (12.09 percent plus or minus one standard deviation, 22.43 percent) is about $^2/_3$. This range is illustrated in Figure 1.7. In other words, there is about one chance in three that the return will be *outside* this range. This literally tells you that, if you buy stocks in large companies, you should expect to be outside this range in one year out of every three. This reinforces our earlier observations about stock market volatility. However, there is only a 5 percent chance (approximately) that we would end up outside the range of −32.77 percent to 56.95 percent (12.09 percent plus or minus 2 × 22.43%). These points are also illustrated in Figure 1.7.

The Second Lesson

Our observations concerning the year-to-year variability in returns are the basis for our second lesson from capital market history. On average, bearing risk is handsomely rewarded, but, in a given year, there is a significant chance of a dramatic change in value. Thus, our second lesson is this: The greater the potential reward, the greater is the risk.

Thus far in this chapter, we have emphasized the year-to-year variability in returns. We should note that even day-to-day movements can exhibit considerable volatility. For example, not long ago, on September 17, 2001, the Dow Jones Industrial Average (DJIA) plummeted 684.81 points, or 7.13 percent. By historical standards, it was a bad day for the 30 stocks that comprise the DJIA (as well as for a majority of stocks in the market). Still, while the drop was the largest one-day decrease in the DJIA ever in terms of points, it actually wasn't quite in the top 12 largest one-day percentage decreases in history, as illustrated in the following table:

Top 12 One-Day Percentage Declines in the Dow-Jones Industrial Average			
December 12, 1914	−24.4%	August 12, 1932	−8.4%
October 19, 1987	−22.6	March 14, 1907	−8.3
October 28, 1929	−12.8	October 26, 1987	−8.0
October 29, 1929	−11.7	July 21, 1933	−7.8
November 6, 1929	−9.9	October 18, 1937	−7.7
December 18, 1899	−8.7	February 1, 1917	−7.2

Source: *Dow Jones.*

This discussion highlights the importance of looking at returns in terms of percentages rather than dollar amounts or index points. For example, prior to 2001, the biggest one-day loss in terms of points was on April 14, 2000, when the DJIA declined by 618 points. The second worst was the 554-point drop of October 27, 1987. By contrast, the 5.57-point drop in the DJIA on December 18, 1899, marked the fifth worst day in the history of the index, but a 5.6-point loss in the DJIA in today's market would hardly be noticed. This is precisely why we relied on percentage returns when we examined market history in this chapter.[3]

INVESTING IN GROWTH STOCKS

EXAMPLE 1.3

As a practical matter, the phrase *growth stock* is frequently a euphemism for small-company stock. Are such investments suitable for "widows and orphans"? Before answering, you should consider historical volatility. For example, from the historical record, what is the approximate probability that you will actually lose 12 percent or more of your money in a single year if you buy stocks from a group of such companies?

The historical average return on a small-company stock portfolio is about 13.28 percent, with an annual standard deviation of about 22.72 percent. From our rule of thumb, there is about a $\frac{1}{3}$ probability that you will experience a return outside the range −9.44 percent to 36 percent (−22.72% + 13.28% to 22.72% + 13.28%).

The odds of being above or below this range are about equal. There is thus about a $\frac{1}{6}$ chance (half of $\frac{1}{3}$) that you will lose more than 12 percent. So you should expect this to happen once in every six years, on average. Such investments can thus be very volatile, and they are not well-suited for those who cannot afford to bear the risk.

Now that you know how to calculate and, more importantly, interpret average returns and standard deviations, the nearby *Spreadsheet Analysis* box shows how to do the calculations using Excel, which can really speed up things when we have a lot of data.

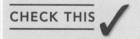

CHECK THIS

1.4a In words, how do we calculate a variance? A standard deviation?

1.4b What is the first lesson from financial market history? The second lesson?

---

[3]By the way, as you may have noticed, what's kind of weird is that 6 of the 12 worst days in the history of the DJIA occurred in October, including the top 3. We have no clue as to why. Furthermore, looking back at the Mark Twain quote near the beginning of the chapter, how do you suppose he knew? Sounds like a case for the X-Files.

SPREADSHEET ANALYSIS

Using a Spreadsheet to Calculate Average Returns and Volatilities

Here is an Excel spreadsheet summarizing the formulas and analysis needed to calculate average returns and standard deviations using the 1990s as an example.

	A	B	C	D	E	F	G	H
1								
2			Using a Spreadsheet to Calculate Average Returns and Standard Deviations					
3								
4	We will calculate the average returns and standard deviations for this period. Here are the							
5	year-by-year returns on S&P/TSX 60 Index.							
6								
7		Year	Return (%)	Year	Return (%)			
8		1990	−9.06	1995	11.05			
9		1991	2.06	1996	11.27			
10		1992	0.21	1997	40.81			
11		1993	11.05	1998	5.67			
12		1994	7.26	1999	2.98			
13								
14		Average return (%):		8.35				
15		Standard Deviation (%):		13.01				
16								
17	The formulas we used to do the calculations are = AVERAGE(F13:F22)							
18	and = STDEV(F13:F22).							

Source: Datastream Database.

1.5   More on Average Returns

Thus far in this chapter, we have looked closely at simple average returns. But there is another way of computing an average return. The fact that average returns are calculated two different ways leads to some confusion, so our goal in this section is to explain the two approaches and also the circumstances under which each is appropriate.

Arithmetic versus Geometric Averages

Let's start with a simple example. Suppose you buy a particular stock for $100. Unfortunately, the first year you own it, it falls to $50. The second year you own it, it rises back to $100, leaving you where you started (no dividends were paid).

What was your average return on this investment? Common sense seems to say that your average return must be exactly zero since you started with $100 and ended with $100. But if we calculate the returns year-by-year, we see that you lost 50 percent the first year (you lost half of your money). The second year, you made 100 percent (you doubled your money). Your average return over the two years was thus (−50% + 100%) / 2 = 25%!

geometric average return The average compound return earned per year over a multiyear period.

arithmetic average return The return earned in an average year over a multiyear period.

So which is correct, 0 percent or 25 percent? The answer is that both are correct; they just answer different questions. The 0 percent is called the **geometric average return**. The 25 percent is called the **arithmetic average return**. The geometric average return answers the question "*What was your average compound return per year over a particular period?*" The arithmetic average return answers the question "*What was your return in an average year over a particular period?*"

Notice that, in previous sections, the average returns we calculated were all arithmetic averages, so we already know how to calculate them. What we need to do now is (1) learn how to calculate geometric averages and (2) learn the circumstances under which one average is more meaningful than the other.

Calculating Geometric Average Returns

First, to illustrate how we calculate a geometric average return, suppose a particular investment had annual returns of 10 percent, 12 percent, 3 percent, and −9 percent over the last four years. The geometric average return over this four-year period is calculated as $(1.10 \times 1.12 \times 1.03 \times .91)^{1/4} - 1 = 3.66\%$. In contrast, the average arithmetic return we have been calculating is $(.10 + .12 + .03 - .09) / 4 = 4.0\%$.

In general, if we have N years of returns, the geometric average return over these N years is calculated using this formula:

$$\text{Geometric average return} = [(1+R_1) \times (1+R_2) \times \ldots \times (1+R_N)]^{1/N} - 1 \quad (1.5)$$

This formula tells us that four steps are required:

1. Take each of the N annual returns $R_1, R_2, \ldots, R_N$ and add a one to each (after converting them to decimals!).
2. Multiply all the numbers from step 1 together.
3. Take the result from step 2 and raise it to the power of $1/N$.
4. Finally, subtract one from the result of step 3. The result is the geometric average return.

CALCULATING THE GEOMETRIC AVERAGE RETURN

EXAMPLE 1.4

Calculate the geometric average return for S&P/TSX 60 stocks for the first five years in Table 1.1, 1983–1987.

First, convert percentages to decimal returns, add one, and then calculate their product.

S&P/TSX 60 Returns	Product
69.33	1.6933
−5.51	× 0.9449
21.50	× 1.2150
−1.64	× 0.9836
42.66	× 1.4266
	2.727845

(continued)

Notice that the number 2.7278 is what our investment is worth after five years if we started with a one dollar investment. The geometric return is then calculated as

Geometric average return = 2.7278$^{1/5}$ − 1 = 0.2223 or 22.23%.

Thus the geometric average return is about 22.23 percent in this example. In contrast, in Example 1.2, the average arithmetic return was calculated as 25.27 percent. Here is a tip: if you are using a financial calculator, you can put $1 in as the present value, $2.7228 as the future value, and 5 as the number of periods. Then, solve for the unknown rate. You should get the same answer we did.

One thing you may have noticed in our examples thus far is that the geometric average returns seem to be smaller. It turns out that this will always be true (as long as the returns are not all identical, in which case the two "averages" would be the same). To illustrate, Table 1.4 shows the arithmetic averages and standard deviations from Figure 1.6, along with the geometric average returns.

As shown in Table 1.4, the geometric averages are generally smaller, but the magnitude of the difference varies quite a bit. The reason is that the difference is greater for more volatile investments. In fact, there is useful approximation. Assuming all the numbers are expressed in decimals (as opposed to percentages), the geometric average return is approximately equal to the arithmetic average return minus half the variance. For example, looking at the large-company stocks, the arithmetic average is 0.1209 and the standard deviation is 0.2243, implying that the variance is 0.0503. The approximate geometric average is thus 0.1209 − 0.0503/2 = 0.09575, which is close to the actual value.

MORE GEOMETRIC AVERAGES

EXAMPLE 1.5

In Figure 1.1, the large company investment grew to $10.8653 over 25 years. The geometric average return is thus

Geometric average return = 10.8653$^{1/25}$ − 1 = 0.1001 or 10.01%.

This 10.01% is the value shown in Table 1.4.

Arithmetic Average Return or Geometric Average Return?

When we look at historical returns, the difference between the geometric and arithmetic average returns isn't too hard to understand. To put it slightly differently, the geometric

TABLE 1.4	Geometric versus Arithmetic Average Returns: 1983–2007		
Series	**Geometric Mean**	**Arithmetic Mean**	**Standard Deviation**
Large-company stocks	10.01	12.09	22.43
Treasury bills	6.30	6.35	3.26
Inflation	2.87	2.88	1.52

Source: Author calculations based on the data obtained from Datastream Database.

average tells you what you actually earned per year on average, compounded annually. The arithmetic average tells you what you earned in a typical year. You should use whichever one answers the question you want answered.

A somewhat trickier question concerns forecasting the future, and there's a lot of confusion about this point among analysts and financial planners. The problem is this. If we have *estimates* of both the arithmetic and geometric average returns, then the arithmetic average is probably too high for longer periods and the geometric average is probably too low for shorter periods.

This concludes our discussion of geometric versus arithmetic averages. One last note: In the future, when we say "average return," we mean arithmetic average unless we explicitly say otherwise.

CHECK THIS 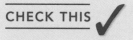   **1.5**   Over a five-year period, an investment in a broad market index yielded annual returns of 10, 16, −5, −8, and 7 percent. What were the arithmetic and geometric average annual returns for this index?

A Note on Annualizing Returns

We've talked about the need to compute percentage returns, but, so far, we've only considered annual returns. Of course, the actual length of time you own an investment will almost never be exactly a year. To compare investments, however, we will usually need to express returns on a per-year or "annualized" basis, so we need to do a little bit more work.

For example, suppose you bought 200 shares of Scotiabank at a price of $50 per share. In three months, you sell your stock for $54. You didn't receive any dividends. What is your return for the three months? What is your annualized return?

In this case, we say that your *holding period*, which is the length of time you own the stock, is three months. The percentage return can be calculated as:

$$\text{Percentage return} = (P_{t+1} - P_t) / P_t = (\$54 - \$50) / \$50 = 0.0800 = 8.00\%$$

This 8.00 percent is your return for the three-month holding period, but what does this return amount to on a per-year basis? To find out, we need to convert this to an annualized return, meaning a return expressed on a per-year basis. Such a return is often **effective annual** called an **effective annual return**, or EAR for short. The general formula is this:

return (EAR) The
return on an
investment expressed
on a per-year, or
"annualized," basis.

$$1 + EAR = (1 + \text{holding period percentage return})^m \qquad (1.6)$$

where m is the number of holding periods in a year.

In our example, the holding period percentage return is 8.00 percent, or 0.0800. The holding period is three months, so there are four (12 months / 3 months) periods in a year. The annualized return, or *EAR*, is thus:

$$1 + EAR = (1 + \text{holding period percentage return})^m$$
$$= (1 + 0.0800)^4$$
$$= 1.3605$$

So, your annualized return is 36.05 percent.

A "RIM" FOR RETURNS

EXAMPLE 1.6

Suppose you buy some stock in RIM at a price of $77 per share. Four months later, you sell it for $81. No dividend is paid. What is your annualized return on this investment?

For the four-month holding period, your return is:

Percentage return $= (P_{t+1} - P_t) / P_t = (\$81 - \$77) / \$77 = 0.0519 = 5.19\%$

There are three four-month periods in a year, so the annualized return is:

$$1 + \textbf{\textit{EAR}} = (1 + \textbf{holding period percentage return})^m$$
$$= (1 + 0.0519)^3$$
$$= 1.1639$$

Subtracting the one, we get an annualized return of 0.1639 or 16.39 percent.

MORE ANNUALIZED RETURNS

EXAMPLE 1.7

Suppose you buy some stock in Enbridge Inc at a price of $34 per share. Two years later, you sell it for $40. No dividend is paid. What is your annualized return on this investment?

The situation here is a bit different because your holding period is now longer than a year, but the calculation is basically the same. For the two-year holding period, your return is:

Percentage return $= (P_{t+1} - P_t) / P_t = (\$40 - \$34) / \$34 = 0.1765 = 17.65\%$

How many two-year holding periods are there in a single year? The answer is one-half, so *m* in this case is 1/2. The annualized return is:

$$1 + \textbf{\textit{EAR}} = (1 + \textbf{holding period percentage return})^m$$
$$= (1 + 0.1765)^{1/2}$$
$$= 1.0847$$

Subtracting the one, we get an annualized return of 0.0847 or 8.47 percent.

1.6　Risk and Return

In previous sections we explored financial market history to see what we could learn about risk and return. In this section we summarize our findings and then conclude our discussion by looking ahead at the subjects we will be examining in later chapters.

The Risk-Return Trade-Off

Figure 1.8 is a way of putting together our findings on risk and return. What it shows is that there is a risk-return trade-off. At one extreme, if we are unwilling to bear any risk at all, but we are willing to forgo the use of our money for a while, then we can earn the risk-free rate. Because the risk-free rate represents compensation for just waiting, it is often called the *time value of money*.

If we are willing to bear risk, then we can expect to earn a risk premium, at least on average. Further, the more risk we are willing to bear, the greater is the risk

FIGURE 1.8	**Risk–Return Trade Off**

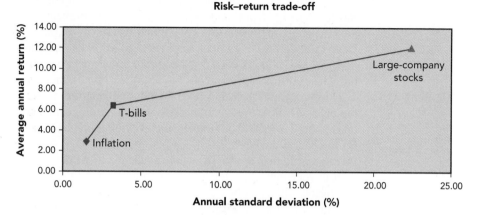

Source: Author calculations based on the data obtained from Datastream Database.

premium. Investment advisers like to say that an investment has a "wait" component and a "worry" component. In our figure, the time value of money is the compensation for waiting, and the risk premium is the compensation for worrying.

There are two important caveats to this discussion. First, risky investments do not *always* pay more than risk-free investments. Indeed, that's precisely what makes them risky. In other words, there is a risk premium *on average*, but, over any particular time interval, there is no guarantee. Second, we've intentionally been a little imprecise about what we mean exactly by risk. As we will discuss in the chapters ahead, not all risks are compensated. Some risks are cheaply and easily avoidable, and there is no expected reward for bearing them. It is only those risks that cannot be easily avoided that are compensated (on average).

1.7   Tulipmania and Stock Market Crashes

We conclude this chapter by examining some market crashes created by the speculative actions of investors. These crashes caused some small investors and businessmen to lose big amounts of money. In this chapter we have examined the average returns and risks that various instruments carry. It is important to examine the extreme losses that investors have suffered at certain periods. We begin with a 17th century event and then we examine two recent stock market crashes.

Tulips were very popular native flowers in the Ottoman Empire during the 13th and 14th centuries. When we look at Turkish ceramic tiles of that period, we see that tulips were used very frequently as motifs. European diplomats sent tulip bulbs back to Germany and the Netherlands in the 15th century and some farmers started growing tulips. In the Netherlands the public started to grow special types of tulips and trade these tulips. As demand for tulips increased very rapidly, so did the prices. In the 1600s tulips began to be traded at exchanges. In the 1630s, tulip bulbs were traded in multiples of 10,000 florins. However, within a decade tulip prices fell tremendously, creating a chaotic situation. Growers and businessmen couldn't sell their tulips and suffered huge losses. This investment bubble is referred to as *tulipmania*, reflecting the manic buying and selling of tulips that occurred.

One of the biggest crashes in history occurred in October 1929 in the United States. The value of the Dow Jones Industrial Average fell more than 50 percent within a month. Millions of shares were traded and although the bankers and the New York Stock Exchange representatives bought shares to prevent mass selling and to support the exchange, the index level continued to fall. In 1932, the beginning of the Great Depression followed the stock market crash. Millions of dollars were lost, bankruptcies occurred, and it took over a decade for the economy to recover. Many investors lost not only their portfolio investments, but also their homes, their cars, and their livelihoods.

Despite various measures taken by the stock markets to prevent crashes and to avoid big drops in price levels and massive selling by the public, another big crash occurred on October 19, 1987. The stock index level fell more than 20 percent on that single day. By the end of the week, the index had recovered to its original level. However, some investors sold their stocks in a panic and lost a lot of money.

It is very important for investors to understand the risk–return characteristics of the various financial instruments and check not only the average returns but also the minimum returns, and to invest only if they can accept these minimum returns if they occur.

A Look Ahead

In the remainder of this text, we focus exclusively on financial assets. An advantage of this approach is that it is limited to four major types: stocks, bonds, options, and futures, in the order that we cover them. This means that we won't be discussing collectibles such as classic automobiles, baseball cards, coins, fine art, or stamps. We also won't be discussing real estate or precious metals such as gold and platinum. It's not that these are unimportant; rather, they are very specialized. So, instead of treating them superficially, we leave a discussion of them for another day (and another book).

As we've indicated, to understand the potential reward from an investment, it is critical to first understand the risk involved. There is an old saying that goes like this: It's easy to make a small fortune investing in _____ (put your favourite investment here)—just start with a large fortune! The moral is that the key to successful investing is to make informed, intelligent decisions about risk. For this reason, we are going to pay particular attention to the things that determine the value of the different assets we discuss and the nature of the associated risks.

One common characteristic that these assets have is that they are bought and sold around the clock and around the world in vast quantities. The way they are traded can be very different, however. We think it is important and interesting to understand exactly what happens when you buy or sell one of these assets, so we will be discussing the different trading mechanisms and the way the different markets function. We will also describe actual buying and selling at various points along the way to show you the steps involved and the results of placing buy and sell orders and having them executed.

1.8   Summary and Conclusions

This chapter explores financial market history. Such a history lesson is useful because it tells us what to expect in the way of returns from risky assets. We summarized our study of market history with two key lessons:

1. Risky assets, on average, earn a risk premium. There is a reward for bearing risk.

2. The greater the potential reward from a risky investment, the greater is the risk.

When we put these two lessons together, we concluded that there is a risk-return trade-off: The only way to earn a higher return is to take on greater risk.

REAL WORLD

This chapter took you through some basic, but important, investment-related calculations. We then walked through the modern history of risk and return. How should you, as an investor or investment manager, put this information to work?

The answer is that you now have a rational, objective basis for thinking about what you stand to make from investing in some important broad asset classes. For the stock market as a whole, as measured by the performance of large-company stocks, you know that you might realistically expect to make 12 percent or so per year on average.

Equally important, you know that you won't make 12 percent in any one year; instead, you'll make more or less. You know that the standard deviation is about 22 percent per year, and you should know what that means in terms of risk. In particular, you need to understand that in one year out of every six, you should expect to lose more than 10 percent (12 percent minus one standard deviation), so this will be a relatively common event. The good news is that in one year out of six, you can realistically expect to earn more than 34 percent (12 percent plus one standard deviation).

The other important, practical thing to understand from this chapter is that a strategy of investing in very low risk assets (such as T-bills) has historically barely kept up with inflation. This might be sufficient for some investors, but if your goal is to do better than that, then you will have to bear some amount of risk to achieve it.

Key Terms

total dollar return 3
dividend yield 4
capital gains yield 4
total percent return 4
risk-free rate 11
risk premium 12

variance 15
standard deviation 15
normal distribution 17
geometric average return 21
arithmetic average return 21
effective annual return (EAR) 23

Chapter Review Problems and Self-Test

1. **Calculating Returns** You bought 400 shares of Metallica Heavy Metal, Inc., at $30 per share. Over the year, you received $.75 per share in dividends. If the stock sold for $33 at the end of the year, what was your dollar return? Your percentage return?

2. **Calculating Returns and Variability** Using the following returns, calculate the arithmetic average returns, the variances, the standard deviations, and the geometric returns for the following stocks:

Year	Michele, Inc.	Janicek Co.
1	12%	5%
2	−4	−15
3	0	10
4	20	38
5	2	17

Answers to Self-Test Problems

1. Your dollar return is just your gain or loss in dollars. Here, we receive $.75 in dividends on each of our 400 shares, for a total of $300. In addition, each share rose from $30 to $33, so we make $3 × 400 shares = $1,200. Our total dollar return is thus $300 + $1,200 = $1,500.

   Our percentage return (or just "return" for short) is equal to the $1,500 we made divided by our initial outlay of $30 × 400 shares = $12,000; so $1,500 / 12,000 = .125 = 12.5%. Equivalently, we could have just noted that each share paid a $.75 dividend and each share gained $3, so the total dollar gain per share was $3.75. As a percentage of the cost of one share ($30), we get $3.75 / 30 = .125 = 12.5%.

2. First, calculate arithmetic averages as follows:

Michele, Inc.	Janicek Co.
12%	5%
−4	−15
0	10
20	38
2	17
30%	55%
Average return: 30 / 5 = 6%	55 / 5 = 11%

   Using the arithmetic averages above, calculate the squared deviations from the arithmetic average returns and sum the squared deviations as follows:

Michele, Inc.	Janicek Co.
$(12 − 6)^2 = 36$	$(5 − 11)^2 = 36$
$(−4 − 6)^2 = 100$	$(−15 − 11)^2 = 676$
$(0 − 6)^2 = 36$	$(10 − 11)^2 = 1$
$(20 − 6)^2 = 196$	$(38 − 11)^2 = 729$
$(2 − 6)^2 = 16$	$(17 − 11)^2 = 36$
384	1,478

   Calculate return variances by dividing the sums of squared deviations by four, which is the number of returns less one.

$$\text{Michele: } 384 / 4 = 96 \qquad \text{Janicek: } 1,478 / 4 = 369.5$$

   Standard deviations are then calculated as the square root of the variance.

$$\text{Michele: } \sqrt{96} = 9.8\% \qquad \text{Janicek: } \sqrt{369.5} = 19.22\%$$

   Geometric returns are then calculated as:

$$\text{Michele: } [(1 + .12)(1 − .04)(1 + .00)(1 + .20)(1 + .02)]^{1/5} − 1 = 5.65\%$$

$$\text{Janicek: } [(1 + .05)(1 − .15)(1 + .10)(1 + .38)(1 + .17)]^{1/5} − 1 = 9.65\%$$

Test Your Investment Quotient

1. **Prices and Returns** You plan to buy a common stock and hold it for one year. You expect to receive both $1.50 from dividends and $26 from the sale of the stock at the end of the year. If you wanted to earn a 15 percent rate of return, what is the maximum price you would pay for the stock today?

   a. $22.61
   b. $23.91

    c. $24.50

    d. $27.50

2. **Returns** A portfolio of non-dividend-paying stocks earned a geometric mean return of 5 percent between January 1, 1994, and December 31, 2000. The arithmetic mean return for the same period was 6 percent. If the market value of the portfolio at the beginning of 1995 was $100,000, the market value of the portfolio at the end of 2000 was *closest* to:

    a. $135,000

    b. $140,710

    c. $142,000

    d. $150,363

3. **Standard Deviation** Which of the following statements about standard deviation is true? Standard deviation

    a. Is the square of the variance.

    b. Can be a positive or negative number.

    c. Is denominated in the same units as the original data.

    d. Is the arithmetic mean of the squared deviations from the mean.

4. **Normal Distribution** An investment strategy has an expected return of 12 percent and a standard deviation of 10 percent. If the investment returns are normally distributed, the probability of earning a return less than 2 percent is closest to:

    a. 10 percent

    b. 16 percent

    c. 32 percent

    d. 34 percent

5. **Normal Distribution** What are the mean and standard deviation of a standard normal distribution?

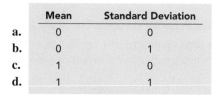

	Mean	Standard Deviation
a.	0	0
b.	0	1
c.	1	0
d.	1	1

6. **Normal Distribution** Given a data series that is normally distributed with a mean of 100 and a standard deviation of 10, about 95 percent of the numbers in the series will fall within which of the following ranges?

    a. 60 to 140

    b. 70 to 130

    c. 80 to 120

    d. 90 to 110

7. **Asset Types** Stocks, bonds, options, and futures are the four major types of

    a. Debt

    b. Real assets

    c. Equity

    d. Financial assets

8. **Investment Returns** Suppose the value of an investment doubles in a one-year period. In this case, the rate of return on this investment over that one-year period is what amount?

    a. 100 percent even if the gain is not actually realized.

    b. 200 percent even if the gain is not actually realized.

    c. 100 percent only if the gain is actually realized.

    d. 200 percent only if the gain is actually realized.

www.mcgrawhill.ca/olc/Jordan

9. **Historical Returns** Which of the following asset categories has an annual returns history most closely linked to historical annual rates of inflation?

   a. Treasury bills
   b. Corporate bonds
   c. Large-company stocks
   d. Small-company stocks

10. **Historical Returns** Based on the annual returns since 1983, which asset category, on average, has yielded the highest risk premium?

    a. Treasury bills
    b. Inflation
    c. Preferred stocks
    d. Large-company stocks

11. **Stat 101** Over a four-year period, an investment in Outa'Synch common stock yields returns of $-10, 40, 0$, and 20. What is the arithmetic return over this period?

    a. 5 percent
    b. 7.5 percent
    c. 10 percent
    d. 12.5 percent

12. **Stat 101** You calculate an average historical return of 20 percent and a standard deviation of return of 10 percent for an investment in Stonehenge Construction Co. You believe these values well represent the future distribution of returns. Assuming that returns are normally distributed, what is the probability that Stonehenge Construction will yield a negative return?

    a. 17 percent
    b. 33 percent
    c. 5 percent
    d. 2.5 percent

13. **Stat 101** Which of the following statements about a normal distribution is incorrect?

    a. A normal distribution is symmetrically centred on its mean.
    b. The probability of being within one standard deviation from the mean is about 68 percent.
    c. The probability of being within two standard deviations from the mean is about 95 percent.
    d. The probability of a negative value is always one-half.

14. **Normal Distribution** Based on a normal distribution with a mean of 500 and a standard deviation of 150, the z-value for an observation of 200 is closest to:

    a. -2.00
    b. -1.75
    c.   1.75
    d.   2.00

15. **Normal Distribution** A normal distribution would least likely be described as:

    a. Asymptotic.
    b. A discreet probability distribution.
    c. A symmetrical or bell-shaped distribution.
    d. A curve that theoretically extends from negative infinity to positive infinity.

Concept Questions

1. **Risk versus Return** Based on the historical record, rank the following investments in increasing order of risk. Rank the investments in increasing order of average returns.

What do you conclude about the relationship between the risk of an investment and the return you expect to earn on it?

a. Large stocks

b. Treasury bills

2. **Return Calculations** A particular stock had a return last year of 4 percent. However, you look at the stock price and notice that it actually didn't change at all last year. How is this possible?

3. **Returns Distributions** What is the probability that the return on small stocks will be less than −100 percent in a single year (think about it)? What are the implications for the distribution of returns?

4. **Arithmetic versus Geometric Returns** What is the difference between arithmetic and geometric returns? Suppose you have invested in a stock for the last 10 years. Which number is more important to you, the arithmetic or geometric return?

5. **Inflation and Returns** Look at Table 1.1 and Figures 1.3 and 1.4. When were T-bill rates at their highest? Why do you think they were so high during this period?

6. **Inflation and Returns** The returns we have examined are not adjusted for inflation. What do you suppose would happen to our estimated risk premiums if we did account for inflation?

7. **Taxes and Returns** The returns we have examined are not adjusted for taxes. What do you suppose would happen to our estimated returns and risk premiums if we did account for taxes? What would happen to our volatility measures?

8. **Taxes and Treasury Bills** As a practical matter, most of the return you earn from investing in Treasury bills is taxed right away as ordinary income. Thus, if you are in a 40 percent tax bracket and you earn 5 percent on a Treasury bill, your aftertax return is only $.05 \times (1 - .40) = .03$, or 3 percent. In other words, 40 percent of your return goes to pay taxes, leaving you with just 3 percent. Once you consider inflation and taxes, how does the long-term return from Treasury bills look?

9. **The Long Run** Given your answer to the last question and the discussion in the chapter, why would any rational person do anything other than load up on 100 percent small stocks?

Questions and Problems

Core Questions

1. **Calculating Returns** Suppose you bought 100 shares of stock at an initial price of $89 per share. The stock paid a dividend of $1.20 per share during the following year, and the share price at the end of the year was $97. Compute your total dollar return on this investment. Does your answer change if you keep the stock instead of selling it? Why or why not?

2. **Calculating Yields** In the previous problem, what is the capital gains yield? The dividend yield? What is the total rate of return on the investment?

3. **Calculating Returns** Rework Problems 1 and 2 assuming that you buy 750 shares of the stock and the ending share price is $81.50.

4. **Calculating Average Returns** The rate of return on Jurassic Jalopies, Inc., stock over the last five years was −8 percent, 34 percent, −16 percent, 8 percent, and 19 percent. Over the same period, the return on Stonehenge Construction Company's stock was −18 percent, 27 percent, −9 percent, 24 percent, and 17 percent. What was the arithmetic average return on each stock over this period?

5. **Calculating Returns and Variability** Using the following returns, calculate the arithmetic average returns, the variances, and the standard deviations for stocks A and B.

Year	A	B
1	24%	32%
2	6	2
3	−8	−15
4	19	21
5	15	11

6. **Return Calculations** A particular stock has a dividend yield of 2.4 percent. Last year, the stock price fell from $74 to $66. What was the return for the year?

7. **Geometric Returns** A stock has had returns of 11 percent, −6 percent, −12 percent, 19 percent, and 37 percent over the last five years. What is the geometric return for the stock?

8. **Arithmetic and Geometric Returns** A stock has had returns of 29 percent, 11 percent, 18 percent, −6 percent, −19 percent, and 34 percent over the last six years. What are the arithmetic and geometric returns for the stock?

Intermediate
Questions

9. **Returns and the Bell Curve** An investment has an expected return of 12 percent per year with a standard deviation of 28 percent. Assuming that the returns on this investment are at least roughly normally distributed, how frequently do you expect to earn between −16 percent and 40 percent? How often do you expect to earn less than −16 percent?

10. **Returns and the Bell Curve** An investment has an expected return of 8 percent per year with a standard deviation of 4 percent. Assuming that the returns on this investment are at least roughly normally distributed, how frequently do you expect to lose money?

11. **Using Returns Distributions** Based on the historical record, if you invest in T-bills, what is the approximate probability that your return will be less than −3.4 percent in a given year? What range of returns would you expect to see 95 percent of the time? 99 percent of the time?

12. **Using Returns Distributions** Based on the historical record, what is the approximate probability that an investment in large stocks will double in value in a single year? How about triple in a single year?

13. **Risk Premiums** Refer to Table 1.1 for large-stock and T-bill returns for the period 1983–1987:
    a. Calculate the observed risk premium in each year for the common stocks.
    b. Calculate the average returns and the average risk premium over this period.
    c. Calculate the standard deviation of returns and the standard deviation of the risk premium.
    d. Is it possible that the observed risk premium can be negative? Explain how this can happen and what it means.

14. **Geometric Return** Your grandfather invested $1,000 in a stock 48 years ago. Currently the value of his account is $197,000. What is his geometric return over this period?

15. **Forecasting Returns** You have found an asset with a 12.60 percent arithmetic average return and a 10.15 percent geometric return. Your observation period is 40 years. What is your best estimate of the return of the asset over the next 5 years? 10 years? 20 years?

16. **Geometric Averages** Look back to Figure 1.1 and find the value of $1 invested in each asset class over this 25-year period. Calculate the geometric return for large company stocks, Treasury bills, and inflation.

17. **Arithmetic and Geometric Returns** A stock has returns of 21 percent, 7 percent, −19 percent, 16 percent, and 13 percent. What are the arithmetic and geometric returns?

18. **Arithmetic and Geometric Returns** A stock has had the following year-end prices and dividends:

Year	Price	Dividend
0	$58.12	$ —
1	61.56	0.55
2	54.32	0.60
3	64.19	0.63
4	74.13	0.72
5	79.32	0.81

What are the arithmetic and geometric returns for the stock?

19. Arithmetic versus Geometric Returns You are given the returns for the following three stocks:

Year	Stock A	Stock B	Stock C
1	11%	8%	−15%
2	11	15	34
3	11	10	16
4	11	9	8
5	11	13	12

Calculate the arithmetic return, geometric return, and standard deviation for each stock. Do you notice anything about the relationship between an asset's arithmetic return, standard deviation, and geometric return? Do you think this relationship will always hold?

Spreadsheet Problems

20. Return and Standard Deviation The 1990s was a good decade for investors in S&P/TSX 60 stocks. To find out how good, construct a spreadsheet that calculates the arithmetic average return, variance, and standard deviation for the S&P/TSX 60 returns during the 1990s using spreadsheet functions.

STANDARD &POOR'S

S&P Problems

www.mcgrawhill.ca/edumarketinsight

1. **Industry Comparison** On the Market Insight Home Page, follow the "Industry" link to go to the industry home page. The drop down menu allows you to select different industries. Answer the following questions for these industries: Air Freight & Logistics, Apparel Retail, Department Stores, Electric Utilities, Home Improvement Retail, Investment Banking & Brokerage, and Regional Banks.

   a. How many companies are in each industry?
   b. What are the total sales in each industry?
   c. Do the industries with the largest total sales have the most companies in the industry? What does this tell you about competition in the various industries?

2. **Calculating Returns** Download the historical stock prices for Biomira (BIOM) under the "Mthly. Adj. Prices" link. Use the closing stock prices to calculate the monthly return each month for the last twelve months. Do your calculations match the return calculations given in the file? Why or why not? Now calculate the dividends paid each month.

3. **Calculating Standard Deviation** Download the historical stock prices for Alliance Atlantis Communication (AACB) under the "Mthly. Adj. Prices" link. Using the monthly returns in the file, calculate the monthly standard deviation of Alliance stock for the past twelve months.

What's on the Web?

1. **Ticker Symbols** Go to finance.yahoo.com and look up the ticker symbols for the following companies: Research In Motion, Shaw Communications, Magna, 3M Corporation, IBM, Dell, American Standard Company.

2. **Average Return and Standard Deviation** Go to finance.yahoo.com and enter the ticker symbol for your favourite stock. Now, look for the historical prices and find the monthly closing stock price for the last six years. Calculate the annual arithmetic average return, the standard deviation, and the geometric return for this period.

3. **Stock Performance** What are the best-performing stocks over the past year? Go to finance.yahoo.com and select the "Stock Screener" link. You will see a "Performance" category and a pull-down menu labelled "1 Yr Stock Perf." Select "Up more than 200%" and "Find Stocks." How many stocks have increased more than 200 percent over the past year? Now go back and select "Down more than 90%." How many stocks have dropped more than 90 percent in value over the past year?

CHAPTER 2

Diversification and Asset Allocation

"Out of this nettle, danger,
We pluck this flower, safety."

—Shakespeare, *Henry IV*

Intuitively, we all know that diversification is important for managing investment risk. But how exactly does diversification work, and how can we be sure we have an efficiently diversified portfolio? Insightful answers can be gleaned from the modern theory of diversification and asset allocation. ■

In this chapter, we examine the role of diversification and asset allocation in investing. Most of us have a strong sense that diversification is important. After all, "Don't put all your eggs in one basket" is a bit of folk wisdom that seems to have stood the test of time quite well. Even so, the importance of diversification has not always been well understood. Diversification is important because portfolios with many investments usually produce a more consistent and stable total return than portfolios with just one investment. When you own many stocks, even if some of them decline in price, others are likely to increase in price (or stay at the same price).

The role and impact of diversification were first formally explained in the early 1950s by financial pioneer Harry Markowitz, who shared the 1986 Nobel Prize in Economics for his insights. Surprisingly, Professor Markowitz's insights are not related to how investors feel about risk or return. In fact, we can talk about the benefits of diversification without having to know how investors feel about risk. In reality, however, it is investors who care about the benefits of diversification. Therefore, to help you understand

Professor Markowitz's insights, we make two assumptions. First, we assume that investors prefer more return to less return, and second, we assume that investors prefer less risk to more risk. In this chapter, variance and standard deviation are measures of risk.

2.1 Expected Returns and Variances

In Chapter 1, we discussed how to calculate average returns and variances using historical data. We now begin to discuss how to analyze returns and variances when the information we have concerns future possible returns and their probabilities.

Expected Returns

We start with a straightforward case. Consider a period of time such as a year. We have two stocks, say, Netcap and Jmart. Netcap is expected to have a return of 25 percent in the coming year; Jmart is expected to have a return of 20 percent during the same period.

Find analyst expectations and estimates of Canadian stocks at www.globe investor. com and www. globefund.com

In a situation such as this, if all investors agreed on these expected return values, why would anyone want to hold Jmart? After all, why invest in one stock when the expectation is that another will do better? Clearly, the answer must depend on the different risks of the two investments. The return on Netcap, although it is *expected* to be 25 percent, could turn out to be significantly higher or lower. Similarly, Jmart's *realized* return could be significantly higher or lower than expected.

For example, suppose the economy booms. In this case, we think Netcap will have a 70 percent return. But if the economy tanks and enters a recession, we think the return will be −20 percent. In this case, we say that there are *two states of the economy*, which means that there are two possible outcomes. This scenario is oversimplified, of course, but it allows us to illustrate some key ideas without a lot of computational complexity.

Suppose we think boom and recession are equally likely to happen, that is, a 50–50 chance of each outcome. Table 2.1 illustrates the basic information we have described and some additional information about Jmart. Notice that Jmart earns 30 percent if there is a recession and 10 percent if there is a boom.

Obviously, if you buy one of these stocks, say, Jmart, what you earn in any particular year depends on what the economy does during that year. Suppose these probabilities stay the same through time. If you hold Jmart for a number of years, you'll earn 30 percent about half the time and 10 percent the other half. In this case, we say your

expected return on Jmart, $E(R_J)$, is 20 percent:

expected return
Average return on a risky asset expected in the future.

$$E(R_J) = .50 \times 30\% + .50 \times 10\% = 20\%$$

In other words, you should expect to earn 20 percent from this stock, on average.

TABLE 2.1	States of the Economy and Stock Returns		
	Probability of State of	**Security Returns if State Occurs**	
State of Economy	**Economy**	**Netcap**	**Jmart**
Recession	.50	−20%	30%
Boom	.50	70	10
	1.00		

		Netcap		Jmart	
(1)	**(2)**	**(3)** Return if	**(4)**	**(5)** Return if	**(6)**
State of Economy	**Probability of State of Economy**	**State Occurs**	**Product (2) × (3)**	**State Occurs**	**Product (2) × (5)**
Recession	.50	−20%	−.10	30%	.15
Boom	.50	70	.35	10	.05
	1.00		$E(R_N) = 25\%$		$E(R_J) = 20\%$

TABLE 2.2 Calculating Expected Returns

For Netcap, the probabilities are the same, but the possible returns are different. Here we lose 20 percent half the time, and we gain 70 percent the other half. The expected return on Netcap, $E(R_N)$, is thus 25 percent:

$$E(R_N) = .50 \times -20\% + .50 \times 70\% = 25\%$$

Table 2.2 illustrates these calculations.

In Chapter 1, we defined a risk premium as the difference between the returns on a risky investment and a risk-free investment, and we calculated the historical risk premiums on some different investments. Using our projected returns, we can calculate the *projected* or *expected risk premium* as the difference between the expected return on a risky investment and the certain return on a risk-free investment.

For example, suppose risk-free investments are currently offering 8 percent. We will say that the risk-free rate, which we label R_f, is 8 percent. Given this, what is the projected risk premium on Jmart? On Netcap? Since the expected return on Jmart, $E(R_J)$, is 20 percent, the projected risk premium is

$$\begin{aligned} \text{Risk premium} &= \text{Expected return} - \text{Risk-free rate} \quad (2.1)\\ &= E(R_J) - R_f\\ &= 20\% - 8\%\\ &= 12\% \end{aligned}$$

Similarly, the risk premium on Netcap is $25\% - 8\% = 17\%$.

In general, the expected return on a security or other asset is simply equal to the sum of the possible returns multiplied by their probabilities. So, if we have 100 possible returns, we would multiply each one by its probability and then add up the results. The sum would be the expected return. The risk premium would then be the difference between this expected return and the risk-free rate.

UNEQUAL PROBABILITIES

EXAMPLE 2.1

Look again at Tables 2.1 and 2.2. Suppose you thought a boom would occur 20 percent of the time instead of 50 percent. What are the expected returns on Netcap and Jmart in this case? If the risk-free rate is 10 percent, what are the risk premiums?

The first thing to notice is that a recession must occur 80 percent of the time (1 − .20 = .80) since there are only two possibilities. With this in mind, Jmart has a 30 percent return in 80 percent of the

(continued)

TABLE 2.3		Calculating Expected Returns				
		Netcap		Jmart	
(1)	(2)	(3)	(4)	(5)	(6)
State of Economy	Probability of State of Economy	Return if State Occurs	Product (2) × (3)	Return if State Occurs	Product (2) × (5)
Recession	.80	−.20%	−.16	30%	.24
Boom	.20	70	.14	10	.02
	1.00		$E(R_N) = -.02 = -2\%$		$E(R_J) = .26 = 26\%$

years and a 10 percent return in 20 percent of the years. To calculate the expected return, we just multiply the possibilities by the probabilities and add up the results:

$$E(R_J) = .80 \times 30\% + .20 \times 10\% = 26\%$$

Table 2.3 summarizes the calculations for both stocks. Notice that the expected return on Netcap is −2 percent.

The risk premium for Jmart is 26% − 10% = 16% in this case. The risk premium for Netcap is negative: −2% − 10% = −12%. This is a little unusual, but, as we will see, it's not impossible.

Calculating the Variance

To calculate the variances of the returns on our two stocks, we first determine the squared deviations from the expected return. We then multiply each possible squared deviation by its probability. Next we add these up, and the result is the variance.

To illustrate, one of our stocks above, Jmart, has an expected return of 20 percent. In a given year, the return will actually be either 30 percent or 10 percent. The possible deviations are thus 30% − 20% = 10% or 10% − 20% = −10%. In this case, the variance is

$$\text{Variance} = \sigma^2 = .50 \times (10\%)^2 + .50 \times (-10\%)^2 = .01$$

The standard deviation is the square root of this:

$$\text{Standard deviation} = \sigma = \sqrt{.01} = .10 = 10\%$$

There's more on risk measures at www.investopedia.com

Table 2.4 summarizes these calculations and the expected return for both stocks. Notice that Netcap has a much larger variance. Netcap has the higher return, but Jmart has less risk. You could get a 70 percent return on your investment in Netcap, but you could also lose 20 percent. Notice that an investment in Jmart will always pay at least 10 percent.

Which of these stocks should you buy? We can't really say; it depends on your personal preferences regarding risk and return. We can be reasonably sure, however, that some investors would prefer one and some would prefer the other.

You've probably noticed that the way we calculated expected returns and variances here is somewhat different from the way we did it in Chapter 1 (and, probably, different from the way you learned it in "sadistics"). The reason is that we were examining historical returns in Chapter 1, so we estimated the average return and the variance based on some actual events. Here, we have projected future returns and their associated probabilities, so this is the information with which we must work.

TABLE 2.4	Expected Returns and Variances	
	Netcap	**Jmart**
Expected return, $E(R)$	25%	20%
Variance, σ^2	.2025	.0100
Standard deviation, σ	45%	10%

MORE UNEQUAL PROBABILITIES

Going back to Table 2.3 in Example 2.1, what are the variances on our two stocks once we have unequal probabilities? What are the standard deviations?

We can summarize the needed calculations as follows:

(1)	(2)	(3)	(4)	(5)
			Squared	
			Return	**Product**
State of	**Probability of State of**	**Return Deviation from**	**Deviation**	**(2) × (4)**
Economy	**Economy**	**Expected Return**		
Netcap				
Recession	.80	$-.20 - (-.02) = -.18$	.0324	.02592
Boom	.20	$.70 - (-.02) = .72$	.5184	.10368
				$\sigma_N^2 = .12960$
Jmart				
Recession	.80	$.30 - .26 = .04$	.0016	.00128
Boom	.20	$.10 - .26 = -.16$	.0256	.00512
				$\sigma_J^2 = .00640$

Based on these calculations, the standard deviation for Netcap is $\sigma_N = \sqrt{.1296} = 36\%$. The standard deviation for Jmart is much smaller, $\sigma_J = \sqrt{.0064}$, or 8 percent.

CHECK THIS ✓ **2.1a** How do we calculate the expected return on a security?

2.1b In words, how do we calculate the variance of an expected return?

2.2 Portfolios

portfolio Group of assets such as stocks and bonds held by an investor.

Thus far in this chapter, we have concentrated on individual assets considered separately. However, most investors actually hold a **portfolio** of assets. All we mean by this is that investors tend to own more than just a single stock, bond, or other asset. Given that this is so, portfolio return and portfolio risk are of obvious relevance. Accordingly, we now discuss portfolio expected returns and variances.

Portfolio Weights

portfolio weight Percentage of a portfolio's total value invested in a particular asset.

There are many equivalent ways of describing a portfolio. The most convenient approach is to list the percentages of the total portfolio's value that are invested in each portfolio asset. We call these percentages the **portfolio weights**.

For example, if we have $50 in one asset and $150 in another, then our total portfolio is worth $200. The percentage of our portfolio in the first asset is $50/$200 = .25. The percentage of our portfolio in the second asset is $150/$200 = .75. Notice that the weights sum up to 1.00 since all of our money is invested somewhere.[1]

Portfolio Expected Returns

Let's go back to Netcap and Jmart. You put half your money in each. The portfolio weights are obviously .50 and .50. What is the pattern of returns on this portfolio? The expected return?

To answer these questions, suppose the economy actually enters a recession. In this case, half your money (the half in Netcap) loses 20 percent. The other half (the half in Jmart) gains 30 percent. Your portfolio return, R_p, in a recession will thus be

$$R_P = .50 \times -20\% + .50 \times 30\% = 5\%$$

Table 2.5 summarizes the remaining calculations. Notice that when a boom occurs, your portfolio would return 40 percent:

$$R_P = .50 \times 70\% + .50 \times 10\% = 40\%$$

As indicated in Table 2.5, the expected return on your portfolio, $E(R_p)$, is 22.5 percent.

We can save ourselves some work by calculating the expected return more directly. Given these portfolio weights, we could have reasoned that we expect half our money to earn 25 percent (the half in Netcap) and half of our money to earn 20 percent (the half in Jmart). Our portfolio expected return is thus

$$E(R_P) = .50 \times E(R_N) + .50 \times E(R_J)$$
$$= .50 \times 25\% + .50 \times 20\%$$
$$= 22.5\%$$

This is the same portfolio return that we calculated in Table 2.5.

This method of calculating the expected return on a portfolio works no matter how many assets there are in the portfolio. Suppose we had n assets in our portfolio, where n is any number at all. If we let x_i stand for the percentage of our money in Asset i, then the expected return is

$$E(R_P) = x_1 \times E(R_1) + x_2 \times E(R_2) + \cdots + x_n \times E(R_n) \qquad (2.2)$$

TABLE 2.5		Expected Portfolio Return	
(1)	**(2)**	**(3)**	**(4)**
State of Economy	**Probability of State of Economy**	**Portfolio Return if State Occurs**	**Product (2) × (3)**
Recession	.50	$.50 \times -20\% + .50 \times 30\% = 5\%$	.025
Boom	.50	$.50 \times 70\% + .50 \times 10\% = 40\%$	.200
		$E(R_p) = .225 = 22.5\%$	

---

[1]Some of it could be in cash, of course, but we would then just consider cash to be another of the portfolio assets.

This says that the expected return on a portfolio is a straightforward combination of the expected returns on the assets in that portfolio. This seems somewhat obvious, but, as we will examine next, the obvious approach is not always the right one.

THREE-STOCK PORTFOLIO

EXAMPLE 2.3

Suppose we had the following projections on three stocks:

State of Economy	Probability of State of Economy	Returns Stock A	Stock B	Stock C
Boom	.50	10%	15%	20%
Bust	.50	8	4	0

We want to calculate portfolio expected returns in two cases. First, what would be the expected return on a portfolio with equal amounts invested in each of the three stocks? Second, what would be the expected return if half of the portfolio were in A, with the remainder equally divided between B and C?

From our earlier discussion, the expected returns on the individual stocks are

$$E(R_A) = 9.0\% \quad E(R_B) = 9.5\% \quad E(R_C) = 10.0\%$$

(Check these for practice.) If a portfolio has equal investments in each asset, the portfolio weights are all the same. Such a portfolio is said to be *equally weighted*. Since there are three stocks in this case, the weights are all equal to 1/3. The portfolio expected return is thus

$$E(R_P) = 1/3 \times 9.0\% + 1/3 \times 9.5\% + 1/3 \times 10.0\% = 9.5\%$$

In the second case, check that the portfolio expected return is 9.375%.

Portfolio Variance

From the preceding discussion, the expected return on a portfolio that contains equal investments in Netcap and Jmart is 22.5 percent. What is the standard deviation of return on this portfolio? Simple intuition might suggest that half of our money has a standard deviation of 45 percent, and the other half has a standard deviation of 10 percent. So the portfolio's standard deviation might be calculated as follows:

$$\sigma_P = 0.50 \times 45\% + 0.50 \times 10\% = 27.5\%$$

Unfortunately, this approach is *completely incorrect*.

Let's see what the standard deviation really is. Table 2.6 summarizes the relevant calculations. As we see, the portfolio's variance is about .031, and its standard deviation is less than we thought—it's only 17.5 percent. What is illustrated here is that the variance on a portfolio is *not* generally a simple combination of the variances of the assets in the portfolio.

We can illustrate this point a little more dramatically by considering a slightly different set of portfolio weights. Suppose we put 2/11 (about 18 percent) in Netcap

TABLE 2.6		Calculating Portfolio Variance		
(1)	(2)	(3)	(4)	(5)
State of Economy	Probability of State of Economy	Portfolio Returns if State Occurs	Squared Deviation from Expected Return	Product (2) × (4)
Recession	.50	5%	$(.05 - .225)^2 = .030625$	.0153125
Boom	.50	40	$(.40 - .225)^2 = .030625$	.0153125
			$\sigma_P^2 = .030625$	
			$\sigma_P = \sqrt{.030625} = 17.5\%$	

and the other 9/11 (about 82 percent) in Jmart. If a recession occurs, this portfolio will have a return of

$$R_P = 2/11 \times -20\% + 9/11 \times 30\% = 20.91\%$$

If a boom occurs, this portfolio will have a return of

$$R_P = 2/11 \times 70\% + 9/11 \times 10\% = 20.91\%$$

Notice that the return is the same no matter what happens. No further calculation is needed: This portfolio has a *zero* variance and no risk!

This is a nice bit of financial alchemy. We take two quite risky assets and, by mixing them just right, we create a riskless portfolio. It seems very clear that combining assets into portfolios can substantially alter the risks faced by an investor. This is a crucial observation, and we will begin to explore its implications in the next section.[2]

PORTFOLIO VARIANCE AND STANDARD DEVIATIONS

EXAMPLE 2.4

In Example 2.3, what are the standard deviations of the two portfolios?

To answer, we first have to calculate the portfolio returns in the two states. We will work with the second portfolio, which has 50 percent in Stock A and 25 percent in each of stocks B and C. The relevant calculations are summarized as follows:

State of Economy	Probability of State of Economy	Returns			
		Stock A	Stock B	Stock C	Portfolio
Boom	.50	10%	15%	20%	13.75%
Bust	.50	8	4	0	5.00

The portfolio return when the economy booms is calculated as

$$R_P = .50 \times 10\% + .25 \times 15\% + .25 \times 20\% = 13.75\%$$

(continued)

---

[2]Earlier, we had a risk-free rate of 8 percent. Now we have, in effect, a 20.91 percent risk-free rate. If this situation actually existed, there would be a very profitable opportunity! In reality, we expect that all riskless investments would have the same return.

The return when the economy goes bust is calculated the same way. Check that it's 5 percent and also check that the expected return on the portfolio is 9.375 percent. The variance is thus

$$\sigma_P^2 = .50 \times (.1375 - .09375)^2 + .50 \times (.05 - .09375)^2 = .0019141$$

The standard deviation is thus about 4.375 percent. For our equally weighted portfolio, redo these calculations and check that the standard deviation is about 5.5 percent.

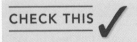

CHECK THIS

2.2a   What is a portfolio weight?

2.2b   How do we calculate the variance of an expected return?

2.3   Diversification and Portfolio Risk

Our discussion to this point has focused on some hypothetical securities. We've seen that portfolio risks can, in principle, be quite different from the risks of the assets that make up the portfolio. We now look more closely at the risk of an individual asset versus the risk of a portfolio of many different assets. As we did in Chapter 1, we will examine some stock market history to get an idea of what happens with actual investments in capital markets.

The Effect of Diversification: Another Lesson from Market History

In Chapter 1, we saw that the standard deviation of the annual return on a portfolio of large common stocks was about 22.4 percent per year. Does this mean that the standard deviation of the annual return on a typical stock in that group is about 22.4 percent? As you might suspect by now, the answer is no. This is an extremely important observation.

Copp and Cleary (see source of Figure 2.1) examined diversification characteristics of the Canadian portfolios by forming portfolios of 222 randomly chosen Canadian stocks. Table 2.7 illustrates their results of standard deviation of monthly portfolio returns.

In column 3 of Table 2.7 we see that the standard deviation for a "portfolio" of one security is 13.47 percent. What this means is that if you randomly select a Canadian stock listed on Toronto Stock Exchange and put all your money into it, your standard deviation of return would typically have been about 13 percent per month. Obviously, such a strategy has significant risk! If you were to randomly select two securities and put half your money in each, your average standard deviation would have been 11 percent.

The important thing to notice in Table 2.7 is that the standard deviation declines as the number of securities is increased. By the time we have 100 randomly chosen stocks (and 1 percent invested in each), the portfolio's volatility has declined by 64 percent, from 13.47 percent to 4.86 percent. Two-thirds of the total risk associated with a random stock can be eliminated in an equally weighted portfolio of 222 stocks. Portfolio risk is reduced by 46 percent for a 10 stock portfolio and 53 percent for a 20 stock portfolio.

TABLE 2.7	Portfolio Standard Deviations			
Number of Stocks in Portfolio	Average Monthly Portfolio Returns (%)	Standard Deviation of Average Monthly Portfolio Returns (%)	Ratio of Portfolio Standard Deviation to Standard Deviation of a Single Stock	Percentage of Total Achievable Risk Reduction
1	1.51	13.47	1.00	0.00
2	1.51	10.99	0.82	27.50
3	1.52	9.91	0.74	39.56
4	1.53	9.30	0.69	46.37
5	1.52	8.67	0.64	53.31
6	1.52	8.30	0.62	57.50
7	1.51	7.95	0.59	61.35
8	1.52	7.71	0.57	64.02
9	1.52	7.52	0.56	66.17
10	1.51	7.33	0.54	68.30
11	1.52	7.17	0.53	70.02
12	1.51	7.03	0.52	71.58
13	1.51	6.91	0.51	72.90
14	1.51	6.80	0.50	74.19
15	1.52	6.72	0.50	75.07
16	1.52	6.63	0.49	76.04
17	1.52	6.56	0.49	76.82
18	1.52	6.51	0.48	77.41
19	1.52	6.45	0.48	78.00
20	1.52	6.39	0.47	78.65
21	1.52	6.32	0 47	79.48
22	1.52	6.25	0.46	80.30
23	1.52	6.20	0.46	80.79
24	1.52	6.15	0.46	81.32
25	1.52	6.11	0.45	81.80
26	1.52	6.07	0.45	82.25
27	1.52	6.03	0.45	82.66
28	1.52	5.99	0.44	83.18
29	1.52	5.94	0.44	83.66
30	1.52	5.91	0.44	84.06
35	1.52	5.76	0.43	85.68
40	1.52	5.62	0.42	87.24
45	1.52	5.50	0.41	88.56
50	1.52	5.41	0.40	89.64
60	1.52	5.25	0.39	91.40
70	1.51	5.12	0.38	92.86
80	1.51	5.02	0.37	94.00
90	1.51	4.93	0.37	94.94
100	1.51	4.86	0.36	95.70
150	1.51	4.64	0.34	98.18
200	1.51	4.51	0.34	99.58
222	1.51	4.48	0.33	100.00

Source: Table 1 in "Diversification with Canadian Stocks: How Much is Enough?" S. Cleary and D. Copp, *Canadian Investment Review*, Fall 1999.

FIGURE 2.1

Portfolio Diversification

Source: Adapted from Figure 1 in "Diversification with Canadian Stocks: How Much is Enough?" S. Cleary and D. Copp, Canadian Investment Review, Fall 1999.

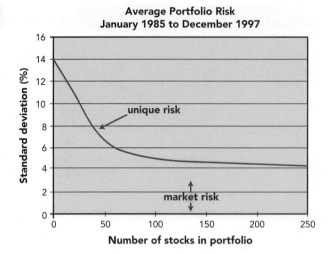

Average Portfolio Risk
January 1985 to December 1997

A 200 stock portfolio will provide 99.6 percent risk reduction. The nearby *Investment Updates* box offers further historical perspective on the need for diversification.

The Principle of Diversification

Figure 2.1 illustrates the point we've been discussing. What we have plotted is the standard deviation of the return versus the number of stocks in the portfolio. Notice in Figure 2.1 that the benefit in terms of risk reduction from adding securities drops off as we add more and more. By the time we have 10 securities, most of the diversification effect is already realized, and by the time we get to 30 or so, there is very little remaining benefit. In other words, the benefit of further diversification increases at a decreasing rate, so the "law of diminishing returns" applies here as it does in so many other places. Investors should be thinking in terms of 30 to 50 randomly chosen stocks when they are building a diversified portfolio.

Figure 2.1 illustrates two key points. First, some of the riskiness associated with individual assets can be eliminated by forming portfolios. The process of spreading an investment across assets (and thereby forming a portfolio) is called *diversification*. The **principle of diversification** tells us that spreading an investment across many assets will eliminate some of the risk. Not surprisingly, risks that can be eliminated by diversification are called "diversifiable" risks.

The second point is equally important. There is a minimum level of risk that cannot be eliminated by simply diversifying. This minimum level is labelled "nondiversifiable risk" in Figure 2.1. Taken together, these two points are another important lesson from financial market history: Diversification reduces risk, but only up to a point. Put another way, some risk is diversifiable and some is not.

principle of diversification
Spreading an investment across a number of assets will eliminate some, but not all, of the risk.

 **CHECK THIS**

2.3a What happens to the standard deviation of return for a portfolio if we increase the number of securities in the portfolio?

2.3b What is the principle of diversification?

Why a Broad Mix Helps in the Long Term

Stock-market diversification is sold as a short-term sedative for antsy investors. But it's also your best bet for ensuring decent long-run returns. In recent columns, I've written a lot about diversification. There's a good reason for that: If this bear market has anything to teach us, it is the value of spreading your stock-market bets widely. Over the past year, the hardest-hit investors have been those who pooh-poohed diversification and loaded up on technology stocks, only to see their portfolios decimated by Nasdaq's implosion. Clearly, these folks would have fared far better with a broader array of stocks. But diversification is more than just a defense against short-run market gyrations. To understand why, consider the performance of large, small and foreign stocks over the past 30 years.

At first blush, the results seem to encourage investors to shun diversification and instead stick with the big blue-chip stocks they know and love. After all, over the 30 years, large, small and foreign stocks generated almost exactly the same average annual total return. According to Chicago researchers Ibbotson Associates, Standard & Poor's 500-stock index of large-company stocks was up an average 13.2% a year, smaller U.S. companies gained 14.7% and Morgan Stanley's Europe, Australasia and Far East index climbed 13.1%. In other words, if all you owned was a smattering of blue-chip stocks, you should have done just fine over the past 30 years.

But the raw data don't tell the whole story. Here's why:

Tenacity Tested: Suppose that in 1970 you settled on a portfolio consisting exclusively of large U.S. stocks. Would you have hung onto that portfolio through the entire 30 years? I doubt it. For starters, you had to sit tight through the unnerving stock-market declines of 1973–74, 1976–78, 1980–82, 1987 and 1990. That would have been tough with an all-stock portfolio. But even if you had an unflinching determination to stick with stocks, you would have been constantly second-guessing your commitment to blue-chip companies. For instance, in the 1970s, you would have been tempted to swap into small companies and foreign shares, both of which outpaced U.S. large-company stocks. In the 1980s, foreign markets again outstripped U.S. large companies. Indeed, it was only in the 1990s that these blue-chip stocks reigned supreme.

Out of Time: Planning on sticking with U.S. large-company stocks for the next three decades? Circumstances may intervene. Maybe you will be forced to liquidate your stock portfolio early because you get divorced, lose your job or get hit with hefty medical bills. Alternatively, maybe your time horizon isn't quite as long as you imagine. For instance, you might be looking at a 30-year retirement. But if you are living off your portfolio, you will probably have to sell many of your stocks before the 30 years are up.

In that case, you will definitely want to be globally diversified, because that will provide vital portfolio protection over this shorter period. For proof, check out the accompanying table. It takes the past 30 years,

(continued)

2.4 Correlation and Diversification

We've seen that diversification is important. What we haven't discussed is how to get the most out of diversification. For example, in our previous section, we investigated what happens if we simply spread our money evenly across randomly chosen stocks. We saw that significant risk reduction resulted from this strategy, but you might wonder whether even larger gains could be achieved by a more sophisticated approach. As we begin to examine that question here, the answer is yes.

Why Diversification Works

Why diversification reduces portfolio risk as measured by the portfolio standard deviation is important and worth exploring in some detail. The key concept is

Why a Broad Mix Helps in the Long Term

picks out the roughest 5, 10, 15 and 20-year stretches for large-company stocks and then shows how other investments fared.

"In each of these bad periods, small stocks and international stocks did better," notes William Reichenstein, an investments professor at Baylor University. "There's a lot to be said for a portfolio that includes a little bit of everything."

On Target: Diversification won't just limit your losses during rough markets. When it's combined with regular rebalancing, it can also boost returns. When you rebalance, you set targets for what percentage of your portfolio is in different investments. Then, every so often, you re-jigger your portfolio to get back to these targets. If you invest in two market sectors, "a rebalanced portfolio may actually do better than the two assets on their own, because rebalancing forces you to buy low and sell high," says William Bernstein, an investment adviser in North Bend, Ore., and author of "The Intelligent Asset Allocator." "Rebalancing is the only form of market timing that works."

Suppose you held a portfolio that was one-third large stocks, one-third small stocks and one-third foreign stocks. At the end of each year, you rebalanced to get back to these portfolio targets. Result? According to Ibbotson, over the past 30 years, your portfolio would have gained 14.2% a year before taxes and trading costs, compared with 13.7% if you had never rebalanced. You are most likely to get this performance bonus when you rebalance among different stock-market sectors, which should have roughly comparable long-run returns. But sometimes, you can also bolster returns by rebalancing between stocks and bonds. Consider, for instance, the 10 years through December 1981. Over that stretch, large stocks struggled, climbing just 6.5% a year, but they still outpaced intermediate government bonds, which returned 5.8%. But an annually rebalanced mix of 50% stocks and 50% bonds did even better, gaining 6.6% a year, Mr. Reichenstein calculates.

Source: Jonathan Clements, *The Wall Street Journal*, April 3, 2001.
© 2001 Dow Jones & Company, Inc. All Rights Reserved Worldwide

Hiding Places How various investments fared during the roughest patches for large-company stocks over the past 30

| | Worst | | | | 30 Years |
	5 Years*	10 Years*	15 Years*	20 Years*	(through Dec. 2000)
Large companies	−0.2%	+6.5%	+9.9%	+11.2%	+13.2%
Small companies	+10.8	+17.3	+16.2	+13.3	+14.7
Foreign stocks	+2.6	+10.6	+15.6	+15.4	+13.1
Intermediate bonds	+6.4	+5.8	+9.2	+9.1	+8.5
Inflation	+7.9	+8.6	+6.9	+6.3	+5.0

Note: The results shown are annual averages and include reinvested dividends.
*Through year-end 1977, 1981, 1987, and 1990, respectively.
Source: Ibbotson Associates.

correlation
The tendency of the returns on two assets to move together.

Measure portfolio diversification using Portfolio X-ray at www.morningstar.ca

correlation, which is the extent to which the returns on two assets move together. If the returns on two assets tend to move up and down together, we say they are *positively* correlated. If they tend to move in opposite directions, we say they are *negatively* correlated. If there is no particular relationship between the two assets, we say they are *uncorrelated.*

The *correlation coefficient*, which we use to measure correlation, ranges from −1 to +1, and we will denote the correlation between the returns on two assets, say A and B, as $\text{Corr}(R_A, R_B)$. The Greek letter ρ (rho) is often used to designate correlation as well. A correlation of +1 indicates that the two assets have a *perfect* positive correlation. For example, suppose that whatever return Asset A realizes, either up or down, Asset B does the same thing by exactly twice as much. In this case, they are perfectly correlated because the movement on one is completely predictable from the movement on the other. Notice, however, that perfect correlation does not necessarily mean they move by the same amount.

FIGURE 2.2   **Correlations**

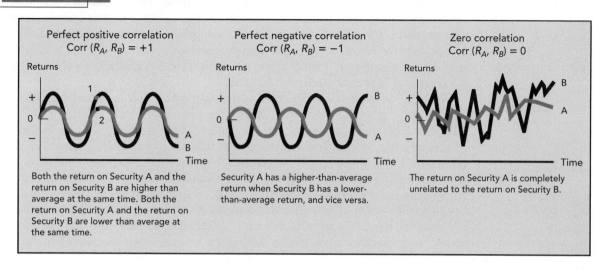

Perfect positive correlation
Corr $(R_A, R_B) = +1$

Returns

Both the return on Security A and the return on Security B are higher than average at the same time. Both the return on Security A and the return on Security B are lower than average at the same time.

Perfect negative correlation
Corr $(R_A, R_B) = -1$

Returns

Security A has a higher-than-average return when Security B has a lower-than-average return, and vice versa.

Zero correlation
Corr $(R_A, R_B) = 0$

Returns

The return on Security A is completely unrelated to the return on Security B.

A zero correlation means that the two assets are uncorrelated. If we know that one asset is up, then we have no idea what the other one is likely to do; there simply is no relation between them. Perfect negative correlation [Corr$(R_A, R_B) = -1$] indicates that they always move in opposite directions. Figure 2.2 illustrates the three benchmark cases of perfect positive, perfect negative, and zero correlation.

Diversification works because security returns are generally not perfectly correlated. We will be more precise about the impact of correlation on portfolio risk in just a moment. For now, it is useful to simply think about combining two assets into a portfolio. If the two assets are highly correlated (the correlation is near $+1$), then they have a strong tendency to move up and down together. As a result, they offer limited diversification benefit. For example, two stocks from the same industry, say, General Motors and Ford, will tend to be relatively highly correlated since the companies are in essentially the same business, and a portfolio of two such stocks is not likely to be very diversified.

In contrast, if the two assets are negatively correlated, then they tend to move in opposite directions; whenever one zigs, the other tends to zag. In such a case, there will be substantial diversification benefit because variation in the return on one asset tends to be offset by variation in the opposite direction from the other. In fact, if two assets have a perfect negative correlation [Corr$(R_A, R_B) = -1$], then it is possible to combine them such that all risk is eliminated. Looking back at our example involving Jmart and Netcap in which we were able to eliminate all of the risk, what we now see is that they must be perfectly negatively correlated.

To further illustrate the impact of diversification on portfolio risk, suppose we observed the actual annual returns on two stocks, A and B, for the years 1999–2003. We summarize these returns in Table 2.8. In addition to actual returns on stocks A and B, we also calculated the returns on an equally weighted portfolio of A and B in Table 2.8. We label this portfolio as AB. In 1999, for example, Stock A returned 10 percent and Stock B returned 15 percent. Since Portfolio AB is half invested in each, its return for the year was

$$1/2 \times 10\% + 1/2 \times 15\% = 12.5\%$$

The returns for the other years are calculated similarly.

At the bottom of Table 2.8, we calculated the average returns and standard deviations on the two stocks and the equally weighted portfolio. These averages and standard deviations are calculated just as they were in Chapter 1 (check a couple just to refresh your memory). The impact of diversification is apparent. The two stocks have standard deviations in the 13 percent to 14 percent per year range, but the portfolio's volatility is only 2.2 percent. In fact, if we compare the portfolio to Stock B, it has a higher return (11 percent vs. 9 percent) and much less risk.

Figure 2.3 illustrates in more detail what is occurring with our example. Here we have three bar graphs showing the year-by-year returns on Stocks A and B and Portfolio AB. Examining the graphs, we see that in 2000, for example, Stock A earned 30 percent while Stock B lost 10 percent. The following year, Stock B earned 25 percent while A lost 10 percent. These ups and downs tend to cancel out in our portfolio, however, with the result that there is much less variation in return from year to year. In other words, the correlation between the returns on stocks A and B is relatively low.

Covariance is very closely related to correlation coefficient. The covariance between two assets shows how returns of these two assets relate to each other and move with respect to each other. A negative covariance indicates two assets' returns move

TABLE 2.8	Annual Returns on Stocks A and B		
Year	Stock A	Stock B	Portfolio AB
1999	10%	15%	12.5%
2000	30	−10	10
2001	−10	25	7.5
2002	5	20	12.5
2003	10	15	12.5
Average returns	9	13	11
Standard deviations	14.3	13.5	2.2

FIGURE 2.3   **Impact of Diversification**

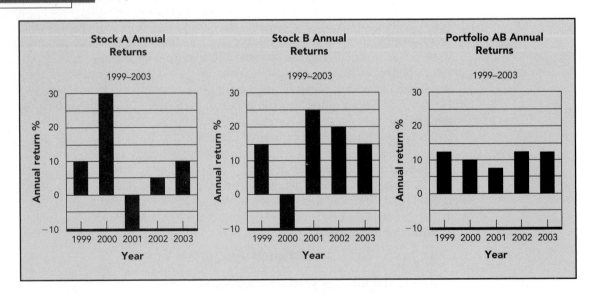

opposite to each other, in other words when the return of the first asset increases the return of the other decreases. On the other hand if two assets have positive covariance, when the return of the first asset increases then the second asset's return will also increase. The following formula shows how to calculate the covariance between two assets:

$$\text{Cov}(R_A, R_B) = \sum_{s=1} P_s(R_{A,s} - E(R_A))(R_{B,s} - E(R_B)) \tag{2.3}$$

In this equation Ps shows probability of state of s. After calculating covariance between two assets, we can calculate the correlation coefficient between two assets using the following formula.

$$\text{Cov}(R_A, R_B) = \frac{\text{Cov}(R_A, R_B)}{\sigma_A \sigma_B} \tag{2.4}$$

Calculating Portfolio Risk

We've seen that correlation is an important determinant of portfolio risk. To further pursue this issue, we need to know how to calculate portfolio variances directly. For a portfolio of two assets, A and B, the variance of the return on the portfolio, σ_P^2, is given by Equation 2.5.

$$\sigma_P^2 = x_A^2 \sigma_A^2 + x_B^2 \sigma_B^2 + 2x_A x_B \sigma_A \sigma_B \text{Corr}(R_A, R_B) \tag{2.5}$$

In this equation, x_A and x_B are the percentages invested in assets A and B. Notice that $x_A + x_B = 1$. (Why?)

For a portfolio of three assets, the variance of the return on the portfolio, $\sigma_P{}^2$, is given in Equation 2.6:

$$\sigma_P^2 = x^2{}_A \sigma_A{}^2 + x^2{}_B \sigma_B{}^2 + x^2{}_C \sigma_C{}^2 + 2x_A x_B \sigma_A \sigma_B \text{Corr}(R_A, R_B) \\ + 2x_A x_C \sigma_A \sigma_C \text{Corr}(R_A, R_C) + 2x_B x_C \sigma_B \sigma_C \text{Corr}(R_B R_C) \tag{2.6}$$

Note that six terms appear in Equation 2.6. There is a term involving the squared weight and the variances of the return for each of the three assets (A, B, and C) as well as a *cross-term* for each pair of assets. The cross-term involves pairs of weights, pairs of standard deviations of returns for each asset, and the correlation between the returns of the asset pair. If you had a portfolio of six assets, you would have an equation with 21 terms. (Can you write this equation?) If you had a portfolio of 50 assets, the equation for the variance of this portfolio would have 1,275 terms. Let's return to Equation 2.5.

Equation 2.5 looks a little involved, but its use is straightforward. For example, suppose Stock A has a standard deviation of 40 percent per year and Stock B has a standard deviation of 60 percent per year. The correlation between them is .15. If you put half your money in each, what is your portfolio standard deviation?

To answer, we just plug the numbers into Equation 2.5. Note that x_A and x_B are each equal to .50, while σ_A and σ_B are .40 and .60, respectively. Taking $\text{Corr}(R_A, R_B) = .15$, we have

$$\sigma_P^2 = .50^2 \times .40^2 + .50^2 \times .60^2 + 2 \times .50 \times .50 \times .40 \times .60 \times .15$$
$$= .25 \times .16 + .25 \times .36 + .018$$
$$= .148$$

Thus, the portfolio variance is .148. As always, variances are not easy to interpret since they are based on squared returns, so we calculate the standard deviation by taking the square root:

$$\sigma_P = \sqrt{.148} = .3847 = 38.47\%$$

Once again, we see the impact of diversification. This portfolio has a standard deviation of 38.47 percent, which is less than either of the standard deviations on the two assets that are in the portfolio.

PORTFOLIO VARIANCE AND STANDARD DEVIATION

EXAMPLE 2.5

In the example we just examined, Stock A has a standard deviation of 40 percent per year and Stock B has a standard deviation of 60 percent per year. Suppose now that the correlation between them is .35. Also suppose you put one-fourth of your money in Stock A. What is your portfolio standard deviation?

If you put 1/4 (or .25) in Stock A, you must have 3/4 (or .75) in Stock B, so $x_A = .25$ and $x_B = .75$. Making use of our portfolio variance equation (2.5), we have

$$\sigma_P^2 = .25^2 \times .40^2 + .75^2 \times .60^2 + 2 \times .25 \times .75 \times .40 \times .60 \times .35$$
$$= .0625 \times .16 + .5625 \times .36 + .0315$$
$$= .244$$

Thus the portfolio variance is .244. Taking the square root, we get

$$\sigma_P = \sqrt{.244} = .49396 \approx 49\%$$

This portfolio has a standard deviation of 49 percent, which is between the individual standard deviations. This shows that a portfolio's standard deviation isn't necessarily less than the individual standard deviations.

PORTFOLIO VARIANCE AND STANDARD DEVIATION

EXAMPLE 2.6

Karen Wilson forms a portfolio of the following three assets:

	Koc	Sabah	Al
Expected Return	10%	20%	30%
Standard Deviation	2%	10%	40%

The correlation coefficients between the assets are as follows:

Koc and Sabah   +0.4
Koc and Al   −0.4
Sabah and Al   −0.2

Karen has $100,000 for investment. She decides to allocate 30% of the funds to Koc, 30% to Sabah, and 40% to Al. Find the variance and standard deviation of her portfolio.

(continued)

$$\sigma_p^2 = x_{KOC}^2 \sigma_{KOC}^2 + x_{SABAH}^2 \sigma_{SABAH}^2 + x_{AL}^2 \sigma_{AL}^2$$
$$+ 2x_{KOC} x_{SABAH} \sigma_{KOC} \sigma_{SABAH} Corr(R_{KOC}, R_{SABAH})$$
$$+ 2x_{KOC} x_{AL} \sigma_{KOC} \sigma_{AL} Corr(R_{KOC}, R_{AL})$$
$$+ 2x_{SABAH} x_{AL} \sigma_{SABAH} \sigma_{AL} Corr(R_{SABAH} R_{AL})$$

$$\sigma_p^2 = (0.3)^2 (0.02)^2 + (0.3)^2 (0.1)^2 + (0.4)^2 (0.4)^2 + 2(0.3)(0.3)(0.02)(0.1)(0.4)$$
$$+ 2(0.3)(0.4)(0.02)(0.4)(-0.4) + 2(0.3)(0.4)(0.1)(0.4)(-0.2)$$
$$= 0.000036 + 0.0009 + 0.0256 + 0.000144 - 0.000768 - 0.00192$$
$$= 0.023992$$

$$\sigma_p = \sqrt{\sigma_p^2}$$
$$= 0.15489$$

The Importance of Asset Allocation, Part 1

asset allocation
How an investor spreads portfolio dollars among assets.

To illustrate why correlation and **asset allocation** are important practical real-world considerations, suppose that as a very conservative, risk-averse investor, you decide to invest all of your money in a bond mutual fund. Based on your analysis, you think this fund has an expected return of 6 percent with a standard deviation of 10 percent per year. A stock fund is available, however, with an expected return of 12 percent, but the standard deviation of 15 percent is too high for your taste. Also, the correlation between the returns on the two funds is about .10.

Is the decision to invest 100 percent in the bond fund a wise one, even for a very risk-averse investor? The answer is no; in fact, it is a bad decision for any investor. To see why, Table 2.9 shows expected returns and standard deviations available from different combinations of the two mutual funds. In constructing the table, we begin with 100 percent in the stock fund and work our way down to 100 percent in the bond fund by reducing the percentage in the stock fund in increments of .05. These calculations are all done just like our examples just above; you should check some (or all) of them for practice.

Beginning on the first row in Table 2.9, we have 100 percent in the stock fund, so our expected return is 12 percent, and our standard deviation is 15 percent. As we begin to move out of the stock fund and into the bond fund, we are not surprised to see both the expected return and the standard deviation decline. However, what might be surprising to you is the fact that the standard deviation falls only so far and then begins to rise again. In other words, beyond a point, adding more of the lower risk bond fund actually *increases* your risk!

investment opportunity set
Collection of possible risk–return combinations available from portfolios of individual assets.

The best way to see what is going on is to plot the various combinations of expected returns and standard deviations calculated in Table 2.9 as we do in Figure 2.4. We simply placed the standard deviations from Table 2.9 on the horizontal axis and the corresponding expected returns on the vertical axis.

Examining the plot in Figure 2.4, we see that the various combinations of risk and return available all fall on a smooth curve (in fact, for the geometrically inclined, it's a hyperbola). This curve is called an **investment opportunity set** because it shows the possible combinations of risk and return available from portfolios of these two assets. One important thing to notice is that, as we have shown, there is a portfolio that has the smallest standard deviation (or variance—same thing) of all. It is labelled "minimum variance portfolio" in Figure 2.4. What are (approximately) its expected return and standard deviation?

TABLE 2.9		Risk and Return with Stocks and Bonds	
Portfolio Weights			
Stocks	**Bonds**	**Expected Return**	**Standard Deviation**
1.00	.00	12.00%	15.00%
.95	.05	11.70	14.31
.90	.10	11.40	13.64
.85	.15	11.10	12.99
.80	.20	10.80	12.36
.75	.25	10.50	11.77
.70	.30	10.20	11.20
.65	.35	9.90	10.68
.60	.40	9.60	10.21
.55	.45	9.30	9.78
.50	.50	9.00	9.42
.45	.55	8.70	9.12
.40	.60	8.40	8.90
.35	.65	8.10	8.75
.30	.70	7.80	8.69
.25	.75	7.50	8.71
.20	.80	7.20	8.82
.15	.85	6.90	9.01
.10	.90	6.60	9.27
.05	.95	6.30	9.60
.00	1.00	6.00	10.00

FIGURE 2.4

Risk and Return with Stocks and Bonds

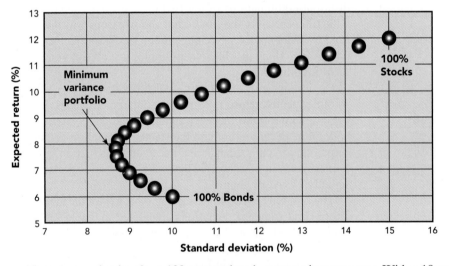

Review modern portfolio theory at www.moneychimp.com

Now we see clearly why a 100 percent bonds strategy is a poor one. With a 10 percent standard deviation, the bond fund offers an expected return of 6 percent. However, Table 2.9 shows us that a combination of about 60 percent stocks and 40 percent bonds has almost the same standard deviation, but a return of about 9.6 percent. Comparing 9.6 percent to 6 percent, we see that this portfolio has a return that is fully 60 percent greater ($6\% \times 1.6 = 9.6\%$) with the same risk. Our conclusion? Asset allocation matters.

Going back to Figure 2.4, notice that any portfolio that plots below the minimum variance portfolio is a poor choice because, no matter which one you pick, there is another portfolio with the same risk and a much better return. In the jargon of finance, we say that these undesirable portfolios are *dominated* and/or *inefficient*. Either way, we mean that given their level of risk, the expected return is inadequate compared to some other portfolio of equivalent risk. A portfolio that offers the highest return for its level of risk is said to be an **efficient portfolio**. In Figure 2.4, the minimum variance portfolio and all portfolios that plot above it are therefore efficient.

efficient portfolio
A portfolio that offers the highest return for its level of risk.

MORE PORTFOLIO VARIANCE AND STANDARD DEVIATION

EXAMPLE 2.7

Looking at Table 2.9, suppose you put 57.627 percent in the stock fund. What is your expected return? Your standard deviation? How does this compare with the bond fund?

If you put 57.627 percent in stocks, you must have 42.373 percent in bonds, so x_A = .57627 and x_B = .42373. Making use of our portfolio variance equation (2.3), we have

$$\sigma_P^2 = .57627^2 \times .15^2 + .42373^2 \times .10^2 + 2 \times .57627 \times .42373 \times .15 \times .10 \times .10$$
$$= .332 \times .0225 + .180 \times .01 + .0007325$$
$$= .01$$

Thus, the portfolio variance is .01, so the standard deviation is .1, or 10 percent. Check that the expected return is 9.46 percent. Compared to the bond fund, the standard deviation is now identical, but the expected return is almost 350 basis points higher.

More on Correlation and the Risk-Return Trade-Off

Given the expected returns and standard deviations on the two assets, the shape of the investment opportunity set in Figure 2.4 depends on the correlation. The lower the correlation, the more bowed to the left the investment opportunity set will be. To illustrate, Figure 2.5 shows the investment opportunity for correlations of −1, 0, and +1 for two stocks, A and B. Notice that Stock A has an expected return of 12 percent and a standard deviation of 15 percent, while Stock B has an expected return of 6 percent and a standard deviation of 10 percent. These are the same expected returns and standard deviations we used to build Figure 2.4, and the calculations are all done the same way; just the correlations are different. Notice also that we use the symbol ρ to stand for the correlation coefficient.

In Figure 2.5, when the correlation is +1, the investment opportunity set is a straight line connecting the two stocks, so, as expected, there is little or no diversification benefit. As the correlation declines to zero, the bend to the left becomes pronounced. For correlations between +1 and zero, there would simply be a less pronounced bend.

Finally, as the correlation becomes negative, the bend becomes quite pronounced, and the investment opportunity set actually becomes two straight-line segments when the correlation hits −1. Notice that the minimum variance portfolio has a *zero* variance in this case.

It is sometimes desirable to be able to calculate the percentage investments needed to create the minimum variance portfolio. We will just state the result here, but a problem

FIGURE 2.5

Risk and Return
with Two Assets

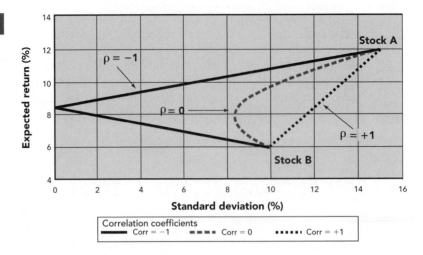

FIGURE 2.5

Risk and Return
with Two Assets

at the end of the chapter asks you to show that the weight on Asset A in the minimum variance portfolio, x_A^*, is

$$x_A^* = \frac{\sigma_B^2 - \sigma_A \sigma_B \, \text{Corr}(R_A, R_B)}{\sigma_A^2 + \sigma_B^2 - 2\sigma_A \sigma_B \, \text{Corr}(R_A, R_B)} \tag{2.7}$$

In Equation 2.7, we will take Asset A to be the one with the larger standard deviation. If the standard deviations happened to be the same, then Asset A could be either.

FINDING THE MINIMUM VARIANCE PORTFOLIO

EXAMPLE 2.8

Looking back at Table 2.9, what combination of the stock fund and the bond fund has the lowest possible standard deviation? What is the minimum possible standard deviation?

Recalling that the standard deviations for the stock fund and bond fund were .15 and .10, respectively, and noting that the correlation was .1, we have

$$x_A^* = \frac{.10^2 - .15 \times .10 \times .10}{.15^2 + .10^2 - 2 \times .15 \times .10 \times .10}$$

$$= .288136$$

$$\approx 28.8\%$$

Thus, the minimum variance portfolio has 28.8 percent in stocks and the balance, 71.2 percent, in bonds. Plugging these into our formula for portfolio variance, we have

$$\sigma_P^2 = .288^2 \times .15^2 + .712^2 \times .10^2 + 2 \times .288 \times .712 \times .15 \times .10 \times .10$$

$$= .007551$$

The standard deviation is the square root of .007551, about 8.7 percent. Notice that this is where the minimum occurs in Figure 2.5.

CHECK THIS ✓

2.4a   Fundamentally, why does diversification work?

2.4b   If two stocks have positive correlation, what does this mean?

2.4c   What is an efficient portfolio?

2.5 The Markowitz Efficient Frontier

In the previous section, we looked closely at the risk-return possibilities available when we consider combining two risky assets. Now we are left with an obvious question: What happens when we consider combining three or more risky assets? As we will see, at least on a conceptual level, the answer turns out to be a straightforward extension of our previous analysis.

The Importance of Asset Allocation, Part 2

As you saw in Equation 2.6, the formula to compute a portfolio variance with three assets is a bit cumbersome. Indeed, the amount of calculation increases greatly as the number of assets in the portfolio grows. The calculations are not difficult, but using a computer is highly recommended for portfolios consisting of more than three assets!

We can, however, illustrate the importance of asset allocation using only three assets. How? Well, a mutual fund that holds a broadly diversified portfolio of securities counts as only one asset. So, with three mutual funds that hold diversified portfolios, we can construct a diversified portfolio with these three assets. Suppose we invest in three index funds—one that represents U.S. stocks, one that represents U.S. bonds, and one that represents foreign stocks. Then we can see how the allocation among these three diversified portfolios matters.

Figure 2.6 shows the result of calculating the expected returns and portfolio standard deviations when there are three assets. To illustrate the importance of asset allocation, we calculated expected returns and standard deviations from portfolios composed of three key investment types: U.S. stocks, foreign (non-U.S.) stocks, and U.S. bonds. These asset classes *are not* highly correlated in general; therefore, we assume a zero

FIGURE 2.6 Markowitz Efficient Portfolio

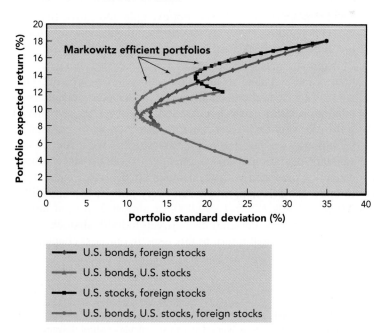

correlation in all cases. When we assume that all correlations are zero, the return to this portfolio is still:

$$R_P = x_F R_F + x_S R_S + x_B R_B \qquad (2.8)$$

But when all correlations are zero, the variance of the portfolio becomes:

$$\sigma_P^2 = x_F^2 \sigma_F^2 + x_S^2 \sigma_S^2 + x_B^2 \sigma_B^2 \qquad (2.9)$$

Suppose the expected returns and standard deviations are as follows:

	Expected Returns	Standard Deviations
Foreign stocks, *F*	18%	35%
U.S. stocks, *S*	12	22
U.S. bonds, *B*	8	14

We can now compute risk-return combinations as we did in our two-asset case. We create tables similar to Table 2.9, and then we can plot the risk-return combinations.

In Figure 2.6, each point plotted is a possible risk-return combination. Comparing the result with our two-asset case in Figure 2.4, we see that now not only do some assets plot below the minimum variance portfolio on a smooth curve, but we have portfolios plotting inside as well. Only combinations that plot on the upper left-hand boundary are efficient; all the rest are inefficient. This upper left-hand boundary is called the **Markowitz efficient frontier**, and it represents the set of risky portfolios with the maximum return for a given standard deviation.

Figure 2.6 makes it clear that asset allocation matters. For example, a portfolio of 100 percent U.S. stocks is highly inefficient. For the same standard deviation, there is a portfolio with an expected return almost 400 basis points, or 4 percent, higher. Or, for the same expected return, there is a portfolio with about half as much risk!

The analysis in this section can be extended to any number of assets or asset classes. In principle, it is possible to compute efficient frontiers using thousands of assets. As a practical matter, however, this analysis is most widely used with a relatively small number of asset classes. For example, most investment banks maintain so-called model portfolios. These are simply recommended asset allocation strategies typically involving three to six asset categories.

A primary reason that the Markowitz analysis is not usually extended to large collections of individual assets has to do with data requirements. The inputs into the analysis are (1) expected returns on all assets; (2) standard deviations on all assets; and (3) correlations between every pair of assets. Moreover, these inputs have to be measured with some precision, or we just end up with a garbage-in, garbage-out (GIGO) system.

Suppose we just look at 2,000 stocks. We need 2,000 expected returns and standard deviations. This is already a problem since returns on individual stocks cannot be predicted with precision at all. To make matters worse, however, we need to know the correlation between every *pair* of stocks. With 2,000 stocks, there are 2,000 × 1,999 / 2 = 1,999,000, or almost 2 million unique pairs![3] Also, as with expected returns, correlations between individual stocks are very difficult to predict accurately. We will return to this issue in our next chapter, where we show that there may be an extremely elegant way around the problem.

Markowitz efficient frontier
The set of portfolios with the maximum return for a given standard deviation.

Check out the online journal at www. efficientfrontier.com

---

[3] With 2,000 stocks, there are $2,000^2 = 4,000,000$ possible pairs. Of these, 2,000 involve pairing a stock with itself. Further, we recognize that the correlation between A and B is the same as the correlation between B and A, so we only need to actually calculate half of the remaining 3,998,000 correlations.

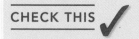

CHECK THIS		**2.5a**	What is the Markowitz efficient frontier?
		2.5b	Why is Markowitz portfolio analysis most commonly used to make asset allocation decisions?

2.6 Asset Allocation and Security Selection Decisions of Portfolio Formation

The current investment environment provides investors many asset classes and many securities within each asset class. Traditionally investors used to allocate their capital between domestic stocks and domestic bonds. The following are asset classes available for investors in today's investment world: (a) domestic stocks, (b) domestic bonds (government, municipal, provincial bonds, corporate bonds), (c) derivative instruments (options, futures, swaps), (d) money market instruments (T-bills, certificates of deposit, repurchase agreements, etc.), and (e) foreign stocks and bonds.

Investors face two problems when they form portfolios of multiple securities from different asset classes. These are as follows: (1) an asset allocation problem, and (2) a security selection problem. The asset allocation problem involves a decision regarding what percentage of an investor's portfolio should be allocated among different asset classes (stocks, bonds, derivatives, money market instruments, and foreign securities). On the other hand, the security selection problem involves deciding which securities to pick in each class and what percentage of funds to allocate to these securities (for example, choosing different stocks and their percentages within the asset class).

Suppose you have $100,000 for investment. First you have to decide which assets you want to hold. You may decide to invest $20,000 in money market instruments, $30,000 in bonds and $50,000 in domestic stocks. Your portfolio consists of 20 percent money market instruments, 30 percent bonds and 50 percent stocks. This is your asset allocation decision.

Then you may decide within the stock part of your portfolio to allocate $50,000 equally among the following five stocks: Nortel, Research In Motion, Royal Bank, Bombardier, and Molson Coors. That decision, your security selection decision, indicates that you will buy $10,000 worth of the stocks of each company.

Analysts claim that the asset allocation decision is the most important decision and determines return and risk level of your portfolio. Investors can use Markowitz's efficient frontier analysis in their asset allocation decisions to find the optimal portfolios at different risk levels. If they want to take minimum risk, they should increase their money market holdings.

Investors and fund managers change the composition of their portfolios for expected bull or bear markets. In a bear market, money market and bonds perform better than stocks. The opposite is true for bull markets. The nearby *Investment Updates* box investigates a fund manager's expectations of a bull market and his portfolio decisions.

Many small investors may leave these decisions to professionals and buy shares of mutual funds. These investors should examine the investment policies of the mutual fund they invest in and find out the composition of the mutual fund portfolios.

In the previous section we examined the efficient frontiers with only domestic assets and with a combination of foreign and domestic assets. Efficient frontiers with

With Cash, Investors Must Find a Happy Medium

Cash doesn't pay much, but when stock markets around the world plunge, as they have recently, an investor begins to look longingly at assets that hold their value no matter what.

For the record, the past two weeks have taken S&P/TSX composite index down almost 7 percent. Around the world, almost every other market tumbled. There was nowhere to hide—except in cash.

The problem is, of course, that while cash holds its value in the short term, keeping it for the long run means giving up a great deal of potential gain in riskier but more profitable stocks and other assets.

Professional investors disdain cash as a long-term investment. "It is a performance drag," says Elizabeth Lunney, senior vice-president and portfolio manager for Fiduciary Trust Co. of Canada, a unit of Toronto-based Franklin Templeton Investments Corp.

Hanif Mamdani, chief investment officer at money manager Phillips Hager & North in Vancouver, points out that the long-term annual return on U.S. stocks is about 8 percent, bonds 4 to 5 percent and cash 3 percent.

In practice, given the 5-percent net difference in returns between stocks and cash, if a portfolio holds 10-percent cash, it will suffer a 0.5-percent average annual reduction in total returns. A small number, but it adds up over time. Over 20 years, a 10-percent cash allocation would cut portfolio gains by 10 percent, using Mr. Mamdani's numbers.

Yet many investors do hold significant amounts of cash. What each investor needs is to find a happy medium between holding too much cash and holding enough cash to protect against excessive short-term risk and perhaps

to take advantage of buying opportunities in market downturns.

Investors differ in trading style, anticipated holding period and needs for cash in daily life. Moreover, there are times when stocks are expensive and a bigger weighting in cash is defensive. Probably the biggest factor though, is risk tolerance. As the accompanying pie chart shows, holding assets other than stocks reduces short-term risk. But the chart also shows that an increase in risk adds to potential gains.

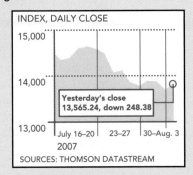

INDEX, DAILY CLOSE

Yesterday's close
13,565.24, down 248.38

July 16–20   23–27   30–Aug. 3
2007

SOURCES: THOMSON DATASTREAM

Over the long term, stocks pay out better returns than bonds or cash, but are much more volatile. "You have to have a good stomach to go through the ups and downs of the market," says Moshe Milevsky, professor of finance at York University. "If you will be in a coma for 20 years, then you would be at 100-percent equity."

The appetite for risk depends on the individual's personality, but also on the individual's situation, Prof. Milevsky adds. "I am a tenured professor and have a

(continued)

foreign assets are superior to those with domestic assets only. This is especially true for Canadian investors, because of the existence of semi-liquid Canadian stock markets. Canadian investors can get better risk-return combinations if they include foreign assets in their portfolios and diversify internationally. We investigate international portfolio investment in our last chapter.

2.7   Summary and Conclusions

In this chapter, we covered the basics of diversification and portfolio risk and return. From this material we saw that:

1. A portfolio's expected return is a simple weighted combination of the expected returns on the assets in the portfolio, but the standard deviation on a portfolio is not.

guaranteed income for life," he explains. "That makes me a bond. If my total income in my life as a teacher will be $2.5-million, should my asset allocation not be affected?" With the foundation of an annuity income, the investor can take more market risk, Prof. Milevsky suggests.

Timing is another big factor when deciding how much cash to carry in a portfolio. Markets can have long periods dominated by a single asset class. In the 1970s, stocks were stuck in a rut, interest rates soared and existing bond prices collapsed.

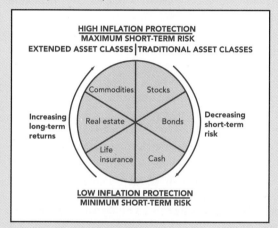

Cash had the best annual returns until 1981 when central banks in the United States and Canada jacked up short-term interest rates and broke the back of inflation. Today, it's anyone's guess as to whether stocks will continue their upward climb, or there will be many days like July 24 when the Toronto Stock Exchange lost 400 points.

"If you think that the stock market is in a period of excess risk, then you want to hold bonds," says Tom Czitron, managing director for income and structured products at Sceptre Investment Counsel Ltd. in Toronto.

That period could be right now, depending on the investor tolerance for the volatile stock market. Normally, an investor need only have a little cash in an investment portfolio, but today, long bonds are paying yields that are about the same as cash equivalents like treasury bills, so an investor can hold cash, explains Brad Bondy, vice-president of investment operations for Genus Capital Management Inc. in Vancouver. In other words, why buy a long-term bond when it is paying less yield than a short-term bond?

Diversification is the key to risk control. A rational investor should have money in stocks, bonds and cash and even the less traditional, but still important, sectors, of real estate, commodities and life insurance, he said.

Over the long term, which is at least as long as several boom-to-bust-to-boom market cycles that traditionally last 36 months each, stocks tend to beat other asset classes. But there is enough variation in those returns to make one want to hedge bets by holding other asset classes, including cash. How much cash depends on one's taste for buying on dips and perhaps on one's need for cash to pay bills for kids in university or a down payment on a house.

In the end, having everything invested in stocks may be a way to make the most of capital, but it also courts higher short-term volatility and the emotional pain of wishing one had more cash when, as it has recently, the market turns risk into loss.

Andrew Allentuck—reprinted with the permission of the author.

2. Diversification is a very important consideration. The principle of diversification tells us that spreading an investment across many assets can reduce some, but not all, of the risk.

3. Diversification works because asset returns are not perfectly correlated. All else the same, the lower the correlation, the greater is the gain from diversification.

4. When we consider the possible combinations of risk and return available from portfolios of assets, we find that some are inefficient (or dominated), meaning that they offer too little return for their risk.

5. Finally, for any group of assets, there is a set that is efficient. That set is known as the Markowitz efficient frontier.

The most important thing to carry away from this chapter is an understanding of diversification and why it works. Once you understand this, then the importance of asset allocation follows immediately.

REAL WORLD

This chapter explained diversification, a very important consideration for real-world investors and money managers. The chapter also explored the famous Markowitz efficient portfolio concept, which shows how (and why) asset allocation affects portfolio risk and return.

Building a diversified portfolio is not a trivial task. Mutual funds provide one way for investors to build diversified portfolios, but there are some significant caveats concerning mutual funds as a diversification tool. First of all, investors sometimes assume a fund is diversified simply because it holds a relatively large number of stocks. However, with the exception of some index funds, most mutual funds will reflect a particular style of investing, either explicitly, as stated in the fund's objective, or implicitly, as favoured by the fund manager. For example, in the mid- to late-1990s, stocks as a whole did very well, but mutual funds that concentrated on smaller stocks generally did not do well at all.

It is tempting to buy a number of mutual funds to ensure broad diversification, but even this may not work. Within a given fund family, the same manager may actually be responsible for multiple funds. In addition, managers within a large fund family frequently have similar views about the market and individual companies.

Thinking just about stocks for the moment, what does an investor need to consider to build a well-diversified portfolio? At a minimum, such a portfolio probably needs to be diversified across industries, with no undue concentrations in particular sectors of the economy; it needs to be diversified by company size (small, midcap, and large), and it needs to be diversified across "growth" (i.e., high-P/E) and "value" (low-P/E) stocks. Perhaps the most controversial diversification issue concerns international diversification. The correlation between international stock exchanges is surprisingly low, suggesting large benefits from diversifying globally.

Perhaps the most disconcerting fact about diversification is that it leads to the following paradox: A well-diversified portfolio will always be invested in something that does not do well! Put differently, such a portfolio will almost always have both winners and losers. In many ways, that's the whole idea. Even so, it requires a lot of financial discipline to stay diversified when some portion of your portfolio seems to be doing poorly. The payoff is that, over the long run, a well-diversified portfolio should provide much steadier returns and be much less prone to abrupt changes in value.

Key Terms

expected return 35
portfolio 38
portfolio weight 38
principle of diversification 44
correlation 46

asset allocation 51
investment opportunity set 51
efficient portfolio 53
Markowitz efficient frontier 56

Chapter Review Problems and Self-Test

Use the following table of states of the economy and stock returns to answer the review problems:

State of Economy	Probability of State of Economy	Security Returns if State Occurs	
		Roten	Bradley
Bust	.40	−10%	30%
Boom	.60	40	10
	1.00		

1. **Expected Returns** Calculate the expected returns for Roten and Bradley.
2. **Standard Deviations** Calculate the standard deviations for Roten and Bradley.
3. **Portfolio Expected Returns** Calculate the expected return on a portfolio of 50 percent Roten and 50 percent Bradley.
4. **Portfolio Volatility** Calculate the volatility of a portfolio of 50 percent Roten and 50 percent Bradley.

Answers to Self-Test Problems

1. We calculate the expected return as follows:

		Roten		Bradley	
(1)	(2)	(3)	(4)	(5)	(6)
State of Economy	Probability of State of Economy	Return if State Occurs	Product (2) × (3)	Return if State Occurs	Product (2) × (5)
Bust	.40	−10%	−.04	30%	.12
Boom	.60	40	.24	10	.06
			$E(R) = 20\%$		$E(R) = 18\%$

2. We calculate the standard deviation as follows:

(1)	(2)	(3)	(4)	(5)
State of Economy	Probability of State of Economy	Return Deviation from Expected Return	Squared Return Deviation	Product (2) × (4)
Roten				
Bust	.40	−.30	.09	.036
Boom	.60	.20	.04	.024
				$\sigma^2 = .06$
Bradley				
Bust	.40	.12	.0144	.00576
Boom	.60	−.08	.0064	.00384
				$\sigma^2 = .0096$

Taking square roots, the standard deviations are 24.495 percent and 9.798 percent.

3. We calculate the expected return on a portfolio of 50 percent Roten and 50 percent Bradley as follows:

(1) State of Economy	(2) Probability of State of Economy	(3) Portfolio Return if State Occurs	(4) Product (2) × (3)
Bust	.40	10%	.04
Boom	.60	25	.15
			$E(R_p) = 19\%$

4. We calculate the volatility of a portfolio of 50 percent Roten and 50 percent Bradley as follows:

(1) State of Economy	(2) Probability of State of Economy	(3) Portfolio Return if State Occurs	(4) Squared Deviation from Expected Return	(5) Product (2) × (4)
Bust	.40	.10	.0081	.00324
Boom	.60	.25	.0036	.00216
				$\sigma_p^2 = .0054$
				$\sigma_p = 7.3485\%$

Test Your Investment Quotient

1. **Diversification** Netcap has an expected return of 25 percent and Jmart has an expected return of 20 percent. What is the likely investment decision for a risk-averse investor?

   a. Invest all funds in Netcap.
   b. Invest all funds in Jmart.
   c. Do not invest any funds in Netcap and Jmart.
   d. Invest funds partly in Netcap and partly in Jmart.

2. **Return Standard Deviation** Netcap experiences returns of 5 percent or 45 percent, each with an equal probability. What is the return standard deviation for Netcap?

   a. 30 percent
   b. 25 percent
   c. 20 percent
   d. 10 percent

3. **Return Standard Deviation** Jmart experiences returns of 0 percent, 25 percent, or 50 percent, each with a one-third probability. What is the approximate return standard deviation for Jmart?

   a. 30 percent
   b. 25 percent
   c. 20 percent
   d. 10 percent

4. **Expected Return** An analyst estimates that a stock has the following return probabilities and returns depending on the state of the economy:

State of Economy	Probability	Return
Good	.1	15%
Normal	.6	13
Poor	.3	7

What is the expected return of the stock?

a. 7.8 percent

b. 11.4 percent

c. 11.7 percent

d. 13.0 percent

5. **Risk Aversion** Which of the following statements best reflects the importance of the asset allocation decision to the investment process? The asset allocation decision

a. Helps the investor decide on realistic investment goals.

b. Identifies the specific securities to include in a portfolio.

c. Determines most of the portfolio's returns and volatility over time.

d. Creates a standard by which to establish the appropriate investment time horizon.

6. **Efficient Frontier** The Markowitz efficient frontier is best described as the set of portfolios that has

a. The minimum risk for every level of return.

b. Proportionally equal units of risk and return.

c. The maximum excess rate of return for every given level of risk.

d. The highest return for each level of beta used on the capital asset pricing model.

7. **Diversification** An investor is considering adding another investment to a portfolio. To achieve the maximum diversification benefits, the investor should add an investment that has a correlation coefficient with the existing portfolio closest to

a. −1.0

b. −.5

c. .0

d. +1.0

8. **Risk Premium** Netcap has an expected return of 25 percent, Jmart has an expected return of 20 percent, and the risk-free rate is 5 percent. You invest half your funds in Netcap and the other half in Jmart. What is the risk premium for your portfolio?

a. 20 percent

b. 17.5 percent

c. 15 percent

d. 12.5 percent

9. **Return Standard Deviation** Both Netcap and Jmart have the same return standard deviation of 20 percent, and Netcap and Jmart returns have zero correlation. You invest half your funds in Netcap and the other half in Jmart. What is the return standard deviation for your portfolio?

a. 20 percent

b. 14.14 percent

c. 10 percent

d. 0 percent

10. **Return Standard Deviation** Both Netcap and Jmart have the same return standard deviation of 20 percent, and Netcap and Jmart returns have a correlation of +1. You invest half your funds in Netcap and the other half in Jmart. What is the return standard deviation for your portfolio?

a. 20 percent

b. 14.14 percent

c. 10 percent

d. 0 percent

11. **Return Standard Deviation** Both Netcap and Jmart have the same return standard deviation of 20 percent, and Netcap and Jmart returns have a correlation of −1.

You invest half your funds in Netcap and the other half in Jmart. What is the return standard deviation for your portfolio?

   a. 20 percent
   b. 14.14 percent
   c. 10 percent
   d. 0 percent

12. **Minimum Variance Portfolio** Both Netcap and Jmart have the same return standard deviation of 20 percent, and Netcap and Jmart returns have zero correlation. What is the minimum attainable return variance for a portfolio of Netcap and Jmart?

   a. 20 percent
   b. 14.14 percent
   c. 10 percent
   d. 0 percent

13. **Minimum Variance Portfolio** Both Netcap and Jmart have the same return standard deviation of 20 percent, and Netcap and Jmart returns have a correlation of -1. What is the minimum attainable return variance for a portfolio of Netcap and Jmart?

   a. 20 percent
   b. 14.14 percent
   c. 10 percent
   d. 0 percent

14. **Minimum Variance Portfolio** Stocks A, B, and C each have the same expected return and standard deviation. The following shows the correlations between returns on these stocks:

	Stock A	Stock B	Stock C
Stock A	+1.0		
Stock B	+0.9	+1.0	
Stock C	+0.1	−0.4	+1.0

Given these correlations, which of the following portfolios constructed from these stocks would have the lowest risk?

   a. One equally invested in stocks A and B.
   b. One equally invested in stocks A and C.
   c. One equally invested in stocks B and C.
   d. One totally invested in stock C.

15. **Markowitz Efficient Frontier** Which of the following portfolios cannot lie on the efficient frontier as described by Markowitz?

	Portfolio	Expected Return	Standard Deviation
a.	W	9%	21%
b.	X	5	7
c.	Y	15	36
d.	Z	12	15

Concept Questions

1. **Diversification and Market History** Based on market history, what is the average annual standard deviation of return for a single, randomly chosen stock? What is the average annual standard deviation for an equally weighted portfolio of many stocks?

2. **Interpreting Correlations** If the returns on two stocks are highly correlated, what does this mean? If they have no correlation? If they are negatively correlated?

CFA® PROBLEMS

CFA® PROBLEMS

3. **Efficient Portfolios** What is an efficient portfolio?

4. **Expected Returns** True or false: If two stocks have the same expected return of 12 percent, then any portfolio of the two stocks will also have an expected return of 12 percent.

5. **Portfolio Volatility** True or false: If two stocks have the same standard deviation of 45 percent, then any portfolio of the two stocks will also have a standard deviation of 45 percent.

6. **Diversification** You are an investment adviser and a client makes the following statement: I do not want a diversified portfolio since I will never get the highest possible return. How do you respond to your client?

7. **Investment Opportunity Set** You have a portfolio created from two assets. As you add more of the lower risk asset to your portfolio, the risk of your portfolio increases. What do you know about your current portfolio?

8. **Minimum Variance Portfolio** Why is the minimum variance portfolio important in regard to the Markowitz efficient frontier?

9. **Markowitz Efficient Frontier** True or false: It is impossible for a single asset to lie on the Markowitz efficient frontier.

10. **Portfolio Variance** Suppose two assets have zero correlation and the same standard deviation. What is true about the minimum variance portfolio?

Questions and Problems

Core Questions

1. **Expected Returns** Use the following information on states of the economy and stock returns to calculate the expected return for Dingaling Telephone:

State of Economy	Probability of State of Economy	Security Return if State Occurs
Recession	.20	−10%
Normal	.60	14
Boom	.20	27

2. **Standard Deviations** Using the information in the previous question, calculate the standard deviation of returns.

3. **Expected Returns and Deviations** Repeat Questions 1 and 2 assuming that all three states are equally likely.

Use the following information on states of the economy and stock returns to answer Questions 4–7:

State of Economy	Probability of State of Economy	Security Returns if State Occurs	
		Roll	Ross
Bust	.40	−10%	21%
Boom	.60	28	8

4. **Expected Returns** Calculate the expected returns for Roll and Ross by filling in the following table (verify your answer by expressing returns as percentages as well as decimals):

(1) State of Economy	(2) Probability of State of Economy	Roll		Ross	
		(3) Return if State Occurs	(4) Product (2) × (3)	(5) Return if State Occurs	(6) Product (2) × (5)
Bust					
Boom					

5. **Standard Deviations** Calculate the standard deviations for Roll and Ross by filling in the following table (verify your answer using returns expressed in percentages as well as decimals):

(1) State of Economy	(2) Probability of State of Economy	(3) Return Deviation from Expected Return	(4) Squared Return Deviation	(5) Product (2) × (4)
Roll				
Bust				
Boom				
Ross				
Bust				
Boom				

6. **Portfolio Expected Returns** Calculate the expected return on a portfolio of 40 percent Roll and 60 percent Ross by filling in the following table:

(1) State of Economy	(2) Probability of State of Economy	(3) Portfolio Return if State Occurs	(4) Product (2) × (3)
Bust			
Boom			

7. **Portfolio Volatility** Calculate the volatility of a portfolio of 70 percent Roll and 30 percent Ross by filling in the following table:

(1) State of Economy	(2) Probability of State of Economy	(3) Portfolio Return if State Occurs	(4) Squared Deviation from Expected Return	(5) Product (2) × (4)
Bust				
Boom				
$\sigma_P^2 =$				
$\sigma_P =$				

8. **Calculating Returns and Standard Deviations** Based on the following information, calculate the expected return and standard deviation for the two stocks.

State of Economy	Probability of State of Economy	Rate of Return if State Occurs	
		Stock A	Stock B
Recession	.15	.04	−.20
Normal	.70	.09	.13
Boom	.15	.12	.33

9. **Returns and Standard Deviations** Consider the following information:

State of Economy	Probability of State of Economy	Rate of Return if State Occurs		
		Stock A	Stock B	Stock C
Boom	.20	.30	.45	.33
Good	.40	.12	.10	.15
Poor	.30	.01	−.15	−.05
Bust	.10	−.06	−.30	−.09

a. Your portfolio is invested 25 percent each in A and C, and 50 percent in B. What is the expected return of the portfolio?

b. What is the variance of this portfolio? The standard deviation?

10. **Portfolio Returns and Volatilities** Fill in the missing information in the following table. Assume that Portfolio AB is 30 percent invested in Stock A.

	Annual Returns		
Year	Stock A	Stock B	Portfolio AB
2001	18%	50%	
2002	40	−30	
2003	−15	45	
2004	20	2	
2005	4	20	
Average returns			
Standard deviations			

Intermediate Questions

11. **Portfolio Returns and Volatilities** Given the following information, calculate the expected return and standard deviation for a portfolio that has 20 percent invested in Stock A, 35 percent in Stock B, and the balance in Stock C.

State of Economy	Probability of State of Economy	Returns		
		Stock A	Stock B	Stock C
Boom	.70	15%	18%	20%
Bust	.30	10	0	−10

12. **Portfolio Variance** Use the following information to calculate the expected return and standard deviation of a portfolio that is 40 percent invested in 3 Doors, Inc., and 60 percent invested in Down Co.:

	3 Doors, Inc.	Down Co.
Expected return, $E(R)$	15%	10%
Standard deviation, σ	50	38
Correlation		.15

13. **More Portfolio Variance** In the previous question, what is the standard deviation if the correlation is +1? 0? −1? As the correlation declines from +1 to −1 here, what do you see happening to portfolio volatility? Why?

14. **Minimum Variance Portfolio** In Problem 12, what are the expected return and standard deviation on the minimum variance portfolio?

15. **Asset Allocation** Fill in the missing information assuming a correlation of .15.

Portfolio Weights		Expected Return	Standard Deviation
Stocks	Bonds		
1.00		12%	21%
.80			
.60			
.40			
.20			
.00		6%	9%

16. **Minimum Variance Portfolio** Consider two stocks, Stock D with an expected return of 13 percent and a standard deviation of 54 percent and Stock I, an international company, with an expected return of 16 percent and a standard deviation of 78 percent. The correlation between the two stocks is $-.10$. What is the weight of each stock in the minimum variance portfolio?

17. **Minimum Variance Portfolio** What are the expected return and standard deviation of the minimum variance portfolio in the previous problem?

18. **Minimum Variance Portfolio** Asset K has an expected return of 15 percent and a standard deviation of 53 percent. Asset L has an expected return of 6 percent and a standard deviation of 10 percent. The correlation between the assets is .02. What are the expected return and standard deviation of the minimum variance portfolio?

19. **Minimum Variance Portfolio** The stock of Bruin, Inc., has an expected return of 17 percent and a standard deviation of 43 percent. The stock of Wildcat Co. has an expected return of 15 percent and a standard deviation of 52 percent. The correlation between the two stocks is .25. Is it possible for there to be a minimum variance portfolio since the highest-return stock has the lowest standard deviation? If so, calculate the expected return and standard deviation of the minimum variance portfolio. Graph the investment opportunity set for these two stocks.

20. **Portfolio Variance** You have a three-stock portfolio. Stock A has an expected return of 12 percent and a standard deviation of 41 percent, Stock B has an expected return of 16 percent and a standard deviation of 58 percent, and Stock C has an expected return of 13 percent and a standard deviation of 48 percent. The correlation between Stocks A and B is .30, between Stocks A and C is .20, and between Stocks B and C is .05. Your portfolio consists of 30 percent Stock A, 50 percent Stock B, and 20 percent Stock C. Calculate the expected return and standard deviation of your portfolio. The formula for calculating the variance of a three-stock portfolio is:

$$\sigma_P^2 = x_A^2\sigma_A^2 + x_B^2\sigma_B^2 + x_C^2\sigma_C^2 + 2x_Ax_B\sigma_A\sigma_B\text{Corr}(R_A, R_B)$$
$$+ 2x_Ax_C\sigma_A\sigma_C\,\text{Corr}(R_A, R_C) + 2x_Bx_C\sigma_B\sigma_C\,\text{Corr}(R_B, R_C)$$

21. **Minimum Variance Portfolio** You are going to invest in Asset J and Asset S. Asset J has an expected return of 15 percent and a standard deviation of 58 percent. Asset S has an expected return of 9 percent and a standard deviation of 24 percent. The correlation between the two assets is .60. What are the standard deviation and expected return of the minimum variance portfolio? What is going on here?

22. **Portfolio Variance** Suppose two assets have perfect positive correlation. Show that the standard deviation on a portfolio of the two assets is simply:

$$\sigma_P = x_A \times \sigma_A + x_B \times \sigma_B$$

(*Hint:* Look at the expression for the variance of a two-asset portfolio. If the correlation is $+1$, the expression is a perfect square.)

23. **Portfolio Variance** Suppose two assets have perfect negative correlation. Show that the standard deviation on a portfolio of the two assets is simply:

$$\sigma_P = \pm(x_A \times \sigma_A - x_B \times \sigma_B)$$

(*Hint:* See previous problem.)

24. **Portfolio Variance** Using the result in Problem 23, show that whenever two assets have perfect negative correlation it is possible to find a portfolio with a zero standard deviation. What are the portfolio weights? (*Hint*: Let x be the percentage in the first asset and $(1 - x)$ be the percentage in the second. Set the standard deviation to zero and solve for x.)

25. **Portfolio Variance** Derive our expression in the chapter for the portfolio weight in the minimum variance portfolio. (Danger! Calculus required!) (*Hint*: Let x be the percentage in the first asset and $(1 - x)$ the percentage in the second. Take the derivative with respect to x, and set it to zero. Solve for x.)

Use the data given in Example 2.6 to solve questions 26, 27 and 28.

26. **Portfolio Expected Return and Variance** Karen Wilson's friend Ed examined Karen's portfolio and told her he would have invested 10% of the funds to Koc, 20% to Sabah and the rest of it to Al. Calculate the expected return and variance of this portfolio.

27. **Portfolio Expected Return and Variance** Compare Karen's portfolio with Ed's portfolio in terms of expected return and variance. Is one of them better than the other?

28. **Portfolios versus Single Assets** Compare expected returns and variances of the two portfolios with those of the single assets. What would you prefer? Do you think there are better combinations of these assets in a portfolio? Show an example.

CHAPTER 3

Buying and Selling Securities

"Don't gamble! Take all your savings and buy some good stock and hold it till it goes up. If it don't go up, don't buy it."

—Will Rogers

You might wish to try Will Rogers's well-known stock market advice, but first you must know the basics of securities trading. Fortunately, trading is a relatively simple task, as attested to by the billions of shares of stocks that trade among investors on a typical day. Essentially, you begin the process by opening a trading account with a brokerage firm and then submitting trading orders. But you should know about some important details beforehand. ■

To help you get started, this chapter covers the basics of the investing process. We begin by describing how you go about buying and selling securities such as stocks and bonds. We then outline some of the most important considerations and constraints to keep in mind as you get more involved in the investing process.

3.1   Getting Started

Suppose you have some money that you want to invest. One way to get started is to open an account with a securities broker, such as Scotia McLeod or TD Waterhouse. Such accounts are often called *brokerage* or *trading accounts*. Opening a trading account is straightforward and really much like opening a bank account. You will be asked to supply some basic information about yourself and sign an agreement (often simply called a customer's agreement) that spells out your rights and obligations and those of your broker. You then give your broker a cheque and instructions on how you want the money invested.

Suppose you want to invest in Magna Corporation. You therefore open an account with $10,000. You instruct your broker to purchase 100 shares of Magna stock and to retain any remaining funds in your account. Your broker will locate a seller and purchase the stock on your behalf. If the share price of Magna is $88, you will pay $8,800. In addition, for providing this service, your broker will charge you a commission. How much depends on a number of things, including the type of broker and the size of your order, but for this order, $25 wouldn't be an unusual commission charge. After paying for the stock and paying the commission, you would have $1,175 left in your account. Your broker will hold your stock for you or deliver the shares to you, whichever you wish. At a later date, you can sell your stock by instructing your broker to do so. You would receive the proceeds from the sale, less another commission charge. You can always add money to your account and purchase additional securities, and you can withdraw money from your account or even close it altogether.

In broad terms, this basic explanation is really all there is to it. As we begin to discuss in the next section, however, there is a range of services available to you, and there are important considerations that you need to take into account before you actually begin investing.

Choosing a Broker

The first step in opening an account is choosing a broker. Brokers are traditionally divided into three groups: full-service brokers, discount brokers, and deep-discount brokers. What distinguishes the three groups is the level of service they provide and the resulting commissions they charge.

With a deep-discount broker, essentially the only services provided are account maintenance and order execution—that is, buying and selling. You generally deal with a deep-discount broker over the telephone or, increasingly, using a Web browser (see the next section on online brokers for a discussion).

At the other extreme, a full-service broker will provide investment advice regarding the types of securities and investment strategies that might be appropriate for you to consider (or avoid). The larger brokerage firms do extensive research on individual companies and securities and maintain lists of recommended (and not recommended) securities. They maintain offices throughout the country, so, depending on where you live, you can actually stop in and speak to the person assigned to your account. A full-service broker will even manage your account for you if you wish.

Discount brokers fall somewhere between the two cases we have discussed so far, offering more investment counselling than the deep-discounters and lower commissions than the full-service brokers. Which type of broker should you choose? It depends on how much advice and service you need or want. If you are the do-it-yourself type, then you may seek out the lower commissions. If you are not, then a full-service broker might be more suitable. Often investors begin with a full-service broker, and then, as they gain experience and confidence, move on to a discount broker.

We should note that the brokerage industry is very competitive, and differences between broker types seem to be blurring. Full-service brokers frequently discount commissions to attract new customers (particularly those with large accounts), and you should not hesitate to ask about commission rates. Similarly, discount brokers have begun to offer securities research and extensive account management services. Basic brokerage services have become almost commodity-like, and, more and more, brokerage firms are competing by offering financial services such as retirement planning, credit cards, and cheque-writing privileges, to name a few.

Online Brokers

The most important recent change in the brokerage industry is the rapid growth of online brokers, also known as e-brokers or cyberbrokers. With an online broker, you place buy and sell orders over the Internet using a Web browser. If you are currently participating in a portfolio simulation such as Stock-Trak, then you already have a very good idea of how an online account looks and feels.

Before 1995, online accounts essentially did not exist; by 2000, many millions of investors were buying and selling securities online. The industry is growing so rapidly that it is difficult to even count the number of online brokers.

Online investing has fundamentally changed the discount and deep-discount brokerage industry by slashing costs dramatically. In a typical online trade, no human intervention is needed by the broker as the entire process is handled electronically, so operating costs are held to a minimum. As costs have fallen, so have commissions. Even for relatively large trades, online brokers typically charge less than $10 per trade. For budget-minded investors and active stock traders, the attraction is clear.

Competition among online brokers is fierce. Some take a no-frills approach, offering only basic services and very low commission rates. Others, particularly the larger ones, charge a little more but offer a variety of services, including research and various banking services such as cheque-writing privileges, credit cards, debit cards, and even mortgages. As technology continues to improve and investors become more comfortable using it, online brokerages will almost surely become the dominant form because of their enormous convenience—and the low commission rates.

When online brokers first appeared they were generally just discount and deep-discount brokers. Today, however, even full-service brokers offer extensive online services. Table 3.1 lists full-service and discount brokerage houses in alphabetical order. The majority of these brokers are rated by the Globeinvestor's website.

Canadian Investor Protection Fund

Canadian Investor Protection Fund
Insurance fund covering investors' brokerage accounts with member firms.

As you are probably aware, when you deposit money in a bank, your account is normally protected (up to $100,000) by the Canadian Deposit Insurance Corporation (CDIC) which is a federal Crown corporation. However, brokerage firms, even though they are often called investment banks, cannot offer CDIC coverage. Most brokerage firms do belong to the **Canadian Investor Protection Fund**, or **CIPF** which was created in 1969. The CIPF insures your account for up to $1,000,000 for losses of securities, commodity and futures contracts, segregated insurance funds and cash. Unlike the CDIC, the CIPF is not a government agency; it is a private insurance fund supported by the securities industry. Almost all brokerage firms are members of the CIPF.

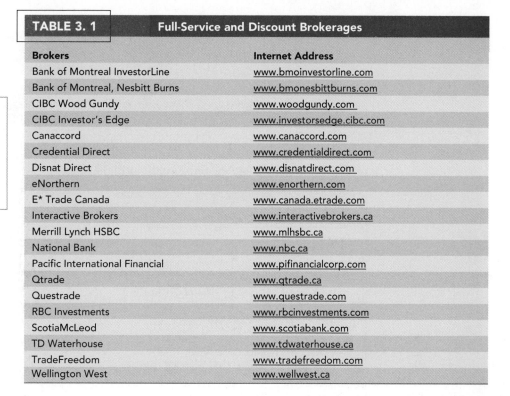

TABLE 3.1	Full-Service and Discount Brokerages
Brokers	**Internet Address**
Bank of Montreal InvestorLine	www.bmoinvestorline.com
Bank of Montreal, Nesbitt Burns	www.bmonesbittburns.com
CIBC Wood Gundy	www.woodgundy.com
CIBC Investor's Edge	www.investorsedge.cibc.com
Canaccord	www.canaccord.com
Credential Direct	www.credentialdirect.com
Disnat Direct	www.disnatdirect.com
eNorthern	www.enorthern.com
E* Trade Canada	www.canada.etrade.com
Interactive Brokers	www.interactivebrokers.ca
Merrill Lynch HSBC	www.mlhsbc.ca
National Bank	www.nbc.ca
Pacific International Financial	www.pifinancialcorp.com
Qtrade	www.qtrade.ca
Questrade	www.questrade.com
RBC Investments	www.rbcinvestments.com
ScotiaMcLeod	www.scotiabank.com
TD Waterhouse	www.tdwaterhouse.ca
TradeFreedom	www.tradefreedom.com
Wellington West	www.wellwest.ca

Which online broker is the best? See ratings at www.globeinvestor.com/series/brokersurvey

There is a very important difference between CIPF coverage and CDIC coverage. Up to the maximum coverage, the value of whatever you deposit in a bank is fully guaranteed by the CDIC; you will not lose a cent under any circumstances with CDIC coverage. In contrast, the CIPF insures only that you will receive whatever cash and securities were held for you by your broker in the event of fraud or other failure. The value of any securities, however, is not guaranteed. In other words, you can lose everything in an CIPF-covered account if the value of your securities falls to zero.

Broker–Customer Relations

There are several other important things to keep in mind when dealing with a broker. First, any advice you receive is *not* guaranteed. Far from it—buy and sell recommendations carry the explicit warning that you rely on them at your own risk. Your broker does have a duty to exercise reasonable care in formulating recommendations and not recommend anything grossly unsuitable, but that is essentially the extent of it.

Second, your broker works as your agent and has a legal duty to act in your best interest; however, brokerage firms are in the business of generating brokerage commissions. This fact will probably be spelled out in the account agreement that you sign. There is, therefore, the potential for a conflict of interest. On rare occasions, a broker is accused of "churning" an account, which refers to extensive trading for the sole purpose of generating commissions. In general, you are responsible for checking your account statements and notifying your broker in the event of any problems, and you should certainly do so.

Finally, in the unlikely event of a significant problem, your account agreement will probably specify very clearly that you must waive your right to sue and/or seek

To learn more about dispute resolution, visit www.ida.ca

WORK THE WEB

In order to participate in e-trading, investors should open an online account for electronic trading. After that they can go to the website of their broker and give buy or sell orders, track their accounts, and trade on margin. The following website shows an online trade for an investor at HSBC's InvestDirect site. The investor entered an order to buy 50 shares of Nortel Stock at market price. Once the investor hits Submit, the order will be entered and the broker will fulfill the order.

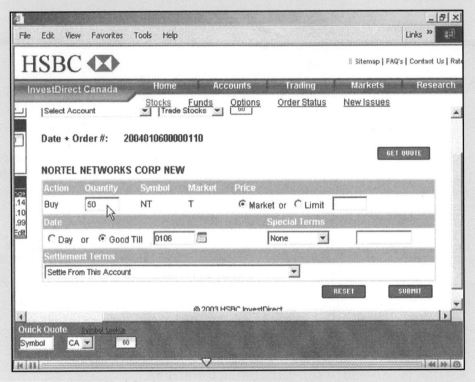

Source: Courtesy of HSBC Bank Canada.

a jury trial. Instead, you agree that any disputes will be settled by arbitration and that arbitration is final and binding. Arbitration is not a legal proceeding, and the rules are much less formal. In essence, a panel is appointed by a self-regulatory body of the securities industry to review the case. The panel will be composed of a small number of individuals who are knowledgeable about the securities industry, but a majority of them will not be associated with the industry. The panel makes a finding, and, absent extraordinary circumstances, its findings cannot be appealed. The panel does not have to disclose factual findings or legal reasoning.

CHECK THIS

3.1a   What are the differences between full-service and deep-discount brokers?

3.1b   What is the CIPF? How does CIPF coverage differ from CDIC coverage?

3.2   Brokerage Accounts

The account agreement that you sign has a number of important provisions and de-tails specifying the types of trades that can be made and who can make them. Another important concern is whether the broker will extend credit and the terms under which credit will be extended. We discuss these issues next.

Cash Accounts

cash account
A brokerage account in which all transac-tions are made on a strictly cash basis.

A **cash account** is the simplest arrangement. Securities can be purchased to the extent that sufficient cash is available in the account. If additional purchases are desired, then the needed funds must be promptly supplied.

Margin Accounts

margin account A brokerage account in which, subject to limits, securities can be bought and sold on credit.

With a **margin account**, you can, subject to limits, purchase securities on credit using money loaned to you by your broker. Such a purchase is called a *margin purchase*. The interest rate you pay on the money you borrow is based on the broker's **call money rate**, which is, loosely, the rate the broker pays to borrow the money. You pay some amount over the call money rate, called the *spread*; the exact spread depends on your broker and the size of the loan. Suppose the call money rate has been hovering around 7 percent. If a brokerage firm charges a 2.5 percent spread above this rate on loan amounts under $10,000, then you would pay a total of about 9.5 percent. However, this is usually reduced for larger loan amounts. For example, the spread may decline to .75 percent for amounts over $100,000.

call money rate The interest rate brokers pay to borrow bank funds for lending to customer margin accounts.

There are several important concepts and rules involved in a margin purchase. For concreteness, we focus on stocks in our discussion. The specific margin rules for other in-vestments can be quite different, but the principles and terminology are usually similar.

margin The portion of the value of an investment that is *not* borrowed.

In general, when you purchase securities on credit, some of the money is yours and the rest is borrowed. The amount that is yours is called the **margin**. Margin is usually expressed as a percentage. For example, if you take $7,000 of your own money and bor-row an additional $3,000 from your broker, your total investment will be $10,000. Of this $10,000, $7,000 is yours, so the margin is $7,000 / $10,000 = .70, or 70 percent.

It is useful to create an account balance sheet when thinking about margin purchases (and some other issues we'll get to in just a moment). To illustrate, suppose you open a margin account with $10,000. You tell your broker to buy 200 shares of Canadian Tire (CTC). Canadian Tire is selling for $91 per share, so the total cost will be $18,200. Since you have only $10,000 in your account, you borrow the remaining $8,200. Im-mediately following the purchase, your account balance sheet would look like this:

Assets		Liabilities and Account Equity	
200 shares of Canadian Tire	$18,200	Margin loan	$ 8,200
		Account equity	10,000
Total	$18,200	Total	$18,200

On the left-hand side of this balance sheet we list the account assets, which, in this case, consist of the $18,200 in Canadian Tire you purchased. On the right-hand side we list the $8,200 loan you took to partially pay for the stock: this is a liability because, at some point, the loan must be repaid. The difference between the value of the assets held in the account and the loan amount is $10,000. This amount is your *account equity*, that is the net value of your investment. Notice that your margin is equal to the account equity divided by the value of the stock owned and held in the account: $10,000 / $18,200 = 0.5495 or 54.95 percent.

THE ACCOUNT BALANCE SHEET

EXAMPLE 3.1

You want to buy 1,000 shares of Loblaws at a price of $48 per share. You put up $30,000 and borrow the rest. What does your account balance sheet look like? What is your margin?

The 1,000 shares of Loblaws cost $48,000. You supply $30,000, so you must borrow $18,000. The account balance sheet looks like this:

Assets		Liabilities and Account Equity	
100 shares of Loblaws	$48,000	Margin loan	$18,000
		Account equity	30,000
Total	$48,000	Total	$48,000

Your margin is the account equity divided by the value of the stock owned:

$$\text{Margin} = \$30,000 \, / \, \$48,000$$
$$= 0.625$$
$$= 62.50 \text{ percent}$$

Initial Margin   When you first purchase securities on credit, there is a minimum margin that you must supply. This percentage is called the **initial margin**. In Canada, Investment Dealers Association of Canada sets the margin requirements. But individual brokerage firms may require higher amounts.

initial margin The minimum margin that must be supplied on a securities purchase.

Currently initial margin requirement for stocks with prices higher than $5.00 is 30 percent, and for stocks with prices between $3.00 and $5.00 it is 50 percent. In other words, if you have $10,000 in cash that is not borrowed, you can borrow up to an additional $10,000, but no more.

We emphasize that these initial margin requirements apply to stocks. In contrast, for the most part, there is little initial margin requirement for government bonds. On the other hand, margin is not allowed at all on certain other types of securities.

CALCULATING INITIAL MARGIN

EXAMPLE 3.2

Suppose you have $6,000 in cash in a trading account with a 50 percent initial margin requirement. What is the largest order you can place (ignoring commissions)? If the initial margin were 60 percent, how would your answer change?

When the initial margin is 50 percent, you must supply half of the total, so $12,000 is the largest order you could place. When the initial margin is 60 percent, your $6,000 must equal 60 percent of the total. In other words, it must be the case that

$$\$6,000 = 0.60 \times \text{Total order}$$
$$\text{Total order} = \$6,000 \, / \, .60$$
$$= \$10,000$$

As this example illustrates, the higher the initial margin required, the less you can borrow.

Maintenance Margin In addition to the initial margin requirement, brokerage firms and exchanges generally have a **maintenance margin** requirement. This amount is the minimum margin required at all times after the purchase.

maintenance margin The minimum margin that must be present at all times in a margin account.

The maintenance margin set by your broker is sometimes called the "house" margin requirement. The level is established by your broker, who may vary it depending on what you are buying. For low-priced and very volatile stocks, the house margin can be as high as 100 percent, meaning no margin at all.

margin call A demand for more funds that occurs when the margin in an account drops below the maintenance margin.

A typical maintenance margin would be 30 percent. If your margin falls below 30 percent, then you may be subject to a **margin call**, which is a demand by your broker to add to your account, pay off part of the loan, or sell enough securities to bring your margin back up to an acceptable level. If you do not or cannot comply, your securities may be sold. The loan will be repaid out of the proceeds, and any remaining amounts will be credited to your account.

To illustrate, suppose your account has a 50 percent initial margin requirement and a 30 percent maintenance margin. A particular stock is selling for $50 per share. You have $20,000, and you want to buy as much of this stock as you possibly can. With a 50 percent initial margin, you buy up to $40,000 worth, or 800 shares. The account balance sheet looks like this:

Assets		Liabilities and Account Equity	
800 shares @$50 / share	$40,000	Margin loan	$20,000
		Account equity	20,000
Total	$40,000	Total	$20,000

Unfortunately, right after you buy it, the company reveals that it has been artificially inflating earnings for the last three years (this is not good), and the share price falls to $35 per share. What does the account balance sheet look like when this happens? Are you subject to a margin call?

To create the new account balance sheet, we recalculate the total value of the stock. The margin loan stays the same, so the account equity is adjusted as needed:

Assets		Liabilities and Account Equity	
800 shares @$35 / share	$28,000	Margin loan	$20,000
		Account equity	8,000
Total	$28,000	Total	$28,000

As shown, the total value of your "position" (i.e., the stock you hold) falls to $28,000, a $12,000 loss. You still owe $20,000 to your broker, so your account equity is $28,000 − $20,000 = $8,000. Your margin is therefore $8,000 / $28,000 = .286, or 28.6 percent. You are below the 30 percent minimum, so you are undermargined and subject to a margin call.

The Effects of Margin Margin is a form of *financial leverage*. Any time you borrow money to make an investment, the impact is to magnify both your gains and losses, hence the use of the term "leverage." The easiest way to see this is through an example. Imagine that you have $30,000 in an account with a 60 percent initial margin. You now know that you can borrow up to an additional $20,000 and buy $50,000 worth of stock (why?). The call money rate is 5.50 percent; you must pay this rate plus a .50 percent spread. Suppose you buy 10,000 shares of Ballard Power Systems at $5 per share. One year later, Ballard is selling at $6 per share. Assuming the call money rate does not change and ignoring dividends, what is the return on this investment?

At the end of the year, your 10,000 shares are worth $60,000. You owe 6 percent interest on the $20,000 you borrowed, or $1,200. If you pay off the loan with interest, you will have $60,000 − $21,200 = $38,800. You started with $30,000 and ended with $38,800, so your net gain is $8,800. In percentage terms, your return was $8,800 / $30,000 = .2933, or 29.33 percent.

How would you have done without the financial leverage created from the margin purchase? In this case, you would have invested just $30,000. At $5 per share, you would have purchased 6000 shares. At the end of the year, your 6000 shares would be worth $6 apiece, or $36,000 total. Your dollar profit is $6,000, so your percentage return would be $6,000 / $30,000 = .20, or 20 percent. If we compare this to the 29.33 percent that you made above, it's clear that you did substantially better by leveraging.

The downside is that you would do much worse if Ballard Power's stock price fell (or didn't rise very much). For example, if Ballard Power had fallen to $4 a share, you would have lost (check these calculations for practice) $11,200, or 37.33 percent on your margin investment, compared to $6,000, or 20 percent on the unmargined investment. This example illustrates how leveraging an investment through a margin account can cut both ways.

A MARGINAL INVESTMENT

EXAMPLE 3.3

A year ago, you bought 3,000 shares of Canfor at $12 per share. You put up the 50 percent initial margin. The call money rate plus the spread you paid was 8 percent. What is the return if the price today is $10? Compare this to the return you would have earned if you had not invested on margin. Your total investment was 3,000 shares at $12 per share, or $36,000. You supplied 50 percent, or $18,000, and you borrowed the remaining $18,000. At the end of the year, you owe $18,000 plus 8 percent interest, or $19,440. If the stock sells for $10, then your position is worth 3000 × 10 = $30,000. Deducting the $19,440 leaves $10,560 for you. Since you originally invested $18,000, your dollar loss is $18,000 − $10,560 = −$7,440. Your percentage return is −$7,440 / 18,000 = −0.41.33 or −41.33 percent.

If you had not leveraged your investment, you would have purchased $18,000 / $12 = 1,500 shares. These would have been worth 1,500 × $10 = $15,000. You therefore would have lost $3,000; your percentage return would have been −$3,000 / $18,000 = −16.67 percent, compared to the −36.57 percent that you lost on your leveraged position.

HOW LOW CAN IT GO?

EXAMPLE 3.4

In our previous example (Example 3.3), suppose the maintenance margin was 40 percent. At what price per share would you have been subject to a margin call?

To answer, let P^* be the critical price. You own 3,000 shares, so, at that price, your stock is worth $3,000 \times P^*$. You borrowed $18,000, so your account equity is equal to the value of your stock less the $18,000 you owe, or $3,000 \times P^* - \$18,000$. We can summarize this information as follows:

> **Amount borrowed = $18,000**
> **Value of stock = $3,000 × P***
> **Account equity = 3,000 × P* − $18,000**

(continued)

From our preceding discussion, your percentage margin is your dollar margin (or account equity) divided by the value of the stock:

$$\text{Margin} = \frac{\text{Account equity}}{\text{Value of stock}}$$

$$= \frac{3{,}000 \times P* \times \$18{,}000}{3{,}000 \times P*}$$

To find the critical price, we will set this margin to the maintenance margin and solve for $P*$:

$$\text{Maintenance margin} = \frac{\text{Number of shares} \times P* - \text{Amount borrowed}}{\text{Number of shares} \times P*}$$

Solving for $P*$ yields

$$P* = \frac{\text{Amount borrowed} / \text{Number of shares}}{1 - \text{Maintenance margin}}$$

Finally, setting the maintenance margin equal to 40 percent, we obtain this critical price for $P*$:

$$P* = \frac{\$18{,}000 / 3{,}000}{1 - 0.40}$$

$$= \frac{\$6}{0.6} = \$10$$

At any price below $10.00, your margin will be less than 40 percent, and you will be subject to a margin call, so this is the lowest possible price that could be reached before that occurs.

As Example 3.4 shows, you can calculate the critical price (the lowest price before you get a margin call) as follows:

$$P* = \frac{\text{Amount borrowed} / \text{Number of shares}}{1 - \text{Maintenance margin}} \qquad (3.1)$$

For example, suppose you had a margin loan of $40,000, which you used to purchase, in part, 1,000 shares. The maintenance margin is 37.5 percent. What's the critical stock price, and how do you interpret it?

See if you don't agree that the critical stock price, $P*$, is $40 / .625 = $64. The interpretation is straightforward: If the stock price falls below $64, you're subject to a margin call.

Hypothecation and Street Name Registration

As part of your margin account agreement, you must agree to various conditions. We discuss two of the most important next.

Hypothecation   Any securities you purchase in your margin account will be held by your broker as collateral against the loan made to you. This practice protects the broker because the securities can be sold by the broker if the customer is unwilling or unable to meet a margin call. Putting securities up as collateral against a loan is called **hypothecation**. In fact, a margin agreement is sometimes called a hypotheca-tion agreement. In addition, to borrow the money that it loans to you, your broker will often *re*-hypothecate your securities, meaning that your broker will pledge them as collateral with its lender, normally a bank.

hypothecation
Pledging securities as collateral against a loan.

street name An
arrangement under
which a broker is the
registered owner of a
security.

Street Name Registration   Securities in a margin account are normally held in **street name**. This means that the brokerage firm is actually the registered owner. If this were not the case, the brokerage firm could not legally sell the securities should a customer refuse to meet a margin call or otherwise fail to live up to the terms of the margin agreement. With this arrangement, the brokerage firm is the "owner of record," but the account holder is the "beneficial owner."

When a security is held in street name, anything mailed to the security owner, such as an annual report or a dividend cheque, goes to the brokerage firm. The brokerage firm then passes these on to the account holder. Street name ownership is actually a great convenience to the owner. In fact, because it is usually a free service, even customers with cash accounts generally choose street name ownership. Some of the benefits are:

1. Since the broker holds the security, there is no danger of theft or other loss of the security. This is important because a stolen or lost security cannot be easily or cheaply replaced.

2. Any dividends or interest payments are automatically credited, and they are often credited more quickly (and conveniently) than they would be if the owner received the cheque in the mail.

3. The broker provides regular account statements showing the value of securities held in the account and any payments received. Also, for tax purposes, the broker will provide all the needed information on a single form at the end of the year, greatly reducing the owner's record-keeping requirements.

Other Account Issues

If you do not wish to manage your account yourself, you can set up an *advisory account*. In this case, you pay someone else to make buy and sell decisions on your behalf. You are responsible for paying any commissions or other costs, as well as a management fee.

In a relatively recent innovation, brokerage firms have begun to offer *wrap accounts*. In such an account, you choose a money manager or set of money managers from a group offered by the brokerage firm. All of the costs, commissions, and expenses associated with your account are "wrapped" into a single fee that you pay, hence the name. If you simply authorize your broker to trade for you, then there is no management fee, but you are still responsible for any commissions. This arrangement is termed a *discretionary account*.

Most of the large brokerage firms offer accounts that provide for complete money management, including cheque-writing privileges, credit cards, and margin loans, especially for larger investors. Such accounts are generally called *asset management accounts*. The terms of these accounts differ from broker to broker, and the services provided frequently change in response to competition.

Finally, if you want to buy and sell a broad variety of individual securities, then a brokerage account is almost a requirement. It is true that some companies and other entities do sell directly to the public, at least at certain times and subject to various restrictions, so you can buy securities directly in some cases. In fact, you could buy and sell through the want ads in your local paper if you were so inclined, but given the modest commissions charged by deep-discount brokers, this hardly seems worth the trouble.

However, you should be aware that if you do not wish to actively buy and sell securities, but you do want to own stocks, bonds, or other financial assets, there is an alternative to a brokerage account: a *mutual fund*. Mutual funds are a means of combining or pooling the funds of a large group of investors. The buy and sell decisions for the resulting pool are then made by a fund manager, who is compensated for the service. Mutual funds have become so important that we will devote an entire chapter to them rather than give them short shrift here.

CHECK THIS ✓

3.2a   What is the difference between a cash and margin account?

3.2b   What is the effect of a margin purchase on gains and losses?

3.2c   What is a margin call?

3.3   Short Sales

An investor who buys and owns shares of stock is said to be *long* in the stock or to have a *long position*. An investor with a long position will make money if the price of the stock increases and lose money if it goes down. In other words, a long investor hopes that the price will increase.

Now consider a different situation. Suppose you thought, for some reason, that the stock in a particular company was likely to *decrease* in value. You obviously wouldn't want to buy any of it. If you already owned some, you might choose to sell it.

short sale A sale in which the seller does not actually own the security that is sold.

Beyond this, you might decide to engage in a **short sale**. In a short sale, you actually sell a security that you do not own. This is referred to as *shorting* the stock. After the short sale, the investor is said to have a *short position* in the security.

Financial assets of all kinds are sold short, not just shares of stock, and the terms "long" and "short" are universal. However, the mechanics of a short sale differ quite a bit across security types. Even so, regardless of how the short sale is executed, the essence is the same. An investor with a long position benefits from price increases, and, as we will see, an investor with a short position benefits from price decreases. For the sake of illustration, we focus here on shorting shares of stock. Procedures for shorting other types of securities are discussed in later chapters.

Basics of a Short Sale

How can you sell stock you don't own? It is easier than you might think: You borrow the shares of stock from your broker and then you sell them. At some future date, you will buy the same number of shares that you originally borrowed and return them, thereby eliminating the short position. Eliminating the short position is often called *covering the position* or, less commonly, *curing the short*.

You might wonder where your broker will get the stock to loan you. Normally, it will simply come from other margin accounts. Often, when you open a margin account, you are asked to sign a loan-consent agreement, which gives your broker the right to loan shares held in the account. If shares you own are loaned out, you still receive any dividends or other distributions and you can sell the stock if you wish. In other words, the fact that some of your stock may have been loaned out is of little or no consequence as far as you are concerned.

For example, assume that you short 1,000 shares of CanWest Global Communications at a price of $12 per share. You receive $12,000 from the sale (more on this in a moment). A month later, the stock is selling for $8 per share. You buy 1,000 shares for $8,000 and return the stock to your broker, thereby covering your position. You received $12,000 from the sale, and it costs you only $8,000 to cover, so you made $4,000.

Conventional Wall Street wisdom states that the way to make money is to "buy low, sell high." With a short sale, we hope to do exactly that, just in opposite order—sell high, buy low. If a short sale strikes you as a little confusing, it might help to think about the everyday use of the terms. Whenever we say that we are "running short" on something, we mean we don't have enough of it. Similarly, when someone says "don't sell me short" they mean don't bet on them not to succeed.

THE LONG AND SHORT OF IT

EXAMPLE 3.5

Suppose you short 2,000 shares of Barrick Gold at $30 per share. Three months later you cover your short. If Barrick is selling for $26 per share at that time, did you make or lose money? How much? What if you covered at $32?

If you shorted at $30 per share and covered at $26, you originally sold 2,000 shares at $30 and later bought them back at $26, so you made $4 per share, or $8,000. If you covered at $32, you lost $4,000.

Short Sales: Some Details

When you short a stock, you must borrow it from your broker, so there are various requirements you must fulfill. First, there is an initial margin and a maintenance margin. Second, after you sell the borrowed stock, the proceeds from the sale are credited to your account, but you cannot use them. They are, in effect, frozen until you return the stock. Finally, if there are any dividends paid on the stock while you have a short position, you must pay them.

To illustrate, we will again create an account balance sheet. Suppose you want to short 100 shares of Aber Diamond when the price is $30 per share. This means you will borrow shares of stock worth a total of $30 × 100 = $3,000. Your broker has a 50 percent initial margin and a 40 percent maintenance margin on short sales.

An important thing to keep in mind with a margin purchase of securities is that margin is calculated as the value of your account equity relative to the value of the securities purchased. With a short sale, margin is calculated as the value of your account equity relative to the value of the securities sold short. Thus, in both cases margin is equal to equity value divided by security value.

In our example here, the initial value of the securities sold short is $3,000 and the initial margin is 50 percent, at a minimum, so you must deposit half of $3,000, or $1,500, in your account. With this in mind, after the short sale, your account balance sheet is as follows:

Assets		**Liabilities and Account Equity**	
Proceeds from sale	$3,000	Short position	$3,000
Initial margin deposit	1,500	Account equity	1,500
Total	$4,500	Total	$4,500

There are many sites devoted to the fine art of short selling. Try www.bearmarket central.com

As shown, there are four items on the account balance sheet:

1. *Proceeds from sale.* This is the $3,000 you received when you sold the stock. This amount will remain in your account until you cover your position. Note that you will not earn interest on this amount—it will just sit there as far as you are concerned.

2. *Margin deposit.* This is the 50 percent margin that you had to post. This amount will not change unless there is a margin call. Depending on the circumstances and your particular account agreement, you may earn interest on the initial margin deposit.

3. *Short position.* Because you must eventually buy back the stock and return it, you have a liability. The current cost of eliminating that liability is $3,000.

4. *Account equity.* As always, the account equity is the difference between the total account value ($4,500) and the total liabilities ($3,000).

We now examine two scenarios: (1) the stock price falls to $20 per share, and (2) the stock price rises to $40 per share.

If the stock price falls to $20 per share, then you are still liable for 100 shares, but the cost of those shares is now just $2,000. Your account balance sheet becomes:

Assets		Liabilities and Account Equity	
Proceeds from sale	$3,000	Short position	$2,000
Initial margin deposit	1,500	Account equity	2,500
Total	$4,500	Total	$4,500

Notice that the left-hand side doesn't change. The same $3,000 you originally received is still held, and the $1,500 margin you deposited is still there also. On the right-hand side, the short position is now a $2,000 liability, down from $3,000. Finally, the good news is that the account equity rises by $1,000, so this is your gain. Your margin is equal to account equity divided by the security value (the value of the short position), $2,500 / $2,000 = 1.25, or 125 percent.

However, if the stock price rises to $40, things are not so rosy. Now the 100 shares for which you are liable are worth $4,000:

Assets		Liabilities and Account Equity	
Proceeds from sale	$3,000	Short position	$4,000
Initial margin deposit	1,500	Account equity	500
Total	$4,500	Total	$4,500

Again, the left-hand side doesn't change. The short liability rises by $1,000, and, unfortunately for you, the account equity declines by $1,000, the amount of your loss.

To make matters worse, when the stock price rises to $40, you are severely under-margined. The account equity is $500, but the value of the stock sold short is $4,000. Your margin is $500 / $4,000 = 12.5 percent. Since this is well below the 40 percent maintenance margin, you are subject to a margin call. You have two options: (1) buy back some or all of the stock and return it, or (2) add funds to your account.

We can graphically show the profit and loss position of an investor short selling 100 shares of stock at stock price $30. Figure 3.1 illustrates profit and loss excluding the transaction and brokerage fees as a function stock price. The investor will get the maximum profit if stock price falls to $0. On the other hand, if stock price exceeds $30, then the investor will get loss.

FIGURE 3.1   **Profit and Loss Positions as a Function of Stock Price**

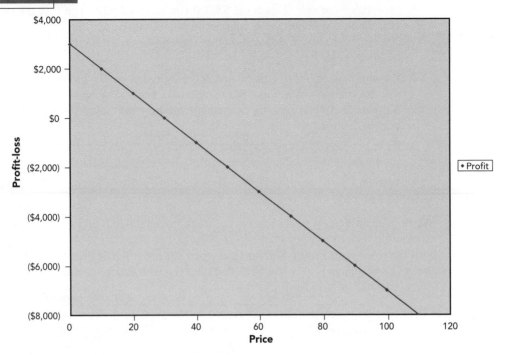

A CASE OF THE SHORTS

EXAMPLE 3.6

You shorted 5,000 shares of a particular stock at a price of $30 per share. The initial margin is 50 percent, and the maintenance margin is 40 percent. What does your account balance sheet look like following the short?

Following the short, your account becomes:

Assets		Liabilities and Account Equity	
Proceeds from sale	$150,000	Short position	$150,000
Initial margin deposit	75,000	Account equity	75,000
Total	$225,000	Total	$225,000

Notice that you shorted $150,000 worth of stock, so, with a 50 percent margin requirement, you deposited $75,000.

Please find below the Top 20 Largest Consolidated Short Position Report Highlights. The report is produced twice monthly, effective the 15th and the end of each month. The report below covers the 2-week period ending July 31th 2007.

TSX Datalinx collects this information on behalf of Market Regulation Services Inc. Participating Organizations are required to file this information pursuant to Universal Market Integrity Rule 10.10.

Issue Name	Symbol	As of July 31	As of July 15	Net Change
BOMBARDIER INC. CL B SV	BBD.B	80,789,751	88,791,612	−7,992,861
ABIBITI-CONSOLIDATED INC.	A	48,974,124	50,490,742	−1,516,618
ROGERS COMMUNICATIONS INC. CL B	RCI.B	34,864,945	35,727,137	−862,192
KINROSS GOLD CORPORATION	K	32,502,833	31,197,514	1,305,319
CELESTICA INC. SV	CLS	27,821,518	26,021,943	1,799,575
CGI GROUP INC. CL A SV	GIB.A	27,753,695	24,804,778	2,498,917
ROYAL BANK OF CANADA	RY	23,692,091	23,664,415	27,676
NORTEL NETWORKS CORPORATION	NT	22,673,809	22,035,632	638,177
CAMECO CORPORATION	CCO	20,525,987	20,735,640	−209,653
NORBORD INC.	NBD	20,102,598	20,106,617	−4,019
BCE INC.	BCE	18,865,171	15,355,031	3,510,140
ISHARES CDN S&P/TSX 60 INDEX FUND UN	XIU	18,414,287	18,557,093	−142,806
NORTHERN ORION RESOURCES INC. J	NNO	17,813,608	18,094,648	−281,040
CANWEST GLOBAL COMMUNICATIONS SV	CGS	16,802,553	15,491,668	1,310,885
MANULIFE FINANCIAL CORPORATION	MFC	15,763,568	15,273,161	490,407
IAMGOLD CORPORATION	IMG	14,841,631	14,436,181	405,450
GILDAN ACTIVEWEAR INC.	GIL	13,713,395	13,166,125	547,270
BANK OF NOVA SCOTIA (THE)	BNS	13,592,958	13,269,758	323,200
DOMTAR CORPORATION	DTC	13,110,516	17,704,067	−4,593,551
CANADIAN IMPERIAL BANK OF COMMERCE	CM	12,591,092	13,196,334	−605,242

For further information please call Catherine McGravey at (416) 947-4655 or, to subscribe to the complete report, call Datalinx at (416) 947-4681.

The information on this page is collected with care but TSX Inc. does not guarantee either the completeness or the accuracy of this information. The data contained in this report is provided for informational purposes only. This is not an invitation to purchase any security mentioned herein. You agree not to rely upon the information contained in this report for any trading, business or financial purpose. By using this report, you expressly agree to the condition that TSX Inc. assumes no liability nor responsibility for any errors or inaccuracies in this report.

WORK THE WEB

You can find the short interest for the current month in many financial publications. But what if you want a longer history of the shares sold short for a particular company? At www.nasdaq.com, you can find the short interest for companies listed on the NASDAQ for the previous 12 months. We went to the site and looked up Yahoo!, and this is what we found:

YHOO - Yahoo! Inc. - Common Stock				
Month	Short Interest	Percent Change	Average Daily Share Volume	Days to Cover
March 2008	73,504,478	(5.44)	19,773,403	3.72
February 2008	77,733,246	(5.67)	35,735,179	2.18
January 2008	82,408,380	3.05	17,052,680	4.83
December 2005	79,969,085	(7.78)	21,970,649	3.64
November 2005	86,717,343	9.55	20,807,599	4.17
October 2005	79,159,966	(0.40)	16,222,850	4.88
September 2005	79,475,645	(4.57)	14,150,721	5.62
August 2005	83,281,872	10.00	21,326,788	3.91
July 2005	75,713,736	(1.55)	15,053,534	5.03
June 2005	76,903,469	(2.30)	16,894,098	4.55
May 2005	78,710,903	2.06	21,136,816	3.72
April 2005	77,123,611	2.71	20,931,176	3.68

As you can see, the short interest in Yahoo! has risen from about 17 million shares in September 2004 to about 21 million shares in August 2005. Why would you want a history of short sales? Some investors use short sales as a technical indicator, which we discuss in a later chapter. Here's a question for you: What do you think "Days to Cover" means?

short interest The amount of common stock held in short positions.

At this point you might wonder whether short selling is a common practice among investors. Actually it is quite common and a substantial volume of stock sales are initiated by short sellers. The nearby *Investment Updates* box is a report from the TSX website reporting short interest. **Short interest** is the amount of common stock held in short positions. As shown on page 85, the amount of stock held short for some companies can be several tens of millions of shares, and the total number of shares held short across all companies can be several billion shares. A nearby *Work the Web* box shows how to find short interest for a particular company.

We conclude our discussion of short sales with a *very* important observation. With a long position, the most you can ever lose is your total investment. In other words, if you buy $10,000 worth of stock, $10,000 is the most you can lose because the worst that can happen is the stock price drops to zero. However, if you short $10,000 in stock, you can lose *much more* than $10,000 because the stock price can keep rising without any particular limit. Potential short sellers should remember the following classic bit of Wall Street wisdom: "He that sells what isn't his'n, must buy it back or go to prison!"[1]

---

[1] Of course, the same is true for "she that sells what isn't hers'n"; it just doesn't rhyme as well.

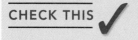

CHECK THIS

3.3a   What is a short sale?

3.3b   Why might an investor choose to short a stock?

3.3c   What is the maximum possible loss on a short sale? Explain.

3.4   Investor Objectives, Constraints, and Strategies

Different investors will have very different investment objectives and strategies. For example, some will be very active, buying and selling frequently; others will be relatively inactive, buying and holding for long periods of time. Some will be willing to bear substantial risk in seeking out returns; for others, safety is a primary concern. In this section, we describe, in general terms, some strategies that are commonly pursued and their relationship to investor constraints and objectives.

In thinking about investor objectives, the most fundamental question is: Why invest at all? For the most part, the only sensible answer is that we invest today to have more tomorrow. In other words, investment is simply deferred consumption; instead of spending today, we choose to wait because we wish to have (or need to have) more to spend later. There is no difference, really, between investing and saving.

Given that we invest now to have more later, the particular investment strategy chosen will depend on, among other things, willingness to bear risk, the time horizon, and taxes. We discuss these and other issues next.

Risk and Return

Probably the most fundamental decision that an investor must make concerns the amount of risk that she is willing to bear. Most investors are *risk-averse*, meaning that, all other things the same, they dislike risk and want to expose themselves to the minimum risk level possible. However, as our previous chapter indicated, larger returns are generally associated with larger risks, so there is a trade-off. In formulating investment objectives, the individual must therefore balance return objectives with risk tolerance.

Attitudes toward risk are strictly personal preferences, and individuals with very similar economic circumstances can have very different degrees of risk aversion. For this reason, the first thing that must be assessed in evaluating the suitability of an investment strategy is risk tolerance. Unfortunately, this is not an easy thing to do. Most individuals have a difficult time articulating in any precise way their attitude toward risk (what's yours?). One reason is that risk is not a simple concept; it is not easily defined or measured. Nevertheless, the nearby *Investment Updates* box contains an article from *The Wall Street Journal* about risk tolerance that has a short quiz that might help you assess your attitude toward risk. When you take the quiz, remember there are no right or wrong answers. Afterwards, score your risk tolerance as shown at the end of the article.

Bumpy Market Reminds Investors to Assess Their Risk Tolerance

Do-It-Yourself Crowd Has Quizzes to Rate Courage on Finances

Risk

For many investors, it's a word that has all but disappeared from the lexicon. Throughout much of the 1990s, stocks mostly went up. And even when they went down, many investors saw the slump as just another buying opportunity because stocks soon would go up again.

But the bumpy ride of the past six months finally has woken investors up to the fact that, with stocks more volatile these days than anytime in history, risk is playing an increasingly significant role in their lives.

Did you root the Nasdaq Composite Index higher when it bested 5000 earlier this year, but secretly fear for your overbloated technology shares? Did you panic when the Nasdaq subsequently plummeted in March and April, then kick yourself for not investing more when the market rebounded days later?

These dueling visions of fear and greed reflect the fact that many of today's do-it-yourself investors haven't assessed their own tolerance for risk, captivated instead by the lure of what seems to be easy, almost riskless, riches.

The current, and often myopic, quest for market wealth has spawned "a willingness to take risks that [average investors] haven't had in the past," says Robert J. Shiller, an economics professor at Yale University and author of a new market tome, "Irrational Exuberance." In the process, he says, "investors haven't stopped to think about what risk is at all."

Until the recent market drop, "people had no clue what [risk] is about," agrees Joanna Bickel, a project manager at TIAA-CREF, the big New York provider of retirement services, which is working to bring a more sophisticated risk-assessment tool to its Web site later this year so that its investors can better gauge their own risk profile.

There once was a time when risk assessment was the duty of stockbrokers or financial planners, who questioned clients to gauge their comfort level for volatility and potential losses. But with the explosion of online trading, investors have taken control of their own finances. In the process, they have cast aside the mental due diligence that ultimately determines whether they're sleepless in Cisco or bored by Boeing.

It's an age-old quest for balance. Investors who structure their portfolios so that they are comfortable with both the rewards and risks are the ones who sleep best when market downdrafts keep others awake at night. Moreover, they aren't the ones berating themselves for missing out on big gains when the market rebounds.

To help investors determine the level of risk they're most comfortable with, here's a statistically based risk-tolerance quiz constructed with the help of Investment Technologies Inc., a New York firm that provides investment tools and risk-assessment instruments to financial institutions such as banks and investment firms.

Financial companies increasingly rely on risk quizzes similar to this one, though often far more detailed, to better assess a client's true tolerance for market vicissitudes. As investors continue to take on increasing responsibility for their own money—through online trading or in self-managed 401(k) and IRA retirement accounts—"the issue of how individual investors make investment decisions is becoming a huge issue," says Brian Rom, president of Investment Technologies.

All manner of risk-assessment quizzes are available. Some are posted on financial Web sites, others are available from financial planners and investment companies. Some are relatively simple and are designed to match an investor with particular mutual funds or annuities.

The more sophisticated quizzes are based on statistical research that quantifies the psychological behavior of people and their money habits. Such "behavioral finance" studies have determined that many people typically aren't rational but are irrational when it comes to money and risk.

For example, research has shown that most people fear loss more than they value comparable gain. Offer someone a sure $50 or, on the flip of a coin, the possibility of winning $100 or winning nothing, and chances are they'll pocket the sure thing. Conversely, penalize them $50 to start, then offer a flip of a coin to lose $100 or lose nothing, and they'll invariably take the coin toss. Both scenarios are statistically equivalent, yet people tend to view "the possibility of recouping a loss as more important than the possibility of greater gain," even though the coin flip could mean an even greater loss, says James Corter, associate professor of statistics and education at New York's Columbia University.

The accompanying quiz is based on research done by Mr. Corter. At just eight questions, it is short, but it is backed by empirical studies and "has adequate reliability and validity," says Mr. Corter.

The quiz is designed to reveal where an individual falls along the risk spectrum. It is accompanied by a chart detailing where a variety of stock and bond investments, based on historical performance and volatility, fall along the risk spectrum, to give quiz takers an idea of the class of investments most likely to match an investor's temperament.

(continued)

Certainly, no risk quiz can tell you everything about your financial courage, and your score here doesn't mean that if you fall into a more conservative category that you can't stomach a little exposure to volatile tech stocks. "But if you answer the questions candidly," says Ms. Bickel at TIAA-CREF, "and don't worry about whether you come out conservative or a swinger, you'll have" an accurate portrayal of your risk level that you can use when building your portfolio.

Risk Adviser

Do you know your risk tolerance? This short questionnaire can help you gain a better understanding of your tolerance for market vicissitudes. Answer the questions, tally the results and match the score to the Suitable Investments.*

1 Choose the statement that best describes your interests in an investment program.
   A My primary aim is to achieve high long-term return in the value of my portfolio, even if that means accepting some significant short-term swings in values.
   B My primary interest is in stable growth in the value of my portfolio, even if that means somewhat lower returns over time.
   C I attach equal value to maximizing long-term returns and minimizing fluctuations in value.

2 How important are the following factors when you decide to purchase a stock or mutual fund?
   a) Short-term potential for the price to appreciate.
   b) Long-term potential for the price to appreciate.
   c) If a stock, the potential that the company will be bought or taken over.
   d) Gain or loss in the price over the past six months.
   e) Gain or loss in the price over the past five years.
   f) Stock was recommended by a friend or coworker.
   g) Risk that the price could drop.
   h) Potential that the investment will pay dividends.

Very Important	Somewhat Important	Not At All Important
A	B	C
A	B	C
A	B	C
A	B	C
A	B	C
A	B	C
A	B	C
A	B	C

3 a) Would you put $5,000 of your assets into an investment where you have a 70% chance of doubling your money (to $10,000) and a 30% chance of losing the entire $5,000?

   Yes _____   No _____

   b) How about an 80% chance of doubling to $10,000 and a 20% chance of losing the entire $5,000?

   Yes _____   No _____

   c) How about a 60% chance of doubling to $10,000 and a 40% chance of losing the entire $5,000?

   Yes _____   No _____

4 Suppose you have a choice between two mutual funds, both of which are broadly diversified into 6 asset classes (e.g., stocks, bonds, real estate, etc.). The charts below show the changes in value over the past 12 months for the assets in each portfolio. Which portfolio of assets do you prefer to invest in?

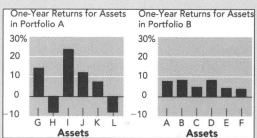

5 Assume that you have made an investment that has dropped in value by $2,000 and you find yourself faced with the following choice (please circle only one option):
   A Sell and take the immediate $2,000 loss (a 100% chance of loss).
   B Hold on to it with a 50% chance of recouping the $2,000 and a 50% chance of losing an additional $2,000.
   C No preference.

6 Assume that you have recently invested $10,000 in a stock and that the value of this stock has dropped 15% in value in one week. You can discover no reason for this decline, and the broader market has not dipped accordingly. Which of the following actions would you be most likely to take? (Circle one answer only.)

(continued)

A Buy more.

B Sell all your holdings in the fund immediately and put the money into a less volatile investment.

C Sell half of your holdings in the fund immediately and put the money elsewhere.

D Wait for the price to recover and then sell all your holdings in the fund.

E Do nothing (occasional dips in price are to be expected).

7 The following charts show quarterly performance of two equity mutual funds over the past two years. Which do you prefer to invest in?

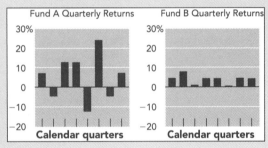

8 As an investor in stock and bond markets, how would you rate your degree of experience relative to other individual investors? (Please circle one.)

A Extremely experienced

B More than average experience

C Average experience

D Less than average experience

E Little or no experience

Source: Investment Technologies Inc.

Scoring

1 – A. 15; B. 0; C. 7

FOR EACH QUESTION:
2a) – A. 0; B. 1; C. 2
2b) through 2e) A. 2; B. 1; C. 0

FOR EACH QUESTION:
2f) through 2h) A. 0; B. 1; C. 2

FOR EACH QUESTION:
3a) through 3c) Yes. 5; No. 0

4 – A. 10; B. 0
5 – A. 0; B. 10; C. 10
6 – A. 15; B. 0; C. 5; D. 0; E. 10

7 – A. 10; B. 0
8 – A. 20; B. 15; C. 10; D. 5; E. 0

Score In Points	Suitable Investments*
0–11	Avoid risk! Open a money-market account—or buy a bigger mattress.
12–33	Gentlemen (and ladies) prefer bonds, and are most at home with high-grade corporate and government bonds of an intermediate duration.
34–55	You're still a bond buyer. But you're willing to live a bit closer to the edge with interest-only U.S. Treasury STRIPS.
56–77	Mix it up. Convertible bonds and stocks are to your liking. But safer utilities and large blue chips are as risky as you go. Real-estate investment trusts fit too.
78–99	Stock up on stocks. At the low end, you're comfortable with larger value stocks; at the high end, riskier midcap and growth stocks work.
100+	Viva Las Vegas, baby! Place your bets on 'Net stocks and new-tech issues. Risks are high, but so are the payoffs.

*Suitable investments are based upon an analysis of the volatility of 75 various bond and stock indices, and apply to investment horizons of between 10 and 15 years.

Source: Jeff D. Opdyke, *The Wall Street Journal*, © 2003 Dow Jones & Company. All Rights Reserved Worldwide.

Investor Constraints

In addition to attitude toward risk, an investor's investment strategy will be affected by various constraints. We discuss five of the most common and important constraints next.

Resources Probably the most obvious constraint, and the one to which many students can most easily relate, is *resources*. Obviously, if you have no money, you cannot invest at all! Beyond that, certain types of investments and investment strategies either explicitly or effectively have minimum requirements.

What is the minimum resource level needed? It depends on the investment strategy, and there is no precise answer. Through mutual funds, investments in the stock market can be made for as little as $500 to start, with subsequent investments as small as $100 or less. However, since there are frequently minimum commission levels, account fees, and other costs associated with buying and selling securities, an investor interested in actively trading on her own would probably need more like $5,000 to $50,000.

Horizon The investment *horizon* refers to the planned life of the investment. For example, individuals frequently save for retirement, where the investment horizon, depending on your age, can be very long. On the other hand, you might be saving to buy a house in the near future, implying a relatively short horizon.

The reason horizon is important is evident in our previous chapter. It is true that stocks outperformed the other investments in the long run, but there were short periods over which they did much worse. Consequently, if you have to pay tuition in 30 days, stocks are probably not the best investment for that money. Thus, in thinking about the riskiness of an investment, one important consideration is when the money will be needed.

Liquidity For some investors, there is the possibility that an asset will need to be sold quickly. In such cases, the asset's *liquidity* is particularly important. An asset with a high degree of liquidity is one that can be sold quickly without a significant price concession. Such an asset is said to be liquid.

Notice that liquidity has two related dimensions. After all, any asset can be sold quickly and easily if the price is cut sufficiently, so it's not just a question of the ease with which an asset can be sold. Liquidity is difficult to measure precisely, but some assets are clearly much more liquid than others. A good way to think about liquidity is to imagine buying an asset and then immediately reselling it. The less you would lose on this "round-trip" transaction, the more liquid is the asset.

Taxes Different types of investments are taxed very differently. When we talk about the return on an investment, what is really relevant is the *aftertax* return. As a result, taxes are a vital consideration. Higher tax bracket investors will naturally seek investment strategies with favourable tax treatments, while lower tax bracket (or tax-exempt) investors will focus more on pretax returns.

In addition, the way in which an investment is held can dramatically affect its tax status. The tax laws and other rules are in a constant state of flux, so we will stick to broad principles. The general idea is that certain types of accounts, particularly retirement savings accounts, receive preferential tax treatment. The tax break can be enormous, and, as a result, the amount you can invest each year in these accounts is strictly limited. There are also lots of rules regarding when you can withdraw the money, and it is important to pay careful attention to them.

Learn how risk-averse you are by visiting the Investing Basics section of http://finance.sympatico.msn.ca

Investors can open an RRSP (Registered Retirement Savings Plan) account and contribute their savings into the plan. They choose the type of investment instruments they want (e.g., stocks, bonds, GICs, mutual funds, etc.). No matter what type of investment instruments investors choose, their contributions are tax-deductible. Later, when they retire, they owe income taxes on whatever they take out of the account. We will discuss RRSP accounts in detail in Chapter 5.

Special Circumstances   Beyond the general constraints we have discussed, essentially everyone will have some special or unique requirements or opportunities. For example, many companies will match certain types of investments made by employees on a dollar-for-dollar basis (typically up to some maximum per year). In other words, you double your money immediately with complete certainty. Since it is difficult to envision any other investment with such a favourable payoff, such an opportunity should probably be taken even though there may be some undesirable liquidity, tax, or horizon considerations.

A list of possible special circumstances would be essentially endless, so we make no attempt to produce one here. Just to give a few examples, however, the number of dependents and their needs will vary from investor to investor, and the need to provide for dependents will be an important constraint. Some investors want to invest only in companies whose products and activities they consider to be socially or politically suitable, and some investors want to invest primarily in their own community or state. Finally, some investors, such as corporate insiders, face regulatory and legal restrictions on their investing, and others, such as political officeholders, may have to avoid (or at least ethically *should* avoid) some types of investments out of concern for conflicts of interest.

Strategies and Policies

In formulating an investment strategy or policy, the four key areas that must be addressed are investment management, market timing, asset allocation, and security selection. We discuss each of these next.

Investment Management   A basic decision that you and every other investor must make is whether you will manage your investments yourself or hire someone else to do it. At the one extreme, you can open an account with a broker and make all of the buy and sell decisions yourself. At the other extreme, you can invest all of your money in a managed account, such as a wrap account, and make no buy and sell decisions at all.

Often investors partially manage their investments themselves and partially use professional managers. For example, you might divide your money between, say, four different mutual funds. In this case, you have hired four different money managers. However, you decided what types of funds to buy, you chose the particular funds within each type, and you decided how to divide your money between the funds.

It might appear that managing your money by yourself is the cheapest way to go because you save on the management fees. Appearances can be deceiving, however. First of all, you should consider the value of your time. For some, researching investments and making investment decisions is something of a hobby; for many of us, however, it is too time-consuming, and this is a powerful incentive to hire professional management. Also, for some strategies, the costs of doing it yourself can exceed those of hiring someone even after considering fees simply because of the higher commissions and other fees that individual investors frequently pay. For example, it might not be a bad idea for some of your investment to be in real estate, but a small investor will find it very difficult to directly acquire a sound real estate investment at reasonable cost.

An interesting question regarding professional management concerns the possibility of generating superior returns. It would seem logical to argue that by hiring a professional investor to manage your money, you would earn more, at least on average. Surely the pros make better investment decisions than the amateurs! Surprisingly, this isn't necessarily true. We will return to this subject in later chapters, but, for now, we simply note that the possibility of a superior return may not be a compelling reason to prefer professional management.

Market Timing   A second basic investment decision you must make is whether you will try to buy and sell in anticipation of the future direction of the overall market. For example, you might move money into the stock market when you thought it was going to rise, and move money out when you thought it was going to fall. This activity is called **market timing**. Some investors very actively move money around to try to time short-term market movements; others are less active but still try to time longer-term movements. A fully passive strategy is one in which no attempt is made to time the market.

Market timing certainly seems like a reasonable thing to do; after all, why leave money in an investment if you expect it to decrease in value? You might be surprised that a common recommendation is that investors *not* try to time the market. As we discuss in more detail in a later chapter, the reason is that successful market timing is, to put it mildly, very difficult. To outperform a completely passive strategy, you must be able to very accurately predict the future; if you make even a small number of bad calls, you will likely never catch up.

Asset Allocation   As we have examined in Chapter 2, in formulating your investment strategy, you must decide what percentage of your money will be placed in each of these broad categories. This is your **asset allocation** decision.

An important asset allocation decision for many investors is how much to invest in common stocks and how much to invest in bonds. There are some basic rules of thumb for this decision, one of the simplest being to split the portfolio into 60 percent stocks and 40 percent bonds. This popular 60–40 mix is generally a reasonable allocation strategy, but you should read the article in the nearby *Investment Updates* box before you finally decide. Most of the major investment firms and many Web sites maintain recommended asset allocation schemes, which can be custom-tailored for individuals depending on their risk tolerance, wealth, and retirement goals.

Security Selection   After the asset allocation you must decide on **security selection**, that is, you must decide which specific securities to buy within each class.

For example, you might decide that you want 30 percent of your money in small stocks. This is an asset allocation decision. Next, however, you must decide *which* small stocks to buy. Here again there is an active strategy and a passive strategy. With an active strategy, we try to identify those small stocks that we think will do the best in the future; in other words, we try to pick "winners." Investigating particular securities within a broad class in an attempt to identify superior performers is often called *security analysis*.

With a passive security selection strategy, we might just acquire a diverse group of small stocks, perhaps by buying a mutual fund that holds shares in hundreds of small companies.

market timing Buying and selling in anticipation of the overall direction of a market.

asset allocation The distribution of investment funds among broad classes of assets.

security selection Selection of specific securities within a particular class.

Popular 60–40 Mix Is No Panacea

Why do so many investors hold a mix of 60% stocks and 40% bonds?

As it turns out, there are three main arguments for the 60–40 mix. *But none of them clinch the case.*

It Produces Good Returns in Bad Times

The 1930s and 1940s were a nightmare for investors. In the 1930s, stocks were trounced by deflation. In the 1940s, bonds were battered by inflation. But in both decades, a mix of 60% U.S. stocks and 40% U.S. longer-term government bonds outpaced inflation by a healthy margin.

"What 60–40 has done is kept people whole over an extended period, especially a deflationary period," says Keith Ambachtsheer, a pension consultant in Toronto. "Where 60–40 runs into problems is in the 1970s," when inflation was much higher than in the 1940s. That high inflation not only wreaked havoc on bonds, but also hurt stocks, which were vulnerable because of rich valuations.

It Offers a Decent Mix of Income and Capital Gains

If you are retired and living off your portfolio, you might have been told to buy a 60–40 mix, because you get a moderate amount of income and your portfolio should keep growing along with inflation.

Right now, for instance, stocks yield less than 2%, but bonds kick off around 6%, giving a 60–40 portfolio an overall yield of some 3½%.

Meanwhile, for capital appreciation, you have to rely on your stocks. Over the long haul, these might climb at 7% a year, assuming share price-to-earnings multiples hold steady and earnings per share rise at their historic 7% annual clip. If you have 60% in stocks, that translates into overall portfolio growth of more than 4%, nicely ahead of today's 2% inflation rate.

But in truth, you could keep up with inflation—and generate a much higher yield—by putting far less into stocks and keeping even more in bonds. For retirees, it seems, there is nothing magical about the 60–40 mix.

It Generates the Best Risk-Adjusted Return

Derek Sasveld, a senior consultant with Chicago's Ibbotson Associates, says the theoretical justification for the 60–40 mix came in the mid-1960s. At that time, there was keen interest among some institutional investors in building portfolios that produced good risk-adjusted returns. To find the right mix, they looked at the past 40 years of U.S. stock and bond returns.

"That 60–40 portfolio from 1926 through 1965 was terrific," Mr. Sasveld notes. "The correlation between stocks and bonds at that point was virtually zero."

But times have changed. "Stocks and bonds are now more correlated," Mr. Sasveld says. "People shouldn't think about the 60–40 mix as being a good place to start."

Source: Jonathan Clements, *The Wall Street Journal*, December 16, 1997. © Dow Jones & Company, Inc. All Rights Reserved Worldwide.

A useful way to distinguish asset allocation from security selection is to note that asset allocation is essentially a macro-level activity because the focus is on whole markets or classes of assets. Security selection is a much more micro-level activity because the focus is on individual securities.

If we simultaneously consider the active versus passive aspects of asset allocation and security selection, four distinct investment strategies emerge, which we summarize in the following two-by-two table:

Asset Allocation	Security Selection	
	Active	Passive
Active	I	II
Passive	III	IV

With strategy I, we actively move money between asset classes based on our beliefs and expectations about future performance and we also try to pick the best performers in each class. This is a fully active strategy. At the other extreme, strategy IV, we follow a fully passive strategy, neither changing asset allocation very much nor choosing individual securities in an attempt to identify the likely best performers.

With strategy II, we actively vary our holdings by class, but we don't try to choose particular securities within each class. With this strategy, we might move back and forth between short-term government bonds and small stocks in an attempt to time the market. Finally, with strategy III, we don't vary our asset allocations, but we do select individual securities. A diehard stock picker would fall into this category; such an investor holds 100 percent stocks and concentrates solely on buying and selling individual companies.

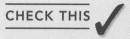

CHECK THIS

3.4a   What does the term "risk-averse" mean?

3.4b   What are some of the constraints investors face in making investment decisions?

3.4c   What is asset allocation?

3.5   Summary and Conclusions

This chapter explores the investing process. We discuss how to choose a broker and various aspects of broker–customer relations, including hypothecation, street name registration, and arbitration. The use of margin to purchase securities is covered, and the financial leverage effect of a margin purchase is emphasized. We describe short sales in some detail and stress the potentially unlimited losses that can arise from a short position. Finally, we cover some of the constraints faced by investors, and we briefly describe some basic investment strategy considerations, including market timing, asset allocation, and security selection.

REAL WORLD

This chapter covered the basics of brokerage accounts, some important trade types, and, finally, some big-picture issues regarding investment strategies and objectives. How should you, as an investor or investment manager, put this information to work?

The answer is that you need to open a brokerage account! Investing is like many activities; the best way to learn is by making mistakes. Unfortunately, making mistakes with real money is an expensive way to learn, so we don't recommend trying things like short sales with real money, at least not at first.

Instead, to learn about how to trade and gain some experience with making (and losing) money, you should open a Stock-Trak account (or a similar simulated brokerage account). Take it seriously. Try various trade types and strategies and see how they turn out. The important thing to do is to follow your trades and try to understand why you made or lost money and also why you made or lost the amount you did.

In a similar vein, you should carefully review your account statements to make sure you understand exactly what each item means and how your account equity is calculated.

After you have gained some experience trading "on paper," you should open a real account as soon as you can pull together enough money. Try visiting the various online brokers we list in Table 3.1 to find out the minimum amount you need to open an account. The amount has been declining.

Looking back at Chapter 1, you know that it's important to get started early. Once you have a real account, however, it's still a good idea to keep a separate "play money" account to test trading ideas to make sure you really understand them before committing your precious real money.

Key Terms

Canadian Investor Protection Fund (CIPF) 72

cash account 75

margin account 75

call money rate 75

margin 75

initial margin 76

maintenance margin 77

margin call 77

hypothecation 79

street name 80

short sale 81

short interest 86

market timing 93

asset allocation 93

security selection 93

Chapter Review Problems and Self-Test

1. **The Account Balance Sheet** Suppose you want to buy 3,000 shares of Magna International at a price of $85 per share. You put up $200,000 and borrow the rest. What does your account balance sheet look like? What is your margin?

2. **Short Sales** Suppose that in the previous problem you shorted 3,000 shares instead of buying. The initial margin is 60 percent. What does the account balance sheet look like following the short?

3. **Margin Calls** You purchased 500 shares of stock at a price of $90 per share on a 50 percent margin. If the maintenance margin is 30 percent, what is the critical stock price?

Answers to Self-Test Problems

1. The 3,000 shares of Magna cost $255,000. You supply $200,000, so you must borrow $55,000. The account balance sheet looks like this:

Assets		Liabilities and Account Equity	
3,000 shares of Magna	$255,000	Margin loan	$55,000
		Account equity	200,000
Total	$255,000	Total	$255,000

    Your margin is the account equity divided by the value of the stock owned:

    $$\text{Margin} = \$200,000 / \$255,000$$
    $$= 0.7843\ldots$$
    $$= 78.43\%$$

2. Following the short, your account is as follows:

Assets		Liabilities and Account Equity	
Proceeds from sale	$255,000	Short position	$255,000
Initial margin deposit	153,000	Account equity	153,000
Total	$408,000	Total	$408,000

    Notice that you shorted $255,000 worth of stock, so, with a 60 percent margin requirement, you deposited $153,000.

3. The lowest price the stock can drop before you receive a margin call is:

    $$P^* = \frac{\text{Amount borrowed / Number of shares}}{1 - \text{Maintenance margin}}$$

    You borrowed $500 \times \$90 \times 0.50 = \$22,500$. Therefore:

    $$P^* = \frac{\$22,500 / 500}{1 - 0.3} = \$64.29$$

    You will receive a margin call if the stock drops below $64.29.

Test Your Investment Quotient

1. **Investment Objectives** An individual investor's investment objectives should be expressed in terms of:

   a. Risk and return.
   b. Capital market expectations.
   c. Liquidity needs and time horizon.
   d. Tax factors and legal and regulatory constraints.

2. **Asset Allocation** Which of the following best reflects the importance of the asset allocation decision to the investment process? The asset allocation decision:

   a. Helps the investor decide on realistic investment goals.
   b. Identifies the specific securities to include in a portfolio.
   c. Determines most of the portfolio's returns and volatility over time.
   d. Creates a standard by which to establish an appropriate investment horizon.

3. **Leverage** You deposit $100,000 cash in a brokerage account and purchase $200,000 of stocks on margin by borrowing $100,000 from your broker. Later, the value of your stock holdings falls to $150,000, whereupon you get nervous and close your account. What is the percentage return on your investment (ignore interest paid)?

   a. 0 percent
   b. −25 percent
   c. −50 percent
   d. −75 percent

4. **Leverage** You deposit $100,000 cash in a brokerage account and short sell $200,000 of stocks. Later, the value of the stocks held short rises to $250,000, whereupon you get nervous and close your account. What is the percentage return on your investment?

   a. 0 percent
   b. −25 percent
   c. −50 percent
   d. −75 percent

5. **Account Margin** You deposit $100,000 cash in a brokerage account and purchase $200,000 of stocks on margin by borrowing $100,000 from your broker. Later, the value of your stock holdings falls to $175,000. What is your account margin in dollars?

   a. $50,000
   b. $75,000
   c. $100,000
   d. $150,000

6. **Account Margin** You deposit $100,000 cash in a brokerage account and purchase $200,000 of stocks on margin by borrowing $100,000 from your broker. Later, the value of your stock holdings falls to $150,000. What is your account margin in percent?

   a. 25 percent
   b. 33 percent
   c. 50 percent
   d. 75 percent

7. **Account Margin** You deposit $100,000 cash in a brokerage account and short sell $200,000 of stocks on margin. Later, the value of the stocks held short rises to $225,000. What is your account margin in dollars?

   a. $50,000
   b. $75,000
   c. $100,000
   d. $150,000

8. **Account Margin** You deposit $100,000 cash in a brokerage account and short sell
$200,000 of stocks on margin. Later, the value of the stocks held short rises to $250,000.
What is your account margin in percent?

   a. 20 percent
   b. 25 percent
   c. 33 percent
   d. 50 percent

9. **Margin Calls** You deposit $100,000 cash in a brokerage account and purchase $200,000
of stocks on margin by borrowing $100,000 from your broker, who requires a mainte-
nance margin of 30 percent. Which of the following is the largest value for your stock
holdings for which you will still receive a margin call?

   a. $200,000
   b. $160,000
   c. $140,000
   d. $120,000

10. **Margin Calls** You deposit $100,000 cash in a brokerage account and short sell $200,000
of stocks. Your broker requires a maintenance margin of 30 percent. Which of the following is the lowest value for the stocks you are holding short for which you will still receive
a margin call?

   a. $260,000
   b. $240,000
   c. $220,000
   d. $200,000

11. **Investment Decisions** Which of the following investment factors, strategies, or tactics is
the least relevant to a passive investment policy?

   a. Market timing
   b. Asset allocation
   c. Political environment
   d. Tax status

12. **Investment Decisions** Which of the following investment factors, strategies, or tactics is
most associated with an active investment policy?

   a. Market timing
   b. Asset allocation
   c. Security selection
   d. Tax status

13. **Investment Decisions** Which of the following investment strategies or tactics will likely
consume the greatest amount of resources, time, effort, and so on, when implementing an
active investment policy?

   a. Market timing
   b. Asset allocation
   c. Security selection
   d. Tax strategy

14. **Investment Decisions** Which of the following investment strategies or tactics is likely
the most relevant in the decision to short sell a particular stock?

   a. Market timing
   b. Asset allocation
   c. Security selection
   d. Tax strategy

15. **Investment Constraints** Which of the following investment constraints is expected
to have the most fundamental impact on the investment decision process for a typical
investor?

    a. Investor's tax status
    b. Investor's time horizon
    c. Investor's need for liquidity
    d. Investor's attitude toward risk

Concept Questions

1. **Margin** What does it mean to purchase a security on margin? Why might you do it?

2. **Short Sales** What does it mean to sell a security short? Why might you do it?

3. **Margin Requirements** What is the reason margin requirements exist?

4. **Allocation versus Selection** What is the difference between asset allocation and security selection?

5. **Allocation versus Timing** Are market timing and active asset allocation similar? Why or why not?

6. **Street Name Registration** Why is street name registration advantageous to investors? Under what circumstances is it required?

7. **Broker–Customer Relations** Suppose your broker tips you on a hot stock. You invest heavily, but, to your considerable dismay, the stock plummets in value. What recourse do you have against your broker?

8. **Long Profits** An important difference between a long position in stock and a short position concerns the potential gains and losses. Suppose a stock sells for $18 per share, and you buy 500 shares. What are your potential gains and losses?

9. **Liquidity** The liquidity of an asset directly affects the risk of buying or selling that asset during adverse market conditions. Describe the liquidity risk you face with a short stock position during a market rally, and a long stock position during a market decline.

10. **Short Sale Profits** Suppose you sell short 1,000 shares of a stock at $60 per share. Ignoring borrowing costs and fees, what is the maximum profit you can earn from this investment? What is the potential maximum loss?

Questions and Problems

Core Questions

1. **Calculating Margin** Simmons Corporation stock sells for $83 per share, and you've decided to purchase as many shares as you possibly can. You have $13,000 available to invest. What is the maximum number of shares you can buy if the initial margin is 50 percent?

2. **Margin** You purchase 400 shares of Omni Co. stock on margin at a price of $65. Your broker requires you to deposit $15,000. What is your margin loan amount? What is the initial margin requirement?

3. **Margin Return** In the previous problem, suppose you sell the stock at a price of $75. What is your return? What would your return have been had you purchased the stock without margin? What if the stock price is $65 when you sell the stock?

4. **Margin** Repeat the previous two problems assuming the initial margin requirement is 40 percent. Does this suggest a relationship between the initial margin and returns?

5. **Margin Purchases** You have $13,000 and decide to invest on margin. If the initial margin requirement is 60 percent, what is the maximum dollar purchase you can make?

6. **Margin Calls** You buy 900 shares of stock at a price of $85 and an initial margin of 60 percent. If the maintenance margin is 35 percent, at what price will you receive a margin call?

7. **Margin Calls** You decide to buy 400 shares of stock at a price of $49 and an initial margin of 50 percent. What is the maximum percentage decline in the stock before you will receive a margin call if the maintenance margin is 25 percent?

8. **Margin Calls on Short Sales** The stock of Cruize Industries is trading at $64. You feel the stock price will decline, so you short 900 shares at an initial margin of 50 percent. If the maintenance margin is 30 percent, at what share price will you receive a margin call?

9. **Margin Calls on Short Sales** You short sold 1,000 shares of stock at a price of $56 and an initial margin of 50 percent. If the maintenance margin is 30 percent, at what share price will you receive a margin call? What is your account equity at this stock price?

10. **Taxes and Returns** You purchase a stock at the beginning of the year at a price of $86. At the end of the year the stock pays a dividend of $1.40 and you sell the stock for $98. What is your return for the year? Now suppose that dividends are taxed at your marginal tax rate of 31 percent and long-term capital gains (over 11 months) are taxed at 20 percent. What is your aftertax return for the year?

Intermediate Questions

11. **Calculating Margin** Using the information in Problem 1, construct your equity account balance sheet at the time of your purchase. What does your balance sheet look like if the share price rises to $90? What if it falls to $65 per share? What is your margin in both cases? Round the number of shares down to the nearest number of whole shares.

12. **Calculating Margin** You've just opened a margin account with $10,000 at your local brokerage firm. You instruct your broker to purchase 450 shares of Smolira Golf stock, which currently sells for $41 per share. What is your initial margin? Construct the equity account balance sheet for this position.

13. **Margin Call** Suppose you purchase 400 shares of stock at $72 per share with an initial cash investment of $15,000. If your broker requires a 30 percent maintenance margin, at what share price will you be subject to a margin call? If you want to keep your position open despite the stock price plunge, what alternatives do you have?

14. **Margin and Leverage** In the previous problem, suppose the call money rate is 5 percent and you are charged a 1.5 percent premium over this rate. Calculate your return on investment for each of the following share prices one year later. What would your rate of return be in each case if you purchased $15,000 of stock with no margin? Ignore dividends.

 a. $96
 b. $72
 c. $64

15. **Margin and Leverage** Suppose the call money rate is 6.8 percent, and you pay a spread of 1.9 percent over that. You buy 1,000 shares at $46 per share with an initial margin of 50 percent. One year later, the stock is selling for $53 per share, and you close out your position. What is your return assuming no dividends are paid?

16. **Margin and Leverage** Suppose the call money rate is 5.8 percent, and you pay a spread of 2.5 percent over that. You buy 800 shares of stock at $32 per share. You put up $15,000. One year later, the stock is selling for $37 per share, and you close out your position. What is your return assuming a dividend of $.64 per share is paid?

17. **Margin Interest** Suppose you take out a margin loan for $45,000. The rate you pay is an 8.7 percent effective rate. If you repay the loan in six months, how much interest will you pay?

18. **Margin Interest** Suppose you take out a margin loan for $32,000. You pay a 6.9 percent effective rate. If you repay the loan in two months, how much interest will you pay?

19. **Calculating Returns** Looking back at Problem 12, suppose the call money rate is 6 percent and your broker charges you a spread of 1.25 percent over this rate. You hold the stock for six months and sell at a price of $46 per share. The company paid a dividend of $.25 per share the day before you sold your stock. What is your total dollar return from this investment? What is your effective annual rate of return?

20. **Short Sales** You believe that Culligan, Inc., stock is going to fall and you've decided to sell 2,000 shares short. If the current share price is $54, construct the equity account balance sheet for this trade. Assume the initial margin is 100 percent.

21. **Short Sales** Repeat the previous problem assuming you short the 2,000 shares on 75 percent margin.

22. **Calculating Short Sale Returns** You just sold short 1,200 shares of Wetscope, Inc., a fledgling software firm, at $86 per share. You cover your short when the price hits $73 per share one year later. If the company paid $1.20 per share in dividends over this period, what is your rate of return on the investment? Assume an initial margin of 50 percent.

23. **Short Sales** You believe the stock in Freeze Frame Co. is going to fall, so you short 1,600 shares at a price of $83. The initial margin is 50 percent. Construct the equity balance sheet for the original trade. Now construct an equity balance sheet for a stock price of $73 and a stock price of $93. What is your margin at each of these stock prices? What is your effective annual return if you cover your short position at each of these prices in five months?

STANDARD &POOR'S

S&P Problems

www.mcgrawhill.ca/edumarketinsight

1. **Margin** Download the historical stock prices for Telus Corporation (T) under the "Mthly. Adj. Prices" link. Assume you purchased 400 shares of Telus Corporation stock at the closing price six months ago. The initial margin requirement is 50 percent and the maintenance margin is 30 percent. Show the account balance sheet based on monthly closing prices for the last five months. At what stock price will you receive a margin call? Are any margin deposits required over this period? What is your return on this investment?

2. **Short Sales** Download the historical stock prices for Celestica Inc. (CLS) under the "Mthly. Adj. Prices" link. Assume you short sold 200 shares of Celestica stock at the closing price six months ago. The initial margin requirement is 50 percent and the maintenance margin is 30 percent. Show the account balance sheet based on monthly closing prices for the last five months. At what stock price will you receive a margin call? Are any margin deposits required over this period? What is your return on this investment?

What's on the Web

1. **Risk Tolerance** As we discussed in the chapter, risk tolerance is based on an individual's personality and investment goals. There are numerous risk tolerance questionnaires on the Web. One, provided by Merrill Lynch, is located at individual.ml.com. Go to the website, locate the questionnaire and take the quiz. How conservative or aggressive are you?

2. **Short Interest** You can find the number of short sales on a particular stock at ca.finance. yahoo.com. Go to the site and find the number of shares sold for Quebecor (IQW) under the "Key Statistics" link. How many shares are sold short in the current month? What about the previous month? What do the "Percent of Float" and "Short Ratio" mean?

3. **Broker Call Money Rate** What is the current call rate? To find out, go to www.canada.etrade.com and look up "Interest/Margin Rates."

4. **Margin Purchases** Suppose you have a margin account with Scotiabank. You purchase 1,000 shares of Rogers Communication on 50 percent margin at today's price. Go to ca.finance.yahoo.com to find your purchase price. Ignoring transaction costs, how much will you borrow? Next go to www.canada.etrade.com to find the current broker call money rate. If you keep your investment for one year, how much will you pay in interest assuming the margin rate stays the same? What does the stock price have to be in one year for you to break even on your investment?

CHAPTER 4

Overview of Security Types

"An investment operation is one which upon thorough analysis promises safety of principal and an adequate return. Operations not meeting these requirements are speculative."

—Benjamin Graham

You invest $4,000 in Nortel common stock and just months later sell the shares for $6,000, realizing a 50 percent return. Not bad! At the same time, your neighbour invests $4,000 in Nortel stock options, which are worth $12,000 at expiration—a 200 percent return. Alternatively your Nortel shares fall in value to $2,000, and you realize a 50 percent loss. Too bad! But at the same time your neighbour's Nortel stock options are now worthless. Clearly there is a big difference between stock shares and stock options. Security type matters. ■

Our goal in this chapter is to introduce you to some of the different types of securities that are routinely bought and sold in financial markets around the world. As we mentioned in Chapter 1, we will be focusing on financial assets such as bonds, stocks, options, and futures in this book, so these are the securities we briefly describe here. The securities we discuss are covered in much greater detail in the chapters ahead, so we touch on only some of their most essential features in this chapter.

For each of the securities we examine, we ask three questions. First, what is its basic nature and what are its distinguishing characteristics? Second, what are the potential gains and losses from owning it? Third, how are its prices quoted in the financial press?

4.1 Classifying Securities

To begin our overview of security types, we first develop a classification scheme for the different securities. As shown in Table 4.1, financial assets can be grouped into three broad categories, and each of these categories can be further subdivided into a few major subtypes. This classification is not exhaustive, but it covers the major types of financial assets. In the sections that follow, we describe these assets in the order they appear in Table 4.1.

When we examine some of these security types in more detail, we will see that the distinctions can become a little blurred, particularly with some recently created financial instruments; as a result, some financial assets are hard to classify. The primary reason is that some instruments are hybrids, meaning that they are combinations of the basic types.

As you may have noticed in our discussion, financial assets, such as bonds and stocks, are often called securities. They are often called financial "instruments" as well. In certain contexts, there are distinctions between these terms, but they are used more or less interchangeably in everyday discussion, so we will stick with common usage.

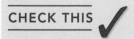 CHECK THIS

	4.1a	What are the three basic types of financial assets?
	4.1b	Why are some financial assets hard to classify?

4.2 Interest-Bearing Assets

Broadly speaking, interest-bearing assets (as the name suggests) pay interest. Some pay interest implicitly and some pay it explicitly, but the common denominator is that the value of these assets depends, at least for the most part, on interest rates. The reason that these assets pay interest is that they all begin life as a loan of some sort, so they are all debt obligations of some issuer.

There are many types of interest-bearing assets. They range from the relatively simple to the astoundingly complex. We discuss some basic types and their features next. The more complex types are discussed in later chapters.

TABLE 4.1	Classification of Financial Assets
Basic Types	**Major Subtypes**
Interest-bearing	Money market instruments
	Fixed-income securities
Equities	Common stock
	Preferred stock
Derivatives	Options
	Futures

Money Market Instrument

For the most part, **money market instruments** are the simplest form of interest-bearing asset. Money market instruments generally have the following two properties:

1. They are essentially IOUs sold by large corporations or governments to borrow money.

2. They mature in less than one year from the time they are sold, meaning that the loan must be repaid within one year.

Most money market instruments trade in very large denominations, and most, but not all, are quite liquid.

The most familiar example of a money market instrument is a Treasury bill, or T-bill for short. The Bank of Canada borrows billions of dollars by selling T-bills to the public bi-weekly. Like many (but not all) money market instruments, T-bills are sold on a *discount basis*. This simply means that T-bills are sold at a price that is less than their stated face value. In other words, an investor buys a T-bill at one price and later, when the bill matures, receives the full face value. The difference is the interest earned.

Treasury bills are the most liquid type of money market instrument—that is, the type with the largest and most active market. Other types of money market instruments traded in active markets include bank certificates of deposit (or CDs) and corporate, provincial and municipal money market instruments.

The potential gain from buying a money market instrument is fixed because the owner is promised a fixed future payment. The most important risk is the risk of default, which is the possibility that the borrower will not repay the loan as promised. With a T-bill, there is no possibility of default, so, as we saw in Chapter 1, T-bills are essentially risk-free. In fact, most money market instruments have relatively low risk, but there are exceptions, and a few spectacular defaults have occurred in the past.

Prices for different money market instruments are quoted in the financial press in different ways. In fact, usually interest rates are quoted, not prices, so some calculation is necessary to convert rates to prices. The procedures are not complicated, but they involve a fair amount of detail, so we save them for another chapter.

Fixed-Income Securities

Fixed-income securities are exactly what the name suggests: securities that promise to make fixed payments according to some preset schedule. The other key characteristic of a fixed-income security is that, like a money market instrument, it begins life as a loan of some sort. Fixed-income securities are therefore debt obligations. They are typically issued by corporations and governments. Unlike money market instruments, fixed-income securities have lives that exceed 12 months at the time they are issued.

The words "note" and "bond" are generic terms for fixed-income securities, but "fixed income" is more accurate. This term is being used more frequently as securities are increasingly being created that don't fit within traditional note or bond frameworks but are nonetheless fixed-income securities.

Examples of Fixed-Income Securities   To give one particularly simple example of a fixed-income security, suppose you invest in a two-year Canada bond. If you buy a two-year bond when it is issued, you will receive a cheque every six months for two years for a fixed amount, called the bond's *coupon*, and in two years you will receive the face amount on the bond.

Suppose you buy $1 million in face amount of a 6 percent, two-year bond. The 6 percent is called the *coupon rate*, and it tells you that you will receive 6 percent of the $1 million face value each year, or $60,000, in two $30,000 semiannual "coupon" payments. In two years, in addition to your final $30,000 coupon payment, you will receive the $1 million face value. The price you would pay for this bond depends on market conditions.

current yield Annual coupon divided by the current bond price.

You must be careful not to confuse the *coupon rate* with the **current yield**. The current yield is the annual coupon rate divided by the current bond price. For most bonds, the coupon rate never changes. But the current yield fluctuates with the price of the bond.

A "NOTE-WORTHY" INVESTMENT?

EXAMPLE 4.1

Suppose you buy $100,000 in face amount of a just-issued five-year Government of Canada Benchmark bond. If the coupon rate is 3.75 percent, what will you receive over the next five years if you hold on to your investment?

You will receive 3.75 percent of $100,000, or $3,750, per year, paid in two semiannual coupons of $1,875. In five years, in addition to the final $1,875 coupon payment, you will receive the $100,000 face amount.

To give a slightly different example, suppose you take out a 48-month car loan. Under the terms of the loan, you promise to make 48 payments of $400 per month. It may not look like it to you, but in taking out this loan, you have issued a fixed-income security to your bank. In fact, your bank may turn around and sell your car loan (perhaps bundled with a large number of other loans) to an investor. Actually, car loans are not sold all that often, but there is a very active market in student loans, which are routinely bought and sold in huge quantities.

Bond quotes have become more available with the rise of the internet. One site where you can find bond prices and yield is CBI's website at www.pfin.ca. Check the nearby Work the Web site to examine price and yield data of government, provincial, and corporate bonds as listed on August 10, 2007.

Check out bond basics at www.investing inbonds.com

Live Markets Wholesale Pricing	10Aug07 01:14PM EDT		Provincials	Price	Yield	Corporates	Price	Yield
			BC 6.0/Jun08	101.12	4.57	Shaw Commun 7.4/Oct07	100.29	5.50
Cda T-Bills	Price	Yield	Ontario 4.4/Nov08	99.63	4.70	BNS 4.515/Nov08	99.58	4.85
1 Month 20Sep	99.56	4.29	NewBrunswick 5.25/Jun09	101.10	4.60	BMO 4.66/Mar09	99.66	4.87
2 Month 18Oct	99.21	4.42	Fin Quebec 4.75/Dec09	100.21	4.65	HFC 4.2/Apr09	98.54	5.13
3 Month 15Nov	98.86	4.47	Ontario 4.0/May10	98.32	4.65	Bell CDA 6.15/Jun09	101.58	5.23
6 Month 07Feb	97.84	4.53	Ontario 4.4/Dec11	99.02	4.65	BMO 4.3/Sep09	98.92	4.86
1 Year 07Aug	95.72	4.54	Alberta 4.25/Jun12	98.31	4.65	BCE Inc. 7.35/Oct09	102.46	6.13
Cda Benchmarks	Price	Yield	Ontario 5.375/Dec12	103.21	4.68	BNS 3.93/Feb10	97.74	4.90
2 Year	98.73	4.49	Ontario 4.75/Jun13	100.41	4.67	HSBC Finl Co 4.0/May10	97.16	5.13
5 Year	96.85	4.49	Ontario 5.0/Mar14	101.47	4.74	HSBC Finl Co 4.8/Apr11	98.07	5.39
10 Year	96.17	4.49	Ontario 4.5/Mar15	98.09	4.80	HSBC Finl Co 4.35/Oct11	96.01	5.44
30 Year	119.69	4.46	Manitoba 4.3/Mar16	96.23	4.84	Bell CDA 6.25/Apr12	97.08	6.99
			AltaCapFinAu 4.35/Jun16	96.95	4.78	BMO 4.65/Mar13	97.98	5.07
			Quebec 4.5/Dec16	96.88	4.92	Royal Bank 4.71/Dec14	97.09	5.19
			Ontario 6.5/Mar29	119.87	4.99	Bell CDA 5.0/Feb17	84.99	7.21

Fixed-Income Price Quotes Prices for fixed-income securities are quoted in different ways, depending on, among other things, what type of security is being priced. As with money market instruments, there are various details that are very important (and often overlooked), so we will defer an extensive discussion of these price quotes to later chapters. However, just to get an idea of how fixed-income prices look, Figure 4.1 presents an example of *Globe and Mail* corporate bond quotes.

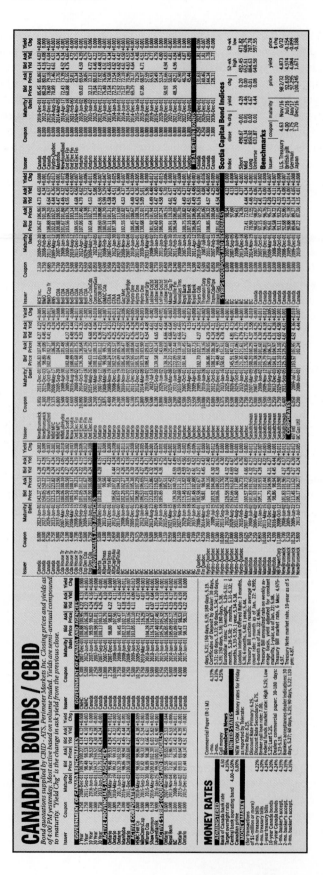

FIGURE 4.1

Perimeter CBID (www.canadianfixedincome.ca)

In Figure 4.1, locate the Hydro One bond issue with a 6.40 coupon rate. The bond was issued by Hydro One. The 6.40 is the bond's annual coupon rate. If you own $1 million in the face amount of these bonds, then you will receive 6.40 percent per year on the $1 million, or $64,000 per year in two semiannual payments. This bond will mature on December 1, 2011. The "Bid Price" is the dealer's buying price and the "Ask Price" is the dealer's selling price. Bond prices are quoted as percentages of bond face value. In this particular case, the bid price is 108.47 percent of $1000, or $1084.7 and the ask price is 108.78 percent, or $1087.8. "Bid Yield" and "Ask Yield" are calculated using bid and ask prices. We discuss how to calculate this yield in Chapter 11.

Finally, the last column, "Yield Change" represents the change in ask yield from the previous close. Compared to yesterday the yield has increased by 0.005.

CORPORATE BOND QUOTES

EXAMPLE 4.2

In Figure 4.1, which Bell CDA bond has the longest maturity? Assuming a face value of $1,000 each, how much would you have to pay for 100 of these?

The bond with the longest maturity is the Bell CDA with a 6.550 coupon and May 1, 2029, maturity. It is sold at 110.380. You will pay $1,103.80 per bond and $110,380 for 100 bonds.

The potential gains from owning a fixed-income security come in two forms. First, there are the fixed payments promised and the final payment at maturity. In addition, the prices of most fixed-income securities rise when interest rates fall, so there is the possibility of a gain from a favourable movement in rates. An unfavourable change in interest rates will produce a loss.

Another significant risk for many fixed-income securities is the possibility that the issuer will not make the promised payments. This risk depends on the issuer. It doesn't exist for Canadian government bonds but for many other issuers the possibility is very real. Finally, unlike most money market instruments, fixed-income securities are often quite illiquid, again depending on the issuer and the specific type.

CHECK THIS ✓

4.2a What are the two basic types of interest-bearing assets?

4.2b What are the two basic features of a fixed-income security?

4.3 Equities

Equities are probably the most familiar type of security. They come in two forms: common stock and preferred stock. Of these, common stock is much more important, so we discuss it first.

Are you a Foolish investor? Go to "Fool School" at www.fool.com

Common Stock

Common stock represents ownership in a corporation. If you own 1,000 shares of Husky Energy (HSE) for example, you own about 0.00024 percent of Husky Energy (Husky has roughly 424 million shares outstanding). It's really that simple. As a part owner, you are entitled to your pro rata share of anything paid out by Husky, and you have the right to vote on important matters regarding Husky Energy. If Husky were to be sold or liquidated, you would receive your share of whatever was left over after all of Husky's debts and other obligations (such as wages) are paid.

The potential benefits from owning common stock come primarily in two forms. First, many companies (but not all) pay cash dividends to their shareholders. However, neither the timing nor the amount of any dividend is guaranteed. At any time, it can be increased, decreased, or omitted altogether. Dividends are paid strictly at the discretion of a company's board of directors, which is elected by shareholders.

The second potential benefit from owning stock is that the value of your stock may rise because share values in general increase or because the future prospects for your particular company improve (or both). The downside is just the reverse: your shares may lose value if either the economy or your particular company falters. As we saw back in Chapter 1, both the potential rewards and the risks from owning common stock have been substantial, particularly shares of stock in smaller companies.

Preferred Stock

The other type of equity security, preferred stock, differs from common stock in several important ways. First, the dividend on a preferred share is usually fixed at some amount and never changed. Further, in the event of liquidation, preferred shares have a particular face value. The reason preferred stock (or preference stock, as it is sometimes termed) is called "preferred" is that a company must pay the fixed dividend on its preferred stock before any dividends can be paid to common shareholders. In other words, preferred shareholders must be paid first.

The dividend on a preferred stock can be omitted at the discretion of the board of directors, so, unlike a debt obligation, there is no legal requirement that the dividend be paid (as long as the common dividend is also skipped). However, some preferred stock is *cumulative*, meaning that any and all skipped dividends must be paid in full (although without interest) before common shareholders can receive a dividend.

Potential gains from owning preferred stock consist of the promised dividend plus any gains from price increases. The potential losses are just the reverse: the dividend may be skipped, and the value of your preferred shares may decline from either marketwide decreases in value or diminished prospects for your particular company's future business (or both).

Preferred stock issues are not rare, but they are much less frequently encountered than common stock issues. Most preferred stock is issued by large companies, particularly banks and public utilities. The nearby *Investment Updates* box provides more information on preferreds.

Finally, an ETF for the little guy. New exchange-traded funds continue to rain down on investors this year, but most of these products are too obscure to generate, or deserve, much attention from the average small investor. Today, a new ETF with much broader appeal begins trading on the Toronto Stock Exchange.

It's called the Claymore S&P/TSX Cdn Preferred Share ETF and it offers an ideal entry into the attractive but deceptively complex world of preferred shares.

Preferred shares are a conservative, income-generating type of investment and they're getting more popular in the aftermath of the federal government's crackdown on income trusts. Preferreds pay quarterly dividends, and they're less volatile than common share. "A preferred share is effectively like a bond that pays dividends," said Som Seif, president of Claymore Investments, the ETF company that is challenging market leader Barclays Global Investments.

The yield on preferred shares is unspectacular at 4 to 5 percent in most cases, but you get preferential tax treatment through the newly enhanced dividend tax credit. In fact, a 4.5-percent dividend yield is equivalent to a bond yield of about 6 percent on an after-tax basis.

This explains why the new Claymore preferred share ETF is designed primarily to be used in taxable accounts. You can certainly hold it in your registered retirement savings plan if you want, but you won't get nearly the same bang for your buck.

The new ETF—the stock symbol is CPD—is based on the S&P/TSX preferred share index. A total of 52 companies are represented in the index and the top five holdings are Great-West Lifeco, BCE Inc., Canadian Imperial Bank of Commerce, Toronto-Dominion Bank and Sun Life Financial.

The yield for the preferred share index is about 4.66 percent. Factor in the 0.45-percent management expense ratio of the Claymore preferred share ETF and you're left with a real-world yield of about 4.21 percent. To put this in context, short-term cash earns about 3.5 to 4 percent today, while federal and provincial government bonds might offer something in the area of 3.9 to 4.1 percent for terms of one through five years.

The problem with preferreds is how difficult it is for individual investors to buy them. Many preferred share issues don't trade much, which means you may have to pay a premium that has the effect of squeezing your yield (preferred share prices move inversely to their yield). Plus, there are hidden complexities. Yields are hard to calculate because you have to factor in not only the purchase price and dividend, but also the earliest date on which the issuer can call in the shares for redemption.

Claymore's Mr. Seif said the new Claymore ETF addresses all these issues. The shares in the fund are purchased at better prices than individual investors can get, which enhances the yield. And professional management reduces the risk in selecting preferreds to buy.

Mr. Seif suggested a portfolio have a weighting of 5 to 10 percent in preferred shares, which seems reasonable. Preferreds are considered fixed income, so you'd be mixing them in with your bonds and guaranteed investment certificates, and not your common stocks and equity funds.

Investors who favour ETFs can easily use these securities to build the entire fixed-income portfolio of their holdings. Barclays offers a range of six ETFs that focus on areas such as long bonds, corporate bonds, government bonds and real-return bonds (they offer a premium above the inflation rate). If you want to keep things simple, there's an all-in-one product called the iShares CDN Bond Index Fund (XBB-TSX).

ETFs are an ideal way to get broad exposure to a sector because they're cheap to own and transparent in that they mirror the holdings of a particular stock or bond index. But there are also several closed-end funds listed on the TSX that invest in preferred shares. Closed-end funds are similar to ETFs in that they trade like stocks, but they employ managers to select stocks rather than mirroring indexes.

An example of a preferred share closed-end fund is Advantaged Preferred Share Trust (PFR.UN-TSX), which holds an equally weighted portfolio of 50 preferred, share issues. You'll find other funds if you do a search under "pref" or "preferred" on both Globeinvestor.com and Globefund.com

Always read the prospectus for closed-end funds because they often use sophisticated investing strategies like leveraging (borrowing money in an attempt to magnify returns) and derivatives. The new Claymore preferred share ETF is pretty simple stuff, which is another reason why it's an ETF for the little guy.

Reprinted with permission from the Globe and Mail.

In many ways, preferred stock resembles a fixed-income security; in fact, it is sometimes classified that way. In particular, preferred stocks usually have a fixed payment and a fixed liquidation value (but no fixed maturity date). The main difference is that preferred stock is not a debt obligation. Also, for accounting and tax purposes, preferred stock is treated as equity.

Having said this, preferred stock is a good example of why it is sometimes difficult to neatly and precisely classify every security type. To further complicate matters, there are preferred stock issues with dividends that are not fixed, so it seems clear that these are not fixed-income securities, but there are also bond issues that do not make fixed payments and allow the issuer to skip payments under certain circumstances. As we mentioned earlier, these are examples of hybrid securities.

To give a more difficult example, consider a *convertible bond*. Such a bond is an ordinary bond in every way except that it can be exchanged for a fixed number of shares of stock anytime at the bondholder's discretion. Whether this is really a debt or equity instrument is difficult (or even impossible) to say.

Common Stock Price Quotes

Unlike fixed-income securities, the price quotes on common and preferred stock are fairly uniform. Part of the common stock page from *The Globe and Mail* can be seen in Figure 4.2. Locate the entry for Enbridge Inc. The column labelled "Close" is the closing price, meaning the last price at which a trade occurred before regular trading hours ended at 4:00 P.M. EST. This price is $41.90 for the Enbridge Inc Corporation. The "Chg" column shows the change between closing price and the previous day's closing price. The closing price has increased 99 cents and 2.42 percent from yesterday.

The information contained in *The Globe and Mail* can be obtained online in many places, of course. The nearby *Work the Web* box describes one way.

Stock price information is also available all day long on television and on the Web. Our nearby *Investment Updates* box explains how to interpret a very common site on television, the on-air ticker. As explained there, once you understand the display, you can actually create your own ticker to track the investments that interest you the most.

FIGURE 4.2   **TSX Trading**

ROB 100 » LARGEST STOCKS FROM THE TSX COMPOSITE BY MARKET CAPITALIZATION

Company	Close	Chg	% Chg	Company	Close	Chg	% Chg	Company	Close	Chg	% Chg	Company	Close	Chg	% Chg	Company	Close	Chg	% Chg
Addax Petroleum	44.20	-.41	-.92	Canadian Oil Sands	45.48	3.16	7.47	George Weston Ltd.	44.48	-1.11	-2.43	National Bank of Ca	48.42	1.28	2.72	Shaw Communications	18.28	.01	.05
Aeroplan Income Fun	17.10	-.97	-5.37	Canadian Pacific Ra	70.44	.74	1.06	Gerdau AmeriSteel	14.30	.05	.35	Nexen Inc.	32.34	.36	1.13	Sherritt Internatio	15.33	-.81	-5.02
Agnico-Eagle Mines	72.37	3.15	4.55	Canadian Tire Corpo	63.44	.52	.83	Gildan Activewear	36.38	.01	.03	Niko Resources	89.83	.58	.65	Shoppers Drug Mart	50.00	-.10	-.20
Agrium	73.41	2.11	2.96	Canadian Utilities	44.63	-.67	-1.48	Goldcorp Inc.	43.88	1.41	3.32	Nortel Networks Cor	7.55	-.18	-2.33	Silver Wheaton	18.01	.82	4.77
Alimentation Couche	16.49	-.10	-.60	Centerra Gold	14.90	.25	1.71	Great-West Lifeco	30.72	.25	.82	Oilexco Inc.	15.48	.84	5.74	Sino-Forest Corp.	19.65	.59	3.10
ARC Energy Trust	24.39	.51	2.14	CGI Group	10.84	.09	.84	Harvest Energy Trus	23.36	-.07	-.30	Onex Corporation	33.84	-.08	-.24	SNC-Lavalin Group	43.00	.48	1.13
ATCO Ltd.	46.50	-2.25	-4.62	CI Financial Income	21.93	.11	.50	Husky Energy	42.51	.53	1.26	OPTI Canada	16.86	.33	2.00	Sun Life Financial	46.26	.22	.48
Bank of Montreal	45.02	-1.87	-3.99	CIBC	64.35	-.84	-1.29	IGM Financial	42.52	.78	1.87	Pan American Silver	40.35	1.21	3.09	Suncor Energy	107.70	2.89	2.76
Bank of Nova Scotia	45.86	.27	.59	Crescent Point Ener	27.25	.55	2.06	Imperial Oil	57.24	1.37	2.45	Pengrowth Energy Tr	18.60	.25	1.36	Talisman Energy	17.62	.67	3.95
Barrick Gold Corp.	52.15	1.25	2.46	Eastern Platinum	4.07	.19	4.90	Industrial Alliance	34.83	.69	2.02	Penn West Energy Tr	28.15	.47	1.70	TD Bank	64.29	.03	.05
BCE Inc.	36.58	.72	2.01	Enbridge Inc.	41.90	.99	2.42	ING Canada	38.64	-.83	-2.10	Petro-Canada	46.37	-.53	-1.13	Teck Cominco Ltd.	41.54	1.14	2.82
Bell Aliant	29.25	.05	.17	EnCana Corp.	76.77	1.06	1.40	Inmet Mining	88.08	4.30	5.13	Petrobank Energy an	55.74	1.11	2.03	TELUS Corp.	44.35	-.02	-.05
Bombardier Inc.	5.48	.00	.00	Enerplus Resources	43.64	.64	1.49	Ivanhoe Mines	12.83	.43	3.47	Potash Corp. of Sas	158.56	2.56	1.64	Thomson Corp.	32.91	.53	1.64
Bonavista Energy Tr	30.30	.99	3.38	Ensign Energy Servi	18.65	.36	1.97	Kinross Gold	26.05	1.19	4.79	Power Corp of Canad	33.07	.13	.39	Tim Hortons	34.72	.32	.93
Brookfield Asset Ma	28.45	-.16	-.56	Equinox Minerals Li	5.54	-.26	-4.48	Loblaw Companies	27.60	-1.01	-3.53	Power Financial Cor	33.85	.03	.09	TransCanada Corp.	40.38	.45	1.13
Brookfield Properti	18.56	-.29	-1.54	Fairfax Financial H	271.01	-3.99	-1.45	Lundin Mining	8.24	-.04	-.48	Research in Motion	100.43	-3.82	-3.66	TSX Group	42.80	-.94	-2.15
CAE Inc.	11.62	-.35	-2.92	Finning Internation	28.31	.46	1.65	Magna International	71.00	.41	.58	RioCan Real Estate	19.72	.02	.10	Vermilion Energy Tr	38.66	.16	.42
Cameco Corp.	38.93	.44	1.14	First Quantum Miner	90.54	.57	.63	Manitoba Telecom Se	41.06	.06	.15	Rogers Communicatio	39.21	-.01	-.03	Yamana Gold Inc.	19.05	.68	3.70
Canadian National R	52.92	1.18	2.28	Fording Canadian Co	51.87	.49	.95	Manulife Financial	37.85	.30	.80	Royal Bank of Canad	47.56	-.43	-.90	Yellow Pages Income	10.56	.16	1.54
Canadian Natural Re	76.45	1.50	2.00	Fortis Inc.	27.88	-.12	-.43	Methanex Corp.	29.30	.49	1.70	Saputo Inc.	25.84	-.34	-1.30				

♣ Free annual reports and if available, quarterly reports, for companies with this symbol. Reports mailed next business day, subject to availability. Open 24 hours, including weekends. To order, call 1-800-965-6199 or visit globeandmail.ar.wilink.com or fax 1-800-617-7678. When ordering by fax, please give ticker symbols for companies you require. Companies wishing to participate in this service, please contact Kirk Brouse at 416-865-3358.

Source: *The Globe and Mail*, January 27, 2007

The on-air "ticker tape" is a familiar sight on television, particularly on financially oriented shows and networks. In Canada, BNN (Business News Network) provides stock price quotes for both Canadian and U.S. stocks continuously. All day long, at the bottom of the screen, two rows of information scroll by.

The display is called a "ticker tape" because, at one time, it was printed on a thin strip of paper by a "ticker" machine (so named because of the sound it made while printing). In fact, the reason for ticker symbols in the first place was to make information quicker and easier to print. Perhaps you have seen old film footage of a "ticker tape parade" in New York. The paper that rains down on the celebrities and dignitaries is ticker tape.

Ticker machines date to an era before television (if you can imagine such a thing). The first one was introduced in 1867 and was later improved by none other than Thomas Edison. To learn more, visit the website www.stocktickercompany.com.

A typical stock quote on BNN ticker looks like this:

This quote tells that a trade in Canfor has just occurred and then provides details about the trade. First we observe the ticker symbol CFP that represents Canfor Company. The trade occurred at 12.43 and the downward pointing "Change Direction" arrow indicates that this price is down compared to yesterday's closing price. The "Change Amount" tells us how much, $0.96 in this case.

In CNBC screens, the upper band shows trading on the New York Stock Exchange, and the lower band shows trading on the Nasdaq Stock Market. In ROBTV, the upper band shows the Toronto Stock Exchange trading and the lower band shows New York Stock Exchange trading then the Nasdaq trading. To learn more, visit www.bnn.ca and link to globeinvestor.com Stock Ticker. As you will see, you can create your own ticker for display on your computer screen just by following the directions given. A personalized ticker allows you to track just the things that interest you the most.

CHECK THIS ✓

4.3a What are the two types of equity securities?

4.3b Why is preferred stock sometimes classified as a fixed-income security?

4.4 Derivatives

primary asset
Security originally sold by a business or government to raise money.

derivative asset
A financial asset that is derived from an existing traded asset rather than issued by a business or government to raise capital. More generally, any financial asset that is not a primary asset.

There is a clear distinction between real assets, which are essentially tangible items, and financial assets, which are pieces of paper describing legal claims. Financial assets can be further subdivided into primary and derivative assets. A **primary asset** (sometimes called a *primitive asset*) is a security that was originally sold by a business or government to raise money, and a primary asset represents a claim on the assets of the issuer. Thus, stocks and bonds are primary financial assets.

In contrast, as the name suggests, a **derivative asset** is a financial asset that is derived from an existing primary asset rather than issued by a business or government to raise capital. As we will see, derivative assets usually represent claims either on other financial assets, such as shares of stock or even other derivative assets, or on the future price of a real asset such as gold. Beyond this, it is difficult to give a general definition of the term "derivative asset" because there are so many different types, and new ones are created almost every day. On the most basic level, however, any financial asset that is not a primary asset is a derivative asset.

WORK THE WEB

Throughout this chapter, we have looked at information from *The Globe and Mail.* One problem is that prices reported in the financial press are always from the previous day. Before you trade, you'll want more up-to-date pricing, particularly in fast-moving markets. Using an Internet server, such as Yahoo!, let's do this. We have entered a ticker symbol of CFP to represent Canfor Company and obtained the following box:

Most of the information here is self-explanatory. The abbreviation "Mkt Cap" is short for "market capitalization" which is the total value of all outstanding shares. Notice, on this particular day, Canfor stock was $12.43 (down 0.96 percent), compared to $12.55 ("Prev Cls") that you would see in newspapers. We will discuss other unfamiliar terms, such as "Bid" and "Ask," a little later in the book. For now, a good exercise is to select a detailed quote yourself and find out what information is in the links below the stock quote.

To give a simple example of a derivative asset, imagine that you and a friend buy 1,000 shares of a dividend-paying stock, perhaps the Bank of Montreal stock we discussed. You each put up half the money, and you agree to sell your stock in one year. Furthermore, the two of you agree that you will get all the dividends paid while your friend gets all the gains or absorbs all the losses on the 1,000 shares.

This simple arrangement takes a primary asset, shares of Bank of Montreal stock, and creates two derivative assets, the dividend-only shares that you hold and the no-dividend shares held by your friend. Derivative assets such as these actually exist, and there are many variations on this basic theme.

There are two particularly important types of derivative assets, futures and options. Many other types exist, but they can usually be built up from these two basic types, possibly by combining them with other primary assets. Futures are the simpler of the two, so we discuss them first.

Futures Contracts

futures contract
An agreement made today regarding the terms of a trade that will take place later.

In many ways, a futures contract is the simplest of all financial assets. A **futures contract** is just an agreement made today regarding the terms of a trade that will take place later. For example, suppose you know that you will want to buy 100 ounces of gold in six months. One thing you could do is to strike a deal today with a seller in which you promise to pay, say, $400 per ounce in six months for the 100 ounces of gold. In other words, you and the seller agree that six months from now, you will exchange $40,000 for 100 ounces of gold. The agreement that you have created is a futures contract.

With your futures contract, you have locked in the price of gold six months from now. Suppose that gold is actually selling for $450 per ounce in six months. If this occurs, then you benefit from having entered into the futures contract because you have to pay only $400 per ounce. However, if gold is selling for $350, you lose because you are forced to pay $400 per ounce. Thus, a futures contract is essentially a bet on the future price of whatever is being bought or sold. Notice that with your futures contract, no money changes hands today.

You can download lots of basic futures info from the Education Centre at www.cbot.com

After entering into the futures contract, what happens if you change your mind in, say, four months, and you want out of the contract? The answer is that you can sell your contract to someone else. You would generally have a gain or a loss when you sell. The contract still has two months to run. If market participants generally believe that gold will be worth more than $400 when the contract matures in two months, then your contract is valuable, and you would have a gain if you sold it. If, on the other hand, market participants think gold will not be worth $400, then you would have a loss on the contract if you sold it because you would have to pay someone else to take it off your hands.

Futures contracts are traded all over the world on many types of assets, and futures contracts can be traced back to ancient civilizations. As we discuss in detail in later chapters, there are two broad categories of futures contracts: *financial futures* and *commodity futures*. The difference is that, with financial futures, the underlying asset is intangible, usually stocks, bonds, currencies, or money market instruments. With commodity futures, the underlying asset is a real asset, typically either an agricultural product (such as cattle or wheat) or a natural resource product (such as gold or oil).

Futures Price Quotes

An important feature of traded futures contracts is that they are *standardized*, meaning that one contract calls for the purchase of a specific quantity of the underlying asset. Further, the contract specifies in detail what the underlying asset is and where it is to be delivered. For example, with a wheat contract, one contract specifies that such-and-such a quantity of a particular type of wheat will be delivered at one of a few approved locations on a particular date in exchange for the agreed-upon futures price.

In Figure 4.3 futures price quotations for 10-year Canada bonds are seen as they appear in *The Globe and Mail*. Looking at Figure 4.3, we see these are quotes for delivery of Canada bonds with a total par, or face, value of $100,000.

FIGURE 4.3

Futures Trading

Source: *The Globe and Mail*, April 19, 2007

The "sea hi" and "sea low" columns refer to the highest and lowest prices over the life of this contact. The "Mth" tells us the delivery date for the bond specified by the contract. The first contract is to be delivered in June 2007. In order, we have the open price, the high price, the low price, and the settle price. The open price is the price at the start of the trading day, the high and low are highest and lowest prices for the day, and the settle is the price on the final trade of the day. The "CHG" is the change in the settle price from the previous trading day. Finally, the "OPEN INT" tells us how many contracts are currently outstanding.

To get a better idea of how futures contracts work, suppose you buy one June contract at the settle price. What you have done is agree to buy 10-year Canada bonds with a total par value of $100,000 in June at a price of 112.74 per $100 of par value which represents $112,740 per $100,000 par value.

Actually, most futures contracts don't result in delivery. Most buyers and sellers close out their contracts before the delivery date. To close out a contract, you take the opposite side. For example, suppose that with your one Canada bond contract, you later decide you no longer wish to be in it. To get out, you simply sell one contract, thereby cancelling your position.

Gains and Losses on Futures Contracts

Futures contracts have the potential for enormous gains and losses. To see why, let's consider again buying Canada bond contracts based on the settle prices in Figure 4.3. To make matters somewhat more interesting, suppose you buy 20 June contracts at the settle price of 112.74 per $100 of par value.

One month later, because of falling inflation, the futures price of Canada bonds for June delivery rises five dollars to 117.74. This may not seem like a huge increase, but it generates a substantial profit for you. You have locked in a price of 112.74 per $100 par value. The price has risen to 117.74, so you make a profit of $5 per $100 of par value, or $5,000 per $100,000 face value. With 20 contracts, each of which calls for delivery of $100,000 in face value of Canada bonds, you make 20 × $5,000 = $100,000, so your profit is a tidy $100,000. Of course, if the price had decreased by five dollars, you would have lost $100,000 on your 20-contract position.

FUTURE SHOCK

EXAMPLE 4.3

Suppose you purchase five June Canada bond contracts at a settle price of 112.74. How much will you pay today? Suppose in one month you close your position and the June futures price at that time is 109.74. Did you make or lose money? How much?

When you purchase the five contracts, you pay nothing today because the transaction is for June. However, you have agreed to pay 112.74 per $100 par value. If the futures price is 109.74 when you close your position in a month, you have a loss of 112.74 − 109.74 = 3 per $100 par value, or 3 × 1,000 = $3,000 per contract. Your total loss is thus $3,000 × 5 contracts, or $15,000 in all (ouch!).

CHECK THIS

4.4a What is a futures contract?

4.4b What are the general types of futures contracts?

4.4c Explain how you make or lose money on a futures contract.

4.5 Option Contracts

option contract An agreement that gives the owner the right, but not the obligation, to buy or sell a specific asset at a specified price for a set period of time.

An **option contract** is an agreement that gives the owner the right, but not the obligation, to buy or sell (depending on the type of option) a specific asset at a specific price for a specific period of time. The most familiar options are stock options. These are options to buy or sell shares of stock, and they are the focus of our discussion here. Options are a very flexible investment tool, and a great deal is known about them. We present some of the most important concepts here; our detailed coverage begins in later chapters.

Option Terminology

call option An option that gives the owner the right, but not the obligation, to buy an asset.

Options come in two flavours, calls and puts. The owner of a **call option** has the right, but not the obligation, to *buy* an underlying asset at a fixed price for a specified time. The owner of a **put option** has the right, but not the obligation, to *sell* an underlying asset at a fixed price for a specified time.

put option An option that gives the owner the right, but not the obligation, to sell an asset.

Options occur frequently in everyday life. Suppose, for example, that you are interested in buying a used car. You and the seller agree that the price will be $3,000. You give the seller $100 to hold the car for one week, meaning that you have one week to come up with the $3,000 purchase price, or else you lose your $100.

This agreement is a call option. You paid the seller $100 for the right, but not the obligation, to buy the car for $3,000. If you change your mind because, for example, you find a better deal elsewhere, you can just walk away. You'll lose your $100, but that is the price you paid for the right, but not the obligation, to buy. The price you pay to purchase an option, the $100 in this example, is called the **option premium**.

option premium
The price you pay to buy an option.

strike price The price specified in an option contract at which the underlying asset can be bought (for a call option) or sold (for a put option). Also called the striking price or exercise price.

A few other definitions will be useful. First, the specified price at which the underlying asset can be bought or sold with an option contract is called the **strike price**, the *striking price*, or the *exercise price*. Using an option to buy or sell an asset is called *exercising* the option. The last day on which an option can be exercised is the day before the *expiration date* on the option contract. Finally, an *American option* can be exercised anytime up to and including the expiration date, whereas a *European option* can be exercised only on the expiration date.

Options versus Futures

Our discussion thus far illustrates the two crucial differences between an option contract and a futures contract. The first is that the purchaser of a futures contract is *obligated* to buy the underlying asset at the specified price (and the seller of a futures contract is obligated to sell). The owner of a call option is not obligated to buy, however, unless she wishes to do so; she has the right, but not the obligation.

The second important difference is that when you buy a futures contract, you pay no money (and you receive none if you sell). However, if you buy an option contract, you pay the premium; if you sell an option contract, you receive the premium.

Option Price Quotes

Like futures contracts, most option contracts are standardized. One call option contract, for example, gives the owner the right to buy 100 shares (one round lot) of stock. Similarly, one put option contract gives the owner the right to sell 100 shares.

To learn more about option visit the Learning Centre at www.cboe.com

Figure 4.4 represents Aber Diamond's stock call and put option quotes taken from the Montreal Exchange. We visited the Montreal Exchange site at www.m-x.ca and under the Trading title clicked the Quotes link. Under the Equity Derivatives sign, we entered the ABZ symbol for the Aber Diamond and got the following box. The left side of the box lists all the call options and the right hand lists the put options. The first column lists expiration months and the second column the strike prices. So, for example, Aber Diamond's call options listing has striking prices ranging from $34 to $50 and expiration months of August 2007, September 2007, October 2007 and January 2008. The third and fourth columns list bid and ask prices respectively. After the last trading price column comes trading volume information.

Referring to August call options with 38.000, we see that 15 call option contracts were traded. The bid and last price is $0.45. Because each contract actually involves 100 shares, the buying price per contract is 100 × 0.45 = $45. The last column shows the implied volatility.

Suppose you wanted the right to buy 500 shares of Aber Diamond for $34 some time between now and September. What would you buy? Based on the information in Figure 4.4 how much would you have to pay?

From Figure 4.4, the option premium for the contract with a $34 strike and a September expiration is $4.45, so one contract would cost $4.45 × 100 = $445. The cost for five contracts would therefore be 5 × $445 = $2,225.

FIGURE 4.4

Options Trading

ABZ - Aber Diamond Corp.

Last update: Aug. 14, 2007 17:00 Montréal time   Refresh | Print

Calls

Month / Strike	Bid Price	Ask Price	Last Price	Vol.	Impl. Vol.
+ 07 AU 36.000	1.700	1.950	1.950	0	31.23
+ 07 AU 38.000	0.300	0.450	0.450	15	24.22
+ 07 AU 40.000	0.000	0.150	0.150	0	32.17
+ 07 AU 42.000	0.000	0.030	0.030	0	0.00
+ 07 AU 44.000	0.000	0.100	0.100	0	0.00
+ 07 AU 46.000	0.000	0.100	0.100	0	0.00
+ 07 AU 48.000	0.000	0.100	0.100	0	0.00
+ 07 SE 34.000	4.200	4.450	4.450	0	0.00
+ 07 SE 36.000	2.600	2.850	2.850	0	34.30
+ 07 SE 38.000	1.350	1.550	1.550	0	30.64
+ 07 SE 40.000	0.550	0.750	0.750	0	28.80
+ 07 SE 42.000	0.150	0.350	0.350	0	28.03
+ 07 SE 44.000	0.000	0.200	0.200	0	28.78
+ 07 SE 46.000	0.000	0.150	0.150	0	0.00
+ 07 OC 34.000	4.400	4.650	4.650	0	0.00
+ 07 OC 36.000	2.900	3.150	3.150	0	31.17
+ 07 OC 38.000	1.700	1.950	1.950	0	29.12
+ 07 OC 40.000	0.900	1.100	1.100	0	28.00
+ 07 OC 42.000	0.400	0.600	0.600	0	27.40
+ 07 OC 44.000	0.100	0.350	0.350	0	26.92
+ 07 OC 46.000	0.000	0.200	0.200	0	27.02
+ 07 OC 48.000	0.000	0.150	0.150	0	0.00
+ 07 OC 50.000	0.000	0.150	0.150	0	0.00
+ 08 JA 34.000	5.450	5.650	5.650	0	0.00
+ 08 JA 36.000	4.100	4.350	4.350	0	32.81
+ 08 JA 38.000	3.000	3.300	3.300	0	31.95
+ 08 JA 40.000	2.100	2.400	2.400	3	30.97
+ 08 JA 42.000	1.450	1.700	1.700	0	30.44
+ 08 JA 44.000	0.950	1.150	1.150	0	29.73
+ 08 JA 46.000	0.600	0.800	0.800	0	29.50
+ 08 JA 48.000	0.400	0.550	0.550	0	29.65
+ 08 JA 50.000	0.250	0.400	0.400	0	29.94
Total				18	

Puts

Month / Strike	Bid Price	Ask Price	Last Price	Vol.	Impl. Vol.
+ 07 AU 36.000	0.010	0.150	0.150	0	27.96
+ 07 AU 38.000	0.500	0.700	0.700	0	21.10
+ 07 AU 40.000	2.150	2.450	2.450	0	0.00
+ 07 AU 42.000	4.050	4.450	4.450	0	0.00
+ 07 AU 44.000	6.050	6.450	6.450	0	0.00
+ 07 AU 46.000	8.050	8.450	8.450	0	0.00
+ 07 AU 48.000	10.050	10.450	10.450	0	0.00
+ 07 SE 34.000	0.300	0.450	0.450	0	0.00
+ 07 SE 36.000	0.650	0.850	0.850	0	29.51
+ 07 SE 38.000	1.400	1.600	1.600	2	27.10
+ 07 SE 40.000	2.600	2.800	2.800	0	24.82
+ 07 SE 42.000	4.150	4.450	4.450	0	21.28
+ 07 SE 44.000	6.100	6.400	6.400	0	0.00
+ 07 SE 46.000	8.100	8.400	8.400	0	0.00
+ 07 OC 34.000	0.600	0.750	0.750	0	0.00
+ 07 OC 36.000	1.100	1.300	1.300	0	30.90
+ 07 OC 38.000	1.850	2.100	2.100	0	28.74
+ 07 OC 40.000	3.050	3.350	3.350	0	28.70
+ 07 OC 42.000	4.550	4.850	4.850	0	28.64
+ 07 OC 44.000	6.300	6.600	6.600	0	29.93
+ 07 OC 46.000	8.150	8.450	8.450	0	31.22
+ 07 OC 48.000	10.100	10.400	10.400	0	34.66
+ 07 OC 50.000	12.100	12.400	12.400	0	39.94
+ 08 JA 34.000	1.500	1.600	1.600	0	0.00
+ 08 JA 36.000	2.150	2.350	2.350	0	32.68
+ 08 JA 38.000	3.000	3.300	3.300	0	31.98
+ 08 JA 40.000	4.100	4.350	4.350	0	31.15
+ 08 JA 42.000	5.400	5.700	5.700	0	31.05
+ 08 JA 44.000	6.900	7.200	7.200	0	31.22
+ 08 JA 46.000	8.550	8.900	8.900	0	32.15
+ 08 JA 48.000	10.350	10.700	10.700	0	33.84
+ 08 JA 50.000	12.200	12.550	12.550	0	35.64
Total				2	

∴ Top

Gains and Losses on Option Contracts

As with futures contracts, option contracts have the potential for large gains and losses. To examine this, let's consider our previous example in which you paid $2,225 for five Aber Diamond September 34 call contracts. Suppose you hold on to your contracts until September rolls around and they are just about to expire. What are your gains (or losses) if Aber Diamond is selling for $64 per share? $24 per share?

PUT POINTS

EXAMPLE 4.4

Suppose you want the right to sell 200 shares of Aber Diamond between now and September at $34.000. In light of the information in Figure 4.4, what contract should you buy? How much will it cost you?

You want the right to sell stock at a fixed price, so you want to buy put options. Specifically, you want to buy two September 34 put contracts. In Figure 4.4, the premium for this contract is given as $0.45. Recalling that this is the premium per share, one contract will cost you $45, so two contracts would be $90.

If Aber Diamond is selling for $64 per share, you will profit handsomely. You have the right to buy 500 shares at a price of $34 per share. Since the stock is worth $64, your options are worth $30 per share, or $15,000 in all. So you invested $2,225 and ended up with more than 6 times that. Not bad.

If the stock ends up at $24 per share, however, the result is not so pretty. You have the right to buy the stock for $34, when it is selling for $24, so your call options expire worthless. You lose the entire $2,225 you originally invested. In fact, if the stock price is anything less than $34, you lose it all.

MORE ON PUTS

EXAMPLE 4.5

In Example 4.4, you bought two Aber Diamond September 34 put options for $90. Suppose in September, Aber Diamond is selling at $24 per share. How did you do? What is the break-even stock price, that is, the stock price at which you just make enough to cover your $90 cost?

Your put options give you the right to sell 200 shares of Aber Diamond at $34 per share. If the stock is worth only $24 per share, your put options are worth $10 per share, or $2,000 in all. To determine the break-even stock price, notice that you paid $0.45 per share for the option, so this is what you must make per share to break even. The break-even stock price is thus $34 − $0.45 = $33.55.

Investing in Stocks versus Options

To get a better idea of the potential gains and losses from investing in stocks compared to investing in options, let's suppose you have $10,000 to invest. You're looking at Macron Technology, which is currently selling for $50 per share. You also notice that a call option with a $50 strike price and three months to maturity is available. The premium is $4. Macron pays no dividends.

You're considering investing all $10,000 either in the stock or in the call options. What is your return from these two investments, if, in three months, Macron is selling for $55 per share? What about $45 per share?

First, if you buy the stock, your $10,000 will purchase two round lots, meaning 200 shares. A call contract costs $400 (why?), so you can buy 25 of them. Notice that your 25 contracts give you the right to buy 2,500 shares at $50 per share.

If, in three months, Macron is selling for $55, your stock will be worth 200 shares × $55 = $11,000. Your dollar gain will be $11,000 less the $10,000 you invested, or

$1,000. Since you invested $10,000, your return for the three-month period is $1,000 / $10,000 = 10%. If Macron is going for $45 per share, then you lose $1,000, and your return is −10 percent.

At the $55 price, your call options are worth $55 − $50 = $5 each, but now you control 2,500 shares, so your options are worth 2,500 shares × $5 = $12,500 total. You invested $10,000, so your dollar return is $12,500 − $10,000 = $2,500, and your percentage return is $2,500 / $10,000 = 25%, compared to 10 percent on the stock investment. However, if Macron is selling for $45 when your options mature, then you lose everything, and your return is −100 percent.

PUT RETURNS

EXAMPLE 4.6

In our example for Macron Technology, suppose a put option is also available with a premium of $2.50. Calculate your percentage return for the three-month holding period if the stock price declines to $47 per share. What is your annualized return?

One put contract costs $250, so you can buy 40 of them. Notice that your 40 contracts give you the right to *sell* 4,000 shares at $50 per share.

If, in three months, Macron is selling for $47, your put options are worth $50 − $47 = $3 each. You control 4,000 shares, so your options are worth 4,000 shares × $3 = $12,000 total. You invested $10,000, so your dollar return is $12,000 − $10,000 = $2,000, and your percentage return is $2,000/ $10,000 = 20%.

To annualize your return, we need to compute the effective annual return, recognizing that there are 4 three-month periods in a year:

$$1 + EAR = 1.20^4$$
$$= 2.0736$$
$$EAR = 1.0736 = 107.36\%$$

Your annualized return is thus about 107 percent.

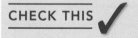

CHECK THIS

4.5a   What is a call option? A put option?

4.5b   If you buy a call option, what do you hope will happen to the underlying stock? What if you buy a put option?

4.5c   What are the two key differences between a futures contract and an option contract?

4.6   Summary and Conclusions

This chapter examines the basic types of financial assets. It discusses three broad classes: interest-bearing assets, equities, and derivative assets. Each of these major groups can be further subdivided. Interest-bearing assets include money market instruments and fixed-income securities. The two major equity types are common stock and preferred stock. The two most important types of derivative assets are options and futures.

For each of the major types of financial assets, we cover three topics. We first describe the basic nature of the asset with an emphasis on what the owner of the asset is entitled to receive. We then illustrate how prices are quoted in the financial press, and we show how to interpret information presented in the newspaper. Finally, we indicate, in fairly broad terms, the potential gains and losses from buying and selling each type of asset.

REAL WORLD

This chapter covered the basics of the four main types of financial assets: stocks, bonds, options, and futures. In addition to discussing basic features, we alerted you to some of the risks associated with these instruments. We particularly stressed the large potential gains and losses possible with derivative assets. How should you, as an investor or investment manager, put this information to work?

Following up on our previous chapter, you need to execute each of the possible transaction types suggested by this chapter in a simulated brokerage account. Your goal is to experience some of the large gains (and losses) to understand them on a personal level. Try to do at least the following:

1. Buy a corporate or government bond.
2. Buy put and call option contracts.
3. Sell put and call option contracts.
4. Buy agriculture, and financial futures contracts.
5. Sell agriculture, and financial futures contracts.

In each case, once you have created the position, be sure to monitor it regularly by checking prices, trading activity, and relevant news using the newspapers or an online information service to understand why it changes in value.

One thing you will discover if you execute these trades is that some of these investments carry relatively low risk and some relatively high risk. Which are which? Under what circumstances is each of these investments appropriate? We will have more to say about these investments later, but you'll get a lot more out of our discussion (and have some fun stories to tell) if you already have some personal experience. As always, it's better to become educated about these things with play money before you commit real money.

Key Terms

money market instruments 104
fixed-income securities 104
current yield 105
primary asset 111
derivative asset 111
futures contract 113

option contract 115
call option 115
put option 115
option premium 116
strike price 116

Chapter Review Problems and Self-Test

1. **Corporate Bond Quotes** In Figure 4.1, locate the Sears Canada bond. What is the coupon rate on this issue? Suppose you purchase $100,000 in face value. How much will this cost? Assuming semiannual payments, what will you receive in coupon payments?

2. **Call Options** Go to the Montreal Exchange's website, under Trading, click Quotes and enter Goldcorp's symbol G in Equity Derivatives, then find Goldcorp September 28 call option. If you buy 10 contracts, how much will you pay? Suppose that in September, just as the option is about to expire, Goldcorp is selling for $40 per share. What is your net profit?

3. **Government Bonds** In Figure 4.1, locate the Province of British Columbia bond that matures in 2023. What is the coupon rate on this issue? Suppose you purchase $1,000,000 face value. How much will it cost? What is the amount of the semiannual payment?

4. **Put Options** Go to Montreal Exchange's website, under Trading and click Quotes and enter BCE's symbol BCE in Equity Derivatives, and find BCE November 32 put option. If you buy 100 contracts, how much will you pay? Suppose that in November, just as the option is about to expire, BCE is selling for $40 per share. What are your options worth?

Answers to Self-Test Problems

1. Based on Figure 4.1, the Sears Canada issue has a 7.45 percent coupon rate. The price, as a percentage of face value, is 104.75, or 104.75 percent. If you buy $100,000 in face value, you would thus pay $104,750. You will receive 7.45 percent of $100,000, or $7,450, in coupon payments every year, paid in two $3,725 semiannual instalments.

2. The Goldcorp September 28 call option was traded at 0.600 on August 14, 2007. Because one contract involves 100 shares, the cost of a contract is $60, and 10 contracts would cost $600. In September, if Goldcorp is selling for $40 per share, then you have the right to buy 10 contracts × 100 shares = 1,000 shares at $28. Your contracts are thus worth $40 − $28 = $12 per share, or $12,000 total. Since they cost you $600, your net profit is $11,400.

3. This bond has 8.00 percent coupon rate. The price, as a percentage of face value, is 140.72 percent. If you buy $1,000,000 in face value, you would pay $1,407,200. The amount of semi-annual coupon payment is $40,000.

4. The BCE November 32 put options were worth $0.25 on August 14, 2007. A contract has 100 shares and costs 100 × $0.25 = $25. 100 contracts will cost $25 × 100 = $2,500. In November, if BCE shares cost $40, then your put options will be worthless.

Test Your Investment Quotient

1. **Money Market Securities** Which of the following is not a common characteristic of money market securities?

   a. Sold on a discount basis.
   b. Mature in less than one year.
   c. Most important risk is default risk.
   d. All of the above are characteristics.

2. **Money Market Securities** Which of the following money market securities is the most liquid?

   a. Treasury bills.
   b. Bank certificates of deposit.
   c. Corporate money market debt.
   d. Municipality money market debt.

3. **Options** A European option can be exercised

   a. Only after American options.
   b. Anytime up to and including the expiration date.
   c. Only on the day before the expiration date.
   d. Only on a European exchange.

4. **Fixed-Income Securities** Your friend told you she just received her semiannual coupon payment on a Canada bond with a $100,000 face value that pays a 6 percent annual coupon. How much money did she receive from this coupon payment?

    a. $3,000
    b. $6,000
    c. $30,000
    d. $60,000

5. **Common Stock** A corporation with common stock issued to the public pays dividends

    a. At the discretion of management, who are elected by the shareholders.
    b. At the discretion of shareholders, since they own the corporation.
    c. At the discretion of the company's board of directors, who are elected by shareholders.
    d. At the discretion of the company's board of directors, who are appointed by management.

6. **Futures Contracts** You buy (go long) five copper futures contracts at 100 cents per pound, where the contract size is 25,000 pounds. At contract maturity, copper is selling for 102 cents per pound. What is your profit (+) or loss (−) on the transaction?

    a. −$2,500
    b. +$2,500
    c. −$25,000
    d. +$25,000

7. **Futures Contracts** You sell (go short) 10 gold futures contracts at $400 per ounce, where the contract size is 100 ounces. At contract maturity, gold is selling for $410 per ounce. What is your profit (+) or loss (−) on the transaction?

    a. −$1,000
    b. +$1,000
    c. −$10,000
    d. +$10,000

8. **Option Contracts** You buy 100 CJC call option contracts with a strike price of 95 at a quoted price of $1. At option expiration, CJC sells for $97. What is your net profit on the transaction?

    a. $2,000
    b. $5,000
    c. $10,000
    d. $20,000

9. **Option Contracts** You buy 100 CJC put option contracts with a strike price of 92 at a quoted price of $8. At option expiration, CJC sells for $83.80. What is your net profit on the transaction?

    a. $200
    b. $1,000
    c. $2,000
    d. $10,000

10. **Short Sales** Which of the following statements about short selling is true?

    a. A short position may be hedged by writing call options.
    b. A short position may be hedged by purchasing put options.
    c. Short sellers may be subject to margin calls if the stock price increases.
    d. Stocks that pay large dividends should be sold short before the ex-dividend date and bought afterward to take advantage of the large price declines in a short time period.

CFA®
PROBLEMS

Concept Questions

1. **Money Market Instruments** What are the distinguishing features of a money market instrument?

2. **Preferred Stock** Why is preferred stock "preferred"?

3. **Stock Quotes** What is the PE ratio reported for stocks in the newspaper? In particular, how is it computed?

4. **Yields** The current yield on a bond is very similar to what number reported for common and preferred stocks?

5. **Volume Quotations** Explain how volume is quoted for stocks, corporate bonds, futures, and options.

6. **Futures Contracts** Changes in what price lead to gains and/or losses in futures contracts?

7. **Futures Contracts** What is the open interest on a futures contract? What do you think will usually happen to open interest as maturity approaches?

8. **Futures versus Options** What is the difference between a futures contract and an option contract? Do the buyer of a futures contract and the buyer of an option contract have the same rights? What about the seller?

9. **Asset Types** What is the distinction between a real asset and a financial asset? What are the two basic types of financial assets, and what does each represent?

10. **Puts versus Calls** Suppose a share of stock is selling for $100. A put and a call are offered, both with $100 strike prices and nine months to maturity. Intuitively, which do you think is more valuable?

Questions and Problems

Core Questions

1. **Stock Quotations** You found the following stock quote for DRK Enterprises, Inc., at your favorite Web site. What was the closing price for this stock yesterday? How many round lots of stock were traded yesterday?

| YTD | 52 Weeks | | | | | Yld | | Vol | | Net |
% Chg	Hi	Lo	Stock	(SYM)	Div	%	PE	100s	Close	Chg
−16.7	32.37	18.90	DRK	(DRK)	.30	1.30	16	2855	??	0.26

2. **Stock Quotations** In the previous problem, assume the company has 25 million shares of stock outstanding. What was net income for the most recent four quarters?

3. **Dividend Yields** The following stock quote for Ehrhardt-Daves Corporation (EDC) appeared on an online quote server:

| YTD | 52 Weeks | | | | | Yld | | Vol | | Net |
% Chg	Hi	Lo	Stock	(SYM)	Div	%	PE	100s	Close	Chg
14.8	91.12	64.13	Ehrdt-Daves	(EDC)	??	3.8	21	3186	84.12	−0.86

What was the last quarterly dividend paid by EDC?

4. **Earnings per Share** In the previous problem, what is the earnings per share (EPS) for the company?

5. **Bonds** You purchase 4,000 bonds with a par value of $1,000 for $920 each. The bonds have a coupon rate of 8.4 percent paid semiannually, and mature in 10 years. How much will you receive on the next coupon date? How much will you receive when the bonds mature?

6. **Futures Profits** The contract size for platinum futures is 50 troy ounces. Suppose you need 700 troy ounces of platinum and the current futures price is $860 per ounce. How many contracts do you need to purchase? How much will you pay for your platinum? What is your dollar profit if platinum sells for $895 a troy ounce when the futures contract expires? What if the price is $840 at expiration?

7. **Option Profits** You purchase 10 call option contracts with a strike price of $70 and a premium of $3.20. If the stock price at expiration is $78.14, what is your dollar profit? What if the stock price is $67.56?

8. **Stock Quotations** You found the following stock quote for Gigantus Corporation in today's newspaper. What was the stock selling for on January 1?

YTD	52 Weeks					Yld		Vol		Net
% Chg	Hi	Lo	Stock	(SYM)	Div	%	PE	100s	Close	Chg
-1.5	55.66	44.94	Gigantus	(GIG)	1.30	2.5	16	12690	51.80	0.13

Use the following bond quote for the next two questions:

Company (Ticker)	Coupon	Maturity	Last Price	Last Yield	EST Spread	UST	EST $ Vol (000's)
Int'l Systems (ISU)	7.700	May 1, 2032	126.326	5.768	141	30	46,206

9. **Bond Quotations** What is the current yield of the bond? What is the yield to maturity of the comparable U.S. Treasury bond?

10. **Bond Quotations** If you currently own 25 of the bonds, how much will you receive on the next coupon date?

11. **Futures Quotations** The following quotations for canola futures trading on the Winnipeg Commodity Exchange appeared in the newspaper dated November 2, 2006. How many of the January 2008 contracts are currently open? How many of these contracts should you sell if you wish to deliver 400 tonnes of canola in January? If you actually make delivery, how much will you receive? Assume you locked in the settle price.

Globe and Mail, November 2, 2006

12. **Futures Quotations** In the previous problem, approximately how many canola futures contracts of all maturities were traded the day before?

13. **Using Futures Quotations** In Problem 11, suppose you buy 15 of the March 2008 canola futures contacts. One month from now, the futures price of this contract is 388.00, and you close out your position. Calculate your dollar profit on this investment.

Use the following cotton futures quote for the next three problems:

| GNR | | | Call | | Put | |
Option/Strike		Exp.	Vol.	Last	Vol.	Last
75.25	65	June	3	10.40	1	0.15
75.25	70	June	21	5.30	16	0.25
75.25	70	July	42	6.00	67	0.45
75.25	75	June	85	1.11	89	0.85
75.25	75	July	8	2.30	124	1.65
75.25	75	Oct	160	3.80	193	2.80
75.25	75	Jan	35	5.10	68	3.70
75.25	80	June	28	0.10	19	9.90
75.25	80	July	9	0.50	4	5.05
75.25	85	June	2	0.05	7	9.95

14. **Options Quotations** What was the closing share price of the underlying stock? If you wanted to purchase the right to sell 2,000 shares of GNR stock in July at a strike price of $75 per share, how much would this cost you?

15. **Options Quotations** Which put contract sells for the lowest price? Which one sells for the highest price? Explain why these respective options trade at such extreme prices.

16. **Using Options Quotations** In Problem 14, suppose GNR stock sells for $71.85 per share immediately prior to your options' expiration. What is the rate of return on your investment? What is your rate of return if the stock sells for $78.45 per share (think about it)? Assume your holding period for this investment is exactly three months.

17. **Options versus Stock** You've located the following option quote for Eric-Cartman, Inc. (ECI):

| ECI | | | Call | | Put | |
Option/Strike		Exp.	Vol.	Last	Vol.	Last
20.25	10	Sep	29	5.50	…	…
20.25	15	Sep	333	7	69	1
20.25	25	Dec	5	2	…	…
20.25	30	Sep	76	2	188	8.75
20.25	35	Oct	89	0.50	…	…

Two of the premiums shown can't possibly be correct. Which two? Why?

18. **Annualized Returns** Suppose you have $20,000 to invest. You're considering Miller-Moore Equine Enterprises (MMEE), which is currently selling for $40 per share. You also notice that a call option with a $40 strike price and six months to maturity is available. The premium is $4.00. MMEE pays no dividends. What is your annualized return from these two investments if, in six months, MMEE is selling for $46 per share? What about $35 per share?

19. **Annualized Returns** In the previous question, suppose a dividend of $.50 per share is paid. Comment on how the returns would be affected.

20. **Option Returns** In Problem 18, suppose a put option with a $40 strike is also available with a premium of $2.50. Calculate your percentage return for the six-month holding period if the stock price declines to $36.40 per share.

What's on the Web?

1. **Option Prices** You want to find the option prices for Nortel Networks (NT). Go to www.m-x.ca to the Montreal Exchange's Web page and enter the ticker symbol for Nortel. What is the option premium and strike price for the highest and lowest strike price options that are nearest to expiring? What are the option premium and strike price for the highest and lowest strike price options expiring next month?

2. **Futures Quotes** Go to www.theice.com/wce and find the contract specifications for western barley futures. What is the size of the western barley futures contract? On the Ice Futures Canada Exchange website, find the settle price for the western barley futures contract that will expire the soonest. If you go long 10 contracts, how much will the western barley cost at the current price?

3. **LEAPS** Go to www.cboe.com, highlight the "Products" tab, then follow the "LEAPS" link. What are LEAPS? What are the two types of LEAPS? What are the benefits of equity LEAPS? What are the benefits of index LEAPS?

www.mcgrawhill.ca/olc/Jordan

CHAPTER 5

Mutual Funds

"And the trouble is, if you don't risk anything, you risk even more."
—Erica Jong

With only $2,000 to invest, you can easily own shares in RIM, Loblaws, Molson, Alcan, and many more stocks through a mutual fund. Or, you can invest in a portfolio of government bonds or other investments. Indeed, there are many thousands of different mutual funds available to investors. In fact, there are about as many mutual funds as there are different stocks traded on the Toronto Stock Exchange. There are funds for aggressive investors, conservative investors, short-term investors, and long-term investors. There are bond funds, stock funds, international funds, and you-name-it funds. Is there a right fund for you? This chapter will help you find out. ∎

As we discussed in an earlier chapter, if you do not wish to actively buy and sell individual securities on your own, you can invest in stocks, bonds, or other financial assets through a *mutual fund*. Mutual funds are simply a means of combining or pooling the funds of a large group of investors. The buy and sell decisions for the resulting pool are then made by a fund manager, who is compensated for the service provided.

Since mutual funds provide indirect access to financial markets for individual investors, they are a form of financial intermediary.

For mutual fund
facts and figures,
visit
www.globefund.com
www.ific.ca

As of the end of 2006, Canadian investors held an estimated 49 million mutual fund accounts, up from 9 million accounts twelve years ago. Similarly total net assets of the mutual fund industry grew from $21 billion to $661 billion from 1993 to 2006.

One of the reasons for the proliferation of mutual funds and fund types is that mutual funds have become, on a very basic level, consumer products. They are created and marketed to the public in ways that are intended to promote buyer appeal. As every business student knows, product differentiation is a basic marketing tactic, and in recent years mutual funds have become increasingly adept at practicing this common marketing technique.

In fact, if you are not already a mutual fund investor, it is very likely that you will be in the near future. The reason has to do with a fundamental change in the way businesses of all types provide retirement benefits for employees. It used to be that most large employers offered so-called defined benefit pensions. With such a plan, when you retire, your employer pays you a pension typically based on years of service and salary. The key is that the pension benefit you receive is based on a predefined formula, hence the name.

Defined benefit plans are rapidly being replaced by "defined contribution" plans. With a defined contribution plan, your employer will contribute money each pay period to a retirement account on your behalf, but you have to select where the funds go. With this arrangement, the benefit you ultimately receive depends entirely on how your investments do; your employer only makes contributions. Most commonly, you must choose from a group of mutual funds for your investments, so it is very important that you understand the different types of mutual funds, as well as their risks and returns.

5.1   Investment Companies and Fund Types

investment company
A business that specializes in pooling funds from individual investors and investing them.

At the most basic level, a company that pools funds obtained from individual investors and invests them is called an **investment company**. In other words, an investment company is a business that specializes in managing financial assets for individual investors. All mutual funds are, in fact, investment companies. As we will see, however, not all investment companies are mutual funds.

In the sections that follow, we will be discussing various aspects of mutual funds and related entities. Figure 5.1 is a big-picture overview of some of the different types of funds and how they are classified. It will serve as a guide for the next several sections. We will define the various terms that appear as we go along.

Open-End versus Closed-End Funds

open-end fund An investment company that stands ready to buy and sell shares at any time.

closed-end fund An investment company with a fixed number of shares that are bought and sold only in the open stock market.

As Figure 5.1 shows, there are two fundamental types of investment companies, *open-end funds* and *closed-end funds*. The difference is very important. Whenever you invest in a mutual fund, you do so by buying shares in the fund. However, how shares are bought and sold depends on which type of fund you are considering.

With an **open-end fund**, the fund itself will sell new shares to anyone wishing to buy and will redeem (i.e., buy back) shares from anyone wishing to sell. When an investor wishes to buy open-end fund shares, the fund simply issues them and then invests the money received. When someone wishes to sell open-end fund shares, the fund sells some of its assets and uses the cash to redeem the shares. As a result, with an open-end fund, the number of shares outstanding fluctuates through time.

With a **closed-end fund**, the number of shares is fixed and never changes. If you want to buy shares, you must buy them from another investor. Similarly, if you wish to sell shares that you own, you must sell them to another investor.

FIGURE 5.1   Fund Types

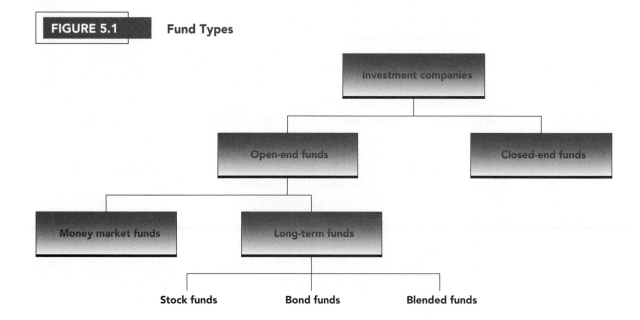

Thus, the key difference between an open-end fund and a closed-end fund is that, with a closed-end fund, the fund itself does not buy or sell shares. In fact, as we discuss below, shares in closed-end funds are listed on stock exchanges just like ordinary shares of stock, where their shares are bought and sold in the same way. Open-end funds are more popular among individual investors than closed-end funds.

Strictly speaking, the term "mutual fund" actually refers only to an open-end investment company. Thus the phrase "closed-end fund" is a bit of an oxymoron, kind of like jumbo shrimp, and the phrase "open-end mutual fund" is a redundancy, an unnecessary repetition, or restatement. Nonetheless, particularly in recent years, the term "investment company" has all but disappeared from common use, and investment companies are now generically called mutual funds. We will stick with this common terminology whenever it won't lead to confusion.

Net Asset Value

net asset value The value of assets less liabilities held by a mutual fund, divided by the number of shares outstanding. Abbreviated NAV.

A mutual fund's **net asset value** is an important consideration. Net asset value is calculated by taking the total value of the assets held by the fund less any liabilities and then dividing by the number of outstanding shares. For example, suppose a mutual fund has $105 million in assets and $5 million in liabilities based on current market values and a total of 5 million shares outstanding. Based on the value of net assets held by the fund, $100 million, each share has a value of $100 million / 5 million = $20. This $20 is the fund's net asset value, often abbreviated as NAV.

NET ASSET VALUE

EXAMPLE 5.1

The BMO Monthly Income Fund has $6,053 million net assets (as of the end of July 2007). It had about 538 million shares outstanding. What is the net asset value?

The net asset value is simply the asset value per share, or $6,053 million / 538 million shares = $11.25

With one important exception, the net asset value of a mutual fund will change essentially every day simply because the value of the assets held by the fund fluctuates. The one exception concerns money market mutual funds, which we discuss in a later section.

As we noted, an open-end fund will generally redeem or buy back shares at any time. The price you will receive for shares you sell is the net asset value. Thus, in our example just above, you could sell your shares back to the fund and receive $20 each. Because the fund stands ready to redeem shares at any time, shares in an open-end fund are always worth their net asset value.

In contrast, because the shares of closed-end funds are bought and sold in the stock markets, their share prices at any point in time may or may not be equal to their net asset values. We examine this issue in more detail in a later section.

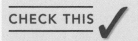

CHECK THIS

5.1a   What is an investment company?

5.1b   What is the difference between an open-end fund and a closed-end fund?

5.2   Mutual Fund Operations

In this section, we discuss some essentials of mutual fund operations. We focus on how mutual funds are created, marketed, regulated, and taxed. Our discussion here deals primarily with open-end funds, but much of it applies to closed-end funds as well. Further details on closed-end funds are provided in a later section.

Mutual Fund Organization and Creation

A mutual fund is simply a corporation. Like a corporation, a mutual fund is owned by its shareholders. The shareholders elect a board of directors; the board of directors is responsible for hiring a manager to oversee the fund's operations. Although mutual funds often belong to a larger "family" of funds, every fund is a separate company owned by its shareholders.

Most mutual funds are created by banks or by investment advisory firms, which are businesses that specialize in managing mutual funds. Investment advisory firms are also called mutual fund companies. Increasingly, such firms have additional operations such as discount brokerages and other financial services.

All the major fund families have websites. Try, e.g., www.manulife.ca

In Canada different mutual funds are offered by banks, insurance companies and investment advisory firms. The largest provider is the RBC Asset Management Inc. with more than 50 different mutual funds and $80 billion in assets under management. Investors Group, CIBC Asset Management, and AIM Trimark Investments are some well-known examples.

Investment advisory firms create mutual funds, simply because they wish to manage them to earn fees. A typical management fee might be 1.5 percent of the total assets in the fund per year. A fund with $200 million in assets would not be large but nonetheless generate management fees of $3.0 million per year. Thus, there is significant economic incentive to create funds and attract investors to them.

For example, a company like RBC might one day decide that there is a demand for a fund that buys stock in companies that grow and process lumber. RBC could form a mutual fund that specializes in such companies and call it something like the RBC Lumber Fund. A fund manager would be appointed, and shares in the fund would be offered to the public. As shares are sold, the money received is invested. If the fund is a success, a large amount of money will be attracted and RBC would benefit from the fees it earns. If the fund is not a success, the board can vote to liquidate it and return shareholders' money or merge it with another fund.

As our hypothetical example illustrates, an investment advisory firm such as RBC can (and often will) create new funds from time to time. Through time, this process leads to a family of funds all managed by the same advisory firm. Each fund in the family will have its own fund manager, but the advisory firm will generally handle the record keeping, marketing, and much of the research that underlies the fund's investment decisions.

In principle, the directors of a mutual fund in a particular family, acting on behalf of the fund shareholders, could vote to fire the investment advisory firm and hire a different one. As a practical matter, this rarely, if ever, occurs. At least part of the reason is that the directors are originally appointed by the fund's founder, and they are routinely reelected. Unhappy shareholders generally "vote with their feet"—that is, sell their shares and invest elsewhere.

Taxation of Investment Companies

As long as an investment company meets certain rules set by the Canada Revenue Agency, it is treated as a "flow-through entity" for tax purposes. This is important because a mutual fund does not pay taxes on its investment income. Instead, the fund passes through all realized investment income to fund shareholders, who then pay taxes on these distributions as though they owned the securities directly. Essentially, the fund simply acts as a conduit, funneling gains and losses to fund owners.

The Fund Prospectus and Annual Report

Mutual funds are required by law to produce a document known as a *prospectus*. The prospectus must be supplied to any investor wishing to purchase shares. Mutual funds must also provide an annual report to their shareholders. The annual report and the prospectus, which are sometimes combined, contain financial statements along with specific information concerning the fund's expenses, gains and losses, holdings, objectives, and management. We discuss many of these items in the next few sections.

CHECK THIS

> **5.2a**   How do mutual funds usually get started?
>
> **5.2b**   How are mutual funds taxed?

5.3   Mutual Fund Costs and Fees

All mutual funds have various expenses that are paid by the fund's shareholders. These expenses can vary considerably from fund to fund, however, and one of the most important considerations in evaluating a fund is its expense structure. All else the same, lower expenses are preferred, of course, but, as we discuss, matters are not quite that cut-and-dried.

Types of Expenses and Fees

There are basically four types of expenses or fees associated with buying and owning mutual fund shares:

1. Sales charges or "loads."
2. Special fees.
3. Management fees.
4. Trading costs.

We discuss each of these in turn.

front-end load A sales charge levied on purchases of shares in some mutual funds.

Sales Charges   Many mutual funds charge a fee whenever shares are purchased. These fees are generally called **front-end loads**. Funds that charge loads are called *load funds*. Funds that have no such charges are called *no-load funds*.

When you purchase shares in a load fund, you pay a price in excess of the net asset value, called the *offering price*. The difference between the offering price and the net asset value is the *load*. Shares in no-load funds are sold at net asset value.

Front-end loads can range as high as 8.5 percent, but 5 percent or so would be more typical. Some funds, with front-end loads in the 2 percent to 3 percent range, are described as *low-load funds*.

Front-end loads are expressed as a percentage of the offering price, not the net asset value. For example, suppose a load fund has an offering price of $100 and a net asset value of $98. The front-end load is $2, which, as a percentage of the $100 offering price, is $2 / $100 = 2 percent. The way front-end loads are calculated understates the load slightly. In our example here, you are paying $100 for something worth only $98, so the load is really $2 / $98 = 2.04 percent.

FRONT-END LOADS

EXAMPLE 5.2

On a particular day, according to *The Globe and Mail,* the Common Sense Growth fund had a net asset value of $13.91. The offering price was $15.20. Is this a load fund? What is the front-end load?

Since the offering price, which is the price you must pay to purchase shares, exceeds the net asset value, this is definitely a load fund. The load can be calculated by taking the difference between the offering price and the net asset value, $1.29, and dividing by the $15.20 offering price. The result is a hefty front-end load of 8.5 percent.

Some funds have "back-end" loads, which are charges levied on redemptions. These loads are often called *deferred sales charges* and abbreviated DSC. The DSC usually declines through time. It might start out at 6 percent for shares held less than one year, then drop to 3 percent for shares held for two years, and disappear altogether on shares held for three or more years.

Special Fees   are charged for certain funds and under certain conditions. These fees include:

1. Annual RRSP, RRIF or RESP trustee fee.
2. Account set-up fee.

3. Short-term trading fee.

4. Processing fees.

Some mutual funds charge these fees under certain conditions.

Management Fees   We briefly discussed management fees in an earlier section. Fees are usually based first on the size of the fund. Beyond this, there is often an incentive provision that increases the fee if the fund outperforms some benchmark, often the S&P/TSX. Management fees generally range from 1.0 percent to 2.0 percent of total fund assets every year.

Trading Costs   Mutual funds have brokerage expenses from trading just like individuals do. As a result, mutual funds that do a lot of trading will have relatively high trading costs.

Trading costs can be difficult to get a handle on because they are not reported directly. However, in the prospectus, funds are required to report something known as **turnover**. A fund's turnover is a measure of how much trading a fund does. It is calculated as the lesser of a fund's total purchases or sales during a year, divided by average daily assets.[1]

turnover A measure of how much trading a fund does, calculated as the lesser of total purchases or sales during a year divided by average daily assets.

TURNOVER

EXAMPLE 5.3

Suppose a fund had average daily assets of $50 million during 2007. It bought $80 million worth of stock and sold $70 million during the year. What is its turnover?

The lesser of purchases or sales is $70 million, and average daily assets are $50 million. Turnover is thus $70 / $50 = 1.4 times.

A fund with a turnover of 1.0 has, in effect, sold off its entire portfolio and replaced it once during the year. Similarly, a turnover of .50 indicates that, loosely speaking, the fund replaced half of its holdings during the year. All else the same, a higher turnover indicates more frequent trading and higher trading costs.

Expense Reporting

Mutual funds are required to report expenses in a fairly standardized way in the prospectus. The exact format varies, but the information reported is generally the same. Figure 5.2 shows the policies and expense statements of the BMO (Bank of Montreal) Equity Index Fund.

The first paragraph shows the type of fund and the investment policies of the fund. This is an equity fund. We learn that all Bank of Montreal Funds are no-load funds. Under the Expenses and Fees section, you will notice that the management fees are 2.00 percent of net asset value.

The second section illustrates the management expense ratio (MER) of the fund, giving information on what types of expenses are covered. The MER for this fund is 2.30 percent as of September 30, 2006.

To see a fund that really discloses information, try www.cibc.com/ca/mutual-funds or CIBC Funds website

---

[1]Purchases and sales for a fund are usually different because of purchases and redemptions of fund shares by shareholders. For example, if a fund is growing, purchases will exceed sales.

FIGURE 5.2

Mutual Fund Policies and Expenses

Source: www.bmo.com, reprinted with permission.

BMO Equity Fund

Overview   Expenses and Fees   Minimum Investment

All BMO Mutual Funds are no-load.

Management Fee, per year, as a percentage (%) of Net Asset Value: (10/05/2006) 2.00%

All mutual funds - including no-load funds - pay management fees. The management fee is a percentage of each investor's holdings in each Fund. For example, if you hold $1,000 in our Equity Index Fund, your management fee is 1%, or $10 per year.

The management fee is calculated daily and paid by the Fund to us monthly.

Management Expense Ratio: (30/09/2006) 2.30%

The management expense ratio is based on the total expenses in the Statement of Operations expressed as an annualized percentage of the average net asset value of the Funds. The definition of the management expense ratio was revised by the Canadian Securities Administrators effective February 1, 2000. The principal change is to include GST paid in expenses for purposes of this calculation.

Securities regulations stipulate that the MER we publish must be for the latest financial year. This means that we cannot publish MERs for Funds launched after the most recent year-end (September).

The MER tells you what you're paying for the professional management of your money. Some fund categories, like emerging market funds, have higher average MERs than others because it's more costly to operate in those markets. The MER is paid out of the fund's earnings before we calculate the fund's unit price. If two funds have the same earnings before the MER is paid, the one with a higher MER will have a lower net return.

You pay an annual trustee or administration fee (plus applicable taxes) only if you hold Funds in the following plans:

Registered Retirement Savings Plan	$10 a year
Registered Education Savings Plan	$10 a year
Systematic Withdrawal Plan	$10 a year

There are special fees for those investors who hold funds in a Registered Retirement Savings Plan, Registered Education Savings Plan, Registered Retirement Income Plan, and/or Systematic Withdrawal Plan.

Why Pay Loads and Fees?

Given that pure no-load funds exist, you might wonder why anyone would buy load funds or funds with substantial DSC or fees. It is becoming increasingly difficult to give a good answer to this question. At one time, there simply weren't many no-load funds, and those that existed weren't widely known. Today, there are many good no-load funds, and competition among funds is forcing many funds to lower or do away with loads and other fees.

Having said this, there are basically two reasons that you might want to consider a load fund or a fund with above-average fees. First, you may simply want a fund run by a particular manager. A good example of this is the Fidelity Magellan Fund. For many years, it was run by Peter Lynch, who is widely regarded as one of the most successful managers in the history of the business. The Magellan Fund was (and is) a load fund, leaving you no choice but to pay the load to obtain Lynch's expertise.

The other reason to consider paying a load is that you want a specialized type of fund. For example, you might be interested in investing in a fund that invests only in a particular foreign country, such as Brazil. We'll discuss such specialty funds in a later section, but for now we note that there is little competition among specialty funds, and, as a result, loads and fees tend to be higher.

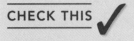

CHECK THIS		
	5.3a	What is the difference between a load fund and a no-load fund?
	5.3b	What are deferred sales charges?

5.4   Short-Term Funds

Mutual funds are usually divided into two major groups, short-term funds and long-term funds. Short-term funds are collectively known as *money market mutual funds*. Long-term funds essentially include everything that is not a money market fund. We discuss long-term funds in our next section; here we focus on money market funds.

Money Market Mutual Funds

money market mutual fund A mutual fund specializing in money market instruments.

As the name suggests, **money market mutual funds**, or MMMFs, specialize in money market instruments. As we have already described, these are short-term debt obligations issued by governments and corporations. Money market funds were introduced in the early 1970s and have grown tremendously. By July 2007, Canadian money market funds managed more than $49 billion in assets. All money market funds are open-end funds.

Most money market funds invest in high-quality, low-risk instruments with maturities of less than 90 days. As a result, they have relatively little risk. However, some buy riskier assets or have longer maturities than others, so they do not all carry equally low risk. For example, some buy only very short-term government securities and are therefore essentially risk-free. Others buy mostly securities issued by corporations which entail some risk. We discuss the different types of money market instruments and their relative risks in later chapters.

Visit the website of IFIC www.ific.ca for info on thousands of funds, including MMMFs.

Money Market Fund Accounting   A unique feature of money market funds is that their net asset values are always $10 per share. This is purely an accounting gimmick, however. A money market fund simply sets the number of shares equal to the fund's asset value divided by ten. In other words, if the fund has $100 million in assets, then it has 10 million shares. As the fund earns interest on its investments, the fund owners are simply given more shares.

The reason money market mutual funds always maintain a $10 net asset value is to make them resemble bank accounts. As long as a money market fund invests in very safe, interest-bearing, short-maturity assets, its net asset value will not drop below $10 per share. However, there is no guarantee that this will not happen. This is a very rare occurrence, but, in 1994, several large money market funds experienced substantial losses because they purchased relatively risky derivative assets, so it definitely can happen.

Money Market Deposit Accounts

Most banks offer what are called "money market" deposit accounts, or MMDAs, which are much like money market mutual funds. For example, both money market funds and money market deposit accounts generally have limited cheque-writing privileges.

There is a very important distinction between such a bank-offered money market account and a money market fund, however. A bank money market account is a bank deposit and offers CDIC protection, whereas a money market fund does not. A money market fund will generally offer CIPF protection, but this is not a perfect substitute. Confusingly, some banks offer both money market accounts and, through a separate, affiliated entity, money market funds.

CHECK THIS

5.4a What is a money market mutual fund? What are the two types?

5.4b How do money market mutual funds maintain a constant net asset value?

5.5 Long-Term Funds

There are many different types of long-term funds. Historically, mutual funds were classified as stock, bond, or income funds. As a part of the rapid growth in mutual funds, however, it is becoming increasingly difficult to place all funds into these three categories. Also, providers of mutual fund information do not use the same classification schemes.

Mutual funds have different goals, and a fund's objective is the major determinant of the fund type. All mutual funds must state the fund's objective in the prospectus. For example, the Scotia Canadian Growth Fund states:

> The fund's objective is long-term capital growth. It invests primarily in a broad range of Canadian equity securities.

Thus, this fund invests in different types of stocks with the goal of capital appreciation. This is clearly a stock fund, and it might further be classified as a "capital appreciation" fund or "aggressive growth" fund, depending on whose classification scheme is used.

Mutual fund objectives are an important consideration; unfortunately, the truth is they frequently are too vague to provide useful information. For example, a very common objective reads like this: "The Big Bucks Fund seeks capital appreciation, income, and capital preservation." Translation: The fund seeks to (1) increase the value of its shares, (2) generate income for its shareholders, and (3) not lose money. Well, don't we all! More to the point, funds with very similar-sounding objectives can have very different portfolios and, consequently, very different risks. As a result, it is a mistake to look only at a fund's stated objective: Actual portfolio holdings speak louder than prospectus promises.

Stock Funds

Stock funds exist in great variety. We consider nine separate general types and some subtypes. We also consider some new varieties that don't fit in any category.

One of the best mutual fund sites is www.morningstar.ca

Capital Appreciation versus Income   The first four types of stock funds trade off capital appreciation and dividend income.

1. *Capital appreciation.* As in our example just above, these funds seek maximum capital appreciation. They generally invest in companies that have, in the opinion of the fund manager, the best prospects for share price appreciation without regard to dividends, company size, or, for some funds, country. Often this means investing in unproven companies or perceived out-of-favour companies.

2. *Growth.* These funds also seek capital appreciation, but they tend to invest in larger, more established companies. Such funds may be somewhat less volatile as a result. Dividends are not an important consideration.

3. *Growth and income.* Capital appreciation is still the main goal, but at least part of the focus is on dividend-paying companies.

4. *Equity income.* These funds focus almost exclusively on stocks with relatively high dividend yields, thereby maximizing the current income on the portfolio.

Among these four fund types, the greater the emphasis on growth, the greater the risk, at least as a general matter. Again, however, these are only rough classifications. Equity income funds, for example, frequently invest heavily in public utility stocks; such stocks had heavy losses in the first part of the 1990s.

Company Size–Based Funds   These next two fund types focus on companies in a particular size range.

1. *Small company.* As the name suggests, these funds focus on stocks in small companies, where "small" refers to the total market value of the stock. Such funds are often called "small-cap" funds, where "cap" is short for total market value or capitalization. In Chapter 1, we saw that small stocks have traditionally performed very well, at least over the long run, hence the demand for funds that specialize in such stocks. With small-company mutual funds, what constitutes small is variable, ranging from perhaps $10 million up to $1 billion or so in total market value, and some funds specialize in smaller companies than others. Since most small companies don't pay dividends, these funds necessarily emphasize capital appreciation.

2. *Midcap.* These funds usually specialize in stocks that are too small to be in the index but too large to be considered small stocks.

International Funds   The next two fund groups invest internationally. Research has shown that diversifying internationally can significantly improve the risk-return trade-off for investors, and international funds have been among the most rapidly growing. However, that growth slowed sharply in the late 1990s.

1. *Global.* These funds have substantial international holdings but also maintain significant investments in domestic stocks.

2. *International.* These funds are like global funds, except they focus on non-Canadian equities.

Among international funds, some specialize in specific regions of the world, such as Europe, the Pacific Rim, or South America. Others specialize in individual countries. Today, there is at least one mutual fund specializing in essentially every country in the world that has a stock market, however small.

International funds that specialize in countries with small or recently established stock markets are often called *emerging markets funds*. Almost all single-country funds, and especially emerging markets funds, are not well-diversified and have historically been extremely volatile.

Many funds that are not classified as international funds may actually have substantial overseas investments, so this is one thing to watch out for. It is not unusual for a fund to call itself a "growth" fund and actually invest heavily outside the domestic market.

Sector Funds   Sector funds specialize in specific sectors of the economy and often focus on particular industries or particular commodities. There are far too many different types to list here. There are funds that only buy software companies, and funds that only buy hardware companies. There are funds that specialize in natural gas producers, oil producers, and precious metals producers. In fact, essentially every major industry in the economy is covered by at least one fund.

One thing to notice about sector funds is that, like single-country funds, they are obviously not well-diversified. Every year, many of the best performing mutual funds (in terms of total return) are sector funds simply because whatever sector of the economy is hottest will generally have the largest stock price increases. Funds specializing in that sector will do well. In the same vein, and for the same reason, the worst performing funds are also almost always some type of sector fund. When it comes to mutual funds, past performance is almost always an unreliable guide to future performance; nowhere is this more true than with sector funds.

Other Fund Types and Issues   Three other types of stock funds that don't fit easily into one of the above categories bear discussing: *index funds*, so-called *social conscience funds*, and *tax-managed funds*.

1. *Index funds.* Index funds simply hold the stocks that make up a particular index in the same relative proportions as the index. The most important index funds are S&P/TSX funds, which are intended to track the performance of the S&P/TSX. By their nature, index funds are passively managed, meaning that the fund manager trades only as necessary to match the index. Such funds are appealing in part because they are generally characterized by low turnover and low operating expenses. Another reason index funds have grown rapidly is that there is considerable debate over whether mutual fund managers can consistently beat the averages. If they can't, the argument runs, why pay loads and management fees when it's cheaper just to buy the averages by indexing? See our nearby *Investment Updates* box for more.

To learn more about "social conscience" funds, visit
www.socialinvest.org
www.domini.com

2. *Social conscience funds.* These funds are a relatively new creation. They invest only in companies whose products, policies, or politics are viewed as socially desirable. The specific social objectives range from environmental issues to personnel policies. The ethical funds provide some examples of these funds. Of course, consensus on what is socially desirable or responsible is hard to find. In fact, there are so-called sin funds (and sector funds) that specialize in these very industries!

Is vice nice? Visit
www.vicefund.com
to find out.

3. *Tax-managed funds.* Taxable mutual funds are generally managed without regard for the tax liabilities of fund owners. Fund managers focus on (and are frequently rewarded based on) total pretax returns. However, recent research has shown that some fairly simple strategies can greatly improve the aftertax returns to shareholders and that focusing just on pretax returns is not a good idea for taxable investors. Tax-managed funds try to hold down turnover to minimize realized capital gains, and they try to match realized gains with realized losses. Such strategies work

High Fliers at Risk of Falling Hardest

What Are We Looking For?

An answer to the question of whether high-flying mutual funds are at risk of falling hardest when the stock market tanks.

Today's Search

We started with the funds in all categories that produced the highest returns over the 12 months to July 31. Then, we ranked them according to the size of their loss for the 30 days to Aug. 13. Call it a quick stress test for the fund industry's leaders.

So What Did We Turn Up?

A definite correlation between up-market success and down-market vulnerability. In other words, what goes up highest might just fall hardest, although there are exceptions (we'll look at them next week).

Latin American funds offer a good illustration of how investors need to be vigilant about losing money in high fliers. These funds turned in gains in the 40- to 50- percent range in the past year, and they've typically lost about 10 to 11 per cent in the past 30 days. Our chart suggests that natural resource and small-cap funds may offer a similar profile. Given any thought to locking in at least some of the profits you made in these funds over the past few years?

You expect sector funds to be twitchy, of course. But our screen shows that even more mainstream funds can fall hard after delivering outsize gains. Sceptre Equity Growth, which made 33.4 percent in the past year under now-departed star manger Allan Jacobs, has fallen 9.2 percent in the past 30 days. You have to be able to block out moves like this if you own a fund like Sceptre Equity Growth, which has an outstanding 15-year average annual return of 19.1 per cent.

Another high-flier that has fallen lately is HBP S&P/TSX 60 Bull Plus, which gives you double exposure to whatever the S&P/TSX 60 does. This formula works well in strong markets, but it can sting you when things deteriorate (there is a bear version of this fund for down markets).

What's Next?

Globefund.com's 15-year fund reviews show annual returns dating back to 1992, so you can get a picture of how a fund performed during such down-market periods as 2000–2002.

Fund name	(As of Jul 2007) Net Assets ('000)	Last MER reported date	MER	Asset class	(As of Jul 2007) 1-yr ret %	(As of Aug 13) 30-day % return
Resolute Performance	761,005	7/31/2006	2.97	Cdn. Small or Mid Cap Equity	47.33	-14.42
HBP S&P/TSX 60 Bull Plus - A	2,188	7/31/2007	2.50	Alternative Strategies	35.48	-14.16
Sentry Select Mining Opportunity Cl	78,525	12/29/2006	2.43	Natural Resources Equity	48.63	-13.09
Caldwell Canada	8,999	7/31/2007	2.75	Cdn. Small or Mid Cap Equity	43.15	-12.84
TD Latin American Growth	235,765	7/31/2007	2.80	Miscellaneous	47.25	-11.94
Scotia Latin American Growth	84,939	7/31/2007	2.63	Miscellaneous	45.43	-11.29
Fidelity Latin America-A	36,858	3/30/2007	2.82	Miscellaneous	44.84	-11.13
Fidelity Latin America-B	69,001	3/30/2007	2.56	Miscellaneous	45.15	-11.11
CIBC Latin American	40,013	12/29/2006	2.94	Miscellaneous	43.17	-10.85
Dynamic FocusPlus Resource	333,513	12/29/2006	2.90	Natural Resources Equity	39.47	-10.72
Mavrix Strategic Small Cap	27,402	7/31/2007	2.36	Cdn. Focused Sm/Mid Cap Eq	42.13	-10.53
Mavrix Small Companies	75,612	7/31/2007	3.46	Cdn. Small or Mid Cap Equity	36.33	-10.39
BMO Resource	326,665	7/31/2007	2.29	Natural Resources Equity	34.05	-10.20
imaxx Canadian Small Cap	1,773	7/31/2007	2.93	Cdn. Small or Mid Cap Equity	32.46	-10.15
RBC Global Resources	227,438	7/31/2007	2.40	Natural Resources Equity	63.30	-10.04
TDK Resource Fund Inc.	57,820	7/31/2007	4.19	Miscellaneous	37.20	-9.67
HBP NASDAQ-100 Bull Plus - A	124	7/31/2007	2.50	Alternative Strategies	38.33	-9.53
Tmpltn BRIC CC	174,505	7/31/2007	2.93	Emerging Markets Equity	47.25	-9.22
Dynamic Power Canadian Growth-T	16,539	12/29/2006	3.12	Cdn. Focused Sm/Mid Cap Eq	33.73	-9.19
Sceptre Equity Growth - A	758,124	12/29/2006	1.58	Cdn. Small or Mid Cap Equity	33.39	-9.17
Dynamic Power Canadian Growth	1,535,953	12/29/2006	3.09	Cdn. Focused Sm/Mid Cap Eq	34.05	-9.16
Acuity All Cap 30 Canadian Equity	320,474	1/31/2007	2.85	Canadian Equity	35.64	-9.01
iShares CDN Tech Sector Index	88,480	7/31/2007	0.55	Science and Tech. Equity	55.05	-8.88
Investors Euro Mid-Cap Equity-B		7/31/2007	2.87	European Equity	37.70	-8.87
Investors Euro Mid-Cap Equity-A	1,184,882	7/31/2007	2.72	European Equity	37.91	-8.85
Investors Euro Mid-Cap Equity-C		7/31/2007	2.89	European Equity	37.66	-8.83
Renaissance Developing Cap Markets	24,910	2/28/2007	2.90	Emerging Markets Equity	34.91	-8.83
Investors Euro Mid-Cap Equity Cl-B		7/31/2007	2.92	European Equity	36.91	-8.82
Investors Euro Mid-Cap Equity Cl-A	161,068	7/31/2007	2.77	European Equity	37.11	-8.81
CIBC Canadian Resource	111,957	12/29/2006	2.48	Natural Resources Equity	32.98	-8.77
imaxx Canadian Equity Growth	19,394	7/31/2007	2.76	Canadian Equity	35.56	-8.56
TD Emerging Markets-A		7/31/2007	2.88	Emerging Markets Equity	41.15	-8.54
TD Emerging Markets	232,892	7/31/2007	2.88	Emerging Markets Equity	41.44	-8.52
BMO Emerging Markets	145,748	7/31/2007	2.83	Emerging Markets Equity	37.08	-8.52

SOURCE: GLOBEFUND

Reprinted with permission from the Globe and Mail.

particularly well for index funds. For example, the RBC Funds have recently introduced the Royal Tax Managed Return Fund. The fund emphasizes on earnings and cash flows, but the fund will also try to avoid realizing taxable gains. We predict funds promoting such strategies will become increasingly common as investors become more aware of the tax consequences of fund ownership.

Taxable and Municipal Bond Funds

Most bond funds invest in domestic corporate and government securities, although some invest in foreign government and non-domestic corporate bonds as well. As we will see, there are a relatively small number of bond fund types.

There are basically five characteristics that distinguish bond funds:

1. **Maturity range.** Different funds hold bonds of different maturities, ranging from quite short (2 years) to quite long (25–30 years).
2. **Credit quality.** Some bonds are much safer than others in terms of the possibility of default. Canadian government bonds have no default risk, while so-called junk bonds have significant default risk.
3. **Type of bond.** Some funds specialize in particular types of fixed-income instruments such as mortgages.
4. **Country.** Most bond funds buy only domestic issues, but some buy foreign company and government issues.

Short-Term and Intermediate-Term Funds As the names suggest, these two fund types focus on bonds in a specific maturity range. Short-term maturities are generally considered to be less than five years. Intermediate-term would be less than 10 years.

One thing to be careful of with these types of funds is that the credit quality of the issues can vary from fund to fund. One fund could hold very risky intermediate-term bonds, while another might hold only the government issues with similar maturities.

General Funds Funds in this category simply don't specialize in any particular way. Our warning just above concerning varied credit quality applies here. Maturities can differ substantially as well.

High-Yield Funds High-yield funds specialize in low-credit quality issues. Such issues have higher yields because of their greater risks. As a result, high-yield bond funds can be quite volatile.

Mortgage Funds A number of funds specialize in so-called mortgage-backed securities. We discuss this important type of security in detail in later chapters.

World Funds A relatively limited number of funds invest worldwide. Some specialize in only government issues; others buy a variety of non-domestic issues.

Stock and Bond Funds

This last major fund group includes a variety of funds. The only common feature is that these funds don't invest exclusively in either stocks or bonds. For this reason, they are often called "blended" or "hybrid" funds. We discuss a few of the main types.

Balanced Funds Balanced funds maintain a relatively fixed split between stocks and bonds. They emphasize relatively safe, high-quality investments. Such funds provide a kind of "one-stop" shopping for fund investors, particularly smaller investors, because they diversify into both stocks and bonds.

Asset Allocation Funds   Two types of funds carry this label. The first is an extended version of a balanced fund. Such a fund holds relatively fixed proportional investments in stocks, bonds, money market instruments, and perhaps real estate or some other investment class. The target proportions may be updated or modified periodically.

The other type of asset allocation fund is often called a *flexible portfolio fund*. Here, the fund manager may hold up to 100 percent in stocks, bonds, or money market instruments, depending on her views about the likely performance of these investments. These funds essentially try to time the market, guessing which general type of investment will do well (or least poorly) over the months ahead.

Convertible Funds   Some bonds are convertible, meaning they can be swapped for a fixed number of shares of stock at the option of the bondholder. Some mutual funds specialize in these bonds.

Income Funds   An income fund emphasizes generating dividend and coupon income on its investments, so it would hold a variety of dividend-paying common, as well as preferred, stocks and bonds of various maturities.

Mutual Fund Objectives: Recent Developments

As we mentioned earlier, a mutual fund's stated objective may not be all that informative. In recent years, there has been a trend toward classifying a mutual fund's objective based on its actual holdings. For example, Figure 5.3 illustrates the classifications used by *The Wall Street Journal*.

A key thing to notice in Figure 5.3 is that most general-purpose funds (as opposed to specialized types such as sector funds) are classified based on the market "cap" of the stocks they hold (small, midsize, or large) and also on whether the fund tends to invest in either "growth" or "value" stocks (or both). We will discuss growth versus value stocks in a later chapter; for now, it is enough to know that "growth" stocks are those considered more likely to grow rapidly. "Value" stocks are those that look to be relatively undervalued and thus may be attractive for that reason. Notice that, in this scheme, *all* stocks are "growth," "value," or a blend of the two, a classic example of the Lake Wobegon effect.[2]

The mutual fund "style" box is an increasingly common sight. A style box is a way of visually representing a fund's investment focus by placing the fund into one of nine boxes like this:

---

[2]Lake Wobegon is a mystical place in Minnesota made famous by Garrison Keillor where "the men are strong, the women are beautiful, and all the children are above average." See www.phc.mpr.org for more.

FIGURE 5.3 Mutual Fund Objectives

MUTUAL-FUND OBJECTIVES

Categories compiled by The Wall Street Journal, based on classifications by Lipper Inc.

STOCK FUNDS

Emerging Markets (EM): Funds that invest in emerging-market equity securities, where the "emerging market" is defined by a country's GNP per capita and other economic measures.

Equity Income (EI): Funds that seek high current income and growth of income through investment in equities.

European Region (EU): Funds that invest in markets or operations concentrated in the European region.

Global Stock (GL): Funds that invest in securities traded outside of the U.S. and may own U.S. securities as well.

Gold Oriented (AU): Funds that invest in gold mines, gold-oriented mining finance houses, gold coins or bullion.

Health/Biotech (HB): Funds that invest in companies related to health care, medicine and biotechnology.

International Stock (IL) (non-U.S.): Canadian; International; International Small Cap.

Latin American (LT): Funds that invest in markets or operations concentrated in the Latin American region.

Large-Cap Growth (LG): Funds that invest in large companies with long-term earnings that are expected to grow significantly faster than the earnings of stocks in major indexes. Funds normally have above-average price-to-earnings ratios, price-to-book ratios and three-year earnings growth.

Large-Cap Core (LC): Funds that invest in large companies, with wide latitude in the type of shares they buy. On average, the price-to-earnings ratios, price-to-book ratios, and three-year earnings growth are in line with those of the U.S. diversified large-cap funds' universe average.

Large-Cap Value (LV): Funds that invest in large companies that are considered undervalued relative to major stock indexes based on price-to-earnings ratios, price-to-book ratios or other factors.

Midcap Growth (MG): Funds that invest in midsize companies with long-term earnings that are expected to grow significantly faster than the earnings of stocks in major indexes. Funds normally have above-average price-to-earnings ratios, price-to-book ratios and three-year earnings growth.

Midcap Core (MC): Funds that invest in midsize companies, with wide latitude in the type of shares they buy. On average, the price-to-earnings ratios, price-to-book ratios, and three-year earnings growth are in line with those of the U.S. diversified midcap funds' universe average.

Midcap Value (MV): Funds that invest in midsize companies that are considered undervalued relative to major stock indexes based on price-to-earnings ratios, price-to-book ratios or other factors.

Multicap Growth (XG): Funds that invest in companies of various sizes, with long-term earnings that are expected to grow significantly faster than the earnings of stocks in major indexes. Funds normally have above-average price-to-earnings ratios, price-to-book ratios, and three-year earnings growth.

Multicap Core (XC): Funds that invest in companies of various sizes with average price-to-earnings ratios, price-to-book ratios and earnings growth.

Multicap Value (XV): Funds that invest in companies of various size, normally those that are considered undervalued relative to major stock indexes based on price-to-earnings ratios, price-to-book ratios or other factors.

Natural Resources (NR): Funds that invest in natural-resource stocks.

Pacific Region (PR): Funds that invest in China Region; Japan; Pacific Ex-Japan; Pacific Region.

Science & Technology (TK): Funds that invest in science and technology stocks. Includes Telecommunication funds.

Sector (SE): Funds that invest in financial services; real estate; specialty & miscellaneous.

S&P 500 Index (SP): Funds that are passively managed, and are designed to replicate the performance of the Standard & Poor's 500-stock Index on a reinvested basis.

Small-Cap Growth (SG): Funds that invest in small companies with long-term earnings that are expected to grow significantly faster than the earnings of stocks in major indexes. Funds normally have above-average price-to-earnings ratios, price-to-book ratios, and three-year earnings growth.

Small-Cap Core (SC): Funds that invest in small companies, with wide latitude in the type of shares they buy. On average, the price-to-earnings ratios, price-to-book ratios, and three-year earnings growth are in line with those of the U.S. diversified small-cap funds' universe average.

Small-Cap Value (SV): Funds that invest in small companies that are considered undervalued relative to major stock indexes based on price-to-earnings ratios, price-to-book ratios or other factors.

Specialty Equity (SQ): Funds that invest in all market capitalization ranges, with no restrictions for any one range. May have strategies that are distinctly different from other diversified stock funds.

Utility (UT): Funds that invest in utility stocks.

TAXABLE BOND FUNDS

Short-Term Bond (SB): Ultra-short Obligation; Short Investment Grade Debt; Short-Intermediate Investment Grade Debt.

Short-Term U.S. (SU): Short U.S. Treasury; Short U.S. Government; Short-Intermediate U.S. Government debt.

Intermediate Bond (IB): Funds that invest in investment-grade debt issues (rated in the top four grades) with dollar-weighted average maturities of five to 10 years.

Intermediate U.S. (IG): Intermediate U.S. Government; Intermediate U.S. Treasury.

Long-Term Bond (AB): Funds that invest in corporate and government debt issues in the top grades.

Long-Term U.S. (LU): General U.S. Government; General U.S. Treasury; Target Maturity.

General U.S. Taxable (GT): Funds that invest in general bonds.

High-Yield Taxable (HC): Funds that aim for high current yields from fixed-income securities and tend to invest in lower-grade debt.

Mortgage (MT): Adjustable Rate Mortgage; GNMA; U.S. Mortgage.

World Bond (WB): Emerging Markets Debt; Global Income; International Income; Short World Multi-Market Income.

MUNICIPAL DEBT FUNDS

Short-Term Muni (SM): California Short-Intermediate Muni Debt; Other States Short-Intermediate Muni Debt; Short-Intermediate Muni Debt; Short Muni Debt.

Intermediate Muni (IM): Intermediate-term Muni Debt including single states.

General Muni (GM): Funds investing in muni-debt issues in the top four credit ratings.

Single-State Municipal (SS): Funds that invest in debt of individual states.

High-Yield Municipal (HM): Funds that invest in lower rated muni debt.

Insured Muni (NM): California Insured Muni Debt; Florida Insured Muni Debt; Insured Muni Debt; New York Insured Muni Debt.

STOCK & BOND FUNDS

Balanced (BL): Primary objective is to conserve principal, by maintaining a balanced portfolio of both stocks and bonds.

Stock/Bond Blend (MP): Multipurpose funds such as Balanced Target Maturity; Convertible Securities; Flexible Income; Flexible Portfolio; Global Flexible and Income funds, that invest in both stocks and bonds.

Source: Reprinted by permission of The *Wall Street Journal*, October 4, 2005. © 2005 Dow Jones & Company, Inc. All Rights Reserved Worldwide.

As shown, this particular fund focuses on large-cap, value stocks.

These newer mutual fund objectives are also useful for screening mutual funds. As our nearby *Work the Web* box shows, many websites have mutual fund selectors that allow you to find funds with particular characteristics.

 CHECK THIS

5.5a What are the three major types of long-term funds? Give several examples of each and describe their investment policies.

5.5b What are the distinguishing characteristics of a bond fund?

5.6 Mutual Fund Performance

We close our discussion of open-end mutual funds by looking at some of the performance information reported in the financial press. We then discuss the usefulness of such information for selecting mutual funds.

WORK THE WEB

As we discussed in the chapter, there are thousands of mutual funds, so how do you pick one? One answer is to visit one of the many mutual fund sites on the Web and use a fund selector. Most of the websites we mention in the chapter have one. Here is an example of how they are used. We went to www.morningstar.ca and clicked on the "Fund Selector." We then indicated that we were interested in a Canadian equity fund that has expense ratio less than 0.5 percent with minimum initial purchase requirement of $3,000. Here is what we got.

Change Criteria	Results of Search	New Search	Definitions			

Fund Name (Click to select all)	▼Morningstar Rating	Tax Adj. Rank	Equity Style	Fixed Inc. Style	Analyst Report
TD US Index Currency Neutral - e	★★★★★	▨	---	---	---
TD NASDAQ Index - e	★★★★★	▨	---	---	---
TD International Indx Currency Neutral-e	★★★★★	▨	---	---	---
Professionals Qc Short Term	★★★★★	▨	---	---	---
FMOQ Money Market	★★★★★	▨	---	---	---
Equitable Life Canada Accum Income	★★★★★	---	---	▦	---
Templeton Treasury Bill GIF	★★★★	---	---	---	---
TD US Index - e	★★★★	▨	---	---	---
TD International Index - e	★★★★	▨	---	---	---
TD European Index - e	★★★★	▨	---	---	---
TD Canadian Index - e	★★★★	▨	---	---	---
TD Canadian Bond Index - e	★★★★	▨	---	---	---
iShares CDN Composite Index	★★★★	▨	▦	---	---
Concordia Balanced	★★★★	---	▦	▦	---
Accumulus Short Term Income	★★★★	▨	---	---	---
TD Dow Jones Industrial Avg Index - e	★★★	▨	---	---	---
Templeton Canadian Balanced GIF	★★	---	---	---	---
Templeton Canadian Stock GIF	★	---	---	---	---
TD Japanese Index - e	−	---	---	---	---
Excel Income and Growth	−	---	▦	▦	---

Results: 1-20 of 20				Click column heading to ran

This search narrowed things down in a hurry! Now we have a list of 20 funds. Clicking on the name of a fund takes you to the Morningstar website on the fund where you can learn more about the fund. Note that the majority of these funds are index funds which have low expense ratios.

Mutual Fund Performance Information

Mutual fund performance is very closely tracked by a number of organizations. Financial publications of all types periodically provide mutual fund data, and many provide lists of recommended funds. We examine *Globe and Mail* information in this section, but by no means is this the only source or the most comprehensive.[3] However, *The Globe and Mail* is a particularly timely source because it reports mutual fund year-to-date returns on a daily basis, and it provides a summary of average investment performance by fund category on a regular basis. The information we consider here applies only to open-end funds.

Figure 5.4 reproduces *The Globe and Mail's* top 180 largest funds. We can learn their Net Asset Values and returns for 1, 3 and 5 years as well as rankings.

Figure 5.5 is a small section of the mutual fund price quotations reported in *The Globe and Mail* each month. All of the funds are Canadian Equity funds. The first piece of information is the stars or the ratings given by the Globefund. Following the fund name is RSP column indicating whether or not the fund is eligible for registered retirement plans. R indicates a fund is 100 percent eligible. NAVPS is the net asset value per share.

MER is the management expense ratio. The "Load/Fees" column shows whether or not front-end or deferred loads exist. O indicates load is optional, N indicates no sales fees and F indicates front-end load.

The next columns show one-month, three month, and one-year to ten-year returns on this fund. For example, AGF Canada Class fund has a $13.60 net asset value per share, and 2.86 percent MER. It is an optional load fund, 100 % RSP eligible. The Fund has earned a 19.7 percent return in one year, but last month it had a 0.1 percent loss.

How Useful Are Fund Performance Ratings?

If you look at the performance ratings reported in Figure 5.5, you might wonder why anyone would buy a fund in a category other than those with the highest returns. Well, the lessons learned in Chapter 1 suggest the answer that these historical returns do not consider the riskiness of the various fund categories. For example, if the market has done well, the best ranked funds may simply be the riskiest funds, since the riskiest funds normally perform the best in a rising market. In a market downturn, however, these best ranked funds are most likely to become the worst ranked funds, since the riskiest funds normally perform the worst in a falling market.

These problems with performance measures deal with the evaluation of historical performance. However, there is an even more fundamental criterion. Ultimately, we don't care about historical performance; we care about *future* performance. Whether historical performance is useful in predicting future performance is the subject of ongoing debate. However, one thing we can say is that some of the poorest-performing funds are those with very high costs. These costs act as a constant drag on performance, and such funds tend to have persistently poorer returns than otherwise similar funds. The accompanying *Investment Update* box gives advice on how to find good funds.

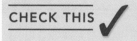

| CHECK THIS | 5.6a | Which mutual fund in Figure 5.5 had the best year-to-date return? The worst? |
| | 5.6b | What are some of the problems with comparing historical performance numbers? |

[3]For more detailed information, publications from companies such as Morningstar, Weisenberger, and Value Line are often available in the library or online. Of course, a mutual fund's prospectus and annual report contain a great deal of information as well.

FIGURE 5.4 The Top 180 Funds By Assets

THE BIG PICTURE » THE TOP 180 FUNDS BY ASSETS

	Close NAV	Week % Chg	YTD % Chg	Perf. 1 yr.	Perf. 3 yr.	Perf. 5 yr.	MER	Assets $Blns	Globe 5 star rating
Acuity High Income	15.24	-3.80	-6.55	-3.88	10.32	13.05	2.3	1.63	★★★
AGF Canadian Balanced	23.63	-2.56	-3.51	5.49	9.47	8.86	2.51	1.07	★★★
AGF Canadian Growth Equity	64.08	-6.45	1.04	10.83	18.46	15.03	2.92	1.07	★★★★
AGF Canadian Large Cap Div-Classic	45.58	-2.46	1.78	10.93	16.85	14.59	1.84	3.38	★★★★
AGF Canadian Stock	52.15	-1.84	.42	9.65	16.07	13.90	2.39	2.43	★★★
AGF Cdn Real Value Balanced	6.92	-1.00	-1.53	5.45	7.23	n-a	2.41	1.28	★★★
AGF European Equity Class	37.70	-1.15	-7.94	8.74	16.68	14.35	2.93	1.87	★★★★
AGF International Stock Class	14.69	-1.67	-5.77	10.87	15.88	11.25	2.85	1.88	★★★★★
AGF International Value	42.25	-1.10	-6.30	9.20	4.78	3.98	2.8	3.40	★★★
AIC Advantage	96.62	-4.06	-3.98	10.27	14.36	10.24	2.47	1.14	★★★
AIC Diversified Canada	44.58	-.85	-5.13	1.94	8.08	6.60	2.47	1.48	★
AIM Canadian First Class	13.03	-2.46	-4.67	.50	14.58	13.53	2.4	1.36	★★
Allegro Moderate Portfolio-A	10.79	-.85	-1.87	4.86	7.69	n-a	2.71	1.09	★★★
Bissett Bond-A	12.53	.72	-1.05	1.29	3.03	4.12	1.44	3.62	★★★
Bissett Canadian Equity-A	85.90	-1.77	1.32	9.64	13.28	11.26	2.59	3.21	★★
BMO Bond	12.74	.45	-1.16	1.30	3.05	3.77	1.54	2.01	★★★
BMO Dividend	49.19	-1.26	-.57	7.40	14.08	14.11	1.73	5.92	★★★★★
BMO Equity	31.70	-2.90	1.77	9.33	15.62	13.53	2.3	2.23	★★★★
BMO Monthly Income	9.71	-.83	-.46	4.53	8.35	8.19	1.51	6.03	★★★
Brandes Global Equity	13.26	-1.61	-8.94	5.18	5.76	6.64	2.7	3.78	★★★
Brandes International Equity	14.09	-1.89	-8.32	5.15	8.85	8.85	2.7	1.52	★★★
Capital Intl - Global Equity D	15.64	-2.01	-4.92	8.73	10.12	n-a	1.66	1.06	★★★★
Capital Intl - Global Equity F	15.92	-2.00	-4.57	9.37	10.70	n-a	1.17	1.06	★★★★
CI Canadian Bond	5.47	.55	-.65	1.72	3.17	3.71	1.62	1.78	★★★
CI Canadian Investment	26.40	-2.04	-1.57	5.21	14.95	13.39	2.3	6.56	★★★
CI Global	13.43	-2.82	-9.44	2.68	6.69	6.68	2.37	1.85	★★★
CI Harbour	21.30	-1.43	1.96	8.67	17.19	12.98	2.35	4.93	★★★
CI Harbour Growth & Income	18.14	-.77	.72	5.30	12.63	9.71	2.35	5.41	★★★★
CI Portfolio Series Balanced	23.56	-1.22	-3.32	4.02	9.07	8.28	2.35	2.16	★★★
CI Portfolio Series Balanced Growth	12.94	-1.45	-3.43	4.36	7.88	7.23	2.37	1.07	★★★
CI Signature Canadian Balanced	15.93	-1.24	-.09	8.43	13.30	11.28	2.35	1.58	★★★★
CI Signature Dividend	13.87	-.93	-3.15	2.38	8.53	8.09	1.81	2.11	★
CI Signature High Income	14.95	-1.45	-1.17	-.14	10.95	12.81	1.55	4.32	★★★
CI Signature Income & Growth	5.53	-1.25	-.29	5.87	12.13	11.30	2.35	2.58	★★★★
CI Signature Select Canadian	20.20	-2.23	-.20	11.50	18.34	15.00	2.35	4.28	★★★
CI Synergy Canadian Corporate Class	14.78	-2.57	-.07	9.48	17.47	16.97	2.36	1.53	★★★★
CI Value Trust Corporate Class	11.22	-.36	-12.34	3.41	-.24	2.09	2.63	1.11	★
CIBC Money Market	10.00	.00	1.88	3.22	2.26	2.03	1.16	3.20	★★★
CIBC Monthly Income	15.45	-.88	-.03	4.32	12.92	11.81	1.43	7.16	★★★★
CIBC Premium T-Bill	10.00	.00	2.18	3.75	2.78	2.52	.59	1.58	★★★
Desjardins Canadian Bond	5.33	.59	-.96	1.35	2.76	3.59	1.63	1.39	★★★
Desjardins Dividend	25.21	-1.56	.63	6.15	11.74	11.62	2.13	1.06	★★★★★
Desjardins Short-Term Income	4.41	.39	.88	2.20	1.71	2.36	1.62	1.31	★★★★
Dynamic Canadian Dividend Fund	17.88	-2.72	2.07	9.84	16.28	15.58	2.44	1.24	★★★
Dynamic Dividend Income	14.13	-1.26	.17	3.20	10.59	n-a	2.31	1.22	★★
Dynamic FocusPls Diversifd Income	17.00	-2.58	2.27	-3.12	12.05	15.26	2.18	1.62	★★★
Dynamic FocusPlus Balanced	11.61	-1.94	-1.87	2.28	6.15	8.53	2.49	1.30	★★
Dynamic Power Canadian Growth	25.18	-6.60	2.19	21.48	26.38	21.49	3.09	1.54	★★★★
Elliott & Page Monthly High Income	15.93	-1.07	2.07	5.16	10.69	12.18	2.11	3.68	★★★★
Fidelity Canadian Asset Alloc.-A	24.82	-1.42	.95	8.13	11.69	10.06	2.43	2.67	★★★★★
Fidelity Canadian Asset Alloc.-B	24.86	-1.41	1.09	8.38	11.91	10.18	2.2	3.62	★★★★★
Fidelity Canadian Balanced-A	18.96	-1.09	2.21	8.91	10.85	9.78	2.28	1.32	★★★★
Fidelity Canadian Growth Company-B	31.31	-3.15	3.46	9.78	13.61	12.56	2.24	1.28	★★★
Fidelity Global - B	32.24	-1.27	-7.24	2.55	6.63	5.37	2.32	1.78	★★★
Fidelity NorthStar-A	15.21	-2.84	-4.89	4.56	8.49	n-a	2.5	1.81	★★★
Fidelity NorthStar-B	15.22	-2.84	-4.78	4.77	8.69	n-a	2.28	1.62	★★★
Fidelity True North-A	29.48	-2.38	4.07	14.56	18.88	15.21	2.45	1.41	★★★★
Fidelity True North-B	29.58	-2.38	4.22	14.82	19.13	15.35	2.21	1.92	★★★★
IA Clarington Canadian Dividend	7.36	-2.20	-.85	6.01	9.53	8.82	2.73	1.80	★★★★★
IG Mackenzie Maxxum Dividend Gro-A	18.99	-.44	-.76	7.36	10.02	n-a	2.71	1.38	★★
Investors Canadian Balanced-A	14.42	-.57	1.83	4.96	10.88	n-a	2.71	1.61	★★★★
Investors Canadian Bond	10.36	.73	-.67	1.49	2.55	4.20	2.01	1.22	★★★
Investors Canadian Equity-A	21.41	-2.32	.90	6.16	15.72	n-a	2.71	3.16	★★★
Investors Cdn Large Cap Value-A	23.85	-1.23	2.14	7.38	16.58	n-a	2.71	2.88	★★★
Investors Dividend-A	23.60	-.66	-3.16	3.61	9.84	n-a	2.71	13.62	★★★
Investors Euro Mid-Cap Equity-A	26.20	-.89	-4.40	24.28	20.48	n-a	2.72	1.18	★★★★★
Investors European Equity-A	15.42	-.55	-5.17	9.29	12.87	n-a	2.72	1.81	★★★★

	Close NAV
MD Bond	7.06
MD Dividend	21.39
MD Equity	25.76
MD Growth	11.34
Mutual Beacon	7.47
National Bank Bond	10.93
National Bank Dividend	18.24
PH&N Canadian Equity-A(08/16)	93.91
PH&N Dividend Income-A(08/16)	87.25
RBC Balanced	12.81
RBC Balanced Growth	13.10
RBC Bond	5.87
RBC Canadian Dividend	48.23
RBC Canadian Money Market	10.00
RBC Canadian Short-Term Income	10.58
RBC Canadian T-Bill	10.00
RBC Cdn Equity	27.55
RBC DS Canadian Focus	16.55
RBC European Equity	21.59
RBC Monthly Income	13.81
RBC North American Growth	26.04
RBC O'Shaughnessy Canadian Equity	19.63
RBC O'Shaughnessy Int'l Equity	12.83
RBC O'Shaughnessy U.S. Value	13.07
RBC Premium Money Market	10.00
RBC Select Balanced	22.37
RBC Select Conservative	18.60
RBC Select Growth	24.12
RBC Tax Managed Return	9.68
RBC U.S. Equity	24.13
Scotia Canadian Balanced	21.88
Scotia Canadian Dividend	39.77
Scotia Canadian Income	12.60
Scotia Money Market	10.00
Scotia Partners Balanced Inc & Gwth(08/16)	13.17
Scotia Partners Conservative Growth(08/16)	14.71
SEI Canadian Equity-O	23.74
SEI Canadian Fixed Income-O	11.24
SEI E.A.F.E. Equity-O	6.64
SEI U.S. Large Co. Equity-O	7.08
Sprott Canadian Equity	35.99
Standard Life Cdn Dividend Growth-A	53.08
Talvest Millennium High Income(08/16)	13.20
TD Balanced Growth	24.45
TD Canadian Blue Chip Equity	34.91
TD Canadian Bond	12.70
TD Canadian Equity	30.00
TD Canadian Money Market	10.00
TD Dividend Growth	54.65
TD Dividend Income	28.76
TD Dividend Income-H	14.84
TD Dividend Income-T	14.82
TD Global Select	15.61
TD High Yield Income	7.41
TD Income Advantage Portfolio - I	10.59
TD Income Advantage Portfolio-H	14.25
TD Income Advantage Portfolio-T	14.23
TD Mgd Aggress Growth Port-I(08/16)	10.48
TD Mgd Aggressive Growth Port - P(08/16)	10.58
TD Mgd Bal Growth Portfolio-I(08/16)	11.07
TD Mgd Balanced Growth Port - P(08/16)	10.34
TD Mgd Inc&Mod Growth Portfolio-I(08/16)	11.13
TD Mgd Income Portfolio-I(08/16)	10.26
TD Monthly Income	16.68
TD Monthly Income-H	14.71
TD Monthly Income-T	14.70
TD Premium Money Market	10.00

FIGURE 5.5   **Mutual Funds**

globefund.com   Page 1

Asset Class: **Canadian Equity**
Date: **July 31, 2007**

Stars Prospectus	Fund Name	RSP	Assets	NAVPS	Distributions	MER	Load /Fees	1month	3month	Returns 1year	3year	5year	10year
***	Acker Finley Canada Focus	R	14.4	21.60		3.26	O	-1.4	5.2	12.8	17.4	–	–
***	Acker Finley Select CanFocus-A	R	53.4	10.51		2.07	O	-1.1	5.7	14.9	19.1	–	–
	Acker Finley Select CanFocus-F	R	14.2	10.19		2.07	N	-1.1	5.8	–	–	–	–
*****	Acuity All Cap 30 Canadian Equ	R	320.5	30.25		2.85	O	2.6	11.6	35.6	23.2	28.8	–
*****	Acuity Pooled Pure Cdn Equity	R	56.1	26.49		*0.15	N	0.5	4.3	28.3	27.5		–
****	Acuity Pooled Soc Val Cdn Equ	R	11.9	20.02		*0.15	N	0.9	5.5	19.0	19.8	–	–
***	Acuity Social Values Cdn Equ	R	52.0	18.84		2.85	O	0.7	4.8	15.9	17.4	19.3	–
****	AGF Canada Class	R	100.0	13.60		2.86	O	-0.1	2.3	19.7	17.4	14.8	7.6
*****	Altafund Investment Corp.	R	71.9	38.51		2.72	N	-0.4	4.1	14.5	21.9	20.8	4.8
****	Altamira Capital Growth	R	91.2	25.09		2.15	N	0.0	4.3	19.3	18.6	15.4	5.7
*****	Altamira Precision Cdn Index	R	191.4	22.41		0.53	N	0.0	4.9	21.5	21.0	18.2	–
***	APEX Canadian Growth (AGF)	R	13.0	14.20		3.19	D	0.1	2.2	18.7	16.4	13.4	7.9
***	Assumption Cdn Equity Plus	R	5.7	25.26		2.13	N	0.3	2.7	14.1	16.4	16.1	–
**	Assumption Cdn Equity Plus-B	R		13.32		3.75	N	0.2	2.3	12.4	14.6	14.5	–
**	Assumption Cdn Equity Plus-C	R		13.48		3.48	R	0.2	2.4	12.6	14.9	14.7	–
***	Assumption Life Cdn Equity	R	8.2	40.59		2.08	N	0.3	2.2	13.9	15.1	12.9	–
**	Assumption Life Cdn Equity-B	R		18.70	0.016	3.80	N	0.2	1.9	12.4	13.6	11.5	–
**	Assumption Life Cdn Equity-C	R		18.93	0.016	3.48	R	0.2	1.9	12.7	13.8	11.8	–
****	Assumption/FDI True North	R	8.1	30.43		2.95	N	-0.6	4.1	23.1	20.1	15.8	–
****	Assumption/FDI True North-B	R		28.33		4.20	N	-0.7	3.8	21.6	18.5	14.3	–
****	Assumption/FDI True North-C	R		28.67		3.80	R	-0.7	3.8	21.8	18.8	14.6	–
******	Assumption/MB TSX 100 Momentum	R	4.1	53.65		1.36	N	3.9	16.7	36.7	34.0	26.0	–
*****	Assumption/MB TSX 100 Moment-B	R		34.05		3.22	N	3.8	16.3	34.6	31.9	24.0	–
*****	Assumption/MB TSX 100 Moment-C	R		34.46		2.84	R	3.8	16.4	34.9	32.2	24.3	–
***	Astra Canadian Index	R	16.7	13.71		2.54	O	-0.3	3.3	17.2	17.5	15.4	–

Reprinted with permission from *The Globe and Mail*.

PORTFOLIO STRATEGY

A Buy-low Guide for Quality Funds

A fund down on its luck can be more rewarding than the latest stars, **ROB CARRICK** *writes*

If you want to become a better mutual fund investor, get tough.

Sell your mistakes. Ignore the pull of a fund with a fabulously successful one-year return. And, last but not least, have the guts to buy good funds when they're down.

Successful stock market investors make cold calculations like these all the time, but things are different with funds. Blame it on the fund industry and its propaganda that funds should be bought and held indefinitely, and that any time you have money is a good time to buy funds. More blame goes to the many investors who ask nothing more from a fund they're buying than that it be on a hot streak.

These people have it backwards: The best time to buy funds is when they're on sale, just like with stocks.

As you read on, you'll find some examples of quality funds that present buy-low opportunities as you ready your portfolio for the year ahead. But first, let's consider the sense in buying on the dips as opposed to the peaks.

The key concept here is a bit of investing theory called reversion to the mean, which suggests that fund ups and downs will balance out to returns that approach the middle point. If a fund has done brilliantly in 2004, chances are it will hit a slump at some point that will bring overall returns down.

The converse is true, too. If you buy a fund that has had a below-average year, chances are good that you'll enjoy a compensating period of better-than-average gains.

Don't just buy any struggling fund, though. To stack the odds of a rebound in your favour, focus on funds with solid long-term results that are working through a slump. Good past returns are no guarantee of future success,

Bottom fishing

The past year has been a good one for mutual fund investors, but there have been disappointments. Here are a few recent laggards that look good because of their solid long-term records.

Fund Name	Asset Class	Net Assets ($million)	MER	Minimum Investment	1-year Return	1-year Category Average	5-year Return	5-year Category Average
Beutel Goodman Canadian Equity	Canadian equity (Pure)	$290.6	1.4%	$10,000	15.4%	16.3%	11.5%	6.9%
Mackenzie Ivy Canadian	Canadian equity	5,235.4	2.5	500	9.7	13.9	6.8	6.4
Mackenzie Ivy Enterprise	Canadian equity	278.0	2.5	500	7.5	13.9	9.8	6.4
Mackenzie Universal Precious Metals	Precious metals	237.3	2.6	500	−17.9	−15.3	27.5	21.0
PH&N Dividend Income-A	Canadian dividend	2,534.8	1.2	25,000	15.1	14.2	16.7	10.6
Saxon High Income	Canadian income trusts	156.5	1.3	5,000	16.2	23.1	17.4	17.9
Trimark Canadian-SC	Canadian equity	1,519.3	1.6	500	10.9	13.9	7.2	6.4
Trimark Fund-SC	Global equity	2,954.7	1.6	500	2.1	6.2	5.7	−2.9
Trimark Select Growth	Global equity	5,342.4	2.4	500	1.5	6.2	4.9	−2.9

Source: www.globefund.com, Article from August 18, 2007 *The Globe and Mail*. Reprinted with permission of *The Globe and Mail*.

(continued)

but a fund that has consistently delivered good performance over 10 years obviously has something going for it.

Buying low suggests a strategy of waiting until a fund hits rock bottom before buying it, but market-timing exercises like this are guesswork. An easier approach is to look at quality funds that haven't been their usual strong selves in 2004.

Screening for funds like these can easily be done on the Globefund.com website. Using the filter function, select an asset class (Canadian equity, for example) and choose the "standard" report. When you get your list of funds, click on the column heading for one-year returns and then click again to order the list from worst performer to best. Next, click on the "quartile ranking" tab at the top of the chart. This will tell you whether a fund has ranked in the first, second, third or fourth quarter of funds in its category on an annual basis in the current year and the previous seven years.

I ran a screen like this for the major fund categories and came up with a few well-established funds that you can buy low right now.

Mackenzie Ivy Canadian, which I've owned for a lot longer than I've been an investment writer, is the definitive example. This $5.2-billion fund has been in the fourth quartile for both 2004 and 2003, which means it has ranked in the bottom 25 percent of its peers in the Canadian equity fund category. For the 12 months to Nov. 30, its 9.7 percent return is a little more than four percentage points below the category average and almost five points below the return of the S&P/TSX 60 index, which I also own through an investment in exchange-traded funds (now you see why actively managed and index funds are a good pairing).

Going on gut instinct, an investor looking for a conservative Canadian equity fund would probably avoid Ivy Canadian because it's clearly in a rut. If you take a long-term view, you might well conclude that this fund's latest numbers are only a temporary setback.

First, its five- and 10-year compound average annual returns are comfortably above average. Second, the fund was in the first quartile four times from 1997 to 2002, a period that includes several bear-market years. If the stock markets were to bog down next year, then Ivy Canadian could be a good way to get some comparatively safe exposure to the equity market. Best of all, it's on sale right now.

The Trimark Fund (SC version) hasn't had the best time of it in 2004, partly because star manager Bill Kanko left and partly because returns have sunk below average. Still, it's another buy-low possibility for 2005.

The bad news with this fund is that the return for the 12 months to Nov. 30 was 2 percent, while the average fund made 6.2 percent. The good news is a 20-year history of beating the daylights out of the average foreign equity fund. If Mr. Kanko's departure worries you, just remember that his co-managers remain, and so does the Trimark philosophy of value investing.

A subtler example of a fund on sale is Phillips Hager & North Dividend Income, which beat the average dividend fund return by a percentage point over the past 12 months, but more recently it slipped below the average.

There are times when a good fund's slump is the beginning of a long and painful slide, but this hardly seems likely with PH&N Dividend Income. This is a fund that has demonstrated the consistent ability to outperform the category average by several percentage points over long periods, and there's no one star manager to pin this success on because of PH&N's team approach.

Here are a few other buy-low opportunities.

- Saxon High Income. This small fund is a contentious pick as a buy-low opportunity because it lacks the definitive long-term record of success. That said, the five-year average annual return is very close to the category average.

- Beutel Goodman Canadian Equity. An interesting choice if you want to invest in big, blue-chip stocks. This fund looked great through the tough market years earlier this decade, and its recent weakness hasn't been too pronounced.

- Mackenzie Universal Precious Metals. If you want exposure to gold through a fund with a proven manager, then this entry has to be a serious contender despite subpar results lately. The five- and 10-year returns are well above average.

The byword with buy-low fund investing is patience. It might take a year or two for a slumping fund to rebound, just as it might take a high-flying fund a while to cool out if you bought it now. The difference with buy-low investing is that the best is yet to come, whereas with buying high you generally have nowhere to go but down.

5.7   Closed-End Funds, Exchange Traded Funds, and Hedge Funds

As we will see, closed-end funds and exchange traded funds have some unusual aspects.

Closed-End Funds Performance Information

As we described earlier, the major difference between a closed-end fund and an open-end fund is that closed-end funds don't buy and sell shares. Instead, there is a fixed number of shares in the fund, and these shares are bought and sold on the open market. About 250 closed-end funds have their shares traded on stock exchanges, which is far fewer than the roughly 5,000 long-term, open-end mutual funds available to investors.

Figure 5.6 shows some quotes for the Canadian closed-end funds. The table lists the first 50 funds of 250 closed-end funds.

Examining the entry for Aberdeen Asia-Pacific Fund, the first column shows the ticker symbol. Next, we have the net asset value, followed by the closing price and the amount of discount/premium. For the Aberdeen fund NAV is $7.87 and the closing price is $7.21. Notice that the closing price per share is less than the net asset value. On a percentage basis, the difference is ($7.21 − $7.87) / $7.87 = −8.39 percent. We will say more about this discount in a moment.

The Closed-End Fund Discount Mystery

Bay Street has many unsolved puzzles, and one of the most famous and enduring has to do with prices of shares in closed-end funds. As we noted earlier, shares in closed-end funds trade in the marketplace. Furthermore, as the Aberdeen Fund shows, share prices can differ from net asset values. In fact, most closed-end funds sell at a discount relative to their net asset values, and the discount is sometimes substantial.

For example, suppose a closed-end fund owns $100 million worth of stock. It has 10 million shares outstanding, so the NAV is clearly $10. It would not be at all unusual, however, for the share price to be only $9, indicating a 10 percent discount. What is puzzling about this discount is that you can apparently buy $10 worth of stock for only $9!

To make matters even more perplexing, the typical discount fluctuates over time. Sometimes the discount is very wide; at other times, it almost disappears. Despite a great deal of research, the closed-end fund discount phenomenon remains largely unexplained.

Because of the discount available on closed-end funds, it is often argued that funds with the largest discounts are attractive investments. The problem with this argument is that it assumes that the discount will narrow or disappear. Unfortunately, this may or may not happen; the discount might get even wider.

Sometimes, certain closed-end funds sell at a premium, implying that investors are willing to pay more than the NAV for shares. This case is not quite as perplexing; however, after all, investors in load funds do the same thing. The reasons we discussed for paying loads might apply to these cases.

One last comment on closed-end funds seems appropriate. When a closed-end fund is first created, its shares are offered for sale to the public. For example, a closed-end fund might raise $50 million by selling 5 million shares to the public at $10 per share (the original offer price is almost always $10), which is the fund's NAV.

If you pay $10, then you are very likely to shortly discover two unpleasant facts. First, the fund promoter will be paid, say, 7 percent of the proceeds right off the top, or about $3.5 million (this will be disclosed in the prospectus). This fee will come out of the fund, leaving a total value of $46.5 million and a NAV of $9.30. Further, as we

| FIGURE 5.6 | Closed-End Funds |

Sort by : Name (Click on a column heading to sort up or down)

Name	Ticker	Net Asset Value	Price	Discount/Premium
5Banc Split Inc B (NAV as of August 16, 2007,Price as of August 22, 2007)	FBS.B-T	18.15	18.94	4.37
AIC Diversified Canada Split Corp. (NAV as of August 17, 2007,Price as of August 21, 2007)	ADC-T	37.31	31.25	-16.24
AIC Global Financial Split Corp. (NAV as of August 17, 2007,Price as of August 22, 2007)	ASC-T	13.96	14.44	3.44
Aberdeen Asia-Pacific	FAP-T	7.87	7.21	-8.44
Aberdeen G7 Trust	GSV.UN-T	9.91	9.67	-2.42
Aberdeen SCOTS Trust (NAV as of August 22, 2007,Price as of August 21, 2007)	SCO.UN-T	22.31	20.91	-6.28
Acuity All Cap & Income Trust (NAV as of August 16, 2007,Price as of August 22, 2007)	AAI.UN-T	10.37	10.30	-0.71
Acuity Diversified Total Return Tru (NAV as of August 16, 2007,Price as of August 22, 2007)	ADF.UN-T	8.05	8.04	-0.14
Acuity Focused Total Return Trust (NAV as of August 16, 2007,Price as of August 22, 2007)	AFU.UN-T	7.75	7.50	-3.28
Acuity Growth & Income Trust (NAV as of August 16, 2007,Price as of August 22, 2007)	AIG.UN-T	11.64	11.65	0.10
Acuity Multi-Cap Total Return Trust (NAV as of August 16, 2007,Price as of August 22, 2007)	ART.UN-T	8.08	7.85	-2.85
Acuity Small Cap Corporation (NAV as of August 16, 2007,Price as of)	-	8.50	-	-
Adjustable Rate MBS Trust (NAV as of August 16, 2007,Price as of August 22, 2007)	ADJ.UN-T	20.10	17.58	-12.54
Advantaged Preferred Share Trust (NAV as of August 15, 2007,Price as of August 22, 2007)	PFR.UN-T	22.44	20.86	-7.04
Alberta Focused Income & Growth (NAV as of August 16, 2007,Price as of August 22, 2007)	AFZ.UN-T	7.20	7.10	-1.39
AllBanc Split Corp. (NAV as of August 16, 2007,Price as of August 21, 2007)	ABK.A-T	195.87	190.81	-2.58
AllBanc Split Corp. II (NAV as of August 16, 2007,Price as of August 22, 2007)	ALB-T	48.70	49.75	2.16
Alliance Split Income Trust (NAV as of August 16, 2007,Price as of August 21, 2007)	ASI.UN-T	15.46	14.36	-7.12
B Split II Corp. (NAV as of August 16, 2007,Price as of August 17, 2007)	BXN-T	25.98	26.25	1.04
BCX Split Corp. (NAV as of August 16, 2007,Price as of August 22, 2007)	BCX.A-T	38.38	39.16	2.03
BG Advantaged Corporate Bond (NAV as of August 16, 2007,Price as of August 22, 2007)	BAC.UN-T	8.22	7.97	-3.04
BG Advantaged Equal Weighted Income (NAV as of August 16, 2007,Price as of August 22, 2007)	BAE.UN-T	10.40	10.44	0.37
BG Advantaged S&P/TSX Income Tr Idx (NAV as of August 16, 2007,Price as of August 22, 2007)	BAI.UN-T	13.13	12.94	-1.42
BG Inc & Growth Split Trust Pfd (NAV as of August 16, 2007,Price as of August 22, 2007)	BDS.PR.A-T	10.01	10.00	-0.08
BG Income & Growth Split Trust (NAV as of August 16, 2007,Price as of August 22, 2007)	BDS.UN-T	11.62	11.11	-4.37
BG Top 100 Equal Weighted Income (NAV as of August 16, 2007,Price as of August 22, 2007)	BTH.UN-T	9.45	9.42	-0.33
BMONT Split Corp. (NAV as of August 16, 2007,Price as of August 20, 2007)	BMT-T	64.91	65.33	0.65
BNS Split Corp. II (NAV as of August 16, 2007,Price as of August 22, 2007)	BSC-T	48.41	50.41	4.13
Bayshore Floating Rate Senior Loan (NAV as of July 27, 2007,Price as of August 22, 2007)	BIF.UN-T	8.63	8.05	-6.72
Big 8 Split Inc (NAV as of August 16, 2007,Price as of August 22, 2007)	BIG.A-T	74.85	77.71	3.82
Big Bank Big Oil Split Corp. (NAV as of August 16, 2007,Price as of August 22, 2007)	BBO-T	25.14	24.56	-2.29
BluMont MAN Alternative Yield (NAV as of June 29, 2007,Price as of August 20, 2007)	BMY.UN-T	8.91	8.70	-2.41
Brascan Adjustable Rate Trust I (NAV as of August 16, 2007,Price as of August 22, 2007)	BAO.UN-T	18.89	17.10	-9.48
Brascan SoundVest Total Return (NAV as of August 17, 2007,Price as of August 22, 2007)	BST.UN-T	9.32	9.01	-3.29
Brascan Soundvest Diversified Inc. (NAV as of August 17, 2007,Price as of August 22, 2007)	BSI.UN-T	10.70	10.64	-0.54
Brascan Soundvest Focused Business (NAV as of August 17, 2007,Price as of August 22, 2007)	BSF.UN-T	8.27	8.10	-2.02
Brascan Soundvest Rising Dist Split (NAV as of August 17, 2007,Price as of August 22, 2007)	BSD.UN-T	7.56	8.02	6.12
Brompton Advantaged Oil & Gas (NAV as of August 16, 2007,Price as of August 22, 2007)	AOG.UN-T	6.22	6.08	-2.19
Brompton Advantaged Tracker (NAV as of August 16, 2007,Price as of August 22, 2007)	ATF.UN-T	7.70	7.79	1.16

Source: Reprinted with permission from *The Globe and Mail.*

have seen, the shares will probably trade at a discount relative to NAV in the market, so you would lose another piece of your investment almost immediately. In short, newly offered closed-end funds are generally very poor investments.

Exchange Traded Funds

Exchange traded funds, or ETFs, are a relatively recent innovation. Although they have been around since 1993, they really began to grow in the late 1990s. As of 2007, there were over 230 traded ETFs at Toronto, New York and American Stock Exchanges. Among these, approximately thirty two of them traded at Toronto. Basically, an ETF is an index fund, and, when you buy an ETF, you are buying the particular basket of stocks in the index. For example, the best known ETF is a "Standard and Poor's Depositary Receipt," or SPDR (pronounced "spider"), which is simply the S&P 500 index. In Canada the most popular ETF is i60 which contains units of S&P/TSX 60 Index Fund.

What makes an ETF different from an index fund is that, as the name suggests, an ETF actually trades like a closed-end fund. ETFs can be bought and sold during the day, and they can be sold short. They generally have very low expenses, lower even than index funds, but you must pay a commission when you buy and sell shares.

The fact that ETFs trade like shares in closed-end funds raises the possibility that they too could sell at a discount to their net asset values, but this probably won't happen. The reason is a little complicated, but, in essence, the fund will buy and sell directly like an open-end fund, but there is usually a minimum size of, say, 50,000 shares. Furthermore, an ETF will redeem shares in kind, meaning that if you sell a block of 50,000 shares to the fund, you actually receive the underlying stock instead of cash. So, if an ETF were to sell for a discount, big investors would buy up shares, redeem them in exchange for stock, and then sell the stock, thereby capturing the discount.

Which is better, an ETF or a more traditional index fund? It's hard to say. For an index like the S&P 500, it probably doesn't make much difference. However, one place where ETFs seem to have an edge is with some of the more specialized indexes. Similarly, there are ETFs that track industry indexes for which few ordinary index funds are available.

Hedge Funds

Hedge funds are a special type of investment company. They are like mutual funds in that a fund manager invests a pool of money obtained from investors. However, unlike mutual funds, hedge funds are not required to register with securities exchange commissions. They are only lightly regulated and are generally free to pursue almost any investment style they wish. In contrast, as we have discussed, mutual funds are regulated and are relatively limited in their permitted investment strategies. For example, mutual funds are usually not allowed to do things like sell short or use large degrees of leverage.

Hedge funds are also not required to maintain any particular degree of diversification or liquidity. They don't have to redeem shares on demand, and they have little in the way of disclosure requirements. The reason that hedge funds avoid many of the restrictions placed on mutual funds is that they only accept "financially sophisticated" investors, and they do not offer their securities for sale to the public. A financially sophisticated investor is, as a practical matter, usually either an institution or a high net worth (i.e., rich) individual. Some types of hedge funds are limited to no more than 100 investors.

For more on ETFs, visit www.morningstar.ca

hedge fund An unregistered investment company not accessible by the general public and significantly less regulated than a mutual fund.

Extensive information about hedge funds is available on the Internet. Try Canadian-hedge watch www.canadian-hedgewatch.com and Hedge World at www.hedgeworld.com

Hedge fund fees Hedge funds typically have a special fee structure, where, in addition to a general management fee of one to two percent of fund assets, the manager is paid a special performance fee. This special performance fee is often in the range from 20 to 40 percent of profits realized by the fund's investment strategy. A modest fee structure might be one that charges an annual management fee of 1 percent of the fund's assets plus 20 percent of any profits realized; however, more elaborate fee structures are common.

Hedge fund styles Worldwide there are thousands of hedge funds, and the number keeps growing. Big hedge funds may require a minimum investment of $1 million or more. Small hedge funds may only require a minimum investment of $50,000 or less. Whether large or small, each fund develops its own investment style or niche.

For example, a hedge fund may focus on a particular sector, like technology, or a particular global region, like Asia or Eastern Europe. Alternatively, a hedge fund may pursue a particular investment strategy, like the "market neutral strategy" in which the fund maintains a portfolio approximately equally split between long and short positions. By being long in some securities and short in others, the portfolio is hedged against market risk and hence the term "market neutral." Incidentally, this is often thought to be the source of the term "hedge fund," originally referring to funds that were hedged against market risk. Today, however, the term hedge fund refers to any unregistered fund pursuing any type of investment style.

Information about starting your own hedge fund is available at Blumont Capital Hedge Funds www.blumontcapital.com

Starting your own hedge fund Ever dreamed about becoming an investment portfolio manager? You can by starting your own hedge fund. It may be easier than you think. A hedge fund is typically structured as a limited partnership in which the manager is a general partner and the investors are limited partners. Rather than stumble through the legal details, we simply advise that you will need the services of a lawyer familiar with investment companies, but the bottom line is that it's not difficult to do. Actually, the hardest part about setting up your own hedge fund is finding willing investors. Essentially, you need to find well-to-do individuals who have faith in your investment ideas. Getting a grade of "A" from your investments course could be a helpful step.

CHECK THIS ✓

5.7a What is a closed-end fund and how does it differ from a mutual fund?

5.7b What is meant by the Net Asset Value (NAV) of a closed-end fund?

5.7c What is a hedge fund? What are the important differences between a hedge fund and a mutual fund?

5.7d What is a market neutral investment strategy? Why is this strategy available to hedge funds but not to mutual funds?

5.8 Registered Retirement Savings Plan (RRSP)

In this part of the chapter we will examine Registered Retirement Savings Plans (RRSP). Every year more and more Canadians choose to invest in registered retirement savings plans as part of their long-term investment portfolios. Although RRSPs can be invested in individual securities or portfolios designed by individual investors, many investors prefer to invest in mutual funds offered by investment brokerage houses or banks.

Got Some RRSP Room? A Loan can Mean a Bigger Pot in the Golden Years

Okay, we all make questionable judgment calls sometimes. Consider Barry Cooper, a former narcotics officer in Texas, who arrested more than 800 drug criminals and has released his new DVD *Never Get Busted Again*. And we remember former chairman of the Canadian Broadcasting Corp., Guy Fournier, who resigned after making comments last year about the joys of bowel movements.

Some things deserve a little more thinking before acting. This applies to your personal finances as well. Registered retirement savings plan season is upon us, and before you decide to pass on the opportunity to contribute to your plan this year because you simply don't have the cash, consider borrowing to contribute instead. It's a questionable judgment call to delay saving for retirement.

The Facts

Canadians have been accumulating RRSP contribution room since 1991. It's not uncommon today to meet someone who has well over $50,000 of unused RRSP room. This unused contribution room can be carried forward indefinitely, it becomes increasingly difficult to make up that room as you fail to make RRSP contributions.

And don't forget, tax laws can change. I'm not going to suggest that the government will soon do away with RRSP carry-forwards, but it's not inconceivable that a cap could be placed on the amount of room accumulating if the government ever feels overexposed to potential RRSP deductions in the hands of Canadians.

Time is also a critical factor when saving for retirement. The longer your money grows, the more you'll have later. So, it's good sense to use up your RRSP contribution room sooner than later.

The Math

Let's suppose that you have a little over $20,000 of unused RRSP contribution room, but haven't got the cash to contribute. Also, let's assume you have $400 a month you can devote to your retirement savings. Consider two options: (1) Contribute $400 monthly to your RRSP for the next five years, or (2) take out a five-year $20,000 loan to contribute to your RRSP today.

You can generally get an RRSP loan at prime rate—currently 6 percent—if the term is a year or less and you're a good customer. For longer-term loans—say, five years—you can generally get prime rate if it's a variable-rate loan.

In our example, contributing $400 monthly to your RRSP will provide RRSP assets at the end of five years worth $28,160, assuming an 8-percent return annually. Add to this $13,066 in tax savings from the RRSP deductions, and growth on the tax savings, for a total value of $41,226 at the end of five years.

If, instead, you use the $400 to make the payment on a loan, at 6 percent, from your financial institution, you'd be able to borrow $20,690 to contribute this year to your RRSP. You'd have $30,401 in the RRSP at the end of five years, assuming the same 8-percent return, plus $14,106 in tax savings (including the growth on those tax savings), for a total value of $44,507 at the end of five years.

Even though you can't deduct the loan interest, you're better off by $3,281 at the end of five years by borrowing up front rather than contributing each month in my example. It's also easier for most to be disciplined to make monthly loan payments than it is to contribute $400 monthly over a five-year period. The $3,281 benefit of borrowing in this example widens to over $15,000 after a 25-year period. So, speak to your financial institution about loans available.

Tim Cestnick is managing director at WaterStreet Group Inc. and author of 101 Tax Secrets for Canadians, among other titles.

The registered retirement savings plan is, as its name suggests, a retirement plan. Investors can open an RRSP account and contribute throughout the year. All contributions are tax deductible; thus, investors can use their contributions to these plans to reduce their income taxes. As long as their savings stay in the plan, investors do not pay tax. Once they withdraw their money, however, they do pay tax.

RRSP funds can be invested in stocks, bonds, and mutual funds. The article above explains that Canadian investors choose mutual funds as the most popular RRSP investment option. You can get more information on registered retirement plans by studying books and websites on personal finance. For the different types of RRSP-eligible mutual funds, check the websites of banks and mutual fund companies.

Top up the RRSP or Pay Down Debt? Most Canadians Just Don't Get it

INVESTMENT UPDATES

In a country where RRSPs are as sacred as hockey and maple syrup, David Trahair is something of a heretic.

"I stopped making RRSP contributions three or four years ago," the Toronto chartered accountant says. Excuse me? You stopped contributing to a registered retirement savings plan? Did you stop eating fibre, too, and exercising regularly?

Are you feeling okay?

Mr. Trahair, 48, is feeling fine. But a few years ago the author of *Smoke and Mirrors: Financial Myths that will Ruin Your Retirement Dreams* felt like he'd been kicked in the stomach. It happened when he sat down to figure out the rate of return on his RRSP. When he looked at the numbers, his jaw dropped.

"It was pathetic. It was about 3 per cent a year," he says. And no wonder: His portfolio was stuffed with fee-laden mutual funds and labour-sponsored investments that lined his financial adviser's pockets but dragged down his returns. That's when he started thinking that maybe contributing to an RRSP wasn't the magic bullet the financial industry made it out to be.

After crunching some numbers, he overhauled his retirement strategy. Now, instead of making RRSP contributions, he uses extra cash to pay down his mortgage. RRSPs have their place, he says. But most Canadians—particularly those with mortgages, car loans and hefty credit card balances—are better off eliminating household debts before putting a penny into an RRSP.

Why? Because paying down debt, unlike investing in the stock market, provides a guaranteed after-tax return.

The financial industry doesn't want people to think that way, of course.

Every year it spends millions on ads to convince consumers that a topped-up RRSP is the surest route to a secure retirement. Buy the right mutual funds and you'll be able to send your kids to university and enjoy the good life.

"Basically they play off people's emotions of fear and greed," Mr. Trahair says. "If you don't [contribute to an RRSP] you're going to be living in a cardboard shack and eating macaroni and cheese three times a day."

That's nonsense, he says. To prove his point, he uses a fictitious couple, Joe and Karen Hart, and examines two scenarios—one in which they dump $4,000 each into their RRSPs every year, and the other in which they use the $8,000 to make an annual lump-sum payment on their $200,000 mortgage.

(His calculations rest on several assumptions: The 20-year mortgage has an average interest rate of 6 percent; the RRSP grows at an average rate of 5 percent; and the tax savings from making RRSP contributions—based on a marginal rate of 31 percent—are reinvested in the RRSP.) The result? After 20 years, the Harts would have come out more than $17,000 ahead by paying off their mortgage first and *then* focusing on RRSP contributions. So much for the idea of contributing early and often to RRSPs. In fact, by making $8,000 lump-sum payments over and above their regular mortgage costs, the Harts would own their home free and clear after less than 11 years.

True, if the RRSP returned more than 5 percent a year, it might make sense to focus on the RRSP instead of whittling down the mortgage. But the beauty of paying down debt is that it's risk-free; one can't say the same of the stock market, particularly when the financial industry is skimming a couple of percentage points off the top of fund returns in the form of fees and commissions.

"There's no way you're going to beat a 20-percent after-tax rate of return which you can get by paying off a credit card," he says.

And yet, every January and February, consumers will rush out to make RRSP payments, even if they're buried in mortgage and personal debts and don't have a clue about the investments they're buying. Some will even borrow more money to max out their contributions, which only compounds the problem.

"The vast majority of Canadians just don't get it," Mr. Trahair says.

You don't have to be one of them.

jheinzl@globeandmail.com
Reprinted with permission from the Globe and Mail.

Investors can make only a limited amount of contributions to RRSP plans each year. The Canada Revenue Agency specifies the amounts for every investor. Also there is a deadline for investors to make their RRSP-eligible contributions. Canadian newspapers publish RRSP supplements every February and analysts and financial advisers recommend the best plans for investors at that time of the year.

Registered retirement savings plans have to follow guidelines set by the government. To learn the restrictions on these plans examine the Canada Revenue Agency's website. You will find two different viewpoints about RRSP investments in the Investment Updates section.

For more information on tax policy regarding RRSPs, check the Canada Revenue Agency website: www.cra-arc.gc.ca/tax/individuals/topics/rrsp

5.9   Income Trusts

We conclude this chapter with a discussion of income trusts. Income trusts started in 1985 with gas and oil company trusts and have become very popular in Canada since that time. Recently, Canadian mutual funds have started to invest heavily (similar to individual investors) in income trusts.

Income trusts are created as asset-holding entities by companies. A trust creates units and offers these units to the public in exchange for money. Trusts can use money collected from unitholders to pay debt and to purchase back the publicly traded shares of the original companies. In Canada income trusts enjoy tax advantages and do not pay corporate taxes.

Income trusts distribute their earnings as cash flows to the unitholders. Cash distributions are taxed differently from dividends. In the 1990s income trusts became very popular among Canadian investors because of tax deduction and tax deferral of cash distributions provided by them.

Income Trusts pay little or no corporate tax, and distribute the majority of their earnings to their unitholders. Because of this tax advantage many investors began to invest in the trusts. This increased demand caused the unit prices to increase further and more and more companies applied to be restructured as income trusts.

On October 31, 2006, the Finance Minister announced that the administration had decided to introduce income trust tax. The tax would be effective immediately for the new income trusts and in 2011 for the pre-existing income trusts. According to the announcement, the effective tax rate on trust distributions would be 34 percent immediately and would fall to 31.5 percent after 2011.

After the announcement, applications to become income trusts decreased. The income trust prices decreased and S&P/TSX fell by 300 points. Some income trusts were acquired by others. Experts think the strong income trusts will survive and continue being viable investment instruments.

You can examine the "Trust Centre" at Globeinvestor's website (www.globeinvestor. com) to find the top 50 income trusts. Enclosed you will find the Income Trust prices and dividend yields, annual high and low prices as reported by the July 7, 2007 *Globe and Mail*.

5.10   Summary and Conclusions

We have covered many aspects of mutual fund investing in this chapter. We have seen that there are thousands of mutual funds and dozens of types. A few of the more important distinctions we made can be summarized as follows:

1. Some funds are open-end and some are closed-end. Open-end funds stand ready to buy or sell shares. Closed-end funds do not; instead, their shares trade on the stock exchanges.

2. Some open-end funds have front-end loads, meaning that there is a fee tacked on to the fund's net asset value when you buy. Other funds are no-load. Various costs and fees exist, including back-end loads and special fees.

3. Funds have very different objectives and, as a result, very different risk and return potentials. Furthermore, funds with similar-sounding objectives can, in fact, be quite different. It is important to consider a fund's actual holdings and investment policies, not just read its stated objective.

4. Mutual fund information is widely available, but performance information should be used with caution. The best performing funds are often the ones with the greatest risks or the ones that just happened to be in the right investment at the right time.

FIGURE 5.7

Income Trust Prices

INCOME TRUST ⌂ .99% OR 1.54 POINTS (WEEK CHANGE)

	157.55	.03	53.96	8.85	177.31	134.95	.99	6.40		
	Close	Friday Net Chg	P/E	Div Yield	52 Wk High	52 Wk Low	Week %Chg	YTD %Chg	Market Cap (billions)	* Sector Influence
ENERGY AND PIPELINES										
Advantage Energy In	14.95	.11	33.22	12.04	19.23	11.46	-.33	20.27	1.72	-.01
AltaGas Income Trus	26.97	.35	13.62	7.56	29.79	21.55	5.72	2.94	1.48	.08
ARC Energy Trust	22.20	-.04	10.18	10.81	31.20	19.05	2.12	-.45	4.57	.09
Baytex Energy Trust	21.25	.01	11.07	10.16	28.66	18.83	-.42	-4.62	1.61	-.01
Bonavista Energy Tr	30.80	-.05	11.04	11.69	38.34	24.52	.65	9.41	2.62	.02
Canadian Oil Sands	31.89	-.41	14.90	5.02	38.75	24.32	-3.19	-2.21	15.28	-.47
Canetic Resources T	17.40	.00	22.60	13.10	23.80	13.70	.46	5.84	3.95	.02
CCS Income Trust	45.50	.05	18.13	4.62	46.12	31.50	-.66	20.53	2.37	-.01
Crescent Point Ener	19.95	.07	6.98	12.03	23.91	15.08	1.63	13.35	2.00	.03
Daylight Resources	10.24	.02	n-a	17.58	14.58	8.74	-.10	.29	.78	-.00
Enerflex Systems	10.58	.27	11.76	9.45	17.08	8.75	.38	-4.25	.49	.00
Enerplus Resources	50.01	-1.30	11.71	10.08	66.00	43.86	-.12	-1.32	6.17	-.01
Fairborne Energy Tr	8.30	.06	9.76	13.01	15.75	7.97	-.12	-20.57	.40	-.00
Focus Energy Trust	17.66	.31	15.91	9.51	25.09	16.00	-.79	-2.86	1.39	-.01
Fort Chicago Energy	10.70	.02	17.83	8.69	12.33	9.50	2.00	-6.71	1.40	.03
Freehold Royalty Tr	15.05	.05	16.01	11.96	23.06	12.43	3.58	1.62	.74	.02
Harvest Energy Trus	33.80	.30	15.58	13.49	34.85	23.20	2.58	28.86	4.40	.11
Inter Pipeline Fund	9.46	.20	15.26	8.88	10.49	7.55	.75	4.65	1.91	.01
Keyera Facilities I	18.48	-.19	15.79	8.12	23.06	15.51	-.32	11.06	1.13	-.00
Mullen Group Income	21.00	-.29	10.99	8.57	28.71	17.00	-1.41	12.36	1.72	-.02
NAL Oil & Gas Trust	13.22	.32	19.73	14.52	21.70	10.86	5.17	7.39	1.04	.05
Paramount Energy Tr	11.05	-.05	n-a	15.20	20.97	8.40	-5.15	-10.89	.95	-.04
Pembina Pipeline In	16.04	-.18	20.30	8.23	18.35	12.88	.50	1.33	2.06	.01
Pengrowth Energy Tr	20.38	-.01	25.80	14.72	27.25	16.81	.54	2.21	4.99	.03
Penn West Energy Tr	35.35	-.14	12.40	11.54	47.77	31.60	-.76	-.62	8.41	-.06
Peyto Energy Trust	18.81	.20	9.60	8.93	26.00	15.36	3.35	6.27	1.99	.05
Precision Drilling	26.59	.35	6.52	5.87	41.80	24.40	2.27	-1.52	3.34	.07
PrimeWest Energy Tr	22.37	.21	12.78	13.41	35.77	19.98	-.09	4.05	2.02	-.00
Progress Energy Tru	13.07	.53	11.27	9.18	17.50	10.60	1.08	3.98	.99	.01
Provident Energy Tr	12.70	-.01	15.68	11.34	14.50	10.05	1.44	-1.09	2.70	.04
Shiningbank Energy	13.80	.15	23.79	13.04	23.30	11.90	.36	7.39	1.19	.00
Trilogy Energy Trus	10.12	.22	10.02	11.86	20.70	8.88	5.31	-11.23	.94	.02
Trinidad Energy Ser	15.13	.14	10.02	9.12	18.38	11.03	.87	9.64	1.27	.01
True Energy Trust	5.85	.02	n-a	16.41	15.64	4.87	1.74	-21.90	.41	.01
Vermilion Energy Tr	36.73	.02	17.24	5.55	37.99	29.56	2.03	4.94	2.41	.05
OTHER BUSINESS										
Aeroplan Income Fun	22.50	.06	53.57	3.73	22.80	12.47	5.98	32.59	4.49	.17
Algonquin Power Inc	8.79	.09	23.76	10.46	10.48	8.25	-.11	-11.48	.64	-.00
Bell Aliant	32.20	.22	24.58	8.76	35.95	26.41	2.71	19.44	4.35	.11
BFI Canada Income F	28.40	.01	39.44	6.40	30.72	22.01	.71	5.58	1.53	.01
CI Financial Income	28.06	.53	15.42	7.70	31.18	22.95	3.54	5.01	7.86	.13
Cineplex Galaxy Inc	17.00	-.06	43.59	7.06	18.40	10.01	-3.41	25.46	.58	-.02
Cinram Internationa	26.06	-.01	23.91	12.47	30.00	19.92	-3.48	13.55	1.52	-.04
CML Healthcare Inco	15.80	.00	13.62	6.58	16.75	10.61	4.22	13.26	1.36	.05
Connors Bros. Incom	11.03	.01	11.03	12.24	12.44	8.88	-2.39	5.05	.56	-.01
Consumers Waterheat	17.15	.29	18.64	7.52	18.25	11.27	3.00	27.79	.85	.02
Davis & Henderson I	19.44	-.01	12.15	8.13	19.80	13.80	.67	25.74	.85	.01
Energy Savings Inco	15.70	.10	17.84	7.39	19.75	11.66	2.61	16.73	1.68	.04
EPCOR Power L.P.	26.27	.02	13.34	9.59	33.74	22.51	-.11	-1.79	1.31	-.00
Fording Canadian Co	35.88	-.18	12.91	7.25	37.01	21.50	2.51	49.19	5.27	.13
GMP Capital Trust	24.50	-.11	11.89	6.12	25.98	17.20	2.73	12.39	1.54	.03
Labrador Iron Ore R	34.90	.05	11.95	4.01	36.23	22.35	5.60	40.73	1.12	.06
Newalta Income Fund	25.69	-.07	13.38	8.64	35.00	22.71	-.04	-8.74	1.03	-.00
North West Company	18.74	-.31	16.30	5.76	20.93	12.25	-.85	20.67	.91	-.01
Northland Power Inc	13.60	.05	21.94	7.94	15.67	11.39	1.64	4.06	.85	.01
Superior Plus Incom	15.73	-.24	n-a	9.92	16.01	9.26	.19	46.87	1.35	.00
TimberWest Forest C	17.90	.04	77.83	6.03	19.65	11.81	-.56	18.78	1.39	-.01
Transalta Power Lp	7.95	.09	19.88	10.00	8.70	6.05	.13	6.43	.60	.00
TransForce Income F	14.69	.24	8.44	10.82	17.99	12.05	-1.61	8.90	1.27	-.02
Westshore Terminals	14.05	.16	15.97	7.12	14.17	9.25	.72	19.17	1.04	.01
Yellow Pages Income	13.89	-.28	15.26	7.85	16.20	11.55	-.07	7.93	7.40	-.00
REAL ESTATE										
Boardwalk REIT	49.29	.19	129.71	3.25	50.95	25.75	1.32	19.38	2.78	.03
Calloway REIT	26.09	.04	96.63	5.75	30.39	23.85	3.78	-5.47	2.36	.06
CAP REIT	19.74	.15	1,974.00	5.47	21.89	16.45	1.02	6.24	1.20	.01
Cdn. Real Estate In	29.70	.16	22.33	4.48	33.78	23.50	1.96	-5.62	1.72	.03
Chartwell Seniors H	15.77	.27	n-a	6.79	17.89	11.50	5.27	13.13	1.18	.07
Cominar REIT	21.65	.02	21.44	5.82	26.04	18.65	.51	-3.78	.81	.00
Dundee REIT	45.07	-.33	118.61	4.88	47.39	28.03	-2.02	16.61	2.20	-.04
Extendicare REIT	16.48	.08	n-a	6.74	19.72	12.65	5.30	13.42	1.16	.05
H&R Real Estate Inv	24.25	.35	29.22	5.65	26.99	20.83	5.71	.66	2.86	.17
S InnVest REIT	12.95	.10	4.68	8.69	14.90	11.25	5.80	-6.16	.72	.04
Legacy Hotels Real	12.10	.07	86.43	2.64	15.00	8.00	1.68	27.64	1.40	.02
Primaris Retail REI	20.05	.05	87.17	5.89	22.23	15.66	2.87	6.20	1.17	.03
RioCan Real Estate	24.93	.28	30.78	5.29	27.34	21.30	5.41	-.87	5.19	.26

REAL WORLD

This chapter covered the essentials of mutual funds. How should you, as an investor or investment manager, put this information to work?

The first thing to do is to start looking at mutual fund prospectuses. These are written to be accessible to novice investors (or, at least, they are *supposed* to be written that way). The best way to begin exploring is to visit websites. Almost any large mutual fund company will have extensive online information available. Links to some of the better known families are available at our Web page. It is important to look at different funds within a given family and also to look across families. Compare growth funds to growth funds, for example. This adventure will give you some of the real-life background you need to select the types of funds most suitable for you or someone else.

Once you have examined prospectuses on different funds, it's time to invest. Beginning with your simulated account, pick a few funds, invest, and observe the outcomes. Open-end mutual funds are probably the place most of you will begin investing real dollars. An initial purchase can be made with a relatively small amount, perhaps $500, and subsequent purchases can be made in amounts of as little as $100 or less.

Most important of all, as we discussed to start the chapter, most employers now provide employees with retirement plans. The way these work is that, typically, your employer will make a contribution to a mutual fund you select (often from a fairly limited set). Your employer may even match, or more than match, a contribution you make. Such plans may be the only retirement benefit offered, but they can be an extraordinary opportunity for those who take full advantage of them by getting the largest possible match and then investing in a suitable fund. It's an important choice, so the more knowledge you have regarding mutual funds, the better your outcome is likely to be.

Key Terms

investment company 127
open-end fund 127
closed-end fund 127
net asset value 128

front-end load 131
turnover 132
money market mutual fund 134
hedge fund 150

Chapter Review Problems and Self-Test

1. **Front-End Loads** The Madura HiGro Fund has a net asset value of $50 per share. It charges a 3 percent load. How much will you pay for 100 shares?

2. **Turnover** The Starks Income Fund's average daily total assets were $100 million for the year just completed. Its stock purchases for the year were $20 million, while its sales were $12.5 million. What was its turnover?

Answers to Self-Test Problems

1. You will pay 100 times the offering price. Since the load is computed as a percentage of the offering price, we can compute the offering price as follows:

$$\text{Net asset value} = (1 - \text{Front-end load}) \times \text{Offering Price}$$

In other words, the NAV is 97 percent of the offering price. Since the NAV is $50, the offering price is $50 / .97 = $51.55. You will pay $5,155 in all, of which $155 is a load.

2. Turnover is the lesser of purchases or sales divided by average daily assets. In this case, sales are smaller at $12.5, so turnover is $12.5 / $100 = .125 times.

Test Your Investment Quotient

1. **Investment Companies** Which of the following statements typically does not characterize the structure of an investment company?

   a. An investment company adopts a corporate form of organization.
   b. An investment company invests a pool of funds belonging to many investors in a portfolio of individual investments.
   c. An investment company receives an annual management fee ranging from 3 to 5 percent of the total value of the fund.
   d. The board of directors of an investment company hires a separate investment management company to manage the portfolio of securities and handle other administrative duties.

2. **Expense Statement** Which of the following is not part of the expense statement?

   a. Shareholder transactions expenses
   b. Shareholder demographic profile
   c. Annual operating expenses
   d. A hypothetical example of expenses

3. **Mutual Fund Investing** Which of the following is the least likely advantage of mutual fund investing?

   a. Diversification
   b. Professional management
   c. Convenience
   d. Mutual fund returns are normally higher than market average returns

4. **Open-End Funds** An open-end mutual fund is owned by which of the following?

   a. An investment company
   b. An investment advisory firm
   c. A "family of funds" mutual fund company
   d. Its shareholders

5. **Closed-End Funds** Which of the following is most true of a closed-end investment company?

   a. The fund's share price is usually greater than net asset value.
   b. The fund's share price is set equal to net asset value.
   c. Fund shares outstanding vary with purchases and redemptions by shareholders.
   d. Fund shares outstanding are fixed at the issue date.

6. **Closed-End Funds** A closed-end fund is owned by which of the following?

   a. An investment company
   b. An investment advisory firm
   c. A "family of funds" mutual fund company
   d. Its shareholders

7. **Investment Advisory Firms** Which of the following is not true about the typical relationship between a mutual fund and an investment advisory firm? The investment advisory firm

   a. Owns the mutual fund.
   b. Manages the mutual fund's assets.
   c. Manages shareholder purchase and redemption operations.
   d. Receives a management fee for services rendered.

8. **Fund Types** Which mutual fund type is most likely to own stocks paying the highest dividend yields?

   a. Capital appreciation fund
   b. Equity income fund
   c. Growth and income fund
   d. Growth fund

9. **Fund Types** Which mutual fund type is most likely to own stocks paying the lowest dividend yields?

   a. Capital appreciation fund
   b. Equity income fund
   c. Growth and income fund
   d. Growth fund

10. **Fund Types** Which mutual fund type will most likely incur the greatest overall risk levels for its investors?

    a. Large-cap index fund
    b. Insured provincial bond fund
    c. Money market mutual fund
    d. Small-cap growth fund

Concept Questions

1. **Fund Ownership** Who actually owns a mutual fund? Who runs it?

2. **Loads** Given that no-load funds are widely available, why would a rational investor pay a front-end load? More generally, why don't fund investors always seek out funds with the lowest loads, management fees, and other fees?

3. **Money Market Funds** Is it true that the NAV of a money market mutual fund never changes? How is this possible?

4. **Money Market Deposit Accounts** What is the difference between a money market deposit account and a money market mutual fund? Which is riskier?

5. **Fund Goals** What is a capital appreciation fund? An equity income fund? Which is likely to be riskier? Why?

6. **Front-End Loads** You are interested in investing in a mutual fund that charges a front-end load of 5 percent. If the length of your investment is one year, would you invest in this fund? Suppose the length of your investment is 20 years? How are the length of your investment and front-end loads related?

7. **Open versus Closed-End Funds** An open-end mutual fund typically keeps a percentage, often around 5 percent, of its assets in cash or liquid money market assets. How does this affect the fund's return in a year in which the market increases in value? How about during a bad year? Closed-end funds do not typically hold cash. What is it about the structure of open-end and closed-end funds that would influence this difference?

8. **Special Fees** What are special fees?

9. **Open versus Closed-End Funds** If you were concerned about the liquidity of mutual funds shares that you held, would you rather hold shares in a closed-end fund or an open-end fund? Why?

10. **Performance** Refer to Figure 5.5. Look at the 5-year performance for the funds listed. Why do you suppose there are so few poor performers? Hint: Think about the hit TV show *Survivor*.

Questions and Problems

www.mcgrawhill.ca/olc/Jordan

Core Questions

1. **Net Asset Value** The World Income Appreciation Fund has current assets with a market value of $4.5 billion and has 130 million shares outstanding. What is the net asset value (NAV) for this mutual fund?

2. **Front-End Loads** Suppose the mutual fund in the previous problem has a current market price quotation of $34.10. Is this a load fund? If so, calculate the front-end load.

3. **Calculating NAV** The Tiki Growth and Equity Fund is a "low-load" fund. The current offer price quotation for this mutual fund is $48.65, and the front-end load is 1.5 percent. What is the NAV? If there are 13.4 million shares outstanding, what is the current market value of assets owned by the Tiki fund?

4. **Money Market Funds** The Hydro Liquid Assets Money Market Mutual Fund has a NAV of $1 per share. During the year, the assets held by this fund appreciated by 4.6 percent. If you had invested $15,000 in this fund at the start of the year, how many shares would you own at the end of the year? What will the NAV of this fund be at the end of the year? Why?

5. **NAV** An open-end mutual fund has the following stocks:

Stock	Shares	Stock Price
A	4,000	$68
B	9,000	32
C	6,500	44
D	8,400	56

If there are 50,000 shares of this mutual fund, what is its NAV?

6. **NAV** Suppose the fund in the previous problem has liabilities of $75,000. What is the NAV of the fund now?

7. **Front-End Load** In the previous problem, assume the fund is sold with a 5 percent front-end load. What is the offering price of the fund?

8. **Turnover** A mutual fund sold $75 million of assets during the year and purchased $68 million in assets. If the average daily assets of the fund was $120 million, what was the fund turnover?

9. **Closed-End Funds** A closed-end fund has total assets of $350 million and liabilities of $800,000. Currently, 20 million shares are outstanding. What is the NAV of the fund? If the shares currently sell for $15.27, what is the premium or discount on the fund?

10. **Mutual Fund Returns** You invested $10,000 in a mutual fund at the beginning of the year when the NAV was $41.86. At the end of the year the fund paid $.34 in short-term distributions and $1.25 in long-term distributions. If the NAV of the fund at the end of the year was $43.51, what was your return for the year?

Intermediate Questions

11. **Calculating Turnover** A sector fund specializing in commercial bank stocks had average daily assets of $2.7 billion during the year. This fund sold $1.45 billion worth of stock during the year, and its turnover ratio was .47. How much stock did this mutual fund purchase during the year?

12. **Calculating Fees** In the previous problem, suppose the annual operating expense ratio for the mutual fund is 1.25 percent, and the management fee is .85 percent. How much money did the fund's management earn during the year? If the fund doesn't charge any 12b-1 fees, how much were miscellaneous and administrative expenses during the year?

13. **Calculating Fees** You purchased 2,000 shares in the New Pacific Growth Fund on January 2, 2006, at an offering price of $41.20 per share. The front-end load for this fund is 5 percent, and the back-end load for redemptions within one year is 2 percent. The underlying assets in this mutual fund appreciate (including reinvested dividends) by 12 percent

during 2006, and you sell back your shares at the end of the year. If the operating expense ratio for the New Pacific Fund is 1.65 percent, what is your total return from this investment? What do you conclude about the impact of fees in evaluating mutual fund performance?

14. **Calculating Fees** Suppose in the previous problem that the mutual fund has no front-end load or back-end load. Further suppose that the operating expense ratio for the fund is .95 percent. What is your return on investment now?

Refer to Figure 5.5 to answer Questions 15–18.

15. **Fund Objectives** Locate the AGF Canada Class. Is it RSP eligible? What is its one-year return? How does this compare to other mutual funds?

16. **Fund Loads** Of the funds listed, what is the highest load?

17. **Fund Costs** Of the funds listed, what types have the lowest costs? The highest?

18. **Purchase Prices** Locate the Apex Canadian Growth fund. If you buy 1,000 shares, what would you pay?

19. **Front-End Loads and Returns** You are considering an investment in a mutual fund with a 5 percent front-end load. Assuming the fund return is 11 percent per year, what is your return in 1 year? 2 years? 5 years? 10 years? 20 years? 50 years? Graph and explain your answers.

20. **Expenses and Returns** You are going to invest in a stock mutual fund with a 5 percent front-end load and a 1.40 percent expense ratio. You also can invest in a money market mutual fund with a 4 percent return and an expense ratio of .20 percent. If you plan to keep your investment for two years, what annual return must the stock mutual fund earn to exceed an investment in the money market fund? What if your investment horizon is 10 years?

21. **Closed-End Funds** The Argentina Fund has $360 million in assets and sells at a 12.8 percent discount to NAV. If the quoted share price for this closed-end fund is $18.43, how many shares are outstanding? If you purchase 1,000 shares of this fund, what will the total shares outstanding be now?

22. **Closed-End Fund Discounts** Suppose you purchase 5,000 shares of a closed-end mutual fund at its initial public offering; the offer price is $25 per share. The offering prospectus discloses that the fund promoter gets an 8 percent fee from the offering. If this fund sells at a 10 percent discount to NAV the day after the initial public offering, what is the value of your investment?

What's on the Web?

1. **Bond Funds** One of the best Internet sites for information on mutual funds is www.morningstar.ca. Go to the website and find the ticker symbol for the BMO Bond Fund. Find all of the following information on the website for this fund: loads, expense ratio, top five holdings, bond quality ratings, the fund's rank in its category for the last seven years, and the Morningstar rating. Next, find out how the Morningstar star ranking system works.

2. **Stock Funds** Go to www.morningstar.ca and find the ticker symbol for a domestic stock fund. Enter the ticker symbol and find the following information for the fund: manager and manager start date, year-to-date return, three-year return, five-year return, front-end or back-end loads, management fees, expense ratio, the top 25 holdings, and the fund address and phone number.

3. **Morningstar Fund Selector** Find the Mutual Fund Selector on the Morningstar website. How many funds fit the following criteria: domestic stock fund, minimum initial purchase equal to or less than $500, expense ratio less than or equal to category average, and turnover less than 75 percent?

CHAPTER 6

The Stock Market

"One of the funny things about the stock market is that every time one man buys, another sells, and both think they are astute."

—William Feather

"If you don't know who you are, the stock market is an expensive place to find out."

—Adam Smith
(pseud. for George J. W. Goodman)

On July 26, 1852, a group of businessmen met to form an "Association of Brokers." Several years later, on October 25, 1861, twenty-four men gathered at the Masonic Hall and passed a resolution which established the Toronto Stock Exchange. In 1977 the Toronto Stock Exchange launched the world's first Computer Assisted Trading System (CATS) and by January 2004 monthly trading had reached over 7.2 billion shares. Meanwhile the Alberta and Vancouver exchanges formed to list west coast stocks, especially mining and petroleum companies. Canada's markets were eventually consolidated in 1999 when the Alberta and Vancouver Exchanges merged to form the Canadian Venture Exchange, which started to list junior Canadian stocks. By 2001, having been acquired by the Toronto Stock Exchange, the west coast exchange was renamed the TSX Venture Exchange. Canada's two major stock exchanges, then, are the Toronto Exchange which trades senior equities and the Venture Exchange which trades junior issues. ■

With this chapter, we begin in earnest our study of stock markets. This chapter presents a "big picture" overview of how a stock market works and how to read and understand stock market information reported in the financial press.

6.1   The Primary and Secondary Stock Markets

primary market
The market in which new securities are originally sold to investors.

secondary market
The market in which previously issued securities trade among investors.

initial public offering (IPO)
An initial public offering occurs when a company offers stock for sale to the public for the first time.

investment banking firm A firm specializing in arranging financing for companies.

underwrite To assume the risk of buying newly issued securities from a company and reselling them to investors.

fixed commitment Underwriting arrangement in which the investment banker guarantees the firm a fixed amount for its securities.

best effort
Arrangement in which the investment banker does not guarantee the firm a fixed amount for its securities.

For more on IPOs, check out Canadian IPO site
ipo.investcom.com

The stock market consists of a **primary market** and a **secondary market**. In the primary, or new-issue market, shares of stock are first brought to the market and sold to investors. In the secondary market, existing shares are traded among investors.

In the primary market, companies issue new securities to raise money. In the secondary market, investors are constantly appraising the values of companies by buying and selling shares previously issued by these companies. We next discuss the operation of the primary market for common stocks, and then we turn our attention to the secondary market for stocks.

The Primary Market for Common Stock

The primary market for common stock is how new securities are first brought to market. It is best known as the market for **initial public offerings (IPOs)**. An IPO occurs when a company offers stock for sale to the public for the first time. Typically, the company is small and growing, and it needs to raise capital for further expansion.

To illustrate how an IPO occurs, suppose that several years ago you started a software company. Your company was initially set up as a privately held corporation with 100,000 shares of stock, all sold for one dollar per share. The reason your company is privately held is that shares were not offered for sale to the general public. Instead, you bought 50,000 shares for yourself and sold the remaining 50,000 shares to a few supportive friends and relatives.

Fortunately, your company has prospered beyond all expectations. However, company growth is now hampered by a lack of capital. At an informal stockholders' meeting, it is agreed to take the company public. Not really knowing how to do this, you consult your accountant, who recommends an **investment banking firm** or an investment dealer in Canada. These firms, among other things, specialize in arranging financing for companies by finding investors to buy newly issued securities.

After lengthy negotiations, including an examination of your company's current financial condition and plans for future growth, your investment banker suggests an issue of 4 million shares of common stock. Two million shares will be distributed to the original stockholders (you and your original investors) in exchange for their old shares. These 2 million shares distributed to the original stockholders ensure that effective control of the corporation will remain in their hands.

After much haggling, your investment banker agrees to **underwrite** the stock issue by purchasing the other 2 million shares from your company for $10 per share. The net effect of this transaction is that you have sold half the company to the underwriter for $20 million. The proceeds from the sale will allow your company to construct its own headquarters building and double its staff of programmers and sales consultants.

Your investment banker will not keep the 2 million shares but instead will resell them in the primary market. She thinks the stock can probably be sold for $12 per share in an IPO. The difference between the $12 the underwriter sells the stock for and the $10 per share you received is called the *underwriter spread* and is a basic part of the underwriter's compensation.

This agreement, under which the underwriter pays the firm a fixed amount, is called a **fixed commitment**. With a fixed (or firm) commitment, the underwriter assumes the risk that investors cannot be persuaded to buy the stock at a price above $10 per share. The other major type of arrangement, called a **best effort**, is just that. Here, the investment banker devotes a best effort to sell as many shares of the issue as possible at the stated fixed offering price. Strictly speaking, a best-effort arrangement is therefore *not* underwritten, but the phrase "best-effort underwriting" is often used nonetheless. Fixed commitment is, by far, the more common type.

As is common with an IPO, some restrictions are imposed on you as part of the underwriting contract. Most important, you and the other original stockholders agree not to sell any of your personal stockholdings for six months after the underwriting. This ties most of your wealth to the company's success and makes selling the stock to investors a more credible undertaking by the underwriter. Essentially, investors are assured that you will be working hard to expand the company and increase its earnings.

After the underwriting terms are decided, much of your time will be devoted to the mechanics of the offering. In particular, before shares can be sold to the public, the issue must obtain an approved registration with the **Ontario Securities Commission (OSC)**. The OSC is the provincial regulatory agency charged with regulating Toronto Stock Exchange listed securities. In Canada there are security exchange commissions in different provinces. Companies must get permission from these commissions as well as the OSC before they sell their securities.

OSC regulations governing IPOs are especially strict. To gain OSC approval, you must prepare a **prospectus**, normally with the help of outside accounting, auditing, and legal experts. The prospectus contains a detailed account of your company's financial position, its operations, and investment plans for the future. Once the prospectus is prepared, it is submitted to the OSC for approval. The OSC makes no judgement about the quality of your company or the value of your stock. Instead, it only checks to make sure that various rules regarding full disclosure and other issues have been satisfied.

While awaiting OSC approval, your investment banker will circulate a preliminary prospectus among investors to generate interest in the stock offering. This document is commonly called a **red herring** because the cover page is stamped in red ink, indicating that final approval for the stock issue has not yet been obtained. The preliminary prospectus is essentially complete except for the final offering price and a few other pieces of information. These are not set because market conditions might change while OSC approval is being sought. Upon obtaining OSC approval, the prospectus will be updated and completed, and your underwriter can begin selling your company's shares to investors.

To publicize an offering, the underwriter will usually place announcements in newspapers and other outlets. Because of their appearance, these announcements are known as *tombstones*, and they are a familiar sight in the financial press.

Figure 6.1 shows a preliminary short-form prospectus of Glencairn Gold Corporation. The short-form prospectus states the name of the company, some information about the issue being sold and the underwriters for the issue. All but very small issues generally involve more than one underwriter. This form shows that Glencairn Gold Corporation seeks to qualify the distribution of 13,700,000 units at a price of $0.73 per unit. Each unit consists of one common share and a one-half of one common share purchase warrant of the corporation. The underwriters are Orion Securities Inc., McFarlane Gordon Inc., RBC Dominion Securities, and Desjardins Securities Inc.

Initial public stock offerings vary in size a great deal. The 2 million share issue for your hypothetical software company discussed above is a fairly small issue. One of the largest initial public offerings in Canada was of Sun Life Financial Services in 2000. The offering raised $2.0 billion. On the other hand, the largest public offering in Canada was the government's sale of Petro-Canada shares in 2004. The offering raised $3.2 billion.

Ontario Securities Commission (OSC) The provincial regulatory agency charged with regulating Toronto Stock Exchange listed securities and the companies.

prospectus Document prepared as part of a security offering detailing a company's financial position, its operations, and investment plans for the future.

red herring A preliminary prospectus not yet approved by the Ontario Securities Commission.

FIGURE 6.1   **Short-Form Prospectus**

PRELIMINARY SHORT FORM PROSPECTUS

New Issue   November 22, 2004

GLENCAIRN GOLD CORPORATION
Cdn$10,001,000
13,700,000 Units

This short form prospectus is being filed to qualify the distribution (the "Offering") of 13,700,000 units (the "Units") of Glencairn Gold Corporation ("Glencairn" or the "Corporation") at a price of Cdn$0.73 per Unit (the "Offering Price"), each Unit consisting of one common share (a "Common Share") of the Corporation and one-half of one Common Share purchase warrant of the Corporation. Each whole Common Share purchase warrant (a "Warrant") will entitle the holder to purchase one Common Share at a price of Cdn$1.25 at any time before 5:00 p.m. (Toronto time) on November 26, 2008. The Units will be issued pursuant to an underwriting agreement (the "Underwriting Agreement") dated as of November 22, 2004 between Glencairn and Orion Securities Inc., McFarlane Gordon Inc., RBC Dominion Securities Inc. and Desjardins Securities Inc. (collectively, the "Underwriters"). The Offering Price has been determined by negotiation between the Corporation and the Underwriters. The distribution of the Common Shares and Warrants comprising the Units is qualified hereunder.

The outstanding Common Shares and Warrants are listed and posted for trading on the Toronto Stock Exchange (the "TSX") under the symbol "GGG" and "GGG.WT", respectively. On November 19, 2004, the last trading day prior to the date of this short form prospectus, the closing price of the Common Shares and the Warrants on the TSX was Cdn$0.67 and Cdn$0.25, respectively. The Corporation has applied to list the Common Shares and Warrants distributed under this short form prospectus and the Common Shares issuable upon exercise of the Warrants on the TSX. Listing will be subject to the Corporation fulfilling all of the listing requirements of the TSX.

Price: Cdn$0.73 per Unit

	Price to the Public[1]	Underwriters' Fee[2]	Net Proceeds to the Corporation[3]
Per Unit	Cdn$0.73	Cdn$0.0438	Cdn$0.6862
Total	Cdn$10,001,000	Cdn$600,060	Cdn$9,400,940

(1) Of the Offering Price, the Corporation will allocate Cdn$0.62 to each Common Share and Cdn$0.11 to each one-half of one Warrant comprising the Units.

(2) In consideration for the services rendered by the Underwriters in connection with the Offering, the Corporation has agreed to pay the Underwriters a fee of Cdn$600,060, representing 6% of the gross proceeds of the Offering.

(3) After deducting the Underwriters' fee, but before deducting expenses of the Offering, including the preparation and filing of this short form prospectus, which are estimated to be Cdn$300,000 and which will be paid from the general funds of the Corporation.

An investment in the Units is subject to certain risks. Prospective investors should carefully consider the risk factors described in this short form propectus under "Risk Factors".

The Underwriters, as principals, conditionally offer the Units, subject to prior sale, if, as and when issued by the Corporation and accepted by the Underwriters in accordance with the conditions contained in the Underwriting Agreement referred to under "Plan of Distribution", subject to the approval of certain legal matters on behalf of the Corporation by Cassels Brock & Blackwell LLP and on behalf of the Underwriters by Wildeboer Dellelce LLP. Subscriptions will be received subject to rejection in whole or in part and the right is reserved to close the subscription books at any time without notice. It is expected that certificates evidencing the Common Shares and the Warrants will be available for delivery at the closing of the Offering, which is expected to take place on or about December 9, 2004, or such other date as may be agreed upon by the Corporation and the Underwriters.

The Underwriters may effect transactions intended to stabilize or maintain the market price for the Common Shares or the Warrants at levels above which might otherwise prevail in the open market. See "Plan of Distribution".

All monetary amounts used herein are stated in United States dollars, unless otherwise indicated. On November 19, 2004, the closing exchange rate for Canadian dollars in terms of the United States dollar, as quoted by the Bank of Canada, was US$1.00=Cdn$1.1930 or Cdn$1.00=US$0.8382. On November 19, 2004, the closing afternoon fixing gold price in United States dollars per troy ounce, as quoted on the London Bullion Market, was $446.

Courtesy of Glencairn Gold Corporation.

The Secondary Market for Common Stock

In the secondary market for common stock, investors buy and sell shares with other investors. If you think of the primary market as the new-car showroom at an automotive dealer, where cars are first sold to the public, then the secondary market is just the used-car lot.

Secondary market stock trading among investors is directed through three channels. An investor may trade:

1. Directly with other investors.
2. Indirectly through a broker who arranges transactions for others.
3. Directly with a dealer who buys and sells securities from inventory.

As we discussed before for individual investors, almost all common stock transactions are made through a broker. However, large institutional investors, such as pension funds and mutual funds, trade through both brokers and dealers, and also trade directly with other institutional investors.

Dealers and Brokers

Since most securities transactions involve dealers and brokers, it is important that you understand exactly what these terms mean. A **dealer** maintains an inventory and stands ready to buy and sell at any time. By contrast, a **broker** brings buyers and sellers together but does not maintain an inventory. Thus, when we speak of used-car dealers and real estate brokers, we recognize that the used-car dealer maintains an inventory, whereas the real estate broker normally does not.

In the securities markets, a dealer stands ready to buy securities from investors wishing to sell them and sell securities to investors wishing to buy them. An important part of the dealer function involves maintaining an inventory to accommodate temporary buy and sell order imbalances. The price a dealer is willing to pay is called the **bid price**. The price at which a dealer will sell is called the **ask price** (sometimes called the offer or offering price). The difference between the bid and ask prices is called the **spread**.

A dealer attempts to profit by selling securities at a higher price than the average price paid for them. Of course, this is a goal for all investors, but the distinguishing characteristic of securities dealers is that they hold securities in inventory only until the first opportunity to resell them. Essentially, trading from inventory is their business.

Dealers exist in all areas of the economy, of course, not just in the stock markets. For example, your local university bookstore is both a primary and secondary market textbook dealer. If you buy a new book, then this is a primary market transaction. If you buy a used book, this is a secondary market transaction, and you pay the store's ask price. If you sell the book back, you receive the store's bid price, often half the ask price. The bookstore's spread is the difference between the bid and ask prices.

In contrast, a securities broker arranges transactions between investors, matching investors wishing to buy securities with investors wishing to sell securities. Brokers may match investors with other investors, investors with dealers, and sometimes even dealers with dealers. The distinctive characteristic of securities brokers is that they do not buy or sell securities for their own account. Facilitating trades by others is their business.

Most common stock trading is directed through an organized stock exchange or a trading network. Whether a stock exchange or a trading network, the goal is to match investors wishing to buy stocks with investors wishing to sell stocks. The largest,

dealer A trader who buys and sells securities from inventory.

broker An intermediary who arranges security transactions among investors.

bid price The price a dealer is willing to pay.

ask price The price at which a dealer is willing to sell. Also called the offer or offering price.

spread The difference between the bid and ask prices.

most active organized stock exchange in the world is the New York Stock Exchange (NYSE). The Toronto Stock Exchange (TSX) is one of the leading North American stock exchanges and it is the largest stock exchange in Canada. The major competitor to the organized stock exchanges is the vast trading network known as Nasdaq. Examine Figure 6.2 to find out the market capitalization of the world equity markets in the last decade. We next discuss the organization of the NYSE, and then examine that of the TSX and Nasdaq.

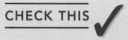

CHECK THIS ✓

6.1a   Is an IPO a primary or secondary market transaction?

6.1b   Which is bigger, the bid price or the ask price? Why?

6.1c   What is the difference between a securities broker and a securities dealer?

6.2   The New York Stock Exchange

The New York Stock Exchange (NYSE, pronounced "Ny-see"), popularly known as the Big Board, celebrated its bicentennial in 1992. It has occupied its current building on Wall Street since the turn of the century. The New York Stock Exchange has operated as a for-profit organization since 2007. On April 4, 2007, the New York Stock Exchange and Euronext announced their merger and thus the creation of the NYSE Euronext group. NYSE Euronext currently operates various equity and derivatives exchanges as well as New York Stock Exchange LLC, a limited liability company.

NYSE-Listed Stocks

For up-to-date info on the NYSE, hit
www.nyse.com

A company is said to be "listed" on the NYSE if its stock is traded there. In 2007, stocks from about 2,300 companies were listed on the "Big Board," with a market value of about $16 trillion. This total includes many large companies so well known that we easily recognize them by their initials—for example, IBM, AT&T, GE, and GM. This total also includes many companies that are not so readily recognized. For example, relatively few would instantly recognize AEP as American Electric Power, but AEX might be recognized as American Express.

The NYSE has minimum requirements for companies wishing to apply for listing on the Big Board. Although the requirements might change from time to time, some example minimum requirements in effect in 2007 included:

1. The company's total number of shareholders must be at least 2,200, and stock trading in the previous six months must have been at least 100,000 shares a month on average.

2. At least 1.1 million stock shares must be held in public hands.

3. Publicly held shares must have at least $100 million in market value ($60 million for IPOs).

4. The company must have annual earnings of $10 million before taxes in the most recent year and $2 million pretax earnings in each of the preceding two years.

In practice, most companies with stock listed on the NYSE easily exceed these minimum listing requirements.

FIGURE 6.2   Market Capitalization of the World Stock Markets

(Market value excludes investment funds)

Exchange	2007						% Change / Jun. 06 (in USD)	% Change / Jun. 06 (in local cur.)
	January	February	March	April	May	June		
Americas								
American SE	281 321,0	280 657,0	281 481,0	284 397,0	284 276,0	284 582,0	5,2%	5,2%
Bermuda SE	2 759,3	2 777,9	2 779,3	2 844,8	2 863,7	2 857,8	17,3%	17,3%
Buenos Aires SE	52 699,3	51 590,3	51 473,5	53 397,6	56 867,2	56 800,8	35,8%	36,0%
Colombia SE	55 769,6	54 910,6	57 920,7	59 504,0	64 186,3	65 011,2	64,1%	24,4%
Lima SE	42 297,2	45 820,9	51 815,1	61 290,3	60 376,5	64 810,9	109,8%	104,1%
Mexican Exchange	356 051,2	343 098,1	373 698,5	385 177,6	424 729,6	422 300,6	72,5%	65,0%
Nasdaq	3 946 426,8	4 014 721,8	3 906 898,8	4 060 657,1	4 163 091,9	4 182 155,2	18,1%	18,1%
NYSE Group	15 549 020,7	15 922 158,2	15 467 745,0	16 111 659,2	16 492 448,9	16 603 601,2	19,1%	19,1%
Santiago SE	177 084,8	179 092,1	184 756,4	201 562,5	203 735,7	214 515,4	55,7%	51,9%
Sao Paulo SE	740 279,2	725 282,3	784 389,9	845 178,7	980 908,5	1 007 839,9	72,5%	53,5%
TSX Group [1]	1 675 553,7	1 699 555,1	1 749 649,8	1 823 352,2	1 985 344,0	1 980 838,5	21,3%	16,0%
Asia - Pacific								
Australian SE	1 100 030,2	1 124 238,4	1 200 715,7	1 282 270,6	1 324 541,1	1 355 556,1	51,1%	32,3%
Bombay SE	856 792,7	787 455,2	815 608,2	931 695,6	1 005 441,5	1 023 454,0	73,1%	53,2%
Bursa Malaysia	257 388,5	262 648,6	278 044,7	301 014,8	304 646,4	306 960,0	59,2%	49,6%
Colombo SE	8 375,2	8 529,5	7 974,9	8 045,9	7 259,3	7 437,9	19,8%	28,4%
Hong Kong Exchanges	1 709 108,3	1 692 266,7	1 734 117,4	1 821 416,6	1 918 475,6	2 027 997,7	60,1%	61,1%
Jakarta SE	135 153,4	132 751,5	140 288,1	153 645,2	163 595,2	166 685,1	71,4%	67,1%
Korea Exchange [2]	787 131,8	815 061,9	842 443,4	904 577,8	1 000 513,1	1 042 158,6	42,4%	38,6%
National Stock Exchange India	809 585,7	744 060,2	774 726,8	888 383,5	961 894,7	976 829,1	78,1%	57,6%
New Zealand Exchange	44 377,4	44 180,7	46 502,7	49 256,6	50 751,3	51 991,1	48,8%	17,5%
Osaka SE	189 071,4	190 027,9	205 097,5	188 376,1	188 333,4	191 644,2	8,8%	17,6%
Philippine SE	74 515,5	73 448,4	76 710,7	79 430,2	88 255,0	94 117,3	112,1%	84,7%
Shanghai SE	1 084 222,0	1 142 917,6	1 297 377,9	1 613 413,5	1 792 223,0	1 693 017,3	335,2%	314,5%
Shenzhen SE	277 865,0	314 133,5	358 896,9	472 922,9	531 989,4	490 463,9	199,2%	184,9%
Singapore Exchange [3]	411 558,8	413 250,5	435 974,5	465 039,6	481 880,6	505 588,6	71,5%	65,9%
Taiwan SE Corp.	578 411,6	594 032,2	589 475,5	585 089,9	610 443,2	668 969,8	32,2%	34,2%
Thailand SE	140 312,1	151 523,9	144 812,4	151 295,4	161 146,8	172 652,0	33,6%	20,9%
Tokyo SE	4 645 319,2	4 893 101,1	4 737 540,4	4 653 107,0	4 679 155,4	4 681 045,7	3,5%	11,8%
Europe - Africa - Middle East								
Athens Exchange	210 173,4	204 073,4	209 211,6	218 037,4	224 195,8	232 665,5	41,1%	33,6%
BME Spanish Exchanges	1 345 061,3	1 332 188,3	1 393 605,6	1 432 074,2	1 515 208,8	1 519 587,6	36,8%	29,5%
Borsa Italiana	1 035 028,3	1 032 398,8	1 066 187,7	1 146 797,4	1 122 939,5	1 099 723,3	22,6%	16,1%
Budapest SE	38 956,8	39 134,1	39 837,0	44 520,8	44 195,2	50 626,6	59,6%	31,0%
Cairo & Alexandria SEs	88 468,8	94 370,2	96 193,1	97 828,8	104 591,0	105 722,6	61,4%	59,6%
Cyprus SE	21 766,0	21 504,3	21 774,5	23 894,2	25 256,2	26 322,1	157,5%	143,8%
Deutsche Börse	1 659 669,6	1 676 445,6	1 756 025,3	1 904 926,1	1 973 227,4	1 956 078,6	42,6%	35,0%
Euronext	3 668 161,4	3 692 137,8	3 882 199,1	4 155 997,5	4 199 679,3	4 240 062,1	33,5%	26,4%
Irish SE	157 526,5	164 229,7	170 928,3	176 954,9	180 967,9	174 357,6	38,4%	31,0%
Istanbul SE	173 037,7	173 223,3	185 364,3	196 591,6	218 633,7	221 282,4	74,7%	43,6%
JSE [4]	715 559,6	716 355,9	793 318,8	806 690,5	802 390,6	795 970,1	32,7%	31,2%
Ljubljana SE	16 991,3	16 672,6	17 823,1	20 273,0	21 502,1	23 801,3	145,5%	132,4%
London SE	3 758 823,1	3 744 426,3	3 842 567,0	3 969 311,8	4 023 059,3	4 036 985,8	20,6%	11,2%
Luxembourg SE	80 140,4	85 685,6	91 205,6	95 757,3	96 061,3	96 863,2	47,9%	40,0%
Malta SE	4 598,8	4 498,8	4 512,8	4 786,4	4 575,9	5 136,5	6,4%	0,7%
Mauritius SE [5]	5 024,6	5 214,8	5 408,4	5 587,1	5 531,9	5 780,6	112,4%	115,4%
OMX Nordic Exchange [6]	1 152 662,6	1 139 082,0	1 194 433,7	1 288 602,1	1 295 984,0	1 289 738,3	46,9%	39,1%
Oslo Bors	292 184,3	284 257,1	300 797,1	318 863,3	320 754,8	339 723,5	39,7%	32,6%
Swiss Exchange	1 232 552,7	1 221 588,4	1 258 552,9	1 341 763,1	1 318 455,5	1 290 048,0	23,8%	23,9%
Tehran SE	37 684,0	38 248,7	41 356,7	41 883,4	38 949,2	38 272,6	12,0%	13,2%
Tel Aviv SE	170 029,9	175 323,7	182 274,5	199 419,5	206 606,7	202 742,4	55,7%	49,1%
Warsaw SE	157 262,4	153 684,9	175 908,5	191 691,7	199 296,6	211 936,2	99,1%	74,0%
Wiener Börse	197 667,1	194 428,3	206 868,3	218 134,6	223 903,2	224 034,3	43,5%	35,8%
Total [7]	51 208 855,1	51 978 376,6	52 555 445,8	55 261 629,2	57 005 110,9	57 360 869,7		

[1] TSX Group also includes TSX Venture market cap
[2] Korea Exchange includes Kosdaq market data
[3] Include Singapore-incorporated companies, foreign-incorporated companies with a primary listing, and foreign-incorporated companies with a secondary listing but with the majority of their trading taking place on SGX
[4] JSE's figures include the market capitalization of all listed companies, but exclude listed warrants, convertibles and investment funds
[5] From Aug. 2006, data includes Development & Enterprise Market
[6] OMX includes Copenhagen, Helsinki, Iceland, Stockholm, Tallinn, Riga and Vilnius Stock Exchanges
[7] Total excludes Osaka and National Stock Exchange of India to avoid double counting with Tokyo and Bombay SE respectively
NA : Not Available
Source : World Federation of Exchanges members

Source: World Federation of Exchanges.

6.3   The Toronto Stock Exchange and TSX Venture Exchange

The Toronto Stock Exchange (TSX), unlike the NYSE, is a computerized exchange. In 2002, the Toronto Stock Exchange celebrated its 150th birthday having started its operations in 1861 with 18 securities and 14 member firms. In 1861, approximately twenty-five businessmen decided to form a stock exchange in Toronto in their meeting at Toronto's Masonic Temple. At that time, members paid $250 to purchase a seat. In 1901, the price of membership had risen to $12,000 and trading volume became approximately 1 million shares per year. The stock exchange stopped its operations in 1914 for a period, because of the First World War. Immediately afterwards, the administration issued bonds to sponsor the ongoing war and opened the exchange one more time. The Toronto Stock Exchange experienced solid growth and became the third largest North American exchange in the 1940s. By 1955 a membership seat cost $100,000 and trading volume reached 1 billion shares. In 1977, the Toronto Stock Exchange introduced the world's first Computer Assisted Trading System (CATS) and closed its trading floor to become the largest electronic North American Exchange.

The Toronto Stock Exchange, with Canadian exchange restructuring in 1999, became the major stock exchange for trading senior equities. Canadian derivatives trading were transferred to the Montreal Exchange. The Vancouver and Alberta Exchanges merged to become the Canadian Venture Exchange (CDNX). Later the TSX purchased the CDNX and called it the TSX Venture Exchange. The Winnipeg Exchange continued its operations as the major Canadian commodity exchange.

Today the TSX has over 100 participating organizations and member firms. These organizations help companies in underwriting their new issues, in listing and in providing corporate financial services. Different customer orders (market, limit or stop orders) are entered into the system by these organizations.

The majority of investors give market orders when they want to buy or sell stocks. A market order is a customer order asking to buy or sell a certain amount of securities at the current market price. When the order is entered, the exchange will execute it immediately. For example if you give an order to buy 100 shares of Nortel Stock traded at the TSX at the market price, you have to choose the market order section for buying 100 shares.

In contrast to a **market order**, in a **limit order** the customer specifies a maximum price he or she is willing to pay for the security in the case of a buy order, or a minimum price he or she is willing to accept in the case of a sell order.

A **stop order** may appear similar to a limit order, but there is an important difference. With a stop order, the customer specifies a "stop" price. This stop price serves as a trigger point. No trade can occur until the stock price reaches this stop price. When the stock price reaches the stop price, the stop order is immediately converted into a market order. Since the order is now a market order, the customer may get a price that is better or worse than the stop price. Thus, the stop price only serves as a trigger point for conversion into a market order. Unlike a limit price, the stop price places no limit on the price at which a trade can occur. Once converted to a market order, the trade is executed just like any other market order.

The most common type of stop order is a *stop-sell* order, which is an order to sell shares if the stock price falls to a specified stop price below the current stock price. This type of order is generally called a *stop-loss* because it is usually intended to limit losses

market order
A customer order to buy or sell securities marked for immediate execution at the current market price.

limit order
A customer order to buy or sell securities with a specified "limit" price. The order can be executed only at the limit price or better.

stop order Customer order to buy or sell securities when a preset "stop" price is reached.

WORK THE WEB

Below is an online equity quote for Nortel Networks using Scotiabank's online brokerage services.

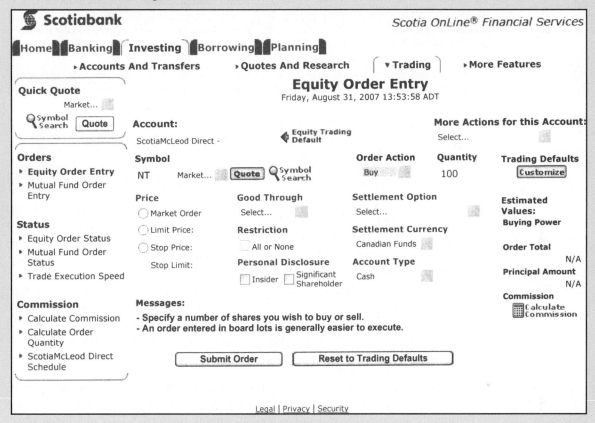

on a long position. The other type is a *stop-buy* order, which is an order to buy shares if the price rises to a specified stop price above the current stock price. Stop-buy orders are often placed in conjunction with short sales, again as means of limiting losses.

Placing stop-loss orders is frequently touted as a smart trading strategy, but there are a couple of issues we should mention. For concreteness, suppose you buy 1,000 shares of GoGo Corp. at $20. You simultaneously place a stop-sell order at $15. Thus you seem to have limited your potential loss to $5 per share.

Unfortunately, after the market closes, a rumor circulates that GoGo has uncovered a significant accounting fraud. The next morning, the stock opens at $8, meaning the first trade occurs at $8 per share. Because this price is below your $15 stop price, a market order to sell your stock will be placed and executed, and you'll lose much more than $5 per share. What you discover is that your stop-loss guarantees only that a market order to sell will be placed as soon as the stock trades at $15 *or below.*

TABLE 6.1	Stock Market Order Types	
Order Type	**Buy**	**Sell**
Market order	Buy at best price available for immediate execution.	Sell at best price available for immediate execution.
Limit order	Buy at best price available, but not more than the preset limit price. Forgo purchase if limit is not met.	Sell at best price available, but not less than the preset limit price. Forgo sale if limit is not met.
Stop order	Convert to a market order to buy when the stock price crosses the stop price from below.	Convert to a market order to sell when the stock price crosses the stop price from above. Also known as a "stop-loss."
Stop-limit order	Convert to a limit order to buy when the stock price crosses the stop price from below.	Convert to a limit order to sell when the stock price crosses the stop price from above.

Adding insult to injury, after your stock is sold, a creditable announcement is made indicating that the rumor is false. GoGo shares promptly bounce back to $20, but you were sold out at a big loss. Thus, a second danger in blindly using stop-loss orders is that volatile conditions can lead to an unfavorable stop sale. Table 6.1 summarizes the characteristics of limit and stop orders.

A limit price can be attached to a stop order to create a *stop-limit order*. This is different from a simple stop order in that once the stock price reaches the preset stop price the order is converted into a limit order. By contrast, a simple stop order is converted into a market order. At this point, the limit order is just like any other limit order. Notice that with a stop-limit order you must specify two prices, the stop and the limit. The two prices can be the same, or they can be different. In our GoGo Corp. example, you could place a stop-limit sell order at $15 stop, $12 limit. This order converts to a limit order to sell at $12 or better if the price ever hits $15 or below. Thus you will never sell below $12. Of course, you may never sell at all unless your limit price is reached! Our nearby *Work the Web* box shows how these orders are entered in an actual online brokerage account.

Another type of order that requires special attention is the *short-sale order*. As explained elsewhere, a short sale involves borrowing stock shares and then selling the borrowed shares in the hope of buying them back later at a lower price. Short-sale loans are normally arranged through the customer's broker. New York Stock Exchange rules require that when shares are sold as part of a short-sale transaction, the order must be marked as a short-sale transaction when it is transmitted to the NYSE floor.

uptick rule Rule for short sales requiring that before a short sale can be executed, the last price change must be an uptick.

Sell orders marked as short sales are subject to the **uptick rule**. According to the uptick rule, a short sale can be executed only if the last price change was an uptick. For example, suppose the last two trades were executed at 55.50 and then 55.63. The last price change was an uptick of .13, and a short sale can be executed at a price of 55.63 or higher. Alternatively, suppose the last two trades were executed at 55.50 and 55.25, where the last price change was a downtick of .25. In this case, a short sale can be executed only at a price higher than 55.25. This rule has been eliminated at the NYSE as of July 2007. In Canada, the uptick rule continues to be applied.

To be listed on the Toronto Stock Exchange, technology companies must have a minimum of one million free shares with total market value of $4 million or

WORK THE WEB

You can actually watch trading take place on the Web by visiting one of the biggest ECNs, INET at www.island.com. (INET used to be called Island.) INET is somewhat unusual in that the "order book," meaning the list of buy and sell orders, is public in real time.

As shown, we have captured a sample of orders for Intel Corporation. On the left-hand side are the buy orders. On the right-hand side are sell orders. All orders are limit orders, and both the limit price and quantity are shown. The inside quotes (the highest bid, or buy, and the lowest ask, or sell, order) in this market are at the top, so we sometimes hear the expression "top of the book" quotes.

If you visit the site, you can see trading take place as limit orders are entered and executed. Notice that on this particular day, by 5:16 P.M., Island had traded more than 21 million shares of Intel. At that time, the inside quotes were a bid price of $23.75 and an ask price of $23.82. In addition to the orders shown, there were also 19 more buy orders and one more sell order.

INET home	System stats	help

inet

INTC

GET STOCK	
INTC	go

☐ Aggregate by price

LAST MATCH		TODAY'S ACTIVITY	
Price	23.7600	Orders	261,945
Time	17:08:09	Volume	21,357,760

BUY ORDERS		SELL ORDERS	
SHARES	PRICE	SHARES	PRICE
752	23.7500	3,750	23.8200
7,000	23.7200	4,000	23.8500
1,000	23.7100	1,000	23.8700
300	23.7000	500	23.8700
2,400	23.6800	1,000	23.8800
2,400	23.6800	100	24.2900
500	23.6800	1,000	24.3500
2,000	23.6700	300	24.4300
2,000	23.6600	500	24.4900
600	23.6600	2,000	24.6800
1,000	23.6500	500	24.7000
2,000	23.6400	300	24.8500
1,000	23.6400	81	26.0000
100	23.6200	100	27.0000
300	23.5700	300	29.9000
(19 more)		(1 more)	

$10 million held by at least 300 public shareholders. There are separate financial criteria for industrial, oil and gas and mining sectors.

Investors can use their brokers or investment dealers to give orders, buy on margin or short sell. In short sales the Toronto Stock exchange applies an uptick rule.

Small and emerging Canadian companies are listed at the TSX Venture Exchange. The majority are mining, oil and technology companies. New companies seeking access to the venture capital marketplace prefer the TSX Venture Exchange. As companies get bigger they apply for listing on senior exchanges.

Companies are listed in three different tiers at the TSX Venture Exchange. Each tier has different listing requirements: (a) initial public offering; (b) reverse takeover; and (c) the Capital Pool Company Program. Currently, there are more than 2,500 companies listed on TSX Venture Exchange.

To get more information on the Toronto Stock Exchange and TSX Venture Exchange, visit www.tsx.com

6.4   Nasdaq

In terms of total dollar volume of trading, the second largest stock market in the world is Nasdaq (say "Naz-dak"). In fact, in terms of companies listed and, on most days recently, number of shares traded, Nasdaq is bigger than the NYSE. The somewhat odd name is derived from the acronym NASDAQ, which stands for National Association of Securities Dealers Automated Quotations system. But Nasdaq is now a name in its own right.

Introduced in 1971, the Nasdaq market is a computer network of securities dealers who disseminate timely security price quotes to Nasdaq subscribers. These dealers act as market makers for securities listed on Nasdaq. As market makers, Nasdaq dealers post bid and ask prices at which they accept sell and buy orders, respectively. With each price quote, they also post the number of stock shares that they obligate themselves to trade at their quoted prices.

Nasdaq's website is www.nasdaq.com Click on "About Nasdaq."

Like NYSE specialists, Nasdaq market makers trade on an inventory basis, using their inventory as a buffer to absorb buy and sell order imbalances. Unlike the NYSE specialist system, Nasdaq features multiple market makers for actively traded stocks. Thus, there are two key differences between the NYSE and Nasdaq:

1. Nasdaq is a computer network and has no physical location where trading takes place.

2. Nasdaq has a multiple market maker system rather than a specialist system.

over-the-counter (OTC) market
Securities market in which trading is almost exclusively done through dealers who buy and sell for their own inventories.

Traditionally, a securities market largely characterized by dealers who buy and sell securities for their own inventories is called an **over-the-counter (OTC) market**. Consequently, Nasdaq is often referred to as an OTC market. However, in their efforts to promote a distinct image, Nasdaq officials prefer that the term OTC not be used when referring to the Nasdaq market. Nevertheless, old habits die hard, and many people still refer to Nasdaq as an OTC market.

By the year 2003, the Nasdaq had grown to the point that it was, by many measures, bigger than the NYSE. For example, in 2001, some 471 billion shares were traded on the Nasdaq versus 308 billion on the NYSE. In dollars, however, based on the total value of listed securities, the NYSE was still a good deal bigger, $15 trillion versus $3 trillion.

The Nasdaq is actually made up of two separate markets, the Nasdaq National Market (NNM) and the Nasdaq SmallCap Market. As the market for Nasdaq's larger and more actively traded securities, the Nasdaq National Market lists about 4,000 securities, including some of the best-known companies in the world. The Nasdaq SmallCap Market is for small companies and lists about 1,000 individual securities. As you might guess, an important difference in the two markets is that the National Market has more stringent listing requirements. Of course, as SmallCap companies become more established, they may move up to the National Market.

As we mentioned previously, the Nasdaq has historically been a dealer market, characterized by competing market makers. In 2003, there were about 500 such market makers, which amounts to about 15 or so per stock. The biggest market makers cover thousands of stocks.

electronic communications network (ECN) A website that allows investors to trade directly with each other.

In a very important development, in the late 1990s, the Nasdaq system was opened to so-called **electronic communications networks (ECNs)**. ECNs are basically websites that allow investors to trade directly with one another. Our nearby *Work the Web* box describes one of the biggest ECNs, Island (www.island.com), and contains important information about ECN "order books." Be sure to read it. In 2003, about 10 ECNs were integrated into the Nasdaq, including Archipelago and Instinet, which are two of the better known.

Investor buy and sell orders placed on ECNs are transmitted to the Nasdaq and displayed along with market maker bid and ask prices. As a result, the ECNs open up the Nasdaq by essentially allowing individual investors to enter orders, not just market makers. As a result, the ECNs act to increase liquidity and competition.

inside quotes Highest bid quotes and the lowest ask quotes offered by dealers for a security.

If you check prices on the Web for Nasdaq-, NYSE, and TSX-listed stocks, you'll notice an interesting difference. For Nasdaq stocks, you can actually see the bid and ask prices as well as recent transactions information. The bid and ask prices for the Nasdaq listings you see represent **inside quotes**, that is, the highest bid and the lowest ask prices. For a relatively small fee (or possibly even free from your broker), you can even have access to "Level II" quotes, which show all of the posted bid and ask prices and, frequently, the identity of the market maker. Of course, NYSE specialists post bid and ask prices as well, they are just not disclosed to the general public (they may be available by subscription at a cost substantially higher than that for Level II Nasdaq quotes).

The success of the Nasdaq National Market as a competitor to NYSE and other organized exchanges can be judged by its ability to attract stock listings by companies that traditionally might have choosen to be listed on the NYSE. Such well-known companies as Microsoft, Apple Computer, Intel, Dell, Yahoo!, and Starbucks list their securities on Nasdaq.

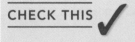
CHECK THIS

6.4a How does Nasdaq differ from the NYSE?

6.4b What are the different levels of access to the Nasdaq network?

6.5   Third and Fourth Market

third market Off-exchange market for securities listed on an organized exchange.

The phrase "**third market**" refers to trading in exchange-listed securities that occurs off the exchange on which the security is listed. For example, a substantial volume of NYSE-listed stock trading is executed through independent securities trading firms.

One well-known example of third-market trading is the securities trading firm of Bernard L. Madoff Investment Securities. Independent trading firms like Madoff Securities lure a large volume of trades away from the New York Stock Exchange by paying a small commission, say, a half-cent per share, to brokerage firms that direct customer orders to them for execution. This practice is called "paying for order flow" and is controversial. Nevertheless, the SEC permits it.

fourth market Market for exchange-listed securities in which investors trade directly with other investors, usually through a computer network.

The term "**fourth market**" refers to direct trading of exchange-listed securities among investors. A good example of fourth-market trading activity is Instinet, an ECN (and one of the oldest) that facilitates trading among its subscribers, particularly after-hours trading. However, as we discussed in our previous section, these fourth-market ECNs are increasingly becoming integrated into the Nasdaq system.

CHECK THIS

6.5a What is the third market for securities?

6.5b What is the fourth market for securities?

6.6   Stock Market Information

Many newspapers publish current price information for a selection of stocks. Investors interested in an overview of stock market activity refer to daily summaries. Among other things, these summaries contain information regarding several stock market indexes. Immediately below, we describe the most important stock market indexes.

The S&P/TSX Composite

The most widely followed barometer of day-to-day stock market activity in Canada is the S&P/TSX Composite Index. The S&P/TSX is a capitalization weighted index of 273 Canadian companies. Figure 6.3 shows the chart of S&P/TSX from the Yahoo Canada Finance website.

Figure 6.3 presents the closing prices and trading volume for the index from August 31, 2006 through August 31, 2007. We see that, based on closing prices, the S&P/TSX reached a high of about 14,626 on July 19, 2007, and then fell to about 12,849 on August 16, 2007.

Stock Market Indexes

A more comprehensive view of stock market trading is contained in Figure 6.4, which is also published daily in *The Globe and Mail*. The excerpt we examine here, "Major Stock Indexes," reports information about a variety of stock market indexes.

FIGURE 6.3   **S&P/TSX Composite**

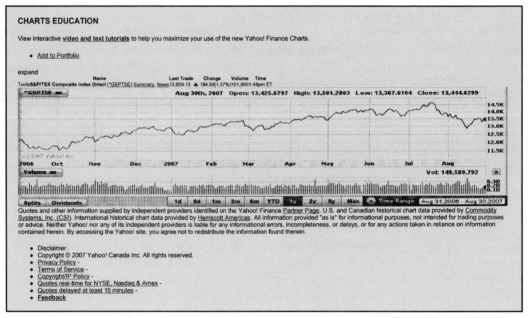

Reproduced with permission of Yahoo! Inc. © 2007 by Yahoo! Inc. YAHOO! and the YAHOO! logo are trademarks of Yahoo! Inc.

FIGURE 6.4 Stock Market Major Indexes

TUESDAY'S MARKETS

WHAT HAPPENED

U.S. indexes erase last week's gains

U.S. stocks posted their biggest drop in three weeks on weaker consumer confidence and speculation tighter credit markets will hurt bank earnings. The S&P 500 slipped 2.4 per cent, while the Dow slid 2.1 per cent and the Nasdaq composite index fell 2.4 per cent.

Raw materials, energy stocks lead composite down

The S&P/TSX composite index fell the most in two weeks, as raw materials and energy producers declined on a drop in consumer confidence in the United States. The index fell 222.56 points, or 1.7 per cent, to 13,264.87, having retreated 9.3 per cent from its July 19 record.

Financial stocks pace retreat in Europe and Asia

Markets in Europe and Asia retreated, led by financial companies on concern the subprime mortgage rout is spreading and will erode global economic growth. The Morgan Stanley Capital International World Index slipped 1.8 per cent to 1,520.88.

S&P/TSX COMPOSITE INDEX

13,264.87 » **–222.56** » **–1.65%** » **149,986,008** VOL » **+2.76%** YTD

DAILY INDEX: LAST 12 MONTHS

DAILY INDEX: 10-MINUTE INTERVAL

S&P 500

1,432.36 » **–34.43** » **–2.35%** » **+0.99%** YTD

DAILY INDEX: LAST 12 MONTHS

DOW JONES INDUSTRIAL AVERAGE

13,041.85 » **–280.28** » **–2.10%** » **230,466,352** VOL » **+4.64%** YTD

DAILY INDEX: LAST 12 MONTHS

MARKET BREADTH

	% change indicates increase/decrease from 13-week average													
	Advance	%Chg	Vol. (000s)	Decline	%Chg	Vol (000s)	Unch.	%Chg	Vol (000s)	Total	New High	%Chg	New Low	%Chg	Vol (000s)	%Chg
TSX	496	-34.02	33,351	1,076	39.12	230,211	667	12.80	21,340	2,239	5	-90.18	55	59.85	284,901	-17.90
Venture	313	-37.67	32,561	702	25.46	79,991	1,329	9.26	16,711	2,344	5	84.97	44	95.78	129,264	-21.71
New York	449	-72.85	139,069	2,912	83.98	2,902,546	233	-24.67	7,964	3,594	8	-95.19	41	-36.58	3,049,559	9.77
Nasdaq	629	-56.39	154,300	2,389	58.16	1,416,951	275	-10.92	45,353	3,293	15	-84.80	57	-17.37	1,617,613	-20.28

TSX

INDEXES

	Close	Chg	% Chg	YTD %Chg
S&P/TSX Composite	13,264.87	-222.56	-1.65	2.76
S&P/TSX 60	769.63	-12.98	-1.66	3.62
S&P/TSX Completion	866.29	-14.31	-1.63	.20
S&P/TSX SmallCap	715.16	-11.96	-1.64	-1.57
S&P/TSX Venture	2,562.93	-69.75	-2.65	-14.20

SUB INDEXES

	Close	Chg	% Chg	YTD %Chg
Cons Discretion	120.61	-2.08	-1.70	4.31
Cons Staples	195.01	-.72	-.37	-.48
Energy	325.45	-4.58	-1.39	.26
Financials	211.69	-2.80	-1.31	-1.16
Health Care	43.63	-.15	-.34	-17.24
Industrials	111.57	-2.17	-1.91	13.13
Info Tech	34.13	-.71	-2.04	-.06
Materials	288.17	-6.65	-2.26	9.96
Metals & Mining	754.18	-35.23	-4.46	17.29
Real Estate	225.55	-4.15	-1.81	-6.26
S&P/TSX Global Gold	257.26	-2.95	-1.13	-20.82
S&P/TSX Global Mini	96.07	-2.95	-2.98	n-a
S&P/TSX Income Trus	142.22	-1.55	-1.08	-3.96
S&P/TSX Preferred S	930.13	2.03	.22	n-a
Telecom Serv	107.98	-1.36	-1.24	17.40
Utilities	213.07	-2.51	-1.16	-1.87

INDEX LIFTERS

Stocks that moved the index the most on the day

	Close	% Chg	Mrkt Cap (billions)	Influence*
Alcan Inc.	103.73	.46	38.35	1.7
Transcontinental In	20.54	3.48	1.75	.5
Metro Inc.	35.11	1.42	4.05	.4
Nova Chemicals Corp	37.96	1.23	3.15	.4
Empire Company	49.69	2.69	3.26	.3

Influence: How many points the stock moved the index

INDEX DRAGS

Stocks that moved the index the most on the day

	Close	% Chg	Mrkt Cap (billions)	Influence*
Research In Motion	82.30	-3.91	45.93	-14.8
Royal Bank of Canad	53.59	-1.62	68.22	-10.5
Teck Cominco Ltd.	42.64	-5.01	17.88	-9.4
Barrick Gold Corp.	32.84	-3.07	28.41	-8.4
Manulife Financial	40.01	-1.36	60.78	-7.9

Influence: How many points the stock moved the index

INTERNATIONAL INDEXES

	Close	Chg	% chg	YTD %
Amsterdam AEX	508.01	-10.11	-1.95	+2.56
DJ Europe STOXX 50	3656.63	-65.31	-1.75	-1.10
DJ Pacific Pan-Asia	154.43	+0.41	+0.27	+5.66
Frankfurt Xetra DAX	7430.24	-55.75	-0.74	+12.63
Hong Kong Hang Seng	23363.76	-213.97	-0.91	+17.03
London FTSE 100	6102.20	-117.90	-1.90	-1.91
Madrid IBEX 35	14124.80	-180.70	-1.26	-0.15
Mexico C IPC	29326.76	-949.08	-3.13	+10.88
Milan S&P/MIB	39158.00	-778.00	-1.95	-5.49
Mumbai Sensitive	14919.19	+76.81	+0.52	+8.21
Nasdaq	2500.64	-60.61	-2.37	+3.53
Paris CAC40	5474.17	-116.37	-2.08	-1.22
Russell 2000	767.83	-21.62	-2.74	-2.52
Russia RTS	1877.10	-18.61	-0.98	-2.33
Sao Paulo BOVESPA	51645.33	-1432.82	-2.70	+16.13
Seoul Kospi	1829.31	+26.28	+1.46	+27.53
Shanghai Composite	5194.68	+44.57	+0.87	+94.16
Singapore Straits T	3343.00	-45.44	-1.34	+11.96
Sydney All Ord	6177.30	-7.60	-0.12	+9.44
Tokyo Nikkei 275	16287.49	-13.90	-0.09	-5.45
Zurich Swiss Mkt	8714.69	-131.51	-1.49	-0.81

Source: *The Globe and Mail*, August 29, 2007. Reprinted with permission from *The Globe and Mail*.

If you were to scrutinize the various indexes in Figure 6.4, you would quickly find that there are essentially four differences between them: (1) the market covered; (2) the types of stocks included; (3) how many stocks are included; and (4) how the index is calculated.

The first three differences are straightforward. Some indexes listed in Figure 6.4, such as the S&P/TSX Energy Index, focus on specific industries. Others, such as the Nasdaq Composite, focus on particular markets. Some have a small number of stocks, like the S&P/TSX 60 which contains only 60 stocks. Some indexes contain small companies, like the S&P/TSX Cdn Small Cap.

How stock market indexes are computed is not quite so straightforward, but it is important to understand. There are two major types of stock market index: price-weighted and value-weighted. With a **price-weighted index**, stocks are held in the index in proportion to their share prices. With a **value-weighted index**, stocks are held in proportion to their total company market values.

The best way to understand the difference between price and value weighting is to consider an example. To keep things relatively simple, we suppose that there are only two companies in the entire market. We have the following information about their shares outstanding, share prices, and total market values:

	Shares Outstanding	Price per Share		Total Market Value	
		Beginning of Year	End of Year	Beginning of Year	End of Year
Company A	50 million	$10	$14	$500 million	$700 million
Company B	1 million	$50	$40	$50 million	$40 million

As shown, Company A has a lower share price but many more shares outstanding. Ignoring dividends, notice that Company A's stock price rose by 40 percent ($10 to $14) while Company B's stock price fell by 20 percent ($50 to $40).

The question we want to answer here is simply: How did the market do for the year? There are several ways we could answer this question. We could first focus on what happened to the average share price. The average share price was ($10 + $50) / 2 = $30 at the beginning of the year, and ($14 + $40) / 2 = $27 at the end, so the average share price fell. If we take the average share price as our index, then our index fell from 30 to 27, for a change of −3 points. Since the index began at 30, this is a −3 / 30 = −10% decrease. We might therefore say that the market was "off" by 10 percent.

This is an example of a price-weighted index. Because Company B's stock price is five times bigger than Company A's, it carries five times as much weight in the index. This explains why the index was down even though Company A's stock gained 40 percent whereas Company B's stock only lost 20 percent. The Dow Jones indexes are price weighted.

Alternatively, instead of focusing on the price of a typical share, we could look at what happened to the total value of a typical company. Here we notice that the average total value, in millions, rose from ($500 + $50) / 2 = $275 to ($700 + $40) / 2 = $370. If we take average total company value as our index, then our index rose from 275 to 370, a 35 percent *increase*.

This is an example of a value-weighted index. The influence a company has in this case depends on its overall change in total market value, not just its stock price change. Because Company A has a much larger total value, it carries a much larger weight in the index.

Now we have a problem. One index tells us the market was down by 10 percent, while the other tells us it was up by 35 percent. Which one is correct? The answer seems fairly obvious. The total value of the market as a whole grew from $550 million to $740 million, so the market as a whole increased in value. Put differently, investors as a whole owned stock worth $550 million at the beginning of the year and $740 million

Take a look at the "value" and "growth" indexes at
www.barra.com
Click on S&P/Barra Indexes

at the end of the year. So, on the whole, stock market investors earned 35 percent, even though the average share price went down.

This example shows that a price-weighted index can be misleading as an indicator of total market value. The basic flaw in a price-weighted index is that the effect a company has on the index depends on the price of a single share. However, the price of a single share is only part of the story. Unless the number of shares is also considered, the true impact on the overall market isn't known, and a distorted picture can emerge.

CAUTION: INDEXES UNDER CONSTRUCTION

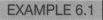

Suppose there are only two stocks in the market and the following information is given:

	Shares Outstanding	Price per Share	
		Beginning of Year	End of Year
Quark Co.	10 million	$10	$11
Bashir, Inc	20 million	$20	$25

Construct price- and value-weighted indexes and calculate the percentage changes in each.

The average share price rose from $15 to $18, or $3, so the price-weighted index would be up by 3 / 15 = 20 percent. Average total market value, in millions, rose from $250 to $305, so the value-weighted index rose by 55 / 250 = 22 percent.

More on Price-Weighted Indexes

The popular Dow Jones averages are price-weighted averages of 30 stocks. Given this, you may wonder why the Dow Jones Industrial Average has such a high value when the stock prices used to calculate the average are much smaller. To answer this question, we must explain one last detail about price-weighted indexes.

The extra detail concerns the effects of stock splits on price-weighted indexes. For example, in a 2-for-1 stock split, all current shareholders receive two new shares in exchange for each old share that they own. However, the total value of the company does not change because it is still the same company after the stock split. There are just twice as many shares, each worth half as much.

A stock split has no effect on a value-weighted index since the total value of the company does not change. But it can have a dramatic effect on a price-weighted index. To see this, consider what happens to the price-weighted and value-weighted indexes we created above when Company B enacts a 2-for-1 stock split. Based on beginning prices, with a 2-for-1 split, Company B's shares fall to $25. The price-weighted index falls to (10 + 25) / 2 = 17.50 from 30, even though nothing really happened.

For a price-weighted index, the problem of stock splits can be addressed by adjusting the divisor each time a split occurs. Once again, an example is the best way to illustrate. In the case stated just above, suppose we wanted the index value to stay at 30 even though B's price per share fell to $25 as a result of the split. The only way to accomplish this is to add together the new stock prices and divide by something less than 2.

This new number is called the *index divisor*, and it is adjusted as needed to remove the effect of stock splits. To find the new divisor in our case, the stock prices are \$25 and \$10, and we want the index to equal 30. We solve for the new divisor, d, as follows:

$$\text{Index level} = \frac{\text{Sum of stock prices}}{\text{Divisor}}$$

$$30 = \frac{25 + 10}{d}$$

$$d = \frac{35}{30} = 1.16666\ldots$$

The new divisor is thus approximately 1.17.

Adjusting the divisor takes care of the problem in one sense, but it creates another problem. Since we are no longer dividing the sum of the share prices by the number of companies in the index, we can no longer interpret the change in the index as the change in price of an average share.

ADJUSTING THE DIVISOR

EXAMPLE 6.2

Take a look back at Example 6.1. Suppose that Bashir splits 5-for-1. Based on beginning information, what is the new divisor?

Following a 5-for-1 split, Bashir's share price will fall from \$20 to \$4. With no adjustment to the divisor, the price-weighted index would drop from 15 to (10 + 4) / 2 = 7. To keep the index at its old level of 15, we need to solve for a new divisor such that (10 + 4) / d = 15. In this case, the new divisor would be 14 / 15 = .93333 . . . , illustrating that the divisor can drop below 1.0.

The Dow Jones Divisors

The method we described of adjusting the divisor on a price-weighted index for stock splits is the method used to adjust the Dow Jones averages. Through time, with repeated adjustments for stock splits, the divisor becomes smaller and smaller. As of February 20, 2003, the divisor was a nice, round .14279922. Since there are 30 stocks in the index, the divisor on the DJIA would be 30 if it were never adjusted, so it has declined substantially. The other Dow Jones averages have similarly odd values.

Given its shortcomings, you might wonder why the financial press continues to report the Dow Jones averages. The reason is tradition; the Dow Jones averages have been around for more than 100 years, and each new generation of investors becomes accustomed to its quirks.

More on Index Formation: Base-Year Values

We next discuss one or two more details about indexes. First, to ease interpretation, the starting value of an index is usually set equal to some simple base number, like 100 or 1,000. For example, if you were to create a value-weighted index for the NYSE, the actual value of the index would be very large and cumbersome, so adjusting it makes sense.

To illustrate, suppose we have a value-weighted index with a starting value of 1.4 million. If we want the starting value to be 100, we just divide the starting value, and every subsequent value, by 1.4 million and then multiply by 100. So, if the next value of the index is 1.6 million, the "reindexed" value would be 1.6 million/1.4 million $\times$ 100 = 114.29, which is easily interpreted as a 14.29 percent increase over a base of 100.

REINDEXING

EXAMPLE 6.3

You've calculated values for an index over a four-year period as follows:

Year 1:   1,687 million

Year 2:   1,789 million

Year 3:   1,800 million

Year 4:   1,700 million

Suppose you wanted the index to start at 1,000. What would the reindexed values be?

To reindex these numbers, we need to (1) divide each of them by the starting value, 1,687 million, and then (2) multiply each by 1,000. Thus, we have:

Year 1:   1,687 million/1,687 million × 1,000 = 1,000.00

Year 2:   1,789 million/1,687 million × 1,000 = 1,060.46

Year 3:   1,800 million/1,687 million × 1,000 = 1,066.98

Year 4:   1,700 million/1,687 million × 1,000 = 1,007.71

Finally, an important consideration in looking at indexes is whether dividends are included. Most indexes don't include them. As a result, the change in an index measures only the capital gain (or loss) component of your return. When you're trying to evaluate how a particular type of stock market investment has done over time, dividends have to be included to get an accurate picture.

index staleness
Condition that occurs when an index does not reflect all current price information because some of the stocks in the index have not traded recently.

You might wonder why popular indexes limit the number of companies included. The answer is timeliness and accuracy. Almost all stocks in the S&P/TSX Composite Index trade every day. Stocks that do not trade every day can cause **index staleness**. Index staleness occurs when an index does not reflect all current price information because some of the stocks in the index have not traded recently.

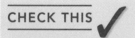

CHECK THIS

6.6a   What is the difference between price- and value-weighting in the construction of stock market indexes? Give an example of a well-known index of each type.

6.6b   Which is better, price or value weighting? Why?

6.6c   Which stock market index is likely to contain the greater degree of index staleness, the S&P 500 or the Wilshire 5000 index?

6.7   Summary and Conclusions

This chapter introduced you to stock markets. We discussed who owns stocks, how the stock exchanges operate, and how stock market indexes are constructed and interpreted. Along the way we saw that:

1. Individual investors, directly or through mutual funds, own over half of all traded stocks. The rest are owned mostly by financial institutions such as pension funds and insurance companies.

2. The stock market is composed of a primary market, where stock shares are first sold, and a secondary market, where investors trade shares among themselves. In the primary market, companies raise money for investment projects. Investment bankers specialize in arranging financing for companies in the primary market. Investment bankers often act as underwriters, buying newly issued stock from the company and then reselling the stock to the public. The primary market is best known as the market for initial public offerings (IPOs).

3. In the secondary market, investors trade securities with other investors. Secondary market transactions are directed through three channels: directly with other investors, indirectly through a broker, or directly with a dealer. We saw that a broker matches buyers and sellers; a dealer buys and sells out of inventory.

4. Most common stock trading is directed through an organized stock exchange or through a trading network. The largest organized stock exchange in the world is the New York Stock Exchange (NYSE). Popularly known as the Big Board, NYSE is owned by its members. There are four major types of NYSE members: commission brokers, specialists, floor brokers, and floor traders. In Canada the senior equities are traded on the Toronto Stock Exchange (TSX) and the junior equities are traded on the TSX Venture Exchange.

5. The second largest stock market in the world is Nasdaq. Nasdaq is a computer network of securities dealers and electronic communications networks (ECNs).

6. The major exchanges face strong competition from securities trading firms operating in the third and fourth markets. The third market refers to off-exchange trading of exchange-listed securities by securities firms. The fourth market refers to direct trading among investors.

7. The most widely followed barometer of day-to-day stock market activity in Canada is the S&P/TSX Composite Index. It is an index of 273 Canadian stocks. We described how these indexes are computed, with particular attention to some of the problems encountered.

REAL WORLD

This chapter covered the operations and organization of the major stock markets. It also covered some of the most important order types and the construction of stock market indexes. How should you, as an investor or investment manager, put this information to work?

As in some previous chapters, you need to submit as many as possible of the different order types suggested by this chapter in a simulated brokerage account (note that not all simulated brokerage accounts allow all trade types). Your goal is to gain experience with the different order types and what they mean and accomplish for you as an investor or investment manager.

Key Terms

primary market 162
secondary market 162
initial public offering (IPO) 162
investment banking firm 162
underwrite 162
fixed commitment 162
best effort 162
Ontario Securities and Exchange
    Commission (OSC) 163
prospectus 163
red herring 163
dealer 165
broker 165
bid price 165
ask price 165

spread 165
market order 168
limit order 168
stop order 168
uptick rule 170
over-the-counter (OTC) market 172
electronic communications
    network (ECN) 172
inside quotes 173
third market 173
fourth market 173
price-weighted index 176
value-weighted index 176
index staleness 179

Chapter Review Problems and Self-Test

1. **Index Construction** Suppose there are only two stocks in the market and the following information is given:

		Price per Share	
	Shares Outstanding	Beginning of Year	End of Year
Ally Co.	100 million	$60	$66
McBeal, Inc.	400 million	$120	$100

Construct price- and value-weighted indexes and calculate the percentage changes in each.

2. **Stock Splits** In the previous problem, suppose that McBeal splits 3-for-1. Based on beginning information, what is the new divisor?

Answers to Self-Test Problems

1. The average share price at the beginning of the year is ($60 + 120) / 2 = $90. At the end of the year, the average price is $83. Thus, the average price declined by $7 from $90, a percentage drop of −$7 / $90 = −7.78%. Total market cap at the beginning of the year is $60 × 100 + $120 × 400 = $54 billion. It falls to $46.6 billion, a decline of $7.4 billion. The percentage decline is −$7.4 billion / $54 billion = −13.7%, or almost twice as much as the price-weighted index.

2. Following a 3-for-1 split, McBeal's share price falls from $120 to $40. To keep the price-weighted index at its old level of 90, we need a new divisor such that (60 + 40) / d = 90. In this case, the new divisor would be 100 / 90 = 1.1111.

Test Your Investment Quotient

1. **Stop-Loss Order** If you place a stop-loss order to sell 100 shares of stock at $55 when the current price is $62, how much will you receive for each share if the price drops to $52?

   a. $50
   b. $55
   c. $54.87
   d. Cannot tell from the information given.

2. **Uptick Rule** You wish to sell short 100 shares of XYZ Corporation stock. If the last two transactions were $34.12 followed by $34.25, you can short on the next transaction only at a price of

   a. $34.12 or higher.
   b. $34.25 or higher.
   c. $34.25 or lower.
   d. $34.12 or lower.

3. **Uptick Rule** Which of the following is false regarding the uptick rule?

   a. The rule does not apply to short sales executed on other exchanges.
   b. The rule is implemented to make it more difficult for speculators to drive down a stock's price by repeated short sales.
   c. The rule has become less of a constraint than it once was.
   d. The rule applies when shorting a stock or when covering a short.

4. **Value-Weighted Index** An analyst gathered the following data about stocks J, K, and L, which together form a value-weighted index:

	December 31, Year 1		December 31, Year 2	
Stock	Price	Shares Outstanding	Price	Shares Outstanding
J	$40	10,000	$50	10,000
K	$30	6,000	$20	12,000*
L	$50	9,000	$40	9,000

*2-for-1 stock split.

   The ending value-weighted index (base index = 100) is closest to:

   a. 92.31
   b. 93.64
   c. 106.80
   d. 108.33

5. **Dow Jones Index** The divisor for the Dow Jones Industrial Average (DJIA) is most likely to decrease when a stock in the DJIA

   a. Has a stock split.
   b. Has a reverse split.
   c. Pays a cash dividend.
   d. Is removed and replaced.

6. **New York Stock Exchange** Which of the following activities are *not* conducted by specialists on the NYSE?

   a. Acting as dealers for their own accounts.
   b. Monitoring compliance with margin requirements.
   c. Providing liquidity to the market.
   d. Monitoring and executing unfilled limit orders.

7. **Stock Markets** What is a securities market characterized by dealers who buy and sell securities for their own inventories called?

   a. A primary market.
   b. A secondary market.
   c. An over-the-counter market.
   d. An institutional market.

8. **Stock Markets** What is the over-the-counter market for exchange-listed securities called?

   a. Third market
   b. Fourth market
   c. After-market
   d. Block market

9. **Stock Indexes** If the market prices of each of the 30 stocks in the Dow Jones Industrial Average all change by the same percentage amount during a given day, which stock will have the greatest impact on the DJIA?

   a. The one whose stock trades at the highest dollar price per share.
   b. The one whose total equity has the highest market value.
   c. The one having the greatest amount of equity in its capital structure.
   d. The one having the lowest volatility.

10. **Stock Indexes** In calculating the Standard & Poor's stock price indexes, how are adjustments for stock splits made?

    a. By adjusting the divisor.
    b. Automatically, due to the manner in which the index is calculated.
    c. By adjusting the numerator.
    d. Quarterly, on the last trading day of each quarter.

11. **Stock Indexes** Which of the following indexes includes the largest number of actively traded stocks?

    a. The Nasdaq Composite Index.
    b. The NYSE Composite Index.
    c. The Wilshire 5000 Index.
    d. The Value Line Composite Index.

12. **Stock Trading** An institutional investor wishing to sell a very large block of stock, say, 10,000 shares or more, is most likely to get the best price in which market?

    a. The primary market
    b. The secondary market
    c. The third market
    d. The fourth market

13. **Stock Indexes** Which one of the following statements regarding the Dow Jones Industrial Average is false?

    a. The DJIA contains 30 well-known large-company stocks.
    b. The DJIA is affected equally by dollar changes in low- and high-priced stocks.
    c. The DJIA is affected equally by percentage changes in low- and high-priced stocks.
    d. The DJIA divisor must be adjusted for stock splits.

Concept Questions

1. **Primary and Secondary Markets** If you were to visit your local Chevrolet retailer, there is both a primary and a secondary market in action. Explain. Is the Chevy retailer a dealer or a broker?

www.mcgrawhill.ca/olc/Jordan

2. **Market and Limit Orders** What is the difference between a market order and a limit order? What is the potential downside to each type of order?

3. **Stop That!** What is a stop-loss order? Why might it be used? Is it sure to stop a loss?

4. **Order Types** Suppose RIM is currently trading at $90. You want to buy it if it reaches $100. What type of order should you submit?

5. **Order Types** Suppose Nortel is currently trading at $8.00. You think that if it reaches $10.00, it will continue to climb, so you want to buy it if and when it gets there. Should you submit a limit order to buy at $10.00?

6. **Nasdaq Quotes** With regard to the Nasdaq, what are inside quotes?

7. **Index Composition** There are basically four factors that differentiate stock market indexes. What are they? Comment on each.

8. **Index Composition** Is it necessarily true that, all else the same, an index with more stocks is better? What is the issue here?

9. **Upticks** What is the uptick rule? Where does it apply? Why does it exist?

Questions and Problems

Core Questions

1. **Price-Weighted Divisor** Able, Baker, and Charlie are the only three stocks in an index. The stocks sell for $46, $128, and $75, respectively. If Baker undergoes a 2-for-1 stock split, what is the new divisor for the price-weighted index?

2. **Price-Weighted Divisor** In the previous problem, assume that Baker undergoes a 3-for-1 stock split. What is the new divisor now?

3. **Order Books** You find the following order book on a particular stock. The last trade on the stock was at $70.54.

Buy Orders		Sell Orders	
Shares	Price	Shares	Price
250	$70.53	100	$70.56
100	70.52	400	70.57
900	70.51	1,000	70.59
75	70.49	700	70.60
		900	70.61

   a. If you place a market buy order for 100 shares, at what price will it be filled?
   b. If you place a market sell order for 100 shares, at what price will it be filled?
   c. Suppose you place a market order to buy 400 shares. At what price will it be filled?

4. **Price-Weighted Index** You are given the following information concerning two stocks that make up an index. What is the price-weighted return for the index?

	Shares Outstanding	Price per Share	
		Beginning of Year	End of Year
Kirk, Inc.	45,000	$84	$93
Picard Co.	60,000	41	49

5. **Value-Weighted Index** Calculate the index return for the information in the previous problem using a value-weighted index.

6. **Reindexing** In Problem 5, assume that you want to reindex with the index value at the beginning of the year equal to 100. What is the index level at the end of the year?

7. **Index Level** In Problem 5, assume the value-weighted index level was 408.16 at the beginning of the year. What is the index level at the end of the year?

8. **Reindexing** You have calculated the following values for an index over a five-year period:

   Year 1: 6,251 million
   Year 2: 6,483 million
   Year 3: 6,124 million
   Year 4: 6,503 million
   Year 5: 6,698 million

   Suppose you wanted the index to start at 500. What would the reindexed values be?

Intermediate Questions

9. **Price-Weighted Divisor** Look back at Problem 1. Assume that Able undergoes a 1-for-3 reverse stock split. What is the new divisor?

10. **DJIA** On August 30, 2005, the DJIA closed at 10,412.82. The divisor at that time was 0.12560864. Suppose the next day the prices for 29 of the stocks remained unchanged and one stock increased by $5.00. What would the DJIA level be the next day?

11. **DJIA** In August 2005, IBM was one of the highest priced stocks in the DJIA and Disney was one of the lowest. The closing price for IBM on August 30, 2005, was $80.54 and the closing price for Disney was $25.29. Suppose the next day the other 29 stock prices remained unchanged and IBM increased 5 percent. What would the new DJIA level be? Now assume Disney increased by 5 percent and find the new DJIA level.

12. **DJIA** Looking back at the previous problems, what would the new index level be if all stocks on the DJIA increased by $1.00 per share on August 30, 2005?

13. **Price-Weighted Divisor** You construct a price-weighted index of 40 stocks. At the beginning of the day the index is 3,487.25. During the day, 39 stock prices remain the same, and one stock price increases by $5.00. At the end of the day, your index value is 3,502.18. What is the divisor on your index?

14. **Price-Weighted Indexes** Suppose the following three defense stocks are to be combined into a stock index in January 2003 (perhaps a portfolio manager believes these stocks are an appropriate benchmark for his or her performance):

	Shares (millions)	Price		
		1/1/04	1/1/05	1/1/06
Douglas McDonnell	220	$119	$123	$132
Dynamics General	400	35	31	39
International Rockwell	350	62	54	68

   a. Calculate the initial value of the index if a price-weighting scheme is used.
   b. What is the rate of return on this index for the year ending December 31, 2004? For the year ending December 31, 2005?

15. **Price-Weighted Indexes** In the previous problem, suppose that Douglas McDonnell shareholders approve a 3-for-1 stock split on January 1, 2005. What is the new divisor for the index? Calculate the rate of return on the index for the year ending December 31, 2005, if Douglas McDonnell's share price on January 1, 2006, is $44.00 per share.

16. **Value-Weighted Indexes** Repeat Problem 14 if a value-weighted index is used. Assume the index is scaled by a factor of 10 million; that is, if the average firm's market value is $5 billion, the index would be quoted as 500.

17. **Value-Weighted Indexes** In the previous problem, will your answers change if Douglas McDonnell stock splits? Why or why not?

18. **Equally Weighted Indexes** In addition to price-weighted and value-weighted indexes, an equally weighted index is one in which the index value is computed from the average

rate of return of the stocks comprising the index. Equally weighted indexes are frequently used by financial researchers to measure portfolio performance.

   a. Using the information in Problem 14, compute the rate of return on an equally weighted index of the three defense stocks for the year ending December 31, 2004.

   b. If the index value is set to 100 on January 1, 2004, what will the index value be on January 1, 2005? What is the rate of return on the index for 2005?

19. **Equally Weighted versus Value-Weighted Indexes** Historically there have been periods where a value-weighted index has a higher return than an equally weighted index and other periods where the opposite has occurred. Why do you suppose this would happen? Hint: Look back to Chapter 1.

20. **Geometric Indexes** Another type of index is the geometric index. The calculation of a geometric index is similar to the calculation of a geometric return:

$$1 + R_G = [(1 + R_1)(1 + R_2) \ldots (1 + R_N)]^{1/N}$$

The difference in the geometric index construction is the returns used are the returns for the different stocks in the index for a particular period, such as a day or year. Construct the geometric index returns for Problem 14 over each of the two years. Assume the beginning index level is 100.

21. **Geometric Indexes** We have seen the importance of geometric returns through time. A geometric index is across different stocks at a particular point in time, such as a day. Constructing a portfolio that exactly replicates a geometric index is thus impossible. Given this, why would you want to use a geometric index? In other words, what does a geometric index measure? Now consider the Value Line Arithmetic Index (VLA), which is equally weighted, and the Value Line Geometric Index (VLG). On February 1, 1988, both indexes were set to a value of 210.75. As of the close of the market on August 30, 2005, the VLA was at 1,848.80 and the VLG was at 404.67. Why would you expect to see such a disparity in the two index levels?

22. **Interpreting Index Values** Suppose you want to replicate the performance of several stock indexes, some of which are price-weighted, others value-weighted, and still others equally weighted. Describe the investment strategy you need for each of the index types. Are any of the three strategies passive, in that no portfolio rebalancing need be performed to perfectly replicate the index (assuming no stock splits or cash distributions)? Which of the three strategies do you think is most often followed by small investors? Which strategy is the most difficult to implement?

STANDARD &POOR'S

S&P Problem

www.mcgrawhill.ca/edumarketinsight

1. **Index Construction** You have decided that you want a stock market index that tracks oil and gas exploration and production companies. The three constituent companies you have decided to use are Canadian Natural Resources (CNQ), Encana Corp. (ECA) and Nexen Inc. (NXY). For each company, download the monthly stock prices. Under the "Financial Hlts" link you can find the number of shares outstanding. Construct a price-weighted and a value-weighted index for the oil and gas exploration and publishing, industries for the last six months. Use a beginning index value of 100 where appropriate. What are the monthly returns for each index?

What's on the Web?

1. **Specialists** Go to www.nyse.com and find the discussion of NYSE members. What are the five essential functions of the specialist according to the website?

2. **DJIA** As you have seen, in a price-weighted index, a stock with a higher price has a higher weight in the index return. To find out the weight of the stocks in the DJIA, go to www.djindexes.com. Which stock in the DJIA has the highest weight? The lowest weight?

3. **S&P/TSX Composite** Go to www.tsx.com and find the names of 10 companies that are included in the index.

4. **S&P/TSX Venture** At the same site, examine the composition of the S&P/TSX Venture Index. How many stocks are included in the index?

5. **Nikkei 225** The Nikkei 225 Index is a highly followed index that measures the performance of the Japanese stock market. Go to www.nni.nikkei.co.jp and find out if the Nikkei 225 is a price-weighted or value-weighted index. What is the divisor for this index? When was the latest reconstitution of the index? Which stocks were added? Which stocks were deleted?

CHAPTER 7

Common Stock Valuation

"Ignore the stock market, ignore the economy and buy a business you understand."

—Warren Buffett

"Prediction is difficult, especially about the future."

—Niels Bohr[1]

Common stock valuation is one of the most challenging tasks in financial analysis. A fundamental assertion of finance holds that the value of an asset is based on the present value of its future cash flows. Accordingly, common stock valuation attempts the difficult task of predicting the future. Consider that the dividend yield for a typical large-company stock might be about 2 percent. This implies that the present value of dividends to be paid over the next 10 years constitutes only a portion of the current stock price. Thus, much of the value of a typical stock is derived from dividends to be paid more than 10 years away! ■

In this chapter, we examine several methods commonly used by financial analysts to assess the economic value of common stocks. These methods are grouped into two categories: dividend discount models and price ratio models. After studying these models, we provide an analysis of a real company to illustrate the use of the methods discussed in this chapter.

---

[1]This quote has also been attributed to Yogi Berra, Samuel Goldwyn, and Mark Twain.

7.1 Security Analysis: Be Careful Out There

It may seem odd that we start our discussion with an admonition to be careful, but in this case, we think it is a good idea. The methods we discuss in this chapter are examples of those used by many investors and security analysts to assist in making buy and sell decisions for individual stocks. The basic idea is to identify both "undervalued" or "cheap" stocks to buy and "overvalued" or "rich" stocks to sell. In practice, however, many stocks that look cheap may in fact be correctly priced for reasons not immediately apparent to the analyst. Indeed, the hallmark of a good analyst is a cautious attitude and a willingness to probe further and deeper before committing to a final investment recommendation.

fundamental analysis
Examination of a firm's accounting statements and other financial and economic information to assess the economic value of a company's stock.

The type of security analysis we describe in this chapter falls under the heading of **fundamental analysis**. Numbers such as a company's earnings per share, cash flow, book equity value, and sales are often called *fundamentals* because they describe, on a basic level, a specific firm's operations and profits (or lack of profits).

Fundamental analysis represents the examination of these and other accounting statement–based company data used to assess the value of a company's stock. Information regarding such things as management quality, products, and product markets is often examined as well.

Our cautionary note is based on the skepticism these techniques should engender, at least when applied simplistically. As our later chapter on market efficiency explains, there is good reason to believe that too-simple techniques that rely on widely available information are not likely to yield systematically superior investment results. In fact, they could lead to unnecessarily risky investment decisions. This is especially true for ordinary investors (like most of us) who do not have timely access to the information that a professional security analyst working for a major securities firm would possess.

Visit the Toronto Society of Financial Analysts at www.torontocfa.ca

As a result, our goal here is not to teach you how to "pick" stocks with a promise that you will become rich. Certainly, one chapter in an investments text is not likely to be sufficient to acquire that level of investment savvy. Instead, an appreciation of the techniques in this chapter is important simply because buy and sell recommendations made by securities firms are frequently couched in the terms we introduce here. Much of the discussion of individual companies in the financial press relies on these concepts as well, so some background is necessary just to interpret commonly presented investment information. In essence, you must learn both the lingo and the concepts of security analysis.

CHECK THIS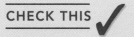

7.1a What is fundamental analysis?

7.1b What is a "rich" stock? What is a "cheap" stock?

7.1c Why does valuing a stock necessarily involve predicting the future?

7.2 The Dividend Discount Model

A fundamental principle of finance holds that the economic value of a security is properly measured by the sum of its future cash flows, where the cash flows are adjusted for risk and the time value of money. For example, suppose a risky security will pay either

$100 or $200 with equal probability one year from today. The expected future payoff is $150 = ($100 + $200) / 2, and the security's value today is the $150 expected future value discounted for a one-year waiting period.

If the appropriate discount rate for this security is, say, 5 percent, then the present value of the expected future cash flow is $150 / 1.05 = $142.86. If instead the appropriate discount rate is 15 percent, then the present value is $150 / 1.15 = $130.43. As this example illustrates, the choice of a discount rate can have a substantial impact on an assessment of security value.

dividend discount model (DDM) Method of estimating the value of a share of stock as the present value of all expected future dividend payments.

A popular model used to value common stock is the **dividend discount model**, or **DDM**. The dividend discount model values a share of stock as the sum of all expected future dividend payments, where the dividends are adjusted for risk and the time value of money.

For example, suppose a company pays a dividend at the end of each year. Let $D(t)$ denote a dividend to be paid t years from now, and let $V(0)$ represent the present value of the future dividend stream. Also, let k denote the appropriate risk-adjusted discount rate. Using the dividend discount model, the present value of a share of this company's stock is measured as this sum of discounted future dividends:

$$V(0) = \frac{D(1)}{(1+k)} + \frac{D(2)}{(1+k)^2} + \frac{D(3)}{(1+k)^3} + \cdots + \frac{D(T)}{(1+k)^T} \qquad (7.1)$$

This expression for present value assumes that the last dividend is paid T years from now, where the value of T depends on the specific valuation problem considered. Thus, if $T = 3$ years and $D(1) = D(2) = D(3) = $100, the present value, $V(0)$, is stated as

$$V(0) = \frac{\$100}{(1+k)} + \frac{\$100}{(1+k)^2} + \frac{\$100}{(1+k)^3}$$

If the discount rate is $k = 10$ percent, then a quick calculation yields $V(0) = $248.69, so the stock price should be about $250 per share.

USING THE DIVIDEND DISCOUNT MODEL

EXAMPLE 7.1

Suppose again that a stock pays three annual dividends of $100 per year and the discount rate is $k = 15$ percent. In this case, what is the present value $V(0)$ of the stock?

With a 15 percent discount rate, we have

$$V(0) = \frac{\$100}{(1.15)} + \frac{\$100}{(1.15)^2} + \frac{\$100}{(1.15)^3}$$

Check that the answer is $V(0) = $228.32.

MORE DIVIDEND DISCOUNT MODEL

EXAMPLE 7.2

Suppose instead that the stock pays three annual dividends of $10, $20, and $30 in years 1, 2, and 3, respectively, and the discount rate is $k = 10$ percent. What is the present value $V(0)$ of the stock?

(continued)

In this case, we have

$$V(0) = \frac{\$10}{(1.10)} + \frac{\$20}{(1.10)^2} + \frac{\$30}{(1.10)^3}$$

Check that the answer is $V(0) = \$48.16$.

Constant Dividend Growth Rate Model

constant growth rate model A version of the dividend discount model that assumes a constant dividend growth rate.

For many applications, the dividend discount model is simplified substantially by assuming that dividends will grow at a constant growth rate. This is called a **constant growth rate model**. Letting a constant growth rate be denoted by g, then successive annual dividends are stated as $D(t + 1) = D(t)(1 + g)$.

For example, suppose the next dividend is $D(1) = \$100$, and the dividend growth rate is $g = 10$ percent. This growth rate yields a second annual dividend of $D(2) = \$100 \times 1.10 = \$110$ and a third annual dividend of $D(3) = \$100 \times 1.10 \times 1.10 = \$100 \times (1.10)^2 = \$121$. If the discount rate is $k = 12$ percent, the present value of these three sequential dividend payments is the sum of their separate present values:

$$V(0) = \frac{\$100}{(1.12)} + \frac{\$110}{(1.12)^2} + \frac{\$121}{(1.12)^3}$$
$$= \$263.10$$

Try surfing to the Association for Investment Management and Research website at www.cfainstitute.org

If the number of dividends to be paid is large, calculating the present value of each dividend separately is tedious and possibly prone to error. Fortunately, if the growth rate is constant, some simplified expressions are available to handle certain special cases. For example, suppose a stock will pay annual dividends over the next T years and these dividends will grow at a constant growth rate g and be discounted at the rate k. The current dividend is $D(0)$, the next dividend is $D(1) = D(0)(1 + g)$, the following dividend is $D(2) = D(1)(1 + g) = D(0)(1 + g)^2$, and so forth. The present value of the next T dividends, that is, $D(1)$ through $D(T)$, can be calculated using this relatively simple formula:

$$V(0) = \frac{D(0)(1+g)}{k-g}\left[1 - \left(\frac{1+g}{1+k}\right)^T\right] \quad g \neq k \qquad (7.2)$$

Notice that this expression requires that the growth rate and the discount rate not be equal to each other, that is, $k \neq g$, since this requires division by zero. Actually, when the growth rate is equal to the discount rate, that is, $k = g$, the effects of growth and discounting cancel exactly, and the present value $V(0)$ is simply the number of payments T times the current dividend $D(0)$:

$$V(0) = T \times D(0) \quad g = k$$

As a numerical illustration of the constant growth rate model, suppose that the growth rate is $g = 8$ percent, the discount rate is $k = 10$ percent, the number of future annual dividends is $T = 20$ years, and the current dividend is $D(0) = \$10$. In this case, a present value calculation yields this amount:

$$V(0) = \frac{\$10(1.08)}{.10 - .08}\left[1 - \left(\frac{1.08}{1.10}\right)^{20}\right]$$
$$= \$165.88$$

USING THE CONSTANT GROWTH MODEL

EXAMPLE 7.3

Suppose that the dividend growth rate is 10 percent, the discount rate is 8 percent, there are 20 years of dividends to be paid, and the current dividend is $10. What is the value of the stock based on the constant growth model?

Plugging in the relevant numbers, we have

$$V(0) = \frac{\$10(1.10)}{.08 - .10}\left[1 - \left(\frac{1.10}{1.08}\right)^{20}\right]$$
$$= \$243.86$$

Thus the price should be $V(0) = \$243.86$.

Constant Perpetual Growth

A particularly simple form of the dividend discount model occurs in the case where a firm will pay dividends that grow at the constant rate g forever. This case is called the **constant perpetual growth model**. In the constant perpetual growth model, present values are calculated using this relatively simple formula:

constant perpetual growth model
A version of the dividend discount model in which dividends grow forever at a constant rate, and the growth rate is strictly less than the discount rate.

$$V(0) = \frac{D(0)(1+g)}{(k-g)} \quad g < k \tag{7.3}$$

Since $D(0)(1 + g) = D(1)$, we could also write the constant perpetual growth model as

$$V(0) = \frac{D(1)}{(k-g)} \quad g < k \tag{7.4}$$

Either way, we have a very simple, and very widely used, expression for the value of a share of stock based on future dividend payments.

Notice that the constant perpetual growth model requires that the growth rate be strictly less than the discount rate, that is, $g < k$. It looks like the share value would be negative if this were not true. Actually, the formula is simply not valid in this case. The reason is that a perpetual dividend growth rate greater than a discount rate implies an *infinite* value because the present value of the dividends keeps getting bigger and bigger. Since no security can have infinite value, the requirement that $g < k$ simply makes good economic sense.

To illustrate the constant perpetual growth model, suppose that the growth rate is $g = 4$ percent, the discount rate is $k = 9$ percent, and the current dividend is $D(0) = \$10$. In this case, a simple calculation yields

$$V(0) = \frac{\$10(1.04)}{.09 - .04} = \$208$$

USING THE CONSTANT PERPETUAL GROWTH MODEL

EXAMPLE 7.4

Suppose dividends for a particular company are projected to grow at 5 percent forever. If the discount rate is 15 percent and the current dividend is $10, what is the value of the stock?

(continued)

$$V(0) = \frac{\$10(1.05)}{.15 - .05} = \$105$$

As shown, the stock should sell for $105.

Applications of the Constant Perpetual Growth Model

In practice, the simplicity of the constant perpetual growth model makes it the most popular dividend discount model. Certainly, the model satisfies Einstein's famous dictum: "Simplify as much as possible, but no more." However, experienced financial analysts are keenly aware that the constant perpetual growth model can be usefully applied only to companies with a history of relatively stable earnings and dividend growth expected to continue into the distant future.

 Visit the AEP and Transalta websites at www.aep.com and www.transalta.com

A standard example of an industry for which the constant perpetual growth model can often be usefully applied is the electric utility industry. Consider American Electric Power, which is traded on the New York Stock Exchange under the ticker symbol AEP. In mid-2003, AEP's annual dividend was $1.40; thus we set $D(0) = \$1.40$.

To use the constant perpetual growth model, we also need a discount rate and a growth rate. An old quick and dirty rule of thumb for a risk-adjusted discount rate for electric utility companies is the yield to maturity on 20-year maturity U.S. Treasury bonds, plus 2 percent. At the time this example was written, the yield on 20-year maturity T-bonds was about 5.3 percent. Adding 2 percent, we get a discount rate of $k = 7.3$ percent.

In 2005, AEP had not increased its dividend in over a decade. However, a future growth rate of zero percent for AEP might be unduly pessimistic because earnings growth in the electric utilities industry was projected to be about 2 percent per year. Thus, a rate of, say, 1.5 percent might be more realistic as an estimate of future growth for AEP.

Putting it all together, we have $k = 7.3$ percent, $g = 1.5$ percent, and $D(0) = \$1.40$. Using these numbers, we obtain this estimate for the value of a share of AEP stock:

$$V(0) = \frac{\$1.40(1.015)}{.073 - .015} = \$24.50$$

This estimate is somewhat below the mid-2005 AEP stock price of $38.80, possibly suggesting that AEP stock was overvalued.

We emphasize the word "possibly" here because we made several assumptions in the process of coming up with this estimate. A change in any of these assumptions could easily lead us to a different conclusion. We will return to this point several times in future discussions.

VALUING TRANSALTA CORPORATION

EXAMPLE 7.5

In 2006, the utility company TransAlta (TA) Company paid a $1.00 dividend. TransAlta had not increased its dividend in 5 years, but previously increased the dividend by 2%. If we make an assumption of a 3% growth rate, take k as the yield on 30-year Canada Bonds plus 2% (4.46 + 2 = 6.46%), and use the constant perpetual growth model we will find the following result.

(continued)

Using $D(0) = \$1.00$, $k = 6.46$, $g = 3\%$,

$$V(0) = \frac{\$1.00(1.03)}{0.0643 - 0.03} = \$30.03$$

We see that our estimated price is very close to the stock price at TSX which is $29.00 on September 1, 2007.

Historical Growth Rates

In the constant growth model, a company's historical average dividend growth rate is frequently taken as an estimate of future dividend growth. Sometimes historical growth rates are provided in published information about the company. Other times it is necessary to calculate a historical growth rate yourself. There are two ways to do this: (1) using a **geometric average dividend growth rate** or (2) using an **arithmetic average dividend growth rate**. Both methods are relatively easy to implement, as we will now illustrate.

To illustrate the difference between a geometric average and an arithmetic average of historical dividend growth, suppose that the Kwik Kiwi Company paid the following dividends at the end of each of the years indicated immediately below.

2007:	$2.20	2004:	$1.75
2006:	2.00	2003:	1.70
2005:	1.80	2002:	1.50

geometric average dividend growth rate
A dividend growth rate based on a geometric average of historical dividends.

arithmetic average dividend growth rate
A dividend growth rate based on an arithmetic average of historical dividends.

We begin with a geometric average growth rate because it is the easiest to calculate. Notice that five years elapsed between the $1.50 dividend paid at the end of 2002 and the $2.20 dividend paid at the end of 2007. A geometric average growth rate is equivalent to a constant rate of growth over the five-year period that would grow the dividend from $1.50 to $2.20. That is, it is the growth rate that solves this growth equation:

$$\$2.20 = \$1.50(1 + g)^5$$

$$g = \left(\frac{\$2.20}{\$1.50}\right)^{1/5} - 1 = .08$$

Thus, in this case, the five-year geometric average dividend growth rate is 8 percent. Notice that this calculation is similar to our calculation of the geometric average return in Chapter 1.

In general, if $D(0)$ is the earliest dividend and $D(N)$ is the latest dividend to be used, to calculate a geometric average dividend growth rate over N years, the general equation used is:

$$g = \left[\frac{D(N)}{D(0)}\right]^{1/N} - 1 \qquad (7.5)$$

In the above example, $D(0) = \$1.50$, $D(N) = \$2.20$, and $N = 5$, which yields $g = 8\%$.

An arithmetic average growth rate takes a little more effort to calculate, since it requires that we first calculate each year's dividend growth rate separately and then calculate an arithmetic average of these annual growth rates. For our Kwik Kiwi example, the arithmetic average of five years of dividend growth is calculated as follows:

Year	Dividend	Yearly Growth Rates
2007	$2.20	10.00% = (2.20 − 2.00) / 2.00
2006	2.00	11.11% = (2.00 − 1.80) / 1.80
2005	1.80	2.86% = (1.80 − 1.75) / 1.75
2004	1.75	2.94% = (1.75 − 1.70) / 1.70
2003	1.70	13.33% = (1.70 − 1.50) / 1.50
2002	1.50	
		40.24 / 5 = 8.05%

Summing the five yearly growth rates yields 40.24, and dividing by five yields an arithmetic average growth rate of 40.24 / 5 = 8.05%. Notice that this arithmetic average growth rate is close to the geometric average growth rate of 8.0 percent that we first calculated. This is usually the case for dividend growth rates, but not always. A large difference means that the dividend grew erratically, which makes the use of the constant growth formula a little questionable in the first place.

NON-CONSTANT DIVIDEND GROWTH

EXAMPLE 7.6

To illustrate how the geometric average and the arithmetic average of historical dividend growth can differ, consider the following dividends paid by the Kwerky Kiwi Company:

2007:	$2.20	2004:	$2.00
2006:	2.00	2003:	1.50
2005:	1.80	2002:	1.50

For Kwerky Kiwi, the arithmetic average of five years of dividend growth is calculated as follows:

Year	Dividend	Yearly Growth Rates
2003	$2.20	10.00% = (2.20 − 2.00) / 2.00
2002	2.00	11.11% = (2.00 − 1.80) / 1.80
2001	1.80	−10.00% = (1.80 − 2.00) / 2.00
2000	2.00	33.33% = (2.00 − 1.50) / 1.50
1999	1.50	0.00% = (1.50 − 1.50) / 1.50
1998	1.50	
		44.44 / 5 = 8.89%

In this case, summing the five yearly growth rates yields 44.44, and dividing by five yields an arithmetic average growth rate of 44.44 / 5 = 8.89%. Notice that this arithmetic average growth rate is somewhat larger than the geometric average growth rate of 8.0 percent.

As this example shows, sometimes the arithmetic and geometric growth rate averages can yield rather different results. In practice, most analysts prefer to use a geometric average when calculating an average historical dividend growth rate. In any case, a historical average growth rate may or may not be a reasonable estimate of future dividend growth. Many analysts adjust their estimates to reflect other information available to them, for example, whether the growth rate appears to be sustainable.

The Sustainable Growth Rate

As we have seen, when using the constant perpetual growth model, it is necessary to come up with an estimate of g, the growth rate in dividends. In our previous discussions, we described two ways to do this: (1) using the company's historical average growth rate or (2) using an industry median or average growth rate. We now describe a third way, known as the **sustainable growth rate**, which involves using a company's earnings to estimate g.

sustainable growth rate A dividend growth rate that can be sustained by a company's earnings.

As we have discussed, a limitation of the constant perpetual growth model is that it should be applied only to companies with stable dividend and earnings growth. Essentially, a company's earnings can be paid out as dividends to its stockholders or kept as **retained earnings** within the firm to finance future growth. The proportion of earnings paid to stockholders as dividends is called the **payout ratio**. The proportion of earnings retained for reinvestment is called the **retention ratio**.

retained earnings Earnings retained within the firm to finance growth.

If we let D stand for dividends and EPS stand for earnings per share, then the payout ratio is simply D/EPS. Since anything not paid out is retained, the retention ratio is just one minus the payout ratio. For example, if a company's current dividend is $4 per share, and its earnings per share are currently $10, then the payout ratio is $4 / $10 = .40, or 40 percent, and the retention ratio is $1 - .40 = .60$, or 60 percent.

payout ratio Proportion of earnings paid out as dividends.

retention ratio Proportion of earnings retained for reinvestment.

A firm's sustainable growth rate is equal to its return on equity (ROE) times its retention ratio.[2]

$$\text{Sustainable growth rate} = \text{ROE} \times \text{Retention ratio} \qquad (7.6)$$
$$= \text{ROE} \times (1 - \text{Payout ratio})$$

Return on equity is commonly computed using an accounting-based performance measure and is calculated as a firm's net income divided by stockholders' equity:

$$\text{Return on equity (ROE)} = \text{Net Income / Equity} \qquad (7.7)$$

CALCULATING SUSTAINABLE GROWTH

EXAMPLE 7.7

In 2005, American Electric Power (AEP) had a return on equity (ROE) of 14.59 percent, earnings per share (EPS) of $2.94, and paid dividends of $D(0) = $1.40. What was AEP's retention rate? Its sustainable growth rate?

AEP's dividend payout was $1.40 / $2.94 = .476, or 47.6 percent. Its retention ratio was thus $1 - .476 = .524$, or 52.4 percent. Finally, AEP's sustainable growth rate was $.1459 \times 52.4\% = 7.645\%$.

---

[2]Strictly speaking, this formula is correct only if ROE is calculated using beginning-of-period stockholders' equity. If ending figures are used, then the precise formula is ROE × Retention ratio / $[1 - (\text{ROE} \times \text{Retention ratio})]$. However, the error from not using the precise formula is usually small, so most analysts do not bother with it.

VALUING AMERICAN ELECTRIC POWER (AEP)

EXAMPLE 7.8

Using AEP's sustainable growth rate of 7.645 percent (see Example 7.7) as an estimate of perpetual dividend growth and its current dividend of $1.40, what is the value of AEP's stock assuming a discount rate of 7.3 percent?

If we plug the various numbers into the perpetual growth model, we obtain a value of $V(0) =$ $1.40(1.07645) / (.073 − .07645) = −436.82! Clearly, something is wrong because we have a negative price. The problem is that the estimate of the sustainable growth rate (7.645%) is greater than the discount rate (7.3%). So, if the discount rate is appropriate, we conclude the estimate of the sustainable growth rate is too high.

VALUING TRANSALTA (TA)

EXAMPLE 7.9

In 2003, TransAlta had a return on equity of ROE = 10.29 percent, earnings per share of EPS = $1.26, and a per-share dividend of $D(0) = 1.00. Assuming a 7.19 percent discount rate, what is the value of TransAlta's stock?

TransAlta's payout ratio was $1.00 / $1.26 = 0.794, or 79.4 percent. Thus, TransAlta's retention ratio was 1 − 0.794 = 0.206, or 20.6 percent. TransAlta's sustainable growth rate was thus 10.29% × 0.206 = 0.0212, or 2.12%. Finally using the constant growth model, we obtain a value of $1.00(1.0212) / (0.0719 − 0.0212) = $20.14. This is higher than the $16.50 stock price at 2003, suggesting that TA stock was undervalued or the growth rate was too high.

As illustrated by Example 7.9, a common problem with sustainable growth rates is that they are sensitive to year-to-year fluctuations in earnings. As a result, security analysts routinely adjust sustainable growth rate estimates to smooth out the effects of earnings variations. Unfortunately, there is no universally standard method to adjust a sustainable growth rate, and analysts depend a great deal on personal experience and their own subjective judgment. Our nearby *Work the Web* box contains more information on analyst-estimated growth rates.

CHECK THIS ✓

7.2a Compare the dividend discount model, the constant growth model, and the constant perpetual growth model. How are they alike? How do they differ?

7.2b What is a geometric average growth rate? How is it calculated?

7.2c What is a sustainable growth rate? How is it calculated?

WORK THE WEB

We discussed use of the sustainable growth formula to estimate a company's growth rate; however, the formula is not foolproof. Changes in the variables of the model can have a dramatic effect on growth rates. One of the most important tasks of an equity analyst is estimating future growth rates. These estimates entail a detailed analysis of the company. One place to find earnings and sales growth rates on the Web is Yahoo! Finance at <u>finance.yahoo.ca</u>. Here we pulled up a quote for Toronto-Dominion Bank (TD) and followed the "Research" link. Below you will see an abbreviated look at the results.

Earnings Est	Current Qtr Jul-07	Next Qtr Oct-07	Current Year Oct-07	Next Year Oct-08
Avg. Estimate	1.31	1.33	5.2	5.71
No. of Analysts	2	2	2	2
Low Estimate	1.26	1.27	5.1	5.62
High Estimate	1.36	1.38	5.31	5.8
Year Ago EPS	1.08	1.07	4.16	5.2
Revenue Est	Current Qtr Jul-07	Next Qtr Oct-07	Current Year Oct-07	Next Year Oct-08
Avg. Estimate	N/A	N/A	N/A	N/A
No. of Analysts	0	0	0	
Low Estimate	N/A	N/A	N/A	N/A
High Estimate	N/A	N/A	N/A	N/A
Year Ago EPS	2.93B	N/A	N/A	N/A
Sales Growth (year/est)	N/A	N/A	N/A	N/A
Earnings History	Jul-06	Oct-06	Jan-07	Apr-07
EPS Est	1.02	1.05	1.08	1.18
EPS Actual	1.08	1.07	1.2	1.17
Difference	0.06	0.02	0.12	−0.01
Surprise %	5.9%	1.9%	11.1%	−0.8%
EPS Trends	Current Qtr Jul-07	Next Qtr Oct-07	Current Year Oct-07	Next Year Oct-08
Current Estimate	1.31	1.33	5.2	5.71
7 Days Ago	1.31	1.33	5.2	5.71
30 Days Ago	1.24	1.26	4.9	5.41
60 Days Ago	1.21	1.24	4.79	5.29
90 Days Ago	1.16	1.19	4.6	5.08

(continued)

As shown, analysts expected earnings per share of 5.2 in 2006 to grow to 5.71 in 2008, an increase of 9.8 percent. We also have the following table comparing TD bank with its competitors within the industry.

	TD	BMO	BNS	RY	Industry
Market Cap:	49.10B	30.69B	48.59B	65.67B	31.89B
Employees:	51.147	N/A	53.251	70.00	37.02K
Rev. Growth (ttm):	7.40%	2.60%	14.90%	9.70%	23.30%
Revenue (ttm):	12.10B	8.88B	11.06B	20.02B	10.60B
Gross Margin (ttm):	N/A	N/A	N/A	N/A	0.00%
EBITDA (ttm):	N/A	N/A	N/A	N/A	N/A
Oper. Margins (ttm):	45.38%	39.19%	49.30%	36.03%	50.49%
Net Income (ttm):	3.13B	2.24B	3.62B	4.84B	3.02B
EPS (ttm):	4.316	4.397	3.621	3.728	3.94
PE (ttm):	15.84	14.01	13.66	13.81	11.69
PEG (ttm):	1.14	1.73	1.23	1.49	1.25
PS (ttm):	3.49	3.40	4.14	3.19	3.09

BMO = Bank of Montreal

BNS = Bank of Nova Scotia

RY = Royal Bank of Canada

Industry = Money Center Bank

7.3 The Two-Stage Dividend Growth Model

In the previous section, we examined dividend discount models based on a single growth rate. You may have already thought that a single growth rate is often unrealistic, since companies experience temporary periods of unusually high or low growth, with growth eventually converging to an industry average or an economywide average. In such cases as these, financial analysts frequently use a **two-stage dividend growth model**.

two-stage dividend growth model
Dividend model that assumes a firm will temporarily grow at a rate different from its long-term growth rate.

A two-stage dividend growth model assumes that a firm will initially grow at a rate g_1 during a first stage of growth lasting T years and thereafter grow at a rate g_2 during a perpetual second stage of growth. The present value formula for the two-stage dividend growth model is stated as follows:

$$V(0) = \frac{D(0)(1+g_1)}{k-g_1}\left[1 - \left(\frac{1+g_1}{1+k}\right)^T\right] + \left(\frac{1+g_1}{1+k}\right)^T \frac{D(0)(1+g_2)}{k-g_2} \tag{7.8}$$

At first glance, this expression looks a little complicated. However, it simplifies if we look at its two distinct parts individually. The first term on the right-hand side measures the present value of the first T dividends and is the same expression we used earlier for the constant growth model. The second term then measures the present value of all subsequent dividends.

Using the formula is mostly a matter of "plug and chug" with a calculator. For example, suppose a firm has a current dividend of $2, and dividends are expected to grow at the rate $g_1 = 20$ percent for $T = 5$ years, and thereafter grow at the rate $g_2 = 5$ percent. With a discount rate of $k = 12$ percent, the present value $V(0)$ is calculated as

$$V(0) = \frac{\$2(1.20)}{.12 - .20}\left[1 - \left(\frac{1.20}{1.12}\right)^5\right] + \left(\frac{1.20}{1.12}\right)^5 \frac{\$2(1.05)}{.12 - .05}$$

$$= \$12.36 + \$42.36$$

$$= \$54.72$$

In this calculation, the total present value of $54.72 is the sum of a $12.36 present value for the first five dividends plus a $42.36 present value for all subsequent dividends.

USING THE TWO-STAGE MODEL

EXAMPLE 7.10

Suppose a firm has a current dividend of $D(0) = \$5$, which is expected to "shrink" at the rate $g_1 = -10$ percent for $T = 5$ years and thereafter grow at the rate $g_2 = 4$ percent. With a discount rate of $k = 10$ percent, what is the value of the stock?

Using the two-stage model, present value, $V(0)$, is calculated as

$$V(0) = \frac{\$5(.90)}{.10 - (-.10)}\left[1 - \left(\frac{.90}{1.10}\right)^5\right] + \left(\frac{.90}{1.10}\right)^5 \frac{\$5(1.04)}{.10 - .04}$$

$$= \$14.25 + \$31.78$$

$$= \$46.03$$

The total present value of $46.03 is the sum of a $14.25 present value of the first five dividends plus a $31.78 present value of all subsequent dividends.

The two-stage growth formula requires that the second-stage growth rate be strictly less than the discount rate, that is, $g_2 < k$. However, the first-stage growth rate g_1 can be greater, smaller, or equal to the discount rate. In the special case where the first-stage growth rate is equal to the discount rate, that is, $g_1 = k$, the two-stage formula reduces to this form:

$$V(0) = D(0) \times T + \frac{D(0)(1 + g_2)}{k - g_2}$$

You may notice with satisfaction that this two-stage formula is much simpler than the general two-stage formula. However, a first-stage growth rate is rarely exactly equal to a risk-adjusted discount rate, so this simplified formula sees little use.

VALUING AMERICAN EXPRESS (AXP)

EXAMPLE 7.11

American Express trades on the New York Stock Exchange under the ticker symbol AXP. In 2005, AXP was paying a dividend of $.48 and analysts forecast five-year growth rates of 13.3 percent for AXP and 11.65 percent for the financial services industry. Assume the growth rate for the financial services industry will remain constant. Then, assuming AXP's growth rate will revert to the industry average after five years, what value would we place on AXP, if we use a discount rate of 13 percent?

(continued)

$$V(0) = \frac{\$.48 \times 1.133}{.13 - .133}\left[1 - \left(\frac{1.133}{1.13}\right)^5\right] + \left(\frac{1.133}{1.13}\right)^5\frac{\$.48 \times 1.1165}{.13 - .1165}$$

$$= (-\$181.28) \times (-.013345) + 1.013345 \times \frac{\$.48 \times 1.1165}{.13 - .1165}$$

$$= \$2.42 + \$40.23$$

$$= \$42.65$$

This present value estimate is less than AXP's mid-2005 share price of $53.40. Is AXP overvalued? What other factors could explain the difference?

HAVE A PEPSI? (PEP)

EXAMPLE 7.12

Pepsi shares trade on the New York Stock Exchange under the ticker symbol PEP. In 2005, Pepsi was paying a dividend of $.95 and analysts forecast a five-year growth rate of 10 percent for Pepsi and a 9 percent growth rate for the soft-drink industry. Suppose Pepsi grows at 10 percent for five years and then at 9 percent thereafter. Assuming a 10.5 percent discount rate, what value would we place on PEP?

Plugging this information into the two-stage dividend growth model, we get:

$$V(0) = \frac{\$.95 \times 1.10}{.105 - .10}\left[1 - \left(\frac{1.10}{1.105}\right)^5\right] + \left(\frac{1.10}{1.105}\right)^5\frac{\$.95 \times 1.09}{.105 - .09}$$

$$= \$4.69 + \$67.49$$

$$= \$72.18$$

This estimate is about 30 percent higher than PEP's mid-2005 share price of $55.54. Suppose we try a second-stage growth rate of 8.50 percent. Then, we get:

$$V(0) = \frac{\$.95 \times 1.10}{.105 - .10}\left[1 - \left(\frac{1.10}{1.105}\right)^5\right] + \left(\frac{1.10}{1.105}\right)^5\frac{\$.95 \times 1.085}{.105 - .085}$$

$$= \$4.69 + \$50.38$$

$$= \$55.07$$

This yields a much more realistic stock price estimate and illustrates how sensitive dividend growth price formulas can be to small changes in estimated growth rates.

The last case we consider is nonconstant growth in the first stage. As a simple example of nonconstant growth, consider the case of a company that is currently not paying dividends. You predict that, in five years, the company will pay a dividend for the first time. The dividend will be $.50 per share. You expect that this dividend will then grow at a rate of 10 percent per year indefinitely. The required return on companies such as this one is 20 percent. What is the price of the stock today?

To see what the stock is worth today, we first find out what it will be worth once dividends are paid. We can then calculate the present value of that future price to get today's price. The first dividend will be paid in five years, and the dividend will grow steadily from then on. Using the dividend growth model, we can say that the price in four years will be:

$$V(4) = D(4) \times (1 + g) / (k - g)$$

$$= D(5) / (k - g)$$

$$= \$.50 / (.20 - .10)$$

$$= \$5$$

If the stock will be worth $5 in four years, then we can get the current value by discounting this price back four years at 20 percent:

$$V(0) = \$5 \, / \, 1.20^4 = \$5 \, / \, 2.0736 = \$2.41$$

The stock is therefore worth $2.41 today.

The problem of nonconstant growth is only slightly more complicated if the dividends are not zero for the first several years. For example, suppose that you have come up with the following dividend forecasts for the next three years:

Year	Expected Dividend
1	$1.00
2	2.00
3	2.50

After the third year, the dividend will grow at a constant rate of 5 percent per year. The required return is 10 percent. What is the value of the stock today?

In dealing with nonconstant growth, a time line can be very helpful. Figure 7.1 illustrates one for this problem. The important thing to notice is when constant growth starts. As we've shown, for this problem, constant growth starts at Time 3. This means that we can use our constant growth model to determine the stock price at Time 3, $V(3)$. By far the most common mistake in this situation is to incorrectly identify the start of the constant growth phase and, as a result, calculate the future stock price at the wrong time.

As always, the value of the stock is the present value of all future dividends. To calculate this present value, we first have to compute the present value of the stock price three years down the road, just as we did before. We then have to add in the present value of the dividends that will be paid between now and then. So, the price in three years is

$$V(3) = D(3) \times (1 + g) \, / \, (k - g)$$
$$= \$2.50 \times 1.05 \, / \, (.10 - .05)$$
$$= \$52.50$$

We can now calculate the total value of the stock as the present value of the first three dividends plus the present value of the price at Time 3, $V(3)$.

$$V(0) = \frac{D(1)}{(1+k)^1} + \frac{D(2)}{(1+k)^2} + \frac{D(3)}{(1+k)^3} + \frac{V(3)}{(1+k)^3}$$
$$= \frac{\$1}{1.10} + \frac{2}{1.10^2} + \frac{2.50}{1.10^3} + \frac{52.50}{1.10^3}$$
$$= \$.91 + 1.65 + 1.88 + 39.44$$
$$= \$43.88$$

The value of the stock today is thus $43.88.

FIGURE 7.1

Time Line

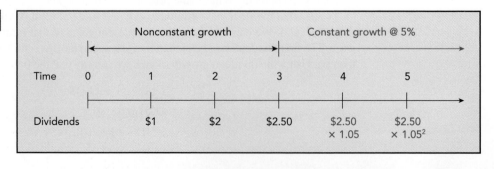

"SUPERNORMAL" GROWTH

EXAMPLE 7.13

Chain Reaction, Inc., has been growing at a phenomenal rate of 30 percent per year because of its rapid expansion and explosive sales. You believe that this growth rate will last for three more years and that the rate will then drop to 10 percent per year. If the growth rate then remains at 10 percent indefinitely, what is the total value of the stock? Total dividends just paid were $5 million, and the required return is 20 percent.

Chain Reaction's situation is an example of supernormal growth. It is unlikely that a 30 percent growth rate can be sustained for any extended length of time. To value the equity in this company, we first need to calculate the total dividends over the supernormal growth period:

Year	Total Dividends (in millions)
1	$5.00 × 1.3 = $6.500
2	6.50 × 1.3 = 8.450
3	8.45 × 1.3 = 10.985

The price at Time 3 can be calculated as

$$V(3) = D(3) \times (1 + g) / (k - g)$$

where g is the long-run growth rate. So we have

$$V(3) = \$10.985 \times 1.10 / (.20 - .10) = \$120.835$$

To determine the value today, we need the present value of this amount plus the present value of the total dividends:

$$V(0) = \frac{D(1)}{(1+k)^1} + \frac{D(2)}{(1+k)^2} + \frac{D(3)}{(1+k)^3} \frac{V(3)}{(1+k)}$$

$$= \frac{\$6.50}{1.20} + \frac{8.45}{1.20^2} + \frac{10.985}{1.20^3} + \frac{120.835}{1.20^3}$$

$$= \$5.42 + 5.87 + 6.36 + 69.93$$

$$= \$87.58$$

The total value of the stock today is thus $87.58 million. If there were, for example, 20 million shares, then the stock would be worth $87.58 / 20 = $4.38 per share.

Discount Rates for Dividend Discount Models

You may wonder where the discount rates used in the preceding examples come from. The answer is that they come from the *capital asset pricing model* (CAPM). Although a detailed discussion of the CAPM is deferred to a later chapter, we can point out here that, based on the CAPM, the discount rate for a stock can be estimated using this formula:

Discount rate = T-bill rate + (Stock beta × Stock market risk premium) (7.9)

The components of this formula, as we use it here, are defined as follows:

T-bill rate:	Return on 90-day T-bills
Stock beta:	Risk relative to an average stock
Stock market risk premium:	Risk premium for an average stock

The basic intuition for this approach can be traced back to Chapter 1. There we saw that the return we expect to earn on a risky asset had two parts, a "wait" component and a "worry" component. We labelled the wait component as the *time value of money*, and we noted that it can be measured as the return we earn from an essentially riskless investment. Here we use the return on a 90-day T-bill as the riskless return.

We called the worry component the *risk premium*, and we noted that the greater the risk, the greater the risk premium. Depending on the exact period studied, the risk premium for the market as a whole over the past 25 or so years has averaged about 5.74 percent. This 5.74 percent can be interpreted as the risk premium for bearing an average amount of stock market risk, and we use it as the stock market risk premium.

beta Measure of a stock's risk relative to the stock market average.

Finally, when we look at a particular stock, we recognize that it may be more or less risky than an average stock. A stock's **beta** is a measure of a single stock's risk relative to an average stock, and we discuss beta at length in a later chapter. For now, it suffices to know that the market average beta is 1.0. A beta of 1.5 indicates that a stock has 50 percent more risk than the average stock, so its risk premium is 50 percent higher. A beta of .50 indicates that a stock is 50 percent less risky than average and has a smaller risk premium.

When this chapter was written, the T-bill rate was 4.50 percent. Taking it as given for now, a stock beta of .8 yields an estimated discount rate of $4.50\% + (0.8 \times 5.74\%) =$ 9.09% or approximately 9%. Similarly, a stock beta of 1.2 yields the discount rate $4.50\% + (1.2 \times 5.74\%) = 11.39\%$. For the remainder of this chapter, we use discount rates calculated according to this CAPM formula.

Observations on Dividend Discount Models

We have examined three dividend discount models: the constant perpetual growth model, the two-stage dividend growth model, and the nonconstant growth model. Each model has advantages and disadvantages. Certainly, the main advantage of the constant perpetual growth model is that it is simple to compute. However, it has several disadvantages: (1) it is not usable for firms not paying dividends, (2) it is not usable when a growth rate is greater than a discount rate, (3) it is sensitive to the choice of growth rate and discount rate, (4) discount rates and growth rates may be difficult to estimate accurately, and (5) constant perpetual growth is often an unrealistic assumption.

The two-stage dividend growth model offers several improvements: (1) it is more realistic, since it accounts for low, high, or zero growth in the first stage, followed by constant long-term growth in the second stage, and (2) it is usable when a first-stage growth rate is greater than a discount rate. However, the two-stage model is also sensitive to the choice of discount rate and growth rates, and it is not useful for companies that don't pay dividends. The nonconstant growth model is more flexible in this regard, but it still remains sensitive to the discount and growth rates assumed.

Financial analysts readily acknowledge the limitations of dividend discount models. Consequently, they also turn to other valuation methods to expand their analyses. In the next section, we discuss some popular stock valuation methods based on price ratios.

CHECK THIS ✓

7.3a　What are the three parts of a CAPM-determined discount rate?

7.3b　Under what circumstances is a two-stage dividend discount model appropriate?

7.4   The Residual Income Model

To this point, we have been valuing only firms that pay dividends. What about the many companies that don't pay dividends? As it turns out, there is an elegant and simple model that we can use.

Residual Income

At the beginning of any period, we can think of the book, or the accounting, equity in a firm as representing the total amount that stockholders have tied up in the company. Let B_{t-1} stand for the book equity per share at the beginning of a period that ends at time t. Over the period, the stockholders have a required return on that investment of k. Thus, the required return in dollars, or required earnings per share (EPS), during the period that ends at time t, or $REPS_t$, is just:

$$REPS_t = B_{t-1} \times k$$

The difference between actual earnings, EPS_t, and required earnings, $REPS_t$, during a period is called the *residual income*, *RI*, and is given by:

$$RI_t = EPS_t - REPS_t = EPS_t - B_{t-1} \times k$$

Economic Value Added (EVA) A financial performance measure based on the difference between a firm's actual earnings and required earnings.

Residual income is sometimes called **Economic Value Added**, or **EVA** for short. It is also called "abnormal" earnings. Whatever it is called, it is the excess of actual earnings over required earnings. We can also think of it as the value created by a firm in period t. Next, we can write the value of a share of stock as the sum of two parts. The first part is the current book value of the firm (i.e., what is currently invested). The second part is the present value of all future residual earnings. That is,

$$P_0 = B_0 + \frac{EPS_1 - B_0 \times k}{(1+k)^1} + \frac{EPS_2 - B_1 \times k}{(1+k)^2} + \frac{EPS_3 - B_2 \times k}{(1+k)^3} + \cdots \quad (7.10)$$

To learn more above Economic Value Added (EVA) visit www.eva.com

When we developed the constant perpetual growth model for dividend-paying stocks, we made the simplifying assumption that *dividends* grow at a constant rate of g. Here we make the similar assumption that *earnings* grow at a constant rate of g. With this assumption, we can simplify equation (7.10) to:

$$P_0 = B_0 + \frac{EPS_0(1+g) - B_0 \times k}{k - g} \quad (7.11)$$

residual income model (RIM) A method for valuing stock in a company that does not pay dividends.

Equation (7.11) is known as the **residual income model**, or **RIM**. If we write both terms in equation (7.11) with a common denominator, we get another way to write the residual income model:

$$P_0 = \frac{EPS_1 - B_0 \times g}{k - g} \quad (7.12)$$

The Rim Versus The Constant Growth DDM

The RIM is closely related to the constant perpetual growth dividend model. To see the connection, assume that the change in book value per share on a stock is equal to earnings per share minus dividends. This is known as the **clean surplus relationship (CSR)**, written as:

$$EPS_1 - D_1 = B_1 - B_0 \text{ or } D_1 = EPS_1 + B_0 - B_1$$

Note that in practice the CSR does not exactly hold because various "dirty" surplus changes to book equity are allowed. But it is usually a good approximation, particularly over the long run.

Assuming that earnings and dividends per share grow at rate g, the CSR shows that book value per share must also grow at rate g, so we can write:

$$D_1 = EPS_1 + B_0 - B_1 = EPS_1 + B_0 - B_0(1 + g) = EPS_1 - B_0 \times g \qquad (7.13)$$

Plugging the expression for D_1 in equation (7.13) into equation (7.12), we see right away that the residual income model is mathematically the same as the constant perpetual growth model:

$$P_0 = \frac{EPS_1 - B_0 \times g}{k - g} = \frac{D_1}{k - g}$$

So these two approaches are really the same, but the RIM is more flexible because we can apply it to any stock, not just dividend payers.

Although we do not present them, there are other forms of the RIM. For example, a two-stage residual income model incorporates two different periods of growth. And the assumption of nonconstant growth for a number of years followed by constant growth can be handled by another form of the residual income model.

THE PRICE OF FIZ

EXAMPLE 7.14

Shares of National Beverage Corporation trade on the American Stock Exchange with the ticker symbol FIZ. National Beverage Corporation does not pay dividends. It is July 1, 2005, and shares of FIZ are trading at $7.98. We have the following data:

	July 1, 2005 (time 0)
EPS_0	$0.47
DIV	$0
Book value, B_0	$4.271

Assume $g = 9$ percent and $k = 10.3$ percent. Using the residual income model,

$$P_0 = B_0 + \frac{EPS_0(1 + g) - B_0 \times k}{k - g}$$

$$= \$4.271 + \frac{\$.47(1 + .09) - \$4.271 \times .103}{.103 - .09}$$

$$= \$4.271 + \frac{\$.5123 - \$.4399}{\$.013} = \$9.84.$$

Verify this price using equation (7.12). Be careful to use g, not $(1 + g)$. Is the market price for FIZ shares too low? If you say yes, what are you saying about the assumed values for g and k?

THE GROWTH OF FIZ

EXAMPLE 7.15

Using the relevant data in Example 7.14 and the residual income model, what growth rate g results in a price of $7.98?

$$P_0 = B_0 + \frac{EPS_0(1+g) - B_0 \times k}{k - g}$$

$$\$7.98 = 4.271 + \frac{.47(1+g) - 4.271 \times .103}{.103 - g}$$

$$\$3.709 \times (.103 - g) = .47 + .47g - .4399$$

$$\$.3820 - 3.709g = .47g + .0301$$

$$.3519 = 4.179\ g$$

$$g = .0842, \text{ or } 8.42\%$$

CHECK THIS ✓

7.4a What does the residual income model do that the perpetual constant growth model cannot do?

7.4b What is the critical assumption that makes the residual income model mathematically equal to the perpetual constant growth model?

7.5 Price Ratio Analysis

Price ratios are widely used by financial analysts, more so even than dividend discount models. Of course, all valuation methods try to accomplish the same thing, which is to appraise the economic value of a company's stock. However, analysts readily agree that no single method can adequately handle this task on all occasions. In this section, we therefore examine several of the most popular price ratio methods and provide examples of their use in financial analysis.

Price-Earnings Ratios

price-earnings (P/E) ratio Current stock price divided by annual earnings per share (EPS).

earnings yield Inverse of the P/E ratio: earnings per share divided by price per share (E/P).

The most popular price ratio used to assess the value of common stock is a company's **price-earnings ratio**, abbreviated as **P/E ratio**. In fact, as we saw in Chapter 4, P/E ratios are reported in the financial press every day. As we discussed, a price-earnings ratio is calculated as the ratio of a firm's current stock price divided by its annual earnings per share (EPS).

The inverse of a P/E ratio is called an **earnings yield**, and it is measured as earnings per share divided by a current stock price (E/P). Clearly, an earnings yield and a price-earnings ratio are simply two ways to measure the same thing. In practice, earnings yields are less commonly stated and used than P/E ratios.

Since most companies report earnings each quarter, annual earnings per share can be calculated either as the most recent quarterly earnings per share times four or as the sum of the last four quarterly earnings per share figures. Most analysts prefer the first method of multiplying the latest quarterly earnings per share value times four. However, some published data sources, including *The Wall Street Journal*, report annual earnings per share as the sum of the last four quarters' figures. The difference is usually small, but it can sometimes be a source of confusion.

Financial analysts often refer to high-P/E stocks as **growth stocks**. To see why, notice that a P/E ratio is measured as a *current* stock price over *current* earnings per share. Now, consider two companies with the same current earnings per share, where one company is a high-growth company and the other is a low-growth company. Which company do you think should have a higher stock price, the high-growth company or the low-growth company?

This question is a no-brainer. All else equal, we would be surprised if the high-growth company did not have a higher stock price, and therefore a higher P/E ratio. In general, companies with higher expected earnings growth will have higher P/E ratios, which is why high-P/E stocks are often referred to as growth stocks.

To give an example, Research in Motion is a high-tech company with a history of aggressive sales growth. Its stock trades on the Toronto Stock Exchange under the ticker symbol RIM. In September 2007, RIM stock traded at $90.21 with earnings per share of EPS = $1.51, and therefore had a P/E ratio of $ 90.21 / $1.51 = 59.74. This value was very high. RIM has never paid dividends and instead reinvests all earnings. So far this strategy has been successful.

The reasons high-P/E stocks are called growth stocks seems obvious enough; however, in a seeming defiance of logic, low-P/E stocks are often referred to as **value stocks**. The reason is that low-P/E stocks are often viewed as "cheap" relative to *current* earnings. (Notice again the emphasis on "current.") This suggests that these stocks may represent good investment values, and hence the term value stocks.

In mid-2005, shares of the well-known S&P 500 auto company Ford (F) were trading at a price of $10.84. With earnings per share of EPS = $1.39, the P/E ratio is $10.84 / $1.39 = 7.80. This is well below the S&P 500 average, and so Ford might be considered a value stock.

Having said all this, we want to emphasize that the terms "growth stock" and "value stock" are mostly just commonly used labels. Of course, only time will tell whether a high-P/E stock turns out to actually be a high-growth stock, or whether a low-P/E stock is really a good value. The nearby *Investment Updates* box contains additional discussion of P/E ratios.

Price-Cash Flow Ratios

Instead of price-earnings (P/E) ratios, many analysts prefer to look at price-cash flow (P/CF) ratios. A **price-cash flow (P/CF) ratio** is measured as a company's current stock price divided by its current annual cash flow per share. Like earnings, cash flow is normally reported quarterly and most analysts multiply the last quarterly cash flow figure by four to obtain annual cash flow. Again, like earnings, many published data sources report annual cash flow as a sum of the latest four quarterly cash flows.

There are a variety of definitions of **cash flow**. In this context, the most common measure is simply calculated as net income plus depreciation, so this is the one we use here. In the next chapter, we examine in detail how cash flow is calculated in a firm's financial statements. Cash flow is usually reported in a firm's financial statements and labelled as cash flow from operations (or operating cash flow).

The difference between earnings and cash flow is often confusing, largely because of the way that standard accounting practice defines net income. Essentially, net income is measured as revenues minus expenses. Obviously, this is logical. However, not all expenses are actually cash expenses. The most important exception is depreciation.

When a firm acquires a long-lived asset such as a new factory facility, standard accounting practice does not deduct the cost of the factory all at once, even though it is

---

Sidebar (left margin):

growth stocks A term often used to describe high-P/E stocks.

Visit the Research in Motion and Ford websites at www.rim.net and www.ford.com

value stocks A term often used to describe low-P/E stocks.

price-cash flow (P/CF) ratio Current stock price divided by current cash flow per share.

cash flow In the context of the price-cash flow ratio, usually taken to be net income plus depreciation.

actually paid for all at once. Instead, the cost is deducted over time. These deductions do not represent actual cash payments, however. The actual cash payment occurred when the factory was purchased. At this point you may be a little confused about why the difference is important, but hang in there for a few more paragraphs.

Most analysts agree that in examining a company's financial performance, cash flow can be more informative than net income. To see why, consider the hypothetical example of two identical companies: Twiddle-Dee Co. and Twiddle-Dum Co. Suppose that both companies have the same constant revenues and expenses in each year over a three-year period. These constant revenues and cash expenses (excluding depreciation) yield the same constant annual cash flows, and they are stated as follows:

	Twiddle-Dee	Twiddle-Dum
Revenues	$5,000	$5,000
Cash expenses	−3,000	−3,000
Cash flow	$2,000	$2,000

Thus, both companies have the same $2,000 cash flow in each of the three years of this hypothetical example.

Next, suppose that both companies incur total depreciation of $3,000 spread out over the three-year period. Standard accounting practice sometimes allows a manager to choose among several depreciation schedules. Twiddle-Dee Co. chooses straight-line depreciation, and Twiddle-Dum Co. chooses accelerated depreciation. These two depreciation schedules are tabulated below:

	Twiddle-Dee	Twiddle-Dum
Year 1	$1,000	$1,500
Year 2	1,000	1,000
Year 3	1,000	500
Total	$3,000	$3,000

Note that total depreciation over the three-year period is the same for both companies. However, Twiddle-Dee Co. has the same $1,000 depreciation in each year, while Twiddle-Dum Co. has accelerated depreciation of $1,500 in the first year, $1,000 in the second year, and $500 depreciation in the third year.

Now, let's look at the resulting annual cash flows and net income figures for the two companies, recalling that in each year, Cash flow = Net income + Depreciation:

	Twiddle-Dee		Twiddle-Dum	
	Cash Flow	Net Income	Cash Flow	Net Income
Year 1	$2,000	$1,000	$2,000	$ 500
Year 2	2,000	1,000	2,000	1,000
Year 3	2,000	1,000	2,000	1,500
Total	$6,000	$3,000	$6,000	$3,000

Note that Twiddle-Dum Co.'s net income is lower in the first year and higher in the third year than Twiddle-Dee Co.'s net income. This is purely a result of Twiddle-Dum Co.'s accelerated depreciation schedule, and has nothing to do with Twiddle-Dum Co.'s actual profitability. However, an inexperienced analyst observing Twiddle-Dum Co.'s rapidly rising annual earnings figures might incorrectly label Twiddle-Dum as a growth

Small Stocks May Offer Investors Huge Returns

Let others fret about the recession. Smart investors should focus on the recovery. Nobody knows when the economy and the stock market will revive. But when the turn comes, history's lesson is clear: Small stocks, and especially small, growth companies, are likely to be huge winners. With that in mind, now could be a great time to start spooning money into some small-stock mutual funds. But make no mistake: This strategy isn't for the faint of heart.

"Coming off market bottoms and coming out of recessions, small stocks historically lead," says John Laporte, manager of the $4 billion-in-assets T. Rowe Price New Horizons Fund. "That's the good news. The bad news is, in down markets and going into recessions, small caps typically underperform." So far, however, the bad news hasn't been all that bad. "Going into this recession, small stocks have done inexplicably well," says David Booth, co-chairman of Dimensional Fund Advisors in Santa Monica, Calif.

Indeed, after being scorned for much of the late 1990s, small stocks have outpaced larger companies over the past 2½ years. Small-company "growth" stocks dazzled in the year running up to the March 2000 market peak. Since then, the big winners in the small-cap sector have been bargain-priced "value" stocks. But even after that relatively strong performance, small stocks still look cheap. Consider some numbers from Leuthold Group in Minneapolis, which keeps tabs on the share price/earnings multiple for 3,000 stocks.

To measure the valuation put on large companies, Leuthold calculates a P/E that is weighted by each company's stock-market capitalization. That produces an earnings multiple of 28.3, based on the past year's operating earnings. But Leuthold also keeps tabs on the valuation of small and midsize companies by looking at the P/E for the median, or typical, stock in its 3,000-stock universe. That generates a P/E of just 14.8. Because of their greater risk, smaller stocks typically trade at lower earnings multiples. But historically, the P/E discount has averaged 18% less, far less than today's 48% haircut.

"Everything is in place for small caps to be the better performers once the recovery starts," argues Andrew Engel, a senior research analyst at Leuthold. "And they should hold up better until then, because they're so much cheaper." In the 12 months following each of the last eight recessions, small stocks have outperformed large companies, according to Baltimore's T. Rowe Price Associates. But investors shouldn't wait for signs of economic recovery before buying small companies. The fact is, the spurt of outperformance usually starts before the recession ends.

(continued)

company. An experienced analyst would observe that there was no cash flow growth to support this naive conclusion.

Financial analysts typically use both price-earnings ratios and price-cash flow ratios. They point out that when a company's earnings per share is not significantly larger than its cash flow per share (CFPS), this is a signal, at least potentially, of good-quality earnings. The term "quality" means that the accounting earnings mostly reflect actual cash flow, not just accounting numbers. When earnings are bigger than cash flow, this may be a signal of poor quality earnings.

Going back to some of our earlier examples, RIM had a cash flow per share of CFPS = $3.66 in US dollars, using the exchange rate 1US \$ = $1.0621 Canadian, CFPS = $3.66 \times 1.0621 = \$3.89$, yielding a P/CF ratio of $\$90.21 / \$3.89 = 23.19$. This ratio was a lot smaller than the P/E ratio, an indication of poor quality of earnings.

Price-Sales Ratios

price-sales (P/S) ratio
Current stock price divided by annual sales per share.

An alternative view of a company's performance is provided by its **price-sales (P/S) ratio**. A price-sales ratio is calculated as the current price of a company's stock divided by its current annual sales revenue per share. A price-sales ratio focuses on a company's ability to generate sales growth. Essentially, a high P/S ratio would suggest high sales growth, while a low P/S ratio might indicate sluggish sales growth.

"Stocks generally start to rally halfway through the recession," says Steven DeSanctis, director of small-cap research at Prudential Securities. "And in that second half, small beats large by almost five percentage points. In the next couple of months, you should position your portfolio to take advantage of the recovery." Even if small stocks don't outperform in the year ahead, they still deserve a place in your portfolio, both for the added diversification and also for the potentially higher long-run return. According to Chicago's Ibbotson Associates, over the past 75 years, small stocks have clocked average annual gains of 12.4%, handily ahead of the 11% a year notched by the Standard & Poor's 500-stock index.

That higher return seems to be a reward for taking on the extra risk involved in buying smaller stocks. "It's not just an American thing," Mr. Booth says. "Everywhere you look around the world, you see this size effect going on." The superior performance of U.S. small stocks is built on some long stretches of dazzling results. Two of the most dazzling winning streaks followed severe economic downturns. In the five years following the 1932 stock-market trough, small stocks outpaced larger companies by 18 percentage points a year, calculates Ibbotson. Meanwhile, in the five years after the 1974 market bottom, small stocks beat large companies by 21.8 percentage points annually.

Will we get the same sort of sparkling performance coming out of the current recession? For small-stock aficionados, that's the big hope. The No-Load Fund Analyst, a newsletter in Orinda, Calif., typically allocates 15% of its model stock portfolio to smaller U.S. companies. But right now, Steve Savage, the newsletter's editor, favours a 19% weighting. "We increased our weighting to small caps in September," Mr. Savage says. "Small caps still offer a valuation advantage. They consistently outperform coming out of a recession. And this time, they've also outperformed on the downside."

Mr. Savage recommends small and midcap funds such as ABN Amro/Veredus Aggressive Growth, Artisan Mid Cap and Rainier Small/Mid Cap. But because there is still so much uncertainty, investors might want to take it slowly with these funds, building up positions over the next three to six months. "There are some compelling reasons to think small caps will do better," Mr. Savage says. "But if there's another terrorist attack or if the recession lasts longer than expected, the danger is that people won't want to own small stocks because they're more illiquid. If the market gets hit again, my fear is that small caps could really underperform."

Source: Jonathan Clements, *The Wall Street Journal*, October 2, 2001. © 2001 Dow Jones & Company, Inc. All Rights Reserved Worldwide.

RIM had sales per share of $5.85 in US dollars, using the exchange rate 1US $ = $1.0621 Canadian, SPS = $5.85 × 1.0621 = $ 6.21, yielding a P/CF ratio of $90.21 / $6.21 = 14.53.

Ford had sales per share of $90.42 for a price-sales ratio of P/S = $10.84 / $90.42 = .12. Notice the large variation in price-sales ratios for the two companies. The main reason for this difference is that the two companies are in very different kinds of businesses. Security analysts recognize that price-sales ratios cannot be compared in isolation from other important information.

Price-Book Ratios

price-book (P/B) ratio Market value of a company's common stock divided by its book (or accounting) value of equity.

A very basic price ratio for a company is its **price-book (P/B) ratio**, sometimes called the market-book ratio. A price-book ratio is measured as the market value of a company's outstanding common stock divided by its book value of equity.

Price-book ratios are appealing because book values represent, in principle, historical cost. The stock price is an indicator of current value, so a price-book ratio simply measures what the equity is worth today relative to what it cost. A ratio bigger than 1.0 indicates that the firm has been successful in creating value for its stockholders. A ratio smaller than 1.0 indicates that the company is actually worth less than it cost.

This interpretation of the price-book ratio seems simple enough, but the truth is that because of varied and changing accounting standards, book values are difficult to interpret. For this and other reasons, price-book ratios may not have as much information value as they once did.

Applications of Price Ratio Analysis

Check out the Tim Hortons website at www.timhortons.com

Price-earnings ratios, price-cash flow ratios, and price-sales ratios are commonly used to calculate estimates of expected future stock prices. This is done by multiplying a historical average price ratio by an expected future value for the price-ratio denominator variable. For example, Table 7.1 summarizes such a price ratio analysis for Tim Hortons company based on 2006 information.

In Table 7.1, the current value row contains values for earnings per share, cash flow per share, and sales per share. The historical ratio row contains the historical P/E, P/CF, and P/S ratios, and the growth rate row contains projected growth rates for EPS, CFPS and SPS.

The expected price row contains expected stock prices one year hence. The basic idea is this. Since Tim Hortons has had an average P/E ratio of 20.43, we will assume that Tim Hortons' stock price will be 20.43 times its earnings one year from now. To estimate Tim Hortons' earnings one year from now, we note that Tim Hortons' earnings are projected to grow at 14.40 percent per year. If earnings continue to grow at this rate, then next year's earnings will be equal to this year's earnings multiplied by 1.1440. Putting it all together, we have

$$
\begin{aligned}
\text{Expected price} &= \text{Historical P/E ratio} \times \text{Projected EPS} \\
&= \text{Historical P/E ratio} \times \text{Current EPS} \times \\
&\quad (1 + \text{Projected EPS Growth rate}) \\
&= 20.43 \times 1.22 \times (1.1440) \\
&= \$28.51
\end{aligned}
$$

The same procedure is used to calculate an expected price based on cash flow per share.

$$
\begin{aligned}
\text{Expected price} &= \text{Historical P/CF ratio} \times \text{Projected CFPS} \\
&= \text{Historical P/CF ratio} \times \text{Current CFPS} \times \\
&\quad (1 + \text{Projected CFPS growth rate}) \\
&= 30.11 \times 0.50 \times (1.1440) \\
&= \$17.22
\end{aligned}
$$

TABLE 7.1	**Price Ratio Analysis For Tim Hortons** **September 2007 Stock Price: US $ 33.11**		
	Earnings (P/E)	**Cash Flow (P/CF)**	**Sales (P/S)**
Historical price ratio	$20.43	$30.11	$4.94
Current value per share	1.22	0.50	5.78
Growth rate	14.40%	14.40%	14.40%
Expected stock price	$28.51	$17.22	$32.66

Even before last week's impressive rally, the stock market was outrageously expensive. At least that's what some key market yardsticks show.

But hold on to your sell orders. Many investment experts reckon the fault lies not with the market, but with the measuring sticks. In particular, these experts see serious shortcomings in three popular stock-market gauges: the price-to-book value ratio, dividend yield, and the price-to-earnings multiple.

The three standard measures "are all flawed in some way," says Frazier Evans, senior economist at Colonial Group, the Boston mutual-fund company. "You have to look under the surface. I'd say that the market is not as expensive as it looks."

Dwindling Dividends

Consider, for instance, the market's dividend yield. The companies in the Standard & Poor's 500-stock index are paying annual dividends amounting to 2.8% of their current stock prices. That's well below the historical average dividend yield of 4.7% and not far above the all-time low of 2.64%, which was hit in 1987, just before that year's stock-market crash.

A danger signal? Maybe not. The reason is that corporations seem to be paying out far less of their earnings as dividends these days. Instead, companies are using profits to expand their businesses and buy their own shares—actions designed to boost stock prices.

The shift should please most investors. Because dividend income is taxed more heavily than capital gains, shareholders benefit more if returns come in the form of higher stock prices, rather than big dividends.

The dividend-yield gauge also is being thrown out of whack by other factors, says Arnold Kaufman, editor of Standard & Poor's Outlook, a weekly newsletter. For instance, "dividends are being held down by the special problems of large dividend-paying industry groups, such as telephones, utilities, and drugs," he says.

Effect on Book Value

At first blush, the market's price-to-book value also suggests shares are richly priced. Bargain hunters often look for stocks that are trading below book value, which is the difference between a company's assets and its liabilities expressed on a per-share basis.

But these days, precious few stocks trade below book value. Indeed, Mr. Kaufman figures stocks on average are trading at more than three times book value, compared with just 1.2 times book in the late 1970s.

But once again, the measuring gauge may be faulty. Book value has been distorted by share repurchases, special charges due to corporate restructurings, and the adoption of a new accounting rule concerning retiree health benefits. "Price-to-book value has lost a lot of its usefulness," Mr. Kaufman concludes.

What about price-to-earnings multiples? Right now, the market is trading at about 15 times expected 1995 earnings, a tad above the historical average. "There are fewer problems with P/E ratios than with the other two measures," says Kathleen Crowley, a senior vice president with Chicago's Stratford Advisory Group.

Even so, earnings multiples also can mislead. In recent years, reported earnings have been depressed by special charges. In addition, experts say the market's earnings multiple shouldn't be viewed in isolation, but instead should be considered in the context of items like interest rates and inflation.

Finally, an expected price based on sales per share is calculated as

$$\text{Expected price} = \text{Historical P/S ratio} \times \text{Projected SPS}$$
$$= \text{Historical P/S ratio} \times \text{Current SPS}$$
$$\times (1 + \text{Projected SPS growth rate})$$
$$= 4.94 \times 5.78 \times (1.1440)$$
$$= \$32.66$$

Notice that each price ratio method yields a different expected price, sometimes with rather large differences.

TABLE 7.2	Price Ratio Analysis for Disney Corporation (DIS) Mid-2005 Stock Price: $26.67		
	Earnings	**Cash Flow**	**Sales**
Five-year average price ratio	31.38 (P/E)	16.51 (P/CF)	1.99 (P/S)
Current value per share	$1.09 (EPS)	$1.70 (CFPS)	$15.05 (SPS)
Growth rate	18.0%	14.0%	7.0%
Expected stock price	$40.36	$31.99	$32.05

GOING TO DISNEYLAND

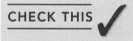

EXAMPLE 7.16

See Mickey's website at
www.disney.go.com

Table 7.2 contains information about Walt Disney Corporation. Calculate expected share prices using each of the three price ratio approaches we have discussed.

For example, using the P/E approach, we come up with the following estimates of the price of Walt Disney stock in one year:

$$\text{Expected price} = \text{Historical P/E ratio} \times \text{Current EPS}$$
$$\times (1 + \text{projected EPS growth})$$
$$= 31.38 \times \$1.09 \times 1.18$$
$$= \$40.36$$

CHECK THIS ✓

7.5a   Why are high-P/E stocks sometimes called growth stocks?

7.5b   Why might an analyst prefer a price-cash flow ratio to a price-earnings ratio?

7.6   An Analysis of the McGraw-Hill Company

Stock market investors have available to them many sources of information about the financial performance of companies with publicly traded stock shares. Indeed, the sheer volume of information available can often be overwhelming. For this reason, several sources publish reference summaries for individual companies.

Visit the McGraw-Hill website at
www.mcgraw-hill.
com

One well-known example is the *Value Line Investment Survey*, a published reference with frequent updates. *Value Line* provides what many investors consider to be the best one-page company summaries available. Current updates to the *Value Line Investment Survey* are available at most stock brokerage offices and many public libraries. Figure 7.2 presents a one-page summary for the McGraw-Hill Corporation published by *Value Line* in 2006. We will make frequent reference to information found in the *Value Line* summary in the discussion of McGraw-Hill.

As shown in the title bar of Figure 7.2, McGraw-Hill stock trades on the New York Stock Exchange (NYSE) under the ticker symbol MHP. When this survey went to press in August 2005, McGraw-Hill's stock price was $47.04, with a P/E ratio of 20.9. *Value Line* calculates a P/E ratio as the most recent stock price divided by the latest six months' earnings per share plus earnings per share estimated for the next six months. McGraw-Hill's relative P/E ratio of 1.11 is obtained by dividing its current P/E by the median P/E

FIGURE 7.2 *Value Line* Analysis Chart

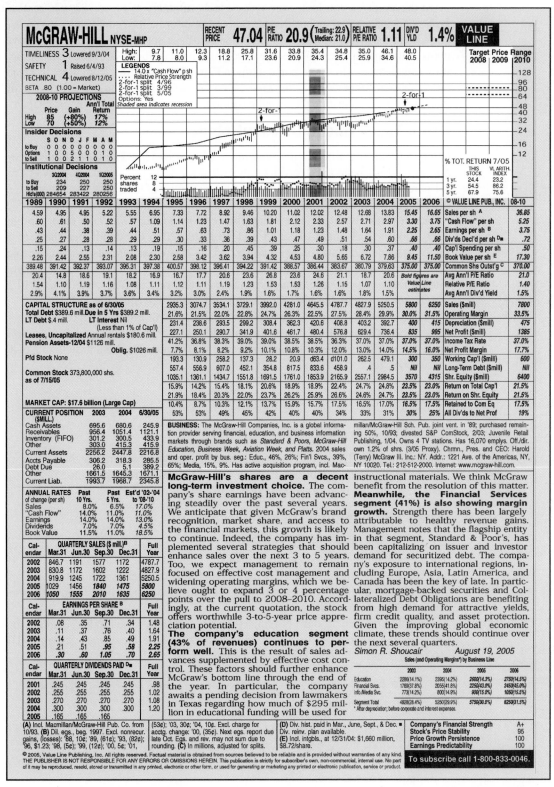

Source: *Value Line* Investment Survey, 2006.

ratio of all stocks under review by *Value Line*. The dividend yield of 1.4 percent is cal-culated by dividing estimated dividends for the coming year by the current stock price.

At this point, as you look over *Value Line*'s summary in Figure 7.2, you realize that *Value Line* has packed a considerable amount of information onto a single page. We ac-knowledge the efficiency of the *Value Line* one-page surveys by not trying to cover all items on the entire page. Most items are well-explained in Figure 7.3, which contains a com-plete sample page. However, some items in Figure 7.2 may differ from those in Figure 7.3 reflecting changes made by *Value Line*. In the following discussion, we refer only to infor-mation needed to illustrate the analytic methods discussed previously in this chapter.

Using The Dividend Discount Model

Our first task is to estimate a discount rate for McGraw-Hill. The *Value Line Investment Survey* reports a beta of .80 for McGraw-Hill stock. Using a current Treasury bill rate of 3.1 percent and a historical stock market risk premium of 9 percent, we obtain a CAPM discount rate estimate for McGraw-Hill of $3.1\% + .80 \times 9\% = 10.3\%$.

Our next task is to calculate a sustainable growth rate. *Value Line* reports projected 2006 earnings per share of $2.65 and projected 2006 dividends per share of $.66, implying a retention ratio of $1 - \$.66 / \$2.65 = .751$. *Value Line* also reports a projected 2006 return on equity of ROE = 23.0 percent (reported as "Return on Shr. Equity"). Putting these together yields a sustainable growth rate of $.751 \times 23.0\% = 17.27\%$, which may be somewhat high for a mature company like McGraw-Hill.

Finally, with a discount rate and sustainable growth rate we can calculate a share price for McGraw-Hill. Using a constant dividend growth rate model with the 2005 dividend of $D(0) = \$.66$, a discount rate of $k = 10.3$ percent, and a growth rate of 17.27 percent, we get:

$$V(0) = \frac{\$0.66 \times 1.1727}{.103 - .1727}$$
$$= -\$11.10$$

which cannot be. The negative price is due to a growth rate greater than the discount rate, indicating we cannot use the constant dividend growth rate model. As a good analyst would, we'll try something else.

Using The Residual Income Model

In reality, a sustainable growth rate of over 17 percent is not feasible. *Value Line* reports that the actual dividend growth rate over the previous five years was 7 percent (from the box labeled "Annual Rates"). You can audit this number by calculating a simple or geometric average dividend growth rate using dividends per share from 2000 through 2005. (Which one rounds to 7 percent?)

Let's assume that "today" is January 1, 2005. Also, let's keep the 7 percent growth rate and 10.3 percent discount rate. From the *Value Line Investment Survey* (VL), we can fill in columns two and three of the table below:

	2005 (time 0)	2006 (VL)	2006 (CSR)
Beginning BV per share	NA	$9.45	$9.45
EPS	2.25	2.65	2.4075*
DIV	0.66	0.66	1.7460**
Ending BV per share	9.45	11.50	10.1115*

*2.25 × 1.07; 9.45 × 1.07.

**"Plug" = 2.4075 − (10.1115 − 9.45).

FIGURE 7.3 *Value Line* **Analysis Chart**

Getting the Most from the Value Line Page

The LEGENDS box contains the "Cash Flow" multiple as well as the amounts and dates of recent stock splits and dividends. Also shows if options are traded on the stock.

Monthly price ranges of the stock—plotted on a ratio (logarithmic) grid to show percentage changes in true proportion.

The "Cash Flow" line—a graphic presentation of cash flow per share, multiplied by a number selected so that the line correlates with a stock's monthly price range.

P/E ratio—the stock's recent price divided by the latest six months' earnings per share plus earnings estimated for the next six months.

Trailing P/E —the recent price divided by the sum of earnings per share during the past 12 months.

Median P/E —the mean of the four middle values of the average annual price-earnings ratios over the past ten years.

Relative P/E ratio—the stock's P/E divided by the median P/E for all stocks under Value Line review.

Dividend yield—cash dividends estimated to be declared in the next 12 months divided by the recent price.

Here is the core of Value Line's advice—the rank for Timeliness; the rank for Safety; the Technical rank. And next to each is normally the date each last changed. Beta shows the stock's sensitivity to fluctuations in the market as a whole.

Projected stock price returns to 2003-05, both absolute (gain/loss without dividends) and total (annual, including dividends).

The record of insider decisions—decisions by officers and directors to buy or sell as reported to the SEC.

The number of large institutions —including banks, insurance companies, mutual funds—buying or selling during the past three quarters and the total number of shares owned.

The capital structure as of recent date showing the percentage of capital in long-term debt and shareholders' equity. Also, Market Capitalization.

Current position—current assets and current liabilities, the components of working capital.

Annual rates of change (on a per-share basis). Actual past, estimated future.

Sales and earnings are shown for each quarter, with earnings on a per share basis.

Quarterly dividends paid are actual payments. The total of dividends paid in four quarters may not equal the figure shown in the annual series on dividends declared. (Sometimes a dividend declared at the end of the year will be paid in the first quarter of the following year).

Footnotes explain a number of things, such as the way earnings are reported, and the net effect of nonrecurring items.

The stock's highest and lowest prices of the year.

The 3- to 5-year Target Price Range, estimated. These are the same ranges shown numerically in the "2003-05 Projections" box on the left side of the price chart.

The % Total Return shows price appreciation (plus dividends) of the stock for the past 1, 3, and 5 years and also for the stock market, as measured by the Value Line Arithmetic Index.

The number of shares traded monthly as a percentage of the total outstanding.

Statistical array that reveals significant long-term trends. Note that the statistics for the current and future years are estimated. The estimates are revised when necessary in the weekly *Summary & Index*.

A condensed summary of the business, significant shareholders (holding over 5%) and the company's address, telephone number, and Internet address.

Analyst's Commentary is a 350-word report on recent developments and prospects, issued once every three months on a preset schedule.

The date of delivery to the subscribers. *The Investment Survey* is mailed on a schedule that aims for delivery to every subscriber on Friday.

Value Line's Indexes of Financial Strength, Price Stability, Price Growth Persistence, and Earnings Predictability.

Source: *Value Line*, "How to Invest in Common Stocks: A Guide to Using the Value Line Investment Survey," 2003.

The fourth column comes from using the clean surplus relationship (CSR). Here, we grow EPS and book value per share using a growth rate of 7 percent. Then we calculate the dividend "plug" that makes the change in book value equal to EPS minus dividends.

Now we can estimate two prices for McGraw-Hill shares using the RIM—one from data provided by *Value Line* and one from data using the clean surplus relationship. In addition, we can compare these values using a constant dividend growth rate model that uses a dividend growth rate of 7 percent. Using the RIM, we get:

$$P_0 = 9.45 + \frac{2.4075 - 9.45 \times .103}{.103 - .07} = \$52.91 \quad \text{(CSR)}$$

$$P_0 = 9.45 + \frac{2.65 - (11.50 - 9.45)}{.103 - .07} = \$27.63 \quad \text{(VL)}$$

Using the DDM, we get:

$$P_0 = \frac{1.7460}{.103 - .07} = \$52.91 \quad \textit{(CSR)}$$

$$P_0 = \frac{.66}{.103 - .07} = \$20.00 \quad \textit{(VL)}$$

The $.66 used is *Value Line*'s estimate of next year's dividend, D_1, because *Value Line* forecasts no dividend growth between 2005 and 2006. As you would expect, both the RIM and the DDM indicate a price of $52.91 for McGraw-Hill when we use the CSR. This share value is reasonably close to McGraw-Hill's recently reported stock price of $47.04. RIM and DDM prices using data from *Value Line* differ, however, because of "dirty surplus."

Using Price Ratio Analysis

Value Line reports annual growth rates for sales, cash flow, earnings, dividends, and book values in the box labeled "Annual Rates." These include historical five-year and ten-year growth rates, along with expected growth rates for the next three to five years. We will estimate expected future stock prices using five-year average price ratios that we will calculate along with expected growth rates supplied by *Value Line*.

The *Value Line* survey reports annual average price-earnings ratios, but it does not report average price to cash flow per share ratios, P/CF, or average price to sales per share ratios, P/S. In this case, because all these numbers are on a per-share basis, a quick way to calculate an average P/CF ratio is to multiply an average P/E ratio by the ratio of earnings per share to cash flow per share. That is, P/CFPS = P/E × EPS/CFPS (recall that the "E" in P/E stands for EPS, so they cancel).

For example, McGraw-Hill's 2004 average P/E was 20.60, EPS was $1.91, CFPS was $2.97, and SPS was $13.83. Thus, a quick calculation of McGraw-Hill's 2004 average P/CF ratio is 20.60 × $1.91 / $2.97 = 13.25. Similarly, the average P/S ratio is 20.60 × $1.91 / $13.83 = 2.84. In Table 7.3, we provide average price ratio calculations for P/CF and P/S ratios for the years 2000 through 2004, along with five-year averages for each price ratio.

We use the five-year average price ratios calculated in Table 7.3 in the price ratio analysis presented in Table 7.4. We use the expected growth rates for earnings, cash flow, and sales provided by *Value Line* (from the "Annual Rates" box) to calculate

TABLE 7.3	Price Ratio Calculations for McGraw-Hill Co. (MHP)					
	2000	**2001**	**2002**	**2003**	**2004**	**Average**
EPS	1.18	1.23	1.48	1.64	1.91	1.49
P/E	23.60	24.60	21.10	18.70	20.60	21.72
CFPS	2.12	2.33	2.57	2.71	2.97	2.54
P/CF	13.14	12.99	12.15	11.32	13.25	12.57
SPS	11.02	12.02	12.48	12.68	13.83	12.41
P/S	2.53	2.52	2.50	2.42	2.84	2.56

TABLE 7.4	Price Ratio Analysis for McGraw-Hill Co. (MHP) August 2005 Stock Price: $47.04		
	Earnings	**Cash Flow**	**Sales**
Five-year average price ratio	21.72 (P/E)	12.57 (P/CF)	2.56 (P/S)
Current value per share	$1.91 (EPS)	$2.97 (CFPS)	$13.83 (SPS)
Growth rate	13.0%	11.0%	17.0%
Expected share price	$46.88	$41.44	$41.42

expected share prices for McGraw-Hill *one year from now*. For ease, we restate the three formulas used to calculate expected prices below. As an exercise, you should verify the expected share prices in Table 7.4.

Expected share price = P/E ratio × EPS × (1 + EPS growth rate)

Expected share price = P/CF ratio × CFPS × (1 + CFPS growth rate)

Expected share price = P/S ratio × SPS × (1 + SPS growth rate)

We can now summarize our analysis by listing the stock prices obtained by the different ways we have described in this chapter, along with the model used to derive them.

DDM, with calculated sustainable growth rate:	Not defined
DDM, historical growth rate, Value Line input:	$20.00
DDM, historical growth rate, CSR:	$52.91
RIM, historical growth rate, Value Line input:	$27.63
RIM, historical growth rate, CSR:	$52.91
Price-earnings model:	$46.88
Price-cash flow model:	$41.44
Price-sales model:	$41.42

Notice the wide range of share values we obtained by our various ways. This is not uncommon in security analysis, and it suggests how daunting a task security analysis sometimes can be. In this case, the price-earnings model yields a value closest to the observed stock price of $47.04. However, the goal is not to find a model that yields a value closest to the current price. Rather, the goal is to find a model about which we are confident, For example, if we were confident in the RIM and assumed the clean surplus relationship, then we would conclude that McGraw-Hill stock is fairly priced. But if we use the RIM but did not assume the clean surplus relationship holds, then we would conclude that McGraw-Hill shares are somewhat overpriced.

CHECK THIS ✔

7.6a Locate *Value Line*'s projected growth rate in dividends. How does it compare to the sustainable growth rate we estimated? The historical growth rates? Revalue the stock using the constant perpetual dividend model and this growth rate.

7.6b Assume that the sustainable growth rate we calculated is the growth rate for the next five years only and that dividends will grow thereafter at the rate projected by *Value Line* analysts. Using these growth rates, revalue the stock using the two-stage dividend growth model.

7.7 Summary and Conclusions

In this chapter, we examined several methods of fundamental analysis used by financial analysts to value common stocks. The methods examined were various dividend discount models, residual income models, and price ratio models. We saw that:

1. Dividend discount models value common stock as the sum of all expected future dividend payments, where the dividends are adjusted for risk and the time value of money.

2. The dividend discount model is often simplified by assuming that dividends will grow at a constant growth rate. A particularly simple form of the dividend discount model is the case in which dividends grow at a constant perpetual growth rate. The simplicity of the constant perpetual growth model makes it the most popular dividend discount model. However, it should be applied only to companies with stable earnings and dividend growth.

3. Dividend models require an estimate of future growth. We described the sustainable growth rate, which is measured as a firm's return on equity times its retention ratio, and illustrated its use.

4. Companies often experience temporary periods of unusually high or low growth, where growth eventually converges to an industry average. In such cases, analysts frequently use a two-stage dividend growth model.

5. The difference between actual and required earnings in any period is called residual income. Residual income is sometimes called Economic Value Added or, sometimes, abnormal earnings.

6. The residual income model is a method that can be used to value a share of stock in a company that does not pay dividends. To derive the residual income model, a series of constant growth assumptions are made for EPS, assets, liabilities, and equity. Together, these growth assumptions result in a sustainable growth rate.

7. The residual income model breaks the value of a share of stock into two parts: the current book value of the firm and the present value of all residual earnings (i.e., income).

8. The clean surplus relationship is an accounting relationship that says earnings minus dividends equals the change in book value per share. The clean surplus relationship might not hold in actual practice. But if the clean surplus relationship is true, then the residual income model is mathematically equivalent to the constant perpetual growth model.

9. Price ratios are widely used by financial analysts. The most popular price ratio is a company's price-earnings ratio. A P/E ratio is calculated as the ratio of a firm's stock price divided by its earnings per share (EPS).

10. Financial analysts often refer to high-P/E stocks as growth stocks and low-P/E stocks as value stocks. In general, companies with high expected earnings growth will have high P/E ratios, which is why high-P/E stocks are referred to as growth stocks. Low-P/E stocks are referred to as value stocks because they are viewed as cheap relative to current earnings.

11. Instead of price-earnings ratios, many analysts prefer to look at price-cash flow (P/CF) ratios. A price-cash flow ratio is measured as a company's stock price divided by its cash flow per share. Most analysts agree that cash flow can provide more information than net income about a company's financial performance.

12. An alternative view of a company's performance is provided by its price-sales (P/S) ratio. A price-sales ratio is calculated as the price of a company's stock divided by its annual sales revenue per share. A price-sales ratio focuses on a company's ability to generate sales growth. A high P/S ratio suggests high sales growth, while a low P/S ratio suggests low sales growth.

13. A basic price ratio for a company is its price-book (P/B) ratio. A price-book ratio is measured as the market value of a company's outstanding common stock divided by its book value of equity. A high P/B ratio suggests that a company is potentially expensive, while a low P/B value suggests that a company may be cheap.

14. A common procedure using price-earnings ratios, price-cash flow ratios, and price-sales ratios is to calculate estimates of expected future stock prices. However, each price ratio method yields a different expected future stock price. Since each method uses different information, each makes a different prediction.

REAL WORLD

This chapter introduced you to some of the basics of common stock valuation and fundamental analysis. It focused on two important tools used by stock analysts in the real world to assess whether a particular stock is "rich" or "cheap": dividend discount models and price ratio analysis. How should you, as an investor or investment manager, put this information to use?

The answer is that you need to pick some stocks and get to work! As we discussed in the chapter, experience and judgment are needed to use these models, and the only

(continued)

way to obtain these is through practice. Try to identify a few stocks that look cheap and buy them in a simulated brokerage account such as Stock-Trak. At the same time, find a few that look rich and short them. Start studying P/E ratios. Scan *The Globe and Mail* (or a similar source of market information) and look at the range of P/Es. What's a low P/E? What's a high one? Do they really correspond to what you would call growth and value stocks?

The Internet is a copious source for information on valuing companies. Try for example, GlobeInvestor (www.globeinvestor.com), Yahoo Canada Finance (ca.yahoo.finance.com), and Hoovers Online (www.hoovers.com). Don't forget to check out the Motley Fool (www.fool.com).

Several trade associations have informative websites that can be helpful. For professional security analysts there is Toronto Society of Financial Analysts website (www.tsfa.ca). The CFA Institute (www.cfainstitute.org) provides a financial analyst's certification that is highly respected among security analysts.

Key Terms

fundamental analysis 189
dividend discount model (DDM) 190
constant growth rate model 191
constant perpetual growth model 192
geometric average dividend growth rate 194
arithmetic average dividend growth rate 194
sustainable growth rate 196
retained earnings 196
payout ratio 196
retention ratio 196
two-stage dividend growth model 199

beta 204
Economic Value Added (EVA) 205
residual income model (RIM) 205
clean surplus relationship (CSR) 206
price-earnings (P/E) ratio 207
earnings yield 207
growth stocks 208
value stocks 208
price-cash flow (P/CF) ratio 208
cash flow 208
price-sales (P/S) ratio 210
price-book (P/B) ratio 211

Chapter Review Problems and Self-Test

1. **The Perpetual Growth Model** Suppose dividends for Tony's Pizza company are projected to grow at 6 percent forever. If the discount rate is 16 percent and the current dividend is $2, what is the value of the stock?

2. **The Two-Stage Growth Model** Suppose the Titanic Ice Cube Co.'s dividend grows at a 20 percent rate for the next three years. Thereafter, it grows at a 12 percent rate. What value would we place on Titanic assuming a 15 percent discount rate? Titanic's most recent dividend was $3.

3. **Residual Income Model** Suppose Al's Infrared Sandwich Company has a current book value of $10.85 per share. The most recent earnings per share were $2.96 per share, and earnings are expected to grow at 6 percent forever. The appropriate discount rate is 8.2 percent. Assume the clean surplus relationship is true. Assuming the company maintains a constant retention ratio, what is the value of the company according to the residual income model if (a) there are no dividends, and (b) there are dividends of $1.00 per share?

4. **Price Ratio Analysis** The table below contains some information about the Jordan Air Co. Provide expected share prices using each of the three price ratio approaches we have discussed.

www.mcgrawhill.ca/olc/Jordan

PRICE RATIO ANALYSIS FOR JORDAN AIR (CURRENT STOCK PRICE: $40)			
	Earnings	Cash Flow	Sales
Five-year average price ratio	25 (P/E)	7 (P/CF)	1.5 (P/S)
Current value per share	$2.00 (EPS)	$6.00 (CFPS)	$30.00 (SPS)
Growth rate	10%	16%	14%

Answers to Self-Test Problems

1. Plugging the relevant numbers into the constant perpetual growth formula results in:

$$V(0) = \frac{\$2(1.06)}{.16 - .06} = \$21.20$$

As shown, the stock should sell for $21.20.

2. Plugging all the relevant numbers into the two-stage formula gets us:

$$V(0) = \frac{\$3(1.20)}{.15 - .20}\left[1 - \left(\frac{1.20}{1.15}\right)^3\right] + \left(\frac{1.20}{1.15}\right)^3 \frac{\$3(1.12)}{.15 - .12}$$
$$= \$9.81 + \$127.25$$
$$= \$137.06$$

Thus, the stock should sell for about $137.

3. Recall the formula for the residual income model when the clean surplus relationship is true:

$$P_0 = B_0 + \frac{EPS_0(1+g) - B_0 \times k}{k - g}$$

Next, make a table of all the information that you need to put into the formula:

Al's Infrared Sandwich Company	Time 0, i.e., Now
Beginning book value, B_0	10.85
Earnings per share, EPS_0	2.96
Growth rate, g	6%
Discount rate, k	8.2%

We can now solve the problem.

$$P_0 = 10.85 + \frac{2.96(1 + .06) - 10.85 \times .082}{.082 - .06}$$
$$P_0 = \$113.03$$

4. Using the P/E approach, we come up with the following estimate of the price of Jordan Air in one year:

$$\text{Estimated price} = \text{Average P/E} \times \text{Current EPS} \times (1 + \text{Growth rate})$$
$$= 25 \times \$2 \times 1.10$$
$$= \$55$$

Using the P/CF approach, we get:

$$\text{Estimated price} = \text{Average P/CF} \times \text{Current CFPS} \times (1 + \text{Growth rate})$$
$$= 7 \times \$6 \times 1.16$$
$$= \$48.72$$

www.mcgrawhill.ca/olc/Jordan

Finally, using the P/S approach, we get:

$$\text{Estimated price} = \text{Average P/S} \times \text{Current SPS} \times (1 + \text{Growth rate})$$
$$= 1.5 \times \$30 \times 1.14$$
$$= \$51.30$$

Test Your Investment Quotient

1. **Sustainable Growth** A company has a return on equity of ROE = 20 percent, and from earnings per share of EPS = $5, it pays a $2 dividend. What is the company's sustainable growth rate?

   a. 8 percent
   b. 10 percent
   c. 12 percent
   d. 20 percent

2. **Sustainable Growth** If the return on equity for a firm is 15 percent and the retention ratio is 40 percent, the sustainable growth rate of earnings and dividends is which of the following?

   a. 6 percent
   b. 9 percent
   c. 15 percent
   d. 40 percent

3. **Dividend Discount Model** A common stock pays an annual dividend per share of $2.10. The risk-free rate is 7 percent and the risk premium for this stock is 4 percent. If the annual dividend is expected to remain at $2.10, the value of the stock is closest to:

   a. $19.09
   b. $30.00
   c. $52.50
   d. $70.00

4. **Dividend Discount Model** Suppose a security pays a current dividend of $5 and all future dividends will grow at a rate of 8 percent per year forever. Assuming the appropriate discount rate is 12 percent, what is the value of this security?

   a. $135
   b. $270
   c. $13.50
   d. $1,350

5. **Dividend Discount Model** The constant-growth dividend discount model will not produce a finite value if the dividend growth rate is which of the following?

   a. Above its historical average.
   b. Above the required rate of return.
   c. Below its historical average.
   d. Below the required rate of return.

6. **Dividend Discount Model** In applying the constant-growth dividend discount model, a stock's intrinsic value will do which of the following when the required rate of return is lowered?

   a. Decrease.
   b. Increase.
   c. Remain unchanged.
   d. Decrease or increase, depending on other factors.

7. **Dividend Discount Model** The constant-growth dividend discount model would typically be most appropriate for valuing the stock of which of the following?

a. New venture expected to retain all earnings for several years.
b. Rapidly growing company.
c. Moderate growth, mature company.
d. Company with valuable assets not yet generating profits.

8. **Dividend Discount Model** A stock has a required return of 15 percent, a constant growth rate of 10 percent, and a dividend payout ratio of 50 percent. What should the stock's P/E ratio be?

a. 3.0
b. 4.5
c. 9.0
d. 11.0

9. **Dividend Discount Model** Which of the following assumptions does the constant growth dividend discount model require?

  I. Dividends grow at a constant rate.
 II. The dividend growth rate continues indefinitely.
III. The required rate of return is less than the dividend growth rate.

a. I only
b. III only
c. I and II only
d. I, II, and III

10. **Dividend Discount Model** A stock will not pay dividends until three years from now. The dividend then will be $2.00 per share, the dividend payout ratio will be 40 percent, and return on equity will be 15 percent. If the required rate of return is 12 percent, which of the following is closest to the value of the stock?

a. $27
b. $33
c. $53
d. $67

11. **Dividend Discount Model** Assume that at the end of the next year, Company A will pay a $2.00 dividend per share, an increase from the current dividend of $1.50 per share. After that, the dividend is expected to increase at a constant rate of 5 percent. If you require a 12 percent return on the stock, what is the value of the stock?

a. $28.57
b. $28.79
c. $30.00
d. $31.78

12. **Dividend Discount Model** A share of stock will pay a dividend of $1.00 one year from now, with dividend growth of 5 percent thereafter. In the context of a dividend discount model, the stock is correctly priced at $10 today. According to the constant dividend growth model, if the required return is 15 percent, what should the value of the stock be two years from now?

a. $11.03
b. $12.10
c. $13.23
d. $14.40

13. **Cash Flow** Which of the following implies the highest quality earnings?

a. Cash flow less than earnings.
b. Cash flow greater than depreciation.
c. Cash flow less than earnings minus depreciation.
d. Cash flow greater than earnings.

www.mcgrawhill.ca/olc/Jordan

14. **Price Ratios** Two similar companies have the same price-sales and price-earnings ratios. However, company A has a lower price-cash flow ratio than company B. This most likely indicates that

   a. A has lower quality earnings than B.
   b. A has lower quality cash flow than B.
   c. A uses straight-line depreciation, while B uses accelerated depreciation.
   d. A uses accelerated depreciation, while B uses straight-line depreciation.

15. **Price Ratios** Two similar companies acquire substantial new production facilities, which they both will depreciate over a 10-year period. However, Company A uses accelerated depreciation while Company B uses straight-line depreciation. In the first year that the assets are depreciated, which of the following is most likely to occur?

   a. A's P/CF ratio will be higher than B's.
   b. A's P/CF ratio will be lower than B's.
   c. A's P/E ratio will be higher than B's.
   d. A's P/E ratio will be lower than B's.

16. **Price Ratios** An analyst estimates the earnings per share and price-to-earnings ratio for a stock market series to be $43.50 and 26 times, respectively. The dividend payout ratio for the series is 65 percent. The value of the stock market series is closest to

   a. 396
   b. 735
   c. 1131
   d. 1866

17. **P/E Ratio** An analyst gathered the following information about a stock market index:

Required rate of return:	16%
Expected dividend payout ratio:	30%
Expected return on equity investment:	20%

   The expected price-earnings (P/E) ratio of the index is closest to

   a. 3.5
   b. 7.0
   c. 15.0
   d. 35.00

18. **P/E Ratio** A company's return on equity is greater than its required return on equity. The earnings multiplier (P/E) for that company's stock is most likely to be positively related to the

   a. Risk-free rate.
   b. Market risk premium.
   c. Earnings retention ratio.
   d. Stock's capital asset pricing model beta.

19. **Residual Income Model** The residual income model separates the value of the firm into two basic components. What are these two components?

   a. The current book value and the present value of future earnings.
   b. The value of earnings per share and the value of cash flow per share.
   c. The current value of the firm's shares and the future value of its shares.
   d. The time value of money and the value of bearing risk.

20. **Residual Income** Residual income is the difference between

   a. Actual earnings less expected earnings.
   b. Any increase in the value of the firm.
   c. The value of profitable investment projects.
   d. The value added by economical use of assets.

21. **Clean Surplus Relation** The clean surplus relation says that
    a. Assets minus liabilities minus shareholder's equity equals the change in current assets plus debt payments.
    b. The difference between earnings and dividends equals the change in book value.
    c. Dividends minus earnings equals one minus the payout ratio.
    d. The difference between earnings and dividends equals the change in surplus inventory.

Concept Questions

1. **Dividend Discount Model** What is the basic principle behind dividend discount models?
2. **P/E Ratios** Why do growth stocks tend to have higher P/E ratios than value stocks?
3. **Earnings Yields** What is the earnings yield on a stock?
4. **Cash Flow** In computing the price-cash flow ratio, how is cash flow per share usually measured?
5. **Stock Valuation** Why does the value of a share of stock depend on dividends?
6. **Stock Valuation** A substantial percentage of the companies listed on the TSX don't pay dividends, but investors are nonetheless willing to buy shares in them. How is this possible given your answer to the previous question?
7. **Dividends** Referring to the previous two questions, under what circumstances might a company choose not to pay dividends?
8. **Constant Perpetual Growth Model** Under what two assumptions can we use the constant perpetual growth model presented in the chapter to determine the value of a share of stock? Comment on the reasonableness of these assumptions.
9. **Dividend Growth Models** Based on the dividend growth models presented in the chapter, what are the two components of the total return of a share of stock? Which do you think is typically larger?
10. **Constant Perpetual Growth Model** In the context of the constant perpetual growth model, is it true that the growth rate in dividends and the growth rate in the price of the stock are identical?

Questions and Problems

Core Questions

1. **Dividend Valuation** CJ Industries will pay a regular dividend of $3.25 per share for each of the next four years. At the end of the four years, the company will also pay out a $50 per share liquidating dividend, and the company will cease operations. If the discount rate is 11 percent, what is the current value of the company's stock?
2. **Dividend Valuation** In the previous problem, suppose the current share price is $50. If all other information remains the same, what must the liquidating dividend be?
3. **Dividend Discount Model** Trust Bankers just paid an annual dividend of $2 per share. The expected dividend growth rate is 6 percent, the discount rate is 12 percent, and the dividends will last for 5 more years. What is the value of the stock? What if the dividends last for 10 more years? 30 years? 100 years?
4. **Dividend Discount Model** Apple Grove, Inc., will pay dividends for the next 10 years. The expected dividend growth rate for this firm is 7 percent, the discount rate is 14 percent, and the stock currently sells for $30 per share. How much must the most recent dividend payment have been?
5. **Dividend Growth Model** Suppose that McKenzie, Inc., just paid a dividend of $4.00 per share. The company will continue to pay dividends for the next 25 years, and then go out

www.mcgrawhill.ca/olc/Jordan

of business. If the discount rate is 10 percent per year, what is the value of the stock for a dividend growth rate of 20 percent? 12 percent? 6 percent? 0 percent? −5 percent?

6. **Perpetual Dividend Growth** A company just paid a dividend of $1.80. If the dividends will grow at 6.2 percent per year and you require a return of 11.8 percent, what is the most you should be willing to pay for the stock?

7. **Perpetual Dividend Growth** Atlantis Seafood Company stock currently sells for $60 per share. The company is expected to pay a dividend of $4.10 per share next year, and analysts project that dividends should increase at 4 percent per year for the indefinite future. What must the relevant discount rate be for Atlantis stock?

8. **Perpetual Dividend Growth** Xytex Products just paid a dividend of $1.80 per share, and the stock currently sells for $35. If the discount rate is 12 percent, what is the dividend growth rate?

9. **Perpetual Dividend Growth** Star Light & Power increases its dividend 4.5 percent per year every year. This utility is valued using a discount rate of 9 percent, and the stock currently sells for $48 per share. If you buy a share of stock today and hold on to it for at least three years, what do you expect the value of your dividend check to be three years from today?

10. **Sustainable Growth** Johnson Products earned $2.20 per share last year and paid a $.75 per share dividend. If ROE was 18 percent, what is the sustainable growth rate?

11. **Sustainable Growth** Joker stock has a sustainable growth rate of 6 percent, ROE of 17 percent, and dividends per share of $1.40. If the P/E ratio is 23, what is the value of a share of stock?

12. **Capital Asset Pricing Model** A certain stock has a beta of .7. If the risk-free rate of return is 4.5 percent and the market risk premium is 8.5 percent, what is the expected return of the stock? What is the expected return of a stock with a beta of 1.25?

13. **Residual Income Model** Bill's Bakery expects *earnings* per share of $EPS = \$5$ next year. Current book value is $4.50 per share. The appropriate discount rate for Bill's Bakery is 12 percent. Calculate the share price for Bill's Bakery if earnings grow at 4 percent forever.

14. **Residual Income Model** For Bill's Bakery described in the previous question, suppose instead that current earnings per share are $5. Calculate the share price for Bill's Bakery if earnings grow at 4 percent forever.

Intermediate Questions

15. **Two-Stage Dividend Growth Model** Underwood Industries just paid a dividend of $1.45 per share. The dividends are expected to grow at a 25 percent rate for the next eight years and then level off to a 7 percent growth rate indefinitely. If the required return is 14 percent, what is the value of the stock today?

16. **Two-Stage Dividend Growth Model** The dividend for Weaver, Inc., is expected to grow at 21 percent for the next 12 years before leveling off at a 6 percent rate indefinitely. If the firm just paid a dividend of $1.34 and you require a return of 12 percent on the stock, what is the most you should pay per share?

17. **Multiple Growth Rates** Netscape Communications does not currently pay a dividend. You expect the company to begin paying a $5 per share dividend in 10 years, and you expect dividends to grow perpetually at 7 percent per year thereafter. If the discount rate is 15 percent, how much is the stock currently worth?

18. **Multiple Growth Rates** PerfectlySoft Corp. is experiencing rapid growth. Dividends are expected to grow at 25 percent per year during the next three years, 20 percent over the following year, and then 7 percent per year thereafter indefinitely. The required return on this stock is 13 percent, and the stock currently sells for $62.10 per share. What is the projected dividend for the coming year?

19. **Multiple Growth Rates** Callaway Corporation is expected to pay the following dividends over the next four years: $9.00, $11.00, $7.00, $1.50. Afterwards, the company

pledges to maintain a constant 7 percent growth rate in dividends forever. If the required return on the stock is 14 percent, what is the current share price?

20. **Multiple Required Returns** My Money, Inc., just paid a dividend of $3.50 per share on its stock. The growth rate in dividends is expected to be a constant 6.5 percent per year indefinitely. Investors require a 19 percent return on the stock for the first three years, then a 14 percent return for the next three years, and then an 11 percent return thereafter. What is the current share price for My Money?

21. **Price Ratio Analysis** Given the information below for Seger Corporation, compute the expected share price at the end of 2006 using price ratio analysis.

Year:	2000	2001	2002	2003	2004	2005
Price	$64.00	$72.00	$77.00	$89.00	$86.00	$108.00
EPS	2.55	2.70	2.80	2.90	3.40	3.75
CFPS	5.20	5.75	6.12	6.53	6.75	7.14
SPS	47.00	50.80	55.43	60.27	64.96	67.85

22. **Dividend Growth Analysis** In the previous problem, suppose the dividends per share over the same period were $.77, $.82, $.89, $.94, $1.01, and $1.09, respectively. Compute the expected share price for 2006 using the perpetual growth method. Assume the market risk premium is 8.5 percent, Treasury bills yield 5 percent, and the projected beta of the firm is .85.

23. **Price Ratio Analysis for Internet Companies** Given the information below for HooYah! Corporation, compute the expected share price at the end of 2006 using price ratio analysis.

Year:	2000	2001	2002	2003	2004	2005
Price	$18.00	$53.00	$143.00	$208.00	$101.00	$9.00
EPS	−6.00	−3.20	−2.10	−1.40	0.03	0.05
CFPS	−8.00	−5.20	−2.60	−0.85	0.04	0.08
SPS	8.00	13.00	17.00	19.40	20.50	17.45

24. **Price Ratio Analysis for Internet Companies** Given the information below for StartUp.Com, compute the expected share price at the end of 2006 using price ratio analysis.

Year:	2002	2003	2004	2005
Price	N/A	$93.12	$43.05	$11.50
EPS	N/A	−8.10	−6.50	−5.20
CFPS	N/A	−10.20	−7.10	−5.05
SPS	N/A	3.60	7.10	10.20

25. **Price Ratio Analysis** The current price of Parador Industries stock is $70 per share. Current earnings per share are $4.50, the earnings growth rate is 10 percent, and Parador does not pay a dividend. The expected return on Parador stock is 14 percent. What one-year ahead P/E ratio is consistent with Parador's expected return and earnings growth rate?

26. **Price Ratio Analysis** The current price of Parador Industries stock is $70 per share. Current sales per share are $23, the sales growth rate is 9 percent, and Parador does not pay a dividend. The expected return on Parador stock is 14 percent. What one-year ahead P/S ratio is consistent with Parador's expected return and sales growth rate?

Use the following information to answer Problems 27–31.

Abbott Laboratories (ABT) engages in the discovery, development, manufacture, and sale of a line of health care and pharmaceutical products. Below you will find selected information from *Value Line*. Use the *Value Line* estimated 2005 figures as the actual year-end figures for the company. The beta reported was 0.85 and the risk-free rate was 3.79 percent. Assume a market risk premium of 8 percent.

2001	2002	2003	2004	2005	2006	©VALUE LINE PUB., INC.
10.48	11.31	12.45	12.49	14.45		Sales per sh
2.65	2.83	3.01	3.05	3.40		"Cash Flow" per sh
1.88	2.06	2.21	2.27	2.50		Earnings per sh[A]
.84	.94	.98	1.04	1.10		Div'ds Decl'd per sh[B]
.75	.83	.79	.82	.85		Cap'l Spending per sh
5.83	6.82	8.27	9.09	9.50		Book Value per sh[C]
1554.5	1563.1	1580.2	1575.1	1550.0		Common Shs Outst'g[D]
26.6	22.3	18.7	18.7	*Bold figures are*		Avg Ann'l P/E Ratio
1.36	1.22	1.07	1.00	*Value Line*		Relative P/E Ratio
1.6%	2.0%	2.3%	2.4%	*estimates*		Avg Ann'l Div'd Yield
16285	17683	19678	19678	22400		Sales ($mill)
27.0%	28.9%	27.0%	28.2%	28.0%		Operating Margin
1168.0	1177.3	1274.0	1288.7	1375		Depreciation ($mill)
2944.1	3242.4	3479.2	3522.8	3925		Net Profit ($mill)
8.4%	24.5%	22.0%	21.4%	24.0%		Income Tax Rate
18.1%	18.3%	17.7%	17.9%	17.5%		Net Profit Margin
492.4	2119.6	2650.9	3908.9	2595		Working Cap'l ($mill)
4335.5	4274.0	3452.3	4787.9	3050		Long-Term Debt ($mill)
9059.4	10665	13072	14326	14700		Shr. Equity ($mill)
22.8%	22.3%	21.5%	18.8%	22.5%		Return on Total Cap'l
32.5%	30.4%	26.6%	24.6%	26.5%		Return on Shr. Equity
18.5%	17.0%	15.0%	13.4%	15.0%		Retained to Com Eq
43%	44%	44%	45%	43%		All Div'ds to Net Prof

The high and low share price each year were:

	2001	2002	2003	2004	2005
High	$57.20	$58.00	$47.20	$47.60	$50.00
Low	42.00	29.80	33.80	38.30	38.10

27. **Constant Perpetual Growth Model** What is the sustainable growth rate and required return for Abbott Laboratories? Using these values, calculate the 2006 share price of Abbott Laboratories Industries stock according to the constant dividend growth model.

28. **Price Ratios** Using the P/E, P/CF, and P/S ratios, estimate the 2006 share price for Abbott Laboratories. Use the average stock price each year to calculate the price ratios.

29. **Residual Income Model** Assume the sustainable growth rate and required return you calculated in Problem 27 are valid. Use the clean surplus relationship to calculate the share price for Abbott Laboratories with the residual income model.

30. **Clean Surplus Dividend** Use the information from the previous problem and calculate the stock price with the clean surplus dividend. Do you get the same stock price as in the previous problem? Why or why not?

31. **Stock Valuation** Given your answers in the previous questions, do you feel Abbott Laboratories is overvalued or undervalued at its current price of around $40? At what price do you feel the stock should sell?

32. **Residual Income Model and Nonconstant Growth** When a stock is going through a period of nonconstant growth for T periods, followed by constant growth forever, the residual income model can be modified as follows:

$$V(0) = \sum_{t=1}^{T} \frac{EPS_T + B_{t-1} - B_1}{(1+k)^t} + \frac{V(T)}{(1+k)^T}$$

where:

$$V(T) = B_T + \frac{EPS_T(1+g) - B_T \times k}{k-g}$$

Al's Infrared Sandwich Company had a book value of $10.85 at the beginning of the year, and the earnings per share for the past year were $2.88. Molly Miller, a research analyst at Miller, Moore & Associates, estimates that the book value and earnings per share will grow at 12.5 and 11 percent per year for the next four years, respectively. After four years, the growth rate is expected to be 6 percent. Molly believes the required return for the company is 8.2 percent. What is the value per share?

The following questions are from the 2000 Level II CFA®Exam. Use this information to answer Problems 33–38.

The management of Telluride, an international diversified conglomerate based in the United States, believes the recent strong performance of its wholly owned medical supply subsidiary, Sundanci, has gone unnoticed. In order to realize Sundanci's full value, Telluride has announced that it will divest Sundanci in a tax-free spinoff.

Sue Carroll, CFA, is the Director of Research at Kesson and Associates. In developing an investment recommendation for Sundanci, Carroll has directed her analysts to determine a valuation of Sundanci using various disciplines. To assist her analysis, Carroll has gathered the following information.

Sundanci Actual 1999 and 2000 Financial Statements for Fiscal Years Ending May 31 ($ in millions except per-share data)		
Income Statement	**1999**	**2000**
Revenue	$ 474	$ 598
Depreciation	20	23
Other operating expenses	368	460
Income before taxes	86	115
Taxes	26	35
Net income	60	80
Dividends	18	24
Earnings per share	$0.714	$0.952
Dividend per share	$0.214	$0.286
Common shares outstanding	84.0	84.0
Balance sheet		
Current assets	$ 201	$ 326
Net property, plant and equipment	474	489
Total assets	675	815
Current liabilities	57	141
Long-term debt	0	0
Total liabilities	57	141
Shareholder equity	618	674
Total liabilities and equity	**675**	**815**
Capital expenditures	34	38
Selected Financial Information		
Required rate of return on equity	14%	
Growth rate of industry	13%	
Industry P/E ratio	26	

33. Sustainable Growth Rate Calculate the ROE for 2000. What is the sustainable growth rate?

34. Sustainable Growth Rate Carroll learns that Sundanci's Board of Directors is considering the following policy changes that will affect Sundanci's sustainable growth rate: Director A proposes an increase in the quarterly dividend to $.15 per share. This would increase the annual dividend to $.60.

Director B proposes a two-for-one stock split.

Would each of these changes increase, decrease, or not affect Sundanci's sustainable growth rate, given that the other factors remain unchanged? Identify which component of the sustainable growth rate model, if any, is affected by each proposal.

35. Two-Stage Dividend Growth Model Helen Morgan, CFA, has been asked by Carroll to determine the potential valuation for Sundanci using the dividend discount model. Morgan anticipates that Sundanci's earnings and dividends will grow at 32 percent for two years and 13 percent thereafter. Calculate the current value of a share of Sundanci stock using the two-stage dividend discount model.

36. P/E Ratio Valuation Christie Johnson, CFA, has been assigned by Carroll to analyze Sundanci using the constant dividend growth price-earnings ratio model. Johnson assumes that Sundanci's earnings and dividends will grow at a constant rate of 13 percent. Note: The constant dividend growth price-earnings ratio using next year's earnings is P/E ratio = Payout ratio/$(k - g)$. Calculate the P/E ratio based on the information given and Johnson's assumptions.

37. P/E Ratio Identify, within the context of the constant dividend growth model, how each of the following factors will affect the P/E ratio of Sundanci. In other words, will each of the following factors increase, decrease, or possibly increase or decrease the P/E ratio? Assume all other factors remain constant.

a. The beta of Sundanci increases substantially.
b. The estimated growth rate of Sundanci's earnings and dividends increases.
c. The dividend payout ratio of Sundanci increases.
d. The market risk premium increases.

38. Payout Ratio and P/E Explain why an increase in the dividend payout ratio may not have the effect that the constant dividend growth P/E model suggests.

S&P Problems

www.mcgrawhill.com/edumarketinsight

1. Constant Perpetual Growth Model Locate the information for Corel Corporation (CORL) If you follow the "Financial Hlts" link you will find the current stock price, most recent dividend, and the five-year growth rate for dividends. Assuming the five-year dividend growth rate is equal to the perpetual growth rate, what is the implied required return for Corel shareholders? Does this number make sense?

2. Sustainable Growth What is the sustainable growth rate for Inco Ltd (N)? Under "Excel Analytics" you will find a link for annual ratios. This report shows return on equity and the payout ratio. Calculate the sustainable growth rate for Inco each year for the past five years. Is the sustainable growth rate the same every year? Why or why not?

STANDARD
&POOR'S

3. **Price Ratio Analysis** Locate the information for Canwest Global Com (CWG). All of the information used in this problem is found under "Excel Analytics." Use the "Mthly. Adj. Prices" link and find the year-end stock price for Canwest for all available years. Next, find the earnings per share for the last five years using EPS Basic from Operations. Locate the balance sheet for each of the past five years and record the Common Equity and Common Shares Outstanding. Use the Annual Cash Flow Statement to find the Net Cash Flow from Operating Activities. Divide both common equity and cash flow by the shares outstanding each year to find the annual book value per share and cash flow per share. Record these numbers. Calculate the price-earnings ratio, price-cash flow ratio, and price-book value ratio for each year. Using this information, compute the expected share price for Canwest at the end of the next year using price ratio analysis.

What's on the Web?

1. **Sustainable Growth Rate** You can find the home page for Magna International at www.magna.com. Go to this page and find the most recent annual report for Magna. Calculate the sustainable growth rate for each of the past two years. Are these values the same? Why or why not?

2. **Sustainable Growth Rate** Go to ca.finance.yahoo.com and get the information for Nova Chemical. Under the "Research" link you should find analysts' estimates for Nova's growth rate over the next five years. How does this compare to the industry, sector, and S&P 500 growth rates? Now find the EPS and dividends per share for Nova and calculate the sustainable growth rate. How does your number compare to analysts' estimates for the company? Why might these estimates differ?

3. **Perpetual Dividend Growth Model** Go to ca.finance.yahoo.com and find the following information for Noranda: the beta, the most recent annual dividend, and analysts' estimated growth rate. Next, find the three-month Treasury bill yield on ca.finance.yahoo.com. Assuming the market risk premium is 9 percent, what is the required return for Noranda? What is the value of Noranda stock using the perpetual dividend growth model? Does Noranda appear overpriced, underpriced, or correctly priced? Why might this analysis be inappropriate, or at least misleading?

CHAPTER 8

Stock Price Behaviour and Market Efficiency

"A market is the combined behaviour of thousands of people responding to information, misinformation, and whim."

—Kenneth Chang

"If you want to know what's happening in the market, ask the market."

—Japanese Proverb

Controversial, intriguing, and baffling issues are at the heart of this chapter. We begin by investigating a very basic question: Can you, as an investor, consistently "beat the market"? You may be surprised to learn that evidence strongly suggests that the answer to this question is probably not. We show that even professional money managers have trouble beating the market. At the end of the chapter, we describe some market phenomena that sound more like carnival side shows, such as the "amazing January effect." ∎

8.1   Introduction to Market Efficiency

efficient markets hypothesis (EMH)
The hypothesis stating that, as a practical matter, investors cannot consistently "beat the market."

For more on market efficiency, go to http://www.e-m-h.org

Market efficiency is probably the most controversial and intriguing issue in investments. The debate that has raged around market efficiency for decades shows few signs of abating. The central issue in the market efficiency debates is: Can you (or anyone else) consistently "beat the market"?

If the answer to this question is no, then the market is said to be efficient. The **efficient markets hypothesis (EMH)** asserts that, as a practical matter, organized financial markets are efficient. The controversy surrounding the EMH centres on this assertion.

In the sections that follow, we discuss many issues surrounding the EMH. You will notice that we focus our discussion on stock markets. The reason is that the EMH debate and associated research have largely centred on these markets. However, the same principles and arguments would also apply to any organized financial market, such as the markets for government bonds, corporate bonds, commodity futures, and options.

CHECK THIS   **8.1a**   What is the central issue in the market efficiency debate?
                8.1b   How would you state the efficient market hypothesis?

8.2   What Does "Beat the Market" Mean?

Good question. As we discussed in Chapter 1 and elsewhere, there is a risk-return trade-off. On average at least, we expect riskier investments to have larger returns than less risky assets. So the fact that an investment appears to have a high or low return doesn't tell us much. We need to know if the return was high or low relative to the risk involved.

excess return
A return in excess of that earned by other investments having the same risk.

Instead, to determine if an investment is superior to another, we need to compare **excess returns**. The excess return on an investment is the difference between what that investment earned and what other investments with the same risk earned. A positive excess return means that an investment has outperformed other investments of the same risk. Thus, *consistently earning a positive excess return* is what we mean by "beating the market."

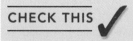
CHECK THIS   **8.2a**   What is an excess return?
                8.2b   What does it mean to "beat the market"?

8.3   Foundations of Market Efficiency

Three economic forces can lead to market efficiency: (1) investor rationality, (2) independent deviations from rationality, and (3) arbitrage. These conditions are so powerful that any one of them can result in market efficiency. We discuss aspects of these conditions in detail throughout this chapter. Given their importance, however, we briefly introduce each of them here. In our discussions, we use the term "rational" to mean only that investors do not systematically overvalue or undervalue financial assets in light of the information that they possess.

If every investor always made perfectly rational investment decisions, earning an excess return would be difficult, if not impossible. The reason is simple: If everyone were fully rational, equivalent risk assets would all have the same expected returns. Put differently, no bargains would be there to be had, because relative prices would all be correct.

However, even if the investor rationality condition does not hold, the market could still be efficient. Suppose that many investors are irrational, and a company makes a relevant announcement about a new product. Some investors will be overly optimistic, some will be overly pessimistic, but the net effect might be that these investors cancel each other out. In a sense, the irrationality is just noise that is diversified away. As a result, the market could still be efficient (or nearly efficient). What is important here is that irrational investors don't all (or mostly all) have similar beliefs. However, even under this condition, called "independent deviations from rationality," the market still may be efficient.

Let us now think of a market with many irrational traders and further suppose that their collective irrationality does not balance out. In this case, observed market prices can be too high or too low relative to their risk. Now suppose there are some well-capitalized, intelligent, and rational investors. This group of traders would see these high or low market prices as a profit opportunity and engage in arbitrage—buying relatively inexpensive stocks and selling relatively expensive stocks.

If these rational arbitrage traders dominate irrational traders, the market will still be efficient. We sometimes hear the expression "Market efficiency doesn't require that *everybody* be rational, just that *somebody* is." In our next section, we look more closely at market efficiency and discuss several different forms.

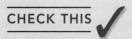 **CHECK THIS**

8.3a   What three economic conditions cause market efficiency?

8.3b   How would well-capitalized, intelligent, and rational investors profit from market inefficiency?

8.4 Forms of Market Efficiency

Now that we have a more precise notion of what beating the market means, we can be a little more precise about market efficiency. A market is efficient *with respect to some particular information* if that information is not useful in earning a positive excess return. Notice the emphasis we place on "with respect to some particular information."

For example, it seems unlikely that knowledge of Shaquille O'Neal's free-throw shooting percentage (low) would be of any use in beating the market. If so, we would say that the market is efficient with respect to the information in Shaq's free-throw percentage. On the other hand, if you have prior knowledge concerning impending takeover offers, you could most definitely use that information to earn a positive excess return. Thus, the market is not efficient with regard to this information. We hasten to add that such information is probably "insider" information, and insider trading is generally, though not always, illegal. As we discuss later in the chapter, using insider information illegally might well earn you a stay in a jail cell and a stiff financial penalty.

FIGURE 8.1

Information
Sets for Market
Efficiency

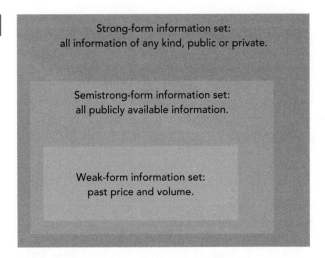

Strong-form information set:
all information of any kind, public or private.

Semistrong-form information set:
all publicly available information.

Weak-form information set:
past price and volume.

Thus, the question of whether a market is efficient is meaningful only relative to some type of information. Put differently, if you are asked whether a particular market is efficient, you should always reply, "With respect to what information?" Three general types of information are particularly interesting in this context, and it is traditional to define three forms of market efficiency: weak, semistrong, and strong.

The particular sets of information used in the three forms of market efficiency are *nested*. That is, the information set in the strong form includes the information set in the semistrong form, which in turn includes the information set in the weak form. Figure 8.1 shows the relationships among the information sets.

A weak-form efficient market is one in which the information reflected in past prices and volume figures is of no value in beating the market. As we discuss in our next chapter, one form of stock market analysis, called "technical analysis," is based on using past prices and volume to predict future prices. If a market is weak-form efficient, however, then technical analysis is of no use whatsoever. You might as well read tea leaves as stock price charts if the market is weak-form efficient.

In a semistrong-form efficient market, publicly available information of any and all kinds is of no use in beating the market. If a market is semistrong-form efficient, then the fundamental analysis techniques we described in a previous chapter are useless. Also, notice that past prices and volume data are publicly available information, so if a market is semistrong-form efficient, it is also weak-form efficient.

The implications of semistrong-form efficiency are, at a minimum, semistaggering. What it literally means is that nothing in the library, for example, is of any value in earning a positive excess return. How about a firm's financial statement? Useless. How about information in the financial press? Worthless. This book? Sad to say, if the market is semistrong-form efficient, there is nothing in this book that will be of any use in beating the market. You can imagine that this form of market efficiency is hotly disputed.

Finally, in a strong-form efficient market no information of any kind, public or private, is useful in beating the market. Notice that if a market is strong-form efficient, it is necessarily weak- and semistrong-form efficient as well. Ignoring the issue of legality, possession of nonpublic inside information of many types clearly would enable you to earn essentially unlimited returns, so this case is not particularly interesting. Instead, the market efficiency debate focuses on the first two forms.

CHECK THIS ✔   **8.4a**   What role does information play in determining whether markets are
                efficient?

                8.4b   What are the forms of market efficiency?

8.5   Why Would a Market Be Efficient?

The driving force toward market efficiency is simply competition and the profit motive. Investors constantly try to identify superior-performing investments. Using the most advanced information processing tools available, investors and security analysts constantly appraise stock values, buying those stocks that look even slightly undervalued and selling those that look even slightly overvalued. This constant appraisal and subsequent trading activity (as well as all the research behind these activities) act to ensure that prices never differ much from their efficient market price.

To give you an idea of how strong the incentive is to identify superior investments, consider a large mutual fund. Suppose this fund has $100 billion under management. If the fund was able through its research to improve the performance by 20 basis points (a basis point is 1 percent of 1 percent, i.e., 0.0001) for one year only, how much would this one time 20-basis point improvement be worth?

The answer is 0.0020 times $100 billion, or $200 million. Thus, the fund would be willing to spend up to $200 million to boost the performance of this one fund by as little as one-fifth of one percent for a single year only. As this example shows, even relatively small performance enhancements are worth tremendous amounts of money and thereby create the incentive to unearth relevant information and use it.

Because of this incentive, the fundamental characteristic of an efficient market is that prices are correct in the sense that they fully reflect relevant information. If and when new information comes to light, prices may change, and they may change by a lot. It just depends on the nature of the new information. However, in an efficient market, right here, right now, price is a consensus opinion of value, where that consensus is based on the information and intellect of hundreds of thousands, or even millions, of investors around the world.

CHECK THIS ✔   **8.5a**   What is the driving force behind market efficiency?
                8.5b   Why does this driving force work?

8.6   Some Implications of Market Efficiency

Does Old Information Help Predict Future Stock Prices?

In its weakest form, the efficient market hypothesis is the simple statement that stock prices fully reflect all past information. If this is true, this means that studying past price movements in the hopes of predicting future stock price movements is really a waste of time.

In addition, a very subtle prediction is at work here. That is, no matter how often a particular stock price path has related to subsequent stock price changes in the past, there is no assurance that this relationship will occur again in the future.

Researchers have used sophisticated statistical techniques to test whether past stock price movements are of any value in predicting future stock price movements. This turns out to be a surprisingly difficult question to answer clearly and without qualification.

In short, although some researchers have been able to show that future returns are partly predictable by past returns, the predicted returns are not *economically* important, which means that predictability is not sufficient to earn an excess return. In addition, trading costs generally swamp attempts to build a profitable trading system on the basis of past returns. Researchers have been unable to provide evidence of a superior trading strategy that uses only past returns. That is, trading costs matter, and buy-and-hold strategies involving broad market indexes are extremely difficult to outperform. (If you know how to outperform a broad market index after accounting for trading costs, please share it with us.)

Random Walks and Stock Prices

If you were to ask people you know whether stock market prices are predictable, many of them would say yes. To their surprise, and perhaps yours, it is very difficult to predict stock market prices. In fact, considerable research has shown that stock prices change through time as if they are random. That is, stock price increases are about as likely as stock price decreases. When the path that a stock price follows shows no discernible pattern, then the stock's price behaviour is largely consistent with the notion of a **random walk**. A random walk is related to the weak-form version of the efficient market hypothesis because past knowledge of the stock price is not useful in predicting future stock prices.

random walk
No discernible pattern to the path that a stock price follows through time.

Figure 8.2 illustrates daily price changes for Magna stock from September 7, 2006, through September 7, 2007. To qualify as a true random walk, Magna stock price changes would have to be truly independent from day to day. In addition, the distribution of possible stock prices each day must be the same. Even so, the graph of daily price changes for Magna stock is essentially what a random walk looks like. It is certainly hard to see any pattern in the daily price changes of Magna.

How Does New Information Get Into Stock Prices?

In its semistrong form, the efficient market hypothesis is the simple statement that stock prices fully reflect publicly available information. Stock prices change when traders buy and sell shares based on their view of the future prospects for the stock. The future prospects for the stock are influenced by unexpected news announcements. Examples of unexpected news announcements might include an increase or decrease in the dividend paid by a stock, an increase or decrease in the forecast for future earnings, lawsuits over company practices, or changes in the leadership team. As shown in Figure 8.3, prices could adjust to a positive news announcement in three basic ways.

- *Efficient market reaction:* The price instantaneously adjusts to, and fully reflects, new information. There is no tendency for subsequent increases or decreases to occur.

- *Delayed reaction:* The price partially adjusts to the new information, but days elapse before the price completely reflects new information.

- *Overreaction and correction:* The price overadjusts to the new information; it overshoots the appropriate new price but eventually falls to the new price.

FIGURE 8.2   **Daily Price Change for Magna Stock**

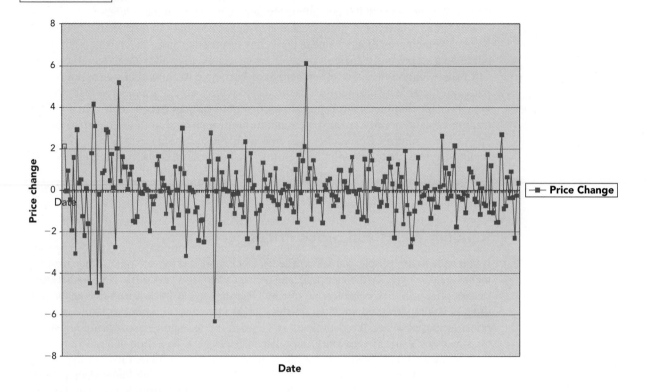

FIGURE 8.3   **Possible Market Price Reactions to a News Announcement**

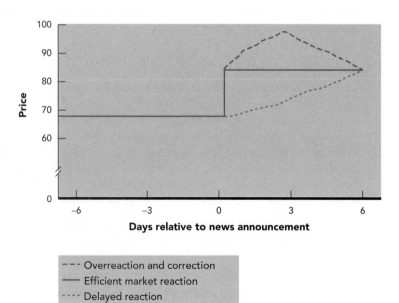

Event Studies

Researchers have examined the effects of many types of news announcements on stock prices. Such researchers are interested in the adjustment process itself as well as the size of the stock price reaction to a news announcement. To test for the effects of new information on stock prices, researchers use an approach called an **event study**. As an illustration of the implications of market efficiency, let us look at how researchers use this method.

event study
A research method designed to help study the effects of news on stock prices.

On Friday, February 25, 2005, executives of Elan Corporation, one of the makers of a new drug used to treat multiple sclerosis, announced that the company was voluntarily halting the supply and marketing of the drug. In addition, the company advised doctors to stop prescribing the drug. Even though the drug had approval from the U.S. Food and Drug Administration, executives of Elan Corporation felt that potentially serious side effects of the drug meant that sales of the drug should be suspended. On Monday, February 28, 2005, Elan shares plummeted $18.10, or more than 69 percent, to $8.00. Figure 8.4 is a graph of the price per share of Elan Corporation in the days surrounding this news announcement.

When researchers look for effects of news on stock prices, however, they must make sure that overall market news is accounted for in their analysis. The reason is simple. Suppose the whole market had fallen drastically on February 28, 2005. How would you be able to separate the overall market decline from the isolated news concerning Elan Corporation?

abnormal returns
The remaining return on a stock after overall market returns have been removed.

To answer this question, researchers calculate **abnormal returns**. The equation to calculate an abnormal return is simply:

$$\text{Abnormal return} = \text{Observed return} - \text{Expected return} \qquad (8.1)$$

The expected return can be calculated using a market index (like the NASDAQ 100 Index, the S&P 500 Index, or the S&P/TSX Composite for Canadian Companies) or by using a long-term average return on the stock. Researchers then align the abnormal

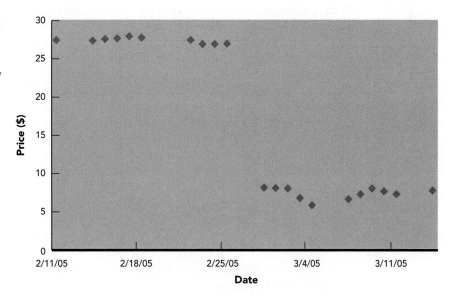

FIGURE 8.4

The Price of Shares in Elan Corporation, February 11, 2005, through March 14, 2005

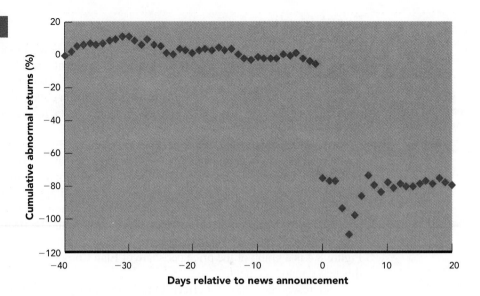

FIGURE 8.5

Cumulative Abnormal Returns for Elan Corporation, December 30, 2004, through March 29, 2005

return on a stock to the days relative to the news announcement. Usually, researchers assign the value of zero to the day a news announcement is made. One day after the news announcement is assigned a value of +1, two days after the news announcement is assigned a value of +2, and so on. Similarly, one day before the news announcement is assigned the value of −1.

According to the efficient market hypothesis, the abnormal return today should relate only to information released on that day. Any previously released information should have no effect on abnormal returns because this information has been available to all traders. Also, the return today cannot be influenced by information that traders do not yet know.

To evaluate abnormal returns, researchers usually accumulate them over some period. Figure 8.5 is a plot of the cumulative abnormal returns for Elan beginning 40 days before the announcement. The first cumulative abnormal return, or CAR, is just equal to the abnormal return on day −40. The CAR on day −39 is the sum of the first two abnormal returns, the CAR on day −38 is the sum of the first three, and so on. By examining CARs, we can see if there was an over- or under-reaction to an announcement.

As you can see in Figure 8.5, Elan's cumulative abnormal return hovered around zero before the announcement. After the news was released, there was a large, sharp downward movement in the CAR. The stock price gyrated as additional news was released, but the overall pattern of cumulative abnormal returns is essentially what the efficient market hypothesis would predict. That is, there is a flat area of cumulative abnormal returns, a sharp break in cumulative abnormal returns, and another flat area of cumulative abnormal returns.

CHECK THIS	8.6a	How is a random walk affiliated with the efficient market hypothesis?
	8.6b	What are the possible market price reactions to a news announcement?
	8.6c	How do researchers use event studies to examine the effects of news announcements on stock prices?

8.7 Informed Traders and Insider Trading

Recall that if a market is strong-form efficient, no information of any kind, public or private, is useful in beating the market. However, inside information of many types clearly would enable you to earn essentially unlimited returns. This fact generates an interesting question: Should any of us be able to earn returns based on information that is not known to the public?

In many countries, though not all, making profits on nonpublic information is illegal. This ban is said to be necessary if investors are to have trust in the stock markets. Various securities exchange commissions in the world are charged with enforcing laws concerning illegal trading activities. As a result, it is important for you to be able to distinguish between informed trading, insider trading, and legal insider trading.

Informed Trading

informed trader An investor who makes a buy or sell decision based on public information and analysis.

When an investor makes a decision to buy or sell a stock based on publicly available information and analysis, this investor is said to be an **informed trader**. The information that an informed trader possesses might come from reading newspapers, reading quarterly reports issued by a company, gathering financial information from the Internet, talking to other traders, or a host of other sources.

Insider Trading

Some informed traders are also insider traders. When you hear the term *insider trading*, you most likely think that such activity is illegal. However, as you will see at the end of this section, not all insider trading is illegal.

material nonpublic information Private knowledge that can substantially influence the share price of a stock.

Who is an Insider?   For the purposes of defining illegal insider trading, an insider is someone who has **material nonpublic information**. Such information is both not known to the public and, if it were known, would impact the stock price. A person can be charged with insider trading when he or she acts on such information in an attempt to make a profit.

Frequently, when an illegal insider trade occurs, there is a *tipper* and a *tippee*. The tipper is the person who has, on purpose, divulged material nonpublic information. The tippee is the person who has knowingly used such information in an attempt to make a profit. For example, a tipper could be a CEO who spills some inside information to a friend who does not work for the company. If the friend then knowingly uses this inside information to make a trade, this tippee is guilty of insider trading.

Proving that a trader is a tippee is difficult for the authorities, because keeping track of insider information flows and subsequent trades is difficult. For example, suppose a person makes a trade based on the advice of a stockbroker. Even if the broker based this advice on material nonpublic information, the trader might not have been aware of the broker's knowledge. The authorities must prove that the trader was, in fact, aware that the broker's information was based on material nonpublic information.

Sometimes, people accused of insider trading claim that they just "overheard" someone talking. Suppose, for example, you are at a restaurant and overhear a conversation between Bill Gates and his CFO concerning some potentially explosive news regarding Microsoft, Inc. If you then go out and make a trade in an attempt to profit from what you overheard, you would be violating the law (even though the information was "innocently obtained"). When you take possession of material nonpublic information, you become an insider and are bound to obey insider trading laws. Note that in this case, Bill Gates and his CFO, although careless, are not necessarily in violation of insider trading laws.

Legal Insider Trading   A company's corporate insiders can make perfectly legal trades in the stock of their company. To do so, they must comply with the reporting rules. When they make a trade and report it to the securities exchange commissions, these trades are reported to the public. In addition, corporate insiders must declare that trades that they made were based on public information about the company, rather than "inside" information. Most public companies also have guidelines that must be followed. For example, companies commonly allow insiders to trade only during certain windows throughout the year, often sometime after earnings have been announced.

It's Not a Good Thing: What Did Martha Do?   Martha Stewart became one of North America's most successful entrepreneurs by telling people how to entertain, cook, and decorate their homes. She built her superhomemaker personality into a far-flung international enterprise. When her company went public in 1999, the initial public offering raised $873 million. Today, Martha Stewart Living Omnimedia, Inc. (MSO), has a market capitalization of well over $1 billion and employs about 500 people (including interns). Stewart owns more than 10 percent of the shares in the company.

Stewart was in the legal news because the U.S. Securities and Exchange Commission believed that Martha Stewart was told by her friend Sam Waksal, who founded a company called ImClone, that a cancer drug being developed by ImClone had been rejected by the Food and Drug Administration. This development was bad news for ImClone. Martha Stewart sold her 3,928 shares in ImClone on December 27, 2001. On that day, ImClone traded below $60 per share, a level that Stewart claimed triggered an existing stop-loss order. However, the SEC believed that Stewart illegally sold her shares because she had information concerning FDA rejection before it became public.

The FDA rejection was announced after the market closed on Friday, December 28, 2001. This news was a huge blow to ImClone shares, which closed at about $46 per share on the following Monday (the first trading day after the information became public). Shares in ImClone subsequently fell to under $10 per share about six months later, in mid-2002. Ironically, shares of ImClone rallied to sell for more than $80 per share in mid-2004.

In June 2003, Stewart and her stockbroker, Peter Bacanovic, were indicted on nine federal counts. They both pleaded not guilty. Stewart's trial began in January 2004. Just days before the jury began to deliberate, however, Judge Miriam Cedarbaum dismissed the most serious charge—securities fraud. Stewart, however, was convicted on all four counts of obstructing justice and lying to investigators.

Judge Cedarbaum fined Stewart $30,000 and sentenced her to five months in prison, two years of probation, and five months of home confinement after her release. The fine was the maximum allowed under federal rules; the sentence was the minimum the judge could impose. Peter Bacanovic, Stewart's broker, was fined $4,000 and was sentenced to five months in prison and two years of probation.

So, to summarize, Martha Stewart was accused, but not convicted, of insider trading. She was accused, and convicted, of obstructing justice and lying to investigators. Although her conviction bars her from taking on the duties of an executive officer, MSO still paid Martha over $5 million in 2005 (base pay plus perks).

CHECK THIS ✓

8.7a   What makes a stock trader an informed trader?

8.7b   What traders are considered to be insiders?

8.7c   What is the difference between legal insider trading and illegal insider trading?

8.8 How Efficient Are Markets?

Are Financial Markets Efficient?

Financial markets are one of the most extensively documented human endeavours. Colossal amounts of financial market data are collected and reported every day. These data, particularly stock market data, have been exhaustively analyzed to test market efficiency.

You would think that with all this analysis going on, we would know whether markets are efficient, but really we don't. Instead, what we seem to have, at least in the minds of many researchers, is a growing realization that beyond a point, we just can't tell.

For example, it is not difficult to program a computer to test trading strategies that are based solely on historic prices and volume figures. Many such strategies have been tested, and the bulk of the evidence indicates that such strategies are not useful.

More generally, market efficiency is difficult to test for four basic reasons:

1. The risk-adjustment problem.
2. The relevant information problem.
3. The dumb luck problem.
4. The data snooping problem.

We briefly discuss each in turn.

The first issue, the risk-adjustment problem, is the easiest to understand. Earlier, we noted that beating the market means consistently earning a positive excess return. To determine whether an investment has a positive excess return, we have to adjust for its risk. As we discuss elsewhere in this book, the truth is that we are not even certain exactly what we mean by risk, much less how to measure it precisely and then adjust for it. Thus, what appears to be a positive excess return may just be the result of a faulty risk-adjustment procedure.

The second issue, the relevant information problem, is even more troublesome. Remember that the concept of market efficiency is meaningful only relative to some particular information. As we look back in time and try to assess whether some particular market behaviour was inefficient, we have to recognize that we cannot possibly know all the information that may have been underlying that market behaviour.

For example, suppose we see that 10 years ago the price of a stock shot up by 100 percent over a short period of time, and then subsequently collapsed. We dig through all the historical information we can find, but we can find no reason for this behaviour. What can we conclude? Nothing, really. For all we know, an undocumented rumour existed of a takeover that never materialized, and relative to this information, the price behaviour was perfectly efficient.

In general, there is no way to tell whether we have all the relevant information. Without *all* the relevant information, we cannot tell if some observed price behaviour is inefficient. Put differently, any price behaviour, no matter how bizarre, might be efficient, and therefore explainable, with respect to *some* information.

The third problem has to do with evaluating investors and money managers. One type of evidence frequently cited to prove that markets can be beaten is the enviable track record of certain legendary investors. For example, *The Wall Street Journal* article reproduced in the nearby *Investment Updates* box gives some information on the track record of superstar investor Warren Buffett.

A hidden argument in the *Investment Updates* box is that because some investors seem to be able to beat the market, it must be the case that there are market inefficiencies.

Warren Buffett, Unplugged

Warren Buffett, the billionaire investor and insurance executive, was in his office here this summer when he received a faxed letter about a company he'd never heard of.

The letter was from an adviser to Forest River Inc., an Elkhart, Ind., recreational vehicle maker. He proposed that Mr. Buffett buy the company for $800 million.

Mr. Buffett liked what he saw: The company had a big market share and little debt.

The next day, Mr. Buffett offered to buy Forest River and to let its founder, Peter Liegl, continue running it. He sealed the deal, at an undisclosed price, in a 20-minute meeting one week later. As the meeting wrapped up, Mr. Buffett told Mr. Liegl not to expect to hear from him more than once a year. Says Mr. Liegl: "It was easier to sell my business than to renew my driver's license."

Mr. Buffett says he knows an attractive acquisition candidate when he sees it. "If I don't know it in five to 10 minutes," Mr. Buffett says, "then I'm not going to know it in 10 weeks."

Mr. Buffett, an Omaha native, learned about investing under the tutelage of the classic "value" investor Benjamin Graham, who preached buying beaten-down stocks with good underlying value. He became a broker in 1951 at Buffett-Falk & Co., his father's stock-brokerage firm in Omaha, before going to work for Mr. Graham in New York three years later. In 1965, Mr. Buffett bought control of Berkshire, a foundering New Bedford, Mass., fabric mill. He soon purchased National Indemnity Cos., an Omaha insurer, which gave Berkshire $20 million of assets.

Mr. Buffett calculates that since 1951, he has generated an average annual return of about 31%. The average return for the Standard & Poor's 500 over that period is 11% a year. A $1,000 investment in Berkshire in 1965 would be worth about $5.5 million today. Over the past decade, Berkshire shares have tripled in price, returning twice as much, in percentage terms, as the S&P 500.

Mr. Buffett, with a personal net worth of $43 billion, is the [United States'] second-richest man, after Bill Gates. His nearly 55-year record has brought him recognition as one of the best investors ever, earned him fierce loyalty from Berkshire shareholders, and inspired legions of investors who attempt to ape his moves.

Though his empire has grown, Mr. Buffett says his routine has changed little over the years. He says he spends the better part of most workdays thinking and reading. He fields a handful of phone calls, and on most days, he confers with the chiefs of a few Berkshire subsidiaries. He seldom holds meetings. "There isn't much going on here," he says of his office on a typical day.

Around midday, a call came in from David Sokol, chief executive of Berkshire's MidAmerican Energy subsidiary. Mr. Buffett put his hands behind his head and cradled the phone against his shoulder, nodding when Mr. Sokol told him that MidAmerican had received a government approval for its pending acquisition of PacificCorp (a utility) for $5.1 billion in cash, plus $4.3 billion of assumed debt. Mr. Buffett, sipping a Coke from a Styrofoam cup, soon ended the conversation.

Mr. Buffett tends to stick to investments for the long haul, even when the going gets bumpy. Mr. Sokol recalls bracing for an August 2004 meeting at which he planned to break the news to Mr. Buffett that the Iowa utility needed to write off about $360 million for a soured zinc project. Mr. Sokol says he was stunned by Mr. Buffett's response: "David, we all make mistakes." Their meeting lasted only 10 minutes.

"I would have fired me if I was him," Mr. Sokol says.

"If you don't make mistakes, you can't make decisions," Mr. Buffett says. "You can't dwell on them."

Mr. Buffett has relied on gut instinct for decades to run Berkshire Hathaway Inc. Watch him at work inside his $136 billion investment behemoth, and what you see resembles no other modern financial titan. He spends most of his day alone in an office with no computer, no stock-quote machine or stock-data terminal. He keeps a muted television set tuned to CNBC, the financial-news network. Although he occasionally carries a cell phone on the road, he does not use one in Omaha. He keeps no calculator on his desk, preferring to do most calculations in his head. "I deplore false precision in math," he says, explaining that he does not need exact numbers for most investment decisions. On the cabinet behind his desk are two black phones with direct lines to his brokers on Wall Street.

On a recent Wednesday morning, Mr. Buffett had barely settled into his seat when one of them rang. It was John Freund, his longtime broker from Citigroup Inc.'s investment-banking unit. Mr. Freund briefed Mr. Buffett on a stock position he had been building for Berkshire. "If we bought a couple million, that would be fine," Mr. Buffett said, giving Mr. Freund a parameter for how many shares he wanted to buy that day. (Mr. Buffett declines to identify the stock.)

By the end of the day, Mr. Buffett had bought $140 million of the stock for Berkshire's investment portfolio—equal to the entire asset value of many mutual funds.

Even with such heavy trading, Mr. Buffett's desk isn't littered with stock research. "I don't use analysts or fortune tellers," he says. "If I had to pick one, I don't know which it would be."

Source: Susan Pulliam and Karen Richardson, *The Wall Street Journal*, November 12, 2005. Reprinted by permission of Dow Jones & Company, Inc. © 2005 Dow Jones & Company, Inc. All Rights Reserved Worldwide.

Is this correct? Maybe yes, maybe no. You may be familiar with the following claim: "If you put an immortal monkey in front of a typewriter, this monkey will eventually produce *Hamlet*." In a similar manner, suppose we have thousands of monkeys who are tasked with picking stocks for a portfolio. We would find that some of these monkeys would appear to be amazingly talented and rack up extraordinary gains. As you surely recognize, however, this is just caused by random chance.

Similarly, if we track the performance of thousands of money managers over some period of time, some managers will accumulate remarkable track records and a lot of publicity. Are they good or are they lucky? If we could track them for many decades, we might be able to tell, but for the most part, money managers are not around long enough for us to accumulate sufficient data. We discuss the performance of money managers as a group later in the chapter.

Our final problem has to do with what is known as "data snooping." Instead of monkeys at typewriters, think of what can happen if thousands of finance researchers with thousands of computers are all studying the same data and are looking for inefficiencies. Apparent patterns, or anomalies, will surely be found.

In fact, researchers *have* discovered extremely simple patterns that, at least historically, have been both highly successful and very hard to explain. We discuss some of these later in the chapter. These discoveries raise another problem: ghosts in the data. If we look long enough and hard enough at any data, we are bound to find some apparent patterns by sheer chance. But are these patterns real? Only time will tell.

Notwithstanding the four problems we have discussed, based on the last 20 to 30 years of scientific research, three generalities about market efficiency seem in order. First, short-term stock price and market movements appear to be very difficult, or even impossible, to predict with any accuracy (at least with any objective method of which we are aware). Second, the market reacts quickly and sharply to new (i.e., unanticipated) information, and the vast majority of studies of the impact of new information find little or no evidence that the market underreacts or overreacts to new information in a way that can be profitably exploited. Third, *if* the stock market can be beaten, the way to do it is at least not *obvious,* so the implication is that the market is not grossly inefficient.

Consequences of Market Efficiency

To the extent that you think a market is efficient, there are some important investment implications. We saw that the investment process can be viewed as having two parts: asset allocation and security selection. Even if all markets are efficient, asset allocation is still important because the way you divide your money among the various types of investments will strongly influence your overall risk-return relation.

However, if markets are efficient, then security selection is less important, and you do not have to worry too much about overpaying or underpaying for any particular security. In fact, if markets are efficient, you would probably be better off just buying a large basket of stocks and following a passive investment strategy. Your main goal would be to hold your costs to a minimum while maintaining a broadly diversified portfolio. We discussed index funds, which exist for just this purpose, in Chapter 5.

In broader terms, if markets are efficient, then little role exists for professional money managers. You should not pay load fees to buy mutual fund shares, and you should shop for low management fees. You should not work with full-service brokers, and so on.

If markets are efficient, there is one other thing that you should not do: You should not try to time the market. Recall that market timing amounts to moving money in and out of the market based on your expectations of future market direction. By trying to time the market, all you will accomplish is to guarantee that you will, on average, underperform the market.

In fact, market efficiency aside, market timing is hard to recommend. Historically, most of the gains earned in the stock market have tended to occur over relatively short periods of time. If you miss even a single one of these short market runups, you will likely never catch up. Put differently, successful market timing requires phenomenal accuracy to be of any benefit, and anything less than that will, based on the historical record, result in underperforming the market.

CHECK THIS

    8.8a   What are the four basic reasons market efficiency is difficult to test?

    8.8b   What are the implications to investors if markets are efficient?

8.9   Market Efficiency and the Performance of Professional Money Managers

Let's have a stock market investment contest in which you are going to take on professional money managers. Of course, the professional money managers have at their disposal their skill, banks of computers, and scores of analysts to help pick their stocks. Does this sound like an unfair match? Well, it is—you have a terrific advantage.

It's true. You can become an expert investor by using the following investment strategy: Hold a broad-based market index. One such index that you can easily buy is a mutual fund called the Vanguard 500 Index Fund (there are other market index mutual funds, too). This low-fee mutual find is designed to produce investment results that correspond to the price and yield performance of the S&P 500 Index. The fund tracks the performance of the S&P 500 Index by investing its assets in the stocks that make up the S&P 500 Index. By the way, this fund is popular—as of April 2006, the Vanguard 500 Index Fund was the largest stock mutual fund in the United States, with over $111 billion in assets.

As discussed in a previous chapter, a general equity mutual fund (GEF) is simply a pool of money invested in stocks that is overseen by a professional money manager. The number of GEFs has grown substantially during the past 20 years. Figure 8.6 shows the growth in the number of GEFs from 1986 through 2003. The solid blue line shows the total number of funds that have existed for at least one year, while the solid red line shows the number of funds that have existed for at least 10 years. From Figure 8.6, you can see that it is difficult for professional money managers to keep their funds in existence for 10 years (if it were easy, there would not be much difference between the solid blue line and the solid red line).

Figure 8.6 also shows the number of these funds that beat the performance of the Vanguard 500 Index Fund. You can see that there is much more variation in the dashed blue line than in the dashed red line. What this means is that in any given year, it is hard to predict how many professional money managers will beat the Vanguard 500 Index Fund. But the low level and low variation of the dashed red line means that the percentage of professional money managers who can beat the Vanguard 500 Index Fund over a 10-year investment period is low and stable.

Figures 8.7 and 8.8 are bar charts that show the percentage of managed equity funds that beat the Vanguard 500 Index Fund. Figure 8.7 uses return data for the previous year only, while Figure 8.8 uses return data for the previous 10 years. As you can see from

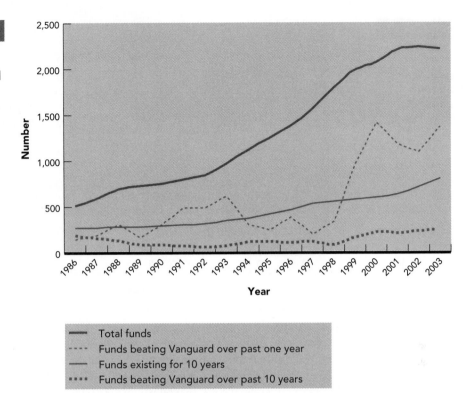

FIGURE 8.6

The Growth of Actively Managed Equity Funds, 1986–2003

Legend:
— Total funds
--- Funds beating Vanguard over past one year
— Funds existing for 10 years
▪▪▪ Funds beating Vanguard over past 10 years

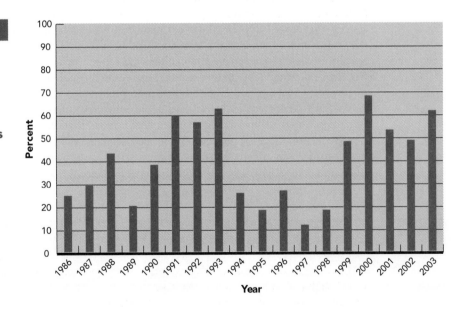

FIGURE 8.7

Percentage of Managed Equity Funds Beating the Vanguard 500 Index Fund, One-Year Returns

Figure 8.7, in only 6 of the 18 years spanning 1986 through 2003 did more than half the professional money managers beat the Vanguard 500 Index Fund. The performance is worse when it comes to 10-year investment periods (1977–1986 through 1994–2003). As shown in Figure 8.8, in only 2 of these 18 investment periods did more than half the professional money managers beat the Vanguard 500 Index Fund.

FIGURE 8.8

Percentage of
Managed Equity
Funds Beating
the Vanguard
500 Index Fund,
10-Year Returns

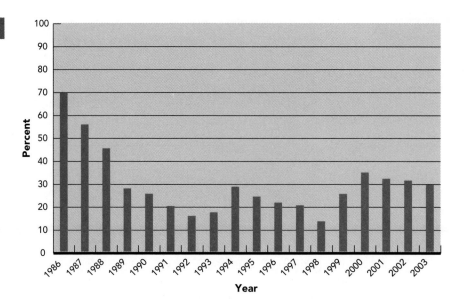

Table 8.1 presents more evidence concerning the performance of professional money managers. Using data from 1977 through 2003, we divide this time period into 1-year investment periods, rolling 3-year investment periods, rolling 5-year investment periods, and rolling 10-year investment periods. Then, after we calculate the number of investment periods, we ask two questions: (1) what percentage of the time did half the professionally managed funds beat the Vanguard 500 Index Fund? and (2) what percentage of the time did three-fourths of the professionally managed funds beat the Vanguard 500 Index Fund?

As you see in Table 8.1, the performance of professional money managers is generally quite poor relative to the Vanguard Index 500 Fund. In addition, the performance of professional money managers declines the longer the investment period.

The figures and table in this section raise some difficult and uncomfortable questions for security analysts and other investment professionals. If markets are inefficient, and tools like fundamental analysis are valuable, why don't mutual fund managers do better? Why can't mutual fund managers even beat a broad market index?

The performance of professional money managers is especially troublesome when we consider the enormous resources at their disposal and the substantial survivorship bias that exists. The survivorship bias comes into being because managers and

TABLE 8.1 The Performance of Professional Money Managers Versus the Vanguard 500 Index Fund

Length of Each Investment Period (Years)	Span	Number of Investment Periods	Number of Investment Periods Half the Funds Beat Vanguard	Percent	Number of Investment Periods Three-Fourths of the Funds Beat Vanguard	Percent
1	1977–2003	27	12	44.4%	3	11.1%
3	1979–2003	25	11	44.0	3	12.0
5	1981–2003	23	6	26.1	3	13.0
10	1986–2003	18	2	11.1	0	0.0

Source: Author calculations.

funds that do especially poorly disappear. If beating the market was possible, then this Darwinian process of elimination should lead to a situation in which the survivors, as a group, are capable of outperforming a broad market index. The fact that professional money managers seem to lack this ability is consistent with the notion that, overall, the equity market is efficient.

So if the market is this efficient, what is the role for portfolio managers? The role of a portfolio manager in an efficient market is to build a portfolio to meet the specific needs of individual investors. You have learned that a basic principle of investing is to hold a well-diversified portfolio. However, exactly which diversified portfolio is optimal varies by investor.

Some factors that influence portfolio choice include the investor's age, tax bracket, risk aversion, and even employer. Employer? Sure, suppose you work for Starbucks and part of your compensation is stock options. Like many companies, Starbucks offers its employees the opportunity to purchase company stock at less than market value. Of course, you would take advantage of this opportunity. You can imagine that you could wind up with a lot of Starbucks stock in your portfolio, which means you are not holding a diversified portfolio. The role of your portfolio manager would be to help you add other assets to your portfolio so that it is once again well diversified.

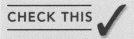

CHECK THIS

8.9a How well do professional money managers perform, on average, against a broad market index?

8.9b What are the implications of this performance to investors?

8.10 Anomalies

In this section, we discuss some aspects of stock price behaviour that are both baffling and potentially hard to reconcile with market efficiency. Researchers call these *market anomalies*. Keep three facts in mind as you read about market anomalies. First, anomalies are generally "small," in that they do not involve many dollars relative to the overall size of the stock market. Second, many anomalies are fleeting and tend to disappear when discovered. Finally, anomalies are not easily used as the basis for a trading strategy, because transaction costs render many of them unprofitable.

The Day-of-the-Week Effect

In the stock market, which day of the week has, on average, the biggest return? The question might strike you as silly; after all, what would make one day different from any other on average? On further reflection, though, you might realize that one day is different: Monday.

When we calculate a daily return for the stock market, we take the percentage change in closing prices from one trading day to the next. For every day except Monday this is a 24-hour period. However, because the markets are closed on the weekends, the average return on Monday is based on the percentage change from Friday's close to Monday's close, a 72-hour period. Thus, the average Monday return would be computed over a three-day period, not just a one-day period. Therefore, because of this longer time period, we would predict that Monday should have the highest return; in fact Monday's average return should be three times as large.

TABLE 8.2	Average Daily S&P 500 Returns, by Day of the Week (Dividends Included)				
			Weekday		
Time Period	**Monday**	**Tuesday**	**Wednesday**	**Thursday**	**Friday**
1950–2004	−0.072%	0.032%	0.089%	0.041%	0.080%
1950–1979	−0.137	0.001	0.094	0.061	0.115
1980–2004	0.006	0.069	0.083	0.018	0.039

Source: Author calculations.

day-of-the-week effect The tendency for Monday to have a negative average return.

Given this reasoning, it may come as a surprise to you to learn that Monday has the lowest average return. In fact, Monday is the only day with a *negative* average return. This is the **day-of-the-week effect**. Table 8.2 shows the average return by day of the week for the S&P 500 for the period January 1950 through December 2004.

In the 54 years spanning 1950 to 2004, the negative return on Monday is significant, both in a statistical sense and in an economic sense. This day-of-the-week effect appears not to be a fluke; it exists in other markets, such as the bond market, and it exists in stock markets outside North America. It has defied explanation since it was first documented in the early 1980s. Interestingly, the effect is much stronger in the 1950–1979 time period than in the 1980–2004 time period.

Still, critics of the efficient markets hypothesis point to this strange return behaviour as evidence of market inefficiency. While this return behaviour is odd, exploiting it presents a problem. That is, how this return behaviour can be used to earn a positive excess return is not clear. This is especially true in the 1980–2004 time period (i.e., in the period following the time when the effect was first documented). So whether this strange return behaviour points to inefficiency is hard to say.

The Amazing January Effect

Beginning in the early 1980s, researchers reported that the difference between large stock returns and small stock returns was too large even to be explained by differences in risk. In other words, small stocks appeared to earn positive excess returns.

Further research found that, in fact, a substantial percentage of the return on small stocks has historically occurred early in the month of January, particularly in the few days surrounding the turn of the year. Even closer research documents that this peculiar phenomenon is more pronounced for stocks that have experienced significant declines in value, or "losers."

Thus, we have the famous "small-stock-in-January-especially-around-the-turn-of-the-year-for-losers effect," or SSIJEATTOTYFLE for short. For obvious reasons, this phenomenon is usually just dubbed the **January effect**. To give you an idea of how big this effect is, we first plotted average returns by month going back to 1926 for large stocks in Figure 8.9A. As shown, the average return per month has been just under 1 percent.

January effect Tendency for small stocks to have large returns in January.

In Figure 8.9A, there is nothing remarkable about January; the largest average monthly return for large stocks occurred in July (followed closely by December); the lowest in September. From a statistical standpoint, there is nothing too exceptional about these large stock returns. After all, some month has to be the highest, and some month has to be the lowest.

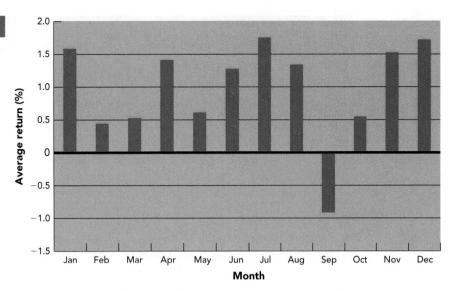

FIGURE 8.9A

Large Stocks'
Average
Monthly Returns,
1926–2004,
Dividends Included

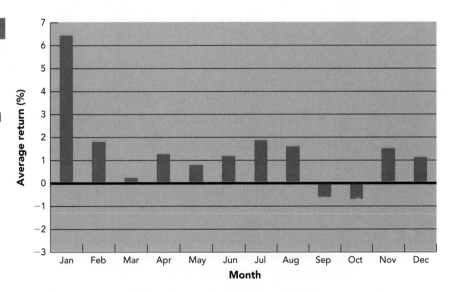

FIGURE 8.9B

Small Stocks'
Average
Monthly Returns,
1926–2004,
Dividends Included

Figure 8.9B, however, shows average returns by month for small stocks (notice the difference in vertical axis scaling between Figures 8.9A and 8.9B). The month of January definitely jumps out. Over the 79 years covered, small stocks gained, on average, about 6.5 percent in the month of January alone! Comparing Figures 8.9A and 8.9B, we see, outside the month of January, small stocks have not done especially well relative to large stocks. To a lesser extent, we see that small stocks have done better than large stocks in February, but large stocks have done better than small stocks by about the same amount in October.

The January effect appears to exist in many major markets around the world, so it's not unique to North America (it's actually more pronounced in some other markets). It also exists in some markets other than stock markets. Critics of market efficiency

TABLE 8.3	Monthly Returns of Small Stocks Minus Monthly Returns of Large Stocks, by Various Time Periods, 1926–2004		
Time Period	Best Difference (%) Month	Next Best Difference (%) Month	Worst Difference (%) Month
1926–2004	4.84% January	1.35% February	−1.26% October
1926–1951	6.73 January	1.51 February	−1.64 December
1952–1977	5.42 January	0.87 February	−1.37 October
1978–2004	2.46 January	1.67 February	22.47 October

Source: Author calculations.

point to enormous gains to be had from simply investing in January and ask: How can an efficient market have such unusual behaviour? Why don't investors take advantage of this opportunity and thereby drive it out of existence?

In Table 8.3, you can see that, on average, small stock returns were 4.84 percent higher than large stock returns in the 1926–2004 time period. The next best month in this period (February) is essentially cancelled out by the worst month (October). When we break the 1926–2004 time period into smaller time intervals, you can see that the January effect has diminished over time. In fact, in the 1978–2004 time period, the *best* monthly difference of 2.46 percent (January) is essentially cancelled out by the worst monthly difference of −2.47 percent (October).

Unlike the day-of-the-week effect, the January effect is at least partially understood. Two factors are thought to be important. The first is tax-loss selling. Investors have a strong tax incentive to sell stocks that have gone down in value to realize the loss for tax purposes. This trading leads to a pattern of selling in these stocks near the end of the year and buying after the turn of the year. In large stocks, this activity wouldn't have much effect, but in the smaller stocks, it could.

The tax-loss selling argument is plausible because researchers have looked to see whether the January effect existed in the United States before there was an income tax—and they found no January effect. However, the January effect has been found in other countries that didn't (or don't) have calendar tax years or didn't (or don't) have capital gains taxes. However, foreign investors in those markets (such as U.S. investors) did (or do). So, debate continues about the tax-loss selling explanation.

The second factor has to do with institutional investors. The argument here has several pieces, but the gist of it is that these large investors compensate portfolio managers based on their performance over the calendar year. Portfolio managers therefore pile into small stocks at the beginning of the year because of their growth potential, bidding up prices. Over the course of the year, they shed the stocks that do poorly because they don't want to be seen as having a bunch of "losers" in their portfolio (this is called "window dressing"). Also, because performance is typically measured relative to the S&P 500, portfolio managers who begin to lag because of losses in small stocks have an incentive to sell them and buy S&P 500 stocks to make sure they don't end up too far behind the S&P 500. Managers who are well ahead late in the year also have an incentive to move into S&P 500 stocks to preserve their leads (this is called "bonus lock-in").

In evaluating the oddity that is known as the January effect, keep in mind that, unlike the day-of-the-week effect, the January effect does not even exist for the market as a whole, so, in big-picture terms, it is not all that important. Also, it doesn't happen every year, so attempts to exploit it will occasionally result in substantial losses.

Turn-of-the-Year Effect

Researchers have delved deeply into the January effect to see whether the effect is due to returns during the whole month of January or to returns bracketing the end of the year. Researchers look at returns over a specific three-week period and compare these returns to the returns for the rest of the year. In Table 8.4, we calculated daily market returns from 1962 through 2004. The specific three-week period we call "Turn-of-the-Year Days" is the last week of daily returns in a calendar year and the first two weeks of daily returns in the next calendar year. Any daily return that does not fall into this three-week period is put into the "Rest-of-the-Days" category.

As you can see in Table 8.4, the returns in the "Turn-of-the-Year Days" category are higher than returns in the "Rest-of-the-Days" category. Further, the difference is apparent in the 1984–2004 period. However, the difference was more than twice as large in the 1962–1983 period.

Turn-of-the-Month Effect

Financial market researchers have also investigated whether a turn-of-the-month effect exists. In Table 8.5, we took daily stock market returns and separated them into two categories. If the daily return is from the last day of any month or the following three days of the following month, it is put into the "Turn-of-the-Month-Days" category. All other daily returns are put into the "Rest-of-the-Days" category.

As you can see in Table 8.5, the returns in the "Turn-of-the-Month" category are higher than the returns in the "Rest-of-the-Days" category. As with the turn-of-the-year anomaly, the turn-of-the-month effect is apparent in each of the three time periods we report. Interestingly, the effect appears to be stronger in the 1984–2004 period than in the 1962–1983 period. Again, the fact that this effect exists is puzzling to proponents of the EMH.

The day-of-the-week, turn-of-the-month, turn-of-the-year, and the January effect are examples of calendar anomalies. There are noncalendar anomalies as well. Two well-known noncalendar anomalies have to do with earnings announcements and price/earnings ratios.

TABLE 8.4	The Turn-of-the-Year Effect	
	Market Return on the:	
Time Period	Turn-of-the-Year Days (%)	Rest-of-the-Days (%)
1962–2004	0.144%	0.039%
1962–1983	0.172	0.031
1984–2004	0.116	0.047

Source: Author calculations.

TABLE 8.5	The Turn-of-the-Month Effect	
	Market Return on the:	
Time Period	Turn-of-the-Month Days (%)	Rest-of-the-Days (%)
1962–2004	0.138%	0.024%
1962–1983	0.126	0.020
1984–2004	0.151	0.028

Source: Author calculations.

The Earnings Announcement Puzzle

As you saw earlier in this chapter, unexpected news releases can have a dramatic impact on the price of a stock. One news item that is particularly important to investors is an earnings announcement. These announcements contain information about past earnings and future earnings potential.

Researchers have shown that substantial price adjustments do occur in anticipation of the actual earnings. According to the EMH, stock prices should then respond very quickly to unanticipated news, or the earnings "surprise." However, researchers have found that it takes days (or even longer) for the market price to adjust fully. In addition, some researchers have found that buying stocks after positive earnings surprises is a profitable investment strategy.

The Price/Earnings (P/E) Puzzle

As we have discussed elsewhere, the P/E ratio is widely followed by investors and is used in stock valuation. Researchers have found that, on average, stocks with relatively low P/E ratios outperform stocks with relatively high P/E ratios, even after adjusting for other factors, like risk. Because a P/E ratio is publicly available information, according to the EMH, it should already be reflected in stock prices. However, purchasing stocks with relatively low P/E ratios appears to be a potentially profitable investment strategy.

There are many other noncalendar anomalies. For example, the market appears to do worse on cloudy days than sunny days. But rather than continuing with a laundry list of anomalies—however much fun they might provide—we will instead turn to some spectacular events in market history.

CHECK THIS

8.10a	What is the day-of-the-week effect?
8.10b	What is the amazing January effect?
8.10c	What is the turn-of-the-year effect?

8.11 Bubbles and Crashes

bubble A situation where observed prices soar far higher than fundamentals and rational analysis would suggest.

crash A situation where market prices collapse significantly and suddenly.

As a famous songwriter penned, "History shows again and again, how nature points up the folly of men."[1] Nowhere is this statement seemingly more appropriate in finance than in a discussion of bubbles and crashes.

A **bubble** occurs when market prices soar far in excess of what normal and rational analysis would suggest. Investment bubbles eventually pop because they are not based on fundamental values. When a bubble does pop, investors find themselves holding assets with plummeting values.

A **crash** is a significant and sudden drop in marketwide values. Crashes are generally associated with a bubble. Typically, a bubble lasts much longer than a crash. A bubble

---

[1]Lyrics from "Godzilla," by Donald "Buck Dharma" Roeser (as performed by Blue Oyster Cult).

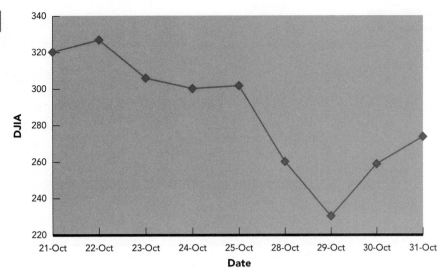

FIGURE 8.10

Dow Jones Industrial Average, October 21, 1929 to October 31, 1929

can form over weeks, months, or even years. Crashes, on the other hand, are sudden, generally lasting less than a week. However, the disastrous financial aftermath of a crash can last for years.

The Crash of 1929

During the Roaring Twenties, the stock market was supposed to be the place where everyone could get rich. The market was widely believed to be a no-risk situation. Many people invested their life savings without learning about the potential pitfalls of investing. At the time, investors could purchase stocks by putting up 10 percent of the purchase price and borrowing the remainder from a broker. This level of leverage was one factor that led to the sudden market downdraft in October 1929.

As you can see in Figure 8.10, on Friday, October 25, the Dow Jones Industrial Average closed up about a point, at 301.22. On Monday, October 28, it closed at 260.64, down 13.5 percent. On Tuesday, October 29, the Dow closed at 230.07, with an interday low of 212.33, which is about 30 percent lower than the closing level on the previous Friday. On this day, known as "Black Tuesday," the NYSE volume of 16.4 million shares was more than four times normal levels.

Although the Crash of 1929 was a large decline, it pales with respect to the ensuing bear market. As shown in Figure 8.11, the DJIA rebounded about 20 percent following the October 1929 crash. However, the DJIA then began a protracted fall, reaching the bottom at 40.56 on July 8, 1932. This level represents about a 90 percent decline from the record high level of 386.10 on September 3, 1929. By the way, the DJIA did not surpass its previous high level until November 24, 1954, more than 25 years later.

The Crash of October 1987

Once, when we spoke of *the* Crash, we meant October 29, 1929. That was until October 1987. The Crash of 1987 began on Friday, October 16. On huge volume (at the time) of about 338 million shares, the DJIA fell 108 points to close at 2,246.73. It was the first time in history that the DJIA fell by more than 100 points in one day.

FIGURE 8.11

Dow Jones Industrial Average, October 1928 to October 1932

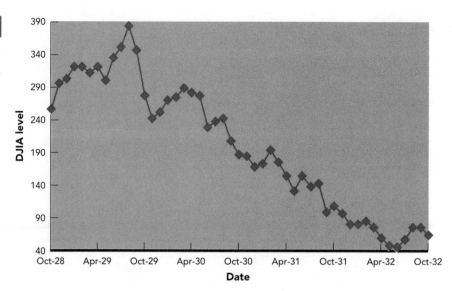

FIGURE 8.12

Dow Jones Industrial Average, October 1986 to October 1990

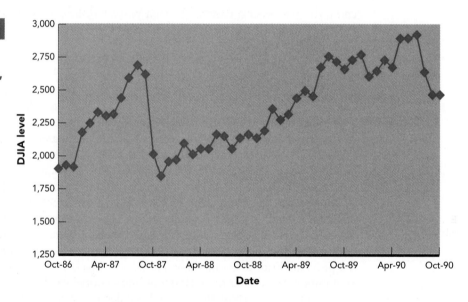

October 19, 1987, now wears the mantle of "Black Monday," and this day was indeed a dark and stormy one on Wall Street; the market lost about 22.6 percent of its value on a new record volume of about 600 million shares traded. The DJIA plummeted 508.32 points to close at 1,738.74.

During the day on Tuesday, October 20, the DJIA continued to plunge in value, reaching an intraday low of 1,616.21. But the market rallied and closed at 1,841.01, up 102 points. From the then market high on August 25, 1987, of 2,746.65 to the intraday low on October 20, 1987, the market had fallen over 40 percent.

After the Crash of 1987, however, there was no protracted depression. In fact, as you can see in Figure 8.12, the DJIA took only two years to surpass its previous market high made in August 1987.

What happened? It's not exactly ancient history, but, here again, debate rages. One faction says that irrational investors had bid up stock prices to ridiculous levels until

Black Monday, when the bubble burst, leading to panic selling as investors dumped their stocks. The other faction says that before Black Monday, markets were volatile, volume was heavy, and some ominous signs about the economy were filtering in. From the close on October 13 to the close on October 16, 1987, for example, the market fell by over 10 percent, the largest three-day drop since May 1940 (when German troops broke through French lines near the start of World War II). To top it all off, market values had risen sharply because of a dramatic increase in takeover activity, but Congress was in session and was actively considering antitakeover legislation.

Another factor is that beginning a few years before the Crash of 1987, large investors had developed techniques known as *program trading* designed for very rapid selling of enormous quantities of shares of stock following a market decline. These techniques were still largely untested because the market had been strong for years. However, following the huge sell-off on October 16, 1987, sell orders came pouring in on Monday at a pace never before seen. In fact, these program trades were (and are) blamed by some for much of what happened.

One of the few things we know for certain about the Crash of 1987 is that the stock exchanges suffered a meltdown. The NYSE simply could not handle the volume. Posting of prices was delayed by hours, so investors had no idea what their positions were worth. The specialists couldn't handle the flow of orders, and some specialists actually began selling. NASDAQ went off-line when it became impossible to get through to market makers. It has even been alleged that many stopped answering the phone.

On the same day stock markets all over the world experienced dramatic falls in their values. The Hong Kong stock market suspended trading for approximately one week. The Toronto Stock Exchange index lost 11.3% of its value and approximately $40 billion in investor money on October 19, 1987. The TSE experienced a 22.63% loss for the whole the month of October.

On the two days following the crash, prices *rose* by about 14 percent, one of the biggest short-term gains ever. Prices remained volatile for some time, but as antitakeover talk in Congress died down, the market recovered.

NYSE circuit breakers Rules that kick in to slow or stop trading when the DJIA declines by more than a preset amount in a trading session.

The Crash of 1987 led to some significant market changes. Upgrades have made it possible to handle much heavier trading volume, for example. One of the most interesting changes was the introduction of **NYSE circuit breakers**. Different circuit breakers are triggered if the DJIA drops by 10, 20, or 30 percent. These 10, 20, and 30 percent decline levels in the DJIA, respectively, will result in the following actions:

1. A 10 percent drop in the DJIA will halt trading for one hour if the decline occurs before 2 P.M.; for one half hour if the decline occurs between 2 and 2:30 P.M.; and it will have no effect if the decline occurs between 2:30 and 4:00 P.M.

2. A 20 percent drop in the DJIA will halt trading for two hours if the decline occurs before 1 P.M.; for one hour if the decline occurs between 1 and 2 P.M.; and for the remainder of the day if it occurs between 2 and 4 P.M.

3. A 30 percent drop will halt trading for the remainder of the day regardless of when the decline occurs.

These specific circuit breaker trigger levels were implemented in 1998. Because circuit breakers are designed to slow a market decline, they are often called "speed bumps." Naturally, how well they work is a matter of debate.

One of the most remarkable things about the crash is how little impact it seems to have had. The postcrash period was one of the better times to be in the market, and the Crash of 1987 increasingly looks like a blip in one of the most spectacular market increases that U.S. investors have ever seen. One thing is clearly true: October is the cruellest month for market investors. Indeed two years after the Crash of 1987, a minicrash occurred on October 13, 1989, as the DJIA fell 190 points in the afternoon (following the collapse of a proposed buyout of United Airlines).

The Asian Crash

The crash of the Nikkei Index, which began in 1990, lengthened into a particularly long bear market. It is quite like the Crash of 1929 in that respect.

The Asian crash started with a booming bull market in the 1980s. Japan and emerging Asian economies seemed to be forming a powerful economic force. The "Asian economy" became an investor outlet for those wary of the U.S. market after the Crash of 1987.

To give you some idea of the bubble that was forming in Japan between 1955 and 1989, real estate prices in Japan increased 70 times, and stock prices increased 100 times over. In 1989, price-earnings ratios of Japanese stocks climbed to unheard of levels as the Nikkei index soared past 39,000. In retrospect, there were numerous warning signals about the Japanese market. At the time, however, optimism about the continued growth in the Japanese market remained high. Crashes never seem to occur when the outlook is poor, so, as with other crashes, many people did not see the impending Nikkei crash.

As you can see in Figure 8.13, in three years from December 1986 to the peak in December 1989, the Nikkei 225 Index rose 115 percent. Over the next three years, the index lost 57 percent of its value. In April 2003, the Nikkei Index stood at a level that was 80 percent off its peak in December 1989.

The growth of the World Wide Web is documented at www.zakon.org/ robert/internet/ timeline

The "Dot-Com" Bubble and Crash

How many Web sites do you think existed at the end of 1994? Would you believe only about 10,000? By the end of 1999, the number of Web sites stood at about 9,500,000 and by 2008, there were over 101,000,000 Web sites.

FIGURE 8.13

Nikkei 225 Index, January 1984 to June 2005

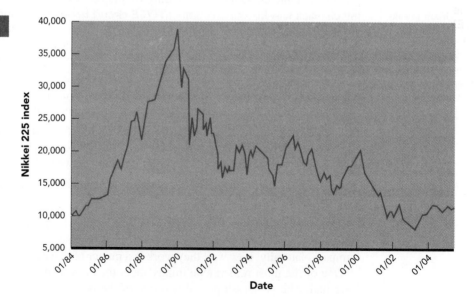

By the mid-1990s, the rise in Internet use and its international growth potential fuelled widespread excitement over the "new economy." Investors did not seem to care about solid business plans—only big ideas. Investor euphoria led to a surge in Internet IPOs, which were commonly referred to as "dot-coms" because so many of their names ended in ".com." Of course, the lack of solid business models doomed many of the newly formed companies. Many of them suffered huge losses and some folded relatively shortly after their IPOs.

The extent of the dot-com bubble and subsequent crash is presented in Table 8.6 and Figure 8.14, which compare the Amex Internet Index and the S&P 500 Index. As shown in Table 8.6, the Amex Internet Index soared from a level of 114.68 on October 1, 1998, to its peak of 688.52 in late March 2000, an increase of 500 percent. The Amex Internet Index then fell to a level of 58.59 in early October 2002, a drop of 91 percent. By contrast, the S&P 500 Index rallied about 31 percent in the same 1998–2000 time period and fell 40 percent during the 2000–2002 time period.

TABLE 8.6	Values of the Amex Internet Index and the S&P 500 Index					
Date	Amex Internet Index Value	Gain to Peak from Oct. 1, 1998 (%)	Loss from Peak to Trough (%)	S&P 500 Index Value	Gain to Peak from Oct. 1, 1998 (%)	Loss from Peak to Trough (%)
October 1, 1998	114.68			986.39		
Late March 2000 (peak)	688.52	500%		1,293.72	31%	
Early October 2002 (trough)	58.59		−91%	776.76		−40%

Source: Author calculations.

FIGURE 8.14

Values of the AMEX Internet Index and the S&P 500 Index, October 1995 through May 2005

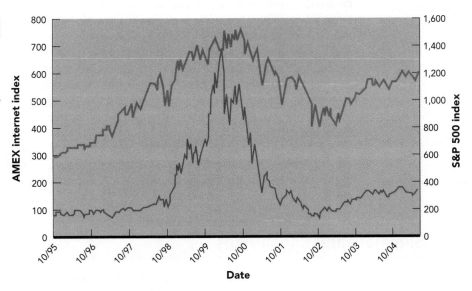

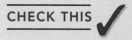

CHECK THIS ✔

8.11a   What is a stock market bubble? A stock market crash?

8.11b   What is a major difference between the Crash of October 1929 and the Crash of October 1987?

8.11c   What are NYSE circuit breakers? What are they intended to do?

8.12 Tests of Different Types of Market Efficiency

Finally in this section we will examine the tests of different types of market efficiency. If a stock market is weak-form efficient, then there should be no exploitable trends and patterns in past stock price and volume information. Otherwise investors can use these trends to consistently earn abnormal positive returns. To test weak-form efficiency, researchers use run-tests and autocorrelation tests among others to find out that prices exhibit short-run persistence (in the short run winners continue to win and losers continue to lose), and long-run reversals. The results of these tests and run-tests indicate that there are indeed trends in stock prices. However when we take transaction costs into consideration it is impossible to earn continuous positive abnormal returns.

Studies demonstrate that different types of anomalies (January effect, small-firm effect, weekend effect) exist in stock markets. We also know that low-price earnings stocks produce higher returns than high P/E ratio stocks. Similarly stocks with high book-to-market value ratios earn higher returns than those with low ratios. These anomalies and the October 19, 1987, crash are evidence against semistrong-form market efficiency of stock markets. Researchers show that previous period's loser portfolios become winner portfolios in the following three-year period. The observed reversal effect is interpreted to mean that stock market participants overreact to stock market news and that contrarian portfolio strategies can earn abnormal positive returns. However once again when we examine whether these inconsistencies can be exploited to earn positive abnormal returns, we conclude that this information does not produce them. Most importantly in different countries mutual fund managers using all the publicly available information generally do not consistently outperform the market index portfolio.

You can examine activities of Canadian company insiders by visiting the site of SEDI at www.csa-acvm.ca

On the other hand many papers demonstrate that not only insiders, but also investors who mimic insiders' actions with a lag consistently earn abnormal returns. In recent years security exchange commissions increased their pressure on insider activities and many lawsuits were filed.

According to the results of these tests, no stock market is strong-form efficient. Many traders believe that major developed stock exchanges are semistrong-form efficient, in the sense that investors cannot consistently earn abnormal returns using past and publicly available stock information.

8.13 Summary and Conclusions

In this chapter, we examined market price behaviour and market efficiency. The efficient markets hypothesis (EMH) asserts that, as a practical matter, organized financial markets are efficient. Researchers who study efficient markets often ask whether it is possible to "beat the market." We say that you beat the market if you can consistently earn returns in excess of those earned by other investments having the same risk. If a market is efficient, earning these excess returns is not possible, except by luck. The controversy surrounding the EMH centres on this assertion.

The EMH states that the market is efficient with respect to some particular information if that information is not useful in earning a positive excess return. The forms of market efficiency and their information sets are:

1. *Weak Form:* past price and volume information.
2. *Semistrong Form:* all publicly available information.
3. *Strong Form:* all information of any kind, public or private.

You learned how information affects market prices by influencing traders to act on the arrival of information. You then learned how to distinguish among informed trading, illegal insider trading, and legal insider trading.

Testing market efficiency is difficult. We discussed four reasons for this: (1) the risk-adjustment problem, (2) the relevant information problem, (3) the dumb luck problem, and (4) the data-snooping problem.

We then presented evidence concerning tests of market efficiency. One lesson you should learn is that professional money managers have been unable to beat the market consistently. This is true despite their tremendous resources, experience, opportunities, and incentives. Also, this is true despite patterns and other oddities that have occurred historically in the stock market. The fact that professional money managers have been unable to beat the market supports the notion that markets are generally rather efficient.

We close the chapter by discussing some aspects of stock price behaviour that are both baffling and hard to reconcile with market efficiency. We discussed the day-of-the-week effect, the amazing January effect, the turn-of-the-year effect, the turn-of-the-month effect, the earnings announcement puzzle, and the price/earnings (P/E) puzzle. Finally, we talked about some famous bubbles and crashes, including the Crash of October 1929, the Crash of October 1987, the Asian crisis, and the dot-com bubble and crash.

REAL WORLD

This chapter covered market efficiency. In it, we raised a significant question: Can you, or indeed anyone, consistently beat the market? In other words, is the market efficient? This is a question that every investor needs to think about because it has direct, practical implications for investing and portfolio management.

If you think the market is relatively efficient, then your investment strategy should focus on minimizing costs and taxes. Asset allocation is your primary concern, and you will still need to establish the risk level you are comfortable with. But beyond this, you should be a buy-and-hold investor, transacting only when absolutely necessary. Investments such as low-cost, low-turnover mutual funds make a lot of sense. Tools for analyzing the market are irrelevant at best. Thus, in some ways, the appropriate investment strategy is kind of boring, but it's the one that will pay off over the long haul in an efficient market.

In contrast, if you think the market is not particularly efficient, then you've got to be a security picker. You also have to decide what market analyzing tools will be the ones you use. This is also true if you are in the money management business; you have to decide which specific stocks or bonds to hold.

In the end, the only way to find out if you've got what it takes to beat the market is to try, and the best way to try is with a simulated brokerage account such as Stock-Trak. Be honest with yourself: You think you can beat the market; most novice investors do. Some change their minds and some don't. As to which tools to use, you will just have to find out which ones work (or don't work) for you.

Key Terms

efficient markets hypothesis (EMH) 235
excess return 235
random walk 239
event study 241
abnormal returns 241
informed trader 243

material nonpublic information 243
day-of-the-week effect 252
January effect 252
bubble 256
crash 256
NYSE circuit breakers 259

Chapter Review Problems and Self-Test

1. **Market Research** Smolira Investment Trust (SIT) runs a retirement account for professors, with a current market value of $2 billion. Alchemy, Inc., offers to conduct market research in an attempt to sift through the market data to find a way to increase the return to SIT's portfolio by 30 basis points per year. Alchemy is offering to conduct the research for the sum of $9 million. Is this price too high or too low?

2. **Picking a Money Manager** You are helping your very rich aunt Molly to decide where to invest her portfolio. She is planning to take a 10-year world tour after she invests the bulk of her portfolio. She thinks that-picking a money manager is unimportant because she believes any professional money manager must be able to beat the market. She's just planning to pick a professional money manager at random. What do you tell her?

Answers to Self-Test Problems

1. Assuming that Alchemy, Inc., actually can conduct research that allows Smolira Investment Trust (SIT) to increase its portfolio return by 30 basis points, SIT would be willing to pay up to $2,000,000,000 times 0.0030 = $6,000,000 for this research. So the price of $9 million is too high.

2. You could show her Figure 8.8. In this figure, it is clear that picking a professional manager at random gives her about a 25 to 30 percent chance of beating a market fund like the Vanguard 500 Index Fund. If she invests her sizable portfolio in the Vanguard 500 Index Fund, she has about a 70 to 75 percent chance of beating a professional money manager picked at random.

Test Your Investment Quotient

1. **Efficient Markets Hypothesis** A market anomaly refers to
   a. An exogenous shock to the market that is sharp but not persistent.
   b. A price or volume event that is inconsistent with historical price or volume trends.
   c. A trading or pricing structure that interferes with efficient buying or selling of securities.
   d. Price behaviour that differs from the behaviour predicted by the efficient markets hypothesis.

2. **Efficient Markets Hypothesis** Which of the following assumptions does not imply an informationally efficient market?
   a. Security prices adjust rapidly to reflect new information.
   b. The timing of one news announcement is independent of other news announcements.
   c. The risk-free rate exists, and investors can borrow and lend unlimited amounts at the risk-free rate.

    d. Many profit-maximizing participants, each acting independently of the others, analyze and value securities.

3. **Efficient Markets Hypothesis** After lengthy trial and error, you discover a trading system that would have doubled the value of your investment every six months if applied over the last three years. Which of the following problems makes it difficult to conclude that this is an example of market inefficiency?

    a. Risk-adjustment problem
    b. Relevant information problem
    c. Dumb luck problem
    d. Data snooping problem

4. **Efficient Markets Hypothesis** In discussions of financial market efficiency, which of the following is not one of the stylized forms of market efficiency?

    a. Strong form
    b. Semistrong form
    c. Weak form
    d. Economic form

5. **Beating the Market** Which of the following is not considered a problem when evaluating the ability of a trading system to "beat the market"?

    a. Risk-adjustment problem
    b. Relevant information problem
    c. Data measurement problem
    d. Data snooping problem

6. **Calendar Anomalies** Which month of the year, on average, has had the highest stock market returns as measured by a small-stock portfolio?

    a. January
    b. March
    c. June
    d. December

7. **Circuit Breakers** Which of the following intraday changes in the Dow Jones Industrial Average (DJIA) will trigger a circuit breaker halting NYSE trading for one hour?

    a. 10 percent drop before 2 P.M.
    b. 10 percent drop after 2 P.M.
    c. 10 percent rise before 2 P.M.
    d. 10 percent rise after 2 P.M.

8. **Efficient Markets Hypothesis** The Ontario Securities Commission (OSC) has regulations that prohibit trading on inside information. If the market is _____ -form efficient, such regulation is not needed.

    a. weak
    b. semistrong
    c. technical
    d. strong

9. **The January Effect** Which of the following is a possible explanation of the January effect?

      I. Institutional window dressing
      II. Bonus demand
      III. Tax-loss selling

    a. I only
    b. I and II only
    c. I and III only
    d. I, II, and III

www.mcgrawhill.ca/olc/Jordan

10. **NYSE Circuit Breakers** Circuit breakers implemented by the NYSE were designed to
    a. Reduce the January effect.
    b. Reduce the effect of technical trading.
    c. Eliminate program trading.
    d. Slow a market decline.

11. **Market Efficiency Implications** Assume the market is semistrong-form efficient. The best investment strategy is to
    a. Examine the past prices of a stock to determine the trend.
    b. Invest in an actively managed mutual fund whose manager searches for underpriced stocks.
    c. Invest in an index fund.
    d. Examine the financial statements for a company to find stocks that are not selling at intrinsic value.

12. **Market Efficiency Implications** Assume the market is weak-form efficient. If this is true, technical analysts _____ earn excess returns and fundamental analysts _____ earn excess returns.
    a. could; could
    b. could; could not
    c. could not; could not
    d. could not; could

13. **Efficient Markets Hypothesis** Which of the following is *not* true concerning the efficient markets hypothesis?
    a. Markets that are less organized are not as likely to be efficient.
    b. Markets with wide fluctuations in prices cannot be efficient.
    c. The efficient markets hypothesis deals only with the stock market.
    d. Prices in an efficient market are fair on average.

14. **Efficient Markets Hypothesis** You purchase a stock that you expect to increase in value over the next year. One year later, after the discovery that the CEO embezzled funds and the company is close to bankruptcy, the stock has fallen in price. Which of the following statements is true?
    a. This is a violation of weak-form efficiency.
    b. This is a violation of semistrong-form efficiency.
    c. This is a violation of all forms of market efficiency.
    d. This is not a violation of market efficiency.

15. **Efficient Markets Hypothesis** Which of the following statements concerning market efficiency is true?
    a. If the market is weak-form efficient, it is also semistrong-form efficient.
    b. If the market is semistrong-form efficient, it is also strong-form efficient.
    c. If the market is weak-form efficient, it is also strong-form efficient.
    d. If the market is semistrong-form efficient, it is also weak-form efficient.

Concept Questions

1. **Efficient Markets** A stock market analyst is able to identify mispriced stocks by comparing the average price for the last 10 days to the average price for the last 60 days. If this is true, what do you know about the market?

2. **Efficient Markets** Critically evaluate the following statement: "Playing the stock market is like gambling. Such speculative investing has no social value, other than the pleasure people get from this form of gambling."

3. **Misconceptions about Efficient Markets** Several celebrated investors and stock pickers have recorded huge returns on their investments over the past two decades. Is the success of these particular investors an invalidation of an efficient stock market? Explain.

4. **Interpreting Efficient Markets** For each of the following scenarios, discuss whether profit opportunities exist from trading in the stock of the firm under the conditions that (1) the market is not weak-form efficient, (2) the market is weak-form but not semistrong-form efficient, (3) the market is semistrong-form but not strong-form efficient, and (4) the market is strong-form efficient.

   a. The stock price has risen steadily each day for the past 30 days.
   b. The financial statements for a company were released three days ago, and you believe you've uncovered some anomalies in the company's inventory and cost control reporting techniques that are understating the firm's true liquidity strength.
   c. You observe that the senior management of a company has been buying a lot of the company's stock on the open market over the past week.
   d. Your next-door neighbour, who happens to be a computer analyst at the local steel plant, casually mentions that a German steel conglomerate hinted yesterday that it might try to acquire the local firm in a hostile takeover.

5. **Performance of the Pros** In the mid- to late-1990s, the performance of the pros was unusually poor—on the order of 90 percent of all equity mutual funds underperformed a passively managed index fund. How does this bear on the issue of market efficiency?

6. **Efficient Markets** A hundred years ago or so, companies did not compile annual reports. Even if you owned stock in a particular company, you were unlikely to be allowed to see the balance sheet and income statement for the company. Assuming the market is semistrong-form efficient, what does this say about market efficiency then compared to now?

7. **Efficient Markets Hypothesis** You invest $10,000 in the market at the beginning of the year, and by the end of the year your account is worth $15,000. During the year the market return was 10 percent. Does this mean that the market is inefficient?

8. **Efficient Markets Hypothesis** Which of the following statements are true about the efficient market hypothesis?

   a. It implies perfect forecasting ability.
   b. It implies that prices reflect all available information.
   c. It implies an irrational market.
   d. It implies that prices do not fluctuate.
   e. It results from keen competition among investors.

9. **Semistrong Efficiency** If a market is semistrong-form efficient, is it also weak-form efficient? Explain.

10. **Efficient Markets Hypothesis** What are the implications of the efficient markets hypothesis for investors who buy and sell stocks in an attempt to "beat the market"?

11. **Efficient Markets Hypothesis** Aerotech, an aerospace technology research firm, announced this morning that it hired the world's most knowledgeable and prolific space researchers. Before today, Aerotech's stock had been selling for $100. Assume that no other information is received over the next week and the stock market as a whole does not move.

    a. What do you expect will happen to Aerotech's stock?
    b. Consider the following scenarios:

       i. The stock price jumps to $118 on the day of the announcement. In subsequent days it floats up to $123, then falls back to $116.
       ii. The stock price jumps to $116 and remains at that level.
       iii. The stock price gradually climbs to $116 over the next week.

    Which scenario(s) indicate market efficiency? Which do not? Why?

12. **Efficient Markets Hypothesis** When the 56-year-old founder of Gulf & Western, Inc., died of a heart attack, the stock price immediately jumped from $18.00 a share to $20.25, a 12.5 percent increase. This is evidence of market inefficiency, because an efficient stock market would have anticipated his death and adjusted the price beforehand. Assume that no other information is received and the stock market as a whole does not move. Is this statement about market efficiency true or false? Explain.

13. **Efficient Markets Hypothesis** Today, the following announcement was made: "Early today the Justice Department reached a decision in the Universal Product Care (UPC) case. UPC has been found guilty of discriminatory practices in hiring. For the next five years, UPC must pay $2 million each year to a fund representing victims of UPC's policies." Assuming the market is efficient, should investors not buy UPC stock after the announcement because the litigation will cause an abnormally low rate of return? Explain.

14. **Efficient Markets Hypothesis** Newtech Corp. is going to adopt a new chip-testing device that can greatly improve its production efficiency. Do you think the lead engineer can profit from purchasing the firm's stock before the news release on the device? After reading the announcement in the newspaper, should you be able to earn an abnormal return from purchasing the stock if the market is efficient?

15. **Efficient Markets Hypothesis** TransTrust Corp. has changed how it accounts for inventory. Taxes are unaffected, although the resulting earnings report released this quarter is 20 percent higher than what it would have been under the old accounting system. There is no other surprise in the earnings report and the change in the accounting treatment was publicly announced. If the market is efficient, will the stock price be higher when the market learns that the reported earnings are higher?

16. **Efficient Markets Hypothesis** The Durkin Investing Agency has been the best stock picker for the past two years. Before this rise to fame occurred, the Durkin newsletter had 200 subscribers. Those subscribers beat the market consistently, earning substantially higher returns after adjustment for risk end transaction costs. Subscriptions have skyrocketed to 10,000. Now, when the Durkin Investing Agency recommends a stock, the price instantly rises several points. The subscribers currently earn only a normal return when they buy recommended stock because the price rises before anybody can act on the information. Briefly explain this phenomenon. Is Durkin's ability to pick stocks consistent with market efficiency?

17. **Efficient Markets Hypothesis** Your broker commented that well-managed firms are better investments than poorly managed firms. As evidence, your broker cited a recent study examining 100 small manufacturing firms that eight years earlier had been listed in an industry magazine as the best-managed small manufacturers in the country. In the ensuing eight years, the 100 firms listed have not earned more than the normal market return. Your broker continued to say that if the firms were well managed, they should have produced better-than-average returns. If the market is efficient, do you agree with your broker?

18. **Efficient Markets Hypothesis** A famous economist just announced in *The Globe and Mail* his findings that the recession is over and the economy is again entering an expansion. Assume market efficiency. Can you profit from investing in the stock market after you read this announcement?

19. **Efficient Markets Hypothesis** Suppose the market is semistrong-form efficient. Can you expect to earn excess returns if you make trades based on
    a. Your broker's information about record earnings for a stock?
    b. Rumors about a merger of a firm?
    c. Yesterday's announcement of a successful new product test?

20. **Efficient Markets Hypothesis** The efficient markets hypothesis implies that all mutual funds should obtain the same expected risk-adjusted returns. Therefore, we can simply pick mutual funds at random. Is this statement true or false? Explain.

21. **Efficient Markets Hypothesis** Assume that markets are efficient. During a trading day, Evergreen Golf, Inc., announces that it has lost a contract for a large golfing project, which, prior to the news, it was widely believed to have secured. If the market is efficient, how should the stock price react to this information if no additional information is released?

22. **Efficient Markets Hypothesis** Prospectors, Inc., is a publicly traded gold prospecting company in Alaska. Although the firm's searches for gold usually fail, the prospectors occasionally find a rich vein of ore. What pattern would you expect to observe for Prospector's cumulative abnormal returns if the market is efficient?

Questions and Problems

Core Questions

1. **Cumulative Abnormal Returns** On November 14, Thorogood Enterprises announced that the public and acrimonious battle with its current CEO had been resolved. Under the terms of the deal, the CEO would step down from his position immediately. In exchange, he was given a generous severance package. Given the information below, calculate the cumulative abnormal return (CAR) around this announcement. Assume the company has an expected return equal to the market return. Graph and interpret your results. Do your results support market efficiency?

Date	Market Return (%)	Company Return (%)
11/7	0.3%	0.2%
11/8	−0.2	0.0
11/9	0.2	0.3
11/10	0.9	0.7
11/11	0.1	0.1
11/14	−0.1	1.8
11/15	1.3	1.1
11/16	−0.6	−0.5
11/17	−0.2	−0.3
11/18	0.3	0.4
11/21	0.5	0.4

2. **Cumulative Abnormal Returns** The following diagram shows the cumulative abnormal returns (CAR) for oil exploration companies announcing oil discoveries over a 30-year period. Month 0 in the diagram is the announcement month. Assume that no other information is received and the stock market as a whole does not move. Is the diagram consistent with market efficiency? Why or why not?

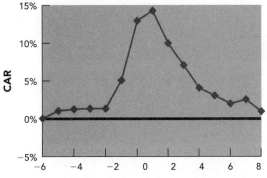

3. **Cumulative Abnormal Returns** The following figures present the results of four cumulative abnormal returns (CAR) studies. Indicate whether the results of each study support, reject, or are inconclusive about the semistrong form of the efficient market hypothesis. In each figure, time 0 is the date of an event.

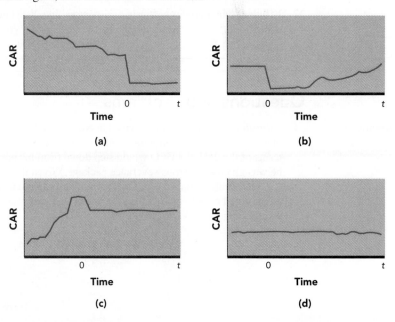

4. **Cumulative Abnormal Returns** A study analyzed the behaviour of the stock prices of firms that had lost antitrust cases. Included in the diagram are all firms that lost the initial court decision, even if the decision was later overturned on appeal. The event at time 0 is the initial, pre-appeal court decision. Assume no other information was released, aside from that disclosed in the initial trial. The stock prices all have a beta of 1. Is the diagram consistent with market efficiency? Why or why not?

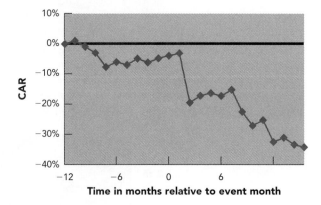

Intermediate Questions

5. **Cumulative Abnormal Returns** Ross Co., Westerfield, Inc., and Jaffe Company announced a new agreement to market their respective products in China on July 18 (7/18), February 12 (2/12), and October 7 (10/7), respectively. Given the information below, calculate the cumulative abnormal return (CAR) for these stocks as a group. Assume all companies have an expected return equal to the market return. Graph and interpret your results. Do your results support market efficiency?

| | Ross Co. | | | Westerfield, Inc. | | | Jaffe Company | |
| | Market | Company | | Market | Company | | Market | Company |
Date	Return (%)	Return (%)	Date	Return (%)	Return (%)	Date	Return (%)	Return (%)
7/12	−0.3%	−0.5%	2/8	−0.9%	−1.1%	10/1	0.5%	0.3%
7/13	0.0	0.2	2/9	−1.0	−1.1	10/2	0.4	0.6
7/16	0.5	0.7	2/10	0.4	0.2	10/3	1.1	1.1
7/17	−0.5	−20.3	2/11	0.6	0.8	10/6	0.1	−0.3
7/18	−2.2	1.1	2/12	−0.3	−0.1	10/7	−2.2	−0.3
7/19	−0.9	−0.7	2/15	1.1	1.2	10/8	0.5	0.5
7/20	−1.0	−1.1	2/16	0.5	0.5	10/9	−0.3	−0.2
7/23	0.7	0.5	2/17	−0.3	−0.2	10/10	0.3	0.1
7/24	0.2	0.1	2/18	0.3	0.2	10/13	0.0	−0.1

CHAPTER 9

Behavioural Finance and the Psychology of Investing

"The investor's chief problem, and even his worst enemy, is likely to be himself."

—Benjamin Graham

"There are three factors that influence the market: Fear, Greed, and Greed."

—Market folklore

Be honest: Do you think of yourself as a better than average driver? If you do, you are not alone. About 80 percent of the people who are asked this question will say yes. Evidently, we tend to overestimate our abilities behind the wheel. Is the same thing true when it comes to making investment decisions? ∎

You will probably not be surprised when we say that human beings sometimes make errors in judgment. How these errors, and other aspects of human behaviour, affect investors and asset prices falls under the general heading of "behavioural finance." In the first part of this chapter, our goal is to acquaint you with some common types of mistakes investors make and their financial implications. As you will see, researchers have identified a wide variety of potentially damaging behaviours. In the second part of the chapter, we describe a trading strategy known as "technical analysis." Some investors use technical analysis as a tool to try to exploit patterns in prices. These patterns are thought to exist (by advocates of technical analysis) because of predictable behaviour by investors.

9.1 Introduction to Behavioural Finance

Sooner or later, you are going to make an investment decision that winds up costing you a lot of money. Why is this going to happen? You already know the answer. Sometimes you make sound decisions, but you just get unlucky when something happens that you could not have reasonably anticipated. At other times (and painful to admit) you just make a bad decision, one that could have (and should have) been avoided. The beginning of investment wisdom is to recognize the circumstances that lead to poor decisions and thereby cut down on the damage done by investment blunders.

behavioural finance The area of finance dealing with the implications of investor reasoning errors on investment decisions and market prices.

As we previously noted, the area of research known as **behavioural finance**[1] attempts to understand and explain how reasoning errors influence investor decisions and market prices. Much of the research done in the area of behavioural finance stems from work in the area of cognitive psychology, which is the study of how people, including investors, think, reason, and make decisions. Errors in reasoning are often called *cognitive errors*.

Some proponents of behavioural finance believe that cognitive errors by investors will cause market inefficiencies. Recall that in a previous chapter, we identified three economic conditions that lead to market efficiency: (1) investor rationality, (2) independent deviations from rationality, and (3) arbitrage. For a market to be inefficient, all three of these conditions must be absent. That is, it must be the case that a substantial portion of investors make irrational investment decisions, and the collective irrationality of these investors then must lead to an overly optimistic or pessimistic market situation that cannot be corrected via arbitrage by rational, well-capitalized investors. Whether this actually occurs in financial markets is the subject of a raging debate, and we are not going to take sides. Instead, our goal is to introduce you to the ideas and issues.

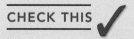 CHECK THIS

9.1a What is behavioural finance?

9.1b What three conditions must be absent for a market to be inefficient?

9.2 Prospect Theory

prospect theory An alternative theory to classical, rational economic decision making, which emphasizes, among other things, that investors tend to behave differently when they face prospective gains and losses.

Prospect theory, developed in the late 1970s, is a collection of ideas that provides an alternative to classical, rational economic decision making. The foundation of prospect theory rests on the idea that investors are much more distressed by prospective losses than they are happy about prospective gains. Researchers have found that a typical investor considers the pain of a $1 loss to be about twice as great as the pleasure received from the gain of $1. Also, researchers have found that investors respond in different ways to identical situations. The difference depends on whether the situation is presented in terms of losses or in terms of gains.

Investors seem to be willing to take more risk to avoid the loss of a dollar than they are to make a dollar profit. Also, if an investor has the choice between a sure gain and

---

[1]The following researchers have conducted pioneering work in behavioural finance: Shiller, De Bondt, Thaler, Odean, Kahneman and Tuersky.

a gamble that could increase or decrease the sure gain, the investor is likely to choose the sure gain. Choosing a sure gain over a gamble is called *risk-averse behaviour.* If the same investor is faced with a sure loss and a gamble that could increase or decrease the sure loss, the investor is likely to take the gamble. Choosing the gamble over the sure loss is called *risk-taking behaviour.*

This focus on gains and losses and the tendency of investors to be risk-averse with regard to gains, but risk-taking when it comes to losses, is the essence of prospect theory. In contrast, a fully rational investor (in an economic sense) is presumed to care only about his or her overall wealth, not the gains and losses associated with individual pieces of that wealth.

To give a simple example, suppose you own just two stocks (which is, of course, a bad idea from a diversification standpoint). On a particular day, one stock goes up sharply, but the other goes down so that your total wealth is unchanged. On another day, neither stock changes price at all. In both cases, your total wealth was unaffected, but in the first case you would probably be upset that your big gain was cancelled out. If you are, you are focusing on the individual pieces, not the big picture. As we will see in the next few subsections, this kind of thinking can lead to potentially damaging errors in judgment.

Frame Dependence

If an investment problem is presented in two different (but really equivalent) ways, investors often make inconsistent choices. That is, how a problem is described, or framed, seems to matter to people. Some people believe that frames are transparent; that is, investors should be able to see through the way the question is asked. Do they? Do you? Try this: Jot down your answers in the following two scenarios.

Scenario One. Suppose we give you $1,000. You have the following choice:

A. You can receive another $500 for sure.

B. You can flip a fair coin. If the coin-flip comes up heads, you get another $1,000, but if it comes up tails, you get nothing.

Scenario Two. Suppose we give you $2,000. You have the following choice:

A. You can lose $500 for sure.

B. You can flip a fair coin. If the coin-flip comes up heads, you lose $1,000, but if it comes up tails, you lose nothing.

What were your answers? Did you choose option A in the first scenario and option B in the second? If that's what you did, you are guilty of just focusing on gains and losses, and not paying attention to what really matters, namely, the impact on your wealth. However, you are not alone. About 85 percent of the people who are presented with the first scenario choose option A, and about 70 percent of the people who are presented with the second scenario choose option B.

If you look closely at the two scenarios, you will see that they are actually identical. You end up with $1,500 for sure if you pick option A, or else you end up with a 50-50 chance of either $1,000 or $2,000 if you pick option B. So you should pick the same option in both scenarios. Which option you prefer is up to you, but the point is that you should never pick option A in one scenario and option B in the other. But people do this because the phrasing, or framing, of the question leads people to answer the questions differently. This phenomenon is known as *frame dependence*.

Our frame dependence example offers several important investment lessons. First, an investor can always frame a decision problem in broad terms (like wealth) or in narrow terms (like gains and losses). Second, broad and narrow frames often lead the investor to make different choices. Although using a narrow frame (like gains and losses) is human nature, doing so can lead to irrational decisions. Therefore, using broad frames, like overall wealth, results in better investment decisions.

Mental Accounts and Loss Aversion

mental accounting
Associating a stock with its purchase price.

When you add a new stock to your portfolio, it is human nature for you to associate the stock with its purchase price. As the price of the stock changes through time, you will have unrealized gains or losses when you compare the current price to the purchase price. Through time, you will mentally account for these gains and losses, and how you feel about the investment depends on whether you are ahead or behind. This behaviour is known as **mental accounting**.

When you engage in mental accounting, you unknowingly have a personal relationship with each of your stocks. As a result, selling one of them becomes more difficult. It is as if you have to "break up" with this stock, or "fire" it from your portfolio. As with personal relationships, these "stock relationships" can be complicated and, believe it or not, make selling stocks difficult at times.

loss aversion
A reluctance to sell investments after they have fallen in value. Also known as the *breakeven* or *disposition effect*.

In fact, you may have particular difficulty selling a stock at a price lower than your purchase price. If you sell a stock at a loss, you may have a hard time thinking that purchasing the stock in the first place was correct. You may feel this way even if the decision to buy was actually a very good decision. A further complication is that you will also think that if you can just somehow "get even," you will be able to sell the stock without any hard feelings. This phenomenon is known as **loss aversion**, which is the reluctance to sell investments such as shares of stock after they have fallen in value. Loss aversion is also called the "break-even" or "disposition effect," and those suffering from it are sometimes said to have "get-evenitis." Legendary investor Warren Buffett offers the following advice: "The stock doesn't know you own it. You have feelings about it, but it has no feelings about you. The stock doesn't know what you paid. People shouldn't get emotionally involved with their stocks."

To see if you are likely to suffer from loss aversion, consider the following two investments:

> **Investment One**. A year ago, you bought shares in Fama Enterprises for $40 per share. Today, these shares are worth $20 each.

> **Investment Two**. A year ago, you bought shares in French Company for $5 per share. Today, these shares are worth $20 each.

What will you do? Will you (1) sell one of these stocks; (2) sell both of these stocks; (3) hold one of these stocks; or (4) hold both of these stocks?

Because you are reading about loss aversion, you will undoubtedly recognize that if you choose to keep the shares in Fama Enterprises, you might be suffering from loss aversion. Why do we say might? Well, consider this. Suppose you are considering a new investment in Fama Enterprises. Does your rational analysis say that it is reasonable to purchase shares at $20? If the rational answer is no, then you should sell. If the rational answer is yes, then you do not suffer from loss aversion. However, if you argued to yourself that if shares in Fama Enterprises were a good buy at $40, then they must be a steal at $20, you probably have a raging case of loss aversion. So, to summarize, there are two important lessons from this example:

- **Lesson One**: The market says that shares in Fama Enterprises are worth $20. The market does not care that you paid $40 a year ago.

- **Lesson Two**: You should not care about your purchase price of Fama Enterprises either. You must evaluate your shares at their current price.

How about the shares in French Company? Do you sell them and take the profit? Once again, the lessons are the same. The market says that shares in French Company are worth $20 per share today. The fact that you paid $5 a year ago is not relevant. Note that selling either of these stocks has tax consequences. Your careful analysis should acknowledge the existence of taxes and transaction fees, and their impact on the net proceeds available to you after you sell a security.

How destructive is loss aversion? Perhaps the most famous case of loss aversion, or "get-evenitis," occurred in 1995, when 28-year-old Nicholas Leeson caused the collapse of his employer, the 233-year-old Barings Bank. At the end of 1992, Leeson had lost about £2 million, which he hid in a secret account. By the end of 1993, his losses were about £23 million, and they mushroomed to £208 million at the end of 1994 (at the time, this was $512 million). Instead of admitting to these losses, Leeson gambled more of the bank's money in an attempt to "double-up and catch-up." On February 23, 1995, Leeson's losses were about £827 million ($1.3 billion) and his trading irregularities were uncovered. Although he attempted to flee from prosecution, he was caught, arrested, tried, convicted, and imprisoned. Also, his wife divorced him.

It is unlikely that you will suffer from a case of loss aversion as severe as Nicholas Leeson's, but loss aversion does affect everyday investors. For example, we know that individual investors sell "winners" more frequently than they sell "losers." If a typical individual investor had 100 stocks with unrealized gains, the investor might sell 15 of them and keep 85. If the same investor had 100 stocks with unrealized losses, the investor would tend to sell 10 of them and keep 90. That is, individual investors are typically about 1.5-times more likely to sell a stock that has gone up in price than they are to sell a stock that has fallen in price.

This effect is worse when investors hold mutual funds. With mutual funds, when investors choose to sell, they are more than 2.5 times as likely to sell a winning fund than a losing fund. How about professional money managers who manage the mutual funds? They also suffer from loss aversion.

House Money

Casinos in Las Vegas (and elsewhere) know all about a concept called "playing with house money." The casinos have found that gamblers are far more likely to take big risks with money that they have won from the casino (i.e., the "house money"). Also, casinos have found that gamblers are not as upset about losing house money as they are about losing the money they brought with them to gamble.

It may seem natural for you to feel that some money is precious because you earned it through hard work, sweat, and sacrifice, whereas other money is less precious because it came to you as a windfall. But these feelings are plainly irrational because any dollar you have buys the same amount of goods and services no matter how you obtained that dollar. The lessons are:

- **Lesson One**. There are no "paper profits." Your profits are yours.

- **Lesson Two**. All your money is your money. That is, you should not separate your money into bundles labelled "house money" and "my money."

Let us return to the shares of Fama Enterprises and French Company. Suppose both were to decline to $15. You might feel very differently about the decline depending on which stock you looked at. With Fama Enterprises, the decline makes a bad situation even worse. Now you are down $25 per share on your investment. On the other hand, with French Company, you only "give back" some of your "paper profit." You are still way ahead. This kind of thinking is playing with house money. Whether you lose from your original investment or from your investment gains is irrelevant.

Frame dependence, mental accounting, and the house money effect are all consistent with the predictions of prospect theory. Many other types of judgment errors have been documented. Here are a few examples:

- **Myopic loss aversion**: This behaviour is the tendency to focus on avoiding short-term losses, even at the expense of long-term gains. For example, you might fail to invest "retirement" money into stocks because you have a fear of loss in the near term.

- **Regret aversion**: This aversion is the tendency to avoid making a decision because you fear that, in hindsight, the decision would have been less than optimal. Regret aversion relates to myopic loss aversion.

- **Sunk cost fallacy**: This mistake is the tendency to "throw good money after bad." An example is to keep buying a stock or mutual fund in the face of unfavourable developments.

- **Endowment effect**: This effect is the tendency to consider something that you own to be worth more than it would be if you did not own it. Because of the endowment effect, people sometimes demand more money to give up something than they would be willing to pay to acquire it.

- **Money illusion**: If you suffer from a money illusion, you are confused between real buying power and nominal buying power (i.e., you do not account for the effects of inflation).

CHECK THIS

9.2a   What is the basic prediction of prospect theory?

9.2b   What is frame dependence?

9.2c   How are mental accounting and loss aversion related?

9.3   Overconfidence

A serious error in judgment you can make as an investor is to be overconfident. We are all overconfident about our abilities in many areas (recall our question about your driving ability at the beginning of the chapter). Here is another example. Ask yourself: What grade will I receive in this course (in spite of the arbitrary and capricious nature of the professor)? In our experience, almost everyone will either say A or, at worst, B. Sadly, when we ask our students this question, we always feel confident (but not overconfident) that at least some of our students are going to be disappointed.

Concerning investment behaviour, overconfidence appears in several ways. The classic example is diversification, or the lack of it. Investors tend to invest too heavily in the company for which they work. When you think about it, this loyalty can be very bad financially. This is because both your earning power (your income) and your retirement nest egg depend on one company.

Other examples of the lack of diversification include investing too heavily in the stocks of local companies. You might also do this because you read about them in the local news or you know someone who works there. That is, you might be unduly confident that you have a high degree of knowledge about local companies versus distant companies.

Overconfidence and Trading Frequency

If you are overconfident about your investment skill, you are likely to trade too much. You should know that researchers have found that investors who make relatively more trades have lower returns than investors who trade less frequently. Based on brokerage account activity over a particular period, researchers found that the average household earned an annual return of 16.4 percent. However, those households that traded the most earned an annual return of only 11.4 percent. The moral is clear: Excessive trading is hazardous to your wealth.

Overtrading and Gender: "It's (basically) a guy thing"

In a study published in 2001, Professors Brad Barber and Terrance Odean examined the effects of overconfidence. Two possible effects of overconfidence are that it leads to more trading and more trading leads to lower returns. If investors could be divided into groups that differed in overconfidence, then these effects could be examined.

Barber and Odean use the fact that psychologists have found that men are more overconfident than women in the area of finance. So, do men trade more than women? Do portfolios of men underperform the portfolios of women? Barber and Odean show that the answer to both questions is yes.

Barber and Odean examine the trading accounts of men and women and find that men trade about 50 percent more than women. They find that both men and women reduce their portfolio returns through excessive trading. However, men do so by 94 basis points more per year than women. The difference is even bigger between single men and single women. Single men trade 67 percent more than single women, and single men reduce their return by 144 basis points compared to single women.

Using four risk measures, and accounting for the effects of marital status, age, and income, Professors Barber and Odean also find that men invested in riskier positions than women. Young and single people held portfolios that displayed more return volatility and contained a higher percentage of stocks in small companies. Investors with higher incomes also accepted more market risk. These results are comforting because it seems to make sense that the relatively young and the relatively wealthy should be willing to take more investment risk, particularly if they do not have dependents. Professors Yuce and Yap (2006) examined the investment behaviour of male and female Canadian students who participated in an investment game and invested $1,000,000 and formed portfolios of different financial assets. Risk aversion levels showed that female students are statistically more risk averse than the male students. All female students avoided futures and options investments, the risky derivative instruments. Their results also showed that female groups did not get the top 5 returns or the bottom 5 returns; instead they obtained middle range returns, because they invested in safer instruments.

What is a Diversified Portfolio to the Everyday Investor?

It is clear to researchers that most investors have a poor understanding of what constitutes a well-diversified portfolio. Researchers have discovered that the average number of stocks in a household portfolio is about four, and the median is about three.

Ask yourself: What percentage of these households beat the market? If you are like most people, your answer is too low. Researchers have found, however, that even when accounting for trading costs, about 43 percent of the households outperformed the market. Surprised? The lack of diversification is the source of your surprise.

Think about it like this. Suppose all investors held just one stock in their account. If there are many stocks, about half the individual stock returns outperform the market average. Therefore, about half the investors will beat the market. Quickly: Did you think that you would certainly be in that half that would beat the market? If you did, this should show you that you might be prone to overconfidence.

**CHECK THIS**

9.3a How does overconfidence appear in investment behaviour?

9.3b What are the effects of trading frequency on portfolio performance?

9.4 Misperceiving Randomness and Overreacting to Chance Events

representativeness heuristic Concluding that causal factors are at work behind random sequences.

Cognitive psychologists have discovered that the human mind is a pattern-seeking device. As a result, we conclude that causal factors or patterns are at work behind sequences of events even when the events are truly random. In behavioural finance, this is known as the **representativeness heuristic**, which says that if something is random, it should look random. But what does random look like?

Suppose we flip a coin 20 times and write down whether we get a head or a tail. Then we do it again. The results of our two sets of 20 flips are:

First 20: T T T H T T T H T T H H H T H H T H H H

Second 20: T H T H H T T H T H T H T T H T H T H H

Do these sequences of heads and tails both look random to you? Most people would say that the first 20 and the second 20 somehow look "different," even though both are random sequences and both have 10 heads and 10 tails.

Let's look at this a bit differently by graphing the results. We'll start at zero. If a head occurs, we will subtract one; if a tail occurs, we will add one. Table 9.1 lists the results. Suppose we graph the two sets of 20 flips in Figure 9.1. Do the two series look different to you? Do you think the line labelled First 20 has a pattern to it, but the line labelled Second 20 appears to be random? If you do, your mind saw a pattern in a random sequence of coin flips, even though both patterns are the result of random coin flips with 10 heads and 10 tails.

The "Hot-Hand" Fallacy

Basketball fans generally believe that success breeds success. Suppose we look at the recent performance of two basketball players named LeBron and Shaquille. Both of these players make half of their shots. But LeBron just made two shots in a row, while Shaquille just missed two shots in a row. Researchers have found that if they ask 100 basketball fans which player has the better chance of making the next shot, 91 of them will say LeBron, because he has a "hot hand." Further, 84 of these fans believe that it is important for team-mates to pass the ball to LeBron after he has made two or three shots in a row.

But—and the sports fans among you will have a hard time with this—researchers have found that the hot hand is an illusion. That is, players really do not deviate much from their long-run shooting averages, although fans, players, announcers, and coaches think they do. Cognitive psychologists actually studied the shooting percentage of one professional basketball team for a season. The findings are presented in Table 9.2. Detailed analysis of shooting data failed to show that players make or miss shots more or less frequently than what would be expected by chance. That is, statistically speaking, all the shooting percentages in Table 9.2 are the "same."

TABLE 9.1			The Results of Two Sets of 20 Coin Flips			
	First 20 Flips			**Second 20 Flips**		
Flip Number	**Result**	**+1/−1**	**Accumulated Sum**	**Result**	**+1/−1**	**Accumulated Sum**
			0			0
1	T	1	1	T	1	1
2	T	1	2	H	−1	0
3	T	1	3	T	1	1
4	H	−1	2	H	−1	0
5	T	1	3	H	−1	−1
6	T	1	4	T	1	0
7	T	1	5	T	1	1
8	H	−1	4	H	−1	0
9	T	1	5	T	1	1
10	T	1	6	H	−1	0
11	H	−1	5	T	1	1
12	H	−1	4	H	−1	0
13	H	−1	3	T	1	1
14	T	1	4	T	1	2
15	H	−1	3	H	−1	1
16	H	−1	2	T	1	2
17	T	1	3	H	−1	1
18	H	−1	2	T	1	2
19	H	−1	1	H	−1	1
20	H	−1	0	H	−1	0
Number of heads	10			10		
Number of tails	10			10		

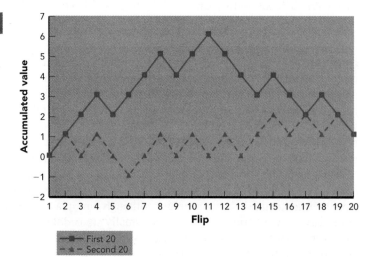

FIGURE 9.1

The Pattern of Two-Different Sets of 20 Coin Flips

TABLE 9.2	Shooting Percentages and the History of Previous Attempts
Shooting Percentage on Next Shot	**History of Previous Attempts**
46%	Made 3 in a row
50	Made 2 in a row
51	Made 1
52	First shot of the game
54	Missed 1
53	Missed 2 in a row
56	Missed 3 in a row

The shooting percentages in Table 9.2 may suggest that teams will try harder to stop a shooter who has made the last two or three shots. To take this into account, researchers have also studied free throw percentages. Researchers told fans that a certain player was a 70 percent free throw shooter and was about to shoot two foul shots. They asked fans to predict what would happen on the second shot if the player

1. Made the first free throw.
2. Missed the first free throw.

Fans thought that this 70 percent free throw shooter would make 74 percent of the second free throws after making the first free throw, but would only make 66 percent of the second free throws after missing the first free throw. Researchers studied free throw data from a professional basketball team over two seasons. They found that the result of the first free throw does not matter when it comes to making or missing the second free throw. On average, the shooting percentage on the second free throw was 75 percent when the player made the first free throw. On average, the shooting percentage on the second free throw was also 75 percent when the player missed the first free throw.

It is true that basketball players shoot in streaks. But these steaks are within the bounds of long-run shooting percentages. So it is an illusion that players are either "hot" or "cold." If you are a believer in the "hot hand," however, you are likely to reject these facts because you "know better" from watching your favourite teams over the years. You are being fooled by randomness, because randomness often appears in clusters.

clustering illusion
Human belief that random events that occur in clusters are not really random.

The **clustering illusion** is our human belief that random events that occur in clusters are not really random. For example, it strikes most people as very unusual if heads comes up four times in a row during a series of coin flips. However, if a fair coin is flipped 20 times, there is about a 50 percent chance of getting four heads in a row. Ask yourself, if you flip four heads in a row, do you think you have a "hot hand" at coin flipping?

Mutual fund investing is one area where investors seem to fall prey to the clustering illusion. Every year, funds that have had exceptionally good performance receive large inflows of investor money. Despite the universal disclaimer that "past performance is no guarantee of future results," investors nonetheless clearly chase past returns.

The Gambler's Fallacy

People commit the gambler's fallacy when they assume that a departure from what occurs on average, or in the long run, will be corrected in the short run. Another way to think about the gambler's fallacy is that because an event has not happened recently, it has become "overdue" and is more likely to occur. People sometimes refer (wrongly) to the "law of averages" in such cases.

Roulette is a random gambling game where gamblers can make various bets on the spin of the wheel. There are 38 numbers on a roulette table; two green ones, 18 red ones, and 18 black ones. One possible bet is to bet whether the spin will result in a red number or in a black number. Suppose a red number has appeared five times in a row. Gamblers will often become confident that the next spin will be black, when the true chance remains at about 50 percent (of course, it is exactly 18 in 38).

The misconception arises from the human intuition that the overall odds of the wheel must be reflected in a small number of spins. That is, gamblers often become convinced that the wheel is "due" to hit a black number after a series of red numbers. Gamblers do know that the odds of a black number appearing are always unchanged: 18 in 38. But gamblers cannot help but feel that after a long series of red numbers, a black one must appear to restore the "balance" between red and black numbers over time. Thousands of betting systems exist that claim to be able to generate money by betting opposite to recent outcomes. One simple example in roulette is to wait until four red numbers in a row appear—then bet on black. Internet hucksters sell "guaranteed" betting systems that are basically based on the gambler's fallacy. None of them work. Think about it. If these betting systems actually worked, why would they be for sale?

Of course, there are many other related investor errors and biases. Here is a partial list:

- **Law of small numbers**: If you believe in the law of small numbers, you believe that a small sample of outcomes always resembles the long-run distribution of outcomes. If your investment guru has been right five out of seven times recently, you might believe that his long-run average of being correct is also five out of seven. The law of small numbers is related to recency bias and to the gambler's fallacy.

- **Recency bias**: Humans tend to give recent events more importance than less recent events. For example, during the great bull market that occurred from 1995 to 1999, many investors thought the market would continue its big gains for a long time—forgetting that bear markets also occur (which happened from 2000 to 2002). Recency bias is related to the law of small numbers.

- **Self-attribution bias**: This bias occurs when you attribute good outcomes to your own skill, but blame bad outcomes on luck.

- **Wishful thinking bias**: You suffer from wishful thinking bias when you believe what you want to believe. Wishful thinking bias relates to self-attribution bias.

- **False consensus**: This is the tendency to think that other people are thinking the same thing about a stock we own (or are going to buy). False consensus relates to overconfidence and loss aversion.

- **Availability bias**: You suffer from availability bias when you put too much weight on information that is easily available and place too little weight on information that is hard to attain. Your financial decisions will suffer if you consider only information that is easy to obtain.

Visit
www.behaviouralfi-
nance.net
for many other
terms and concepts
of behavioural
finance.

CHECK THIS ✔

9.4a   What is the representativeness heuristic?

9.4b   What is the hot-hand fallacy? How could it affect investor decisions?

9.4c   What is the gambler's fallacy? How could it affect investor decisions?

Behavioural finance is clearly working its way from academia into the nitty-gritty business of running mutual-fund portfolios.

Lewis Sanders, chief executive of Alliance Capital Management, held forth on the subject at Morningstar's annual investment conference in June, and JP Morgan Asset Management has launched a stable of funds whose investment framework exploits the concept. Basically, behavioural finance looks at why investors make bad, irrational decisions—whether it's holding on to losing stocks for too long or selling-winners too early. These poor decisions create market inefficiencies that savvy investors can capitalize on.

"Chasing strong investment performance, whether through asset classes or investment managers, seems to be a permanent feature of investor decision-making," Sanders pointed out. He walked the audience through a number of blind spots, one being that investors tend to focus disproportionately on the part of their portfolio that's not performing well.

Sanders concluded that investors "systematically buy high and sell low"—adding that in most cases, they are unaware of their biases. There's no doubt that irrational investment decisions are common, but does behavioural finance form the underpinning of a worthy portfolio management style?

There are some skeptics. "I'm not personally aware of any models that would allow analysts to scientifically or precisely choose their entry points based on behavioural finance," says Don Cassidy, senior research analyst at Lipper, who is a student of the discipline. What's more, many money-management shops already watch for behavioural-finance moves. Value investing, for example, holds that the market can become too pessimistic about certain stocks, creating buying opportunities.

JPMorgan Asset Management, which is trying to raise its profile as a fund manager, insists that behavioural finance is a sound investment framework, having launched four of its Intrepid funds in February 2003. It has run similar portfolios in Europe for about a decade.

Silvio Tarca, who heads the U.S. behavioural-finance team at JPMorgan Asset Management, says the funds look for "securities that have been mispriced by irrational investor behaviour. We're looking for securities with attractive valuations and improving earnings expectations where the investment sentiment has turned favourable."

Intrepid managers focus on three behavioural patterns:

- Investors are too optimistic about past winners and too pessimistic about past losers.

- Analysts tend to underreact to earnings information when they revise their forecasts, thereby underestimating a stock's intrinsic worth.

- Investors tend to hold recent losing stocks for too long and sell their winners too quickly.

The combination of value and momentum investing should balance each other. Emphasizing valuation provides some downside protection, notes Morningstar's Dan McNeela.

Tarca acknowledges that there are other portfolio managers incorporating behavioural-finance tenets into their strategies. But many managers "spend a good deal of their time meeting with company management and sell-side analysts trying to make qualitative assessments about a company's business prospects, as opposed to [our] more quantitative approach," he says.

The JPMorgan Intrepid Mid Cap (PECAX), previously under the BancOne fund stable until it was acquired, came into the fold late last year. So far this year the portfolio has gained 14.51%, placing it in the top 5% of Morningstar's mid-cap blend category. The other funds are off to a good start, for the most part. Intrepid Value Fund (JPIVX) gained 17.5% last year, besting 90% of its Morningstar peers. Intrepid Contrarian Fund (JIISX) was up 16% last year, landing it in the bottom half of its group. Intrepid Growth Fund (JPGSX) gained 10.50% last year, surpassing 74% of its peers. Intrepid American Fund (JPIAX) notched a 12.7% gain, placing it in the top 17% of its group. Intrepid European (VEUAX), launched in 2000, has a five-year return of 7.77%, ranking it in the top 27% of its group.

Other firms have tried to incorporate behavioural finance. Take AllianceBernstein Wealth Appreciation Strategies (AWAAX), which automatically rebalances the portfolio if it strays five percentage points from the targeted 50-50 split between growth and value stocks.

"We're really trimming from the outperforming asset class and buying the underperforming asset class, which is exactly the thing people can't do by themselves," says Tom Fontaine, senior portfolio manager at Alliance-Bernstein Investment Research and Management.

Source: Lawrence C. Strauss, *Barron's Online*, September 19, 2005.

9.5 Sentiment-Based Risk and Limits to Arbitrage

It is important to realize that the efficient markets hypothesis does not require every investor to be rational. As we have noted, all that is required for a market to be efficient is that at least some investors are smart and well-financed. These investors are prepared to buy and sell to take advantage of any mispricing in the marketplace. This activity is what keeps markets efficient. Sometimes, however, a problem arises in this context.

Limits to Arbitrage

limits to arbitrage
The notion that the price of an asset may not equal its correct value because of barriers to arbitrage.

The term **limits to arbitrage** refers to the notion that under certain circumstances, rational, well-capitalized traders may not be able to correct a mispricing, at least not quickly. The reason is that strategies designed to eliminate mispricings are often risky, costly, or somehow restricted. Three important impediments are:

- *Firm-specific risk*: This issue is the most obvious risk facing a would-be arbitrageur. Suppose that you believe that observed price on General Motors stock is too low, so you purchase many, many shares. Then, some unanticipated negative news drives the price of General Motors stock even lower. Of course, you could try to hedge some firm-specific risk by shorting shares in another stock, say, Ford. But there is no guarantee that the price of Ford will fall if some firm-specific event triggers a decline in the price of General Motors. It might even rise, leaving you even worse off. Furthermore, in many, if not most, cases there might not even be a stock that could be considered a close substitute.

noise trader A trader whose trades are not based on information or meaningful financial analysis.

- *Noise trader risk*: A **noise trader** is someone whose trades are not based on information or financially meaningful analysis. Noise traders could, in principle, act together to worsen a mispricing in the short run. Noise trader risk is important because the worsening of a mispricing could force the arbitrageur to liquidate early and sustain steep losses. As Keynes once famously observed, "Markets can remain irrational longer than you can remain solvent."[2] Noise trader risk is also called **sentiment-based risk**, meaning the risk that an asset's price is being influenced by sentiment (or irrational belief) rather than fact-based financial analysis. If sentiment-based risk exists, then it is another source of risk beyond the systematic and unsystematic risks we discussed in an earlier chapter.

sentiment-based risk A source of risk to investors above and beyond firm-specific risk and overall market risk.

- *Implementation costs*: These costs include transaction costs such as bid-ask spreads, brokerage commissions, and margin interest. In addition, there might be some short-sale constraints. One short-sale constraint arises when there are not enough shares of the security to borrow so that the arbitrageur can take a large short position. Another short-sale constraint stems from legal restrictions. Many money managers, especially pension fund and mutual fund managers, are not allowed to sell short.

When these or other risks and costs are present, a mispricing may persist because arbitrage is too risky or too costly. Collectively, these risks and costs create barriers or limits to arbitrage. How important these limits are is difficult to say, but we do know that mispricings occur, at least on occasion. To illustrate, we next consider two well-known examples.

---

[2]This remark is generally attributed to Keynes, but whether he actually said it is not known.

The 3Com/Palm Mispricing

On March 2, 2000, a profitable provider of computer networking products and services, 3Com, sold 5 percent of one of its subsidiaries to the public via an initial public offering (IPO). At the time, the subsidiary was known as Palm (now it is known as palmOne).

3Com planned to distribute the remaining Palm shares to 3Com shareholders at a later date. Under the plan, if you owned 1 share of 3Com, you would receive 1.5 shares of Palm. So, after 3Com sold part of Palm via the IPO, investors could buy Palm shares directly, or they could buy them indirectly by purchasing shares of 3Com.

What makes this case interesting is what happened in the days that followed the Palm IPO. If you owned one 3Com share, you would be entitled, eventually, to 1.5 shares of Palm. Therefore, each 3Com share should be worth *at least* 1.5 times the value of each Palm share. We say "at least" because the other parts of 3Com were profitable. As a result, each 3Com share should have been worth much more than 1.5 times the value of one Palm share. But, as you might guess, things did not work out this way.

The day before the Palm IPO, shares in 3Com sold for $104.13. After the first day of trading, Palm closed at $95.06 per share. Multiplying $95.06 by 1.5 results in $142.59, which is the minimum value one would expect to pay for 3Com. But the day Palm closed at $95.06, 3Com shares closed at $81.81, more than $60 lower than the price implied by Palm. It gets stranger.

A 3Com price of $81.81 when Palm is selling for $95.06 implies that the market values the rest of 3Com's businesses (per share) at $81.81 − $142.59 = −$60.88. Given the number of 3Com shares outstanding at the time, this means the market placed a *negative* value of about −$22 billion for the rest of 3Com's businesses. Of course, a stock price cannot be negative. This means, then, that the price of Palm relative to 3Com was much too high.

To profit from this mispricing, investors would purchase shares of 3Com and short shares of Palm. In a well-functioning market, this action would force the prices into alignment quite quickly. What happened?

As you can see in Figure 9.2, the market valued 3Com and Palm shares in such a way that the non-Palm part of 3Com had a negative value for about two months, from March 2, 2000, until May 8, 2000. Even then, it took approval by the IRS for 3Com to proceed with the planned distribution of Palm shares before the non-Palm part of 3Com once again had a positive value.

The Royal Dutch/Shell Price Ratio

Another fairly well known example of a mispricing involves two large oil companies. In 1907, Royal Dutch of the Netherlands and Shell of the United Kingdom agreed to merge their business enterprises and pay dividends on a 60-40 basis. So, whenever the stock prices of Royal Dutch and Shell are not in a 60-40 ratio, there is a potential opportunity to make an arbitrage profit. If, for example, the ratio were 50-50, you would buy Royal Dutch, and short sell Shell.

Figure 9.3 plots the daily deviations from the 60-40 ratio of the Royal Dutch price to the Shell price. If the prices of Royal Dutch and Shell are in a 60-40 ratio, there is a zero percentage deviation. If the price of Royal Dutch is too high compared to the Shell price, there is a positive deviation. If the price of Royal Dutch is too low compared to the price of Shell, there is a negative deviation. As you can see in Figure 9.3, there have been large and persistent deviations from the 60-40 ratio. In fact, the ratio is seldom at 60-40 for most of the time from 1962 through 2004.

FIGURE 9.2

The Percentage Difference between 1 Share of 3Com and 1.5 Shares of Palm, March 2, 2000 to July 27, 2000

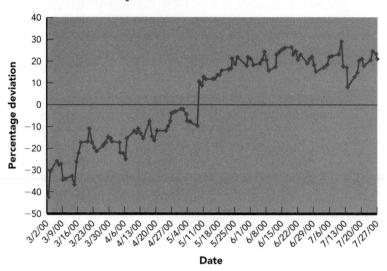

FIGURE 9.3

Royal Dutch and Shell 60–40 Price Ratio Deviations, 1962 to 2004

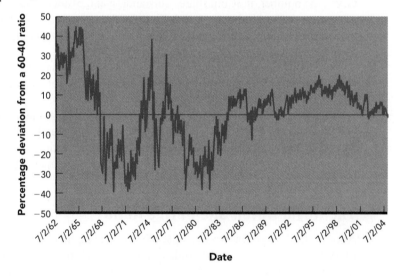

CHECK THIS ✓

9.5a   What does the term *limits to arbitrage* mean?

9.5b   If there were no limits to arbitrage, what would have been the relationship between 1 share of 3Com and 1.5 shares of Palm?

9.5c   If there were no limits to arbitrage, what would have been the relationship between the prices of Royal Dutch and Shell?

9.6   Technical Analysis

technical analysis
Using past price data and other nonfinancial data to identify future trading opportunities.

Many investors try to predict future stock price movements based on investor sentiment, errors in judgment, and/or historical price movements. These investors are using **technical analysis**. Unlike fundamental analysis, technical analysis does not rely on traditional valuation techniques like those presented in our earlier chapters.

Why Does Technical Analysis Continue to Thrive?

Proponents of the efficient markets hypothesis do not believe that technical analysis can assist investors in predicting future stock price movements. If that is the case, why is technical analysis still used? In fact, in this Internet and computer age, technical analysis is actually thriving. Why?

One possible reason that technical analysis still exists is that an investor can derive thousands of successful technical analysis systems by using historical security prices. Past movements of security prices are easy to fit into a wide variety of technical analysis systems. As a result, proponents of technical analysis can continuously tinker with their systems and find methods that fit historical prices. This process is known as "backtesting." Alas, successful investment is all about future prices.

Another possible reason that technical analysis still exists is simply that it sometimes works. Again, given a large number of possible technical analysis systems, it is possible that many of them will work (or appear to work) in the short run.

To give an example of a technical analysis tool, or a technical "indicator," consider trying to analyze market sentiment. The term "market sentiment" refers to the prevailing mood among investors about the future outlook of an individual security or the market. Market sentiment is generally classified as optimistic (bullish), neutral (undecided), or pessimistic (bearish).

Market sentiment usually takes time to change. That is, it takes time for, say, 80 percent of the investors to become bullish if only 50 percent of the investors are currently bullish. Investors who rely on market sentiment often believe that once 80 percent of the investors are bullish or bearish, a consensus has been reached. Further, once a consensus is reached, investors take this as a sign of an impending turn in the direction of the market. One way to measure market sentiment is to ask investors whether they think the market is going up or down. Suppose you ask 50 investors whether they are "bullish" or "bearish" on the market over the next month. Twenty say that they are bearish. The market sentiment index (MSI) can then be calculated as:

$$MSI = \frac{\text{Number of bearish investors}}{\text{Number of bullish investors} + \text{Number of bearish investors}}$$

$$MSI = \frac{20}{30 + 20} = 0.40$$

The MSI has a maximum value of 1.00, which occurs when every investor you ask is bearish on the market. The MSI has a minimum value of 0.00, which occurs when every investor you ask is bullish on the market. Note that if you are constructing a sentiment index, you will have to decide how many investors to ask, the identity of these investors, and their investment time frame, that is, daily, weekly, monthly, quarterly, or longer. You can construct a sentiment index for any financial asset for any investment time interval you choose.

People who calculate and use sentiment indexes often view them as "contrarian indicators." This means that if most other investors are bearish, perhaps the market is "oversold" and prices are due to rebound. Or if most other investors are bullish, perhaps the market is "overbought" and prices will be heading down.

The following saying is useful when you are trying to remember how to interpret the MSI: "When the MSI is high, it is time to buy; when the MSI is low, it is time to go." Note that there is no theory to guide investors as to what level of the MSI is "high" and what level is "low." This lack of precise guidance is a common problem with a technical indicator like the MSI.

Technical analysis techniques are centuries old, and their number is enormous. Many, many books on the subject have been written. For this reason, we only touch on the subject and introduce some of its key ideas in the next few sections. Although we focus on the use of technical analysis in the stock market, you should be aware that it is very widely used in commodity markets, and most comments herein apply to those markets as well.

Recall that investors with a positive outlook on the market are often called "bulls," and their outlook is characterized as "bullish." A rising market is called a "bull market." In contrast, pessimistic investors are called "bears," and their dismal outlook is characterized as "bearish." A falling market is called a "bear market." Technical analysts essentially search for bullish or bearish signals, meaning positive or negative indicators about stock prices or market direction.

Dow Theory

Dow theory
A method for predicting market direction that relies on the Dow Industrial and the Dow Transportation averages.

Dow theory is a method of analyzing and interpreting stock market movements that dates back to the turn of the twentieth century. The theory is named after Charles Dow, a cofounder of the Dow Jones Company and an editor of the Dow Jones–owned newspaper, *The Wall Street Journal.*

The essence of Dow theory is that there are, at all times, three forces at work in the stock market: (1) a primary direction or trend, (2) a secondary reaction or trend, and (3) daily fluctuations. According to the theory, the primary direction is either bullish (up) or bearish (down), and it reflects the long-run direction of the market.

Learn more about Dow theory at www.dowtheory. com and www.thedowtheory. com

However, the market can, for limited periods of time, depart from its primary direction. These departures are called secondary reactions or trends and may last for several weeks or months. These are eliminated by *corrections,* which are reversions to the primary direction. Daily fluctuations are essentially noise and are of no real importance.

The basic purpose of the Dow theory is to signal changes in the primary direction. To do this, two stock market averages, the Dow Jones Industrial Average (DJIA) and the Dow Jones Transportation Average (DJTA), are monitored. If one of these departs from the primary trend, the movement is viewed as secondary. However, if a departure in one is followed by a departure in the other, then this is viewed as a *confirmation* that the primary trend has changed. The Dow theory was, at one time, very well known and widely followed. It is less popular today, but its basic principles underlie more contemporary approaches to technical analysis.

Elliott Waves

Elliott wave theory
A method for predicting market direction that relies on a series of past market price swings (i.e., waves).

In the early 1930s, an accountant named Ralph Nelson Elliott developed the **Elliott wave theory**. While recuperating from life-threatening anemia (as well as his disastrous losses in the Crash of October 1929), Elliott read a book on Dow theory and began to study patterns of market price movements. Elliott discovered what he believed to be a persistent and recurring pattern that operated between market tops

| **FIGURE 9.4** | **Basic Elliott Wave Pattern** |

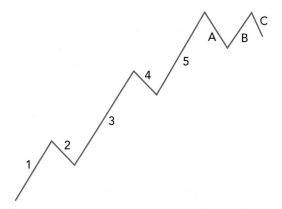

and bottoms. His theory was that these patterns, which he called "waves," collectively expressed investor sentiment. Through use of sophisticated measurements that he called "wave counting," a wave theorist could forecast market turns with a high degree of accuracy.

In 1935, Elliott published his theory in his book called *The Wave Principle.* His main theory was that there was a repeating eight-wave sequence. The first five waves, which he called "impulsive," were followed by a three-wave "corrective" sequence. Figure 9.4 shows the basic Elliott wave pattern. The impulse waves are labelled numerically, 1 through 5, while the corrective waves are labelled A, B, and C.

The basic Elliott wave theory gets very complicated because, under the theory, each wave can subdivide into finer wave patterns that are classified into a multitude of structures. Notwithstanding the complex nature of the Elliott wave theory, it is still a widely followed indicator.

Learn more about the Elliott-wave at www.elliottwave.com

Support and Resistance Levels

A key concept in technical analysis is the identification of support and resistance levels. A **support level** is a price or level below which a stock or the market as a whole is unlikely to fall. A **resistance level** is a price or level above which a stock or the market as a whole is unlikely to rise.

The idea behind these levels is straightforward. As a stock's price (or the market as a whole) falls, it reaches a point where investors increasingly believe that it can fall no further—the point at which it "bottoms out." Essentially, purchases by bargain-hungry investors ("bottom feeders") pick up at that point, thereby "supporting" the price. A resistance level is formed by reverse logic. As a stock's price (or the market as a whole) rises, it reaches a point where investors increasingly believe that it can go no higher—the point at which it "tops out." Once it does, sales by profit-hungry investors ("profit takers") pick up, thereby "resisting" further advances.

Resistance and support areas are usually viewed as psychological barriers. As the DJIA approaches levels with three zeros, such as 11,000, increased talk of "psychologically important" prices appears in the financial press. A "breakout" occurs when a stock (or the market as a whole) closes below a support level or above a resistance level. A breakout is usually interpreted to mean that the price move will continue in that direction.

As this discussion illustrates, much colourful language is used under the heading of technical analysis. We will see many more examples just ahead.

support level
Price or level below which a stock or the market as a whole is unlikely to fall.

resistance level
Price or level above which a stock or the market as a whole is unlikely to rise.

Technical Indicators

Learn more about charting at www.stockcharts. com Select "Chart School."

Technical analysts rely on a variety of technical indicators to forecast the direction of the market. Every day, The *Globe and Mail* publishes a variety of such indicators. An excerpt of the "Market Breadth" section appears in Figure 9.5.

Much, but not all, of the information presented is self-explanatory. We see the number of price advances, the number of price declines, and the number of unchanged prices. The number of stock prices reaching new highs and new lows as of that day is also listed. Figure 9.6 shows the Market Health section of the September 15, 2007, *Globe and Mail*. You can find the bull–bear ratio, the insider line, and the bullish percent index line. Each graph is followed by an explanation of how to interpret the figures.

For a trader's glossary, check out www.traders.com then click on Traders' Resource

One popular technical indicator is called the *advance/decline line*. This indicator shows, for some given period, the cumulative difference between advancing issues and declining issues. For example, Table 9.3 contains advance and decline information for the August 1, 2005, to August 5, 2005, trading week.

In Table 9.3, notice how we take the difference between the number of issues advancing and declining on each day and then cumulate the difference through time. For example, on Monday, 302 more issues advanced than declined. On Tuesday, 1,125 more issues advanced than declined. Over the two days, the cumulative advance/decline is thus $302 + 1,125 = 1,427$.

This cumulative advance/decline number, once plotted, is the advance/decline line. A downward-sloping advance/decline line would be considered a bearish signal, whereas an upward-sloping advance/decline line is a bullish signal. The advance/decline line is often used to measure market "breadth." If the market is going up, for example, then technical analysts view it as a good sign if there is market breadth. That is, the signal is more bullish if the advance is accompanied by a steeply upwardly sloping advance/decline line.

"Closing Arms" is the ratio of average trading volume in declining issues to average trading volume in advancing issues. It is calculated as follows:

$$\text{Arms} = \frac{\text{Declining Volume/Declining Issue}}{\text{Advancing Volume/Advancing Issues}} \tag{9.1}$$

FIGURE 9.5

Market Breadth

MARKET BREADTH

% change indicates increase/decrease from 13-week average

	TSX	Venture	NYSE	Nasdaq
Advance	686	572	1,836	1,629
% Chg	-9.01	13.76	10.66	12.71
Adv. Vol (000s)	113,910	239,571	1,549,001	818,012
Decline	822	550	1,496	1,312
% Chg	6.44	-1.43	-5.37	-13.03
Decl. Vol (000s)	166,094	69,041	1,158,210	748,963
Unchanged	730	1,229	270	351
% Chg	22.81	.75	-12.10	13.71
Unch. Vol (000s)	34,009	20,908	17,078	30,803
Total	2,238	2,351	3,602	3.292
New High	9	18	62	50
% Chg	-81.91	-44.73	-61.82	-48.50
New Low	32	36	79	96
% Chg	6.93	57.84	22.82	39.37
Vol (000s)	314,014	329,519	2,724,289	1,597,777
% Chg	-9.37	99.31	-2.15	-20.99

FIGURE 9.6

Globe and Mail

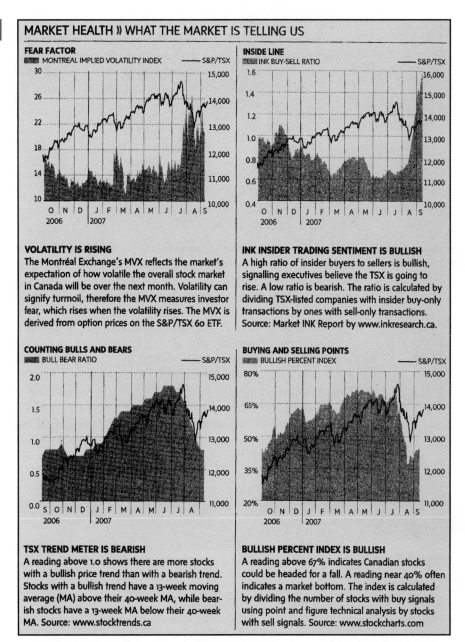

MARKET HEALTH » WHAT THE MARKET IS TELLING US

FEAR FACTOR

MONTREAL IMPLIED VOLATILITY INDEX — S&P/TSX

VOLATILITY IS RISING
The Montréal Exchange's MVX reflects the market's expectation of how volatile the overall stock market in Canada will be over the next month. Volatility can signify turmoil, therefore the MVX measures investor fear, which rises when the volatility rises. The MVX is derived from option prices on the S&P/TSX 60 ETF.

INSIDE LINE

INK BUY-SELL RATIO — S&P/TSX

INK INSIDER TRADING SENTIMENT IS BULLISH
A high ratio of insider buyers to sellers is bullish, signalling executives believe the TSX is going to rise. A low ratio is bearish. The ratio is calculated by dividing TSX-listed companies with insider buy-only transactions by ones with sell-only transactions. Source: Market INK Report by www.inkresearch.ca.

COUNTING BULLS AND BEARS

BULL BEAR RATIO — S&P/TSX

TSX TREND METER IS BEARISH
A reading above 1.0 shows there are more stocks with a bullish price trend than with a bearish trend. Stocks with a bullish trend have a 13-week moving average (MA) above their 40-week MA, while bearish stocks have a 13-week MA below their 40-week MA. Source: www.stocktrends.ca

BUYING AND SELLING POINTS

BULLISH PERCENT INDEX — S&P/TSX

BULLISH PERCENT INDEX IS BULLISH
A reading above 67% indicates Canadian stocks could be headed for a fall. A reading near 40% often indicates a market bottom. The index is calculated by dividing the number of stocks with buy signals using point and figure technical analysis by stocks with sell signals. Source: www.stockcharts.com

Courtesy of StockCharts.com, Inc.

TABLE 9.3	Advance/Decline Line Calculation			
Weekday	**Issues Advancing**	**Issues Declining**	**Difference**	**Cumulative Difference**
Monday	1,777	1,475	+302	+302
Tuesday	2,192	1,067	+1,125	1,427
Wednesday	1,546	1,724	−178	1,249
Thursday	1,079	2,207	−1,128	+121
Friday	738	2,532	−1,794	−1,673

The ratio is named after its inventor, Richard Arms; it is often called the "trin," which is an acronym for "tr(ading) in(dex)." Notice that the numerator in this ratio is just the average volume for issues that declined on that day. The denominator is the average volume for advancing issues. Values greater than 1.00 are considered bearish because the indication is that declining shares had heavier volume. Using the number from Figure 9.5 we can calculate the Arms value as follows:

$$\text{Arms} = \frac{166{,}094/822}{113{,}910/686} = 1.215$$

A caveat: Some sources reverse the numerator and the denominator when they calculate this ratio.

Relative Strength Charts

relative strength
A measure of the performance of one investment relative to another.

Relative strength charts illustrate the performance of one company, industry, or market relative to another. If you look back at the *Value Line* exhibit in Chapter 7, you will see a plot labelled "relative strength." Very commonly, such plots are created to analyze how a stock has done relative to its industry or the market as a whole.

To illustrate how such plots are constructed, suppose that on some particular day, we invest equal amounts, say $100, in both Ford and GM (the amount does not matter; what matters is that the original investment is the same for both). On every subsequent day, we take the ratio of the value of our Ford investment to the value of our GM investment, and we plot it. A ratio bigger than 1.0 indicates that, on a relative basis, Ford has outperformed GM, and vice versa. Thus, a value of 1.20 indicates that Ford has done 20 percent better than GM over the period studied. Notice that if both stocks are down, a ratio bigger than 1.0 indicates that Ford is down by less than GM.

RELATIVE STRENGTH

EXAMPLE 9.1

Consider the following series of monthly stock prices for two hypothetical companies:

Month	Stock A	Stock B
1	$25	$50
2	24	48
3	22	45
4	22	40
5	20	39
6	19	38

On a relative basis, how has stock A done compared to stock B?

To answer, suppose we had purchased four shares of A and two shares of B for an investment of $100 in each. We can calculate the value of our investment in each month and then take the ratio of A to B as follows:

(continued)

| | Investment Value | | |
Month	Stock A (4 shares)	Stock B (2 shares)	Relative Strength
1	$100	$100	1.00
2	96	96	1.00
3	88	90	0.98
4	88	80	1.10
5	80	78	1.03
6	76	76	1.00

What we see is that over the first four months both stocks were down, but A outperformed B by 10 percent. However, after six months the two had done equally well (or equally poorly).

Charting

Technical analysts rely heavily on charts showing recent market activity in terms of either prices or, less frequently, volume. In fact, technical analysis is sometimes called "charting," and technical analysts are often called "chartists." There are many types of charts, but the basic idea is that by studying charts of past market prices (or other information), the chartist identifies particular patterns that signal the direction of a stock or the market as a whole. We briefly describe some charting techniques next.

Open-High-Low-Close Charts (OHLC)   Perhaps the most popular charting method is the bar chart. The most basic bar chart uses the stock's opening, high, low, and closing prices for the period covered by each bar. If the technician is constructing a daily bar chart, the technician will use the daily opening high, daily low, and daily closing prices of the stock. The high and low prices are represented by the top and bottom of the vertical bar and the opening and closing prices are shown by short horizontal lines crossing the vertical bar. The example of a bar chart in Figure 9.7 for RIM is from www.stockcharts.com.

Price Channel   A price channel is a chart pattern using OHLC data that can slope upward, downward, or sideways. Price channels belong to the group of price patterns known as *continuation patterns*. A continuation pattern is a pattern where the price of the stock is expected to continue along its main direction. A price channel has two boundaries, an upper trendline and a lower trendline. The upper trendline marks resistance and the lower trendline marks support. If the overall price movement of the stock is downward, the upper trendline is called the main trendline, and the lower trendline is called the channel line. The example of a price channel for ChevronTexaco in Figure 9.8 is from the Web site www.stockcharts.com.

Head and Shoulders   A head and shoulders chart pattern belongs to a group of price charts known as *reversal patterns*. Reversal pattern charts also use OHLC data. These chart patterns signal that a reversal from the main trendline is possibly going to occur. Because it belongs to the reversal pattern group, a head and shoulders pattern is identified as either a *head and shoulders top* or a *head and shoulders bottom*. The example of a head and shoulders top for CNET Networks in Figure 9.9 is also from the Web site www.stockcharts.com.

FIGURE 9.7   **Open-High-Low-Close Bar Chart for RIM**

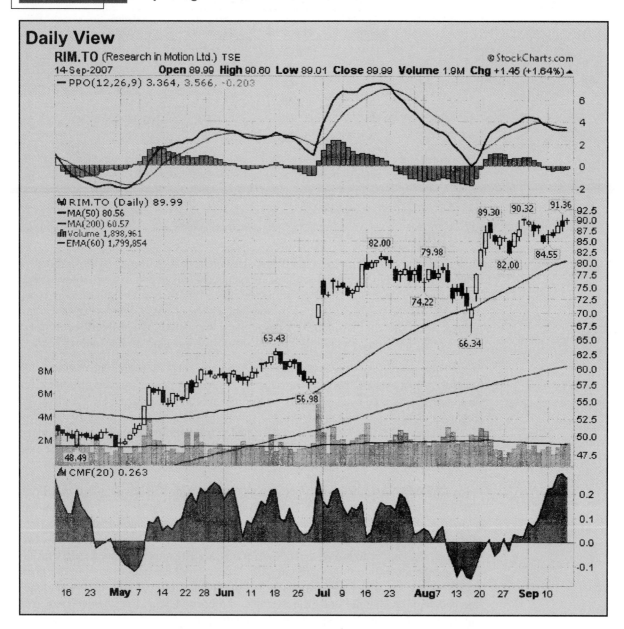

As you can see in Figure 9.9, the head and shoulders top formation has three components: the *left shoulder,* the *head,* and the *right shoulder.* To qualify as a head and shoulders top pattern, the shoulders must be lower than the head. Then, a *neckline support* is drawn between the valleys formed by the left and right shoulders. The reversal signal is generated when the neckline is *pierced.* In the case of CNET, once the stock price fell below $45, the stock plunged to $25. Of course, there are *false piercings,* which do not result in a sudden downdraft of the stock.

Moving Averages   Moving averages are used to generate price reversal signals. As the name implies, a moving average is simply the average closing price of a stock over

FIGURE 9.8

Price Channel Chart for ChevronTexaco

FIGURE 9.9

Head and Shoulders Chart for CNET Networks, Inc.

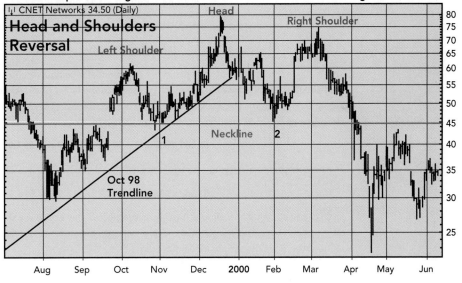

For more technical analysis charts and explanations, visit www.bigcharts.com www.stockcharts. com www.incredible-charts.com

a fixed length of time, say 20 days. Each day, the new closing price is added to the calculation, and the oldest closing price is dropped from the calculation.

Moving averages are either simple or exponential. In a *simple moving average,* all days are given equal weighting. In an *exponential moving average,* more weight is given to the most recently observed price. Market technicians, like many investors, often believe that the latest price observed for a stock is the most important piece of information about the stock. In Example 9.2, we present data for a three-day simple moving average and data for a three-day exponential moving average, where two-thirds of the average weight is placed on the most recent price.

THREE-DAY SIMPLE MOVING AVERAGE AND THREE-DAY EXPONENTIAL MOVING AVERAGE

EXAMPLE 9.2

Day	Closing Price	Three-Day Simple Moving Average	Three-Day Exponential Moving Average
1	$89.00		
2	88.44		$88.72
3	87.60	$88.35	87.97
4	86.20	87.41	86.79
5	85.75	86.52	86.10
6	84.57	85.51	85.08
7	83.64	84.65	84.12
8	76.70	81.64	79.17
9	76.65	79.00	77.49
10	75.48	76.28	76.15

To calculate the first three-day simple moving average, we need three closing prices. The first simple moving average entry is simply:

($89.00 + $88.44 + $87.60)/3 = $88.35

The second simple moving average entry is:

($88.44 + $87.60 + $86.20)/3 = $87.41

To calculate a three-day exponential moving average, we begin by averaging the first two days:

($89.00 + $88.44)/2 = $88.72

This is the first number that appears in the exponential moving average column. To obtain the next one, you must decide how much weight is placed on the latest price. As noted above, we selected a 2/3, or 0.667, weight. To calculate the next exponential moving average entry, we multiply the latest closing price by 0.667 and the previous exponential moving average entry by 0.333:

(0.667)($87.60) + (0.333)($88.72) = $87.97

The next exponential moving average entry is:

(0.667)($86.20) + (0.333)($87.97) = $86.79

You can see that the simple moving average and the exponential moving average generate different numbers. The exponential moving average responds more quickly to the latest price information than does the simple moving average.

For a description of many technical indicators, including other moving average indicators, see www.incredible-charts.com.

In practice, 50-day moving averages are frequently compared to 200-day moving averages. The 200-day moving average might be thought of as indicative of the long-run trend, while the 50-day average might be thought of as a short-run trend. If the 200-day average was rising while the 50-day average was falling, the indication might be that price declines are expected in the short term, but the long-term outlook is favourable. Alternatively, the indication might be that there is a danger of a change in the long-term trend. Our nearby *Work the Web* box gives an example.

WORK THE WEB

Charts are easy to draw online. Two of the best sites are stockcharts.com and www.bigcharts.com. Here is an example from finance.yahoo.com:

As illustrated, we have drawn a moving average chart for Microsoft. The jagged line tracks Microsoft's daily stock price over the past year. The two smoother lines are the 50-day and 200-day moving averages. Notice the 50-day average crosses the 200-day average in August from below. Such a crossing is sometimes interpreted as a signal to buy. In this case, the signal was false in the short run because the stock subsequently fell in price. Despite the fall, the 50-day moving average remained above the 200-day moving average. Investors who stayed in have made a profit.

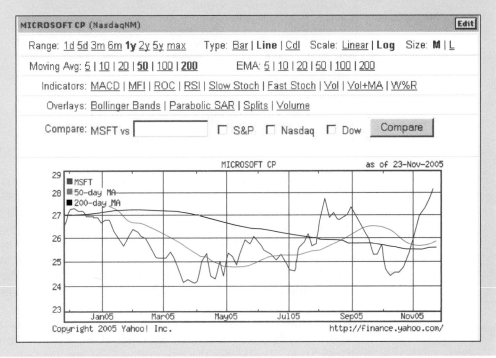

Putting it All Together   Quite often, a market technician will be using multiple chart indicators to help in making trading decisions. Let's examine the collection of technical information available from the Web site www.bigcharts.com. We set the Web site controls to give us three months of daily data for General Motors (GM). In addition, we asked the Web site to provide us with 9-day and 18-day exponential moving averages, Bollinger bands, volume, *MACD*, and *money flow*. The results appear in Figure 9.10.

Bollinger Bands   John Bollinger created Bollinger bands in the early 1980s. The purpose of Bollinger bands is to provide *relative* levels of high and low prices. Bollinger bands represent a 2-standard deviation bound calculated from the moving average (this is why Bollinger bands do not remain constant). In Figure 9.10, the Bollinger bands surround a 20-day moving average. The Bollinger bands are the maroon bands that appear in the top chart. Bollinger bands have been interpreted in many ways by their users. For example, when the stock price is relatively quiet, the Bollinger bands are tight, which indicates a possible pent-up tension that must be released by a subsequent price movement.

FIGURE 9.10

Technical Analysis Data for General Motors

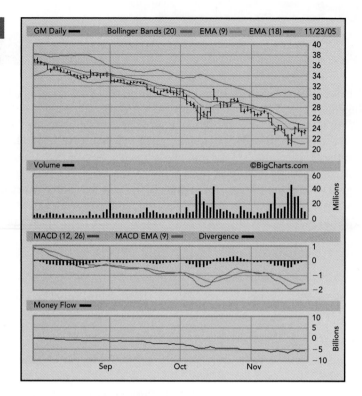

MACD   MACD stands for moving average convergence divergence. The MACD indicator shows the relationship between two moving averages of prices. The MACD is derived by dividing one moving average by another and then comparing this ratio to a third moving average, the signal line. In the GM example, the MACD uses a 12-day and a 26-day moving average and a 9-day signal line. The convergence/divergence of these three averages is represented by the solid black bars in the third chart of Figure 9.10. The basic MACD trading rule is to sell when the MACD falls below its signal line and to buy when the MACD rises above its signal line.

Money Flow   The idea behind money flow is to identify whether buyers are more eager to buy the stock than sellers are to sell it. In its purest form, money flow looks at each trade. To calculate the money flow indicator, the technician multiplies price and volume for the trades that occur at a price higher than the previous trade price.

CALCULATING MONEY FLOW

EXAMPLE 9.3

Price	Up (+); Down (−); Unchanged (0)	Volume	Price × Volume	Money Flow (+)	Money Flow (−)	Net Money Flow
10						
11	+	1,000	11,000	11,000		
12	+	100	1,200	12,200		
12	0	500	6,000			
11	−	500	5,500		5,500	
10	−	50	500		6,000	
	At the end of the day:					6,200

The technician then sums this money flow. From this sum, the technician subtracts another money flow: the accumulated total of price times volume for trades that occur at prices lower than the previous trade. Example 9.3 shows how to calculate money flow.

Traders using money flow look for a divergence between money flow and price. If price remains stable but money flow becomes highly positive, this is taken as an indicator that the stock price will soon increase. Similarly, if the stock price remains stable but the money flow becomes quite negative, this is taken as an indicator that the stock price will soon decrease. In Figure 9.10, the negative accumulation of money flow for GM signals to followers of money flow that further price declines for GM are in order.

Fibonacci Numbers

Traders using technical analysis are interested in timing their purchase or sale of a stock. As you know by now, these traders look for support or resistance stock price levels. As strange as it may seem, one source that traders use is known as the *golden mean*. The golden mean is sometimes abbreviated by the greek letter phi (ϕ). The golden mean, ϕ, is approximately equal to 1.618 (it is precisely equal to $(\sqrt{5}+1)/2$). The golden mean is mathematically interesting, because, among other things, $\phi^2 = \phi + 1$.

The golden mean also results from a series of numbers known as *Fibonacci numbers*. The infinite Fibonacci series grows as follows:

$$1,1,2,3,5,8,13,21,34,55,89,144,233,377,610,987\ldots$$

Note that the series begins with 1,1 and grows by adding the two previous numbers together (for example, $21 + 34 = 55$). Let's look at the ratio of some number to their predecessor in the series:

$$21/13 = 1.6154$$
$$34/21 = 1.6190$$
$$55/34 = 1.6176$$
$$89/55 = 1.6182$$

For an excellent source on Fibonacci numbers and the golden mean, visit www.mcs.surrey. ac.uk/Personal/ R.Knott/Fibonacci/ fib.html

The ratio converges to 1.618, or ϕ. Market technicians are interested in ϕ because:

$$(\phi - 1)/\phi = 0.618/1.618 = 0.382$$
$$1/\phi = 1.000/1.618 = 0.618 = \phi - 1$$

Market technicians use these numbers to predict support and resistance levels. For example, as a stock increases in value over time, it will occasionally pull back in value. Suppose a stock has increased from $40 to $60, and has recently begun to fall a bit in value. Using the $(\phi - 1)/\phi$ ratio, market technicians would predict the primary support area would occur at $52.36 ($60 − $40 = $20; $20 × 0.382 = $7.64; $60 − $7.64 = $52.36). A similar calculation that uses the $1/\phi$ ratio of 0.618 instead of 0.382 results in the secondary support area of $47.64. If the stock were to pierce this secondary support level and close below it, the rally would be declared over. Market technicians would then begin to look for opportunities to sell the stock short if it subsequently rallied.

Nature provides many instances involving Fibonacci numbers. The number of petals on a flower is often a Fibonacci number. For example, black-eyed susans have 13 petals and ordinary daisies have 34. Also, pinecones and pineapples have spirals containing 8 or 13 scales. There are so many other examples that some observers classify Fibonacci numbers as a "law of nature." Because of this, some market technicians believe that the Fibonacci numbers should also apply to market prices.

Other Technical Indicators

We close our discussion of technical analysis by describing a few additional technical indicators. The "odd-lot" indicator looks at whether odd-lot purchases (purchases of fewer than 100 shares) are up or down. One argument is that odd-lot purchases represent the activities of smaller, unsophisticated investors, so when they start buying, it's time to sell. This is a good example of a "contrarian" indicator. In contrast, some argue that because short selling is a fairly sophisticated tactic, increases in short selling are a negative signal.

Some indicators can seem a little silly. For example, there is the "hemline" indicator, which is also known as the "bull markets and bare knees" indicator. Through much of the nineteenth century, long skirts dominated women's fashion and the stock market experienced many bear markets. In the 1920s, flappers revealed their knees and the stock market boomed. Even the stock market crash of October 1987 was predicted by hemlines. During the 1980s, miniskirts flourished, but by October 1987, a fashion shift had women wearing longer skirts.

One of the more famous (or fatuous, depending on how you look at it) indicators is the Super Bowl indicator, which forecasts the direction of the market based on whether the National Football Conference or the American Football Conference wins. A Super Bowl win by a National Football Conference team or an American Football Conference team that used to be in the old National Football League (e.g., Pittsburgh Steelers, Baltimore Colts) is bullish. This probably strikes you as absurd, so you might be surprised to learn that for the period 1967–1988, the Super Bowl indicator forecast the direction of the stock market with more than 90 percent accuracy. A nearby *Investment Updates* box contains more details about this indicator.

CHECK THIS ✓

9.6a What is technical analysis?

9.6b What is the purpose of charting a stock's past price?

9.6c What is the purpose of using technical indicators?

There are lots of other technical trading rules. How seriously should you take them? That's up to you, but our advice is to keep in mind that life is full of odd coincidences. Just because a bizarre stock market predictor seems to have worked well in the past doesn't mean that it's going to work in the future.

9.7 Summary and Conclusions

In this chapter, we examined behavioural finance and technical analysis. We learned that a key to becoming a wise investor is to avoid certain types of behaviour. By studying behavioural finance, you can see the potential damage to your (or your client's) portfolio from overconfidence and psychologically induced errors.

The evidence is relatively clear on one point: Investors probably make mistakes. A much more difficult question, and one where the evidence is not at all clear, is whether risks stemming from errors in judgment by investors can influence market prices and lead to market inefficiencies. Market efficiency does not require that all investors behave in a rational fashion. It just requires that some do.

The Super Guide to Investing

Every January, about 90 million people in the United States watch television for a prediction of how well the stock market is going to do in the upcoming year. So you missed it this year? Maybe not. The stock market predictor we are talking about is the Super Bowl!

The Super Bowl indicator has become one of the more famous (or infamous) technical indicators of stock market performance. Here's how it works. In the 1960s, the original National Football League (NFL) and the upstart American Football League (AFL) were fighting for dominance. The Super Bowl indicator says that if a team from the original AFL wins the Super Bowl, the market posts a negative return for the year, and if a team from the original NFL wins, the market will post a gain for the year.

So how has the Super Bowl predictor performed? Take a look at the chart we obtained from www.cnn.com.

For the first 31 Super Bowls, the indicator was correct 28 out of 31 times! The Miami Dolphins are perhaps the best market predictor. When Miami won the Super Bowl in 1973, the market proceeded to drop by 14.7 percent. The next year was an even better indicator. The next year, the Dolphins beat the Minnesota Vikings and the S&P 500 lost 26.5 percent, the worst one-year performance in its history. When the Dolphins lost the Super Bowl in 1972, 1983, and 1985, the S&P 500 posted double-digit gains in each of those years.

So you are not ready to bet the ranch on the Super Bowl indicator? It's probably a good thing. Since 1997, the Super Bowl indicator has been right only twice, in 2002 and 2005. The New England Patriots, an AFL team, won the Super Bowl in both of these years and the S&P 500 dropped 30 percent in 2002 (but only 0.6 percent in 2005). The performance in 2001 is not as clear. The Baltimore Ravens won the Super Bowl that year and the market lost 7.6 percent. The Ravens are the descendants of the original Cleveland Browns, a member of the original NFL. In this case, the Super Bowl indicator was incorrect. However, purists (especially in Cleveland) argue that

since the Browns have been revived, the Ravens cannot be considered a member of the original NFL. But the Ravens did beat the New York Giants, an old NFL team. In 2003, the expansion Tampa Bay Buccaneers beat an original AFL team, the Oakland Raiders, and the market went up about 28 percent.

The Predictor (30-7-2)

Bullish years (22)
49ers - '82, '85, '89, '95
Bears- '86
Colts - '71
Cowboys - '72, '93, '94, '96
Giants - '87, '91
Packers, '67, '68, '97
Redskins - '83, '88, '92
Steelers - '75, '76, '79, '80

Bearish years (8)
Dolphins - '73, '74
Jets, '69
Patriots, '02, '05
Raiders - '77, '81, '84

Indicator missed (7)
Broncos - '98, '99
Chiefs - '70
49ers - '90
Cowboys - '78
Rams -'00
Patriots - '04

Inconclusive (2)
Ravens - '01*
Buccaneers - '03**

*Created when the old NFL Cleveland Browns moved to Baltimore, the NFL says the Ravens started life as an AFC team in 1996, which would mean the predictor was accurate.
**Expansion team

Nonetheless, many investors try to predict future stock price movements based on investor sentiment, errors in judgment, or historical price movements. Such investors rely on the tools of technical analysis, and we present numerous specific methods used by technical analysts. Whether these tools or methods work is much debated. We close this chapter by noting that it is possible that market prices are influenced by factors like errors in judgment by investors, sentiment, emotion, and irrationality. If they are, however, we are unaware of any scientifically proven method investors such as you can use to profit from these influences.

REAL WORLD

This chapter deals with various aspects of behavioural finance. How do you go about incorporating these concepts into the management of your portfolio? First, recall that one of the major lessons from this chapter is that, at times, you may be your own worst enemy when you are investing.

But suppose that you are able to harness your own psychological flaws that unduly influence your investment decisions. To profit from insights from behavioural finance, you might try to shift your portfolio to take advantage of situations where you perceive other market participants have incorrectly valued certain stocks, bonds, derivatives, market sectors, or even countries. Shifting portfolio weights to take advantage of these opportunities is called a "dynamic" trading strategy.

Here is one example of using a dynamic trading strategy. Consider a typical value/growth portfolio weight-shifting scheme. When there is a great deal of market overreaction, perhaps signalled by high market volatility, you would increase, or tilt, your relative portfolio weight toward value stocks. When there is a great deal of market underreaction, perhaps signalled by low market volatility, you would increase your relative weighting in growth stocks. The problem, of course, is knowing when and how to tilt your portfolio to take advantage of what you perceive to be market overreactions and underreactions. At times, you can do very well when you tilt your portfolio. Other times, to use an old commodity market saying, "you get your head handed to you."

There is a great amount of information available on the Internet about behavioural finance and building portfolios. One interesting place to start is the research section at www.psychonomics.com. Make sure that the money that you are using to test any trading scheme is only a small portion of your investment portfolio.

Key Terms

behavioural finance 273
prospect theory 273
mental accounting 275
loss aversion 275
representativeness heuristic 279
clustering illusion 281
limits to arbitrage 284
noise trader 284

sentiment-based risk 284
technical analysis 287
Dow theory 288
Elliott wave theory 288
support level 289
resistance level 289
relative strength 292

Chapter Review Problems and Self-Test

1. **It's All Relative** Consider the following series of monthly stock prices for two companies:

Week	Phat Co	GRRL Power
1	$10	$80
2	12	82
3	16	80
4	15	84
5	14	85
6	12	88

On a relative basis, how has Phat done compared to GRRL Power?

2. **Simple Moving Averages** Using the prices from the previous problem, calculate the three-month simple moving average prices for both companies.

Answers to Self-Test Problems

1. Suppose we had purchased eight shares of Phat and one share of GRRL Power. We can calculate the value of our investment in each month and then take the ratio of Phat to GRRL Power as follows:

Week	Investment Value		Relative Strength
	Phat Co (8 shares)	GRRL Power (1 share)	
1	$80	$80	1.00
2	96	82	1.17
3	128	80	1.60
4	120	84	1.43
5	112	85	1.32
6	96	88	1.09

Phat Co. has significantly outperformed GRRL Power over much of this period; however, after six weeks, the margin has fallen to about 9 percent from as high as 60 percent.

2. The moving averages must be calculated relative to the share price; also note that results cannot be computed for the first two weeks because of insufficient data.

Week	Phat Co	Phat Co. Moving Average	GRRL Power	GRRL Power Moving Average
1	$10	—	$80	—
2	12	—	82	—
3	16	$12.67	80	$80.67
4	15	14.33	84	82.00
5	14	15.00	85	83.00
6	12	13.67	88	85.67

Test Your Investment Quotient

CFA®
PROBLEMS

1. **Technical Analysis** Which of the following is a basic assumption of technical analysis in contrast to fundamental analysis?

   a. Financial statements provide information crucial in valuing a stock.
   b. A stock's market price will approach its intrinsic value over time.
   c. Aggregate supply and demand for goods and services are key determinants of stock value.
   d. Security prices move in patterns, which repeat over long periods.

2. **Technical Analysis** Which of the following is least likely to be of interest to a technical analyst?

   a. A 15-day moving average of trading volume.
   b. A relative strength analysis of stock price momentum.
   c. Company earnings and cash flow growth.
   d. A daily history of the ratio of advancing issues over declining issues.

3. **Dow Theory** Dow theory asserts that three forces are at work in the stock market at any time. Which of the following is not one of these Dow theory forces?

   a. Daily price fluctuations
   b. A secondary reaction or trend
   c. A primary direction or trend
   d. Reversals or overreactions

4. **Technical Indicators** The advance/decline line is typically used to

a. Measure psychological barriers.
b. Measure market breadth.
c. Assess bull market sentiment.
d. Assess bear market sentiment.

5. **Technical Indicators** The Closing Arms (trin) ratio is the ratio of

a. Average trading volume in declining issues to advancing issues.
b. Average trading volume in NYSE issues to NASDAQ issues.
c. The number of advancing issues to the number of declining issues.
d. The number of declining issues to the number of advancing issues.

6. **Technical Indicators** Resistance and support areas for a stock market index are viewed as technical indicators of

a. Economic barriers
b. Psychological barriers
c. Circuit breakers
d. Holding patterns

7. **Technical Analysis** Which of the following are used by technical analysts?
   I. Historical prices
  II. Financial statements
 III. Historical volume
  IV. Investor sentiment

a. I and II only
b. I and III only
c. I, III, and IV only
d. I, II, III, and IV

8. **Technical Analysis** Which of the following technical measures has the effect of smoothing out day-to-day price fluctuations?

a. Moving average charts
b. Advance/decline lines
c. Candlestick charts
d. Point-and-figure charts

9. **Technical Analysis** Which of the following statements would a technical analyst agree with?

a. Financial statements provide invaluable information concerning a company's stock price.
b. The value of a share of stock should always be the present value of future dividends.
c. The stock market is at least weak-form efficient.
d. Stock prices follow patterns which repeat over time.

10. **Technical Analysis** Suppose a stock breaks through a support level. According to technical analysis, you should

a. Buy the stock.
b. Sell the stock.
c. Do nothing since this is a congestion area.
d. Buy the stock on margin.

11. **Advance/Decline Lines** An upward-sloping advance/decline line is considered_____, and a heavy advancing volume is considered _____.

a. bearish; bearish
b. bearish; bullish
c. bullish; bullish
d. bullish; bearish

12. **Behavioural Finance Concepts** Which of the following topics related to behavioural finance deals with the idea that investors experience more pain from a loss than pleasure from a comparable gain?

    a. Frame dependence
    b. Prospect theory
    c. Loss aversion
    d. Mental accounting

13. **Limits to Arbitrage** Which of the following is not a reason that rational, well-capitalized investors can correct a mispricing, at least not immediately?

    a. Firm-specific risk
    b. Implementation costs
    c. Aversion risk
    d. Noise trader risk

14. **Technical Indicators** Which of the following techniques deals with the breadth of the market?

    a. Price channels
    b. Advance/decline lines
    c. Bollinger bands
    d. Support and resistance lines

15. **Technical Indicators** Which of the following techniques does not assume there are psychologically important barriers in stock prices?

    a. Price channels
    b. Advance/decline lines
    c. Bollinger bands
    d. Support and resistance lines

Concept Questions

1. **Dow Theory** In the context of Dow theory, what are the three forces at work at all times? Which is the most important?

2. **Technical Analysis** To a technical analyst, what are support and resistance areas?

3. **Dow Theory** In the context of Dow theory, what are corrections and confirmations?

4. **Bad Breadth?** On a particular day, the stock market as a whole is up; however, losers outnumber gainers by 2,000 to 1,600. What might a technical analyst conclude?

5. **A Call to Arms** How is the Arms ratio computed? What is it designed to capture?

6. **Bad Timing?** A key concern in technical analysis such as the Dow theory is to identify turning points in market direction and thereby time the market. What are the implications of market efficiency for market timing?

7. **Dow Theory** Why do you think the industrial and transportation averages are the two that underlie Dow theory?

8. **Limits to Arbitrage** In the chapter, we discussed the 3Com/Palm and Royal Dutch/Shell mispricings. Which of the limits to arbitrage would least likely be the main reason for these mispricings? Explain.

9. **Contrarian Investing** What does it mean to be a contrarian investor? How would a contrarian investor use technical analysis?

10. **Technical Analysis** A frequent argument against the usefulness of technical analysis is that trading on a pattern has the effect of destroying the pattern. Explain what this means.

www.mcgrawhill.ca/olc/Jordan

11. **Gaps** Gaps are another technical analysis tool used in conjunction with open-high-low-close charts. A gap occurs when either the low price for a particular day is higher than the high price from the previous day, or the high price for a day is lower than the low price from the previous day. Do you think gaps are a bullish or bearish signal? Why?

12. **Probabilities** Suppose you are flipping a fair coin in a coin-flipping contest and have flipped eight heads in a row. What is the probability of flipping a head on your next coin flip? Suppose you flipped a head on your ninth toss. What is the probability of flipping a head on your tenth toss?

13. **Prospect Theory** How do prospect theory and the concept of a rational investor differ?

14. **Frame Dependence** How can frame dependence lead to irrational investment decisions?

15. **Noise Trader Risk** What is noise trader risk? How can noise trader risk lead to market inefficiencies?

16. **Overconfidence** Do you think there are differences in female and male investors' behaviour? Which group exhibit higher overconfidence? Explain.

17. **Hot-Hand Fallacy** Explain hot-hand fallacy.

18. **Behavioural Finance** How do financial managers use behavioural finance in their decision making?

Questions and Problems

Core Questions

1. **Advance/Decline Lines** Use the data below to construct the advance/decline line for the stock market. Volume figures are in thousands of shares.

	Advancing	Adv. Vol.	Declining	Dec. Vol.
Monday	1,893	1,077,176	1,159	542,400
Tuesday	1,833	1,172,094	1,211	733,082
Wednesday	1,705	987,314	1,411	845,305
Thursday	1,821	1,042,316	1,305	750,318
Friday	1,784	1,258,634	1,187	645,847

2. **Calculating Arms Ratio** Using the data in the previous problem, construct the Arms ratio on each of the five trading days.

3. **Simple Moving Averages** The table below shows the closing monthly stock prices for Amazon.com and Walt Disney. Calculate the simple three-month moving average for each month for both companies.

	AMZN	DIS
February	$35.18	$27.94
March	34.27	29.73
April	32.36	26.40
May	35.51	27.44
June	33.09	25.18
July	45.15	25.64
August	42.70	25.19
September	45.30	24.13
October	39.86	24.37
November	47.99	25.05

4. **Exponential Moving Averages** Using the stock prices in the previous problem, calculate the exponential three-month moving average for both stocks where two-thirds of the average weight is placed on the most recent price.

5. **Exponential Moving Averages** Calculate the exponential three-month moving average for Amazon.com and Walt Disney where 50 percent of the average weight is placed on the most recent price. How does this exponential moving average compare to your result from the previous problem?

6. **Market Sentiment Index** A group of investors was polled each week for the last five weeks about whether they were bullish or bearish concerning the market. Construct the market sentiment index for each week based on these polls. Assuming the market sentiment index is being used as a contrarian indicator, which direction would you say the market is headed?

Week	Bulls	Bears
1	72	78
2	70	80
3	79	71
4	68	82
4	63	87

7. **Money Flow** You are given the following information concerning the trades made on a particular stock. Calculate the money flow for the stock based on these trades. Is the money flow a positive or negative signal in this case?

Price	Volume
$84.12	
84.16	5,000
84.15	2,400
84.17	1,800
84.19	3,400
84.23	1,700
84.20	4,600

8. **Moving Averages** Suppose you are given the following information on the S&P 500:

Date	Close
8-Nov-05	1218.59
9-Nov-05	1220.65
10-Nov-05	1230.96
11-Nov-05	1234.72
14-Nov-05	1233.76
15-Nov-05	1229.01
16-Nov-05	1231.21
17-Nov-05	1242.80
18-Nov-05	1248.27
21-Nov-05	1254.85

Calculate the simple three-day moving average for the S&P 500 and the exponential three-day moving average where two-thirds of the weight is placed on the most recent close. Why would you want to know the moving average for an index? If the close on November 22, 2005, was above the three-day moving average, would it be a buy or sell signal?

9. **Support and Resistance Levels.** Below you will see a stock price chart for Encana from co.finance.yahoo.com. Do you see any resistance or support levels? What do support and resistance levels mean for the stock price?

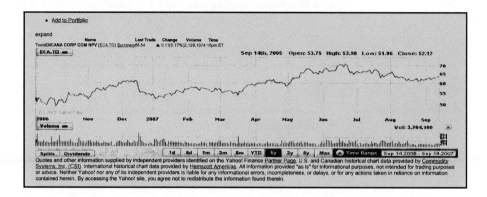

10. **Advance/Decline Lines and Arms Ratio** Use the data below to construct the advance/decline line and Arms ratio for the market. Volume is in thousands of shares.

	Advancing	Advancing Vol.	Declining	Declining Vol.
Monday	1,132	987,064	2,205	1,203,543
Tuesday	1,287	843,456	2,103	1,356,406
Wednesday	1,451	864,056	1,978	1,135,056
Thursday	1,682	1,013,168	1,796	980,673
Friday	1,508	990,731	1,834	1,206,650

11. **Money Flow** A stock had the following trades during a particular period. What was the money flow for the stock? Is the money flow a positive or negative signal in this case?

Price	Volume
$43.87	
43.89	1,600
43.88	1,200
43.90	600
43.90	1,400
43.88	1,100
43.86	800
43.84	1,300
43.83	1,400
43.82	1,000

Intermediate Questions

12. **Fibonacci Numbers** A stock recently increased in price from $78 to $95. Using ϕ, what are the primary and secondary support areas for the stock?

13. **Simple Moving Averages** Below you will find the closing stock prices for eBay over a three-week period. Calculate the simple three-day and five-day moving averages for the stock and graph your results. Are there any technical indications of the future direction of the stock price?

Date	Close
31-Oct-05	$39.61
1-Nov-05	40.27
2-Nov-05	41.08
3-Nov-05	41.55
4-Nov-05	41.58
7-Nov-05	41.87
8-Nov-05	42.30
9-Nov-05	42.08
10-Nov-05	43.31
11-Nov-05	43.89
14-Nov-05	43.53
15-Nov-05	43.05
16-Nov-05	42.54
17-Nov-05	43.80
18-Nov-05	44.67

14. **Exponential Moving Averages** Use the information from the previous problem to calculate the three-day and five-day exponential moving averages for eBay and graph your results. Place two-thirds of the average weight on the most recent stock price. Are there any technical indications of the future direction of the stock price?

15. **Put/Call Ratio.** Another technical indicator is the put/call ratio. The put/call ratio is the number of put options traded divided by the number of call options traded. The put/call ratio can be constructed on the market or an individual stock. Below you will find the number of puts and calls traded over a four-week period for all stocks:

Week	Puts	Calls
1	467,152	645,132
2	508,612	497,163
3	498,344	532,628
4	520,197	625,981

How would you interpret the put/call ratio? Calculate the put/call ratio for each week. From this analysis, does it appear the market is expected to be upward trending or downward trending?

What's on the Web?

1. **Bollinger Bands** You can learn more about Bollinger bands at www.chartsmart.com. What does the site say about using Bollinger bands in technical analysis? Now go to finance.yahoo.com, and enter your favourite stock. Find the technical analysis section and view the Bollinger band for your stock. What does the chart tell you about this stock?

2. **Relative Strength** Relative strength measures the performance of a stock against a "bogey," which is either another stock or suitable index. Pick your favourite stock and go to the technical analysis area of finance.yahoo.com. Compare the relative strength of your stock against a close competitor and the TSX / S&P Composite Index. How is this stock performing relative to these bogeys?

3. **Triangles** Go to www.borsanaliz.com/eng. How many different types of triangles are listed on the site? What does each type of triangle mean to a technical analyst?

4. **Market Volume** An important tool for most technical traders is market volume. Go to www.marketvolume.com. Look on the site to find the reasons market volume is considered important.

PART 3

Interest Rates and
Bond Valuation

CHAPTER 10

Interest Rates

"Remember that time is money."

—Benjamin Franklin

Benjamin Franklin stated a fundamental truth of commerce when he sagely advised young tradesmen that time is money. In finance, we call this the time value of money. But how much time corresponds to how much money? Interest constitutes a rental payment for money, and an interest rate tells us how much money for how much time. But there are many interest rates, each corresponding to a particular money market. Interest rates state money prices in each of these markets. ■

This chapter is the first dealing specifically with interest-bearing assets. As we discussed before, there are two basic types of interest-bearing assets, money market instruments and fixed-income securities. For both types of assets, interest rates are a key determinant of asset values. Furthermore, since there are trillions of dollars in interest-bearing assets outstanding, interest rates play a pivotal role in financial markets and the economy.

Because interest rates are one of the most closely watched financial market indicators, we devote this entire chapter to them. We first discuss the many different interest rates that are commonly reported in the financial press, along with some of the different ways interest rates are calculated and quoted. We then go on to describe the basic determinants and separable components of interest rates.

10.1 Interest Rate History and Money Market Rates

Recall from Chapter 4 that money market instruments are debt obligations that have a maturity of less than one year at the time they are originally issued. Each business day, newspapers publish a list of current interest rates for several categories of money market securities in their Money Rates reports. We will discuss each of these interest rates and the securities they represent immediately below. First, however, we take a quick look at the history of interest rates.

Interest Rate History

In Chapter 1, we saw how looking back at the history of returns on various types of investments gave us a useful perspective on rates of return. Similar insights are available from interest rate history. For example, in 2007, short-term interest rates were about 4.54 percent. We might ask, "Are these rates unusually high or low?" To find out, we examine Figure 10.1, which graphically illustrates historical interest rates in Canada.

Interest rate of returns are plotted in Figure 10.1 for two instruments, one for bills and one for bonds. Both rates are based on government securities, or close substitutes. We discuss bills and bonds in detail in this chapter and the next chapter. For now, it is enough to know that bills are short term and bonds are long term, so what are plotted in Figure 10.1 are short- and long-term interest rate of returns.

FIGURE 10.1   **Interest Rate History (Canadian Rate of Returns on T-Bills and Bonds)**

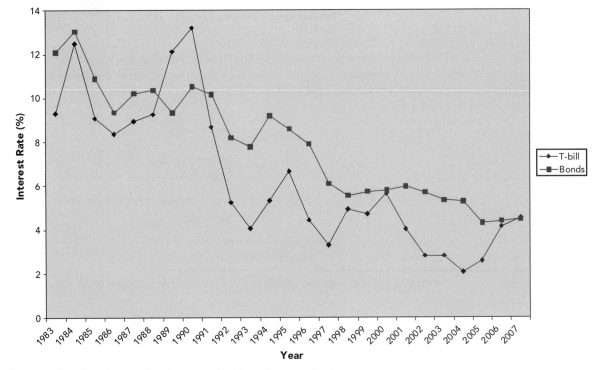

Source: Author calculations based on the data obtained from Datastream Database.

A QUICK REVIEW OF THE TIME VALUE OF MONEY

EXAMPLE 10.1

Undoubtedly, your instincts tell you that $1,000 received in three years is not the same as $1,000 received today. But if you are going to receive $1,000 today, what is an equivalent amount of money received in three years?

Fortunately, an equation tells us exactly what this is:

$$\text{Future value} = \text{Present value} \times (1 + r)^N \tag{10.1}$$

In this equation, the r represents a periodic interest rate (expressed as a decimal), and the N represents the number of periods (expressed as an integer). Although the periods could be weeks, months, or years, the important thing to remember is that the interest rate must be expressed as an interest rate *per period*.

Suppose you have $1,000 to invest and you can invest at an annual rate of 3.5 percent per year. In Equation 10.1 the per period interest rate enters as 0.035. If you invest for three years ($N = 3$), the amount you will have in three years is:

$$\$1,108.718 = \$1,000 \times (1 + 0.035)^3 \tag{10.2}$$

which would be rounded to $1,108.72.

You can also use Equation 10.1 to tell you how much a future amount is worth today. If we divide both sides of Equation 10.1 by $(1 + r)^N$ and rearrange terms, we get:

$$\text{Present value} = \frac{\text{Future value}}{(1 + r)^N} \tag{10.3}$$

which, by the rules of exponents, can be written as:

$$\text{Present value} = \text{Future value} \times (1 + r)^{-N} \tag{10.4}$$

That is, $(1 + r)^{-N}$ is just another way to write $1 / (1 + r)^N$.

If you remember the relationship between Equations 10.1 and 10.4, you will soon become very comfortable with *compounding*, which is Equation 10.1, and *discounting*, which is Equation 10.4.

To continue with our numerical example, first note that $(1 + 0.035)^3 = 1.108718$. Therefore, using Equation 10.3,

$$\text{Present value} = \frac{\text{Future value}}{(1 + r)^N}$$

$$\$1,000 = \frac{\$1,081.718}{1.081718}$$

Suppose you invest $500 for 4 percent for six years. How much money will you have at the end of six years?

$$\text{Future value} = \text{Present value} \times (1 + r)^N$$

$$\$632.66 = \$500 \times (1.04)^6$$

Now suppose you will be getting $800 in four years. What is an equivalent amount today if you discount at 3.7 percent?

$$\text{Present value} = \text{Future value} \times (1 + r)^{-N}$$

$$\$691.79 = \$800 \times (1 + 0.037)^{-4}$$

Probably the most striking feature in Figure 10.1 is the fact that the highest interest rates occurred in the not-too-distant past. Rates began rising sharply in the 1970s, and then peaked at extraordinary levels in the early 1980s. They have generally declined since then. The other striking aspect is the very low short-term interest rates that prevailed from the 1930s to the 1960s. This was the result, in large part, of deliberate actions by the US Fed and Bank of Canada to keep short-term rates low—a policy that ultimately proved unsustainable and even disastrous. Much was learned by the experience, however, and now the central bank is more concerned with controlling inflation.

With long-term rates around 4.5 percent as this chapter was written, many market observers have commented that these interest rate levels are extraordinarily low.

Money Market Rates

Figure 10.2 reproduces a Bank of Canada "Money Rates" report of interest rates for the most important money market instruments. A commonly quoted interest rate is the **prime rate**. The prime rate is a key short-term interest rate since it is the basis for interest rates that large commercial banks charge on short-term loans (rates are quoted as prime plus or minus a spread). The prime rate is well known as a **bellwether rate** of bank lending to business.

The Bank of Canada's bank rate is a pivotal interest rate for commercial banks. The discount rate is the interest rate that the bank offers to commercial banks for overnight reserve loans. You might recall from your Money and Banking class that banks are required to maintain reserves equal to some fraction of their deposit liabilities. When a bank cannot supply sufficient reserves from internal sources, it must borrow reserves from other banks through the Bank of Canada.

The Bank of Canada is the central bank of Canada. It is charged with the responsibility of managing interest rates and the money supply to control inflation and promote stable economic growth. The **bank rate** is a basic tool of monetary policy for the Bank of Canada. An announced change in the discount rate is often interpreted as a signal of the Bank of Canada's intentions regarding future monetary policy. For example, by increasing the discount rate, the bank may be signalling that it intends to pursue a tight-money policy, most likely to control budding inflationary pressures. Similarly, by decreasing the discount rate, the bank may be signalling an intent to pursue a

prime rate The basic interest rate on short-term loans that the largest commercial banks charge to their most creditworthy corporate customers.

bellwether rate Interest rate that serves as a leader or as a leading indicator of future trends, e.g., interest rates as a bellwether of inflation.

bank rate The interest rate that the Bank of Canada offers to commercial banks for-overnight reserve-loans.

For the latest on money market rates visit www.bankofcanada.ca

---

FIGURE 10.2	**Money Market Interest Rates**

EXCHANGE RATES [+ MORE]	21/12/07	24/12/07	+/−	INFLATION [+ MORE]	10/07	11/07	+/−
$Can/US closing rate	0.9927	0.9850	−0.0077	Inflation-control target range	1–3	1–3	–
$Can/US noon rate	0.9944	0.9871	−0.0073				
$US/Canada noon rate	1.0056	1.0131	+0.0075	Total consumer price index**	2.4%	2.5%	+0.1
CERI*	120.78	121.66	+0.88	Core consumer price index**	1.8%	1.6%	−0.2
MONEY MARKET [+ MORE]	20/12/07	21/12/07	+/−	INTEREST RATES [+ MORE]	12/12/07	19/12/07	+/−
Overnight rate	4.2530%	4.2607%	+0.0077	Prime business rate	6.00%	6.00%	0.00
Target for the overnight rate	4.25%	4.25%	0.00	Conventional mortgage, 5 year	7.39%	7.39%	0.00
Overnight repo rate (CORRA)	4.2446%	4.2670%	+0.0224	BOND YIELDS [+ MORE]	20/12/07	21/12/07	+/−
Corporate paper, 1 month	4.61%	4.61%	0.00	GoC marketable bonds, +10 yr	4.10%	4.17%	+0.07
Treasury bill, 1 month	3.70%	3.71%	+0.01				
Bankers' Acceptances, 1 month	4.58%	4.58%	0.00	GoC benchmark bonds, 3 yr	3.85%	3.92%	+0.07

Source: Bank of Canada, http://www.bankofcanada.ca

loose-money policy to stimulate economic activity. Of course, many times a bank rate change is simply a case of the Bank of Canada catching up to financial market conditions rather than leading them. Indeed, the Bank of Canada often acts like the lead goose, who, upon looking back and seeing the flock heading in another direction, quickly flies over to resume its position as "leader" of the flock. The Bank Rate is closely related to the target for the Overnight Rate.

call money rate The interest rate broker-age firms pay for call money loans, which are bank loans to brokerage firms. This rate is used as the basis for customer rates on margin loans.

The **call money rate**, or simply the call rate, refers to loans from banks to security brokerage firms, and the call rate is the interest rate that brokerage firms pay on call money loans. As we discussed in Chapter 3, brokers use funds raised through call money loans to make margin loans to customers to finance leveraged stock and bond purchases. The call money rate is the basic rate that brokers use to set interest rates on customer call money loans. Brokers typically charge their customers the call money rate plus a premium, where the broker and the customer may negotiate the premium. For example, a broker may charge a customer the basic call money rate plus 1 percent for a margin loan to purchase common stock.

commercial paper Short-term, unsecured debt issued by the largest corporations.

Commercial paper is short-term, unsecured debt issued by the largest corporations. The commercial paper market is dominated by financial corporations, such as banks and insurance companies, or financial subsidiaries of large corporations. Commercial paper is a popular investment vehicle for portfolio managers and corporate treasurers with excess funds on hand that they wish to invest on a short-term basis. "Euro" commercial paper refers to commercial paper denominated in euros rather than dollars.

certificate of deposit (CD) Large-denomination deposits of $100,000 or more at commercial banks for a specified term.

Certificates of deposit, or **CDs**, represent large-denomination deposits of $100,000 or more at commercial banks for a specified term. The interest rate paid on CDs usually varies according to the term of the deposit. For example, a one-year CD may pay a higher interest rate than a six-month CD, which in turn may pay a higher interest rate than a three-month CD.

Large-denomination certificates of deposit are generally negotiable instruments, meaning that they can be bought and sold among investors. Consequently, they are often called negotiable certificates of deposit, or negotiable CDs. Negotiable CDs can be bought and sold through a broker. The large-denomination CDs described here should not be confused with the small-denomination CDs that banks offer retail customers. These small-denomination CDs are simply bank time deposits. They normally pay a lower interest rate than large-denomination CDs and are not negotiable instruments.

In Canada, certificates issued by trust companies used to be called "guaranteed investment certificates (GIC)s." Currently both banks and trust companies issue guaranteed investment certificates. In fact, all short-term certificates are called guaranteed investment certificates in Canada. Over the recent years GICs became very popular short-term liquid investment instruments.

banker's acceptance A postdated cheque on which a bank has guaranteed payment; commonly used to finance international trade transactions.

A **banker's acceptance** is essentially a postdated cheque upon which a commercial bank has guaranteed payment. Banker's acceptances are normally used to finance international trade transactions. For example, as an importer, you wish to purchase computer components from a company in Singapore and pay for the goods three months after delivery, so you write a postdated cheque. You and the exporter agree, however, that once the goods are shipped, your bank will guarantee payment on the date specified on the cheque.

After your goods are shipped, the exporter presents the relevant documentation, and, if all is in order, your bank stamps the word *ACCEPTED* on your cheque. At this point your bank has created an acceptance, which means it has promised to pay the acceptance's face value (the amount of the cheque) at maturity (the date on the cheque). The exporter can then hold on to the acceptance or sell it in the money market. The banker's acceptance rate published in "Money Rates" is the interest rate for acceptances issued by the largest commercial banks.

Banker's acceptances (BAs) are short-term, marketable securities and they are guaranteed by both the borrower and the bank. In Canada BAs are issued in bearer forms and sold at discount prices.

Eurodollars are certificates of deposit denominated in US dollars at commercial banks outside the USA. Eurodollar rates are interest rates paid for large-denomination deposits. Eurodollar CDs are negotiable and are traded in a large, very active Eurodollar money market. The "Money Rates" report lists Eurodollar rates for various maturities obtained from transactions occurring late in the day.

Eurodollars
Certificates of deposit denominated in US dollars at commercial banks outside the USA.

The **London Interbank Offered Rate (LIBOR)** is the interest rate offered by London commercial banks for dollar deposits from other banks. The LIBOR rate is perhaps the most frequently cited rate used to represent the London money market. Bank lending rates are often stated as LIBOR plus a premium, where the premium is negotiated between the bank and its customer. For example, a corporation may be quoted a loan rate from a London bank at LIBOR plus 2 percent. Euro LIBOR refers to deposits denominated in euros rather than eurodollars. Euribor is the rate in "euroland" rather than London.

London Interbank Offered Rate (LIBOR)
Interest rate that international banks charge one another for overnight Eurodollar loans.

Treasury bills, or just **T-bills**, represent short-term government debt issues. The Treasury bill market is the largest market for short-term debt securities in the world. As such, the Treasury bill market leads all other credit markets in determining the general level of short-term interest rates. "Money Rates" reports Treasury bill interest rates set during the most recent bi-weekly Treasury bill auction. Interest rates determined at each Treasury bill auction are closely watched by professional money managers throughout the world. The overnight repurchase, or "repo," rate is essentially the rate charged on overnight loans that are collateralized by government securities.

Treasury bill (T-bill)
A short-term government debt instrument.

For more on LIBOR, visit
www.bba.org.uk

CHECK THIS ✔

10.1a Which money market interest rates are most important to commercial banks?

10.1b Which money market interest rates are most important to nonbank corporations?

10.2 Money Market Prices and Rates

pure discount security
An interest-bearing asset that makes a single payment of face value at maturity with no payments before maturity.

Money market securities typically make a single payment of face value at maturity and make no payments before maturity. Such securities are called **pure discount securities** because they sell at a discount relative to their face value. In this section, we discuss the relationship between the price of a money market instrument and the interest rate quoted on it.

One of the things you will notice in this section is that there are several different ways market participants quote interest rates. This presents a problem when we wish to compare rates on different investments. But before we can do this, we must put them on a common footing.

After going through the various interest rate conventions and conversions needed to compare them, you might wonder why everybody doesn't just agree to compute interest rates and prices in some uniform way. Well perhaps they should, but they definitely do not. As a result, we must review some of the various procedures actually used in money markets. We hope you come to recognize that the calculations are neither mysterious nor even especially difficult, although they are rooted in centuries-old procedures and may sometimes be tedious. However, given the billions of dollars of securities traded every day based on these numbers, it is important to understand them.

One other thing to notice is that the word "yield" appears frequently. For now, you can take it as given that the yield on an interest-bearing asset is simply a measure of the interest rate being offered by the asset. We will discuss the topic of yields in greater detail in the next chapter.

basis point With regard to interest rates or bond yields, one basis point is 1 percent of 1 percent.

Bond yields and many interest rates are quoted as a percentage with two decimal places, such as 11.82 percent. With this quote, the smallest possible change would be .01 percent, or .0001. This amount, which is 1 percent of 1 percent, is called a **basis point**. So, if our 11.82 percent rose to 11.94 percent, we would say rates rose by $94 - 82 = 12$ basis points. The quantity to the left of the decimal point (the "11") is called the "handle." Traders frequently omit the handle when quoting or discussing rates since, presumably, anyone actively trading would know it.

Bank Discount Rate Quotes

bank discount basis A method for quoting interest rates on money market instruments.

Interest rates for some key money market securities, including Treasury bills and banker's acceptances, are quoted on a **bank discount basis**, or simply discount basis. An interest rate quoted on a discount basis is often called a discount yield. If we are given an interest rate quoted on a bank discount basis for a particular money market instrument, then we calculate the price of that instrument as follows:

$$\text{Current price} = \text{Face value} \times \left(1 - \frac{\text{Days to maturity}}{360} \times \text{Discount yield}\right) \quad (10.5)$$

The term "discount yield" here simply refers to the quoted interest rate.

To give an example, suppose a banker's acceptance has a face value of $1 million that will be paid in 90 days. If the interest rate, quoted on a discount basis, is 5 percent, what is the current price of the acceptance?

As the following calculation shows, a discount yield of 5 percent and maturity of 90 days gives a current price of $987,500.

$$\$987{,}500 = \$1{,}000{,}000 \times \left(1 - \frac{90}{360} \times .05\right)$$

The difference between the face value of $1 million and the price of $987,500 is $12,500 and is called the "discount." This discount is the interest earned over the 90-day period until the acceptance matures.

Notice that the formula used to calculate the acceptance price assumes a 360-day business year. This practice dates back to a time when calculations were performed manually. Assuming a 360-day business year, with exactly four 90-day quarters rather than a true 365-day calendar year, made manual discount calculations simpler and less subject to error. Consequently, if $1 million is discounted over a full calendar year of 365 days using a bank discount yield of 5 percent and an assumed 360-day business year, the resulting price of $949,305.56 is calculated as follows:

$$\$949,305.56 \times \$1,000,000 \times \left(1 - \frac{365}{360} \times .05\right)$$

MONEY MARKET PRICES

EXAMPLE 10.2

The rate on a particular money market instrument, quoted on a discount basis, is 6 percent. The instrument has a face value of $100,000 and will mature in 71 days. What is its price? What if it had 51 days to maturity?

Using the bank discount basis formula, we have

$$\textbf{Current price} = \textbf{Face value} \times \left(1 - \frac{\textbf{Days to maturity}}{\textbf{360}} \times \textbf{Discount yield}\right)$$

$$\$98,816.67 = \$100,000 \times \left(1 - \frac{71}{360} \times .06\right)$$

Check for yourself that the price in the second case of a 51-day maturity is $99,150.

bond equivalent yield
A method for quoting Canadian treasury bills.

Canadian T-bills rates are quoted using **bond equivalent yield** instead of bank discount yield. As we will explain in later sections, bond equivalent yield uses 365 days instead of 360 days and the bond price instead of $1,000 par value. Bond equivalent yield is given by the following formula:

$$\text{Bond Equivalent Yield} = \frac{(\$1000 - \text{Price})}{\text{Price}} \times \frac{365}{\text{Days till Maturity}} \quad (10.6)$$

We will give the conversion formula between bank discount yield and bond equivalent yield in the next section.

Treasury Bill Quotes

The Wall Street Journal reports current interest rates on US Treasury bills each business day. Figure 10.3 reproduces a "Treasury Bills" interest rate report. The maturity of each bill issue is stated in month-day-year format, followed by the number of days remaining until the bill matures. The two columns following the days to maturity give the bid and asked discounts for each bill issue. The bid discount is used by Treasury bill dealers to state what they are willing to pay for a Treasury bill, and the asked discount is used to state what price a dealer will accept to sell a Treasury bill. The next column shows the change in the asked discount from the previous day.

For example, consider the bill issue with 155 days to maturity, with a bid discount rate of 3.52 percent and an asked discount rate of 3.51 percent. For a $1 million face value Treasury bill, the corresponding bid and asked prices can be calculated by using the discounts shown along with our bank discount basis pricing formula. For example, the bid price would be:

For price and yield data on Canadian Treasury securities visit
www.bankofcanada.ca/en/tbill-look.html
www.fin.gc.ca

$$\text{Bid price} = \$984,844.44 = \$1,000,000 \times \left(1 - \frac{155}{360} \times .0352\right)$$

Check that the ask price would be $984,887.50.

FIGURE 10.3

U.S. Treasury Bills

Source: *The Wall Street Journal*, September 7, 2005. Reprinted by permission of Dow Jones, Inc. via Copyright Clearance Center, Inc., © 2005 Dow Jones and Company, Inc. All Rights Reserved Worldwide.

Treasury Bills

MATURITY	DAYS TO MAT	BID	ASKED	CHG	ASK YLD
Sep 08 05	1	3.26	3.25	0.01	3.30
Sep 15 05	8	3.45	3.44	-0.01	3.49
Sep 22 05	15	3.32	3.31	...	3.36
Sep 29 05	22	3.32	3.31	...	3.36
Oct 06 05	29	3.29	3.28	0.02	3.33
Oct 13 05	36	3.26	3.25	-0.01	3.31
Oct 20 05	43	3.27	3.26	...	3.32
Oct 27 05	50	3.27	3.26	0.01	3.32
Nov 03 05	57	3.33	3.32	0.02	3.38
Nov 10 05	64	3.34	3.33	0.02	3.40
Nov 17 05	71	3.36	3.35	0.02	3.42
Nov 25 05	79	3.40	3.39	0.04	3.46
Dec 01 05	85	3.42	3.41	0.04	3.49
Dec 08 05	92	3.43	3.42	0.02	3.50
Dec 15 05	99	3.39	3.38	-0.02	3.46
Dec 22 05	106	3.42	3.41	0.03	3.49
Dec 29 05	113	3.45	3.44	0.03	3.53
Jan 05 06	120	3.48	3.47	0.04	3.56
Jan 12 06	127	3.49	3.48	0.04	3.57
Jan 19 06	134	3.50	3.49	0.04	3.59
Jan 26 06	141	3.51	3.50	0.04	3.60
Feb 02 06	148	3.53	3.52	0.05	3.62
Feb 09 06	155	3.52	3.51	0.04	3.61
Feb 16 06	162	3.54	3.53	0.04	3.64
Feb 23 06	169	3.55	3.54	0.06	3.65
Mar 02 06	176	3.57	3.56	0.06	3.67

T-BILL PRICES

EXAMPLE 10.3

Suppose you wanted to buy a T-bill with 85 days to maturity and a face value of $5,000,000. How much would you have to pay if the asked discount is 3.41 percent?

Because you are buying, you must pay the asked price. To calculate the asked price, we use the asked discount in the bank discount basis formula:

$$\text{Asked price} = \$4,959,743.06 = \$5,000,000 \times \left(1 - \frac{85}{360} \times .0341\right)$$

Calculate a bid price for this T-bill assuming a bid discount of 3.42 percent. Notice that the asked price is higher than the bid price even though the asked discount is lower than the bid discount. The reason is that a bigger discount produces a lower price.

Treasury bill prices may be calculated using a built-in spreadsheet function. An example of how to use an Excel™ spreadsheet to calculate a Treasury bill price is shown in the nearby *Spreadsheet Analysis* box.

The last column in Figure 10.3 lists the asked yield ("ASK YLD") for each Treasury bill issue. It is important to realize that the asked yield is *not* quoted on a discount basis. Instead, it is a "bond equivalent yield." Unlike a discount rate, a bond equivalent yield assumes a 365-day calendar year. Bond equivalent yields are principally used to

SPREADSHEET ANALYSIS

	A	B	C	D	E	F	G	H
1								
2			Treasury Bill Price and Yield Calculations					
3								
4	A Treasury bill traded on March 14, 2006, pays $100 on June 1, 2006. Assuming a							
5	discount rate of 6 percent, what are its price and bond equivalent yield?							
6	Hint: Use the Excel function TBILLPRICE and TBILLEQ.							
7								
8		$98.6833	= TBILLPRICE("3/14/2006","6/1/2006",0.06)					
9								
10		6.164%	= TBILLEQ("3/14/2006","6/1/2006",0.06)					
11								
12								
13	A credit card charges a nominal annual interest rate of 15 percent. With interest							
14	charged monthly, what is the effective annual rate (EAR) on this credit card?							
15	Hint: Use the Excel function EFFECT.							
16								
17		16.075%	= EFFECT(0.15,12)					
18								

compare yields on Treasury bills with yields on other money market instruments as well as government bonds and other bonds (we discuss these long-term yields in the next chapter).

Bank Discount Yields versus Bond Equivalent Yields

A bank discount yield is converted to a bond equivalent yield using the following formula:

$$\text{Bond equivalent yield} = \frac{365 \times \text{Discount yield}}{360 - \text{Days to maturity} \times \text{Discount yield}} \quad (10.7)$$

This conversion formula is correct for maturities of six months or less. Calculation of bond equivalent yields for maturities greater than six months is a little more complicated, and we will not discuss it here, particularly since T-bills with maturities greater than six months are no longer sold.

For example, suppose the asked discount rate on a T-bill with 170 days to maturity is 3.22 percent. What is the bond equivalent yield? Plugging into the conversion formula, a 3.22 percent discount is converted into a bond equivalent yield as follows:

$$3.315\% = \frac{365 \times .0322}{360 - 170 \times .0322}$$

The bond equivalent yield is thus 3.315 percent.

BOND EQUIVALENT YIELDS

EXAMPLE 10.4

Suppose a T-bill has 45 days to maturity and an asked discount of 5 percent. What is the bond equivalent yield?

Using the bond equivalent yield conversion formulas, we have

$$5.101\% = \frac{365 \times .05}{360 - 45 \times .05}$$

The bond equivalent yield is thus 5.101 percent.

Bond equivalent yields may be calculated using a built-in spreadsheet function. An example of how to use an Excel™ spreadsheet to calculate a bond equivalent yield is shown in the nearby *Spreadsheet Analysis* box.

One common cause of confusion about bond equivalent yield calculations is the way that leap years are handled. The rule is that we must use 366 days if February 29 occurs within the next 12 months. For example, 2012 will be a leap year. So, beginning on March 1, 2011, we must use 366 days in Equation 10.6. Then beginning on March 1, 2012, we must revert back to using 365 days.

BACK TO THE FUTURE: LEAP YEAR BOND EQUIVALENT YIELDS

EXAMPLE 10.5

Calculate the asked yield (bond equivalent yield) for a T-bill price quoted in December 2011 with 119 days to maturity and an asked discount of 5.41 percent.

Since the 12-month period following the date of the price quote includes February 29, we must use 366 days. Plugging this into the conversion formula, we get:

$$5.60\% = \frac{366 \times .0541}{360 - 119 \times .0541}$$

This 5.60 percent is the ask yield stated as a bond equivalent yield.

We can calculate a Treasury bill asked price using the asked yield, which is a bond equivalent yield, as follows:

$$\text{Bill price} = \frac{\text{Face value}}{1 + \text{Bond equivalent yield} \times \text{Days to maturity} / 365} \tag{10.8}$$

For example, just above we calculated the 3.315 percent bond equivalent yield on a T-bill with 170 days to maturity and a 3.22 percent asked discount rate. If we calculate its price using this bond equivalent yield, we get

$$\$984,795 = \frac{\$1,000,000}{1 + .03315 \times 170 / 365}$$

Check that, ignoring a small rounding error, you get the same price using the bank discount formula.

Bond Equivalent Yields, APRs, and EARs

Money market rates not quoted on a discount basis are generally quoted on a "simple" interest basis. Simple interest rates are calculated just like the annual percentage rate (APR) on a consumer loan. So, for the most part, money market rates are either bank discount rates or APRs. For example, CD rates are APRs.

In fact, the bond equivalent yield on a T-bill with less than six months to maturity is also an APR. As a result, like any APR, it understates the true interest rate, which is usually called the *effective annual rate*, or EAR. In the context of the money market, EARs are sometimes referred to as effective annual yields, effective yields, or annualized yields. Whatever it is called, to find out what a T-bill, or any other money market instrument, is *really* going to pay you, yet another conversion is needed. We will get to the needed conversion in a moment.

First, however, recall that an APR is equal to the interest rate per period multiplied by the number of periods in a year. For example, if the rate on a car loan is 1 percent per month, then the APR is $1\% \times 12 = 12\%$. In general, if we let m be the number of periods in a year, an APR is converted to an EAR as follows:

$$1 + EAR = \left(1 + \frac{APR}{m}\right)^m \tag{10.9}$$

For example, on our 12 percent APR car loan, the EAR can be determined by

$$1 + EAR = \left(1 + \frac{.12}{12}\right)^{12}$$
$$= 1.01^{12}$$
$$= 1.126825$$
$$EAR = 12.6825\%$$

Thus, the rate on the car loan is really 12.6825 percent per year.

APRS AND EARS

EXAMPLE 10.6

A typical credit card may quote an APR of 18 percent. On closer inspection, you will find that the rate is actually 1.5 percent per month. What annual interest rate are you really paying on such a credit card?

With 12 periods in a year, an APR of 18 percent is converted to an EAR as follows:

$$1 + EAR = \left(1 + \frac{.18}{12}\right)^{12}$$
$$= 1.015^{12}$$
$$= 1.1956$$
$$EAR = 19.56\%$$

Thus, the rate on this credit card is really 19.56 percent per year.

Effective annual rates may be calculated using a built-in spreadsheet function. An example of how to use an Excel™ spreadsheet to calculate an effective annual rate is shown in a previous *Spreadsheet Analysis* box.

Now, to see that the bond equivalent yield on a T-bill is just an APR, we can first calculate the price on the bill we considered earlier (3.22 percent asked discount, 170 days to maturity). Using the bank discount formula, the asked price, for $1 million in face value, is

$$\text{Asked price} = \$984{,}794 = 1{,}000{,}000 \times \left(1 - \frac{170}{360} \times .0322\right)$$

The discount is $15,206. Thus, on this 170-day investment, you earn $15,206 in interest on an investment of $984,794. On a percentage basis, you earned

$$1.544\% = \frac{\$15{,}206}{\$984{,}794}$$

In a 365-day year, there are 365 / 170 = 2.147 periods of 170-day length. So if we multiply what you earned over the 170-day period by the number of 170-day periods in a year, we get

$$3.315\% = 2.147 \times 1.544\%$$

This is precisely the bond equivalent yield we calculated earlier.

Finally, for this T-bill we can calculate the EAR using this 3.315 percent:

$$1 + EAR = \left(1 + \frac{.03315}{2.147}\right)^{2.147}$$
$$= 1.03344$$
$$EAR = 3.344\%$$

In the end, we have three different rates for this simple T-bill. The last one, the EAR, finally tells us what we really want to know: What are we actually going to earn?

DISCOUNTS, APRS, AND EARS

EXAMPLE 10.7

A money market instrument with 60 days to maturity has a quoted ask price of 99, meaning $99 per $100 face value. What are the banker's discount yield, the bond equivalent yield, and the effective annual return?

First, to get the discount yield, we have to use the bank discount formula and solve for the discount yield:

$$\$99 = \$100 \times \left(1 - \frac{60}{360} \times \text{Discount yield}\right)$$

With a little algebra, we see that the discount yield is 6 percent.

We convert this to a bond equivalent yield as follows:

$$6.145\% = \frac{365 \times .06}{360 - 60 \times .06}$$

The bond equivalent yield is thus 6.145 percent.

(continued)

Finally, to get the EAR, note that there are 6.0833 sixty-day periods in a year, so

$$1 + EAR = \left(1 + \frac{.06145}{6.0833}\right)^{6.0833}$$
$$= 1.06305$$
$$EAR = 6.305\%$$

This example illustrates the general result that the discount rate is lower than the bond equivalent yield, which in turn is less than the EAR.

CHECK THIS

10.2a What are the three different types of interest rate quotes that are important for money market instruments?

10.2b How are T-bill rates quoted? How are CD rates quoted?

10.2c Of the three different types of interest rate quotes, which is the largest? Which is the smallest? Which is the most relevant?

10.3 Rates and Yields on Fixed-Income Securities

Thus far we have focused on short-term interest rates, where "short-term" means one year or less. Of course, these are not the only interest rates we are interested in, so we now begin to discuss longer-term rates by looking at fixed-income securities. To keep this discussion to a manageable length, we defer the details of how some longer-term rates are computed to Chapter 11.

Fixed-income securities include long-term debt contracts from a wide variety of issuers. The largest single category of fixed-income securities is debt issued by the Canadian government. The second largest category of fixed-income securities is mortgage debt issued to finance real estate purchases. The two other large categories of fixed-income securities are debt issued by corporations and debt issued by municipal and provincial governments. Each of these categories represents several trillion dollars of outstanding debt.

Because of its sheer size, the government bond market attracts more investors than the stock market. In the nearby *Investment Updates* box, you will read an article on government bond markets. Interest rates for government bonds are closely watched and daily reports can be found in most major newspapers.

The Yield Curve

Canadian yield curve
A graph of Canadian government bond yields against maturities.

A **Canadian yield curve** plots yields of Canadian government bonds against maturities. Yields are measured along the vertical axis, and maturities are measured along the horizontal axis. The next *Investment Updates* box shows an example of a Canadian yield curve as well as a market overview reported by Fidelity Investments.

WORK THE WEB

What does the current Treasury yield curve look like? You can find the answer on the Web many different places. We went to www.bloomberg.com, and here is what we found after the market close on September 9, 2005:

As you can see, Bloomberg shows you the yield curve for today and yesterday. For this day, the yield curve shifted upward, as can be seen from the increase in the yield (or decrease in price) for each maturity. This yield curve would be considered a normal, upward-sloping yield curve. The short-term rates are about 3.6 percent, and the six-month rate is about 4.0 percent. Here's a question for you: This yield curve is from September 9, 2005. The 2-, 5- and 10-year maturity notes are dated 2, 5, and 10 years from this date. However the 30-year maturity is actually only 26 years. Why would the 26-year maturity Treasury bond be used for the 30-year interest rate?

U.S. TREASURIES

Bills

	COUPON	MATURITY DATE	CURRENT PRICE/YIELD	PRICE/YIELD CHANGE	TIME
3-Month	N.A.	12/08/2005	3.40/3.48	0.02/.020	09/09
6-Month	N.A.	03/09/2006	3.60/3.72	0.03/.004	09/09

Notes/Bonds

	COUPON	MATURITY DATE	CURRENT PRICE/YIELD	PRICE/YIELD CHANGE	TIME
2-Year	4.000	08/31/2007	100-07/3.87	0-00/-.001	09/09
3-Year	4.125	08/15/2008	100-20/3.88	0-00/-.004	09/09
5-Year	3.875	09/15/2010	99-24/3.93	0-02/-.019	09/09
10-Year	4.250	08/15/2015	101-01/4.12	0-06/-.025	09/09
30-Year	5.375	02/15/2031	114-27/4.40	0-18/-.034	09/09

© Bloomberg L.P.

Too Much Doom and Gloom? Seek Safety in Bonds

This was a good week for the doom and gloom crowd, the ones who maintain an unshakeable confidence that the U.S. economy is heading to hell in a hand basket, that stocks and bonds are doomed to suffer a great fall and that the slumping U.S. dollar is not even close to its bottom.

Fed chief Ben Bernanke confirmed their darkest thoughts by unexpectedly slashing interest rates half a percentage point. Others praised what they saw as Mr. Bernanke's decisive response to a deteriorating credit situation.

But the pessimists regarded it as an inflation-stoking move that only proved things must be a lot worse than the unwary public had been led to believe by various Wall Street soothsayers and senior government officials, including the guy in charge at the Fed.

Gold climbed to its highest level since 1980, the greenback fell sharply against major and exceedingly minor currencies and 30-year U.S. government bonds plunged. Some investment-grade U.S. corporate debt was priced as a greater risk than the stuff issued by the likes of Colombia.

But while the naysayers batten down the hatches to wait out the deluge, along comes someone like Robert Kessler to pour cold water on their cherished views about inflation (it's not a concern), commodities (the wrong place to be when consumption is falling) and the future of the U.S. dollar (not as grim as people think, because there aren't a lot of other options, and as the price of U.S. assets falls, foreign money will be plowed into them).

Mr. Kessler, whose Kessler Investment Advisors Inc. of Denver devises and runs. Treasury portfolios for major corporations and financial institutions, is no Pollyanna when it comes to current economic and market conditions.

He, too, is firmly convinced that the United States is headed toward a recession and that it will suck the wind out of the rest of the global economy, unless the Fed takes even more drastic action now—including slashing interest rates to 1 percent. And don't get him started on Wall Street firms or the people they employ to keep tabs on the economy. "Why would anyone listen to these idiots?"

But he had not begun loading up his Colorado home with survival gear just yet.

"People keep asking where the fed funds rate will go," Mr. Kessler said. "If the goal is to stimulate the American consumer or the housing market, we shouldn't be surprised if it ends up at 1 percent."

Which is where it stood back in 2003 and remained for a year.

"I would argue that if they went to 1 percent, it would not trigger inflation unless someone is stupid enough to loan money at a rate that doesn't make credit sense."

Indeed, as Mr. Kessler eagerly pointed out, if inflation was going to be a problem, it would have happened when the credit cycle was at its peak, not when businesses have stopped investing and consumers are tapped out.

(continued)

Check out the "living yield curve" at www.smartmoney.com/bonds

The yield curve is fundamental to bond market analysis because it represents the interest rates that financial markets are charging to the Canadian government, the debtor with the highest credit ranking. In essence, the curve represents interest rates for default-free lending across the maturity spectrum. As such, almost all other domestic interest rates are determined with respect to Canadian government interest rates. Our nearby *Work the Web* box shows how to get yield curves online.

CHECK THIS ✓ **10.3a** What is the yield curve? Why is it important?

Central Bank Rates

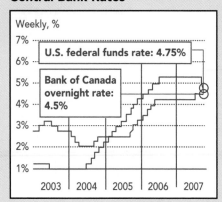

Weekly, %

SOURCE: THOMSON DATASTREAM

What he has been seeing on main Street doen't jibe with the everything-is-just-fine comments spewed out by government officials and Wall Street prognosticators as recently as six weeks ago.

"Have they been watching the same stuff that I'm watching? Because Main Street America is going through a really serious problem. This is not news to anyone who's out there looking at it."

Mr. Kessler, 65, began his career on Wall Street four decades ago as a gung-ho equity trader, but gave up on stocks when the market was flattened in the mid-1970s. He switched to the fixed-income side, where he played the mortgage and credit markets, before abandoning both after their woes of the early 1990s. He then turned exclusively to government bonds. He also climbs mountains, which is why he lives in Colorado. It helps give him an acute understanding of risk.

Explaining how a risk-taker ended up in fixed income, the most conservative part of the market, Mr. Kessler said: "It's transparent, liquid and pays a pretty good return of 4 to 5 per cent. And if you're good on timing, you can make 15 to 20 per cent." So we also know he's good at timing.

And since he doesn't believe that the financial world as we know it is about to end, where would he put his money? Well, U.S. Treasuries and cash, because that's his turf.

But he also likes Canada and Singapore, because of their stability, lack of deficits, competent central banks and reasonable prices.

"This is one of those times I would probably be short emerging markets and I'd be long something that has some sort of credit guarantee to it," he said, listing Treasuries, Canadian government bonds and Singapore dollars as havens to wait out the credit market storms.

Reprinted with permission from the Globe and Mail.

10.4   The Term Structure of Interest Rates

term structure of interest rates
Relationship between time to maturity and interest rates for default-free, pure discount instruments.

The yield curve tells us the relationship between Canadian bond yields and time to maturity. The **term structure of interest rates** (or just "term structure") is a similar, but not identical, relationship. Recall that a pure discount instrument has a single payment of face value at maturity with no other payments until then. Canadian bonds are *not* pure discount instruments because they pay coupons every six months. Pure discount instruments with more than a year to maturity are often called "zero coupon bonds," or just "zeroes," because they are, in effect, bonds with a zero coupon rate.

The term structure of interest rates is the relationship between time to maturity and interest rates for default-free, pure discount instruments. So, the difference between the yield curve and the term structure is that the yield curve is based on coupon bonds, whereas the term structure is based on pure discount instruments. The term structure is sometimes called the "zero coupon yield curve" to distinguish it from the Canadian yield curve.

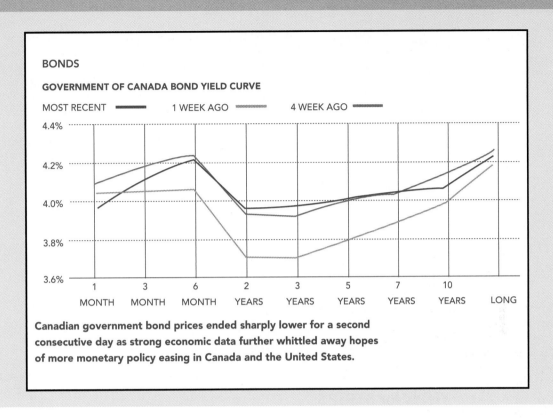

BONDS

GOVERNMENT OF CANADA BOND YIELD CURVE

MOST RECENT ▬▬▬   1 WEEK AGO ▬ ▬ ▬   4 WEEK AGO ▬ ▬ ▬

Canadian government bond prices ended sharply lower for a second consecutive day as strong economic data further whittled away hopes of more monetary policy easing in Canada and the United States.

STRIP BONDS

STRIP BONDS Pure discount securities created by stripping coupons and principal payments of bonds. Stands for Separate Trading of Registered Interest and Principal of Securities.

Read more about STRIPS at www.publicdebt.treas.gov

Until about 1987, the term structure of interest rates was not directly observable simply because default-free, pure discount instruments with maturities greater than one year did not exist or reliable data on them were not available. Today, however, the term structure of interest rates can be easily seen by examining yields on **STRIP BONDS**.

STRIPS are pure discount instruments created by "stripping" the coupons and principal payments of bonds into separate parts and then selling the parts separately. The term STRIPS stands for Separate Trading of Registered Interest and Principal of Securities. For example, a bond with 10 years to maturity will make 20 semiannual coupon payments during its life and will also make a principal payment at maturity. This bond can therefore be stripped into 21 separate parts, and each part can be bought and sold separately.

Figure 10.4 is a sample STRIPS daily report of individual STRIPS prices and yields as it appeared in *The Globe and Mail*. The first column shows the name of the issuer. The third column gives the maturity date. The next two columns contain bid and asked prices for each STRIPS. As always, the bid price is a quote of what dealers were willing to pay to buy STRIPS, and the asked price is a quote of what dealers were willing to accept to sell STRIPS.

The last column in Figure 10.4 lists changes in the asked prices from the previous day's prices.

327

FIGURE 10.4

STRIPS

Source: *The Globe and Mail*, February 12, 2005. Reprinted with permission from *The Globe and Mail*.

STRIPS (COUPONS AND RESIDUALS)	Coupon	Maturity	Bid	Ask	Bid Yld	Ask Yld	Chg
BC	0.000	2007-Jun-09		93.29		3.03	+0.011
BC	0.000	2007-Sep-05	92.11	92.37	3.25	3.14	+0.016
BC	0.000	2008-Jun-09		89.22		3.47	+0.013
BC	0.000	2013-Dec-18		67.06		4.57	+0.009
BC	0.000	2014-Jun-09	65.17	65.30	4.65	4.63	+0.012
Bell CDA	0.000	2031-Nov-15		18.89		6.33	+0.004
Bell CDA	0.000	2047-Dec-01		6.63		6.44	+0.006
Canada	0.000	2005-Jun-01	99.27	99.29	2.55	2.48	-0.005
Canada	0.000	2005-Dec-01	97.92	98.01	2.70	2.57	-0.002
Canada	0.000	2006-Mar-01	97.18	97.30	2.78	2.66	+0.002
Canada	0.000	2006-Jun-01	96.50	96.59	2.78	2.71	+0.008
Canada	0.000	2007-Jun-01	93.26	93.36	3.07	3.03	+0.011
Canada	0.000	2007-Oct-01	91.96	92.23	3.22	3.11	+0.016
Canada	0.000	2008-Jun-01	89.42	89.60	3.43	3.37	+0.013
Canada	0.000	2012-Jun-01	73.84	74.02	4.21	4.17	+0.009
Canada	0.000	2014-Dec-01	65.05	65.38	4.44	4.39	+0.003
Canada	0.000	2017-Jun-01	56.81	57.42	4.66	4.57	-0.001
Canada	0.000	2022-Jun-01	43.02	43.68	4.94	4.85	+0.004
Manitoba	0.000	2014-Mar-05		66.68		4.53	+0.003
Newfoundland	0.000	2014-Apr-17		65.36		4.69	+0.004
Ont Elec Fin	0.000	2017-Aug-18		53.50		5.07	+0.009
Ont Elec Fin	0.000	2021-Feb-06		43.78		5.24	+0.006
Ont Elec Fin	0.000	2024-Nov-26		35.08		5.37	+0.006
Ont Elec Fin	0.000	2027-Apr-11		30.91		5.37	+0.006
Ontario	0.000	2005-Dec-01	97.91	98.02	2.71	2.57	-0.002
Ontario	0.000	2015-Jun-02	61.26	61.69	4.82	4.75	+0.004
Ontario	0.000	2023-Jul-13		37.85		5.35	+0.006
Ontario	0.000	2031-Jun-02	25.14	26.00	5.32	5.19	+0.006
Quebec	0.000	2013-Dec-01		66.51		4.69	+0.004
Quebec	0.000	2015-Jan-16		62.91		4.73	+0.004
Quebec	0.000	2018-Jun-01		51.03		5.13	+0.006
Quebec	0.000	2018-Dec-01		49.55		5.16	+0.006
Quebec	0.000	2019-Jun-01		47.91		5.22	+0.006
Quebec	0.000	2019-Dec-01		46.49		5.25	+0.006
Quebec	0.000	2020-Jun-01		45.10		5.28	+0.006
Quebec	0.000	2020-Dec-01		43.73		5.31	+0.006
Quebec	0.000	2021-Jun-01		42.47		5.33	+0.006
Quebec	0.000	2021-Dec-01		41.23		5.35	+0.006
Quebec	0.000	2022-Jun-01		39.95		5.38	+0.005
Quebec	0.000	2022-Dec-01		38.77		5.40	+0.006
Quebec	0.000	2023-Jan-16		39.25		5.29	+0.004
Quebec	0.000	2023-Jun-01		37.62		5.42	+0.006
Quebec	0.000	2023-Dec-01		36.49		5.44	+0.006
Quebec	0.000	2024-Jun-01		35.39		5.46	+0.006
Quebec	0.000	2024-Dec-01		34.38		5.47	+0.006
Quebec	0.000	2025-Jun-01		33.58		5.45	+0.006
Quebec	0.000	2025-Dec-01		32.69		5.45	+0.006
Quebec	0.000	2027-Jun-01		30.44		5.41	+0.004
Quebec	0.000	2032-Jun-01		23.37		5.40	+0.004

Yields for STRIPS

An asked yield for a STRIPS is an APR (APRs were discussed earlier in this chapter). It is calculated as two times the true semiannual rate. Calculation of the yield on a STRIPS is a standard time value of money calculation. The price today of the STRIPS is the *present value*; the face value received at maturity is the *future value.* As you probably know, the relationship between present values and futures values is

$$\text{Present value} = \frac{\text{Future value}}{(1+r)^N}$$

In this equation, r is the rate per period and N is the number of periods. Notice that a period is not necessarily one year long.[1] For Treasury STRIPS, the number of periods is two times the number of years to maturity, here denoted by $2M$, and the interest rate is the "yield to maturity" (*YTM*) divided by 2:

$$\text{STRIPS price} = \frac{\text{Face value}}{(1 + YTM/2)^{2M}} \qquad (10.10)$$

---

[1] Any financial calculator can perform these calculations, but we will work them the hard way for the benefit of those who don't have financial calculators.

Consider a STRIPS with an asked price of 42.72, a reported yield of 6.40, and 13.5 years to maturity. The actual semiannual rate is 6.40% / 2 = 3.20%. Also, 13.5 years to maturity converts to 2 × 13.5, or 27, semiannual periods. To check that the reported price is correct given the reported yield, we plug in future value, rate per period, and number of periods:

$$\text{STRIPS price} = \frac{\$100}{(1+.032)^{27}}$$
$$= 42.72$$

If we need to go the other way and calculate the asked yield on a STRIPS given its price, we can rearrange the basic present value equation to solve it for r:

$$r = \left(\frac{\text{Future value}}{\text{Present value}}\right)^{\frac{1}{N}} - 1$$

For STRIPS, $N = 2M$ is the number of semiannual periods, and $r = YTM / 2$ is the semiannual interest rate, so the formula is:

$$YTM = 2 \times \left[\left(\frac{\text{Face value}}{\text{STRIPS price}}\right)^{\frac{1}{2M}} - 1\right] \qquad (10.11)$$

Consider a STRIPS maturing in six years with an asked price of 73.03125. Its yield to maturity of 5.3072 percent as calculated immediately below becomes 5.31 percent after rounding to two decimal places.

$$5.3072\% = 2 \times \left[\left(\frac{100}{73.03125}\right)^{\frac{1}{12}} - 1\right]$$

As another example, consider a STRIPS maturing in 20 years with an asked price of 26.1875. As calculated immediately below, its yield to maturity of 6.8129 percent becomes 6.81 percent after rounding to two decimal places.

$$6.8129\% = 2 \times \left[\left(\frac{100}{26.1875}\right)^{\frac{1}{40}} - 1\right]$$

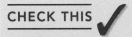
CHECK THIS

10.4a What is the yield to maturity (YTM) on a STRIPS maturing in five years if its asked price quote is 77.24?

10.4b What is the YTM of a STRIPS maturing in 15 years if its asked price quote is 38.26?

10.4c What is the YTM of a STRIPS maturing in 25 years if its asked price quote is 18.21?

10.5 Nominal versus Real Interest Rates

nominal interest rates Interest rates as they are normally observed and quoted, with no adjustment for inflation.

There is a fundamental distinction between *nominal* and *real* interest rates. **Nominal interest rates** are interest rates as we ordinarily observe them. Thus, all the money market rates we discussed earlier in this chapter and the STRIPS yields we discussed just above are nominal rates.

Real Interest Rates

real interest rates Interest rates adjusted for the effect of inflation, calculated as the nominal rate less the rate of inflation.

Real interest rates are nominal rates adjusted for the effects of price inflation. To obtain a real interest rate, simply subtract an inflation rate from a nominal interest rate:

$$\text{Real interest rate} = \text{Nominal interest rate} - \text{Inflation Rate} \quad (10.12)$$

The real interest rate is so-called because it measures the real change in the purchasing power of an investment. For example, if the nominal interest rate for a one-year certificate of deposit is 7 percent, then a one-year deposit of $100,000 will grow to $107,000. But if the inflation rate over the same year is 4 percent, you would need $104,000 after one year passes to buy what cost $100,000 today. Thus, the real increase in purchasing power for your investment is only $3,000, and, therefore, the real interest rate is only 3 percent.

Figure 10.5 displays real interest rates based on annual rates of return on Canadian T-bills and inflation rates over the 25-year period 1983 through 2007. The Bank

FIGURE 10.5   **Real T-Bill Rates**

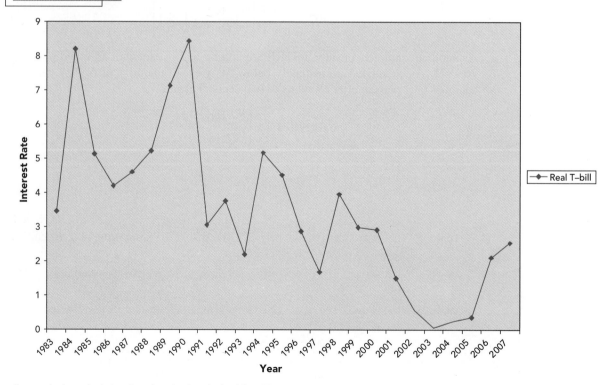

Source: Author calculations based on the data obtained from Datastream Database.

of Canada initiated a tight-money policy to fight an inflationary spiral in the late 1970s. The tight-money policy caused the 1980s to begin with historically high real interest rates. Throughout the 1980s, real Treasury bill rates were falling as inflation subsided. During this period the average real Treasury bill interest rate was approximately 3.47 percent.

The Fisher Hypothesis

Fisher hypothesis
Assertion that the general level of nominal interest rates follows the general level of inflation.

The relationship between nominal interest rates and the rate of inflation is often couched in terms of the *Fisher hypothesis*, which is named for the famous economist Irving Fisher, who formally proposed it in 1930. The **Fisher hypothesis** simply asserts that the general level of nominal interest rates follows the general level of inflation.

According to the Fisher hypothesis, interest rates are on average higher than the rate of inflation. Therefore, it logically follows that short-term interest rates reflect current inflation, while long-term interest rates reflect investor expectations of future inflation. Figure 10.6 graphs nominal interest rates and inflation rates used to create Figure 10.5. Notice that when inflation rates were high, Treasury bill returns tended to be high also, as predicted by the Fisher hypothesis.

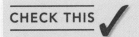

CHECK THIS

10.5a What is the difference between a nominal interest rate and a real interest rate?

10.5b What does the Fisher hypothesis assert?

FIGURE 10.6   **Inflation and T-Bill Rates**

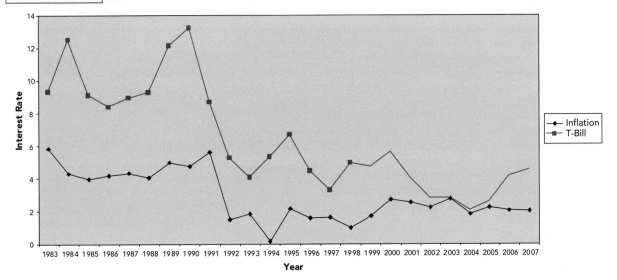

Source: Author calculations based on the data obtained from Datastream Database.

Fed Sees Bond Market Hampering Its Steps to Keep Inflation in Check

As the U.S Federal Reserve prepares to raise short-term interest rates again next week, officials there increasingly believe the bond market, which sets long-term rates, is diluting their efforts to tighten credit and contain inflation.

The result: The longer the bond market keeps long-term rates unusually low, the further the Fed is likely to raise the short-term rates it controls in an effort to keep the economy from overheating. Conversely, sharply higher bond yields would encourage the Fed to stop raising short-term rates.

This dynamic marks a striking break from the past when the Fed typically saw sharply higher bond yields as a reason to lift short-term rates further and low yields as a reason to worry about the economy.

Fed officials say future rate moves mostly depend on what data indicate about growth and inflation. With inflation low but the economy steadily using up unused capacity, officials plan to keep raising short-term rates to "neutral," a level thought to be between 3% and 5% that neither stimulates nor restrains economic growth. The bond market's unusual behavior is complicating that strategy by making it harder to know where neutral is.

Some policy makers worry that bond yields are being kept in check by overly complacent investor sentiment which could rapidly dissipate, pushing up mortgage rates and shaking the housing market. Indeed, some Fed officials see similarities between the attitudes of bond investors today and of stock investors in the late 1990s.

The Fed influences economic conditions by changing the target for the federal-funds rate, which is the rate charged on overnight loans between banks. That affects short-term consumer and business loans, including adjustable-rate mortgages. But longer-term rates, such as those for fixed-rate 30-year mortgages, are set by bond-market investors and have a bigger impact on the economy.

Low bond yields "are telling the Fed their job isn't done and they have to keep going," said Laurence Meyer, a former Fed governor and now an analyst at forecasting firm Macroeconomic Advisers. Mr. Meyer thinks the Fed eventually will raise its short-term rate to 4% from today's 3.25%, if bond yields rise significantly. If long-term rates don't rise, the Fed will have to raise short-term rates above 4.5%, he said.

The Fed is expected to raise the short-term rate to 3.5% on Tuesday. Since June of last year, the Fed has raised the Fed funds rate target from a 46-year low of 1% to 3.25%.

Yet, over the same period, the yield on the benchmark 10-year Treasury bond has declined. It fell from 4.7% to below 4% a month ago, although it has bounced back up to 4.3%. Yields have remained low even as the economy has been strong, inflation has drifted up, and the Fed has steadily raised short-term rates.

For months, Fed officials have debated the reasons long-term rates have declined. In February, Chairman Alan Greenspan labelled it a "conundrum." In a speech last week, Federal Reserve Bank of San Francisco President Janet Yellen said the debate "boils down to whether the [drop] is due to various 'special factors' operating independently of the current business cycle, or instead augurs bad economic news on the horizon."

If "special factors," such as increased investor confidence that inflation will remain low, or purchases of bonds by foreign central banks, are the reason for low bond yields, "the federal-funds rate probably needs to be somewhat higher than would otherwise be appropriate," Ms. Yellen said. But if the market is anticipating hard economic times, "a somewhat easier policy may be appropriate," she said.

In the past month, other key Fed policy makers have come to view special factors as the likelier explanation for low long-term rates than economic weakness. Many factors influence bond yields: expected inflation, which erodes an investor's purchasing power; the worldwide supply and demand for credit; what economists call a "term premium," the extra yield that investors demand for the many risks of lending money over a longer term, including fluctuations in economic growth and inflation; and Fed actions.

10.6 Traditional Theories of the Term Structure

Yield curves have been studied by financial economists for well over a century. During this period a number of different theories have been proposed to explain why yield curves may be upward sloping at one point in time and then downward sloping or flat at another point in time. We discuss three of the most popular traditional theories of the term structure in this section. We then present a modern perspective on the term structure in the following section.

Expectations Theory

expectations theory
The term structure of interest rates is a reflection of financial market beliefs regarding future interest rates.

According to the **expectations theory** of the term structure of interest rates, the shape of a yield curve expresses financial market expectations regarding future interest rates. Essentially, an upward-sloping yield curve predicts an increase in interest rates, and a downward-sloping yield curve predicts a decrease in interest rates. A flat yield curve expresses the sentiment that interest rates are not expected to change in the near future.

Expectations and Forward Rates The basic principles of the expectations theory can be explained with a two-period example. Let r_1 stand for the current market interest rate on a one-year investment, and let r_2 be the current market interest rate on a two-year investment. Also, let $r_{1,1}$ be the market interest rate on a one-year investment that will be available in one year. Of course, this rate is not known today.

For a two-year investment, you have two strategies available. First, you can invest for two years at the rate r_2. In this case, $1 invested today will become $\$(1 + r_2)^2$ in two years. For example, if $r_2 = 10$ percent, you would have $\$1 \times (1.10)^2 = \$1.21$ in two years for every dollar you invest.

Alternatively, you can invest for one year at the rate r_1, and, at the end of one year, you can reinvest the proceeds at the rate $r_{1,1}$. In this case, $1 invested today will become $\$(1 + r_1)(1 + r_{1,1})$ in two years. For example, suppose $r_1 = 10$ percent and, after a year passes, it turns out that $r_{1,1} = 8$ percent. Then you would end up with $\$1 \times 1.10 \times 1.08 = \$1.19$. Alternatively, suppose that after a year passes it turns out that $r_{1,1} = 12$ percent; then you would have $\$1 \times 1.10 \times 1.12 = \$1.232$. Notice that this second strategy entails some uncertainty since the next year's interest rate, $r_{1,1}$, is not known when you originally select your investment strategy.

forward rate An expected future interest rate implied by current interest rates.

The expectations theory of the term structure of interest rates asserts that, on average, the two-year investment proceeds, $\$(1 + r_2)^2$ and $\$(1 + r_1)(1 + r_{1,1})$, will be equal. In fact, we can obtain what is known as the implied **forward rate**, $f_{1,1}$, by setting the two total proceeds equal to each other:

$$(1 + r_2)^2 = (1 + r_1)(1 + f_{1,1})$$

Solving for the forward rate, $f_{1,1}$, we see that

$$f_{1,1} = \frac{(1 + r_2)^2}{1 + r_1} - 1$$

Notice that this forward interest rate is simply a future interest rate implied by current interest rates.

According to expectations theory, the forward rate $f_{1,1}$ is an accurate predictor of the rate $r_{1,1}$ to be realized one year in the future. Thus, if $r_2 = 10$ percent and $r_1 = 8$ percent, then $f_{1,1} = 12$ percent, approximately, which predicts that the one-year interest rate will increase from its current value of 10 percent to 12 percent. Alternatively, if $r_2 = 10$ percent and $r_1 = 12$ percent, then $f_{1,1} = 8$ percent, approximately, which predicts that the one-year interest rate will decrease from its current value of 10 percent to 8 percent.

In general, if $r_2 > r_1$, such that the term structure is upward sloping, then expectations theory predicts an interest rate increase. Similarly, if $r_2 < r_1$, indicating a downward-sloping term structure, then expectations theory predicts an interest rate decrease. Thus, the slope of the term structure points in the predicted direction of future interest rate changes.

LOOKING FORWARD

EXAMPLE 10.8

Suppose the yield on a two-year STRIPS is 7 percent and the yield on a one-year STRIPS is 6 percent. Based on the expectations theory, what will the yield on a one-year STRIPS be one year from now?

According to the expectations theory, the implied forward rate is an accurate predictor of what the interest rate will be. Thus, solving for the forward rate, we have

$$(1 + r_2)^2 = (1 + r_1)(1 + f_{1,1})$$

$$(1 + 0.7)^2 = (1 + .06)(1 + f_{1,1})$$

and the forward rate is

$$f_{1,1} = \frac{1.07^2}{1.06} - 1 = 8.00943\%$$

Based on the expectations theory, the rate next year will be about 8 percent. Notice that this is higher than the current rate, as we would predict since the term structure is upward sloping.

Expectations Theory and the Fisher Hypothesis The expectations theory is closely related to the Fisher hypothesis we discussed earlier. The relationship between the expectations theory of interest rates and the Fisher hypothesis is stated as follows. If expected future inflation is higher than current inflation, then we are likely to see an upward-sloping term structure where long-term interest rates are higher than short-term interest rates. Similarly, if future inflation is expected to be lower than its current level, we would then be likely to see a downward-sloping term structure where long rates are lower than short rates.

In other words, taken together, the expectations theory and the Fisher hypothesis assert that an upward-sloping term structure tells us that the market expects that nominal interest rates and inflation are likely to be higher in the future.

Maturity Preference Theory

Another traditional theory of the term structure asserts that lenders prefer to lend short-term to avoid tying up funds for long periods of time. In other words, they have a preference for shorter maturities. At the same time, borrowers prefer to borrow long-term to lock in secure financing for long periods of time.

maturity preference theory Long-term interest rates contain a maturity premium necessary to induce lenders into making longer-term loans.

According to the **maturity preference theory**, then, borrowers have to pay a higher rate to borrow long-term rather than short-term to essentially bribe lenders into loaning funds for longer maturities. The extra interest is called a *maturity premium*.[2]

The Fisher hypothesis, maturity preference theory, and expectations theory can coexist without problem. For example, suppose the shape of a yield curve is basically determined by expected future interest rates according to expectations theory. But where do expected future interest rates come from? According to the Fisher hypothesis, expectations regarding future interest rates are based on expected future rates of inflation. Thus, expectations theory and the Fisher hypothesis mesh quite nicely.

Furthermore, a basic yield curve determined by inflationary expectations could also accommodate maturity preference theory. All we need to do is add a maturity premium to longer term interest rates. In this view, long-term, default-free interest rates have three components: a real rate, an anticipated future inflation rate, and a maturity premium.

Market Segmentation Theory

market segmentation theory Debt markets are segmented by maturity, with the result that interest rates for various maturities are determined separately in each segment.

An alternative theory of the term structure of interest rates is the **market segmentation theory**, which asserts that debt markets are segmented according to the various maturities of debt instruments available for investment. By this theory, each maturity represents a separate, distinct market. For example, one group of lenders and borrowers may prefer to lend and borrow using securities with a maturity of 10 years, while another group may prefer to lend and borrow using securities with a maturity of 5 years. Segmentation theory simply states that interest rates corresponding to each maturity are determined separately by supply and demand conditions in each market segment.

Another theory of the term structure, known as the *preferred habitat theory*, is essentially a compromise between market segmentation and maturity preference. In the preferred habitat theory, as in the market segmentation theory, different investors have different preferred maturities. The difference is that they can be induced to move to less preferred maturities by a higher interest rate. In the maturity preference theory, the preferred habitat is always toward shorter maturities rather than longer maturities.

CHECK THIS ✓

10.6a According to the expectations theory, what does an upward-sloping term structure indicate?

10.6b What basic assertion does maturity preference theory make about investor preferences? If this assertion is correct, how does it affect the term structure of interest rates?

10.6c What is a maturity premium?

---

[2]Traditionally, maturity preference theory has been known as "liquidity" preference theory and the maturity premium was termed a "liquidity" premium. However, as we discussed before the term "liquidity" is universally used to indicate the relative ease with which an asset can be sold. Also, the term "liquidity premium" now has a different meaning. To avoid confusion and to make this theory more consistent with modern views of liquidity, interest rates, and the term structure, we have adopted the more descriptive name of maturity premium.

10.7 Determinants of Nominal Interest Rates: A Modern Perspective

Our understanding of the term structure of interest rates has increased significantly in the last few decades. Also, the evolution of fixed-income markets has shown us that, at least to some extent, traditional theories discussed in our previous section may be inadequate to explain the term structure. We discuss some problems with these theories next and then move on to a modern perspective.

Problems with Traditional Theories

To illustrate some problems with traditional theories, we could examine the behaviour of the term structure in the last two decades. What we would find is that the term structure is almost always upward sloping. But contrary to the expectations hypothesis, interest rates have not always risen. Furthermore, as we saw with STRIPS term structure, it is often the case that the term structure turns down at very long maturities. According to the expectations hypothesis, market participants apparently expect rates to rise for 20 or so years and then decline. This seems to be stretching things a bit.

In terms of maturity preference, governments borrow much more heavily short term than long term. Furthermore, many of the biggest buyers of fixed-income securities, such as pension funds, have a strong preference for *long* maturities. It is hard to square these facts with the behavioural assumptions underlying the maturity preference theory.

Finally, in terms of market segmentation, governments borrow at all maturities. Many institutional investors, such as mutual funds, are more than willing to move among maturities to obtain more favourable rates. At the same time, there are bond trading operations that do nothing other than buy and sell various maturity issues to exploit even very small perceived premiums. In short, in the modern fixed-income market, market segmentation does not seem to be a powerful force.

Modern Term Structure Theory

Going back to Chapter 1, we saw that long-term government bonds had higher returns, on average, than short-term T-bills. They had substantially more risk as well. In other words, there appears to be a risk-return trade-off for default-free bonds as well, and long-term bonds appear to have a risk premium.

Notice that this risk premium doesn't result from the possibility of default since it exists on default-free government debt. Instead, it exists because longer-term bond prices are more volatile than shorter-term prices. As we discuss in detail in the next chapter, the reason is that, for a given change in interest rates, long-term bond prices change more than short-term bonds. Put differently, long-term bond prices are much more sensitive to interest rate changes than short-term bonds. This is called *interest rate risk,* and the risk premium on longer-term bonds is called the *interest rate risk premium.*

The interest rate risk premium carried by long-term bonds leads us to a modern reinterpretation of the maturity preference hypothesis. All other things the same, investors do prefer short-term bonds to long-term bonds. The reason is simply that short-term bonds are less risky. As a result, long-term bonds have to offer higher yields to compensate investors for the extra interest rate risk.

Putting it together, the modern view of the term structure suggests that nominal interest rates on default-free securities can be stated as follows:

$$NI = RI + IP + RP \qquad (10.13)$$

where: NI = Nominal interest rate
RI = Real interest rate
IP = Inflation premium
RP = Interest rate risk premium

In this decomposition, the real rate of interest is assumed to be the same for all securities, and, on average, the real interest rate is positive, as predicted by the Fisher hypothesis.

As we discussed above, the inflation premium (IP) reflects investor expectations of future price inflation. The inflation premium may be different for securities with different maturities because expected inflation may be different over different future horizons. For example, the expected average rate of inflation over the next two years may be different from the expected average rate of inflation over the next five years.

In addition to the real rate and the inflation premium, nominal rates reflect an interest rate risk premium (RP) which increases with the maturity of the security being considered. As a result, if interest rates are expected to remain constant through time, the term structure would have a positive slope. This is consistent with maturity preference theory. Indeed, for zero coupon bonds the interest rate risk premium and the maturity premium are the same thing.

The separate effects of the inflation premium and the interest rate risk premium are difficult to distinguish. For example, the yields for U.S. Treasury STRIPS reveal a substantial yield premium for long-maturity STRIPS over short-term STRIPS. This yield premium for long-maturity STRIPS reflects the combined effects of the inflation premium and the risk premium. However, it is unclear how much of the total premium is caused by an inflation premium and how much is caused by a risk premium. Figure 10.7 shows how nominal interest rates can be separated into the real interest rate, the inflation premium, and the interest rate risk premium.

Liquidity and Default Risk

Thus far we have examined the components of interest rates on default-free, highly liquid securities such as STRIPS. We now expand our coverage to securities that are less liquid, not default-free, or both, to present a more detailed decomposition of nominal interest rates. When we are finished, what we will see is that nominal interest rates for individual securities can be decomposed into five basic components as follows:

$$NI = RI + IP + RP + LP + DP \qquad (10.14)$$

where: NI = Nominal interest rate
RI = Real interest rate
IP = Inflation premium
RP = Interest rate risk premium
LP = Liquidity premium
DP = Default premium

FIGURE 10.7   The Term Structure of Interest Rates

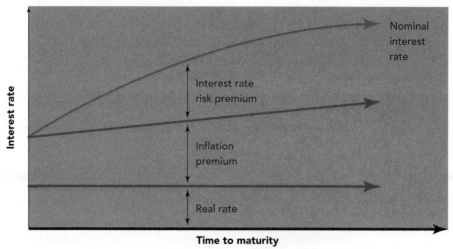

(a) Upward-sloping term structure

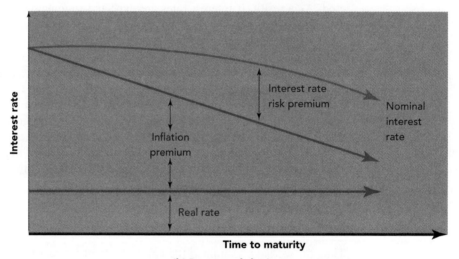

(b) Downward-sloping term structure

We have already discussed the first three components of the nominal interest rate. We now consider the two new ones on our list, the default and liquidity premiums.

The *liquidity premium* (LP) is a reflection of the fact that two otherwise identical securities may have very different degrees of liquidity. All else the same, the one with less liquidity would have to offer a higher yield as compensation.

The fifth, and final, component of a nominal interest rate is a *default premium* (DP). Investors demand a default premium to assume the risk of holding a security that might default on its promised payments. Naturally, the greater is the risk of default for a particular bond issue, the larger is the default premium required by investors. The topic of default risk is discussed in detail for corporate bonds in later chapters.

10.8 Summary and Conclusions

The time value of money is arguably the most important principle of finance. Interest rates are a convenient way to measure and state the time value of money. Furthermore, understanding interest rates is essential for understanding money market and fixed-income securities. In this chapter, we covered a number of topics relating to interest rates, including:

1. Important short-term money market rates include the prime rate and the Bank of Canada rate. The prime rate is a bellwether of bank lending to business, while the Bank of Canada rate is the interest rate that the bank offers to commercial banks for overnight reserve loans.

2. A yield curve graphs the relationship between yields on government securities and their maturities. The yield curve is fundamental to bond market analysis because it represents the interest rates that financial markets are charging to governments.

3. The term structure of interest rates is the fundamental relationship between time to maturity and interest rates for default-free, pure discount instruments such as STRIPS.

4. A number of different theories—including the expectations theory, the maturity preference theory, and the market segmentation theory—have been proposed to explain why the term structure of interest rates and yield curves may be upward sloping at one point in time and then downward sloping or flat at another time. In a modern view of the term structure, yields on default-free, pure discount bonds are determined by the real rate of interest, expectations of future inflation, and an interest rate risk premium.

5. Interest rates have five basic components: the real rate, an inflation premium, an interest rate risk premium, a liquidity premium, and a default premium. Treasury securities are free of default risk and are very liquid, so the last two components are absent from such instruments. For other issues, however, these components are very important.

REAL WORLD

This chapter covered the essentials of interest rates. How should you, as an investor or investment manager, put this information to work?

The best thing to do is to buy a variety of instruments discussed in this chapter. STRIPS, in particular, are an important investment vehicle both for institutional and individual investors. To gain some practical experience with the risks and rewards from STRIPS investing, you should invest equal dollar amounts in several different STRIPS with different maturities. Pick short-term (a few years), intermediate-term (10 or so years), and long-term (25 years or longer), for example. Once you make these investments, monitor their yields and prices.

A good place to start with a study of interest rates is to visit some federal government websites. Try the Bank of Canada (www.bankofcanada.ca) and the Department of Finance (www.fin.gc.ca).

Key Terms

Chapter Review Problems and Self-Test

1. **Money Market Prices** The rate on a particular money market instrument, quoted on a discount basis, is 5 percent. The instrument has a face value of $100,000 and will mature in 40 days. What is its price?

2. **Bond Equivalent Yields** Suppose a T-bill has 75 days to maturity and an asked discount of 4 percent. What is the bond equivalent yield?

Answers to Self-Test Problems

1. Using the bank discount basis formula, we have

$$\text{Current price} = \text{Face value} \times \left(1 - \frac{\text{Days to maturity}}{360} \times \text{Discount yield}\right)$$

$$\$99,444.44 = \$100,000 \times \left(1 - \frac{40}{360} \times .05\right)$$

You would pay $99,444.44.

2. Using the bond equivalent yield conversion formula, we have

$$4.09\% = \frac{365 \times .04}{360 - 75 \times .04}$$

The bond equivalent yield is thus 4.09 percent.

Test Your Investment Quotient

1. **Interest Rates** Which of the following interest rates is a bellwether (leading indicator) rate of bank lending to business?

   a. Unsecured business loan rate.
   b. Prime rate.
   c. Commercial paper rate.
   d. Banker's acceptance rate.

2. **T-Bill Yields** A Treasury bill with 180 days to maturity has a discount yield of 5 percent and a face value of $100,000. What is its current price?

   a. $97,500
   b. $95,000
   c. $92,500
   d. $90,000

3. **T-Bill Yields** A Treasury bill with 90 days to maturity has a price of $95,000. What is its discount yield?

   a. 5 percent
   b. 10 percent
   c. 15 percent
   d. 20 percent

4. **T-bill Yields** A 30-day Treasury bill is selling at a 12 percent yield on a discount basis. Which of the following is the approximate bond equivalent yield?

   a. 6.0 percent
   b. 11.7 percent
   c. 12.0 percent
   d. 12.3 percent

5. **Effective Annual Rates** A credit card company states an annual percentage rate (APR) of 12 percent, which is actually a rate of 1 percent per month. What is the EAR?

   a. 12 percent
   b. 12.68 percent
   c. 13.08 percent
   d. 13.76 percent

6. **STRIPS Yields** A Treasury STRIPS maturing in 10 years has a current price of $502.57 for $1,000 of face value. What is the yield to maturity of this STRIPS?

   a. 7.0 percent
   b. 7.12 percent
   c. 8.0 percent
   d. 8.12 percent

7. **STRIPS Yields** A Treasury STRIPS with $1,000 face value maturing in 5 years has a yield to maturity of 7 percent. What is the current price of this STRIPS?

   a. $930
   b. $712.99
   c. $708.92
   d. $650

8. **Bond Yields** An analyst finds that the semiannual interest rate that equates the present value of the bond's cash flow to its current market price is 3.85 percent. Consider the following possible alternatives:
   I. The bond equivalent yield on this security is 7.70 percent.
   II. The effective annual yield on the bond is 7.85 percent.
   III. The bond's yield-to-maturity is 7.70 percent.
   IV. The bond's horizon return is 8.35 percent.
   Which of these alternatives are true?

   a. I and II only
   b. II, III, and IV only
   c. I, II, and III only
   d. III only

9. Forward Rates An analyst gathered the following spot rates:

Time (years)	Annual Spot Rate
1	15.0%
2	12.5
3	10.0
4	7.5

The one-year forward rate two years from now is closest to

a. −4.91 percent
b. 5.17 percent
c. 10.05 percent
d. 7.5 percent

10. Zeroes If an investor's required return is 12 percent, the value of a 10-year maturity zero coupon bond with a maturity value of $1,000 is closest to:

a. $312
b. $688
c. $1,000
d. $1,312

11. Fisher Hypothesis The Fisher hypothesis essentially asserts which of the following?

a. Nominal interest rates follow inflation.
b. Real interest rates follow inflation.
c. Inflation follows real interest rates.
d. Inflation follows nominal interest rates.

12. Term Structure Theory Which one of the following statements about the term structure of interest rates is true?

a. The expectations hypothesis indicates a flat yield curve if anticipated future short-term rates exceed current short-term rates.
b. The expectations hypothesis contends that the long-term rate is equal to the anticipated short-term rate.
c. The liquidity premium theory indicates that, all else being equal, longer maturities will have lower yields.
d. The market segmentation theory contends that borrowers and lenders prefer particular segments of the yield curve.

13. Term Structure Theory Which one of the following is not an explanation of the relationship between a bond's interest rate and its term to maturity?

a. Default (credit) risk hypothesis
b. Expectations hypothesis
c. Liquidity preference hypothesis
d. Segmentation hypothesis

14. Term Structure Theory Which theory explains the shape of the yield curve by considering the relative demands for various maturities?

a. Relative strength theory
b. Segmentation theory
c. Unbiased expectations theory
d. Liquidity premium theory

15. **Term Structure Theory** The concepts of spot and forward rates are most closely associated with which one of the following explanations of the term structure of interest rates?

   a. Expectations hypothesis
   b. Liquidity premium theory
   c. Preferred habitat hypothesis
   d. Segmented market theory

16. **Forward Rates** The current one-year interest rate is 6 percent and the current two-year interest rate is 7 percent. What is the implied forward rate for next year's one-year rate?

   a. 9 percent
   b. 8 percent
   c. 7 percent
   d. 6 percent

17. **Forward Rates** The current one-year interest rate is 7 percent and the current two-year interest rate is 6 percent. What is the implied forward rate for next year's one-year rate?

   a. 7 percent
   b. 6 percent
   c. 5 percent
   d. 4 percent

18. **Forward Rates** The 6-month Treasury bill spot rate is 4 percent, and the 1-year Treasury bill spot rate is 5 percent. The implied 6-month forward rate 6 months from now is which of the following?

   a. 3.0 percent
   b. 4.5 percent
   c. 5.5 percent
   d. 5.9 percent

19. **Forward Rates** An analyst gathers the following information:

Years to Maturity	Spot Rate
1	5.00%
2	6.00
3	6.50

Based on the data above, the one-year implied forward rate two years from now is *closest* to:

   a. 6.25 percent
   b. 7.01 percent
   c. 7.26 percent
   d. 7.51 percent

Concept Questions

1. **Interest Rate History** Based on the history of interest rate of returns, what is the range of returns on short-term and long-term interest rates in Canada? The range of long-term rates? What is a typical value for each?

2. **Discount Securities** What are pure discount securities? Give two examples.

3. **Commercial Paper** Compare and contrast commercial paper and Treasury bills. Which would typically offer a higher interest rate? Why?

4. **LIBOR** What is LIBOR? Why is it important?

5. **Bank Discount Rates** Why do you suppose rates on some money market instruments are quoted on a bank discount basis? (*Hint:* Why use a 360-day year?)

6. **Nominal and Real Rates** When we observe interest rates in the financial press, do we see nominal or real rates? Which are more relevant to investors?

7. **Provincial versus Government of Canada** Which would have a higher yield, a provincial bond or a Government of Canada bond of the same maturity?

8. **Term Structure** Discuss how each of the following theories for the term structure of interest rates could account for a downward-sloping term structure of interest rates:
   a. Pure expectations
   b. Liquidity preference
   c. Market segmentation

9. **Banker's Acceptance** Compare T-bill rates with BA rates. Which would typically offer a higher interest rate? why?

Questions and Problems

Core Questions

1. **STRIPS** What is the price of a STRIPS with a face value of $100 that matures in seven years and has a yield to maturity of 5.6 percent?

2. **STRIPS** A STRIPS matures in 7.5 years and has a yield to maturity of 6.9 percent. If the par value is $100,000, what is the price of the STRIPS? What is the quoted price?

3. **STRIPS** A STRIPS is quoted at 75.89 and has six years until maturity. What is the yield to maturity?

4. **STRIPS** What is the yield to maturity on a Treasury STRIPS with 10 years to maturity and a quoted price of 50.12?

5. **Fisher Effect** A stock had a return of 12.2 percent last year. If the inflation rate was 4.3 percent, what was the approximate real return?

6. **Fisher Effect** Your investments increased in value by 11.4 percent last year but your purchasing power increased by only 5.8 percent. What was the inflation rate?

7. **Treasury Bill Prices** What is the price of a Treasury bill with 84 days to maturity quoted at a discount yield of 4.70 percent? Assume a $1 million face value.

8. **Treasury Bill Prices** In the previous problem, what is the bond-equivalent yield?

9. **Treasury Bill Prices** How much would you pay for a Treasury bill with 27 days to maturity quoted at a discount yield of 3.85 percent? Assume a $1 million face value.

10. **Treasury Bill Prices** In the previous problem, what is the bond-equivalent yield?

Intermediate Questions

11. **Treasury Bills** A Treasury bill with 35 days to maturity is quoted at 99.43. What is the bank discount yield, the bond equivalent yield, and the effective annual return?

12. **Treasury Bills** A Treasury bill purchased in December 2007 has 49 days until maturity and a bank discount yield of 4.68 percent. What is the price of the bill as a percentage of face value? What is the bond equivalent yield?

13. **Money Market Prices** The treasurer of a large corporation wants to invest $20 million in excess short-term cash in a particular money market investment. The prospectus quotes the instrument at a true yield of 6.70 percent; that is, the EAR for this investment is 6.70 percent. However, the treasurer wants to know the money market yield on this instrument to make it comparable to the T-bills and CDs she has already bought. If the term of the instrument is 120-days, what are the bond-equivalent and discount yields on this investment?

Use the following information to answer the next six questions:

U.S. Treasury STRIPS, close of business February 15, 2006:

Maturity	Price	Maturity	Price
Feb 07	95:21	Feb 10	81:10
Feb 08	90:27	Feb 11	76:05
Feb 09	85:24	Feb 12	71:18

14. **Zero Coupon Bonds** Calculate the quoted yield for each of the STRIPS given in the table above. Does the market expect interest rates to go up or down in the future?

15. **Zero Coupon Bonds** What is the yield of the two-year STRIPS expressed as an EAR?

16. **Forward Interest Rates** According to the pure expectations theory of interest rates, how much do you expect to pay for a one-year STRIPS on February 15, 2007? What is the corresponding implied forward rate? How does your answer compare to the current yield on a one-year STRIPS? What does this tell you about the relationship between implied forward rates, the shape of the zero coupon yield curve, and market expectations about future spot interest rates?

17. **Forward Interest Rates** According to the pure expectations theory of interest rates, how much do you expect to pay for a five-year STRIPS on February 15, 2007? How much do you expect to pay for a two-year STRIPS on February 15, 2009?

18. **Forward Interest Rates** This problem is a little harder. Suppose the term structure is set according to pure expectations and the maturity preference theory. To be specific, investors require no compensation for holding investments with a maturity of one year, but they demand a premium of .30 percent for holding investments with a maturity of two years. Given this information, how much would you pay for a one-year STRIPS on February 15, 2011? What is the corresponding implied forward rate? Compare your answer to the solutions you found in Problem 16. What does this tell you about the effect of a maturity premium on implied forward rates?

19. **Bond Price Changes** Suppose the (quoted) yield on each of the six STRIPS increases by .25 percent. Calculate the percentage change in price for the one-year, three-year, and six-year STRIPS. Which one has the largest price change? Now suppose that the quoted price on each STRIPS decreases by 16/32. Calculate the percentage change in (quoted) yield for the one-year, three-year, and six-year STRIPS. Which one has the largest yield change? What do your answers tell you about the relationship between prices, yields, and maturity for discount bonds?

20. **Inflation and Returns** You observe that the current interest rate on short-term Treasury bills is 4.24 percent. You also read in the newspaper that the GDP deflator, which is a common macroeconomic indicator used by market analysts to gauge the inflation rate, currently implies that inflation is 3.5 percent. Given this information, what is the

approximate real rate of interest on short-term Treasury bills? Is it likely that your answer would change if you used some alternative measure for the inflation rate, such as the CPI? What does this tell you about the observability and accuracy of real interest rates compared to nominal interest rates?

21. **Forward Interest Rates** Consider the following spot interest rates for maturities of one, two, three, and four years.

$$r_1 = 4.9\% \qquad r_2 = 5.7\% \quad r_3 = 6.4\% \qquad r_4 = 7.1\%$$

What are the following forward rates, where $f_{1,k}$ refers to a forward rate for the period beginning in one year and extending for k years?

$$f_{1,1} = \qquad ; f_{1,2} = \qquad ; f_{1,3} =$$

Hint: Use the equation $(1 + r_1)(1 + f_{1,k})k = (1 + r_{k+1})^{k+1}$ to solve for $f_{1,k}$.

22. **Forward Interest Rates** Based on the spot interest rates in the previous question, what are the following forward rates, where $f_{k,1}$ refers to a forward rate beginning in k years and extending for 1 year?

$$f_{2,1} = \qquad ; f_{3,1} =$$

Hint: Use the equation $(1 + r_k)^k(1 + f_{k,1}) = (1 + r_{k+1})^{k+1}$ to solve for $f_{k,1}$.

23. **Expected Inflation Rates** Based on the spot rates in Question 21, and assuming a constant real interest rate of 2 percent, what are the expected inflation rates for the next four years?

Hint: Use the Fisher hypothesis and the unbiased expectations theory.

Spreadsheet Problems

24. **Treasury Bills** A Treasury bill that settles on July 17, 2010, pays $100,000 on August 16, 2010. Assuming a discount rate of 4.98 percent, what is the price and bond equivalent yield?

25. **Effective Annual Rate** You have a car loan with a nominal rate of 7.2 percent. With interest charged monthly, what is the effective annual rate (EAR) on this loan?

What's on the Web

1. **Yield Curve** What is the shape of the Treasury yield curve today? Go to www.bloomberg.com and find out. Is the yield curve upward sloping or downward sloping? According to the expectations theory, are interest rates in the future expected to be higher or lower than they are today?

2. **STRIPS** Go to http://www.stripbonds.info. Answer the following questions: Which securities are stripped? How do I buy strip bonds? Why do investors hold strips?

3. **STRIPS** Go to www.canada.etrade.com/bonds and find the quotes for strip bonds that are offered for sale on the site. How many strip bonds are offered for sale? What is the lowest and highest yield to maturity? Are there strips with the same maturity that have different prices? How could this happen?

CHAPTER 11

Bond Prices and Yields

"More money has been lost reaching for yield than at the point of a gun."
—Raymond Devoe

Interest rates go up and bond prices go down. But which bonds go down the most and which go down the least? Interest rates go down and bond prices go up. But which bonds go up the most and which go up the least? For bond portfolio managers, these are important questions about interest rate risk. For anyone managing a bond portfolio, an understanding of interest rate risk rests on an understanding of the relationship between bond prices and yields. ■

In the preceding chapter on interest rates, we introduced the subject of bond yields. As we promised there, we now return to this subject and discuss bond prices and yields in some detail. We first describe how bond yields are determined and how they are interpreted. We then go on to examine what happens to bond prices as yields change. Finally, once we have a good understanding of the relation between bond prices and yields, we examine some of the fundamental tools of bond risk analysis used by fixed-income portfolio managers.

11.1 Bond Basics

A bond essentially is a security that offers the investor a series of fixed interest payments during its life, along with a fixed payment of principal when it matures. So long as the bond issuer does not default, the schedule of payments does not change. When originally issued, bonds normally have maturities ranging from 2 years to 30 years, but bonds with maturities of 50 or 100 years also exist. Bonds issued with maturities of less than 10 years are usually called notes. A very small number of bond issues have no stated maturity, and these are referred to as perpetuities or consols.

Straight Bonds

The most common type of bond is the so-called straight bond. By definition, a straight bond is an IOU that obligates the issuer to pay the bondholder a fixed sum of money at the bond's maturity along with constant, periodic interest payments during the life of the bond. The fixed sum paid at maturity is referred to as bond principal, par value, stated value, or face value. The periodic interest payments are called coupons. Perhaps the best example of straight bonds are Canadian bonds issued by the federal government to finance the national debt. However, business corporations and municipal governments also routinely issue debt in the form of straight bonds.

In addition to a straight bond component, many bonds have additional special features. These features are sometimes designed to enhance a bond's appeal to investors. For example, convertible bonds have a conversion feature that grants bondholders the right to convert their bonds into shares of common stock of the issuing corporation. As another example, "retractable" bonds have a put feature that grants bondholders the right to sell their bonds back to the issuer at a special put price.

These and other special features are attached to many bond issues, but we defer discussion of special bond features until later chapters. For now, it is only important to know that when a bond is issued with one or more special features, strictly speaking, it is no longer a straight bond. However, bonds with attached special features will normally have a straight bond component, namely, the periodic coupon payments and fixed principal payment at maturity. For this reason, straight bonds are important as the basic unit of bond analysis.

The typical example of a straight bond pays a series of constant semiannual coupons, along with a face value of $1,000 payable at maturity. This example is used in this chapter because it is common and realistic. For example, most corporate bonds are sold with a face value of $1,000 per bond, and most bonds pay constant semiannual coupons.

Coupon Rate and Current Yield

A familiarity with bond yield measures is important for understanding the financial characteristics of bonds. As we briefly discussed in Chapter 4, two basic yield measures for a bond are its coupon rate and current yield.

coupon rate A bond's annual coupon divided by its par value. Also called *coupon yield* or *nominal yield*.

A bond's **coupon rate** is defined as its annual coupon amount divided by its par value, or, in other words, its annual coupon expressed as a percentage of face value:

$$\text{Coupon rate} = \frac{\text{Annual coupon}}{\text{Par value}} \qquad (11.1)$$

For example, suppose a $1,000 par value bond pays semiannual coupons of $40. The annual coupon is then $80, and, stated as a percentage of par value, the bond's coupon rate is $80 / $1,000 = 8%. A coupon rate is often referred to as the *coupon yield* or the *nominal yield*. Notice that the word "nominal" here has nothing to do with inflation.

current yield A bond's annual coupon divided by its market price.

A bond's **current yield** is its annual coupon payment divided by its current market price:

$$\text{Current yield} = \frac{\text{Annual coupon}}{\text{Bond price}} \quad (11.2)$$

For example, suppose a $1,000 par value bond paying an $80 annual coupon has a price of $1,032.25. The current yield is $80 / $1,032.25 = 7.75%. Similarly, a price of $969.75 implies a current yield of $80 / $969.75 = 8.25%. Notice that whenever there is a change in the bond's price, the coupon rate remains constant. However, a bond's current yield is inversely related to its price, and it changes whenever the bond's price changes.

CHECK THIS

11.1a What is a straight bond?

11.1b What is a bond's coupon rate? Its current yield?

11.2 Straight Bond Prices and Yield to Maturity

yield to maturity (YTM) The discount rate that equates a bond's price with the present value of its future cash flows. Also called *promised yield* or just *yield*.

The single most important yield measure for a bond is its **yield to maturity**, commonly abbreviated as **YTM**. By definition, a bond's yield to maturity is the discount rate that equates the bond's price with the computed present value of its future cash flows. A bond's yield to maturity is sometimes called its *promised yield*, but, more commonly, the yield to maturity of a bond is simply referred to as its *yield*. In general, if the term "yield" is being used with no qualification, it means yield to maturity.

Straight Bond Prices

For straight bonds, the following standard formula is used to calculate a bond's price given its yield:

$$\text{Bond price} = \frac{C/2}{YTM/2}\left[1 - \frac{1}{(1 + YTM/2)^{2M}}\right] + \frac{FV}{(1 + YTM/2)^{2M}}$$

This formula can be simplified just a bit as follows:

$$= \frac{C}{YTM}\left[1 - \frac{1}{(1 + YTM/2)^{2M}}\right] + \frac{FV}{(1 + YTM/2)^{2M}} \quad (11.3)$$

where:
$$C = \text{Annual coupon, the sum of two semiannual coupons}$$
$$FV = \text{Face value}$$
$$M = \text{Maturity in years}$$
$$YTM = \text{Yield to maturity}$$

In this formula, the coupon used is the annual coupon, which is the sum of the two semiannual coupons. As discussed in our previous chapter for STRIPS, the yield on a bond is an annual percentage rate (APR), calculated as twice the true semiannual yield. As a result, the yield on a bond somewhat understates its effective annual rate (EAR).

The straight bond pricing formula has two separate components. The first component is the present value of all the coupon payments. Since the coupons are fixed and paid on a regular basis, you may recognize that they form an ordinary annuity, and the first piece of the bond pricing formula is a standard calculation for the present value of an annuity. The other component represents the present value of the principal payment at maturity, and it is a standard calculation for the present value of a single lump sum.

Calculating bond prices is mostly "plug and chug" with a calculator. In fact, a good financial calculator or spreadsheet should have this formula built into it. In any case, we will work through a few examples the long way just to illustrate the calculations.

Suppose a bond has a $1,000 face value, 20 years to maturity, an 8 percent coupon rate, and a yield of 9 percent. What's the price? Using the straight bond pricing formula, the price of this bond is calculated as follows:

1. Present value of semiannual coupons:

$$\frac{\$80}{.09}\left[1-\frac{1}{(1.045)^{40}}\right] = \$736.06337$$

2. Present value of $1,000 principal:

$$\frac{\$1,000}{(1.045)^{40}} = \$171.92871$$

The price of the bond is the sum of the present values of coupons and principal:

$$\text{Bond price} = \$736.06 + \$171.93 = \$907.99$$

So, this bond sells for $907.99.

CALCULATING STRAIGHT BOND PRICES

EXAMPLE 11.1

Suppose a bond has 20 years to maturity and a coupon rate of 8 percent. The bond's yield to maturity is 7 percent. What's the price?

In this case, the coupon rate is 8 percent and the face value is $1,000, so the annual coupon is $80. The bond's price is calculated as follows:

1. Present value of semiannual coupons:

$$\frac{\$80}{0.07}\left[1-\frac{1}{(1.035)^{40}}\right] = \$854.20289$$

2. Present value of $1,000 principal:

$$\frac{\$1,000}{(1.035)^{40}} = \$252.57247$$

The bond's price is the sum of coupon and principal present values:

$$\text{Bond price} = \$854.20 + \$252.57 = \$1,106.77$$

(continued)

SPREADSHEET ANALYSIS

	A	B	C	D	E	F	G	H
1								
2			Calculating the Price of a Coupon Bond					
3								
4	A bond traded on March 30, 2004 matures in 20 years on March 30, 2024.							
5	Assuming an 8 percent coupon rate and a 7 percent yield to maturity, what is the							
6	price of this bond?							
7	Hint: Use the Excel function PRICE.							
8								
9		$110.6775	= PRICE("3/30/2004","3/30/2024",0.08,0.07,100,2,3)					
10								
11	For a bond with $1,000 face value, multiply the price by 10 to get $1,106.78.							
12								
13	This function uses the following arguments:							
14								
15		=PRICE("Now","Maturity", Coupon,Yield,100,2,3)						
16								
17	The 100 indicates redemption value as a percent of face value.							
18	The 2 indicates semiannual coupons.							
19	The 3 specifies an actual day count with 365 days per year.							
20								
21								
22								
23								

This bond sells for $1,106.77.

Straight bond prices may be calculated using a built-in spreadsheet function. An example of how to use an Excel™ spreadsheet to calculate a bond price is shown in the nearby *Spreadsheet Analysis* box.

Premium and Discount Bonds

Bonds are commonly distinguished according to whether they are selling at par value or at a discount or premium relative to par value. These three relative price descriptions—premium, discount, and par bonds—are defined as follows:

1. **Premium bonds:** Bonds with a price greater than par value are said to be selling at a premium. The yield to maturity of a premium bond is less than its coupon rate.
2. **Discount bonds:** Bonds with a price less than par value are said to be selling at a discount. The yield to maturity of a discount bond is greater than its coupon rate.
3. **Par bonds:** Bonds with a price equal to par value are said to be selling at par. The yield to maturity of a par bond is equal to its coupon rate.

The important thing to notice is that whether a bond sells at a premium or discount depends on the relation between its coupon rate and its yield. If the coupon rate exceeds the yield, the bond will sell at a premium. If the coupon is less than the yield, the bond will sell at a discount.

PREMIUM AND DISCOUNT BONDS

EXAMPLE 11.2

Consider two bonds, both with eight years to maturity and a 7 percent coupon. One bond has a yield to maturity of 5 percent while the other has a yield to maturity of 9 percent. Which of these bonds is selling at a premium and which is selling at a discount? Verify your answer by calculating each bond's price.

For the bond with a 9 percent yield to maturity, the coupon rate of 7 percent is less than the yield, indicating a discount bond. The bond's price is calculated as follows:

$$\frac{\$70}{.09}\left[1-\frac{1}{(1.045)^{16}}\right]+\frac{\$1,000}{(1.045)^{16}}=\$877.66$$

For the bond with a 5 percent yield to maturity, the coupon rate of 7 percent is greater than the yield, indicating a premium bond. The bond's price is calculated as follows:

$$\frac{\$70}{.05}\left[1-\frac{1}{(1.025)^{16}}\right]+\frac{\$1,000}{(1.025)^{16}}=\$1,130.55$$

The relationship between bond prices and bond maturities for premium and discount bonds is graphically illustrated in Figure 11.1 for bonds with an 8 percent coupon rate. The vertical axis measures bond prices, and the horizontal axis measures bond maturities.

Figure 11.1 also describes the paths of premium and discount bond prices as their maturities shorten with the passage of time, assuming no changes in yield to maturity. As shown, the time paths of premium and discount bond prices follow smooth curves. Over time, the price of a premium bond declines and the price of a discount bond rises. At maturity, the price of each bond converges to its par value.

FIGURE 11.1   **Premium, Par, and Discount Bond Prices**

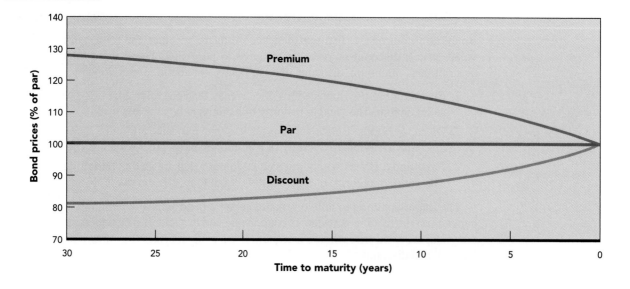

Figure 11.1 illustrates the general result that, for discount bonds, holding the coupon rate and yield to maturity constant, the longer the term to maturity of the bond the greater is the discount from par value. For premium bonds, holding the coupon rate and yield to maturity constant, the longer the term to maturity of the bond the greater is the premium over par value.

PREMIUM BONDS

EXAMPLE 11.3

Consider two bonds, both with a 9 percent coupon rate and the same yield to maturity of 7 percent, but with different maturities of 5 and 10 years. Which has the higher price? Verify your answer by calculating the prices.

First, since both bonds have a 9 percent coupon and a 7 percent yield, both bonds sell at a premium. Based on what we know, the one with the longer maturity will have a higher price. We can check these conclusions by calculating the prices as follows:

5-year maturity premium bond price:

$$\frac{\$90}{.07}\left[1-\frac{1}{(1.035)^{10}}\right]+\frac{\$1,000}{(1.035)^{10}}=\$1,083.17$$

10-year maturity premium bond price:

$$\frac{\$90}{.07}\left[1-\frac{1}{(1.035)^{20}}\right]+\frac{\$1,000}{(1.035)^{20}}=\$1,142.12$$

Notice that the longer maturity premium bond has a higher price, as we predicted.

DISCOUNT BONDS

EXAMPLE 11.4

Now consider two bonds, both with a 9 percent coupon rate and the same yield to maturity of 11 percent, but with different maturities of 5 and 10 years. Which has the higher price? Verify your answer by calculating the prices.

These are both discount bonds. (Why?) The one with the shorter maturity will have a higher price. To check, the prices can be calculated as follows:

5-year maturity discount bond price:

$$\frac{\$90}{.11}\left[1-\frac{1}{(1.055)^{10}}\right]+\frac{\$1,000}{(1.055)^{10}}=\$924.62$$

10-year maturity discount bond price:

$$\frac{\$90}{.11}\left[1-\frac{1}{(1.055)^{20}}\right]+\frac{\$1,000}{(1.055)^{20}}=\$880.50$$

In this case, the shorter maturity discount bond has the higher price.

Relationships among Yield Measures

We have discussed three different bond rates or yields in this chapter—the coupon rate, the current yield, and the yield to maturity. We've seen the relationship between coupon rates and yields for discount and premium bonds. We can extend this to include current yields by simply noting that the current yield is always between the coupon rate and the yield to maturity (unless the bond is selling at par, in which case all three are equal).

Putting together our observations about yield measures, we have the following:

Premium bonds:	Coupon rate > Current yield > Yield to maturity
Discount bonds:	Coupon rate < Current yield < Yield to maturity
Par value bonds:	Coupon rate = Current yield = Yield to maturity

Thus, when a premium bond and a discount bond both have the same yield to maturity, the premium bond has a higher current yield than the discount bond. However, as shown in Figure 11.1, the advantage of a high current yield for a premium bond is offset by the fact that the price of a premium bond must ultimately fall to its face value when the bond matures. Similarly, the disadvantage of a low current yield for a discount bond is offset by the fact that the price of a discount bond must ultimately rise to its face value at maturity. For these reasons, current yield is not a reliable guide to what an actual yield will be.

If you wish to get current price and yield information for government bond issues, try the Internet. The nearby *Work the Web* box displays a typical search query and the search results from a popular website for U.S. Treasury bond and notes.

A Note on Bond Price Quotes

clean price The price of a bond net of accrued interest; this is the price that is typically quoted.

dirty price The price of a bond including accrued interest, also known as the *full* or *invoice price*. This is the price the buyer actually pays.

If you buy a bond between coupon payment dates, the price you pay will usually be more than the price you are quoted. The reason is that standard convention in the bond market is to quote prices net of "accrued interest," meaning that accrued interest is deducted to arrive at the quoted price. This quoted price is called the **clean price**. The price you actually pay, however, includes the accrued interest. This price is the **dirty price**, also known as the "full" or "invoice" price.

An example is the easiest way to understand these issues. Suppose you buy a bond with a 12 percent annual coupon, payable semiannually. You actually pay $1,080 for this bond, so $1,080 is the dirty, or invoice, price. Further, on the day you buy it, the next coupon is due in four months, so you are between coupon dates. Notice that the next coupon will be $60.

The accrued interest on a bond is calculated by taking the fraction of the coupon period that has passed, in this case two months out of six, and multiplying this fraction by the next coupon, $60. So, the accrued interest in this example is 2 / 6 × $60 = $20. The bond's quoted price (i.e., its clean price) would be $1,080 − $20 = $1,060.[1]

---

[1]The way accrued interest is calculated actually depends on the type of bond being quoted, for example, government or corporate. The difference has to do with exactly how the fractional coupon period is calculated. In our example just above, we implicitly treated the months as having exactly the same length (i.e., 30 days each, 360 days in a year), which is consistent with the way corporate bonds are quoted. In contrast, for government bonds, actual day counts are used. If you look back at our *Spreadsheet Analysis* exhibit, you'll see that we had to specify this treatment to value our government bond.

WORK THE WEB

Current information on Treasury bond prices and yields is available at the search tool at Bondpage.com (www.bondpage.com). An example query definition and the search results is shown below.

Notice that three of the bonds have a much higher yield to maturity than the rest. The reason is that these bonds are the "Callable" bonds (also note the "C" after the maturity date). We will have more to say about callable bonds later.

Keep in mind that clean prices and accrued interest are purely a quoting convention. The price that matters to you is the invoice price, because that is what you will actually pay for the bond. The only thing that's important about accrued interest on a bond is that it may impact the taxes you owe on the first coupon you receive.

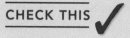

CHECK THIS	**11.2a**	A straight bond's price has two components. What are they?
	11.2b	What do you call a bond that sells for more than its face value?
	11.2c	What is the relationship between a bond's price and its term to maturity when the bond's coupon rate is equal to its yield to maturity?
	11.2d	Does current yield more strongly overstate yield to maturity for long-maturity or short-maturity premium bonds?

11.3 More on Yields

In the previous section, we focused on finding a straight bond's price given its yield. In this section, we reverse direction to find a bond's yield given its price. We then discuss the relationship among the various yield measures we have seen. We finish the section with some additional yield calculations.

Calculating Yields

To calculate a bond's yield given its price, we use the same straight bond formula used previously. The only way to find the yield is by trial and error. Financial calculators and spreadsheets do it this way at very high speed.

To illustrate, suppose we have a 6 percent bond with 10 years to maturity. Its price is 90, meaning 90 percent of face value. Assuming a $1,000 face value, the price is $900 and the coupon is $60 per year. What's the yield?

To find out, all we can do is try different yields until we come across the one that produces a price of $900. However, we can speed things up quite a bit by making an educated guess using what we know about bond prices and yields. We know the yield on this bond is greater than its 6 percent coupon rate because it is a discount bond. So let's first try 8 percent in the straight bond pricing formula:

$$\frac{\$60}{.08}\left[1 - \frac{1}{(1.04)^{20}}\right] + \frac{\$1,000}{(1.04)^{20}} = \$864.10$$

The price with an 8 percent yield is $864.10, which is somewhat less than the $900 price, but not too far off.

To finish, we need to ask whether the 8 percent we used was too high or too low. We know that the higher the yield, the lower is the price, thus 8 percent is a little too high. So let's try 7.5 percent:

$$\frac{\$60}{.075}\left[1 - \frac{1}{(1.0375)^{20}}\right] + \frac{\$1,000}{(1.0375)^{20}} = \$895.78$$

Now we're very close. We're still a little too high on the yield (since the price is a little low). If you try 7.4 percent, you'll see that the resulting price is $902.29, so the yield is between 7.4 and 7.5 percent (it's actually 7.435 percent).

SPREADSHEET ANALYSIS

	A	B	C	D	E	F	G	H
1								
2		Calculating the Yield to Maturity of a Coupon Bond						
3								
4	A bond traded on March 30, 2004, matures in 8 years on March 30, 2012.							
5	Assuming an 8 percent coupon rate and a price of 110, what is this bond's yield							
6	to maturity?							
7	Hint: Use the Excel function YIELD.							
8								
9		6.3843%	= YIELD("3/30/2004","3/30/2012",0.08,110,100,2,3)					
10								
11	This function uses the following arguments:							
12								
13			= YIELD("Now","Maturity",Coupon,Price,100,2,3)					
14								
15	Price is entered as a percent of face value.							
16	The 100 indicates redemption value as a percent of face value.							
17	The 2 indicates semiannual coupons.							
18	The 3 specifies an actual day count with 365 days per year.							
19								
20								

CALCULATING YTM

EXAMPLE 11.5

Suppose a bond has eight years to maturity, a price of 110, and a coupon rate of 8 percent. What is its yield?

This is a premium bond, so its yield is less than the 8 percent coupon. If we try 6 percent, we get (check this) $1,125.61. The yield is therefore a little bigger than 6 percent. If we try 6.5 percent, we get (check this) $1,092.43, so the answer is slightly less than 6.5 percent. Check that 6.4 percent is almost exact (the exact yield is 6.3843 percent).

Yields to maturity may be calculated using a built-in spreadsheet function. An example of how to use an Excel™ spreadsheet to calculate a yield to maturity is shown in the nearby *Spreadsheet Analysis* box.

Yield to Call

callable bond A bond is callable if the issuer can buy it back before it matures.

call price The price the issuer of a callable bond must pay to buy it back.

The discussion in this chapter so far has assumed that a bond will have an actual maturity equal to its originally stated maturity. However, this is not always so since most bonds are **callable bonds**. When a bond issue is callable, the issuer can buy back outstanding bonds before the bonds mature. In exchange, bondholders receive a special **call price**, which is often equal to face value, although it may be slightly higher. When a call price is equal to face value, the bond is said to be *callable at par*.

Bonds are called at the convenience of the issuer, and a call usually occurs after a fall in market interest rates allows issuers to refinance outstanding debt with new bonds paying lower coupons. However, an issuer's call privilege is often restricted so that outstanding bonds cannot be called until the end of a specified **call protection period**, also termed a *call deferment period*. As a typical example, a bond issued with a 20-year maturity may be sold to investors subject to the restriction that it is callable anytime after an initial five-year call protection period.

If a bond is callable, its yield to maturity may no longer be a useful number. Instead, the **yield to call**, commonly abbreviated **YTC**, may be more meaningful. Yield to call is a yield measure that assumes a bond issue will be called at its earliest possible call date.

We calculate a bond's yield to call using the straight bond pricing formula we have been using with two changes. First, instead of time to maturity, we use time to the first possible call date. Second, instead of face value, we use the call price. The resulting formula is thus:

$$\text{Callable bond price} = \frac{C}{YTC}\left[1 - \frac{1}{(1 + YTC/2)^{2T}}\right] + \frac{CP}{(1 + YTC/2)^{2T}} \quad (11.4)$$

where:
$$C = \text{Constant annual coupon}$$
$$CP = \text{Call price of the bond}$$
$$T = \text{Time in years until earliest possible call date}$$
$$YTC = \text{Yield to call assuming semiannual coupons}$$

Calculating a yield to call requires the same trial-and-error procedure as calculating a yield to maturity. Most financial calculators will either handle the calculation directly or can be tricked into it by just changing the face value to the call price and the time to maturity to time to call.

To give a trial-and-error example, suppose a 20-year bond has a coupon of 8 percent, a price of 98, and is callable in 10 years. The call price is 105. What are its yield to maturity and yield to call?

Based on our earlier discussion, we know the yield to maturity is slightly bigger than the coupon rate. (Why?) After some calculation, we find it to be 8.2 percent.

To find the bond's yield to call, we pretend it has a face value of 105 instead of 100 ($1,050 versus $1,000) and will mature in 10 years. With these two changes, the procedure is exactly the same. We can try 8.5 percent, for example:

$$\frac{\$80}{.085}\left[1 - \frac{1}{(1.0425)^{20}}\right] + \frac{\$1,050}{(1.0425)^{20}} = \$988.51$$

Since this $988.51 is a little too high, the yield to call is slightly bigger than 8.5 percent. If we try 8.6, we find that the price is $981.83, so the yield to call is about 8.6 percent (it's 8.6276 percent).

A natural question comes up in this context. Which is bigger, the yield to maturity or the yield to call? The answer depends on the call price. However, if the bond is callable at par (as many are), then, for a premium bond, the yield to maturity is greater. For a discount bond, the reverse is true.

---

call protection period
The period during which a callable bond cannot be called. Also called a *call deferment period*.

yield to call (YTC)
Measure of return that assumes a bond will be redeemed at the earliest call date.

SPREADSHEET ANALYSIS

	A	B	C	D	E	F	G	H
1								
2				Calculating Yield to Call				
3								
4		A bond traded on March 30, 2004 matures in 15 years on March 30, 2019 and may						
5		be called anytime after March 30, 2009 at a call price of 105. The bond pays an						
6		8.5 percent coupon and currently trades at par. What are the yield to maturity						
7		and yield to call for this bond?						
8								
9		Yield to maturity is based on the 2019 maturity and the current price of 100.						
10								
11		8.500%	= YIELD("3/30/2004","3/30/2019",0.085,100,100,2,3)					
12								
13		Yield to call is based on the 2009 call date and the call price of 105.						
14								
15		9.308%	= YIELD("3/30/2004","3/30/2009",0.085,100,105,2,3)					
16								
17								

YIELD TO CALL

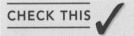
EXAMPLE 11.6

An 8.5 percent coupon bond maturing in 15 years is callable at 105 in 5 years. If the price is 100, which is bigger, the yield to call or the yield to maturity?

Since this is a par bond callable at a premium, the yield to call is bigger. We can verify this by calculating both yields. Check that the yield to maturity is 8.50 percent, whereas the yield to call is 9.308 percent.

Yields to call may be calculated using a built-in spreadsheet function. An example of how to use an Excel™ spreadsheet to calculate a yield to call is shown in the nearby *Spreadsheet Analysis* box.

CHECK THIS ✔

11.3a What does it mean for a bond to be callable?

11.3b What is the difference between yield to maturity and yield to call?

11.3c Yield to call is calculated just like yield to maturity except for two changes. What are the changes?

11.4 Interest Rate Risk and Malkiel's Theorems

interest rate risk The possibility that changes in interest rates will result in losses in a bond's value.

Bond yields are essentially interest rates, and, like interest rates, they fluctuate through time. When interest rates change, bond prices change. This is called **interest rate risk**. The term "interest rate risk" refers to the possibility of losses on a bond from changes in interest rates.

Promised Yield and Realized Yield

realized yield The yield actually earned or "realized" on a bond.

The terms *yield to maturity* and *promised yield* both seem to imply that the yield originally stated when a bond is purchased is what you will actually earn if you hold the bond until it matures. Actually, this is not generally correct. The return or yield you actually earn on a bond is called the **realized yield**, and an originally stated yield to maturity is almost never exactly equal to the realized yield.

The reason a realized yield will almost always differ from a promised yield is that interest rates fluctuate, causing bond prices to rise or fall. One consequence is that if a bond is sold before maturity, its price may be higher or lower than originally anticipated, and, as a result, the actually realized yield will be different from the promised yield.

Another important reason why realized yields generally differ from promised yields relates to the bond's coupons. We will get to this in the next section. For now, you should know that, for the most part, a bond's realized yield will equal its promised yield only if its yield doesn't change at all over the life of the bond, an unlikely event.

Interest Rate Risk and Maturity

While changing interest rates systematically affect all bond prices, it is important to realize that the impact of changing interest rates is not the same for all bonds. Some bonds are more sensitive to interest rate changes than others. To illustrate, Figure 11.2 shows how two bonds with different maturities can have different price sensitivities to changes in bond yields.

In Figure 11.2, bond prices are measured on the vertical axis, and bond yields are measured on the horizontal axis. Both bonds have the same 8 percent coupon rate, but one bond has a 5-year maturity while the other bond has a 20-year maturity. Both bonds display the inverse relationship between bond prices and bond yields. Since both bonds have the same 8 percent coupon rate, and both sell for par, their yields are 8 percent.

FIGURE 11.2 **Bond Prices and Yields**

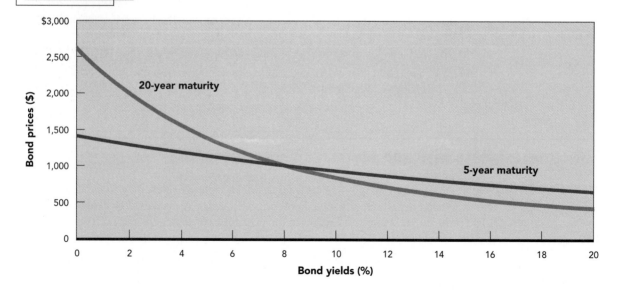

However, when bond yields are greater than 8 percent, the 20-year maturity bond has a lower price than the 5-year maturity bond. In contrast, when bond yields are less than 8 percent, the 20-year maturity bond has a higher price than the 5-year maturity bond. Essentially, falling yields cause both bond prices to rise, but the longer maturity bond experiences a larger price increase than the shorter maturity bond. Similarly, rising yields cause both bond prices to fall, but the price of the longer maturity bond falls by more than the price of the shorter maturity bond.

Malkiel's Theorems

The effect illustrated in Figure 11.2, along with some other important relationships among bond prices, maturities, coupon rates, and yields, is succinctly described by Burton Malkiel's five bond price theorems.[2] These five theorems are:

1. Bond prices and bond yields move in opposite directions. As a bond's yield increases, its price decreases. Conversely, as a bond's yield decreases, its price increases.

2. For a given change in a bond's yield to maturity, the longer the term to maturity of the bond, the greater will be the magnitude of the change in the bond's price.

3. For a given change in a bond's yield to maturity, the size of the change in the bond's price increases at a diminishing rate as the bond's term to maturity lengthens.

4. For a given change in a bond's yield to maturity, the absolute magnitude of the resulting change in the bond's price is inversely related to the bond's coupon rate.

5. For a given absolute change in a bond's yield to maturity, the magnitude of the price increase caused by a decrease in yield is greater than the price decrease caused by an increase in yield.

The first, second, and fourth of these theorems are the simplest and most important. The first one says that bond prices and yields move in opposite directions. The second one says that longer-term bonds are more sensitive to changes in yields than shorter-term bonds. The fourth one says that lower coupon bonds are more sensitive to changes in yields than higher coupon bonds.

The third theorem says that a bond's sensitivity to interest rate changes increases as its maturity grows, but at a diminishing rate. In other words, a 10-year bond is much more sensitive to changes in yield than a 1-year bond. However, a 30-year bond is only slightly more sensitive than a 20-year bond. Finally, the fifth theorem says essentially that the loss you would suffer from, say, a 1 percent increase in yields is less than the gain you would enjoy from a 1 percent decrease in yields.

Table 11.1 illustrates the first three of these theorems by providing prices for 8 percent coupon bonds with maturities of 5, 10, and 20 years and yields to maturity of 7 percent and 9 percent. Be sure to check these for practice. As the first theorem says, bond prices are lower when yields are higher (9 percent versus 7 percent). As the

---

[2]Burton C. Malkiel, "Expectations, Bond Prices, and the Term Structure of Interest Rates," *Quarterly Journal of Economics,* May 1962, pp. 197–218.

TABLE 11.1	Bond Prices and Yields		
	Time to Maturity		
Yields	**5 Years**	**10 Years**	**20 Years**
7%	$1,041.58	$1,071.06	$1,106.78
9%	960.44	934.96	907.99
Price difference	$ 81.14	$ 136.10	$ 198.79

TABLE 11.2	Twenty-Year Bond Prices and Yields		
	Coupon Rates		
Yields	**6 Percent**	**8 Percent**	**10 Percent**
6%	$1,000.00	$1,231.15	$1,462.30
8%	802.07	1,000.00	1,197.93
10%	656.82	828.41	1,000.00

second theorem indicates, the differences in bond prices between yields of 7 percent and 9 percent are greater for bonds with a longer term to maturity. However, as the third theorem states, the effect increases at a diminishing rate as the maturity lengthens. To see this, notice that $136.10 is 67.7 percent larger than $81.14, while $198.79 is only 46.1 percent larger than $136.10.

To illustrate the last two theorems, we present prices for 20-year maturity bonds with coupon rates and yields to maturity of 6 percent, 8 percent, and 10 percent (again, calculate these for practice) in Table 11.2. To illustrate the fourth theorem, compare the loss on the 6 percent and the 8 percent bonds as yields move from 8 percent to 10 percent. The 6 percent bond loses ($656.82 − $802.07) / $802.07 = −18.1%. The 8 percent bond loses ($828.41 − $1,000) / $1,000 = −17.2%, showing that the bond with the lower coupon is more sensitive to a change in yields. You can (and should) verify that the same is true for a yield increase.

Finally, to illustrate the fifth theorem, take a look at the 8 percent coupon bond in Table 11.2. As yields decrease by 2 percent from 8 percent to 6 percent, its price climbs by $231.15. As yields rise by 2 percent, the bond's price falls by $171.59.

As we have discussed, bond maturity is an important factor determining the sensitivity of a bond's price to changes in interest rates. However, bond maturity is an incomplete measure of bond price sensitivity to yield changes. For example, we have seen that a bond's coupon rate is also important. An improved measure of interest rate risk for bonds that accounts both for differences in maturity and differences in coupon rates is our next subject. A nearby *Investment Updates* box discusses tips for investing in bonds.

CHECK THIS

11.4a True or false: A bond price's sensitivity to interest rate changes increases at an increasing rate as maturity lengthens.

11.4b Which is more sensitive to an interest rate shift: a low-coupon bond or a high-coupon bond?

BY ANDREW ALLENTUCK

Globe Investor Magazine Online, Dec. 6. 2007

The world is having a debt crisis and Canadian capital markets are caught in the middle. Old stalwarts like bank stocks have been knocked down as investors recognize that banks are exposed to billions of dollars worth of risky derivatives. There are few places to hide, but don't forget to consider bonds.

Bond returns have been so low for so long that many investors may have overlooked them. But here are six tips to remember when parking your money in bonds.

1. Learn the alphabet soup of credit rating.

Corporate bonds vary in quality from AAA ultrasafe to single B dubious to C close to default. See www.moodys.com for ratings on 170.000 bonds and other credit instruments. Registration is required, but most of the info is free. For safety, pick the survivors, that is, bonds from companies with strong earnings and manageable depth.

There are bargains these days in senior bonds of major banks. You can pick up a five-year bond from Royal Bank or Bank of Montreal that pays 5 percent to maturity compared to 3.8 percent to maturity for a government of Canada bond. There is a theoretical risk that either bank could go up in smoke by 2012, but most investors will take the extra yield boost as a gift.

"It is hard to lose money buying Canadian big five bank bonds; and if you hold them to maturity, you get a great return." says Tom Czitron, who runs fixed income portfolios as a managing director of Sceptre Investment Council Ltd. in Toronto.

2. Understand the importance of interest rates.

Government bonds do not default; instead, they fluctuate in response to interest rate changes. Here is how it works. Let's say you have a bond that yields 5-percent. If interest rates fall to 3 percent, then the value of your 5-percent bond is going rise. After all, your old bond now has a higher yield compared to new bonds that can only offer 3 percent.

Conversely, if interest rates rise to 7 percent, then your 5-percent bond will fall in value because no one wants a bond that pays only 5 percent. The old bond will fall in price until it produces a yield of 7 percent.

So if you think interest rates are about to fall, it is a good time to buy bonds.

3. Frame the safety you want in terms of the time you need it.

Treasury bills, which government bonds due in one year or less, are safe but are good for only their time remaining to maturity. If you think that interest rates are headed down, you may want to buy a bond with a longer term. The problem is that very long bonds with terms of 20 to 30 years not only lock in a rate, but can penalize you should interest rates rise.

Rather than speculate on the future course of rates, which even the best economists do not do well, buy bonds for your natural holding period—say the five years before junior will need money for university the sequence of years when you will be retired.

"You may not be able to predict where interest rates will be in 10 years, but you can predict when you will need money. That makes bond buying a lot simple," says Craig Allardyee, a fixed income manager at Mavrix Fund Management Inc. in Toronto.

Alternatively, you can build what bond dealers call a "ladder." Say you need a some of money, perhaps $50.000, in 20 years. What you do is ladder your exposer by dividing up the money into chunks and putting perhaps $10.000 down on a bond due in five years, $10.000 down on a due in 10 years, $10.000 down on 15 years and the balance $20.000 down on the bond with the 20-year maturity.

When each "rung" of the ladder comes due, you reinvest and roll on to the 20-year target.

4. Government bond price changes can be estimated with accuracy.

The amount a bond will gain or loss when interest rates change is called duration. You can calculate duration via the differential equations financial types study in university or look up durations for major federal and most provincial bonds at a website like the Globe and Mail's http://gold.globeinvestor.com. A very short bond has a duration close to zero. Its price will vary little from that based on the interest rate at which it was issued.

On the other hand, a 30-year strip bond that pays no interest until its term is up has a duration of 30; it will rise 30 percent in value for every 1-percent drop in interest rates. With stocks this kind of precise risk calibration is impossible.

5. Don't be a yield pig.

Be careful with anything that isn't A rated. That's because after you leave the relatively safe world of bonds with

(continued)

Income and Yield: Six Tips for Investing in Bonds

various numbers of A's for ratings, default rates soar. Canadian corporate bonds rated single B, which is way below investment grade, have a cumulative 28.3-percent default record over 10 years in comparison to AAA Canada corporates that have a zero-percent default record over 10 years.

"Low-rated bonds are buyer beware territory; you have to do your homework before you buy," says Chris Kresic, senior vice-president for investments at Mackenzie Financial Corporation in Toronto.

6. Buying bond funds.
If you want to leave the details of bond trading to prose, buy into a bond fund with a manager with a strong track record over at least five years, "Investors who pile into bonds they don't understand can lose badly," Mr. Czitron says.

And pay attention to fees. Bond returns are usually mid-single digits annually. The average management fee

on a bond fund, almost 2 percent a year can really eat into returns if bond yields are low like they are now.

Also, be aware of what kind of bond fund you're buying. Canadian fixed income funds turned in an average 0.48-percent return for the 12 months ended Oct. 31. 2007. But over the 10 years ended Oct. 31, they had an average annual compound return of 4.56 percent. By comparison, high-yield bond funds paid 0.99-percent for the last 12 months but generated an average annual compound return of 3.68 percent for the decade.

Either way, look for funds with performance justified by fees. You are entitled to get what you pay for.

Special to The Globe and Mail

Reprinted with permission from the Globe and Mail & Andrew Allentuck.

11.5 Duration

duration A widely used measure of a bond's sensitivity to changes in bond yields.

To account for differences in interest rate risk across bonds with different coupon rates and maturities, the concept of **duration** is widely applied. As we will explore in some detail, duration measures a bond's sensitivity to interest rate changes. The idea behind duration was first presented by Frederick Macaulay.[3] Today, duration is a very widely used measure of a bond's price sensitivity to changes in bond yields.

Macaulay Duration

There are several duration measures. The original version is called *Macaulay duration*. The usefulness of Macaulay duration stems from the fact that it satisfies the following approximate relationship between percentage changes in bond prices and changes in bond yields:

$$\text{Percentage change in bond price} \approx -\,\text{Duration} \times \frac{\text{Change in } YTM}{(1 + YTM/2)} \quad (11.5)$$

As a consequence, two bonds with the same duration, but not necessarily the same maturity, have approximately the same price sensitivity to a change in bond yields. This approximation is quite accurate for relatively small changes in yields, but it becomes less accurate when large changes are considered.

---

[3]Frederick Macaulay, *Some Theoretical Problems Suggested by the Movements of Interest Rates, Bond Yields, and Stock Prices in the United States since 1856* (New York: National Bureau of Economic Research, 1938).

To see how we use this result, suppose a bond has a Macaulay duration of six years, and its yield decreases from 10 percent to 9.5 percent. The resulting percentage change in the price of the bond is calculated as follows:

$$-6 \times \frac{.095 - .10}{1.05} = 2.86\%$$

Thus, the bond's price rises by 2.86 percent in response to a yield decrease of 50 basis points.

MACAULAY DURATION

EXAMPLE 11.7

A bond has a Macaulay duration of 11 years, and its yield increases from 8 percent to 8.5 percent. What will happen to the price of the bond?

The resulting percentage change in the price of the bond can be calculated as follows:

$$-11 \times \frac{.085 - .08}{1.04} = -5.29\%$$

The bond's price declines by approximately 5.29 percent in response to a 50 basis point increase in yields.

Modified Duration

Some analysts prefer to use a variation of Macaulay duration called *modified duration*. The relationship between Macaulay duration and modified duration for bonds paying semiannual coupons is simply:

$$\text{Modified duration} = \frac{\text{Macaulay duration}}{(1 + YTM / 2)} \qquad (11.6)$$

As a result, based on modified duration, the approximate relationship between percentage changes in bond prices and changes in bond yields is just:

$$\text{Percentage change in bond price} \approx -\text{Modified duration} \times \text{Change in } YTM$$

$$(11.7)$$

In other words, to calculate the percentage change in the bond's price, we just multiply the modified duration by the change in yields.

MODIFIED DURATION

EXAMPLE 11.8

A bond has a Macaulay duration of 8.5 years and a yield to maturity of 9 percent. What is its modified duration?

The bond's modified duration is calculated as follows:

$$\frac{8.5}{1.045} = 8.134$$

Notice that we divided the yield by 2 to get the semiannual yield.

MODIFIED DURATION

EXAMPLE 11.9

A bond has a modified duration of seven years. Suppose its yield increases from 8 percent to 8.5 percent. What happens to its price?

We can very easily determine the resulting percentage change in the price of the bond using its modified duration:

$$-7 \times (.085 - .08) = -3.5\%$$

The bond's price declines by about 3.5 percent.

Calculating Macaulay Duration

Macaulay duration is often described as a bond's *effective maturity*. For this reason, duration values are conventionally stated in years. The first fundamental principle for calculating the duration of a bond concerns the duration of a zero coupon bond. Specifically, the duration of a zero coupon bond is equal to its maturity. Thus, on a pure discount instrument, such as the STRIPS we discussed in Chapter 10, no calculation is necessary to come up with Macaulay duration.

The second fundamental principle for calculating duration concerns the duration of a coupon bond with multiple cash flows. The duration of a coupon bond is a weighted average of individual maturities of all the bond's separate cash flows. The weights attached to the maturity of each cash flow are proportionate to the present values of each cash flow.

A sample duration calculation for a bond with three years until maturity is illustrated in Table 11.3. The bond sells at par value. It has an 8 percent coupon rate and an 8 percent yield to maturity.

As shown in Table 11.3, calculating a bond's duration can be laborious—especially if the bond has a large number of separate cash flows. Fortunately, relatively simple formulas are available for many of the important cases. For example, if a bond is selling for par value, its duration can be calculated easily using the following formula:

$$\text{Par value bond duration} = \frac{(1 + YTM/2)}{YTM}\left[1 - \frac{1}{(1 + YTM/2)^{2M}}\right] \quad (11.8)$$

TABLE 11.3	Calculating Bond Duration			
Years	Cash Flow	Discount Factor	Present Value	Years × Present Value ÷ Bond Price
0.5	$ 40	.96154	$ 38.4615	.0192 years
1	40	.92456	36.9822	.0370
1.5	40	.88900	35.5599	.0533
2	40	.85480	34.1922	.0684
2.5	40	.82193	32.8771	.0822
3	1,040	.79031	821.9271	2.4658
			$1,000.00	2.7259 years
			Bond Price	Bond Duration

where: M = Bond maturity in years

YTM = Yield to maturity assuming semiannual coupons

For example, using YTM = 8% and M = 3 years we obtain the same duration value (2.7259 years) computed in Table 11.3.

DURATION FOR A PAR VALUE BOND

EXAMPLE 11.10

Suppose a par value bond has a 6 percent coupon and 10 years to maturity. What is its duration?

Since the bond sells for par, its yield is equal to its coupon rate, 6 percent. Plugging this into the par value bond duration formula, we have:

$$\text{Par value bond duration} = \frac{(1+.06/2)}{.06}\left[1 - \frac{1}{(1+.06/2)^{20}}\right]$$

After a little work on a calculator, we find that the duration is 7.66 years.

The par value bond duration formula (Equation 11.8) is useful for calculating the duration of a bond that is actually selling at par value. Unfortunately, the general formula for bonds not necessarily selling at par value is somewhat more complicated. The general duration formula for a bond paying constant semiannual coupons is:

$$\text{Duration} = \frac{1+YTM/2}{YTM} - \frac{(1+YTM/2) + M(CPR - YTM)}{YTM + CPR[(1+YTM/2)^{2M} - 1]} \quad (11.9)$$

where: CPR = Constant annual coupon rate

M = Bond maturity in years

YTM = Yield to maturity assuming semiannual coupons

Although somewhat tedious for manual calculations, this formula is used in many computer programs that calculate bond durations. Some popular personal computer spreadsheet packages also have a built-in function to perform this calculation.

DURATION FOR A DISCOUNT BOND

EXAMPLE 11.11

A bond has a yield to maturity of 7 percent. It matures in 12 years. Its coupon rate is 6 percent. What is its modified duration?

We first must calculate the Macaulay duration using the unpleasant-looking formula just above. We finish by converting the Macaulay duration to modified duration. Plugging into the duration formula, we have:

$$\begin{aligned} \text{Duration} &= \frac{1+.07/2}{.07} - \frac{(1+.07/2) + 12(.06 - .07)}{.07 + .06[(1+.07/2)^{24} - 1]} \\ &= \frac{1.035}{.07} - \frac{1.035 + 12(-.01)}{.07 + .06(1.035^{24} - 1)} \end{aligned}$$

After a little button pushing, we find that the duration is 8.56 years. Finally, converting to modified duration, we find that the modified duration is equal to 8.56 / 1.035 = 8.27 years.

(continued)

SPREADSHEET ANALYSIS

	A	B	C	D	E	F	G	H
1								
2		Calculating Macaulay and Modified Durations						
3								
4	A bond traded on March 30, 2004, matures in 12 years on March 30, 2016.							
5	Assuming a 6 percent coupon rate and a 7 percent yield to maturity, what are the							
6	Macaulay and Modified durations of this bond?							
7	Hint: Use the Excel functions DURATION and MDURATION.							
8								
9		8.561	= DURATION("3/30/2004","3/30/2016",0.06,0.07,2,3)					
10								
11		8.272	= MDURATION("3/30/2004","3/30/2016",0.06,0.07,2,3)					
12								
13	These functions use the following arguments convention:							
14								
15		= DURATION("Now","Maturity",Coupon,Yield,2,3)						
16								
17	The 2 indicates semiannual coupons.							
18	The 3 specifies an actual day count with 365 days per year.							
19								
20								

Bond durations may be calculated using a built-in spreadsheet function. An example of how to use an Excel™ spreadsheet to calculate a Macaulay duration and modified duration is shown above.

Properties of Duration

Macaulay duration has a number of important properties. For straight bonds, the basic properties of Macaulay duration can be summarized as follows:

1. All else the same, the longer a bond's maturity, the longer is its duration.

2. All else the same, a bond's duration increases at a decreasing rate as maturity lengthens.

3. All else the same, the higher a bond's coupon, the shorter is its duration.

4. All else the same, a higher yield to maturity implies a shorter duration, and a lower yield to maturity implies a longer duration.

As we saw earlier, a zero coupon bond has a duration equal to its maturity. The duration on a bond with coupons is always less than its maturity. Because of the second principle, durations much longer than 10 or 15 years are rarely seen. There is an exception to some of these principles that involves very long maturity bonds selling at a very steep discount. This exception rarely occurs in practice, so these principles are generally correct.

A graphical illustration of the relationship between duration and maturity is presented in Figure 11.3, where duration is measured on the vertical axis and maturity is measured on the horizontal axis. In Figure 11.3, the yield to maturity for all bonds is 10 percent. Bonds with coupon rates of 0 percent, 5 percent, 10 percent, and 15 percent are presented. As the figure shows, the duration of a zero coupon

FIGURE 11.3   **Bond Duration and Maturity**

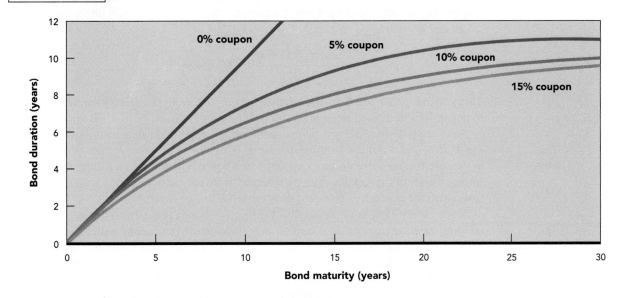

bond rises step for step with maturity. For the coupon bonds, however, the duration initially moves closely with maturity, as our first duration principle suggests, but, consistent with the second principle, the lines begin to flatten out after four or five years. Also, consistent with our third principle, the lower coupon bonds have higher durations.

CHECK THIS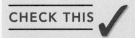

11.5a   What does duration measure?

11.5b   What is the duration of a zero coupon bond?

11.5c   What happens to a bond's duration as its maturity grows?

11.6   Dedicated Portfolios and Reinvestment Risk

Duration has another property that makes it a vital tool in bond portfolio management. To explore this subject, we first need to introduce two important concepts, dedicated portfolios and reinvestment risk.

Dedicated Portfolios

dedicated portfolio
A bond portfolio created to prepare for a future cash outlay.

Bond portfolios are often created for the purpose of preparing for a future liability payment or other cash outlay. A portfolio formed for such a specific purpose is called a **dedicated portfolio**. When the future liability payment of a dedicated portfolio is due on a known date, that date is commonly called the portfolio's *target date*.

Pension funds provide a good example of dedicated portfolio management. A pension fund normally knows years in advance the amount of benefit payments it must make to its beneficiaries. The fund then purchases bonds in the amount needed to prepare for these payments.

To illustrate, suppose the Safety First pension fund estimates that it must pay benefits of about $100 million in five years. Using semiannual discounting, and assuming that bonds currently yield 8 percent, the present value of Safety First's future liability is calculated as follows:

$$\frac{\$100,000,000}{(1.04)^{10}} \approx \$67,556,417$$

This amount, about $67.5 million, represents the investment necessary for Safety First to construct a dedicated bond portfolio to fund a future liability of $100 million.

Next, suppose the Safety First pension fund creates a dedicated portfolio by investing exactly $67.5 million in bonds selling at par value with a coupon rate of 8 percent to prepare for the $100 million payout in five years. The Safety First fund decides to follow a maturity matching strategy whereby it invests only in bonds with maturities that match the portfolio's five-year target date.

Since Safety First is investing $67.5 million in bonds that pay an 8 percent annual coupon, the fund receives $5.4 million in coupons each year, along with $67.5 million of principal at the bonds' five-year maturity. As the coupons come in, Safety First reinvests them. If all coupons are reinvested at an 8 percent yield, the fund's portfolio will grow to about $99.916 million on its target date. This is the future value of $67.5 million compounded at 4 percent semiannually for five years:

$$\$67.5 \text{ million} \times (1.04)^{10} \approx \$100 \text{ million}$$

This amount is also equal to the future value of all coupons reinvested at 8 percent, plus the $67.5 million of bond principal received at maturity. To see this, we calculate the future value of the coupons (using the standard formula for the future value of an annuity) and then add the $67.5 million:

$$\frac{\$5.4 \text{ million}}{.08}[(1.04)^{10} - 1] + \$67.5 \text{ million} \approx \$100 \text{ million}$$

Thus, as long as the annual coupons are reinvested at 8 percent, Safety First's bond fund will grow to the amount needed.

Reinvestment Risk

As we have seen, the bond investment strategy of the Safety First pension fund will be successful if all coupons received during the life of the investment can be reinvested at a constant 8 percent yield. However, in reality, yields at which coupons can be reinvested are uncertain, and a target date surplus or shortfall is therefore likely to occur.

The uncertainty about future or target date portfolio value that results from the need to reinvest bond coupons at yields that cannot be predicted in advance is called **reinvestment rate risk**. Thus, the uncertain portfolio value on the target date represents reinvestment risk. In general, more distant target dates entail greater uncertainty and reinvestment risk.

To examine the impact of reinvestment risk, we continue with the example of the Safety First pension fund's dedicated bond portfolio. We will consider two cases, one in which all bond coupons are reinvested at a higher 9 percent yield, and one in which all coupons are reinvested at a lower 7 percent yield. In this case, the payment of the

reinvestment rate risk The uncertainty about future or target date portfolio value that results from the need to reinvest bond coupons at yields not known in advance.

fixed $67.5 million principal plus the future value of the 10 semiannual coupons compounded at an uncertain rate, either 9 percent or 7 percent, comprises the total five-year target date portfolio value.

For 9 percent and 7 percent yields, these target date portfolio values are calculated as follows:

$$\frac{\$5.4 \text{ million}}{.09}[(1.045)^{10} - 1] + \$67.5 \text{ million} = \$100.678 \text{ million}$$

and

$$\frac{\$5.4 \text{ million}}{.07}[(1.035)^{10} - 1] + \$67.5 \text{ million} = \$99.175 \text{ million}$$

As shown, a target date portfolio value of $100.678 million is realized through a 9 percent reinvestment rate, and a value of $99.175 million is realized by a 7 percent reinvestment rate. The difference between these two amounts, about $1.5 million, represents reinvestment risk.

As this example illustrates, a maturity matching strategy for a dedicated bond portfolio entails substantial reinvestment risk. Indeed, this example understates a pension fund's total reinvestment risk since it considers only a single target date. In reality, pension funds have a series of target dates, and a shortfall at one target date typically coincides with shortfalls at other target dates as well.

A simple solution for reinvestment risk is to purchase zero coupon bonds that pay a fixed principal at a maturity chosen to match a dedicated portfolio's target date. Since there are no coupons to reinvest, there is no reinvestment risk! However, a zero coupon bond strategy has its drawbacks. As a practical matter, STRIPS are the only zero coupon bonds issued in sufficient quantity to even begin to satisfy the dedicated portfolio needs of pension funds, insurance companies, and other institutional investors. However, government securities have lower yields than even the highest quality corporate bonds. A yield difference of only .25 percent between government and corporate bonds can make a substantial difference in the initial cost of a dedicated bond portfolio.

For example, suppose that STRIPS have a yield of 7.75 percent. Using semiannual compounding, the present value of these zero coupon bonds providing a principal payment of $100 million at a five-year maturity is calculated as follows:

$$\frac{\$100 \text{ million}}{(1.03875)^{10}} \approx \$68.374 \text{ million}$$

This cost of $68.374 million based on a 7.75 percent yield is significantly higher than the previously stated cost of $67.556 million based on an 8 percent yield. From the perspective of the Safety First pension fund, this represents a hefty premium to pay to eliminate reinvestment risk. Fortunately, as we discuss in the next section, other methods are available at lower cost.

CHECK THIS ✓

11.6a What is a dedicated portfolio?

11.6b What is reinvestment rate risk?

11.7 Immunization

immunization Constructing a portfolio to minimize the uncertainty surrounding its target date value.

Constructing a dedicated portfolio to minimize the uncertainty in its target date value is called **immunization**. In this section, we show how duration can be used to immunize a bond portfolio against reinvestment risk.

Price Risk versus Reinvestment Rate Risk

To understand how immunization is accomplished, suppose you own a bond with eight years to maturity. However, your target date is actually just six years from now. If interest rates rise, are you happy or unhappy?

price risk The risk that bond prices will decrease, which arises in dedicated portfolios when the target date value of a bond or bond portfolio is not known with certainty.

Your initial reaction is probably "unhappy" because you know that as interest rates rise, bond values fall. However, things are not so simple. Clearly, if interest rates rise, then, in six years, your bond will be worth less than it would have been at a lower rate. This is called **price risk**. However, it is also true that you will be able to reinvest the coupons you receive at a higher interest rate. As a result, your reinvested coupons will be worth more. In fact, the net effect of an interest rate increase might be to make you *better* off.

As our simple example illustrates, for a dedicated portfolio, interest rate changes have two effects. Interest rate increases act to decrease bond prices (price risk) but increase the future value of reinvested coupons (reinvestment rate risk). In the other direction, interest rate decreases act to increase bond values but decrease the future value of reinvested coupons. The key observation is that these two effects—price risk and reinvestment rate risk—tend to offset each other.

You might wonder if it is possible to engineer a portfolio in which these two effects offset each other more or less precisely. As we illustrate next, the answer is most definitely yes.

Immunization by Duration Matching

The key to immunizing a dedicated portfolio is to match its duration to its target date. If this is done, then the impacts of price and reinvestment rate risk will almost exactly offset, and interest rate changes will have a minimal impact on the target date value of the portfolio. In fact, immunization is often simply referred to as duration matching.

To see how a duration matching strategy can be applied to reduce target date uncertainty, suppose the Safety First pension fund initially purchases $67.5 million of par value bonds paying 8 percent coupons with a maturity of 6.2 years. From the par value duration formula we discussed earlier, a maturity of 6.2 years corresponds to a duration of 5 years. Thus, the duration of Safety First's dedicated bond portfolio is now matched to its five-year portfolio target date.

Suppose that immediately after the bonds are purchased, a one-time shock causes bond yields to either jump up to 10 percent or jump down to 6 percent. As a result, all coupons are reinvested at either a 10 percent yield or a 6 percent yield, depending on which way rates jump.

This example is illustrated in Figure 11.4, where the left vertical axis measures initial bond portfolio values, and the right vertical axis measures bond portfolio values realized by holding the portfolio until the bonds mature in 6.2 years. The horizontal axis measures the passage of time from initial investment to bond maturity. The positively sloped lines plot bond portfolio values through time for bond yields that have jumped to

FIGURE 11.4   **Bond Price and Reinvestment Rate Risk**

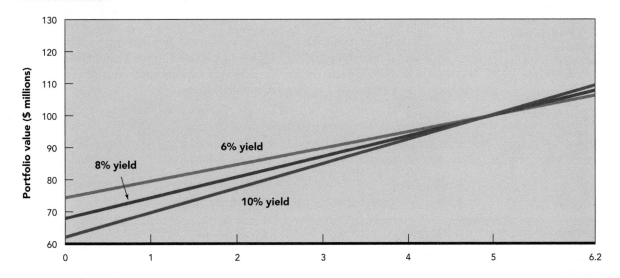

either 10 percent or 6 percent immediately after the initial investment of $67.5 million in par value 8 percent coupon bonds. This example assumes that after their initial jump, bond yields remain unchanged.

As shown in Figure 11.4, the initial jump in yields causes the value of Safety First's bond portfolio to jump in the opposite direction. If yields increase, bond prices fall, but coupons are reinvested at a higher interest rate, thereby leading to a higher portfolio value at maturity. In contrast, if yields decrease, bond prices rise, but a lower reinvestment rate reduces the value of the portfolio at maturity.

However, what is remarkable is that regardless of whether yields rise or fall, there is almost no difference in Safety First's portfolio value at the duration-matched five-year target date. Thus, the immunization strategy of matching the duration of Safety First's dedicated portfolio to its portfolio target date has almost entirely eliminated reinvestment risk.

Dynamic Immunization

The example of the Safety First pension fund immunizing a dedicated bond portfolio by a duration matching strategy assumed that the bond portfolio was subject to a single yield shock. In reality, bond yields change constantly. Therefore, successful immunization requires that a dedicated portfolio be rebalanced frequently to maintain a portfolio duration equal to the portfolio's target date.

For example, by purchasing bonds with a maturity of 6.2 years, the Safety First pension fund had matched the duration of the dedicated portfolio to the fund's 5-year target date. One year later, however, the target date is 4 years away, and bonds with a duration of 4 years are required to maintain a duration matching strategy. Assuming interest rates haven't changed, the par value duration formula shows that a maturity of 4.7 years corresponds to a duration of 4 years. Thus, to maintain a duration-matched target date, the Safety First fund must sell its originally purchased bonds now with a maturity of 5.2 years and replace them with bonds having a maturity of 4.7 years.

dynamic immunization Periodic rebalancing of a dedicated bond portfolio to maintain a duration that matches the target maturity date.

The strategy of periodically rebalancing a dedicated bond portfolio to maintain a portfolio duration matched to a specific target date is called **dynamic immunization**. The advantage of dynamic immunization is that reinvestment risk caused by continually changing bond yields is greatly reduced. The drawback of dynamic immunization is that each portfolio rebalancing incurs management and transaction costs. Therefore, portfolios should not be rebalanced too frequently. In practice, rebalancing on an intermittent basis, say, each quarter, is a reasonable compromise between the costs of rebalancing and the benefits of dynamic immunization.

CHECK THIS ✓

11.7a What are the two effects on the target date value of a dedicated portfolio of a shift in yields? Explain why they tend to offset.

11.7b How can a dedicated portfolio be immunized against shifts in yields?

11.7c Why is rebalancing necessary to maintain immunization?

11.8 Convexity

If we examine Figure 11.2, which graphs bond prices as a function of bond yields, we see that we do not have a line, but a convex curve. Remember Equation 11.7 is only an approximate formula to calculate percentage change in bond price as a function of change in YTM.

Figure 11.5 shows the percentage price change of a bond as the function of yield change. As we can see from the graph, duration formula becomes inadequate for big changes in the yield.

In order to get a more precise formula we need to calculate convexity of a bond and revise Equation 11.7 to include convexity.

Convexity of a bond is calculated as follows:

$$\text{Convexity} = \frac{1}{P \times (1 + YTM/2)^2} \sum_{t=1}^{n} \left[\frac{C_t}{(1 + YTM/2)t} (t + t^2) \right] \quad (11.10)$$

P = Price of the bond, C_t = Cash Flow at time t, t = time period

CONVEXITY

EXAMPLE 11.12

Calculate the convexity of a province of Saskatchewan bond that has a 6.25 percent coupon rate and two-year maturity. The bond has 3 percent yield to maturity and a price of 106.263 percent.

$$\text{Convexity} = \frac{1}{1062.263 \times (1.015)^2} \left[\frac{31.25 \times (1+1)}{(1.015)} + \frac{31.25 \times (2+4)}{(1.015)^2} + \frac{31.25 \times (3+9)}{(1.015)^3} + \frac{1031.25 \times (4+16)}{(1.015)^4} \right]$$

$$= 18.30$$

FIGURE 11.5

Bond Price Changes

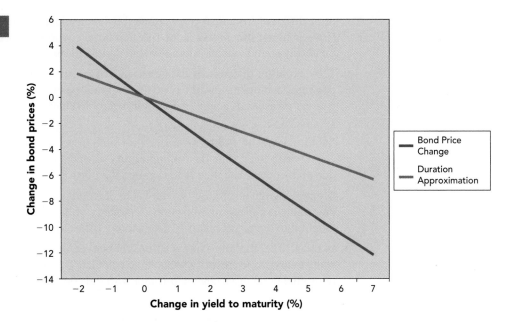

Bonds with high convexity values experience a higher price increase when interest rates fall and a lower price decrease when interest rates increase. Investors prefer bonds with high convexity values.

If we add the convexity correction to Equation 11.7, we get the following formula:

$$\text{Percentage change in bond price} = -\text{Modified duration} \times \text{Change in YTM} + \frac{1}{2}\text{convexity} \times (\text{Change in YTM})^2$$

(11.11)

11.9 Summary and Conclusions

This chapter covers the basics of bonds, bond yields, duration, and immunization. In this chapter we saw that:

1. Bonds are commonly distinguished according to whether they are selling at par value or at a discount or premium relative to par value. Bonds with a price greater than par value are said to be selling at a premium; bonds with a price less than par value are said to be selling at a discount.

2. There are three different yield measures: coupon yield or rate, current yield, and yield to maturity. Each is calculated using a specific equation, and which is the biggest or smallest depends on whether the bond is selling at a discount or premium.

3. Important relationships among bond prices, maturities, coupon rates, and yields are described by Malkiel's five bond price theorems.

4. A stated yield to maturity is almost never equal to an actually realized yield because yields are subject to bond price risk and coupon reinvestment rate risk. Bond price risk is the risk that a bond sold before maturity must be sold at a

price different from the price predicted by an originally stated yield to maturity. Coupon reinvestment risk is the risk that bond coupons must be reinvested at yields different from an originally stated yield to maturity.

5. To account for differences in interest rate risk across bonds with different coupon rates and maturities, the concept of duration is widely applied. Duration is a direct measure of a bond's price sensitivity to changes in bond yields.

6. Bond portfolios are often created for the purpose of preparing for a future liability payment. Portfolios formed for such a specific purpose are called dedicated portfolios. When the future liability payment of a dedicated portfolio is due on a known date, that date is called the portfolio's target date.

7. Minimizing the uncertainty of the value of a dedicated portfolio's future target date value is called immunization. A strategy of matching a bond portfolio's duration to the target maturity date accomplishes this goal.

8. In order to capture the exact relationship between bond price change and change in yield to maturity we need to calculate the convexity of a bond and revise the bond price change formula with the convexity term.

REAL WORLD

This chapter covered bond basics. How should you, as an investor or investment manager, put this information to work?

Now that you've been exposed to basic facts about bonds, their prices, and their yields, you might try applying the various principles we have discussed. Do this by buying some bonds and then observing the behaviour of their prices and yields. Buying Treasury bonds is the best place to start.

With a simulated brokerage account (such as Stock-Trak), buy two Treasury bonds with the same maturity but different coupons. This will let you see the impact of coupon rates on price volatility. Similarly, buy two bonds with very different maturities but similar coupon rates. You'll see firsthand how maturity determines the risk of a bond.

While you're at it, calculate the durations of the bonds you buy. As their yields fluctuate, check that the percentage change in price is very close to what your calculated duration suggests it should be.

To learn more about bond prices and yields, visit some interesting websites such as Bonds Online (www.bondsonline.com), Investing in Bonds (www.investinginbonds.com), and James Baker & Assoc. (www.jamesbaker.com).

Key Terms

coupon rate 348
current yield 349
yield to maturity (YTM) 349
clean price 354
dirty price 354
callable bond 357
call price 357
call protection period 358
yield to call (YTC) 358

interest rate risk 359
realized yield 360
duration 364
dedicated portfolio 369
reinvestment rate risk 370
immunization 372
price risk 372
dynamic immunization 374

Chapter Review Problems and Self-Test

1. **Straight Bond Prices** Suppose a bond has 10 years to maturity and a coupon rate of 6 percent. The bond's yield to maturity is 8 percent. What's the price?

2. **Premium Bonds** Suppose we have two bonds, both with a 6 percent coupon rate and the same yield to maturity of 4 percent, but with different maturities of 5 and 15 years. Which has the higher price? Verify your answer by calculating the prices.

3. **Macaulay Duration** A bond has a Macaulay duration of nine years, and its yield increases from 6 percent to 6.25 percent. What will happen to the price of the bond?

Answers to Self-Test Problems

1. Here, the coupon rate is 6 percent and the face value is $1,000, so the annual coupon is $60. The bond's price is calculated as follows:

   Present value of semiannual coupons:

   $$\frac{\$60}{.08}\left[1 - \frac{1}{(1.04)^{20}}\right] = \$407.70979$$

   Present value of $1,000 principal:

   $$\frac{\$1,000}{(1.04)^{20}} = \$456.38695$$

   The bond's price is the sum of coupon and principal present values:

   $$\text{Bond price} = \$407.71 + \$456.39 = \$864.10$$

2. Because both bonds have a 6 percent coupon and a 4 percent yield, both bonds sell at a premium, and the one with the longer maturity will have a higher price. We can verify these conclusions by calculating the prices as follows:

   5-year maturity premium bond price:

   $$\frac{\$60}{.04}\left[1 - \frac{1}{(1.02)^{10}}\right] + \frac{\$1,000}{(1.02)^{10}} = \$1,089.83$$

   15-year maturity premium bond price:

   $$\frac{\$60}{.04}\left[1 - \frac{1}{(1.02)^{30}}\right] + \frac{\$1,000}{(1.02)^{30}} = \$1,223.96$$

   Notice that the longer maturity premium bond has a higher price, just as we thought.

3. The resulting percentage change in the price of the bond can be calculated as follows:

   $$-9 \times \frac{.0625 - .06}{1.03} = -2.18\%$$

   The bond's price declines by approximately 2.18 percent in response to a 25 basis point increase in yields.

Test Your Investment Quotient

1. **Yield to Maturity** The yield to maturity on a bond is
   a. Below the coupon rate when the bond sells at a discount and above the coupon rate when the bond sells at a premium.
   b. The interest rate that makes the present value of the payments equal to the bond price.
   c. Based on the assumption that all future payments received are reinvested at the coupon rate.
   d. Based on the assumption that all future payments received are reinvested at future market rates.

2. **Bond Yields** In which one of the following cases is the bond selling at a discount?
   a. Coupon rate is greater than current yield, which is greater than yield to maturity.
   b. Coupon rate, current yield, and yield to maturity are all the same.
   c. Coupon rate is less than current yield, which is less than yield to maturity.
   d. Coupon rate is less than current yield, which is greater than yield to maturity.

3. **Bond Yields** When are yield to maturity and current yield on a bond equal?
   a. When market interest rates begin to level off.
   b. If the bond sells at a price in excess of its par value.
   c. When the expected holding period is greater than one year.
   d. If the coupon and market interest rate are equal.

4. **Bond Yields** Which of the following states the correct relationship among yield measures for discount bonds?
   a. Coupon rate < Current yield < Yield to maturity
   b. Current yield < Coupon rate < Yield to maturity
   c. Coupon rate < Yield to maturity < Current yield
   d. Yield to maturity < Coupon rate < Current yield

5. **Bond Yields** Which of the following states the correct relationship among yield measures for premium bonds?
   a. Coupon rate > Current yield > Yield to maturity
   b. Current yield > Coupon rate > Yield to maturity
   c. Coupon rate > Yield to maturity > Current yield
   d. Yield to maturity > Coupon rate > Current yield

6. **Bond Prices** Consider a five-year bond with a 10 percent coupon that is presently trading at a yield to maturity of 8 percent. If market interest rates do not change, one year from now the price of this bond
   a. Will be higher
   b. Will be lower
   c. Will be the same
   d. Cannot be determined

7. **Bond Prices** Using semiannual compounding, what would be the price of a 15-year, zero coupon bond that has a par value of $1,000 and a required return of 8 percent?
   a. $308
   b. $315
   c. $464
   d. $555

8. **Bond Prices** If an investor's required return is 12 percent, the value of a 10-year maturity zero coupon bond with a maturity value of $1,000 is *closest* to
   a. $312
   b. $688

    c. $1,000
    d. $1,312

9. **Duration** Another term for bond duration is

    a. Actual maturity
    b. Effective maturity
    c. Calculated maturity
    d. Near-term maturity

10. **Duration** Which of the following is not a property of duration?

    a. A longer maturity generally yields a longer duration.
    b. Duration generally increases at a decreasing rate as maturity lengthens.
    c. A bigger coupon generally yields a longer duration.
    d. A higher yield to maturity generally yields a shorter duration.

11. **Duration** Which statement is true for the Macaulay duration of a zero coupon bond?

    a. It is equal to the bond's maturity in years.
    b. It is equal to one-half the bond's maturity in years.
    c. It is equal to the bond's maturity in years divided by its yield to maturity.
    d. It cannot be calculated because of the lack of coupons.

12. **Duration** Which of the following states the correct relationship between Macaulay duration and modified duration?

    a. Modified duration = Macaulay duration $/ (1 + YTM / 2)$
    b. Modified duration = Macaulay duration $\times (1 + YTM / 2)$
    c. Modified duration = Macaulay duration $/ YTM$
    d. Modified duration = Macaulay duration $\times YTM$

13. **Duration** Which one of the following bonds has the shortest duration?

    a. Zero coupon, 10-year maturity.
    b. Zero coupon, 13-year maturity.
    c. 8 percent coupon, 10-year maturity.
    d. 8 percent coupon, 13-year maturity.

14. **Duration** Identify the bond that has the longest duration (no calculations necessary).

    a. 20-year maturity with an 8 percent coupon.
    b. 20-year maturity with a 12 percent coupon.
    c. 15-year maturity with a 0 percent coupon.
    d. 10-year maturity with a 15 percent coupon.

15. **Duration** Which bond has the longest duration?

    a. 8-year maturity, 6 percent coupon.
    b. 8-year maturity, 11 percent coupon.
    c. 15-year maturity, 6 percent coupon.
    d. 15-year maturity, 11 percent coupon.

16. **Duration** The duration of a bond normally increases with an increase in

    a. Term to maturity
    b. Yield to maturity
    c. Coupon rate
    d. All of the above

17. **Duration** When interest rates decline, what happens to the duration of a 30-year bond selling at a premium?

    a. It increases.
    b. It decreases.
    c. It remains the same.
    d. It increases at first, then declines.

18. **Duration** An 8 percent, 20-year corporate bond is priced to yield 9 percent. The Macaulay duration for this bond is 8.85 years. Given this information, how many years is the bond's modified duration?

   a. 8.12
   b. 8.47
   c. 8.51
   d. 9.25

19. **Using Duration** A 9-year bond has a yield to maturity of 10 percent and a modified duration of 6.54 years. If the market yield changes by 50 basis points, what is the change in the bond's price?

   a. 3.27 percent
   b. 3.66 percent
   c. 6.54 percent
   d. 7.21 percent

20. **Using Duration** A 6 percent coupon bond paying interest semiannually has a modified duration of 10 years, sells for $800, and is priced at a yield to maturity (YTM) of 8 percent. If the YTM increases to 9 percent, the predicted change in price, using the duration concept, is which of the following amounts?

   a. $76.56
   b. $76.92
   c. $77.67
   d. $80.00

21. **Immunization** Which of the following strategies is most likely to yield the best interest rate risk immunization results for a bond portfolio?

   a. Maturity matching.
   b. Duration matching.
   c. Buy and hold.
   d. Investing in interest rate-sensitive stocks.

22. **Immunization** Consider two dedicated bond portfolios both with the same 10-year target dates. One is managed using a buy-and-hold strategy with reinvested coupons. The other is managed using a dynamic immunization strategy. The buy-and-hold portfolio is most likely to outperform the immunized portfolio under what kind of interest rate environment?

   a. Steadily rising interest rates.
   b. Steadily falling interest rates.
   c. Constant interest rates.
   d. Performance will be the same under any environment.

23. **Bond Yields** A zero coupon bond paying $100 at maturity 10 years from now has a current price of $50. Its yield to maturity is *closest* to which of the following?

   a. 5 percent
   b. 6 percent
   c. 7 percent
   d. 8 percent

24. **Bond Price** A newly issued 10-year option-free bond is valued at par on June 1, 2000. The bond has an annual coupon of 8.0 percent. On June 1, 2003, the bond has a yield to maturity of 7.1 percent. The first coupon is reinvested at 8.0 percent and the second coupon is reinvested at 7.0 percent. The price of the bond on June 1, 2003, is closest to

   a. 100.0 percent of par
   b. 102.5 percent of par
   c. 104.8 percent of par
   d. 105.4 percent of par

25. **Interest Rate Risk** The interest rate risk of a noncallable bond is most likely to be positively related to the
    a. Risk-free rate
    b. Bond's coupon rate
    c. Bond's time to maturity
    d. Bond's yield to maturity

Concept Questions

1. **Bond Prices** What are premium, discount, and par bonds?

2. **Bond Features** What is the normal face value for corporate and government bonds? How are coupons calculated? How often are coupons paid?

3. **Coupon Rates and Current Yields** What are the coupon rate and current yield on a bond? What happens to these if a bond's price rises?

4. **Interest Rate Risk** What is interest rate risk? What are the roles of a bond's coupon and maturity in determining its level of interest rate risk?

5. **Bond Yields** For a premium bond, which is greater, the coupon rate or the yield to maturity? Why? For a discount bond? Why?

6. **Bond Yields** What is the difference between a bond's promised yield and its realized yield? Which is more relevant? When we calculate a bond's yield to maturity, which of these are we calculating?

7. **Interpreting Bond Yields** Is the yield to maturity (YTM) on a bond the same thing as the required return? Is YTM the same thing as the coupon rate? Suppose that today a 10 percent coupon bond sells at par. Two years from now, the required return on the same bond is 8 percent. What is the coupon rate on the bond now? The YTM?

8. **Interpreting Bond Yields** Suppose you buy a 9 percent coupon, 15-year bond today when it's first issued. If interest rates suddenly rise to 15 percent, what happens to the value of your bond? Why?

9. **Bond Prices versus Yields** (a) What is the relationship between the price of a bond and its YTM? (b) Explain why some bonds sell at a premium to par value, and other bonds sell at a discount. What do you know about the relationship between the coupon rate and the YTM for premium bonds? What about discount bonds? For bonds selling at par value? (c) What is the relationship between the current yield and YTM for premium bonds? For discount bonds? For bonds selling at par value?

10. **Yield to Call** For callable bonds, the financial press generally reports either the yield to maturity or the yield to call. Often yield to call is reported for premium bonds, and yield to maturity is reported for discount bonds. What is the reasoning behind this convention?

Questions and Problems

Core Questions

1. **Bond Prices** Reynolds Inc. has 9 percent coupon bonds on the market that have 15 years left to maturity. If the YTM on these bonds is 8.2 percent, what is the current bond price?

2. **Bond Yields** Corpstein Company bonds have a coupon rate of 8 percent, 19 years to maturity, and a current price of $904. What is the YTM? The current yield?

3. **Bond Prices** A bond has a coupon rate of 7.5 percent and 13 years until maturity. If the yield to maturity is 6.3 percent, what is the price of the bond?

4. **Bond Prices** A bond with 25 years until maturity has a coupon rate of 9 percent and a yield to maturity of 6.5 percent. What is the price of the bond?

5. **Yield to Maturity** A bond sells for $864.50 and has a coupon rate of 8 percent. If the bond has 16 years until maturity, what is the yield to maturity of the bond?

6. **Yield to Maturity** A bond with a maturity of 19.5 years sells for $913. If the coupon rate is 6 percent, what is the yield to maturity of the bond?

7. **Yield to Maturity** Shane Industries has a bond outstanding that sells for $1,118. The bond has coupon rate of 7.5 percent and nine years until maturity. What is the yield to maturity of the bond?

8. **Yield to Maturity** Sealord Fisheries issues zero coupon bonds on the market at a price of $180 per bond. Each bond has a face value of $1,000 payable at maturity in 20 years. What is the yield to maturity for these bonds?

9. **Yield to Call** Sealord Fisheries zero coupon bonds referred to above are callable in 10 years at a call price of $500. Using semiannual compounding, what is the yield to call for these bonds?

10. **Yield to Call** If instead the Sealord Fisheries zero coupon bonds referred to above are callable in 10 years at a call price of $475, what is their yield to call?

Intermediate Questions

11. **Coupon Rates** Raider Corporation has bonds on the market with 13 years to maturity, a YTM of 7.5 percent, and a current price of $1,082.20. What must the coupon rate be on the company's bonds?

12. **Bond Prices** Perry's Pizzeria issued 20-year bonds one year ago at a coupon rate of 9.40 percent. If the YTM on these bonds is 9.02 percent, what is the current bond price?

13. **Bond Yields** Soprano's Spaghetti Factory issued 30-year bonds two years ago at a coupon rate of 8.5 percent. If these bonds currently sell for 78 percent of par value, what is the YTM?

14. **Bond Price Movements** A zero coupon bond with an 8 percent YTM has 20 years to maturity. Two years later, the price of the bond remains the same. What's going on here?

15. **Realized Yield** For the bond referred to in the previous question, what would be the realized yield if it were held to maturity?

16. **Bond Price Movements** Bond P is a premium bond with a 9 percent coupon, a YTM of 7 percent, and 15 years to maturity. Bond D is a discount bond with a 9 percent coupon, a YTM of 11 percent, and also 15 years to maturity. If interest rates remain unchanged, what do you expect the price of these bonds to be 1 year from now? In 5 years? In 10 years? In 14 years? In 15 years? What's going on here?

17. **Interest Rate Risk** Both bond A and bond B have 8 percent coupons and are priced at par value. Bond A has 2 years to maturity, while bond B has 15 years to maturity. If interest rates suddenly rise by 2 percent, what is the percentage change in price of bond A? Of bond B? If rates were to suddenly fall by 2 percent instead, what would the percentage change in price of bond A be now? Of bond B? Illustrate your answers by graphing bond prices versus YTM. What does this problem tell you about the interest rate risk of longer term bonds?

18. **Interest Rate Risk** Bond J is a 5 percent coupon bond. Bond K is a 9 percent coupon bond. Both bonds have 10 years to maturity and have a YTM of 7 percent. If interest rates suddenly rise by 2 percent, what is the percentage price change of these bonds? What if rates suddenly fall by 2 percent instead? What does this problem tell you about the interest rate risk of lower-coupon bonds?

19. **Finding the Bond Maturity** Crosby Co. has 7.5 percent coupon bonds with a YTM of 6.98 percent. The current yield on these bonds is 7.22 percent. How many years do these bonds have left until they mature?

20. **Finding the Bond Maturity** You've just found a 10 percent coupon bond on the market that sells for par value. What is the maturity on this bond?

21. **Realized Yields** Suppose you buy a 9 percent coupon bond today for $1,080. The bond has 15 years to maturity. What rate of return do you expect to earn on your investment? Two years from now, the YTM on your bond has increased by 2 percent, and you decide to sell. What price will your bond sell for? What is the realized yield on your investment? Compare this yield to the YTM when you first bought the bond. Why are they different? Assume interest payments are reinvested at the original YTM.

22. **Yield to Call** Fooling Company has a 12 percent callable bond outstanding on the market with 20 years to maturity, call protection for the next 5 years, and a call premium of $80. What is the yield to call (YTC) for this bond if the current price is 118 percent of par value?

23. **Calculating Duration** What is the Macaulay duration of a 7 percent coupon bond with nine years to maturity and a current price of $1,130.60? What is the modified duration?

24. **Using Duration** In the previous problem, suppose the yield on the bond suddenly increases by 2 percent. Use duration to estimate the new price of the bond. Compare your answer to the new bond price calculated from the usual bond pricing formula. What do your results tell you about the accuracy of duration?

25. **Calculating Duration** A bond with a coupon rate of 9 percent sells at a yield to maturity of 10 percent. If the bond matures in 17 years, what is the Macaulay duration of the bond? What is the modified duration?

26. **Calculating Duration** Assume the bond in the previous problem has a yield to maturity of 8 percent. What is the Macaulay duration now? What does this tell you about the relationship between duration and yield to maturity?

27. **Calculating Duration** You find a bond with 25 years until maturity that has a coupon rate of 8 percent and a yield to maturity of 7 percent. What is the Macaulay duration? The modified duration?

28. **Using Duration** Suppose the yield to maturity on the bond in the previous problem increases by .25 percent. What is the new price of the bond using duration? What is the new price of the bond using the bond pricing formula? What if the yield to maturity increases by 1 percent? By 2 percent? By 5 percent? What does this tell you about using duration to estimate bond price changes for large interest rate changes?

29. **Using Duration** Noah Kramer, a fixed-income portfolio manager based in the country of Sevista, is considering the purchase of Sevista government bonds. Sevista currently has government bonds evenly distributed among 5-, 10-, and 25-year maturities. Noah decides to evaluate two strategies for investing in Sevista bonds. The following table shows the details of the two strategies.

Strategy	5-Year Maturity Modified Duration = 4.83	15-Year Maturity Modified Duration = 14.35	25-Year Maturity Modified Duration = 23.81
I	$5 million	$0	$5 million
II	$0	10 million	$0

The market value of the bonds purchased will be $10 million and the target modified duration is 15 years. Before choosing one of the two bond investment strategies, Kramer wants to study how the market value of the bonds will change if an instantaneous interest rate shift occurs immediately after his investment. The details of the interest rate shift are shown below.

Interest Rate Maturity (years)	Interest Rate Change (basis points)
5	Down 75
15	Up 25
25	Up 50

Calculate, for this instantaneous interest rate shift, the percentage change in the market value of the bonds that will occur under each investment strategy.

30. Bootstrapping One method of obtaining an estimate of the term structure of interest rates is called bootstrapping. Suppose you have a one-year zero coupon bond with a rate of r_1 and a two-year bond with an annual coupon payment of C. To bootstrap the two-year rate, you can set up the following equation for the price (P) of the coupon bond:

$$P = \frac{C_1}{1 + r_1} + \frac{C_2 + \text{Par value}}{(1 + r_2)^2}$$

Since you can observe all of the variables except r_2, the spot rate for two years, you can solve for this interest rate. Suppose there is a zero coupon bond with one year to maturity that sells for $952 and a two-year bond with a 7 percent coupon paid annually that sells for $1,032. What is the interest rate for two years? Suppose a bond with three years until maturity and an 8 percent annual coupon sells for $1,060. What is the interest rate for three years?

31. Bootstrapping You find that the one-, two-, three-, and four-year interest rates are 5.20 percent, 5.85 percent, 6.15 percent, and 6.75 percent. What is the yield to maturity of a four-year bond with an annual coupon rate of 8 percent? *Hint*: Use the bootstrapping technique in the previous problem to find the price of the bond.

Spreadsheet Problems

32. Yield to Maturity A Treasury bond that settles on August 10, 2006, matures on April 15, 2011. The coupon rate is 5.6 percent and the quoted price is 106:17. What is the bond's yield to maturity? Use an actual day count with 365 days per year.

33. Bond Yields A bond that settles on June 7, 2006, matures on July 1, 2030, and may be called at any time after July 1, 2010, at a price of 108. The coupon rate on the bond is 8 percent and the price is 111.50. What is the yield to maturity and yield to call on this bond? Use the NASD 30/360-day count basis.

34. Duration A Treasury bond that settles on October 18, 2006, matures on March 30, 2021. The coupon rate is 8.2 percent and the bond has a 6.85 yield to maturity. What are the Macaulay duration and modified duration?

35. Convexity Caterpillar Corporation's 5.25% coupon, 10 year maturity bond is selling for 97.303 and is providing a 5.6% yield. Calculate the convexity of this bond.

36. Convexity GE has issued a 5.00% coupon bond. The bond has a 12-year maturity. The price and yield of the bond are 94.55 and 5.663%. Calculate the convexity of this bond.

PART 4

Portfolio Management

CHAPTER 12

Return, Risk, and the Security Market Line

"To be alive at all involves some risk."

—Harold MacMillan

An important insight of modern financial theory is that some investment risks yield an expected reward, while other risks do not. Essentially, risks that can be eliminated by diversification do not yield an expected reward, and risks that cannot be eliminated by diversification do yield an expected reward. Thus, financial markets are somewhat fussy regarding what risks are rewarded and what risks are not. ■

Chapter 1 presented some important lessons from capital market history. The most noteworthy, perhaps, is that there is a reward, on average, for bearing risk. We called this reward a *risk premium*. The second lesson is that this risk premium is positively correlated with an investment's risk.

In this chapter, we return to an examination of the reward for bearing risk. Specifically, we have two tasks to accomplish. First, we have to define risk more precisely and then discuss how to measure it. Second, once we have a better understanding of just what we mean by "risk," we will go on to quantify the relation between risk and return in financial markets.

When we examine the risks associated with individual assets, we find there are two types of risk: systematic and unsystematic. This distinction is crucial because, as we will see, systematic risk affects almost all assets in the economy, at least to some degree, whereas unsystematic risk affects at most only a small number of assets. This observation allows us to say a great deal about the risks and returns on individual assets. In particular, it is the basis for a famous relationship between risk and return called the *security market line*, or SML. To develop the SML, we introduce the equally famous beta coefficient, one of the centrepieces of modern finance. Beta and the SML are key concepts because they supply us with at least part of the answer to the question of how to go about determining the expected return on a risky investment.

12.1 Announcements, Surprises, and Expected Returns

We now begin to describe more carefully the risks and returns associated with individual securities. Thus far, we have measured volatility by looking at the difference between the actual return on an asset or portfolio, R, and the expected return, $E(R)$. We now look at why those deviations exist.

Expected and Unexpected Returns

To begin, consider the return on the stock of a hypothetical company called Flyers. What will determine this stock's return in, say, the coming year?

The return on any stock traded in a financial market is composed of two parts. First, the normal, or expected, return from the stock is the part of the return that investors predict or expect. This return depends on the information investors have about the stock, and it is based on the market's understanding today of the important factors that will influence the stock in the coming year.

The second part of the return on the stock is the uncertain, or risky, part. This is the portion that comes from unexpected information revealed during the year. A list of all possible sources of such information would be endless, but here are a few basic examples:

News about Flyers's product research.

Government figures released on gross domestic product.

The results from the latest arms control talks.

The news that Flyers's sales figures are higher than expected.

A sudden, unexpected drop in interest rates.

Based on this discussion, one way to express the return on Flyers stock in the coming year would be

$$\text{Total return} - \text{Expected return} = \text{Unexpected return} \qquad (12.1)$$

or

$$R - E(R) = U$$

where R stands for the actual total return in the year, $E(R)$ stands for the expected part of the return, and U stands for the unexpected part of the return. What this says is that the actual return, R, differs from the expected return, $E(R)$, because of surprises that occur during the year. In any given year, the unexpected return will be positive or negative, but, through time, the average value of U will be zero. This simply means that, on average, the actual return equals the expected return.

Announcements and News

We need to be careful when we talk about the effect of news items on stock returns. For example, suppose Flyers's business is such that the company prospers when gross domestic product (GDP) grows at a relatively high rate and suffers when GDP is relatively stagnant. In this case, in deciding what return to expect this year from owning stock in Flyers, investors either implicitly or explicitly must think about what GDP is likely to be for the coming year.

When the government actually announces GDP figures for the year, what will happen to the value of Flyers stock? Obviously, the answer depends on what figure is released. More to the point, however, the impact depends on how much of that figure actually represents new information.

At the beginning of the year, market participants will have some idea or forecast of what the yearly GDP figure will be. To the extent that shareholders have predicted GDP, that prediction will already be factored into the expected part of the return on the stock, $E(R)$. On the other hand, if the announced GDP is a surprise, then the effect will be part of U, the unanticipated portion of the return.

As an example, suppose shareholders in the market had forecast that the GDP increase this year would be .5 percent. If the actual announcement this year is exactly .5 percent, the same as the forecast, then the shareholders don't really learn anything, and the announcement isn't news. There will be no impact on the stock price as a result. This is like receiving redundant confirmation about something that you suspected all along; it reveals nothing new.

To give a more concrete example, Nabisco once announced it was taking a massive $300 million charge against earnings for the second quarter in a sweeping restructuring plan. The company also announced plans to cut its workforce sharply by 7.8 percent, eliminate some package sizes and small brands, and relocate some of its operations. This all seems like bad news, but the stock price didn't even budge. Why? Because it was already fully expected that Nabisco would take such actions, and the stock price already reflected the bad news.

A common way of saying that an announcement isn't news is to say that the market has already discounted the announcement. The use of the word "discount" here is different from the use of the term in computing present values, but the spirit is the same. When we discount a dollar to be received in the future, we say it is worth less to us today because of the time value of money. When an announcement or a news item is discounted into a stock price, we say that its impact is already a part of the stock price because the market already knew about it.

Going back to Flyers, suppose the government announces that the actual GDP increase during the year has been 1.5 percent. Now shareholders have learned something, namely, that the increase is 1 percentage point higher than they had forecast. This difference between the actual result and the forecast, 1 percentage point in this example, is sometimes called the *innovation* or the *surprise*.

This distinction explains why what seems to be bad news can actually be good news. For example, Gymboree, a retailer of children's apparel, had a 3 percent decline in same-store sales for a particular month, yet its stock price shot up 13 percent on the news. In the retail business, same-store sales, which are sales by existing stores in operation at least a year, are a crucial barometer, so why was this decline good news? The reason was that analysts had been expecting significantly sharper declines, so the situation was not as bad as previously thought.

A key fact to keep in mind about news and price changes is that news about the future is what matters. For example, America Online (AOL) once announced third-quarter earnings that exceeded Wall Street's expectations. That seems like good news, but America Online's stock price promptly dropped 10 percent. The reason was that America Online also announced a new discount subscriber plan, which analysts took as an indication that future revenues would be growing more slowly. Similarly, shortly thereafter, Microsoft reported a 50 percent jump in profits, exceeding projections. That seems like *really* good news, but Microsoft's stock price proceeded to decline sharply. Why? Because Microsoft warned that its phenomenal growth could not be sustained indefinitely, so its 50 percent increase in current earnings was not such a good predictor of future earnings growth.

See recent earnings surprises at earnings.nasdaq.com

To summarize, an announcement can be broken into two parts, the anticipated, or expected, part plus the surprise, or innovation:

$$\text{Announcement} = \text{Expected part} + \text{Surprise} \qquad (12.2)$$

The expected part of any announcement is the part of the information that the market uses to form the expectation, $E(R)$, of the return on the stock. The surprise is the news that influences the unanticipated return on the stock, U.

Our discussion of market efficiency in Chapter 9 bears on this discussion. We are assuming that relevant information known today is already reflected in the expected return. This is identical to saying that the current price reflects relevant publicly available information. We are thus implicitly assuming that markets are at least reasonably efficient in the semistrong-form sense. Henceforth, when we speak of news, we will mean the surprise part of an announcement and not the portion that the market had expected and therefore already discounted.

IN THE NEWS

EXAMPLE 12.1

Suppose Intel were to announce that earnings for the quarter just ending were up by 40 percent relative to a year ago. Do you expect that the stock price would rise or fall on the announcement?

The answer is that you can't really tell. Suppose the market was expecting a 60 percent increase. In this case, the 40 percent increase would be a negative surprise, and we would expect the stock price to fall. On the other hand, if the market was expecting only a 20 percent increase, there would be a positive surprise, and we would expect the stock to rise on the news.

CHECK THIS

12.1a   What are the two basic parts of a return on common stock?

12.1b   Under what conditions will an announcement have no effect on common stock prices?

12.2 Efficient Frontier and Capital Asset Line

Markowitz is one of the founders of Modern Portfolio Theory. He examined relationships between return and risk characteristics of various financial instruments and tried to identify those portfolios that investors choose. He assumed that investors are risk averse and rational. Given these assumptions, he concluded that investors would choose at every expected return level the assets and portfolios with minimum risk. According to his theory total risk level (standard deviation or variance) is the important factor in rewards of portfolios and therefore portfolio preference of investors.

He claims that investors find the minimum risk portfolios at every return level and choose these portfolios over the others. Investors plot every financial instrument and portfolio in an economy in an expected return-risk graph and try to find the minimum risk portfolios at every return level.

When investors minimize risk for every return level they obtain a parabola and the upper part of the parabola is called the efficient frontier. Figure 12.1 shows the Markowitz efficient frontier prepared with Canadian data.

In every economy, when investors combine the risk-free asset with efficient frontier, they obtain a line called the CAL (Capital Asset Line). Markowitz states that every rational investor will choose his or her optimal portfolio on CAL according to his or her preferred risk level.

Later, Sharpe, Lintner, Mossin and Tobin developed the Capital Asset Pricing Model. They claimed that systematic risk, not total risk, is the key factor in determining investment rewards. In the next section we will describe systematic risk and the Capital Asset Pricing Model (CAPM).

FIGURE 12.1   **Markowitz Efficient Frontier**

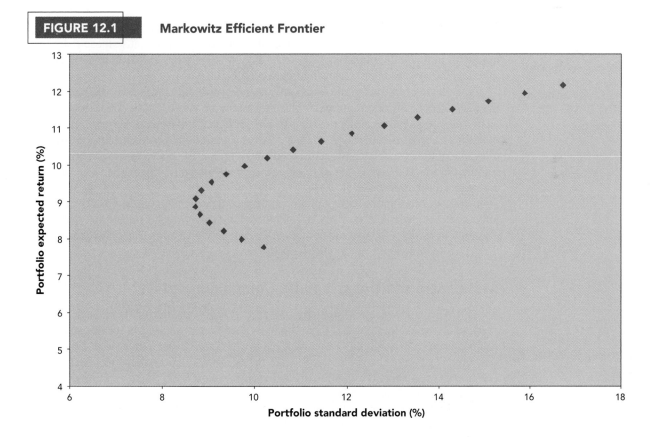

12.3 Risk: Systematic and Unsystematic

It is important to distinguish between expected and unexpected returns because the unanticipated part of the return, that portion resulting from surprises, is the significant risk of any investment. After all, if we always receive exactly what we expect, then the investment is perfectly predictable and, by definition, risk-free. In other words, the risk of owning an asset comes from surprises—unanticipated events.

There are important differences, though, among various sources of risk. Look back at our previous list of news stories. Some of these stories are directed specifically at Flyers, and some are more general. Which of the news items are of specific importance to Flyers?

Announcements about interest rates or GDP are clearly important for nearly all companies, whereas the news about Flyers's president, its research, or its sales is of specific interest to Flyers investors only. We distinguish between these two types of events, because, as we will see, they have very different implications.

Systematic and Unsystematic Risk

systematic risk Risk that influences a large number of assets. Also called *market risk*.

unsystematic risk Risk that influences a single company or a small group of companies. Also called *unique* or *asset-specific risk*.

The first type of surprise, the one that affects most assets, we label **systematic risk**. A systematic risk is one that influences a large number of assets, each to a greater or lesser extent. Because systematic risks have marketwide effects, they are sometimes called *market risks*.

The second type of surprise we call **unsystematic risk**. An unsystematic risk is one that affects a single asset, or possibly a small group of assets. Because these risks are unique to individual companies or assets, they are sometimes called *unique* or *asset-specific risks*. We use these terms interchangeably.

As we have seen, uncertainties about general economic conditions, such as GDP, interest rates, or inflation, are examples of systematic risks. These conditions affect nearly all companies to some degree. An unanticipated increase, or surprise, in inflation, for example, affects wages and the costs of supplies that companies buy; it affects the value of the assets that companies own; and it affects the prices at which companies sell their products. Forces such as these, to which all companies are susceptible, are the essence of systematic risk.

In contrast, the announcement of an oil strike by a particular company will primarily affect that company and, perhaps, a few others (such as primary competitors and suppliers). It is unlikely to have much of an effect on the world oil market, however, or on the affairs of companies not in the oil business, so this is an unsystematic event.

Systematic and Unsystematic Components of Return

Analyze risk at www.portfolioscience. com

The distinction between a systematic risk and an unsystematic risk is never really as exact as we would like it to be. Even the most narrow and peculiar bit of news about a company ripples through the economy. This is true because every enterprise, no matter how tiny, is a part of the economy. It's like the tale of a kingdom that was lost because one horse lost a shoe. This is mostly hairsplitting, however. Some risks are clearly much more general than others.

The distinction between the two types of risk allows us to break down the surprise portion, U, of the return on the Flyers stock into two parts. Earlier, we had the actual return broken down into its expected and surprise components: $R - E(R) = U$.

We now recognize that the total surprise component for Flyers, U, has a systematic and an unsystematic component, so

$$R - E(R) = \text{Systematic portion} + \text{Unsystematic portion} \qquad (12.3)$$

Because it is traditional, we will use the Greek letter epsilon, ϵ, to stand for the unsystematic portion. Because systematic risks are often called "market" risks, we use the letter m to stand for the systematic part of the surprise. With these symbols, we can rewrite the formula for the total return:

$$R - E(R) = U = m + \epsilon \qquad (12.4)$$

The important thing about the way we have broken down the total surprise, U, is that the unsystematic portion, ϵ, is unique to Flyers. For this reason, it is unrelated to the unsystematic portion of return on most other assets. To see why this is important, we need to return to the subject of portfolio risk.

SYSTEMATIC VERSUS UNSYSTEMATIC EVENTS

EXAMPLE 12.2

Suppose Intel were to unexpectedly announce that its latest computer chip contains a significant flaw in its floating point unit that left it unable to handle numbers bigger than a couple of gigatrillion (meaning that, among other things, the chip cannot calculate Intel's quarterly profits). Is this a systematic or unsystematic event?

Obviously, this event is for the most part unsystematic. However, it would also benefit Intel's competitors to some degree and, at least potentially, harm some users of Intel products such as personal computer makers. Thus, as with most unsystematic events, there is some spillover, but the effect is mostly confined to a relatively small number of companies.

CHECK THIS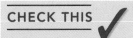

12.3a What are the two basic types of risk?

12.3b What is the distinction between the two types of risk?

12.4 Diversification, Systematic Risk, and Unsystematic Risk

In Chapter 2, we introduced the principle of diversification. What we saw was that some of the risk associated with individual assets can be diversified away and some cannot. We are left with an obvious question: Why is this so? It turns out that the answer hinges on the distinction between systematic and unsystematic risk.

Diversification and Unsystematic Risk

By definition, an unsystematic risk is one that is particular to a single asset or, at most, a small group of assets. For example, if the asset under consideration is stock in a single company, such things as successful new products and innovative cost savings will tend to increase the value of the stock. Unanticipated lawsuits, industrial accidents, strikes, and similar events will tend to decrease future cash flows and thereby reduce share values.

Here is the important observation: If we hold only a single stock, then the value of our investment will fluctuate because of company-specific events. If we hold a large portfolio, on the other hand, some of the stocks in the portfolio will go up in value because of positive company-specific events, and some will go down in value because of negative events. The net effect on the overall value of the portfolio will be relatively small, however, because these effects will tend to cancel each other out.

Now we see why some of the variability associated with individual assets is eliminated by diversification. When we combine assets into portfolios, the unique, or unsystematic, events—both positive and negative—tend to "wash out" once we have more than just a few assets. This is an important point that bears repeating:

> **Unsystematic risk is essentially eliminated by diversification, so a portfolio with many assets has almost no unsystematic risk.**

In fact, the terms *diversifiable risk* and *unsystematic risk* are often used interchangeably.

Diversification and Systematic Risk

We've seen that unsystematic risk can be eliminated by diversification. What about systematic risk? Can it also be eliminated by diversification? The answer is no because, by definition, a systematic risk affects almost all assets. As a result, no matter how many assets we put into a portfolio, systematic risk doesn't go away. Thus, for obvious reasons, the terms *systematic risk* and *nondiversifiable risk* are used interchangeably.

Because we have introduced so many different terms, it is useful to summarize our discussion before moving on. What we have seen is that the total risk of an investment can be written as

$$\text{Total risk} = \text{Systematic risk} + \text{Unsystematic risk} \qquad (12.5)$$

Systematic risk is also called *nondiversifiable risk* or *market risk*. Unsystematic risk is also called *diversifiable risk*, *unique risk*, or *asset-specific risk*. Most important, for a well-diversified portfolio, unsystematic risk is negligible. For such a portfolio, essentially all risk is systematic.

 CHECK THIS

12.4a   Why is some risk diversifiable? Why is some risk not diversifiable?

12.4b   Why can't systematic risk be diversified away?

12.5 Systematic Risk and Beta

We now begin to address another question: What determines the size of the risk premium on a risky asset? Put another way, why do some assets have a larger risk premium than other assets? The answer, as we discuss next, is also based on the distinction between systematic and unsystematic risk.

The Systematic Risk Principle

Thus far, we've seen that the total risk associated with an asset can be decomposed into two components: systematic and unsystematic risk. We have also seen that unsystematic risk can be essentially eliminated by diversification. The systematic risk present in an asset, on the other hand, cannot be eliminated by diversification.

Based on our study of capital market history in Chapter 1, we know that there is a reward, on average, for bearing risk. However, we now need to be more precise about what we mean by risk. The **systematic risk principle** states that the reward for bearing risk depends only on the systematic risk of an investment.

systematic risk principle The reward for bearing risk depends only on the systematic risk of an investment.

The underlying rationale for this principle is straightforward: Because unsystematic risk can be eliminated at virtually no cost (by diversifying), there is no reward for bearing it. In other words, the market does not reward risks that are borne unnecessarily.

The systematic risk principle has a remarkable and very important implication:

The expected return on an asset depends only on its systematic risk.

There is an obvious corollary to this principle: No matter how much total risk an asset has, only the systematic portion is relevant in determining the expected return (and the risk premium) on that asset.

Measuring Systematic Risk

beta coefficient (β) Measure of the relative systematic risk of an asset. Assets with betas larger (smaller) than 1 have more (less) systematic risk than average.

Because systematic risk is the crucial determinant of an asset's expected return, we need some way of measuring the level of systematic risk for different investments. The specific measure we will use is called the **beta coefficient**, designated by the Greek letter β. A beta coefficient, or just beta for short, tells us how much systematic risk a particular asset has relative to an average asset. By definition, an average asset has a beta of 1.0 relative to itself. An asset with a beta of .50, therefore, has half as much systematic risk as an average asset. Likewise, an asset with a beta of 2.0 has twice as much systematic risk.

Table 12.1 presents the estimated beta coefficients for the stocks of some well-known companies. The range of the betas in Table 12.1 is typical for stocks of large Canadian companies. Betas outside this range occur, but they are less common.

The important thing to remember is that the expected return, and thus the risk premium, on an asset depends only on its systematic risk. Because assets with larger betas have greater systematic risks, they will have greater expected returns. Thus, from Table 12.1, an investor who buys stock in BCE, with a beta of 1.05, should expect to earn less, on average, than an investor who buys stock in Quebecor, with a beta of about 3.04.

TABLE 12.1	Beta Coefficients	
	Company	**Beta β**
	Barrick Gold	1.11
	Quebecor Inc	3.04
	Toronto Dominion Bank	1.25
	Nova Chemicals	1.96
	BCE	1.05
	TELUS	1.96
	Biovail Corp	1.96
	Rogers Communication Inc	1.40

Source: Betas are obtained from the Yahoo webpage: finance.yahoo.com, December 28, 2007.

One cautionary note is in order: Not all betas are created equal. Different sources report different betas. Also betas change with time. The difference results from the different procedures used to come up with beta coefficients. We will have more to say on this subject when we explain how betas are calculated in a later section. Our nearby *Work the Web* box shows one way to get betas online.

TOTAL RISK VERSUS BETA

EXAMPLE 12.3

Consider the following information on two securities. Which has greater total risk? Which has greater systematic risk? Greater unsystematic risk? Which asset will have a higher risk premium?

	Standard Deviation	Beta
Security A	40%	.50
Security B	20	1.50

From our discussion in this section, Security A has greater total risk, but it has substantially less systematic risk. Because total risk is the sum of systematic and unsystematic risk. Security A must have greater unsystematic risk. Finally, from the systematic risk principle, Security B will have a higher risk premium and a greater expected return, despite the fact that it has less total risk.

Portfolio Betas

Earlier, we saw that the riskiness of a portfolio has no simple relation to the risks of the assets in the portfolio. By contrast, a portfolio beta can be calculated just like a portfolio expected return. For example, looking at Table 12.1, suppose you put half of your money in BCE and half in TELUS. What would the beta of this combination be? Because BCE has a beta of 1.05 and TELUS has a beta of 1.96, the portfolio's beta, β_p would be

$$\beta_p = .50 \times \beta_{BCE} + 0.5 \times \beta_{TELUS}$$
$$= 0.5 \times 1.05 + 0.5 \times 1.96$$
$$= 1.505$$

In general, if we had a large number of assets in a portfolio, we would multiply each asset's beta by its portfolio weight and then add the results to get the portfolio's beta.

PORTFOLIO BETAS

EXAMPLE 12.4

Suppose we have the following information:

Security	Amount Invested	Expected Return	Beta
Stock A	$1,000	8%	.80
Stock B	2,000	12	.95
Stock C	3,000	15	1.10
Stock D	4,000	18	1.40

(continued)

WORK THE WEB

Suppose you want to find the beta for a company like Rogers Communications. One way is to work the Web. We went to <u>finance.yahoo.com</u>, entered the ticker symbol RCI for the company, and followed the "Key Statistics" link.

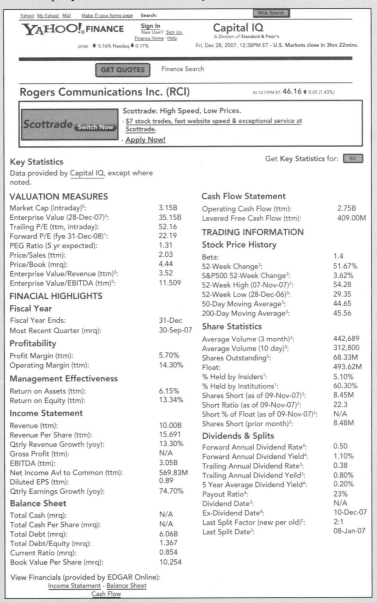

The reported beta for Rogers Communications is 1.40, which means that Rogers Communications has about 1.40 times the systematic risk of a typical stock. Notice that the stock price change within the 52 weeks is 51.67%.

WORK THE WEB

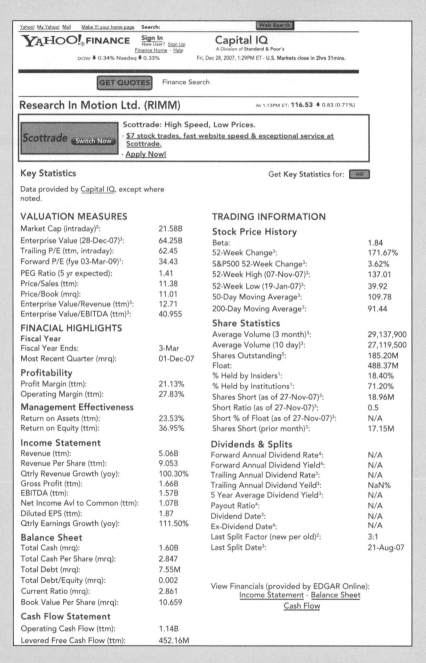

Our second example is the Research In Motion Company. The company has a beta of 1.84 indicating that the company returns will increase by 1.84% (similar to the market index portfolio) when the market index experiences a 1% return increase.

What is the expected return on this portfolio? What is the beta of this portfolio? Does this portfolio have more or less systematic risk than an average asset?

To answer, we first have to calculate the portfolio weights. Notice that the total amount invested is $10,000. Of this, $1,000 / $10,000 = 10% is invested in Stock A. Similarly, 20 percent is invested in Stock B, 30 percent is invested in Stock C, and 40 percent is invested in Stock D. The expected return, $E(R_p)$, is thus

$$E(R_p) = .10 \times E(R_A) + .20 \times E(R_B) + .30 \times E(R_C) + .40 \times E(R_D)$$
$$= .10 \times 8\% + .20 \times 12\% + .30 \times 15\% \times .40 \times 18\%$$
$$= 14.9\%$$

Similarly, the portfolio beta, β_p, is

$$\beta_p = .10 \times \beta_A + .20 \times \beta_B + .30 \times \beta_C + .40 \times \beta_D$$
$$= .10 \times .80 + .20 \times .95 + .30 \times 1.10 + .40 \times 1.40$$
$$= 1.16$$

This portfolio thus has an expected return of 14.9 percent and a beta of 1.16. Because the beta is larger than 1, this portfolio has greater systematic risk than an average asset.

CHECK THIS ✓

12.5a   What is the systematic risk principle?

12.5b   What does a beta coefficient measure?

12.5c   How do you calculate a portfolio beta?

12.5d   True or false: The expected return on a risky asset depends on that asset's total risk. Explain.

12.6 The Security Market Line

We're now in a position to see how risk is rewarded in the marketplace. To begin, suppose that Asset A has an expected return of $E(R_A) = 20\%$ and a beta of $\beta_A = 1.6$. Further suppose that the risk-free rate is $R_f = 8\%$. Notice that a risk-free asset, by definition, has no systematic risk (or unsystematic risk), so a risk-free asset has a beta of zero.

Beta and the Risk Premium

Consider a portfolio made up of Asset A and a risk-free asset. We can calculate some different possible portfolio expected returns and betas by varying the percentages invested in these two assets. For example, if 25 percent of the portfolio is invested in Asset A, then the expected return is

$$E(R_p) = .25 \times E(R_A) + (1 - .25) \times R_f$$
$$= .25 \times 20\% + .75 \times 8\%$$
$$= 11\%$$

Similarly, the beta on the portfolio, β_p, would be

$$\beta_p = .25 \times \beta_A + (1 - .25) \times 0$$
$$= .25 \times 1.6$$
$$= .40$$

Notice that, because the weights have to add up to 1, the percentage invested in the risk-free asset is equal to 1 minus the percentage invested in Asset A.

One thing that you might wonder about is whether it is possible for the percentage invested in Asset A to exceed 100 percent. The answer is yes. This can happen if the investor borrows at the risk-free rate and invests the proceeds in stocks. For example, suppose an investor has $100 and borrows an additional $50 at 8 percent, the risk-free rate. The total investment in Asset A would be $150, or 150 percent of the investor's wealth. The expected return in this case would be

$$E(R_p) = 1.50 \times E(R_A) + (1 - 1.50) \times R_f$$
$$= 1.50 \times 20\% - .50 \times 8\%$$
$$= 26\%$$

The beta on the portfolio would be

$$\beta_p = 1.50 \times \beta_A + (1 - 1.50) \times 0$$
$$= 1.50 \times 1.6$$
$$= 2.4$$

We can calculate some other possibilities, as follows:

Percentage of Portfolio in Asset A	Portfolio Expected Return	Portfolio Beta
0%	8%	.0
25	11	.4
50	14	.8
75	17	1.2
100	20	1.6
125	23	2.0
150	26	2.4

In Figure 12.2A, these portfolio expected returns are plotted against portfolio betas. Notice that all the combinations fall on a straight line.

The Reward-to-Risk Ratio

What is the slope of the straight line in Figure 12.2A? As always, the slope of a straight line is equal to the rise over the run. In this case, as we move out of the risk-free asset into Asset A, the beta increases from zero to 1.6 (a run of 1.6). At the same time, the expected return goes from 8 percent to 20 percent, a rise of 12 percent. The slope of the line is thus 12% / 1.6 = 7.5%.

FIGURE 12.2

**Betas and
Portfolio Returns**

A. Portfolio expected returns and betas for Asset A

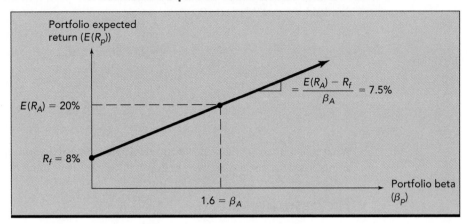

B. Portfolio expected returns and betas for Asset B

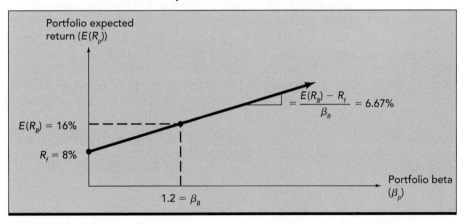

C. Portfolio expected returns and betas for both assets

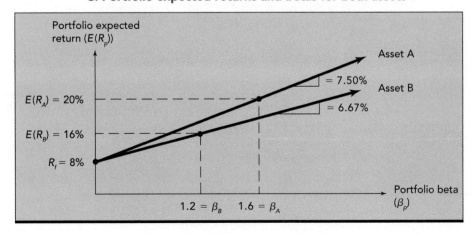

Notice that the slope of our line is just the risk premium on Asset A, $E(R_A) - R_f$ divided by Asset A's beta, β_A:

$$\text{Slope} = \frac{E(R_A) - R_f}{\beta_A}$$

$$= \frac{20\% - 8\%}{1.6}$$

$$= 7.50\%$$

What this tells us is that Asset A offers a *reward-to-risk* ratio of 7.5 percent.[1] In other words, Asset A has a risk premium of 7.50 percent per "unit" of systematic risk.

The Basic Argument

Now suppose we consider a second asset, Asset B. This asset has a beta of 1.2 and an expected return of 16 percent. Which investment is better, Asset A or Asset B? You might think that we really cannot say—some investors might prefer A; some investors might prefer B. Actually, however, we can say: A is better because, as we will demonstrate, B offers inadequate compensation for its level of systematic risk, at least relative to A.

To begin, we calculate different combinations of expected returns and betas for portfolios of Asset B and a risk-free asset, just as we did for Asset A. For example, if we put 25 percent in Asset B and the remaining 75 percent in the risk-free asset, the portfolio's expected return will be

$$E(R_p) = .25 \times E(R_B) + (1 - .25) \times R_f$$

$$= .25 \times 16\% + .75 \times 8\%$$

$$= 10\%$$

Similarly, the beta on the portfolio, β_p, would be

$$\beta_p = .25 \times \beta_B + (1 - .25) \times 0$$

$$= .25 \times 1.2$$

$$= .30$$

Some other possibilities are as follows:

Percentage of Portfolio in Asset B	Portfolio Expected Return	Portfolio Beta
0%	8%	.0
25	10	.3
50	12	.6
75	14	.9
100	16	1.2
125	18	1.5
150	20	1.8

---

[1]This ratio is sometimes called the *Treynor index*, after one of its originators.

When we plot these combinations of portfolio expected returns and portfolio betas in Figure 12.2B, we get a straight line, just as we did for Asset A.

The key thing to notice is that when we compare the results for Assets A and B, as in Figure 12.2C, the line describing the combinations of expected returns and betas for Asset A is higher than the one for Asset B. What this tells us is that for any given level of systematic risk (as measured by beta), some combination of Asset A and the risk-free asset always offers a larger return. This is why we were able to state that Asset A is a better investment than Asset B.

Another way of seeing that Asset A offers a superior return for its level of risk is to note that the slope of our line for Asset B is

$$\text{Slope} = \frac{E(R_B) - R_f}{\beta_B}$$
$$= \frac{16\% - 8\%}{1.2}$$
$$= 6.67\%$$

Thus, Asset B has a reward-to-risk ratio of 6.67 percent, which is less than the 7.5 percent offered by Asset A.

The Fundamental Result

The situation we have described for Assets A and B could not persist in a well-organized, active market because investors would be attracted to Asset A and away from Asset B. As a result, Asset A's price would rise and Asset B's price would fall. Because prices and expected returns move in opposite directions, A's expected return would decline and B's would rise.

This buying and selling would continue until the two assets plotted on exactly the same line, which means they would offer the same reward for bearing risk. In other words, in an active, competitive market, we must have the situation that

$$\frac{E(R_A) - R_f}{\beta_A} = \frac{E(R_B) - R_f}{\beta_B} \tag{12.6}$$

This is the fundamental relation between risk and return.

Our basic argument can be extended to more than just two assets. In fact, no matter how many assets we had, we would always reach the same conclusion:

> **The reward-to-risk ratio must be the same for all assets in a competitive financial market.**

This result is really not too surprising. What it says is that, for example, if one asset has twice as much systematic risk as another asset, its risk premium will simply be twice as large.

Because all assets in the market must have the same reward-to-risk ratio, they all must plot on the same line. This argument is illustrated in Figure 12.3, where the subscript i on the return R_i and beta β_i indexes Assets A, B, C, and D. As shown, Assets A and B plot directly on the line and thus have the same reward-to-risk ratio. If an asset plotted above the line, such as C in Figure 12.3, its price would rise and its expected return would fall until it plotted exactly on the line. Similarly, if an asset plotted below the line, such as D in Figure 12.3, its price would fall, and its expected return would rise until it too plotted directly on the line.

FIGURE 12.3

Expected Returns and Systematic Risk

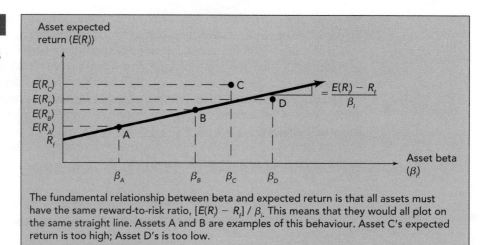

The fundamental relationship between beta and expected return is that all assets must have the same reward-to-risk ratio, $[E(R_i) - R_f] / \beta_i$. This means that they would all plot on the same straight line. Assets A and B are examples of this behaviour. Asset C's expected return is too high; Asset D's is too low.

The arguments we have presented apply to active, competitive, well-functioning markets. Active financial markets, such as the TSX, best meet these criteria. Other markets, such as real asset markets, may or may not. For this reason, these concepts are most useful in examining active financial markets.

BUY LOW, SELL HIGH

EXAMPLE 12.5

A security is said to be *overvalued* relative to another security if its price is too high given its expected return and risk. Suppose you observe the following situation:

Security	Beta	Expected Return
Melan Co.	1.3	14%
Choly Co.	.8	10

The risk-free rate is currently 6 percent. Is one of the two securities overvalued relative to the other?

To answer, we compute the reward-to-risk ratio for both. For Melan, this ratio is (14% − 6%) / 1.3 = 6.15%. For Choly, this ratio is 5 percent. What we conclude is that Choly offers an insufficient expected return for its level of risk, at least relative to Melan. Because its expected return is too low, its price is too high. In other words, Choly is overvalued relative to Melan, and we would expect to see its price fall relative to Melan. Notice that we could also say Melan is *undervalued* relative to Choly.

security market line (SML) Graphical representation of the linear relationship between systematic risk and expected return in financial markets.

The Security Market Line

The line that results when we plot expected returns and beta coefficients is obviously of some importance, so it's time we gave it a name. This line, which we use to describe the relationship between systematic risk and expected return in financial markets, is usually called the **security market line (SML)**, and it is one of the most important concepts in modern finance.

Market Portfolios   We will find it very useful to know the equation of the SML. Although there are many different ways we could write it, we will discuss the most frequently seen version. Suppose we consider a portfolio made up of all of the assets in the market. Such a portfolio is called a *market portfolio*, and we will express the expected return on this market portfolio as $E(R_M)$.

Because all the assets in the market must plot on the SML, so must a market portfolio made up of those assets. To determine where it plots on the SML, we need to know the beta of the market portfolio, β_M. Because this portfolio is representative of all of the assets in the market, it must have average systematic risk. In other words, it has a beta of 1. We could therefore express the slope of the SML as

$$\text{SML slope} = \frac{E(R_M) - R_f}{\beta_M} = \frac{E(R_M) - R_f}{1} = E(R_M) - R_f$$

market risk premium The risk premium on a market portfolio, i.e., a portfolio made of all assets in the market.

The term $E(R_M) - R_f$ is often called the **market risk premium** because it is the risk premium on a market portfolio.

The Capital Asset Pricing Model   To finish up, if we let $E(R_i)$ and β_i stand for the expected return and beta, respectively, on any asset in the market, then we know that asset must plot on the SML. As a result, we know that its reward-to-risk ratio is the same as that of the overall market:

$$\frac{E(R_i) - R_f}{\beta_i} = E(R_M) - R_f$$

If we rearrange this, then we can write the equation for the SML as

$$E(R_i) = R_f + [E(R_M) - R_f] \times \beta_i \tag{12.7}$$

capital asset pricing model (CAPM) A theory of risk and return for securities in a competitive capital market.

This result is the famous **capital asset pricing model (CAPM)**.[2]

What the CAPM shows is that the expected return for an asset depends on three things:

1. *The pure time value of money.* As measured by the risk-free rate, R_f, this is the reward for merely waiting for your money, without taking any risk.

2. *The reward for bearing systematic risk.* As measured by the market risk premium, $E(R_M) - R_f$, this component is the reward the market offers for bearing an average amount of systematic risk.

3. *The amount of systematic risk.* As measured by β_i, this is the amount of systematic risk present in a particular asset relative to that in an average asset.

By the way, the CAPM works for portfolios of assets just as it does for individual assets. In an earlier section, we saw how to calculate a portfolio's beta in the CAPM equation.

Figure 12.4 summarizes our discussion of the SML and the CAPM. As before, we plot expected return against beta. Now we recognize that, based on the CAPM, the slope of the SML is equal to the market risk premium, $E(R_M) - R_f$.

There's a CAPM calculator (if you really need it!) at www.moneychimp.com

---

[2]Our discussion of the CAPM is actually closely related to the more recent development, arbitrage pricing theory (APT). The theory underlying the CAPM is more complex than we have indicated here, and it has implications beyond the scope of this discussion. As we present it here, the CAPM has essentially identical implications to those of the APT, so we don't distinguish between them.

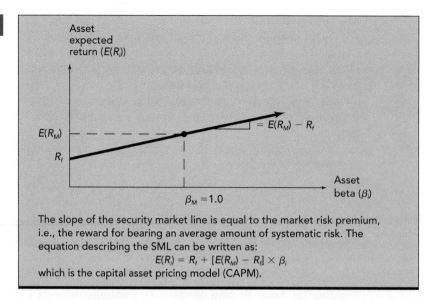

FIGURE 12.4

Security Market Line (SML)

The slope of the security market line is equal to the market risk premium, i.e., the reward for bearing an average amount of systematic risk. The equation describing the SML can be written as:

$$E(R_i) = R_f + [E(R_M) - R_f] \times \beta_i$$

which is the capital asset pricing model (CAPM).

TABLE 12.2   **Risk and Return Summary**

1. **Total risk.** The *total risk* of an investment is measured by the variance or, more commonly, the standard deviation of its return.

2. **Total return.** The *total return* on an investment has two components: the expected return and the unexpected return. The unexpected return comes about because of unanticipated events. The risk from investing stems from the possibility of an unanticipated event.

3. **Systematic and unsystematic risks.** *Systematic risks* (also called *market risks*) are unanticipated events that affect almost all assets to some degree because the effects are economywide. *Unsystematic risks* are unanticipated events that affect single assets or small groups of assets. Unsystematic risks are also called *unique* or *asset-specific risks*.

4. **The effect of diversification.** Some, but not all, of the risk associated with a risky investment can be eliminated by diversification. The reason is that unsystematic risks, which are unique to individual assets, tend to wash out in a large portfolio, but systematic risks, which affect all of the assets in a portfolio to some extent, do not.

5. **The systematic risk principle and beta.** Because unsystematic risk can be freely eliminated by diversification, the *systematic risk principle* states that the reward for bearing risk depends only on the level of systematic risk. The level of systematic risk in a particular asset, relative to the average, is given by the *beta* of that asset.

6. **The reward-to-risk ratio and the security market line.** The *reward-to-risk ratio* for Asset i is the ratio of its risk premium, $E(R_i) - R_f$, to its beta, β_i.

$$\frac{E(R_i) - R_f}{\beta_i}$$

In a well-functioning market, this ratio is the same for every asset. As a result, when asset expected returns are plotted against asset betas, all assets plot on the same straight line, called the *security market line* (SML).

7. **The capital asset pricing model.** From the SML, the expected return on Asset i can be written

$$E(R_i) = R_f + [E(R_M) - R_f] \times \beta_i$$

This is the *capital asset pricing model* (CAPM). The expected return on a risky asset thus has three components. The first is the pure time value of money (R_f), the second is the market risk premium, $E(R_M) - R_f$, and the third is the beta for that asset (β_i).

This concludes our presentation of concepts related to the risk-return trade-off. Table 12.2 summarizes the various concepts in the order in which we discussed them.

RISK AND RETURN

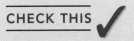

Suppose the risk-free rate is 4 percent, the market risk premium is 8.6 percent, and a particular stock has a beta of 1.3. Based on the CAPM, what is the expected return on this stock? What would the expected return be if the beta were to double?

With a beta of 1.3, the risk premium for the stock is 1.3 × 8.6%, or 11.18 percent. The risk-free rate is 4 percent, so the expected return is 15.18 percent. If the beta were to double to 2.6, the risk premium would double to 22.36 percent, so the expected return would be 26.36 percent.

CHECK THIS ✓

12.6a What is the fundamental relationship between risk and return in active markets?

12.6b What is the security market line (SML)? Why must all assets plot directly on it in a well-functioning market?

12.6c What is the capital asset pricing model (CAPM)? What does it tell us about the required return on a risky investment?

12.7 More on Beta

In our last several sections, we discussed the basic economic principles of risk and return. We found that the expected return on a security depends on its systematic risk, which is measured using the security's beta coefficient, β. In this final section, we examine beta in more detail. We first illustrate more closely what it is that beta measures. We then show how betas can be estimated for individual securities, and we discuss why it is that different sources report different betas for the same security.

A Closer Look at Beta

Going back to the beginning of the chapter, we discussed how the actual return on a security, R, could be written as follows:

$$R - E(R) = m + \epsilon \qquad (12.8)$$

Recall that in Equation 12.8, m stands for the systematic or marketwide portion of the unexpected return. Based on our discussion of the CAPM, we can now be a little more precise about this component.

Specifically, the systematic portion of an unexpected return depends on two things. First, it depends on the size of the systematic effect. We will measure this as $R_M - E(R_M)$, which is simply the difference between the actual return on the overall market and the expected return. Second, as we have discussed, some securities have greater systematic risk than others, and we measure this risk using beta. Putting it together, we have

$$m = [R_M - E(R_M)] \times \beta \qquad (12.9)$$

In other words, the marketwide, or systematic, portion of the return on a security depends on both the size of the marketwide surprise, $R_M - E(R_M)$, and the sensitivity of the security to such surprises, β.

Now, if we combine Equations 12.8 and 12.9, we have

$$R - E(R) = m + \epsilon$$
$$= [R_M - E(R_M)] \times \beta + \epsilon \qquad (12.10)$$

Equation 12.10 gives us some additional insight into beta by telling us why some securities have higher betas than others. A high-beta security is simply one that is relatively sensitive to overall market movements, whereas a low-beta security is one that is relatively insensitive. In other words, the systematic risk of a security is just a reflection of its sensitivity to overall market movements.

A hypothetical example is useful for illustrating the main point of Equation 12.10. Suppose a particular security has a beta of 1.2, the risk-free rate is 5 percent, and the expected return on the market is 12 percent. From the CAPM, we know that the expected return on the security is

$$E(R) = R_f + [E(R_M) - R_f] \times \beta$$
$$= .05 + (.12 - .05) \times 1.2$$
$$= .134$$

Thus, the expected return on this security is 13.4 percent. However, we know that in any year the actual return on this security will be more or less than 13.4 percent because of unanticipated systematic and unsystematic events.

Columns 1 and 2 of Table 12.3 list the actual returns on our security, R, for a five-year period along with the actual returns for the market as a whole, R_M, for the same period. Given these actual returns and the expected returns on the security (13.4 percent) and the market as a whole (12 percent), we can calculate the unexpected returns on the security, $R - E(R)$, along with the unexpected return on the market as a whole, $R_M - E(R_M)$. The results are shown in columns 3 and 4 of Table 12.3.

Next we decompose the unexpected returns on the security—that is, we break them down into their systematic and unsystematic components in columns 5 and 6. From Equation 12.9, we calculate the systematic portion of the unexpected return by taking the security's beta, 1.2, and multiplying it by the market's unexpected return:

$$\text{Systematic portion} = m = [R_M - E(R_M)] \times \beta$$

TABLE 12.3			Decomposition of Total Returns into Systematic and Unsystematic Portions			
	Actual Returns		Unexpected Returns		Systematic Portion	Unsystematic Portion (ϵ)
Year	R	R_M	$R - E(R)$	$R_M - E(R_M)$	$[R_M - E(R_M)] \times \beta$	$[R - E(R)] - [R_M - E(R_M)] \times \beta$
2001	20%	15%	6.6%	3%	3.6%	3%
2002	−24.6	−3	−38	−15	−18	−20
2003	23	10	9.6	−2	−2.4	12
2004	36.8	24	23.4	12	14.4	9
2005	3.4	7	−10	−5	−6	−4

FIGURE 12.5

Unexpected Returns and Beta

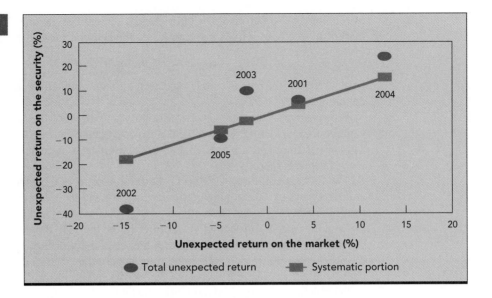

Finally, we calculate the unsystematic portion by subtracting the systematic portion from the total unexpected return:

$$\text{Unsystematic portion} = \epsilon = [R - E(R)] - [R_M - E(R_M)] \times \beta$$

Notice that the unsystematic portion is essentially whatever is left over after we account for the systematic portion. For this reason, it is sometimes called the "residual" portion of the unexpected return.

Figure 12.5 illustrates the main points of this discussion by plotting the unexpected returns on the security in Table 12.3 against the unexpected return on the market as a whole. These are the individual points in the graph, each labelled with its year. We also plot the systematic portions of the unexpected returns in Table 12.3 and connect them with a straight line. Notice that the slope of the straight line is equal to 1.2, the beta of the security. As indicated, the distance from the straight line to an individual point is the unsystematic portion of the return, ϵ, for a particular year.

Where Do Betas Come From?

As our discussion to this point shows, beta is a useful concept. It allows us to estimate the expected return on a security, it tells how sensitive a security's return is to unexpected market events, and it lets us separate out the systematic and unsystematic portions of a security's return. In our example just above, we were given that the beta was 1.2, so the required calculations were all pretty straightforward. Suppose, however, that we didn't have the beta ahead of time. In this case, we would have to estimate it.

A security's beta is a measure of how sensitive the security's return is to overall market movements. That sensitivity depends on two things: (1) how closely correlated the security's return is with the overall market's return and (2) how volatile the security is relative to the market. Specifically, going back to our previous chapter, let $\text{Corr}(R_i, R_M)$ stand for the correlation between the return on a particular security i and the overall market. As before, let σ_i and σ_M be the standard deviations on the security and the market, respectively. Given these numbers, the beta for the security, β_i, is simply

$$\beta_i = \text{Corr}(R_i, R_M) \times \sigma_i / \sigma_M \qquad (12.11)$$

In other words, the beta is equal to the correlation multiplied by the ratio of the standard deviations.

From previous chapters, we know how to calculate the standard deviations in Equation 12.11. However, we have not yet discussed how to calculate correlations. This is our final task for this chapter. The simplest way to proceed is to construct a worksheet like Table 12.4.

The first six columns of Table 12.4 are familiar from Chapter 1. The first two contain five years of returns on a particular security and the overall market. We add these up and divide by 5 to get the average returns of 10 percent and 12 percent for the security and the market, respectively, as shown in the table. In the third and fourth columns we calculate the return deviations by taking each individual return and subtracting out the average return. In columns 5 and 6 we square these return deviations. To calculate the variances, we total these squared deviations and divide by $5 - 1 = 4$.

We calculate the standard deviations by taking the square roots of the variances, and we find that the standard deviations for the security and the market are 18.87 percent and 15.03 percent, respectively.

Now we come to the part that's new. In the last column of Table 12.4, we have calculated the *product* of the return deviations by simply multiplying columns 3 and 4. When we total these products and divide by $5 - 1 = 4$, the result is called the **covariance**.

covariance A measure of the tendency of two things to move or vary together.

Covariance, as the name suggests, is a measure of the tendency of two things to vary together. If the covariance is positive, then the tendency is to move in the same direction, and vice versa for a negative covariance. A zero covariance means there is no particular relation. For our security in Table 12.4, the covariance is $+.0204$, so the security tends to move in the same direction as the market.

| TABLE 12.4 | Calculating Beta |

	Returns		Return Deviations		Squared Deviations		
Year	Security (1)	Market (2)	Security (3)	Market (4)	Security (5)	Market (6)	Product of Deviations (7)
2001	.10	.08	.00	−.04	.0000	.0016	.0000
2002	−.08	−.12	−.18	−.24	.0324	.0576	.0432
2003	−.04	.16	−.14	.04	.0196	.0016	−.0056
2004	.40	.26	.30	.14	.0900	.0196	.0420
2005	.12	.22	.02	.10	.0004	.0100	.0020
Totals	.50	.60	0	0	.1424	.0904	.0816

	Average Returns	Variances	Standard Deviations
Security	$.50/5 = .10 = 10\%$	$.1424/4 = .0356$	$\sqrt{.0356} = .1887 = 18.87\%$
Market	$.60/5 = .12 = 12\%$	$.0904/4 = .0226$	$\sqrt{.0226} = .1503 = 15.03\%$

Covariance $= \text{Cov}(R_i, R_M) = .0816 / 4 = .0204$

Correlation $= \text{Corr}(R_i, R_M) = .0204 / (.1887 \times .1503) = .72$

Beta $= \beta = .72 \times (.1887 / .1503) = .9031 \approx .9$

SPREADSHEET ANALYSIS

	A	B	C	D	E	F	G	H
1								
2			**Using a Spreadsheet to Calculate Beta**					
3								
4	To illustrate how to calculate betas, correlations, and covariances using a spreadsheet,							
5	we have entered the information from Table 12.4 into the spreadsheet below. Here, we							
6	use Excel functions to do all the calculations.							
7								
8				Returns				
9				Security	Market			
10			2001	10%	8%	Note: The Excel Format is		
11			2002	−8%	−12%	set to percent, but the		
12			2003	−4%	16%	numbers are entered as		
13			2004	40%	26%	decimals.		
14			2005	12%	22%			
15								
16			Average:	10%	12%	(Using the =AVERAGE function)		
17			Std. Dev.:	18.87%	15.03%	(Using the =STDEV function)		
18			Correlation:	0.72		=CORREL(D10:D14,E10:E14)		
19								
20			Beta:	0.90				
21								
22	Excel also has a covariance function, =COVAR, but we do not use it because it divides							
23	by n instead of n −1. Verify that you get a Beta of about 0.72 if you use the COVAR							
24	function divided by the variance of the Market Returns (Use the Excel function, =VAR).							
25								
26	Question 1: How would you correct the covariance calculation?							
27	Question 2: What happens when you use =SLOPE, an Excel function?							
28								

A problem with covariances is that, like variances, the actual numbers are hard to interpret (the sign, of course, is not). For example, our covariance is .0204, but, just from this number, we can't really say if the security has a strong tendency to move with the market or only a weak one. To fix this problem, we divide the covariance by the product of the two standard deviations. The result is the correlation coefficient, introduced in the previous chapter.

From Table 12.4, the correlation between our security and the overall market is .72. Recalling that correlations range from −1 to +1, this .72 tells us that the security has a fairly strong tendency to move with the overall market, but that tendency is not perfect.

Now, we have reached our goal of calculating the beta coefficient. As shown in the last row of Table 12.4, from Equation 12.11, we have

$$\beta_i = \text{Corr}(R_i, R_M) \times \sigma_i / \sigma_M$$
$$= .72 \times (.1887 / .1503)$$
$$= .90$$

We find that this security has a beta of .9, so it has slightly less than average systematic risk. As our nearby *Spreadsheet Analysis* box shows, these calculations can be done easily with a spreadsheet.

Why Do Betas Differ?

Now, we consider why different sources report different betas. The important thing to remember is that betas are estimated from actual data. Different sources estimate differently, possibly using different data. We discuss some of the key differences next.

First, there are two issues concerning data. Betas can be calculated using daily, weekly, monthly, quarterly, or annual returns. In principle, it does not matter which is chosen, but with real data, different estimates will result. Second, betas can be estimated over relatively short periods such as a few weeks or over long periods of 5 to 10 years or even more.

The trade-off here is not hard to understand. Betas obtained from high-frequency returns, such as daily returns, are less reliable than those obtained from less frequent returns, such as monthly returns. This argues for using monthly or longer returns. On the other hand, any time we estimate something, we would like to have a large number of recent observations. This argues for using weekly or daily returns. There is no ideal balance; the most common choices are three to five years of monthly data or a single year of weekly data. The betas we get from a year of weekly data are more current in the sense that they reflect only the previous year, but they tend to be less stable than those obtained from longer periods.

Another issue has to do with choice of a market index. All along, we have discussed the return on the "overall market," but we have not been very precise about how to measure this. Different sources use different indexes to capture the overall market, and different indexes will lead to different beta estimates.

You might wonder whether some index is the "correct" one. The answer is yes, but a problem comes up. In principle, in the CAPM, when we speak of the overall market, what we really mean is the market for *every* risky asset of every type. In other words, what we would need is an index that included all the stocks, bonds, real estate, precious metals, and everything else in the entire world. Obviously, no such index exists, so instead we must choose some smaller index to proxy for this much larger one.

Last, a few sources calculate betas the way we described in Table 12.4, but then they go on to adjust them for statistical reasons. The nature of the adjustment goes beyond our discussion, but such adjustments are another reason why betas differ across sources.

12.8 Multifactor Models

In the 1980s, researchers recognized that there was no single factor (market risk) that determined systematic risk and developed multifactor models. If we apply this principle we obtain the following formula:

$$E(R_i) = R_f + [E(R_m) - R_f] \times \beta_{i1} + [\text{Second Factor Premium}] \times \beta_{i2} \qquad (12.12)$$
$$+ [\text{Third Factor Premium}] \times \beta_{i3} \ldots$$

where β_{i2} = sensitivity of stock i to factor 2.

The Arbitrage Pricing Model was developed in 1976. The model advocates that various economic factors affect stock returns and that stock returns reach their equilibrium level because of the arbitrage principle. If equilibrium is violated, investors can earn abnormal returns by forming risk-free arbitrage portfolios. Since many investors will form these portfolios, prices will increase and decrease until equilibrium is reached. The model was theoretically correct and easy to understand; however, it did not specify which factors affect stock returns significantly. Different researchers use various statistical methods to identify these factors.

Unfortunately, no researcher identified exactly how many factors we should use and which factors we should employ. Some models used various macroeconomic factors (inflation, GDP), others used a combination of macroeconomic and company specific factors (company size, book value/market value ratio, and so on).

We will discuss the tests of CAPM in the next section and afterwards we will introduce one very popular multifactor model, the Fama and French three factor model.

12.9 A (Very) Brief History of Testing CAPM

The CAPM was introduced in the mid-1960s (but, perhaps surprisingly, tests of this model began to appear only in the early 1970s). When researchers test the CAPM, they essentially look to see whether average returns are linearly related to beta. That is, they want to know if asset returns and beta line up as shown in Figure 12.3. The earliest tests of the CAPM suggested that return and risk (as measured by beta) showed a reasonable relationship. However, the relationship was not so strong that financial researchers were content to move on and test other theories.

To summarize years of testing, the relationship between returns and beta appeared to vary depending on the time period that was studied. Over some periods, the relationship was strong. In others, it was apparent but not strong. In others, it was seemingly nonexistent. Over the years, researchers refined their techniques to measure betas. In addition, the question was raised whether researchers could calculate betas at all. The basic argument was that betas could not be calculated relative to the overall market portfolio because we cannot observe the true market portfolio. Nonetheless, despite this insightful critique, researchers continue to test CAPM and debate the findings of CAPM research to this day.

Despite the debate between CAPM critics and CAPM champions, some important ideas have emerged. Few researchers question these general principles:

- Investing has two dimensions: risk and return.
- It is inappropriate to look at the risk of an individual security. What is appropriate is how the individual security contributes to the risk of a diversified portfolio.
- Risk can be decomposed into systematic risk and nonsystematic risk.
- Investors will be compensated only for taking systematic risk.

12.10 The Fama-French Three-Factor Model

To illustrate some aspects of the debate surrounding CAPM, we now briefly explore the Fama-French three-factor model, which gets its name from its creators, Gene Fama and Ken French. Table 12.5 illustrates an important finding from years of research into stock market returns. As shown, two groups of stocks have tended to do noticeably better than the market as a whole: (1) stocks with a small-market capitalization (small-cap stocks) and (2) stocks that have a higher than average ratio of book (or accounting) value to market value of equity (so-called value stocks).

Small Cap Value May No Longer Be a Value

Good things come in small packages. Just ask investors in small-cap value stocks.

Value stocks in the Russell 2000 Index, a benchmark for small stocks, have done twice as well as the Standard & Poor's 500 has over the last 24 months.

And over the past decade small-cap value stocks are up an eye-popping 168%, easily outpacing the S&P's 103% advance and the Russell 2000 Growth index's mere 44% gain.

So, not surprisingly, some small value stocks are starting to look pricey.

The Russell 2000, whose median market cap is about $576 million, fetches 23.4 times earnings estimates for the next four quarters. That's far richer than the S&P 500's 15.5 times forward earnings, according to Thomson Financial/Baseline.

That's why some money managers advise taking profits in the priciest value small caps and replacing them with shares of larger companies.

"We think it would be a good idea for investors to sell some of their small cap-stocks," says Ned Notzon, chairman of the asset allocation committee at T. Rowe Price Associates.

Small caps (which typically have a market capitalization of $1 billion or less) can be great long-term investments, even though their returns can fluctuate much more than shares of large, well-known companies.

For the last 78 years, small caps have generated compound annual returns of 12.7%, compared with 10.4% for large caps, according to Ibbotson Associates. Historically, small-cap value stocks do best—they've risen nearly 15% compared with the 9.6% returns for small-cap growth.

Value stocks typically have stable earnings growth and lower price-to-book and price-to-earnings ratios. Growth stocks tend to have higher growth rates and valuations.

The question is, how long can the current run for small caps last?

Small-cap stocks outperformed others for nearly a decade during the bull market that began in 1974, says Roger Ibbotson, chief executive officer of the Chicago research firm Ibbotson Associates.

But in the fourth year of the two most recent bull markets (which is where we are in the current one), small caps have underperformed big-cap stocks, according to Sam Stovall, chief investment strategist at S&P.

"I would not be optimistic about small caps in 2006," Ibbotson says. "The run has got to be about over, even though momentum is working for the seventh year in a row."

Barry James, a portfolio manager at James Investment Research near Dayton, Ohio, recommends that investors cut their allocations for small caps to 10 to 15% of their portfolios, from 25%.

He's looking for small caps in the technology sector to hold up well, however, and expects smaller energy stocks to resist a broader market decline, even if oil prices drop.

Arthur Nunes, at IMS Capital, says that in the past 20 years, mid-cap stocks—those whose market capitalization is between $1 billion and $5 billion—have been silent winners, offering 15.2% returns with a lower risk than small caps.

Ultimately, investors who have profited by thinking small over the last few years may now need to look at the bigger picture.

Source: Dimitra Defotis, *Barron's Online*, October 11, 2005.

Table 12.5 is formed as follows. First, for each year of historical data, a large set of stocks are ranked on the basis of their market cap, or size. The smallest 20 percent of the stocks are placed into the market cap quintile number 1, the next smallest 20 percent are placed into market cap quintile number 2, and so on. Then, the same set of stocks are ranked on the basis of their book/market (B/M) ratio. The smallest 20 percent are placed into B/M quintile number 1, the next smallest 20 percent are placed into B/M quintile number 2, and so on.

Let's look at the cell with an average annual return of 8.42 percent. This number is calculated as follows. After the sorting described above, we put stocks into portfolios according to both of their quintile scores, for a total of 25 (= 5 × 5) portfolios. So, for example, the stocks with both the smallest cap and the lowest B/M end up in the quintile 1–1 portfolio. As shown in Table 12.5, over the time period 1926 to 2004, the average annual return for stocks in the quintile 1–1 portfolio is 8.42 percent.

TABLE 12.5	Average Annual Percentage Returns from 25 Portfolios Formed on Size (Cap) and Book to Market, 1926–2004				
Quintile	1 (Lowest B/M)	2	3	4	5 (Highest B/M)
1 (smallest cap)	8.42	14.34	18.09	22.06	22.95
2	11.57	16.20	18.06	19.02	19.76
3	12.99	15.83	16.48	17.27	18.47
4	12.44	13.57	15.64	16.51	17.75
5 (largest cap)	11.64	11.32	12.84	13.29	14.92

Source: Author calculations using data from the Web site of Ken French.

www
You can download lots of data behind the Fama-French model at http://mba.tuck. dartmouth.edu/ pages/ faculty/ken.french/

Three things should jump out at you in Table 12.5. Notice that the cell 1-5, which contains stocks with the smallest cap and highest B/M, has had the highest returns. Looking down each column, you can see that in three columns the highest return belongs to the smallest cap quintile (this happens in columns 3, 4, and 5). Looking across each row, you can see that in every row, the highest return belongs to the highest B/M quintile.

Based on further analysis of these data, Professors Fama and French concluded that differences in beta were not sufficient to explain the differences in returns in Table 12.5. They therefore argue that two additional factors beyond beta must be considered to understand differences in expected returns on stocks, namely, market cap and B/M. Thus, their model of stock returns has a total of three factors. Whether these extra factors are truly sources of systematic risk is a subject of ongoing debate.

12.11 Summary and Conclusions

This chapter has covered the essentials of risk and return. Along the way, we have introduced a number of definitions and concepts. The most important of these is the security market line, or SML. The SML is important because it tells us the reward offered in financial markets for bearing risk.

Because we have covered quite a bit of ground, it's useful to summarize the basic economic logic underlying the SML as follows:

1. Based on capital market history, there is a reward for bearing risk. This reward is the risk premium on an asset.

2. The total risk associated with an asset has two parts: systematic risk and unsystematic risk. Unsystematic risk can be freely eliminated by diversification (this is the principle of diversification), so only systematic risk is rewarded. As a result, the risk premium on an asset is determined by its systematic risk. This is the systematic risk principle.

3. An asset's systematic risk, relative to the average, can be measured by its beta coefficient, β_i. The risk premium on an asset is then given by the market risk premium multiplied by the asset's beta coefficient, $[E(R_M) - R_f] \times \beta_i$.

4. The expected return on an asset, $E(R_i)$, is equal to the risk-free rate, R_f, plus the asset's risk premium:

$$E(R_i) = R_f + [E(R_M) - R_f] \times \beta_i$$

This is the equation of the SML, and it is often called the capital asset pricing model (CAPM).

Finally, to close out the chapter we showed how betas are calculated, and we discussed some of the main reasons different sources report different beta coefficients.

REAL WORLD

This chapter introduced you to the famous capital asset pricing model, or CAPM for short. For investors, the CAPM has a stunning implication: What you earn, through time, on your portfolio depends only on the level of systematic risk you bear. The corollary is equally striking: As a diversified investor, you don't need to be concerned with the total risk or volatility of any individual asset in your portfolio—it is simply irrelevant.

An immediate implication of the CAPM is that you, as an investor, need to be aware of the level of systematic risk you are carrying. Look up the betas of the stocks you hold in your simulated brokerage account and compute your portfolio's systematic risk. Is it bigger or smaller than 1.0? More important, is the portfolio's beta consistent with your desired level of portfolio risk?

Betas are particularly useful for understanding mutual fund risk and return. Since most mutual funds are at least somewhat diversified (the exceptions being sector funds and other specialized funds), they have relatively little unsystematic risk, and their betas can be measured with some precision. Look at the funds you own and learn their betas (www.morningstar.ca is a good source). Are the risk levels what you intended? As you study mutual fund risk, you will find some other measures exist, most of which are closely related to the measures discussed in this chapter. Take a few minutes to understand these as well.

Of course, we should note that the CAPM is a theory, and, as with any theory, whether it is correct or not is a question for the data. So does the CAPM work or not? Put more directly, does expected return depend on beta, and beta alone, or do other factors come into play? There is no more hotly debated question in all of finance, and the research that exists to date is inconclusive. (Some researchers would dispute this!) At a minimum, it appears that beta is a useful measure of market-related volatility, but whether it is a useful measure of expected return (much less a comprehensive one) awaits more research. Lots more research.

Key Terms

systematic risk 390
unsystematic risk 390
systematic risk principle 393
beta coefficient (β) 393

security market line (SML) 402
market risk premium 403
capital asset pricing model (CAPM) 403
covariance 408

Chapter Review Problems and Self-Test

1. **Risk and Return** Suppose you observe the following situation:

Security	Beta	Expected Return
Sanders	1.8	22.00%
Janicek	1.6	20.44

If the risk-free rate is 7 percent, are these two stocks correctly priced relative to each other? What must the risk-free rate be if they are correctly priced?

2. **CAPM** Suppose the risk-free rate is 8 percent. The expected return on the market is 16 percent. If a particular stock has a beta of .7, what is its expected return based on the CAPM? If another stock has an expected return of 24 percent, what must its beta be?

Answers to Self-Test Problems

1. If we compute the reward-to-risk ratios, we get $(22\% - 7\%) / 1.8 = 8.33\%$ for Sanders versus 8.4% for Janicek. Relative to Sanders, Janicek's expected return is too high, so its price is too low.

   If they are correctly priced, then they must offer the same reward-to-risk ratio. The risk-free rate would have to be such that

   $$\frac{22\% - R_f}{1.8} = \frac{20.44\% - R_f}{1.6}$$

   With a little algebra, we find that the risk-free rate must be 8 percent:

   $$22\% - R_f = (20.44\% - R_f)(1.8 / 1.6)$$
   $$22\% - 20.44\% \times 1.125 = R_f - R_f \times 1.125$$
   $$R_f = 8\%$$

2. Because the expected return on the market is 16 percent, the market risk premium is $16\% - 8\% = 8\%$ (the risk-free rate is also 8 percent). The first stock has a beta of .7, so its expected return is $8\% + 8\% \times .7 = 13.6\%$.

   For the second stock, notice that the risk premium is $24\% - 8\% = 16\%$. Because this is twice as large as the market risk premium, the beta must be exactly equal to 2. We can verify this using the CAPM:

   $$E(R_i) = R_f + [E(R_M) - R_f] \times \beta_i$$
   $$24\% = 8\% + (16\% - 8\%) \times \beta_i$$
   $$\beta_i = 16\% / 8\% = 2.0$$

Test Your Investment Quotient

CFA®
PROBLEMS

1. **Portfolio Return** According to the CAPM, what is the rate of return of a portfolio with a beta of 1?
   a. Between R_M and R_f
   b. The risk-free rate, R_f
   c. Beta $\times (R_M - R_f)$
   d. The return on the market, R_M

2. **Stock Return** The return on a stock is said to have which two of the following basic parts?
   a. An expected return and an unexpected return.
   b. A measurable return and an unmeasurable return.
   c. A predicted return and a forecast return.
   d. A total return and a partial return.

3. **News Components** A news announcement about a stock is said to have which two of the following parts?

   a. An expected part and a surprise.
   b. Public information and private information.
   c. Financial information and product information.
   d. A good part and a bad part.

4. **News Effects** A company announces that its earnings have increased 50 percent over the previous year, which matches analysts' expectations. What is the likely effect on the stock price?

   a. The stock price will increase.
   b. The stock price will decrease.
   c. The stock price will rise and then fall after an overreaction.
   d. The stock price will not be affected.

5. **News Effects** A company announces that its earnings have decreased 25 percent from the previous year, but analysts expected a small increase. What is the likely effect on the stock price?

   a. The stock price will increase.
   b. The stock price will decrease.
   c. The stock price will rise and then fall after an overreaction.
   d. The stock price will not be affected.

6. **News Effects** A company announces that its earnings have increased 25 percent from the previous year, but analysts actually expected a 50 percent increase. What is the likely effect on the stock price?

   a. The stock price will increase.
   b. The stock price will decrease.
   c. The stock price will rise and then fall after an overreaction.
   d. The stock price will not be affected.

7. **News Effects** A company announces that its earnings have decreased 50 percent from the previous year, but analysts only expected a 25 percent decrease. What is the likely effect on the stock price?

   a. The stock price will increase.
   b. The stock price will decrease.
   c. The stock price will rise and then fall after an overreaction.
   d. The stock price will not be affected.

8. **Security Risk** The systematic risk of a security is also called its

   a. Perceived risk.
   b. Unique or asset-specific risk.
   c. Market risk.
   d. Fundamental risk.

9. **Security Risk** Which type of risk is essentially eliminated by diversification?

   a. Perceived risk
   b. Market risk
   c. Systematic risk
   d. Unsystematic risk

10. **Security Risk** The systematic risk principle states that

   a. Systematic risk doesn't matter to investors.
   b. Systematic risk can be essentially eliminated by diversification.
   c. The reward for bearing risk is independent of the systematic risk of an investment.
   d. The reward for bearing risk depends only on the systematic risk of an investment.

11. **Security Risk** The systematic risk principle has an important implication, which is that
    a. Systematic risk is preferred to unsystematic risk.
    b. Systematic risk is the only risk that can be reduced by diversification.
    c. The expected return on an asset is independent of its systematic risk.
    d. The expected return on an asset depends only on its systematic risk.

12. **CAPM** A financial market's security market line (SML) describes
    a. The relationship between systematic risk and expected returns.
    b. The relationship between unsystematic risk and expected returns.
    c. The relationship between systematic risk and unexpected returns.
    d. The relationship between unsystematic risk and unexpected returns.

13. **Risk Aversion** Which of the following is not an implication of risk aversion for the investment process?
    a. The security market line is upward sloping.
    b. The promised yield on AAA-rated bonds is higher than on A-rated bonds.
    c. Investors expect a positive relationship between expected return and risk.
    d. Investors prefer portfolios that lie on the efficient frontier to other portfolios with equal rates of return.

14. **Unsystematic Risk** In the context of capital market theory, unsystematic risk
    a. Is described as unique risk.
    b. Refers to nondiversifiable risk.
    c. Remains in the market portfolio.
    d. Refers to the variability in all risk assets caused by macroeconomic factors and other aggregate market-related variables.

15. **Security Market Line** Which of the following statements about the security market line (SML) is false?
    a. Properly valued assets plot exactly on the SML.
    b. The SML leads all investors to invest in the same portfolio of risky assets.
    c. The SML provides a benchmark for evaluating expected investment performance.
    d. The SML is a graphic representation of the relationship between expected return and beta.

Concept Questions

1. **Diversifiable Risk** In broad terms, why is some risk diversifiable? Why are some risks nondiversifiable? Does it follow that an investor can control the level of unsystematic risk in a portfolio, but not the level of systematic risk?

2. **Announcements and Prices** Suppose the government announces that, based on a just-completed survey, the growth rate in the economy is likely to be 2 percent in the coming year, compared to 5 percent for the year just completed. Will security prices increase, decrease, or stay the same following this announcement? Does it make any difference whether the 2 percent figure was anticipated by the market? Explain.

3. **Announcements and Risk** Classify the following events as mostly systematic or mostly unsystematic. Is the distinction clear in every case?
    a. Short-term interest rates increase unexpectedly.
    b. The interest rate a company pays on its short-term debt borrowing is increased by its bank.
    c. Oil prices unexpectedly decline.
    d. An oil tanker ruptures, creating a large oil spill.
    e. A manufacturer loses a multimillion-dollar product liability suit.
    f. A court decision substantially broadens producer liability for injuries suffered by product users.

4. **Announcements and Risk** Indicate whether the following events might cause stocks in general to change price, and whether they might cause Big Widget Corp.'s stock to change price.

   a. The government announces that inflation unexpectedly jumped by 2 percent last month.

   b. Big Widget's quarterly earnings report, just issued, generally fell in line with analysts' expectations.

   c. The government reports that economic growth last year was at 3 percent, which generally agreed with most economists' forecasts.

   d. The directors of Big Widget die in a plane crash.

   e. Parliament approves changes to the tax code that will increase the top marginal corporate tax rate. The legislation had been debated for the previous six months.

5. **Diversification and Risk** True or false: The most important characteristic in determining the expected return of a well-diversified portfolio is the variances of the individual assets in the portfolio. Explain.

6. **Announcements** As indicated by examples in this chapter, earnings announcements by companies are closely followed by, and frequently result in, share price revisions. Two issues should come to mind. First, earnings announcements concern past periods. If the market values stocks based on expectations of the future, why are numbers summarizing past performance relevant? Second, these announcements concern accounting earnings. Such earnings may have little to do with cash flow, so, again, why are they relevant?

7. **Beta** Is it possible that a risky asset could have a beta of zero? Explain. Based on the CAPM, what is the expected return on such an asset? Is it possible that a risky asset could have a negative beta? What does the CAPM predict about the expected return on such an asset? Can you give an explanation for your answer?

8. **Relative Valuation** Suppose you identify a situation in which one security is overvalued relative to another. How would you go about exploiting this opportunity? Does it matter if the two securities are both overvalued relative to some third security? Are your profits certain in this case?

9. **Reward-to-Risk Ratio** Explain what it means for all assets to have the same reward-to-risk ratio. How can you increase your return if this holds true? Why would we expect that all assets have the same reward-to-risk ratio in liquid, well-functioning markets?

10. **Systematic versus Firm-Specific Risk** Dudley Trudy, CFA, recently met with one of his clients. Trudy typically invests in a master list of 30 securities drawn from several industries. After the meeting concluded, the client made the following statement: "I trust your stock-picking ability and believe that you should invest my funds in your five best ideas. Why invest in 30 companies when you obviously have stronger opinions on a few of them?" Trudy plans to respond to his client within the context of Modern Portfolio Theory.

    a. Contrast the concept of systematic and firm-specific risk and give one example of each.

    b. Critique the client's suggestion. Discuss the impact of the systematic risk and firm-specific risk on portfolio risk as the number of securities in a portfolio is increased.

Questions and Problems

Core Questions

1. **Stock Betas** A stock has an expected return of 13.6 percent, the risk-free rate is 4 percent, and the market risk premium is 7.5 percent. What must the beta of this stock be?

2. **Market Returns** A stock has an expected return of 12 percent, its beta is .85, and the risk-free rate is 5 percent. What must the expected return on the market be?

3. **Risk-Free Rates** A stock has an expected return of 11 percent, a beta of .70, and the expected return on the market is 13 percent. What must the risk-free rate be?

4. **Market Risk Premium** A stock has a beta of 1.3 and an expected return of 16 percent. If the risk-free rate is 5.5 percent, what is the market risk premium?

5. **Portfolio Betas** You own a stock portfolio invested 15 percent in Stock Q, 20 percent in Stock R, 25 percent in Stock S, and 40 percent in Stock T. The betas for these four stocks are 1.2, .6, 1.5, and .9, respectively. What is the portfolio beta?

6. **Portfolio Betas** You own 200 shares of Stock A at a price of $60 per share, 300 shares of Stock B at $85 per share, and 100 shares of Stock C at $25 per share. The betas for the stocks are 1.2, .9, and 1.6, respectively. What is the beta of your portfolio?

7. **Stock Betas** You own a portfolio equally invested in a risk-free asset and two stocks. If one of the stocks has a beta of 1.2, and the total portfolio is exactly as risky as the market, what must the beta be for the other stock in your portfolio?

8. **Expected Returns** A stock has a beta of 1.15, the expected return on the market is 12 percent, and the risk-free rate is 5.8 percent. What must the expected return on this stock be?

9. **CAPM and Stock Price** A share of stock sells for $48 today. The beta of the stock is 1.2, and the expected return on the market is 11 percent. The stock is expected to pay a dividend of $1.10 in one year. If the risk-free rate is 4.5 percent, what will the share price be in one year?

10. **Portfolio Weights** A stock has a beta of 1.1 and an expected return of 15 percent. A risk-free asset currently earns 6 percent.

    a. What is the expected return on a portfolio that is equally invested in the two assets?
    b. If a portfolio of the two assets has a beta of .5, what are the portfolio weights?
    c. If a portfolio of the two assets has an expected return of 12 percent, what is its beta?
    d. If a portfolio of the two assets has a beta of 1.80, what are the portfolio weights? How do you interpret the weights for the two assets in this case? Explain.

Intermediate Questions

11. **Portfolio Risk and Return** Asset W has an expected return of 15 percent and a beta of 1.2. If the risk-free rate is 7 percent, complete the following table for portfolios of Asset W and a risk-free asset. Illustrate the relationship between portfolio expected return and portfolio beta by plotting the expected returns against the betas. What is the slope of the line that results?

Percentage of Portfolio in Asset W	Portfolio Expected Return	Portfolio Beta
0%		
25		
50		
75		
100		
125		
150		

12. **Relative Valuation** Stock Y has a beta of 1.5 and an expected return of 18 percent. Stock Z has a beta of .80 and an expected return of 11 percent. If the risk-free rate is 6 percent and the market risk premium is 7 percent, are these stocks correctly priced?

13. **Relative Valuation** In the previous problem, what would the risk-free rate have to be for the two stocks to be correctly priced relative to each other?

14. **CAPM** Using the CAPM, show that the ratio of the risk premiums on two assets is equal to the ratio of their betas.

15. **Relative Valuation** Suppose you observe the following situation:

Security	Beta	Expected Return
Oxy Co.	1.10	16%
More-On Co.	.75	12

Assume these securities are correctly priced. Based on the CAPM, what is the expected return on the market? What is the risk-free rate?

16. **Calculating Beta** Show that another way to calculate beta is to take the covariance between the security and the market and divide by the variance of the market's return.

17. **Calculating Beta** Fill in the following table, supplying all the missing information. Use this information to calculate the security's beta.

	Returns		Returned Deviations		Squared Deviations		Product of
Year	Security	Market	Security	Market	Security	Market	Deviations
2001	12%	6%					
2002	−9	−12					
2003	−6	0					
2004	30	−4					
2005	18	30					
Totals	45	20					

18. **Analyzing a Portfolio** You have $100,000 to invest in a portfolio containing Stock X, Stock Y, and a risk-free asset. You must invest all of your money. Your goal is to create a portfolio that has an expected return of 15 percent and that has only 90 percent of the risk of the overall market. If X has an expected return of 19 percent and a beta of 1.5, Y has an expected return of 12.2 percent and a beta of 1.1, and the risk-free rate is 6 percent, how much money will you invest in Stock Y? How do you interpret your answer?

19. **Systematic versus Unsystematic Risk** Consider the following information on Stocks I and II:

			Rate of Return if State Occurs	
State of Economy	Probability of State of Economy	Stock I	Stock II	
Recession	.25	.04	−.20	
Normal	.50	.21	.11	
Irrational exuberance	.25	.16	.34	

The market risk premium is 8 percent, and the risk-free rate is 5 percent. Which stock has the most systematic risk? Which one has the most unsystematic risk? Which stock is "riskier"? Explain.

20. **Systematic and Unsystematic Risk** The beta for a certain stock is 1.20, the risk-free rate is 6 percent, and the expected return on the market is 13 percent. Complete the following table to decompose the stock's return into the systematic return and the unsystematic return.

	Actual Returns		Unexpected Portion		Systematic Portion	Unsystematic Portion (ϵ)
Year	R	R_M	$R - E(R)$	$R_M - E(R_M)$	$[R_M - E(R_M)] \times \beta$	$R - E(R)] - [R_M - E(R_M)] \times \beta$
2001	26%	19%				
2002	12	8				
2003	−21	−13				
2004	−3	4				
2005	38	22				

21. **CAPM** John Wilson, a portfolio manager, is evaluating the expected performance of two common stocks, Furhman Labs, Inc., and Garten Testing, Inc. The risk-free rate is 5 percent, the expected return on the market is 11.5 percent, and the betas of the two stocks are 1.5 and .8, respectively. Wilson's own forecasts of the returns on the two stocks are 13.25 percent for Furhman Labs and 11.25 percent for Garten. Calculate the required return for each stock. Is each stock undervalued, fairly valued, or overvalued?

Use the following information for the next four questions: Abigail Grace has a $900,000 fully diversified portfolio. She subsequently inherits ABC Company common stock worth $100,000. Her financial adviser provided her with the forecasted information below:

	Monthly Expected Returns	Expected Standard Deviation of Monthly Returns
Original portfolio	.67%	2.37%
ABC Company	1.25	2.95

The expected correlation coefficient of ABC stock returns and the original portfolio is .40. The inheritance changes her overall portfolio and she is deciding whether to keep the ABC stock.

22. **Portfolio Return and Standard Deviation** Assuming Grace keeps the ABC stock, calculate the expected return of the new portfolio, the covariance of ABC stock with the original portfolio, and the expected standard deviation of the new portfolio.

23. **Portfolio Return and Standard Deviation** If Grace sells the ABC stock, she will invest the proceeds in risk-free government securities yielding .42 percent monthly. Calculate the expected return of the new portfolio, the covariance of the government security returns with the original portfolio, and the expected standard deviation of the new portfolio.

24. **Beta** Determine whether the beta of Grace's new portfolio, which includes the government securities, will be higher or lower than the beta of her original portfolio. Justify your response with one reason. No calculations are necessary.

25. **Diversification** Based on a conversation with her husband, Grace is considering selling the $100,000 of ABC stock and acquiring $100,000 of XYZ Company common stock instead. XYZ stock has the same expected return and standard deviation as ABC stock. Her husband comments, "It doesn't matter whether you keep all of the ABC stock or replace it with $100,000 of the XYZ stock." Are her husband's comments correct or incorrect? Justify your response.

Spreadsheet Problem

26. **Calculating Correlation** You are given the following information concerning a stock and the market:

	Returns	
Year	Market	Stock
2000	34%	49%
2001	27	24
2002	11	6
2003	19	10
2004	−12	−25
2005	8	3

Calculate the average return and standard deviation for the market and the stock. Next, calculate the correlation between the stock and the market. Use a spreadsheet to calculate your answers.

STANDARD &POOR'S

S&P Problem

Note: These problems can be calculated manually, but a spreadsheet program such as Excel is recommended for use in calculations.

1. **Return Correlations** Go to the "Excel Analytics" link for Canadian Pacific (CP) and Thompson Corporation (TOC) and download the monthly adjusted stock prices. Copy the monthly returns for each stock into a new spreadsheet. Calculate the correlation between the two stock returns. Would you expect a higher or lower correlation if you had chosen Canadian National Railways instead of Thompson in the two stocks? What is the standard deviation of a portfolio 75 percent invested in CP and 25 percent in TOC? What about a portfolio equally invested in the two stocks? What about a portfolio invested 25 percent in CP and 75 percent in TOC?

2. **Beta** Go to the "Excel Analytics" link for Abitibi (ABY) and download the monthly adjusted stock prices. Copy the monthly returns for Abitibi and monthly TSX composite returns into a new spreadsheet. Calculate the beta of Abitibi for the entire period of data available. Now download the monthly stock prices for Nortel (NT) and calculate the beta for this company. Are the betas similar? Would you have expected the beta of Abitibi to be higher or lower than the beta for Nortel? Why?

What's on the Web?

1. **Expected Return** You want to find the expected return for BCE using the CAPM. First you need the market risk premium. Go to www.bankofcanada.ca. Find the current interest rate for three-month Treasury Bills. Use the average large-company stock return in Chapter 1 to calculate the market risk premium. Next, go to finance.yahoo.com, enter the ticker symbol BCE, and follow the "Key Statistics" link. In the Statistics at a Glance section you will find the beta for BCE. What is the expected return for BCE using the CAPM? What assumptions have you made to arrive at this number?

2. **Portfolio Beta** You have decided to invest in an equally-weighted portfolio consisting of American Express, Procter & Gamble, Johnson and Johnson, and United Technologies, and you need to find the beta of your portfolio. Go to finance.yahoo.com and follow the "Global Symbol Lookup" link to find the ticker symbols for each of these companies. Next, go back to finance.yahoo.com, enter one of the ticker symbols, and get a stock quote. Follow the "Profile" link to find the beta for this company. You will then need to find the beta for each of the companies. What is the beta for your portfolio?

3. **Beta** Which stock has the highest and lowest beta? Go to www.hoovers.com and follow the "StockScreener" link. Enter 0 as the maximum beta and enter search. How many stocks currently have a beta less than 0? Which stock has the lowest beta? Go back to the stock screener and enter 3 as the minimum value. How many stocks have a beta greater than 3? What about 4? Which stock has the highest beta?

4. **Security Market Line** Go to finance.yahoo.com and enter the ticker symbol TU for Telus. Follow the "Profile" link to get the beta for the company. Next, follow the "Research" link to find the estimated price in 12 months according to market analysts. Using the current share price and the mean target price, compute the expected return for this stock. Don't forget to include the expected dividend payments over the next year. Now go to www.bloomberg.com, follow the "Bonds & Rates" link, then the "Latest Rates" link, and find the current interest rate for three-month Treasury bills. Using this information, calculate the expected return on the market using the reward-to-risk ratio. Does this number make sense? Why or why not?

CHAPTER 13

Performance Evaluation and Risk Management

"It is not the return on my investment that I am concerned about; it is the return of my investment!"

—Will Rogers

"The stock market will fluctuate!"

—J. P. Morgan

Humourist Will Rogers expressed concern about "the return *of* [his] investment." Famed financier J. P. Morgan, when asked by a reporter what he thought the stock market would do, replied, "The stock market will fluctuate!" Both Will Rogers and J. P. Morgan understood a basic fact of investing—investors holding risky assets worry: How well are my investments doing? How much money am I making (or losing)? and What are my chances of incurring a significant loss? ∎

This chapter examines methods of dealing with two related problems faced by investors in risky assets. These are (1) evaluating risk-adjusted investment performance and (2) assessing and managing the risks involved with specific investment strategies. Both subjects have come up previously in our text, but we have deferred a detailed discussion of them until now.

We first consider the problem of performance evaluation. Specifically, suppose we have investment returns data for several portfolios covering a recent period, and we wish to evaluate how well these portfolios have performed relative to other portfolios or some investment benchmark. The need for this form of scrutiny arises in a number of situations, including:

- An investor wishing to choose a mutual fund wants to first compare the investment performance of several dozen candidate funds.

- A pension fund administrator wants to select a money manager and thus needs to compare the investment performance of a group of money managers.

- An employer wants to compare the performance of several investment companies before selecting one for inclusion in her company-sponsored retirement plan.

In the first section of this chapter, we examine several useful evaluation measures of portfolio performance and discuss how they might be applied to these and similar situations.

In the second part of the chapter, we discuss the important problem of risk management from the perspective of an investor or money manager concerned with the possibility of a large loss. Specifically, we examine methods to assess the probabilities and magnitudes of losses we might expect to experience during a set future time period. These risk assessment techniques are commonly employed in a number of situations, including:

- A dealer wants to know how much of a loss is possible with a 5 percent probability during the coming day's trading from the firm's inventory.

- The foreign currency manager of a commercial bank wants to know how much of a loss is possible with a 2 percent probability on the bank's foreign currency portfolio during the coming week.

- A futures exchange clearinghouse wants to know how much margin funds should be deposited by exchange members to cover extreme losses that might occur with a "once in a century" probability.

Methods used to assess risk in these and similar scenarios fall into the category commonly referred to as "Value-at-Risk." Value-at-Risk techniques are widely applied by commercial banks, securities firms, and other financial institutions to assess and understand the risk exposure of portfolios under their management.

13.1 Active and Passive Portfolio Management

Investors can either follow an active strategy or a passive strategy after they form their portfolio. Investors who choose passive management do not change the composition of their portfolio. A *Buy and Hold* strategy involves buying financial instruments, forming the portfolio, and then holding the chosen securities in the original percentage of the portfolio and not changing the composition of the portfolio. Another technique of passive portfolio management is buying shares of a *market index fund* that mimics a market index (e.g., S&P/TSX Composite Index) and holding it. Investors do not pay transaction fees for frequent buying and selling. They also do not spend a lot of time gathering information to find underpriced securities.

In contrast to passive management, active management involves changing the composition of portfolios. Some active managers follow *market timing* strategy. There are mutual fund managers who specialize in market timing. This strategy involves using various techniques and predicting future movements in financial instruments, especially stocks, and buying and selling them at the right time. Also, market timers may advocate moving into a stock market or an industry at a particular time. Other managers attempt to find undervalued and overvalued securities, buy the undervalued ones and short sell the overvalued ones to try and obtain abnormal profits. Active management is costly, time consuming, and risky. Investors need to evaluate managers of actively managed funds to find out whether or not their strategies are successful. The Sharpe ratio, Treynor ratio, and all the other risk measures are important tools for these investors.

13.2 Performance Evaluation

performance evaluation The assessment of how well a money manager achieves a balance between high returns and acceptable risks.

Investors have a natural (and very rational) interest in how well particular investments have done. This is true whether the investor manages his or her own portfolio or has money managed by a professional. Concern with investment performance motivates the topic of **performance evaluation**. In general terms, performance evaluation focuses on assessing how well a money manager achieves high returns balanced with acceptable risks.

Going back to our discussion of efficient markets in Chapter 8, we raised the question of risk-adjusted performance and whether anyone can consistently earn an "excess" return, thereby "beating the market." The standard example is an evaluation of investment performance achieved by the manager of a mutual fund. Such a performance evaluation is more than an academic exercise, since its purpose is to help investors decide whether they would entrust investment funds with this fund manager. Our goal here is to introduce you to the primary tools used to make this assessment.

Performance Evaluation Measures

raw return States the total percentage return on an investment with no adjustment for risk or comparison to any benchmark.

A variety of measures are used to evaluate investment performance. Here, we examine four of the best-known and most popular measures: the Sharpe ratio, the Treynor ratio, Jensen's alpha and M^2 Measure. But before we do so, let us first briefly discuss a naive measure of performance evaluation—the **raw return** on a portfolio.

The raw return on an investment portfolio, here denoted by R_p, is simply the total percentage return on the portfolio with no adjustment for risk or comparison to any benchmark. Calculating percentage returns was discussed in Chapter 1. The fact that a raw portfolio return does not reflect any consideration of risk suggests that its usefulness is limited when making investment decisions. After all, risk is important to almost every investor.

The Sharpe Ratio

Sharpe ratio Measures investment performance as the ratio of portfolio risk premium over portfolio return standard deviation.

A basic measure of investment performance that includes an adjustment for risk is the Sharpe ratio, originally proposed by Nobel laureate William F. Sharpe. The **Sharpe ratio** is computed as a portfolio's risk premium divided by the standard deviation of the portfolio's return:

$$\text{Sharpe ratio} = \frac{R_p - R_f}{\sigma_p} \qquad (13.1)$$

Visit Professor
Sharpe at
www.wsharpe.com

In this case, the portfolio risk premium is the raw portfolio return less a risk-free return, that is, $R_p - R_f$, which we know is the basic reward for bearing risk. The return standard deviation, σ_p, is a measure of risk, which we discussed in Chapter 1 and again in Chapter 2.

More precisely, return standard deviation is a measure of the *total* risk (as opposed to systematic risk) for a security or a portfolio. Thus, the Sharpe ratio is a reward-to-risk ratio that focuses on total risk. Because total risk is used to make the adjustment, the Sharpe ratio is probably most appropriate for evaluating relatively diversified portfolios.

The Sharpe ratio measures whether or not a portfolio produces extra return over the risk-free rate. A negative Sharpe ratio indicates that a portfolio fails to earn a return above and beyond the risk-free rate. Mor0eover, the ratio ranks the portfolios according to their portfolio risk level by dividing the extra return to standard deviation. Investors expect higher-risk portfolios to earn higher returns. Portfolios with high Sharpe ratios are managed well. Investors choose the highest Sharpe ratio portfolios among different portfolios.

LOOK SHARPE

EXAMPLE 13.1

Over a recent three-year period, the average annual return on a portfolio was 20 percent, and the annual return standard deviation for the portfolio was 25 percent. During the same period, the average return on 90-day Treasury bills was 5 percent. What is the Sharpe ratio for this portfolio during this three-year period?

Referring to the equation above, we calculate

$$\text{Sharpe ratio} = \frac{.20 - .05}{.25} = .6$$

This indicates that the Sharpe ratio of portfolio excess return to total risk is .6.

The Treynor Ratio

Another standard measure of investment performance that includes an adjustment for systematic risk is the Treynor ratio (or index), originally suggested by Jack L. Treynor. The **Treynor ratio** is computed as a portfolio's risk premium divided by the portfolio's beta coefficient:

Treynor ratio
Measures investment performance as the ratio of portfolio risk premium over portfolio beta.

$$\text{Treynor ratio} = \frac{R_p - R_f}{\beta_p} \tag{13.2}$$

As with the Sharpe ratio, the Treynor ratio is a reward-to-risk ratio. The key difference is that the Treynor ratio looks at systematic risk only, not total risk.

THE TREYNOR RATIO

EXAMPLE 13.2

Over a three-year period, the average return on a portfolio was 20 percent, and the beta for the portfolio was 1.25. During the same period, the average return on 90-day Treasury bills was 5 percent. What is the Treynor ratio for this portfolio during this period?

(continued)

Referring to the Treynor ratio equation above, we calculate

Treynor ratio $= \dfrac{.20 - .05}{1.25} = .12$

This reveals that the Treynor ratio of portfolio excess return to portfolio beta is .12.

You may recall that we saw the Treynor ratio in our previous chapter. There we said that in an active, competitive market, a strong argument can be made that all assets (and portfolios of those assets) should have the same Treynor ratio, that is, the same reward-to-risk ratio, where "risk" refers to systematic risk. To the extent that they don't, then there is evidence that at least some portfolios have earned excess returns.

Jensen's Alpha

Jensen's alpha
Measures investment performance as the raw portfolio return less the return predicted by the Capital Asset Pricing Model.

A third common measure of investment performance that draws on capital asset pricing theory for its formulation is Jensen's alpha, proposed by Michael C. Jensen. **Jensen's alpha** is computed as the raw portfolio return less the expected portfolio return predicted by the Capital Asset Pricing Model (CAPM).

Recall from our previous chapter that, according to the CAPM, the expected return on a portfolio, $E(R_p)$, can be written as:

$$E(R_p) = R_f + [E(R_M) - R_f] \times \beta_p \tag{13.3}$$

To compute Jensen's alpha, we compare the actual return, R_p, to the predicted return. The difference is the alpha, denoted α_p:

$$\begin{aligned}\alpha_p &= R_p - E(R_p) \\ &= R_p - \{R_f + [E(R_M) - R_f] \times \beta_p\}\end{aligned} \tag{13.4}$$

Jensen's alpha is easy to understand. It is simply the excess return above or below the security market line, and, in this sense, it can be interpreted as a measure of how much the portfolio "beat the market." This interpretation is illustrated in Figure 13.1, which

FIGURE 13.1

Jensen's Alpha

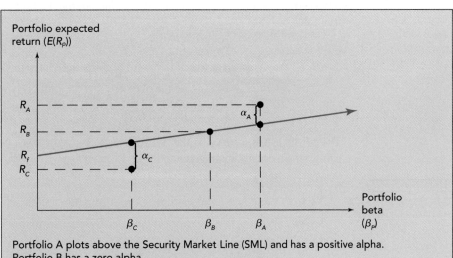

Portfolio A plots above the Security Market Line (SML) and has a positive alpha.
Portfolio B has a zero alpha.
Portfolio C plots below the SML and has a negative alpha.

shows a portfolio with a positive (A), zero (B), and negative (C) alpha, respectively. As shown, a positive alpha is a good thing because the portfolio has a relatively high return given its level of systematic risk.

JENSEN'S ALPHA

EXAMPLE 13.3

Over a three-year period, the average annual return on a portfolio was 20 percent, and the beta for the portfolio was 1.25. During the same period, the average annual return on 90-day Treasury bills was 5 percent, and the average return on the market portfolio was 15 percent. What is Jensen's alpha for this portfolio during this period?

Referring to the Jensen-alpha equation above, we calculate

$$.20 - [.05 + (.15 - .05)1.25] = .025$$

This shows that the portfolio had an alpha measure of portfolio excess return of 2.5 percent.

M^2 Measure

Leah Modigliani and Franco Modigliani developed a new measure which compares the performance of managed portfolio with the same risk level hypothetical portfolio. M^2 Measure gives us the excess return of a hypothetical portfolio over the market portfolio. For a portfolio p, we can create a hypothetical portfolio by combining a percentage of portfolio p with a risk-free asset (T-bill) such that the hypothetical portfolio will have the same standard deviation as the market portfolio. We can then compare two same-risk portfolios using their returns.

$$M^2 = R_{hp} - R_m \tag{13.5}$$

where hp represents the hypothetical portfolio and m represents the market index.

For example, assume that portfolio A has 12 percent return and 40 percent standard deviation. Market portfolio has a 15 percent return and 15 percent standard deviation. Our hypothetical portfolio consists of w percentage of portfolio p and $1 - w$ percentage of risk-free asset. A ninety-day T-bill has the annual average return of 5 percent (risk-free rate).

$$R_{hp} = w \times 0.12 + (1 - w) \times 0.05$$

$$\sigma_{hp} = w \times 0.4 = 0.15, w = 0.15/0.4 = 0.375$$

$$R_{hp} = 0.375 \times 0.12 + 0.625 \times 0.05 = 0.0763$$

$$M^2 = 0.0763 - 0.15 = -0.0737$$

The M^2 measure shows that the portfolio's excess return was negative (-0.0737) indicating unsuccessful management.

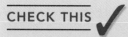

CHECK THIS

13.1a What is the Sharpe ratio of portfolio performance?

13.1b What is the Treynor ratio of portfolio performance?

13.1c What is Jensen's alpha?

13.1d Why can Jensen's alpha be interpreted as measuring by how much an investment portfolio beat the market?

13.3 Comparing Performance Measures

Table 13.1 presents investment performance data for three risky portfolios, A, B, and C, along with return data for the market portfolio and a risk-free portfolio, denoted by M and F, respectively. Based on the performance data in Table 13.1, Table 13.2 provides computed performance measures for portfolios A, B, and C, along with a market portfolio, M. The market portfolio is a benchmark of investment performance.

As shown in Table 13.2, the Sharpe ratio ranks the three risky portfolios in the ascending order of performance A, B, and C. By contrast, the Treynor ratio ranks these three risky portfolios in the reversed order of performance C, B, and A. Jensen's alpha yields another portfolio ranking altogether, with the ascending order of performance C, A, and B. According to M^2 measure the best portfolio is C with positive return of 0.23%, followed by B and A.

The example above illustrates that the four performance measures can yield substantially different performance rankings. The fact that each of the three performance measures can produce such different results leaves us with the burning question: "Which performance measure should we use to evaluate portfolio performance?"

Well, the simple answer is: "it depends." If you wish to select a performance measure to evaluate an entire portfolio held by an investor, then the Sharpe ratio is appropriate. But if you wish to choose a performance measure to individually evaluate securities or portfolios for possible inclusion in a broader (or "master") portfolio, then either the Treynor ratio or Jensen's alpha is appropriate.

In broader terms, all measures have strengths and weaknesses. Jensen's alpha is, as we have seen, easy to interpret. Comparing Jensen's alpha and the Treynor ratio, they are really very similar. The only difference is that the Treynor ratio standardizes everything, including any excess return, relative to beta. If you were to take Jensen's alpha and divide it by beta, then you would have a Jensen-Treynor alpha, which measures excess return relative to beta.

A common weakness of the Jensen and Treynor measures is that both require a beta estimate. As we discussed in our last chapter, betas from different sources can

TABLE 13.1	Investment Performance Data		
Portfolio	R_P	σ_P	β_P
A	12%	40%	.5
B	15%	30%	.75
C	20%	22%	1.4
M	15%	15%	1
F	5%	0%	0

TABLE 13.2	Portfolio Performance Measurement		
Portfolio	**Sharpe Ratio**	**Treynor Ratio**	**Jensen Alpha**	**M^2**
A	.175	.14	2%	−7.37%
B	.333	.133	2.5%	−5%
C	.682	.107	1%	−0.23%
M	.667	.10	0%	0%

differ a lot, and, as a result, what appears to be a positive alpha might just be due to a mismeasured beta.

The Sharpe ratio has the advantage that no beta is necessary, and standard deviations can be calculated unambiguously. The drawback is that total risk is frequently not what really matters. However, for a relatively well-diversified portfolio, most of the risk is systematic, so there's not much difference between total risk and systematic risk. For this reason, for doing things like evaluating mutual funds, the Sharpe ratio is probably the most commonly used. Furthermore, if a mutual fund is not very diversified, then its standard deviation would be larger, resulting in a smaller Sharpe ratio. Thus, the Sharpe ratio, in effect, penalizes a portfolio for being undiversified.

To see how these performance measures are used in practice, have a look at our nearby *Work the Web* box, which shows some actual numbers for a mutual fund.

PICKING PORTFOLIOS

EXAMPLE 13.4

Suppose you are restricted to investing all of your money in only a single portfolio from among the choices A, B, and C presented in Table 13.1. Which portfolio should you choose?

Since you can only select a single portfolio, the Sharpe-ratio measure of portfolio performance should be used. Referring to Table 13.2, we see that portfolio C has the highest Sharpe ratio of excess return per unit of total risk. Therefore, portfolio C should be chosen.

PICKING PORTFOLIOS AGAIN

EXAMPLE 13.5

Suppose you are considering whether portfolios A, B, and C presented in Table 13.1 should be included in a master portfolio. Should you select one, two, or all three portfolios for inclusion in your master portfolio?

Since you are selecting portfolios for inclusion in a master portfolio, either the Treynor ratio or Jensen's alpha should be used. Suppose you decide to consider any portfolio that outperforms the market portfolio M, based on either the Treynor ratio or Jensen's alpha. Referring to Table 13.2, we see that all three portfolios have Treynor ratios and Jensen alphas greater than the market portfolio. Therefore, you decide to include all three portfolios in your master portfolio.

CHECK THIS ✓

13.2a Explain the difference between systematic risk measured by beta and total risk measured by standard deviation. When are they essentially the same?

13.2b Alter the returns data in Table 13.1 so that portfolios A, B, and C all have a raw return of 15 percent. Which among these three portfolios then have a Treynor ratio or Jensen alpha greater than that of the market portfolio M?

WORK THE WEB

The various performance measures we've discussed are frequently used to evaluate mutual funds, or, more accurately, mutual fund managers. For example, the information below concerns the Fidelity Low-Priced Stock Fund, which is a small-cap value fund. We obtained the numbers from www.morningstar.com by entering the fund's ticker symbol (FLPSX) and following the "Risk Measures" link. By the way, you'll see the abbreviation "MPT" in this context quite a bit. MPT is an acronym for "Modern Portfolio Theory," which is the general label for things related to Markowitz-type portfolio analysis and the CAPM.

For this fund, the beta is .97, so the degree of market risk is about average. The fund's alpha is 7.47 percent, a relatively high number. The fund's standard deviation is 12.44 percent. The mean reported, 24.85 percent, is the geometric return of the fund over the past three years. The Sharpe ratio for the fund is 1.72. Of course we can't judge this value in isolation, but at least we know it is positive. Other measures of risk are reported here, but they are specific to Morningstar. To learn more, visit the Web site.

Fidelity Low-Priced Stock FLPSX   See Fund Family Data ▸▸   🅕 *Fidelity*

Volatility Measurements	Trailing 3-Yr through 09-30-05	*Trailing 5-Yr through 09-30-05	
Standard Deviation	12.44	Sharpe Ratio	1.72
Mean	24.85	Bear Market Decile Rank*	1

Modern Portfolio Theory Statistics		Trailing 3-Yr through 09-30-05
	Standard Index S&P 500	**Best Fit Index** Wil 4500
R-Squared	74	93
Beta	0.97	0.92
Alpha	7.47	1.95

Sharpe-Optimal Portfolios

In this section, we show how to obtain a funds allocation with the highest possible Sharpe ratio. Such a portfolio is said to be "Sharpe optimal." The method is closely related to the procedure of obtaining a Markowitz efficient frontier discussed in Chapter 2. This is no surprise, as both methods are used to achieve an optimal balance of risk and return for investment portfolios.

To illustrate the connection, have a look at Figure 13.2. This figure actually reproduces Figure 2.4, which shows the investment opportunity set of risk-return possibilities for a portfolio of two assets, a stock fund and a bond fund. Now the question is: "Of all of these possible portfolios, which one is Sharpe optimal?" To find out, consider the portfolio labelled A in the figure. Notice that we have drawn a straight line from the risk-free rate running through this point.

What is the slope of this straight line? As always, the slope of a straight line is the "rise over the run." In this case, the return rises from the risk-free rate, R_f, to the

FIGURE 13.2

The Sharpe-Optimal Portfolio

Portfolio *T* has the highest Sharpe ratio of any possible combination of these two assets, so it is Sharpe optimal.

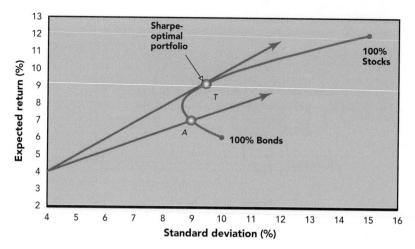

expected return on portfolio *A*, so the rise is $E(R_A) - R_f$. At the same time, risk moves from zero for a risk-free asset up to the standard deviation on portfolio *A*, so the run is $\sigma_A - 0 = \sigma_A$. Thus, the slope is $[E(R_A) - R_f] / \sigma_A$, which is just the Sharpe ratio for portfolio *A*.

So, the slope of a straight line drawn from the risk-free rate to a portfolio in Figure 13.2 tells us the Sharpe ratio for that portfolio. This is always the case, even if there are many assets, not just two. The problem of finding the Sharpe-optimal portfolio thus boils down to finding the line with the steepest slope. Looking again at Figure 13.2, we quickly figure out that the line with the steepest slope is always going to be the one that just touches (i.e., is tangent to) the investment opportunity set. We have labelled this portfolio *T* (for tangent).

We now have an interesting and important result. The Markowitz efficient frontier tells us which portfolios are efficient, but it does not tell us which of the efficient portfolios is the best. What Figure 13.2 shows is that, of those efficient portfolios, one is the very best, at least in the sense of being Sharpe optimal.

To illustrate actually finding the Sharpe optimal portfolio, recall from Chapter 2 that the returns of the stock and bond funds are 12 percent and 6 percent. The standard deviations are 15 percent and 10 percent, respectively, and the correlation is .10. From our discussion in Chapter 2, we know that the expected return on a portfolio of two assets is given by:

$$E(R_P) = x_S E(R_S) + x_B E(R_B)$$

where x_S and x_B are the percentages invested in the stock and bond fund, respectively. Also from Chapter 2, the variance on a portfolio of these two assets is:

$$\sigma_P^2 = x_S^2 \sigma_S^2 + x_B^2 \sigma_B^2 + 2x_S x_B \sigma_S \sigma_B \text{Corr}(R_S, R_B)$$

Putting it all together, the Sharpe ratio for our two-asset portfolio looks like this:

$$\frac{E(R_P) - R_f}{\sigma_P} = \frac{x_S E(R_S) + x_B E(R_B) - R_f}{\sqrt{x_S^2 \sigma_S^2 + x_B^2 \sigma_B^2 + 2x_S x_B \sigma_S \sigma_B \text{Corr}(R_S, R_B)}} \tag{13.6}$$

Our job is to find the values of x_S and x_B that make this ratio as large as possible. This looks like a tough job, but, as our nearby *Spreadsheet Analysis* box shows, it can be

SPREADSHEET ANALYSIS

	A	B	C	D	E	F	G	H
1								
2			**Optimal Sharpe Ratio with Two Risky Assets, Stocks and Bonds**					
3								
4		Expected Returns:						
5		Stocks =	0.12					
6		Bonds =	0.06			Portfolio Return, E(Rp) =		0.102
7								
8		Risk-Free Rate =	0.04			Portfolio Standard Deviation, SD(Rp) =		0.112
9								
10		Standard Deviations:					Sharpe Ratio =	0.553
11		Stocks =	0.15					
12		Bonds =	0.10					
13						Portfolio Weights to Maximize Sharpe Ratio:		
14		Correlation between					Stocks =	0.7000
15		Stocks and Bonds =	0.10				Bonds =	0.3000
16							(= 1 − H15)	
17								
18	Formulas for Portfolio Return, Portfolio Standard Deviation, and Sharpe Ratio:							
19								
20	E(Rp) =	H14*C5+H15*C6						
21								
22	SD(Rp) =	SQRT(H14*H14*C11*C11+H15*H15*C12*C12+2*H14*H15*C15*C11*C12)						
23								
24	Sharpe Ratio = (E(Rp) − RF) / SD(Rp) = (H6−C8) / H8							
25								
26	Using SOLVER® to compute portfolio weights that maximize the Sharpe Ratio:							
27								

Solver Parameters ? ✕

Set Target Cell: `$H$10`

Equal To: ⦿ Max ◯ Min ◯ Value of: `0`

By Changing Cells:

`$H$14`   Guess

Subject to the Constraints:

`$H$14 >= 0`   Add
`$H$15 >= 0`   Change
   Delete

Solve
Close
Options
Reset All
Help

done relatively easily. As shown there, assuming a risk-free interest rate of 4 percent, the highest possible Sharpe ratio is .553 based on a 70–30 mix between stocks and bonds.

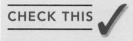

CHECK THIS

13.2c   What is a Sharpe-optimal portfolio?

13.2d   Among the many Markowitz efficient portfolios, which one is Sharpe optimal?

13.4 Investment Risk Management

investment risk management
Concerns a money manager's control over investment risks, usually with respect to potential short-run losses.

In the first part of this chapter, we discussed performance evaluation within a framework of optimizing the trade-off between risk and return for an investment portfolio. In the remainder of this chapter, we examine **investment risk management** within the framework of a money manager's concern over potential losses for an investment portfolio within a specific time horizon. We focus on what is known as the Value-at-Risk approach. However, risk can be viewed in many different ways, and, for some alternative viewpoints, we suggest reading the nearby *Investment Updates* box.

Value-at-Risk (VaR)
Assesses risk by stating the probability of a loss a portfolio might experience within a fixed time horizon with a specified probability.

Value-at-Risk

An important goal of this chapter is to learn how to assess portfolio risk using **Value-at-Risk**. In essence, the Value-at-Risk (usually abbreviated VaR) method involves evaluating the probability of a significant loss. The basic approach we describe here is widely used by many different financial institutions.

VaR RISK STATISTIC

EXAMPLE 13.6

You agree with J. P. Morgan that the stock market will fluctuate and have become concerned with how these fluctuations might affect your stock portfolio. Having read about the VaR method for measuring investment risk, you decide to apply it to your portfolio.

Suppose you believe that there is a 5 percent chance of a return of -18 percent or worse in the coming week. Mathematically, this risk assessment can be stated as:

$$\textit{Prob}(R_p \leq -18\%) = 5\%$$

Taken together, this -18 percent or worse expected loss and 5 percent probability form a VaR "statistic" for your stock portfolio.

normal distribution
A statistical model for assessing probabilities related to many phenomena, including security returns.

The VaR measure of investment risk is closely related to something we discussed way back in Chapter 1. There we said that if the returns on an investment follow a **normal distribution**, then we can state the probability that a portfolio's return will be within a certain range. Since a normal distribution is completely specified by its mean and standard deviation, these are all that we need to state this probability.

For example, suppose you own a S&P/TSX 60 index fund. What is the probability of a return of -10.34 percent or worse in a particular year? As we saw in Chapter 1, since 1983 the return on the S&P/TSX 60 Index has averaged 12.09 percent per year with a standard deviation of about 22.43 percent per year. A return of -4.72 percent is exactly one standard deviation below the average ($12.09 - 0.2243 = -0.1034$). We know from Chapter 1 (and basic statistics) that the odds of being within one standard deviation are about 2/3 or .67. Being within one standard deviation of the mean of 0.1209 means being between 0.1209 plus 0.2243 and 0.1209 minus 0.2243, i.e., between -0.1034 and $+0.3452$.

Learn all about VaR at
www.gloriamundi.org

William F. Sharpe was probably the biggest expert in the room when economists from around the world gathered in Sonoma, Calif., to hash out a pressing problem in July: How to gauge hedge-fund risk.

About 40 years ago, Dr. Sharpe, now a retired professor from Stanford University, created a simple calculation for measuring the return that investors should expect for the level of volatility they are accepting. The so-called Sharpe Ratio became a cornerstone of modern finance, as investors used it to help select money managers and mutual funds. But at the Sonoma meeting, the use of the ratio was criticized by many prominent academics—including Dr. Sharpe himself.

The ratio is commonly used—"misused," Dr. Sharpe says—for promotional purposes by hedge funds. "That is very disturbing," says the 71-year-old Dr. Sharpe. Hedge funds often use complex strategies that are vulnerable to surprise events and elude any simple formula for measuring risk. "Past average experience may be a terrible predictor of future performance," Dr. Sharpe says.

"This is becoming more of a problem because there is a movement to offer retail versions of hedge funds," says Andrew Lo, a Massachusetts Institute of Technology finance professor and a partner in the AlphaSimplex Group, a hedge fund that manages $350 million. "The typical retail investor might very well be misled by amazing looking Sharpe Ratios."

"Hedge funds can manipulate the ratio to misrepresent their performance," adds Dr. Sharpe, a founder of Financial Engines, a Palo Alto, Calif., investment adviser and manager. In a recent study, Dr. Lo found that the annual Sharpe Ratio for hedge funds can be overstated by as much as 65%. "You can legitimately generate very attractive Sharpe Ratios and still, in time, lose money," he says. "People should not take the Sharpe Ratio at face value."

Even if it isn't manipulated, Dr. Sharpe says, it doesn't foreshadow hedge-fund woes because "no number can." The formula can't predict such troubles as the inability to sell off investments quickly if they start to head south, nor can it account for extreme unexpected events. Long-Term Capital Management, a huge hedge fund in Connecticut, had a glowing Sharpe Ratio before it abruptly collapsed in 1998 when Russia devalued its currency and defaulted on debt.

In Hong Kong, the government bars hedge funds from opening unless they can prove they aren't going to fail—and yet there is no adequate measure, says Sally Wong, executive director of the Hong Kong Investment Funds Association. Her problem with the Sharpe Ratio is that it assumes that a fund's returns will remain even over time. "Many hedge-fund strategies have greater downside events," Ms. Wong says. She favors another measure, the Sortino Ratio. That is similar to the Sharpe Ratio, but instead of using the standard deviation as the denominator, it uses downside deviation—the amount a portfolio strays from its average downturns—to distinguish between "good" and "bad" volatility.

But even the namesake of that ratio is troubled by its use for evaluating hedge funds. "I think it's used too much because it makes hedge funds look good," says Frank Sortino, who developed the ratio 20 years ago and is director of the Pension Research Institute in San Francisco. "It's misleading to say the least," he adds. "I hate that they're using my name."

Dr. Sharpe feels similarly. "I never named it the Sharpe Ratio," he says of his formula. "I called it the Reward-to-Variability ratio."

Source: Ianthe Jeanne Dugan, *The Wall Street Journal*, August 31, 2005.

If the odds of being within this range are 2/3, then the odds of being *outside* this range are about 1/3. Finally, if we are outside this range, then half of the time we'll be above and half of the time we'll be below. Half of 1/3 is 1/6, so we'll experience a return of −0.1034 or worse 1/6, or about 17 percent, of the time.

Putting it together, if you own S&P/TSX 60 Index fund, this risk assessment can be stated:

$$Prob(R_p \leq -0.1034) = 17\%$$

Your VaR statistic is thus a return of −0.1034 or worse with a probability of 17 percent. By the way, here is an important note: When we say a loss of −0.1034 or worse, we mean that, *one year from now*, your portfolio value is down by 10 percent or more.

How to Play the Game of Risk When Investing Your Money

If we want our portfolios to go up, we need to spend a little time looking down. Take too much risk with our investments, and we could end up selling in a panic at the worst possible time. Take too little risk, and we will likely clock unnecessarily low returns. So how do we settle on the right amount of risk? Here are some thoughts on this messy notion:

Looking for Danger

High risk is meant to lead to high returns. But what do we mean by "high risk"? If we bet all our money on a couple of hot stocks, we are undoubtedly taking a ton of risk. But there is every chance we will lose our shirts. Instead, when academics talk about risk getting rewarded, they are referring to market risk. When investing in stocks, we can eliminate the risk of owning any one stock by spreading our money across a fistful of different companies. But even if we do that, we will still take a hit if the broad market declines. This market risk, which we can't diversify away, is the risk we get rewarded for taking.

What does this mean for our portfolios? If we want higher long-run returns, we need to take more market risk, by keeping less in conservative investments and more in stocks. But to be confident of getting our reward, we need to ensure that our stock portfolios are well diversified. This diversification has the added advantage of bolstering our tenacity. Have shares just tumbled 20%? If all we own are a couple of stocks, we will no doubt fret over whether our shares will ever bounce back. But if we own a broadly diversified portfolio, we will have greater confidence that our stocks should eventually generate decent gains.

Looking Up

To gauge risk, investment experts have traditionally looked at an investment's volatility, as reflected in statistical measures such as standard deviation and beta. Standard deviation is a gauge of how far an investment's results have strayed from its average performance, while beta measures an investment's price gyrations relative to a broad market index.

But investors often dismiss such statistical measures, complaining that they aren't bothered when volatility works to their advantage and generates big gains. Instead, what they care about is losses, and it is these losses that risk measures should seek to capture. But in fact, upside volatility is a great measure of downside risk. Consider technology stocks. Their dismal performance in the recent bear market was foretold by their equally astonishing rise during the late 1990s bull market.

Looking Out

When measuring risk, some experts don't just look at volatility. They also consider longer-run performance. For

(continued)

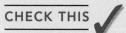
CHECK THIS ✓

13.3a What is the probability of realizing a portfolio return one or more standard deviations below the expected mean return?

13.3b What is the probability of realizing a portfolio return two or more standard deviations below the expected mean return?

13.3c Your portfolio has a mean return of 15 percent and a return standard deviation of 25 percent. What portfolio return is two standard deviations below the mean?

13.5 More on Computing Value-at-Risk

In this section we extend our discussion of computing VaR. Our goal is mainly to examine how to evaluate horizons that are shorter or longer than one year. The easiest way to do this is to take our earlier example concerning the S&P-TSX 60 composite and extend it a bit.

instance, if we hold stocks for 20 years, we are unlikely to lose money and we will almost certainly outpace bonds. That has led some commentators to argue that stocks are less risky than bonds. But this is nonsense. If we look out far enough, the highest-returning investments will always appear to be the least risky. Indeed, I fear such foolishness could lead folks to bet far too much on stocks.

"Over a long enough period, risk and return become the same thing," says William Bernstein, author of "The Intelligent Asset Allocator" and an investment adviser in North Bend, Ore. "The reason stocks have seemed so low risk is because the returns have been so high. But the high returns may not be true going forward." Moreover, not everybody has a 20-year time horizon, and not many investors can ignore short-term market turmoil. "People feel risk in their gut in the short term and in their brain in the long term," Mr. Bernstein says. "Unfortunately, they react to their gut."

Looking Pale

How much risk can each of us stomach? Mutual-fund companies and investment advisers have questionnaires that try to help folks figure out whether they are aggressive or conservative investors. But often, people later discover that their risk tolerance is far higher or lower. What to do? Eleanor Blayney, a financial planner in McLean, Va., says investors should spend time studying their own investment history. "The best indicator of risk tolerance is past behaviour," she argues. In particular, Ms. Blayney likes to ask clients what they believe their best and worst investment decisions were. She says aggressive investors tend to fret about missing out on gains, while conservative investors tend to dwell on their losses.

Looking for Safety

Even if we set out to take a lot of risk, we often gravitate toward investments we perceive to be safe. For instance, we may choose to invest a hefty amount in the stock market. But when it comes to picking individual stocks, we often select companies we view as safe. Indeed, if we didn't think a stock was a pretty safe bet, we probably wouldn't have the courage to buy.

Result? We tend to invest in widely admired corporations or those shares that have lately performed well. Meanwhile, we shy away from companies that have had financial problems or have suffered steep share-price declines, even though studies suggest that these tarnished companies often generate market-beating gains. "People will accept that risk gets rewarded if they are forced to listen to the finance-professor spiel," says Hersh Shefrin, a finance professor at Santa Clara University in California. "They will accept the notion intellectually. But emotionally, they associate good stocks with safe stocks."

Source: Jonathan Clements, *The Wall Street Journal*, February 2, 2002. © 2002 Dow Jones & Company, Inc. All Rights Reserved Worldwide.

Learn about the risk management profession at www.garp.com

Once again, suppose you own an S&P/TSX 60 index fund. What is the probability of a loss of 23 percent or more over the next *two* years? To answer, we need to know the average two-year return and the average two-year return standard deviation. Getting the average two-year return is easy enough; we just have to double the one-year average. So, the two-year average return is $2 \times 0.1209 = 0.2418$ or 24 percent.

The two-year standard deviation is a little trickier. The two-year *variance* is just double the one-year variance. In our case, the one-year variance is $0.2243^2 = 0.0503$, and the two-year variance is thus 0.050. As always, to get the two-year standard deviation, we take the square root of this, which is 0.2243 or 22 percent. The main thing to notice is that the two-year standard deviation is not just double the one-year number. In fact, if you look at it, the two-year number is equal to the one-year number multiplied by the square root of 2, or 1.414.

Now we can answer our question. A two-year loss of 23 percent is equal to the two-year average return of 0.2418 percent less two standard deviations: $0.2418 - (2 \times 0.2243) = -0.2068$. From Chapter 1, we know that the odds of being within two standard deviations are 95 percent, so the odds of being outside this range are 5 percent. The odds of being on the bad side (the loss side) are half that, namely, 2.5 percent.

VaR RISK STATISTIC

EXAMPLE 13.7

The Ned Kelley Hedge Fund focuses on investing in bank and transportation companies in Australia with above-average risk. The average annual return is 15 percent with an annual return standard deviation of 50 percent. What loss level can we expect over a two-year investment horizon with a probability of .17?

We assume a two-year expected return of 30 percent. The one-year variance is $.50^2 = .25$, so the two-year variance is .50. Taking the square root, we get a two-year standard deviation of .7071, or 70.71 percent. A loss probability of .17 corresponds to one standard deviation below the mean, so the answer to our question is $.30 - .7071 = -.4071$, a substantial loss. We can write this succinctly as

$$Prob(R_P \leq -40.71\%) = 17\%$$

Notice that there is a 17 percent chance of a 40.71 percent loss or worse over the next two years.

VaR RISK STATISTIC

EXAMPLE 13.8

Going back to the Ned Kelley Hedge Fund in our previous example, what loss level might we expect over six months with a probability of .17?

The six-month expected return is half of 15 percent, or 7.5 percent. The six-month standard deviation is $.5 \times \sqrt{1/2} = .3536$. So the answer to our question is $.075 - .3536 = -.2786$. Again, we can write this succinctly as

$$Prob(R_P \leq -27.86\%) = 17\%$$

Thus there is a 17 percent chance of a 27.86 percent loss or worse over the next six months.

A ONE-IN-TWENTY LOSS

EXAMPLE 13.9

For the Ned Kelley Hedge Fund specified in our previous examples, what is the expected loss for the coming year with a probability of 5 percent?

In this case, with an annual return mean of 15 percent and an annual return standard deviation of 50 percent, set $T = 1$ for a one-year time horizon and calculate this VaR statistic:

$$Prob[R_{p,1} \leq E(R_p) \times 1 - 1.645\sigma_P \times \sqrt{1}] = Prob(R_{p,1} \leq 15\% - 1.645 \times 50\%)$$
$$= Prob(R_{p,1} \leq -67.25\%) = 5\%$$

Thus we can expect a loss of -67.25 percent or worse over the next year with a 5 percent probability.

A ONE-IN-A-HUNDRED LOSS

EXAMPLE 13.10

For the Ned Kelley Hedge Fund specified in our previous examples, what is the expected loss for the coming month with a 1 percent probability?

Setting $T = 1 / 12$ for a one-month time horizon, we calculate this VaR statistic:

$$\textbf{Prob}[R_{P,T} \leq E(R_P) \times 1 / 12 - 2.326\sigma_P \times \sqrt{1/12}] = \textbf{Prob}(R_{P,T} \leq 1.25\% - 2.326 \times 50\% \times .2887)$$
$$= \textbf{Prob}(R_{P,T} \leq -32.32\%) = \textbf{1\%}$$

Thus we can expect a loss of -32.32 percent or more with a 1 percent probability over the next month.

In general, if we let T stand for the number of years, then the expected return on a portfolio over T years, $E(R_{p,T})$ can be written as:

$$E(R_{p,T}) = E(R_p) \times T \qquad (13.7)$$

Similarly, the standard deviation can be written as:

$$\sigma_{p,T} = \sigma_p \times \sqrt{T} \qquad (13.8)$$

If the time period is less than a year, the T is just a fraction of a year.

When you do a VaR analysis, you have to pick the time horizon and loss level probability. You can pick any probability you want, of course, but the most common are 1, 2.5, and 5 percent. We know that 2.5 percent, which is half of 5 percent, corresponds to two standard deviations (actually 1.96 to be more precise) below the expected return. To get the 1 percent and 5 percent numbers, you would need to find an ordinary "z" table to tell you the number of standard deviations. We'll save you the trouble. The 1 percent level is 2.326 standard deviations below the average, and the 5 percent level is 1.645 "sigmas" below.

Wrapping up our discussion, the VaR statistics for these three levels can be summarized as follows:

$$Prob(R_{p,T} \leq E(R_p) \times T - 2.326 \times \sigma_p \sqrt{T}) = 1\%$$
$$Prob(R_{p,T} \leq E(R_p) \times T - 1.96 \times \sigma_p \sqrt{T}) = 2.5\% \qquad (13.9)$$
$$Prob(R_{p,T} \leq E(R_p) \times T - 1.645 \times \sigma_p \sqrt{T}) = 5\%$$

Notice that if T, the number of years, is equal to 1, the 1 percent level corresponds to once in a century. Similarly, 5 percent is once every 20 years, and 2.5 percent is once every 40 years.

As an application of Value-at-Risk, consider the problem of determining VaR statistics for a Sharpe-optimal stock and bond portfolio. As with any VaR problem for a portfolio, remember that the key to the problem is to first determine the expected return and standard deviation for the portfolio. From our discussion in Chapter 2 and earlier in this chapter, we know that the expected return and standard deviation of a stock and bond portfolio are specified by these two equations:

$$E(R_P) = x_S E(R_S) + x_B E(R_B)$$
$$\sigma_P = \sqrt{x_S^2 \sigma_S^2 + x_B^2 \sigma_B^2 + 2x_S x_B \sigma_S \sigma_B \text{Corr}(R_S, R_B)}$$

Check out risk grades at www.riskmetrics.com

Thus the problem of calculating VaR statistics for a Sharpe-optimal portfolio is the same for any portfolio once the appropriate portfolio weights are determined.

VAR FOR A SHARPE-OPTIMAL PORTFOLIO

EXAMPLE 13.11

Suppose you have the following expected return and risk information for stocks and bonds that will be used to form a Sharpe-optimal portfolio. Calculate VaR risk statistics for a one-year investment horizon.

$$E(R_S) = .12; \quad \sigma_S = .15; \quad E(R_B) = .06; \quad \sigma_B = .10; \quad \text{Corr}(R_S, R_B) = .10; \quad R_F = .04$$

In the case of just two assets, stocks and bonds, the formulas for the portfolio weights for the optimal Sharpe portfolio are:

$$x_S = \frac{\sigma_B^2 \times [E(R_S) - R_F] - \text{Corr}(R_S, R_B) \times \sigma_S \times \sigma_B \times [E(R_B) - R_F]}{\sigma_B^2 \times [E(R_S) - R_F] + \sigma_S^2 \times [E(R_B) - R_F] - [E(R_S) + E(R_B) - 2 \times R_F] \times \text{Corr}(R_S, R_B) \times \sigma_S \times \sigma_B}$$

and

$$x_B = 1 - x_S$$

Inserting the expected return and risk information into these formulas yields these optimal Sharpe portfolio weights for stocks and bonds:

$$x_S = \frac{.10^2 \times [.12 - .04] - .10 \times .15 \times .10 \times [.06 - .04]}{.10^2 \times [.12 - .04] + .15^2 \times [.06 - .04] - [.12 + .06 - 2 \times .04] \times .10 \times .15 \times .10} = .70$$

and

$$x_B = 1 - x_S = 1 - .70 = .30$$

With these results, we now have all the information needed to calculate the expected return and standard deviation for the Sharpe-optimal portfolio.

$$\begin{aligned}
E(R_P) &= x_S E(R_S) + x_B E(R_B) \\
&= .70 \times .12 + .30 \times .06 \\
&= .102, \text{ or } 10.2\%
\end{aligned}$$

$$\begin{aligned}
\sigma_P &= \sqrt{x_S^2 \sigma_S^2 + x_B^2 \sigma_B^2 + 2 x_S x_B \sigma_S \sigma_B \text{Corr}(R_S, R_B)} \\
&= \sqrt{.70^2 \times .15^2 + .30^2 \times .10^2 \times 2 \times .70 \times .30 \times .15 \times .10 \times .10} \\
&= .112, \text{ or } 11.2\%
\end{aligned}$$

Thus, with a one-year investment horizon, you obtain the following VaR risk statistics for 5 percent and 1 percent probabilities:

$$\begin{aligned}
5\% VaR = Prob[R_P \leq E(R_P) - 1.645\sigma_P] &= Prob[R_P \leq 10.2\% - 1.645 \times 11.2\%] \\
&= Prob[R_P \leq -8.22\%]
\end{aligned}$$

$$\begin{aligned}
1\% VaR = Prob[R_P \leq E(R_P) - 2.326\sigma_P] &= Prob[R_P \leq 10.2\% - 2.326 \times 11.2\%] \\
&= Prob[R_P \leq -15.85\%]
\end{aligned}$$

These calculations indicate that over the next year, we can expect a loss of 8.22 percent or more with a 5 percent probability and a loss of 15.85 percent with a 1 percent probability.

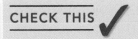

13.4a   Your portfolio allocates 40 percent of funds to ABC stock and 60 percent to XYZ stock. ABC has a return mean and standard deviation of 15 percent and 20 percent, respectively. XYZ stock has a return mean and standard deviation of 25 percent and 30 percent, respectively. What is the portfolio return standard deviation if the return correlation between ABC and XYZ stocks is zero?

13.4b   Based on your answer to the previous question, what is the smallest expected loss for your portfolio in the coming year with a probability of 1 percent? What is the smallest expected loss for your portfolio in the coming month with a probability of 5 percent?

13.6   Summary and Conclusions

In this chapter, we covered the related topics of performance measurement and risk management. Our goal with performance measurement is essentially to rank investments based on their risk-adjusted returns. We introduced and discussed the most common tools used to do this: the Sharpe ratio, the Treynor ratio, Jensen's alpha, and M^2 Measure. As we saw, each has a somewhat different interpretation and which one is the most suitable depends on the specific question.

We then moved over to the issue of risk management by introducing you to the popular and widely used "Value-at-Risk," or VaR, approach. Here the goal is usually to assess the probability of a large loss within a fixed time frame. Investors use this tool both to better understand the risks of their existing portfolios and to assess the risks of potential investments.

REAL WORLD

This chapter covered the essentials of performance evaluation and investment risk management. With thousands of mutual funds and investment companies competing for performance while trying to control risk, these topics are especially important. If you wish to learn more about these subjects, a good place to start is the Internet.

Some useful and informative websites on investment performance analysis are: Performance Analysis (www.andreassteiner.net/performanceanalysis), an informative website on investment performance analysis; Professor William F. Sharpe (www.wsharpe.com), website of the Nobel laureate who created the Sharpe ratio; and FinPlan (www.finplan.com), a financial planning website with a useful section on investment performance analysis. You can also consult www.garp.com, which is the website of the Global Association of Risk Professionals (GARP), an independent organization of financial risk management practitioners and researchers.

Since financial institutions generally prefer that their risk profiles be kept private, a large part of the world of financial risk management is hidden from public view. Nevertheless, the field of risk management is large and growing. If you want to know more about

(continued)

this fascinating subject, some interesting websites that provide a wealth of information are: Gloria Mundi (www.gloriamundi.org), a site that tells you all about Value-at-Risk; Risk Metrics (www.riskmetrics.com), a leading risk management consultancy group; Margrabe (www.margrabe.com), the website of a professional risk management consultant; and E-Risks (www.erisks.com), a general resource site for risk management.

There are various sites that give information on how to measure portfolio performance. Go to the following website for recommendations on portfolio records and monitoring—Investor Education Fund: www.investored.ca.

Key Terms

performance evaluation 425
raw return 425
Sharpe ratio 425
Treynor ratio 426

Jensen's alpha 427
investment risk management 434
Value-at-Risk (VaR) 434
normal distribution 434

Chapter Review Problems and Self-Test

1. **Performance Measures** Compute Sharpe ratios, Treynor ratios, and Jensen alphas for portfolios A, B, and C based on the following returns data, where M and F stand for the market portfolio and risk-free rate, respectively:

Portfolio	R_P	σ_P	β_P
A	10%	30%	0.75
B	15%	25%	1.00
C	20%	40%	1.50
M	15%	15%	1.00
F	5%	0%	0.00

2. **Value-at-Risk (VaR)** A portfolio manager believes her $100 million stock portfolio will have a 10 percent return standard deviation during the coming week and that her portfolio's returns are normally distributed. What is the probability of her losing $10 million or more? What is the dollar loss expected with a 5 percent probability? What is the dollar loss expected with a 1 percent probability?

Answers to Self-Test Problems

1. Using Equations 13.1, 13.2, 13.3 yields these performance measurement values:

Portfolio	Sharpe Ratio	Treynor Ratio	Jensen Alpha
A	.167	.0667	−2.5%
B	.400	.10	0%
C	.375	.10	0%
M	.667	.10	0%

2. Since a mean is not given but the time horizon is only one week, we can simply assume a mean of zero. Thus the probability of a $10 million or greater loss is the probability of a loss of one or more return standard deviations, which for a normal distribution is 15.87 percent. For a normal distribution, a realization 1.645 or more standard deviations below the mean occurs with a 5 percent probability, yielding a potential loss of at least 1.645 × $10 million = $16.45 million. For a normal distribution, a realization 2.326 or more standard deviations below the mean occurs with a 1 percent probability, yielding a potential loss of at least 2.326 × $10 million = $23.26 million.

Test Your Investment Quotient

1. **Beta and Standard Deviation** Beta and standard deviation differ as risk measures in that beta measures
   a. Only unsystematic risk, whereas standard deviation measures total risk.
   b. Only systematic risk, whereas standard deviation measures total risk.
   c. Both systematic and unsystematic risk, whereas standard deviation measures only unsystematic risk.
   d. Both systematic and unsystematic risk, whereas standard deviation measures only systematic risk.

Answer Questions 2 through 8 based on the following information.

Portfolio	Risk and Return Data		
	Average Return	Standard Deviation	Beta
P	17%	20%	1.1
Q	24%	18%	2.1
R	11%	10%	0.5
S	16%	14%	1.5
S&P 500	14%	12%	1.0

A pension fund administrator wants to evaluate the performance of four portfolio managers. Each manager invests only in U.S. common stocks. During the most recent five-year period, the average annual total return on the S&P 500 was 14 percent, and the average annual rate on Treasury bills was 8 percent. The table above shows risk and return measures for each portfolio.

2. **Treynor Ratio** The Treynor portfolio performance measure for Portfolio P is
   a. 8.18
   b. 7.62
   c. 6.00
   d. 5.33

3. **Sharpe Ratio** The Sharpe portfolio performance measure for Portfolio Q is
   a. .45
   b. .89
   c. .30
   d. .57

4. **Jensen Alpha** The Jensen alpha portfolio performance measure for Portfolio R is
   a. 2.4 percent
   b. 3.4 percent
   c. 0 percent
   d. −1 percent

5. **Treynor Ratio** Which portfolio has the highest Treynor ratio?

   a. P
   b. Q
   c. R
   d. S

6. **Sharpe Ratio** Which portfolio has the highest Sharpe ratio?

   a. P
   b. Q
   c. R
   d. S

7. **Jensen Alpha** Which portfolio has the highest Jensen alpha?

   a. P
   b. Q
   c. R
   d. S

8. **Sharpe Ratio** Assuming uncorrelated returns, the Sharpe ratio for a master portfolio with equal allocations to Portfolio S and Portfolio Q is

   a. .71
   b. 1.4
   c. .95
   d. 1.05

9. **Normal Distribution** Given a data series that is normally distributed with a mean of 100 and a standard deviation of 10, about 95 percent of the numbers in the series will fall within

   a. 60 to 140
   b. 70 to 130
   c. 80 to 120
   d. 90 to 110

10. **Normal Distribution** Given a data series that is normally distributed with a mean of 100 and a standard deviation of 10, about 99 percent of the numbers in the series will fall within

    a. 60 to 140
    b. 80 to 120
    c. 70 to 130
    d. 90 to 110

11. **Normal Distribution** A normal distribution is completely specified by its

    a. Mean and correlation
    b. Variance and correlation
    c. Variance and standard deviation
    d. Mean and standard deviation

12. **Standard Normal Distribution** A normal random variable is transformed into a standard normal random variable by

    a. Subtracting its mean and dividing by its standard deviation.
    b. Adding its mean and dividing by its standard deviation.
    c. Subtracting its mean and dividing by its variance.
    d. Adding its mean and multiplying by its standard deviation.

13. **Standard Normal Distribution** The probability that a standard normal random variable is either less than -1 or greater than $+1$ is

    a. 2 percent
    b. 5 percent

    c. 10 percent
    d. 31.74 percent

14. **Standard Normal Distribution** The probability that a standard normal random variable is either less than -1.96 or greater than $+1.96$ is approximately

    a. 2 percent
    b. 5 percent
    c. 10 percent
    d. 31.74 percent

15. **Value-at-Risk (VaR)** The Value-at-Risk statistic for an investment portfolio states

    a. The probability of an investment loss.
    b. The value of the risky portion of an investment portfolio.
    c. The smallest investment loss expected with a specified probability.
    d. The largest investment loss expected with a specified probability.

Concept Questions

1. **Performance Evaluation Ratios** Explain the difference between the Sharpe ratio and the Treynor ratio.

2. **Performance Evaluation Measures** What is a common weakness of Jensen's alpha and the Treynor ratio?

3. **Jensen's Alpha** Explain the relationship between Jensen's alpha and the Security Market Line (SML) of the Capital Asset Pricing Model (CAPM).

4. **Sharpe Ratio** What are an advantage and a disadvantage of the Sharpe ratio?

5. **Normal Distribution** Which two parameters completely specify a normal distribution?

6. **Optimal Sharpe Ratio** What is meant by a Sharpe-optimal portfolio?

7. **Optimal Sharpe Ratio** What is the relationship between the Markowitz efficient frontier and the optimal Sharpe ratio?

8. **Value-at-Risk (VaR) Statistic** Explain the meaning of a Value-at-Risk statistic in terms of a smallest expected loss and the probability of such a loss.

9. **Value-at-Risk (VaR) Statistic** The largest expected loss for a portfolio is -20 percent with a probability of 95 percent. Relate this statement to the Value-at-Risk statistic.

10. **Normal Probabilities** The probability that a normal random variable X is less than x is equal to 50 percent, i.e., $Pr(X < x)$. What is this value of x?

11. **M^2 Measure** Compare M^2 measure with sharpe ratio. Which one is better? Explain.

Questions and Problems

Core Questions

1. **Standard Deviation** You find a particular stock has an annual standard deviation of 54 percent. What is the standard deviation for a two-month period?

2. **Standard Deviation** A portfolio has an annual variance of .0607. What is the standard deviation over a two-month period?

3. **Standard Deviation** You find the monthly standard deviation of a stock is 16.18 percent. What is the annual standard deviation of the stock?

4. **Standard Deviation** The weekly standard deviation of a stock is 7.48 percent. What is the monthly standard deviation? The annual standard deviation?

5. **Performance Evaluation** You are given the following information concerning three portfolios, the market portfolio, and the risk-free asset:

Portfolio	R_P	σ_P	β_P
X	18%	39%	1.3
Y	15	26	1.2
Z	8	17	.8
Market	12	21	1.0
Risk-free	5	0	.0

What is the Sharpe ratio, Treynor ratio, and Jensen's alpha for each portfolio?

6. **Normal Probabilities** What is the probability that a normal random variable is less than one standard deviation below its mean?

7. **Normal Probabilities** What are the probabilities that a normal random variable is less than n standard deviations below its mean for values of n equal to 1.645, 1.96, 2.326?

8. **Normal Probabilities** The probabilities that a normal random variable X is less than various values of x are 5 percent, 2.5 percent, and 1 percent. What are these values of x?

9. **Value-at-Risk (VaR) Statistic** Raybrooks Co. stock has an annual return mean and standard deviation of 13 percent and 25 percent, respectively. What is the smallest expected loss in the coming year with a probability of 5 percent?

10. **Value-at-Risk (VaR) Statistic** Joi, Inc., stock has an annual return mean and standard deviation of 16 percent and 33 percent, respectively. What is the smallest expected loss in the coming month with a probability of 2.5 percent?

11. **Value-at-Risk (VaR) Statistic** Your portfolio allocates equal funds to the Raybrooks Co. and Joi, Inc., stocks referred to in the previous two questions. The return correlation between Raybrooks Co. and Joi, Inc., is zero. What is the smallest expected loss for your portfolio in the coming month with a probability of 2.5 percent?

12. **Value-at-Risk (VaR) Statistic** The stock of Metallica Bearings has an average annual return of 15 percent and a standard deviation of 47 percent. What is the smallest expected loss in the next year with a probability of 1 percent?

13. **Value-at-Risk (VaR) Statistic** Osbourne, Inc., stock has an annual mean return of 18 percent and a standard deviation of 58 percent. What is the smallest expected loss in the next week with a probability of 2.5 percent?

14. **Value-at-Risk (VaR) Statistic** Your portfolio is equally weighted between Metallica Bearings and Osbourne, Inc., stocks in the previous two questions. The return correlation between the two stocks is zero. What is the smallest expected loss on your portfolio in the next month with a probability of 5 percent?

15. **Sharpe Ratio** What is the formula for the Sharpe ratio for a stock and bond portfolio with a zero correlation between stock and bond returns?

Intermediate
Questions

16. **Sharpe Ratio** What is the formula for the Sharpe ratio for an equally weighted portfolio of stocks and bonds?

17. **Sharpe Ratio** What is the formula for the Sharpe ratio for a portfolio of stocks and bonds with equal expected returns, i.e., $E(R_S) = E(R_B)$, and a zero return correlation?

18. **Value-at-Risk (VaR) Statistic** A stock has an annual return of 14 percent and a standard deviation of 63 percent. What is the smallest expected loss over the next year with a probability of 1 percent? Does this number make sense?

19. **Value-at-Risk (VaR) Statistic** For the stock in the previous problem, what is the smallest expected gain over the next year with a probability of 1 percent? Does this number make sense? What does this tell you about stock return distributions?

20. **Value-at-Risk (VaR) Statistic** Tyler Trucks stock has an annual return mean and standard deviation of 12 percent and 41 percent, respectively. Michael Moped Manufacturing stock has an annual return mean and standard deviation of 17 percent and 62 percent, respectively. Your portfolio allocates equal funds to Tyler Trucks stock and Michael Moped

Manufacturing stock. The return correlation between Tyler Trucks and Michael Moped Manufacturing is −.5. What is the smallest expected loss for your portfolio in the coming month with a probability of 5 percent?

21. **Value-at-Risk (VaR) Statistic** Using the same return means and standard deviations as in the previous question for Tyler Trucks and Michael Moped Manufacturing stocks, but assuming a return correlation of −.5, what is the smallest expected loss for your portfolio in the coming month with a probability of 5 percent?

22. **Value-at-Risk (VaR) Statistic** Your portfolio allocates equal amounts to three stocks. All three stocks have the same mean annual return of 16 percent. Annual return standard deviations for these three stocks are 40 percent, 50 percent, and 60 percent. The return correlations among all three stocks are zero. What is the smallest expected loss for your portfolio in the coming year with a probability of 1 percent?

23. **Value-at-Risk (VaR) Statistic** Using the same return means and standard deviations as in the previous question for the three stocks, but assuming a correlation of .2 among returns for all three stocks, what is the smallest expected loss for your portfolio in the coming year with a probability of 1 percent?

24. **Optimal Sharpe Portfolio Value-at-Risk** You are constructing a portfolio of two assets, Asset A and Asset B. The expected returns of the assets are 12 percent and 16 percent, respectively. The standard deviations of the assets are 34 percent and 59 percent, respectively. The correlation between the two assets is .20 and the risk-free rate is 5 percent. What is the optimal Sharpe ratio in a portfolio of the two assets? What is the smallest expected loss for this portfolio over the coming year with a probability of 2.5 percent?

Spreadsheet Problem

25. **Optimal Sharpe Ratio** You are constructing a portfolio of two assets. Asset A has an expected return of 10 percent and a standard deviation of 21 percent. Asset B has an expected return of 15 percent and a standard deviation of 62 percent. The correlation between the two assets is .30 and the risk-free rate is 4 percent. What is the weight of each asset in the portfolio of the two assets that has the largest possible Sharpe ratio?

STANDARD &POOR'S

S&P Problem
www.mcgrawhill.com/edumarketinsight

Note: This problem can be done manually, but a spreadsheet program such as Excel is recommended for use in calculations.

1. **Performance Evaluation** Go to the "Excel Analytics" link for Sun Life Financial (SLF) and download the monthly adjusted stock prices. Copy the monthly returns for SLF and the monthly S&P/TSX Composite returns into a new spreadsheet. Calculate the Sharpe ratio, Jensen's alpha, and the Treynor ratio for this company. Assume a risk-free rate of 5 percent.

What's on the Web?

1. **Morningstar Ratings** Go to www.morningstar.com and find out how to interpret the "Bear Market Decile Rank." While you are at the website, also learn more about the best fit index numbers. What do the best fit index numbers mean?

2. **Morningstar Risk** Go to www.morningstar.com and find out how Morningstar calculates the "Morningstar Risk" category. What percentage of funds are rated as Below Average by Morningstar? What percentage are rated Average?

3. **Modified VaR** Go to www.alternativesoft.com and learn about modified VaR proposed at the website. Why would you want to use a modified VaR?

4. **Morningstar Ratings** Go to www.morningstar.ca and find out the mutual fund performance rankings for Canadian funds.

www.mcgrawhill.ca/olc/Jordan

Options

"Derivatives, like NFL quarterbacks, probably get more credit and more blame than they deserve."

—Gerald Corrigan of Goldman Sachs

Options have fascinated investors for centuries. The option concept is simple. Instead of buying stock shares today, you buy an option to buy the stock at a later date at a price specified in the option contract. You are not obligated to exercise the option, but if doing so benefits you, of course you will. Moreover, the most you can lose is the original price of the option, which is normally only a fraction of the stock price. Sounds good, doesn't it? ■

Options on common stocks have traded in financial markets for about as long as common stocks have. However, it was not until 1973, when the Chicago Board Options Exchange was established, that options trading became a large and important part of the financial landscape. Since then, the success of options trading has been phenomenal.

Much of the success of options trading is attributable to the tremendous flexibility that options offer investors in designing investment strategies. For example, options can be used to reduce risk through hedging strategies or to increase risk through speculative strategies. As a result, when properly understood and applied, options are appealing both to conservative investors and to aggressive speculators.

In this chapter, we discuss options generally, but our primary focus is on options on individual common stocks. However, later in the chapter we also discuss options on stock market indexes, which are options on portfolios of common stocks and on foreign currency. We begin by reviewing some of the ideas we touched on in Chapter 4, where we very briefly discussed options.

14.1 Options on Common Stocks

Option Basics

derivative security
Security whose value is derived from the value of another security. Options are a type of derivative security.

call option On common stock, grants the holder the right, but not the obligation, to buy the underlying stock at a given strike price.

put option On common stock, grants the holder the right, but not the obligation, to sell the underlying stock at a given strike price.

strike price Price specified in an option contract that the holder pays to buy shares (in the case of call options) or receives to sell shares (in the case of put options) if the option is exercised. Also called the *exercise price*.

As we have discussed, options on common stock are a type of **derivative security** because the value of a stock option is "derived" from the value of the underlying common stock. For example, the value of an option to buy or sell EnCana stock is derived from the value of EnCana stock. However, the relationship between the value of a particular stock option and the value of the underlying stock depends on the specific type of option.

Recall that there are two basic option types: **call options** and **put options**. Call options are options to buy, and put options are options to sell. Thus, a call option on EnCana stock is an option to buy EnCana shares, and a put option on EnCana stock is an option to sell EnCana shares. More specifically, a call option on common stock grants the holder the right, but not the obligation, to buy the underlying stock at a given **strike price** before the option expiration date. Similarly, a put option on common stock grants the holder the right, but not the obligation, to sell the underlying stock at a given strike price before the option expiration date. The strike price, also called the *exercise price*, is the price at which stock shares are bought or sold to fulfill the obligations of the option contract.

Options are contracts, and, in practice, option contracts are standardized to facilitate convenience in trading and price reporting. Standardized stock options have a contract size of 100 shares of common stock per option contract. This means that a single call option contract involves an option to buy 100 shares of stock. Likewise, a single put option contract involves an option to sell 100 shares of stock.

Because options are contracts, an understanding of stock options requires that we know the specific contract terms. In general, options on common stock must stipulate at least the following six contract terms:

1. The identity of the underlying stock.
2. The strike price, also called the striking or exercise price.
3. The option contract size.
4. The option expiration date, also called the option maturity.
5. The option exercise style.
6. The delivery or settlement procedure.

First, a stock option contract requires that the specific stock issue be clearly identified. While this may seem to be stating the obvious, in financial transactions it is important that the "obvious" is in fact clearly and unambiguously understood by all concerned parties.

Second, the strike price, also called the exercise price, must be stipulated. The strike price is quite important, since the strike price is the price that an option holder will pay (in the case of a call option) or receive (in the case of a put option) if the option is exercised.

Third, the size of the contract must be specified. As stated earlier, the standard contract size for stock options is 100 stock shares per option.

The fourth contract term that must be stated is the option expiration date. An option cannot be exercised after its expiration date. If an option is unexercised and its expiration date has passed, the option becomes worthless.

Fifth, the option's exercise style determines when the option can be exercised. There are two basic exercise styles: American and European. **American options** can be exercised any time before option expiration, but **European options** can be exercised only on the last day before expiration. Options on individual stocks are normally American style, and stock index options are usually European style.

Finally, in the event that a stock option is exercised, the settlement process must be stipulated. For stock options, standard settlement requires delivery of the underlying stock shares several business days after a notice of exercise is made by the option holder.

Stock options are traded in financial markets in a manner similar to the way that common stocks are traded. For example, there are organized options exchanges, and there are over-the-counter (OTC) options markets. The largest volume of stock options trading in the United States takes place at the Chicago Board Options Exchange (CBOE). In Canada the major exchange for financial options or other financial derivatives is the Montreal Exchange. Stock options are also actively traded at the Philadelphia Stock Exchange (PHLX), the New York Stock Exchange (NYSE), the American Stock Exchange (AMEX), and the Pacific Stock Exchange (PSE). Like a stock exchange, or, for that matter, any securities exchange, an options exchange is a marketplace where customer buy orders and sell orders are matched up with each other.

Option Price Quotes

Current prices for a relatively small number of stock options traded at the major options exchanges are reported each day in major journals. Only the most heavily traded stock options are included. Figure 14.1 reproduces the "Equity Options" section from *The Globe and Mail*.

In Figure 14.1, the table entitled "Five Most Active" reports data on selected option contracts with the highest trading volumes in the previous day's options trading. In the table itself, the first three columns report the name of the option's underlying stock, the expiration month, and the strike price for the option. A "p" following the strike price indicates a put option; otherwise, it is a call option. The next two columns give the previous day's closing bid and ask prices for the contract.

The column labelled "tot vol" reports volume, measured as the number of contracts traded on the previous day. The final column reports open interest, which is the total number of contracts outstanding.

The rest of the "Equity Options" page reports options trading data grouped by the underlying stock. For each underlying stock with options listed in Figure 14.1, the first row shows the underlying stock, previous day's closing price, total volume and total open interest in bold letters. The first column under a stock name states the expiration months of each available option contract. By convention, standardized stock options expire on Saturday following the third Friday of their expiration month. Because of this convention, the exact date that an option expires can be known exactly by referring to a calendar to identify the third Friday of its expiration month. The second column states strike prices of the various options available for each stock. Notice that the range of available strike prices for stock options typically brackets a current stock price.

FIGURE 14.1

Equity Options

Source: *The Globe and Mail*, August 7, 2004. Reprinted with permission from *The Globe and Mail*.

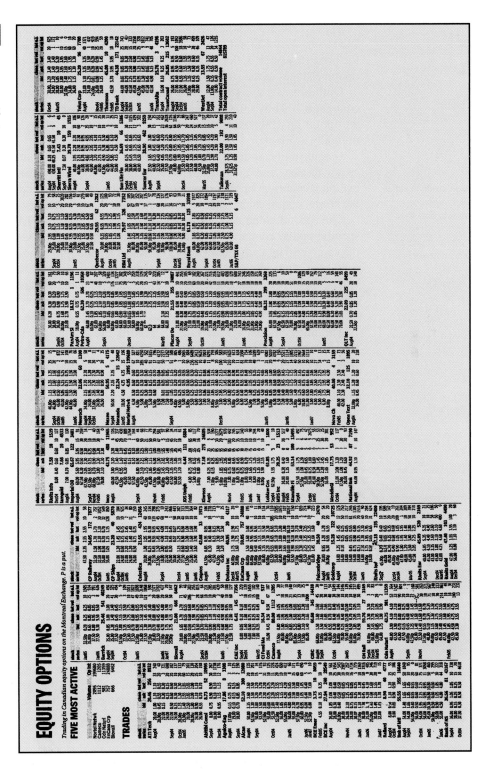

These first three contract terms—the identity of the underlying stock, the strike price, and the expiration month—will not change during the life of the option. However, since the price of a stock option depends on the price of the underlying stock, the price of an option changes as the stock price changes.

Option prices are stated on a per-share basis, but the actual price of an option contract is 100 times the per-share price. This is because each option contract represents an option on 100 shares of stock. Fractional contracts for, say, 50 shares, are not normally available.

Useful online sources for option prices include the Montreal Exchange website (www.m-x.ca) and Yahoo! Finance (finance.yahoo.com). The nearby *Work the Web* exhibit contains an **option chain** for Rogers Inc (RCI) stock options. The box contains the Nortel option chain, with separate sections for call options and put options.

The second column of each section (labelled "Symbol") lists ticker symbols for specific option contracts. The tickers for Rogers options have five letters identifying the contract. The sixth letter (X) is just used by Yahoo! to indicate an option ticker. The first three letters are RCI, which is the ticker symbol for Rogers stock. For the next two letters, the first letter specifies the expiration month and whether the option is a call or a put, while the second letter identifies the strike price. Option tickers are discussed in more detail in the *Stock-Trak* section at the end of this chapter.

The third column ("Last Trade") reports the option price for the last trade. The fourth column ("Chg") states the change in price from the previous day's last trade, where a zero indicates either no change in price or no trade that day. The next two columns ("Bid" and "Ask") contain representative bid and ask price quotes from dealers. Finally, the seventh column ("Vol") reports trading volume as the number of contracts traded that day, and the seventh column ("Open Int") states open interest as the total number of contracts outstanding.

option chain A list of available option contracts and their prices for a particular security arrayed by strike price and maturity.

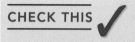
CHECK THIS

14.1a   What is a call option? What is a put option?

14.1b   What are the six basic contract terms that an options contract must specify?

14.1c   What is an option chain?

14.2 Why Options?

As a stock market investor, a basic question you might ask is: "Why buy stock options instead of shares of stock directly?" Good question! To answer it properly, we need to compare the possible outcomes from two investment strategies. The first investment strategy entails simply buying stock. The second strategy involves buying a call option that allows the holder to buy stock any time before option expiration.

For example, suppose you buy 100 shares of RIM stock at a price of $115 per share, representing an investment of $11,500. Afterwards, three things could happen: the stock price could go up, go down, or remain the same. If the stock price goes up, you make money; if it goes down, you lose money. Of course, if the stock price remains the same, you break even.

WORK THE WEB

Here is an option chain for Rogers Communication (RCI) from Yahoo! Finance.

Rogers Communications Inc. (RCI)

100 FREE TRADES E*TRADE Securities | **Active Traders** Fidelity | **AMERITRADE** Transfer today and get up to $300 | **Scottrade** Member FINRA/SIPC Up to $100 BACK when you switch

Options

View By Expiration: **Jan 08** | Feb 08 | Apr 08 | Jul 08

CALL OPTIONS   Expire at close Fri, Jan 18, 2008

Strike	Symbol	Last	Chg	Bid	Ask	Vol	Open Int
35.00	RCIAG.X	16.30	0.00	10.40	10.70	0	69
40.00	RCIAH.X	5.60	↓0.70	5.50	5.80	16	143
45.00	RCIAI.X	1.95	0.00	1.45	1.60	43	952
50.00	RCIAJ.X	0.15	↓0.05	N/A	0.15	40	1,442
55.00	RCIAK.X	0.15	0.00	N/A	0.10	0	301

PUT OPTIONS   Expire at close Fri, Jan 18, 2008

Strike	Symbol	Last	Chg	Bid	Ask	Vol	Open Int
35.00	RCIMG.X	0.15	0.00	N/A	0.10	0	120
40.00	RCIMH.X	0.10	0.00	N/A	0.10	1	177
45.00	RCIMI.X	0.80	0.00	0.85	1.00	1	583
50.00	RCIMJ.X	4.64	0.00	4.40	4.70	3	41

Reproduced with permission of Yahoo! Inc. © 2004 by Yahoo! Inc. YAHOO! and the YAHOO! logo are trademarks of Yahoo! Inc.

Now, consider the alternative strategy of buying a call option with a strike price of $115 expiring in three months at a per-share price of $5. This corresponds to a contract price of $500 since the standard option contract size is 100 shares. The first thing to notice about this strategy is that you have invested only $500, and therefore the most that you can lose is only $500.

To compare the two investment strategies just described, let's examine three possible cases for RIM's stock price at the close of trading on the third Friday of the option's expiration month. In case 1, the stock price goes up to $125. In case 2, the stock price goes down to $105. In case 3, the stock price remains the same at $115.

Case 1: If the stock price goes up to $125, and you originally bought 100 shares at $115 dollars per share, then your profit is $100 \times (\$125 - \$115) = \$1,000$.

As a percentage of your original investment amount of $9,000, this represents a return on investment of $1,000/$9,000 = 11.11%.

Alternatively, if you originally bought the call option, you can exercise the option and buy 100 shares at the strike price of $115 and sell the stock at the $125 market price. After accounting for the original cost of the option contract, your profit is $100 \times (\$125 - \$115) - \$500 = \$500$. As a percentage of your original investment of $500, this represents a return on investment of $500/$500 = 100%.

Case 2: If the stock price goes down to $105, and you originally bought 100 shares at $115 dollars per share, then your loss is $100 \times (\$105 - \$115) = -\$1,000$. As a percentage of your original investment, this represents a return of $-\$1,000/\$9,000 = -11.11\%$.

If instead you originally bought the call option, it would not pay to exercise the option, and it would expire worthless. You would then realize a total loss of your $500 investment, and your return is -100 percent.

Case 3: If the stock price remains the same at $115, and you bought 100 shares, you break even, and your return is zero percent.

However, if you bought the call option, it would not pay to exercise the option, and it would expire worthless. Once again, you would lose your entire $500 investment.

As these three cases illustrate, the outcomes of the two investment strategies differ significantly, depending on subsequent stock price changes. Whether one strategy is preferred over another is a matter for each individual investor to decide. What is important is the fact that options offer an alternative means of formulating investment strategies.

STOCK RETURNS

EXAMPLE 14.1

Suppose you bought 100 shares of stock at $50 per share. If the stock price goes up to $60 per share, what is the percentage return on your investment? If, instead, the stock price falls to $40 per share, what is the percentage return on your investment?

If the stock goes to $60 per share, you make $10 / $50 = 20%. If it falls to $40, you lose $10 / $50 = 20%.

CALL OPTION RETURNS

EXAMPLE 14.2

In Example 14.1 just above, suppose that you bought one call option contract for $200. The strike price is $50. If the stock price is $60 just before the option expires, should you exercise the option? If you exercise the option, what is the percentage return on your investment? If you don't exercise the option, what is the percentage return on your investment?

If the stock price is $60, you should definitely exercise. If you do, you will make $10 per share, or $1,000, from exercising. Once we deduct the $200 original cost of the option, your net profit is $800. Your percentage return is $800 / $200 = 400%. If you don't exercise, you lose your entire $200 investment, so your loss is 100 percent.

MORE CALL OPTION RETURNS

EXAMPLE 14.3

In Example 14.2, if the stock price is $40 just before the option expires, should you exercise the option? If you exercise the option, what is the percentage return on your investment? If you don't exercise the option, what is the percentage return on your investment?

If the stock price is $40, you shouldn't exercise since, by exercising, you will be paying $50 per share. If you did exercise, you would lose $10 per share, or $1,000, plus the $200 cost of the option, or $1,200 total. This would amount to a $1,200 / $200 = 600% loss! If you don't exercise, you lose the $200 you invested, for a loss of 100 percent.

Of course, we can also calculate percentage gains and losses from a put option purchase. Here we make money if the stock price declines. So, suppose you buy a put option with a strike price of $20 for $.50. If you exercise your put when the stock price is $18, what is your percentage gain?

You make $2 per share since you are selling at $20 when the stock is worth $18. Your put contract cost $50, so your net profit is $200 − $50 = $150. As a percentage of your original $50 investment, you made $150 / $50 = 300%.

CHECK THIS

14.2a   If you buy 100 shares of stock at $10 and sell out at $12, what is your percentage return?

14.2b   If you buy one call contract with a strike of $10 for $100 and exercise it when the stock is selling for $12, what is your percentage return?

14.3 Option "Moneyness"

in-the-money option An option that would yield a positive payoff if exercised.

out-of-the-money option An option that would not yield a positive payoff if exercised.

To understand option payoffs and profits, we need to know two important terms related to option value: **in-the-money options** and **out-of-the-money options**. Essentially, an in-the-money option is one that would yield a positive payoff if exercised immediately and an out-of-the-money option is one that would not yield a positive payoff if exercised.

IN-THE-MONEY CALL OPTION

EXAMPLE 14.4

TD stock is currently $70 per share. Let's look at a call option to buy TD stock at $65 ($65 is the strike price). The stock price is greater than the strike price. If the call option were exercised immediately, there would be a positive payoff of $5 = $70 − $65. Because the option has a positive payoff if it is exercised immediately, this option is known as an in-the-money option.

OUT-OF-THE-MONEY CALL OPTION

EXAMPLE 14.5

TD stock is currently $70 per share. Let's look at a call option to buy TD stock at $75 ($75 is the strike price). Because the stock price is less than the strike price, immediate exercise would not benefit the option holder. Because option exercise would not yield a positive payoff, this option is called an out-of-the-money option.

IN-THE-MONEY PUT OPTION

EXAMPLE 14.6

Nortel stock is selling at $15. Let's look at a put option to sell Nortel at a price of $20 per share ($20 is the strike price). Notice that the stock price is less than the strike price. If the put option were exercised immediately, it would yield a payoff of $5 = $20 − $15. Because the option has a positive payoff if exercised immediately, it is known as an in-the-money option.

OUT-OF-THE-MONEY PUT OPTION

EXAMPLE 14.7

Nortel stock is selling at $15. Let's look at a put option to sell Nortel at a price of $10 per share ($10 is the strike price). Because the stock price is greater than the strike price, immediate exercise would not benefit the option holder. Because option exercise would not yield a positive payoff, this option is called an out-of-the-money option.

If this all seems a little complicated, simply remember that if the stock price, S, is greater than the strike price, K, a call option is said to be "in the money" and a put option is said to be "out of the money." Likewise, if the current stock price is less than the strike price, a call option is "out of the money" and a put option is "in the money." The chart immediately below summarizes the relationship between the stock price and the strike price for in-the-money and out-of-the-money options.

	In the Money	Out of the Money
Call option	$S > K$	$S < K$
Put option	$S < K$	$S > K$

CHECK THIS

14.3a All else equal, would an in-the-money option or an out-of-the-money option have a higher price? Why?

14.3b Does an out-of-the-money option ever have value? Why?

14.4 Option Payoffs and Profits

Options are appealing because they offer investors a wide variety of investment strategies. In fact, there is essentially no limit to the number of different investment strategies available using options. However, fortunately for us, only a small number of basic strategies are available, and more complicated strategies are built from these. We discuss the payoffs from basic strategies in this section and the following section.

Option Writing

Thus far, we have discussed options from the standpoint of the buyer only. However, options are contracts, and every contract must link at least two parties. The two parties to an option contract are the buyer and the seller. The seller of an option is called the "writer," and the act of selling an option is referred to as **option writing**.

option writing Taking the seller's side of an option contract.

By buying an option you buy the right, but not the obligation, to exercise the option before the option's expiration date. By selling or writing an option, you take the seller's side of the option contract. As a result, option writing involves receiving the option price and, in exchange, assuming the obligation to satisfy the buyer's exercise rights if the option is exercised.

call writer One who has the obligation to sell stock at the option's strike price if the option is exercised.

For example, a **call writer** is obligated to sell stock at the option's strike price if the buyer decides to exercise the call option. Similarly, a **put writer** is obligated to buy stock at the option's strike price if the buyer decides to exercise the put option.

put writer One who has the obligation to buy stock at the option's strike price if the option is exercised.

Option Payoffs

It is useful to think about option investment strategies in terms of their initial cash flows and terminal cash flows. The initial cash flow of an option is the price of the option, also called the option *premium*. To the option buyer, the option price (or premium) is a cash outflow. To the option writer, the option price (or premium) is a cash inflow. The terminal cash flow of an option is the option's payoff that could be realized from the exercise privilege. To the option buyer, a payoff entails a cash inflow. To the writer, a payoff entails a cash outflow.

To learn more on options, see www.tradingmarkets. com

For example, suppose the current price of RIM stock is $115 per share. You buy a call option on RIM with a strike price of $115. The premium is $4 per share. Thus, the initial cash flow is −$400 for you and +$400 for the option writer. What are the terminal cash flows for you and the option writer if RIM has a price of $125 when the option expires? What are the terminal cash flows if RIM has a price of $105 when the option expires?

If RIM is at $125, then you experience a cash inflow of $10 per share, whereas the writer experiences an outflow of $10 per share. If RIM is at $105, you both have a zero cash flow when the option expires because it is worthless. Notice that in both cases the buyer and the seller have the same cash flows, just with opposite signs. This shows that options are a "zero-sum game," meaning that any gains to the buyer must come at the expense of the seller and vice versa.

Payoff Diagrams

When investors buy options, the price that they are willing to pay depends on their assessment of the likely payoffs (cash inflows) from the exercise privilege. Likewise, when investors write options, an acceptable selling price depends on their assessment of

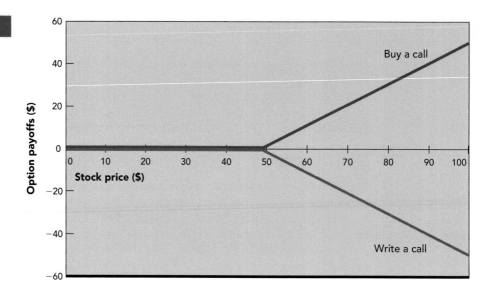

FIGURE 14.2

Call Option Payoffs

the likely payoffs (cash outflows) resulting from the buyers' exercise privilege. Given this, a general understanding of option payoffs is critical for understanding how option prices are determined.

A payoff diagram is a very useful graphical device for understanding option payoffs. The payoffs from buying a call option and the payoffs from writing a call option are seen in the payoff diagram in Figure 14.2. The vertical axis of Figure 14.2 measures option payoffs, and the horizontal axis measures the possible stock prices on the option expiration date. These examples assume that the call option has a strike price of $50 and that the option will be exercised only on its expiration date.

In Figure 14.2, notice that the call option payoffs are zero for all stock prices below the $50 strike price. This is because the call option holder will not exercise the option to buy stock at the $50 strike price when the stock is available in the stock market at a lower price. In this case, the option expires worthless.

In contrast, if the stock price is higher than the $50 strike price, the call option payoff is equal to the difference between the market price of the stock and the strike price of the option. For example, if the stock price is $60, the call option payoff is equal to $10, which is the difference between the $60 stock price and the $50 strike price. This payoff is a cash inflow to the buyer, because the option buyer can buy the stock at the $50 strike price and sell the stock at the $60 market price. However, this payoff is a cash outflow to the writer, because the option writer must sell the stock at the $50 strike price when the stock's market price is $60.

Putting it all together, the distinctive "hockey-stick" shape of the call option payoffs shows that the payoff is zero if the stock price is below the strike price. Above the strike price, however, the buyer of the call option gains $1 for every $1 increase in the stock price. Of course, as shown, the call option writer loses $1 for every $1 increase in the stock price above the strike price.

Figure 14.3 is an example of a payoff diagram illustrating the payoffs from buying a put option and from writing a put option. As with our call option payoffs, the vertical axis measures option payoffs, and the horizontal axis measures the possible stock prices on the option expiration date. Once again, these examples assume that the put has a strike price of $50, and that the option will be exercised only on its expiration date.

In Figure 14.3, the put option payoffs are zero for all stock prices above the $50 strike price. This is because a put option holder will not exercise the option to sell stock

FIGURE 14.3

Put Option
Payoffs

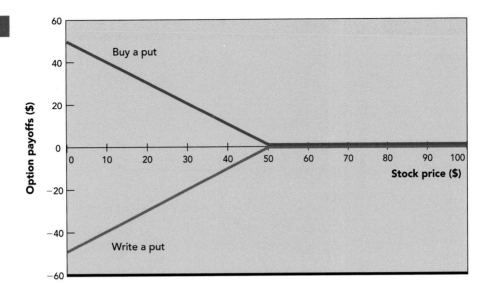

at the $50 strike price when the stock can be sold in the stock market at a higher price. In this case, the option expires worthless.

In contrast, if the stock price is lower than the $50 strike price, the put option payoff is equal to the difference between the market price of the stock and the strike price of the option. For example, if the stock price is $40, the put option payoff is equal to $10, which is the difference between the $40 stock price and the $50 strike price. This payoff is a cash inflow to the buyer, because the option buyer can buy the stock at the $40 market price and sell the stock at the $50 strike price. However, this payoff is a cash outflow to the writer, because the option writer must buy the stock at the $50 strike price when the stock's market price is $40.

Our payoff diagrams illustrate an important difference between the maximum possible gains and losses for puts and calls. Notice that if you buy a call option, there is no upper limit to your potential profit because there is no upper limit to the stock price. However, with a put option, the most you can make is the strike price. In other words, the best thing that can happen to you if you buy a put is for the stock price to go to zero. Of course, whether you buy a put or a call, your potential loss is limited to the option premium you pay.

Similarly, as shown in Figure 14.2, if you write a call, there is no limit to your possible loss, but your potential gain is limited to the option premium you receive. As shown in Figure 14.3, if you write a put, both your gain and loss are limited, although the potential loss could be substantial.

Option Profits

For even more on options, see www.investorlinks. com

Between them, Figures 14.2 and 14.3 tell us essentially everything we need to know about the payoffs from the four basic strategies involving options, buying and writing puts and calls. However, these figures give the payoffs at expiration only and so do not consider the original cash inflow or outflow. Option profit diagrams are an extension of payoff diagrams that do take into account the initial cash flow.

As we have seen, the profit from an option strategy is the difference between the option's terminal cash flow (the option payoff) and the option's initial cash flow (the option price, or premium). An option profit diagram simply adjusts option payoffs for

FIGURE 14.4

Call Option Profits

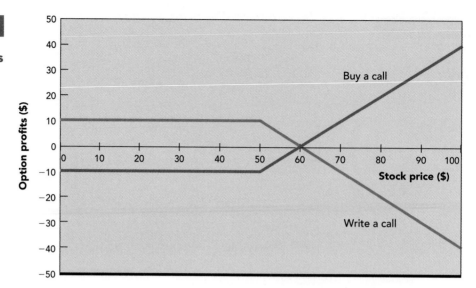

FIGURE 14.5

Put Option Profits

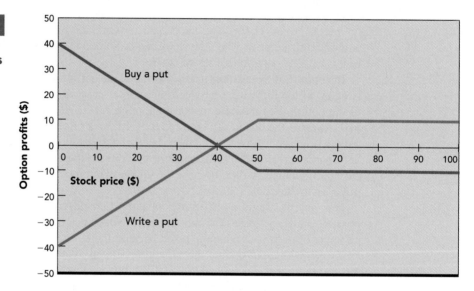

the original price of the option. This means that the option premium is subtracted from the payoffs from buying options and added to payoffs from writing options.

To illustrate, Figures 14.4 and 14.5 are profit diagrams corresponding to the four basic investment strategies for options. In each diagram, the vertical axis measures option profits, and the horizontal axis measures possible stock prices. Each profit diagram assumes that the option's strike price is $50 and that the put and call option prices are both $10. Notice that in each case the characteristic hockey-stick shape is maintained; the "stick" is just shifted up or down.

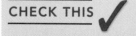

CHECK THIS		
	14.4a	What is option writing?
	14.4b	What are the payoffs from writing call options?
	14.4c	What are the payoffs from writing put options?

14.5 Option Strategies

Thus far, we have considered the payoffs and profits from buying and writing individual calls and puts. In this section, we consider what happens when we start to combine puts, calls, and shares of stock. There are numerous combinations that we could examine, but we will stick to just a few of the most basic and most important strategies.

The Protective Put Strategy

For ideas on option trading strategies, see www. commodityworld.com

Suppose you own a share of TelMex (Teléfonos de México) stock, currently worth $50. Suppose you additionally purchase a put option with a strike price of $50 for $2. What is the net effect of this purchase?

To answer, we can compare what happens if TelMex stock stays at or above $50 to what happens if it drops below $50. If TelMex stays at or above $50, your put will expire worthless since you would choose not to exercise it. You would be out the $2. However, if TelMex falls below $50, you would exercise your put, and the put writer would pay you $50 for your stock. No matter how far below $50 the price falls, you have guaranteed that you will receive $50 for your stock.

Thus, by purchasing a put option, you have protected yourself against a price decline. In the jargon of Wall Street, you have paid $2 to eliminate the "downside risk." For this reason, a strategy of buying a put option on a stock you already own is called a **protective put** strategy.

protective put Strategy of buying a put option on a stock already owned. This protects against a decline in value.

Notice that this use of a put option *reduces* the overall risk faced by an investor, so it is a conservative strategy. This is a good example of how options, or any derivative asset, can be used to decrease risk rather than increase it. Stated differently, options can be used to hedge as well as speculate, so they do not inherently increase risk.

Buying a put option on an asset you own is just like buying term insurance. When you buy car insurance, for example, you are effectively buying a put option on your car. If, because of an accident or theft, your car's value declines, you "exercise" your option, and the insurance company essentially pays for the decline in value.

The Covered Call Strategy

For more on covered calls, see www.writecall.com

Another conservative option strategy is to write call options on stock you already own. For example, again suppose you own some TelMex stock currently selling at $50. Now, instead of buying a put, consider selling a call option for, say, $2, with an exercise price of $55. What is the effect of this transaction?

To answer, we can compare what happens if TelMex stays below $55 (the exercise price on the option you sold) to what happens if it rises above $55. If TelMex stays below $55, the option will expire worthless, and you pocket the $2 premium you received. If the stock rises above $55, the option will be exercised against you, and you will deliver the stock in exchange for $55.

Thus, when you sell a call option on stock you already own, you keep the option premium no matter what. The worst thing that can happen to you is that you will have to sell your stock at the exercise price. Since you already own the stock, you are said to be "covered," and this strategy is known as a **covered call** strategy.

covered call Strategy of selling a call option on stock already owned.

With our covered call strategy, the stock is currently selling for $50. Since the strike price on the option is $55, the net effect of the strategy is to give up the possibility of a profit greater than $5 on the stock in exchange for the certain option premium of $2. This decreases the uncertainty surrounding the return on the investment and therefore decreases its risk.

In the jargon of Wall Street, a covered call exchanges "upside" potential for current income. In contrast, a strategy of selling call options on stock you do not own is a "naked" call strategy and, as we saw earlier, has unlimited potential losses. Thus, selling call options is either quite risky or else acts to reduce risk, depending on whether you are covered or naked. This is important to understand.

Straddles

Suppose a share of stock is currently selling at $50. You think the price is going to make a major move, but you are uncertain about the direction. What could you do? One answer is buy a call *and* buy a put, both with a $50 exercise price. That way, if the stock goes up sharply, your call will pay off; if it goes down sharply, your put will pay off. This is an example of a long **straddle**.

straddle Buying or selling a call and a put of the same security with the same exercise price and the same expiry date. Buying is a long straddle; selling is a short straddle.

This is called a "straddle" because you have, in effect, straddled the current $50 stock price. It is a long straddle because you bought both options. If you thought the stock price was *not* going to move in either direction, you might sell a put and a call, thereby generating some income. As long as the stock price stays at $50, both options would expire worthless. This is an example of a short straddle.

There are many other strategies, with colourful names such as strips, strangles, collars, and spreads, but we need to move on. In our next section, we discuss some upper and lower bounds on option values. For some interesting discussions of option strategies, see our nearby *Investment Updates* box.

OPTION STRATEGIES

EXAMPLE 14.8

You own a share of stock worth $80. Suppose you sell a call option with a strike price of $80 and also buy a put with a strike of $80. What is the net effect of these transactions on the risk of owning the stock?

Notice that what you have done is combine a protective put and a covered call strategy. To see the effect of doing this, suppose that, at option expiration, the stock is selling for more than $80. In this case, the put is worthless. The call will be exercised against you, and you will receive $80 for your stock. If the stock is selling for less than $80, the call is worthless. You would exercise your put and sell the stock for $80. In other words, the net effect is that you have guaranteed that you will exchange the stock for $80 no matter what happens, so you have created a riskless asset!

CHECK THIS ✓

14.5a   What is a protective put strategy? A covered call strategy?

14.5b   What is a short straddle? When might it be appropriate?

14.6 Option Prices, Intrinsic Values, and Arbitrage

There are strict limits to the range of values that an option price can attain in competitive options markets. We will have much to say about the determinants of an option's value in the next chapter. Here we touch on the subject by discussing some basic boundaries for the price of an option.

Some Stock-Option Strategies Win a Guarded Endorsement

Let's start with a concession: Maybe options aren't totally devoid of merit.

I don't like exchange-traded stock options. They are complicated. They are often used for mindless speculation. And the odds are unattractive. For every winner, there is a loser. In fact, after trading costs, investors collectively end up out of pocket. Still, I did manage to find two options strategies that almost pass muster. Options come in two flavours: puts and calls. By buying a put, you acquire the right to sell stock at a fixed price. Similarly, by purchasing a call, you acquire the right to buy stock at a set price.

But these rights don't come cheap. You have to pay a premium to the sellers of these options. Indeed, many folks sell puts and calls as a way of generating extra investment income. But that strategy can backfire if the stock involved has a big move. Sellers of call options may miss out on big gains by the underlying shares, while sellers of puts can be forced to pay a lofty price for a now-battered stock.

Sound confusing? To get a better handle on what is involved, consider these two strategies that may appeal to certain investors.

Easing Out

Suppose you have 1,000 shares of Microsoft that you bought for a pittance. You know you ought to diversify, but you are reluctant to sell because of the resulting tax bill. Options could ease the pain of selling. The idea is to write call options against your Microsoft position. Let's say you sold July calls, with a $75 strike price, somewhat above the current $68.47 share price. By writing the calls, you agree to sell your Microsoft shares for $75 any time between now and the options' expiration date. In return, you will receive $4,200 in option premiums, which will help to offset the tax bill, should your stock get called away.

"The problem is the downside," says Eric Seff, a financial planner in Mamaroneck, N.Y. What if your Microsoft shares plunge? Mr. Seff says the option premiums you collected probably wouldn't compensate for your losses. To guard against a big decline in Microsoft's shares, you could combine the sale of call options with the purchase of Microsoft puts. That would give you downside protection. But the premium you pay for the puts will likely wipe out the income you earned by selling the calls.

What to do? Maybe you should forget the puts and instead sell calls with a strike price very close to today's share price. For instance, you could sell Microsoft calls with a strike price of $70, just above the current stock price. That way, you will earn some extra income, while being almost certain that the options you sold will be exercised and thus your Microsoft stock will get called away. Or maybe you should just dump the shares. "If you know you should get out of the stock, then get out of the stock and forget the options," advises Minneapolis financial planner Ross Levin. "The taxes may hurt. But that's the price of good investment choices you made in the past."

Looking Down

What if a bear market hits when you are retired? If you are already a few years into retirement, you are probably in fine shape, thanks to the cushion created by earlier investment gains. But if you have just retired, you could find yourself in deep trouble, as your portfolio is rapidly depleted through a combination of tumbling stock prices and your own withdrawals.

To protect yourself during the critical first few years of retirement, you might buy put options, says Moshe Milevsky, a finance professor at York University in Toronto and author of "The Probability of Fortune." Suppose you bought puts on the Standard & Poor's 500-stock index that expire in December and that will limit your losses during the next year to 8%. This insurance will currently cost you about 5% of your stock portfolio's value. Sound like a heap of change? To pay for this downside protection, you could sell call options. But those calls will limit your potential gain. To earn enough to pay for the puts, you would probably have to write calls that cap your stock-market earnings during the next year at 8%.

That would be a big mistake if your first year of retirement turns out to be a gangbuster year for stocks. "If you are worried about the upside, sell a call at a higher strike price and finance part of the put out of your own pocket," Prof. Milevsky suggests. Because these calls with a higher strike price won't generate as big a premium, protecting against a one-year market decline of greater than 8% might cost you 3% or 4% of your stock portfolio's value. For antsy investors, that might be money well spent. But I would rather keep the cash and take my chances.

Source: Jonathan Clements, *The Wall Street Journal*, January 15, 2002. © 2002 Dow Jones & Company, Inc. All Rights Reserved Worldwide.

The Upper Bound for a Call Option Price

What is the most a call option could sell for? To answer, suppose we have a call option on a share of stock. The current stock price is $60. Without more information, we can't say a lot about the price of the call option, but we do know one thing: The price of the option must be less than $60!

If you think about it, the right to buy a share of stock cannot be worth more than the share itself. To illustrate, suppose the call option was actually selling for $65 when the stock was selling at $60. What would you do?

What you would do is get very rich, very fast. You would sell call options at $65 and buy stock at $60. You pocket the $5 difference. The worst thing that can happen to you is the options are exercised and you receive the exercise price. In this case, you make an unlimited amount of money at no risk.

This is an example of a true *arbitrage* opportunity. An arbitrage is an opportunity that (1) requires no net investment on your part, (2) has no possibility of loss, and (3) has at least the potential for a gain. The case of a call option selling for more than its underlying asset is a particularly juicy arbitrage because it puts money in your pocket today, and later either leaves you with stock you acquired at no cost or else leaves you with the exercise price on the option. Very nice, indeed! But too good to be true.

The Upper Bound for a Put Option Price

We've seen that a call option cannot sell for more than the underlying stock. How about a put option? To answer, suppose again that the stock price is $60. If a put sells for $65, is there an arbitrage opportunity?

It may look a little odd, but, without more information, we can't tell if there is an arbitrage or not. To see this, suppose the exercise price on the put option is $1,000. The right to sell a share of stock for $1,000 when its current worth is only $60 is obviously valuable, and it is obviously worth more than $65.

As this example suggests, the upper bound on a put option's price depends on the strike price. To illustrate, suppose we have a put option with an exercise price of $50 and a price of $60. What would you do?

This situation is an arbitrage opportunity. You would simply sell puts at $60 and put the money in the bank. The worst thing that could happen to you is that you would have to buy the stock for $50 a share, leaving you with stock and $10 per share in cash (the difference between the $60 you received and the $50 you paid for the stock). So you would either end up with stock that cost you nothing to acquire plus some cash or, if the option expires worthless, you would keep the entire $60. We therefore conclude that a put option must sell for less than its strike price.

The Lower Bounds on Option Prices

Having established the most a call or put could sell for, we now want to know what is the least they could sell for. We observe that an option cannot have a negative value, since, by definition, an option can simply be discarded.

intrinsic value
The payoff that an option holder receives assuming the underlying stock price remains unchanged from its current value.

To further address this question, it is useful to define what is known as the **intrinsic value** of an option. The intrinsic value of an option is the payoff that an option holder receives if the underlying stock price does not change from its current value. Equivalently, it is what the option would be worth if it were expiring immediately.

For example, suppose a certain call option contract specifies a strike price of $50, and the underlying stock price for the option is currently $45. Suppose the option was about to expire. With the stock price at $45 and the strike at $50, this option would have no value. Thus, this call option's intrinsic value is zero.

Alternatively, suppose the underlying stock price is currently $55. If the option was about to expire, it would be exercised, yielding a payoff of $5. This $5, which is simply the difference between the $55 stock price and the $50 strike price, is the call option's intrinsic value.

As another example of intrinsic value, suppose a put option has a strike price of $50, and the current stock price is $55. If the put were about to expire, it would be worthless. In this case, the put option's intrinsic value is zero.

Alternatively, suppose the underlying stock price was $45. The put option would be exercised, yielding a payoff of $5, which is the difference between the $50 strike price and the $45 stock price. In this case, the put option's intrinsic value is $5.

Based on our examples, the intrinsic value of a call option and a put option can be written as follows, where S is the current stock price and K is the option's strike price. The term "*max*" is a shorthand notation for maximum.

$$\text{Call optioin intrinsic value} = max\ [0, S - K] \qquad (14.1)$$
$$\text{Put option intrinsic value} = max\ [0, K - S]$$

This notation simply means that the intrinsic value of a call option is equal to $S - K$ or zero, whichever is bigger. Similarly, the intrinsic value of a put option is equal to $K - S$ or zero, whichever is bigger.

An option with a positive intrinsic value is said to be "in the money," and an option with a zero intrinsic value is said to be "out of the money" or "out the money." If the stock price and the strike price are essentially equal, the option is said to be "at the money." Thus, a call option is in the money when the stock price is greater than the strike price, and a put option is in the money when the stock price is less than the strike price.

Having defined an option's intrinsic value, we now ask: Is it possible for an option to sell for less than its intrinsic value? The answer is no. To see this, suppose a current stock price is $S = \$60$, and a call option with a strike price of $K = \$50$ has a price of $C = \$5$. Clearly, this call option is in the money, and the $5 call price is less than the option's intrinsic value of $S - K = \$10$.

If you are actually presented with these stock and option prices, you have an arbitrage opportunity to obtain a riskless arbitrage profit by following a simple three-step strategy. First, buy the call option at its price of $C = \$5$. Second, immediately exercise the call option and buy the stock from the call writer at the strike price of $K = \$50$. At this point, you have acquired the stock for $55, which is the sum of the call price plus the strike price.

As a third and final step, simply sell the stock at the current market price of $S = \$60$. Since you acquired the stock for $55 and sold the stock for $60, you have earned an arbitrage profit of $5. Clearly, if such an opportunity continued to exist, you would repeat these three steps over and over until you became bored with making easy money (as if that could ever happen!). But realistically, such easy arbitrage opportunities do not exist, and it therefore follows that a call option price is never less than its intrinsic value.

A similar arbitrage argument applies to put options. For example, suppose a current stock price is $S = \$40$, and a put option with a strike price of $K = \$50$ has a price of $P = \$5$. This $5 put price is less than the option's intrinsic value of $K - S = \$10$. To exploit this opportunity, you first buy the put option at its price of $P = \$5$, and then buy the stock at its current price of $S = \$40$. At this point, you have acquired the stock for \$45, which is the sum of the put price plus the stock price. Now you immediately exercise the put option, thereby selling the stock to the option writer at the strike price of $S = \$50$. Since you acquired the stock for \$45 and sold the stock for \$50, you have earned an arbitrage profit of \$5. Again, you would not realistically expect such an easy arbitrage opportunity to actually exist, and therefore we conclude that a put option's price is never less than its intrinsic value.

Our conclusion that call option and put option prices are never less than their intrinsic values can be stated as follows, where the mathematical symbol "$\geq$" means "greater than or equal to:"

$$\text{Call option price} \geq max\ [0, S - K] \qquad (14.2)$$
$$\text{Put option price} \geq max\ [0, K - S]$$

In plain English, these equations simply state that an option's price is never less than the intrinsic value of the option.

There is an important caveat concerning our lower bounds on option values. If you pick up *The Wall Street Journal*, it is relatively easy to find cases in which it appears an option is selling for less than its intrinsic value, at least by a small amount. However, if you tried to actually exploit the apparent arbitrage, you would find that the prices in the *Journal* are not the ones you could actually trade at! There are a variety of reasons for this, but, at a minimum, keep in mind that the prices you see for the stock and the option are probably not synchronous, so the two prices may never have existed at the same point in time.

CHECK THIS ✓

14.6a   What is the most a call option could be worth? The least?

14.6b   What is the most a put option could be worth? The least?

14.6c   What is an out-of-the-money put option?

14.7 Employee Stock Options

employee stock option (ESO) An option granted to an employee by a company giving the employee the right to buy shares of stock in the company at a fixed price for a fixed time.

In this section, we take a brief look at **employee stock options**, or **ESOs**. An ESO is, in essence, a call option that a firm gives to employees giving them the right to buy shares of stock in the company. The practice of granting options to employees has become widespread. It is almost universal for upper management, but some companies, like The Gap and Starbucks, have granted options to almost every employee. Thus, an understanding of ESOs is important. Why? Because you may very soon be an ESO holder!

ESO Features

Since ESOs are basically call options, we have already covered most of the important aspects. However, ESOs have a few features that make them different from regular stock options. The details differ from company to company, but a typical ESO has a 10-year life, which is much longer than most ordinary options. Unlike traded options,

ESOs cannot be sold. They also have what is known as a "vesting" period. Often, for up to three years or so, an ESO cannot be exercised and also must be forfeited if an employee leaves the company. After this period, the options "vest," which means they can be exercised. Sometimes employees who resign with vested options are given a limited time to exercise their options.

Why are ESOs granted? There are basically two reasons. First, the owners of a corporation (the shareholders) face the basic problem of aligning shareholder and management interests and also of providing incentives for employees to focus on corporate goals. ESOs are a powerful motivator because, as we have seen, the payoffs on options can be very large. High-level executives in particular stand to gain enormous wealth if they are successful in creating value for stockholders.

The second reason some companies rely heavily on ESOs is that an ESO has no immediate, upfront, out-of-pocket cost to the corporation. In smaller, possibly cash-strapped, companies, ESOs are simply a substitute for ordinary wages. Employees are willing to accept them instead of cash, hoping for big payoffs in the future. In fact, ESOs are a major recruiting tool, allowing businesses to attract talent that they otherwise could not afford.

ESO Repricing

ESOs are almost always "at the money" when they are issued, meaning that the stock price is equal to the strike price. Notice that, in this case, the intrinsic value is zero, so there is no value from immediate exercise. Of course, even though the intrinsic value is zero, an ESO is still quite valuable because of, among other things, its very long life.

If the stock falls significantly after an ESO is granted, then the option is said to be "underwater." On occasion, a company will decide to lower the strike price on underwater options. Such options are said to be "restruck" or "repriced." This has happened to Nortel company.

The practice of repricing ESOs is very controversial. Companies that do it argue that once an ESO becomes deeply out of the money, it loses its incentive value because employees recognize there is only a small chance that the option will finish in the money. In fact, employees may leave and join other companies where they receive a fresh options grant.

Critics of repricing point out that a lowered strike price is, in essence, a reward for failing. They also point out that if employees know that options will be repriced, then much of the incentive effect is lost. Today, many companies award options on a regular basis, perhaps annually or even quarterly. That way, an employee will always have at least some options that are near the money even if others are underwater. Also, regular grants ensure that employees always have unvested options, which gives them an added incentive to stay with their current employer rather than forfeit the potentially valuable options.

ESOs AT THE GAP, INC.

The Gap, Inc., is a large, well-known company whose stock trades under the ticker symbol GPS (GAP is the ticker symbol for Great Atlantic & Pacific Tea Co., which you probably know as A&P). The Gap grants employee stock options that are fairly standard. This description of The Gap's ESOs is taken from its annual report:

> Under our stock option plans, options to purchase common stock are granted to officers, directors, eligible employees and consultants at exercise prices equal to the fair market value of the stock at the date of grant. Stock options generally expire 10 years from

the grant date, three months after termination, or one year after the date of retirement or death, if earlier. Stock options generally vest over a four-year period, with shares becoming exercisable in equal annual installments of 25 percent.

The GAP's ESOs are not European-style options because they vest in equal increments over a four-year period. By "vest," we mean the holders can exercise these options. If you were granted options on 500 shares of GPS stock, you could exercise options on 125 shares one year after the grant date, another 125 shares two years after the grant date, another 125 shares three years after the grant date, and the last 125 shares four years after the grant date. Of course, you wouldn't have to exercise your options this quickly. As long as you stay with the company you could wait 10 years to exercise your options just before they expire.

CHECK THIS ✓   **14.7a**   What are the key differences between a traded stock option and an ESO?

14.7b   What is ESO repricing? Why is it controversial?

14.8 Put-Call Parity

put-call parity
Theorem asserting a certain parity relationship between call and put prices for European-style options with the same strike price and expiration date.

Put-call parity is perhaps the most fundamental parity relationship among option prices. **Put-call parity** states that the difference between a call option price and a put option price for European-style options with the same strike price and expiration date is equal to the difference between the underlying stock price and the discounted strike price. The put-call parity relationship is algebraically represented as

$$C - P = S - Ke^{-rT} \qquad (14.3)$$

where the variables are defined as follows:

C = Call option price P = Put option price
S = Current stock price K = Option strike price
r = Risk-free interest rate T = Time remaining until option expiration

The logic behind put-call parity is based on the fundamental principle of finance stating that two securities with the same riskless payoff on the same future date must have the same price. To illustrate how this principle is applied to demonstrate put-call parity, suppose we form a portfolio of risky securities by following these three steps:

1. Buy 100 shares of Nortel stock (NT).

2. Write one Nortel call option contract.

3. Buy one Nortel put option contract.

For information on trading options, see www.ino.com

Both Nortel options have the same strike price and expiration date. We assume that these options are European style and, therefore, cannot be exercised before the last day prior to their expiration date.

Table 14.1 states the payoffs to each of these three securities based on the expiration date stock price, denoted by S_T. For example, if the expiration date stock price is greater than the strike price, that is, $S_T > K$, then the put option expires worthless and the call

TABLE 14.1	Put-Call Parity	
	Expiration Date Payoffs	
Expiration Date Stock Price	$S_T > K$	$S_T < K$
Buy stock	S_T	S_T
Write one call option	$-(S_T - K)$	0
Buy one put option	0	$(K - S_T)$
Total portfolio expiration date payoff	K	K

option requires a payment from writer to buyer of $(S_T - K)$. Alternatively, if the stock price is less than the strike price, that is, $S_T < K$, the call option expires worthless and the put option yields a payment from writer to buyer of $(K - S_T)$.

In Table 14.1, notice that no matter whether the expiration date stock price is greater or less than the strike price, the payoff to the portfolio is always equal to the strike price. This means that the portfolio has a risk-free payoff at option expiration equal to the strike price. Since the portfolio is risk-free, the cost of acquiring this portfolio today should be no different from the cost of acquiring any other risk-free investment with the same payoff on the same date. One such riskless investment is a Treasury bill.

To learn more about trading options, see www.optionetics. com

The cost of a Treasury bill paying K dollars at option expiration is the discounted strike price Ke^{-rT}, where r is the risk-free interest rate and T is the time remaining until option expiration, which together form the discount factor e^{-rT}. By the fundamental principle of finance stating that two riskless investments with the same payoff on the same date must have the same price, it follows that this cost is also equal to the cost of acquiring the stock and options portfolio. Since this portfolio is formed by (1) buying the stock, (2) writing a call option, and (3) buying a put option, its cost is the sum of the stock price, plus the put price, less the call price. Setting this portfolio cost equal to the discounted strike price yields this equation:

$$S + P - C = Ke^{-rT}$$

By a simple rearrangement of terms we obtain the originally stated put-call parity equation, thereby validating our put-call parity argument:

$$C - P = S - Ke^{-rT}$$

The put-call parity argument stated above assumes that the underlying stock paid no dividends before option expiration. If the stock does pay a dividend before option expiration, then the put-call parity equation is adjusted as follows, where y represents the dividend yield:

$$C - P = Se^{-yT} - Ke^{-rT} \tag{14.4}$$

The logic behind this adjustment is the fact that a dividend payment reduces the value of the stock, since company assets are reduced by the amount of the dividend payment. When the dividend payment occurs before option expiration, investors adjust the effective stock price determining option payoffs to be made after the dividend payment. This adjustment reduces the value of the call option and increases the value of the put option.

IMPLIED PUT OPTION PRICES

EXAMPLE 14.9

A current stock price is $50, and a call option with a strike price of $55 maturing in two months has a price of $8. The stock has a 4 percent dividend yield. If the interest rate is 6 percent, what is the price implied by put-call parity for a put option with the same strike price and maturity?

Rearranging the put-call parity equations yields the following price for a put option:

$$P = C + Ke^{-rT} - Se^{-yT}$$

Substituting numerical values yields this price for the put option:

$$\$12.78 = \$8 + \$55e^{-.06 \times (2/12)} - \$50e^{-.04 \times (2/12)}$$

CHECK THIS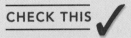

14.8a   The argument supporting put-call parity is based on the fundamental principle of finance that two securities with the same riskless payoff on the same future date must have the same price. Restate the demonstration of put-call parity based on this fundamental principle. (Hint: Start by recalling and explaining the contents of Table 14.1.)

14.8b   Exchange-traded options on individual stock issues are American style, and, therefore, put-call parity does not hold exactly for these options. In the "Equity Options" page of *The Globe and Mail*, compare the differences between selected call and put option prices with the differences between stock prices and discounted strike prices. How closely does put-call parity appear to hold for these American-style options?

14.9   Stock Index Options

Following the tremendous success of stock options trading on the Chicago Board Options Exchange, the exchange looked for other new financial products to offer to investors and portfolio managers. In 1982, the CBOE created stock index options, which, at the time, represented a new type of option contract.

Index Options: Features and Settlement

stock index option
An option on a stock market index.

A **stock index option** is an option on a stock market index. In Montreal Exchange contracts on S&P Canada 60 Index options are traded. The index consists of 60 large companies representative of Canadian industry. This index is simply called the "S&P Canada 60." The S&P Canada 60 index options trade under the ticker symbol SXO.

Before stock index options could be introduced, one very important detail that had to be worked out was what to do when an option is exercised. It was obvious to exchange officials that actual delivery of all stocks comprising a stock index was impractical. Instead, a cash settlement procedure was adopted for stock index options. With cash settlement, when a stock index option is exercised, the option writer pays a cash amount to the option buyer based on the difference between the exercise date index level and the option's strike price. For example, suppose you had purchased an SXO call option with a strike price of $850 and the S&P Canada 60 Index was $800 on the day before option expiration. The difference between the index level and the strike price is $850 − $800 = $50. Since the contract size for SXO options is 100 times the S&P Canada 60 index, the option writer must pay 100 × $50 = $5,000, which you receive as the option holder.

In the example above, the contract size for SXO options was stated to be 100 times the S&P Canada 60 index. In fact, the contract size for almost all standardized stock index options is 100 times the underlying index. Thus, the actual price of a stock index option is 100 times the price stated on an index level basis. There are only a few exceptions to this rule. For example, the CBOE offers so-called Reduced Value index options with a contract size that is one-tenth the size of standard index options. Reduced Value index options are appealing to some individual investors, but they represent only a minuscule share of all index options trading.

Index Option Price Quotes

There now exists a wide variety of stock market indexes for which options are available. Each business day, newspapers provide a summary of the previous day's activity in stock index options. Figure 14.6 shows the prices for call and put contracts for S&P Canada 60 Index options. It is downloaded from the website of the Montreal Exchange. The first column shows the expiration date, the strike price, and the ticker symbols of various contracts. Columns 2, 3, 4 and 5 show bid size, bid price, ask size and ask price of the contacts. The last price column indicates the closing price of the previous day followed by net change and highest and lowest prices. The last two columns report trading volume measured as the number of contracts traded during the previous day's trading and open interest measured by the total number of contracts traded on a given day.

INDEX OPTIONS

EXAMPLE 14.10

Suppose you bought 10 Jan 820 SXO call contacts at a quoted price of $7. How much did you pay in total? At option expiration, suppose the S&P Canada 60 is at 840. What would you receive?

The price per SXO contract is 100 times the quoted price. Since you bought 10 contracts you paid a total of 7 × 100 × 10 = $7,000. If at expiration, the S&P Canada 60 is at 840, you would receive $100 × (840 − 820) = $2,000 per contract or $20,000 in all. This $20,000 would be paid you in cash, since index options feature cash settlement.

CHECK THIS

14.9a In addition to the underlying asset, what is the major difference between any ordinary stock option and a stock index option?

FIGURE 14.6

Index Options Trading

Source: S&P Canadian Index Services.

SXO-S&P Canada 60 Index Options

Last update: Dec. 31, 2007 14:34 Montréal time (DATA 15 MINUTES DELAYED)   Refresh | Print

Calls

Month/Strike	Bid Price	Ask Price	Last Price	Net Change	Vol.
+ 08 JA 750.000	56.250	63.950	63.000	0.000	0
+ 08 JA 760.000	47.450	54.300	53.450	0.000	0
+ 08 JA 770.000	38.900	44.900	44.050	0.000	0
+ 08 JA 780.000	30.800	35.800	35.000	0.000	0
+ 08 JA 790.000	23.250	27.250	26.450	0.000	0
+ 08 JA 800.000	16.750	19.550	18.800	0.000	0
+ 08 JA 810.000	11.000	13.050	12.350	0.000	0
+ 08 JA 820.000	6.300	7.900	7.000	−0.250	5
+ 08 JA 830.000	3.100	4.150	3.650	0.000	0
+ 08 JA 840.000	0.950	1.850	1.500	−0.050	4
+ 08 JA 850.000	0.000	0.750	0.600	0.000	0
+ 08 JA 860.000	0.000	0.300	0.250	0.000	0
+ 08 FE 750.000	65.900	68.550	67.650	0.000	0
+ 08 FE 760.000	54.800	59.750	58.900	0.000	0
+ 08 FE 770.000	46.800	51.250	50.400	0.000	0
+ 08 FE 780.000	41.200	43.100	42.300	0.000	0
+ 08 FE 790.000	33.850	35.550	34.700	0.000	0
+ 08 FE 800.000	27.100	28.550	27.700	0.000	0
+ 08 FE 810.000	21.050	22.300	21.400	0.000	0
+ 08 FE 820.000	15.700	16.750	15.900	0.000	0
+ 08 FE 830.000	11.050	11.950	11.100	0.000	0
+ 08 MR 730.000	90.100	93.900	90.850	0.000	0
+ 08 MR 740.000	81.500	85.250	82.250	0.000	0
+ 08 MR 750.000	73.150	76.800	73.900	0.000	0
+ 08 MR 760.000	65.050	68.550	65.800	0.000	0
+ 08 MR 770.000	57.300	60.650	58.000	0.000	0
+ 08 MR 780.000	49.950	53.100	50.550	0.000	0
+ 08 MR 790.000	42.950	46.150	43.500	0.000	0
+ 08 MR 800.000	36.350	39.500	36.850	0.000	0
+ 08 MR 810.000	30.250	32.800	30.700	0.000	0
+ 08 MR 820.000	24.600	27.500	25.000	0.000	0
+ 08 MR 830.000	19.500	21.850	19.800	0.000	0
+ 08 MR 840.000	14.950	17.150	15.200	0.000	0
+ 08 MR 850.000	11.050	13.300	11.200	0.000	0
+ 08 MR 860.000	7.800	9.950	7.950	0.000	0
+ 08 JN 750.000	88.250	91.900	89.200	0.000	0
+ 08 JN 760.000	80.850	84.100	81.850	0.000	0
+ 08 JN 770.000	73.700	77.050	74.700	0.000	0
+ 08 JN 780.000	66.850	70.150	67.850	0.000	0
+ 08 JN 790.000	60.250	64.000	61.200	0.000	0
+ 08 JN 800.000	53.900	57.650	54.850	0.000	0
+ 08 JN 810.000	47.900	51.050	48.800	0.000	0
+ 08 JN 820.000	42.200	45.200	43.050	0.000	0
+ 08 JN 830.000	36.850	40.000	37.700	0.000	0
+ 08 JN 840.000	31.850	35.000	32.650	0.000	0
+ 08 JN 850.000	27.250	30.350	29.800	0.000	0
+ 08 JN 860.000	23.000	26.000	23.750	0.000	0
+ 08 SE 760.000	93.450	97.450	94.900	0.000	0
+ 08 SE 770.000	86.550	90.600	88.050	0.000	0
+ 08 SE 780.000	79.950	84.150	81.350	0.000	0
+ 08 SE 790.000	73.500	77.400	74.900	0.000	0
+ 08 SE 800.000	67.300	71.300	68.650	0.000	0
+ 08 SE 810.000	61.350	65.300	61.700	−0.950	1
+ 08 SE 820.000	55.650	59.550	56.950	0.000	0
+ 08 SE 830.000	50.250	54.250	0.000	0.000	0

Puts

Month/Strike	Bid Price	Ask Price	Last Price	Net Change	Vol.
+ 08 JA 750.000	0.400	1.150	1.250	0.000	0
+ 08 JA 760.000	0.800	1.700	1.850	0.000	0
+ 08 JA 770.000	1.700	2.500	2.650	0.000	0
+ 08 JA 780.000	2.750	3.650	3.900	0.000	0
+ 08 JA 790.000	4.250	5.400	5.650	0.000	0
+ 08 JA 800.000	6.800	8.000	8.300	0.000	0
+ 08 JA 810.000	10.000	11.850	12.200	0.000	0
+ 08 JA 820.000	14.350	17.050	17.450	0.000	0
+ 08 JA 830.000	20.150	23.750	24.250	0.000	0
+ 08 JA 840.000	25.800	31.950	32.650	0.000	0
+ 08 JA 850.000	33.550	41.200	42.000	0.000	0
+ 08 JA 860.000	46.750	50.950	51.850	0.000	0
+ 08 FE 750.000	3.650	5.000	5.050	0.000	0
+ 08 FE 760.000	4.900	6.250	6.350	0.000	0
+ 08 FE 770.000	7.050	7.850	7.950	0.000	0
+ 08 FE 780.000	9.050	9.850	9.950	0.000	0
+ 08 FE 790.000	11.500	12.350	12.450	0.000	0
+ 08 FE 800.000	14.550	15.500	16.400	0.850	3
+ 08 FE 810.000	18.250	19.350	19.400	0.000	0
+ 08 FE 820.000	22.650	23.950	23.950	0.000	0
+ 08 FE 830.000	27.750	29.250	29.350	0.000	0
+ 08 MR 730.000	6.450	8.350	7.450	0.000	0
+ 08 MR 740.000	7.750	9.750	8.750	0.000	0
+ 08 MR 750.000	9.250	11.600	10.300	0.000	0
+ 08 MR 760.000	11.050	13.450	12.650	0.500	2
+ 08 MR 770.000	13.150	15.300	14.300	0.000	0
+ 08 MR 780.000	15.600	17.850	16.800	0.000	0
+ 08 MR 790.000	18.500	20.900	19.750	0.000	0
+ 08 MR 800.000	21.750	24.400	23.050	0.000	0
+ 08 MR 810.000	25.500	28.250	26.800	0.000	0
+ 08 MR 820.000	29.700	32.550	31.050	0.000	0
+ 08 MR 830.000	34.400	37.450	35.850	0.000	0
+ 08 MR 840.000	39.700	42.950	41.200	0.000	0
+ 08 MR 850.000	45.600	49.000	47.150	0.000	0
+ 08 MR 860.000	52.150	55.300	53.850	0.000	0
+ 08 JN 750.000	19.950	23.300	20.500	−1.050	2
+ 08 JN 760.000	22.350	26.000	23.950	0.000	0
+ 08 JN 770.000	25.000	28.600	26.650	0.000	0
+ 08 JN 780.000	27.900	31.600	29.550	0.000	0
+ 08 JN 790.000	31.050	34.400	32.700	0.000	0
+ 08 JN 800.000	34.500	38.000	36.150	0.000	0
+ 08 JN 810.000	38.250	41.750	39.850	0.000	0
+ 08 JN 820.000	42.300	46.100	43.900	0.000	0
+ 08 JN 830.000	46.700	50.050	48.300	0.000	0
+ 08 JN 840.000	51.500	54.850	53.100	0.000	0
+ 08 JN 850.000	56.650	60.100	58.200	0.000	0
+ 08 JN 860.000	62.150	66.000	63.750	0.000	0
+ 08 SE 760.000	30.500	34.900	32.400	0.000	0
+ 08 SE 770.000	33.300	37.750	35.200	0.000	0
+ 08 SE 780.000	36.300	40.250	38.200	0.000	0
+ 08 SE 790.000	39.500	43.550	39.150	−2.250	1
+ 08 SE 800.000	42.950	47.050	44.850	0.000	0
+ 08 SE 810.000	46.650	50.750	48.550	0.000	0
+ 08 SE 820.000	50.600	54.800	52.500	0.000	0
+ 08 SE 830.000	54.850	59.300	0.000	0.000	0

14.10 Foreign Currency Options

foreign currency options These give holders the right to buy or sell a certain amount of foreign currency at the strike price until the maturity date.

Foreign currency options give holders the right to buy (call) or sell a certain amount of foreign currency at the strike price until the maturity date. In Canada, foreign currency options contracts are not traded. In the United States, the Philadelphia Exchange offers six contracts of the following currencies against the USD: Australian dollar, British pound, Canadian dollar, Euro, Japanese yen and Swiss franc. Each contract has different sizes. The size of the Canadian dollar contracts are 50,000 dollars.

Figure 14.7 shows the volume and the prices of Canadian dollar–US dollar options from the Philadelphia Exchange.

14.11 Warrants

In this section we will discuss warrants which are issued by companies giving the right to buy stock of the company at a specified strike price. Warrants are very similar to call options except they are written by the companies. If a warrant holder decides to exercise the right, then the company has to issue new shares in exchange for the strike price. As a result, the company gets the cash inflow, but increases the number of outstanding shares.

Companies generally issue warrants with other securities to make these securities more attractive. For example many companies attach warrants with their bond issues. Some companies may issue warrants separately, but this is not very common.

14.12 The Canadian Derivatives Clearing Corporation

Suppose that you ordered a new car through a local dealer and paid a $2,000 deposit. Further suppose that two weeks later you receive a letter informing you that your dealer had entered bankruptcy. No doubt, you would be quite upset at the prospect of losing your $2,000 deposit.

Now consider a similar situation where you pay $2,000 for several call options through a broker. On the day before expiration you tell your broker to exercise the options, since they would produce, say, a $5,000 payoff. Then, a few days later, your broker tells you that the call writer entered bankruptcy proceedings and that your $2,000 call premium and $5,000 payoff were lost. No doubt, this would also be quite upsetting. However, if your options were traded through a registered options exchange, the integrity of your options investment would be guaranteed by the **Canadian Derivatives Clearing Corporation (CDCC)**.

Canadian Derivatives Clearing Corporation (CDCC) Corporation that guarantees that the terms of an option contract will be fulfilled if the option is exercised; issues and clears all option contracts trading on Canadian exchanges.

The Canadian Derivatives Clearing Corporation is the clearing agency for all derivatives exchanges in Canada (Montreal and Winnipeg). Most options investors are unaware of the CDCC because only member firms of the Montreal Exchange (ME) deal directly with it. However, in fact, all option contracts traded in Canada are originally issued, guaranteed, and cleared by the CDCC. Brokerage firms merely act as intermediaries between investors and the CDCC.

To better understand the function of the CDCC, let us examine a hypothetical order to buy options. In this example, assume that you instruct your broker to buy, say, 10 January 25 put options on Nortel. For simplicity, let us assume that your broker works for a member firm of ME and can therefore relay your order directly to ME.

FIGURE 14.7

Currency Options

Source: Philadelphia
Stock Exchange
(www.phlx.com).

Products > U.S. Dollar Settled PHLX World Currency Options^SM

PHLX Announces Penny Increment Trading for World Currency Options Beginning January 2, 2008

Click Here to Access PHLX Webinar Series

PHLX US DOLLAR SETTLED WORLD CURRENCY OPTIONS

Currency   Canadian Dollar (XDC)   [Submit]

QUICK QUOTE

(XDC) Canadian Dollar
Last: 100.60 Change: -1.33 (-1.30 %)

CHART

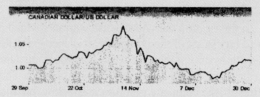

CANADIAN DOLLAR/US DOLLAR

| | 29 Sep | 22 Oct | 14 Nov | 7 Dec | 30 Dec |

DISPLAY PROPERTIES

Chain Type	Options Range	Expiration
Calls & Puts	All	Jan 2008 [View Chain]

CALLS

Symbol	Last Trade	Change	Bid	Ask	Volume	Interest	Strike Price
CEJAJ	6.00	-1.40	6.00	6.30	n.a.	n.a.	94.50
XDCAL	n.a.	n.a.	5.50	5.80	n.a.	220	95.00
CEJAN	5.00	-1.40	5.00	5.30	n.a.	n.a.	95.50
XDCAP	n.a.	n.a.	4.60	4.80	n.a.	9	96.00
CEJAR	4.10	-1.40	4.10	4.30	n.a.	n.a.	96.50
XDCAT	3.70	-1.30	3.70	3.90	n.a.	200	97.00
CEJAV	n.a.	n.a.	3.20	3.50	n.a.	510	97.50
XDCAA	2.85	-1.25	2.85	3.00	n.a.	10	98.00
CEJAC	n.a.	n.a.	2.40	2.55	n.a.	300	98.50
XDCAE	2.10	0.45	2.05	2.20	250	1	99.00
CEJAG	n.a.	n.a.	1.70	1.80	n.a.	6	99.50
XDCAI	1.55	-0.95	1.40	1.50	400	10	100.00
CEJAK	1.30	-0.70	1.15	1.20	201	200	100.50
XDCAM	n.a.	n.a.	0.90	1.00	n.a.	106	101.00
CEJAO	n.a.	n.a.	0.70	0.80	n.a.	25	101.50
XDCAQ	n.a.	n.a.	0.55	0.60	n.a.	403	102.00
CEJAS	0.40	-0.50	0.40	0.50	n.a.	n.a.	102.50
XDCAU	n.a.	n.a.	0.30	0.40	n.a.	106	103.00
CEJAW	n.a.	n.a.	0.20	0.30	n.a.	222	103.50
XDCAB	n.a.	n.a.	0.15	0.25	n.a.	1,012	104.00
CEJAD	n.a.	n.a.	0.10	0.20	n.a.	200	104.50
XDCAF	n.a.	n.a.	0.05	0.15	n.a.	192	105.00
CEJAH	0.05	-0.10	0.05	0.15	n.a.	n.a.	105.50
XDCAJ	n.a.	n.a.	0.05	0.10	n.a.	100	106.00
CEJAL	n.a.	n.a.	0.05	0.10	n.a.	20	106.50
XDCAN	n.a.	n.a.	0.05	0.10	n.a.	263	107.00
CEJAP	n.a.	n.a.	n.a.	0.05	n.a.	150	107.50
XDCAR	n.a.	n.a.	n.a.	0.05	n.a.	820	108.00
CEJAT	n.a.	n.a.	n.a.	0.05	n.a.	830	108.50
XDCAV	n.a.	n.a.	n.a.	0.05	n.a.	42	109.00
CEJAA	n.a.	n.a.	n.a.	0.05	n.a.	200	109.50
XDCAC	n.a.	n.a.	n.a.	0.05	n.a.	622	110.00
CEJME	n.a.	n.a.	9.70	10.00	n.a.	20	110.50
XDCMG	n.a.	n.a.	10.20	10.50	n.a.	200	111.00
CEJMX	n.a.	n.a.	10.70	11.00	n.a.	n.a.	111.50

□ Indicates in-the-money   Scroll down for additional strike prices and quotes

PUTS

Symbol	Last Trade	Change	Bid	Ask	Volume	Interest	Strike Price
CEJMJ	n.a.	n.a.	n.a.	0.10	n.a.	n.a.	94.50
XDCML	n.a.	n.a.	n.a.	0.10	n.a.	60	95.00
CEJMN	n.a.	n.a.	n.a.	0.10	n.a.	10	95.50
XDCMP	0.05	0.00	0.05	0.15	n.a.	20	96.00
CEJMR	n.a.	n.a.	0.05	0.15	n.a.	50	96.50
XDCMT	0.10	0.05	0.10	0.15	n.a.	n.a.	97.00
CEJMV	0.15	0.10	0.15	0.25	n.a.	n.a.	97.50
XDCMA	n.a.	n.a.	0.20	0.30	n.a.	2	98.00
CEJMC	n.a.	n.a.	0.30	0.40	n.a.	200	98.50
XDCME	n.a.	n.a.	0.40	0.50	n.a.	198	99.00
CEJMG	0.55	0.00	0.55	0.65	200	n.a.	99.50
XDCMI	0.70	-1.25	0.75	0.85	200	614	100.00
CEJMK	n.a.	n.a.	0.95	1.05	n.a.	211	100.50
XDCMM	n.a.	n.a.	1.20	1.30	n.a.	399	101.00
CEJMO	n.a.	n.a.	1.50	1.60	n.a.	200	101.50
XDCMQ	1.30	-1.60	1.85	1.95	50	178	102.00
CEJMS	n.a.	n.a.	2.20	2.30	n.a.	200	102.50
XDCMU	n.a.	n.a.	2.55	2.70	n.a.	3	103.00
CEJMW	3.00	1.00	3.00	3.20	n.a.	n.a.	103.50
XDCMB	n.a.	n.a.	3.40	3.60	n.a.	403	104.00
CEJMD	n.a.	n.a.	3.80	4.10	n.a.	10	104.50
XDCMF	n.a.	n.a.	4.30	4.50	n.a.	450	105.00
CEJMH	n.a.	n.a.	4.80	5.00	n.a.	50	105.50
XDCMJ	5.30	1.30	5.30	5.50	n.a.	n.a.	106.00
CEJML	n.a.	n.a.	5.70	6.00	n.a.	310	106.50
XDCMN	n.a.	n.a.	6.20	6.50	n.a.	480	107.00
CEJMP	n.a.	n.a.	6.70	7.00	n.a.	10	107.50
XDCMR	7.30	1.40	7.30	7.50	n.a.	n.a.	108.00
CEJMT	n.a.	n.a.	7.70	8.00	n.a.	10	108.50
XDCMV	n.a.	n.a.	8.20	8.50	n.a.	200	109.00
CEJMA	8.70	1.30	8.70	9.00	n.a.	n.a.	109.50
XDCMC	n.a.	n.a.	9.20	9.50	n.a.	10	110.00
XDCAG	0.05	-0.40	n.a.	0.05	5	1,492	111.00
CEJAX	n.a.	n.a.	n.a.	0.05	n.a.	n.a.	111.50

□ Indicates in-the-money   Scroll down for additional strike prices and quotes

WORK THE WEB

We have examined the one-year price information of Inco company warrants by going to the finance.yahoo.com website and entering N-WT.TO as the symbol. N stands for Inco Company, WT stands for the warrant and TO indicates that the instrument is traded on the Toronto Stock Exchange.

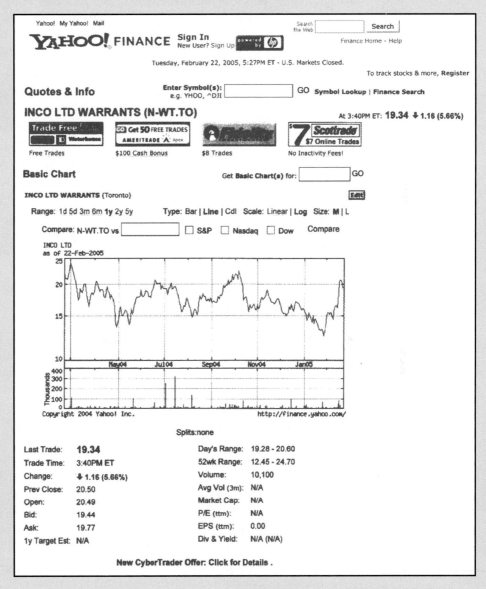

Source: Reproduced with permission of Yahoo! Inc. © 2004 by Yahoo! Inc. YAHOO! and the YAHOO! logo are trademarks of Yahoo! Inc.

When the order arrives at the ME, it is directed to one of several dealers for NT options. The ME dealer accepts the order by taking the position of a writer for the 10 put contracts. The order is then transferred to the CDCC. Once the CDCC verifies that there are matching orders from a buyer and a writer, for a small fee it takes over the dealer's position as the writer for your 10 January 25 puts.

By assuming the writer's obligation, the clearing corporation guarantees that the terms of your put contracts will be fulfilled if you later decide to exercise the options. From the ME dealer's perspective, the clearing corporation becomes the buyer of the 10 January 25 puts. As such, the ME dealer becomes obligated to the clearing corporation as the writer of 10 January 25 put options.

In this way, all dealer default risk is transferred to the clearing corporation. Ultimately, the CDCC ensures the performance of all options traded on all registered options exchanges in Canada.

14.13 Summary and Conclusions

In 1973, organized stock options trading began when the Chicago Board Options Exchange (CBOE) was established. Since then, options trading has grown enormously. In this chapter, we examined a number of concepts and issues surrounding stock options. We saw that:

1. Options on common stock are derivative securities because the value of a stock option is derived from the value of the underlying common stock. There are two basic types of options: call options and put options. Call options are options to buy, and put options are options to sell.

2. Options are contracts. Standardized stock options represent a contract size of 100 shares of common stock per option contract. We saw how standardized option prices are quoted in the financial press.

3. Various strategies exist with options, ranging from buying and selling individual puts and calls to combination strategies involving calls, puts, and the underlying stock. There are many common strategies, including protective puts and covered calls.

4. Option prices have boundaries enforced by arbitrage. A call option cannot sell for more than the underlying asset, and a put option cannot sell for more than the strike price on the option.

5. An option's intrinsic value is a lower bound for an option's price. The intrinsic value of an option is the payoff that an option holder receives if the underlying stock price does not change from its current value.

6. An employee stock option (ESO) is an option granted by a firm to an employee. Such options provide an incentive for employees to work to increase the firm's stock price.

7. Put-call parity states that the difference between a call price and a put price for European-style options with the same strike price and expiration date is equal to the difference between the dividend-adjusted stock price and the discounted strike price.

8. A stock index option is an option on a stock market index such as the S&P 500. All stock index options use a cash settlement procedure when they are

exercised. With a cash settlement procedure, when a stock index option is exercised, the option writer pays a cash amount to the option buyer.

9. The Canadian Derivative Clearing Corporation (CDCC) is the clearing agency for all options exchanges in Canada. It guarantees that the terms of an option contract are fulfilled if the option is exercised.

REAL WORLD

This chapter added to your understanding of put and call options by covering the rights, obligations, and potential gains and losses involved in trading options. How should you put this information to work? You need to buy and sell options to experience the gains and losses that options can provide. So, with a simulated brokerage account (such as *Stock-Trak*), you should first execute each of the basic option transactions: buy a call, sell a call, buy a put, and sell a put.

For help getting started, you can find an enormous amount of information about options on the Internet. Useful places to start are the options exchanges: Montreal Exchange (www.m-x.ca), Chicago Board Options Exchange (www.cboe.com), American Stock Exchange (www.amex.com), and Philadelphia Stock Exchange (www.phlx.com). An excellent website devoted to options education is the Canadian Derivative Clearing Corporation (www.cdcc.ca). You might also look at the options section of Trading Markets (www.tradingmarkets.com), or Investor Links (www.investorlinks.com).

For information on option trading strategies, try entering the strategy name into an Internet search engine. For example, enter the search phrases "covered calls" or "protective puts" for online information about those strategies. For more general information, try the search phrase "options trading strategies" to find sites like Commodity World (www.commodityworld.com). For a sales pitch on writing covered calls, check out Write Call (www.writecall.com) or Global Investor (www.globeinvestor.com).

If you're having trouble understanding options ticker symbols, don't feel alone as most everyone has trouble at first. For help on the net, try the search phrases "option symbols" or "options symbols." Of course, the options exchanges listed above also provide complete information on the option ticker symbols they use.

Key Terms

derivative security 449
call option 449
put option 449
strike price 449
American option 450
European option 450
option chain 452
in-the-money option 455
out-of-the money option 455
option writing 457
call writer 457

put writer 457
protective put 461
covered call 461
straddle 462
intrinsic value 464
employee stock option (ESO) 466
put-call parity 468
stock index option 470
foreign currency options 473
Canadian Derivatives Clearing
　　Corporation (CDCC) 473

Chapter Review Problems and Self-Test

1. **Call Option Payoffs** You purchase 25 call contracts on Blue Ox stock. The strike price is $22, and the premium is $1. If the stock is selling for $24 per share at expiration, what are your call options worth? What is your net profit? What if the stock were selling for $23? $22?

2. **Stock versus Options** Stock in Bunyan Brewery is currently priced at $20 per share. A call option with a $20 strike and 60 days to maturity is quoted at $2. Compare the percentage gains and losses from a $2,000 investment in the stock versus the option in 60 days for stock prices of $26, $20, and $18.

3. **Put-Call Parity** A call option sells for $8. It has a strike price of $80 and six months until expiration. If the underlying stock sells for $60 per share, what is the price of a put option with an $80 strike price and six months until expiration? The risk-free interest rate is 6 percent.

Answers to Self-Test Problems

1. Blue Ox stock is selling for $24. You own 25 contracts, each of which gives you the right to buy 100 shares at $22. Your options are thus worth $2 per share on 2,500 shares, or $5,000. The option premium was $1, so you paid $100 per contract, or $2,500 total. Your net profit is $2,500. If the stock is selling for $23, your options are worth $2,500, so your net profit is exactly zero. If the stock is selling for $22, your options are worthless, and you lose the entire $2,500 you paid.

2. Bunyan stock costs $20 per share, so if you invest $2,000, you'll get 100 shares. The option premium is $2, so an option contract costs $200. If you invest $2,000, you'll get $2,000 / $200 = 10 contracts. If the stock is selling for $26 in 60 days, your profit on the stock is $6 per share, or $600 total. The percentage gain is $600 / $2,000 = 30%.

    In this case, your options are worth $6 per share, or $600 per contract. You have 10 contracts, so your options are worth $6,000 in all. Since you paid $2,000 for the 10 contracts, your profit is $4,000. Your percentage gain is a whopping $4,000 / $2,000 = 200%.

    If the stock is selling for $20, your profit is $0 on the stock, so your percentage return is 0 percent. Your options are worthless (why?), so the percentage loss is −100 percent. If the stock is selling for $18, verify that your percentage loss on the stock is −10 percent and your loss on the options is again −100 percent.

3. Using the put-call parity formula, we have

$$C - P = S - Ke^{-rT}$$

Rearranging to solve for P, the put price, and plugging in the other numbers gets us

$$P = C - S + Ke^{-rT}$$
$$= \$8 - \$60 + \$80e^{-.06(.5)}$$
$$= \$25.64$$

Test Your Investment Quotient

1. **Option Contracts** Which of the following is not specified by a stock option contract?
   a. The underlying stock's price.
   b. The size of the contract.
   c. Exercise style—European or American.
   d. Contract settlement procedure—cash or delivery.

2. **Option Contracts** A July 50 call option contract for SOS stock is identified by which ticker symbol? (*Hint*: See the *Stock-Trak* section at the end of this chapter.)

   a. SOS-JG
   b. SOS-JS
   c. SOS-GJ
   d. SOS-SJ

3. **Option Contracts** An April 40 put option contract for SOS stock is identified by which ticker symbol? (*Hint*: See the *Stock-Trak* section at the end of this chapter.)

   a. SOS-HD
   b. SOS-HP
   c. SOS-DH
   d. SOS-PH

4. **Option Payoffs** All of the following statements about the value of a call option at expiration are true, except the:

   a. Short position in the same call option can result in a loss if the stock price exceeds the exercise price.
   b. Value of the long position equals zero or the stock price minus the exercise price, whichever is higher.
   c. Value of the long position equals zero or the exercise price minus the stock price, whichever is higher.
   d. Short position in the same call option has a zero value for all stock prices equal to or less than the exercise price.

5. **Option Strategies** Which of the following stock option strategies has the greatest potential for large losses?

   a. Writing a covered call
   b. Writing a covered put
   c. Writing a naked call
   d. Writing a naked put

6. **Option Strategies** Which statement does not describe an at-the-money protective put position (comprised of owning the stock and the put)?

   a. Protects against loss at any stock price below the strike price of the put.
   b. Has limited profit potential when the stock price rises.
   c. Returns any increase in the stock's value, dollar for dollar, less the cost of the put.
   d. Provides a pattern of returns similar to a stop-loss order at the current stock price.

7. **Put-Call Parity** Which of the following is not included in the put-call parity condition?

   a. Price of the underlying stock.
   b. Strike price of the underlying call and put option contracts.
   c. Expiration dates of the underlying call and put option contracts.
   d. Volatility of the underlying stock.

8. **Put-Call Parity** According to the put-call parity condition, a risk-free portfolio can be created by buying 100 shares of stock and

   a. Writing one call option contract and buying one put option contract.
   b. Buying one call option contract and writing one put option contract.
   c. Buying one call option contract and buying one put option contract.
   d. Writing one call option contract and writing one put option contract.

9. **Option Strategies** Investor A uses options for defensive and income reasons. Investor B uses options as an aggressive investment strategy. What is an appropriate use of options for Investors A and B, respectively?

   a. Writing covered calls / buying puts on stock not owned.
   b. Buying out-of-the-money calls / buying puts on stock owned.

c. Writing naked calls / buying in-the-money calls.

d. Selling puts on stock owned / buying puts on stock not owned.

10. **Option Strategies** Which one of the following option combinations best describes a straddle? Buy both a call and a put on the same stock with

a. Different exercise prices and the same expiration date.

b. The same exercise price and different expiration dates.

c. The same exercise price and the same expiration date.

d. Different exercise prices and different expiration dates.

11. **Option Strategies** Which of the following strategies is the riskiest options transaction if the underlying stock price is expected to increase substantially?

a. Writing a naked call option.

b. Writing a naked put option.

c. Buying a call option.

d. Buying a put option.

12. **Option Gains and Losses** You create a "strap" by buying two calls and one put on ABC stock, all with a strike price of $45. The calls cost $5 each, and the put costs $4. If you close your position when ABC stock is priced at $55, what is your per-share gain or loss?

a. $4 loss

b. $6 gain

c. $10 gain

d. $20 gain

13. **Option Gains and Losses** A put on XYZ stock with a strike price of $40 is priced at $2.00 per share, while a call with a strike price of $40 is priced at $3.50. What is the maximum per-share loss to the writer of the uncovered put and the maximum per-share gain to the writer of the uncovered call?

	Maximum Loss to Put Writer	Maximum Gain to Call Writer
a.	$38.00	$3.50
b.	$38.00	$36.50
c.	$40.00	$3.50
d.	$40.00	$40.00

14. **Option Pricing** If a stock is selling for $25, the exercise price of a put option on that stock is $20, and the time to expiration of the option is 90 days, what are the minimum and maximum prices for the put today?

a. $0 and $5

b. $0 and $20

c. $5 and $20

d. $5 and $25

15. **Option Strategies** Which of the following strategies is most suitable for an investor wishing to eliminate "downside" risk from a long position in stock?

a. A long straddle position.

b. A short straddle position.

c. Writing a covered call option.

d. Buying a protective put option.

16. **Covered Calls** The current price of an asset is $75. A three-month, at-the-money American call option on the asset has a current value of $5. At what value of the asset will a covered call writer break even at expiration?

    a. $70
    b. $75
    c. $80
    d. $85

17. **Option Strategies** The current price of an asset is $100. An out-of-the-money American put option with an exercise price of $90 is purchased along with the asset. If the break-even point for this hedge is at an asset price of $114 at expiration, then the value of the American put at the time of purchase must have been

    a. $0
    b. $4
    c. $10
    d. $14

18. **Option Strategies** The following diagram shows the value of a put option at expiration:

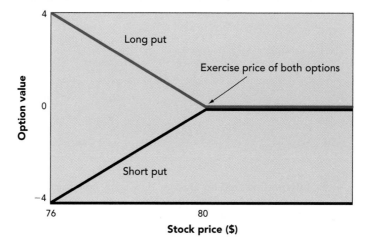

Ignoring transaction costs, which of the following statements about the value of the put option at expiration is true?

    a. The value of the short position in the put is $4 if the stock price is $76.
    b. The value of the long position in the put is −$4 if the stock price is $76.
    c. The long put has value when the stock price is below the $80 exercise price.
    d. The value of the short position in the put is zero for stock prices equalling or exceeding $76.

Concept Questions

1. **Basic Properties of Options** What is a call option? A put option? Under what circumstances might you want to buy each? Which one has greater potential profit? Why?

2. **Calls versus Puts** Complete the following sentence for each of these investors:

    a. A buyer of call options
    b. A buyer of put options
    c. A seller (writer) of call options
    d. A seller (writer) of put options

The (buyer/seller) of a (put/call) option (pays/receives) money for the (right/obligation) to (buy/sell) a specified asset at a fixed price for a fixed length of time.

3. **Option Break-even** In general, if you buy a call option, what stock price is needed for you to break even on the transaction ignoring taxes and commissions? If you buy a put option?

4. **Protective Puts** Buying a put option on a stock you own is sometimes called "stock price insurance." Why?

5. **Defining Intrinsic Value** What is the intrinsic value of a call option? How do we interpret this value?

6. **Defining Intrinsic Value** What is the intrinsic value of a put option? How do we interpret this value?

7. **Arbitrage and Options** You notice that shares of stock in the Patel Corporation are going for $50 per share. Call options with an exercise price of $35 per share are selling for $10. What's wrong here? Describe how you could take advantage of this mispricing if the option expires today.

Use the following options quotations to answer questions 8 through 11:

Option & Close	Strike Price	Expiration	Calls Vol.	Calls Last	Puts Vol.	Puts Last
Milson						
59	55	Mar	98	3.5	66	1.06
59	55	Apr	54	6.25	40	1.94
59	55	Jul	25	8.63	17	3.63
59	55	Oct	10	10.25	5	3.25

8. **Interpreting Options Quotes** How many options contracts on Milson stock were traded with an expiration date of July? How many underlying shares of stock do these options contracts represent?

9. **Interpreting Options Quotes** Are the call options in the money? What is the intrinsic value of a Milson Corp. call option?

10. **Interpreting Options Quotes** Are the put options in the money? What is the intrinsic value of a Milson Corp. put option?

11. **Interpreting Options Quotes** Two of the options are clearly mispriced. Which ones? At a minimum, what should the mispriced options sell for? Explain how you could profit from the mispricing in each case.

12. **Option Strategies** Recall the options strategies of a protective put and covered call discussed in the text. Suppose you have sold short some shares of stock. Discuss analogous option strategies and how you would implement them. (*Hint*: They're called protective calls and covered puts.)

13. **Put-Call Parity** A put and a call option have the same maturity and strike price. If both are at the money, which is worth more? Prove your answer and then provide an intuitive explanation.

14. **Put-Call Parity** A put and a call option have the same maturity and strike price. If they also have the same price, which one is in the money?

15. **Put-Call Parity** One thing the put-call parity equation tells us is that given any three of a stock, a call, a put, and a T-bill, the fourth can be synthesized or replicated using the other three. For example, how can we replicate a share of stock using a put, a call, and a T-bill?

Questions and Problems

Core Questions

1. **Call Option Payoffs** Suppose you purchase eight call contracts on Macron Technology stock. The strike price is $80, and the premium is $3. If, at expiration, the stock is selling for $88 per share, what are your call options worth? What is your net profit?

2. **Put Option Payoffs** Suppose you purchase five put contracts on Testaburger Co. The strike price is $45, and the premium is $3. If, at expiration, the stock is selling for $38 per share, what are your put options worth? What is your net profit?

3. **Stock versus Options** Stock in Cheezy-Poofs Manufacturing is currently priced at $80 per share. A call option with an $80 strike and 90 days to maturity is quoted at $3. Compare the percentage gains and losses from a $12,000 investment in the stock versus the option in 90 days for stock prices of $70, $80, and $90.

Use the following options quotations to answer questions 4 through 7:

Option & N.Y. Close	Strike Price	Expiration	Calls Vol.	Calls Last	Puts Vol.	Puts Last
Hendreeks						
75	70	July	72	5.80	50	.65
75	70	Aug	41	6.70	29	1.20
75	70	Oct	16	7.90	10	2.70
75	70	Jan	8	9.50	2	3.90

4. **Calculating Option Payoffs** Suppose you buy 50 August 70 call option contracts. How much will you pay, ignoring commissions?

5. **Calculating Option Payoffs** In Problem 4, suppose that Hendreeks stock is selling for $84 per share on the expiration date. How much is your options investment worth? What if the terminal stock price is $75?

6. **Calculating Option Payoffs** Suppose you buy 30 January 70 put option contracts. What is your maximum gain? On the expiration date, Hendreeks is selling for $63 per share. How much is your options investment worth? What is your net gain?

7. **Calculating Option Payoffs** In Problem 6, suppose you write 30 of the January 70 put contracts. What is your net gain or loss if Hendreeks is selling for $55 at expiration? For $100? What is the break-even price, that is, the terminal stock price that results in a zero profit?

8. **Put-Call Parity** A call option is currently selling for $6. It has a strike price of $65 and six months to maturity. What is the price of a put option with a $65 strike price and six months to maturity? The current stock price is $61, and the risk-free interest rate is 5 percent.

9. **Put-Call Parity** A call option currently sells for $8. It has a strike price of $80 and six months to maturity. A put with the same strike and expiration date sells for $4. If the risk-free interest rate is 4 percent, what is the current stock price?

10. **Put-Call Parity** A put option with a strike price of $75 sells for $8.90. The option expires in two months, and the current stock price is $78. If the risk-free interest rate is 5 percent, what is the price of a call option with the same strike price?

Intermediate Questions

11. **Put-Call Parity** A call option is currently selling for $9.40. It has a strike price of $55 and five months to maturity. The current stock price is $58, and the risk-free rate is 5 percent. The stock has a dividend yield of 2 percent. What is the price of a put option with the same exercise price?

12. **Put-Call Parity** A call option is currently selling for $3.80. It has a strike price of $70 and three months to maturity. A put option with the same strike price sells for $7.10. The risk-free rate is 6 percent, and the stock has a dividend yield of 3 percent. What is the current stock price?

13. **Put-Call Parity** A put option is currently selling for $6.20. It has a strike price of $80 and seven months to maturity. The current stock price is $83. The risk-free rate is 5 percent, and the stock has a dividend yield of 2 percent. What is the price of a call option with the same strike price?

14. **Call Option Writing** Suppose you write 20 call option contracts with a $50 strike. The premium is $3.50. Evaluate your potential gains and losses at option expiration for stock prices of $40, $50, and $60.

15. **Put Option Writing** Suppose you write 15 put option contracts with a $35 strike. The premium is $2.40. Evaluate your potential gains and losses at option expiration for stock prices of $25, $35, and $45.

16. **Index Options** Suppose you buy one SPX call option contract with a strike of 1300. At maturity, the S&P 500 index is at 1340. What is your net gain or loss if the premium you paid was $21?

17. **Option Strategies** You write a put with a strike price of $70 on stock that you have shorted at $70 (this is a "covered put"). What are the expiration date profits to this position for stock prices of $60, $65, $70, $75, and $80 if the put premium is $3.50?

18. **Option Strategies** You buy a call with a strike price of $70 on stock that you have shorted at $70 (this is a "protective call"). What are the expiration date profits to this position for stock prices of $60, $65, $70, $75, and $80 if the call premium is $5.20?

19. **Option Strategies** You simultaneously write a covered put and buy a protective call, both with strike prices of $70, on stock that you have shorted at $70. What are the expiration date payoffs to this position for stock prices of $60, $65, $70, $75, and $80?

20. **Option Strategies** You simultaneously write a put and buy a call, both with strike prices of $70, naked, i.e., without any position in the underlying stock. What are the expiration date payoffs to this position for stock prices of $60, $65, $70, $75, and $80?

21. **Option Strategies** You buy a straddle, which means you purchase a put and a call with the same strike price. The put price is $2.10 and the call price is $4.60. Assume the strike price is $75. What are the expiration date profits to this position for stock prices of $65, $70, $75, $80, and $85? What are the expiration date profits for these same stock prices? What are the break-even stock prices?

22. **Index Option Positions** Suppose you buy one SPX call option with a strike of 1300 and write one SPX call option with a strike of 1350. What are the payoffs at maturity to this position for S&P 500 index levels of 1250, 1300, 1350, 1400, and 1450?

23. **Index Option Positions** Suppose you buy one SPX put option with a strike of 1300 and write one SPX put option with a strike of 1350. What are the payoffs at maturity to this position for S&P 500 index levels of 1200, 1250, 1300, 1350, and 1400?

24. **Index Option Positions** Suppose you buy one SPX call option with a strike of 1300 and write one SPX put option with a strike of 1300. What are the payoffs at maturity to this position for S&P 500 index levels of 1200, 1250, 1300, 1350, and 1400?

25. **Index Option Positions** Suppose you buy one each SPX call options with strikes of 1200 and 1400 and write two SPX call options with a strike of 1300. What are the payoffs at maturity to this position for S&P 500 index levels of 1100, 1150, 1200, 1250, 1300, 1350, and 1400?

What's on the Web?

1. **Option Prices** You want to find option prices for Biovail (BVF). Go to finance.yahoo.com, get a stock quote, and follow the "Options" link. What is the option premium and strike price for the highest and lowest strike price options that are nearest to expiring? What are the option premium and strike price for the highest and lowest strike price options expiring next month?

2. **Option Symbol Construction** What is the option symbol for a call option on Cisco Systems (CSCO) with a strike price of $25 that expires in July? Go to www.cboe.com, follow the "Trading Tools" link, then the "Symbol Lookup" link. Find the basic ticker symbol for Cisco Systems options. Next, follow the "Strike Price Code" link. Find the codes for the expiration month and strike price and construct the ticker symbol. Now construct the ticker symbol for a put option with the same strike price and expiration.

3. **Option Expiration** Go to www.m-x.ca, highlight the "Quick Links" tab, then follow the "Trading Calendar" link. Which options expire next month?

4. **LEAPS** Go to www.cboe.com, highlight the "Products" tab, then follow the "LEAPS" link. What are LEAPS? What are the two types of LEAPS? What are the benefits of equity LEAPS? What are the benefits of index LEAPS?

5. **FLEX Options** Go to www.cboe.com, highlight the "Institutional" tab, then follow the "FLEX Options" link. What is a FLEX option? When do FLEX options expire? What is the minimum size of a FLEX option?

6. **Option Investment** Go to Royal Bank's website (www.actiondirect.com), then follow the "Education Centre" link. Find the commission and fees for the option investment.

CHAPTER 15

Option Valuation

"I have compared the results of observation with those of theory…to show that the market, unwittingly, obeys a law which governs it, the law of probability."

—Louis Bachelier

Just what is an option worth? Actually, this is one of the more difficult questions in finance. Option valuation is an esoteric area of finance since it often involves complex mathematics. Fortunately, just like most options professionals, you can learn quite a bit about option valuation with only modest mathematical tools. But no matter how far you might wish to delve into this topic, you must begin with the Black-Scholes-Merton option pricing model. This model is the core from which all other option pricing models trace their ancestry. ■

The previous chapter introduced the basics of stock options. From an economic standpoint, perhaps the most important subject was the expiration date payoffs of stock options. Bear in mind that when investors buy options today, they are buying risky future payoffs. Likewise, when investors write options today, they become obligated to make risky future payments. In a competitive financial marketplace, option prices observed each day are collectively agreed on by buyers and writers assessing the likelihood of all possible future payoffs and payments and setting option prices accordingly.

In this chapter, we discuss stock option prices. This discussion begins with the Black-Scholes-Merton option pricing model, which is widely regarded by finance professionals as the premier model of stock option valuation.

15.1 The Black-Scholes-Merton Option Pricing Model

Option pricing theory made a great leap forward in the early 1970s with the development of the Black-Scholes option pricing model by Fischer Black and Myron Scholes. Recognizing the important theoretical contributions by Robert Merton, many finance professionals knowledgeable in the history of option pricing theory refer to an extended version of the model as the Black-Scholes-Merton option pricing model. In 1997, Myron Scholes and Robert Merton were awarded the Nobel Prize in Economics for their pioneering work in option pricing theory. Unfortunately, Fischer Black had died two years earlier and so did not share the Nobel Prize, which cannot be awarded posthumously. The nearby *Investment Updates* box presents *The Wall Street Journal* story of the Nobel Prize award.

The Black-Scholes-Merton option pricing model states the value of a stock option as a function of these six input factors:

1. The current price of the underlying stock.
2. The dividend yield of the underlying stock.
3. The strike price specified in the option contract.
4. The risk-free interest rate over the life of the option contract.
5. The time remaining until the option contract expires.
6. The price volatility of the underlying stock.

Black-Scholes and Merton assumed that stock prices are lognormally distributed and tried to find the formula that expresses value of a call option. Value of a call option increases with increasing stock prices, and with increasing volatility. The longer the time to maturity, the higher will be the value of a call option. On the other hand increasing strike prices will lower values of call options. For put options, increasing volatility and increasing time to maturity have a positive effect in increasing the values. Increasing stock prices decrease the values of put options while increasing strike prices increase them.

The six inputs are algebraically defined as follows:

S = Current stock price

y = Stock dividend yield

K = Option strike price

r = Risk-free interest rate

T = Time remaining until option expiration

σ = Sigma, representing stock price volatility

In terms of these six inputs, the Black-Scholes-Merton formula for the price of a call option on a single share of common stock is

$$C = Se^{-yT}N(d_1) - Ke^{-rT}N(d_2) \qquad (15.1)$$

The Black-Scholes-Merton formula for the price of a put option on a share of common stock is

$$P = Ke^{-rT}N(-d_2) - Se^{-yT}N(-d_1) \qquad (15.2)$$

 The CBOE has a free options calculator that will do most of the calculations in this chapter at www.cboe.com

Two U.S. Economists Win the Nobel Prize for Work on Options

Two economists with close ties to Wall Street, Robert C. Merton and Myron S. Scholes, won the Nobel Memorial Prize in Economic Science for path-breaking work that helped spawn the $148 billion stock-options industry.

The Nobel economics prize is given to innovators whose work breaks new ground and sires whole bodies of economic research. But this year, the prize committee chose laureates not only with distinguished academic records, but also with especially pragmatic bents, to split the $1 million award. Prof. Merton, 53 years old, teaches at Harvard Business School, while Prof. Scholes, 56, has emeritus status from the Stanford Graduate School of Business.

In the early 1970s, Prof. Scholes, with the late mathematician Fischer Black, invented an insightful method of pricing options and warrants at a time when most investors and traders still relied on educated guesses to determine the value of various stock-market products. Prof. Merton later demonstrated the broad applicability of the Black-Scholes options-pricing formula, paving the way for the incredible growth of markets in options and other derivatives.

"Thousands of traders and investors now use this formula every day to value stock options in markets throughout the world," the Royal Swedish Academy of Sciences said yesterday.

The Black-Scholes Formula

In their paper, Black and Scholes obtained exact formulas for pricing options.

$$C = SN(d) - Ke^{-rT}N(d - \sigma\sqrt{T})$$

According to the formula, the value of the call option C is given by the difference between the expected share value (the first term on the right-hand-side of the equation) and the expected cost (the second term) if the option is exercised at maturity.

The Black-Scholes option-pricing model "is really the classic example of an academic innovation that has been adopted widely in practice," said Gregg Jarrell, professor of economics at the University of Rochester's William E. Simon Business School and former chief economist at the Securities and Exchange Commission. "It is one of the most elegant and precise models that any of us has ever seen."

Options allow investors to trade the future rights to buy or sell assets—such as stocks—at a set price. An investor who holds 100 shares of International Business Machines Corp. stock today, for example, might buy an option giving them the right to sell 100 IBM shares at a fixed price in three months' time. The investor is therefore partially protected against a fall in the stock price during the life of the option.

Until the Black-Scholes model gained acceptance, the great minds of economics and finance were unable to develop a method of putting an accurate price on those options. The problem was how to evaluate the risk associated with options, when the underlying stock price changes from moment to moment. The risk of an option depends on the price of the stock underlying the option.

That breakthrough allowed the economists to create a pricing formula that included the stock price, the agreed sale or "strike" price of the option, the stock's volatility, the risk-free interest rate offered with a secure bond, and the time until the option's expiration. They published their work in 1973, the same year the Chicago Board Options Exchange turned the scattered world of options trading into a more formal market.

Prof. Merton himself forged a formal theoretical framework for the Black-Scholes formula, and extended the analysis to other derivative products—financial instruments in which the value of the security depends on the value of another indicator, such as mortgage, interest or exchange rates. More broadly, his work allowed economists and financial professionals to view a wide variety of commonly traded financial instruments—such as corporate bonds—as derivatives and to price them using the ideas first expounded by Dr. Black and Prof. Scholes. "For the most part, the thing was conceived entirely in theory," said Prof. Merton.

The practical implications soon became apparent, however, as market participants flocked to the Black-Scholes-Merton approach to determine how much options are worth. "It's just a terrific yardstick for investors to help make that judgment," said Bill Kehoe, vice president and manager of the options marketing group at Merrill Lynch & Co., and an options trader since 1961.

Options markets have grown astronomically in the quarter century since the formula reached trading floors around the country. The value of U.S. exchange-traded options in 1995 was $118 billion. Last year, it surged to $148 billion, and in the first nine months of 1997, the figure hit $155 billion. More than 100,000 options series are now available. "Even now, we calculate the value of options world-wide using the Black-Scholes formula," said Yair Orgler, chairman of the Tel Aviv Stock Exchange.

In these call and put option formulas, the numbers d_1 and d_2 are calculated as

$$d_1 = \frac{\ln(S/K) + (r - y + \sigma^2/2)T}{\sigma\sqrt{T}} \quad \text{and } d_2 = d_1 - \sigma\sqrt{T}$$

In the formulas above, call and put option prices are algebraically represented by C and P, respectively. In addition to the six input factors S, K, r, y, T, and σ, the following three mathematical functions are used in the call and put option pricing formulas:

1. e^x, or $exp(x)$, denoting the natural exponent of the value of x.
2. $ln(x)$, denoting the natural logarithm of the value of x.
3. $N(x)$, denoting the standard normal probability of the value of x.

COMPUTING BLACK-SCHOLES-MERTON OPTION PRICES

EXAMPLE 15.1

Calculate call and put option prices, given the following inputs to the Black-Scholes-Merton option pricing formula.

Stock price	$S = \$50$
Dividend yield	$y = 2\%$
Strike price	$K = \$45$
Time to maturity	$T = 3$ months
Stock volatility	$\sigma = 25\%$
Interest rate	$r = 6\%$

Referring to equations 15.1 and 15.2, first we compute values for d_1 and d_2:

$$d_1 = \frac{\ln(50/45) + (.06 - .02 + .25^2/2).25}{.25\sqrt{.25}}$$

$$= \frac{.10536 + .07125 \times .25}{.125}$$

$$= .98538$$

$$d_2 = d_1 - .25\sqrt{.25}$$

$$= .86038$$

The following standard normal probabilities are provided (see next example):

$$N(d_1) = N(.98538) = .83778 \qquad N(-d_1) = 1 - N(d_1) = .16222$$
$$N(d_2) = N(.86038) = .80521 \qquad N(-d_2) = 1 - N(d_2) = .19479$$

We can now calculate the price of the call option as

$$C = \$50 \times e^{-.02 \times .25} \times .83778 - \$45 \times e^{-.06 \times .25} \times .80521$$

$$= \$50 \times .99501 \times .83778 - \$45 \times .98511 \times .80521$$

$$= \$5.985$$

and the price of the put option as

$$P = \$45 \times e^{-.06 \times .25} \times .19479 - \$50 \times e^{-.02 \times .25} \times .16222$$

$$= \$45 \times .98511 \times .19479 - \$50 \times .99501 \times .16222$$

$$= \$.565$$

USING A WEB-BASED OPTION CALCULATOR

EXAMPLE 15.2

The purpose of Example 15.1 was to show you that the Black-Scholes-Merton formula is not hard to use—even if at first it looks imposing. If you are in a hurry to price an option or if you simply want to verify the price of an option that you have calculated, a number of option calculators are available on the Web. Let's check our previous answers by using the option calculator we found at www.DerivativesModels.com:

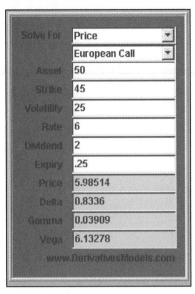
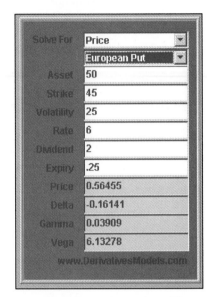

As you can see, our answers in Example 15.1 check out (except for small rounding differences). You might be wondering about the word "expiry." **Expiry** is a shortened way of saying "time to option contract maturity" or "time to maturity" for any contract. You might also be wondering what delta, gamma, and vega represent. We discuss these terms later in the chapter.

CHECK THIS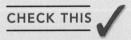

15.1a   Consider the following inputs to the Black-Scholes-Merton option pricing model.

$$S = \$50 \qquad y = 0\%$$
$$K = \$50 \qquad r = 5\%$$
$$T = 60 \text{ days} \qquad \sigma = 25\%$$

These input values yield a call option price of $2.22 and a put option price of $1.81.

Verify these prices from your own calculations.

15.2 Valuing Employee Stock Options

An interesting application of the Black-Scholes-Merton option pricing formula is the valuation of employee stock options, which we discussed in our previous chapter.

Companies issuing stock options to employees must report estimates of their value in financial statements. The Black-Scholes-Merton formula is widely used for this purpose. For example, in December 2002, the Coca-Cola Company granted employee stock options to several executives representing over a half million shares of Coke stock. The options had a stated term of 15 years, but, to allow for the fact that employee stock options are often exercised before maturity, Coca-Cola used two time horizon assumptions to value the options: the longest possible term of 15 years and an expected term of 6 years. The company then adjusted their interest rate, dividend yield, and volatility assumptions to each of these terms.

The different input values assumed and the resulting Black-Scholes option values are summarized in Table 15.1. Notice that Coca-Cola assumed a higher volatility and dividend yield, but a lower riskless interest rate for the six-year time horizon assumption. This seems reasonable given that stock market volatility was high and interest rates were low in 2002 compared to recent historical experience. A *Wall Street Journal* article discussing the valuation of these Coke options is contained in the nearby *Investment Updates* box.

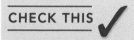

CHECK THIS

15.2a Go to finance.yahoo.com, check the current price of Coca-Cola stock under the ticker symbol KO, and compare it to the stock price on the employee stock option grant data given in Table 15.2.

15.2b Recalculate the Black-Scholes option value for the Coca-Cola employee stock options based on the current stock price for Coke shares.

TABLE 15.1	Coca-Cola Employee Stock Options	
Inputs	**Input Value Assumptions**	
Stock price	$44.55	$44.55
Exercise price	$44.655	$44.655
Time horizon	15 years	6 years
Volatility	25.53%	30.20%
Risk-free interest rate	5.65%	3.40%
Dividend yield	1.59%	1.70%
Black-Scholes-Merton option value	$19.92	$13.06

TABLE 15.2	Six Inputs Affecting Option Prices		
	Sign of Input Effect		
Inputs	**Call**	**Put**	**Common Name**
Underlying stock price (S)	+	−	Delta
Strike price of the option contract (K)	−	+	
Time remaining until option expiration (T)	+	+	Theta
Volatility of the underlying stock price (σ)	+	+	Vega
Risk-free interest rate (r)	+	−	Rho
Dividend yield of the underlying stock (y)	−	+	

Coke Plan for Option Valuing Fizzles Out after Few Months: News Dashes Hopes for Alternative to Black-Scholes Expensing Models

Coca-Cola Co.'s novel plan for valuing its employee stock-option compensation has fizzled out.

The world's biggest soft-drink company made a splash in July by announcing it would begin recognizing stock-option compensation as an expense on its financial statements. But it wasn't just Coke's decision to expense that piqued market interest. Even more noteworthy was the unique valuation method it planned to use, at Coke director Warren Buffett's urging. Instead of using Wall Street's much maligned, but widely used, Black-Scholes mathematical models, Coke said it would solicit quotations from two independent financial institutions to buy and sell Coke shares under the identical terms of the options to be expensed. Coke then would average the quotations to determine the value of the options.

So much for that plan.

Coke now concedes it won't work and that it will use Black-Scholes after all, notwithstanding the method's drawbacks. The disclosure almost certainly will disappoint investors who favour mandatory expensing of option-based compensation, but had been hoping for a feasible alternative to the subjective results often produced by Black-Scholes models.

It also signals that Black-Scholes, like it or not, may remain the norm even should the Financial Accounting Standards Board follow through with its plans to unveil a proposal this year mandating that public companies treat stock-option compensation as an expense.

Coke executives Thursday said they had no choice but to abandon the Buffet-backed plan. They said the company eventually concluded that current accounting standards wouldn't allow the new approach and instead require companies to perform their own value calculations.

In any event, the disclosure in Coke's proxy shows that dealer quotes wouldn't have yielded any different results than a Black-Scholes calculation. Coke says it determined the value of the options through Black-Scholes calculations—and only then obtained independent market quotes from two dealers "to ensure the best market-based assumptions were used." And, as it turned out, "our Black-Scholes value was not materially different from the independent quotes," Coke's proxy says. Coke declined to name the two financial institutions.

Because the dealer quotes were so similar, "you can assume they use Black-Scholes too," says Gary Fayard, Coke's chief financial officer. Asked if an alternative to Black-Scholes is needed, Mr. Fayard says, "I think it's

(continued)

15.3 Varying the Option Price Input Values

An important goal of this chapter is to provide an understanding of how option prices change as a result of varying each of the six input values. Table 15.2 summarizes the sign effects of the six inputs on call and put option prices. A plus sign indicates a positive effect, and a minus sign indicates a negative effect. Where the magnitude of the input impact has a commonly used name, this is stated in the rightmost column.

The two most important inputs determining stock option prices are the stock price and the strike price. However, the other input factors are also important determinants of option value. We next discuss each input factor separately.

Varying the Underlying Stock Price

For option trading strategies and more, see www.numa.com

Certainly, the price of the underlying stock is one of the most important determinants of the price of a stock option. As the stock price increases, the call option price increases and the put option price decreases. This is not surprising, since a call option grants the right to buy stock shares and a put option grants the right to sell stock shares at a fixed strike price. Consequently, a higher stock price at option expiration increases the payoff of a call option. Likewise, a lower stock price at option expiration increases the payoff of a put option.

something that business and the accounting profession need to work on and evaluate."

Given the lack of any meaningful difference, some accounting specialists say future efforts to seek market quotations for employee options likely will be pointless.

"All they did was go to the expense of getting quotes from two independent parties who may have used the Black-Scholes model themselves," says Jack Ciesielski, publisher of the Analyst's Accounting Observer newsletter in Baltimore. "The whole affair winds up being an exercise in circularity."

While expensing options remains voluntary, all public companies are required to disclose what the effect on their earnings would be if they did expense options. Most such disclosures rely on variants of the model published in the 1970s by economists Fischer Black and Myron Scholes.

Like almost all valuation models, Black-Scholes hinges on lots of assumptions. For instance, option-pricing models typically require projections of the underlying security's future volatility, as well as the option's expected life. Those aren't easy to project with any precision. Even small changes in assumptions can make crucial differences in results and, consequently, a company's reported expenses. What's more, the Black-Scholes model wasn't designed to value options that, like the kind companies grant to employees, aren't freely transferable.

For example, SEC proxy rules required Coke to assume the options' time horizon would be the full life of the options' terms, or 15 years. That drove Coke to assume relatively lower volatility, given the lengthy time horizon. Using those assumptions, Coke calculated that the value of its options was $19.92 a share. However, accounting rules required Coke to use the options' "expected life" when calculating the time horizon. Coke assumed six years. That reduced the options' value, though the effect was partly offset by Coke's assumptions that volatility would be higher, given the shorter time span. The result: Under that Black-Scholes calculation, the value was $13.06 a share.

Source: Jonathan Weil and Betsy McKay, *The Wall Street Journal*, March 7, 2003. © 2003 Dow Jones & Company, Inc. All Rights Reserved Worldwide.

For a given set of input values, the relationship between call and put option prices and an underlying stock price is illustrated in Figure 15.1. In Figure 15.1, stock prices are measured on the horizontal axis and option prices are measured on the vertical axis.

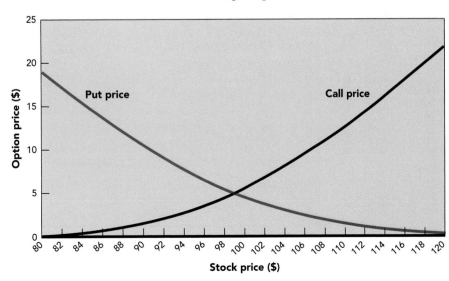

FIGURE 15.1

Put and Call Option Prices

Input values:
$K = \$100$
$T = \frac{1}{4}$ year
$r = 5\%$
$\sigma = 25\%$
$y = 0\%$

Notice that the graph lines describing relationships between call and put option prices and the underlying stock price have a convex (bowed) shape. Convexity is a fundamental characteristic of the relationship between option prices and stock prices.

Varying the Option's Strike Price

As the strike price increases, the call price decreases and the put price increases. This is reasonable, since a higher strike price means that we must pay a higher price when we exercise a call option to buy the underlying stock, thereby reducing the call option's value. Similarly, a higher strike price means that we will receive a higher price when we exercise a put option to sell the underlying stock, thereby increasing the put option's value. Of course, this logic works in reverse also; as the strike price decreases, the call price increases and the put price decreases.

Varying the Time Remaining until Option Expiration

Time remaining until option expiration is an important determinant of option value. As time remaining until option expiration lengthens, both call and put option prices normally increase. This is expected, since a longer time remaining until option expiration allows more time for the stock price to move away from a strike price and increase the option's payoff, thereby making the option more valuable. The relationship between call and put option prices and time remaining until option expiration is illustrated in Figure 15.2, where time remaining until option expiration is measured on the horizontal axis and option prices are measured on the vertical axis.

Varying the Volatility of the Stock Price

Stock price volatility (sigma, σ) plays an important role in determining option value. As stock price volatility increases, both call and put option prices increase. This is as expected, since the more volatile the stock price, the greater is the likelihood that the stock price will move farther away from a strike price and increase the option's payoff, thereby making the option more valuable. The relationship between call and put option prices and stock price volatility is graphed in Figure 15.3, where volatility is measured on the horizontal axis and option prices are measured on the vertical axis.

FIGURE 15.2

Option Prices and Time to Expiration

Input values:
S = $100
K = $100
r = 5%
σ = 25%
y = 0%

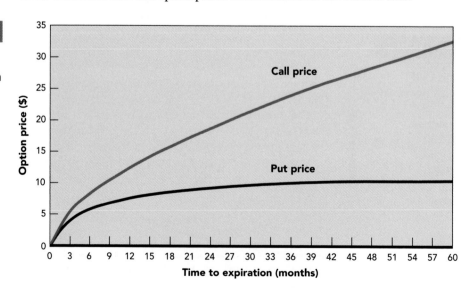

Option Prices and Sigma

Input values:
$S = \$100$
$K = \$100$
$T = \frac{1}{4}$ year
$r = 5\%$
$y = 0\%$

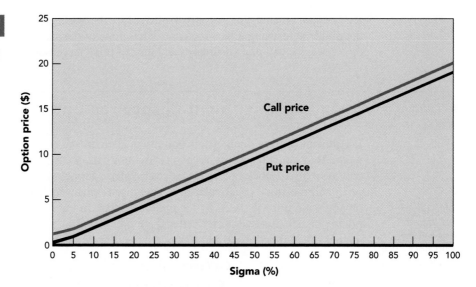

Option Prices and Interest Rates

Input values:
$S = \$100$
$K = \$100$
$T = \frac{1}{4}$ year
$\sigma = 5\%$
$y = 0\%$

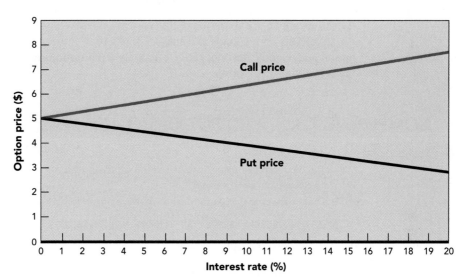

Varying the Interest Rate

Although seemingly not as important as the other inputs, the interest rate still noticeably affects option values. As the interest rate increases, the call price increases and the put price decreases. This is explained by the time value of money. A higher interest rate implies a greater discount, which lowers the present value of the strike price that we pay when we exercise a call option or receive when we exercise a put option. Figure 15.4 graphs the relationship between call and put option prices and interest rates, where the interest rate is measured on the horizontal axis and option prices are measured on the vertical axis.

Varying the Dividend Yield

A stock's dividend yield has an important effect on option values. As the dividend yield increases, the call price decreases and the put price increases. This follows from the fact that when a company pays a dividend, its assets are reduced by the amount of the dividend, causing a like decrease in the price of the stock. Then, as the stock price decreases, the call price decreases and the put price increases.

15.4 Measuring the Impact of Input Changes on Option Prices

delta Measure of the dollar impact of a change in the underlying stock price on the value of a stock option. Delta is positive for a call option and negative for a put option.

Investment professionals using options in their investment strategies have standard methods to state the impact of changes in input values on option prices. The two inputs that most affect stock option prices over a short period, say, a few days, are the stock price and the stock price volatility. The approximate impact of a stock price change on an option price is stated by the option's **delta**. In the Black-Scholes-Merton option pricing model, expressions for call and put option deltas are stated as follows, where the mathematical functions e^x and $N(x)$ were previously defined:

$$\text{Call option delta} = e^{-yT} N(d_1) > 0$$
$$\text{Put option delta} = -e^{-yT} N(-d_1) < 0$$

As shown above, a call option delta is always positive and a put option delta is always negative. This corresponds to Table 15.3, where $+$ indicates a positive effect for a call option and $-$ indicates a negative effect for a put option resulting from an increase in the underlying stock price.

COMPUTING CALL AND PUT OPTION DELTAS

EXAMPLE 15.3

Given the inputs to the Black-Scholes-Merton option pricing formula provided in Example 15.1, calculate call and put option deltas.

The necessary probabilities for d_1 and $-d_1$ were provided in Example 15.1.

$$N(d_1) = N(.98538) = .83778 \quad N(-d_1) = 1 - N(d_1) = .16222$$

Deltas are then calculated as

$$\textit{Call option delta} = .99501 \times .83778 = .83360$$
$$\textit{Put option delta} = -.99501 \times .16222 = -.16141$$

eta Measure of the percentage impact of a change in the underlying stock price on the value of a stock option. Eta is positive for a call option and negative for a put option.

The approximate percentage impact of a stock price change on an option price is stated by the option's **eta**. In the Black-Scholes-Merton option pricing model, expressions for call and put option etas are stated as follows, where the mathematical functions e^x and $N(x)$ were previously defined:

$$\text{Call option eta} = e^{-yT} N(d_1) S / C > 1$$
$$\text{Put option eta} = -e^{-yT} N(-d_1) S / P < -1$$

In the Black-Scholes-Merton option pricing model, a call option eta is greater than $+1$ and a put option eta is less than -1.

COMPUTING CALL AND PUT OPTION ETAS

EXAMPLE 15.4

Given the inputs to the Black-Scholes-Merton option pricing formula provided in Example 15.1, calculate call and put option etas.

As shown above, option etas are simply option deltas multiplied by the stock price and divided by the option price. Thus, in this example, they are calculated from values provided above as follows:

Call option eta $= .83360 \times 50 / 5.985 = 6.964$
Put option eta $= -.16141 \times 50 / .565 = -14.284$

vega Measure of the impact of a change in stock price volatility on the value of a stock option. Vega is positive for both a call option and a put option.

The approximate impact of a volatility change on an option's price is measured by the option's **vega**.[1] In the Black-Scholes-Merton option pricing model, vega is the same for call and put options and is stated as follows, where the mathematical function $n(x)$ represents a standard normal density.

$$Vega = Se^{-yT}n(d_1)\sqrt{T} > 0$$

As shown above, vega is always positive. Again this corresponds with Table 15.2, where $+$ indicates a positive effect for both a call option and a put option from a volatility increase.

COMPUTING CALL AND PUT OPTION VEGAS

EXAMPLE 15.5

Given the inputs to the Black-Scholes-Merton option pricing formula provided in Example 15.1, calculate call and put option vegas.

The vega for a call option is the same as the vega for a put option. Computing vega requires calculation of the standard normal density value for d_1. This is calculated as shown here.

$$n(d_1) = \frac{e^{-d_1^2/2}}{\sqrt{2\pi}} = \frac{e^{-.98538^2/2}}{\sqrt{6.28318}} = .245508$$

Substituting appropriate values into the vega formula above yields this vega value:

Vega $= 50 \times .99501 \times .245508 \times \sqrt{.25} = 6.107$

Refer to the *Spreadsheet Analysis* box on the next page for examples of calculating Black-Scholes-Merton call and put option prices as well as deltas, etas, and vega using a spreadsheet.

---

[1]Those of you who are scholars of the Greek language recognize that "vega" is not a Greek letter like the other option sensitivity measures. (It is a star in the constellation Lyra.) Alas, the term vega has entered the options professionals' vocabulary and is in widespread use.

SPREADSHEET ANALYSIS

	A	B	C	D	E	F	G
1							
2		**Calculating Black-Scholes-Merton Option Prices**					
3							
4	XYZ stock has a price of $50 and an annual return volatility of 25 percent. The riskless						
5	interest rate is 6 percent and the stock pays a 2 percent dividend yield. Calculate						
6	call and put option prices with a strike price of $45 and a 3-month time to expiration.						
7							
8	Stock =	50		d1 =	0.9854	N(d1) =	0.8378
9	Strike =	45				N(−d1) =	0.1622
10	Volatility =	0.25		d2 =	0.8604	N(d2) =	0.8052
11	Yield =	0.02				N(−d2) =	0.1948
12	Time =	0.25				exp(−Yield × Time) =	0.9950
13	Rate =	0.06				exp(−Rate × Time) =	0.9851
14							
15	Call Price =	Stock × exp(−Yield × Time) × N(d1)					
16		−Strike × exp(−Rate × Time) × N(d2) =			5.985		
17							
18	Put Price =	Strike × exp(−Rate × Time) × N(−d2)					
19		−Stock × exp(−Yield × Time) × N(−d1) =			0.565		
20							
21	Formula entered in E8 is =(LN(B8/B9)+(B13−B11+0.5*B10^2)*B12)/(B10*SQRT(B12))						
22	Formula entered in E10 is =E8−B10*SQRT(B12)						
23	Formulas entered in G8 and G9 are =NORMSDIST(E8) and =NORMSDIST(−E8)						
24	Formulas entered in G10 and G11 are =NORMSDIST(E10) and =NORMSDIST(−E10)						
25							
26							
27		**Calculating Black-Scholes-Merton Greeks**					
28							
29	Call Delta =	exp(−Yield × Time) × N(d1) =					0.8336
30	Put Delta =	−exp(−Yield × Time) × N(−d1) =					−0.1614
31	Call Eta =	Call Delta × Stock/Call Price =					6.9639
32	Put Eta =	Put Delta × Stock/Put Price =					−14.2952
33	Gamma =	(exp(−(d1^2/2))/sqrt(2*Pi)) /					
34		(exp(−Yield × Time) × Stock × Volatility × sqrt(Time)) =					0.0395
35	Vega =	(exp(−(d1^2/2))/sqrt(2 × Pi)) ×					
36		exp(−Yield × Time) × Stock × sqrt(Time) =					6.1071
37							
38	Notes: Gamma and Vega are the same for calls and puts using the Black-Scholes-Merton						
39	model. Also, we use the Excel function =PI() in the calculations. (Pi = 3.141592....)						
40							
41							

Interpreting Option Deltas

Interpreting the meaning of an option delta is relatively straightforward. Delta measures the impact of a change in the stock price on an option price, where a $1 change in the stock price causes an option price to change by approximately delta dollars. For example, using the input values stated immediately below, we obtain a call option price of $5.99 and a put option price of $.56. These yield a call option delta of $+.83$ and a put option delta of $-.16$.

$$S = \$50 \qquad y = 2\%$$
$$K = 45 \qquad r = 6\%$$
$$T = .25 \qquad \sigma = 25\%$$

Now if we change the stock price from $50 to $51, we get a call option price of $6.84 and a put option price of $.42. Thus, a +$1 stock price change increased the call option price by $.85 and decreased the put option price by $.14. These price changes are close to, but not exactly equal to, the call option delta value of +.83 and put option delta value of −.16.

Interpreting Option Etas

Eta measures the percentage impact of a change in the stock price on an option price, where a 1 percent change in the stock price causes an option price to change by approximately eta percent. For example, the input values stated above yield a call option price of $5.99, and a put option price of $.56, a call option eta of 6.96, and a put option eta of −14.28. If the stock price changes by 1 percent from $50 to $50.50, we get a call option price of $6.41 and a put option price of $.49. Thus, a 1 percent stock price change increased the call option price by 7.01 percent and decreased the put option price by 12.50 percent. These percentage price changes are close to the call option eta value of +6.96 and put option eta value of −14.28.

Interpreting Option Vegas

Interpreting the meaning of an option vega is also straightforward. Vega measures the impact of a change in stock price volatility on an option price, where a 1 percent change in sigma changes an option price by approximately the amount .01 times vega. For example, using the same input values stated earlier we obtain call and put option prices of $5.99 and $.56, respectively. We also get an option vega of +6.1. If we change the stock price volatility to $\sigma = 26\%$, we then get call and put option prices of $6.05 and $.63. This +1 percent stock price volatility change increased call and put option prices by $.06 and $.07, respectively, as predicted by vega.

Interpreting an Option's Gamma, Theta, and Rho

In addition to delta, eta, and vega, options professionals commonly use three other measures of option price sensitivity to input changes: gamma, theta, and rho.

gamma Measure of delta sensitivity to a stock price change.

Gamma measures delta sensitivity to a stock price change, where a one-dollar stock price change causes delta to change by approximately the amount gamma. In the Black-Scholes-Merton option pricing model, gammas are the same for call and put options.

theta Measure of the impact on an option price from a change in time remaining until option expiration.

Theta measures option price sensitivity to a change in time remaining until option expiration, where a given change in option maturity causes the option price to change by approximately the amount theta. A common convention is to calibrate theta so that it measures an option price change due to a one-week change in option maturity.

rho Measure of option price sensitivity to a change in the interest rate.

Rho measures option price sensitivity to a change in the interest rate, where a 1 percent interest rate change causes the option price to change by approximately the amount rho. Rho is positive for a call option and negative for a put option.

15.5 Implied Standard Deviations

The Black-Scholes-Merton stock option pricing model is based on six inputs: a stock price, a strike price, an interest rate, a dividend yield, the time remaining until option expiration, and the stock price volatility. Of these six factors, only the stock price

implied standard deviation (ISD) An estimate of stock price volatility obtained from an option price.

implied volatility (IVOL) Another term for implied standard deviation.

volatility is not directly observable and must be estimated somehow. A popular method to estimate stock price volatility is to use an implied value from an option price. A stock price volatility estimated from an option price is called an **implied standard deviation** or **implied volatility**, often abbreviated as **ISD** or **IVOL**, respectively. Implied volatility and implied standard deviation are two terms for the same thing.

Calculating an implied volatility requires that all input factors have known values, except sigma, and that a call or put option price be known. For example, consider the following option price input values, absent a value for sigma.

$$S = \$50 \qquad y = 2\%$$
$$K = \$45 \qquad r = 6\%$$
$$T = .25$$

Suppose we also have a call price of $C = \$5.99$. Based on this call price, what is the implied volatility? In other words, in combination with the input values stated above, what sigma value yields a call price of $C = \$5.99$? The answer comes from Example 15.1, which shows that a sigma value of .25, or 25 percent, yields a call option price of $5.99.

Now suppose we wish to know what volatility value is implied by a call price of $C = \$7$. To obtain this implied volatility value, we must find the value for sigma that yields this call price. By trial and error, you can try various sigma values until a call option price of $7 is obtained. This occurs with a sigma value of 39.22 percent, which is the implied standard deviation (ISD) corresponding to a call option price of $7.

COMPUTING IMPLIED VOLATILITY

EXAMPLE 15.6

Options professionals compute implied volatilities using special computer programs. The formula immediately below provides a useful alternative to compute implied volatility when you do not have a special computer program. This formula yields accurate implied volatility values as long as the stock price is not too far from the strike price of the option contract.

$$\sigma \approx \frac{\sqrt{2\pi/T}}{Y + X}\left[C - \frac{Y - X}{2} + \sqrt{\left(C - \frac{Y - X}{2}\right)^2 - \frac{(Y - X)^2}{\pi}}\right]$$
$$Y = Se^{-yT} \qquad X = Ke^{-rT}$$

As an example calculation, substitute the following input values into the above formula:

$$S = \$50 \qquad y = 2\%$$
$$K = \$45 \qquad r = 6\%$$
$$T = .25 \qquad C = \$7$$

The result yields this implied standard deviation value:

$$\frac{\sqrt{6.2832/.25}}{49.75 + 44.33}\left[7 - \frac{49.75 - 44.33}{2} + \sqrt{\left(7 - \frac{49.75 - 44.33}{2}\right)^2 - \frac{(49.75 - 44.33)^2}{3.1416}}\right]$$
$$= .3889 = 38.89\%$$

This is quite close to the exact implied standard deviation of 39.22 percent obtained using a special computer program.

WORK THE WEB

From our discussion of implied standard deviations (ISDs), you know that solving for an ISD when you know the option price can be tedious. Fortunately, most option calculators will do the work for you. Suppose you have a call option with a strike price of $95 that matures in 75 days. The stock currently sells for $98.12, the option sells for $10.25, and the interest rate is 4.5 percent per year, compounded continuously. What is the ISD? To find out, we went to the options calculator at www.numa.com. After entering all this information, here is what we got:

implied volatility for european call option

INPUT DATA	Share Price: 98.120	Strike Price: 95.000	Maturity(yrs): 0.205
	Dividend Yld: 0	Interest Rate: 4.5	Option Price: 10.250

Implied Volatility = 46.73

Intrinsic Value: 3.120	Time Value: 7.130

Notice the calculator changes the days to maturity to .205, which is 75 / 365 of a year. So, the underlying stock has an ISD of 46.73 percent per year.

For applications of implied volatility, see www.ivolatility.com

You can easily obtain an estimate of stock price volatility for almost any stock with option prices reported in newspapers. For example, suppose you wish to obtain an estimate of stock price volatility for Toronto Dominion Bank stock. The following information is obtained from Yahoo Finance and Bank of Canada websites using option and stock quotes for TD Bank and the T-bill quote for the interest rate.

Stock price = $ 69.95   Dividend yield = 2.75%

Exercise price = $ 75.00   Interest rate = 3.77%

Time until contract expiration = 45 days

Call price = $0.85

Substituting these input values into the formula from Example 15.6 yields this implied volatility for TD Bank:

$$\frac{\sqrt{6.2832/0.125}}{69.71+74.647}\left[0.85-\frac{69.71-74.647}{2}\right.$$

$$\left.+\sqrt{\left(0.85-\frac{(69.71-74.647)}{2}\right)^2-\frac{(69.71-74.647)^2}{3.1416}}\right]$$

$$=0.2516=25.16\%$$

This is quite close to the exact implied standard deviation of 25.84 percent obtained using a special computer program. Our nearby *Work the Web* box shows how to get ISDs the easy way.

MVX versus XIU
The dark chart represents MVX numbers and the light chart represents XIU numbers

Implied Volatility Index (MVX)
An index of investor volatility-expectations calculated with at-the-money options on i60 units of the S&P/TSX 60 XIU.

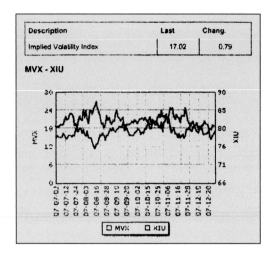

For more information on MVX volatility indexes, visit the Montreal Exchange website at
www.m-x.ca

ME Implied Volatilities for Stock Indexes

The Montreal Exchange (ME) publishes an **Implied Volatility Index (MVX)**. This index shows investor expectations about future stock market volatility. MVX is calculated using at-the-money options on the i60units of S&P/TSX 60 Index Participation Fund (XIU).

Current levels of this volatility index and the underlying stock index are available at the ME website (www.m-x.ca). Figure 15.5 shows the recent MVX and XIU numbers.

CHECK THIS ✓

15.5a In a recent issue of a newspaper, look up the stock price, dividend yield, strike price, interest rate, and time to expiration for an option on Royal Bank common stock. Note the call price corresponding to the selected strike and time values. From these values, use the formula in Example 15.6 to obtain an implied standard deviation estimate for Royal Bank stock price volatility.

15.5b Check the current levels of the volatility and stock indexes MVX, XIU at www.m-x.ca.

15.6 Hedging Stock with Stock Options

Options provide investors with the opportunity to protect themselves against losses. Taking advantage of this opportunity is known as hedging.

Suppose you own 1,000 shares of XYZ stock, the stock we analyzed in the *Spreadsheet Analysis* earlier in the chapter. From the assumptions used in the *Spreadsheet Analysis,* we calculated prices and deltas for call and put options. If we had used all the same assumptions but used a stock price of $49 instead of $50, we would get a different set of prices and deltas for call and put options. Table 15.3 provides a convenient summary (notice we have rounded the option prices to two decimal places). In Table 15.3, all option prices use these inputs: a Strike of $45, Volatility of 25%, Dividend Yield of 2%, Risk-Free Rate of 6%, and three months to maturity.

TABLE 15.3	Using the Black-Scholes-Merton Option Model for Hedging			
XYZ Stock Price	**Call Price**	**Call Delta**	**Put Price**	**Put Delta**
$50	$5.99	0.8336	$0.56	−0.1614
$49	$5.17	0.7910	$0.75	−0.2040
Change in option price:	$−0.81		$0.19	

Further suppose that you want to protect yourself against declines in XYZ stock price. That is, you want to hedge: you want to have a portfolio that does not change in value if the stock price changes. Thus, you want changes in your portfolio value from stock price changes to be equal to changes in the value of your portfolio due to options.

$$\text{Change in stock price} \times \text{Shares} = \text{Change in option price} \quad (15.3)$$
$$\times \text{Number of options}$$

From earlier in the chapter, we know that the delta of an option is a prediction of how the option price will change when the stock price changes. So we can rewrite Equation 15.3 as:

$$\text{Change in stock price} \times \text{Shares} = \text{Option delta} \times \text{Number of options} \quad (15.4)$$

Hedging Using Call Options—the Prediction

As shown in Table 15.2, stock prices and call option prices are directly related. When the stock price increases, so do prices of call options on these shares. From Table 15.3, the call option delta is .8336 when XYZ stock price is $50. The call option delta is a prediction that the call option price will increase (decrease) by about $.83 if the stock price increases (decreases) by $1.00.

So, to hedge declines in XYZ share prices using call options, you need to write, or short sell, call options to protect against a price decline. But notice that if the price of XYZ stock fell by $1.00 and you had 1,000 options, you would gain only $833.60. This would partially, but not fully, offset your loss of $1,000. You can do better by writing more options. Fortunately, you can use Equation 15.4 to tell you how many call options to write:

$$\text{Change in stock price} \times \text{Shares} = \text{Option delta} \times \text{Number of options}$$
$$-1 \times 1,000 = .8336 \times \text{Number of options}$$
$$\text{Number of options} = -1,000 / .8336 = -1,199.62$$

The minus sign confirms that you should write, or sell, call options. Because traded call options have 100 options per contract, you would need to write:

$$1,199.62 / 100 \approx 12$$

call option contracts to create a hedge using call options with a strike of $45.

Hedging Using Call Options—the Results

Suppose you write 12 call option contracts at a price of $5.99 per option, or $599 per contract. Further, just as you feared, XYZ stock fell in value by $1.00, so you suffered a $1,000 loss in the value of your shares. But what happened to the value of the call options you wrote? At the new XYZ stock price of $49, each call option is now worth

$5.17, a decrease of $.81 for each call, or $81 per contract. Because you wrote 12 call option contracts, your call option gain was $972.

Your gain in the call options nearly offsets your loss of $1,000 in XYZ shares. Why isn't it exact? You can see from Table 15.3 that delta also fell when the stock price fell. This means that you did not sell quite enough options. But because options contracts consist of 100 shares, you really did about as well as you could in this case.

Hedging Using Put Options—the Prediction

As shown in Table 15.2, stock prices and put option prices are inversely related. When the stock price increases, put option prices on these shares decrease. From Table 15.3, the put option delta is $-.1614$ when the stock price is $50. The put option delta is a prediction that the put option price will decrease (increase) by about $.16 if the stock price increases (decreases) by $1.00.

This means that you want to purchase put options to profit from their price increase if the stock price decreases. But notice that if the price of XYZ stock fell by $1.00 and if you had 1,000 put options, you would gain only $161.40. This is insignificant when compared to your $1,000 loss in XYZ shares. You will have to purchase more put options if you are going to have a better hedge. Fortunately, Equation 15.4 also tells you how many put options to purchase:

$$\text{Change in stock price} \times \text{Shares} = \text{Option delta} \times \text{Number of options}$$
$$-1 \times 1,000 = -.1614 \times \text{Number of options}$$
$$\text{Number of options} = -1,000 \, / \, -.1614 = 6,195.79$$

Because this number is positive, this confirms that you want to purchase put options. Because traded put options have 100 options per contract, you would need to purchase:

$$6,195.79 \, / \, 100 \approx 62$$

put option contracts to create a hedge using put options with a strike of $45.

Hedging Using Put Options—the Results

Suppose you purchase 62 put option contracts at a price of $.56 per option, or $56 per contract. Again, as you feared, XYZ stock fell in value by $1.00, so you suffered a $1,000 loss in the value of your shares. But what happened to the value of the put options? At the new XYZ stock price of $49, each put option is now worth $.75, an increase of $.19 for each put option, or $19 per contract. Because you purchased 62 put option contracts, your put option gain was $1,178.

Your gain in the put options more than offsets your loss of $1,000 in XYZ shares. Why isn't it exact? You can see from Table 15.3 that the put delta also fell when the stock price fell (but it increased in absolute value). This means that you purchased too many put options. If you had purchased 52 or 53 put option contracts, you would have offset your share loss more closely. How would you have known the 52 or 53 put options make a better hedge than 62 options?

By constructing a table similar to Table 15.3 in advance, you would know that these put options increase in value by $.19 when the stock falls in value by $1. Therefore, each put option contract increases by about $19. Dividing $1,000 by $19 yields 52.63, telling us that 52 or 53 put contracts will provide a good hedge.

CHECK THIS

15.6a What happens to call and put prices when the price of the underlying stock changes?

15.6b What is the goal of a hedger who uses options?

15.7 Hedging a Stock Portfolio with Stock Index Options

Hedging is a common use of stock options among portfolio managers. In particular, many institutional money managers make some use of stock index options to hedge the equity portfolios they manage. In this section, we examine how an equity portfolio manager might hedge a diversified stock portfolio using stock index options.

To begin, suppose that you manage a $10 million diversified portfolio of large-company stocks and that you maintain a portfolio beta of 1 for this portfolio. With a beta of 1, changes in the value of your portfolio closely follow changes in the Standard & Poor's 500 index. Therefore, you decide to use options on the S&P 500 index as a hedging vehicle. S&P 500 index options trade on the Chicago Board Options Exchange (CBOE) under the ticker symbol SPX. SPX option prices are reported daily in the "Index Options Trading" column of *The Wall Street Journal*. Each SPX option has a contract value of 100 times the current level of the S&P 500 index.

For stock option reports, see www.aantix.com

SPX options are a convenient hedging vehicle for an equity portfolio manager because they are European style and because they settle in cash at expiration. For example, suppose you hold one SPX call option with a strike price of 1500 and at option expiration, the S&P 500 index stands at 1507. In this case, your cash payoff is 100 times the difference between the index level and the strike price, or $100 \times (1507 - 1500) = \$700$. Of course, if the expiration date index level falls below the strike price, your SPX call option expires worthless.

Hedging a stock portfolio with index options requires first calculating the number of option contracts needed to form an effective hedge. While you can use either put options or call options to construct an effective hedge, we assume that you decide to use call options to hedge your $10 million equity portfolio. Using stock index call options to hedge an equity portfolio involves writing a certain number of option contracts. In general, the number of stock index option contracts needed to hedge an equity portfolio is stated by the equation

$$\text{Number of option contracts} = \frac{\text{Portfolio beta} \times \text{Portfolio value}}{\text{Option delta} \times \text{Option contract value}} \quad (15.5)$$

In your particular case, you have a portfolio beta of 1 and a portfolio value of $10 million. You now need to calculate an option delta and option contract value.

The option contract value for an SPX option is simply 100 times the current level of the S&P 500 index. Checking the "Index Options Trading" column in *The Wall Street Journal* you see that the S&P 500 index has a value of 1508, which means that each SPX option has a current contract value of $150,800.

To calculate an option delta, you must decide which particular contract to use. You decide to use options with an October expiration and a strike price of 1500, that is, the October 1500 SPX contract. From the "Index Options Trading" column, you find the price for these options is $64^5/_8$, or 64.625. Options expire on the

Saturday following the third Friday of their expiration month. Counting days on your calendar yields a time remaining until option expiration of 73 days. The interest rate on Treasury bills maturing closest to option expiration is 6 percent. The dividend yield on the S&P 500 index is not normally reported in *The Wall Street Journal*. Fortunately, the S&P 500 trades in the form of depository shares on the American Stock Exchange (AMEX) under the ticker SPY. SPY shares represent a claim on a portfolio designed to match the S&P 500 as closely as possible. By looking up information on SPY shares on the Internet, you find that the dividend yield is 1.5 percent.

With the information now collected, you use the input values $S = 1508.80$, $K = 1500$, $T = .2$, $r = 6\%$, and $y = 1.5\%$ and option price $C = 64.625$ to get an implied volatility of 20 percent. This represents a current estimate of S&P 500 index volatility. Using this sigma value of 20 percent then yields a call option delta of .579. You now have sufficient information to calculate the number of option contracts needed to effectively hedge your equity portfolio. By using equation 15.5, we can calculate the number of October 1500 SPX options that you should write to form an effective hedge.

$$\frac{1.0 \times \$10,000,000}{.579 \times \$150,800} \approx 115 \text{ contracts}$$

Furthermore, by writing 115 October 1500 call options, you receive $115 \times 100 \times 64.625 = \$743,187.50$.

To assess the effectiveness of this hedge, suppose the S&P 500 index and your stock portfolio both immediately fall in value by 1 percent. This is a loss of $100,000 on your stock portfolio. After the S&P 500 index falls by 1 percent, its level is 1493.71, which then yields a call option price of $C = 56.21$. Now, if you were to buy back the 115 contracts, you would pay $115 \times 100 \times 56.21 = \$646,415$. Since you originally received $743,187.50 for the options, this represents a gain of $743,187.50 - \$646,415 = \$96,772.50$, which cancels most of the $100,000 loss on your equity portfolio. In fact, your final net loss is only $3,227.50, which is a small fraction of the loss that would have been realized with an unhedged portfolio.

To maintain an effective hedge over time, you will need to rebalance your options hedge on, say, a weekly basis. Rebalancing simply requires calculating anew the number of option contracts needed to hedge your equity portfolio, and then buying or selling options in the amount necessary to maintain an effective hedge. The nearby *Investment Updates* box contains a brief *Wall Street Journal* report on hedging strategies using stock index options.

THE OPTION HEDGE RATIO FOR A STOCK PORTFOLIO

EXAMPLE 15.7

You are managing a $15 million stock portfolio with a beta of 1.1 which you decide to hedge by buying index put options with a contract value of $125,000 per contract and a delta of .4. How many option contracts are required?

Plugging our information into equation 15.3 yields this calculation:

$$\frac{1.1 \times \$15,000,000}{.4 \times \$125,000} = 330 \text{ contracts}$$

Thus, you would need to buy 330 put option contracts.

Money Managers Use Options to Hedge Portfolios

Traders and money managers began using options to hedge their portfolios yesterday after spending the past week ignoring defensive strategies to speculate on earnings and stock price movements.

The turning point came late in the morning when the Standard & Poor's 500 index slid below 1140. This wiped out many S&P 500 index futures positions and market professionals responded by buying S&P 500 index options to protect their portfolios from the market's volatility.

This hedging activity marked a change in the approach they have taken to the market. Many professionals recently stopped hedging their portfolios because the stock market has quickly corrected in the past. They spent money for hedges they ultimately didn't need.

"A lot of people were completely unhedged when the decline began," said Leon Gross, Salomon Smith Barney's options strategist. He noted that the S&P 500 index's rise to 1186 from 1086 took six weeks, while it dropped 50 points in only four days.

The fear in the options market spiked higher as the S&P index fell along with the Dow Jones Industrial Average.

The option market's fear gauge, the Chicago Board Options Exchange Volatility Index, rose 1.72, or 7.5%, to 24.66. "This is an indication that people are getting nervous and paying for puts," Mr. Gross said.

Options prices reflected this discomfort, which made hedging portfolios even more expensive than normal. For more aggressive traders, such as hedge funds, high options prices created opportunities to short sell puts and sectors.

The Nasdaq index of the 100 largest nonfinancial stocks was a popular way to short the technology sector. Other traders sold put options because they think the fear is overdone and they'll be able to buy the contracts back for less money.

Source: Steven M. Sears, *The Wall Street Journal*, July 29, 1998. Reprinted by permission of Dow Jones & Company, Inc., via Copyright Clearance Center, Inc. © 1998 Dow Jones & Company, Inc. All Rights Reserved Worldwide.

 CHECK THIS

15.7a In the hedging example above, suppose instead that your equity portfolio had a beta of 1.5. What number of SXO call options traded on the Montreal Exchange would be required to form an effective hedge?

15.7b Alternatively, suppose that your equity portfolio had a beta of .5. What number of SXO call options would then be required to form an effective hedge?

15.8 Summary and Conclusions

In this chapter, we examined stock option prices. Many important aspects of option pricing were covered, including the following:

1. The Black-Scholes-Merton option pricing formula states that the value of a stock option is a function of the current stock price, the stock dividend yield, option strike price, risk-free interest rate, time remaining until option expiration, and the stock price volatility.

2. The two most important determinants of the price of a stock option are the price of the underlying stock and the strike price of the option. As the stock price increases, call prices increase and put prices decrease. Conversely, as the strike price increases, call prices decrease and put prices increase.

3. Time remaining until option expiration is an important determinant of option value. As time remaining until option expiration lengthens, both call and put option prices normally increase. Stock price volatility also plays an important role in determining option value. As stock price volatility increases, both call and put option prices increase.

4. Although less important, the interest rate can noticeably affect option values. As the interest rate increases, call prices increase and put prices decrease. A stock's dividend yield also affects option values. As the dividend yield increases, call prices decrease and put prices increase.

5. The two input factors that most affect stock option prices over a short period, say, a few days, are the stock price and the stock price volatility. The impact of a stock price change on an option price is measured by the option's delta. The impact of a volatility change on an option's price is measured by the option's vega.

6. A call option delta is always positive, and a put option delta is always negative. Delta measures the impact of a stock price change on an option price, where a one-dollar change in the stock price causes an option price to change by approximately delta dollars.

7. Vega measures the impact of a change in stock price volatility (sigma, σ) on an option price, where a 1 percent change in volatility changes an option price by approximately the amount vega.

8. Of the six input factors to the Black-Scholes-Merton option pricing model, only the stock price volatility is not directly observable and must be estimated somehow. A stock price volatility estimated from an option price is called an implied volatility or an implied standard deviation, which are two terms for the same thing.

9. Options on a market index are a convenient hedging vehicle for an equity portfolio. Hedging a stock portfolio with index options requires calculating the number of option contracts needed to form an effective hedge.

10. To maintain an effective hedge over time, you should rebalance the options hedge on a regular basis. Rebalancing requires recalculating the number of option contracts needed to hedge an equity portfolio and then buying or selling options in the amount necessary to maintain an effective hedge.

11. Volatility skews, or volatility smiles, occur when individual implied volatilities differ across call and put options with different strike prices. Volatility skews commonly appear in implied volatilities for stock index options and also appear in implied volatilities for options on individual stocks. The most important factor causing volatility skews is stochastic volatility, the phenomenon of stock price volatility changing over time in a largely random fashion.

12. The Black-Scholes-Merton option pricing model assumes a constant stock price volatility and yields option prices that may differ from stochastic volatility option prices. Nevertheless, even when volatility is stochastic, the Black-Scholes-Merton option pricing model yields accurate option prices for options with strike prices close to a current stock price. Therefore, when using implied volatility to estimate an underlying stock price volatility, it is best to use at-the-money options.

REAL WORLD

This chapter began by introducing you to the Nobel-Prize-winning Black-Scholes-Merton option pricing formula. We saw that the formula and its associated concepts are fairly complex, but, despite that complexity, the formula is very widely used by traders and money managers. You can find out more about the Black-Scholes-Merton option pricing model on the Internet.

To put into practice some real-world uses for the concepts we discussed, you should gather options trading information off the Web and then use the information to trade options through Stock-Trak. Some suggested websites are the Web Center for Futures and Options (www.ino.com), NUMA Derivatives (www.numa.com), Optionetics (www.optionetics.com), PM Publishing (www.pmpublishing.com), and Antix Stock Option Report (www.aantix.com). Of course, don't forget the most extensive website for options at the Chicago Board Options Exchange (www.cboe.com) and at the Montreal Exchange (www.m-x.ca).

Another important use for option pricing theory is to gain some insight into stock market volatility. Recall that in Chapter 1 we discussed the probabilities associated with returns equal to the average plus or minus a particular number of standard deviations. Implied standard deviations (ISDs) provide a means of broadening this analysis to anything with traded options. Try calculating a few ISDs for both stock index options and some high-flying technology stocks. You can learn a lot about implied volatilities and how they are used by options professionals on the Internet. Enter the search phrases "implied volatility" or "implied standard deviation" into your favourite Internet search engine for links to dozens of websites, like IVolatility (www.ivolatility.com).

Key Terms

delta 496
eta 496
vega 497
gamma 499
theta 499

rho 499
implied standard deviation (ISD) 500
implied volatility (IVOL) 500
Implied Volatility Index (MVX) 502

Chapter Review Problems and Self-Test

1. **Black-Scholes Formula** What is the value of a call option if the underlying stock price is $100, the strike price is $90, the underlying stock volatility is 40 percent, and the risk-free rate is 4 percent? Assume the option has 60 days to expiration.

2. **Black-Scholes Formula** What is the value of a put option using the assumptions from the previous problem?

Answers to Self-Test Problems

1. We will use these input values to calculate the price of the call option.

   S = current stock price = $100
   K = option strike price = $90
   r = risk-free interest rate = .04
   σ = stock volatility = .40
   T = time to expiration = 60 days
   y = stock dividend yield = 0

www.mcgrawhill.ca/olc/Jordan

We first compute values for d_1 and d_2.

$$d_1 = \frac{\ln(100/90) + (.04 + .4^2/2) \times 60/365}{.4\sqrt{60/365}}$$
$$= \frac{.10536 + .12 \times .16438}{.16218}$$
$$= .77130$$
$$d_2 = d_1 - .16218$$
$$= .60912$$

The following standard normal probabilities are given:

$$N(d_1) = N(.7713) = .77973 \qquad N(d_2) = N(.60912) = .72878$$

We can now calculate the price of the call option as

$$C = \$100 \times .77973 - \$90 \times e^{-.04 \times 60/365} \times .72878$$
$$= \$100 \times .77973 - \$90 \times .99345 \times .72878$$
$$= \$12.81$$

2. Since we already know the values for d_1 and d_2, we can solve for $N(-d_1)$ and $N(-d_2)$ as follows:

$$N(-d_1) = 1 - N(d_1) = 1 - .77973 = .22027$$
$$N(-d_2) = 1 - N(d_2) = 1 - .72878 = .27122$$

We can now calculate the price of the put option as

$$P = \$90 \times e^{-.04 \times 60/365} \times .27122 - \$100 \times .22027$$
$$= \$90 \times .99345 \times .27122 - \$100 \times .22027$$
$$= \$2.22$$

Alternatively, using put-call parity from the previous chapter:

$$P = C + Ke^{-rT} - S$$
$$= \$12.81 + \$90 \times e^{-.05 \times 90/365} - \$100$$
$$= \$12.81 + \$90 \times .99345 - \$100$$
$$= \$2.22$$

Test Your Investment Quotient

1. **Black-Scholes-Merton Model** The only variable in the Black-Scholes-Merton option pricing model that cannot be directly observed is the

    a. Stock price volatility
    b. Dividend yield
    c. Stock price
    d. Risk-free rate

2. **Delta** You purchase a call option with a delta of .34. If the stock price decreases by $2.00, the price of the option will

    a. Increase by $.34
    b. Decrease by $.34

    c. Increase by $.68

    d. Decrease by $.68

3. **Black-Scholes-Merton Model** In the Black-Scholes-Merton option pricing model, the value of an option contract is a function of six inputs. Which of the following is not one of these inputs?

    a. The price of the underlying stock.

    b. The strike price of the option contract.

    c. The expected return on the underlying stock.

    d. The time remaining until option expiration.

4. **Black-Scholes Formula** In the Black-Scholes option valuation formula, an increase in a stock's volatility

    a. Increases the associated call option value.

    b. Decreases the associated put option value.

    c. Increases or decreases the option value, depending on the level of interest rates.

    d. Does not change either the put or call option value because put-call parity holds.

5. **Option Prices** Which of the following variables influence the value of options?

    I. Level of interest rates

    II. Time to expiration of the option

    III. Dividend yield of underlying stock

    IV. Stock price volatility

    a. I and IV only

    b. II and III only

    c. I, III, and IV only

    d. I, II, III, and IV

6. **Option Prices** Which of the following factors does not influence the market price of options on a common stock?

    a. Expected return on the underlying stock.

    b. Volatility of the underlying stock.

    c. Relationship between the strike price of the options and the market price of the underlying stock.

    d. Option's expiration date.

7. **Option Prices** Which one of the following will increase the value of a call option?

    a. An increase in interest rates.

    b. A decrease in time to expiration of the call.

    c. A decrease in the volatility of the underlying stock.

    d. An increase in the dividend rate of the underlying stock.

8. **Option Prices** Which one of the following would tend to result in a high value of a call option?

    a. Interest rates are low.

    b. The variability of the underlying stock is high.

    c. There is little time remaining until the option expires.

    d. The exercise price is high relative to the stock price.

9. **Option Price Factors** Which of the following incorrectly states the signs of the impact of an increase in the indicated input factor on call and put option prices?

	Call	Put
a. Risk-free interest rate	+	−
b. Underlying stock price	+	−
c. Dividend yield of the underlying stock	−	+
d. Volatility of the underlying stock price	+	−

10. **Option Price Factors** Which of the following incorrectly states the signs of the impact of an increase in the indicated input factor on call and put option prices?

	Call	Put
a. Strike price of the option contract	+	−
b. Time remaining until option expiration	+	+
c. Underlying stock price	+	−
d. Volatility of the underlying stock price	+	+

11. **Option Price Sensitivities** Which of the following measures the impact of a change in the underlying stock price on the option price?

   a. Vega
   b. Rho
   c. Delta
   d. Theta

12. **Option Price Sensitivities** Which of the following measures the impact of a change in the time remaining until option contract expiration on the option price?

   a. Vega
   b. Rho
   c. Delta
   d. Theta

13. **Option Price Sensitivities** Which of the following measures the impact of a change in the underlying stock's price volatility on the option price?

   a. Vega
   b. Rho
   c. Delta
   d. Theta

14. **Option Price Sensitivities** Which of the following measures the impact of a change in the risk-free interest rate on the option price?

   a. Vega
   b. Rho
   c. Delta
   d. Theta

15. **Hedging with Options** You wish to hedge a $5 million stock portfolio with a portfolio beta equal to 1. The hedging index call option has a delta equal to .5 and a contract value equal to $100,000. Which of the following hedging transactions is required to hedge the stock portfolio?

   a. Write 200 index call option contracts.
   b. Write 100 index call option contracts.
   c. Buy 200 index call option contracts.
   d. Buy 100 index call option contracts.

16. **Hedging with Options** You wish to hedge a $10 million stock portfolio with a portfolio beta equal to 1. The hedging index put option has a delta equal to .5 and a contract value of $200,000. Which of the following hedging transactions is required to hedge the stock portfolio?

   a. Write 200 put option contracts.
   b. Write 100 put option contracts.
   c. Buy 200 put option contracts.
   d. Buy 100 put option contracts.

17. **Implied Volatility** Which of the following provides the best economic interpretation of implied volatility for an underlying stock?

    a. Implied volatility predicts the stock's future volatility.
    b. Implied volatility states the stock's historical volatility.
    c. Implied volatility is unrelated to the underlying stock.
    d. Implied volatility is an accurate measure of interest rate risk.

18. **Implied Volatility** Two call options on the same underlying stock with the same expiration dates have strike prices of $40 and $60 and yield implied volatilities of 45 percent and 35 percent, respectively. The stock price is $50. This means that

    a. The underlying stock has two different volatilities.
    b. Both options are incorrectly priced.
    c. The volatility skew has a negative slope.
    d. The underlying stock will soon pay a dividend.

19. **Implied Volatility** With respect to call options with three months to expiration on a particular underlying stock, in-the-money implied volatilities are higher than out-of-the-money implied volatilities. This means that

    a. The volatility skew is shifting.
    b. The volatility skew is flat.
    c. The volatility skew has a negative slope.
    d. The volatility skew has a positive slope.

20. **Implied Volatility** The implied volatility for an at-the-money call option suddenly jumps from 25 percent to 50 percent. This most likely means that

    a. The underlying stock has just paid a dividend.
    b. The volatility jump is temporary.
    c. The option has a short time to expiration.
    d. An unforeseen event has increased the risk of the underlying stock.

Concept Questions

1. **Option Prices** What are the six factors that determine an option's price?

2. **Options and Expiration Dates** What is the impact of lengthening the time to expiration on an option's value? Explain.

3. **Options and Stock Price Volatility** What is the impact of an increase in the volatility of the underlying stock on an option's value? Explain.

4. **Options and Dividend Yields** How do dividend yields affect option prices? Explain.

5. **Options and Interest Rates** How do interest rates affect option prices? Explain.

6. **Time Value** What is the time value of a call option? Of a put option? What happens to the time value of a call option as the maturity increases? What about a put option?

7. **Delta** What does an option's delta tell us? Suppose a call option with a delta of .60 sells for $5.00. If the stock price rises by $1, what will happen to the call's value?

8. **Eta** What is the difference between an option's delta and its eta? Suppose a call option has an eta of 10. If the underlying stock rises from $100 to $104, what will be the impact on the option's price?

9. **Vega** What does an option's vega tell us? Suppose a put option with a vega of .80 sells for $15.00. If the underlying volatility rises from 40 to 41 percent, what will happen to the put's value?

10. **Rho** What does an option's rho measure? Suppose a call option with a rho of .14 sells for $10.00. If the interest rate rises from 4 to 5 percent, what will happen to the call value?

Questions and Problems

Core Questions

1. **Call Option Prices** What is the value of a call option if the underlying stock price is $108, the strike price is $105, the underlying stock volatility is 62 percent, and the risk-free rate is 4 percent? Assume the option has 270 days to expiration.

2. **Call Option Prices** What is the value of a call option if the underlying stock price is $47, the strike price is $50, the underlying stock volatility is 50 percent, and the risk-free rate is 4 percent? Assume the option has 60 days to expiration and the underlying stock has a dividend yield of 2 percent.

3. **Call Option Prices** What is the value of a call option if the underlying stock price is $81, the strike price is $75, the underlying stock volatility is 60 percent, and the risk-free rate is 5 percent? Assume the option has 45 days to expiration.

4. **Call Option Prices** A stock is currently priced at $87 and has an annual standard deviation of 43 percent. The dividend yield of the stock is 2 percent, and the risk-free rate is 6 percent. What is the value of a call option on the stock with a strike price of $95 and 45 days to expiration?

5. **Call Option Prices** The stock of Nugents Nougats currently sells for $44 and has an annual standard deviation of 45 percent. The stock has a dividend yield of 1.5 percent, and the risk-free rate is 7 percent. What is the value of a call option on the stock with a strike price of $40 and 65 days to expiration?

6. **Put Option Prices** The stock of Lead Zeppelin, a metal manufacturer, currently sells for $86 and has an annual standard deviation of 67 percent. The risk-free rate is 6 percent. What is the value of a put option with a strike price of $85 and 29 days to expiration?

7. **Put Option Prices** What is the value of a put option if the underlying stock price is $75, the strike price is $80, the underlying stock volatility is 47 percent, the dividend yield of the stock is 2 percent, and the risk-free rate is 5 percent? Assume the option has 120 days to expiration.

8. **Put Option Prices** A stock with an annual standard deviation of 60 percent currently sells for $104. The dividend yield of the stock is 1.2 percent, and the risk-free rate is 6 percent. What is the value of a put option with a strike price of $115 and 150 days to expiration?

9. **Hedging with Options** You are managing a pension fund with a value of $200 million and a beta of 1.15. You are concerned about a market decline and wish to hedge the portfolio. You have decided to use SPX calls. How many contracts do you need if the delta of the call option is .55 and the S&P index is currently at 1180?

10. **Hedging with Options** Suppose you have a stock market portfolio with a beta of .95 that is currently worth $300 million. You wish to hedge against a decline using index options. Describe how you might do so with puts and calls. Suppose you decide to use SPX calls. Calculate the number of contracts needed if the contract you pick has a delta of .50, and the S&P 500 index is at 1100.

Intermediate Questions

11. **Black-Scholes-Merton Model** A call option matures in six months. The underlying stock price is $90, and the stock's return has a standard deviation of 20 percent per year. The risk-free rate is 4 percent per year, compounded continuously. If the exercise price is $0, what is the price of the call option?

12. **Black-Scholes-Merton Model** A call option has an exercise price of $90 and matures in six months. The current stock price is $95, and the risk-free rate is 5 percent per year, compounded continuously. What is the price of the call if the standard deviation of the stock is 0 percent per year?

13. **Black-Scholes-Merton Model** A stock is currently priced at $40. A call option with an expiration of one year has an exercise price of $50. The risk-free rate is 12 percent per year, compounded continuously, and the standard deviation of the stock's return is infinitely large. What is the price of the call option?

14. **ISDs** A call option has a price of $7.25. The underlying stock price, strike price, and dividend yield are $108, $115, and 2 percent, respectively. The option has 100 days to expiration, and the risk-free interest rate is 6 percent. What is the implied volatility?

15. **ISDs** A put option has a price of $12.10. The underlying stock price, strike price, and dividend yield are $92, $100, and 2 percent, respectively. The option has 75 days to expiration, and the risk-free interest rate is 6 percent. What is the implied volatility?

16. **Calculating the Greeks** Calculate the price and the following "greeks" for a call and a put option with 60 days to expiration: delta, eta, and vega. The stock price is $82, the strike price is $90, the volatility is 50 percent, the dividend yield is 1.5 percent, and the risk-free interest rate is 5 percent.

17. **Employee Stock Options** In its 10-K dated January 28, 2005, Dell, Inc., had outstanding employee stock options (ESOs) representing over 365 million shares of its stock. Dell accountants estimated the value of these options using the Black-Scholes-Merton formula and the following assumptions:

S = current stock price = $41.06
K = option strike price = $29.70
r = risk-free interest rate = .0289
σ = stock volatility = .36
T = time to expiration = 3.8 years

What was the estimated value of these employee stock options per share of stock?

18. **Employee Stock Options** Suppose you hold Dell employee stock options (ESOs) representing options to buy 10,000 shares of Dell stock. You wish to hedge your position by buying put options with three-month expirations and a $45 strike price. How many put option contracts are required? Use the same assumptions specified in the previous problem. (Note that such a trade may not be permitted by the covenants of many ESO plans. If the trade were permitted, it could be considered unethical.)

19. **Employee Stock Options** Immediately after establishing your put options hedge, volatility for Dell stock suddenly jumps to 45 percent. This changes the number of put options required to hedge your Dell employee stock options (ESOs). How many put option contracts are now required? (Except for the new volatility, use the same assumptions specified in the previous problem.)

20. **Employee Stock Options** Suppose the put option in the previous problem has a price of $6. What is the implied volatility? (Use the same assumptions specified in the previous problems.)

Use the following information for the next three problems: Donna Donie, CFA, has a client who believes the common stock price of TRT Materials (currently $58 per share) could move substantially in either direction in reaction to an expected court decision involving the company. The client currently owns no TRT shares, but asks Donie for advice about implementing a strangle strategy to capitalize on the possible stock price movement. Donie gathers the TRT option pricing data shown below.

Note: A long strangle is similar to a long straddle but involves purchasing a put option at K_1 and purchasing a call option at K_2 where $K_1 < K_2$.

	Call Option	Put Option
Price	$ 5	$ 4
Strike price	$60	$55
Time to expiration	90 days	90 days

Spreadsheet Questions

21. Strangles Should Donie choose a long strangle strategy or a short strangle strategy to achieve the client's objective? Justify your recommendation with one reason.

22. Strangle Payoff For the appropriate strategy in the previous problem, calculate at expiration the maximum possible loss per share, the maximum possible gain per share, and the break-even stock price(s).

23. Delta The delta of the call option in the previous problems is .625, and TRT stock does not pay any dividends. Calculate the approximate change in price for the call option if TRT's stock price immediately increases to $59.

24. Black-Scholes-Merton Model A stock has a price of $78 and an annual return volatility of 55 percent. The risk-free rate is 3.8 percent, and the stock pays a 1.3 percent dividend yield. Using a computer spreadsheet program, calculate the call and put option prices with a strike price of $75 and a 65-day expiration.

25. Greeks Using the information in the previous problem, construct a second spreadsheet that calculates the delta for the put and call, the eta for the put and call, and the vega.

What's on the Web?

1. **Black-Scholes** Go to www.cfo.com and find the options pricing calculator. There is a call and a put option on a stock that expire in 30 days. The strike price is $55 and the current stock price is $58.70. The standard deviation of the stock is 45 percent per year, and the risk-free rate is 4.8 percent per year, compounded continuously. What is the price of the call and the put? What are the delta, gamma, theta, and vega of the call and the put?

2. **Black-Scholes** Go to www.cboe.com and find the options pricing calculator. A stock is currently priced at $98 per share and has a standard deviation of 58 percent per year. Options are available with an exercise price of $95, and the risk-free rate of interest is 5.2 percent per year, compounded continuously. What is the price of the call and the put that expire next month? What are the delta, gamma, seven-day theta, vega, and rho of the call and the put? How do you interpret these numbers? How do your answers change for an exercise price of $100?

3. **Implied Standard Deviation** Go to www.numa.com and find the options pricing calculator. You purchased a call option for $11.50 that matures in 55 days. The strike price is $95 and the underlying stock has a price of $99.50. If the risk-free rate is 5.4 percent, compounded continuously, what is the implied standard deviation of the stock? Using this implied standard deviation, what is the price of a put option with the same characteristics?

4. **Black-Scholes with Dividends** Recalculate the first two problems assuming a dividend yield of 2 percent per year. How does this change your answers?

CHAPTER 16

Futures Contracts

"There are two times in a man's life when he should not speculate: when he can't afford it and when he can."

—Mark Twain

"When you bet on a sure thing—hedge!"

—Robert Half

Futures contracts can be used for speculation or for risk management. For would-be speculators, Mark Twain's advice is well worth considering. In addition to their risk dimension, trading in futures contracts adds a time dimension to commodity markets. A futures contract separates the date of the agreement—when a delivery price is specified—from the date when delivery and payment actually occur. By separating these dates, buyers and sellers achieve an important and flexible tool for risk management. So fundamental is this underlying principle that it has been practised for several millennia and is likely to be around for many more. ■

This chapter covers modern-day futures contracts. The first sections discuss the basics of futures contracts and how their prices are quoted in the financial press. From there, we move into a general discussion of how futures contracts are used and the relationship between current cash prices and futures prices.

16.1 Futures Contracts Basics

forward contract
Agreement between a buyer and a seller, who both commit to a transaction at a future date at a price set by negotiation today.

futures contract
Contract between a seller and a buyer specifying a commodity or financial instrument to be delivered and paid at contract maturity. Futures contracts are managed through an organized futures exchange.

futures price Price negotiated by buyer and seller at which the underlying commodity or financial instrument will be delivered and paid for to fulfill the obligations of a futures contract.

By definition, a **forward contract** is a formal agreement between a buyer and a seller who both commit to a commodity transaction at a future date at a price set by negotiation today. The genius of forward contracting is that it allows a producer to sell a product to a willing buyer before it is actually produced. By setting a price today, both buyer and seller remove price uncertainty as a source of risk. With less risk, buyers and sellers mutually benefit and commerce is stimulated. This principle has been understood and practised for centuries.

Futures contracts represent a step beyond forward contracts. Futures contracts and forward contracts accomplish the same economic task, which is to specify a price today for future delivery. This specified price is called the **futures price**. However, while a forward contract can be struck between any two parties, futures contracts are managed through an organized futures exchange. Sponsorship through a-futures exchange is a major distinction between a futures contract and a forward contract. Futures contracts are standardized in terms of contract size, delivery date, and quality.

Modern History of Futures Trading

The oldest organized futures exchange in the United States is the Chicago Board of Trade (CBOT). The CBOT was established in 1848 and grew with the westward expansion of American ranching and agriculture. Today, the CBOT is the largest, most active futures exchange in the world. Other early American futures exchanges still with us today include the MidAmerica Commodity Exchange (founded in 1868), New York Cotton Exchange (1870), New York Mercantile Exchange (1872), Chicago Mercantile Exchange (1874), New York Coffee Exchange (1882), and the Kansas City Board of Trade (1882).

In Canada the Winnipeg Commodity Exchange started its trading in 1887 with wheat, oats, and barley contracts. Over the years new product contracts were added to the original contracts. Some very popular contracts include canola, flaxseed, and barley.

For more than 100 years, futures exchanges devoted their activities exclusively to commodity futures. However, a revolution began in the 1970s with the introduction of financial futures. Unlike commodity futures, which call for delivery of a physical commodity, financial futures require delivery of a financial instrument. The first financial futures were foreign currency contracts introduced in 1972 at the International Monetary Market (IMM), a division of the Chicago Mercantile Exchange (CME).

Next came interest rate futures, introduced at the Chicago Board of Trade in 1975. An interest rate futures contract specifies delivery of a fixed-income security. In 2007 the Chicago Mercantile Exchange and the Chicago Board of Trade merged to create the CME group. The CME group is currently the world's largest derivative exchange. Canadian financial futures contracts are traded on the Montreal Exchange. The following interest rate futures contracts are available for investors: three-month bankers' acceptance futures, 30-day overnight repo rate futures, two-year government of Canada bond futures and ten-year government of Canada bond futures. Finally, stock index futures were introduced. Various S&P stock index futures are now bought and sold at the Montreal Exchange.

Financial futures have been so successful that they now constitute the bulk of all futures trading. This success is largely attributed to the fact that financial futures have become an indispensable tool for financial risk management by corporations and portfolio managers. As we will see, futures contracts can be used to reduce risk through

Visit these futures exchange websites:
www.cbot.com
www.m-x.ca
www.wce.ca
www.nymex.com
www.cme.com
www.kcbt.com
www.theice.com
www.cmegroup.com

hedging strategies or to increase risk through speculative strategies. In this chapter, we discuss futures contracts generally, but, since this text deals with financial markets, we will ultimately focus on financial futures.

Futures Contract Features

Futures contracts are a type of derivative security because the value of the contract is derived from the value of an underlying instrument. For example, the value of a futures contract to buy or sell gold is derived from the market price of gold. However, because a futures contract represents a zero-sum game between a buyer and a seller, the net value of a futures contract is always zero. That is, any gain realized by the buyer is exactly equal to a loss realized by the seller, and vice versa.

Futures are contracts, and, in practice, exchange-traded futures contracts are standardized to facilitate convenience in trading and price reporting. Standardized futures contracts have a set contract size specified according to the particular underlying instrument. For example, a standard gold futures contract specifies a contract size of 100 troy ounces. This means that a single gold futures contract obligates the seller to deliver 100 troy ounces of gold to the buyer at contract maturity. In turn, the contract also obligates the buyer to accept the gold delivery and pay the negotiated futures price for the delivered gold.

To properly understand a futures contract, we must know the specific terms of the contract. In general, futures contracts must stipulate at least the following five contract terms:

1. The identity of the underlying commodity or financial instrument.

2. The futures contract size.

3. The futures maturity date, also called the expiration date.

4. The delivery or settlement procedure.

5. The futures price.

First, a futures contract requires that the underlying commodity or financial instrument be clearly identified. This is stating the obvious, but it is important that the obvious is clearly understood in financial transactions.

Second, the size of the contract must be specified.

The third contract term that must be stated is the maturity date. Contract maturity is the date on which the seller is obligated to make delivery and the buyer is obligated to make payment.

Fourth, the delivery process must be specified. For commodity futures, delivery normally entails sending a warehouse receipt for the appropriate quantity of the underlying commodity. After delivery, the buyer pays warehouse storage costs until the commodity is sold or otherwise disposed.

Finally, the futures price must be mutually agreed on by the buyer and seller. The futures price is quite important, since it is the price that the buyer will pay and the seller will receive for delivery at contract maturity.

For interest rate futures, delivery is often accomplished by a transfer of registered ownership.

Other financial futures feature cash settlement, which means that the buyer and seller simply settle up in cash with no actual delivery. We discuss cash settlement in more detail when we discuss stock index futures. The important thing to remember for now is that delivery procedures are selected for convenience and low cost. Specific delivery procedures are set by the futures exchange and may change slightly from time to time.

WORK THE WEB

One problem with futures quotes from newspapers is that the prices are from the previous trading day. If you need quotes from today, one of the best places to find current quotes is the exchange website. We wanted to find current prices for the S&P Canada 60 Index futures, so we went to www.m-x.ca, the Montreal Exchange, where they are traded. Here is what we found:

SXF - S&P Canada 60 Index Futures

Last update: Jan. 1, 2008 14:24 Montréal time (DATA 15 MINUTES DELAYED)   Refresh | Print

Month / Strike	Bid Price	Ask Price	Settl. Price	Net Change	Vol.
✦ 08 MR	814.800	814.900	813.500	-1.200	5759
✦ 08 JN	0.000	0.000	815.500	-1.200	0
✦ 08 SE	0.000	0.000	817.500	-1.200	0
✦ 08 DE	0.000	0.000	819.500	-1.200	0
Total					5759

∴ Top

As you can see, most of the information is self-explanatory. There were four futures contracts on the S&P Canada 60 index, they all expire in 2008.

Source: S&P Canadian Index Services.

Futures Prices

The largest volume of futures trading in the United States takes place at the Chicago Board of Trade, which accounts for about half of all domestic futures trading. However, futures trading is also quite active at other futures exchanges. Current futures prices for contracts traded at the major futures exchanges are reported each day in *The Wall Street Journal*. Our nearby *Work the Web* box shows how to get prices online, and Figure 16.1 reproduces a portion of the daily "Futures Prices" report of *The Wall Street Journal*.

This section of the *Journal* contains a box labelled "Exchange Abbreviations," which lists the major world futures exchanges and their exchange abbreviation codes. Elsewhere, the information is divided into sections according to categories of the underlying commodities or financial instruments. For example, the section "Grain and Oilseed Futures" lists futures price information for wheat, oats, soybeans, and similar crops. The sections "Metal Futures" and "Petroleum Futures" report price information for copper, gold, and petroleum products. There are separate sections for financial futures, which include "Currency," "Interest Rate," and "Index" categories.

Each section states the contract name, futures exchange, and contract size, along with price information for various contract maturities. For example, under "Metal Futures" we find the Copper contract traded at the Commodities Exchange (CMX), the COMEX (Division of the New York Mercantile Exchange). The standard contract size for copper is 25,000 pounds per contract. The futures price is quoted in cents per pound.

FIGURE 16.1 Futures Prices

THE WALL STREET JOURNAL.

FUTURES

Tuesday, December 13, 2005

Agriculture Futures

	OPEN	HIGH	LOW	SETTLE	CHG	LIFETIME HIGH	LIFETIME LOW	OPEN INT
Corn (CBT)-5,000 bu.; cents per bu.								
Dec	195.00	195.50	191.00	195.50	1.25	288.50	185.75	3,413
Mr06	207.00	209.00	204.25	208.75	1.00	276.50	199.50	471,834
Oats (CBT)-5,000 bu.; cents per bu.								
Dec	220.00	220.75	220.00	220.50	3.00	220.75	141.25	61
Mr06	205.00	206.00	201.75	205.00	...	206.00	146.50	9,224
Soybeans (CBT)-5,000 bu.; cents per bu.								
Jan	582.25	598.00	579.00	597.50	13.50	777.00	526.00	109,732
Mar	591.00	609.00	588.50	608.25	13.75	760.00	529.00	96,863
Soybean Meal (CBT)-100 tons; $ per ton.†								
Dec	188.50	196.00	188.00	196.00	7.50	244.80	159.20	1,184
Ja06	188.00	195.00	185.90	194.30	6.30	241.00	161.00	37,221
Soybean Oil (CBT)-60,000 lbs.; cents per lb.								
Dec	20.85	20.95	20.70	20.90	.03	26.94	19.50	308
Mr06	21.36	21.58	21.17	21.40	.03	26.45	19.70	70,068
Rough Rice (CBT)-2,000 cwt.; cents per cwt.								
Jan	784.00	785.00	772.00	782.00	-3.50	810.00	670.00	3,989
Mar	813.00	813.00	800.00	808.50	-4.00	823.00	690.00	3,757
Wheat (CBT)-5,000 bu.; cents per bu.								
Dec	300.00	304.00	298.00	304.00	4.50	406.00	292.50	479
Mr06	314.50	319.00	310.50	318.50	3.75	393.00	307.00	224,724
Wheat (KC)-5,000 bu.; cents per bu.								
Dec	355.00	355.00	351.50	353.00	2.00	392.50	321.00	181
Mr06	360.00	362.50	354.00	360.00	-.25	394.00	331.50	69,368
Wheat (MPLS)-5,000 bu.; cents per bu.								
Dec	366.50	369.00	361.00	367.00	7.00	410.00	332.00	42
Mr06	370.00	372.00	366.50	370.50	.50	399.00	340.75	21,651
Cattle-Feeder (CME)-50,000 lbs.; cents per lb.								
Jan	114.975	115.250	114.425	114.825	.650	117.900	95.800	15,666
Mar	113.600	114.500	113.600	114.325	.825	116.100	96.000	8,757
Cattle-Live (CME)-40,000 lbs.; cents per lb.								
Dec	93.500	93.825	92.700	93.725	1.250	94.450	80.200	15,670
Fb06	95.600	96.675	95.500	96.250	1.050	96.950	82.100	118,603
Hogs-Lean (CME)-40,000 lbs.; cents per lb.								
Dec	62.350	62.550	62.250	62.375	.250	65.650	51.000	6,519
Fb06	66.375	67.100	65.750	66.575	.725	68.300	55.100	75,154
Pork Bellies (CME)-40,000 lbs.; cents per lb.								
Feb	84.600	85.600	84.100	84.200	-1.400	98.400	74.500	1,345
Mar	84.850	85.200	83.975	83.975	-.825	98.000	75.000	145
Lumber (CME)-110,000 bd. ft., $ per 1,000 bd. ft.								
Jan	323.20	327.30	322.70	323.80	-3.20	359.50	276.00	2,682
Mar	336.00	342.40	336.00	339.50	-3.30	361.10	288.00	1,843
Milk (CME)-200,000 lbs., cents per lb.								
Dec	13.37	13.44	13.37	13.42	.04	13.65	12.00	2,149
Ja06	12.96	13.04	12.96	13.00	.04	13.30	11.90	2,105
Cocoa (NYBOT)-10 metric tons; $ per ton.								
Dec	1,476	1,487	1,487	1,485	1	1,887	1,315	366
Mr06	1,480	1,497	1,475	1,480	1	1,890	1,344	55,880
Coffee (NYBOT)-37,500 lbs.; cents per lb.								
Dec	96.50	96.15	95.25	95.40	-1.05	147.00	79.00	71
Mr06	100.45	101.20	98.00	98.30	-1.40	148.75	82.60	61,106
Sugar-World (NYBOT)-112,000 lbs.; cents per lb.								
Mar	13.63	13.90	13.63	13.81	-.15	14.06	6.61	298,011
May	13.69	13.93	13.69	13.87	-.08	14.05	7.65	78,829
Sugar-Domestic (NYBOT)-112,000 lbs.; cents per lb.								
Mar	21.20	21.50	21.20	21.40	.17	22.04	20.40	3,207
July	21.40	21.85	21.40	21.83	.36	22.04	20.88	3,539
Cotton (NYBOT)-50,000 lbs.; cents per lb.								
Mar	53.30	53.75	53.30	53.69	.28	69.00	48.30	79,800
May	53.95	54.38	53.95	54.27	.27	61.20	49.25	13,679
Orange Juice (NYBOT)-15,000 lbs.; cents per lb.								
Jan	129.60	130.80	128.50	130.40	-.20	130.80	81.50	21,133
Mar	131.50	132.60	130.50	132.45	-.05	133.00	87.25	11,591

Metal & Petroleum Futures

	OPEN	HIGH	LOW	SETTLE	CHG	LIFETIME HIGH	LIFETIME LOW	OPEN INT
Copper-High (CMX)-25,000 lbs.; cents per lb.								
Dec	216.20	219.90	215.30	217.30	1.75	219.90	99.00	5,363
Mr06	199.00	203.60	198.65	202.65	4.05	204.60	98.00	74,649
Gold (CMX)-100 troy oz.; $ per troy oz.								
Dec	528.40	530.70	519.50	521.00	-7.40	538.50	298.40	1,919
Fb06	530.60	533.00	522.90	524.10	-7.40	544.50	415.00	249,199
Apr	534.40	536.10	527.00	528.40	-7.40	548.40	418.00	12,068
June	538.40	541.00	531.00	532.80	-7.50	551.80	312.00	20,310
Dec	552.50	554.00	544.50	546.40	-7.60	565.60	338.00	10,717
Dc07	580.00	580.00	575.50	573.70	-7.80	592.50	368.00	7,111
Platinum (NYM)-50 troy oz.; $ per troy oz.								
Jan	1018.80	1018.80	984.00	995.90	-22.20	1026.00	870.00	11,093
Apr	1012.00	1012.00	990.00	1000.70	-22.10	1030.00	815.00	1,734
Silver (CMX)-5,000 troy oz.; cnts per troy oz.								
Dec	875.0	877.5	848.0	849.7	-29.5	917.0	447.0	1,236
Mr06	891.0	895.0	851.5	858.5	-29.7	934.5	662.5	105,114
Crude Oil, Light Sweet (NYM)-1,000 bbls.; $ per bbl.								
Jan	61.29	61.90	60.76	61.37	0.07	71.68	25.25	145,304
Feb	62.01	62.85	61.67	62.31	0.05	71.87	25.85	169,368
Mar	62.80	63.45	62.25	62.89	0.03	71.11	25.54	80,167
June	64.00	64.00	63.19	63.69	-0.03	70.30	23.75	46,284
Dec	64.04	64.68	64.04	64.35	-0.13	68.79	19.10	52,824
Dc07	63.45	63.83	63.45	63.46	-0.22	66.35	19.50	50,696
Heating Oil No. 2 (NYM)-42,000 gal.; $ per gal.								
Jan	1.7725	1.8425	1.7626	1.8365	.0640	2.2200	.9730	53,191
Feb	1.8230	1.8825	1.8106	1.8785	.0553	2.2250	1.0350	55,026
Gasoline-NY Unleaded (NYM)-42,000 gal.; $ per gal.								
Jan	1.6474	1.6620	1.6290	1.6459	-.0009	2.0200	1.3260	46,841
Feb	1.6949	1.7085	1.6800	1.6958	-.0011	2.0000	1.3620	36,001
Natural Gas (NYM)-10,000 MMBtu.; $ per MMBtu.								
Jan	14.900	15.780	14.851	15.378	.537	15.780	4.020	63,905
Feb	14.954	15.780	14.920	15.427	.514	15.780	3.850	59,199
Mar	14.815	15.550	14.800	15.287	.483	15.550	3.781	72,395
Apr	11.320	11.650	11.240	11.487	.233	11.680	3.786	38,275
May	10.915	11.154	10.855	11.037	.163	11.266	3.571	27,403
Oct	11.001	11.185	11.001	11.117	.133	11.390	3.732	27,082

Interest Rate Futures

	OPEN	HIGH	LOW	SETTLE	CHG	LIFETIME HIGH	LIFETIME LOW	OPEN INT
Treasury Bonds (CBT)-$100,000; pts 32nds of 100%								
Dec	112-01	112-12	111-30	112-04	3	119-07	106-08	25,520
Mr06	111-23	112-05	111-21	111-28	3	118-19	110-01	516,783
Treasury Notes (CBT)-$100,000; pts 32nds of 100%								
Dec	108-160	108-250	108-155	108-200	4.5	113-205	106-260	99,745
Mr06	108-075	108-190	108-070	108-125	4.5	112-300	106-220	1,611,879
5 Yr. Treasury Notes (CBT)-$100,000; pts 32nds of 100%								
Dec	106-005	106-045	105-310	106-010	3.0	108-295	105-115	25,322
Mr06	105-245	106-025	105-235	105-275	3.0	108-240	105-060	1,118,799
2 Yr. Treasury Notes (CBT)-$200,000; pts 32nds of 100%								
Dec	102-197	102-202	102-190	102-200	.7	103-280	102-097	31,763
Mr06	102-155	102-187	102-145	102-165	1.0	102-272	102-100	321,036
30 Day Federal Funds (CBT)-$5,000,000; 100 - daily avg.								
Dec	95.840	95.840	95.835	95.840	...	96.955	95.830	90,282
Fb06	95.525	95.530	95.520	95.530	...	96.290	95.500	123,646

	OPEN	HIGH	LOW	SETTLE	CHG	YIELD	CHG	OPEN INT
1 Month Libor (CME)-$3,000,000; pts of 100%								
Dec	95.6250	95.6250	95.6200	95.6200	...	4.3800	...	18,611
Ja06	95.5050	95.5125	95.5000	95.5025	-.0025	4.4975	.0025	10,338
Eurodollar (CME)-$1,000,000; pts of 100%								
Dec	95.4950	95.4975	95.4900	95.4925	-.0025	4.5075	.0025	1,114,476
Mr06	95.2150	95.2800	95.1950	95.2200	...	4.7800	...	1,165,170
June	95.0950	95.1900	95.0900	95.1300	.0350	4.8700	-.0350	1,327,539
Dec	95.1200	95.2100	95.1200	95.1600	.0350	4.8400	-.0350	1,093,585

Currency Futures

	OPEN	HIGH	LOW	SETTLE	CHG	LIFETIME HIGH	LIFETIME LOW	OPEN INT
Japanese Yen (CME)-¥12,500,000; $ per 100¥								
Dec	.8355	.8365	.8307	.8342	-.0013	1.0084	.8252	132,895
Mr06	.8442	.8453	.8395	.8429	-.0013	.9660	.8338	85,668
Canadian Dollar (CME)-CAD 100,000; $ per CAD								
Dec	.8692	.8710	.8668	.8696	.0010	.8710	.7480	62,682
Mr06	.8713	.8729	.8690	.8718	.0010	.8729	.7927	75,707
British Pound (CME)-£62,500; $ per £								
Dec	1.7754	1.7782	1.7653	1.7695	-.0062	1.9090	1.7046	59,282
Mr06	1.7759	1.7780	1.7651	1.7692	-.0062	1.8550	1.7050	50,218
Swiss Franc (CME)-CHF 125,000; $ per CHF								
Dec	.7758	.7777	.7717	.7737	-.0012	.8922	.7548	56,612
Mr06	.7822	.7839	.7778	.7799	-.0012	.8888	.7610	53,669
Australian Dollar (CME)-AUD 100,000; $ per AUD								
Dec	.7556	.7568	.7525	.7543	-.0006	.7835	.6664	51,686
Mr06	.7543	.7549	.7506	.7524	-.0006	.7675	.6920	27,901
Mexican Peso (CME)-MXN 500,000; $ per 10MXN								
Dec	.93800	.94175	.93400	.93950	-.00075	96025	.82400	44,845
Mr06	.93100	.93500	.92600	.93175	-.00075	.95150	.81300	63,680
Euro (CME)-€125,000; $ per €								
Dec	1.1957	1.1992	1.1910	1.1957	.0005	1.3740	1.1661	135,566
Mr06	1.2015	1.2047	1.1966	1.2013	.0005	1.3789	1.1719	54,687

Index Futures

	OPEN	HIGH	LOW	SETTLE	CHG	LIFETIME HIGH	LIFETIME LOW	OPEN INT
DJ Industrial Average (CBT)-$10 x index								
Dec	10775	10872	10757	10838	64	11066	10037	31,413
Mr06	10827	10932	10810	10892	65	11029	10257	25,433
Mini DJ Industrial Average (CBT)-$5 x index								
Dec	10776	10877	10758	10838	64	10987	10060	77,356
Mr06	10826	10932	10810	10892	65	11036	10238	31,709
S&P 500 Index (CME)-$250 x index								
Dec	1260.20	1273.00	1259.10	1268.90	7.80	1274.50	1071.50	242,675
Mr06	1269.60	1281.30	1267.20	1277.10	7.90	1282.80	1075.50	491,647
Mini S&P 500 (CME)-$50 x index								
Dec	1261.25	1273.25	1259.25	1269.00	8.00	1274.50	1171.75	735,914
Mr06	1269.50	1281.50	1267.25	1277.00	7.75	1282.50	1179.00	751,490
Nasdaq 100 (CME)-$100 x index								
Dec	1698.50	1712.00	1695.00	1706.50	6.50	1719.50	1430.50	41,825
Mr06	1717.50	1731.00	1711.00	1724.00	7.00	1734.50	1523.50	37,042
Mini Nasdaq 100 (CME)-$20 x index								
Dec	1700.0	1713.5	1694.5	1706.5	6.5	1719.0	1486.0	282,304
Mr06	1717.5	1731.0	1711.5	1724.0	7.0	1745.0	1539.0	187,497
Russell 1000 (NYBOT)-$500 x index								
Dec	686.00	686.15	686.00	690.30	4.00	692.15	636.70	16,882
Mr06	690.75	695.75	690.50	695.00	4.10	695.75	684.00	81,497
U.S. Dollar Index (NYBOT)-$1,000 x index								
Dec	90.32	90.57	90.14	90.34	.03	92.53	81.20	14,516
Mr06	89.98	90.37	89.82	90.06	.03	92.20	86.00	20,103

Electricity Price Indexes

Explanatory Notes

Figures represent weighted average price of electricity traded at the indicated hubs. All indexes quoted in dollars per megawatt hour; volumes in megawatt hours. **Firm:** Electricity that meets the minimum criteria of being Financially Firm and backed by liquidating damages. **Non Firm:** Electricity subject to interruption at any time. **On Peak:** 16-hour period of heavy demand. **Off Peak:** Eight-hour period of light demand. **r:** Revised. **n.q.:** No quote. **s:** Surveyed data. **n.a.:** One-day lag for non-firm, not available for others. **For questions and additional hubs from Dow Jones please call 609-520-4663.**

Tuesday, December 13, 2005

DJ COB California-Oregon and Nevada-Oregon Borders

	DEC 13	DEC 12	DEC 11	DEC 10
FIRM				
On Peak	132.02	134.00	n.q.	136.72
Volume	5,664	6,992	n.q.	7,728
Off Peak	105.58	109.48	n.q.	107.33
Volume	936	2,096	n.q.	2,664
NON FIRM				
On Peak	n.a.	s107.20	n.q.	s109.38
Volume	n.a.	0	n.q.	0
Off Peak	n.a.	s87.58	s98.53	s85.86
Volume	n.a.	0	0	0

Source: Reprinted from *The Wall Street Journal*, December 14, 2005, via Copyright Clearance Center, Inc. © 2005 Dow Jones & Company, Inc. All Rights Reserved Worldwide.

FUTURES QUOTES

EXAMPLE 16.1

In Figure 16.1, locate the gold and wheat contracts. Where are they traded? What are the contract sizes for the gold and wheat contracts and how are their futures prices specified?

The gold contract trades on the CMX, the COMEX Division of the New York Mercantile Exchange. One gold contract calls for delivery of 100 troy ounces. The gold futures price is quoted in dollars per ounce.

Wheat contracts are traded on the Chicago Board of Trade (CBT), the Kansas City Board of Trade (KC), and the Minneapolis Grain Exchange (MPLS). One wheat contract calls for delivery of 5,000 bushels of wheat, and wheat futures prices are quoted in cents per bushel.

For futures prices and price charts, visit these-websites: www.pcquote.com/ futures

The reporting format for each futures contract is similar. For example, the first column of a price listing gives the contract delivery/maturity month. For each maturity month, the next five columns report futures prices observed during the previous day at the opening of trading ("Open"), the highest intraday price ("High"), the lowest intraday price ("Low"), the price at close of trading ("Settle"), and the change in the settle price from the previous day ("Chg").

The next two columns ("Lifetime," "High" and "Low") report the highest and lowest prices for each maturity observed over the previous year. Finally, the last column reports open interest for each contract maturity, which is the number of contracts outstanding at the end of that day's trading. The last row below these eight columns summarizes trading activity for all maturities by reporting aggregate trading volume and open interest for all contract maturities.

By now, we see that four of the contract terms for futures contracts are stated in the futures prices listing. These are:

1. The identity of the underlying commodity or financial instrument.

2. The futures contract size.

3. The futures maturity date.

4. The futures price.

Exact contract terms for the delivery process are available from the appropriate futures exchange on request.

FUTURES PRICES

EXAMPLE 16.2

In Figure 16.1, locate the soybean contract with the greatest open interest. Explain the information provided.

The soybean (or just "bean") contract with the greatest open interest is specified by the contract maturity with the greatest number of contracts outstanding, so the January 2006 contract is the one we seek. One contract calls for delivery of 5,000 bushels of beans (a bushel, of course, is four pecks). The closing price for delivery at that maturity is stated as a quote in cents per bushel. Since there are 5,000 bushels in a single contract, the total contract value is the quoted price per bushel times 5,000, or 597.50 cents × 5000 or $29,875 for the January contracts.

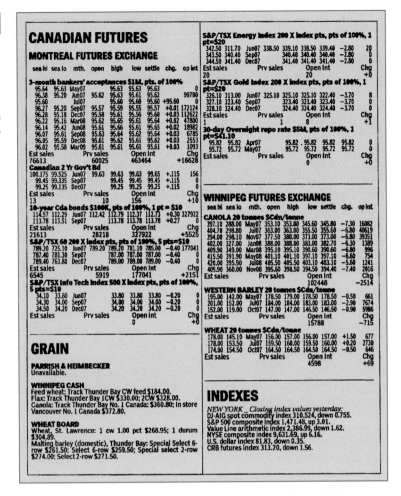

FIGURE 16.2

Canadian Futures Contracts

Source: *The Globe and Mail*, April 8, 2007. Reprinted with permission from *The Globe and Mail*.

To get an idea of the magnitude of financial futures trading, take a look at the first entry under "Interest Rate Futures" in Figure 16.1, the CBT Treasury bond contract. One contract calls for the delivery of $100,000 in par value bonds. The total open interest in this one contract is often close to half a million contracts. Thus, the total face value represented by these contracts is close to half a *trillion* dollars. Figure 16.2 shows the Canadian futures contracts available at the Montreal and Winnipeg Futures Exchanges.

Who does all this trading? The orders originate from money managers around the world and are sent to the various exchanges' trading floors for execution. On the floor, the orders are executed by professional traders who are quite aggressive at getting the best prices. On the floor and off, futures traders can be recognized by their colourful jackets. As *The Wall Street Journal* article in the nearby *Investment Updates* box reports, these garish jackets add a touch of clamour to the trading pits. In the next section we will discuss how and why futures contracts are used for speculation and hedging.

CHECK THIS

16.1a   What is a forward contract?

16.1b   What is a futures contract, and why is it different from a forward contract?

16.1c   What is a futures price?

Garish Jackets Add to Clamour of Chicago Pits

For the inhabitants of Chicago's futures and options trading pits, dressing for success means throwing good taste to the wind.

Take James Oliff, a trader in the Chicago Mercantile Exchange's newly opened Mexican peso futures pit. Daily, he dons a multicoloured jacket bedecked with cacti and sombreros, in keeping, he says, with the "theme" of the product he trades.

Twisting and turning to display his gaudy garb, the veteran currency options trader explains: "I wanted a jacket that would be easy to pick out in the crowd. Runners get orders to me more quickly, and clerks find me faster when I'm trying to do trades."

It's important to have what veterans of the mayhem describe as "pit presence" to make money in the crowded and noisy trading pits of the Merc and the Chicago Board of Trade. That elusive quality, they say, involves such stratagems as finding the best spot in the pit from which to communicate with clerks and other traders, maintaining good posture and using a loud, well-projected voice and forceful hand signals to attract attention.

Increasingly, in places such as the CBOT's bond pit, where hundreds of people cram into a space only slightly larger than a tennis court, garb is being used to grab attention. Hence the insatiable demand for magenta, lime-green, and silver-lamé jackets, featuring designs that run the gamut from the Mighty Morphin Power Rangers to bucolic farmhouses and sunflowers.

"I'd come in buck naked if I could," says Thomas Burke, a trader in the CBOT's overpopulated bond-futures pit. "As it is, the more obnoxious the jacket, the better. The louder it is, the more I can rest my voice and let my jacket draw the attention."

Chicago's exchanges quietly tolerate the proliferation of the garish trading jackets. Dress codes ban jeans and still require members to wear shirts with collars and don ties (although some of these may be little more than strings, having been worn daily for more than a decade). The rules also say that trading jackets must have sleeves that come below the elbow and contain pockets into which the traders stuff their trading cards and other documents. But during the past decade, traders say, exchange efforts to regulate the colour and design of the jackets, or gently encourage their wearers to opt for something in quiet good taste, have been dropped as an exercise in futility.

Robert Pierce, who trades corn options at the CBOT, says the old brown jackets made him look like a UPS delivery man. "When someone gave me a UPS cap on the floor one day as a joke, I decided it was time for a change of style," he says. The switch, to a comparatively tasteful multicoloured geometric pattern, has the added advantage of disguising pen and pencil marks, adds his wife, Cathy.

Dawn Guera, a former clerk at the CBOT, has spun the traders' need to stand out in the crowd into a four-year-old business designing and manufacturing custom trading jackets. Traders wander into her storefront operation next door to the CBOT to choose from dozens of fabrics with designs ranging from a subdued Harvard University crest on a crimson background to a slinky leopard skin pattern or turquoise frogs cavorting on a neon-pink background.

"Everyone has their own hobbies and interests and wants the jackets to reflect that," she explains, pointing to fabrics with designs of dice and cards aimed at traders willing to acknowledge their addiction to gambling in the markets. "It's like a vanity license plate."

And, at $50 a pop, traders are willing, even eager, to order multiple jackets, Ms. Guera says, especially since many believe that washing or dry cleaning a "lucky" jacket will launder out the luck in it. Some, like the CBOT's Gilbert Leistner, take a seasonal approach to jackets: in summer and fall he wears a brightly coloured turquoise and aquamarine jacket decorated with tropical fish, but switches to a Southwestern theme come Thanksgiving.

"It's my version of going south for the winter," he says, adding he's contemplating donning something in gold lamé for New Year's celebrations.

Ms. Guera, a former sportswear designer in New York, says traders have a long way to go before they'll pull themselves off the worst-dressed lists. To be sure, some of the early emphasis on flashiness is easing a bit, she says, and demands for fluorescent geometric patterns are giving way to a new trend favouring subtler paisley-type patterns with lapels, cuffs, and pockets in a contrasting, solid colour.

"I think it would be great if we could really push the fashion envelope here and remove the collar and cuffs from the jackets, or even persuade the exchanges to let traders wear vests instead," she says. "I'm looking for a way of making this whole trading process more artistic and creative."

16.2 Why Futures?

Futures contracts can be used for speculation or for hedging. Certainly, hedging is the major economic purpose for the existence of futures markets. However, a viable futures market cannot exist without participation by both hedgers and speculators. Hedgers transfer price risk to speculators, and speculators absorb price risk. Hedging and speculating are complementary activities. We next discuss speculating with futures; then we discuss hedging with futures.

Speculating with Futures

To learn more about futures, visit www.usafutures.com

Suppose you are thinking about speculating on commodity prices because you believe you can accurately forecast future prices most of the time. The most convenient way to speculate is with futures contracts. If you believe that the price of gold will go up, then you can speculate on this belief by buying gold futures. Alternatively, if you think gold will fall in price, you can speculate by selling gold futures. To be more precise, you think that the current futures price is either too high or too low relative to what gold prices will be in the future.

long position In futures jargon, refers to the contract buyer. A long position profits from a futures price increase.

Buying futures is often referred to as "going long," or establishing a **long position**. Selling futures is often called "going short," or establishing a **short position**. A **speculator** accepts price risk in order to bet on the direction of prices by going long or short.

short position In futures jargon, refers to the seller. A short position profits from a futures price decrease.

To illustrate the basics of speculating, suppose you believe the price of gold will go up. In particular, the current futures price for delivery in three months is $900 per ounce. You think that gold will be selling for more than that three months from now, so you go long 100 three-month gold contracts. Each gold contract represents 100 troy ounces, so 100 contracts represents 10,000 ounces of gold with a total contract value of $10,000 \times \$900 = \$9,000,000$. In futures jargon, this is a $9 million long gold position.

speculator Trader who accepts price risk by going long or short to bet on the future direction of prices.

Now, suppose your belief turns out to be correct, and, at contract maturity, the market price of gold is $920 per ounce. From your long futures position, you accept delivery of 10,000 troy ounces of gold at $900 per ounce and immediately sell the gold at the market price of $920 per ounce. Your profit is $20 per ounce, or $10,000 \times \$20 = \$200,000$, less applicable commissions.

Of course, if your belief turned out wrong and gold fell in price, you would lose money since you must still buy the 10,000 troy ounces at $900 per ounce to fulfill your futures contract obligation. Thus, if gold fell to, say, $890 per ounce, you would lose $10 per ounce, or $10,000 \times \$10 = \$100,000$. As this example suggests, futures speculation is risky, but it is potentially rewarding if you can accurately forecast the direction of future commodity price movements.

As another example of commodity speculation, suppose an analysis of weather patterns has convinced you that the coming winter months will be warmer than usual, and that this will cause heating oil prices to fall as unsold inventories accumulate. You can speculate on this belief by selling heating oil futures.

The standard contract size for heating oil is 42,000 gallons. Suppose you go short 10 contracts at a futures price of 55 cents per gallon. This represents a short position with a total contract value of $10 \times 42,000 \times \$.55 = \$231,000$.

If, at contract maturity, the price of heating oil is, say, 50 cents per gallon, you could buy 420,000 gallons for delivery to fulfill your futures commitment. Your profit would be 5 cents per gallon, or $10 \times 42,000 \times \$.05 = \$21,000$, less applicable commissions. Of course, if heating oil prices rise by 5 cents per gallon, you would lose $21,000 instead. Again, speculation is risky but rewarding if you can accurately forecast the weather.

WHAT WOULD JUAN VALDEZ DO?

EXAMPLE 16.3

After an analysis of political currents in Central and South America, you conclude that future coffee prices will be lower than currently indicated by futures prices. Would you go long or short? Analyze the impact of a swing in coffee prices of 10 cents per pound in either direction if you have a 10-contract position, where each contract calls for delivery of 37,500 pounds of coffee.

You would go short since you expect prices to decline. You're short 10 contracts, so you must deliver $10 \times 37{,}500 = 375{,}000$ pounds of coffee. If coffee prices fall to 10 cents below your originally contracted futures price, then you make 10 cents per pound, or \$37,500. Of course, if you're wrong and prices are 10 cents higher, you lose \$37,500.

Hedging with Futures

Many businesses face price risk when their activities require them to hold a working inventory. For example, suppose you own a regional gasoline distributorship and must keep a large operating inventory of gas on hand, say, 5 million gallons. In futures jargon, this gasoline inventory represents a long position in the underlying commodity.

If gas prices go up, your inventory goes up in value; but if gas prices fall, your inventory value goes down. Your risk is not trivial, since even a 5-cent fluctuation in the gallon price of gas will cause your inventory to change in value by \$250,000. Because you are in the business of distributing gas, and not speculating on gas prices, you would like to remove this price risk from your business operations. Acting as a **hedger**, you seek to transfer price risk by taking a futures position opposite to an existing position in the underlying commodity or financial instrument. In this case, the value of your gasoline inventory can be protected by selling gasoline futures contracts.

hedger Trader who seeks to transfer price risk by taking a futures position opposite to an existing position in the underlying commodity or financial instrument.

Gasoline futures are traded on the New York Mercantile Exchange (NYM), and the standard contract size for gasoline futures is 42,000 gallons per contract. Since you wish to hedge 5 million gallons, you need to sell $5{,}000{,}000 / 42{,}000 = 119$ gasoline contracts. With this hedge in place, any change in the value of your long inventory position is cancelled by an approximately equal but opposite change in value of your short futures position. Because you are using this short position for hedging purposes, it is called a **short hedge**.

short hedge Sale of futures to offset potential losses from falling prices.

Many Canadian companies operate in natural resource industries and therefore depend heavily on commodity prices. These companies can reduce their risk by short-hedging using futures contracts. For example Placer Dome Company can short S&P/TSX Gold Index futures contracts. Airline companies, such as West Jet and Air Canada, can protect their profits against increasing fuel prices by getting into long S&P/TSX Energy Index contracts.

By hedging, you have greatly reduced or even eliminated the possibility of a loss from a decline in the price of gasoline. However, you have also eliminated the possibility of a gain from a price increase. This is an important point. If gas prices rise, you would have a substantial loss on your futures position, offsetting the gain on your inventory. Overall, you are long the underlying commodity because you own it; you offset the risk in your long position with a short position in futures.

Of course, your business activities may also include distributing other petroleum products like heating oil and natural gas. Futures contracts are available for these petroleum products also, and therefore they may be used for inventory hedging purposes.

SHORT HEDGING

Suppose you have an inventory of 1.2 million pounds of soybean oil. Describe how you would hedge this position.

Since you are long in the commodity, bean oil, you need to go short in (sell) futures. A single bean oil contract calls for delivery of 60,000 pounds of oil. To hedge your position, you need to sell 1.2 million / 60,000 = 20 futures contracts.

long hedge Purchase of futures to offset potential losses from rising prices.

The opposite of a short hedge is a **long hedge**. In this case, you do not own the underlying commodity, but you need to acquire it in the future. You can lock in the price you will pay in the future by buying, or going long in, futures contracts. In effect, you are short the underlying commodity because you must buy it in the future. You offset your short position with a long position in futures.

MORE HEDGING

You need to buy 600,000 pounds of orange juice in three months. How can you hedge the price risk associated with this future purchase? What price will you effectively lock in? One orange juice contract calls for delivery of 15,000 pounds of juice concentrate.

You are effectively short orange juice since you don't currently own it but plan to buy it. To offset the risk in this short position, you need to go long in futures. You should buy 600,000 / 15,000 = 40 contracts. The price you lock in is the original futures price.

EVEN MORE HEDGING

Suppose your company will receive payment of £10 million in six months, which will then be converted to US dollars. What is the standard futures contract size for British pounds? Describe how you could use futures contracts to lock in an exchange rate from British pounds to US dollars for your planned receipt of £10 million, including how many contracts are required.

Your company will be receiving £10 million, so you are effectively long pounds. To hedge, you need to short (sell) futures contracts. Put differently, you will want to exchange pounds for dollars. By selling a futures contract, you obligate yourself to deliver the underlying commodity, in this case currency, in exchange for payment in dollars. One British pound contract calls for delivery of £62,500. You will therefore sell £10 million / £62,500 = 160 contracts.

CHECK THIS ✓

16.2a   What is a long position in futures? A short position?

16.2b   For a speculator, when is a long position appropriate and when is a short position appropriate?

16.2c   What is a long hedge? A short hedge?

16.2d   For a hedger, when is a long hedge appropriate and when is a short hedge appropriate?

16.3 Futures Trading Accounts

For a list of online futures brokers visit the Commodities & Futures section of Investor Links at www.investorlinks.com

A futures exchange, like a stock exchange, allows only exchange members to trade on the exchange. Exchange members may be firms or individuals trading for their own accounts, or they may be brokerage firms handling trades for customers. Some firms conduct both trading and brokerage operations on the exchange. In this section, we discuss the mechanics of a futures trading account as it pertains to a customer with a trading account at a brokerage firm.

The biggest customer trading accounts are those of corporations that use futures to manage their business risks and money managers who hedge or speculate with clients' funds. Many individual investors also have futures trading accounts of their own, although speculation by individual investors is not recommended without a full understanding of all risks involved. Whether a futures trading account is large or small, the mechanics of account trading are essentially the same.

There are several essential things to know about futures trading accounts. The first thing is that margin is required. In this way, futures accounts resemble the stock margin accounts we discussed in Chapter 3; however, the specifics are quite different. **Futures margin** is a deposit of funds in a futures trading account dedicated to covering potential losses from an outstanding futures position. An **initial margin** is required when a futures position is first established. The amount varies according to contract type and size, but margin requirements for futures contracts usually range between 2 percent and 5 percent of total contract value. Initial margin is the same for both long and short futures positions.

The second thing to know about a futures trading account is that contract values in outstanding futures positions are marked to market on a daily basis. **Marking-to-market** is a process whereby gains and losses on outstanding futures positions are recognized at the end of each day's trading.

For example, suppose one morning you call your broker and instruct her to go long five Treasury bond contracts for your account. A few minutes later, she calls back to confirm order execution at a futures price of 110. Since the Treasury bond contract size is $100,000 par value, contract value is 110% × $100,000 = $110,000 per contract. Thus, the total position value for your order is $550,000, for which your broker requires $25,000 initial margin. In addition, your broker requires that at least $20,000 in **maintenance margin** be present at all times. The necessary margin funds are immediately wired from a bank account to your futures account.

Now, at the end of trading that day Treasury bond futures close at a price of 108. Overnight, all accounts are marked to market. Your Treasury bond futures position is marked to $108,000 per contract, or $540,000 total position value, representing a loss of $10,000. This loss is deducted from your initial margin to leave only $15,000 of margin funds in your account.

Since the maintenance margin level on your account is $20,000, your broker will issue a **margin call** on your account. Essentially, your broker will notify you that you must immediately restore your margin level to the initial margin level of $25,000, or else she will close out your Treasury bond futures position at whatever trading price is available at the exchange.

This example illustrates what happens when a futures trading account is marked to market and the resulting margin funds fall below the maintenance margin level. The alternative, and more pleasant, experience occurs when a futures price moves in your favour, and the marking-to-market process adds funds to your account. In this case,

futures margin
Deposit of funds in a futures trading account dedicated to covering potential losses from an outstanding futures position.

initial margin
Amount required when a futures contract is first bought or sold. Initial margin varies with the type and size of a contract, but it is the same for long and short futures positions.

marking-to-market
In futures trading accounts, the process whereby gains and losses on outstanding futures positions are recognized on a daily basis.

maintenance margin
The minimum margin level required in a futures trading account at all times.

margin call Notification to increase the margin level in a trading account.

marking-to-market gains can be withdrawn from your account so long as remaining margin funds are not less than the initial margin level.

The third thing to know about a futures trading account is that a futures position can be closed out at any time; you do not have to hold a contract until maturity. A futures position is closed out by simply instructing your broker to close out your position. To actually close out a position, your broker will enter a **reverse trade** for your account.

reverse trade A trade that closes out a previously established futures position by taking the opposite position.

A reverse trade works like this: Suppose you are currently short five Treasury bond contracts, and you instruct your broker to close out the position. Your broker responds by going long five Treasury bond contracts for your account. In this case, going long five contracts is a reverse trade because it cancels exactly your previous five-contract short position. At the end of the day in which you make your reverse trade, your account will be marked to market at the futures price realized by the reverse trade. From then on, your position is closed out, and no more gains or losses will be realized.

This example illustrates that closing out a futures position is no more difficult than initially entering into a position. There are two basic reasons to close out a futures position before contract maturity. The first is to capture a current gain or loss, without realizing further price risk. The second is to avoid the delivery requirement that comes from holding a futures contract until it matures. In fact, over 98 percent of all futures contracts are closed out before contract maturity, which indicates that less than 2 percent of all futures contracts result in delivery of the underlying commodity or financial instrument.

Before closing this section, let's briefly list the three essential things to know about a futures trading account as discussed above:

1. Margin is required.
2. Futures accounts are marked to market daily.
3. A futures position can be closed out any time by a reverse trade.

Understanding the items in this list is important to anyone planning to use a futures trading account.

CHECK THIS ✓

16.3a What are the three essential things you should know about a futures trading account?

16.3b What is meant by initial margin for a futures position? What is meant by maintenance margin for a futures position?

16.3c Explain the process of marking-to-market a futures trading account. What is a margin call, and when is one issued?

16.3d How is a futures position closed out by a reverse trade? What proportion of all futures positions are closed out by reverse trades rather than by delivery at contract maturity?

16.4 Cash Prices versus Futures Prices

We now turn to the relationship between today's price of some commodity or financial instrument and its futures price. We begin by examining current cash prices.

Cash Prices

cash price Price of a commodity or financial instrument for current delivery. Also called the *spot price*.

cash market Market in which commodities or financial instruments are traded for essentially immediate delivery. Also called the *spot market*.

The **cash price** of a commodity or financial instrument is the price quoted for current delivery. The cash price is also called the *spot price*, as in "on the spot." In futures jargon, terms like "spot gold" or "cash wheat" are used to refer to commodities being sold for current delivery in what is called the **cash market** or the *spot market*.

Figure 16.3 reproduces the "Cash Prices" column of *The Wall Street Journal*, published the same day as the "Futures Prices" column seen in Figure 16.1. The column is divided into sections according to commodity categories. For example, the first section, "Grains and Feeds," lists spot price information for wheat, corn, soybeans, and similar crops. Other commodity sections include "Foods," "Fats and Oils," "Metals," and "Precious Metals." Each section gives commodity names along with cash market prices for the last two days of trading and one year earlier.

FIGURE 16.3

Commodity Cash Prices

Source: Reprinted by permission of *The Wall Street Journal*, May 8, 2003, via Copyright Clearance Center, Inc. © 2003 Dow Jones & Company, Inc. All Rights Reserved Worldwide.

Cash Prices December 13, 2005

	LO/HI RANGE TUE	TUE	MON	YEAR AGO
Grains and Feeds				
Barley, top-quality Mpls., bu	u2.8	sp	2.75	2.5
Bran, wheat middlings, KC ton	u76	81	76.5	63
Corn, No. 2 yel. Cent. Ill. bu	bpu1.895	sp	1.885	1.86
Corn Gluten Feed, Midwest, ton	uw48	60	53.5	55
Cottonseed Meal, ton	uw165	sp	155	120
Hominy Feed, Cent. Ill. ton	uw50	60	53	49
Meat-Bonemeal, 50% pro Ill. ton	uw152	157.5	157.5	177.5
Oats, No. 2 milling, Mpls., bu	u2.28	2.3	2.2275	1.81
Sorghum, (Milo) No. 2 Gulf cwt	u4.35	4.44	4.38	4.17
Soybean Meal, Cent. Ill., rail, ton 48%	u196	202	193	166.7
Soybeans, No. 1 yel Cent. Ill., bu	bpu5.84	sp	5.71	5.43
Wheat, Spring 14%-pro Mpls bu.	u4.805	4.955	4.9675	4.755
Wheat, No. 2 sft red, St.Lou. bu	bpu3.075	sp	3.035	3.395
Wheat, hard, KC, bu	4.355	sp	4.3575	4.25
Wheat, No. 1 sft wht, del Port Ore	u3.44	sp	3.41	3.96
Foods				
Beef, Carcass Equiv. Index Value, choice 1-3,600-900 lbs.	u144.89	sp	144.05	129.7
Beef, Carcass Equiv. Index Value, select 1-3,600-900 lbs.	u133.62	sp	133.5	123.09
Broilers, Dressed "A" lb.	ux.7019	sp	.7019	.6756
Broilers, 12-Cty Comp Wtd Av	uw.6442	sp	.6442	.6748
Butter, AA, Chgo., lb.	u1.37	sp	1.37	1.55
Cheddar Cheese, barrels, Chgo lb.	n139.75	sp	139	139.75
Cheddar Cheese, blocks, Chgo lb.	n143.5	sp	143.5	142.25
Milk, Non-fat Dry, Chgo	96.25	sp	96.25	86
Cocoa, Ivory Coast, $metric ton	z	sp	1,686	1,833
Coffee, Brazilian, Comp.	n.9702	sp	.9395	z
Coffee, Colombian, NY lb.	n1.0703	sp	1.0392	z
Eggs, Lge white, Chgo doz.	u.61	.7	.655	.725
Flour, hard winter KC cwt	11.3	sp	11.3	11.3
Hams, 17-20 lbs, Mid-US lb fob	u.82	sp	z	.79
Hogs, Iowa-S.Minn. avg. cwt	u59.93	sp	61.44	68.41
Hogs, Sioux Falls, SD avg cwt	u44	45	45.5	47
Pork Bellies, 12-14 lbs Mid-US lb	u.75	sp	z	.91
Pork Loins, 13-19 lbs, Mid-US lb	u.96	1.04	1	1.125
Steers, Tex.-Okla. ch avg cwt	z	sp	91	83.96
Steers, Feeder, Okl Cty, av cwt	u123.38	sp	122.125	111.94
Sugar, cane, raw, world, lb. fob	14.97	sp	15.08	10.02
Fats and Oils				
Corn Oil, crd wet/dry mill	u-s25.5	26.5	26	27.25
Grease, choice white, Chgo lb.	n.17	sp	a.17	.16625
Lard, Chgo lb.	u.1725	sp	.1725	.26
Soybean Oil, crd, Central Ill. Lb.	u.2055	.2105	.2077	.21535
Tallow, bleachable, Chgo lb.	n.165	sp	.165	.1675
Tallow, edible, Chgo lb.	u.19	sp	.19	.175

	TUE	MON	YEAR AGO
Fibers and Textiles			
Burlap, 10 oz 40-in NY yd	nw.4375	.4375	.4125
Cotton, 1 1/16 str lw-md Mphs lb	.5119	.5116	.4138
Wool, 64s Staple, Terr. Del. Lb.	uw1.4	1.4	2.15
Miscellaneous			
Hides, hvy native steers lb., fob	u78.5-80.5	77.5-80.5	82
Precious Metals			
Gold, troy oz.			
Engelhard indus bullion	524.04	538.06	438.49
Engelhard fabric prods	563.34	578.42	471.38
Handy & Harman base price	522.50	536.50	437.10

Complete futures prices and futures options data can be found at **wsj.com/free**

	TUE	WED	YEAR AGO
Handy & Harman fabric price	564.30	579.42	472.07
London fixing AM 522.80 PM	522.50	536.50	437.10
Krugerrand, whol	ae526.80	533.70	442.25
Maple Leaf, troy oz.	ae542.67	549.85	458.06
American Eagle, troy oz.	ae542.67	549.85	458.06
Platinum, (Free Mkt.)	995.00	1004.00	833.00
Platinum, indust (Engelhard)	998.00	1019.00	833.00
Platinum, fabrc prd (Engelhard)	1098.00	1119.00	933.00
Palladium, indust (Engelhard)	274.00	295.00	190.00
Palladium, fabrc prd (Engelhard)	374.00	395.00	290.00
Silver, troy oz.			
Engelhard indust bullion	8.580	9.170	6.770
Engelhard fabric prods	10.296	11.004	7.989
Handy & Harman base price	8.500	9.110	6.755
Handy & Harman fabric price	10.200	10.932	7.971
London Fixing (in pounds)			
Spot (U.S. equiv. $8.7400)	4.9447	5.2296	3.5106
Coins, whol $1,000 face val	a6,053	6,214	4,845
Metals			
Aluminum Comex lb.	1.037	1.022	0.874
Antimony, RN Spot, $/lb.	d1.85-87	1.85-87	1.38
Copper, high gr lb., Cmx sp price	2.173	2.1555	1.444
Lead, RN NA Solder, cts./lb.	d75.218	75.218	64.663
St. Steel Scrap, US, $/gross ton	d1245	1245	1550
Tin, RN NA Solder, cts./lb.	d457.811	459.344	567.134
Zinc, RN NA Dealer, cts./lb.	d86.031	87.097	55.459

a-Asked. b-Bid. bp-Country elevator bids to producers. c-Corrected. d-Ryan's Notes h-Reuters. e-Manfra, Tordella & Brookes, Inc. n-Nominal. na-Not available. r-Rail bids. s-high price-asked, low price-bid. u-U.S. Dept. of Agriculture. w-weekly price. x-Less than truckloads. z-Not quoted. xx-f.o.b tankcars. sp-Single price.

Oil Prices December 13, 2005

CRUDE GRADES	TUE	MON	YR AGO
Offshore-d			
European "spot" or free market prices			
Forties	59.65	58.22	38.35
Brent	58.85	57.42	37.25
Bonny lt.	59.55	58.12	36.15
Urals-Medit.	55.85	54.27	32.45
Domestic-f			
Spot market			
W. Tex. Int Cush (5550-6082) (Jan)	61.38	61.31	41.83
W. Tex.sour, Midl (5048-5543)	56.08	56.01	38.08
LA sweet St.James (5675-6050)	61.78	61.51	41.83
Al. No. Slope Pacific Del.	59.22	c59.15	35.09

Open-Market crude oil values in Northwest Europe around 17:50 GMT in dlrs per barrel, for main loading ports in country of origin for prompt loading, except as indicated.

	TUE	MON	YR AGO
Refined Products			
Fuel Oil, No. 2 NY gal.	1.7740	1.7098	1.2733
Diesel Fuel, 0.05 S. NY harbor low sulfur	1.8003	1.7338	1.3033
Gasoline, unlded, premium NY gal. non-oxygenated	1.7734	1.7743	1.0905
Gasoline, unlded, premium NY gal. Oxygenated	1.7822	1.7843	1.0855
Gasoline, unlded, reg. NY gal. non-oxygenated	1.6547	1.6468	1.0568
Gasoline, unlded, reg. NY gal. Oxygenated	1.6209	1.6168	1.0568
Gasoline, CARBOB, reg. LA gal.	m1.6550	1.5750	1.1700
Propane, non-tet, Mont Belvieu, Texas, gal.	1.1488	1.0850	.7450
Propane, wet-tet, Mont Belvieu, Texas, gal.	1.1475	1.0863	.7625
Butane, normal, Mont Belvieu, Texas, gal.	1.3675	1.3238	.9050
Raw Products			
Natural gas Henry Hub, $ per mmbtu	15.410	14.800	6.840

a-Asked. b-Bid. c-Corrected. d-As of 11 a.m. ET in Northwest Europe. f-As of 4 p.m. ET. Refiners' posted buying prices are in parentheses. m-Midday price. na-Not available. z-Not quoted. n-Nominal. r-Revised. Source: Dow Jones Energy Service

Cash-Futures Arbitrage

Intuitively, you might think that there is a close relationship between the cash price of a commodity and its futures price. If you do, then your intuition is quite correct. In fact, your intuition is backed up by strong economic argument and more than a century of experience observing the simultaneous operation of cash and futures markets.

As a routine matter, cash and futures prices are closely watched by market professionals. To understand why, suppose you notice that spot gold is trading for $400 per ounce while the two-month futures price is $450 per ounce. Do you see a profit opportunity?

You should, because buying spot gold today at $400 per ounce while simultaneously selling gold futures at $450 per ounce locks in a $50 per ounce profit. True, gold has storage costs (you have to put it somewhere), and a spot gold purchase ties up capital that could be earning interest. However, these costs are small relative to the $50 per ounce gross profit, which works out to be $50 / $400 = 12.5% per two months, or about 100 percent per year (with compounding). Furthermore, this profit is risk-free! Alas, in reality, such easy profit opportunities are the stuff of dreams.

Earning risk-free profits from an unusual difference between cash and futures prices is called **cash-futures arbitrage**. In a competitive market, cash-futures arbitrage has very slim profit margins. In fact, the profit margins are almost imperceptible when they exist at all.

Comparing cash prices for commodities in Figure 16.2 with their corresponding futures prices reported in Figure 16.1, you will find that cash prices and futures prices are seldom equal. In futures jargon, the difference between a cash price and a futures price is called **basis**.[1]

For commodities with storage costs, the cash price is usually less than the futures price. This is referred to as a **carrying-charge market**. Sometimes, however, the cash price is greater than the futures price, and this is referred to as an **inverted market**. We can summarize this discussion of carrying-charge markets, inverted markets, and basis as follows:

Carrying-charge market: Basis = Cash price − Futures price < 0	(16.1)
Inverted market: Basis = Cash price − Futures price > 0	

A variety of factors can lead to an economically justifiable difference between a commodity's cash price and its futures price, including availability of storage facilities, transportation costs, and seasonal price fluctuations. However, the primary determinants of cash-futures bases are storage costs and interest costs. Storage cost is the cost of holding the commodity in a storage facility, and interest cost refers to interest income forgone because funds are being used to buy and hold the commodity.

If a futures price rises far enough above a cash price to more than cover storage costs and interest expense, commodity traders will undertake cash-futures arbitrage by buying in the cash market and selling in the futures market. This drives down the futures price and drives up the cash price until the basis is restored to an economically justifiable level.

Similarly, if a futures price falls far enough relative to a cash price, traders will undertake cash-futures arbitrage by short selling in the cash market and buying in the

---

cash-futures arbitrage Strategy for earning risk-free profits from an unusual difference between cash and futures prices.

basis The difference between the cash price and the futures price for a commodity, i.e., basis = cash price − futures price.

carrying-charge market The case where the futures price is greater than the cash price; i.e., the basis is negative.

inverted market The case where the futures price is less than the cash price; i.e., the basis is positive.

---

[1]Confusingly, basis is sometimes presented as the futures price less the cash price. The official Commodity Trading Manual of the Chicago Board of Trade defines basis as the difference between the cash and the futures price, i.e., basis = cash price − futures price. We will be consistent with the CBOT definition.

futures market. This drives down the cash price and drives up the futures price until an economically justifiable basis is restored. In both cases, arbitrage ensures that the basis is kept at an economically appropriate level.

Spot-Futures Parity

For more information on single-stock futures trading visit www.nqlx.com www.onechicago. com and the Futures Source website at www.futuresource. com

We can be slightly more precise in illustrating the relationship between spot and futures prices for financial futures. Consider the example of futures contracts for shares of stock in a single company. One place such futures contracts are traded in the United States is one Chicago a joint venture of the major Chicago exchanges.

Suppose we are examining a particular single-stock futures contract that calls for delivery of 100 shares of stock in one year. The current (i.e., cash or spot) stock price is $50 per share, and the stock does not pay dividends. Also, 12-month T-bills are yielding 6 percent. What should the futures price be? To answer, notice that you can buy 100 shares of stock for $50 per share, or $5,000 total. You can eliminate all of the risk associated with this purchase by selling one futures contract. The net effect of this transaction is that you have created a risk-free asset. Since the risk-free rate is 6 percent, your investment must have a future value of $5,000 × 1.06 = $5,300. In other words, the futures price should be $53 per share.

Suppose the futures price is, in fact, $52 per share. What would you do? To make money, you would short 100 shares of stock at $50 per share and invest the $5,000 proceeds at 6 percent.[2] Simultaneously, you would buy one futures contract.

At the end of the year, you would have $5,300. You would use $5,200 to buy the stock to fulfill your obligation on the futures contract and then return the stock to close out the short position. You pocket $100. This is just another example of cash-futures arbitrage.

More generally, if we let F be the futures price, S be the spot price, and r be the risk-free rate, then our example illustrates that

$$F = S(1 + r) \qquad (16.2)$$

In other words, the futures price is simply the future value of the spot price, calculated at the risk-free rate. This is the famous **spot-futures parity** condition. This condition must hold in the absence of cash-futures arbitrage opportunities.

spot-futures parity
The relationship between spot prices and futures prices that holds in the absence of arbitrage opportunities.

More generally, if r is the risk-free rate per period, and the futures contract matures in T periods, then the spot-futures parity condition is

$$F_T = S(1 + r)^T \qquad (16.3)$$

Notice that T could be a fraction of one period. For example, if we have the risk-free rate per year, but the futures contract matures in six months, T would be 1/2.

PARITY CHECK

EXAMPLE 16.7

A non–dividend-paying stock has a current price of $12 per share. The risk-free rate is 4 percent per year. If a futures contract on the stock matures in three months, what should the futures price be?

(continued)

---

[2]For the sake of simplicity, we ignore the fact that individual investors don't earn interest on the proceeds from a short sale.

From our spot-futures parity condition, we have

$$F_T = S(1+r)^T$$
$$= \$12(1.04)^{1/4}$$
$$= \$12.12$$

The futures price should be $12.12. Notice that T, the number of periods, is 1/4 because the contract matures in one quarter.

More on Spot-Futures Parity

In our spot-futures parity example just above, we assumed that the underlying financial instrument (the stock) had no cash flows (no dividends). If there are dividends (for a stock future) or coupon payments (for a bond future), then we need to modify our spot-futures parity condition.

For a stock, we let D stand for the dividend, and we assume that the dividend is paid in one period, at or near the end of the futures contract's life. In this case, the spot-futures parity condition becomes

$$F = S(1+r) - D \qquad (16.4)$$

Notice that we have simply subtracted the amount of the dividend from the future value of the stock price. The reason is that if you buy the futures contract, you will not receive the dividend, but the dividend payment will reduce the stock price.

An alternative, and very useful, way of writing the dividend-adjusted spot-futures parity result in Equation 16.4 is to define d as the dividend yield on the stock. Recall that the dividend yield is just the upcoming dividend divided by the current price. In our current notation, this is just $d = D/S$. With this in mind, we can write the dividend-adjusted parity result as

$$F = S(1+r) - D(S/S) \qquad (16.5)$$
$$= S(1+r) - S(D/S)$$
$$= S(1+r) - Sd$$
$$= S(1+r-d)$$

Finally, as above, if there is something other than a single period involved, we would write

$$F_T = S(1+r-d)^T \qquad (16.6)$$

where T is the number of periods (or fraction of a period).

For example, suppose there is a futures contract on a stock with a current price of $80. The futures contract matures in six months. The risk-free rate is 7 percent per year, and the stock has an annual dividend yield of 3 percent. What should the futures price be?

Plugging in the values to our dividend-adjusted parity equation, we have

$$F_T = S(1+r-d)^T$$
$$= \$80(1+.07-.03)^{1/2}$$
$$= \$81.58$$

Notice that we set T equal to 1/2 since the contract matures in six months.

16.4a   What is the spot price for a commodity?

16.4b   With regard to futures contracts, what is the basis?

16.4c   What is an inverted market?

16.4d   What is the spot-futures parity condition?

16.5 Stock Index Futures

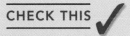

For information on stock index futures visit the CBOT website at www.cbot.com and the Montreal Exchange website at www.m-x.ca CME group website at www.cmegroup.com

There are a number of futures contracts on stock market indexes. Because these contracts are particularly important, we devote this entire section to them. We first describe the contracts and then discuss some trading and hedging strategies involving their use.

Basics of Stock Index Futures

Go to the website of the Montreal Exchange (www.m-x.ca). Here we see various index derivatives. Locate futures contracts and examine the SXF contracts. This contract futures, on the S&P Canada 60 Index, is the most important. With this contract, actual delivery would be very difficult or impossible because the seller of the contract would have to buy all 60 stocks in exactly the right proportions to deliver. Clearly, this is not practical, so this contract features cash settlement.

To understand how stock index futures work, suppose you bought one S&P Canada 60 contract at a futures price of 815. The contract size is $200 times the level of the index. What this means is that, at maturity, the buyer of the contract will pay the seller $200 times the difference between the futures price of 815 and the level of the S&P Canada Index at contract maturity.

For example, suppose that at maturity the S&P had actually fallen to 795. In this case, the buyer of contract must pay $200 \times (815 - 795) = $4,000$ to the seller of the contract. In effect, the buyer of the contract has agreed to purchase 200 "units" of the index at a price of $815 per unit. If the index is below 815, the buyer will lose money. If the index is above that, then the seller will lose money.

INDEX FUTURES

EXAMPLE 16.8

Suppose you are convinced that the Dow stocks are going to skyrocket in value. Consequently, you buy 20 DJIA futures contracts maturing in six months at a price of 10,500. Suppose that the Dow Jones index is at 10,920 when the contracts mature. How much will you make or lose?

The futures price is 10,500, and the contract size is $10 times the level of the index. At maturity, if the index is at 10,920, you make $10 \times (10,920 - 10,500) = $4,200$ per contract. With 20 contracts, your total profit is $84,000.

index arbitrage
Strategy of monitoring the futures price on a stock index and the level of the underlying index to exploit deviations from parity.

Index Arbitrage

The spot-futures parity relation we developed above is the basis for a common trading strategy known as **index arbitrage**. Index arbitrage refers to monitoring the futures price on a stock index along with the level of the underlying index. The trader looks for violations of parity and trades as appropriate.

For example, suppose the S&P 500 futures price for delivery in one year is 1,540. The current level is 1,500. The dividend yield on the S&P is projected to be 3 percent per year, and the risk-free rate is 5 percent. Is there a trading opportunity here?

From our dividend-adjusted parity equation (16.6), the futures price should be

$$F_T = S(1 + r - d)^T$$
$$= 1,500(1 + .05 - .03)^1$$
$$= 1,530$$

Thus, based on our parity calculation, the futures price is too high. We want to buy low, sell high, so we buy the index and simultaneously sell the futures contract.

program trading
Computer-assisted monitoring of relative prices of financial assets; it sometimes includes computer submission of buy and sell orders to exploit perceived arbitrage opportunities.

Index arbitrage is often implemented as a **program trading** strategy. While this term covers a lot of ground, it generally refers to the monitoring of relative prices by computer to more quickly spot opportunities. In some cases it includes submitting the needed buy and sell orders using a computer to speed up the process.

Whether a computer is used in program trading is not really the issue; instead, a program trading strategy is any coordinated, systematic procedure for exploiting (or trying to exploit) violations of parity or other arbitrage opportunities. Such a procedure is a trading "program" in the sense that whenever certain conditions exist, certain trades are made. Thus, the process is sufficiently mechanical that it can be automated, at least in principle.

Technically, the NYSE defines program trading as the simultaneous purchase or sale of at least 15 different stocks with a total value of $1 million or more. Program trading accounts for about 15 percent of total trading volume on the NYSE, and about 20 percent of all program trading involves stock-index arbitrage.

There is another phenomenon often associated with index arbitrage and, more generally, futures and options trading. S&P 500 futures contracts have four expiration months per year, and they expire on the third Friday of those months. On these same four Fridays, options on the S&P index and various individual stock options also expire. These Fridays have been dubbed the "triple witching hour" because all three types of contracts expire, sometimes leading to unusual price behaviour.

For information on program trading, visit www.programtrading.com

In particular, on triple witching hour Fridays, all positions must be liquidated, or "unwound." To the extent that large-scale index arbitrage and other program trading has taken place, enormous buying or selling sometimes occurs late in the day on such Fridays, as positions are closed out. Large price swings and, more generally, increased volatility are often seen. To curtail this problem to a certain extent, the exchanges have adopted rules regarding the size of a position that can be carried to expiration, and other rules have been adopted as well.

Hedging Stock Market Risk with Futures

We earlier discussed hedging using futures contracts in the context of a business protecting the value of its inventory. We now discuss some hedging strategies available to portfolio managers based on financial futures. Essentially, an investment portfolio is an inventory of securities, and financial futures can be used to reduce the risk of holding a securities portfolio.

We consider the specific problem of an equity portfolio manager wishing to protect the value of a stock portfolio from the risk of an adverse movement of the overall stock market. Here, the portfolio manager wishes to establish a short hedge position to reduce risk and must determine the number of futures contracts required to properly hedge a portfolio.

In this hedging example, you are responsible for managing a broadly diversified stock portfolio with a current value of $160 million. Analysis of market conditions leads you to believe that the stock market is unusually susceptible to a price decline during the next few months. Of course, nothing is certain regarding stock market fluctuations, but still you are sufficiently concerned to believe that action is required.

A fundamental problem exists for you, however, in that there is no futures contract that exactly matches your particular portfolio. As a result, you decide to protect your stock portfolio from a fall in value caused by a falling stock market using stock index futures. This is an example of a **cross-hedge**, where a futures contract on a related, but not identical, commodity or financial instrument is used to hedge a particular spot position.

cross-hedge Hedging a particular spot position with futures contracts on a related, but not identical, commodity or financial instrument.

Thus, to hedge your portfolio, you wish to establish a short hedge using stock index futures. To do this, you need to know how many index futures contracts are required to form an effective hedge. There are three basic inputs needed to calculate the number of stock index futures contracts required to hedge a stock portfolio:

1. The current value of your stock portfolio.

2. The beta of your stock portfolio.

3. The contract value of the index futures contract used for hedging.

Based on previous chapters, you are familiar with the concept of beta as a measure of market risk for a stock portfolio. Essentially, beta measures portfolio risk relative to the overall stock market. We will assume that you have maintained a beta of 1.25 for your $160 million stock portfolio.

You believe that the market (and your portfolio) will fall in value over the next three months and you decide to eliminate market risk from your portfolio. That is, you would like to convert your risky portfolio with a beta of 1.25 to a riskless portfolio with a beta of zero. Because you hold a stock portfolio, you know that you will need to establish a short hedge using futures contracts. You decide to use futures contracts on the S&P 500 index, because this is the index you used to calculate the beta for your portfolio.

From the newspaper, you find that the S&P 500 futures price for contracts that mature in three months is currently 1,280. Because the contract size for the S&P 500 futures is 250 times the index level, the current value of a single S&P 500 index futures contract is $250 \times 1,280 = $320,000$.

You now have all the information you need to calculate the number of S&P 500 index futures contracts needed to hedge your $160 million stock portfolio. The number of stock index futures contracts needed to convert the beta of your portfolio from 1.25 to zero is determined by the following formula:

$$\text{Number of contracts} = (\beta_D - \beta_P) \times \frac{V_P}{V_F} \qquad (16.7)$$

where: β_D = Desired beta of the stock portfolio
β_P = Current beta of the stock portfolio
V_p = Value of the stock portfolio
V_F = Value of one stock index futures contract

For your particular hedging problem, $\beta_D = 0$, $\beta_P = 1.25$, $V_p = 160 million, and $V_F = $320,000$, and thereby yielding this calculation:

$$\text{Number of contracts} = (0 - 1.25) \times \frac{160,000,000}{320,000} = -625$$

Thus, you can establish an effective short hedge by going short 625 S&P 500 index futures contracts. This short hedge will protect your stock portfolio against the risk of a general fall in the stock market during the remaining three-month life of the futures contract.

Equation 16.7 reinforces the notion that you want to go short futures contracts to lower the beta of your portfolio. The negative number of contracts is a reminder that you are trying to shed risk, which calls for a short position in the S&P 500 index futures market.

You can see that Equation 16.7 can also be used to change the beta of your portfolio to any level you want. However, any level other than zero is not considered a hedge, because your portfolio will still retain some systematic risk.

HEDGING WITH STOCK INDEX FUTURES

EXAMPLE 16.9

How many stock index futures contracts are required to hedge a $250 million stock portfolio, assuming a portfolio beta of .75 and an S&P 500 index futures level of 1,500?

Using Equation 16.7 and the knowledge that a true hedge reduces the portfolio beta to zero, we have:

$$\text{Number of contracts} = (0 - 0.75) \times \frac{250,000,000}{375,000} = -500$$

Therefore, you need to short 500 stock index futures contracts to hedge this $250 million portfolio. In this example, note that the value of one futures contract is given by $250 \times 1,500 = \$375,000$.

Hedging Interest Rate Risk with Futures

Having discussed hedging a stock portfolio, we now turn to hedging a bond portfolio. As we will see, the bond portfolio hedging problem is similar to the stock portfolio hedging problem. Once again, we will be cross-hedging, but this time using futures contracts on 10-year Canada bonds. Here, our goal is to protect the bond portfolio against changing interest rates.

In this example, you are responsible for managing a bond portfolio with a current value of $100 million. Recently, rising interest rates have caused your portfolio to fall in value slightly, and you are concerned that interest rates may continue to trend upward for the next several months. You decide to establish a short hedge based on 10-year Canada bond futures.

The formula for the number of 10-year Canada bond futures contracts needed to hedge a bond portfolio is

$$\text{Number of contracts} = \frac{D_P \times V_P}{D_F \times V_F} \tag{16.8}$$

where: D_P = Duration of the bond portfolio
V_P = Value of the bond portfolio
D_F = Duration of the futures contract
V_F = Value of a single futures contract

We already know the value of the bond portfolio, which is $100 million. Also, suppose that the duration of the portfolio is given as eight years. Next, we must calculate the duration of the futures contract and the value of the futures contract.

As a useful rule of thumb, the duration of an interest rate futures contract is equal to the duration of the underlying instrument plus the time remaining until contract maturity:

$$D_F = D_U + M_F \qquad (16.9)$$

where: D_F = Duration of the futures contract
D_U = Duration of the underlying instrument
M_F = Time remaining until contract maturity

For simplicity, let us suppose that the duration of the underlying Canada bond is 6 1/2 years and the futures contract has a maturity of 1/2 year, yielding a futures contract duration of 7 years.

The value of a single futures contract is the current futures price times the futures contract size. The standard contract size for Canada bond futures contracts is $100,000 par value. Now suppose that the futures price is 110, or 110 percent of par value. This yields a futures contract value of $100,000 × 1.10 = $110,000.

You now have all inputs required to calculate the number of futures contracts needed to hedge your bond portfolio. The number of Canada bond futures contracts needed to hedge the bond portfolio is calculated as follows:

$$\text{Number of contracts} = \frac{8 \times \$100,000,000}{7 \times \$110,000} = 1,039$$

Thus, you can establish an effective short hedge by going short 1,039 futures contracts for 10-year Canada bonds. This short hedge will protect your bond portfolio against the risk of a general rise in interest rates during the life of the futures contracts.

HEDGING WITH US TREASURY NOTE FUTURES

EXAMPLE 16.10

How many futures contracts are required to hedge a $250 million bond portfolio with a portfolio duration of 5 years using 10-year US Treasury note futures with a duration of 7.5 years and a futures price of 105?

Using the formula for the number of contracts, we have

$$\textbf{Number of contracts} = \frac{\mathbf{5 \times \$250,000,000}}{\mathbf{7.5 \times \$105,000}} = \mathbf{1,587}$$

You therefore need to sell 1,587 contracts to hedge this $250 million portfolio.

Futures Contract Delivery Options

cheapest-to-deliver option Seller's option to deliver the cheapest instrument when a futures contract allows several instruments for delivery. For example, US Treasury note futures allow delivery of any Treasury note with a maturity between 6 1/2 and 10 years.

Many futures contracts have a delivery option, whereby the seller can choose among several different "grades" of the underlying commodity or instrument when fulfilling delivery requirements. Naturally, we expect the seller to deliver the cheapest among available options. In futures jargon, this is called the **cheapest-to-deliver option**. The cheapest-to-deliver option is an example of a broader feature of many futures contracts, known as a "quality" option. Of course, futures buyers know about the delivery option, and therefore the futures prices reflect the value of the cheapest-to-deliver instrument.

As a specific example of a cheapest-to-deliver option, the 10-year Treasury note contract allows delivery of *any* Treasury note with a maturity between 6 1/2 and 10 years. This complicates the bond portfolio hedging problem. For the portfolio manager trying to hedge a bond portfolio with US Treasury note futures, the cheapest-to-deliver feature means that a note can be hedged only based on an assumption about which note will actually be delivered. Furthermore, through time the cheapest-to-deliver note may vary, and, consequently, the hedge will have to be monitored regularly to make sure that it correctly reflects the note issue that is most likely to be delivered. Fortunately, because this is a common problem, many commercial advisory services provide this information to portfolio managers and other investors.

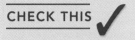

CHECK THIS

16.5a   What is a cross-hedge?

16.5b   What are the three basic inputs required to calculate the number of stock index futures contracts needed to hedge an equity portfolio?

16.5c   What are the basic inputs required to calculate the number of interest rate futures contracts needed to hedge a bond portfolio?

16.5d   What is the cheapest-to-deliver option?

16.6 Summary and Conclusions

This chapter surveyed the basics of futures contracts. In it, we saw that:

1. A forward contract is an agreement between a buyer and a seller for a future commodity transaction at a price set today. Futures contracts are a step beyond forward contracts. Futures contracts and forward contracts accomplish the same task, but a forward contract can be struck between any two parties, while standardized futures contracts are managed through organized futures exchanges.

2. Commodity futures call for delivery of a physical commodity. Financial futures require delivery of a financial instrument or, in some cases, cash. Futures contracts are a type of derivative security, because the value of the contract is derived from the value of an underlying instrument.

3. Hedging is the major economic reason for the existence of futures markets. However, a viable futures market requires participation by both hedgers and speculators. Hedgers transfer price risk to speculators, and speculators absorb price risk. Hedging and speculating are thus complementary activities.

4. Futures trading accounts have three essential features: margin is required, futures accounts are marked to market daily, and a futures position can be closed out any time by a reverse trade.

5. The cash price of a commodity or financial instrument is the price quoted for current delivery. The cash price is also called the spot price.

6. The difference between a cash price and a futures price is called basis. For commodities with storage costs, the cash price is usually less than the futures price. This is referred to as a carrying-charge market. Sometimes the cash price is greater than the futures price, and this case is referred to as an inverted market.

7. There is a simple relationship between cash and futures prices known as spot-futures parity. Violations of parity give rise to arbitrage opportunities, including index arbitrage, which involves stock index futures.

8. Cross-hedging refers to using futures contracts on a related commodity or instrument to hedge a particular spot position. Stock index futures, for example, can be used to hedge an equities portfolio against general declines in stock prices, and interest rate futures can be used to hedge a bond portfolio.

REAL WORLD

This chapter covered the essentials of what many consider to be a complex subject, futures contracts. As we hope you realize, futures contracts per se are not complicated at all; in fact, they are, for the most part, quite simple. This doesn't mean that they're for everybody, of course. Because of the tremendous leverage possible, very large gains and losses can (and do) occur with great speed.

To experience some of the gains and losses from outright speculation, you should buy and sell a variety of contracts in a simulated brokerage account such as Stock-Trak. Be sure to go both long and short and pick a few of each major type of contract.

The Internet offers a rich source for more information on trading futures. Probably the best place to begin is by visiting the websites of the major futures exchanges: the Chicago Board of Trade (www.cbot.com), the Chicago Mercantile Exchange (www.cme.com), the New York Mercantile Exchange (www.nymex.com), the Kansas City Board of Trade (www.kcbt.com), the Montreal Exchange (www.m-x.ca), the Winnipeg Commodity Exchange (www.theice.com), and the CME Group (www.cmegroup.ca). You might also visit the websites of some major international futures exchanges: the London International Financial Futures Exchange (www.liffe.com), Sydney Futures Exchange (www.sfe.com.au), Tokyo International Financial Futures Exchange (www.tfx.co.jp/en), and the Singapore Exchange (www.ses.com.sg). The reference section of Numa Web (www.numa.com) maintains an extensive list of the world's futures exchanges.

Useful websites on trading futures are Futures Trading (www.futures-trading.org), Daily Futures (www.dailyfutures.com), and Trading Markets (www.tradingmarkets.com). For a very large list of links to anything and everything related to futures, visit the commodities and futures section of Investor Links (www.investorlinks.com).

Key Terms

forward contract 518
futures contract 518
futures price 518
long position 525
short position 525
speculator 525
hedger 526
short hedge 526
long hedge 527
futures margin 528
initial margin 528
marking-to-market 528
maintenance margin 528

margin call 528
reverse trade 529
cash price 530
cash market 530
cash-futures arbitrage 531
basis 531
carrying-charge market 531
inverted market 531
spot-futures parity 532
index arbitrage 534
program trading 535
cross-hedge 536
cheapest-to-deliver option 538

Chapter Review Problems and Self-Test

1. **Futures Gains and Losses** Suppose you purchase 10 orange juice contracts today at the settle price of $1 per pound. How much do these 10 contracts cost you? If the settle price is lower tomorrow by 2 cents per pound, how much do you make or lose? The contract size is 15,000 pounds.

2. **Spot-Futures Parity** There is a futures contract on a stock, which is currently selling at $200 per share. The contract matures in two months; the risk-free rate is 5 percent annually. The current dividend yield on the stock is 0 percent. What does the parity relationship imply the futures price should be?

Answers to Self-Test Problems

1. If you go long (purchase) 10 contracts, you pay nothing today (you will be required to post margin, but a futures contract is an agreement to exchange cash for goods later, not today). If the settle price drops by 2 cents per pound, you lose 15,000 pounds (the contract size) $\times$ $.02 = $300 per contract. With 10 contracts, you lose $3,000.

2. The spot-futures parity condition is

$$F_T = S(1 + r - d)^T$$

where S is the spot price, r is the risk-free rate, d is the dividend yield, F is the futures price, and T is the time to expiration measured in years.

Plugging in the numbers we have, with zero for the dividend yield and 1/6 for the number of years (2 months out of 12), gets us

$$F_{1/6} = \$200(1 + .05)^{1/6} = \$201.63$$

Test Your Investment Quotient

1. **Futures Exchanges** Which of the following is the oldest and currently the most active futures exchange in the United States?

   a. Kansas City Board of Trade (KBOT)
   b. Chicago Mercantile Exchange (CME)
   c. New York Mercantile Exchange (NYMX)
   d. Chicago Board of Trade (CBOT)

2. **Futures versus Forward Contracts** Which of the following statements is true regarding the distinction between futures contracts and forward contracts?

   a. Futures contracts are exchange-traded, whereas forward contracts are OTC-traded.
   b. All else equal, forward prices are higher than futures prices.
   c. Forward contracts are created from baskets of futures contracts.
   d. Futures contracts are cash-settled at maturity, whereas forward contracts result in delivery.

3. **Futures versus Forward Contracts** In which of the following ways do futures contracts differ from forward contracts?

   I. Futures contracts are standardized.
   II. For futures, performance of each party is guaranteed by a clearinghouse.
   III. Futures contracts require a daily settling of any gains or losses.

   a. I and II only
   b. I and III only
   c. II and III only
   d. I, II, and III

4. **Futures Contracts** The open interest on a futures contract at any given time is the total number of outstanding

   a. Contracts
   b. Unhedged positions
   c. Clearinghouse positions
   d. Long and short positions

5. **Futures Margin** Initial margin for a futures contract is usually

   a. Regulated by the Montreal Exchange and the Winnipeg Exchange.
   b. Less than 2 percent of contract value.
   c. In the range between 2 percent to 5 percent of contract value.
   d. In the range between 5 percent to 15 percent of contract value.

6. **Futures Margin** In futures trading, the minimum level to which an equity position may fall before requiring additional margin is *most accurately* termed the

   a. Initial margin
   b. Variation margin
   c. Cash flow margin
   d. Maintenance margin

7. **Futures Margin** A silver futures contract requires the seller to deliver 5,000 troy ounces of silver. An investor sells one July silver futures contract at a price of $8 per ounce, posting a $2,025 initial margin. If the required maintenance margin is $1,500, the price per ounce at which the investor would first receive a maintenance margin call is closest to

   a. $5.92
   b. $7.89
   c. $8.11
   d. $10.80

8. **Futures Margin** Which of the following statements is false about futures account margin?

   a. Initial margin is higher than maintenance margin.
   b. A margin call results when account margin falls below maintenance margin.
   c. Marking-to-market of account margin occurs daily.
   d. A margin call results when account margin falls below initial margin.

9. **Futures Contracts** Which of the following contract terms changes daily during the life of a futures contract?

   a. Futures price
   b. Futures contract size
   c. Futures maturity date
   d. Underlying commodity

10. **Futures Trading Accounts** Which of the following is perhaps the least essential thing to know about a futures trading account?

    a. Margin is required.
    b. Futures accounts are marked-to-market daily.
    c. A futures position can be closed by a reverse trade.
    d. A commission is charged for each trade.

11. **Futures Delivery** On the maturity date, stock index futures contracts require delivery of

    a. Common stock.
    b. Common stock plus accrued dividends.
    c. Treasury bills.
    d. Cash.

12. **Futures Delivery** On the maturity date, Treasury note futures contracts require delivery of

    a. Treasury notes plus accrued coupons over the life of the futures contract.
    b. Treasury notes.
    c. Treasury bills.
    d. Cash.

13. **Spot-Futures Parity** A Canada bond futures contract has a quoted price of 100. The underlying bond has a coupon rate of 7 percent, and the current market interest rate is 7-percent. Spot-futures parity then implies a cash bond price of

a. 93
b. 100
c. 107
d. 114

14. **Spot-Futures Parity** A stock index futures contract maturing in one year has a currently traded price of $1,000. The cash index has a dividend yield of 2 percent, and the interest rate is 5 percent. Spot-futures parity then implies a cash index level of

    a. $933.33
    b. $970.87
    c. $1,071
    d. $1,029

15. **Spot-Futures Parity** A stock index futures contract matures in one year. The cash index currently has a level of $1,000 with a dividend yield of 2 percent. If the interest rate is 5 percent, then spot-futures parity implies a futures price of

    a. $943.40
    b. $970.87
    c. $1,060
    d. $1,030

16. **Futures Hedging** You manage a $100 million stock portfolio with a beta of .8. Given a contract size of $100,000 for a stock index futures contract, how many contracts are needed to hedge your portfolio?

    a. 8
    b. 80
    c. 800
    d. 8,000

17. **Futures Hedging** You manage a $100 million bond portfolio with a duration of 9 years. You wish to hedge this portfolio against interest rate risk using Canada bond futures with a contract size of $100,000 and a duration of 12 years. How many contracts are required?

    a. 750
    b. 1,000
    c. 133
    d. 1,333

18. **Futures Hedging** Which of the following is not an input needed to calculate the number of stock index futures contracts required to hedge a stock portfolio?

    a. The value of the stock portfolio.
    b. The beta of the stock portfolio.
    c. The contract value of the index futures contract.
    d. The initial margin required for each futures contract.

Concept Questions

1. **Understanding Futures Quotations** Using Figure 16.1, answer the following questions:

    a. How many exchanges trade wheat futures contracts?
    b. If you have a position in 10 gold futures, what quantity of gold underlies your position?
    c. If you are short 20 oat futures contracts and you opt to make delivery, what quantity of oats must you supply?
    d. Which maturity of the unleaded gasoline contract has the largest open interest? Which one has the smallest open interest?

2. **Hedging with Futures** Kellogg's uses large quantities of corn in its breakfast cereal operations. Suppose the near-term weather forecast for the corn-producing states is droughtlike conditions, so corn prices are expected to rise. To hedge its costs, Kellogg's decides to use the Chicago Board of Trade corn futures contracts. Should the company be a short hedger or a long hedger in corn futures?

3. **Hedging with Futures** Suppose one of RBC's mutual funds closely mimics the S&P Canada 60 Index. The fund has done very well during the year, and in November the fund manager wants to lock in the gains he has made using stock index futures. Should he take a long or short position in the S&P Canada 60 Index futures?

4. **Hedging with Futures** A mutual fund that predominantly holds long-term Canada bonds plans on liquidating the portfolio in three months. However, the fund manager is concerned that interest rates may rise from current levels and wants to hedge the price risk of the portfolio. Should she buy or sell Canada bond futures contracts?

5. **Hedging with Futures** An American electronics firm imports its completed circuit boards from Japan. The company signed a contract today to pay for the boards in Japanese yen upon delivery in four months; the price per board in yen was fixed in the contract. Should the importer buy or sell Japanese yen futures contracts?

6. **Hedging with Futures** Jed Clampett just dug another oil well, and, as usual, it's a gusher. Jed estimates that, in 2 months, he'll have 2 million barrels of crude oil to bring to market. However, Jed would like to lock in the value of this oil at today's prices, since the oil market has been skyrocketing recently. Should Jed buy or sell crude oil futures contracts?

7. **Hedging with Futures** The town of South Park is planning a bond issue in six months and Kenny, the town treasurer, is worried that interest rates may rise, thereby reducing the value of the bond issue. Should Kenny buy or sell Canada bond futures contracts to hedge the impending bond issue?

8. **Futures Markets** Is it true that a futures contract represents a zero-sum game, meaning that the only way for a buyer to win is for a seller to lose, and vice versa?

9. **Program Trading** Program traders closely monitor relative futures and cash market prices, but program trades are not actually made on a fully mechanical basis. What are some of the complications that might make program trading using, for example, the S&P 500 contract more difficult than the spot-futures parity formula indicates?

10. **Short Selling** What are the similarities and differences in short selling a futures contract and short selling a stock? How do the cash flows differ?

Questions and Problems

Core Questions

1. **Understanding Futures Quotations** Using Figure 16.1, answer the following questions:

   a. What was the settle price for March 2006 coffee futures on this date? What is the total dollar value of this contract at the close of trading for the day?

   b. What was the settle price for CBT December 2005 Treasury bond futures on this date? If you held 10 contracts, what is the total dollar value of your futures position?

   c. Suppose you held an open position of 25 March 2006 DJ Industrial Average futures on this day. What is the change in the total dollar value of your position for this day's trading? If you held a long position, would this represent a profit or a loss to you?

   d. Suppose you are short 10 January 2006 soybean meal futures contracts. Would you have made a profit or a loss on this day?

2. **Futures Profits and Losses** You are long 20 March 2006 soybean futures contracts. Calculate your dollar profit or loss from this trading day using Figure 16.1.

3. **Futures Profits and Losses** You are short 15 December 2005 corn futures contracts. Calculate your dollar profit or loss from this trading day using Figure 16.1.

4. **Futures Profits and Losses** You are short 30 March 2006 five-year Treasury note futures contracts. Calculate your profit or loss from this trading day using Figure 16.1.

5. **Open Interest** Referring to Figure 16.1, what is the total open interest on the December 2005 Japanese yen contract? Does it represent long positions, short positions, or both? Based on the settle price on the contract, what is the dollar value of the open interest?

6. **Spot-Futures Parity** A non-dividend-paying stock is currently priced at $64.87. The risk-free rate is 5 percent, and a futures contract on the stock matures in four months. What price should the futures be?

7. **Spot-Futures Parity** A non-dividend-paying stock has a futures contract with a price of $87.62 and a maturity of three months. If the risk-free rate is 4.5 percent, what is the price of the stock?

8. **Spot-Futures Parity** A non-dividend-paying stock has a current share price of $32.17 and a futures price of $33.53. If the maturity of the futures contract is eight months, what is the risk-free rate?

9. **Spot-Futures Parity** A stock has a current share price of $74.13 and a dividend yield of 1.5 percent. If the risk-free rate is 5.4 percent, what is the futures price if the maturity is four months?

10. **Spot-Futures Parity** A stock futures contract is priced at $61.57. The stock has a dividend yield of 1.25 percent, and the risk-free rate is 6.1 percent. If the futures contract matures in six months, what is the current stock price?

Intermediate Questions

11. **Margin Call** Suppose the initial margin on heating oil futures is $1,500, the maintenance margin is $1,250 per contract, and you establish a long position of 10 contracts today, where each contract represents 42,000 gallons. Tomorrow, the contract settles down .02 from the previous day's price. Are you subject to a margin call? What is the maximum price decline on the contract that you can sustain without getting a margin call?

12. **Marking-to-Market** You are long 10 gold futures contracts, established at an initial settle price of $480 per ounce, where each contract represents 100 ounces. Your initial margin to establish the position is $1,000 per contract, and the maintenance margin is $750 per contract. Over the subsequent four trading days, gold settles at $473, $479, $482, and $486, respectively. Compute the balance in your margin account at the end of each of the four trading days, and compute your total profit or loss at the end of the trading period. Assume that a margin call requires you to fund your account back to the initial margin requirement.

13. **Marking-to-Market** You are short 25 gasoline futures contracts, established at an initial settle price of 1.52 per gallon, where each contract represents 42,000 gallons. Your initial margin to establish the position is $6,075 per contract, and the maintenance margin is $4,500 per contract. Over the subsequent four trading days, oil settles at $1.46, $1.55, $1.59, and $1.62, respectively. Compute the balance in your margin account at the end of each of the four trading days, and compute your total profit or loss at the end of the trading period. Assume that a margin call requires you to fund your account back to the initial margin requirement.

14. **Futures Profits** You went long 20 March 2006 crude oil futures contracts at a price of 58.75. Looking back at Figure 16.1, if you closed your position at the settle price on this day, what was your profit?

15. **Futures Profits** You shorted 15 March 2006 British pound futures contracts at the lifetime high of the contract. Looking back at Figure 16.1, if you closed your position at the settle price on this day, what was your profit?

16. **Index Arbitrage** Suppose the CAC-40 index (a widely followed index of French stock prices) is currently at 4,512, the expected dividend yield on the index is 2 percent per year, and the risk-free rate in France is 7 percent annually. If CAC-40 futures contracts

that expire in six months are currently trading at 4,640, what program trading strategy would you recommend?

17. **Cross-Hedging** You have been assigned to implement a three-month hedge for a stock mutual fund portfolio that primarily invests in medium-sized companies. The mutual fund has a beta of 1.15 measured relative to the S&P Midcap 400, and the net asset value of the fund is $300 million. Should you be long or short in the Midcap 400 futures contracts? Assuming the Midcap 400 index is at 740 and its futures contract size is 500 times the index, determine the appropriate number of contracts to use in designing your cross-hedge strategy.

18. **Spot-Futures Parity** Suppose the 180-day S&P 500 futures price is 1,253.80, while the cash price is 1,231.21. What is the *implied difference* between the risk-free interest rate and the dividend yield on the S&P 500?

19. **Spot-Futures Parity** Suppose the 180-day S&P 500 futures price is 1,274.19, while the cash price is 1,243.71. What is the *implied dividend yield* on the S&P 500 if the risk-free interest rate is 7 percent?

20. **Hedging Interest Rate Risk** Suppose you want to hedge a $900 million bond portfolio with a duration of 6.5 years using 10-year Canada bond futures with a duration of 9 years, a futures price of 102, and 3 months to expiration. The multiplier on Canada bond is $100,000. How many contracts do you buy or sell?

21. **Hedging Interest Rate Risk** Suppose you want to hedge a $400 million bond portfolio with a duration of 16.5 years using 10-year Canada bond futures with a duration of 8 years, a futures price of 98, and 70 days to expiration. The multiplier on Canada bond is $100,000. How many contracts do you buy or sell?

22. **Futures Arbitrage** A non-dividend-paying stock is currently priced at $87.12 per share. A futures contract maturing in five months has a price of $88.38 and the risk-free rate is 4 percent. Describe how you could make an arbitrage profit from this situation. How much could you make on a per-share basis?

23. **Futures Arbitrage** A stock is currently priced at $80.34 and the futures on the stock that expire in six months have a price of $82.76. The risk-free rate is 7 percent, and the stock is not expected to pay a dividend. Is there an arbitrage opportunity here? How would you exploit it? What is the arbitrage opportunity per share of stock?

24. **Futures Arbitrage** Joan Tam, CFA, believes she has identified an arbitrage opportunity as indicated by the information given below:

Spot price for commodity:	$120
Futures price for commodity expiring in one year:	$125
Interest rate for one year:	8%

   a. Describe the transactions necessary to take advantage of this specific arbitrage opportunity.
   b. Calculate the arbitrage profit.
   c. Describe two market imperfections that could limit Tam's ability to implement this arbitrage strategy.

25. **Futures Arbitrage** Donna Doni, CFA, wants to explore inefficiencies in the futures market. The TOBEC stock index has a spot value of 185 now. TOBEC futures are settled in cash and underlying contract values are determined by multiplying $100 times the index value. The current annual risk-free interest rate is 6 percent.

   a. Calculate the theoretical price of the futures contract expiring six months from now, using the cost-of-carry model.
   b. The total (round-trip) transaction cost for trading a futures contract is $15. Calculate the lower bound for the price of the futures contract expiring six months from now.

What's on the Web

1. **OneChicago** Go to www.onechicago.com. How many single stock futures and narrow-based indexes are traded at OneChicago? What is the contract size of a single stock future? What is the minimum tick size, contract month, and contract expiration? What is the margin requirement?

2. **Spot-Futures Parity** Go to www.onechicago.com and find the futures quotes for Halliburton Co. Now go to finance.yahoo.com and find the current stock price for Halliburton. What is the implied risk-free rate using these prices? Does each different maturity give you the same interest rate? Why or why not?

3. **Contract Specifications** You want to find the contract specifications for futures contracts. Go to the Winnipeg Commodity Exchange at www.theice.com, and follow the "Contract Specifications" link. Now go to canola futures. What is the contract size?

4. **New York Board of Trade** Go to the Montreal Exchange website at (www.m-x.ca). Follow the "Contract Specification link." Which index futures contracts are traded? Find the characteristics of the S&P/TSX Capped Energy Index futures.

5. **Hedging with Futures** You are working for a company that processes beef and will take delivery of 200,000 pounds of cattle in August. You would like to lock in your costs today because you are concerned about an increase in cattle prices. Go to the Chicago Mercantile Exchange (CME) at www.cme.com, follow the "Products" link, the "Agricultural Commodities" link, and the "Contract Specs" link. How many futures contracts will you need to hedge your exposure? How will you use these contracts? Go back to the CME home page, follow the "Prices" link, the "10-Minute Futures Updates" link, the "Agricultural Commodity Futures" link, and the "Live Cattle Futures" link. What price are you effectively locking in if you traded at the last price? Suppose cattle prices increase 5 percent before the expiration. What is your profit or loss on the futures position? What if the price decreases by 5 percent? Explain how your futures position has eliminated your exposure to price risk in the live cattle market.

CHAPTER 17

Projecting Cash Flow and Earnings

"Financial statements are like fine perfume; to be sniffed, but never swallowed."

—Abraham Briloff

Cash flow is a company's lifeblood, and, for a healthy company, the primary source of cash flow is earnings. Security analysts strive to make accurate predictions about future cash flow and earnings because an analyst who predicts these well has a head start in forecasting future stock performance. ■

Like any security analyst, we must examine financial statements to make cash flow and earnings projections. The quality of our financial statement analysis depends on accurate and timely financial statements. Generally, firms issue financial statements that provide a fair and accurate summary of the firm's financial health. You should know, however, that firms do have some discretion in reporting financial information. In rare cases, firms issue inaccurate, or even fraudulent, financial statements. Therefore, Abraham Briloff offers sound advice when he advocates a critical viewing of financial statements.

In an earlier chapter, we examined the important concepts of stock analysis and valuation. Here we probe deeper into the topic of common stock valuation through an analysis of earnings and cash flow. In particular, we focus on earnings and cash flow forecasting. This chapter will acquaint you with financial accounting concepts necessary to understand basic financial statements and perform earnings and cash flow analysis using these financial statements. You may not become an expert analyst—this requires experience. But you will have a grasp of the fundamentals, which is a good start.

Unfortunately, most investors have difficulty reading financial statements and instead rely on various secondary sources of financial information. Of course, this is good for those involved with publishing secondary financial information. Bear in mind, however, that no one is paid well just for reading such sources of financial information. By reading this chapter, you take an important step toward becoming financial statement literate, and an extra course in financial accounting is also helpful. But ultimately you learn to read financial statements by reading financial statements! Like a good game of golf or tennis, financial statement reading skills require practice. If you have an aptitude for it, financial statement analysis is a skill worth mastering. Good analysts are paid well, but good analysis is expected in return. Maybe you, too, can become one of the few, the proud—a financial analyst.

17.1 Sources of Financial Information

Good financial analysis begins with good financial information. An excellent primary source of financial information about any company is its annual report to stockholders. Most companies expend considerable resources preparing and distributing annual reports. In addition to their stockholders, companies also make annual reports available to anyone requesting a copy. A convenient way to request copies of annual reports from several companies simultaneously is to use the annual reports service provided by *The Globe and Mail*. If you open the newspaper to its daily stock price reports, you will see a shamrock symbol (♣) next to entries for many individual stocks. The shamrock indicates that the company will send annual reports to readers who request them through *The Globe and Mail*. Requests can be submitted by telephone or by fax.

The Internet is a convenient source of financial information about many companies. For example, the Toronto Stock Exchange website (www.tsx.com) provides a directory of websites for companies whose stock trades on the exchange. The content of company websites varies greatly, but many provide recent quarterly or annual financial reports.

Information about Toronto or Canadian Venture Exchange listed companies can be obtained by examining the websites of the Ontario Securities Commission and Toronto Stock Exchange. Also investors can visit the websites of individual companies to get information on past and present financial statements as well as information on recent company events.

In addition to company annual reports, a wealth of primary financial information is available to investors through the Ontario Securities (OSC). The OSC requires publicly traded companies to submit financial statements on a regular basis. Investors can get the financial statements of the Canadian companies from **SEDAR** files. The SEDAR website (www.sedar.com) lists company reports, announcements and other information about public companies and mutual funds since 1997. Investors can use EDGAR files from the Securities and Exchange Commission (SEC) website (www.sec.com) to find financial statements of US stock exchange listed companies.

The majority of big Canadian companies are listed on the US stock markets as well as on the Canadian exchanges. These dually listed companies report their statements calculated in US dollars with the Securities Exchange Commission. These financial statements can be examined using the EDGAR or SEDAR websites.

The Ontario Securities Exchange Commission's **disclosure regulations** require that when a company discloses material nonpublic information to security analysts and stockholders who may well trade on the basis of the information, it must also make a simultaneous disclosure of that information to the general public. Most companies satisfy the regulations by distributing important announcements via e-mail alerts.

Review regulations regarding company disclosure requirements at the Ontario Securities (OSC) website at www.osc.gov.on.ca

Examine the Canadian companies listed on the Toronto Stock Exchange (TSX) and the Canadian Venture Exchange, at the Toronto Stock Exchange website at www.tsx.com

SEDAR Electronic archive of company filings with the Canadian securities regulatory agencies.

disclosure regulation Requires companies making a public disclosure of material nonpublic information to do so fairly without preferential recipients.

Securities and Exchange Commissions require companies to disclose not only financial statements, but also material information about their companies to public. Most companies make announcements at their websites, make press announcements, and also send e-mail alerts. To receive these e-mails automatically, you need to register for the service at the company website.

17.2 Financial Statements

Financial statements reveal the hard facts about a company's operating and financial performance. This is why the OSC requires timely dissemination of financial statements to the public. It's also why security analysts spend considerable time poring over a firm's financial statements before making an investment recommendation. A firm's balance sheet, income statement, and cash flow statement are essential reading for security analysts. Each of these interrelated statements offers a distinct perspective. The **balance sheet** provides a snapshot view of a company's assets and liabilities on a particular date. The **income statement** measures operating performance over an accounting period, usually a quarter or a year, and summarizes company revenues and expenses. The **cash flow statement** reports how cash was generated and where it was used over the accounting period. Understanding the format and contents of these three financial statements is a prerequisite for understanding earnings and cash flow analysis.

We begin by considering the basic structure and general format of financial statements through a descriptive analysis of the balance sheet, income statement, and cash flow statement of a hypothetical intergalactic company—the Borg Corporation.

balance sheet
Accounting statement that provides a snapshot view of a company's assets and liabilities on a particular date.

income statement
Summary statement of a firm's revenues and expenses over a specific accounting period, usually a quarter or a year.

cash flow statement
Analysis of a firm's sources and uses of cash over the accounting period, summarizing operating, investing, and financing cash flows.

The Balance Sheet

Table 17.1 presents year-end 2535 and 2536 balance sheets for Borg Corporation. The format of these balance sheets is typical of that contained in company annual reports. Get used to the accounting practice of specifying subtraction with parentheses and calculating subtotals while moving down a column of numbers. For example, Borg's 2536 fixed assets section is reproduced below, with the left numerical column following standard accounting notation and the right numerical column following standard arithmetic notation:

Fixed Assets	Accounting Style	Numeric Style
Plant facilities	$35,000	$35,000
Production equipment	20,000	+20,000
Administrative facilities	15,000	+15,000
Patents	10,000	+10,000
Accumulated depreciation	(20,000)	−20,000
Total fixed assets	$60,000	$60,000

Common to both numerical columns, an underline indicates that the numbers listed above should be summed. However, accounting notation omits the plus "+" sign and subtraction is indicated by parentheses "( )" instead of the more familiar minus "−" sign. Referring to Table 17.1, notice that total fixed assets is a subtotal used to calculate total assets, which is indicated by a double underline. With these conventions in mind, let us look over these sample balance sheets and try to become familiar with their format and contents.

TABLE 17.1	Borg Corporation Balance Sheets, 2536 and 2535	
	Year 2536	**Year 2535**
Current assets		
Cash	$2,000	$1,356
Accounts receivable	1,200	1,200
Prepaid expenses	500	500
Materials and supplies	300	300
Inventory	6,000	6,000
Total current assets	$10,000	$9,356
Fixed assets		
Plant facilities	$35,000	$35,000
Production equipment	20,000	20,000
Administrative facilities	15,000	15,000
Patents	10,000	10,000
Accumulated depreciation	(20,000)	(17,000)
Total fixed assets	$60,000	$63,000
Investments		
Cardassian Mining		
7% Preferred stock	$10,000	$10,000
Klingon Enterprises		
Common stock	10,000	
Goodwill	5,000	
Total investments	$25,000	$10,000
Other assets	5,000	5,000
Total assets	$100,000	$87,356
Current liabilities		
Short-term debt	$10,000	$10,000
Accounts payable	2,000	2,000
Leasing obligations	3,000	3,000
Total current liabilities	$15,000	$15,000
Long-term debt	$30,000	$20,000
Other liabilities	5,000	5,000
Total liabilities	$50,000	$40,000
Stockholder equity		
Paid-in capital	$10,000	$10,000
Retained earnings	40,000	37,356
Total stockholder equity	$50,000	$47,356
Total liabilities and equity	$100,000	$87,356
Shares outstanding	2,000	2,000
Year-end stock price	$40	$36

asset Anything a company owns that has value.

The Borg Corporation balance sheet has four major **asset** categories: current assets, fixed assets, investments, and other assets. Current assets are cash or items that will be converted to cash or be used within a year. For example, inventory will be sold, accounts receivable will be collected, and materials and supplies will be used within a year. Cash is, of course, the quintessential current asset. Fixed assets have an expected life longer than one year and are used in normal business operations. Fixed assets may be tangible or intangible. Property, plant, and equipment are the most common tangible fixed assets. Rights, patents, and licenses are common intangible assets. Except for land, all fixed assets normally depreciate in value over time. Investments include various securities held for investment purposes. Goodwill measures the premium paid over market value to acquire an asset. For example, a company may pay $50 per share for stock with a market price of $40 per share when acquiring a very large block of stock. Other assets includes miscellaneous items not readily fitting into any of the other asset categories. The sum of these four categories of assets is the firm's total assets.

liability A firm's financial obligation.

The Borg balance sheet has three major **liability** categories: current liabilities, long-term debt, and other liabilities. Current liabilities normally require payment or other action within a one-year period. These include accounts payable and accrued taxes. Long-term debt includes notes, bonds, or other loans with a maturity longer than one year. Other liabilities include miscellaneous items not belonging to any other liability category.

equity An ownership interest in the company.

Stockholder **equity** is the difference between total assets and total liabilities. It includes paid-in capital, which is the amount received by the company from issuing common stock, and retained earnings, which represent accumulated income not paid out as dividends but instead used to finance company growth.

A fundamental accounting identity for balance sheets states that assets are equal to liabilities plus equity:

$$\text{Assets} = \text{Liabilities} + \text{Equity} \qquad (17.1)$$

This identity implies that the balance sheet always "balances" because the left side is always equal in value to the right side. If an imbalance occurs when a balance sheet is created, then an accounting error has been made and needs to be corrected.

Financial analysts often find it useful to condense a balance sheet down to its principal categories. This has the desirable effect of simplifying further analysis while still revealing the basic structure of the company's assets and liabilities. How much a balance sheet can be condensed and still be useful is a subjective judgement of the analyst. When making this decision, recall Albert Einstein's famous dictum: "Simplify as much as possible, but no more."

Table 17.2 is a condensed version of Borg's 2536 balance sheet that still preserves its basic structure. Notice that the current assets rows are reduced to two components, cash and operating assets. We separate cash from operating assets for a good reason. Later, we show that the net cash increase from the cash flow statement is used to adjust cash on the balance sheet. This adjustment is more clearly illustrated by first separating current assets into cash and operating assets.

TABLE 17.2	**Borg Corporation** **Condensed 2536 Balance Sheet**	
Cash	$2,000	Current liabilities	$15,000
Operating assets	8,000	Long-term debt	30,000
Fixed assets	60,000	Other liabilities	5,000
Investments	25,000		
Other assets	5,000	Stockholder equity	50,000
Total assets	$100,000	Total liabilities and equity	$100,000

CHECK THIS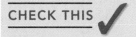

17.2a What are some examples of current assets?

17.2b What are some examples of fixed assets?

17.2c What are some examples of current liabilities?

17.2d Which accounts in Table 17.1 show changes between 2535 and 2536 balance sheets?

The Income Statement

Table 17.3 is a condensed income statement for Borg Corporation. The left column follows standard accounting notation, and the right column follows familiar arithmetic notation. Of course, the right column would not appear in an actual financial statement and is included here for convenience only. This income statement reports revenues and expenses for the corporation over a one-year accounting period. Examine it carefully and be sure you are familiar with its top-down structure.

The income statement begins with net sales, from which cost of goods sold (COGS) is subtracted to yield gross profit. Cost of goods sold represents direct costs of production and sales, that is, costs that vary directly with the level of production and sales. Next, operating expenses are subtracted from gross profit to yield operating **income**. Operating expenses are indirect costs of administration and marketing; that is, costs that do not vary directly with production and sales.

income The difference between a company's revenues and expenses, used to pay dividends to stockholders or kept as retained earnings within the company to finance future growth.

In addition to operating income from its own business operations, Borg Corporation has investment income from stock dividends received from another publicly traded Canadian company. Adding this investment income and then subtracting interest expense on debt yields pretax income. Finally, subtracting income taxes from pretax income yields net income. Net income is often referred to as the "bottom line" because it is normally the last line of the income statement. In this example, however, we have added dividends and retained earnings information, items that often appear in a separate financial statement. To avoid a separate statement, we show here that Borg Corporation paid dividends during the year. The sum of dividends and retained earnings is equal to net income:

$$\text{Net income} = \text{Dividends} + \text{Retained earnings} \qquad (17.2)$$

TABLE 17.3	Borg Corporation Condensed Income Statement	
	Net sales	$90,000
	Cost of goods sold	(70,000)
	Gross profit	$20,000
	Operating expenses	(13,000)
	Operating income	$7,000
	Investment income	700
	Interest expense	(2,000)
	Pretax income	$5,700
	Income tax[a]	(2,000)
	Net income	$3,700
	Dividends	(1,056)
	Retained earnings	$2,644

[a]A tax rate of 40 percent is applied to the total operating income less interest expense. Dividend income received by a company from a publicly traded Canadian company is tax exempt.

The footnote to Table 17.3 explains that dividend income from another publicly traded company is tax-exempt. In this case, Borg receives $700 in dividends from Cardassian Mining and does not pay any tax on that amount.

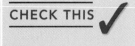

17.2e   What is cost of goods sold (COGS)?

17.2f   What is the difference between gross profit and operating income?

17.2g   What is the difference between net income and pretax income?

17.2h   What is meant by retained earnings?

The Cash Flow Statement

The cash flow statement reports where a company generated cash and where cash was used over a specific accounting period. The cash flow statement assigns all cash flows to one of three categories: operating cash flows, investment cash flows, or financing cash flows.

cash flow Income realized in cash form.

Table 17.4 is a condensed cash flow statement for Borg Corporation. (This is the last appearance of both accounting and arithmetic notation.) The cash flow statement begins with net income, which is the principal accounting measure of earnings for a corporation. However, net income and **cash flow** are not the same and often deviate greatly from each other. A primary reason why income differs from cash flow is that income contains **noncash items**. For example, depreciation is a noncash expense that must be added to net income when calculating cash flow. Adjusting net income for noncash items yields **operating cash flow**.

noncash items Income and expense items not realized in cash form.

operating cash flow Cash generated by a firm's normal business operations.

Operating cash flow is the first of three cash flow categories reported in the cash flow statement. The second and third categories are investment cash flow and financing cash flow. **Investment cash flow** (or "investing" cash flow) includes any purchases or sales of fixed assets and investments. For example, Borg's purchase of Klingon Enterprises common stock reported in footnote "a" is an investment cash flow. **Financing cash flow** includes any funds raised by an issuance of securities or expended by a repurchase of outstanding securities. In this example, Borg's $10,000 debt issue and $1,056 dividend payout reported in footnote "b" are examples of financing cash flows.

investment cash flow Cash flow resulting from purchases and sales of fixed assets and investments.

financing cash flow Cash flow originating from the issuance or repurchase of securities and the payment of dividends.

Standard accounting practice specifies that dividend payments to stockholders are financing cash flows, whereas interest payments to bondholders are operating cash flows. One reason is that dividend payments are discretionary, while interest payments are mandatory. Also, interest payments are tax-deductible expenses, but dividend payouts are not tax deductible. In any case, interest payments are cash expenses reported

TABLE 17.4	Borg Corporation Condensed Cash Flow Statement	
Net income		$3,700
Depreciation		3,000
Operating cash flow		$6,700
Investment cash flow[a]		(15,000)
Financing cash flow[b]		8,944
Net cash increase		$644

[a]December 2536 purchase of 50 percent interest in Klingon Enterprises for $15,000 (including $5,000 goodwill).
[b]Issue of $10,000 par value 8 percent coupon bonds, less a $1,056 dividend payout.

on the income statement. Since they are cash expenses, they do not appear in the cash flow statement to reconcile the difference between income and cash flow.

The sum of operating cash flow, investment cash flow, and financing cash flow yields the net change in the firm's cash. This change is the "bottom line" of the cash flow statement and reveals how much cash flowed into or out of the company's cash account during an accounting period. In this case, $644 of cash flowed into Borg Corporation (you can also see this change by comparing cash columns in Table 17.1).

CHECK THIS ✓

17.2i What is the difference between net income and operating cash flow?

17.2j What are some noncash items used to calculate operating cash flow?

17.2k What is the difference between an investment cash flow and a financing cash flow?

17.2l What is meant by net increase in cash?

17.2m Can you explain why a cash item like interest expense does not appear on the cash flow statement?

Performance Ratios and Price Ratios

Annual reports normally contain various items of supplemental information about the company. For example, certain profitability ratios may be reported to assist interpretation of the company's operating efficiency. For Borg Corporation, some standard profitability ratios for 2536 are calculated as follows.

Ratio	Formula	Calculation
Gross margin	$\dfrac{\text{Gross profit}}{\text{Net sales}}$	$\dfrac{\$20,000}{\$90,000} = 22.22\%$
Operating margin	$\dfrac{\text{Operating income}}{\text{Net sales}}$	$\dfrac{\$7,000}{\$90,000} = 7.78\%$
Return on assets (ROA)	$\dfrac{\text{Net income}}{\text{Total assets}}$	$\dfrac{\$3,700}{\$100,000} = 3.70\%$
Return on equity (ROE)	$\dfrac{\text{Net income}}{\text{Stockholder equity}}$	$\dfrac{\$3,700}{\$50,000} = 7.40\%$

return on assets (ROA) Net income stated as a percentage of total assets.

return on equity (ROE) Net income stated as a percentage of stockholder equity.

Notice that **return on assets (ROA)** and **return on equity (ROE)** are calculated using current year-end values for total assets and stockholder equity. It could be argued that prior-year values should be used for these calculations. However, the use of current year-end values is more common.

Companies calculate and report some valuation ratios. One of the most popular ratios is the Tobin's q ratio. This ratio is calculated by dividing market price of assets into replacement cost of assets. If the ratio value exceeds one then this indicates that company is managed well.

Annual reports may also report per-share calculations of book value, earnings, and operating cash flow, respectively. Per-share calculations require the number of common stock shares outstanding. Borg's balance sheet reports 2,000 shares of common stock outstanding. Thus, for Borg Corporation, these per-share values are calculated as follows:

Ratio	Formula	Calculation
Book value per share (BVPS)	$\dfrac{\text{Stockholder equity}}{\text{Shares outstanding}}$	$\dfrac{\$50,000}{\$2,000} = \$25$
Earnings per share (EPS)	$\dfrac{\text{Net income}}{\text{Shares outstanding}}$	$\dfrac{\$3,700}{\$2,000} = \$1.85$
Cash flow per share (CFPS)	$\dfrac{\text{Operating cash flow}}{\text{Shares outstanding}}$	$\dfrac{\$6,700}{\$2,000} = \$3.35$

Notice that cash flow per share (CFPS) is calculated using operating cash flow—*not* the bottom line on the cash flow statement! Most of the time when you hear the term "cash flow," it refers to operating cash flow.

Recall that previously, we made extensive use of price ratios to analyze stock values. Using the per-share values calculated immediately above, and Borg's year-end stock price of $40 per share, we get the following (rounded) price ratios:

Ratio	Formula	Calculation
Price-book (P/B)	$\dfrac{\text{Stock price}}{\text{BVPS}}$	$\dfrac{\$40}{\$25} = 1.6$
Price-earnings (P/E)	$\dfrac{\text{Stock price}}{\text{EPS}}$	$\dfrac{\$40}{\$1.85} = 21.6$
Price-cash flow (P/CF)	$\dfrac{\text{Stock price}}{\text{CFPS}}$	$\dfrac{\$40}{\$3.35} = 11.9$

We use these price ratios later when assessing the potential impact of a sales campaign on Borg Corporation's future stock price. Our nearby *Work the Web* box shows another use for price ratios.

CHECK THIS

17.2n What is the difference between gross margin and operating margin?

17.2o What is the difference between return on assets and return on equity?

17.2p What is the difference between earnings per share and cash flow per share?

17.2q How is cash flow per share calculated?

17.3 Financial Statement Forecasting

pro forma financial statements
Statements prepared using certain assumptions about future income, cash flow, and other items. Pro forma literally means according to prescribed form.

In December 2536, Borg publicly announced the completed acquisition of a 50 percent financial interest in Ferengi Traders. However, half the acquired shares do not carry voting rights, so the acquisition is treated as a simple investment on the balance sheet. The stated purpose of the acquisition was to expand sales outlets. Complementing the acquisition, Borg also announces plans for a marketing campaign to increase next year's net sales to a targeted $120,000.

As a Borg analyst, you must examine the potential impact of these actions. You immediately contact Borg management to inquire about the details of the acquisition and the marketing campaign. Armed with this additional information, you decide to construct **pro forma financial statements** for Borg Corporation for the year 2537. You also decide to formulate your analysis by considering two scenarios: an optimistic

One of the more common uses of financial ratios is stock screening. Stock screening is the process of selecting stocks based on specific criteria. A popular method used by the legendary investor Warren Buffett, among others, is searching for value stocks that have high growth potential. A value stock has relatively low price ratios. However, low price ratios can also be an indication of low future growth potential, so we also want to determine if these stocks have future growth possibilities. We went to *finance. yahoo.com* and used the stock screener we found there. We used the preset screen named "large, growing, and cheap." This screen looks for stocks with a market cap greater than $5 billion; estimated EPS growth greater than 20 percent; P/E less than 20; and P/S less than 1.3. Here is what we found:

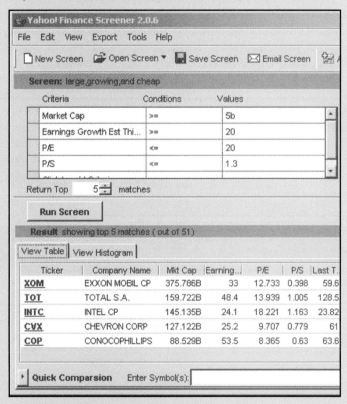

Using stock screening as an investment tool is not really this simple. What we have done here is narrowed the universe of stocks to a few stocks that meet our criteria. It is now up to us to further examine the companies to determine if they are actually good investments. In other words, stock screening is not the end of the investment process—it simply narrows the field of candidates.

sales scenario and a pessimistic sales scenario. Under the optimistic scenario, the marketing campaign is successful and targeted net sales of $120,000 are realized with an assumed cost of goods sold of $90,000. Under the pessimistic scenario, only $100,000 of net sales are realized with a cost of goods sold of $80,000. Operating expenses will be $17,000 under both scenarios, reflecting the costs of the marketing campaign. The appropriate sequence for your analysis is to construct pro forma income statements, then pro forma cash flow statements, followed by pro forma balance sheets.

The Pro Forma Income Statement

Table 17.5 contains side-by-side pro forma income statements for Borg Corporation corresponding to optimistic and pessimistic sales scenarios in the coming year. These begin with the assumed net sales and cost of goods sold values for both scenarios. They then proceed with the standard top-down calculations of income where several calculation methods and additional assumptions are explained in footnotes. The optimistic sales scenario produces a net income of $8,320 of which $1,056 is paid as dividends and $7,264 is kept as retained earnings. Under the pessimistic sales scenario net income is only $820 with $1,056 of dividends and −$236 of retained earnings.

Footnote "a" explains that investment income is $2,200 under optimistic sales and $700 under pessimistic sales. This reflects stock dividends of $700 and assumed noncash investment income from Frengi Traders of $1,500 under optimistic sales and $0 under pessimistic sales. The difference in scenario investment incomes stems from the fact that Frengi is involved with the sales campaign.

Footnote "c" explains that taxes are paid on operating income less interest expense plus the taxable portion of preferred stock dividends. Notice that Borg's noncash investment income from Ferengi Traders is not taxed because Ferengi paid no dividends. In this situation, Borg records the value of its investment in Ferengi as its share of Ferengi's stockholder equity value. Thus, when Ferengi adds retained earnings to its equity value, Borg records its share of the addition as noncash income and changes the balance sheet value of its investment in Ferengi accordingly. The next step of your analysis is construction of pro forma cash flow statements.

TABLE 17.5	Borg Corporation Pro Forma Income Statements	
Sales Growth (%)	**Optimistic**	**Pessimistic**
Net sales	$120,000	$100,000
Cost of goods sold	(90,000)	(80,000)
Gross profit	$30,000	$20,000
Operating expenses	(17,000)	(17,000)
Operating income	$13,000	$3,000
Investment income[a]	2,200	700
Interest expense[b]	(2,800)	(2,800)
Pretax income	$12,400	$900
Income taxes[c]	(4,080)	(80)
Net income	$8,320	$820
Dividends[d]	$(1,056)	$(1,056)
Retained earnings	$7264	$(236)

[a]Stock dividends of $700 plus $1,500 noncash investment income from Ferengi Traders under optimistic sales results and $0 under pessimistic sales results, i.e. $700 + $1,500 = $2,200.

[b]Prior-year interest expense of $2,000 plus payment of 8 percent coupons on the December 2536 debt issue of $10,000, i.e. $2,000 + 8% × $10,000 = $2,800.

[c]Tax rate of 40% applied to the sum of operating income less interest expense. Dividend income is tax-free, i.e. $(13,000−2,800) × 0.4 = $4,080.

[d]Assumes no change in dividends from prior year.

TABLE 17.6	Borg Corporation Pro Forma Cash Flow Statements		
		Optimistic	Pessimistic
Net income		$8,320	$820
Depreciation and amortization[a]		3,200	3,200
Increase in operating assets[b]		(2,000)	(3,000)
Noncash investment income		(1,500)	0
Operating cash flow		$8,020	$1,020
Investment cash flow[c]		$0	$0
Financing cash flow[d]		$(1,056)	$(1,056)
Net increase (decrease) in cash		$6,964	($36)

[a]Assumes the same $3,000 depreciation as in the prior year and annual goodwill amortization of $200.
[b]Assumes an increase in operating assets of $2,000 under optimistic sales and $3,000 under pessimistic sales.
[c]Assumes no new investments.
[d]Assumes no change in dividends.

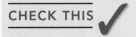

CHECK THIS

17.3a Create a pro forma income statement for Borg Corporation corresponding to pessimistic sales results assuming noncash investment losses of $1,000.

The Pro Forma Cash Flow Statement

Table 17.6 contains side-by-side pro forma cash flow statements for Borg Corporation under optimistic and pessimistic sales scenarios. Under the optimistic sales scenario the net cash increase is $6,964; under the pessimistic scenario the net cash decrease is $36. The net cash change is applied to adjust the cash account on the pro forma balance sheet. This adjustment is now more convenient since you separated cash from operating assets in Borg's condensed balance sheet.

Footnote "a" explains that goodwill amortization is $200 per year based on a 25-year amortization schedule. This amortization is applied to the $5,000 of goodwill on Borg's prior-year balance sheet associated with its purchase of a 50 percent stake in Ferengi Traders. Footnote "b" explains that operating assets are assumed to increase by $2,000 under optimistic sales and $3,000 under pessimistic sales. These increases are realistic since a sales campaign will surely require additional inventory. The increase is bigger under pessimistic sales because more inventory goes unsold. Your next step is to create the pro forma balance sheet for Borg Corporation.

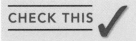

CHECK THIS

17.3b Create a pro forma cash flow statement for Borg Corporation under pessimistic sales results assuming noncash investment losses of $1,000.

The Pro Forma Balance Sheet

Table 17.7 contains side-by-side pro forma balance sheets for Borg Corporation as they might result from optimistic and pessimistic sales scenarios. This balance sheet is created by starting with the prior-year condensed balance sheet and then making the following adjustments consistent with the pro forma income statements and cash flow statements:

1. Cash of $2,000 is adjusted by a net cash change of $6,964 under the optimistic sales scenario and $(36) under the pessimistic sales scenario.

TABLE 17.7	Borg Corporation Pro Forma Balance Sheets		
		Optimistic	**Pessimistic**
Cash[a]		$8,964	$1,964
Operating assets[b]		10,000	11,000
Fixed assets[c]		57,000	57,000
Investments[d]		26,300	24,800
Other assets		5,000	5,000
Total assets		$107,264	$99,764
Current liabilities		$15,000	$15,000
Long-term debt		30,000	30,000
Other liabilities		5,000	5,000
Stockholder equity[e]		57,264	49,764
Total liabilities and equity		$107,264	$99,764

[a]Prior-year cash of $2,000 plus $6,964 (optimistic) and ($36) (pessimistic) net cash change from the pro forma cash flow statement.

[b]Prior-year operating assets of $8,000 plus an additional $2,000 under optimistic sales and $3,000 under pessimistic sales.

[c]Prior-year fixed assets of $60,000 less the assumed $3,000 depreciation.

[d]Prior-year investments of $25,000 plus noncash investment income of $1,500 under optimistic sales only less $200 goodwill amortization.

[e]Prior-year equity of $50,000 plus $7,264 (optimistic) and −$236 (pessimistic) retained earnings from the pro forma income statement.

2. Operating assets of $8,000 are increased by $2,000 under the optimistic sales scenario and increased by $3,000 under the pessimistic sales scenario.

3. Fixed assets of $60,000 are adjusted by depreciation of $3,000, which is the same under both sales scenarios.

4. Investments of $25,000 are increased by the assumed noncash investment income from Ferengi Traders of $1,500 under optimistic sales and $0 under pessimistic sales, less $200 of goodwill amortization. As noted earlier, the difference by scenario is based on the fact that Ferengi is involved with the sales campaign.

5. Equity of $50,000 is adjusted for retained earnings of $7,264 under optimistic sales and $(236) under pessimistic sales.

All other accounts remain unchanged, which is a simplifying assumption made to focus attention on the immediate impact of the sales campaign.

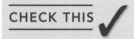

CHECK THIS   **17.3c**   Create a pro forma balance sheet for Borg under a pessimistic sales scenario assuming noncash investment losses of $1,000.

Projected Profitability and Price Ratios

In addition to preparing pro forma financial statements, you also decide to calculate projected profitability ratios and per-share values under optimistic and pessimistic sales scenarios. These are reported immediately below and compared with their original year-end values.

Scenario	Original	Optimistic	Pessimistic
Gross margin	22.22%	25.00%	20.00%
Operating margin	7.78%	10.83%	3.00%
ROA	3.70%	7.75%	0.82%
ROE	7.40%	14.52%	1.65%
Book value per share (BVPS)	$25.00	$28.63	$24.88
Earnings per share	$1.85	$4.16	$0.41
Cash flow per share	$3.35	$4.01	$0.51

One common method of analysis is to calculate projected stock prices under optimistic and pessimistic sales scenarios using prior-period price ratios and projected per-share values from pro forma financial statements. Similar procedures were performed in the previous chapter using prior-period average price ratios and per-share values based on growth rate projections. For Borg Corporation, you decide to take your previously calculated year-end 2536 price ratios and multiply each ratio by its corresponding pro forma per-share value. The results of these projected stock price calculations (rounded) are shown immediately below.

	Projected Stock Prices	
	Optimistic	Pessimistic
BVPS × P/B	$45.81	$39.81
EPS × P/E	$89.86	$17.86
CFPS × P/CF	$47.72	$6.07

These projected stock prices reflect widely varying degrees of sensitivity to optimistic and pessimistic sales scenario outcomes. For example, projected prices based on EPS and CFPS are especially sensitive to which scenario is realized. On the other hand, projected stock prices based on BVPS are far less sensitive to scenario realization.

Which projected stock price is correct? Well, it clearly depends on which sales scenario is realized and which price ratio the financial markets will actually use to value Borg Corporation's stock. This is where experience and breadth of knowledge count immensely. Of course, no one can make perfectly accurate predictions, but the analyst's job is to expertly assess the situation and make an investment recommendation supported by reasonable facts and investigation. But some analysts are better than others. Like professional baseball players, professional stock analysts with better batting averages can do very well financially.

17.4 Barrick Gold Corporation Case Study

After carefully reading the analysis of Borg Corporation, you should have a reasonably clear picture of how earnings and cash flow analyses might proceed using pro forma financial statements. To further illustrate the use of pro forma financial statements in earnings and cash flow analysis, this section presents an analysis based on the 2006 financial statements for Barrick Gold Corporation. Using data for a real company provides a real challenge.

This section begins with a review of Barrick Gold 2006 financial statements. We then proceed to analyze the effects on earnings and cash flow that might result from product sales either rising or falling by 10 percent. The analysis is similar to that for Borg Corporation, but there are a few important differences. Note that amounts shown are in thousands of dollars (except earnings per share).

Visit Barrick
Gold Corporation's
website at
www.barrick.com

Barrick Gold Corporation's 2006 condensed balance sheet is shown in Table 17.8. This balance sheet shows that at year-end 2006 Barrick Gold had $21.373 billion of total assets and $14.199 billion of shareholder equity. In Table 17.9, Barrick Gold's condensed income statement, the bottom line reveals that Barrick earned $1.506 billion in net income from $5.636 billion in net sales. From these values, we calculate Barrick Gold's return on assets as 7.01 percent and return on equity as 10.60 percent. Also, with 868.74 million shares outstanding, Barrick Gold realized earnings per share of $1.54. Finally, based on Barrick Gold's stock price of $45.44, we obtain a price-book ratio of 2.78 and a price-earnings ratio of 29.48.

The operating cash flow section of Barrick Gold's condensed 2006 cash flow statement (Table 17.10) shows that in 2006, Barrick Gold got $ 2.122 billion from sale of operations. The investing cash flow section reveals $1.593 billion is used for investment. The financing cash flow section shows that cash was raised by issuance of debt. The company repaid some long-term debt and settled liabilities of derivative instruments. The cash flow per share is $2.48 and price-cash flow ratio is $18.35.

We now move on to what-if analyses of earnings and cash flow. Specifically, what might happen to earnings and cash flow if product sales increased or decreased by 10 percent? To perform this analysis, we proceed through the same sequence of operations as before. That is, we first create a pro forma income statement, then a pro forma cash flow statement, and finally a pro forma balance sheet.

Pro forma income statements corresponding to a 10 percent increase and a 10 percent decrease in net sales and cost of goods sold for Barrick Gold are shown in Table 17.11. For convenience, italics indicate times for which constant 2006 values are used. The ±10 percent changes in net sales and cost of goods sold cause gross profit to increase and decrease by 10 percent also. However, since operating expenses are assumed to be a constant 2006 value across the two sales scenarios, operating income varies considerably. By assuming the same average tax rate as in 2006, we obtain net income values across both sales scenarios. Then, letting 2006 dividends continue unchanged, we get very different pro forma retained earnings values. These retained earnings values from the pro forma income statement will be used to adjust cumulative retained earnings on the pro forma balance sheet. But first we take these pro forma net income values as starting points to create pro forma cash flow statements.

TABLE 17.8	Barrick Gold Corporation 2006 Balance Sheet ($ in Thousands)		
ASSETS		**LIABILITIES**	
Current Assets		Current liabilities	1,852,000
Cash and cash equivalents	3,043,000	Long term debt	3,244,000
Net receivables	234,000	Other liabilities	1,279,000
Inventory	931,000	Deferred long term liability charges	798,000
Other current assets	588,000	Minority interest	1,000
Total current assets	4,796,000	Total liabilities	7,174,000
Long term investments	1,182,000	Stockholders' equity	
Property plant and equipment	8,703,000	Common stock	13,106,000
Goodwill	5,855,000	Retained earnings	974,000
Intangible assets	75,000	Other stockholder equity	119,000
Other assets	198,000	Total stockholder equity	14,199,000
Deferred long term asset charges	564,000		
Total assets	21,373,000	Total liabilities and stockholder equity	21,373,000

TABLE 17.9	Barrick Gold Corporation 2006 Income Statement ($ in Thousands)
Total revenue	5,636,000
Cost of revenue	2,907,000
Gross profit	2,729,000
Operating expenses	1,137,000
Operating income	1,592,000
Other income/expenses	94,000
Earnings before interest and taxes	1,686,000
Interest expense	126,000
Income before tax	1,560,000
Income tax expense	−348,000
Minority interest	1,000
Equity investees	−4,000
Net income from continuing ops	1,209,000
Discontinued operations	297,000
Net income	1,506,000
Adjustment to Net Income	−167,000
Net income applicable to common shares	$1,339,000
Shares	868,740,000
Earnings per share	$1.54

TABLE 17.10	Barrick Gold Corporation 2006 Cash Flow Statement ($ in Thousands)
Net income	1,506,000
Depreciation	774,000
Adjustments to net income	(167,000)
Changes in accounts receivables	(98,000)
Changes in liabilities	218,000
Changes in inventories	(193,000)
Changes in other operating activities	111,000
Total cash flow from operating activities	2,151,000
Investing Activities, Cash Flows Provided By or Used In	
Capital expenditures	(1,087,000)
Investments	(307,000)
Other cash flows from investing activities	2,589,000
Total cash flows from investing activities	1,195,000
Financing Activities, Cash Flows Provided By or Used In	
Dividends paid	(191,000)
Sale purchase of stock	74,000
Net borrowings	(1,232,000)
Other cash flows from financing activities	13,000
Total cash flows from financing activities	(1,336,000)
Effect of exchange rate changes	(4,000)
Change in cash and cash equivalents, end of year	$2,006,000

TABLE 17.11	Barrick Gold Corporation 2007 Pro Forma Income Statement ($ in Thousands)		
Sales Growth (thousands)	**31-Dec-06**	**+10%**	**−10%**
Total revenue	5,636,000.0	6,199,600.0	5,072,400.0
Cost of revenue[a]	(2,907,000.0)	(3,197,700.0)	(2,616,300.0)
Gross profit	2,729,000.0	3,001,900.0	2,456,100.0
Operating expenses	(1,137,000.0)	(1,137,000.0)	(1,137,000.0)
Operating income	1,592,000.0	1,864,900.0	1,319,100.0
*Other income/expenses**	94,000.0	94,000.0	94,000.0
Earnings before interest and taxes	1,686,000.0	1,958,900.0	1,413,100.0
Interest expense	(126,000.0)	(126,000.0)	(126,000.0)
Income before tax	1,560,000.0	1,832,900.0	1,287,100.0
Income tax expense	(348,000.0)	(408,920.0)	287,152.0
Minority interest	1,000.0	1,000.0	1,000.0
Equity investees	(4,000)	(4,000)	(4,000)
Net income from continuing ops	1,209,000.0	1,420,980.0	996,948.0
Discontinued operations[c]	297,000.0	297,000.0	297,000.0
Net income	1,506,000.0	1,717,980.0	1,293,948.0
Adjustments to net income	(167,000)	(167,000)	(167,000)
Net income applicable to common shares	1,339,000.0	1,550,980.0	1,126,948.0
Dividends	(191,000.0)	(191,000.0)	(191,000.0)
Retained earnings	1,148,000.0	1,359,980.0	935,948.0
Shares	868740000	868740000	868740000
Earnings per share	$1.54	$1.79	$1.30

[a]Assumes a constant 2006 gross margin, which implies that cost of goods sold changes by the same +(−) 10% as net sales.
[b]Assumes a constant 2006 average tax rate of 22.30%.
[c]Assumes income from discontinued operations will be same.
*Italics indicate items with constant 2006 values.

Pro forma cash flow statements for Barrick Gold appear in Table 17.12, where italics indicate that constant 2006 values are used. These statements begin with pro forma net income values, to which we add back constant 2006 depreciation and amortization expenses and also adjust for constant 2006 changes in operating assets and current liabilities. This yields operating cash flows across both sales scenarios. Since our intention is to isolate the impacts of changes in net sales, we set investment cash flow equal to zero in both sales scenarios. Similarly, for financing cash flows, we set the change in long-term debt to zero. Then, summing operating, investment, and financing cash flows yields net cash increases for the two sales scenarios. Now, we move on to the pro forma balance sheets.

To create Barrick Gold pro forma balance sheets as in Table 17.13, the first two steps are:

1. Adjust retained earnings on the balance sheet with retained earnings from the income statement.

2. Adjust cash on the balance sheet with net cash increase from the cash flow statement.

TABLE 17.12	Barrick Gold Corporation 2007 Pro Forma Cash Flow Statement 2008 ($ in Thousands)		
PERIOD ENDING	**31-Dec-06**	**10%**	**−10%**
Net income	1,506,000	1,717,980	1,293,948
*Depreciation**	774,000	774,000	774,000
Adjustments to net income	(167,000)	(167,000)	(167,000)
Changes in accounts receivables	(98,000)	(98,000)	(98,000)
*Changes in liabilities**	218,000	218,000	218,000
Changes in inventories	(193,000)	(193,000)	(193,000)
Changes in other operating activities	111,000	111,000	111,000
Total cash flow from operating activities	2,151,000	2,362,980	1,938,948
Investing Activities, Cash Flows Provided By or Used In			
Capital expenditures	(1,087,000)	0	0
Investments	(307,000)	0	0
Other cash flows from investing activities	2,589,000	0	0
Total cash flows from investing activities	1,195,000	0	0
Financing Activities, Cash Flows Provided By or Used In			
Dividends paid	(191,000)	(191,000)	(191,000)
Sale purchase of stock	74,000	0	0
Net borrowings	(1,232,000)	0	0
Other cash flows from financing activities	13,000	0	0
Total cash flows from financing activities	(1,336,000)	0	0
Effect of exchange rate changes	(4,000)	0	0
Change in cash and cash equivalents, end of year	$2,006,000	$2,171,980	$1,747,948

[a]Assumes zero investment cash flows.
[b]Assumes a zero change in shares outstanding, long-term debt, and other financing, but constant 2006 dividends of $191 Million.
*Italics indicate items with constant 2006 values.

Since retained earnings and the net cash increase are not equal, at this point the balance sheets will not balance. However, all items making up the difference between retained earnings and the net cash increase appear on the cash flow statement. Therefore, all subsequent adjustments will come from the cash flow statement. In this example, two adjustments are needed.

First property, plant, and equipment and goodwill accounts must be adjusted to reflect depreciation and amortization. For realistic detail, notice that constant 2006 depreciation and amortization of $774 million is allocated in 2007 as $5.855 million of amortization (0.1% of 2006 goodwill) and $768.145 million of depreciation as follows:

2006 Property	8,703,000	
2007 Depreciation	768,145	
2007 Property	7,934,855	
2006 Goodwill	5,855,000	
2007 Amortization	5855	.1% Goodwill
2007 Goodwill	5,849,145	

TABLE 17.13	Barrick Gold Corporation 2007 Pro Forma Balance Sheet ($ in Thousands)		
Net Sales Growth	**31-Dec-06**	**+10%**	**−10%**
Assets			
Current assets			
Cash and cash equivalents	3,043,000	5,214,980	4,790,948
Net receivables[a]	234,000	332,000	332,000
Inventory[b]	931,000	1,124,000	1,124,000
Other current assets[c]	588,000	477,000	477,000
Total current assets	4,796,000	7,147,980	6,723,948
*Long term investments**	1,182,000	1,182,000	1,182,000
Property plant and equipment[e]	8,703,000	7,934,855	7,934,855
Goodwill[e]	5,855,000	5,849,145	5,849,145
*Intangible assets**	75,000	75,000	75,000
*Other assets**	198,000	198,000	198,000
*Deferred long term asset charges**	564,000	564,000	564,000
Total assets	21,373,000	22,950,980	22,526,948
Liabilities			
Current liabilities[d]	1,852,000	2,070,000	2,070,000
*Long term debt**	3,244,000	3,244,000	3,244,000
*Other liabilities**	1,279,000	1,279,000	1,279,000
*Deferred long term liability charges**	798,000	798,000	798,000
*Minority interest**	1,000	1,000	1,000
Total liabilities	7,174,000	7,392,000	7,392,000
Stockholders' Equity			
Common stock	13,106,000	13,106,000	13,106,000
Retained earnings	974,000	2,333,980	1,909,948
Other stockholder equity	119,000	119,000	119,000
Total stockholder equity	14,199,000	15,558,980	15,134,948
Total liabilities and equity	21,373,000	22,950,980	22,526,948

[a]2006 net receivables of $234 million plus an increase of $98 million.
[b]2006 inventory of $931 million plus an increase of $193 million.
[c]2006 other current assets of $588 million minus a decrease of $111 million.
[d]2006 current liabilities of $1,852 million plus $218 million.
[e]Depreciation and amortization of $774 million is allocated as $5.855 million of amortization (10 percent of 2006 goodwill) and $768.145 million of depreciation.
*Italics indicate items with constant 2006 values.

Since depreciation and amortization are part of the difference between retained earnings and net cash flow, these adjustments bring the balance sheet to a complete balance.

To complete the analysis of Barrick Gold, projected profitability ratios and per-share values under increased and decreased sales scenarios are reported immediately below and compared with their original year-end 2006 values.

	RATIOS		
Scenario	Original	10%	−10%
Gross margin	48%	48%	48%
Operating margin	106%	109%	102%
ROA	7.0%	7.5%	5.7%
ROE	10.6%	11.0%	8.5%
Stock price	$45.44	$45.44	$45.44
Book value	$16.34	$17.91	$17.42
Price-book	2.7801638	2.537155	2.608238
Price-earnings	29.481363	25.452	35.02872
Earnings per share	$1.54	$1.79	$1.30
Cash flow per share	$2.48	$2.72	$2.23
Price-cash flow ratio	18.352183	16.70583	20.35926

For Barrick Gold Company, taking year-end 2006 price ratios and multiplying each ratio by its corresponding projected 2007 per-share value results in the following projected stock price calculations (subject to minor rounding errors):

	Projected Stock Prices	
	10%	−10%
BVPS × P/B	$49.79	$48.44
EPS × P/E	$52.63	$38.24
CFPS × P/CF	$49.92	$40.96

These projected stock prices reflect widely varying degrees of sensitivity to sales scenario outcomes. Earnings per share and cash flow per share are especially sensitive to which scenario is realized, while book value per share is less sensitive to scenario realization.

17.5 Summary and Conclusions

This chapter focuses on earnings and cash flow analysis using financial statement information. Several important aspects of financial statements and their use were covered. These are summarized as follows:

1. A primary source of financial information is a company's annual report. In addition, the annual reports can be obtained from the OSC website and SEDAR website.

2. Three financial statements are essential reading for securities analysts: the balance sheet, the income statement, and the cash flow statement.

3. The balance sheet has three sections: assets, which are used to generate earnings; liabilities, which are financial obligations; and equity, representing ownership claims. A fundamental accounting identity for balance sheets states that assets are equal to liabilities plus equity:

$$\text{Assets} = \text{Liabilities} + \text{Equity}$$

4. The balance sheet has four major asset categories: current assets, fixed assets, investments, and other assets.

5. The balance sheet has three major liability categories: current liabilities, long-term debt, and other liabilities.

6. The income statement reports revenues and expenses. Income is used to pay dividends or retained to finance future growth. Net income is the "bottom line" for a company.

7. The cash flow statement reports how cash was generated and where it was used. The cash flow statement assigns all cash flows to one of three categories: operating cash flow, investment cash flow, or financing cash flow. The sum of operating cash flow, investment cash flow, and financing cash flow yields the net cash increase.

8. Profitability ratios based on financial statement information are often reported to assist interpretation of a company's operating efficiency. Some standard profitability ratios are calculated as follows:

$$\text{Gross margin} = \frac{\text{Gross profit}}{\text{Net sales}}$$

$$\text{Operating margin} = \frac{\text{Operating income}}{\text{Net sales}}$$

$$\text{Return on assets (ROA)} = \frac{\text{Net income}}{\text{Total assets}}$$

$$\text{Return on equity (ROE)} = \frac{\text{Net income}}{\text{Stockholder equity}}$$

9. Annual reports also report per-share calculations of book value, earnings, and operating cash flow, respectively. These per-share values are calculated as follows:

$$\text{Book value per share (BVPS)} = \frac{\text{Stockholder equity}}{\text{Share outstanding}}$$

$$\text{Earnings per share (EPS)} = \frac{\text{Net income}}{\text{Share outstanding}}$$

$$\text{Cash flow per share (CFPS)} = \frac{\text{Operating cash flow}}{\text{Shares outstanding}}$$

Dividing the common stock price by the preceding per-share values, we get the following price ratios:

$$\text{Price-book ratio (P/B)} = \frac{\text{Stock prices}}{\text{BVPS}}$$

$$\text{Price-earnings ratio (P/E)} = \frac{\text{Stock price}}{\text{EPS}}$$

$$\text{Price-cash flow ratio (P/CF)} = \frac{\text{Stock price}}{\text{CFPS}}$$

10. One common method of analysis is to calculate projected stock prices using prior-period price ratios and projected per-share values from pro forma financial statements. These projected stock prices are calculated as follows:

BVPS $\times$ P/B = Projected price based on pro forma book value
EPS $\times$ P/E = Projected price based on pro forma earnings
CFPS $\times$ P/CF = Projected price based on pro forma cash flow

REAL WORLD

This chapter builds on the preceding chapter by going deeper into earnings and cash flow concepts, which are two of the most important tools of fundamental analysis. It focuses on using financial statement information to develop pro forma numbers to use in stock valuation. How should you, as an investor or investment manager, get started putting this information to work? The answer is you need to get your fingers dirty! Dig into the financial statements of a few companies and develop your own pro forma financial statements.

Excellent sources for financial statement information are the OSC website (www. osc.gov.on.ca) and SEDAR website (www.Sedar.com). Other useful online sources are CanCorp Financials (http://www.micromedia.ca/Corp-SecInfo) and Global Reports (www. global-reports.com).

Download the most recent financial reports for Barrick Gold from SEDAR (www.sedar. com) or the Barrick Gold website (www.barrick.com). Then try your hand at developing pro forma financial statements for Barrick Gold similar to the ones developed in this chapter.

Download the financial reports for the following companies and develop pro forma financial statements.

1. Magna International (www.magnaint.com)
2. Quebecor (www.quebecorworldinc.com)
3. Canfor (www.canfor.com)

A next step is to pick a company you are interested in and examine its financial statements. As you read a company's financial statements, an important exercise is to try to understand what each number really represents. Why is it there? Is it a cash or market value? Or is it just an accounting number (like depreciation)? Once you are familiar with a company's current financial statements, try to develop pro forma statements for various sales scenarios as was done in this chapter. You really can learn a lot by doing this.

Key Terms

SEDAR 549
disclosure regulation 549
balance sheet 550
income statement 550
cash flow statement 550
asset 551
liability 552
equity 552
income 553

cash flow 554
noncash items 554
operating cash flow 554
investment cash flow 554
financing cash flow 554
return on assets (ROA) 555
return on equity (ROE) 555
pro forma financial statements 556

Chapter Review Problems and Self-Test

1. **Margin Calculations** Use the following income statement for Paul Bunyan Lumber Co. to calculate gross and operating margins.

Paul Bunyan Lumber 2006 Income Statement	
Net sales	$8,000
Cost of goods sold	(6,400)
Gross profit	$1,600
Operating expenses	(400)
Operating income	$1,200
Other income	80
Net interest expense	(120)
Pretax income	$1,160
Income tax	(464)
Net income	$696
Earnings per share	$3.48
Recent share price	$76.56

2. **Return Calculations** Use the following balance sheet for Paul Bunyan Lumber Co. along with the income statement in the previous question to calculate return on assets and return on equity.

Paul Bunyan Lumber 2006 Balance Sheet	
Cash and cash equivalents	$400
Operating assets	400
Property, plant, and equipment	3,160
Other assets	216
Total assets	$4,176
Current liabilities	$720
Long-term debt	612
Other liabilities	60
Total liabilities	$1,392
Paid-in capital	$600
Retained earnings	2,184
Total shareholder equity	$2,784
Total liabilities and equity	$4,176

3. **Pro Forma Income Statements** Prepare a pro forma income statement for Paul Bunyan Lumber Co. assuming a 5 percent increase in sales. Based only on the pro forma income statement, what is the projected stock price? (*Hint:* What is the price-earnings ratio?)

Answers to Self-Test Problems

1. Gross margin is $1,600/$8,000 = 20%
   Operating margin is $1,200/$8,000 = 15%

2. Return on assets is $696/$4,176 = 16.67%
   Return on equity is $696/$2,784 = 25%

3. With 5 percent sales growth, sales will rise to $8,400 from $8,000. The pro forma income statement follows. A constant gross margin is assumed, implying that cost of goods sold will also rise by 5 percent. A constant tax rate of 40 percent is used. Items in italics are carried over unchanged.

Paul Bunyan Lumber Pro Forma 2007 Income Statement	
Net sales	$8,400
Cost of goods sold	(6,720)
Gross profit	$1,680
Operating expenses	(400)
Operating income	$1,280
Other income	80
Net interest expense	(120)
Pretax income	$1,240
Income tax	(496)
Net income	$744
Earnings per share	$3.72

To get a projected stock price, notice that the 2006 price-earnings ratio was $76.56 / $3.48 = 22. Using this ratio as a benchmark, the pro forma earnings of $3.72 imply a stock price of 22 × $3.72 = $81.84.

Test Your Investment Quotient

1. Balance Sheet Assets White Company assets as of December 31, 2005:

Cash and cash equivalents	$150
Operating assets	$1,190
Property, plant and equipment	$1,460
Total assets	$2,800

White Co. experienced the following events in 2000:

Old equipment that cost $120 and that was fully depreciated was scrapped

Depreciation expense was $125

Cash payments for new equipment were $200

Based on the information above, what was White Co.'s net amount of property, plant and equipment at the end of 2000?

a. $1,415
b. $1,535
c. $1,655
d. $1,660

2. Cash Flow Cash flow per share is calculated as

a. Net cash flow/Shares outstanding.
b. Operating cash flow/Shares outstanding.
c. Investing cash flow/Shares outstanding.
d. Financing cash flow/Shares outstanding.

3. Cash Flow Which of the following is not an adjustment to net income used to obtain operating cash flow?

a. Changes in operating assets
b. Changes in current liabilities
c. Loss on sale of assets
d. Dividends paid

4. Cash Flow The difference between net income and operating cash flow is at least partially accounted for by which of the following items?

a. Retained earnings
b. Cash and cash equivalents
c. Depreciation
d. Dividends paid

www.mcgrawhill.ca/olc/Jordan

5. **Financial Ratios** Which of the following profitability ratios is incorrect?

   a. Gross margin = Gross profit/Cost of goods sold
   b. Operating margin = Operating income/Net sales
   c. Return on assets = Net income/Total assets
   d. Return on equity = Net income/Stockholder equity

6. **Financial Ratios** Which of the following per-share ratios is incorrect?

   a. Book value per share = Total assets/Shares outstanding
   b. Earnings per share = Net income/Shares outstanding
   c. Cash flow per share = Operating cash flow/Shares outstanding
   d. Dividends per share = Dividends paid/Shares outstanding

7. **Stock Repurchase** A company repurchase of common stock outstanding has which of the following effects on the balance sheet?

   a. An increase in shares outstanding
   b. An increase in stockholder equity
   c. A decrease in paid-in capital
   d. A positive investment cash flow

8. **Dividend Payment** A dividend payment has which of the following effects on the balance sheet?

   a. An increase in shares outstanding
   b. A decrease in stockholder equity
   c. A decrease in paid-in capital
   d. An increase in retained earnings

9. **Stock Split** A 2-for-1 stock split has which of the following effects on the balance sheet?

   a. An increase in shares outstanding
   b. A decrease in stockholder equity
   c. A decrease in paid-in capital
   d. An increase in retained earnings

Use the following raw data to answer the next four questions:

Net income:	$16
Depreciation/amortization:	$4
Repurchase of outstanding common stock:	$10
Issuance of new debt:	$18
Sale of property:	$12
Purchase of equipment:	$14
Dividend payments:	$4

10. **Cash Flow Analysis** Operating cash flow is

    a. $20
    b. $16
    c. $12
    d. $30

11. **Cash Flow Analysis** Investing cash flow is

    a. $2
    b. $(2)
    c. $12
    d. $(12)

12. **Cash Flow Analysis** Financing cash flow is

    a. $8
    b. $(8)
    c. $4
    d. $(4)

13. **Cash Flow Analysis** Net cash increase is
   a. $18
   b. $20
   c. $22
   d. $24

Use the following financial data to answer the next three questions:

Cash payments for interest:	$(12)
Retirement of common stock:	$(32)
Cash payments to merchandise suppliers:	$(85)
Purchase of land:	$(8)
Sale of equipment:	$30
Payments of dividends:	$(37)
Cash payment for salaries:	$(35)
Cash collection from customers:	$260
Purchase of equipment:	$(40)

14. **Cash Flow Analysis** Cash flows from operating activities are
   a. $91
   b. $128
   c. $140
   d. $175

15. **Cash Flow Analysis** Cash flows from investing activities are
   a. $(67)
   b. $(48)
   c. $(18)
   d. $(10)

16. **Cash Flow Analysis** Cash flows from financing activities are
   a. $(81)
   b. $(69)
   c. $(49)
   d. $(37)

17. **Cash Flow Analysis** A firm has net sales of $3,000, cash expenses (including taxes) of $1,400, and depreciation of $500. If accounts receivable increase over the period by $400, cash flow from operations equals
   a. $1,200
   b. $1,600
   c. $1,700
   d. $2,100

18. **Cash Flow Analysis** A firm using straight-line depreciation reports gross investment in fixed assets of $80 million, accumulated depreciation of $45 million, and annual depreciation expense of $5 million. The approximate average age of fixed assets is
   a. 7 years
   b. 9 years
   c. 15 years
   d. 16 years

19. **Preferred Dividends** What proportion of preferred stock dividends received by a corporation is normally exempt from federal income taxation?
   a. 25–35 percent
   b. 50–60 percent
   c. 70–80 percent
   d. 90–100 percent

20. **Price Ratios** All else the same, which of the following ratios is unaffected by an increase in depreciation?

    a. Price-earnings (P/E)

    b. Price-book (P/B)

    c. Price-cash flow (P/CF)

    d. Price-sales (P/S)

Concept Questions

1. **Financial Statements** In very broad terms, what is the difference between an income statement and a balance sheet?

2. **Current Events** What makes current assets and liabilities "current"? Are operating assets "current"?

3. **Income and EPS** What is the relationship between net income and earnings per share (EPS)?

4. **Noncash Items** Why do we say depreciation is a "noncash item"?

5. **Cash Flow** What are the three sections on a standard cash flow statement?

6. **Operating Cash Flow** In the context of the standard cash flow statement, what is operating cash flow?

7. **Pro Forma** What is a pro forma financial statement?

8. **Retained Earnings** What is the difference between the "retained earnings" number on the income statement and the balance sheet?

9. **Gross!** What is the difference between gross margin and operating margin? What do they tell us? Generally speaking, are larger or smaller values better?

10. **More Gross** Which is larger, gross margin or operating margin? Can either be negative? Can both?

11. **Dividends and Taxes** Are dividends paid a tax-deductible expense to the paying company? Suppose a company receives dividends from another. How are these taxed?

12. **Cash Flow** How is the bottom line on a standard cash flow statement calculated? What does cash flow represent?

13. **Retained Earnings** Take a look at the balance sheet for Barrick Gold (Table 17.8). On it, retained earnings are $974 million. How do you interpret this? Does that mean that Barrick Gold has $974 million in cash available to spend?

14. **Price Ratios** George Smith from Alberta wants to learn the valuation method best suited for comparison of companies in the beef industry that has the following characteristics:

    Principal competitors within the industry are located in the United States, Australia, France.

    Because of mad-cow disease the industry is operating at a cyclical low.

    Many small businesses are reporting losses.

John Jones, MBA recommends that the client consider the price-earnings ratio, price-book value ratio, price-sales ratio. Determine which one of the three valuation ratios is most appropriate for comparing companies in this industry. Support your answer with two reasons that make that ratio superior to either of the other two ratios.

Questions and Problems

Core Questions

1. **Income Statements** Given the following information for Smashville, Inc., construct an income statement for the year:

Cost of goods sold:	$135,000
Investment income:	$2,100

Net sales:	$234,000
Operating expense:	$53,000
Interest expense:	$4,600
Dividends:	$5,800
Tax rate:	35%

What are retained earnings for the year?

2. **Balance Sheets** Given the following information for Smashville, Inc., construct a balance sheet:

Current liabilities:	$29,000
Cash:	$26,000
Long-term debt:	$87,000
Other assets:	$27,000
Fixed assets:	$125,000
Other liabilities:	$9,000
Investments:	$26,000
Operating assets:	$69,000

3. **Performance Ratios** Given the information in the previous two problems, calculate the gross margin, the operating margin, return on assets, and return on equity for Smashville, Inc.

4. **Per-Share Ratios** During the year, Smashville, Inc., had 12,000 shares of stock outstanding and depreciation expense of $13,000. Calculate the book value per share, earnings per share, and cash flow per share.

5. **Price Ratios** At the end of the year, Smashville stock sold for $48 per share. Calculate the price-book ratio, price-earnings ratio, and the price-cash flow ratio.

6. **Calculating EFN** The most recent financial statements for Bradley, Inc., are shown here (assuming no income taxes):

Income Statement		Balance Sheet			
Sales	$4,400	Assets	$13,400	Debt	$ 9,100
Costs	(2,685)			Equity	4,300
Net income	$1,715	Total	$13,400	Total	$13,400

Assets and costs are proportional to sales. Debt and equity are not. No dividends are paid. Next year's sales are projected to be $5,192. What is the external financing needed?

7. **Operating Cash Flow** Weston Corporation had earnings per share of $2.14, depreciation expense of $265,000, and 180,000 shares outstanding. What was the operating cash flow per share? If the share price was $34, what was the price-cash flow ratio?

8. **Earnings per Share** Alphonse Inc. has a return on equity of 20 percent, 35,000 shares of stock outstanding, and a net income of $65,000. What are earnings per share?

9. **Addition to Retained Earnings** Lemon Co. has net income of $125,000 and 30,000 shares of stock. If the company pays a dividend of $1.60, what are the additions to retained earnings?

10. **Cash Flow Statement** Given the following information for Hetrich, Inc., calculate the operating cash flow, investment cash flow, financing cash flow, and net cash flow:

Net income:	$128
Depreciation:	45
Issuance of new stock:	12
Repurchase of debt:	15
Sale of property:	16
Purchase of equipment:	50
Dividend payments:	8
Interest payments:	34

Intermediate
Questions

Use the following financial statement information to answer the next five questions.
Amounts are in thousands of dollars (except number of shares and price per share):

Kiwi Fruit Company Balance Sheet	
Cash and cash equivalents	$300
Operating assets	500
Property, plant and equipment	2,100
Other assets	80
Total assets	$2,980
Current liabilities	$400
Long-term debt	1,200
Other liabilities	100
Total liabilities	$1,700
Paid-in capital	$300
Retained earnings	980
Total shareholder equity	$1,280
Total liabilities and equity	$2,980

Kiwi Fruit Company Income Statement	
Net sales	$6,000
Cost of goods sold	(4,700)
Gross profit	$1,300
Operating expenses	(625)
Operating income	$675
Other income	140
Net interest expense	(200)
Pretax income	$615
Income tax	(210)
Net income	$405
Earnings per share	$1.01
Shares outstanding	400,000
Recent price	$18

Kiwi Fruit Company Cash Flow Statement	
Net income	$405
Depreciation and amortization	205
Changes in operating assets	(135)
Changes in current liabilities	(110)
Operating cash flow	$365
Net additions to properties	$405
Changes in other assets	(130)
Investing cash flow	$275
Issuance/redemption of long-term debt	$(250)
Dividends paid	(120)
Financing cash flow	$(370)
Net cash increase	$270

11. **Calculating Margins** Calculate the gross and operating margins for Kiwi Fruit.

12. **Calculating Profitability Measures** Calculate ROA and ROE for Kiwi Fruit and interpret these ratios.

13. **Calculating Per-Share Measures** Calculate the price-book, price-earnings, and price-cash flow ratios for Kiwi Fruit.

14. **Pro Forma Financial Statements** Following the examples in the chapter, prepare a pro forma income statement, balance sheet, and cash flow statement for Kiwi Fruit assuming a 10 percent increase in sales.

15. **Projected Share Prices** Based on the previous two questions, what is the projected stock price assuming a 10 percent increase in sales?

STANDARD &POOR'S

S&P Problems

www.mcgrawhill.com/edumarketinsight

1. **Company Performance** Under the "S&P Stock Reports" for Nortel (NT), download the Stock Report and Industry Outlook. What is the outlook for the industry? What is the outlook for the company? What are the factors mentioned in the stock report that affect the future outlook for Nortel?

2. **Cash Flow Statement** Under the "Excel Analytics" link, download the cash flow statements for Alcan (AL). Using the most recent cash flow statement, explain the various cash flows for Alcan. Make sure you note whether each item is an inflow or an outflow.

3. **Cash Flow Statement** Look up the information for Rogers Communications (RCI). Under "Excel Analytics," you will find the annual income statements, balance sheets, and cash flow statements. Although we covered the basics of the cash flow statement in this chapter, you can see that Rogers' cash flow statement is much more detailed. For the most recent year, use the income statement and balance sheets to reproduce the cash flow statement provided. Confirm the numbers provided on the cash flow statement where possible.

What's on the Web?

1. **Ratio Analysis** Go to www.investor.reuters.com and enter the ticker symbol RY for Royal Bank of Canada. Find the ratios for Royal Bank. Evaluate and compare the bank's performance with those of the industry and the TSX/SP 60.

2. **Ratio Calculation** Go to the Loblaw website at www.loblaw.com and examine their annual reports, calculate the ratios, prepare pro forma statements under 5% increase and decrease in sales scenarios.

3. **Cash Flow Statement** You can find financial statements for Research in Motion in the company's annual report located in the Investor Relations section of the company's website, www.rim.net. Locate the statement of cash flows in the annual report. How have the items changed over the years? Explain RIM's most recent cash flow statement in words.

CHAPTER 18

Corporate Bonds

"If you'd know the value of money, go and borrow some."
—Benjamin Franklin

A corporation issues bonds intending to meet all obligations of interest and repayment of principal. Investors buy bonds believing the corporation intends to fulfill its debt obligation in a timely manner. Although defaults can and do occur, the market for corporate bonds exists only because corporations are able to convince investors of their original intent to avoid default. Reaching this state of trust is not a trivial process, and it normally requires elaborate contractual arrangements. ■

Almost all corporations issue notes and bonds to raise money to finance investment projects. Indeed, for many corporations, the value of notes and bonds outstanding can exceed the value of common stock shares outstanding. Nevertheless, most investors do not think of corporate bonds when they think about investing. This is because corporate bonds represent specialized investment instruments that are usually bought by financial institutions like insurance companies and pension funds. For professional money managers at these institutions, a knowledge of corporate bonds is absolutely essential. This chapter introduces you to the specialized knowledge that these money managers possess.

18.1 Corporate Bond Basics

Corporate bonds represent the debt of a corporation owed to its bondholders. More specifically, a corporate bond is a security issued by a corporation that represents a promise to pay to its bondholders a fixed sum of money at a future maturity date, along with periodic payments of interest. The fixed sum paid at maturity is the bond's *principal*, also called its par or face value. The periodic interest payments are called *coupons*.

From an investor's point of view, corporate bonds represent an investment distinct from common stock. The three most fundamental differences are these:

1. Common stock represents an ownership claim on the corporation, whereas bonds represent a creditor's claim on the corporation.

2. Promised cash flows—that is, coupons and principal—to be paid to bondholders are stated in advance when the bond is issued. By contrast, the amount and timing of dividends paid to common stockholders may change at any time.

3. Most corporate bonds are issued as callable bonds, which means that the bond issuer has the right to buy back outstanding bonds before the maturity date of the bond issue. When a bond issue is called, coupon payments stop and the bondholders are forced to surrender their bonds to the issuer in exchange for the cash payment of a specified call price. By contrast, common stock is almost never callable.

Who owns corporate bonds and why? The answer is that most corporate bond investors belong to only a few distinct categories. The single largest group of corporate bond investors is life insurance companies. Remaining ownership shares are roughly equally balanced among individual investors, pension funds, banks, and foreign investors.

The pattern of corporate bond ownership is largely explained by the fact that corporate bonds provide a source of predictable cash flows. While individual bonds occasionally default on their promised cash payments, large institutional investors can diversify away most default risk by including a large number of different bond issues in their portfolios. For this reason, life insurance companies and pension funds find that corporate bonds are a natural investment vehicle to provide for future payments of retirement and death benefits, since both the timing and amount of these benefit payments can be matched with bond cash flows. These institutions can eliminate much of their financial risk by matching the timing of cash flows received from a bond portfolio to the timing of cash flows needed to make benefit payments—a strategy called cash flow matching. For this reason, life insurance companies and pension funds together own more than half of all outstanding corporate bonds. For similar reasons, individual investors might own corporate bonds as a source of steady cash income. However, since individual investors cannot easily diversify default risk, they should normally invest only in bonds with higher credit quality. Figure 18.1 illustrates a recent bond offering by Qwest Energy. The unsecured bonds that provide 5 percent interest are offered at $100. These bonds will mature on December 31, 2014.

Every corporate bond issue has a specific set of issue terms associated with it. The issue terms associated with any particular bond can range from a relatively simple arrangement, where the bond is little more than an IOU of the corporation, to a complex contract specifying in great detail what the issuer can and cannot do with respect to its obligations to bondholders. Bonds issued with a standard, relatively simple set of features are popularly called **plain vanilla bonds** or "bullet" bonds.

For more information on corporate bonds visit www. investinginbonds. com

---

plain vanilla bonds Bonds issued with a relatively standard set of features. Also known as bullet bonds.

FIGURE 18.1   Bond Offering

This prospectus constitutes a public offering of these securities only in those jurisdictions where they may be lawfully offered for sale and therein only by persons permitted to sell such securities. No securities regulatory authority has expressed an opinion about these securities and it is an offence to claim otherwise.

PROSPECTUS

Initial Public Offering   February 21, 2005

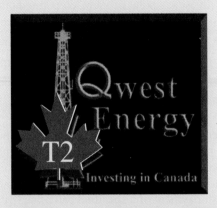

QWEST ENERGY 2005 FLOW-THROUGH LIMITED PARTNERSHIP
Maximum Offering: $50,000,000 (500,000 LP Units)

Minimum Offering: $5,000,000 (50,000 LP Units)

and

QWEST ENERGY 2005 FINANCIAL CORP.
Maximum Offering: $50,000,000 (500,000 Bonds)

Minimum Offering: $1,000,000 (10,000 Bonds)

LP Unit Price: $100.00 per LP Unit	**Bond Price: $100.00 per Bond**
Minimum LP Unit Purchase: 50 LP Units	**Minimum Bond Purchase: 50 Bonds**

The Partnership: Qwest Energy 2005 Flow-Through Limited Partnership (the "Partnership"), a limited partnership established under the laws of British Columbia, proposes to issue limited partnership units (the "LP Units") at a price of $100.00 per LP Unit (the "LP Unit Offering"). **LP Units cannot be purchased or held by "non-residents" as defined in the *Income Tax Act* (Canada) (the "Tax Act") or by individuals who are resident or deemed to be resident in the Province of Quebec for the purposes of the *Taxation Act* (Quebec).** See "The Partnership" and "Description of the LP Units".

Financial Corp.: Qwest Energy 2005 Financial Corp. ("Financial Corp."), a corporation incorporated under the laws of Canada, proposes to issue unsecured redeemable 5.0% bonds (the "Bonds") at a price of $100 per Bond (the "Bond Offering"). The Bonds will mature on December 31, 2014 and will bear interest at a rate per annum of 5.0% from the later of March 31, 2005 and the Final Closing Date (as hereinafter defined). Interest is payable annually on the last day of February of each year (or, if such day is not a business day, the immediately preceding business day) commencing February 28, 2006 and on the maturity date. Financial Corp. may redeem all or any portion of the Bonds at its option, at any time on or after June 30, 2007 and prior to maturity upon not less than 30 nor more than 60 days' notice mailed to each bondholder whose Bonds will be redeemed. Bonds will be so redeemed at a redemption price equal to the face value of the Bonds plus accrued interest up to, but excluding, the redemption date. Financial Corp. is a wholly-owned subsidiary of Knightswood Financial Corp., a reporting issuer in the Provinces of British Columbia and Alberta and whose shares are listed on the TSX Venture Exchange. Knightswood, through its wholly-owned subsidiary companies, provides financing to limited partnerships and investors in limited partnerships. See "Financial Corp." and "Description of the Bonds".

The Partnership's Investment Objective: The Partnership's investment objective is to provide limited partners of the Partnership ("Limited Partners") with a tax-assisted investment in a diversified portfolio of Flow-Through Shares (as hereinafter defined) of Resource Issuers (as hereinafter defined) with a view to achieving capital appreciation and profits for Limited Partners. The principal business of the Resource Issuers will be: (i) oil and gas exploration, development and production; (ii) mineral exploration, development and production; or (iii) certain energy production that may incur certain start-up phase costs of renewable energy and energy efficient projects. The General Partner expects to distribute at least 70% of the Partnership's Available Funds (as hereinafter defined) to Limited Partners for investment in Resource Issuers in the oil and gas sector, and up to 30% of the Available Funds for investment in Resource Issuers in the mining sector. Resource Issuers will agree to incur Canadian Exploration Expense or Canadian Development Expense (hereinafter defined as "Eligible Expenditures") in carrying out resource exploration and development in Canada and renounce Eligible Expenditures to former Limited Partners ("Beneficial Owners"). Subject to certain limitations, Beneficial Owners with sufficient income will be entitled to claim deductions for purposes of the Tax Act with respect to Eligible Expenditures incurred and renounced to them. See "Canadian Federal Income Tax Considerations". All investments will be made in accordance with the Partnership's Investment Strategy and Investment Guidelines, as described in this prospectus. See "Investment Structure" and "Investment Guidelines".

Source: SEDAR website, www.sedar.com, February 28, 2005.

TABLE 18.1	Software Iz Us Five-Year Note Issue	
Issue amount	$20 million	Note issue total face value is $20 million
Issue date	12/15/2003	Notes offered to the public in December 2003
Maturity date	12/31/2008	Remaining principal due December 31, 2008
Face value	$1,000	Face value denomination is $1,000 per note
Coupon interest	$100 per annum	Annual coupons are $100 per note
Coupon dates	6/30, 12/31	Coupons are paid semiannually
Offering price	100	Offer price is 100 percent of face value
Yield to maturity	10%	Based on stated offer price
Call provision	Not callable	Notes may not be paid off before maturity
Security	None	Notes are unsecured
Rating	Not rated	Privately placed note issue

As an illustration of a plain vanilla corporate debt issue, Table 18.1 summarizes the issue terms for a note issue by Software Iz Us. Referring to Table 18.1, we see that the Software Iz Us notes were issued in December 2003 and mature five years later in December 2008. Each individual note has a face value denomination of $1,000. Since the total issue amount is $20 million, the entire issue contains 20,000 notes. Each note pays a $100 annual coupon, which is equal to 10 percent of its face value. The annual coupon is split between two semiannual $50 payments made each June and December. Based on the original offer price of 100, which means 100 percent of the $1,000 face value, the notes have a yield to maturity of 10 percent. The notes are not callable, which means that the debt may not be paid off before maturity.

unsecured debt
Bonds, notes, or other debt issued with no specific collateral pledged as security for the bond issue.

The Software Iz Us notes are **unsecured debt**, which means that no specific collateral has been pledged as security for the notes. In the event that the issuer defaults on its promised payments, the noteholders may take legal action to acquire sufficient assets of the company to settle their claims as creditors.

When issued, the Software Iz Us notes were not reviewed by a rating agency like Moody's or Standard & Poor's. Thus, the notes are unrated. If the notes were to be assigned a credit rating, they would probably be rated as "junk grade." The term "junk," commonly used for high-risk debt issues, is unduly pejorative. After all, your company must repay the debt. However, the high-risk character of the software industry portends an above-average probability that your company may have difficulty paying off the debt in a timely manner.

Reflecting their below-average credit quality, the Software Iz Us notes were not issued to the general public. Instead, the notes were privately placed with two insurance companies. Such private placements are common among relatively small debt issues. Private placements will be discussed in greater detail later in this chapter.

18.2 Types of Corporate Bonds

debentures
Unsecured bonds issued by a corporation.

Debentures are the most frequently issued type of corporate bond. Debenture bonds represent an unsecured debt of a corporation. Debenture bondholders have a legal claim as general creditors of the corporation. In the event of a default by the issuing corporation, the bondholders' claim extends to all corporate assets. However, they may have to share this claim with other creditors who have an equal legal claim or yield to creditors with a higher legal claim.

mortgage bond
Debt secured with a property lien.

collateral trust bond
Debt secured with financial collateral.

equipment trust certificate Shares in a trust with income from a lease contract.

In addition to debentures, there are three other basic types of corporate bonds: mortgage bonds, collateral trust bonds, and equipment trust certificates. **Mortgage bonds** represent debt issued with a lien on specific property, usually real estate, pledged as security for the bonds. A mortgage lien gives bondholders the legal right to foreclose on property pledged by the issuer to satisfy an unpaid debt obligation. However, in actual practice, foreclosure and sale of mortgaged property following a default may not be the most desirable strategy for bondholders. Instead, it is common for a corporation in financial distress to reorganize itself and negotiate a new debt contract with bondholders. In these negotiations, a mortgage lien can be an important bargaining tool for the trustee representing the bondholders.

Collateral trust bonds are characterized by a pledge of financial assets as security for the bond issue. Collateral trust bonds are commonly issued by holding companies, which may pledge the stocks, bonds, or other securities issued by their subsidiaries as collateral for their own bond issue. The legal arrangement for pledging collateral securities is similar to that for a mortgage lien. In the event of an issuer's default on contractual obligations to bondholders, the bondholders have a legal right to foreclose on collateralized securities in the amount necessary to settle an outstanding debt obligation.

Equipment trust certificates represent debt issued by a trustee to purchase heavy industrial equipment that is leased and used by railroads, airlines, and other companies with a demand for heavy equipment. Under this financial arrangement, investors purchase equipment trust certificates, and the proceeds from this sale are used to purchase equipment. Formal ownership of the equipment remains with a trustee appointed to represent the certificate holders. The trustee then leases the equipment to a company. In return, the company promises to make a series of scheduled lease payments over a specified leasing period. The trustee collects the lease payments and distributes all revenues, less expenses, as dividends to the certificate holders. These distributions are conventionally called dividends because they are generated as income from a trust. The lease arrangement usually ends after a specified number of years when the leasing company makes a final lease payment and may take possession of the used equipment. From the certificate holders' point of view, this financial arrangement is superior to a mortgage lien since they actually own the equipment during the leasing period. Thus, if the leasing corporation defaults, the equipment can be sold without the effort and expense of a formal foreclosure process. Since the underlying equipment for this type of financing is typically built according to an industry standard, the equipment can usually be quickly sold or leased to another company in the same line of business.

Figure 18.2 is a *Wall Street Journal* bond announcement for an aircraft equipment trust for Northwest Airlines. Notice that the $243 million issue is split into two parts: $177 million of senior notes paying 8.26 percent interest and $66 million of subordinated notes paying 9.36 percent interest. The senior notes have a first claim on the aircraft in the event of a default by the airline, while the subordinated notes have a secondary claim. In the event of a default, investment losses for the trust will primarily be absorbed by the subordinated noteholders. For this reason the subordinated notes are riskier and, therefore, pay a higher interest rate. Of course, if no default actually occurs, it would turn out that the subordinated notes were actually a better investment. However, there is no way of knowing this in advance.

Visit the Northwest Airlines website at www.nwa.com

FIGURE 18.2   **Equipment Trust Notes Issue**

These securities have not been registered under the Securities Act of 1933 and may not be offered or sold in the United States or to U.S. persons except in accordance with the resale restrictions applicable thereto. These securities having been previously sold, this announcement appears as a matter of record only.

$243,000,000

NWA Trust No. 1

$177,000,000 8.26% Class A Senior Aircraft Notes

$66,000,000 9.36% Class B Subordinated Aircraft Notes

The 8.26% Class A Senior Aircraft Notes and the 9.36% Class B Subordinated Aircraft Notes are secured by, among other things, a security interest in certain aircraft sold by Northwest Airlines, Inc. ("Northwest") to an owner trust for a purchase price of $443 million and the lease relating to such Aircraft, including the right to receive amounts payable by Northwest under such lease. The Noteholders also have the benefit of a liquidity facility, initially provided by General Electric Capital Corporation, to support certain payments of interest on the Notes.

Lehman Brothers   **BT Securities Corporation**

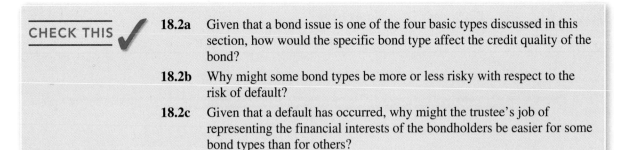

18.2a Given that a bond issue is one of the four basic types discussed in this section, how would the specific bond type affect the credit quality of the bond?

18.2b Why might some bond types be more or less risky with respect to the risk of default?

18.2c Given that a default has occurred, why might the trustee's job of representing the financial interests of the bondholders be easier for some bond types than for others?

18.3 Bond Indentures

A bond indenture is a formal written agreement between the corporation and the bondholders. It is an important legal document that spells out in detail the mutual rights and obligations of the corporation and the bondholders with respect to the bond issue. Indenture contracts are often quite long, sometimes several hundred pages, and make for very tedious reading. In fact, very few bond investors ever read the original indenture, but instead might refer to an **indenture summary** provided in the **prospectus** that was circulated when the bond issue was originally sold to the public. Alternatively, a summary of the most important features of an indenture is published by debt rating agencies.

Companies generally appoint a trustee to represent the interests of bondholders. Also, all responsibilities of a duly appointed trustee must be specified in detail in the indenture. Some corporations maintain a blanket or open-ended indenture that applies to all currently outstanding bonds and any new bonds that are issued, while other corporations write a new indenture contract for each new bond issue sold to the public.

Descriptions of the most important provisions frequently specified in a bond indenture agreement are presented next.

indenture summary
Description of the contractual terms of a new bond issue included in a bond's prospectus.

prospectus
Document prepared as part of a security offering detailing information about a company's financial position, its operations, and investment plans.

Bond Seniority Provisions

A corporation may have several different bond issues outstanding; these issues normally can be differentiated according to the seniority of their claims on the firm's assets. Seniority usually is specified in the indenture contract.

Consider a corporation with two outstanding bond issues: (1) a mortgage bond issue with certain real estate assets pledged as security and (2) a debenture bond issue with no specific assets pledged as security. In this case, the mortgage bond issue has a senior claim on the pledged assets but no specific claim on other corporate assets. The debenture bond has a claim on all corporate assets not specifically pledged as security for the mortgage bond, but it would have only a residual claim on assets pledged as security for the mortgage bond issue. This residual claim would apply only after all obligations to the mortgage bondholders have been satisfied.

As another example, suppose a corporation has two outstanding debenture issues. In this case, seniority is normally assigned to the bonds first issued by the corporation. The bonds issued earliest have a senior claim on the pledged assets and are called **senior debentures**. The bonds issued later have a junior or subordinate claim and are called **subordinated debentures**.

senior debentures
Bonds that have a higher claim on the firm's assets than other bonds.

subordinated debentures Bonds that have a claim on the firm's assets after those with a higher claim have been satisfied.

negative pledge clause Bond indenture provision that prohibits new debt from being issued with seniority over an existing issue.

The seniority of an existing debt issue is usually protected by a **negative pledge clause** in the bond indenture. A negative pledge clause prohibits a new issue of debt with seniority over a currently outstanding issue. However, it may allow a new debt issue to share equally in the seniority of an existing issue. A negative pledge clause is part of the indenture agreement of most senior debenture bonds.

Call Provisions

Most corporate bond issues have a call provision allowing the issuer to buy back all or part of its outstanding bonds at a specified call price sometime before the bonds mature. The most frequent motive for a corporation to call outstanding bonds is to take advantage of a general fall in market interest rates. Lower interest rates allow the corporation to replace currently outstanding high-coupon bonds with a new issue of bonds paying lower coupons. Replacing existing bonds with new bonds is called **bond refunding**.

bond refunding Process of calling an outstanding bond issue and refinancing it with a new bond issue.

From an investor's point of view, a call provision has a distinct disadvantage. For example, suppose an investor is currently holding bonds paying 10 percent coupons. Further suppose that, after a fall in market interest rates, the corporation is able to issue new bonds that only pay 8 percent coupons. By calling existing 10 percent coupon bonds, the issuer forces bondholders to surrender their bonds in exchange for the call price. But this happens at a time when the bondholders can reinvest funds only at lower interest rates. If instead the bonds were noncallable, the bondholders would continue to receive the original 10 percent coupons. For this reason, callable bonds are less attractive to investors than noncallable bonds. Consequently, a callable bond will sell at a lower price than a comparable noncallable bond.

Despite their lower prices, corporations generally prefer to issue callable bonds. However, to reduce the price gap between callable and noncallable bonds, issuers typically allow the indenture contract to specify certain restrictions on their ability to call an outstanding bond issue. Three features are commonly used to restrict an issuer's call privilege:

1. Callable bonds usually have a *deferred call provision* which provides a *call protection period* during which a bond issue cannot be called. For example, a bond may be call-protected for a period of five years after its issue date.

2. A call price often includes a *call premium* over par value. A standard arrangement stipulates a call premium equal to one-year's coupon payments for a call occurring at the earliest possible call date. Over time, the call premium is gradually reduced until it is eliminated entirely. After some future date, the bonds become callable at par value.

3. Some indentures specifically prohibit an issuer from calling outstanding bonds for the purpose of refunding at a lower coupon rate but still allow a call for other reasons. This *refunding provision* prevents the corporation from calling an outstanding bond issue solely as a response to falling market interest rates. However, the corporation can still pay off its bond debt ahead of schedule by using funds acquired from, say, earnings, or funds obtained from the sale of newly issued common stock.

Make-Whole Call Provision   In just the last few years, a new type of call provision, a "make-whole" call, has become common in the corporate bond market. If a callable bond has a make-whole call provision, bondholders receive approximately what the bond is worth if the bond is called. This call provision gets its name because the bondholder does not suffer a loss in the event of a call; that is, the bondholder is "made whole" when the bond is called.

Like a fixed-price call provision, a make-whole call provision allows the borrower to pay off the remaining debt early. Unlike a fixed-price call provision, however, a make-whole call provision requires the borrower to make a lump-sum payment representing the present value of all payments that will not be made because of the call. The discount rate used to calculate the present value is usually equal to the yield on a comparable maturity Treasury security plus a fixed, prespecified *make-whole premium.*

Because the yield of a comparable Treasury security changes over time, the call price paid to bondholders changes over time. As interest rates decrease, the make-whole call price increases because the discount rate used to calculate the present value decreases. As interest rates increase, the make-whole call price decreases. In addition, make-whole call provisions typically specify that the minimum amount received by a bondholder is the par value of the bond.

As interest rates decline, even in the region of low yields, the price of bonds with a make-whole call provision will increase. That is, these bonds exhibit the standard *convex price-yield relationship* in all yield regions. In contrast, recall that bond prices with a fixed-price call provision exhibit *negative convexity* in the region of low yields.

Graphical Analysis of Callable Bond Prices

After a bond's call protection period has elapsed, a rational investor would be unwilling to pay much more than the call price for the bond since the issuer might call the bond at any time and pay only the call price for the bond. Consequently, a bond's call price serves as an effective ceiling on its market price. It is important for bond investors to understand how the existence of a price ceiling for callable bonds alters the standard price-yield relationship for bonds.

The relationship between interest rates and prices for comparable callable and noncallable bonds is illustrated in Figure 18.3. In this example, the vertical axis measures bond prices, and the horizontal axis measures bond yields. In this two-bond example, both bonds pay an 8 percent coupon and are alike in all respects except that one of the bonds is callable any time at par value.

FIGURE 18.3   **Callable and Noncallable Bonds**

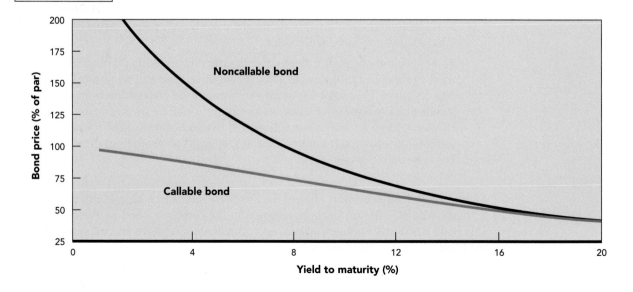

As shown, the noncallable bond has the standard *convex price-yield relationship*, where the price-yield curve is bowed toward the origin. When the price-yield curve is bowed to the origin this is called *positive convexity*. In contrast, the callable bond has a convex or bowed price-yield relationship in the region of high yields, but is bowed away from the origin in the region of low yields. This is called *negative convexity*. The important lesson here is that no matter how low market interest rates might fall, the maximum price of an unprotected callable bond is generally bounded above by its call price.

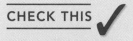

CHECK THIS

18.3a   After a call protection period has elapsed, why is the call price an effective ceiling on the market price of a callable bond?

Put Provisions

put bonds Bonds that can be sold back to the issuer at a prespecified price on any of a sequence of prespecified dates. Also called *extendible bonds*.

A bond issue with a put provision grants bondholders the right to sell their bonds back to the issuer at a special *put price*, normally set at par value. These bonds are called **put bonds** or *putable bonds* in the United States, and *retractable bonds* in Canada. These so-called put bonds are "putable" on each of a series of designated *put dates*. These are often scheduled to occur annually but sometimes occur at more frequent intervals. At each put date, the bondholder decides whether to sell the bond back to the issuer or continue to hold the bond until the next put date. For this reason, put bonds are often called *extendible bonds* because the bondholder has the option of extending the maturity of the bond at each put date.

Notice that by granting bondholders an option to sell their bonds back to the corporation at par value, the put feature provides an effective floor on the market price of the bond. Thus, the put feature offers protection to bondholders from rising interest rates and the associated fall in bond prices.

A put feature also helps protect bondholders from acts of the corporation that might cause a deterioration of the bond's credit quality. However, this protection is not granted without a cost to bond investors, since a putable bond will command a higher market price than a comparable nonputable bond.

CHECK THIS

18.3b   Using Figure 18.3 as a guide, what would the price-yield relationship look like for a noncallable bond putable at par value?

18.3c   Under what conditions would a put feature not yield an effective floor for the market price of a put bond? (*Hint*: Think about default risk.)

Bond-to-Stock Conversion Provisions

convertible bonds Bonds that holders can exchange for common stock according to a prespecified conversion ratio.

Some bonds have a valuable bond-to-stock conversion feature. These bonds are called convertible bonds. **Convertible bonds** grant bondholders the right to exchange each bond for a designated number of common stock shares of the issuing firm. To avoid confusion in a discussion of convertible bonds, it is important to understand some basic terminology.

1. The number of common stock shares acquired in exchange for each converted bond is called the *conversion ratio*:

   Conversion ratio = Number of stock shares acquired by conversion

2. The par value of a convertible bond divided by its conversion ratio is called the bond's *conversion price*:

$$\text{Conversion price} = \frac{\text{Bond par value}}{\text{Conversion ratio}}$$

3. The market price per share of common stock acquired by conversion times the bond's conversion ratio is called the bond's *conversion value*:

$$\text{Conversion value} = \text{Price per share of stock} \times \text{Conversion ratio}$$

For example, suppose a convertible bond with a par value of $1,000 can be converted into 20 shares of the issuing firm's common stock. In this case, the conversion price is $1,000 / 20 = $50. Continuing this example, suppose the firm's common stock has a market price of $40 per share, then the conversion value of a single bond is 20 × $40 = $800.

Figure 18.4 is *The Wall Street Journal* announcement of an issue of convertible subordinated notes by Advanced Micro Devices (AMD). The notes pay a 6 percent coupon rate and matured in 2005. The conversion price for this note issue is $37 per share, which implies a conversion ratio of 27.027 shares of common stock for each $1,000 face value note.

From an investor's perspective, the conversion privilege of convertible bonds has the distinct advantage that bondholders can receive a share of any increase in common stock value. However, the conversion option has a price. A corporation can sell convertible bonds at par value with a coupon rate substantially less than the coupon rate of comparable nonconvertible bonds. This forgone coupon interest represents the price of the bond's conversion option.

When convertible bonds are originally issued, their conversion ratio is customarily set to yield a conversion value 10 percent to 20 percent less than par value. For example, suppose the common stock of a company has a price of $30 per share and the company issues convertible bonds with a par value of $1,000 per bond. To set the original conversion value at $900 per bond, the company would set a conversion ratio of 30 stock shares per bond. Thereafter, the conversion ratio is fixed, but each bond's conversion value becomes linked to the firm's stock price, which may rise or fall in value. The price of a convertible bond reflects the conversion value of the bond. In general, the higher the conversion value the higher is the bond price, and vice versa.

Investing in convertible bonds is more complicated than owning nonconvertible bonds, because the conversion privilege presents convertible bondholders with an important timing decision. When is the best time to exercise a bond's conversion option and exchange the bond for shares of common stock? The answer is that investors should normally postpone conversion as long as possible, because while they hold the bonds they continue to receive coupon payments. After converting to common stock, they lose all subsequent coupons. In general, unless the total dividend payments on stock acquired by conversion are somewhat greater than the forgone bond coupon payments, investors should hold on to their convertible bonds to continue to receive coupon payments.

The rational decision of convertible bondholders to postpone conversion as long as possible is limited, however, since convertible bonds are almost always callable. Firms customarily call outstanding convertible bonds when their conversion value has risen by 10 percent to 15 percent above bond par value, although there are many exceptions to this rule. When a convertible bond issue is called by the issuer, bondholders are forced to make an immediate decision whether to convert to common stock shares or accept a cash payment of the call price. Fortunately, the decision is simple—convertible bondholders should choose whichever is more valuable, the call price or the conversion value.

Find out more about convertible bonds at www.convertbond. com

Visit the AMD website at www.amd.com

Convertible Notes Issue

This announcement is neither an offer to sell, nor a solicitation of an offer to buy, any of these securities.
The offer is made only by the Prospectus and related Prospectus Supplement.

$517,500,000

AMD

Advanced Micro Devices, Inc.

6% Convertible Subordinated Notes due 2005

The 6% Convertible Subordinated Notes due 2005 (the "Notes") will be convertible at the option of the holder into shares of common stock, par value $.01 per share (the "Common Stock"), of Advanced Micro Devices, Inc. (the "Company") at any time at or prior to maturity, unless previously redeemed or repurchased, at a conversion price of $37.00 per share (equivalent to a conversion rate of 27.027 shares per $1,000 principal amount of Notes), subject to adjustment in certain events.

Price 100%

Copies of the Prospectus and related Prospectus Supplement may be obtained in any State from such of the undersigned as may legally offer these securities in compliance with the securities laws of such State.

Donaldson, Lufkin & Jenrette
Securities Corporation

Salomon Smith Barney

CHECK THIS **18.3d** Describe the conversion decision that convertible bondholders must make when the bonds mature.

Graphical Analysis of Convertible Bond Prices

The price of a convertible bond is closely linked to the value of the underlying common stock shares that can be acquired by conversion. A higher stock price implies a higher bond price, and, conversely, a lower stock price yields a lower bond price.

The relationship between the price of a convertible bond and the price of the firm's common stock is depicted in Figure 18.5. In this example, the convertible bond's price is measured on the vertical axis, and the stock price is measured along the horizontal axis. The straight, upward-sloping line is the bond's conversion value; the slope of the line is the conversion ratio. The horizontal line represents the price of a comparable nonconvertible bond with the same coupon rate, maturity, and credit quality.

in-the-money bond
A convertible bond whose conversion value is greater than its call price.

A convertible bond is said to be an **in-the-money bond** when its conversion value is greater than its call price. If an in-the-money convertible bond is called, rational bondholders will convert their bonds into common stock. When the conversion value is less than the call price, a convertible bond is said to be *out of the money*. If an out-of-the-money bond is called, rational bondholders will accept the call price and forgo the conversion option. In practice, however, convertible bonds are seldom called when they are out of the money.

intrinsic bond value
The price below which a convertible bond cannot fall, equal to the value of a comparable nonconvertible bond. Also called *investment value*.

The curved line in Figure 18.5 shows the relationship between a convertible bond's price and the underlying stock price. As shown, there are two lower bounds on the value of a convertible bond. First, a convertible bond's price can never fall below its **intrinsic bond value**, also commonly called its *investment value* or *straight bond value*. This value is what the bond would be worth if it were not convertible, but otherwise identical in terms of coupon, maturity, and credit quality. Second, a convertible bond can never sell for less than its *conversion value* because, if it did, investors could simply buy the bond and convert, thereby realizing an immediate, riskless profit.

FIGURE 18.5 **Convertible Bond Prices**

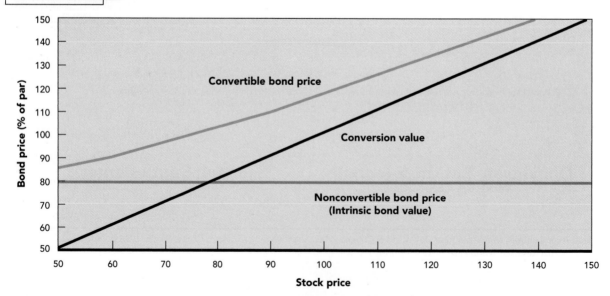

Thus, the *floor value* of a convertible bond is its intrinsic bond value or its conversion value, whichever is larger. As shown in Figure 18.5, however, a convertible bond will generally sell for more than this floor value. This extra is the amount that investors are willing to pay for the right, but not the obligation, to convert the bond at a future date at a potentially much higher stock price.

An interesting variation of a bond-to-stock conversion feature occurs when the company issuing the bonds is different from the company whose stock is acquired by the conversion. In this case, the bonds are called **exchangeable bonds**. Figure 18.6 presents a *Wall Street Journal* announcement of an issue of exchangeable subordinated debentures by the McKesson Corporation. These debentures are exchangeable for common stock shares of Armor All Products Corporation. McKesson is a retail distributor, and Armor All markets consumer chemical products. Exchangeable bonds, while not unusual, are less common than convertible bonds.

exchangeable bonds Bonds that can be converted into common stock shares of a company other than the issuer's.

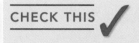

CHECK THIS

18.3e For nonconvertible bonds, the call price is a ceiling on the market price of the bond. Why might the call price not be an effective ceiling on the price of a convertible bond?

Bond Maturity and Principal Payment Provisions

term bonds Bonds issued with a single maturity date.

Term bonds represent the most common corporate bond maturity structure. A term bond issue has a single maturity date. On this date, all outstanding bond principal must be paid off. The indenture contract for a term bond issue normally stipulates the creation of a *sinking fund,* that is, an account established to repay bondholders through a series of fractional redemptions before the bond reaches maturity. Thus, at maturity, only a fraction of the original bond issue will still be outstanding. Sinking fund provisions are discussed in more detail later.

serial bonds Bonds issued with a regular sequence of maturity dates.

An alternative maturity structure is provided by **serial bonds**, where a fraction of an entire bond issue is scheduled to mature in each year over a specified period. Essentially, a serial bond issue represents a collection of subissues with sequential maturities. As an example, a serial bond issue may stipulate that one-tenth of an entire bond issue must be redeemed in each year over a 10-year period, with the last fraction redeemed at maturity. Serial bonds generally do not have a call provision, whereas term bonds usually do have a call provision.

When originally issued, most corporate bonds have maturities of 30 years or less. However, in recent years some companies have issued bonds with 40- and 50-year maturities. In 1993, Walt Disney Company made headlines in the financial press when it sold 100-year maturity bonds. This bond issue became popularly known as the "Sleeping Beauty" bonds, after the classic Disney movie. However, the prince might arrive early for these bonds since they are callable after 30 years. Nevertheless, this was the first time since 1954 that 100-year bonds were sold by any borrower in the United States. Only days later, however, Coca-Cola issued $150 million of 100-year maturity bonds. Both the Disney and Coke bond issues locked in the unusually low interest rates prevailing in 1993. You can examine the suggestions given regarding corporate and government bond investments in the next *Investment Updates box.*

FIGURE 18.6	Exchangeable Debentures Issue

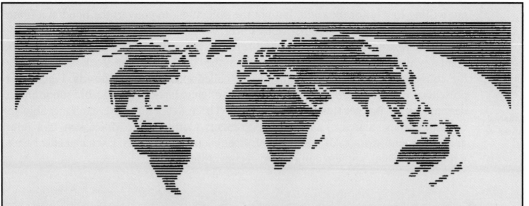

This announcement is neither an offer to sell nor a solicitation of an offer to buy any of these Securities. The offer is made only by the Prospectus.

$180,000,000

McKesson Corporation

4½% Exchangeable Subordinated Debentures Due 2004

Exchangeable for Shares of Common Stock of

Armor All Products Corporation

Interest Payable March 1 and September 1

Price 100% and Accrued Interest, if any

Copies of the Prospectus may be obtained in any State from only such of the undersigned as may legally offer these Securities in compliance with the securities laws of such State.

MORGAN STANLEY & CO.
Incorporated

MONTGOMERY SECURITIES

MONNESS, CRESPI, HARDT & CO. INC.

WHEAT FIRST BUTCHER & SINGER
Capital Markets

Short-term thinking is depriving investors of decent returns from bonds.

Too many people have a one- to five-year mindset when buying fixed-income investments. The explanation may be that this is the way guaranteed investment certificates and mortgages are sold, or maybe not. Whatever the reason, it's shortsighted.

If you want superior returns from bonds these days, you have to go long. Now, how about a 5-percent yield on a fixed-income investment for your registered retirement savings plan?

Your bank won't give it to you on a GIC, that's for sure. The best you'll do is roughly 3.5 percent, assuming you talk your way into a bonus on posted rates, or 4 percent if you go to small independents such as ING Direct. A five-year bond or strip bond are alternatives, but there you're looking at yields of 3.8 percent at best.

A 5-percent yield is available, but you have to go long. Perusing the bond inventory of on-line broker TD Waterhouse, I found a Province of Quebec strip bond maturing Dec. 1, 2016, that was priced to yield 5.02 percent, and an Ontario Hydro strip that matures Nov. 26, 2017, and yields 5.05 percent.

There are risks to buying long bonds like these, but they don't apply to most investors.

The longer a bond's term, the more volatile it is as interest rates move up and down. If rates were to shoot up because of inflationary pressure, then long bonds could fall sharply in price.

If you're the sort of investor who buys and sells bonds for capital gains as well as to collect the semi-annual interest payments, this kind of vulnerability is problematic. But if you're like most and hold bonds until they mature, then moves in prices are just trivia.

"We've taken surveys and we've found that most individual investors hold until maturity when they buy bonds," said Sheldon Dong, vice-president of fixed-income strategy for the research-marketing group of TD Waterhouse.

For this reason, Mr. Dong is a big believer in owning bonds that mature in 10 years or more. Specifically, he likes long Government of Canada, provincial and municipal bonds, but he's not crazy about corporate bonds.

Mr. Dong argues that the chances of default are remote with all three levels of government because their debt obligations are ultimately income taxes, which can be raised if necessary. Corporate bonds are riskier because of the possibility that companies can run into financial problems that affect their ability to meet their obligations to bondholders.

"The problem that most individual investors have is that they don't monitor their bond portfolios," he explained. "They buy, hold and forget. Corporate bonds have to be treated like a stock. If something smells fishy, boom, you have to be able to sell it, whereas with a government bond, you can truly buy and forget."

For this reason, Mr. Dong suggests you buy corporate bonds that mature in five years or less. As for government bonds, you can go out as long as 10, 20 or even 30 years. "For someone who's young, heck, why not own a 30-year bond?"

Why not, indeed. Mr. Dong thinks many investors shun long bonds because they're worried about the volatility. "They read the media and they see all these so-called experts saying, well, this is a bad year for bonds, interest rates may go up. That's a very short-term, myopic trading view. What people don't realize is that, hey, they're in it for the long term."

Another point is that some investment advisers are reluctant to sell long-dated strips. Mr. Dong says that when price swings on long bonds show up on account statements, they tend to generate calls from concerned clients who don't understand that the volatility means nothing.

An adviser who continually rolls over short-term bonds would seem to be in a position to generate more commissions than one who sells a single long bond, but Mr. Dong said long-bond commissions are large enough to offset any disadvantage.

If you plan to buy some long bonds, integrate them into your portfolio using the tried-and-true strategy of laddering. That's where you stagger maturities so that you regularly have money coming due that you can invest at higher rates if the opportunity arises. Similarly, you're protected from lower rates because you'll never have to reinvest a lot of money at one time.

Be sure to consider your life-cycle goals when buying long bonds, too. For example, buying a 20-year bond when you're 55 would limit your flexibility once you retire.

Many investors have responded to today's low returns on bonds by buying income trusts, which currently trade at peak prices. Long bonds don't offer as much yield, but they're still more attractive than short-term bonds and GICs.

"They're a safe road to go, and I don't think people are thinking enough about safety right now," Mr. Dong said.

Source: Rob Carrick, *The Globe and Mail*, January 20, 2005, p. B14. Reprinted with permission from *The Globe and Mail*. rcarrick@globeandmail.com

Sinking Fund Provisions

sinking fund
An account used to provide for scheduled redemptions of outstanding bonds.

The indentures of most term bonds include a **sinking fund** provision that requires the corporation to make periodic payments into a trustee-managed account. Account reserves are then used to provide for scheduled redemptions of outstanding bonds. The existence of a sinking fund is an important consideration for bond investors mainly for two reasons:

1. A sinking fund provides a degree of security to bondholders, since payments into the sinking fund can be used only to pay outstanding obligations to bondholders.

2. A sinking fund provision requires fractional bond issue redemptions according to a preset schedule. Therefore, some bondholders will be repaid their invested principal before the stated maturity for their bonds whether they want repayment or not.

As part of a *scheduled sinking fund redemption*, some bondholders may be forced to surrender their bonds in exchange for cash payment of a special *sinking fund call price*. For this reason, not all bondholders may be able to hold their bonds until maturity, even though the entire bond issue has not been called according to a general call provision. For example, the indenture for a 25-year maturity bond issue may require that one-twentieth of the bond issue be retired annually, beginning immediately after an initial 5-year call protection period.

Typically, when a redemption is due, the sinking fund trustee will select bonds by lottery. Selected bonds are then called, and the affected bondholders receive the call price, which for sinking fund redemptions is usually par value. However, the issuer normally has a valuable option to buy back the required number of bonds in the open market and deliver them to the sinking fund trustee instead of delivering the cash required for a par value redemption. Issuers naturally prefer to exercise this option when bonds can be repurchased in the open market at less than par value.

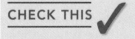 **CHECK THIS**

> **18.3f**   For bond investors, what are some of the advantages and disadvantages of a sinking fund provision?

Coupon Payment Provisions

Coupon rates are stated on an annual basis. For example, an 8 percent coupon rate indicates that the issuer promises to pay 8 percent of a bond's face value to the bondholder each year. However, splitting an annual coupon into two semiannual payments is an almost universal practice. An exact schedule of coupon payment dates is specified in the bond indenture when the bonds are originally issued.

If a company suspends payment of coupon interest, it is said to be in default. Default is a serious matter. In general, bondholders have an unconditional right to the timely payment of interest and principal. They also have a right to bring legal action to enforce such payments. Upon suspension of coupon payments, the bondholders could, for example, demand an acceleration of principal repayment along with all past-due interest. However, a corporation in financial distress has a right to seek protection in bankruptcy court from inflexible demands by bondholders. As a practical matter, it is often in the best interests of both the bondholders and the corporation to negotiate a new debt contract. Indeed, bankruptcy courts normally encourage a settlement that minimizes any intervention on their part.

18.4 Protective Covenants

protective covenants
Restrictions in a bond indenture designed to protect bondholders.

In addition to the provisions already discussed, a bond indenture is likely to contain a number of **protective covenants**. These agreements are designed to protect bondholders by restricting the actions of a corporation that might cause a deterioration in the credit quality of a bond issue. Protective covenants can be classified into two types: negative covenants and positive, or affirmative, covenants.

A *negative covenant* is a "thou shalt not" for the corporation. Here are some examples of negative covenants that might be found in an indenture agreement:

1. The firm cannot pay dividends to stockholders in excess of what is allowed by a formula based on the firm's earnings.

2. The firm cannot issue new bonds that are senior to currently outstanding bonds. Also, the amount of a new bond issue cannot exceed an amount specified by a formula based on the firm's net worth.

3. The firm cannot refund an existing bond issue with new bonds paying a lower coupon rate than the currently outstanding bond issue it would replace.

4. The firm cannot buy bonds issued by other companies, nor can it guarantee the debt of any other company.

A *positive covenant* is a "thou shalt." It specifies things that a corporation must do, or conditions that it must abide by. Here are some common examples of positive covenants:

1. Proceeds from the sale of assets must be used either to acquire other assets of equal value or to redeem outstanding bonds.

2. In the event of a merger, acquisition, or spinoff, the firm must give bondholders the right to redeem their bonds at par value.

3. The firm must maintain the good condition of all assets pledged as security for an outstanding bond issue.

4. The firm must periodically supply audited financial information to bondholders.

CHECK THIS

18.4a Why would a corporation voluntarily include protective covenants in its bond indenture contract?

18.5 Event Risk

event risk The possibility that the issuing corporation will experience a significant change in its bond credit quality.

Protective covenants in a bond indenture help shield bondholders from event risk. **Event risk** is broadly defined as the possibility that some structural or financial change to the corporation will cause a significant deterioration in the credit quality of a bond issue, thereby causing the affected bonds to lose substantial market value.

A classic example of event risk, and what could happen to bondholders without adequate covenant protection, is provided by an incident involving Marriott Corporation, best known for its chain of hotels and resorts. In October 1992, Marriott announced its intention to spin off part of the company. The spinoff, called Host Marriott, would acquire most of the parent company's debt and its poorly performing real estate holdings. The parent, Marriott International, would be left relatively debt-free with possession of most of the better performing properties, including its hotel management division.

On the announcement date, the affected Marriott bonds fell in value by about 30 percent, reflecting severe concern about the impact of the spinoff on the credit quality of the bonds. On the same day, Marriott stock rose in value by about 30 percent, reflecting a large wealth transfer from bondholders to stockholders. A subsequent bondholder legal challenge was unsuccessful. Standard & Poor's later announced that it was formally revising its credit ratings on Marriott bonds to recognize the impact of the spinoff. (Credit ratings are discussed in detail in a later section.) Debt remaining with Marriott International would have an investment-grade rating, while bonds assigned to Host Marriott would have junk bond status. *The Wall Street Journal* report covering the story is reproduced in the nearby *Investment Updates* box.

18.5a   What are some possible protective covenants that would have protected Marriott bondholders from the adverse impact of the spinoff described here?

18.6 Bonds without Indentures

private placement
A new bond issue sold to one or more parties in private transactions not available to the public.

It is possible for bonds to be sold only to one or more financial institutions in what is called a **private placement**. Private placements are exempt from registration requirements with the provincial securities exchange commissions. Nevertheless, even privately placed debt issues often have a formal indenture contract.

When a corporation issues debt without an indenture, it makes an unconditional promise to pay interest and principal according to a simple debt contract. Debt issued without an indenture is basically a simple IOU of the corporation. Bond analysts sometimes reserve the designation "bonds" to mean corporate debt subject to an indenture and refer to corporate debt not subject to an indenture as "notes." However, it is more common to distinguish between bonds and notes on the basis of maturity, where bonds designate relatively long maturities, say, 10 years or longer, and notes designate maturities less than 10 years. Both definitions overlap since most long-term debt is issued subject to an indenture, and most privately placed short-term debt is issued as a simple IOU. In between, however, privately placed intermediate-maturity debt may or may not be issued subject to an indenture and therefore might be referred to as either a bond or a note regardless of the existence of an indenture. As in any profession, the jargon of investments is sometimes ambiguous.

18.7 Preferred Stock

preferred stock
A security with a claim to dividend payments that is senior to common stock.

Preferred stock has some of the features of both bonds and common stock. Preferred stockholders have a claim to dividend payments that is senior to the claim of common stockholders—hence the term "preferred stock." However, their claim is subordinate to the claims of bondholders and other creditors. A typical preferred stock issue has the following basic characteristics:

1. Preferred stockholders do not normally participate with common stockholders in the election of a board of directors. However, a few preferred stock issues do grant voting rights to their holders.

2. Preferred stockholders are promised a stream of fixed dividend payments. Thus, preferred dividends resemble bond coupons.

Marriott Corp. shareholders approved a plan to split the company into a real-estate concern, with most of Marriott's debt, and a high-growth hotel-management company.

The split, approved by 85% of the shares voted, was the main issue at Marriott's annual meeting Friday. Under the plan, which is expected to take effect in September, stockholders will receive a share of Marriott International, Inc., the hotel-management operation, for each Marriott share they own. Then Marriott Corp. will be renamed Host Marriott Corp., an entity that will operate the real-estate side of the business.

The plan stunned bondholders when it was announced in October. They argued that the financial support of their debt was being undermined, and a suit by some of the bondholders is still pending.

Marriott shares have risen 60% since the plan's announcement. In New York Stock Exchange trading Friday, Marriott closed at $27.785, up 12.5 cents. The stock has traded as low as $15.50 in the past year.

The Marriott family controls more than 25% of the 100.8 million shares outstanding as of Jan. 1.

Marriott's directors set a distribution date for the split dividend of Sept. 10 for shares of record Sept. 1.

J. W. Marriott, 61 years old and currently chairman and president of the company, will be chairman, president and chief executive officer of Marriott International, while his brother, Richard E. Marriott, 54, will be chairman of Host Marriott. Richard Marriott is currently vice chairman and executive vice president of the company.

In addition to the bondholders' lawsuit seeking to block the reorganization, Marriott had faced a suit by holders of preferred stock. Marriott said that the holders have agreed to dismiss their case and convert their preferred shares into common stock.

The suit by the group of bondholders, representing about a dozen institutional investors, is still pending, however. Under the reorganization plan, holders of about $1.5 billion in Marriott bonds would have the option to swap their notes for new notes of a unit of the new real-estate entity. The company will retain $2.1 billion of Marriott's $3 billion long-term debt and will own 139 hotels and other real-estate assets.

Larry Kill, attorney for the bondholders, said the suit would proceed despite the shareholder vote. "This was a very unfair transaction," he said.

As a separate company, Host Marriott would have had about $1.2 billion in sales in 1992, according to the company's estimates. Marriott International, Inc., the new hotel concern, will operate more than 760 hotels through Marriott's four hotel-management units and related management services. Marriott International would have had $7.8 billion in sales last year, the company estimates.

In 1992, Marriott had net income of $85 million, or 64 cents a share, on sales of $8.72 billion. It had about $3 billion in long-term debt as of Jan. 1.

Moody's Investors Service, Inc., downgraded its ratings on the senior unsecured debt of Marriott Corp., affecting about $2.3 billion in debt, to Ba-2 from single-B-2. Moody's said the bond-exchange plan will leave a Host Marriott unit highly leveraged "with modest debt protection." Moody's said it expects only gradual improvement in operating earnings, given the sluggish economy and glut of hotel rooms. Moody's said, however, that the Host Marriott unit will be well-positioned for increased earnings when the recovery hits full speed.

Source: Jyoti Thottam, *The Wall Street Journal*, July 26, 1993. Reprinted by permission of Dow Jones & Company, Inc., via Copyright Clearance Center, Inc. © 1993 Dow Jones & Company, Inc. All Rights Reserved Worldwide.

3. Preferred stock normally has no specified maturity, but it is often callable by the issuer.

4. Management can suspend payment of preferred dividends without setting off a bankruptcy process, but only after suspending payment of all common stock dividends.

5. If preferred dividends have been suspended, all unpaid preferred dividends normally become a cumulative debt that must be paid in full before the corporation can resume any payment of common stock dividends. Preferred stock with this feature is termed *cumulative preferred*.

6. Some preferred stock issues have a conversion feature similar to convertible bonds. These are called *convertible preferred stock*.

All else equal, preferred stock normally pays a lower interest rate to investors than do corporate bonds. Companies that issue ordinary preferred stock must treat preferred dividends the same as common stock dividends for tax purposes and, therefore, cannot deduct preferred dividends from their taxable income.

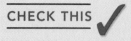

18.7a   From the perspective of common stockholders and management, what are some of the advantages of issuing preferred stock instead of bonds or new shares of common stock?

18.8 Adjustable-Rate Bonds and Adjustable-Rate Preferred-Stock

adjustable-rate bonds Securities that pay coupons that change according to a prespecified rule. Also called *floating-rate bonds* or simply *floaters*.

Many bond, note, and preferred stock issues allow the issuer to adjust the annual coupon according to a rule or formula based on current market interest rates. These securities are called **adjustable-rate bonds**; they are also sometimes called *floating-rate bonds* or *floaters*.

For example, a typical adjustment rule might specify that the coupon rate be reset annually to be equal to the current rate on 180-day maturity Treasury bills plus 2 percent. Alternatively, a more flexible rule might specify that the coupon rate on a bond issue cannot be set below 105 percent of the yield to maturity of newly issued five-year Treasury notes. Thus, if five-year Treasury notes have recently been sold to yield 6 percent, the minimum allowable coupon rate is $1.05 \times 6\% = 6.3\%$.

Adjustable-rate bonds and notes are often putable at par value. For this reason, an issuer may set a coupon rate above an allowable minimum to discourage bondholders from selling their bonds back to the corporation.

18.8a   How does an adjustable coupon rate feature affect the interest rate risk of a bond?

18.8b   How might bondholders respond if the coupon rate on an adjustable-rate putable bond was set below market interest rates?

18.9 Corporate Bond Credit Ratings

credit rating An assessment of the credit quality of a bond issue based on the issuer's financial condition.

When a corporation sells a new bond issue to investors, it usually subscribes to several bond rating agencies for a credit evaluation of the bond issue. Each contracted rating agency then provides a **credit rating**—an assessment of the credit quality of the bond issue based on the issuer's financial condition. Rating agencies charge a fee for this service. As part of the contractual arrangement between the bond issuer and the rating agency, the issuer agrees to allow a continuing review of its credit rating even if the rating deteriorates. Without a credit rating a new bond issue would be very difficult to sell to the public, which is why almost all bond issues originally sold to the general public have a credit rating assigned at the time of issuance. Also, most public bond issues have ratings assigned by several rating agencies.

Established rating agencies include Duff and Phelps, Inc. (D&P); Fitch Investors Service (Fitch); McCarthy, Crisanti and Maffei (MCM); Moody's Investors Service Moody's); and Standard & Poor's Corporation (S&P) and Dominion Bond Rating Service. Of these, the two best known rating agencies are Moody's and Standard & Poor's. These companies publish regularly updated credit ratings for thousands of domestic and international bond issues.

It is important to realize that corporate bond ratings are assigned to particular bond issues and not to the issuer of those bonds. For example, a senior bond issue is likely to have a higher credit rating than a subordinated issue even if both are issued by the same corporation. Similarly, a corporation with two bond issues outstanding may have a higher credit rating assigned to one issue because that issue has stronger covenant protection specified in the bond's indenture contract.

Seniority and covenant protection are not the only things affecting bond ratings. Bond rating agencies consider a number of factors before assigning a credit rating, including an appraisal of the financial strength of the issuer, the calibre of the issuer's management, and the issuer's position in an industry as well as the industry's position in the economy. In general, a bond rating is intended to be a comparative indicator of overall credit quality for a particular bond issue. However, the rating in itself is not a recommendation to buy or sell a bond.

Table 18.2 summarizes corporate bond rating symbols and definitions used by Moody's (first column), Duff and Phelps (second column), and Standard & Poor's (third column). As shown, bond credit ratings fall into three broad categories: investment grade, speculative grade, and extremely speculative grade.

TABLE 18.2		Corporate Bond Credit Rating Symbols	
Rating Agency			
Moody's	**Duff and Phelps**	**Standard & Poor's and Dominion Bond Ratings**	**Credit Rating Description**
Investment-Grade Bond Ratings			
Aaa	1	AAA	Highest credit rating, maximum safety
Aa1	2	AA+	
Aa2	3	AA	High credit quality, investment-grade bonds
Aa3	4	AA−	
A1	5	A+	
A2	6	A	Upper-medium quality, investment-grade bonds
A3	7	A−	
Baa1	8	BBB+	
Baa2	9	BBB	Lower-medium quality, investment-grade bonds
Baa3	10	BBB−	
Speculative-Grade Bond Ratings			
Ba1	11	BB+	Low credit quality, speculative-grade bonds
Ba2	12	BB	
Ba3	13	BB−	
B1	14	B+	Very low credit quality, speculative-grade bonds
B2	15	B	
B3	16	B−	
Extremely Speculative-Grade Bond Ratings			
Caa	17	CCC+	Extremely low credit standing, high-risk bonds
		CCC	
		CCC−	
Ca		CC	Extremely speculative
C		C	
		D	Bonds in default

Why Bond Ratings Are Important

Bond credit ratings assigned by independent rating agencies are quite important to bond market participants. Only a few institutional investors have the resources and expertise necessary to properly evaluate a bond's credit quality on their own. Bond ratings provide investors with reliable, professional evaluations of bond issues at a reasonable cost. This information is indispensable for assessing the economic value of a bond.

prudent investment guidelines
Restrictions on investment portfolios stipulating that securities purchased must meet a certain level of safety.

Furthermore, many financial institutions have **prudent investment guidelines** stipulating that only securities with a certain level of investment safety may be included in their portfolios. For example, bond investments for many pension funds are limited to investment-grade bonds rated at least Baa by Moody's or at least BBB by Standard & Poor's. Bond ratings provide a convenient measure to monitor implementation of these guidelines.

Individual investors investing in bonds also find published bond ratings useful. Individual investors generally do not have the ability to diversify as extensively as do large institutions. With limited diversification opportunities, an individual should invest only in bonds with higher credit ratings.

CHECK THIS ✓

18.9a Does a low credit rating necessarily imply that a bond is a bad investment?

18.9b What factors besides the credit rating might be important in deciding whether a particular bond is a worthwhile investment?

18.10 Junk Bonds

high-yield bonds
Bonds with a speculative credit rating that is offset by a yield premium offered to compensate for higher credit risk. Also called *junk bonds*.

Bonds with a speculative or low grade rating—that is, those rated Ba or lower by Moody's or BB or lower by Standard & Poor's—are commonly called **high-yield bonds**, or, more colourfully, *junk bonds*. The designation "junk" is somewhat misleading and often unduly pejorative, since junk bonds *have* economic value. Junk bonds simply represent debt with a higher than average credit risk. To put the term in perspective, one should realize that most consumer debt and small business debt represents higher than average credit risk. Yet it is generally considered desirable from an economic and social perspective that credit be available to consumers and small businesses.

Junk bonds that were originally issued with an investment-grade credit rating that subsequently fell to speculative grade because of unforeseen economic events are called *fallen angels*. Another type, *original-issue junk*, is defined as bonds originally issued with a speculative-grade rating.

Junk bonds are attractive investments for many institutional investors with well-diversified portfolios. The logic of junk bond investing revolves around the possibility that the *yield premium* for junk bonds might be high enough to justify accepting the higher default rates of junk bonds. As an example of this logic, consider the following back-of-the-envelope calculations.

Suppose that the average yield on junk bonds is 10 percent when Treasury bonds yield 7 percent. In this case, the yield premium of junk bonds over default-free Treasury bonds is 3 percent. Further suppose that an investor expects about 4 percent of all outstanding junk bonds to default each year, and experience suggests that when junk bonds default bondholders on average receive 50 cents for each dollar of bond face value. Based on these rough assumptions, diversified junk bond investors expect to lose 2 percent ($.04 \times .50$) of their portfolio value each year through defaults. But with a junk bond yield premium of 3 percent, the junk bond portfolio is expected to outperform Treasury bonds

WORK THE WEB

One important reason you need the credit rating for a bond is the yield spread. The yield spread is the extra return, in the form of an increased yield to maturity, that investors receive for buying a bond with a lower credit rating. Because of the credit risk, investors demand a risk premium for investing in lower rated bonds. You can create a yield curve for bonds with different credit ratings. We went to www.bondsonline.com and followed the "Corporate Bond Spreads" link. Here is what we got:

Reuters Corporate Spreads for Banks

Spreads compiled using: Reuters Evaluators ▾ Refresh Download spread file

Rating	1 yr	2 yr	3 yr	5 yr	7 yr	10 yr	30 yr
Aaa/AAA	27	36	47	59	77	90	110
Aa1/AA+	33	49	53	68	87	101	121
Aa2/AA	35	54	56	72	90	103	124
Aa3/AA-	37	57	58	77	94	107	133
A1/A+	61	73	77	92	110	125	148
A2/A	64	76	79	94	111	127	151
A3/A-	68	79	82	98	115	130	153
Baa1/BBB+	81	98	104	123	158	184	207
Baa2/BBB	84	106	112	130	163	187	212
Baa3/BBB-	91	111	117	134	168	194	217
Ba1/BB+	605	615	625	635	655	675	695
Ba2/BB	615	625	635	645	665	685	705
Ba3/BB-	625	635	645	655	675	695	715
B1/B+	775	785	795	825	865	905	955
B2/B	785	795	805	835	875	915	965
B3/B-	795	805	815	845	885	925	975
Caa/CCC	1195	1205	1215	1240	1270	1330	1280

Note: Reuters Evaluator spreads for bullet bonds.

Here is how you interpret the table. If you look at the three-year Aaa/AAA-rated bonds, you will find the number 47. This means the yield spread is 47 basis points, or .47 percent greater than the yield to maturity for a three-year Treasury note. If you think credit rating is unimportant, look at the 30-year Caa/CCC bonds, where the spread above a comparable maturity Treasury bond is 12.80 percent!

by 1 percent per year. It is true that a junk bond portfolio is much more expensive to manage than a Treasury bond portfolio. However, for a $1 billion bond portfolio, a junk bond yield premium of 1 percent represents $10 million of additional interest income per year. Our nearby *Work the Web* box has more on credit ratings and yield spreads.

Of course, actual default rates could turn out to be much different than expected. History suggests that the major determinant of aggregate bond default rates is the state of economic activity. During an expansionary economic period, bond default rates are usually low. But in a recession, default rates can rise dramatically. For this reason, the investment performance of a junk bond portfolio largely depends on the health of the economy.

High-Yield Bonds
Tuesday, January 3, 2006

Ten most active fixed-coupon high-yield, or "junk", corporate bonds

COMPANY (TICKER)	COUPON	MATURITY	LAST PRICE	LAST YIELD	*EST SPREAD	UST†	EST VOL (000's)
Ford Motor Credit Co (F)	7.000	Oct 01, 2013	86.250	9.551	518	10	120,757
Dana Corp (DCN)	6.500	Mar 01, 2009	82.500	13.488	915	3	97,448
General Motors Corp (GM)	8.375	Jul 15, 2033	67.500	12.623	807	30	87,977
Ford Motor Credit Co (F)	7.375	Oct 28, 2009	89.500	10.801	650	3	78,943
Ford Motor Credit Co (F)	7.375	Feb 01, 2011	88.250	10.414	611	5	76,837
Pilgrims Pride Corp (PPC)	9.625	Sep 15, 2011	106.250	7.088	277	5	67,190
Ford Motor Co (F)	7.450	Jul 16, 2031	68.625	11.194	664	30	65,349
General Motors Acceptance Corp (GM)	8.000	Nov 01, 2031	98.250	8.162	361	30	64,532
Adelphia Communications Corp (ADELQ)	10.250	Jun 15, 2011	61.500	23.273	1897	5	60,250
Ford Motor Credit Co (F)	7.250	Oct 25, 2011	87.060	10.259	596	5	58,437

Volume represents total volume for the market; price/yield data are for trades of $100,000 and greater. * Estimated spreads, in basis points (100 basis points is one percentage point), over the 2, 3, 5, 10 or 30-year hot run Treasury note/bond. 2-year: 4.250 11/07; 3-year: 4.375 11/08; 5-year: 4.375 12/10; 10-year: 4.500 11/15; 30-year: 5.375 02/31. †Comparable U.S. Treasury issue.

Source: MarketAxess Corporate BondTicker

Prices and yields of selected junk bonds are published regularly in *The Wall Street Journal* in its "High-Yield Bonds" report. A sample report is displayed in Figure 18.7. We discuss the data in Figure 18.7 in more detail in our next section. For an interesting discussion on investing in junk bonds, see the nearby *Investment Updates* box.

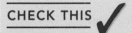

CHECK THIS

18.10a Can junk bond default risk be completely diversified away by large institutional bond investors?

18.10b From an investor's perspective, is there any importance in distinguishing between fallen angels and original-issue junk?

18.11 Bond Market Trading

Consistent with the need to hold bonds for predictable cash flows, most corporate bond investors buy and hold bonds until they mature. However, many investors need to liquidate some bonds before they mature, and others wish to purchase outstanding bonds originally issued by a particular corporation several years earlier. For these and many other reasons, the existence of an active secondary market for corporate bonds is important for most bond investors. Fortunately, an active secondary market with a substantial volume of bond trading does exist to satisfy most of the liquidity needs of investors.

Most of the Canadian debt issues trade in the over-the counter (OTC) market. Transaction prices of Canadian debt-issues are reported on CBID Markets Inc. website.

As shown in Figure 18.8, the CBID website provides a daily snapshot of Canadian bonds. The information reported is largely self-explanatory. After the coupon and maturity date, price and yields are reported for each issue.

CHECK THIS

18.11a All else equal, is an actively traded bond more or less risky as an investment than a thinly traded bond? (*Hint*: Is liquidity a good or a bad thing for a bond?)

18.11b Why might a current yield for a convertible bond be uninformative for the purpose of making a comparison between two or more bonds?

Hungry for healthy stock-market returns? Here's an intriguing suggestion: Buy junk bonds. Like stocks, junk (or "high yield") bonds have had a rough time lately. Mutual funds that invest in junk bonds tumbled an average 8.1% last year and shed an additional 1.8% in this year's first 10 months, according to Chicago researcher Morningstar Inc.

Stocks, of course, have suffered even more. Still, I believe there is a decent chance that high-yield bonds, those risky securities issued by heavily indebted companies, could outpace stocks in the years ahead. As I have argued in many columns this year, expected stock-market returns remain modest, despite the 30% decline in share prices. The outlook seems especially grim for blue-chip U.S. shares, which continue to sport nosebleed share-price-to-earnings multiples and skimpy dividend yields.

By contrast, junk bonds today offer lush 13% yields. Don't believe junk-bond prices will rebound soon? As they say on Wall Street, you are getting paid to wait. "One of the reasons investors may gravitate in this direction is, in part, because they don't see a lot of upside in stocks," says Martin Fridson, chief high-yield strategist at Merrill Lynch & Co. "They might say, 'Ordinarily, I'm not that excited about bonds, but that 12% or 13% looks pretty attractive right now.'"

Today's 13% yield is some nine percentage points higher than the yield on 10-year Treasury notes. How unusual is that? Put it this way: The spread between junk and Treasury yields was only slightly wider during the economic turmoil of 1990–91. That was the last time that junk bonds got really pummelled, and many investors still remember the pain. In the late 1980s, unscrupulous securities salesmen hawked junk-bond funds as higher-yielding certificates of deposit.

That fantasy was shredded in late 1989 and 1990, as junk-bond issuers struggled with an overdose of debt and a slowing economy. Junk-bond funds proved anything but safe, as their rich yields failed to compensate for shrinking fund-share prices. But for those who hung tough, the story had a happy ending. After getting hammered in 1990, both junk bonds and stocks came roaring back in 1991. In fact, in 1991, junk-bond funds soared an average 37.1%, rivalling the performance of diversified U.S.-stock funds. Naysayers might dismiss the parallels, noting that the economy is likely to deteriorate further in 2002, triggering a rash of defaults among junk-bond issuers. But that won't necessarily mean lousy junk-bond

returns, says Ken Gregory, president of Litman/Gregory, a money manager in Orinda, Calif.

For instance, 1991 was a terrible year for junk-bond defaults, and yet the bonds posted fabulous gains. "Like every other financial asset, high-yield bonds discount the future," Mr. Gregory notes. "There are a lot of defaults forecasted for next year, but that's not inconsistent with high returns." In 1990–91, junk bonds and stocks seemed to move in lockstep, first losing money together and then rebounding together. But junk bonds could do well in the next few years, even if stocks don't. Mr. Gregory reckons that the worst-case scenario for junk bonds is "a zero return over the next 12 months," as slumping junk-bond prices and defaults wipe out the entire gain from the 13% yield. "I think the downside in stocks is a lot greater than that," Mr. Gregory says. "It's hard to argue that the stock market is at bargain levels. Over the next five years, I see annual returns of maybe 3% on the low side and 9% on the high side."

By contrast, junk bonds seem to offer far higher potential gains. Historically, junk-bond investors have lost 2% a year to defaults. Even if you subtract two percentage points from today's 13% yield, that still leaves investors collecting 11%. And returns could be much higher, if junk-bond prices bounce back. If you are intrigued by junk bonds, consider no-load funds such as Fidelity Capital & Income, Northeast Investors Trust, T. Rowe Price High-Yield, Strong High-Yield Bond and Vanguard High-Yield Corporate. According to Morningstar, all have expenses below 1%, managers with better-than-average five-year records, and investment minimums of $3,000 and below. Because junk funds are so tax inefficient, they are best held in a retirement account, unless you plan to spend the income.

Here's an added consideration: Don't buy a fund that has done too well this year. Again, cast your mind back to 1990–91. The 50% of funds that held up best in 1990 went on to gain an average 32.8% in 1991. But the funds that got hit hardest in 1990 did even better in 1991, climbing 42.1%. That suggests the best funds to own may be those that have made little or no money this year. "If you look just at the funds that have done best this year, you're limiting yourself to the higher-quality high-yield funds," Mr. Gregory says. "We would rather look at funds that we consider pure plays."

Source: Jonathan Clements, *The Wall Street Journal*, November 13, 2001. © 2001 Dow Jones & Company, Inc. All Rights Reserved Worldwide.

FIGURE 18.8

Canadian Bond Trading

Closing Markets Wholesale Pricing	04Jan08 04:00PM EST	
Cda T-Bills	**Price**	**Yield**
1 Month 07Feb	99.71	3.48
2 Month 06Mar	99.40	3.71
3 Month 03Apr	99.13	3.68
6 Month 26Jun	98.30	3.70
1 Year 24Dec	96.57	3.68
Cda Benchmarks	**Price**	**Yield**
2 Year	100.28	3.54
5 Year	100.26	3.68
10 Year	100.95	3.88
30 Year	126.52	4.07
Provincials	**Price**	**Yield**
Ontario 4.4/Nov08	100.48	3.82
NewBrunswick 4.25/Dec08	100.35	3.85
Alberta 5.0/Dec08	101.20	3.68
Ontario 4.0/May09	100.14	3.89
Fin Quebec 4.75/Dec09	101.48	3.93
Ontario 4.0/May10	100.14	3.94
Ontario 4.4/Dec11	101.34	4.02
Alberta 4.25/Jun12	100.98	4.00
Ontario 4.75/Jun13	103.00	4.12
Manitoba 5.05/Dec13	104.57	4.17
Ontario 5.0/Mar14	104.35	4.19
Ontario 4.4/Mar16	100.61	4.31
Ontario 4.3/Mar17	99.76	4.33
Ontario 6.5/Mar29	125.93	4.57
Ontario 4.7/Jun37	101.73	4.59
Corporates	**Price**	**Yield**
BNS 4.515/Nov08	100.20	4.27
GTAA 4.45/Feb09	99.87	4.57
BMO 4.3/Sep09	99.49	4.62
HSBC Finl Co 4.0/May10	97.95	4.95
HSBC Bk Cda 5.31/Oct10	101.46	4.74
BNS 4.25/Nov10	99.14	4.57
BMO 4.69/Jan11	99.87	4.73
HSBC Finl Co 4.8/Apr11	99.39	5.00
HSBC Finl Co 4.35/Oct11	97.59	5.06
Royal Bank 4.53/May12	99.42	4.68
CIBC 5.0/Sep12	99.73	5.06
Wfargo Cda 4.4/Dec12	97.43	4.99
BMO 4.65/Mar13	98.73	4.93
TD Bank 5.69/Jun13	103.54	4.93
MerrillLynch 5.0/Feb14	96.78	5.63

Perimeter CBID (www.canadianfixedincome.ca)

18.12 Summary and Conclusions

This chapter covers the important topic of corporate bonds, a major source of capital used by corporations. In this chapter we saw that:

1. A corporate bond represents a corporation's promise to pay bondholders a fixed sum of money at maturity, along with periodic payments of interest. The sum paid at maturity is the bond's principal, and the periodic interest payments are coupons. Most bonds pay fixed coupons, but some pay floating coupon rates adjusted regularly according to prevailing market interest rates.

2. Corporate bonds are usually callable, which means that the issuer has the right to buy back outstanding bonds before maturity. When a bond issue is called, bondholders surrender their bonds in exchange for a prespecified call price.

3. The largest category of corporate bond investors is life insurance companies, which own about a third of all outstanding corporate bonds. Remaining ownership shares are roughly equally distributed among individual investors, pension funds, banks, and foreign investors.

4. Debentures are the most common type of corporate bond. Debenture bonds represent the unsecured debt of a corporation. Mortgage bonds represent debt issued with a lien on specific property pledged as security for the bonds. Collateral trust bonds are characterized by a pledge of financial assets as security for a bond issue. Equipment trust certificates are issued according to a lease form of financing, where investors purchase equipment trust certificates and the proceeds from this sale are used to purchase equipment that is leased to a corporation.

5. A bond indenture is a formal agreement between the corporation and bondholders that spells out the legal rights and obligations of both parties with respect to a bond issue. An indenture typically specifies the seniority of a bond issue, along with any call provisions, put provisions, bond-to-stock conversion provisions, and sinking fund provisions.

6. When a corporation sells a new bond issue to the public, it usually has a credit rating assigned by several independent bond rating agencies. Without a credit rating, a new bond issue would be difficult to sell, which is why almost all bond issues sold to the public have credit ratings assigned.

7. Bonds with a speculative or lower grade rating, commonly called high-yield bonds, or junk bonds, represent corporate debt with higher than average credit risk. Credit ratings for junk bonds are frequently revised to reflect changing financial conditions.

8. The existence of an active secondary market for corporate bonds is important to most bond investors. The greatest total volume of bond trading occurs in the OTC market.

REAL WORLD

This chapter explored the world of corporate bonds, an important category of investments for institutions, such as pension funds and life insurance companies, and also for individuals. This category also includes convertible bonds and preferred stock. How should you put this information to work?

Now that you understand the most important features of corporate bonds, you need to buy several different issues to experience the real-world gains and losses that come with managing a bond portfolio. So, with a simulated brokerage account (such as Stock-Trak), try putting roughly equal dollar amounts into three or four different corporate bond issues. Be sure to include some junk bonds in your selections. Check the credit ratings of the bond issues you have selected at a site such as Bonds Online (www.bondsonline.com).

You can find out more information about corporate bonds at the many websites now-specializing in bonds, including Investing In Bonds (www.investinginbonds.com), Bond Markets (www.bondmarkets.com), and Convertible Bonds (www.convertbond.com). The websites of bond rating agencies such as Moody's (www.moodys.com), Standard & Poor's (www.standardandpoors.com), Duff & Phelps (www.duffllc.com), Fitch (www.fitchibca.com) and Dominion Bond Rating Services (www.dbrs.com) are also quite informative.

As you monitor the prices of your bonds, notice how interest rates influence their prices. You may also notice that for bonds with lower credit ratings, the stock price of the issuing company is an important influence. Why do you think this is so?

Of course, with the convertible issues the bond price will definitely be influenced by the underlying stock value, but the impact depends on the specific conversion features of the bond, including whether the bond is in the money or not.

Key Terms

plain vanilla bonds 579	in-the-money bond 590
unsecured debt 581	intrinsic bond value 590
debentures 581	exchangeable bonds 591
mortgage bond 582	term bonds 591
collateral trust bond 582	serial bonds 591
equipment trust certificate 582	sinking fund 594
indenture summary 584	protective covenants 595
prospectus 584	event risk 595
senior debentures 584	private placement 596
subordinated debentures 584	preferred stock 596
negative pledge clause 585	adjustable-rate bonds 598
bond refunding 585	credit rating 598
put bonds 587	prudent investment guidelines 600
convertible bonds 587	high-yield bonds 600

Chapter Review Problems and Self-Test

1. **Callable Bonds** A particular bond matures in 30 years. It is callable in 10 years at 110. The call price is then cut by 1 percent of par each year until the call price reaches par. If the bond is called in 12 years, how much will you receive? Assume a $1,000 face value.

2. **Convertible Bonds** A convertible bond features a conversion ratio of 50. What is the conversion price? If the stock sells for $30 per share, what is the conversion value?

3. **Convertible Bonds** A convertible bond has an 8 percent coupon, paid semiannually, and will mature in 15 years. If the bond were not convertible, it would be priced to yield 9 percent. The conversion ratio on the bond is 40, and the stock is currently selling for $24 per share. What is the minimum value of this bond?

Answers to Self-Test Problems

1. The call price will be $110\% - 2 \times 1\% = 108\%$ of face value, or $1,080.

2. The conversion price is face value divided by the conversion ratio, $1,000 / 50 = $20. The conversion value is what the bond is worth on a converted basis, $50 \times $30 = $1,500.

3. The minimum value is the larger of the conversion value and the intrinsic bond value. The conversion value is $40 \times $24 = $960. To calculate the intrinsic bond value, note that we have a face value of $1,000 (by assumption), a semiannual coupon of $40, an annual yield of 9 percent (4.5 percent per half-year), and 15 years to maturity (30 half-years). Using the standard bond pricing formula from Chapter 10, the bond's price (be sure to verify this) if it were not convertible is $918.56. This convertible bond thus will sell for more than $960.

Test Your Investment Quotient

1. **Trust Certificates** An airline elects to finance the purchase of some new airplanes using equipment trust certificates. Under the legal arrangement associated with such certificates, the airplanes are pledged as collateral, but which other factor applies?

   a. The airline still has legal title to the planes.
   b. Legal title to the planes resides with the manufacturer.
   c. The airline does not get legal title to the planes until the manufacturer is paid off.
   d. Legal title to the planes resides with a third party who then leases the planes to the airline.

2. **Callable Bonds** What does the call feature of a bond mean?

   a. Investor can call for payment on demand.
   b. Investor can only call if the firm defaults on an interest payment.
   c. Issuer can call the bond issue prior to the maturity date.
   d. Issuer can call the issue during the first three years.

3. **Callable Bonds** Who benefits from a call provision on a corporate bond?

   a. The issuer
   b. The bondholders
   c. The trustee
   d. The government regulators

4. **Callable Bonds** Which of the following describes a bond with a call feature?

   a. It is attractive, because the immediate receipt of principal plus premium produces a high return.
   b. It is more likely to be called when interest rates are high, because the interest savings will be greater.
   c. It would usually have a higher yield than a similar noncallable bond.
   d. It generally has a higher credit rating than a similar noncallable bond.

5. **Callable Bonds** Which of the following is not a component of call risk for a bond investor?

   a. The cash flow pattern for the bond is not known with certainty.
   b. When the issuer calls a bond, the investor is exposed to reinvestment risk.
   c. The value of a callable bond drops when expected interest rate volatility decreases.
   d. The capital appreciation potential of a callable bond is lower than a noncallable bond.

6. **Callable Bonds** Two bonds are identical, except one is callable and the other is noncallable. Compared to the noncallable bond, the callable bond has

   a. Negative convexity and a lower price.
   b. Negative convexity and a higher price.
   c. Positive convexity and a lower price.
   d. Positive convexity and a higher price.

7. **Convexity** What does positive convexity on a bond imply?

   a. The direction of change in yield is directly related to the change in price.
   b. Prices increase at a faster rate as yields drop than they decrease as yields rise.
   c. Price changes are the same for both increases and decreases in yields.
   d. Prices increase and decrease at a faster rate than the change in yield.

8. **Convexity** A bond with negative convexity is best described as having a price-yield relationship displaying

   a. Positive convexity at high yields and negative convexity at low yields.
   b. Negative convexity at high yields and positive convexity at low yields.
   c. Negative convexity at low and high yields and positive at medium yields.
   d. Positive convexity at low and high yields and negativity at medium yields.

9. **Convexity and Duration** Which of the following *most accurately* measures interest rate sensitivity for bonds with embedded options?

   a. Convexity
   b. Effective duration
   c. Modified duration
   d. Macaulay duration

10. **Convexity and Duration** Which of the following most accurately measures interest rate sensitivity for bonds *without* embedded options?

   a. Convexity
   b. Effective duration
   c. Modified duration
   d. Macaulay duration

11. Indentures Which of the following is not a responsibility of a corporate trustee with regard to a bond's trust indenture?

 a. Checking compliance
 b. Authenticating the bonds issued
 c. Negotiating the terms
 d. Declaring defaults

12. Refundings The refunding provision of an indenture allows bonds to be retired unless

 a. They are replaced with a new issue having a lower interest cost.
 b. The remaining time to maturity is less than five years.
 c. The stated time period in the indenture has not passed.
 d. The stated time period in the indenture has passed.

13. Debentures Holders of unsecured debentures with a negative pledge clause can claim which of the following assurances?

 a. No additional secured debt will be issued in the future.
 b. If any secured debt is issued in the future, the unsecured debentures must be redeemed at par.
 c. The debentures will be secured, but to a lesser degree than any secured debt issued in the future.
 d. The debentures will be secured at least equally with any secured debt issued in the future.

14. Credit Risk An "original issue junk" bond is *best* described as a bond issued

 a. Below investment grade.
 b. At an original issue discount.
 c. As investment grade, but declined to speculative grade.
 d. As below investment grade, but upgraded to speculative grade.

15. Credit Risk A "fallen angel" bond is *best* described as a bond issued

 a. Below investment grade.
 b. At an original issue discount.
 c. As investment grade, but declined to speculative grade.
 d. As a secured bond, but the collateral value declined below par value.

16. Preferred Stock Nonconvertible preferred stock has which of the following in comparison to common stock?

 a. Preferential claim on a company's earnings.
 b. A predetermined dividend rate.
 c. Preferential voting rights.
 d. All of the above.

17. Preferred Stock A preferred stock that is entitled to dividends in arrears is known as

 a. Convertible
 b. Cumulative
 c. Extendible
 d. Participating

18. Convertible Bonds Which one of the following statements about convertible bonds is true?

 a. The longer the call protection on a convertible, the less the security is worth.
 b. The more volatile the underlying stock, the greater the value of the conversion feature.
 c. The smaller the spread between the dividend yield on the stock and the yield to maturity on the bond, the more the convertible is worth.
 d. The collateral that is used to secure a convertible bond is one reason convertibles are more attractive than the underlying common stocks.

19. Convertible Bonds Which one of the following statements about convertible bonds is false?

    a. The yield on the convertible will typically be higher than the yield on the underlying common stock.

    b. The convertible bond will likely participate in a major upward movement in the price of the underlying common stock.

    c. Convertible bonds are typically secured by specific assets of the issuing company.

    d. A convertible bond can be valued as a straight bond with an attached option.

20. **Convertible Bonds** Consider the possible advantages of convertible bonds for investors:

    I. The conversion feature enables the convertible to participate in major upward moves in the price of the underlying common stock.

    II. The bonds are typically secured by specific assets of the issuing company.

    III. Investors may redeem their bonds at the stated conversion price any time during the life of the issue.

    IV. The yield on the convertible will almost always be higher than the yield on the underlying common stock.

    Which are true?

    a. I and II only.

    b. II and III only.

    c. I and III only.

    d. I and IV only.

21. **Convertible Bonds** A convertible bond sells at $1,000 par with a conversion ratio of 40 and an accompanying stock price of $20 per share. The conversion price and conversion value are, respectively,

    a. $20 and $1,000

    b. $20 and $800

    c. $25 and $1,000

    d. $25 and $800

22. **Convertible Bonds** A convertible bond sells at $1,000 par with a conversion ratio of 25 and conversion value of $800. What is the price of the underlying stock?

    a. $12

    b. $48

    c. $40

    d. $32

23. **Convertible Bonds** A convertible bond has a par value of $1,000 and a conversion ratio of 20. The price of the underlying stock is $40. What is the conversion value?

    a. $20

    b. $800

    c. $1,000

    d. $25

24. **International Bonds** A U.S. investor who buys Japanese bonds will most likely maximize his return if interest rates

    a. Fall and the dollar weakens relative to the yen.

    b. Fall and the dollar strengthens relative to the yen.

    c. Rise and the dollar weakens relative to the yen.

    d. Rise and the dollar strengthens relative to the yen.

Concept Questions

1. **Bond Types** What are the four main types of corporate bonds?

2. **Bond Features** What is a bond refunding? Is it the same thing as a call?

3. **Callable Bonds** With regard to the call feature, what are call protection and the call premium? What typically happens to the call premium through time?

4. **Put Bonds** What is a put bond? Is the put feature desirable from the investor's perspective? The issuer's?

5. **Bond Yields** What is the impact on a bond's coupon rate from
   a. A call feature?
   b. A put feature?

6. **Exchangeable Bonds** What is the difference between an exchangeable bond and a convertible bond?

7. **Event Risk** What is event risk? In addition to protective covenants, what bond feature do you think best reduces or eliminates such risk?

8. **Floaters** From the bondholder's perspective, what are the potential advantages and disadvantages of floating coupons?

9. **Effective Duration** Why is effective duration a more accurate measure of interest rate risk for bonds with embedded options?

10. **Embedded Options** What are some examples of embedded options in bonds? How do they affect the price of a bond?

11. **Junk Bonds** Explain the difference between an original issue junk bond and a fallen angel bond.

12. **Put Bonds** What is the difference between put bonds and extendible bonds?

13. **Callable Bonds** All else the same, callable bonds have less interest rate sensitivity than noncallable bonds. Why? Is this a good thing?

14. **Callable Bonds** Two callable bonds are essentially identical, except that one has a refunding provision while the other has no refunding provision. Which bond is more likely to be called by the issuer? Why?

15. **Inverse Floaters** An "inverse floater" is a bond with a coupon that is adjusted down when interest rates rise and up when rates fall. What is the impact of the floating coupon on the bond's price volatility?

Questions and Problems

Core Questions

1. **Conversion Price** A convertible bond has a $1,000 face value and a conversion ratio of 35. What is the conversion price?

2. **Conversion Price** A convertible bond has a conversion ratio of 18 and a par value of $1,000. What is the conversion price?

3. **Conversion Ratio** A company just sold a convertible bond at par value of $1,000. If the conversion price is $42, what is the conversion ratio?

4. **Conversion Value** A convertible bond has a $1,000 face value and a conversion ratio of 45. If the stock price is $26, what is the conversion value?

5. **Conversion Value** A convertible bond has a conversion ratio of 20 and a par value of $1,000. If the stock is currently priced at $47, what is the conversion value?

6. **Conversion Ratio** You find a convertible bond outstanding with a conversion value of $896. The stock is currently priced at $32. What is the conversion ratio of the bond?

7. **Callable Bonds** A bond matures in 25 years, but is callable in 10 years at 112. The call premium decreases by 2 percent of par per year. If the bond is called in 13 years, how much will you receive?

8. **Call Premium** You own a bond with a 8 percent coupon rate and a yield to call of 8.65 percent. The bond currently sells for $1,029.07. If the bond is callable in five years, what is the call premium of the bond?

9. **Convertible Bonds** A convertible bond has a 9 percent coupon, paid semiannually, and will mature in 10 years. If the bond were not convertible, it would be priced to yield

10 percent. The conversion ratio on the bond is 20, and the stock is currently selling for $53 per share. What is the minimum value of this bond?

10. **Convertible Bonds** You own a convertible bond with a conversion ratio of 30. The stock is currently selling for $38 per share. The issuer of the bond has announced a call; the call price is 110. What are your options here? What should you do?

Intermediate Questions

11. **Convertible Bonds** There is a 30-year bond with an 10 percent coupon and a 7 percent yield to maturity. The bond is callable in 10 years at par value. What is the Macaulay duration of the bond assuming it is not called? What is the Macaulay duration if the bond is called? Which number is more relevant?

Use the following information to answer the next two questions: Rajiv Singh, a bond analyst, is analyzing a convertible bond. The characteristics of the bond are given below.

Convertible Bond Characteristics	
Par value	$1,000
Annual coupon rate (annual pay)	6.5%
Conversion ratio	22
Market price	105% of par
Straight value	99% of par
Underlying Stock Characteristics	
Current market price	$40 per share
Annual cash dividend	$1.20 per share

12. **Convertible Bonds** Compute the bond's conversion value and market conversion price.

13. **Convertible Bonds** Determine whether the value of a callable convertible bond will increase, decrease, or remain unchanged if there is an increase in stock price volatility. What if there is an increase in interest rate volatility? Justify each of your responses.

Use the following information to answer the next two questions: Rich McDonald, CFA, is evaluating his investment alternatives in Ytel Incorporated by analyzing a Ytel convertible bond and Ytel common equity. Characteristics of the two securities are as follows:

Characteristic	Convertible Bond	Common Equity
Par value	$1,000	
Coupon (annual payment)	4%	
Current market price	$980	$35 per share
Straight bond value	$925	
Conversion ratio	25	
Conversion option	At any time	
Dividend		$0
Expected market price in one year	$1,125	$45 per share

14. **Convertible Bonds** Calculate the following:

a. The current market conversion price for the Ytel convertible bond.
b. The expected one-year rate of return for the Ytel convertible bond.
c. The expected one-year rate of return for the Ytel common equity.

15. **Convertible Bonds** One year has passed and Ytel's common equity price has increased to $51 per share. Also, over the year, the interest rate on Ytel's nonconvertible bonds of the same maturity has increased, while credit spreads remained unchanged. Name the two components of the convertible bond's value. Indicate whether the value of each component should increase, stay the same, or decrease in response to the increase on Ytel's common equity and the increase in interest rates.

www.mcgrawhill.ca/olc/Jordan

What's on the Web?

1. **Bond Quotes** Go to www.bondsonline.com and find the corporate bond search. Enter "Ford" for Ford Motor Company in the Issue box and search for Ford bonds. How many bonds are listed for sale? What are the different credit ratings for these bonds? What is the yield to maturity for the longest maturity bond? What is its price?

2. **Credit Spreads** What are the current credit spreads? Go to www.bondsonline.com and look for corporate yield spreads. Are the yield spreads linear? In other words, does the yield spread increase by the same number of basis points for each decline in credit rating? Why or why not? Why are the yield spreads higher for longer term bonds?

3. **Historical Credit Spreads** The St. Louis Federal Reserve Board has files with historical interest rates on its website at www.stls.frb.org. Go to the site and find the monthly Moody's Seasoned Aaa Corporate Bond Yield and the monthly Moody's Seasoned Baa Corporate Bond Yield. You can calculate a credit spread as the difference between these two returns. When was the largest credit spread? The smallest? What factors do you think led to the large credit spreads and the small credit spreads?

4. **Bond Terminology** Go to www.investinginbonds.com and find the definitions for the following terms: bond resolution, cap, collar, defeasance, extraordinary redemption, overcollateralization, and refunding.

5. **Bond Quotes** Go to CBID Markets Inc.'s website at www.pfin.ca and find the corporate bonds. Find the price and yield of the TD Bank bond.

6. **Historical Yields** Go to the Bank of Canada website at www.bankofcanada.ca and find the average yields on corporate bonds from 1994.

www.mcgrawhill.ca/olc/Jordan

CHAPTER 19

Government Bonds and Mortgage-Backed Securities

"Blessed are the young, for they shall inherit the national debt."
—Herbert Hoover

Government bonds are among the safest investments available because they are secured by the considerable resources of the federal government. Many bonds issued by federal government agencies, and by provincial and local municipal governments, are also nearly free of default risk. Consequently, government bonds are generally excellent vehicles for conservative investment strategies seeking predictable investment results. ∎

The largest and most important debt market is that for debt issued by the government. In this chapter, we examine securities issued by federal, provincial, and local governments.

19.1 Government Bond Basics

The Canadian federal government is the largest borrower among different government agencies in Canada. At the end of 2003, the amount of outstanding T-bills was approximately $18,120.7 million.

The Bank of Canada finances government debt by issuing marketable securities and nonmarketable securities. Most of the gross public debt is financed by the sale of marketable securities at regularly scheduled Bank of Canada auctions. Marketable securities include Treasury bills, Government of Canada Bonds or Canada Bonds. Outstanding marketable securities trade among investors in a large, active financial market. Canada Savings Bonds are the nonmarketable securities.

Treasury security ownership is registered with the Bank of Canada. When an investor sells a government security to another investor, registered ownership is officially transferred by notifying the Bank of Canada of the transaction. However, only marketable securities allow registered ownership to be transferred. Nonmarketable securities do not allow a change of registered ownership and therefore cannot trade among investors. For example, a Canada Savings Bond is a nonmarketable security. If an investor wishes to sell a Canada Savings Bond, it must be redeemed by the Bank of Canada. This is normally a simple procedure. For example, most banks handle the purchase and sale of Canada Savings Bonds for their customers.

Another large market for government debt is the market for municipal government debt.

Visit
www.bankofcanada.ca

19.2 Treasury Bills, Notes, Bonds, and STRIPS

face value The value of a bill, note, or bond at its maturity when a payment of principal is made. Also called redemption value.

discount basis Method of selling a Treasury bill at a discount from face value.

imputed interest The interest paid on a Treasury bill determined by the size of its discount from face value.

Treasury bills are short-term obligations that mature in one year or less. They are originally issued with maturities of 4, 13, 26 or 52 weeks. A T-bill entitles its owner to receive a single payment at the bill's maturity, called the bill's **face value** or *redemption value*. The smallest denomination T-bill has a face value of $1,000. T-bills are sold on a **discount basis**, where a price is set at a discount from face value. For example, if a $10,000 bill is sold for $9,500, then it is sold at a discount of $500, or 5 percent. The discount represents the **imputed interest** on the bill.

Treasury notes are medium-term obligations with original maturities of 10 years or less, but more than 1 year. They are normally issued with original maturities of 2, 5, or 10 years, and they have face value denominations as small as $1,000. Besides a payment of face value at maturity, T-notes also pay semiannual coupons.

Canada bonds are long-term obligations with much longer original-issue maturities. Canada bonds can have a maturity of up to 40 years. These marketable bonds pay their face value at maturity, pay semiannual coupons, and have face value denominations as small as $1,000.

The coupon rate for Canada bonds is set according to interest rates prevailing at the time of issuance. For example, if the prevailing interest rate for a bond of a certain maturity is 5 percent, then the coupon rate—that is, the annual coupon as a percentage of par value—for a new issue with that maturity is set at or near 5 percent. Thus, a $1,000 par value Canada bond paying a 5 percent coupon would pay two $25 coupons each year. Coupon payments normally begin six months after issuance and continue to be paid every six months until the last coupon is paid along with the face value at maturity. Once set, the coupon rate remains constant throughout the life of a Canada bond.

STRIPS Treasury program allowing investors to buy individual coupon and principal payments from a whole government. Acronym for *Separate Trading of Registered Interest and Principal of Securities.*

zero coupon bonds A note or bond paying a single cash flow at maturity. Also called zeroes.

Visit the Bank of Canada at www.bankofcanada.ca

STRIPS are derived from long-term Canada bonds. The STRIPS program (an acronym for *Separate Trading of Registered Interest and Principal of Securities*) allows brokers to divide bonds into *coupon strips* and *principal strips*, thereby allowing investors to buy and sell the strips of their choice. Principal strips represent face-value payments, and coupon strips represent coupon payments. For example, a 30-year maturity bond can be separated into 61 strips, representing 60 semiannual coupon payments and a single face value payment. Under the STRIPS program, each of these strips can be separately registered to different owners.

The terms "STRIPS" and "strips" can sometimes cause confusion. The acronym STRIPS is used when speaking specifically about the Treasury STRIPS program. However, the term *strips* now popularly refers to any separate part of a note or bond issue broken down into its component parts. In this generic form, the term strips is acceptable.

Since each strip created under the STRIPS program represents a single future payment, STRIPS securities effectively become **zero coupon bonds** and are commonly called *zeroes*. The unique characteristics of zeroes make them an interesting investment choice.

The yield to maturity of a zero coupon bond is the interest rate that an investor will receive if the bond is held until it matures. Table 19.1 lists bond prices for zero coupon bonds with a face value of $10,000, maturities of 5, 10, 20, and 30 years, and yields from 3 percent to 15 percent. As shown, a $10,000 face-value zero coupon bond with a term to maturity of 20 years and an 8 percent yield has a price of $2,082.89.

TABLE 19.1	Zero Coupon Bond Prices, $10,000 Face Value			
Yield to Maturity	**Bond Maturity**			
	5 Years	**10 Years**	**20 Years**	**30 Years**
3.0%	$8,616.67	$7,424.70	$5,512.62	$4,092.96
3.5	8,407.29	7,068.25	4,996.01	3,531.30
4.0	8,203.48	6,729.71	4,528.90	3,047.82
4.5	8,005.10	6,408.16	4,106.46	2,631.49
5.0	7,811.98	6,102.71	3,724.31	2,272.84
5.5	7,623.98	5,812.51	3,378.52	1,963.77
6.0	7,440.94	5,536.76	3,065.57	1,697.33
6.5	7,262.72	5,274.71	2,782.26	1,467.56
7.0	7,089.19	5,025.66	2,525.72	1,269.34
7.5	6,920.20	4,788.92	2,293.38	1,098.28
8.0	6,755.64	4,563.87	2,082.89	950.60
8.5	6,595.37	4,349.89	1,892.16	823.07
9.0	6,439.28	4,146.43	1,719.29	712.89
9.5	6,287.23	3,952.93	1,562.57	617.67
10.0	6,139.13	3,768.89	1,420.46	535.36
10.5	5,994.86	3,593.83	1,291.56	464.17
11.0	5,854.31	3,427.29	1,174.63	402.58
11.5	5,717.37	3,268.83	1,068.53	349.28
12.0	5,583.95	3,118.05	972.22	303.14
12.5	5,453.94	2,974.55	884.79	263.19
13.0	5,327.26	2,837.97	805.41	228.57
13.5	5,203.81	2,707.96	733.31	198.58
14.0	5,083.49	2,584.19	667.80	172.57
14.5	4,966.23	2,466.35	608.29	150.02
15.0	4,851.94	2,354.13	554.19	130.46

SPREADSHEET ANALYSIS

	A	B	C	D	E	F	G
1							
2			Calculating the Price of a Zero-Coupon STRIPS				
3							
4	A STRIPS traded on March 30, 2002, matures in 20 years on March 30, 2022.						
5	Assuming a 7 percent yield to maturity, what is the STRIPS price?						
6	Hint: Use the Excel function PRICE with the coupon rate set to zero.						
7							
8		$25.2572	=PRICE("3/30/2002","3/30/2022",0,0.07,100,2,3)				
9							
10	For a bond with a $10,000 face value, multiply the price by 100 to get $2,525.72.						
11							
12			Calculating the Yield to Maturity of a STRIPS				
13							
14	A STRIPS traded on March 30, 2002, matures in 10 years on March 30, 2012.						
15	The STRIPS price is $55. What is its yield to maturity?						
16	Hint: Use the Excel function YIELD with the coupon rate set to zero.						
17							
18		6.07%	=YIELD("3/30/2002","3/30/2012",0,55,100,2,3)				
19							
20							

CALCULATING A STRIPS PRICE

EXAMPLE 19.1

What is the price of a STRIPS maturing in 20 years with a face value of $10,000 and a yield to maturity of 7 percent?

The STRIPS price is calculated as the present value of a single cash flow as follows:

$$\text{STRIPS price} = \frac{\$10,000}{(1+0.07/2)^{40}}$$
$$= \$2,525.72$$

You can also calculate a STRIPS price using a built-in spreadsheet function. For example, the nearby *Spreadsheet Analysis* box contains this STRIPS price calculation using an Excel spreadsheet.

CALCULATING A STRIPS YIELD

EXAMPLE 19.2

What is the yield to maturity of a STRIPS maturing in 10 years with a face value of $10,000 and a price of $5,500?

The STRIPS yield is calculated as a yield to maturity of a single cash flow as follows:

$$\text{STRIPS yield} = 2 \times \left[\left(\frac{\$10,000}{\$5,500} \right)^{1/20} - 1 \right]$$
$$= 6.07\%$$

The nearby *Spreadsheet Analysis* box contains an example of this STRIPS yield calculation using an Excel spreadsheet.

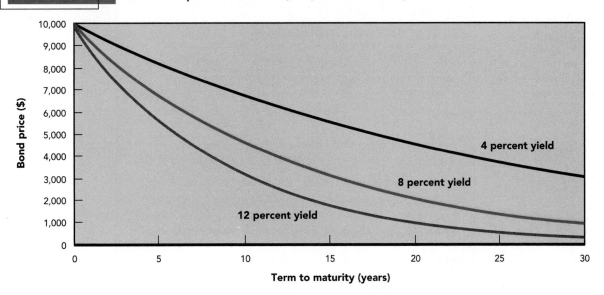

FIGURE 19.1   **Zero Coupon Bond Prices ($10,000 Face Value)**

Figure 19.1 graphs prices of zero coupon bonds with a face value of $10,000. The vertical axis measures bond prices, and the horizontal axis measures bond maturities. Bond prices for yields of 4, 8, and 12 percent are illustrated.

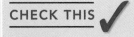

CHECK THIS ✓

19.2a   What are some possible reasons why individual investors might prefer to buy Treasury STRIPS rather than common stocks?

19.2b   What are some possible reasons why individual investors might prefer to buy individual Treasury STRIPS rather than whole bonds?

19.2c   For zero coupon bonds with the same face value and yield to maturity, is the price of a zero with a 15-year maturity larger or smaller than the average price of two zeroes with maturities of 10 years and 20 years? Why?

Canadian Government Bonds

Figure 19.2 displays a partial listing of *The Globe and Mail* prices and other relevant information for Canadian bonds. We discuss the section for Government of Canada and agencies next.

Bond price quotes are stated on a percentage of par basis where, for example, a price of 102 equals par value plus 2 percent. To illustrate, the first column in Figure 19.2 states the maturity of the bonds, the next columns report coupon rate, yield and daily change respectively.

Some bonds are callable. If a particular issue is callable, the issuer has the right to buy it back by paying a call premium or call price which is higher than the maturity value. A **yield to call (YTC)** is the interest rate for a bond assuming the bond will be called at its earliest possible call date and the bondholder will hold the bond until it is called. When a callable bond has a price above par, the reported yield is a yield to call.

yield to call (YTC)
The interest rate on a bond that assumes the bond will be called at its earliest possible call date.

FIGURE 19.2

Canadian Bonds

Source: *The Globe and Mail*, January 8, 2008. Reprinted with permission from *The Globe and Mail*.

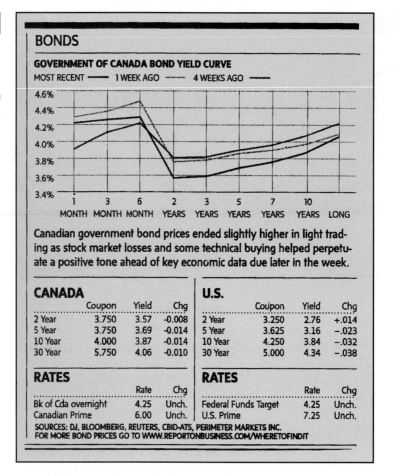

BONDS

GOVERNMENT OF CANADA BOND YIELD CURVE

MOST RECENT ——— 1 WEEK AGO ········ 4 WEEKS AGO ———

Canadian government bond prices ended slightly higher in light trading as stock market losses and some technical buying helped perpetuate a positive tone ahead of key economic data due later in the week.

CANADA	Coupon	Yield	Chg
2 Year	3.750	3.57	-0.008
5 Year	3.750	3.69	-0.014
10 Year	4.000	3.87	-0.014
30 Year	5.750	4.06	-0.010

U.S.	Coupon	Yield	Chg
2 Year	3.250	2.76	+.014
5 Year	3.625	3.16	-.023
10 Year	4.250	3.84	-.032
30 Year	5.000	4.34	-.038

RATES	Rate	Chg
Bk of Cda overnight	4.25	Unch.
Canadian Prime	6.00	Unch.

RATES	Rate	Chg
Federal Funds Target	4.25	Unch.
U.S. Prime	7.25	Unch.

SOURCES: DJ, BLOOMBERG, REUTERS, CBID-ATS, PERIMETER MARKETS INC.
FOR MORE BOND PRICES GO TO WWW.REPORTONBUSINESS.COM/WHERETOFINDIT

You can find more about the amount of Canadian government bonds and public debt by visiting the website of the Department of Finance at www.fin.gc.ca.

Since government bonds pay semiannual coupons, bond yields are stated on a semiannual basis. The relationship between the price of a note or bond and its yield to maturity was discussed in Chapter 11. For convenience, the bond price formula from that chapter is restated here:

$$\text{Bond price} = \frac{\text{Annual coupon}}{YTM} \times \left[1 - \frac{1}{(1 + YTM/2)^{2M}}\right] + \frac{\text{Face value}}{(1 + YTM/2)^{2M}}$$

Figure 19.3 illustrates the relationship between the price of a bond and its yield to maturity for 2-year, 7-year, and 30-year terms to maturity. Notice that each bond has a price of 100 when its yield is 8 percent. This indicates that each bond has an 8 percent coupon rate, because when a bond's coupon rate is equal to its yield to maturity, its price is equal to its par value.

FIGURE 19.3   **Bond Prices ($10,000 Face Value)**

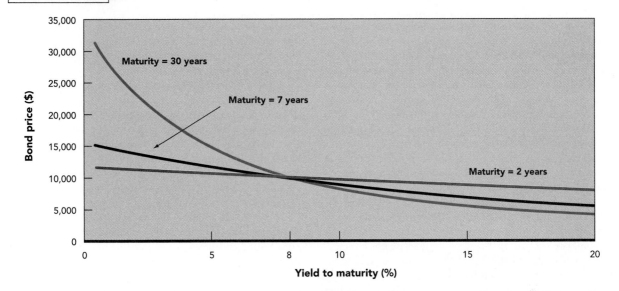

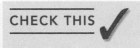

CHECK THIS ✓ | **19.2d** | What would Figure 19.3 look like if the three bonds all had coupon rates of 6 percent? What about 10 percent?

Real Return Canadian Bonds

In recent years, the Bank of Canada has issued securities that guarantee a fixed rate of return in excess of realized inflation rates. These inflation-indexed securities pay a fixed coupon rate on their current principal and adjust their principal semiannually according to the most recent inflation rate.

For example, suppose a real return bond is issued with a coupon rate of 3.5 percent and an initial principal of $1,000. Six months later, the note will pay a coupon of $1,000 × 3.5% / 2 = $17.50. Assuming 2 percent inflation over the six months since issuance, the note's principal is then increased to $1,000 × 102% = $1,020. Six months later, the bond pays $1,020 × 3.5% / 2 = $17.85, and its principal is again adjusted to compensate for recent inflation.

Price and yield information for real return bonds is reported in newspapers in the same section with other Canadian bonds. Listings for real return bonds first show the fixed coupon rate and maturity. The third column shows the price of these bonds. Prices for real return bonds are reported as percentages of current accrued principal. The last column lists an inflation-adjusted yield to maturity.

For investors wanting long-term protection against inflation along with the safety of government security, real return bonds are perhaps the perfect investment. The nearby *Investment Updates* box further discusses the attractive features of inflation-indexed Treasury securities.

"Inflation-Linked Treasurys Hold Surprising Appeal"

Inflation-indexed treasury bonds don't quite rival the Swiss Army Knife. But it's amazing what you can do with them. Need income? Worried about stocks? Want a place to park some cash? Inflation bonds can come in handy. Here's how:

RISING INCOME: Each year, the value of inflation bonds is stepped up along with consumer prices. Investors also collect interest based on this ever-rising principal value. Those twin attributes make the bonds an intriguing investment for retirees.

Suppose you invested $1,000 in inflation bonds at the current yield of 3.8%. If consumer prices rose 2.5% over the next year, your principal would climb to $1,025 and you would earn interest equal to 3.8% of this growing sum. Thus, if you spent the interest but didn't cash in any bonds, you would enjoy a rising stream of income, while keeping your principal's spending power intact.

Retirees should still keep some money in stocks, so they have a shot at even higher returns. After all, many folks won't have a big enough portfolio to live off inflation bonds' 3.8% yield. Still, inflation bonds are a good choice for at least part of your portfolio. "The long-run total return may not be as high as it is from stocks," says Ken Volpert, co-manager of Vanguard Inflation Protected Securities Fund, a no-load fund with $120 million in assets. "But you have greater certainty that the rise in your income and your principal will be in line with inflation."

INFLATION INSURANCE: Need protection against rising consumer prices? Inflation bonds may be just the ticket. "Say you were going to retire next year, and you plan to buy an annuity at that point," Mr. Hammond says. "With inflation bonds, you've protected yourself against a short-term spike in inflation."

Alternatively, suppose you sold your house and won't buy another for a few years. Maybe you are taking a job overseas or planning to rent while you look for the perfect spot to retire. If you plunked your home equity into inflation bonds and earned 3.8 percentage points a year more than inflation, you should have a good shot at keeping pace with real-estate prices.

PORTFOLIO PROTECTION: If inflation takes off or the economy tumbles into recession, stocks will get whacked. Want to cushion that blow? Traditionally, stock investors have added a dollop of regular bonds to their portfolios. That works well in a recession, when interest rates tend to fall, driving up the price of regular bonds, whose fixed-interest payouts now seem more attractive. But when inflation takes off, interest rates climb. Result: Both stocks and regular bonds get crushed.

That is where inflation bonds come in. They won't do as well as regular bonds in a recession. But during periods of rising consumer prices, inflation bonds will sparkle, thus helping to offset your stock-market losses.

PARKING PLACE: Because inflation bonds don't perform as erratically as regular bonds, they can be a good place to stash your emergency money. You never know when you will need this emergency money. Maybe you will have to call on your reserve next month—or maybe the money will sit untouched for the next decade. Because your time horizon is uncertain, you want the money to be readily available, but you also want it to earn healthy returns. Inflation bonds look good on both counts. Mr. Volpert figures your chances of losing money in any given year are slim. "You might even have better downside protection than you would with a short-term bond fund," he says.

19.3 Bank of Canada Auctions

For recent information on Bank of Canada auctions visit
www.bankofcanada.ca

The Bank of Canada conducts regularly scheduled auctions for government securities. At each auction, the Bank of Canada accepts sealed bids of two types: competitive bids and noncompetitive bids. Competitive bids for T-bills specify a bid price and a bid quantity. The bid price is what the bidder is willing to pay, and the bid quantity is the face value amount that the bidder will purchase if the bid is accepted. Noncompetitive bids specify only a bid quantity since the price charged to noncompetitive bidders will be determined by the results of the competitive auction process. Individual investors can submit noncompetitive bids, but only Treasury securities dealers can submit competitive bids.

cut-off yield The lowest yield at which the sum of competitive and noncompetitive bid amounts is greater than or equal to the issuing amount.

At the close of bidding, all sealed bids are forwarded to the Bank of Canada for processing. As a first step, all noncompetitive bids are accepted automatically and are subtracted from the total issue amount. Then a **cut-off yield** is determined; this is the price at which all competitive bids are sufficient to finance the remaining issue amount. Competitive bids at or above the cut-off yield are accepted, and bids below the cut-off yield bid are rejected.

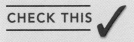 CHECK THIS

19.3a The Bank of Canada announces an offering of Treasury bills with a face value amount of $25 billion. The response is $5 billion of noncompetitive bids, along with the following competitive bids:

Bidder	Price Bid	Quantity Bid
A	$9,500	$5 billion
B	9,550	5 billion
C	9,600	5 billion
D	9,650	5 billion
E	9,700	5 billion

In an auction, which bids are accepted and what prices are paid by each bidder? How much money is raised by the entire offering?

19.4 Canada Savings Bonds

Canada Savings Bonds (CSBs) are non-marketable long-term bonds offered to Canadian investors by the Bank of Canada. Investors can purchase these bonds at all financial institutions in Canada. The bonds are offered on sale for six months from October and April. They must be registered by the investors or institutions in their own names.

Bonds are available in face denominations ranging from $100 to $10,000. There are two different types of bonds: regular interest and compound interest bonds. The bonds provide minimum guaranteed annual interest rates. If market interest rates increase, then the interest rates of Canada Savings Bonds are increased. Canada Savings Bonds can be cashed any time at Canadian financial institutions. The bonds are non-callable and non-transferable. Investors can use Canada Savings Bonds in their RRSP plans and get a tax deduction for their investments.

The Canada Premium Bond (CPB) is very similar to the Canada Savings Bond. However the CPB provides higher rates of return than the CSB. These bonds are redeemable once a year. To get more information on both the Canada Savings Bond and the Canada Premium Bond, visit the Government of Canada website at www.csb.gc.ca. A third type of bond, the Canada Investment Bond, is no longer issued as of April 2004.

 For the latest on Savings Bonds visit www.fin.gc.ca

19.5 Provincial and Municipal Bonds

default risk The risk that a bond issuer will cease making scheduled payments of coupons or principal or both.

Provincial and municipal bonds are intermediate to long-term interest bearing obligations of provincial and local governments. These bonds are typically less complicated investments than corporate bonds. However, while provincial debt often carries a high credit rating, **default risk** does exist. Thus, investing in provincial debt requires more care than investing in federal government securities.

TABLE 19.2	City Of Bedford Falls General Obligation Bonds	
Issue amount	$50 million	Bond issue represents a total face value amount of $50 million
Issue date	12/15/99	Bonds were offered to the public on December 15, 1999
Maturity date	12/31/29	All remaining principal must be paid at maturity on December 31, 2029
Par value	$5,000	Each bond has a face value of $5,000
Coupon rate	6%	Annual coupons of $300 per bond
Coupon dates	12/31, 6/30	Semiannual coupons of $150
Offering price	100	Offer price is 100% of par value
Yield to maturity	6%	Based on stated offer price
Call provision	Callable after 12/31/09	Bonds are call-protected for 10 years
Call price	100	Bonds are callable at par value
Trustee	Potters Bank of Bedford Falls	The trustee is appointed to represent the bondholders and administer the sinking fund
Sinking fund	$2.5 million annual par redemptions after 12/31/09	City must redeem at par value $2.5 million of the bond issue each year beginning in 2010

Provincial and municipal bonds are issued in annual simple interest form or compound interest form. They are RRSP eligible and if used in a retirement plan provide a tax deduction. Otherwise these bonds are taxable.

Some provinces issue step-up and variable rate bonds in addition to fixed-rate bonds.

To illustrate some standard features of a municipal bond issue, Table 19.2 summarizes the issue terms for a hypothetical bond issued by the city of Bedford Falls. We see that the bonds were issued in December 1999 and mature 30 years later in December 2029. Each bond has a face value denomination of $5,000 and pays an annual coupon equal to 6 percent of face value. The annual coupon is split between two semiannual payments each June and December. Based on the original offer price of 100, or 100 percent of par value, the bonds have a yield to maturity of 6 percent. The Bedford Falls bonds are call-protected for 10 years, until January 2009. Thereafter, the bonds are callable any time at par value.

general obligation bonds (GOs) Bonds issued by a municipality that are secured by the full faith and credit of the issuer.

The Bedford Falls bonds are **general obligation bonds** (**GOs**), which means that the bonds are secured by the full faith and credit of the city of Bedford Falls. "Full faith and credit" means the power of the municipality to collect taxes. The trustee for the bond issue is the Potters Bank of Bedford Falls. A trustee is appointed to represent the financial interests of bondholders and administer the sinking fund for the bond issue. A sinking fund requires a bond issuer to redeem for cash a fraction of an outstanding bond issue on a periodic basis. The sinking fund in this example requires that, beginning 10 years after issuance, the city must redeem at par value $2.5 million of the bond issue each year. At each annual redemption, a fraction of the bond issue is called and the affected bondholders receive the par value call price.

call provision Feature of a provincial and municipal bond issue that specifies when the bonds may be called by the issuer and the call price that must be paid.

A **call provision** is a standard feature of most provincial and municipal bond issues. A call provision allows an issuer to retire outstanding bonds before they mature, usually to refund with new bonds after a fall in market interest rates. When the bond is called, each bondholder receives the bond's call price in exchange for the bond. However, two bond features often limit an issuer's call privilege. First, callable provincial and municipal bonds usually offer a period of call protection following their original issue date. Since a bond issue is not callable during this period, the earliest possible call date is the end of the call protection period. Second, a call price is often specified with a call premium. A call premium is the difference between a bond's call price and its par value. A common arrangement is to specify a call premium equal to one year's coupons for a call occurring at the earliest possible call date. This is then followed by a schedule of call premium reductions, until about 5 to 10 years before maturity, when the call premium is eliminated entirely. Thereafter, the bond issue is callable any time at par value.

While most provincial and municipal bonds maintain a constant coupon rate (hence the term fixed-rate bonds), interest rate risk has induced many provinces to issue **variable-rate notes**, often called *floaters*. For these debt issues, the coupon rate is adjusted periodically according to an index-based rule. For example, at each adjustment the coupon rate may be set at 60 percent of the prevailing rate on 91-day maturity Treasury bills. A variable-rate note may also be putable, in which case it is called a *variable-rate demand obligation*, often abbreviated to VRDO. A stipulation attached to most VRDOs allows the issuer to convert an entire variable-rate issue to a fixed-rate issue following a specified conversion procedure. Essentially, the issuer notifies each VRDO holder of the intent to convert the outstanding VRDO issue to a fixed-rate issue on a specific future date. In response, VRDO holders have the option of tendering their VRDOs for cash, or they can accept conversion of their VRDOs into fixed-rate bonds.

variable-rate notes
Securities that pay an interest rate that changes according to market conditions. Also called *floaters*.

Municipal and Provincial Bond Credit Ratings

Municipal and Provincial bond credit rating agencies provide investors with an assessment of the credit quality of individual bond issues. As part of the issuance and credit rating process, the rating agency is paid a fee to assign a credit rating to a new bond issue, to periodically reevaluate the issue, and to make these ratings available to the public. The largest municipal bond credit rating agencies are Moody's Investors Service, Standard & Poor's Corporation, and Dominion Bond Rating Services (DBRS). Among them, they rate thousands of new issues each year. Table 19.3 compares and briefly describes the credit rating codes assigned by these agencies.

Check out these rating agency web-sites: Moody's at www.moodys.com S&P at www. standardandpoors. com Dominion Bond Rating Services at www.dbrs.com

TABLE 19.3	Municipal and Provincial Bond Credit Ratings		
Rating Agency			
Standard & Poor's	**Moody's**	**Dominion Bond Rating Service**	**Credit Rating Description**
Investment-Grade Bond Ratings			
AAA	Aaa	AAA	Highest credit quality
AA	Aa	AA	High credit quality
A	A	A	Good credit quality
BBB	Baa	BBB	Satisfactory credit quality
Speculative-Grade Bond Ratings			
BB	Ba	BB	Speculative credit quality
B	B	B	Highly speculative quality
CCC	Caa	CCC	Poor credit quality
CC	Ca	CC	Probable default
Extremely Speculative-Grade Bond Ratings			
C	C	C	Imminent default
D		DDD	In default
		DD, D	

The highest credit rating that can be awarded is "triple-A," which indicates that interest and principal are exceptionally secure because of the financial strength of the issuer. Notice that "triple-A" and "double-A" ratings are denoted as AAA and AA, respectively, by Standard & Poor's and DBRS, but as Aaa and Aa, respectively, by Moody's. Also notice that "triple-B" and "double-B" ratings—that is, BBB and BB, respectively—by Standard & Poor's and DBRS correspond to "B-double-a" and "B-single-a" ratings—Baa and Ba, respectively—by Moody's. The same pattern holds for C ratings.

The highest four credit ratings, BBB or Baa and above, designate investment-grade bonds. As a matter of policy, many financial institutions will invest only in investment-grade bonds. Lower rankings indicate successively diminishing levels of credit quality. Ratings of BB or Ba and below designate speculative-grade bonds. Individual investors should probably avoid speculative-grade bonds. A rating of C or below indicates that actual or probable default makes the bond issue unsuitable for most investors.

It is not unusual for the ratings assigned to a particular bond issue to differ slightly across credit rating agencies. For example, a bond issue may be rated AA by Standard & Poor's, Aa by Moody's, but only A by DBRS. When this occurs, it usually reflects a difference in credit rating methods rather than a disagreement regarding basic facts. For example, Moody's may focus on the budgetary status of the issuer when assigning a credit rating, while Standard & Poor's may emphasize the economic environment of the issuer. Remember that Standard & Poor's, Moody's, and DBRS are competitors in the bond rating business, and, like competitors in any industry, they try to differentiate their products.

19.6 Mortgage-Backed Securities

Almost all real estate purchases are financed by mortgages. Indeed, most of us become familiar with mortgages by financing the purchase of a home. But did you ever stop to think about what happens to a mortgage after it is originated? Today, they are usually pooled to create mortgage-backed securities. The basic concept is simple. Collect a portfolio of mortgages into a mortgage pool. Then issue securities with pro rata claims on mortgage pool cash flows. These mortgage-backed securities are attractive to investors because they represent a claim on a diversified portfolio of mortgages and, therefore, are considerably less risky than individual mortgage contracts.

Mortgage financing makes home ownership possible for almost everyone. With mortgage financing, a home buyer makes only a down payment and borrows the remaining cost of a home with a mortgage loan. The mortgage loan is obtained from a mortgage originator, usually a local bank or other mortgage broker. Describing this financial transaction, we can say that a home buyer *issues* a mortgage and an originator *writes* a mortgage. A mortgage loan distinguishes itself from other loan contracts by a pledge of real estate as collateral for the loan.

19.7 A Brief History of Mortgage-Backed Securities

Traditionally, savings banks and savings and loans (S&Ls) wrote most home mortgages and then held the mortgages in their portfolios of interest-earning assets. This changed radically during the 1970s and 1980s when market interest rates ascended to their highest levels in history. Entering this financially turbulent period, savings banks and S&Ls held large portfolios of mortgages written at low pre-1970s interest rates. These portfolios were financed from customers' savings deposits. When market interest rates climbed to near 20 percent levels in the early 1980s, customers flocked to withdraw funds from their savings deposits to invest in money market funds that paid higher interest rates. As a result, savings institutions were often forced to sell mortgages at depressed prices to satisfy the onslaught of deposit withdrawals. For this, and other reasons, the ultimate result was the collapse of many savings institutions.

Today, home buyers still commonly turn to local banks for mortgage financing, but few mortgages are actually held by the banks that originate them. After writing a mortgage, an originator usually sells the mortgage to a mortgage repackager who accumulates them into mortgage pools. To finance the creation of a mortgage pool, the mortgage repackager issues mortgage-backed bonds, where each bond claims a pro rata share of all cash flows derived from mortgages in the pool. A pro rata share allocation pays cash flows in proportion to a bond's face value. Essentially, each mortgage pool is set up as a trust fund, and a servicing agent for the pool collects all mortgage payments. The servicing agent then passes these cash flows through to bondholders. For this reason, mortgage-backed bonds are often called **mortgage passthroughs**, or simply *pass-throughs*. However, all securities representing claims on mortgage pools are generically called **mortgage-backed securities** (**MBSs**). The primary collateral for all mortgage-backed securities is the underlying pool of mortgages.

The transformation from mortgages to mortgage-backed securities is called **mortgage securitization**. More than $3 trillion of mortgages have been securitized in mortgage pools. This represents tremendous growth in the mortgage securitization business, since in the early 1980s less than $1 billion of home mortgages were securitized in pools. Yet despite the multi-trillion-dollar size of the mortgage-backed securities market, the risks involved with these investments are often misunderstood even by experienced investors.

In Canada, the Canada Mortgage and Housing Corporation (CMHC) obtained permission to offer Mortgage-Backed Securities (MBS) for residential mortgages in 1984. Today chartered banks, trust companies, insurance companies, credit unions and caisses populaire can issue mortgage-backed securities after getting approval from the CMHC. Currently four types of MBS pools are offered: exclusive homeowner, multi-family, social housing, and mixed.

Visit www. investinginbonds. com for more information on mortgage-backed securities

mortgage passthroughs Bonds representing a claim on the cash flows of an underlying mortgage pool passed through to bondholders.

mortgage-backed securities (MBSs) Securities whose investment returns are based on a pool of mortgages.

mortgage securitization The creation of mortgage-backed securities from a pool of mortgages.

19.8 Fixed-Rate Mortgages

Understanding mortgage-backed securities begins with an understanding of the mortgages from which they are created. Most home mortgages are 15-year or 30-year maturity **fixed-rate mortgages** requiring constant monthly payments. As an example of a fixed-rate mortgage, consider a 30-year mortgage representing a loan of $100,000 financed at an annual interest rate of 8 percent. This translates into a monthly interest rate of 8 percent / 12 months = .67%, and it requires a series of 360 monthly payments. The size of the monthly payment is determined by the requirement that the present value of all monthly payments, based on the financing rate specified in the mortgage contract, be equal to the original loan amount of $100,000. Mathematically, the constant monthly payment for a $100,000 mortgage is calculated using the following formula:

fixed-rate mortgage Loan that specifies constant monthly payments at a fixed interest rate over the life of the mortgage.

$$\text{Monthly payment} = \frac{\text{Mortgage amount} \times r/12}{1 - \dfrac{1}{(1 + r/12)^{T \times 12}}} \tag{19.1}$$

where: r = Annual mortgage financing rate
$r/12$ = Monthly mortgage financing rate
T = Mortgage term in years
$T \times 12$ = Mortgage term in months

In the example of a $100,000, thirty-year mortgage financed at 8 percent, the monthly payment is $733.76. This amount is calculated as follows:

$$\text{Monthly payment} = \frac{\$100,000 \times .08/12}{1 - \dfrac{1}{(1 + .08/12)^{360}}}$$
$$= \$733.76$$

In Canada mortgage payments are compounded semiannually and therefore we have to use an effective annual rate instead of an annual fixed rate. The effective annual rate for semiannual compounding is calculated as follows:

$$\text{Effective annual rate} = \left[1 + \frac{r}{2} \right]^2 - 1 \qquad (19.2)$$

We then substitute this rate instead of r in Equation 19.1 to find monthly payments. For example, a Canada mortgage holder with an 8 percent annual mortgage rate will pay the following monthly amount:

$$\text{Effective annual rate} = \left[1 + \frac{0.08}{2} \right]^2 - 1 = 0.0816 \; or \; 8.16\%$$

$$\text{Monthly payment} = \frac{\$100,000 \times 0.0816/12}{1 - \dfrac{1}{(1 + 0.0816/12)^{360}}} = \$744.96$$

The Canadian mortgage payment period is generally 25 years.

CALCULATING MONTHLY MORTGAGE PAYMENTS

EXAMPLE 19.3

What is the monthly payment for a 15-year, $100,000 mortgage loan financed at 8 percent interest?

A 15-year mortgage specifies 180 monthly payments. Using the monthly payment formula we get a monthly payment of $955.65 as follows:

$$\text{Monthly payment} = \frac{\$100,000 \times 0.08/12}{1 - \dfrac{1}{(1 + .08/12)^{180}}}$$
$$= \$955.65$$

If you wish to calculate mortgage payments for other interest rates, maturities, and loan amounts, we suggest using a built-in spreadsheet function. For example, the nearby *Spreadsheet Analysis* box contains an example mortgage payment calculation using an Excel spreadsheet.

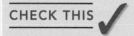

CHECK THIS

19.8a The most popular fixed-rate mortgages among home buyers are those with 15-year and 30-year maturities. What might be some of the comparative advantages and disadvantages of these two mortgage maturities?

19.8b Suppose you were to finance a home purchase using a fixed-rate mortgage. Would you prefer a 15-year or 30-year maturity mortgage? Why?

SPREADSHEET ANALYSIS

	A	B	C	D	E	F	G
1							
2		**Monthly Payments for a 30-year Mortgage**					
3							
4	A 30-year mortgage specifies an annual interest rate of 8 percent and a						
5	loan amount of $100,000.What are the monthly payments?						
6	Hint: Use the Excel function PMT.						
7							
8		−$733.76	=PMT(0.08/12,360,100000,0,0)				
9							
10	Monthly interest is 8% / 12 = .667%						
11	Number of monthly payments is 12 x 30 = 360.						
12	Initial principal is $100,000.						
13	First zero indicates complete repayment after last monthly payment.						
14	Second zero indicates end-of-month payments.						
15							
16	For a 15-year mortgage we get a bigger monthly payment.						
17							
18		−$955.65	=PMT(0.08/12,180,100000,0,0)				
19							
20							

Monthly mortgage payments are sensitive to the interest rate stipulated in the mortgage contract. Table 19.4 provides a schedule of monthly payments required for 5-year, 10-year, 15-year, 20-year, and 30-year mortgages based on annual interest rates ranging from 5 percent to 15 percent in increments of .5 percent. Notice that monthly payments required for a $100,000 thirty-year mortgage financed at 5 percent are only $536.82, while monthly payments for the same mortgage financed at 15 percent are $1,264.44.

Fixed-Rate Mortgage Amortization

mortgage principal
The amount of a mortgage loan outstanding, which is the amount required to pay off the mortgage.

Each monthly mortgage payment has two separate components. The first component represents payment of interest on outstanding **mortgage principal**. Outstanding mortgage principal is also called a mortgage's *remaining balance* or *remaining principal*. It is the amount required to pay off a mortgage before it matures. The second component represents a pay-down, or *amortization*, of mortgage principal. The relative amounts of each component change throughout the life of a mortgage. For example, a 30-year $100,000 mortgage financed at 8 percent requires 360 monthly payments of $733.76.

TABLE 19.4	$100,000 Mortgage Loan Monthly Payments				
Interest Rate	**Mortgage Maturity**				
	30-Year	**20-Year**	**15-Year**	**10-Year**	**5-Year**
5.0%	$536.82	$659.96	$790.79	$1,060.66	$1,887.12
5.5	567.79	687.89	817.08	1,085.26	1,910.12
6.0	599.55	716.43	843.86	1,110.21	1,933.28
6.5	632.07	745.57	871.11	1,135.48	1,956.61
7.0	665.30	775.30	898.83	1,161.08	1,980.12
7.5	699.21	805.59	927.01	1,187.02	2,003.79
8.0	733.76	836.44	955.65	1,213.28	2,027.64
8.5	768.91	867.82	984.74	1,239.86	2,051.65
9.0	804.62	899.73	1,014.27	1,266.76	2,075.84
9.5	840.85	932.13	1,044.22	1,293.98	2,100.19
10.0	877.57	965.02	1,074.61	1,321.51	2,124.70
10.5	914.74	998.38	1,105.40	1,349.35	2,149.39
11.0	952.32	1,032.19	1,136.60	1,377.50	2,174.24
11.5	990.29	1,066.43	1,168.19	1,405.95	2,199.26
12.0	1,028.61	1,101.09	1,200.17	1,434.71	2,224.44
12.5	1,067.26	1,136.14	1,232.52	1,463.76	2,249.79
13.0	1,106.20	1,171.58	1,265.24	1,493.11	2,275.31
13.5	1,145.41	1,207.37	1,298.32	1,522.74	2,300.98
14.0	1,184.87	1,243.52	1,331.74	1,552.66	2,326.83
14.5	1,224.56	1,280.00	1,365.50	1,582.87	2,352.83
15.0	1,264.44	1,316.79	1,399.59	1,613.35	2,378.99

The first monthly payment consists of a $666.67 payment of interest and a $67.10 paydown of principal. The first month's interest payment, representing one month's interest on a mortgage balance of $100,000, is calculated as

$$\$100,000 \times .08/12 = \$666.67$$

After this payment of interest, the remainder of the first monthly payment, that is, $733.76 − $666.67 = $67.10 (there's a small rounding error), is used to amortize outstanding mortgage principal. Thus, after the first monthly payment, outstanding principal is reduced to $100,000 − $67.10 = $99,932.90.

The second monthly payment includes a $666.22 payment of interest calculated as

$$\$99,932.90 \times .08/12 = \$666.22$$

The remainder of the second monthly payment, that is, $733.76 − $666.22 = $67.54, is used to reduce mortgage principal to $99,932.91 − $67.54 = $99,865.37.

This process continues throughout the life of the mortgage. The interest payment component gradually declines, and the payment of principal component gradually increases. Finally, the last monthly payment is divided into a $4.86 payment of interest and a final $728.91 pay-down of mortgage principal. The process of paying down mortgage principal over the life of a mortgage is called **mortgage amortization**.

mortgage amortization The process of paying down mortgage principal over the life of the mortgage.

Mortgage amortization is described by an amortization schedule. An amortization schedule states the remaining principal owed on a mortgage at any point in time and

TABLE 19.5	$100,000 Mortgage Loan Amortization Schedules for 15-year and 30-year Mortgages						
30-Year Mortgage $733.76 Monthly Payment				15-Year Mortgage $955.65 Monthly Payment			
Payment Month	Remaining Principal	Principal Reduction	Interest Payment	Payment Month	Remaining Principal	Principal Reduction	Interest Payment
1	$99,932.90	$67.10	$666.67	1	$99,711.01	$288.99	$666.67
12	99,164.64	72.19	661.58	12	96,402.15	310.90	644.75
24	98,259.94	78.18	655.59	24	92,505.69	336.70	618.95
36	97,280.15	84.67	649.10	36	88,285.81	364.65	591.00
48	96,219.04	91.69	642.07	48	83,715.70	394.91	560.74
60	95,069.86	99.30	634.46	60	78,766.26	427.69	527.96
72	93,825.29	107.55	626.22	72	73,406.02	463.19	492.46
84	92,477.43	116.47	617.29	84	67,600.89	501.64	454.02
96	91,017.70	126.14	607.63	96	61,313.93	543.27	412.38
108	89,436.81	136.61	597.16	108	54,505.16	588.36	367.29
120	87,724.70	147.95	585.82	120	47,131.26	637.20	318.46
132	85,870.50	160.23	573.54	132	39,145.34	690.08	265.57
144	83,862.39	173.53	560.24	144	30,496.58	747.36	208.29
156	81,687.61	187.93	545.84	156	21,129.99	809.39	146.26
168	79,332.33	203.53	530.24	168	10,985.97	876.57	79.08
180	76,781.56	220.42	513.35	180	0.00	949.32	6.33
192	74,019.08	238.71	495.05				
204	71,027.31	258.53	475.24				
216	67,787.23	279.98	453.78				
228	64,278.22	303.22	430.54				
240	60,477.96	328.39	405.38				
252	56,362.29	355.65	378.12				
264	51,905.02	385.16	348.60				
276	47,077.79	417.13	316.63				
288	41,849.91	451.75	282.01				
300	36,188.12	489.25	244.52				
312	30,056.40	529.86	203.91				
324	23,415.75	573.83	159.93				
336	16,223.93	621.46	112.30				
348	8,435.20	673.04	60.72				
360	0.00	728.91	4.86				

also states the scheduled principal payment and interest payment in any month. Amortization schedules for 15-year and 30-year $100,000 mortgages financed at a fixed rate of 8 percent are listed in Table 19.5. The payment month is given in the left-hand column. Then, for each maturity, the first column reports remaining mortgage principal immediately after a monthly payment is made. Columns 2 and 3 for each maturity list the principal payment and the interest payment scheduled for each monthly payment. Notice that immediately after the 180th monthly payment for a 30-year $100,000 mortgage, $76,781.56 of mortgage principal is still outstanding. Notice also that as late as the 252nd monthly payment, the interest payment component of $378.12 still exceeds the principal payment component of $355.65.

MORTGAGE AMORTIZATION

EXAMPLE 19.4

After five years of payments on a mortgage loan financed at 8 percent, what are the remaining balance and interest and principal reduction components of the monthly payment?

For the 30-year mortgage, referring to Table 19.4 we see that the monthly payment is $733.76. Referring to the 60th monthly payment in Table 19.5, we find that the remaining balance on the mortgage is $95,069.86. Principal reduction for this payment is $99.30, and the interest payment is $634.46.

For the 15-year mortgage, the monthly payment is $955.65 and, after the 60th monthly payment, the remaining balance is $78,766.26, principal reduction is $427.69, and the interest payment is $527.96.

If you wish to calculate interest and principal reduction components for other interest rates, maturities, and loan amounts, we suggest using built-in spreadsheet functions. A nearby *Spreadsheet Analysis* box contains an example calculation of interest and principal reduction components for a mortgage using an Excel spreadsheet. Another *Spreadsheet Analysis* box contains an example calculation of the remaining balance on a mortgage.

SPREADSHEET ANALYSIS

	A	B	C	D	E	F	G
1							
2		**Amortization Schedule for a 30-year Mortgage**					
3							
4	A 30-year mortgage specifies an annual interest rate of 8 percent and a						
5	loan amount of $100,000. What are the interest and principal payments?						
6	Hint: Use the Excel function IPMT and PPMT.						
7							
8	For the 120th payment after 10 years, interest and principal payments are						
9							
10		−$585.82	=IPMT(0.08/12,120,360,100000,0)				
11							
12		−$147.95	=PPMT(0.08/12,120,360,100000,0)				
13							
14	For the 240th payment after 20 years, interest and principal payments are						
15							
16		−$405.38	=IPMT(0.08/12,240,360,100000,0)				
17							
18		−$328.39	=PPMT(0.08/12,240,360,100000,0)				
19							
20							

(continued)

	A	B	C	D	E	F	G
1							
2		**Remaining Balance for a 30-year Mortgage**					
3							
4	A 30-year mortgage specifies an annual interest rate of 8 percent and a						
5	loan amount of $100,000. What is the remaining balance?						
6	Hint: Use the Excel function CUMPRINC.						
7							
8	Remaining balance at the 100th payment after 8 years and 4 months is						
9	the present value of payments 101 through 360.						
10							
11		−$90,504.68	=CUMPRINC(0.08/12,360,100000,101,360,0)				
12							
13	Remaining balance at the 200th payment after 16 years and 8 months is						
14	the present value of payments 201 through 360.						
15							
16		−$72,051.18	=CUMPRINC(0.08/12,360,100000,201,360,0)				
17							
18							
19							
20							

The amortization process for a 30-year $100,000 mortgage financed at 8 percent interest is illustrated graphically in Figure 19.4. Figure 19.4A graphs the outstanding mortgage principal over the life of the mortgage. Figure 19.4B graphs the rising principal payment component and the falling interest payment component of the mortgage.

Fixed-Rate Mortgage Prepayment and Refinancing

A mortgage borrower has the right to pay off an outstanding mortgage at any time. This right is similar to the call feature on corporate bonds, whereby the issuer can buy back outstanding bonds at a prespecified call price. Paying off a mortgage ahead of its amortization schedule is called **mortgage prepayment**.

mortgage prepayment Paying off all or part of outstanding mortgage principal ahead of its amortization schedule.

Prepayment can be motivated by a variety of factors. A homeowner may pay off a mortgage in order to sell the property when a family moves because of, say, new employment or retirement. After the death of a spouse, a surviving family member may pay off a mortgage with an insurance benefit. These are examples of mortgage prepayment for personal reasons. However, mortgage prepayments often occur for a purely financial reason: an existing mortgage loan may be refinanced at a lower interest rate when a lower rate becomes available.

Consider a 30-year $100,000 fixed-rate 8 percent mortgage with a monthly payment of $733.76. Suppose that, 10 years into the mortgage, market interest rates have fallen, and the financing rate on new 20-year mortgages is 6.5 percent. After 10 years (120 months), the remaining balance for the original $100,000 mortgage is $87,724.70. The monthly payment on a new 20-year $90,000 fixed-rate 6.5 percent mortgage is $671.02, which is $62.74 less than the $733.76 monthly payment on the old 8 percent mortgage with 20 years of payments remaining. Thus, a homeowner could profit by prepaying the original 8 percent mortgage and refinancing with a new 20-year 6.5 percent mortgage.

FIGURE 19.4

FIGURE 19.4

Mortgage
Principal and
Payments for a
$100,000 30-Year
Mortgage with an
8 Percent Interest
Rate

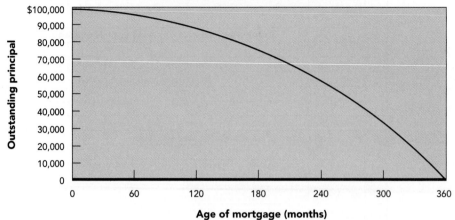

A. Outstanding mortgage principal

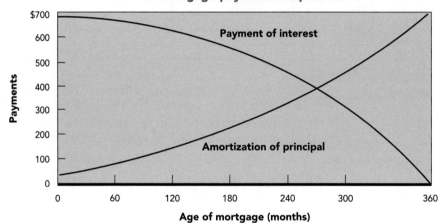

B. Mortgage payment components

Monthly payments would be lower by $62.75, and the $2,275.30 difference between the new $90,000 mortgage balance and the old $87,724.70 mortgage balance would defray any refinancing costs.

As this example suggests, during periods of falling interest rates, mortgage refinancings are an important reason for mortgage prepayments. The nearby *Investment Updates* box presents a *Wall Street Journal* article discussing the merits of mortgage refinancing.

The possibility of prepayment and refinancing is an advantage to mortgage borrowers but a disadvantage to mortgage investors. For example, consider investors who supply funds to write mortgages at a financing rate of 8 percent. Suppose that mortgage interest rates later fall to 6.5 percent, and, consequently, homeowners rush to prepay their 8 percent mortgages so as to refinance at 6.5 percent. Mortgage investors recover their outstanding investment principal from the prepayments, but the rate of return that they can realize on a new investment is reduced because mortgages can now be written only at the new 6.5 percent financing rate. The possibility that falling interest rates will set off a wave of mortgage refinancings is an ever-present risk that mortgage investors must face.

Smart investing begins at home. Many folks diligently nurture their portfolios of stocks, bonds and mutual funds. Got a mortgage on your house? You should manage your home loan with the same sort of investment savvy. Planning to refinance? Considering extra principal payments? Here's how to make smarter decisions when handling your mortgage:

Reducing Your Rate

Imagine you bought your house seven years ago. At the time, you borrowed $200,000 through a 30-year mortgage with a fixed 7% rate, resulting in a monthly mortgage payment of $1,331. Now, a loan officer at the local bank says that, for $2,500 in fees, you could refinance and get a new 30-year loan at 6%.

At first blush, that might seem appealing. Your seven years of mortgage payments has left you with a loan balance of $182,295. If you refinanced that sum at 6% over 30 years, your monthly payment would drop to $1,093.

A sweet deal? It isn't quite as sweet as it seems. Think about it: You are replacing what's now a 23-year loan with a 30-year loan. Even if your mortgage rate stayed the same, your monthly payment would still drop, because you are now paying back the sum borrowed over an additional seven years.

Instead, to make a fair comparison, you have to compare your current 23-year 7% loan with a new 23-year 6% loan. To that end, try playing with mortgage calculators at sites like www.bankrate.com, www.hsh.com, www.mortgage-x.com and www.realestateabc.com.

If you compare the two 23-year loans, you'll find you could save $111 a month by refinancing. Divide that $111 into the $2,500 in fees. Result: Refinancing makes sense, provided you stay in your current house for just over 22 months. Your local bank won't actually offer you a 23-year loan. Instead, you might opt for, say, a 20-year loan. But taking that shorter loan could be a smart move, says Michael Maloon, a financial planner in San Ramon, Calif.

"If people are refinancing and going back to a 30-year mortgage, they're crazy," he contends. "If you do that and you end up with an extra couple of hundred dollars a month in discretionary income, you will get used to spending that amount. Now, you need even more to retire," because you are accustomed to a higher standard of living. Instead, Mr. Maloon argues that folks who refinance should look to shorten the length of their loans, with a view to getting their mortgages paid off before they retire. "To win in the refi game, you want to lower the rate, lower your payments and pay off your mortgage sooner," he says. "I don't know how you retire if you still have a mortgage."

Paying Down Principal

To get your mortgage paid off by the time you retire, you might also want to make extra principal payments.

(continued)

19.9 Canada Mortgage and Housing Corporation

Canada Mortgage and Housing Corporation
Government agency charged with promoting liquidity in the home mortgage market.

fully modified mortgage pool
Mortgage pool that guarantees timely payment of interest and principal.

In 1946, the federal government established the **Canada Mortgage and Housing Corporation** (CMHC). The CMHC was charged with the mission of promoting liquidity in the secondary market for home mortgages. Liquidity is the ability of investors to buy and sell securities quickly at competitive market prices. Essentially, mortgages repackaged into mortgage pools are a more liquid investment product than the original unpooled mortgages. The CMHC sponsored the repackaging of several million dollars' worth of mortgages into hundreds of thousands of mortgage-backed security pools.

Mortgages in CMHC pools are said to be **fully modified mortgage pools** because CMHC guarantees bondholders full and timely payment of both principal and interest even in the event of default of the underlying mortgages. But investors still face **prepayment risk**, the risk that mortgage takers decide to pay mortgage principal and interest early, that is, before maturity of the mortgage.

The CMHC operates in cooperation with private lenders and underwriters certified by the CMHC to create mortgage pools. The underwriters originate or otherwise acquire the mortgages to form a pool. After verifying that the mortgages comply with

Manage Your Home Like an Investment

By adding $100 or $200 to each monthly mortgage check, you could save yourself thousands of dollars in interest and pay off your loan years earlier.

Sound attractive? To figure out whether this is the right strategy for you, consider not only the interest rate on your mortgage, but also your tax situation and what else you might do with the money. Let's say you have a mortgage with a 6.5% interest rate. That 6.5% is the interest expense you avoid by making extra principal payments and thus that is the effective pretax rate of return you earn. You should be able to do better than that 6.5% by buying stocks or bonds within a retirement account or by purchasing stocks in a taxable account.

But what if you have maxed out on your retirement accounts and you already own plenty of stocks? What if the alternative is to buy bonds or certificates of deposit within your taxable account? In that case, making extra principal payments could be a smart strategy. Suppose you are choosing between paying down your 6.5% mortgage and buying a corporate bond for your taxable account that yields 5.5%. If your mortgage interest is tax-deductible and you are in the 27% federal income-tax bracket, the after-tax return from paying down your mortgage is 4.75%. But the after-tax return on the corporate bond would be even lower. After paying federal income taxes on the bond's 5.5% yield, you would be left with just 4.02%.

In fact, paying down your mortgage may garner you an even higher return. Imagine you are married and you file a joint tax return. In 2003, you and your spouse are entitled to a standard deduction of $7,950. But let's assume you don't take the standard deduction. Instead, you itemize your deductions by filing Schedule A along with your federal tax return. This year, you expect to have itemized deductions of $10,000, consisting of $5,000 in mortgage interest and another $5,000 in property taxes, charitable gifts and state income taxes. Because your total of $10,000 in itemized deductions is greater than your $7,950 standard deduction, you save taxes by itemizing.

Even so, the tax benefit you get from your mortgage interest is still fairly modest. Indeed, I would argue that just $2,050 of your mortgage interest is truly tax-deductible. The reason: If you had $2,050 less in annual mortgage interest, you would take the standard deduction instead and thus you wouldn't get any tax benefit from your mortgage. Nonetheless, the after-tax return from adding an extra $100 to your mortgage check would still be 4.75%. How come? The interest you avoid by making extra principal payments is interest you could have deducted. Eventually, however, as you pay down your mortgage and thereby reduce the amount of interest you incur each year, your itemized deductions will fall below $7,950 and you will take the standard deduction instead. At that point, the after-tax return from making extra principal payments jumps to the full 6.5%.

Source: Jonathan Clements, *The Wall Street Journal*, April 27, 2003.
© 2003 Dow Jones & Company, Inc. All Rights Reserved Worldwide.

---

prepayment risk
Uncertainty faced by mortgage investors regarding early payment of mortgage principal and interest.

Visit the CMHC website at
www.cmhc.ca

CMHC requirements, the CMHC authorizes the underwriter to issue mortgage-backed securities with a CMHC guarantee.

As a simplified example of how a CMHC pool operates, consider a hypothetical CMHC fully modified mortgage pool containing only a single mortgage. After obtaining approval from the CMHC, the pool has a CMHC guarantee and is called a CMHC bond. The underwriter then sells the bond, and the buyer is entitled to receive all mortgage payments, less servicing and guarantee fees. If a mortgage payment occurs ahead of schedule, the early payment is passed through to the bondholder. If a payment is late, CMHC makes a timely payment to the bondholder. If any mortgage principal is prepaid, the early payment is passed through to the bondholder. If a default occurs, the CMHC settles with the bondholder by making full payment of the remaining mortgage principal. In effect, to a CMHC bondholder, mortgage default is the same thing as a prepayment.

J. Kyle Bass, a hedge fund manager from Dallas, strode into a New York conference room in August, 2006, to pitch his theory about a looming housing market meltdown to senior executives of a Wall Street investment bank.

Home prices had been on a five-year tear, rising more than 10 per cent annually. Mr. Bass conceived a hedge fund that bet on a crash for residential real estate by trading securities based on subprime mortgages to the least creditworthy borrowers. The investment bank, which Mr. Bass declines to identify, owned billions of dollars in mortgage-backed securities.

"Interesting presentation," Mr. Bass says the firm's chief risk officer said into his ear, his arm draped across Mr. Bass's shoulders. "God, I hope you're wrong."

Within six months, Mr. Bass was right. Delinquencies of home loans made to people with poor credit reached record levels, and prices for the securities backed by these sub-prime mortgages plunged. The world's biggest financial institutions would write off more than $80-billion (U.S.) in sub-prime losses, while Mr. Bass, his allies and a handful of Wall Street trading desks racked up billions in profits.

Mr. Bass and investors like him saw opportunity in a range of new investment tools that banks created to sell sub-prime securities worldwide. These included mortgage bond derivatives, contracts whose values are derived from packages of home loans and are used to hedge risk or for speculation. The vehicles allowed hedge funds like Mr. Bass's to bet against particular pools of mortgages.

From the bankers who expanded the subprime market, to the sales companies that mass-marketed high-risk mortgages, to the ratings companies that blessed investment-grade designations with securities based on such loans, there was money to be made, and everyone charged after it.

The new subprime derivatives, which amplified the risks of the underlying mortgages, were sold to blanks and institutional investors. When borrowers started to default on high-yield, high-risk subprime mortgages by the thousands, the values of these leveraged securities plunged.

Mr. Bass, a former salesman for Bear Stearns Cos. and Legg Mason Inc., had struck out on his own in early 2006. He started Hayman Capital Partners, specializing in corporate turnarounds, restructurings and mortgages. Mr. Bass isn't related to the Texas billionaire Robert Bass.

A former competitive diver who had put himself through Texas Christian University in Fort Worth partly on an athletic scholarship, he was about to take his most ambitious plunge yet: betting home values would decline for the first time since the Great Depression.

"We were saying that there were going to be $i-trillion in loans in trouble," Mr. Bass says. "That had really never happened before. You had to have an imagination to believe us."

Other early converts were Mark Hart of Corriente Capital Management in Fort Worth, Tex., and Alan Fournier of Pennant Capital in Chatham, NJ. In his earlier sales jobs, Mr. Bass had sold securities to Mr. Fournier. Now the two joined forces to research bad loans.

On the other side of their trades would be investors chasing the high yields from securities based on subprime loans. This group included Wall Street firms, German and Japanese banks and U.S. and foreign pension funds. They were reassured by the securities' investment-grade ratings, even as foreclosures started in some parts of the U.S.

The traditional way for a speculator to wager against, or short, the housing market was to sell the stocks of major home-building companies with borrowed money and repurchase them for a lower price if the shares fell.

Mr. Bass had tried that strategy in the past and found there were limits on its effectiveness, he says. There was always a danger that a leveraged buyout firm would bid for the home-building company and cause the stock to rise, which would cost anyone shorting the stock money.

The new, standardized mortgage bond derivative contracts created a strategy with less risk and greater profit potential.

To learn about the contracts, Mr. Bass visited Wall Street trading desks and mortgage servicers. He met with housing lenders and hedge fund analysts.

"What I didn't understand was the synthetic marketplace," Mr. Bass says. "When someone explained to me that it was a synthetic CDO that takes the other side of my trade, it took me a month to understand what the hell was going on."

Mr. Bass and Mr. Fournier hired private detectives, searched news reports, asked Wall Street underwriters which mortgage companies' loans were at risk of default and called those lenders directly.

In this blizzard of research, Mr. Bass turned up the California mortgage lender Quick Loan Funding and its proprietor, Daniel Sadek.

The hedge fund traders learned from a news account that Mr. Sadek was dating a soap opera actress, Nadia Bjor-lin, and using profits from his mortgage company to fund a movie about car racing, in which she starred.

"When they started catapulting Porsche Carrera GTs and he says, 'What the hell, what are a couple of cars being thrown around?' I'm thinking, 'That's the guy you want to bet against,'" Mr. Bass says.

(continued)

Mr. Bass called Quick Loan Funding directly. He says he got on the phone with a senior loan officer, identified himself and said he was interested in the mortgage business. As Mr. Bass tells it, the conversation sealed his determination to short Quick Loan's mortgages.

For his part, Mr. Sadek says he was never told that hedge funds had asked how his firm did business. He disputes Mr. Bass's characterization of Quick Loan's mortgages.

"If my loans were so bad, why did Wall Street keep buying them to securitize?" Mr. Sadek says.

As Mr. Bass and Mr. Fournier executed their trades in August and September, 2006, foreclosures were beginning to spread across the U.S.

In May, two independent researchers, Joshua Rosner of Graham Fisher & Co. and Joseph Mason of Drexel University, concluded in an 84-page study that the U.S. ratings companies Standard & Poor's, Moody's and Fitch had been wrong to bless billions of dollars of mortgage securities with triple-A and triple-B ratings.

For Mr. Bass and Mr. Fournier, it was validation of their trading strategy. As investors worldwide began to panic, they watched the values of their short positions soar.

Mortgage-backed securities are eligible for retirement plans and are exempt from non-resident withholding tax. Each month, CMHC mortgage-backed bond investors receive pro rata shares of cash flows derived from fully modified mortgage pools. Each monthly cash flow has three distinct components:

1. Payment of interest on outstanding mortgage principal.
2. Scheduled amortization of mortgage principal.
3. Mortgage principal prepayments.

19.10 Summary and Conclusions

This chapter covers the topic of government bonds, including Canada Bonds, Canada Savings Bonds and Canadian provincial and local municipal bonds. In the chapter, we saw that:

1. In Canada, the Bank of Canada issues Treasury bills and Canada Bonds are sold at regular auctions to finance government debt.
2. Treasury bills are short-term obligations that are sold on a discount basis. Treasury notes are medium-term obligations that pay fixed semiannual coupons as well as payment of face value at maturity. Government bonds are long-term obligations that pay their face value at maturity and pay fixed semiannual coupons.
3. Under the STRIPS programs government bonds and notes are broken down into principal strips which represent face value payments and coupon strips. Since each strip created under the STRIPS program represents a single future payment, strips effectively become zero coupon bonds.
4. Another large market for government debt is the market for municipal and provincial government debt. Individual investors hold about half this debt, while the remainder is roughly split equally between holdings of property and casualty insurance companies and commercial banks.
5. Most municipal and provincial bonds pay a constant coupon rate, but some pay variable coupon rates that change according to prevailing market interest rates.

Also, a call provision is a standard feature of most municipal bond issues. A call provision allows an issuer to retire outstanding bonds before they mature. When the bond is called, each bondholder receives the bond's call price in exchange for returning the bond to the issuer.

6. Most people finance their homes with mortgages. The buyer makes a down payment and borrows the remaining cost with a mortgage loan. Mortgages are often repackaged into mortgage-backed securities through a process called mortgage securitization. Currently, about half of all mortgages have been securitized, yet the risks involved in these investments are often misunderstood.

7. Most home mortgages are 15- or 30-year fixed-rate mortgages requiring constant monthly payments. In Canada, most mortgages are 25-year fixed-rate mortgages. The present value of all monthly payments is equal to the original amount of the mortgage loan. Each monthly payment has two components: payment of interest on outstanding mortgage principal and a scheduled pay-down of mortgage principal. The relative amounts of each component change throughout the life of a mortgage. The interest payment component gradually declines, and the pay-down of principal component gradually increases.

8. A mortgage borrower has the right to pay off a mortgage early, which is called mortgage prepayment. Borrowers frequently prepay to refinance an existing mortgage at a lower interest rate. Prepayment and refinancing, advantages to mortgage borrowers, are disadvantages to mortgage investors. Thus, mortgage investors face prepayment risk.

9. In 1946, the federal government created the Canadian Mortgage and Housing Corporation as a crown corporation charged with promoting liquidity in the secondary market for home mortgages. The CMHC is the largest single guarantor of mortgage-backed securities.

10. Each month, CMHC mortgage-backed bond investors receive cash flows derived from fully modified mortgage pools. Each monthly cash flow has three distinct components: payment of interest on outstanding mortgage principal, scheduled amortization of mortgage principal, and mortgage principal prepayments.

REAL WORLD

This chapter covered government bonds, a large and important securities market. How should you put your knowledge to work? Begin by purchasing (in a simulated brokerage account like Stock-Trak) the various types of government securities that are available for trading out there. Observe how their prices and yields change over time.

You should also learn more about buying government securities. A great place to start is the Department of Finance website (www.fin.gc.ca). There you can examine and download the forms needed to bid in the regular auctions. You can also obtain current auction information, including forthcoming auctions and the results of previous auctions.

You will probably find that you cannot trade municipal bonds through a simulated brokerage account. The reason is that the market for municipals is so thin that getting timely price information for a particular issue isn't possible. In practice, municipal bonds are best suited for buy-and-hold investors who buy the bonds when originally issued and hold them until maturity. You can now buy municipal bonds online through a number of brokers.

(continued)

Also covered in this chapter is one of the more complex investments available, mortgage-backed securities (MBSs). Ironically, these investments are fairly complicated, but unlike most exotic instruments, the basic types of MBSs are very suitable for ordinary individual investors. In fact, CMHC and similar investments are frequently recommended, and rightly so, for even very conservative investors.

However, as a practical matter, directly buying into mortgage pools is not practical for most individual investors. It is also probably unwise, because not all pools are equally risky in terms of prepayments, and analysis of individual pools is best left to experts. Instead, most investors in MBSs end up in mutual funds specializing in these instruments, and most of the major mutual fund families have such funds.

If you are interested in learning more about these investments, the Internet contains a large amount of information. The first place to visit is the website for CMHC (www.cmhc.gc.ca). Some informative sites with good-to-excellent sections on mortgage-backed securities include Investing in Bonds (www.investinginbonds.com). If you are thinking about a research project and need some data on mortgage-backed securities, look at what's available at Financial Data Services (www.dataonfindata.com).

Key Terms

face value 614
discount basis 614
imputed interest 614
STRIPS 615
zero coupon bonds 615
yield to call (YTC) 617
cut-off yield 621
default risk 621
general obligation bonds (GOs) 622
call provision 622
variable-rate notes 623

mortgage passthroughs 625
mortgage-backed securities (MBSs) 625
mortgage securitization 625
fixed-rate mortgage 625
mortgage principal 627
mortgage amortization 628
mortgage prepayment 631
Canada Mortgage and Housing
  Corporation 633
fully modified mortgage pool 633
prepayment risk 634

Chapter Review Problems and Self-Test

1. **Treasury Yields** A callable Treasury bond's price is 140.25. It has a coupon rate of 10 percent, makes semiannual payments, and matures in 21 years. What yield would be reported in the financial press?

2. **Mortgage Payments** What are the monthly payments on a 30-year $150,000 mortgage if the mortgage rate is 6 percent? What portion of the first payment is interest? Principal?

3. **Mortgage Prepayments** Consider a 15-year $210,000 mortgage with a 7 percent interest rate. After 10 years, the borrower (the mortgage issuer) pays it off. How much will the lender receive?

Answers to Self-Test Problems

1. First, note that this is a callable issue selling above par, so the yield to call will be reported. All callable Treasury bonds are callable at face value five years before they mature. Thus, to calculate the yield to call, all we have to do is pretend that the bond has 16 years to maturity instead of 21. We therefore have a bond with a price of 140.78125 (after converting from thirty-seconds), a coupon of 10 percent paid semiannually, and

a maturity of 16 years (or 32 periods). Verify, using the standard bond formula from Chapter 10, that the semiannual yield to call is 3 percent, so the reported yield would be 6 percent.

2. This is a standard time value of money calculation in which we need to find an annuity-type payment. The present value is $150,000. The interest rate is .06 / 12 = .005, or .5 percent, per month. There is a total of 360 payments. Using the formula from the text, we have

$$\text{Monthly payment} = \frac{\text{Mortgage balance} \times r/12}{1 - \dfrac{1}{(1 + r/12)^{T \times 12}}}$$

Plugging in r = .06 and T = 30, we get a payment of $899.33. The interest portion for a month is equal to the mortgage balance at the beginning of the month ($150,000 in this case) multiplied by the interest rate per month (.5 percent), or $150,000 × .005 = $750. The remaining portion of the payment, $899.33 − $750 = $149.33, goes to reduce the principal balance.

3. We first need to know the monthly payment. Here, the original balance is $210,000, the rate is 7 percent, and the original life is 15 years. Plugging in the numbers using the formula just above, check that we get a monthly payment of $1,887.54. From here, there are two ways to go. One is relatively easy, the other is relatively tedious. The tedious way would be to construct an amortization table for the mortgage and then locate the balance in the table. However, we need only a single balance, so there is a much faster way. After 10 years, we can treat this mortgage as though it were a five-year mortgage with payments of $1,887.54 and an interest rate of 7 percent. We can then solve for the mortgage balance using the same formula:

$$\text{Monthly payment} = \frac{\text{Mortgage balance} \times .07/12}{1 - \dfrac{1}{(1 + .07/12)^{5 \times 12}}} = \$1,887.54$$

Solving for the mortgage balance gets us $95,324.50.

Test Your Investments Quotient

1. **Zero Coupon Bonds** What is the yield to maturity (YTM) on a zero coupon bond?

    a. The interest rate realized if the bond is held to maturity.
    b. The interest rate realized when the bond is sold.
    c. The coupon yield for an equivalent coupon bond.
    d. A fixed rate when the bond is issued.

2. **Treasury Notes** The coupon rate for a Treasury note is set

    a. The same for all Treasury note issues.
    b. By a formula based on the size of the Treasury note issue.
    c. According to prevailing interest rates at time of issuance.
    d. According to the supply and demand for money.

3. **Treasury Notes and Bonds** US Treasury notes and bonds have face value denominations as small as

    a. $1,000
    b. $5,000
    c. $10,000
    d. $25,000

4. **Treasury STRIPS** When originally issued, a 10-year maturity Treasury note can be stripped into how many separate components?

   a. 10
   b. 11
   c. 20
   d. 21

5. **Treasury Bills** Treasury bills are sold on a discount basis, meaning that the difference between their issued price and their redemption value is

   a. The same for all T-bill issues.
   b. The imputed interest on the T-bill.
   c. Never less than the issued price.
   d. The bond equivalent yield for the T-bill.

6. **Dealers** When trading government securities, dealers

   a. Buy at the bid price and sell at the asked price.
   b. Sell at the bid price and buy at the asked price.
   c. Buy at the stop-out bid price and sell at the market price.
   d. Sell at the stop-out bid price and buy at the market price.

7. **Fixed-Rate Mortgages** Which of the following statements about fixed rate mortgages is false?

   a. 15-year mortgages have higher monthly payments than 30-year mortgages.
   b. Scheduled monthly payments are constant over the life of the mortgage.
   c. Actual monthly payments may vary over the life of the mortgage.
   d. Actual monthly payments are never more than scheduled monthly payments.

8. **Fixed-Rate Mortgages** The interest component of a monthly payment for a fixed-rate mortgage is

   a. Highest during the first year of the mortgage.
   b. Highest during the middle year of the mortgage.
   c. Highest during the last year of the mortgage.
   d. Constant throughout the life of the mortgage.

9. **Fixed-Rate Mortgages** The principal reduction component of a monthly payment for a fixed-rate mortgage is

   a. Highest during the first year of the mortgage.
   b. Highest during the middle year of the mortgage.
   c. Highest during the last year of the mortgage.
   d. Constant throughout the life of the mortgage.

10. **Fixed-Rate Mortgages** The remaining balance on a 30-year $100,000 mortgage loan financed at 8 percent after the 180th payment is (no calculation necessary)

    a. $100,000
    b. $50,000
    c. $76,782
    d. $23,219

11. **Fixed-Rate Mortgages** Which of the following mortgages has the lowest monthly payment (no calculation necessary)?

    a. 30-year, 8 percent
    b. 30-year, 10 percent
    c. 15-year, 8 percent
    d. 15-year, 10 percent

12. **Fixed-Rate Mortgages** Which of the following mortgages will pay the smallest total interest over the life of the mortgage (no calculation necessary)?

    a. 30-year, 8 percent
    b. 30-year, 10 percent

    c. 15-year, 8 percent
    d. 15-year, 10 percent

13. **Fixed-Rate Mortgages** Which of the following mortgages will have the largest remaining balance after 180 monthly payments (no calculation necessary)?

    a. 30-year, 8 percent
    b. 30-year, 10 percent
    c. 15-year, 8 percent
    d. 15-year, 10 percent

14. **CMHC Bonds** Mortgages in CMHC pools are said to be fully modified because CMHC guarantees bondholders which of the following?

    a. A minimum rate of return on their investment.
    b. A modified schedule of cash flows over the life of the pool.
    c. Full and timely payment of both principal and interest in the event of default.
    d. Eventual payment of both principal and interest in the event of default.

15. **CMHC Bonds** Which of the following is not a source of risk for CMHC mortgage pool investors?

    a. Prepayment risk
    b. Default risk
    c. Interest rate risk
    d. Reinvestment risk

CFA® PROBLEMS

16. **Mortgage-Backed Bonds** If a mortgage-backed bond is issued as a fully modified passthrough security, it means that

    a. Bondholders will receive full and timely payment of principal and interest even if underlying mortgage payments are not made.
    b. The bond has been structured to include both conforming and nonconforming loans.
    c. The interest rates on the underlying mortgages have been altered so that they equal the weighted-average coupon on the bond.
    d. The security carries a balloon payment to ensure that the bond is fully amortized in a set time frame (12 to 15 years).

Concept Questions

1. **Bills versus Bonds** What are the key differences between T-bills and T-bonds?

2. **Provincials versus Government** From an investor's standpoint, what are the main differences between government and provincial issues?

3. **Callable Bond Issues** For a callable bond selling above par, is it necessarily true that the yield to call will be less than the yield to maturity? Why or why not?

4. **Government versus Municipal Bonds** Why might the yield to maturity on, say, a BBB-rated municipal bond with moderate default risk actually be less than that of a Treasury bond with no default risk?

5. **Canada Savings Bonds** Compare T-bills and Canada Savings Bonds. Which one is better for a long-term investor? Why?

6. **Canada Premium Bonds** What are the characteristics of the Canada Premium Bonds?

7. **Provincial Bonds** Compare provincial bonds with Canada Savings Bonds. What are the advantages of holding provincial bonds?

8. **Mortgage Securitization** How does mortgage securitization benefit borrowers?

9. **Mortgage Securitization** How does mortgage securitization benefit mortgage originators?

10. **Mortgage Payments** All else the same, will the payments be higher on a 15-year mortgage or a 30-year mortgage? Why?

11. **Mortgage Pools** What does it mean for a mortgage pool to be fully modified?

12. **Prepayments** What are some of the reasons that mortgages are paid off early? Under what circumstances are mortgage prepayments likely to rise sharply? Explain.

13. **Prepayments** Explain why the right to prepay a mortgage is similar to the call feature contained in most corporate bonds.

14. **Prepayments** Evaluate the following argument: "Prepayment is not a risk to mortgage investors because prepayment actually means that the investor is paid both in full and ahead of schedule." Is the statement always true or false?

15. **Prepayments** Mortgage pools also suffer from defaults. Explain how defaults are handled in a fully modified mortgage pool. In the case of a fully modified mortgage pool, explain why defaults appear as prepayments to the mortgage pool investor.

Questions and Problems

Core Questions

1. **STRIPS Price** What is the price of a STRIPS with a maturity of 15 years, a face value of $10,000, and a yield to maturity of 8 percent?

2. **STRIPS YTM** A STRIPS with 18 years until maturity and a face value of $10,000 is trading for $3,225. What is the yield to maturity?

3. **Bank of Canada Auctions** The Bank of Canada announces an offering of Treasury bills with a face value of $30 billion. Noncompetitive bids are made for $7 billion, along with the following competitive bids:

Bidder	Price Bid	Quantity Bid
A	$9,250	$10 billion
B	9,300	8 billion
C	9,320	7 billion
D	9,350	6 billion
E	9,400	5 billion
F	9,410	5 billion

In an auction, which bids are accepted and what prices are paid by each bidder? How much money is raised by the entire offering?

4. **Municipal Bonds** A municipal bond with a coupon rate of 4.5 percent has a yield to maturity of 3.8 percent. If the bond has 10 years to maturity, what is the price of the bond?

5. **Yield to Maturity** A provincial bond with a coupon rate of 5.4 percent sells for $5,604 and has eight years until maturity. What is the yield to maturity of the bond?

6. **Yield to Maturity** A provincial bond has 23 years until maturity and sells for $6,120. If the coupon rate on the bond is 6.20 percent, what is the yield to maturity?

7. **Yield to Call** Assume the bond in the previous problem can be called in eight years. What is the yield to call if the call price is 103 percent of par?

8. **Government Prices** A noncallable Treasury bond has a quoted yield of 5.62 percent. It has a 6 percent coupon and 16 years to maturity. What is its dollar price assuming a $1,000 par value? What is its quoted price?

9. **Government Yields** In a recent newspaper, locate the Canada bond with the longest maturity (the so-called bellwether bond). Verify that, given the price, the reported yield is correct.

10. **Callable Government Bonds** In a recent *Globe and Mail*, examine the yields on Canada bonds maturing in 2014 and 2015.

**Spreadsheet
Problems**

11. **Zero Price** A STRIPS traded on May 1, 2004, matures in 25 years on May 1, 2029. Assuming a 6 percent yield to maturity, what is the STRIPS price?

12. **Zero YTM** A STRIPS traded on July 1, 2004, matures in 15 years on July 1, 2019. The STRIPS price is $45. What is its yield to maturity?

13. **Mortgage Payments** What is the monthly payment on a 30-year fixed rate mortgage if the original balance is $175,000 and the rate is 7 percent?

14. **Mortgage Balances** If a mortgage has monthly payments of $1,100, a life of 30 years, and a rate of 5.5 percent per year, what is the mortgage amount?

15. **Mortgage Payments** A homeowner takes out a $210,000, 30-year fixed-rate mortgage at a rate of 6.4 percent. What are the monthly mortgage payments?

16. **Mortgage Balance** You have decided to buy a house. You can get a mortgage rate of 6.8 percent, and you want your payments to be $1,200 or less. How much can you borrow on a 30-year fixed-rate mortgage?

17. **Mortgage Interest** A 30-year $200,000 mortgage has a rate of 6.5 percent. What are the interest and principal portions in the first payment? In the second?

18. **Mortgage Balances** A homeowner takes a 25-year fixed-rate mortgage for $250,000 at 7.8 percent. After seven years, the homeowner sells the house and pays off the remaining principal. How much is the principal payment?

19. **Mortgage Balances** Consider a 30-year $300,000 mortgage with a 6.9 percent interest rate. After 10 years, the borrower (the mortgage issuer) pays it off. How much will the lender receive?

20. **Mortgage Payments** A 30-year mortgage has an annual interest rate of 6.25 percent and a loan amount of $180,000. What are the monthly mortgage payments?

What's on the Web?

1. **Bank of Canada Auctions** Go to www.bankofcanada.ca and find the next auctions scheduled. When are the auctions scheduled? What instruments will be offered at these auctions?

2. **Bank of Canada Auctions** Go to www.bankofcanada.ca and find the recently completed Treasury auctions for bills. When did the auctions occur? What were the yields for each bill sold at these auctions?

3. **Canada Savings Bonds** Go to www.fin.gc.ca, find the rates and characteristics of the latest Canada Savings Bond.

4. **Provincial Bonds** Go to the CBID markets website at www.pfin.ca and compare Ontario bonds. Which bond is the best investment for you? Elaborate.

5. **Canada Benchmarks** Go to the CBID markets website at www.pfin.ca and compare Canada benchmarks with Canada T-bills in terms of rates, yield and prices.

6. **T-Bills** Go to the Yahoo website at www.finance.yahoo.com and find the US T-bill rates. Compare these rates with those of Canadian T-bills.

7. **CMHC** Go to the mortgage-backed security section at www.cmhc.gc.ca. Examine the site, get as much information as you can for investors.

CHAPTER 20

International Portfolio Investment

"Don't put all your eggs in one basket."

—Anonymous

Canadian stock markets are approximately 3 percent of the world stock markets. Can Canadian investors find their optimum portfolio by investing only in Canadian assets, stocks, bonds and mutual funds?

International market stocks, bonds and mutual funds have a very low correlation with Canadian financial instruments and provide higher returns, especially emerging market funds. On the other hand, emerging market securities are extremely risky.

Canadian investors can invest in foreign stocks, bonds, money market funds or mutual funds and both diversify their portfolios and increase their returns. Before 2005, Registered Retirement Savings Plans could contain a maximum of 30 percent foreign content. In 2005, the federal budget removed this restriction making it possible for Canadians to invest up to 100 percent in foreign securities. One should be aware, however, that investing in foreign markets creates both exchange rate risk and political risk. Obviously there are both benefits and costs involved in investing in foreign instruments. ■

Should you allocate your funds domestically or invest part of your funds into foreign stocks, bonds or better yet into mutual funds that invest exclusively in foreign markets?

In this chapter we will examine international portfolio investment. We introduce you to the foreign exchange market, and then investigate portfolio return and risk with investment in foreign stocks. Of particular interest are the questions, "What are the benefits of including foreign stocks and diversifying your portfolio internationally?" and "What are the costs of international diversification?"

20.1 Foreign Exchange Rates

foreign exchange rate A foreign exchange rate shows the price of one country's currency in terms of another country's currency.

spot rate A spot rate between two currencies is the valid rate between them for transactions that require immediate delivery.

forward rate A forward rate indicates the fixed rate for transactions that require future delivery.

cross-rate A cross-rate between two currencies is the calculated separate rate between the currencies by using quotes of each currency against a major currency.

A **foreign exchange rate** shows the price of one country's currency in terms of another country's currency. For example, the exchange rate between the Canadian dollar and the British pound shows how many British pounds one Canadian dollar is worth. Newspapers report spot and forward rates between currencies. A **spot rate** between two currencies is the valid rate between them for transactions that require immediate delivery. A **forward rate** indicates the fixed rate for transactions that require future delivery. For instance, if you need 100,000 Russian rubles in three months and you want to avoid uncertainty regarding future exchange rate, then you can buy a forward contact with a fixed rate between the Canadian dollar and Russian ruble. This contract stipulates you will pay a given amount of Canadian dollars and receive the equivalent of 100,000 Russian rubles.

Generally newspapers and foreign exchange services provide the values of one currency in terms of other major currencies like the U.S. dollar, Euro, British pound, etc. If you want to find out the value of one currency in terms of a minor currency, you will have to calculate the value using quotes of both currencies against the major currency and find a **cross-rate**. This is not a market quoted rate but a calculated rate.

Figure 20.1 shows spot exchange rates on January 5, 2008. One Japanese Yen is equal to 0.011933 Canadian dollars for three-month forward transactions. European Union countries started using the Euro in 1999. If you want to buy a Belgian security, the exchange rate between Euros and Canadian dollars is as follows: Canadian $1.4773 = 1 Euro. At the beginning of the figure you can observe cross-rates between the Canadian dollar and other currencies.

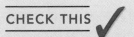 CHECK THIS

20.1a   What does a foreign exchange rate show?

20.1b   What is a forward rate?

20.1c   What is a spot rate?

20.2 Returns on Foreign Investments

If you invest in a foreign stock, your return will depend not only on your company's stock return, but also on the foreign exchange rate between the Canadian dollar and the currency of the country where your company is located. Return in Canadian dollars is given by the following formula:

$$1 + R = (1 + R_{\text{in foreign currency}})(1 + R_{\text{foreign exchange}}) \qquad (20.1)$$

FIGURE 20.1

Foreign Exchange Rate Quotes

Source: *The Globe and Mail*, January 5, 2008. Reprinted with permission of *The Globe and Mail*.

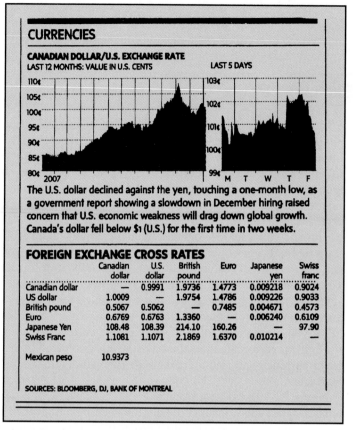

CURRENCIES

CANADIAN DOLLAR/U.S. EXCHANGE RATE
LAST 12 MONTHS: VALUE IN U.S. CENTS   LAST 5 DAYS

The U.S. dollar declined against the yen, touching a one-month low, as a government report showing a slowdown in December hiring raised concern that U.S. economic weakness will drag down global growth. Canada's dollar fell below $1 (U.S.) for the first time in two weeks.

FOREIGN EXCHANGE CROSS RATES

	Canadian dollar	U.S. dollar	British pound	Euro	Japanese yen	Swiss franc
Canadian dollar	—	0.9991	1.9736	1.4773	0.009218	0.9024
US dollar	1.0009	—	1.9754	1.4786	0.009226	0.9033
British pound	0.5067	0.5062	—	0.7485	0.004671	0.4573
Euro	0.6769	0.6763	1.3360	—	0.006240	0.6109
Japanese Yen	108.48	108.39	214.10	160.26	—	97.90
Swiss Franc	1.1081	1.1071	2.1869	1.6370	0.010214	—
Mexican peso	10.9373					

SOURCES: BLOOMBERG, DJ, BANK OF MONTREAL

Your return will magnify if the foreign currency appreciates against the Canadian dollar. On the other hand, you will not get the same return as you would have obtained if the Canadian dollar appreciates against the foreign currency.

RETURN ON FOREIGN STOCK TRANSACTION

EXAMPLE 20.1

You purchased 100 shares of Henkel company shares on the Frankfurt stock exchange paying 32 €/share. One year later Henkel shares are trading at 35 €/share. The exchange rate was 1.53 Canadian $/one €. Now the same exchange rate is 1.48. What is your return? How much profit did you obtain?

Return in € = (35 − 32)/32 = 0.09375

$$\text{Return on foreign exchange} = \frac{1.48 - 1.53}{1.53} = -0.0327$$

Return in Canadian dollars = (1 + 0.09375)(1 − 0.0327) − 1 = 0.05798 or 5.8%

Initially you spent 100 × 32 €/share × 1.53 Canadian $/€ = $4896

At the end of the year you obtained 100 × 35 €/share × 1.48 Canadian $/€ = $5180

Your profit is = $5180 − $4896 = $204

In this example, your company, Henkel, earned a 9.375 percent return. But you earned a 5.79 percent return, because the Euro has depreciated against the Canadian dollar by 3.27 percent.

WORK THE WEB

We visited the Yahoo Finance website at www.finance.yahoo.com and obtained the graph of the Japanese yen–Canadian dollar exchange rate's performance in the previous one-year period.

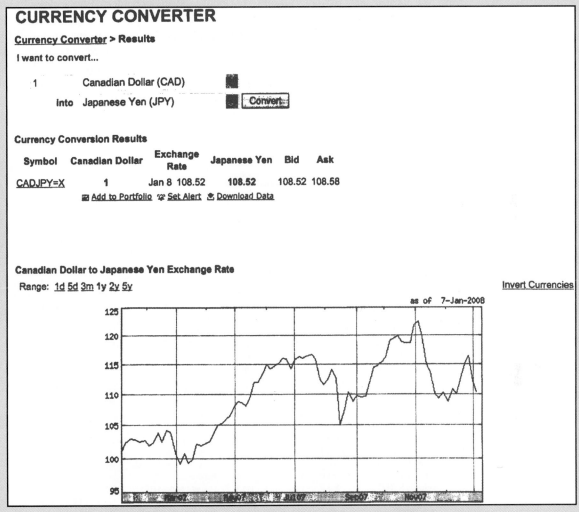

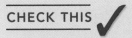

CHECK THIS

20.2a   If you invest in a foreign security, how do you calculate your return?

20.2b   If you invest in a foreign security and if the Canadian dollar appreciates, how will your return be affected?

20.3 Benefits and Risks Involved in International Investment

Traditionally, low correlations among different stock markets are cited as the primary benefits of international diversification. Indeed the correlations among stock exchanges, especially between far-away exchanges had been very low. Recently, with improvements in information technology and in globalization, these correlations started to increase among stock markets. However they are still low and one can reduce portfolio risk significantly by including international securities or international index funds into one's portfolio.

Another benefit of international diversification is the high returns provided by some of the emerging markets. Examine Figure 20.2 to compare returns on various stock markets in 2006. Among developed stock exchanges, Germany had the highest percentage return with 34.6 percent in USD. In the Chinese market, investors earned three times as much return with a 182.2 percent return in 2006. It is not uncommon to witness more than 100 percent in emerging markets.

FIGURE 20.2

Returns on Major Stock Exchanges

The Economist January 5th 2008

Markets

	Index Jan 2nd	one week	% change on Dec 29th 2006 in local currency	in $ terms
United States (DJIA)	13,044.0	-2.4	+4.7	+4.7
United States (S&P 500)	1,447.2	-3.4	+2.0	+2.0
United States (NAScomp)	2,609.6	-4.2	+8.0	+8.0
Japan (Nikkei 225)	15,307.8‡	-2.2	-11.1	-3.5
Japan (Topix)	1,475.7‡	-2.2	-12.2	-4.7
China (SSEA)	5,533.3	+0.8	+96.6	+110.3
China (SSEB, $ terms)	367.2	+1.1	+163.7	+182.2
Britain (FTSE 100)	6,416.7	-1.0	+3.1	+4.3
Canada (S&P TSX)	13,926.8	+1.7	+7.9	+26.1
Euro area (FTSE Euro 100)	1,357.9	-1.1	+6.2	+18.6
Euro area (DJ STOXX 50)	4,339.2	-1.0	+5.3	+17.6
Austria (ATX)	4,509.2	+0.7	+1.0	+12.8
Belgium (Bel 20)	4,114.5	-0.5	-6.2	+4.7
France (CAC 40)	5,550.4	-1.1	+0.2	+11.8
Germany (DAX)*	7,949.1	-0.7	+20.5	+34.6
Greece (Athex Comp)	5,207.4	+1.9	+18.5	+32.3
Italy (S&P/MIB)	38,035.0	-0.4	-8.2	+2.5
Netherlands (AEX)	509.8	-1.2	+2.9	+14.9
Spain (Madrid SE)	1,624.8	-1.9	+4.5	+16.7
Czech Republic (PX)	1,808.6	+2.2	+13.8	+32.8
Denmark (OMXCB)	446.1	-0.3	+5.2	+17.5
Hungary (BUX)	25,889.9	-0.6	+4.2	+15.3
Norway (OSEAX)	570.1	+2.5	+13.5	+30.5
Poland (WIG)	55,521.4	-0.5	+10.1	+30.3
Russia (RTS, $ terms)	2,290.5	+0.3	+10.7	+19.2
Sweden (Aff.Gen)	334.9	-1.3	-8.3	-2.1
Switzerland (SMI)	8,484.5	+0.2	-3.4	+5.4
Turkey (ISE)	54,708.4	-1.2	+39.9	+69.4
Australia (All Ord.)	6,434.1	+0.7	+14.0	+27.8
Hong Kong (Hang Seng)	27,560.5	-2.0	+38.0	+37.4
India (BSE)	20,465.3	+1.4	+48.4	+66.6
Indonesia (JSX)	2,731.5	+0.6	+51.3	+45.1
Malaysia (KLSE)	1,435.7	+0.8	+31.0	+39.6
Pakistan (KSE)	13,353.4	-9.9	+33.0	+30.9
Singapore (STI)	3,461.2	-0.3	+15.9	+23.7
South Korea (KOSPI)	1,853.5	-2.8	+29.2	+28.3
Taiwan (TWI)	8,323.1	+2.0	+6.4	+6.8
Thailand (SET)	843.0	+0.2	+24.0	+33.5
Argentina (MERV)	2,151.7	-1.3	+2.9	+0.3
Brazil (BVSP)	62,815.0	-2.3	+41.2	+70.5
Chile (IGPA)	13,876.0	-1.4	+12.1	+19.9
Colombia (IGBC)	10,648.5	-0.3	-4.6	+6.3
Mexico (IPC)	28,699.1	-4.3	+8.5	+7.8
Venezuela (IBC)	37,903.7	+1.9	-27.4	-55.9
Egypt (Hermes)	94,213.8	+3.7	+53.7	+59.4
Israel (TA-100)	1,159.2	nil	+25.8	+37.7
Saudi Arabia (Tadawul)	10,892.6	-4.6	+37.3	+37.2
South Africa (JSE AS)	29,290.2	-0.7	+17.6	+21.8
Europe (FTSEurofirst 300)	1,487.2	-1.4	+0.3	+12.0
World, dev'd (MSCI)	1,578.1	-1.3	+6.4	+6.4
Emerging markets (MSCI)	1,235.2	-0.7	+35.3	+35.3
World, all (MSCI)	400.5	-1.2	+8.9	+8.9
World bonds (Citigroup)	739.4	+2.7	+12.3	+12.3
EMBI+ (JPMorgan)	434.3	+0.3	+6.6	+6.6
Hedge funds (HFRX)	1,330.6	-0.1	+4.3	+4.3
Volatility, US (VIX)	23.2	18.7	11.6 (levels)	
CDSs, Eur (iTRAXX)†	53.1	nil	+127.9	+154.5
CDSs, N Am (CDX)†	91.3	+5.2	+173.1	+173.1
Carbon trading (EU ETS) €†	22.9	+3.7	+25.8	+40.5

*Total return index. †Credit-default swap spreads, basis points.
Sources: National statistics offices, central banks and stock exchanges; Thomson Datastream; Reuters; WM/Reuters; JPMorgan Chase; Bank Leumi le-Israel; CBOE; CMIE; Danske Bank; EEX; HKMA; Markit; Standard Bank Group; UBS; Westpac. ‡New series. ‡December 28th 2007.

Indicators for more countries, as well as additional series, can be found at
www.economist.com/indicators

Correlation Coefficients Between Different Stock Markets

Upper-Right: Correlations based on 60 months of real dollar returns, 1996–2000, from FTSE World (Ireland and South Africa) and MSCI (all others).

Lower-left: Correlations based on 101 years of real dollar returns, 1900–2000.

	Wld	US	UK	Swi	Swe	Spa	Saf	Neth	Jap	Ita	Ire	Ger	Fra	Den	Can	Bel	Aus
Wld		.93	.77	.59	.62	.67	.54	.73	.68	.52	.69	.69	.73	.57	.82	.54	.69
US	.85		.67	.44	.46	.53	.46	.57	.49	.40	.66	.56	.56	.46	.78	.45	.57
UK	.70	.55		.58	.44	.63	.31	.71	.42	.39	.73	.58	.59	.57	.57	.59	.56
Swi	.68	.50	.62		.39	.60	.19	.72	.36	.45	.57	.53	.64	.58	.35	.63	.37
Swe	.62	.44	.42	.54		.63	.38	.63	.34	.49	.27	.76	.76	.44	.61	.29	.44
Spa	.41	.25	.25	.36	.37		.35	.63	.32	.64	.50	.64	.75	.56	.51	.55	.54
Saf	.55	.43	.49	.39	.34	.26		.30	.44	.24	.31	.42	.37	.25	.62	.10	.66
Neth	.57	.39	.42	.51	.43	.28	.29		.39	.59	.63	.74	.77	.64	.55	.70	.46
Jap	.45	.21	.33	.29	.39	.40	.31	.25		.18	.33	.25	.36	.24	.50	.17	.59
Ita	.54	.37	.43	.52	.39	.41	.41	.32	.34		.33	.55	.71	.50	.40	.51	.38
Ire	.58	.38	.73	.70	.42	.35	.42	.46	.29	.43		.42	.45	.49	.54	.57	.50
Ger	.30	.12	−.01	.22	.09	−.03	.05	.27	.06	.016	.03		.83	.61	.57	.59	.46
Fra	.62	.36	.45	.54	.44	.47	.38	.48	.25	.52	.53	.19		.63	.60	.66	.48
Den	.57	.38	.40	.51	.56	.34	.31	.50	.46	.38	.55	.22	.45		.55	.54	.30
Can	.80	.80	.55	.48	.53	.27	.54	.34	.30	.37	.41	.13	.35	.46		.30	.65
Bel	.58	.38	.40	.57	.43	.40	.29	.60	.25	.47	.49	.26	.68	.42	.35		.30
Aus	.66	.47	.66	.51	.50	.28	.56	.41	.28	.43	.62	.04	.47	.42	.62	.35	

Source: Elroy Dimson, Paul Marsh and Mike Staunton, *Triumph of the Optimists, 101 Years of Global Investment Returns*, Princeton University Press, 2002, p. 115. © 2002 Elroy Dimson, Paul Marsh and Mike Staunton. Published by Princeton University Press. Reprinted by permission of Princeton University Press.

Figure 20.3 exhibits the correlation coefficients between different stock markets using real dollar returns for the period 1900–2000. If we examine the correlations between the Canadian and other markets, we observe that the highest correlation coefficient is with the United States for 0.80 and the lowest correlation is with Germany for 0.13. Can a Canadian investor benefit by investing part of his or her portfolio in the German market? First we have to examine the risk-return characteristics of the German stock market. Figure 20.4 reports that German stocks have an 8.8 percent return and 32.3 percent standard deviation. A Canadian investor may want to increase the return of his or her portfolio by including German equities.

RETURN AND RISK CHARACTERISTICS OF INTERNATIONAL PORTFOLIOS

Calculate the average return and standard deviation of a portfolio consisting of 30 percent German equities and 70 percent Canadian equities using Figure 20.4.

Canadian equities have 0.077 average return and 0.168 standard deviation. German equities have 0.088 average return and 0.323 standard deviation. The portfolio average return is the weighted average of the returns.

$$R_p = 0.7 \times R_{Canada} + 0.3 \times R_{Germany} = 0.7 \times 0.077 + 0.3 \times 0.088 = 0.0803 \text{ or } 8.03\%$$

(continued)

| FIGURE 20.4 | Risk and Return Characteristics of Various Stock Markets |

Country	Equities (%)		Bonds (%)		Bills (%)	
	Mean	S.D.	Mean	S.D.	Mean	S.D.
Australia	9.0	17.7	1.9	13.0	0.6	5.6
Belgium	4.8	22.8	0.3	12.1	0.0	8.2
Canada	7.7	16.8	2.4	10.6	1.8	5.1
Denmark	6.2	20.1	3.3	12.5	3.0	6.4
France	6.3	23.1	0.1	14.4	−2.6	11.4
Germany	8.8	32.3	0.3	15.9	0.1	10.6
Ireland	7.0	22.2	2.4	13.3	1.4	6.0
Italy	6.8	29.4	−0.8	14.4	−2.9	12.0
Japan	9.3	30.3	1.3	20.9	−0.3	14.5
The Netherlands	7.7	21.0	1.5	9.4	0.8	5.2
South Africa	9.1	22.8	1.9	10.6	1.0	6.4
Spain	5.8	22.0	1.9	12.0	0.6	6.1
Sweden	9.9	22.8	3.1	12.7	2.2	6.8
Switzerland	6.9	20.4	3.1	8.0	1.2	6.2
United Kingdom	7.6	20.0	2.3	14.5	1.2	6.6
United States	8.7	20.2	2.1	10.0	1.0	4.7

Source: Elroy Dimson, Paul Marsh and Mike Staunton, *Triumph of the Optimists, 101 Years of Global Investment Returns*, Princeton University Press, 2002. © 2002 Elroy Dimson, Paul Marsh and Mike Staunton. Published by Princeton University Press. Reprinted by permission of Princeton University Press.

The portfolio variance is given by the following formula:

$$\sigma_p^2 = (0.7)^2 \times (0.168)^2 + (0.3)^2 \times (0.323)^2 + 2 \times (0.7) \times (0.3) \times 0.13 \times (0.168) \times (0.323)$$
$$= 0.0262$$

The standard deviation is the square root of variance and equal to

$$\sigma_p = \sqrt{\sigma_p^2} = 0.1617 = 16.17\%$$

This portfolio has a better return and lower risk than a 100 percent Canadian equities portfolio and demonstrates that Canadian investors can get better investment portfolios by diversifying internationally.

political risk The political situation in a foreign country may create risk through things such as nationalization of certain industries by the government, corruption and ethnic strife.

There are two types of risks created by international investing: **political** and **foreign exchange**. The political situation in a foreign country may create risk through things such as nationalization of certain industries by the government, corruption and ethnic strife. There are various websites and books that treat these risk factors. The Transparency International Agency has surveyed multinational company executives about corruption levels in different countries. Table 20.1 exhibits the ranking in 2006. According to the table, Finland has the lowest perceived corruption level and Brazil and China the highest.

| TABLE 20.1 | Corruption Perceptions Index 2006 |

Country Rank	Country	2006 CPI Score	Surveys used	Confidence range	Country Rank	Country	2006 CPI Score	Surveys used	Confidence range
1	Finland	9.6	7	9.4–9.7	36	Bahrain	5.7	5	5.3–6.2
1	Iceland	9.6	6	9.5–9.7	37	Botswana	5.6	6	4.8–6.6
1	New Zealand	9.6	7	9.4–9.6	37	Cyprus	5.6	4	5.2–5.9
4	Denmark	9.5	7	9.4–9.6	39	Oman	5.4	3	4.1–6.2
5	Singapore	9.4	9	9.2–9.5	40	Jordan	5.3	7	4.5–5.7
6	Sweden	9.2	7	9.0–9.3	41	Hungary	5.2	8	5.0–5.4
7	Switzerland	9.1	7	8.9–9.2	42	Mauritius	5.1	5	4.1–6.3
8	Norway	8.8	7	8.4–9.1	42	South Korea	5.1	9	4.7–5.5
9	Australia	8.7	8	8.3–9.0	44	Malaysia	5.0	9	4.5–5.5
9	Netherlands	8.7	7	8.3–9.0	45	Italy	4.9	7	4.4–5.4
11	Austria	8.6	7	8.2–8.9	46	Czech Republic	4.8	8	4.4–5.2
11	Luxembourg	8.6	6	8.1–9.0	46	Kuwait	4.8	5	4.0–5.4
11	United Kingdom	8.6	7	8.2–8.9	46	Lithuania	4.8	6	4.2–5.6
14	Canada	8.5	7	8.0–8.9	49	Latvia	4.7	6	4.0–5.5
15	Hong Kong	8.3	9	7.7–8.8	49	Slovakia	4.7	8	4.3–5.2
16	Germany	8.0	7	7.8–8.4	51	South Africa	4.6	8	4.1–5.1
17	Japan	7.6	9	7.0–8.1	51	Tunisia	4.6	5	3.9–5.6
18	France	7.4	7	6.7–7.8	53	Dominica	4.5	3	3.5–5.3
18	Ireland	7.4	7	6.7–7.9	54	Greece	4.4	7	3.9–5.0
20	Belgium	7.3	7	6.6–7.9	55	Costa Rica	4.1	5	3.3–4.8
20	Chile	7.3	7	6.6–7.6	55	Namibia	4.1	6	3.6–4.9
20	USA	7.3	8	6.6–7.8	57	Bulgaria	4.0	7	3.4–4.8
23	Spain	6.8	7	6.3–7.2	57	El Salvador	4.0	5	3.2–4.8
24	Barbados	6.7	4	6.0–7.2	59	Colombia	3.9	7	3.5–4.7
24	Estonia	6.7	8	6.1–7.4	60	Turkey	3.8	7	3.3–4.2
26	Macao	6.6	3	5.\4–7.1	61	Jamaica	3.7	5	3.4–4.0
26	Portugal	6.6	7	5.9–7.3	61	Poland	3.7	8	3.2–4.4
28	Malta	6.4	4	5.4–7.3	63	Lebanon	3.6	3	3.2–3.8
28	Slovenia	6.4	8	5.7–7.0	63	Seychelles	3.6	3	3.2–3.8
28	Uruguay	6.4	5	5.9–7.0	63	Thailand	3.6	9	3.2–3.9
31	United Arab Emirates	6.2	5	5.6–6.9	66	Belize	3.5	3	2.3–4.0
					66	Cuba	3.5	3	1.8–4.7
32	Bhutan	6.0	3	4.1–7.3	66	Grenada	3.5	3	2.3–4.1
32	Qatar	6.0	5	5.6–6.5	69	Croatia	3.4	7	3.1–3.7
34	Israel	5.9	7	5.2–6.5	70	Brazil	3.3	7	3.1–3.6
34	Taiwan	5.9	9	5.6–6.2	70	China	3.3	9	3.0–3.6

Source: http://www.globalcorruptionreport.org.

foreign exchange risk
Movements in foreign exchange rates can significantly increase or decrease portfolio returns.

In terms of foreign exchange risk, we have already seen that depending on the movement of foreign exchange rates our portfolio returns can be significantly increased or decreased. How big is this risk? With today's floating exchange rate environment, exchange rates change continuously and create significant instability in portfolios depending on the percentage of investment in international markets.

If investors choose to invest part of their portfolio in international stocks, benefits outweigh the costs in the long-term. The question is what percentage of one's portfolio should be allocated to foreign stocks? The nearby *Investment Updates* box discusses this issue for Canadian investors. As mentioned in the article many investors choose to hold 70 percent of their portfolio in domestic issues and 30 percent in foreign markets. Thirty percent foreign content used to be the maximum amount permissible for retirement accounts. Now Canadian investors can invest up to 100 percent of their funds in foreign securities if they choose to do so.

Every investor has a different degree of risk aversion. A very risk-averse investor may prefer to hold a small percentage of the portfolio in foreign markets and may avoid emerging markets. On the other hand a less risk-averse investor may invest heavily in emerging markets.

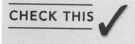

CHECK THIS

20.3a   What are the benefits of international diversification?

20.3b   What are the risks of international diversification?

20.3c   What about you? What percentage of your portfolio will you allocate in foreign funds?

20.4 International Funds

Canadian investors can invest in both short-term and long-term foreign securities. If you want to invest in short-term funds, you can choose among many T-bills or other money market funds. Also long-term debt securities are available as foreign government bonds or foreign company bonds. Many Canadian investors choose to invest in U.S. Treasury bonds.

However, generally investors invest in stocks when the time comes to invest internationally. You can choose to invest in single foreign stocks. This strategy is very risky if you do not know the company or country very well. A better strategy would be to invest in a mutual fund that invests exclusively in a region or a country.

There are single-country funds which form diversified portfolios of a specific country's stocks like the Japan Fund. There are regional funds which form diversified portfolios of regional stocks like the Latin America Fund. Also mutual fund companies combine stocks of emerging countries and form Emerging Country Funds. The nearby article describes the benefits of international mutual funds.

CHECK THIS

20.4a   What type of financial instruments do Canadian investors choose for their international investments?

20.4b   Why is it better to invest in mutual funds with foreign content rather than in single stocks?

The Canadian stock market gets a real vote of confidence when portfolio strategist Wilf Hahn lays out his ideally diversified global portfolio.

"We're a little overweight on Canada," says Mr. Hahn, president of Hahn Investment Stewards & Co. "The [global] benchmark has Canada at a little more than 2 percent of the total, but we're about double-weight. That puts us at about 4 percent of the total portfolio."

Yee-haw. Four percent. Ain't we something.

Like it or not, Canada is borderline insignificant in the global investing universe. In hockey terms, we're the Columbus Blue Jackets. In baseball terms, we're the Toronto Blue Jays.

And yet, we live and work in Canada and the vast majority of us will retire here. It makes sense, then, for us to invest here, too.

Here, we arrive at a question facing every diligent Canadian investor and investment adviser: How much of a balanced portfolio should be invested at home and how much elsewhere?

Unfortunately, that most loathsome of answers applies here: It depends. It depends on who you talk to, what asset allocation tools you use and how much risk you're willing to take on.

One certainty is that you want global exposure in your portfolio. By participating in global markets, you're in a position to make money while the Canadian market struggles. In 1998, the benchmark Canadian stock index lost 1.6 percent while the main index for global stocks outside North America made 28 percent in Canadian-dollar terms. U.S. stocks outperformed Canadian stocks routinely through the 1990s.

You've probably absorbed lessons like this from mutual fund industry hype designed to sell global equity funds. But you've also likely noticed that in the past few years, global and U.S. equity funds have been just awful compared with Canadian equity funds.

The average global equity fund lost a compound average annual 1.8 percent in the five years to Aug. 31, the average U.S. equity fund lost 6 percent and the average Canadian fund gained 5.5 percent. Home sweet home, indeed.

Here are two other recent developments to confuse your thinking about global diversification. First, the Canadian dollar's appreciation against its U.S. counterpart has squeezed the life out of many U.S. equity funds. And while traditionalists talk about breaking your equity holdings into Canadian, U.S. and global portions, the most dynamic markets these days are regional or country-specific. Think of China or India, for example.

So how do you divide up your money internationally?

While Mr. Hahn would only use a sprinkling of Canada for ideal global diversification, his mix for people who live and expect to retire here would be 70 percent Canadian content and 30 percent foreign. The same mix was recommended by Ranga Chand, an economist, mutual fund analyst and author of several financial books.

The 70–30 mix is convenient because the government caps the foreign content in your registered retirement plan at 30 percent of book value. You can go beyond that using so-called clone funds—foreign funds that count as domestic content—but these products cost more than regular funds.

You can mix your 30-percent content between U.S. and global or international equity funds, or you can do as Mr. Chand suggests and just choose a broadly diversified global fund with significant U.S. exposure. One example is the Trimark Fund, with close to 60 percent of its assets invested in the U.S. market.

If you want to focus on a particular region or sub-category, say emerging markets or the Far East, then Mr. Chand suggests you go with a 5-percent weighting. First, though, make sure you can handle the ferocious ups and downs of these sorts of specialty funds.

"Always ask, what's the worst 12-month period this fund has delivered," Mr. Chand said. "What's the biggest loss?"

One other caveat he suggested is to make sure your core global fund doesn't already have a big weighting in whatever region you plan to focus on. Inadvertently bulking up on one particular region can blow a big hole in your portfolio.

Mr. Chand says that if he were to pick one foreign specialty fund to buy, it would be Asia. He's impressed by the maturing economies there that are being fuelled increasingly by domestic demand rather than exports.

"What we really like right now, and it's surprising to me, even, is emerging markets," Mr. Hahn says. Emerging markets are wickedly volatile in general, but he thinks they're as attractively valued as they have been in the past 15 years.

As for humble Canada, there's nothing wrong with having the bulk of your portfolio at home.

"When I look at Canada, what pleases me is that we're the only industrial economy that has both a current account surplus and a fiscal surplus," Mr. Chand said. "I think the fundamentals in Canada are excellent."

Source: Rob Carrick, *The Globe and Mail.* Reprinted with permission from *The Globe and Mail.*

WORK THE WEB

We examined the mutual funds at the Yahoo finance site: www.finance.yahoo.com. Here is what we found for the last year's performance of the Korea Fund. Examine it and decide whether or not to invest in it.

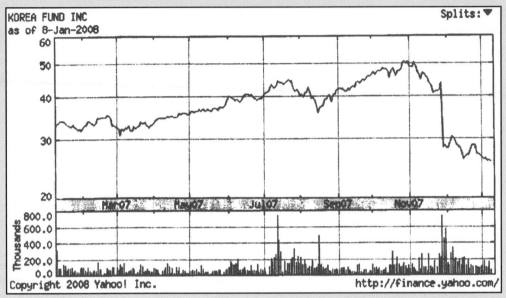

Source: Reproduced with permission of Yahoo! Inc. © 2004 by Yahoo! Inc. Yahoo! and the Yahoo! logo are trademarks of Yahoo! Inc.

20.5 Crosslisting

Lastly we will examine those companies that choose to be listed on more than one stock exchange. For example if you want to buy Royal Bank stocks, you can buy them either from the Toronto Stock Exchange or from the New York Stock Exchange, because the company is crosslisted on both exchanges. There are benefits and costs of crosslisting. Companies should carefully evaluate both advantages and disadvantages and if benefits exceed costs then consider multiple listings. Generally companies operating in countries with less liquid stock markets choose to be listed on more liquid exchanges like the New York Stock Exchange.

Listing on a liquid and prestigious stock exchange increases liquidity of companies and may increase stock prices. Companies may increase their visibility in another country by being listed in that country. Generally Japanese multinationals choose to be listed in all major stock exchanges to increase their visibility and introduce their brand (e.g., Sony, Toyota).

On the other hand, getting listed on another exchange is very costly and time-consuming. Companies have to hire lawyers and accountants and translate their financial

Sunday, September 12, 2004—NEW YORK—There have always been lots of reasons to invest in international stocks: Opportunity abounds beyond our borders. But lately, many on Wall Street have raised their stake overseas as high valuations and slower growth at home make U.S. stocks relatively less attractive.

Small investors can do the same through mutual funds and exchange traded funds, or ETFs, which can diversify the risks associated with volatile foreign markets and currency swings.

"Growth rates around the world are not in synchronicity," said John Krey, senior investment officer with Standard & Poor's. "A number of factors are working against U.S. growth at this time . . . which means investors are looking for opportunities for growth elsewhere."

The waning effects of tax cuts enacted by the Bush administration, higher energy prices and a weak dollar have conspired against domestic equities this year. But while our own indexes have floundered through most of 2004, a number of markets outside the United States have advanced, and some have even posted double-digit returns. Small-cap stocks in Japan are up 30 percent year-to-date; the Dow Jones country index for Austria has surged 25 percent. Mexico is up 14 percent and the Philippines has added 17 percent.

Of course, it's never a good idea to make dramatic changes to your investment strategy based on something as capricious as currency market conditions. But understanding why big traders are sending so much money abroad can be instructive. And if the equity portion of your portfolio is currently dominated by domestic stocks, now might not be such a terrible time to introduce some geographic diversity.

"There are winners and losers for every macroeconomic scenario you could have," said Michael Porter, senior research analyst at Lipper Inc. "But I would say that the weakening dollar . . . has augmented returns on international stocks and might be a reason to consider them, all things being equal."

There are plenty of other reasons to maintain a healthy chunk of exposure to international stocks. Many of the best companies in the world are domiciled outside the United States. If all of your stock exposure came from an S&P 500 fund, you'd never own industry leaders like Taiwan Semiconductor Manufacturing Co., Samsung Corp., Toyota Motor Corp., Nokia Corp., The Royal Dutch/Shell Group of software giant SAP AG.

In addition, a number of foreign markets, including China and other emerging economies in Southeast Asia and Eastern Europe, have attractive valuations and offer opportunities for growth not available in the United States. China and India, the two most-populous na-

tions in the world, are increasingly attractive to foreign investment because of their low-paid, skilled work forces, and are poised to grow far more rapidly than the U.S. economy as a whole in the decades ahead.

"Investors should be flexible enough to go where the best investments can be found," Porter said. "You shouldn't be parochial and limit yourself to the U.S. because you cut out a lot of opportunities."

If you're venturing into foreign markets for the first time, you should start out with a broadly mandated international fund. Once you become more knowledgeable and comfortable with your investment, you can zero in on regions or single countries keeping in mind that his is an aggressive strategy that even the most sophisticated investors might shy away from. Foreign markets, known for being extremely volatile, are notoriously difficult to time.

"Aside from currency changes, the kinds of things that really turn a country upside down are political, economic and social events," Porter said. "That's especially true of smaller, more exotic emerging markets. One way you can protect yourself from that is going for a more broadly diversified fund."

When you're considering a fund that invests in foreign securities, keep an eye on its individual holdings. Global funds invest mostly in foreign companies, but may also include U.S.-based stocks, which could create some redundancy within your portfolio. International funds, meanwhile, invest only outside the United States. If you want to target your investment, there are any number of regional and country funds, including a number of ETFs offered by iShares.

Complicating matters, a number of international mutual funds have recently closed to new investors because their asset levels had grown too high, or because fund managers found a shortage of attractive choices in world securities. A number of good performers remain open, however, and indexing remains a cheap and predictable option.

For small investors, the most important thing is to keep some perspective about the current popularity of international funds. The short-term events that motivate large traders, such as currency fluctuations, really should have little or no bearing on your long-term strategy.

"It's just very difficult to predict currency movements," said Gregg Wolper, senior fund analyst at Morningstar Inc. "Even the experts who do that full-time find themselves surprised by what happens. There are times when it may seem obvious which direction the currency markets are going, but the surprises are not far behind."

statements according to the new country's regulation, increase their disclosure, and meet the stricter requirements of the foreign country's stock exchanges.

Last century brought increased globalization to stock exchanges and many companies chose to be multiple-listed. Although the largest number of foreign companies is listed on the London Stock Exchange, the highest volume of foreign company listings takes place in U.S. stock exchanges. Many Canadian multinational companies are crosslisted on U.S. markets.

20.6 Summary and Conclusions

This chapter investigates international investment. First we discuss different types of exchange rates: forward, spot rates and cross rates, then examine how exchange rate appreciation and depreciation affect portfolio returns. After exploring the benefits and risks of international investment, we investigate how to allocate funds to international funds. We see that low correlations among international markets help in the reduction of portfolio risk. We find out that emerging markets provide very high returns but they have high risk. Investing internationally creates two types of risk: political risk and exchange rate risk. Exchange rate risk creates volatility in portfolio returns.

Although some experts advocate 30 percent foreign content in a portfolio, we discover that the optimum percentage depends on the investor's degree of risk aversion and knowledge about foreign markets.

REAL WORLD

This chapter covered the benefits and costs of international investment. How should you choose your foreign investment? You can use your Stock-Trak account and allocate 10 percent, 20 percent, 30 percent, 40 percent and 50 percent of your portfolio in foreign stocks. Choose various American, German, British and Japanese stocks and check the portfolio performances after one month, then after three months.

What is your optimum portfolio? Which markets would you like to invest in? Which stocks would you choose?

Key Terms

foreign exchange rate 645   cross-rate 645
spot rate 645   political risk 650
forward rate 645   foreign exchange risk 652

Chapter Review Problems and Self-Test

1. **International Stock Return** You invested in an American company called Chup Inc. one year ago, when the exchange rate was $1.37 Canadian/U.S.$. The company earned 10 percent return in a year and the exchange rate became $1.30 Canadian/U.S.$. Calculate your return in one year.

2. **Portfolio Return** You invested 30 percent in Chup Inc. and 70 percent in a Canadian company called Grand, which produced a 3 percent return. What is your annual portfolio return?

3. **Portfolio Variance** You have the following data:

$$\sigma_{\text{Chup}} = 0.42, \quad \sigma_{\text{Grand}} = 0.30 \text{ and the Cov(Grand, Chup)} = -0.1$$

Find the portfolio variance.

Answers to Self-Test Problems

1. $1 + R = (1 + R_{\text{in foreign currency}})(1 + R_{\text{foreign exchange}}) = (1 + 0.1)(1 + R_{\text{foreign exchange}})$

   $R_{\text{foreign exchange}} = (1.30 - 1.37) / 1.37 = -0.051$

   $\text{Return} = (1.1 \times (1 - 0.051)) - 1 = 0.0439 = 4.39\%$

   Although the company earned 10 percent in American dollars, you earned 4.39 percent in Canadian dollars.

2. $R_{\text{portfolio}} = 0.3 \times R_{\text{Chup}} + 0.7 \times R_{\text{Grand}} = 0.3 \times 0.0439 + 0.7 \times 0.03$

   $= 0.03417 = 3.42 \text{ percent}$

3. $\sigma^2_{\text{portfolio}} = (0.3)^2 \times \sigma^2_{\text{Chup}} + (0.7)^2 \times \sigma^2_{\text{Grand}} + 2 \times 0.3 \times 0.7 \times \text{Cov(Grand, Chup)}$

   $= 0.09 \times (0.42)^2 + 0.49 \times (0.30)^2 + 0.42 \times (-0.1)$

   $= 0.015876 + 0.0441 - 0.042$

   $= 0.017976$

   $\sigma_{\text{portfolio}} = 0.1341$

   By adding Chup Inc. into your portfolio you increase your portfolio return and reduce portfolio risk tremendously.

Test Your Investment Quotient

1. **Foreign Exchange** Foreign Exchange rate shows the relationships between:
   a. Two countries' interest rates.
   b. Two countries' currencies.
   c. Two countries' money markets.
   d. Two countries' stock markets.

2. **Foreign Exchange** Foreign Exchange quote for immediate delivery transactions is called:
   a. Spot Rate.
   b. Forward Rate.
   c. Future Rate.
   d. Cross-Rate.

3. **Foreign Exchange** If an investor invested in a foreign stock and if domestic currency appreciates, this will
   a. hurt the return.
   b. increase the return.
   c. does not affect the return.
   d. affect the return, but the direction (negative or positive) depends on the amount of appreciation.

4. **Foreign Exchange** Last year 1 British pound was worth 2.25 Canadian dollars. This year the exchange rate is 2.32 Canadian dollars. The Canadian dollar

   a. appreciated by 3.96 percent.
   b. depreciated by 3.96 percent.
   c. appreciated by 3.02 percent.
   d. depreciated by 3.02 percent.

5. **Foreign Exchange** Last year 1 Australian dollar was worth 0.92 Canadian dollars. This year the exchange rate is 0.91 Canadian dollars. The Canadian dollar

   a. appreciated by 1.10 percent.
   b. depreciated by 1.10 percent.
   c. appreciated by 0.52 percent.
   d. depreciated by 0.52 percent.

6. **Foreign Exchange** Last year 1 Swiss frank was worth 0.99 Canadian dollars. This year the exchange rate is 1.02 Canadian dollars. The Canadian dollar

   a. appreciated by 3.03 percent.
   b. depreciated by 3.03 percent.
   c. appreciated by 2.94 percent.
   d. depreciated by 2.94 percent.

7. **Foreign Exchange** Which of the following statements is true?

   a. One of the benefits of international investment is political benefits.
   b. One of the risks of international investment is exchange rate risk.
   c. One of the benefits of international investment is speculation benefit.
   d. One of the risks of international investment is hedging risk.

8. **Foreign Content** Which percentage of foreign content is optimum for Canadian investors?

   a. 30 percent foreign content.
   b. 50 percent foreign content.
   c. 70 percent foreign content.
   d. depends on the degree of risk aversion of investors.

9. **Emerging Markets** Why are emerging markets attractive to investors?

   a. Generally they provide higher return than developed markets.
   b. They have low correlations with developed market stocks.
   c. They have higher risk than those of developed markets.
   d. Both a and b.

10. **Foreign Stocks** You have a Canadian stock in your portfolio, there are four foreign stocks available for investment. They all provide the same return and risk, except their correlation coefficients with your Canadian stock are different. Which one would you choose?

    a. Stock A correlation coefficient = −0.1.
    b. Stock B correlation coefficient = 0.
    c. Stock C correlation coefficient = 0.5.
    d. Stock D correlation coefficient = 0.7.

11. **Foreign Exchange** Which of the following statements is true?

    a. If you need 1,000,000 Russian rubles in three months, you should buy Russian rubles in the three-month forward market.
    b. If you need 1,000,000 Russian rubles in three months, you should buy Russian rubles in the three-month paying spot market rate.
    c. If you need 1,000,000 Russian rubles in three months, you should sell Russian rubles in the three-month forward market.
    d. Spot rates and three-month forward rates are generally equal.

12. **International Investments** Canadian investors can invest in

    a. foreign stocks.
    b. foreign T-bills.
    c. foreign government bonds.
    d. all of the above.

13. **International Investment** Which of these instruments is the riskiest?

    a. foreign stocks
    b. foreign T-bills
    c. foreign government bonds
    d. all of the above

14. **International Investments** What type of mutual funds are available for international investment?

    a. Single Country Funds
    b. Intercontinental Funds
    c. Double Country Funds
    d. Offshore Funds

15. **International Investment** What is the maximum amount of foreign content in an RRSP fund?

    a. 20 percent
    b. 25 percent
    c. 30 percent
    d. no limit

Concept Questions

1. **Exchange Rate** What is an exchange rate? From which sources can we find daily exchange rates?

2. **Forward and Spot Rates** Compare and contrast forward and spot rates. For which maturities are forward rates quoted?

3. **Foreign Exchange Rates** How does change in foreign exchange rate affect value or return on a foreign investment?

4. **International Investment** Discuss the benefits of international investment and diversification.

5. **International Investment** Discuss two different types of risks of international investment.

6. **International Investment** Compare the benefits of international investments with the risks of international investment.

7. **International Investment** Discuss different types of financial instruments available for international investment.

8. **International Investment** Compare and contrast different types of international mutual funds.

9. **International Investment** Discuss the following statement. "The optimum portfolio for Canadian investors is 30 percent foreign."

10. **International Investment** Suppose two identical international funds exist. Fund A has a correlation coefficient of -0.2, and Fund B has a correlation coefficient of 0 with the rest of the portfolio. Which one would you choose? Why?

11. **Crosslisting** Describe crosslisting. Find two crosslisted Canadian companies.

Questions and Problems

Core Questions

The following data regarding exchange rates are available. Use Table 20.2 to answer questions 1–10.

TABLE 20.2	Canadian Dollar—Foreign Currency Exchange Rates							
Date	Australian Dollar	Chinese Yuan	Hong Kong Dollar	Japanese Yen	Malaysian Ringgit	Singapore Dollar	South Korean Won	Thai Baht
September 2003	1.1362	6.3926	5.9871	85.9955	2.9261	1.3367	895.6709	30.9478
September 2004	1.1430	6.7593	6.3621	90.2720	3.0996	1.3795	939.02	33.8053

Source: Based on data from http://www.oanda.com.

1. **Foreign Exchange** Did the Canadian dollar appreciate or depreciate against the Australian dollar? Calculate the return on foreign exchange for a Canadian investor.

2. **Foreign Exchange** Did the Canadian dollar appreciate or depreciate against the Chinese yuan? Calculate the return on foreign exchange for a Canadian investor.

3. **Foreign Exchange** Did the Canadian dollar appreciate or depreciate against the Hong Kong dollar? Calculate the return on foreign exchange for a Canadian investor.

4. **Foreign Exchange** Did the Canadian dollar appreciate or depreciate against the Japanese yen? Calculate the return on foreign exchange for a Canadian investor.

5. **Foreign Exchange** Did the Canadian dollar appreciate or depreciate against the Malaysian ringgit? Calculate the return on foreign exchange for a Canadian investor.

6. **Foreign Exchange** Did the Canadian dollar appreciate or depreciate against the Singapore dollar? Calculate the return on foreign exchange for a Canadian investor.

7. **Foreign Exchange** Did the Canadian dollar appreciate or depreciate against the Korean won? Calculate the return on foreign exchange for a Canadian investor.

8. **Foreign Exchange** Did the Canadian dollar appreciate or depreciate against the Thai baht? Calculate the return on foreign exchange for a Canadian investor.

9. **Foreign Exchange** If there are securities providing equal return at each of these exchanges, which one would you choose? Why?

10. **Foreign Exchange** In general would you recommend investment in Asian markets to Canadian investors?

Use Table 20.3 for questions 11–14.

TABLE 20.3	Canadian Dollar—Foreign Currency Exchange Rates						
Date	Euro	British Pound	Swiss Frank	U.S. Dollar	Argentine Peso	Brazilian Real	Mexican Peso
September 2003	0.6710	0.4648	1.0420	0.7714	2.2949	2.2548	8.3210
September 2004	0.6652	0.4522	1.0301	0.8157	2.4503	2.3419	9.3339

Source: Based on data from http://www.oanda.com.

11. **Foreign Exchange** How did the Canadian dollar perform against European currencies? Calculate the returns on foreign exchange for a Canadian investor.

12. **Foreign Exchange** How did the Canadian dollar perform against Latin American currencies? Calculate the returns on foreign exchange for a Canadian investor.

13. **Foreign Exchange** How did the Canadian dollar perform against the U.S. dollar? Calculate the return on foreign exchange for a Canadian investor.

14. **Foreign Exchange** Everything else being equal, which country or region is best for a Canadian investor?

Intermediate Questions

Use the following information for questions 15–19.

Your portfolio consists of three funds from different regions with the following proportions:

Latin American Fund	0.2
Asia Fund	0.4
North America	0.4

All funds are traded in Canadian dollars.

The funds have the following expected returns, standard deviations, and correlations between them:

$$E(R_{\text{Latin America}}) = 0.12 \quad E(R_{\text{Asia}}) = 0.15 \quad E(R_{\text{North America}}) = 0.06$$

$$\rho_{\text{Latin America-Asia}} = 0.3 \quad \rho_{\text{Latin America-North America}} = 0.8 \quad \rho_{\text{North America-Asia}} = 0.5$$

$$\text{Standard deviation (Latin American Fund)} = 0.30$$

$$\text{Standard deviation (Asia Fund)} = 0.20$$

$$\text{Standard deviation (North American Fund)} = 0.1$$

15. **Foreign Funds** Calculate the expected return on your portfolio.

16. **Foreign Funds** Calculate variance of the portfolio. *Hint*: Use the portfolio variance formula for three stock portfolios including three correlations.

17. **Foreign Funds** If you had invested 20% in Asia and 40% in Latin America, what would your expected return and variance be?

18. **Foreign Funds** Which portfolio is better? Which portfolio would you prefer in the long-run?

19. **Foreign Funds** Calculate the expected returns on both portfolios if these funds are traded in foreign currencies using Table 20.2 and 20.3 and using the average return on currencies of each region.

20. **Forward Rate** Examine the 6-month forward Euro rates given in Figure 20.1, check whether or not there is a premium or discount and calculate the amount of premium or discount.

21. **Forward Rate** Examine the 6-month forward U.S. rates given in Figure 20.1, check whether or not there is a premium or discount and calculate the amount of premium or discount.

22. **Forward Rate** Examine the 6-month forward British pound rates given in Figure 20.1, check whether or not there is a premium or discount and calculate the amount of premium or discount.

23. **Forward Rate** Which currency provides the best prospects for international investment?

24. **Cross-Rate** Calculate the cross-rate between the Hong Kong dollar and the Russian ruble using Figure 20.2, and their rates against the U.S. dollar at September 8, 2004.

25. **Cross-Rate** Calculate the cross rate between the Brazilian real and Thai baht, using Figure 20.2 and their rates against the U.S. dollar at September 8, 2004.

What's on the Web?

1. **International Investment** Go to *The Economist* web site (www.economist.com) and find the current exchange rates of the Japanese yen and Chinese yuan in terms of U.S. dollars.

2. **International Investment** Go to *The Economist* web site (www.economist.com) and find the return on all stock markets in the last year.

3. **Forward Rates** Go to the Globe Investor's website (www.globeinvestor.com) to find the latest forward rates between the Canadian dollar and other currencies.

4. **Foreign Exchange Trading** Go to the GCI Financial Ltd. website (www.gcitrading.com) and open a free demo account. Now you can trade foreign currencies. Try to get a profit by buying and selling spot and forward foreign currencies.

5. **Foreign Exchange Trading** Go to the OANDA website (www.oanda.com) and open a free demo account. Now you can trade foreign currencies. Try to get a profit by buying and selling spot and forward foreign currencies.

Answers to Selected Questions and Problems

Chapter 1

1-1 $920
1-4 Jurassic average return = 7.40%
Stonehenge average return = 8.20%
1-8 Arithmetic average = 11.17%
Geometric average = 9.50%

Chapter 2

2-1 11.80%
2-5 Roll = 18.62%
Ross = 6.37%
2-9 *a.* 7.93%
b. 0.03419; 18.49%
2-17 Standard deviation = 39.93%
Expected return = 14.13%
2-20 Standard deviation = 37.06%
Expected return = 14.20%

Chapter 3

3-1 313.25 shares
3-5 $23,636.36
3-9 Critical stock price = $64.62
Account equity = $19,380
3-13 $49.29
3-17 $1,916.68
3-22 Effective annual return = 27.44%

Chapter 4

4-1 Closing price = $22.82
Round lots = 2,855
4-5 Next payment = $16,800
Payments at maturity = $416,800
4-9 Current yield = 6.10%
Treasury yield = 4.36%
4-13 $11,700
4-20 107.36%

Chapter 5

5-1 $34.62
5-5 $26.33
5-9 $17.46; −12.54%
5-13 2.74%
5-18 $14,200
5-19 1 year: 5.45%
2 year: 8.19%
5 year: 9.87%
10 years: 10.43%
5-22 $103,500

Chapter 6

6-1 2.22892
6-5 14.18%
6-9 4.10843
6-13 0.334896

Chapter 7

7-1 $43.02
7-5 $374.63
7-9 $2.16; $2.36
7-13 $60.25
7-17 $17.77
7-22 $29.19
7-25 16.42 times
7-29 $87.31
7-33 ROE = 11.87%
g = 8.31%

Chapter 8

None

Chapter 9

9-2 0.822; 0.947; 1.035; 1.001; 0.771
9-6 0.5200; 0.5333; 0.4733; 0.5467; 0.5800
9-15 0.7241; 1.0230; 0.9356; 0.8310

Chapter 10

10-1 68:28
10-5 7.90%
10-9 $997,112.50
10-13 BEY = 6.555%
Discount yield = 6.329%
10-17 5-year STRIP = 74:26
$f_{1,5}$ = 5.976%
2-year STRIP = 88:26
$f_{2,3}$ = 6.112%
10-21 $f_{1,1}$ = 6.51%
$f_{1,2}$ = 7.16%
$f_{1,3}$ = 7.84%

Chapter 11

11-1 $1,068.34
11-5 9.68%
11-9 10.48%
11-13 11.06%
11-19 10.71%
11-21 YTM = 8.07%
Realized yield = 3.20%
11-27 Macaulay duration = 11.844
Modified duration = 11.443
11-31 6.65%

Chapter 12

12-1 1.28
12-5 1.035
12-9 $52.80
12-13 3.00%
12-17 1.27
12-23 Expected return = 0.645%
Standard deviation = 2.13%

Chapter 13

13-1 22.05%
13-4 Monthly standard deviation = 14.96%
Annual standard deviation = 53.94%
13-9 −28.12%
13-13 −15.42%
13-18 −132.56%
13-21 −11.76%

Chapter 14

14-1 *a.* $35,775
b. $1,121,250
c. $16,250
d. −$180
14-5 $13,857,626,125
14-9 $75.08
14-13 Day 1: $214,875
Day 2: $120,375
Day 3: $151,875
Day 4: $120,375
Profit = −$105,000
14-17 923.43
14-21 5334.9
14-25 *a.* 190.55
b. 190.40

Chapter 15

15-1 $4,000
15-5 $70,000; $25,000
15-9 $82.42
15-13 $10.54
15-16 $1,900

Chapter 16

16-1 $25.23
16-5 $5.81
16-9 3,544
16-13 $40
16-17 $18.12
16-21 7,225

Chapter 17

17-1 $19,745
17-5 P/B = 3.89 times
P/E = 22.55 times
P/CF = 14.94 times
17-9 $97,000

17-13 P/B = 5.03 times
P/E = 12.97 times
P/CF = 9.47 times

Chapter 18

18-1 $28.57
18-5 $940
18-8 $84
18-12 Conversion value = $880
Conversion price = $47.73

Chapter 19

19-1 $3,083.19
19-3 Accepted bid = $9,230
Total raised = $27.96 billion
19-5 3.65%
19-7 3.32%
19-11 22.81
19-13 $1,164.28
19-15 $1,313.56
19-16 $184,070.20

Chapter 20

20-1 Appreciate, 0.5985%
20-3 Appreciate, 6.2635%
20-5 Appreciate, 5.9294%
20-7 Appreciate, 4.8398%
20-13 Appreciate, 5.7428%
20-15 10.80%
20-25 14.3448 Thai Baht/Brasilian Real